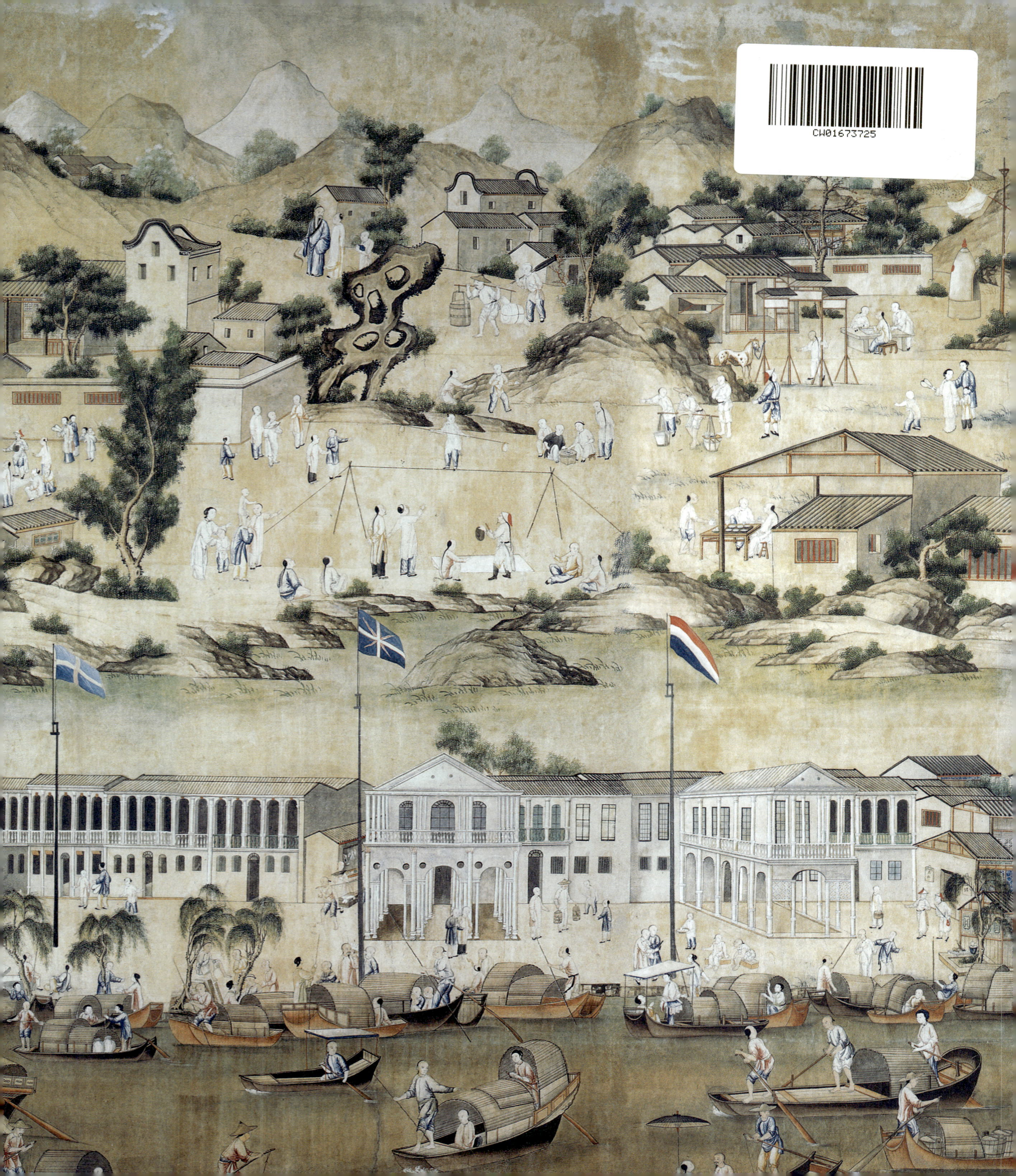

Encounters

THE MEETING OF ASIA AND EUROPE 1500–1800

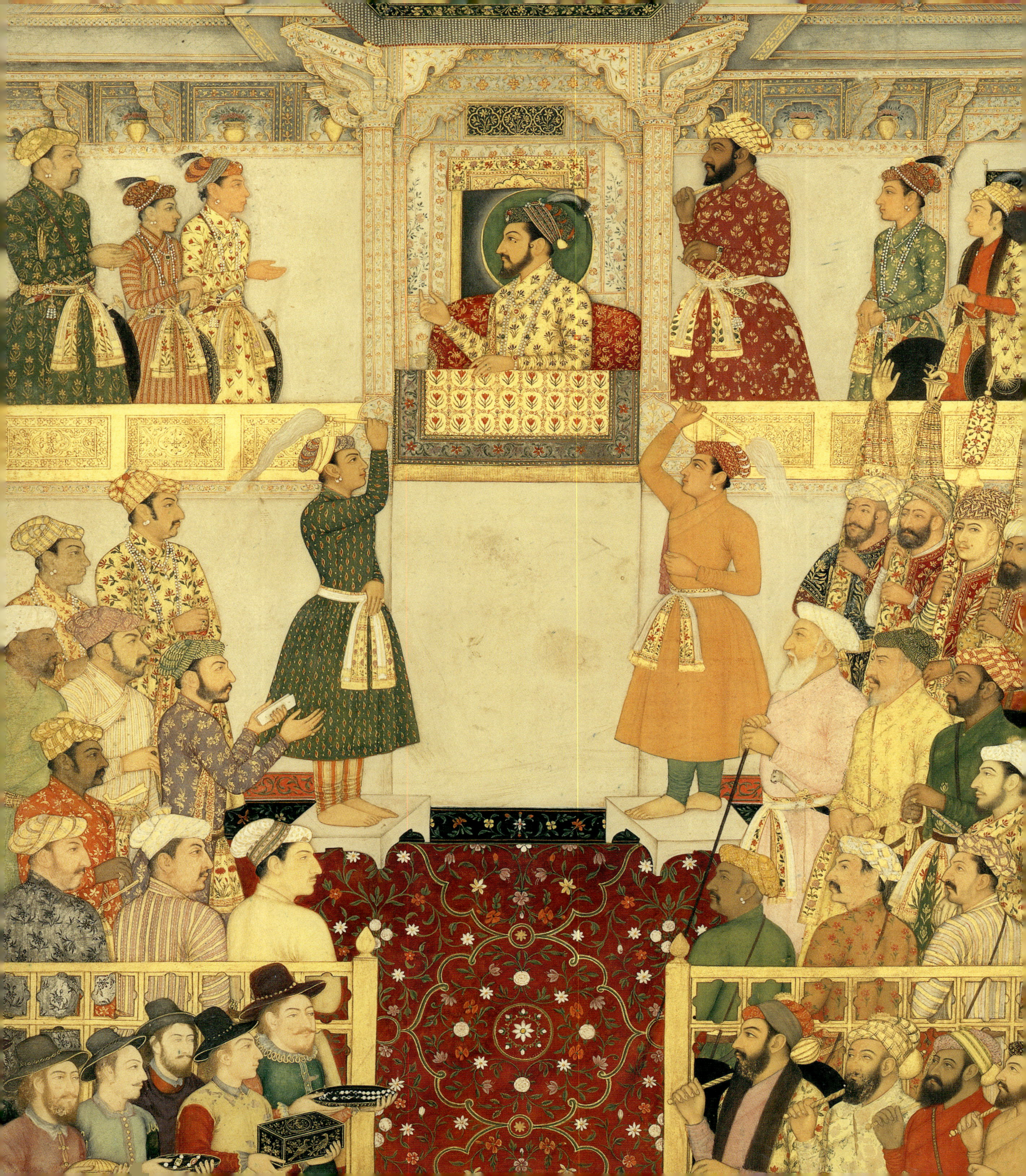

Encounters

THE MEETING OF ASIA AND EUROPE 1500–1800

EDITED BY ANNA JACKSON & AMIN JAFFER

V&A PUBLICATIONS

PART THREE
Exchanges

Nomura Group is very proud to support *Encounters: The Meeting of Asia and Europe 1500–1800*. It is particularly appropriate that Nomura should be identified with an exhibition exploring a period of commercial, cultural, artistic and technological exchange. In the same entrepreneurial spirit with which merchants of old traded the routes between Asia and Europe, so we at Nomura now form a bridge in the financial markets between Japan, Asia and the world.

We hope that all those who see this exhibition share the same sense of excitement experienced by those early pioneers, as they too discover, encounter and exchange.

Nobuyuki Koga
President & CEO
Nomura Holdings, Inc.

NOMURA

ACKNOWLEDGEMENTS

This exhibition and the accompanying book would not have been possible without the kind help and support of a great number of people. We are tremendously indebted to all of them.

Nomura has generously sponsored the exhibition, and we would like to thank the company for its support and for embracing the project so enthusiastically. The initial travel and research for the project were funded by Fidelity Foundation, for which great thanks are due. We are also grateful to Niall Hobhouse and John Leaning, who have offered funds for conservation, photography and travel.

The project was conceived and developed at the Victoria and Albert Museum and we are immensely grateful to all our colleagues for their participation. Above all, we would like to thank Tessa Hore, the Exhibition Coordinator, who has worked tirelessly alongside us throughout the project. Her dedication and meticulous planning have ensured that the exhibition has been realized successfully. We also owe special thanks to our colleagues in the Asian Department who contributed to the book and exhibition and offered considerable help in their areas of specialism.

The broad approach taken in this book has been possible thanks to the expertise of its contributing authors, who have very kindly shared their knowledge and enthusiasm for the subject. Deep thanks are due to these scholars, many of whom also offered critical advice on approach and content.

This book accompanies an exhibition for which the Museum has borrowed extensively. We would like to thank the public institutions and private lenders who have graciously permitted the loan of their works to *Encounters: The Meeting of Asia and Europe, 1500–1800*. In the UK: Her Majesty the Queen; The British Library; British Museum, London; The Royal Pavilion, Libraries and Museums, Brighton and Hove; Trustees of Chicheley Hall; Hobhouse Limited; Collection Howard Hodgkin; Impey Family Collection; The Khalili Collections; Jonathan Lourie, Private Collection; Martyn Gregory Gallery, London; National Maritime Museum, London; National Portrait Gallery, London; Wardens & Scholars of New College, Oxford; Board of Trustees of the Royal Armouries; Tate; Jorge Welsh; York Museum Trust (York Art Gallery); in continental Europe: Bibliothèque nationale de France, Paris; Trustees of the Chester Beatty Library, Dublin; Stift Kremsmuenster Kunstsammlungen; Kunsthistorisches Museum, Wien, Kunstkammer; Musée du Louvre, Paris; Museu Nacional de Arte Antiga, Lisbon; Museu Nacional Soares dos Reis, Porto; National Museum of Ireland; Rijksmuseum, Amsterdam; Staatlich Museen Kassel; Collection KIT/Tropenmuseum, Amsterdam; in the United States: Brooklyn Museum of Art, New York; Chen Art Gallery, Torrance; The Metropolitan Museum of Art; Richard Milhender; Museum of Fine Arts, Boston; Peabody Essex Museum, Salem; Ruth and Sherman Lee Institute, Permanent Collection; in China: Collection of the Palace Museum, Beijing; in Japan: Imperial Household Collection, Tokyo; Kobe City Museum; Kyoto Living Craft Museum; Namban Bunkakan, Osaka; Rinno-ji, Nikko; and all those lenders who wish to remain anonymous.

We are extremely grateful to the many specialists from the lending institutions and to other scholars, curators, collectors and advisers for their time and knowledge. Particular thanks are due to: Kyoko Ando, Hiroo Aoyama, Peter Barber, Luis and Eduardo Barreiros, la Princesse de Beauvau-Craon, David Beevers, Elizabeth Beller, Richard Blurton, Andrew Bolton, Michael Burden, Jan van Campen, Manuel Castilho, Tim Clark, Maria Concecão Borges de Souza, Patrick Conner, Karina Corrigan, Yuji Dainobu, David van Durren, Anthony Farrington, Menno Fitski, Barbara Ford, Matthi Forrer, Jane Gallagher, Francesca Galloway, Gary Garabedian, Paul Greenhalgh, Charles Greig, Yong Han, Victor Harris, Jessica Harrison-Hall, Ebeltje Hartkamp-Jonxis, Esther Ho, Robert Holden, Yoshiya Ishida, Sebastian Izzard, Yoshiro Kitamura, Jun'ichi Kobayashi, Shaoyi Li, Anthony Lin, Christopher Lloyd, Xiao Lan Lui, Pauline Lunsingh Scheurleer, Robert Knox, Forrest McGill, Becky Macguire, Duncan McLaren, David McNeff, Errol Manners, Frederic Marguerre, Jonathan Marsden, Kojima Michihiro, Dan Munro, Hiroko Nishida, Anne Nishimura Morse, Barbara O'Connor, Miles Ogborn, Aya Ohta, Yasumasa Oka, Teresa Parames, José Luis Porfirio, Amy Poster, Simon Ray, Thom Richardson, Robert Riley, Graeme Rimer, Sir Hugh Roberts, Bertrand Rondot, Alan Rubin, Jessica Rutherford, Takamasa Saito, William R. Sargent, Allison Sharpe, Josie Shepherd, Tatsuya Shimokara, Peter Sigmond, Robert Skelton, Nancy Stoddart, Leng Tan, Akiko Terao, David Thompson, Antonia Tozer, Maki Tsuchida, Cheng-Sheng Tu, Nuno Vassallo e Silva, Teresa Viana, John Villiers, Paul Walter, Jorge Welsh, Frances Wood, Iwao Yamaguchi and family, Hongxing Zhang, Xinmiao Zheng and Kees Zandvliet.

A large number of people within the V&A have participated in the project. That many of the objects in the book look so beautiful is thanks to the skills of Christine Smith from the Museum's Photographic Studio. Nigel Bamforth and Pauline Webber have managed the complex conservation programme and we are very grateful to them and to the Technical Services Department. In the Press and Marketing Department we would like to thank Damien Whitmore, Debra Isaac, Sarah Armond, Gareth Harris and Cathy Mason. In the Development Department we would like to extend our gratitude to Nicole Newman, Laura Hingley and Charles McCallum. In the Education Department we would like to thank Eithne Nightingale, Irna Qureshi, Francis Pugh, Clare Goodwin and Lucy Trench, and in the Exhibitions Department, Ruth Cribb.

Our work on the exhibition was undertaken in the Research Department and we would like to thank Carolyn Sargentson, Mark Haworth-Booth, Victoria Coulson, Karen Livingstone, Jane Pavitt, John Styles and Ghislaine Wood. We would also like to thank the volunteers who contributed to the project: Benedict Bull, Mallika Kurana and William Lautenschlager.

The Design Department has played a particularly important role in realizing our ideas and we would like to thank Moira Gemmil, Siddhartha Das, Kirsten Ambrogi and, above all, Line Lund. Thanks also to our graphic designer Suzy McGrath.

For the book, we would like to thank the V&A Publications team: Mary Butler, Monica Woods, Clare Davis, Geoff Barlow, Nina Jacobson, Frances Ambler, Victoria Standing, Claire Sawford; the editor Mandy Greenfield and the designer Isambard Thomas.

Finally, our deep gratitude is due to Mark Jones, Linda Lloyd Jones and Deborah Swallow for their continued and unfailing support throughout the project.

Anna Jackson and Amin Jaffer
2004

CONTRIBUTORS

ANNA JACKSON is acting Deputy Keeper of the Asian Department of the V&A. One of her main research interests is the cultural relationship between East Asia and the West and she has contributed essays to *Art Nouveau 1890–1914* (2000), *The Victorian Vision: Inventing New Britain* (2001) and *Art Deco, 1910–1939* (2003). She is also responsible for the Museum's collection of Japanese textiles and dress, and is the author of *Japanese Country Textiles* (1997) and *Japanese Textiles in the Victoria and Albert Museum* (2000).

DR AMIN JAFFER is a Curator in the Asian Department of the V&A. He is an expert on furniture in early colonial India and is the author of *Furniture from British India and Ceylon* (2001) and *Luxury Goods from India: The Art of the Indian Cabinet Maker* (2002). He has contributed to *Art Deco, 1910–1939* (2003), *La Route des Indes* (1998) and *The Arts of Kutch* (2000).

GAUVIN ALEXANDER BAILEY is Associate Professor of Renaissance and Baroque Art at Clark University in Worcester, Massachusetts. His areas of interest include Renaissance and Baroque art in Italy, as well as the art of Asia and Latin America. His book, *Art on the Jesuit Missions in Asia and Latin America* (1999), won the Bainton Prize in Art History. Recent publications include *Between Renaissance and Baroque: Jesuit Art in Rome, 1565–1610* (2003) and *The Art of Colonial Latin America, 1492–1820* (2004).

NICK BARNARD is a Curator in the Asian Department of the V&A. His interests include South Asian sculpture, architecture and gardens, and architectural models, and he recently co-curated a small exhibition entitled *Buildings in Miniature*. He is currently working on a book about the V&A's collection of Indian jewellery.

LEONARD BLUSSÉ holds the chair for the History of Asian-European relations at Leiden University and also teaches at the Research School of South-East Asian Studies of Xiamen University in China. He has published widely on topics dealing with the maritime history of East and South-East Asia in early modern times. He is presently involved in various Dutch, English and Chinese source publication projects and is heading the Towards a New Age of Partnership (TANAP) project, which aims at familiarizing Asian historians with the rich archival sources of the Dutch East India Company.

KEE IL CHOI, JR. contributes frequently to the literature of Asian export art and advises clients worldwide in the same field. In 2003, he was awarded a research grant from the American Ceramic Circle and was instrumental in the acquisition by the Rijksmuseum, Amsterdam, of the collection of Andreas Everardus van Braam Houckgeest (1739–1801).

ROSEMARY CRILL is Senior Curator (South Asia) at the V&A. She specializes in Indian textiles and Rajasthani paintings. She is the author of *Indian Ikat Textiles* (1998), *Marwar Painting* (1999) and *Indian Embroidery* (1999), co-author of *Trade, Temple and Court: Indian Textiles from the Tapi Collection* (2002) and *Colours of the Indus: Costume and Textiles of Pakistan* (1997), and has contributed to many other books and journals.

WILLIAM DALRYMPLE is a writer, historian and broadcaster. He is a Fellow of the Royal Society of Literature and of the Royal Asiatic Society. His most recent publication is *White Mughals* (1999), which was awarded the Wolfson Prize for History.

RUPERT FAULKNER is Senior Curator in the V&A's Asian Department. His areas of expertise are Japanese ceramics, *ukiyo-e* woodblock prints and Japanese studio crafts. His publications include *Japanese Studio Crafts: Tradition and the Avant-Garde* (1995), *Hiroshige Fan Prints* (2001) and *Tea: East and West* (2003).

PAULO VARELA GOMES teaches architectural history at the University of Coimbra, Portugal. He has published extensively on sixteenth- and seventeenth-century architectural culture. He was in charge of Fundação Oriente's cultural centre in Goa (India) in 1996–98.

JOHN GUY is Senior Curator for South and South-East Asian Art at the V&A, with responsibility for the sculpture collections. His research interests focus on Indian temple arts and India's cultural relations with South-East Asia. He has worked on a number of archaeological excavations, at both land and maritime sites, and has served as an adviser to UNESCO on historical sites in South-East Asia. He has curated and co-curated a number of exhibitions, including *The Peaceful Liberators. Jain Art from India*; recent publications include *Woven Cargoes. Indian Textiles in the East* (1998).

JAMES L. HEVIA is Director of the International Studies programme in the college of the University of Chicago. His most recent publication is *English Lessons: The Pedagogy of Imperialism in Nineteenth-Century China*.

JULIA HUTT is Curator in the Asian Department of the V&A, with particular responsibility for the collection of Japanese lacquerwork, *inrō* and *netsuke*. She is also tutor and lecturer for the MA in East Asian Art at Sotheby's Institute, London. Her main publications include *Understanding Far Eastern Art* (1987), *Japanese Inrō* (1997) and *Japanese Netsuke* (2003).

GREG IRVINE is Curator in the V&A's Asian Department, where he specializes in Japanese metalwork, particularly arms and armour. He regularly lectures and writes on these subjects and on the philosophies and social background behind the use of weaponry in Japan's historical period. He is the author of *The Japanese Sword, the Soul of the Samurai* (2000).

Annemarie Jordan Gschwend is an Independent Research Scholar. She has a PhD in art history from Brown University where she wrote her dissertation on the patronage, collecting and court of Catherine of Austria (1507–78). She is an expert on the history of collecting and court culture at the Habsburg courts (Austria, Spain, Netherlands and Portugal) in the Renaissance. She is the author of numerous articles, essays in exhibition catalogues and books, including *Retrato de Corte em Portugal. O legado de Antonio Moro, 1552–1572* (1994).

Rose Kerr recently retired as Head of the Far Eastern Section in the V&A's Asian Department. An expert in East Asian art, she lectures and publishes internationally. She is the author of ten books, with two further works to be published in 2004: *Song Dynasty Ceramics* and *Ceramic Technology* in the series *Science and Civilization of China.*

J.P. Losty is Head of the Prints, Drawings and Photographs Section in the Asia Pacific and Africa Collections of the British Library. He has published widely on many aspects of painting in India, and is currently working on a new edition of the journal of William Daniell in India.

Sally North is a graduate of SOAS and did her doctoral research (on the architecture and culture of Lucknow) at the London Institute. Her current post is Assistant Curator at the RIBA Drawings Collection. She has a particular interest in the interaction of cultures East and West and how that is expressed in artefacts and the built environment.

Catherine Pagani is Professor of Asian Art History at the University of Alabama. Her research has focused on cross-cultural influences in the arts and sciences between China and Europe in the seventeenth and eighteenth centuries. She is the author of *Eastern Magnificence and European Ingenuity: Clocks of Late Imperial China* (2001).

Steven Parissien is Dean of Arts and Professor of Architectural History at the University of Plymouth. He has written extensively on architectural history, conservation and cultural history; his most recent book, *George IV: The Grand Entertainment*, was published in 2001.

Graham Parlett is Curator in the V&A's Asian Department. He has lectured on Company painting and is currently engaged on a catalogue of pictures by British artists who worked in South Asia. He is also a musicologist and author of *A Catalogue of the Works of Sir Arnold Bax* (1999).

William R. Sargent is curator of Asian Export Art at the Peabody Essex Museum, Salem. He has been with the collection for more than 25 years, has lectured extensively on all aspects of Asian trade arts, and is the author of *The Copeland Collection: Chinese and Japanese Ceramic Figures* and *Views of the Pearl River Delta: Macau, Canton and Hong Kong.*

Timon Screech is Reader in the History of Japanese Art at SOAS, University of London. He is author of some half-dozen books on Edo art, including *Sex and the Floating World* and *The Shogun's Painted Culture.*

Susan Stronge is a Senior Curator in the Asian Department of the V&A, specializing in the courtly arts of North India. Her most recent book, *Painting for the Mughal Emperor: The Art of the Book 1560–1660*, is a survey of the V&A's renowned collection.

Miyoshi Tadayoshi is a specialist in historical geography, specifically the history of cartography. He is currently Chief Curator of the Kobe City Kuboso Memorial Museum of Art. Recent publications include *Illustrated World Old Map Collection* (1999) and *Illustrated Japanese Old Map Collection* (2004).

Ming Wilson is Senior Curator (China) in the Asian Department at the V&A, where she is responsible for the collections of Chinese jades, carvings and graphic art. She is the author of *Rare Marks on Chinese Ceramics* (1998) and *Chinese Jades* (2004); co-editor of *Europe Studies China* (1995) and *Souvenir from Canton, Chinese Export Paintings from the V&A* (2003).

David Woodward is Arthur H. Robinson Professor Emeritus of Geography at the University of Wisconsin, Madison, and editor of the multi-volume *History of Cartography* (1987–). His interests are in medieval and Renaissance cartography and the philosophy of maps. Published works include *Five Centuries of Map Printing* (1975), *The All-American Map* (1977) and *Maps as Prints in the Italian Renaissance* (1995).

I

INTRODUCTION: THE MEETING OF ASIA AND EUROPE 1500–1800

Anna Jackson & Amin Jaffer

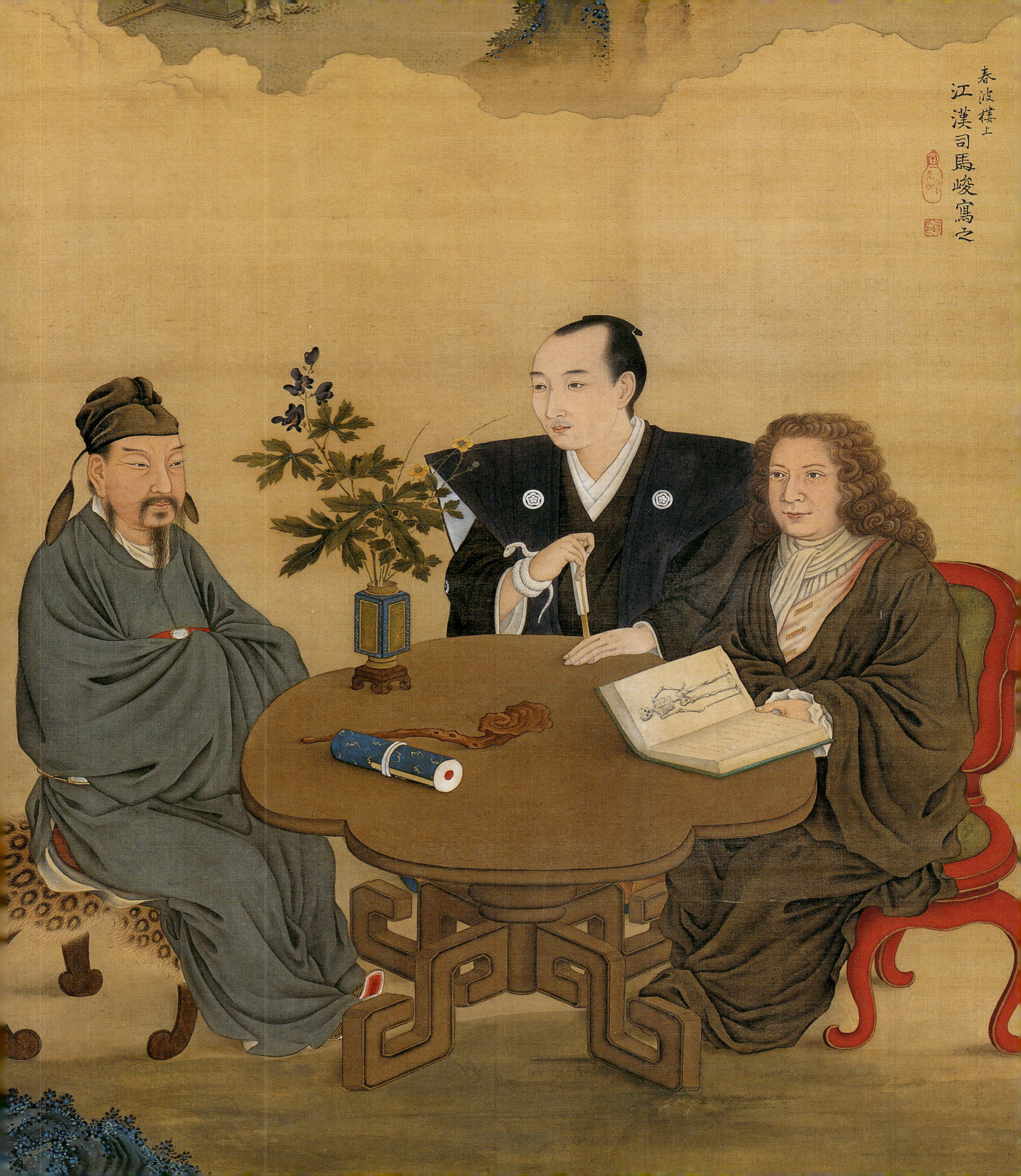
春波樓上
江漢司馬峻寫之

Detail of 1.6 previous page

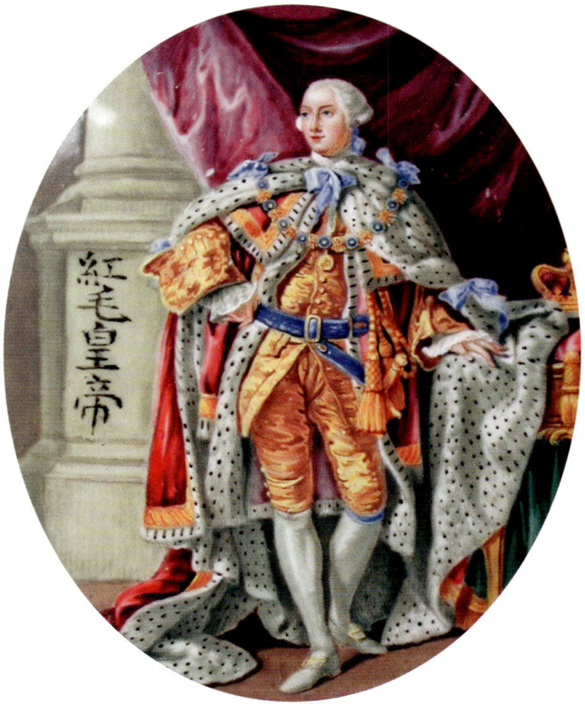

1.1
George III
Miniature portrait, after the painting by Allan Ramsay

Inscribed in Chinese, 'Red-haired Emperor'
Enamel on copper
England, late 18th century

Nour Foundation, London

The Chinese inscription on this enamel is something of a mystery. It appears to have been written under the glaze, suggesting that the piece was made specifically for a Chinese reader, possibly as a diplomatic gift presented at the time of the Macartney mission of 1793.

1.2 below
Joseph Collet
Amoy Chinqua

Painted unfired clay on bamboo armature
China (Canton), 1716

National Portrait Gallery, London

Collet (1673–1725) was not unique in commissioning a portrait of himself from a 'face modeller' at Canton. He sent this likeness to his daughter in 1716, describing it as 'a sort of Picture or Image of my Self. The lineaments and the Features are Esteem'd very just but the complexion is not quite so well hit; the proportion of my body and my habit is very exact.'

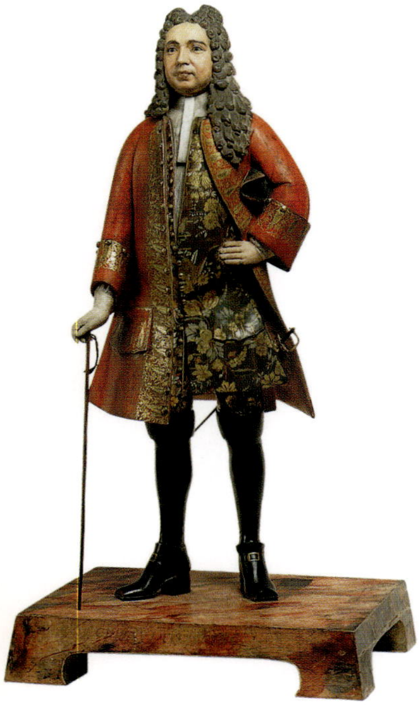

THE FINAL YEARS of the fifteenth century heralded a new era in the relationship between Asia and Europe. In May 1498 the Portuguese explorer Vasco da Gama landed on the west coast of India near Calicut. His arrival established for the first time direct contact between Europe and maritime Asia, ushering in a period of commercial, cultural, artistic and technological exchange. The long voyage from Lisbon had taken him around the Cape of Good Hope and up the east coast of Africa, where, with good fortune, he was able to employ a Gujarati navigator who led his ships to India with the aid of the monsoon winds. The first man ashore was not da Gama himself, but a Portuguese *degredado* (convict-exile) whose role was precisely to bear the risk in such an encounter with the unknown. The first person he met was not an Indian, but a Tunisian Muslim who confronted him, speaking Castilian or Genoese. The convict apparently replied with the now famous words: '*Vimos buscar christãos e especiaria*' – 'We come in search of Christians and spices.'

The Portuguese quest to find the sea route to the Indies was indeed both a religious and a commercial enterprise. Along with the neighbouring kingdoms of Castile and Aragon, Portugal had gradually and systematically repulsed Muslims from the Iberian peninsula. The *Reconquista*, or expulsion of the infidel, was still central to the Portuguese psyche when in 1453 the Turks captured Constantinople, exposing the eastern flank of Christendom and imposing a commercial barrier to the trade in Asian goods. These goods, particularly spices, had previously been brought to Europe through the Red Sea and the Persian Gulf to the Levant, from where they were carried by European traders to the ports of the Mediterranean, chiefly Venice, and then onwards throughout Europe. Ottoman hegemony over the eastern Mediterranean now rendered these shipping lanes virtually impassable. The supply of Asian goods was no longer reliable and those goods that did reach Europe were considerably more expensive. A new route to the Indies was needed.

It was not only spices that were sought after, but also a wide variety of luxury goods – silk, porcelain, precious stones, aromatic woods and such exotic products as ambergris – much prized by European elites. Great wealth seemed assured to the country that could establish direct access to these legendary riches. Even in Antiquity, Europe looked with admiration towards the wondrous civilizations of Asia, but since the time of Alexander the Great had scarcely any knowledge of them. Until the Mongol conquests in the thirteenth century opened the overland routes to the East, Asia remained an almost entirely unknown place of which fantastic tales were told, of strange and monstrous beasts and kingdoms of unimaginable wealth and power. From the thirteenth century onwards the accounts of diplomats and travellers who had actually experienced the courts and cities of the East fired the European imagination. It must be remembered that in 1492 when Columbus set sail, his aim was to find Asia. But the successful discovery of a sea route there was achieved by the Portuguese, who, squeezed between a newly united Spain and the Atlantic, and with a long tradition of maritime enterprise, looked to the ocean for opportunities of enrichment and empire. Supported by royal patronage from the early fifteenth century, Portuguese navigators sailed further and further down the coast of Africa, colonizing Madeira and the Azores en route and returning with much-prized gold and ivory. These voyages were greatly facilitated by important advances made during the fifteenth century in navigational skills, shipbuilding and naval gunnery. Vasco da Gama completed the achievements of his predecessors by making the final crossing from East Africa to the Malabar coast of India.

The story of Vasco da Gama's arrival at Calicut reveals that although he and his crew may have been physically equipped to voyage successfully to Asia, mentally they were totally unprepared for the experience that awaited them. When his attempts to articulate his objectives to local rulers failed – partly due to his inability to understand Asian conventions for conducting business and diplomacy – da Gama resorted to violence and the use of superior firepower. Successive Portuguese explorers, administrators, traders and missionaries arrived in Asia with a firmer grasp of how to negotiate successfully with local princes and merchants alike. However, it was Portuguese military superiority and the ability to control the sea lanes that at first underpinned their success in establishing a presence in Asia. Within 60 years the Portuguese had developed an empire consisting of fortified coastal settlements and trading posts, which secured the passage of their merchandise from and between Nagasaki and Macao in East Asia, Malacca (Melaka) on the Malay Peninsula, the Spice Islands of Banda and the Moluccas in South-East Asia, Hooghly (Hugli), Cochin and Goa in India, Hormuz in the Persian Gulf, Mombasa on the east coast of Africa and back to Lisbon.

The sacks of spices and exotica which the Portuguese were able to acquire in Asia at local market prices yielded handsome returns in Europe. In Asia the Portuguese also discovered a highly evolved network of trade and swiftly realized that, by tapping into it, substantial profits could be made. By operating a crown monopoly, Manuel I of Portugal, 'the grocer king' as François Ier of France unkindly dubbed him, became the richest monarch in Europe. However, Portugal's trade with the East

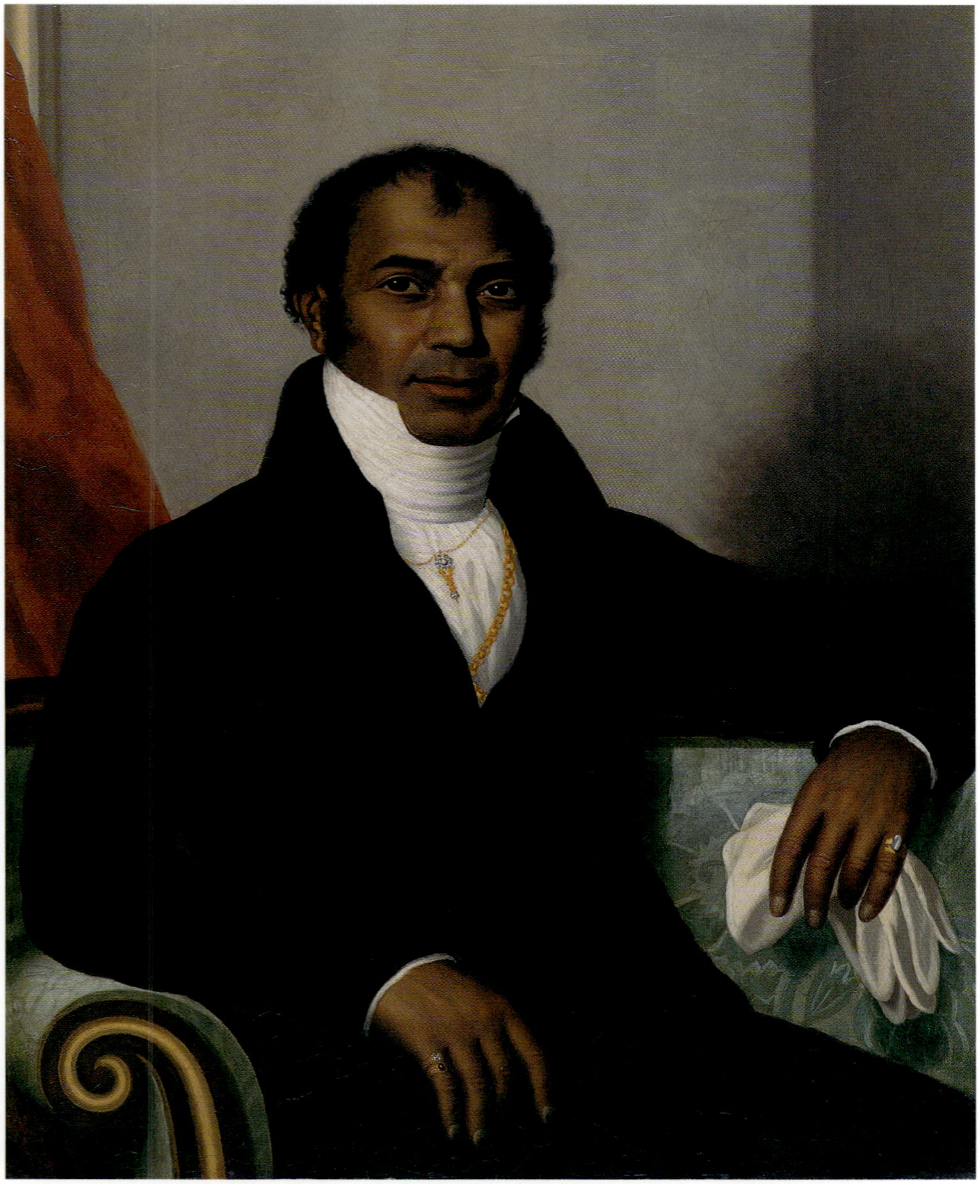

1.3
Sake Dean Mohamed
Thomas Baynes

Oil on canvas
England, early 19th century

Brighton Museums and Art Gallery

Sake Dean Mohamed served in the Bengal Army before leaving India for Cork, Ireland in 1782. In 1793 he published *Travels of Dean Mohomet* ..., becoming the first Indian to write a book in English. He and his Irish wife moved to London and in 1810 opened England's first Indian restaurant, the Hindoostanee Coffee House. They later moved to Brighton where Sake Dean became the famed proprietor of Mahomed's Baths.

was fundamentally imbalanced because the goods they brought from Europe had little appeal in Asian markets. One of the few commodities that Asian merchants were prepared to accept was silver. Vast supplies of the metal became available following the Spanish conquest of the New World and the discovery of rich mines in Mexico and Peru. Silver specie flooded into Europe and triggered rapid inflation. The newly mined precious metal also found its way from Europe to the Asian commodity markets, where it underpinned the acquisition of local goods. Much of the silver that financed the Asian trade arrived directly from the New World in galleons that traversed the Pacific from Acapulco in Mexico to Manila, capital of the Spanish colony of the Philippines. Here it was exchanged for Chinese silk and porcelain shipped from Macao, and smaller quantities of Indonesian spices and Indian textiles. In this way Spanish-American silver was redistributed throughout Asia. This international flow of commodities and currency marks the early development of a global economy in which the markets of Asia, the Americas and Europe were inextricably linked.

By the close of the sixteenth century it was apparent that Portugal did not possess the resources necessary to adequately equip, finance and police its far-flung empire and trade network. By the beginning of the next century the Portuguese royal monopoly over Asian trade had been destroyed by competition from the newly chartered Dutch and English East India Companies. These leaner organizations, directed by bodies of experienced businessmen driven purely by profit and unencumbered by missionary zeal for proselytization, threatened Portuguese power in the East by providing Asian merchants and princes with alternative trading and political partners. In 1638 the Dutch ousted the Portuguese from Ceylon and in 1641 from Malacca. In 1622 English merchants allied with the Persians to throw the Portuguese out of Hormuz, and in 1639 they were expelled from Japan, thus losing their profitable trade. Thereafter the Japanese restricted their trade with Europe to the Dutch. By the late seventeenth century the Portuguese had been driven out of all their trading settlements in Asia except Goa, Timor and Macao and henceforth confined their imperial ambitions chiefly to developing their

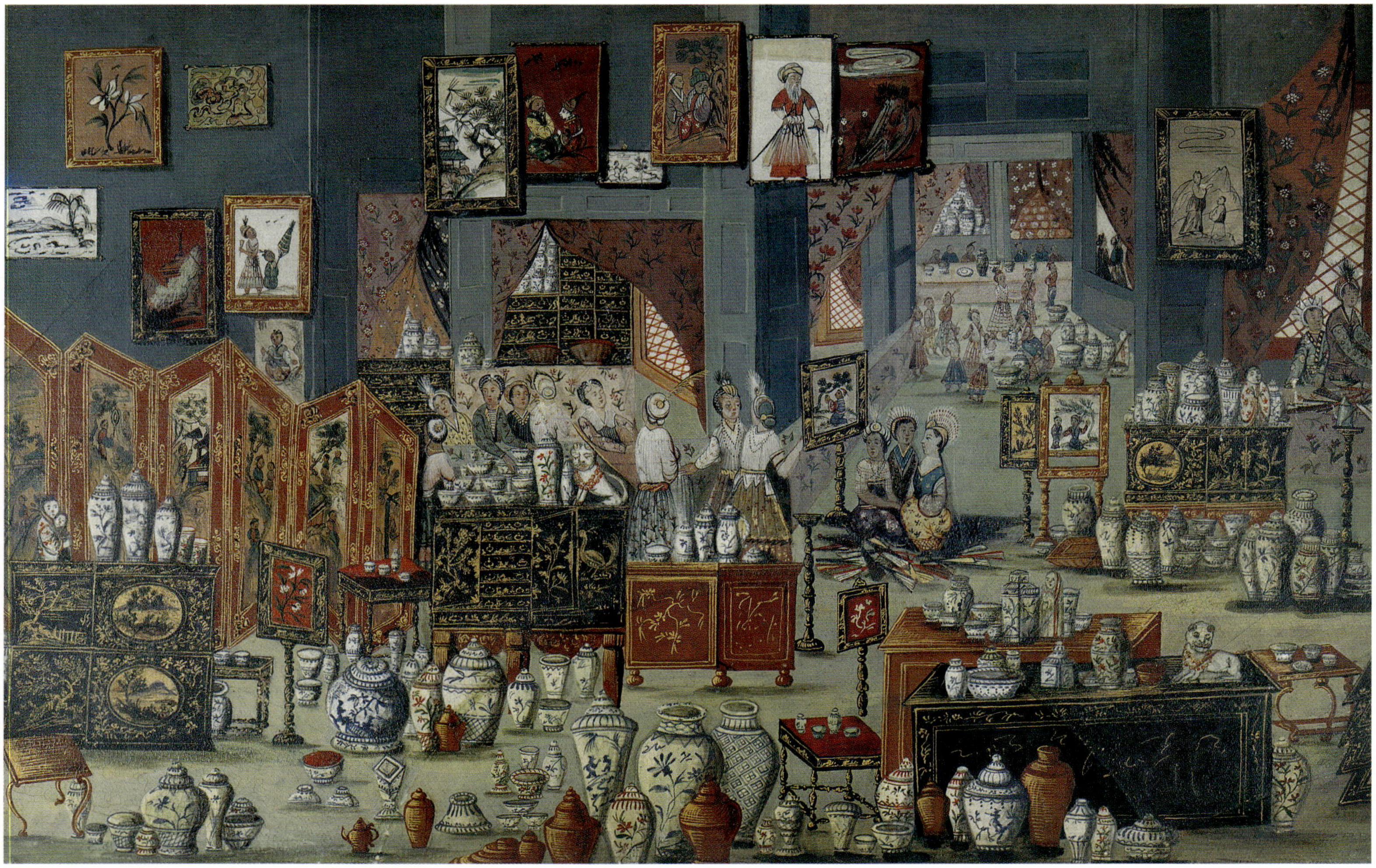

1.4
Design for a fan

Oil on board
Europe, c.1700
V&A: P.35–1926

This fanciful depiction seems to be of a merchant's shop in South or East Asia. While the furniture and porcelain are painted with reasonable accuracy and suggest a familiarity with such goods, the portrayal of the figures is drawn more from the imagination and seems to derive from prints or paintings of Turkish life.

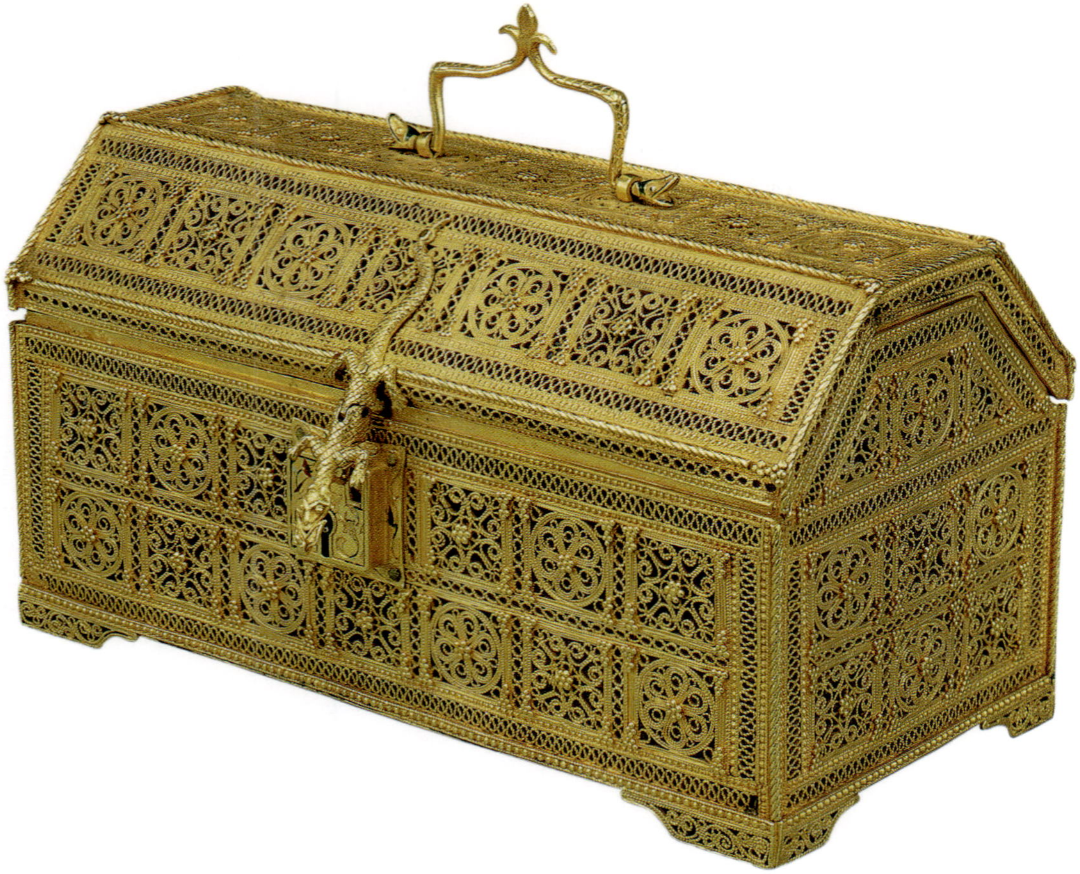

1.5
Casket

Gold filigree
India (Goa), 1575–1600

Museu Nacional de Arte Antiga, Lisbon

The Portuguese form of this casket reveals how swiftly Indian craftsmen were able to adapt their skills to new markets. The floral designs in the panels are typical of western Indian decorative traditions.

1.6
A Meeting of Japan, China and the West
Attributed to Shiba Kōkan

Hanging scroll; ink, colours and gold on silk
Japan, late 18th century

Ruth & Sherman Lee Institute for Japanese Art at the Clark Center, Hanford, CA

This painting depicts three men of learning from Japan, China and Europe discussing scientific matters, while behind them three groups, again Japanese, Chinese and European, use different methods to quell a fire. The artist, probably Shiba Kōkan, the father of western-style painting in Japan, employed a combination of Japanese and European styles to produce this unique image of a cultural and technological encounter.

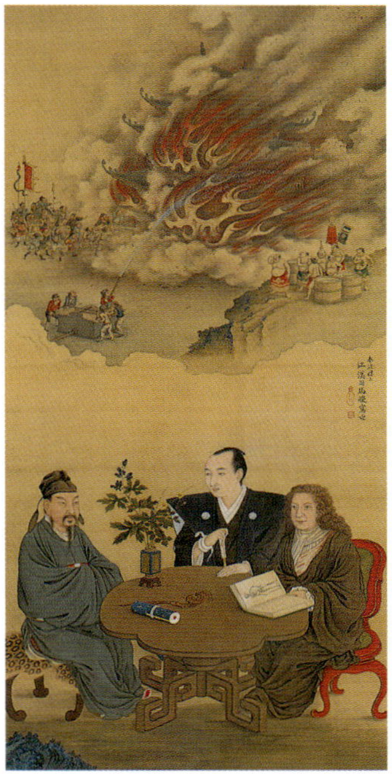

interests in Brazil and their African colonies. With the demise of Portuguese authority, the Dutch Verenigde Oost-Indische Compagnie (VOC) and English East India Company continued to vie with one another for control of Asian trade, the former eventually establishing authority over the Indonesian archipelago with its base at Batavia; and the latter dominating trade with India. Other European powers, among them the French, Swedes and Danes, also entered the scramble for power in the Indian Ocean and Indonesia, but were ultimately confined to their own small trading settlements.

At the time of da Gama's voyage the trading communities of some Asian ports already included small numbers of European merchants from the Mediterranean basin, typically they had arrived there after arduous journeys – sometimes of many years – during which they absorbed something of the successive cultures they encountered, even shedding certain aspects of their European identity as they travelled further.

The arrival of the Portuguese, and later of the Dutch and British, directly by ship made for a rather different encounter. On their voyages their identity remained undiluted; the context and physical environment in which they travelled to Asia was wholly European. The difference between their appearance and manner and those of the people they encountered was therefore immediate and marked, and it is tempting to suppose that these meetings led inevitably to a clash of cultures. However, the notion of a simple dichotomy between East and West is misleading. Maritime Asia was as vast as it was varied, and the response to the European arrival was correspondingly diverse. Such a model also belies the complexities and subtleties of the subsequent period of encounter and exchange. The European experience in Asia was thus not a uniform one.

This book, and the exhibition that it accompanies, addresses the varied nature of these encounters, exploring from a broad perspective the way in which Asians and Europeans responded to one another. The book is in three sections. The first section, *Discoveries*, examines how in the European mind the West 'discovered' Asia. It opens with a study of the cartographic world view from both European and Asian perspectives, and explores how the

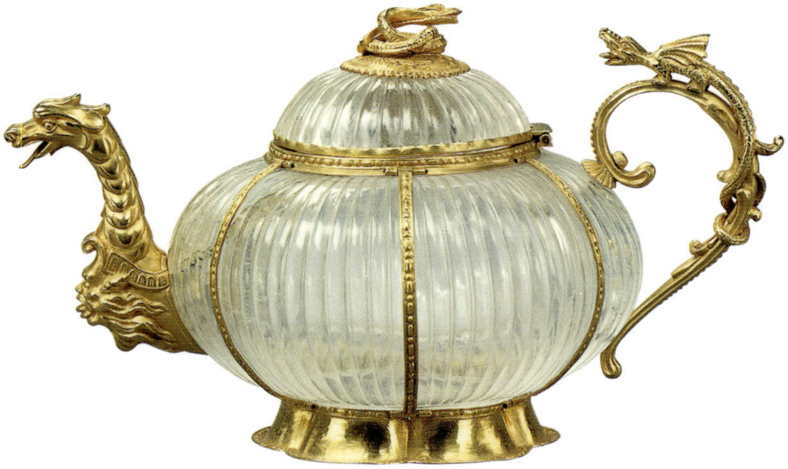

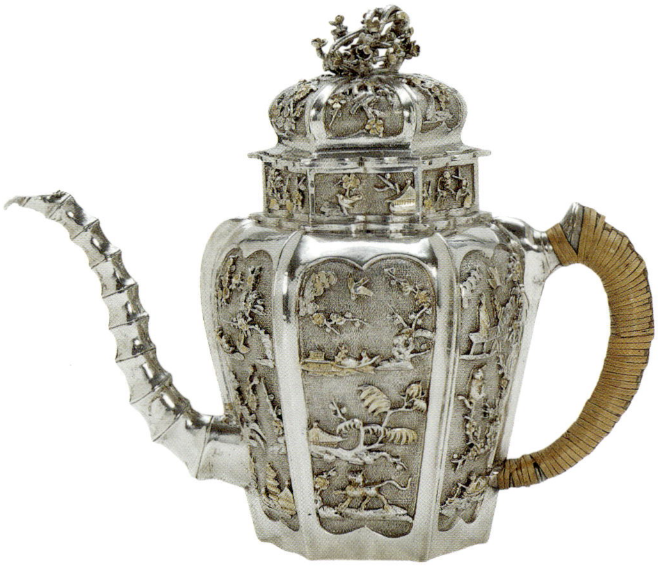

1.7 and 1.8
Teapots

left: Composed of a bowl and cover, later mounted with a spout and handle
Rock crystal, with gold mounts
Mughal India, *c.*1700; mounts: Germany (Dresden), *c.*1720

Metropolitan Museum of Art, New York

right: Composed of a tea canister later mounted with a spout and handle; Silver, partly gilt, with silver-gilt spout and handle
China, 1680; mounts: England, *c.*1750

V&A: M.69–1955

After arriving in Europe, this Mughal covered bowl and Chinese tea canister were transformed into teapots with the addition of mounts. It was perhaps thought that the eastern origin of these pieces rendered them particularly suited to the consumption of tea. Interestingly, the mounts are in a chinoiserie style.

Asian exotica that arrived in Europe before and immediately after the Discoveries fuelled the desire to know the East and its products. The section closes with a revealing look at the sophisticated nature of intra-Asian trade and consumption at the time that the first Europeans arrived in the East. The human dimension of the story is explored in the second section, *Encounters*, which looks at the face-to-face meeting of Asians and Europeans in different spheres: diplomacy, religion and personal life, as well as the physical spaces in which these encounters occurred. Although some Asians did travel to Europe (plate 1.3), the encounters took place almost exclusively in Asia, and in this section the impact which the strangers from the West had on the Asian visual landscape is also explored. The curiosity about and appeal of the exotic are discussed in more detail in the final section, *Exchanges*, which examines the material dimension of the relationship, looking at the mechanism that developed in Asia for producing western-style goods specifically for export (plate 1.4) and at the reverse process, the European goods that were desirable in Asian markets and their impact there. The elaboration and reconfiguration of goods from one culture by another is a further theme that is explored (plates 1.7–9). The final essays address the most potent manifestation of the mutual fascination experienced by Asia and Europe: the creation of fantasies of the other (plates 1.10–11, 1.14–15).

An underlying theme of the book is that both the East and the West considered each other exotic and that this appeal shaped the culture of both. In this post-colonial era the word 'exotic' is sometimes considered a pejorative one, part of the discourse of colonial appropriation and cultural plunder. The term derives from the Greek *exotikos*, literally 'from the outside'. Its first usage in English was by Ben Jonson, who employed it to mean alien or foreign. In *Cynthia's Revels* of 1601 he referred to the gift of 'some parcels of French, or some pretty Commodity of Italian to commence with, if you would be exotick and exquisite'.[1] By the eighteenth century the meaning of the word had broadened to also suggest something outlandish, or something whose appeal lay in being strange. Although the word 'exotic' had no direct translation in South and East Asian languages in the period 1500–1800, the terms used to describe foreigners (*firingi, videshi, yangren, nambanjin*) – be they Europeans or other Asians – often signified more than simply the people themselves.

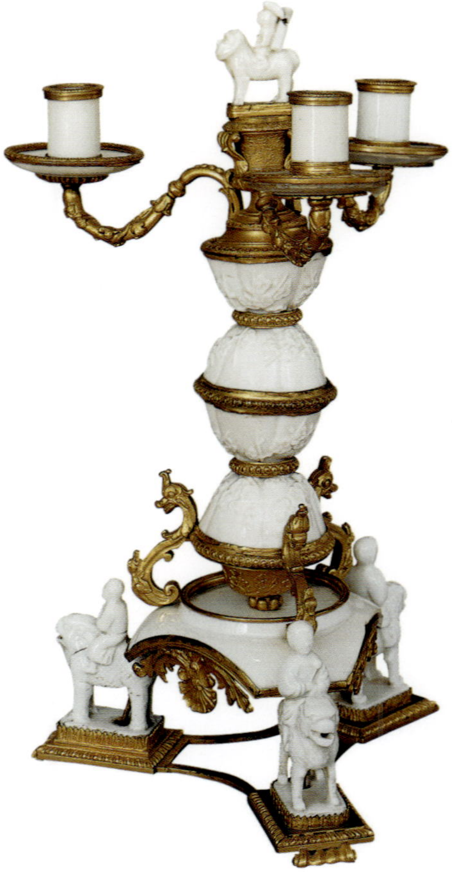

1.9
Candelabrum (one of a pair)

Composed of wine cups and whistles, mounted with saucers and candle cups
Wine cups and whistles: porcelain with a white glaze, China (Dehua), 1690–1710; saucers and candle cups: soft paste porcelain, mounts: gilt-bronze, France 18th century

Peabody Essex Museum, Salem

Here commonplace pieces of Chinese and French porcelain have been ingeniously transformed to create a flamboyant pair of candelabra.

1.10 right
Panel of wallpaper

France, designed *c.* 1806, printed *c.* 1850

Private collection, London

In devising its panoramic wallpaper *L'Indoustan*, French wallpaper-makers Zuber drew freely from the Daniells' picturesque views of India. The design of this panel marries the great Nandi from the Brihadisvara Temple at Tanjore with a section of the famous frieze *The Descent of the Ganges* at Mamallapuram.

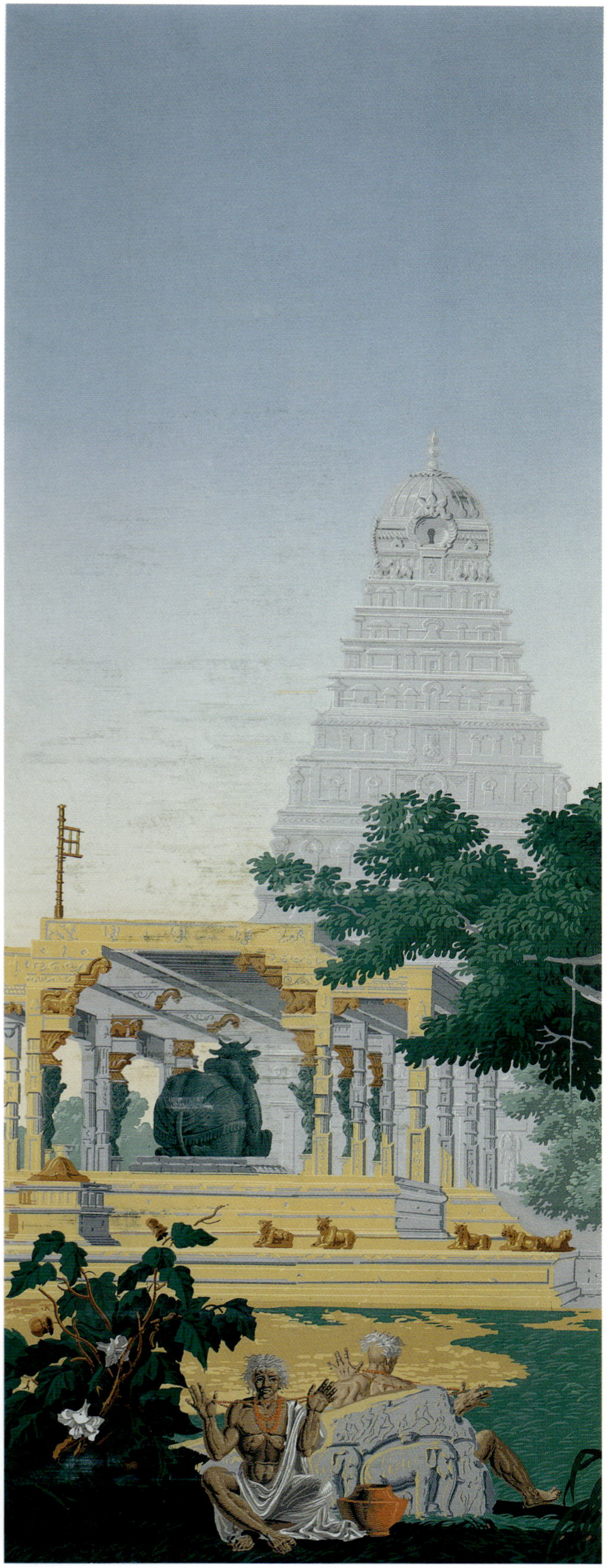

1.11 below
The Great Bull, an Hindoo Idol at Tanjore
Thomas and William Daniell

Aquatint on paper
England, 1798, based on sketches made in India in 1792

V&A: E.909–1902

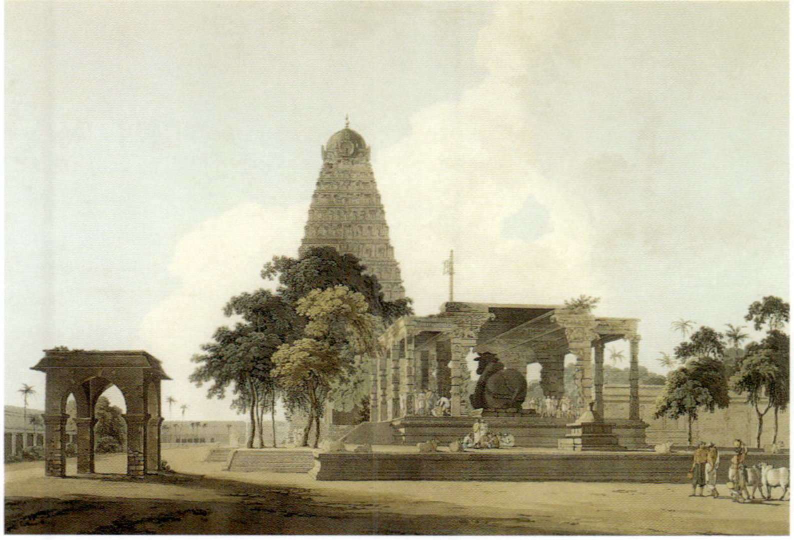

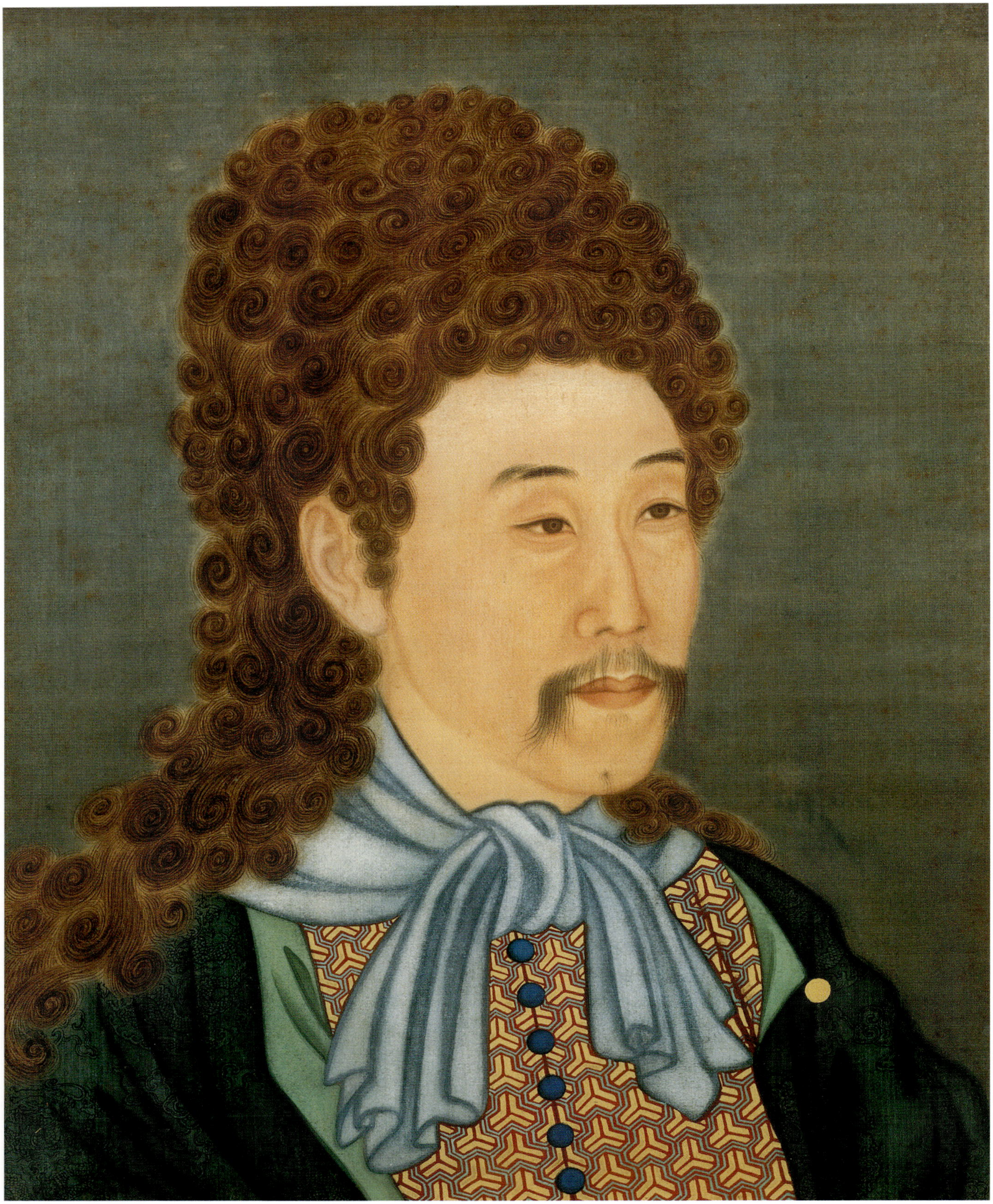

It is interesting to draw parallels between the way in which the concept of the exotic functioned in Asia and in Europe during this period. The new and the different had a genuine appeal in both places; the goods exchanged between East and West – whether tea and cotton or maps and guns – brought about real social, economic and political changes; but the exotic could also be something that was simply enjoyable, wondrous, fashionable or amusing that lent lustre and interest to the domestic scene without being a threat. However, by appropriating the exotic, by extracting and consuming certain elements of it, one could claim emblematic power over the other. The Yongzheng emperor of China did not have himself depicted in European dress because he wanted to be European, or indeed merely for fun, but to signify China's universal sovereignty (plate 1.12). Conversely, Occidentalism or Orientalism could be employed to challenge authority, and could represent a counter-culture by which it was possible to question one's own accepted norms: Enlightenment scholars used the East, specifically China, as a mirror to hold up to western values and criticize them, while in Japan, for example, *Rangaku* (Dutch studies) represented an alternative to dominant intellectual practices derived from China. No less importantly, exoticism offered escape from normality, an opportunity to embrace other modes of being and behaviour and to transgress the boundaries of native and foreign, of reality and fantasy.

Indeed, what is fascinating about this period is that it was characterized by fluidity and hybridity, not by dichotomy. In eighteenth-century Japan, for example, there evolved both a popular and a scholarly interest in Europe, although technically the country was 'closed' to outside influence. Although traditionally seen as uninterested in the West, China adopted elements of European scientific learning, inviting Jesuit scholars to reform the calendar along western lines as early as the 1640s. However, East Asian powers certainly controlled their relationship with foreigners carefully. In the Indian subcontinent and Indonesian archipelago, regions that had historically absorbed a succession of invaders, Europeans were much more integrated and at some places a hybrid society evolved. The period is not marked by overriding feelings of cultural prejudice. Although Europeans regarded Asians as 'heathens' or 'infidels', this did not colour their perception of all aspects of Asian culture; indeed, in some periods Europeans showed a marked interest and appreciation of Asian ideologies (plate 1.16). Likewise in the Asian mind, Europeans were often seen as inferior and as barbarians but this did not necessarily detract from Asian interest in western technology.

In the period from 1500 to 1800 Asians and Europeans often met as equals (plate 1.6). Indeed, at centres of dominance such as Ming and Qing China, Tokugawa Japan and Mughal India, the encounter took place on Asian terms. It was not

1.12 opposite
The Yongzheng Emperor in European Dress

Ink and colour on silk
China (Qing court), Yongzheng period (1724–35)

Palace Museum, Beijing

By commissioning a portrait in western costume, the Yongzheng Emperor was reinforcing the imperial image of himself as the ruler of 'all under heaven'.

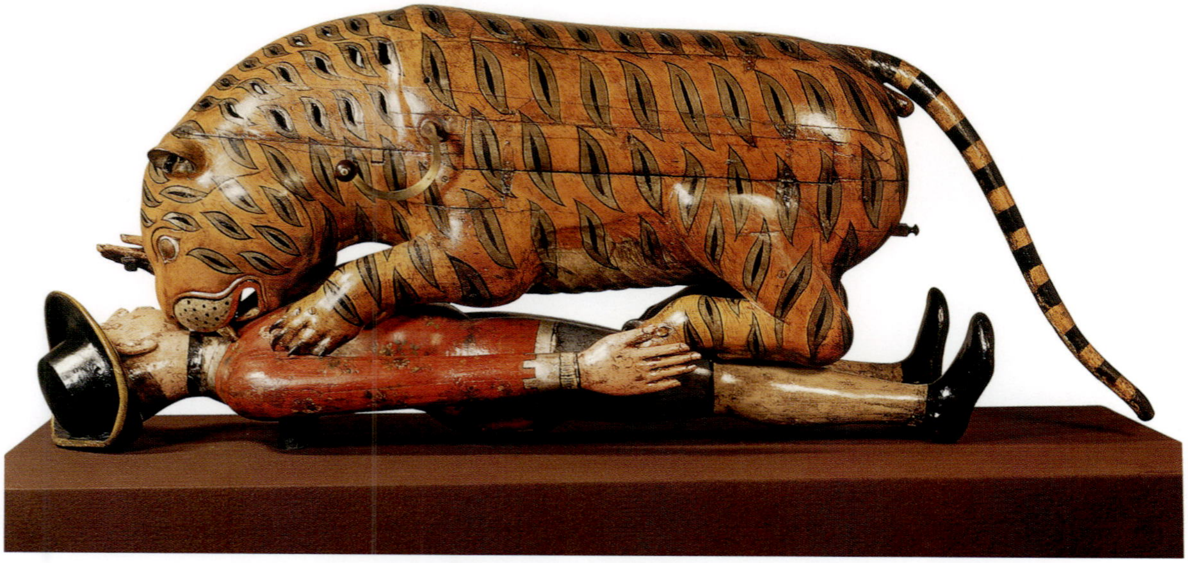

1.13
Tippoo's Tiger

Automaton with mechanical organ; wood, painted; with metal and ivory fixtures
India (Mysore), *c.* 1795

V&A: 2545 (IS)

This extraordinary model of a tiger devouring a European reflects both Tipu Sultan's opposition to the British and his fascination with western technology. The tiger houses an organ, possibly the work of a Frenchman in Tipu's service, which simulates its roar as well as the shrieks of the victim. Taken at the fall of Seringapatam the tiger was displayed in the museum of the East India Company.

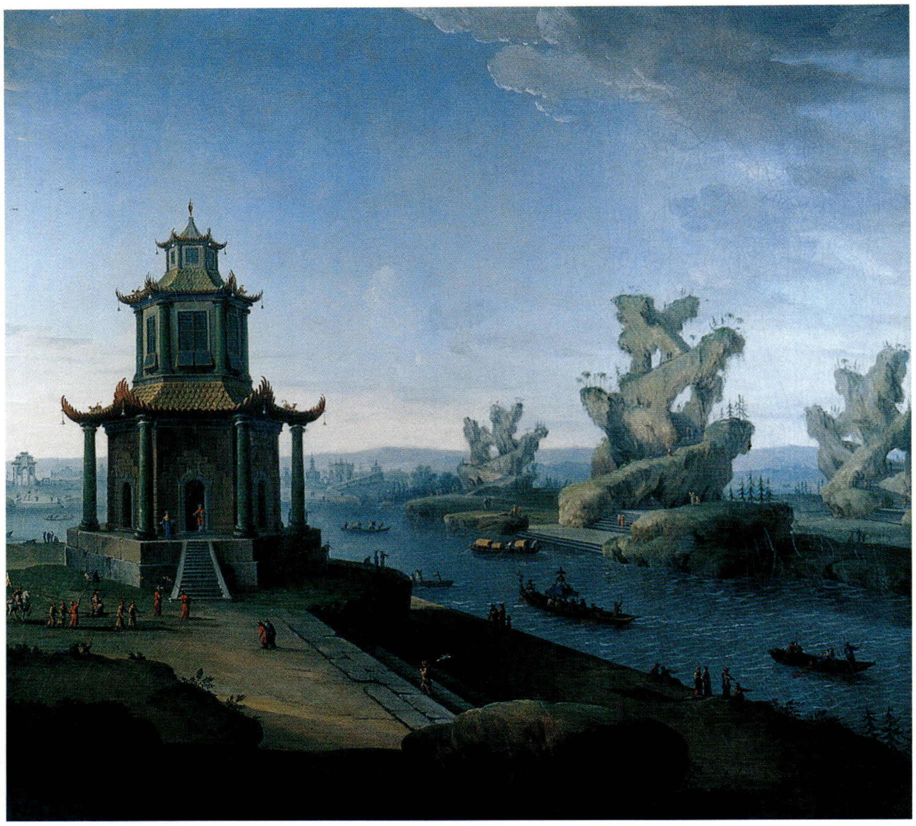

1.14
A Capriccio of Chinese Landscape
Antonio Joli

Oil on canvas
Possibly England, 1744–48

Private collection, Paris

This fantastic scene of China is drawn from two prints in J.B. Fischer von Erlach's *A plan of civil and historical architecture in the representation of the most noted buildings of foreign nations*…vol. 111, published in Leipzig in 1725. The marriage of unusual architecture and strange landscape reinforced the idea of China as an exotic other world.

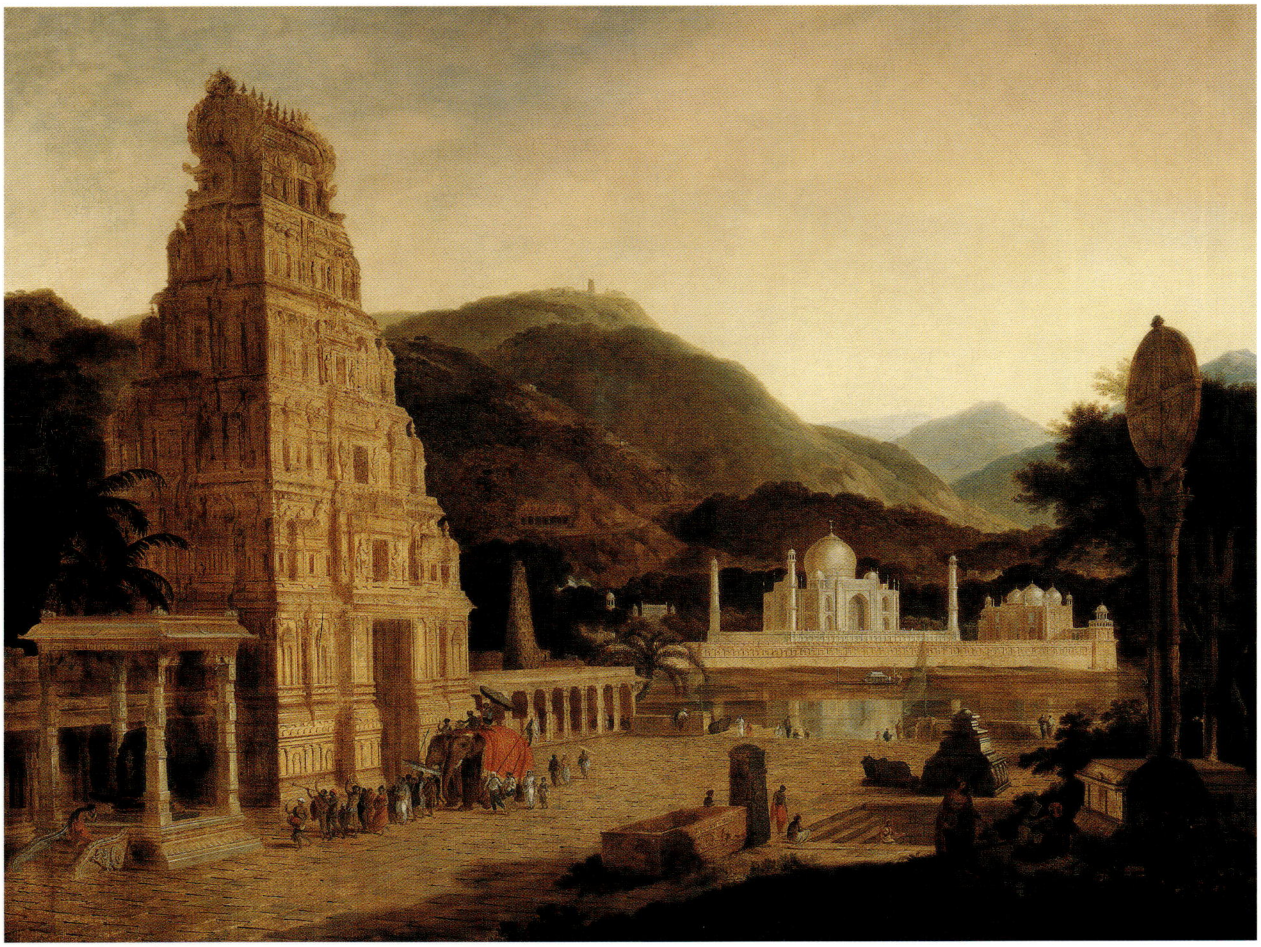

1.15
Large composition of architecture representing some of the most celebrated Hindoo and Moorish buildings in India
Thomas Daniell

Oil on canvas
England, *c.*1799

Private collection, England

Painted for the Indian Drawing Room of Thomas Hope's celebrated Duchess Street mansion, this canvas brings together masterpieces of Indian architecture. The juxtaposition of buildings of different styles and periods echoes the contemporary taste for classical capriccios and illustrates that Europeans of the period often regarded the architectural heritage of India as equal to their own.

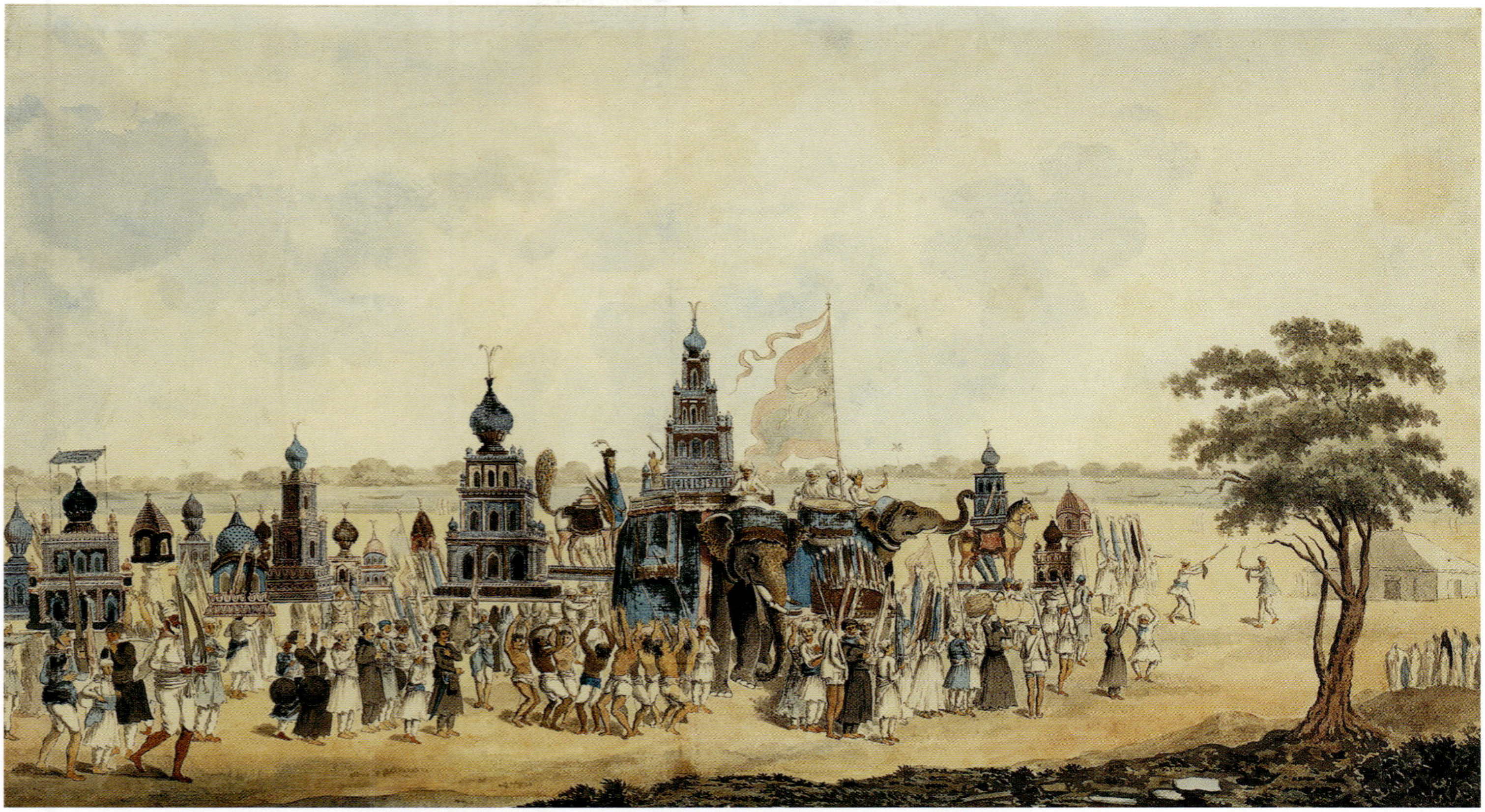

always a positive one, however; it was often marred by greed, misunderstanding and violence. At centres of dependence, such as the coastal kingdoms of south India and the islands of the Indonesian archipelago, Europeans were able to dictate terms, sometimes using their superior firepower to ensure that their goals were achieved. In 1621, for example, 15,000 people in the Banda Islands, then the only known source in the world of nutmeg and mace, were slaughtered by the VOC for failing to comply with the monopolistic contract that the Dutch had imposed on them.

In the late eighteenth century any uncertainty that may have existed as to the position of Europeans in began to evaporate. The British solution to the problem of how to redress the trade imbalance with China was to flood the Middle Kingdom with Indian opium, inflicting damage on both the economy of the country and the health of its people. The tensions that this inevitably created were to lead to the Opium Wars of the nineteenth century, which sealed western economic dominance of East Asia. In India the collapse of the Mughal empire created a power vacuum that was filled by the East India Company, whose administrative and military machine reshaped the subcontinent to suit British priorities. The irony of Tipu Sultan's automaton of an Indian tiger mauling a prone European is that within a few years of its manufacture it was seized by British forces as a trophy of war (plate 1.13). With Tipu Sultan's defeat and death in 1799 came the transformation of the character of the European presence in Asia and a solidifying of hitherto fluid boundaries between different cultures. Hereafter the European attitude towards Asians was inevitably coloured by their perceived position of superiority and by more rigid assumptions of 'East' and 'West'.

1.16
The Muharram Procession

Opaque watercolour on paper
India (Murshidabad), 1795–1805

V&A: IS 11 (12)–1887

This watercolour by an Indian artist for a European patron is probably based on a lost oil by George Farrington (1752–88), who lived at Murshidabad, where he developed a deep interest in portraying religious rites and ceremonies of Hindu and Muslim communities.

PART ONE

Discoveries

2

MAPPING THE WORLD

David Woodward

midiũ duę tenent: Europa & africa:

t

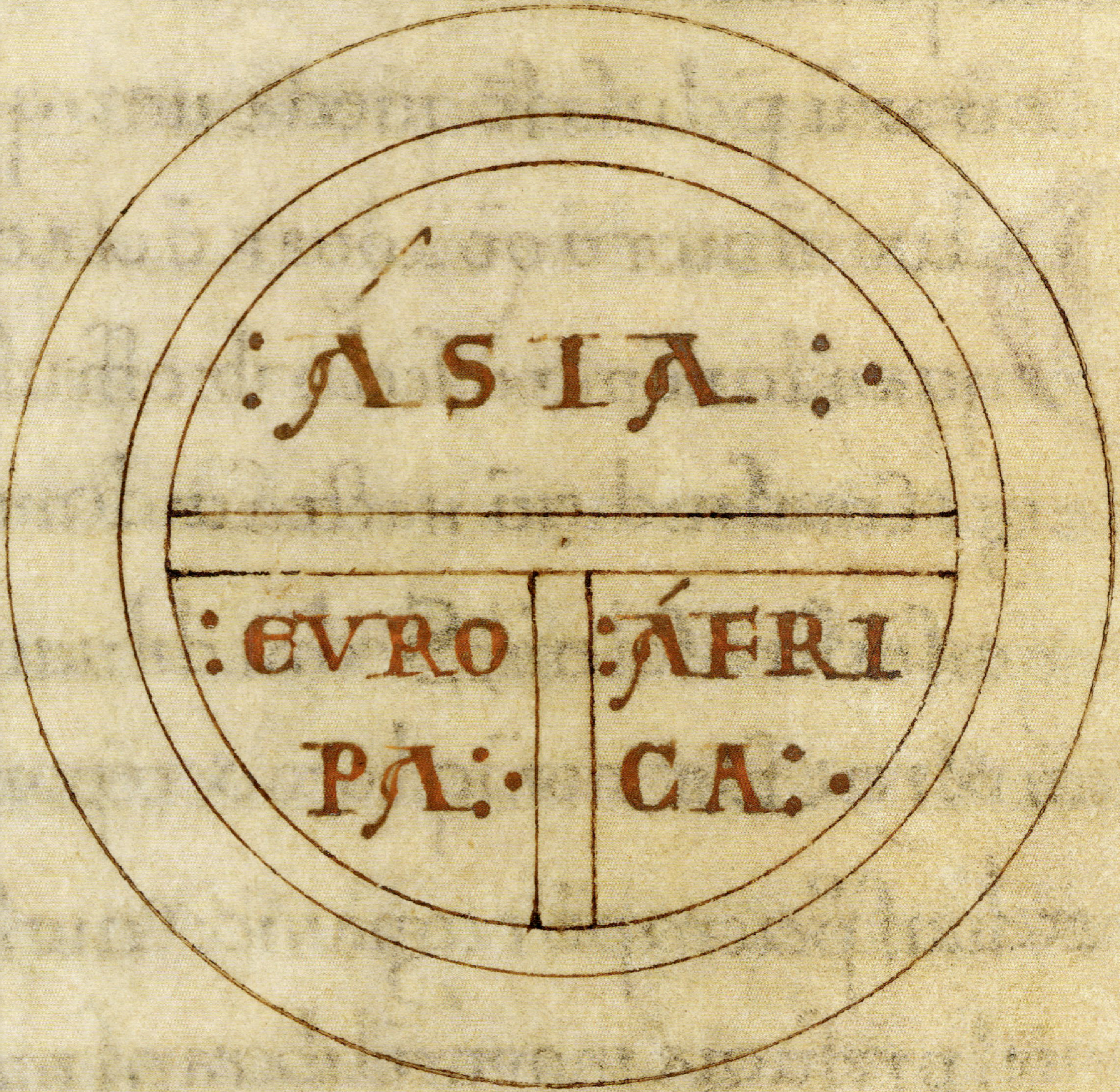

:

c

u

es:

so: Paradysus ÷ locus in orientis partib:

aice eden dr: qd in nr̃am linguã delicię

2.1 previous page
T-O map (detail)
Ink and tempera on vellum
England, ate 13th century
British Library, London

Maps provide a window on the world, but the shape and position of the window and the view that it provides are chosen by the mapmaker. Although it is commonly assumed that maps are objective measured images of the world, this is only partly true. Different cultures map the world in different ways. The purpose of this essay is to review how – in the fifteenth to the seventeenth centuries – Europe mapped Asia, Asia mapped Europe, and the ideas of both became modified as mutual geographical knowledge increased.

EUROPEAN MAPPING OF ASIA AND THE WORLD

Uniting cultures as diverse as those in China, Thailand, Sri Lanka, Turkey and Arabia under the guise of a homogeneous land-mass called 'Asia' has led to many misconceptions and prejudices. It is no wonder that, since the time of Herodotus (?484–25 BC) historians have debated where the boundaries between Europe, Africa and Asia should be drawn.[1] In the Greco-Roman world, the boundary between Europe and Asia was regarded as the Don River, while that between Africa and Asia was thought to be the Nile. Claudius Ptolemy's second-century AD *Geography*, which influenced the way the world was mapped and how maps of different parts of the world were framed, clearly divides the world between Europe, Africa and Asia. Ptolemy divided Africa and Asia by the Red Sea, explicitly 'in order not to split Egypt by dividing [the continents] by the Nile'.[2]

These concepts also found expression in medieval world maps, or *mappaemundi*, which commonly divided the Earth into three parts like a capital letter T inside a capital O, each inhabited by a branch of the families of the three sons of Noah: Shem (Asia), Ham (Africa) and Japheth (Europe). In terms of size, Asia was typically as large as Europe and Africa combined, and so was assigned to the eldest son. It was also at the top of the map, in the east, the Christian sacred direction and the supposed location of the Garden of Eden (plate 2.1).[3]

When Ptolemy's manual was translated from Greek into Latin and reprinted in the fifteenth and sixteenth centuries, it perpetuated the three-part scheme, and the order of Ptolemy's maps became a model for sixteenth-century atlases that otherwise owe little or no debt to his data. As it became clear that North and South America formed a separate land-mass between Europe and Asia, a fourth part was added. By the third quarter of the sixteenth century, sets of the four continent maps were popular as wall-maps in private houses as a 'description of the world in four parts'. By framing the maps in this way, it could be argued that they became *de facto* 'continents', even if they were not routinely called such. The repeated exposure of people to maps of this type may have had an inexorable effect in cementing this division well before the seventeenth century. Such spatial constructions of the world tended to stereotype and over-simplify the huge

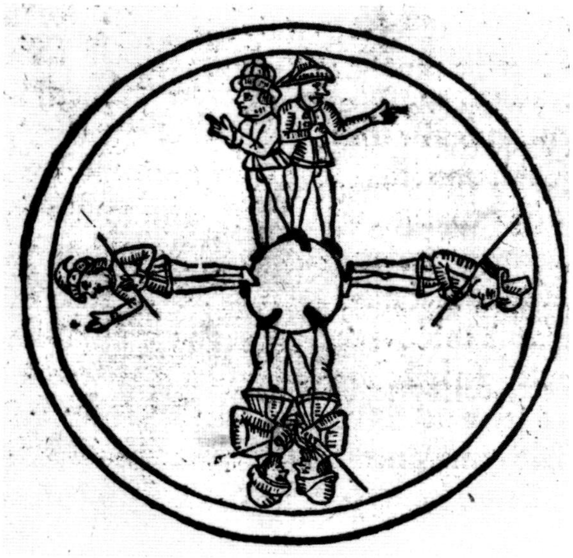

2.2
Diagram of the earth as an apple (detail)
Gautier de Metz, *from Image du Monde,* published by William Caxton, London, 1481
Woodcut on paper
Huntington Library, San Marino

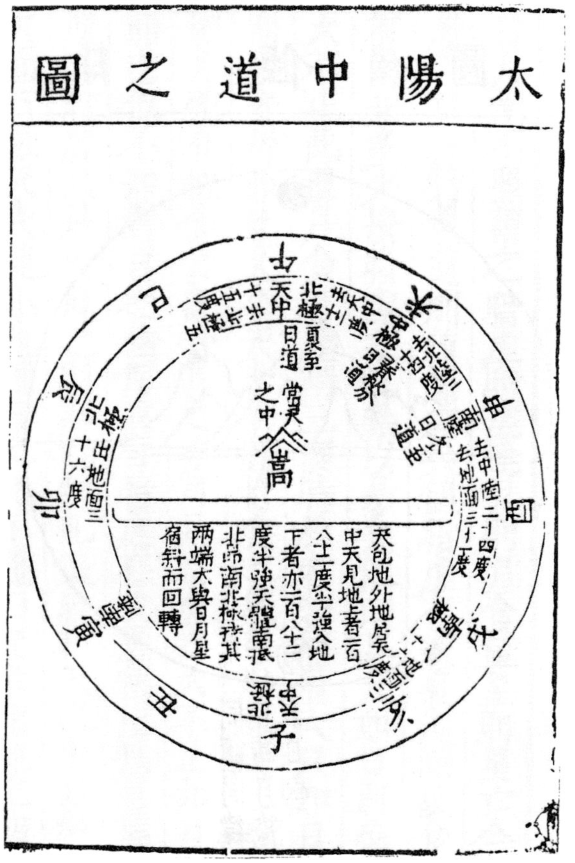

2.3
Depiction of the heavens as round and the earth as square and flat
Wang Qi, from *Sancai tuhui tianwen*, completed 1607, printed 1609
Woodcut on paper
Harvard-Yenching Library, Harvard University, Cambridge, MA

cultural differences within 'Asia' or 'Africa' and regard the divisions as natural.

The term 'India' was employed in a bewildering array of contexts. It was often used to mean Asia or parts of it, commonly in their position relative to Europe. There were at least three main 'Indias': *India citra* (or *intra*) *Gangem* (this side of the Ganges) or 'Greater India'; *India ultra* (or *extra*) *Gangem* (beyond the Ganges) or 'Lesser India'; as well as *India Extrema*, *India superioris* (Upper India), *India meridionalis* (Southern India). In addition, Middle India or Ethiopic India was considered Asiatic because it lay beyond the Nile, although it encompassed the territories of eastern Africa. In general it is possible to say simply that in the late Middle Ages the term 'India' denoted the regions that bordered the Indian Ocean.

Central to Europe's view of Asia was the possibility of a westward route to China and the Spice Islands, which in turn implied a belief in a spherical world. It is commonly assumed that during the Middle Ages Chinese cartography was far in advance of that of Europe. When it came to concepts of the sphericity of the globe, however, the reverse was more likely the case. That the Earth was round had been generally accepted by Greek philosophers since 500 BC, and with the exception of a couple of over-publicized flat-Earthers, no scholar in the Middle Ages who cared about the matter believed that the Earth was flat (plate 2.2).[4] However, the tenacity of the *gaitian* theory in China during the same period, in which it was postulated that the Earth was a flat square in a spherical heaven, suggests a confusion about the shape of the Earth in China that was not as evident in Europe (plate 2.3).[5]

The position of Asia on the globe in turn depended on knowledge of the size of the Earth. As estimates of the Earth's size increased, so did the perceived westward distance between Asia and Europe. The question of the width of the Western Ocean had a pedigree dating back to Aristotle (384–22 BC). Seneca (*c.* 5 BC–AD 65) had stated that 'the end of Spain and the beginning of India are not far distant but close, and it is evident that this sea is navigable in a few days with a fair wind'. And in an often forgotten passage in his thirteenth-century *Opus Maius*, Roger Bacon (*c.* 1214–94) recited this pedigree and its implications for the Christian domination of the world by his patron Pope Clement IV. Some of his manuscripts illustrate this concept with a curious diagram showing the relationship of Asia to Europe (plate 2.4).[6]

Perhaps more dramatic evidence of the exaggerated width of Asia is shown by the globe associated with Martin Behaim (1459–1507) (plate 2.5). Here the globemaker was forced to deal directly with the excess width of the Western Ocean, which on the globe was reduced to 78° of longitude between Gomera in the Canaries and the east coast of Cipangu (Japan). One of the sources used by Behaim seems to have been similar to world maps by Henricus Martellus Germanus (*fl.* 1480–96), a German cartographer working in Florence. The manuscript map that Martellus made in 1489

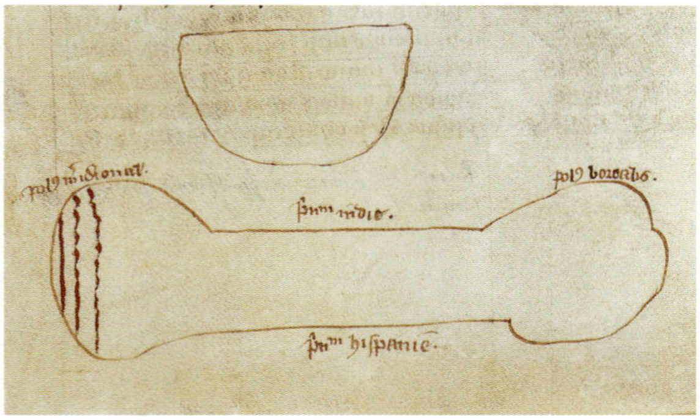

2.4
Diagram showing the relationship of Europe and Asia
Roger Bacon, from *Opus Maius*, 1268
Ink on paper
England (probably Oxford)
British Library, London

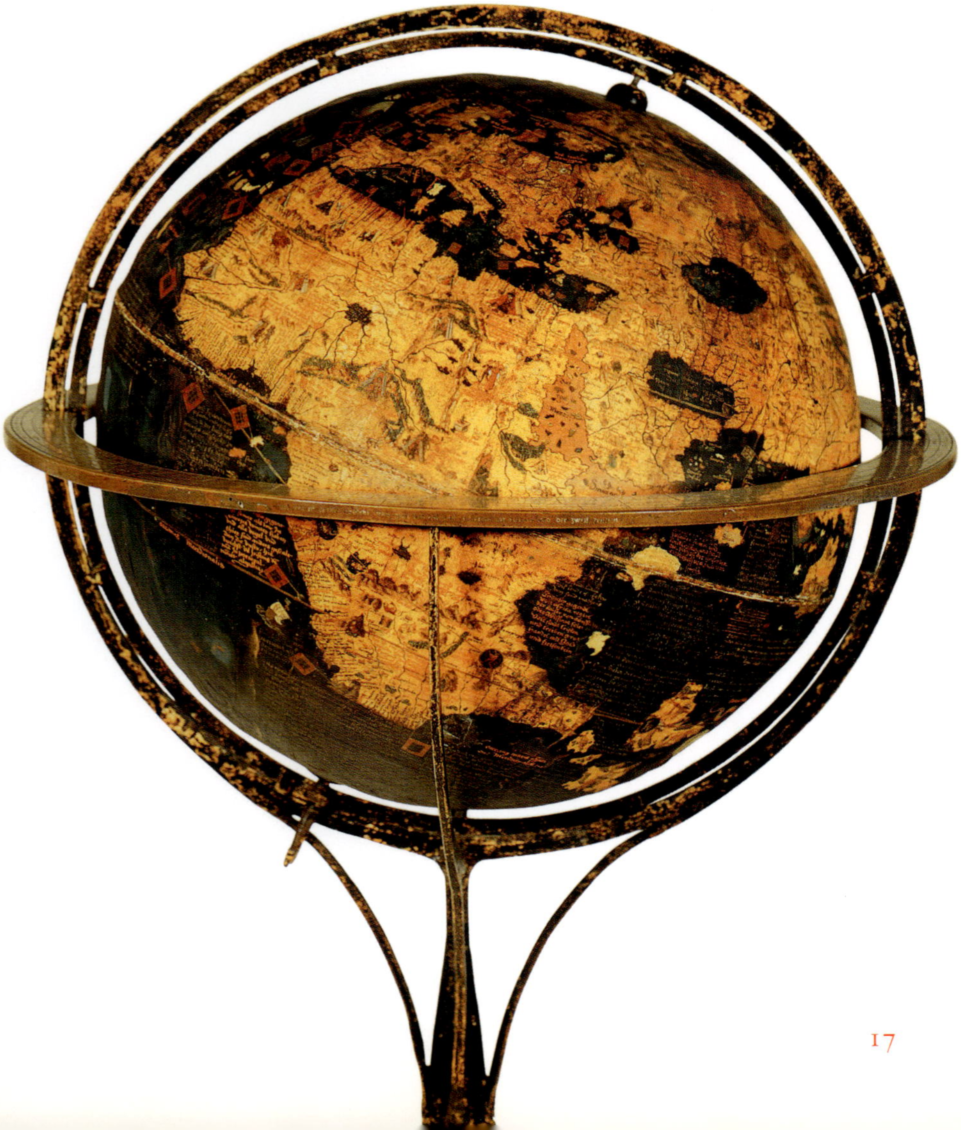

2.5
Globe
Martin Behaim
Colours on vellum
Germany (Nuremberg), 1492
Germanisches Nationalmuseum, Nuremberg

2.6
World Map
Henricus Martellus Germanus

Ink and watercolour on paper
Probably Italy, 1489

British Library, London

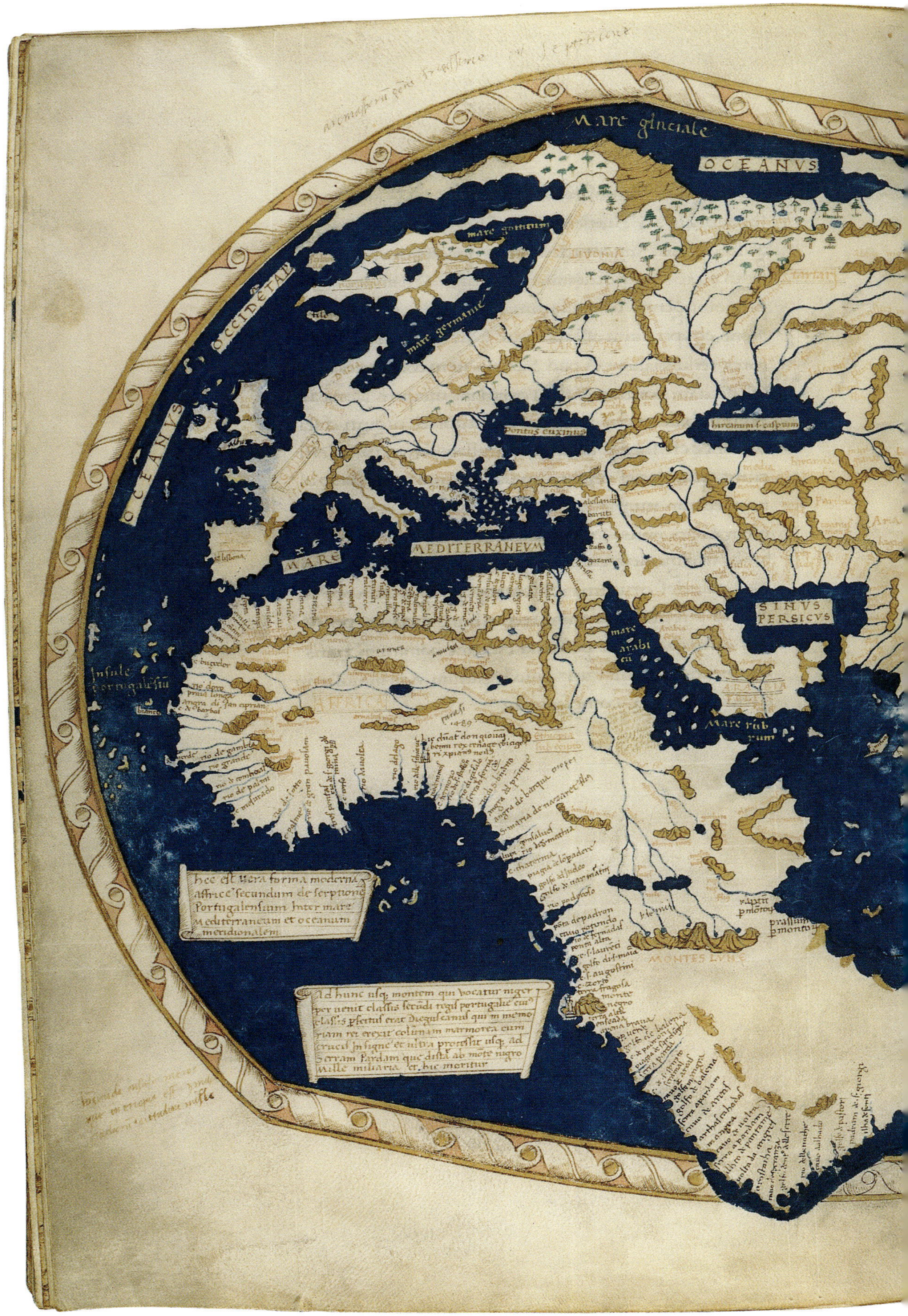

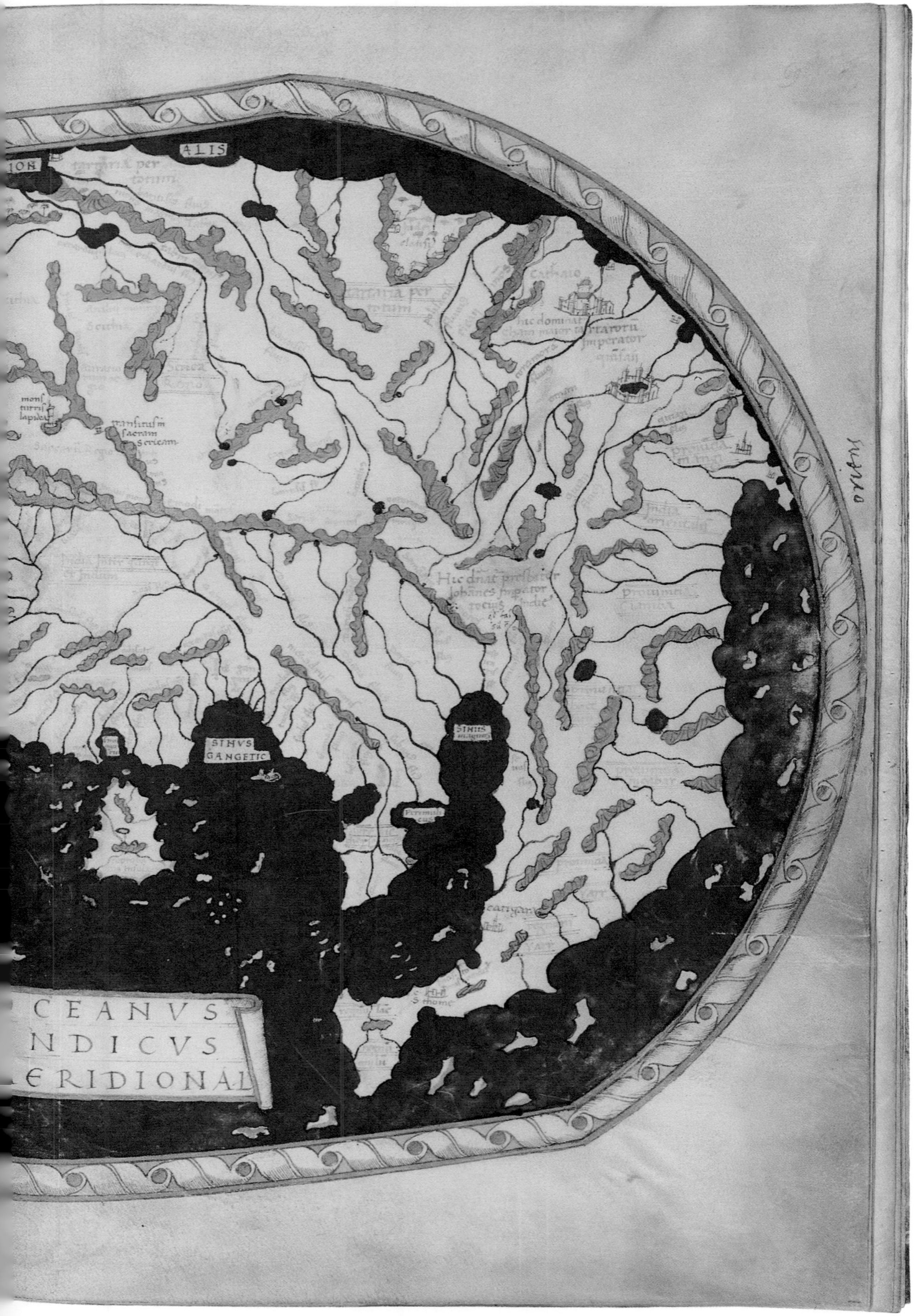
ALIS
SINVS
GANGETIC
CEANVS
NDICVS
ERIDIONAL

is the most dramatic example of how Asia's width was overstated. It omits 85° of the Earth's circuit in the Pacific and implies that 90° exist between the Canary Islands and Cipangu (plate 2.6).

By the time of the Renaissance, a web of land routes to Asia from Europe had been known for many centuries. Alexander the Great's influence had reached the Ganges and legends and stories of his exploits continued to be retold in the Middle Ages. The so-called Silk Road (although more accurately described as a vast network of local trade connections) had been in operation since Roman times. The Crusades (1096–1270) enormously widened the geographical horizons of many classes of people, increased mobility and fostered a culture of travel, although in Donald Lach's words 'the Crusades themselves changed almost nothing in Europe's pictorial image of Asia'.[7]

A key source of new information in thirteenth- and fourteenth-century geographical treatises derived from diplomatic, missionary and mercantile expeditions to the East. In 1245, Pope Innocent IV despatched the Franciscan John of Plano Carpini (1180–1252) to the Mongol court in an attempt to learn about Mongol customs, to convert the Great Khan Güyüg (r. 1246–48) and to cement an alliance with him. John's narrative, *The History of the Mongols*, was largely superseded by accounts by other travellers to Asia, notably William of Rubruck (1253–55), who travelled there for similar missionary purposes, and those of Niccolò Polo, Maffeo Polo and Marco Polo (his journeys of 1260–69 and 1271–95), who went East for very different, mercantile reasons.[8] Although Marco Polo's book yielded a mine of commercial knowledge about Asia, it had a surprisingly limited effect on European geographical theory and cartography. However, findings from Polo's text are represented in the Catalan Atlas (1375) and the Fra Mauro map (1459).[9]

Fra Mauro's *mappamundi* is one of the landmark maps in the history of medieval cartography. It is extremely unusual that such a large – it is almost

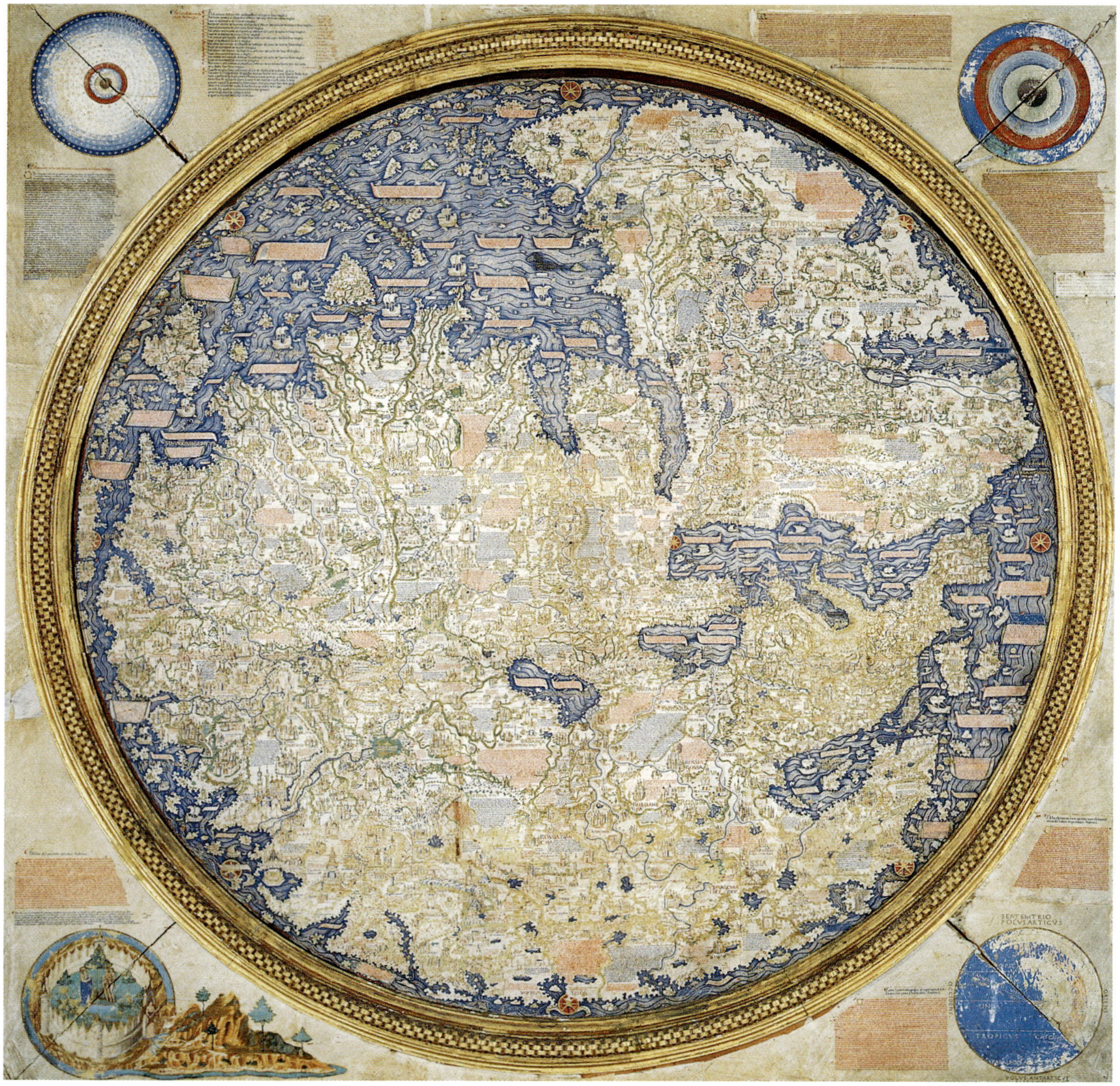

2.7
Mappamundi
Fra Mauro
Ink and colours on vellum pasted on wood
Italy (Venice), 1459
Biblioteca Nazionale Marciana, Venice

two metres square – and detailed map has survived, preserved in the Biblioteca Marciana in Venice (plate 2.7). What seems striking today is the *mappamundi*'s orientation with south at the top, indicating its Arabic influence and ultimate link to an Aristotelian cosmographic tradition. Aristotle censured the Pythagoreans for not recognizing that the heavens had an 'up' and 'down' direction, and explained that the uppermost pole had to be in the south because all motion originates and moves to the right-hand side, 'right' being a nobler and superior direction. Since the heavens appear to turn to the right when we face south, it made sense to orient the world view in this way. Aristotle's philosophy was in favour early in the Islamic world, and Arabic world maps are frequently oriented to the south.

The map that survives is a copy of one that Fra Mauro worked on from 1457 to 1459 as a commission from Afonso V of Portugal. The original sent to Portugal did not survive. Fra Mauro died in 1460 before he could finish a copy of the map for the Venetian Senate, but one of his assistants, possibly Andrea Bianco, produced the map that now resides in the Biblioteca Marciana. Fra Mauro clearly struggled to reconcile three sources of geographical information: Ptolemy's manual of mapmaking (the *Geography*), various medieval *mappaemundi* and nautical charts. Although Fra Mauro did not use Ptolemy's framework of longitude and latitude, he was aware of the *Geography* and used it for those parts of the world for which he believed Ptolemy had good information. This did not extend to the Indian Ocean, which Ptolemy represented as closed. And although Fra Mauro would have liked to centre the world on Jerusalem, as many (but by no means all) medieval world maps had done, he realized that to do so would severely compromise the width of Asia. So he rationalized moving the Holy City to the west by saying that it was more the centre of population than the longitudinal centre.[10]

Since the map was originally made for the Portuguese king, one would expect it to dutifully record the Portuguese progress down the west coast of Africa. This is true until Cape Rosso (which Fra Mauro calls *c[av]o rosso*), explored by the Portuguese by 1441, but the line of the coast then takes an abrupt turn inland into what is called the Sinus Ethiopicus, based perhaps on oral reports of what may have been the Gulf of Guinea. The argument has been advanced that Fra Mauro had been supplied with deliberately censored charts that omitted the latest discoveries beyond Cape Rosso, explored by Alvaro Fernandes in 1445–46. It is known that Fra Mauro was working on a *mappamundi* in 1448, and the one ten years later may have been essentially the same as the first, which would account for its outdated character. It might seem strange that the King of Portugal would want an outdated map. However, it is possible that he was more interested in Fra Mauro's representation of the world as a whole than he was merely in Portuguese progress down the coast.

Fra Mauro's representation of what is now the Cape of Good Hope seems to be based on hearsay evidence. It could be argued that the navigable passage is simply the Mare Oceanus that was commonly found encircling the Earth in medieval world maps. In a text block on the map, Fra Mauro mentions a passage from Solinus, confirmed by Pliny, that 'that ocean and those south and south-western parts were navigable'. Another passage reads as follows:

> Around 1420 a ship or junk from India [possibly China] navigated through the Indian Ocean towards the Islands of Men and Women [possibly, the Seychelles] off the Cape of Diab in between the Green Islands [?] and the darkness and westward and south-westward for 40 days, finding nothing but water and air, and they navigated for 2,000 miles and his fortune declined and they return back to the Cape of Diab in 70 days.

The story derived from either an Arabic tale or reports of one of the voyages of the Chinese admiral Zheng He (1371–1433) between 1405 and 1433.[11] However, despite a recent theory to the contrary, there is no compelling cartographic evidence that confirms any activity by Zheng He's fleets outside the coasts of East and South-East Asia and the Indian Ocean.[12]

Fra Mauro's information on East Asia is largely derived from Ptolemy, Marco Polo's travel narrative and contact with Niccolò de' Conti (*c.* 1395–1469). He followed Ptolemy in placing a large island off the coast of the peninsula of India, which he calls 'Saylam' or Ceylon, complete with a representation of Adam's Peak, a supposed location of the Garden of Eden. He criticized Ptolemy for having confused the island with Taprobana, which Fra Mauro places further east and also calls 'siamotra' or Sumatra. Fra Mauro generally followed Ptolemy's configuration of some of the promontories and peninsulas along the northern coast of the Indian Ocean east of the Persian Gulf, and, like Ptolemy, dramatically omitted the huge Deccan peninsula itself. Where Ptolemy referred to 'terra incognita', as in the far north-east part of China, Fra Mauro supplied ample, if not necessarily reliable, data. The richness of the illuminated cities, towers, columns, rivers and bridges on Fra Mauro's map is extraordinary and reflects the descriptions in the book of Marco Polo. One of the bridges is described as having 300 arches and 6,000 images of lions. Fra Mauro explains in a note that, as Asia was so vast, he had plenty of space to represent the cities, and his artist had embellished them in the Venetian style. But since Marco Polo had been notably unspecific when it came to the exact locations of the places he had seen, Fra Mauro's geography is often confused. The massive rivers, wonderfully represented as shaded blue-grey serpents, wind in and out of the cities, plunge underground and branch magically into deltas and lakes. Recognizable, if not always debouching into the appropriate gulfs, are the Yellow River, the Yangtze, the Irrawaddy, Ganges, Brahmaputra and Indus.

For areas around Java, Sumatra and Burma, Fra Mauro seems to have relied on the account of Niccolò de' Conti, a Venetian merchant who started a series of travels in Asia from 1419. Niccolò's work should be far better known; he was the prime European traveller to Asia of the fifteenth century. His report, which we would not have were it not for a penance required by the pope for Niccolò's renunciation of Christianity during his travels, describes his experiences in Mesopotamia, the Persian Gulf, the coasts of Iran and India, Sumatra, Burma, Java, north-western Vietnam, back to India, Socotra, Aden, Somalia, the Egyptian coast, Mount Sinai, Cairo and his return to Venice in 1444. It is easy to imagine that Niccolò saw Fra Mauro's map in some version in Venice, where he lived until his death in 1469.[13]

For the next chapter of Europe's image of Asia, it is necessary to turn to the voyages of the Portuguese, which pushed ever further down the western coast of Africa during the fifteenth century. These voyages were the result of a combination of economic, political and proselytizing motives. Prominent on the early agenda were the exploitation of the gold mines of West Africa and the search for the mythical Christian king Prester John, who was thought to reign in the East and who, it was hoped, might provide an alliance for a rearguard action against the Muslims. Although this systematic programme of exploration became known as the *plano da India*, there is some controversy as to when 'India' as we know it came into the picture. Proponents of the importance of Prince Henry (1394–1460) in Portuguese navigation plans believe that the goal to reach South Asia was part of these plans from the beginning. Yet the earliest-known author to explicitly attribute the aim of reaching India to Prince Henry was Damião de Góis (1502–74) in 1567.[14]

As we have seen, the Portuguese employed the term 'India' in different ways, often using it to refer to parts of Africa. Even the peoples of West Africa were sometimes referred to as 'Indians'. Part of the confusion arose from the misapprehension that the Nile was somehow connected to a huge westward-flowing river whose mouth lay on the West African coast. Peoples living beyond this westward branch of the Nile might be regarded as living in 'Asia' following the ancient classical boundary. Thus the 'India' sought from the days of Prince Henry was not necessarily the India of the Deccan peninsula reached by Vasco da Gama in 1498. Certainly by the time of João II (r. 1481–95), however, a navigable trade route to the Indian Ocean was a definite part of the agenda of Portuguese explorers. Pero da Covilhão (*c.* 1450–*c.* 1524), who had reached Calicut through the Red Sea, seeing spices for sale there in 1488, suggested that there could be a route to India around the southern tip of Africa. Although some of these ideas had been initiated by Prince Henry, it was mainly João II who integrated this overseas policy into a modern and coherent project. By 1489 Bartolemeu Dias (*c.* 1450–1500) had reached the Cape of Good Hope, and his discovery was dramatically represented on several maps by Henricus Martellus Germanus (plate 2.6); a small printed copy of a Martellus map by Francesco Rosselli (*c.* 1445/7–*c.* 1513); and the globe by Martin Behaim (plate 2.5). The widespread dissemination of the discovery of the Cape indicates that the idea of an open Indian Ocean was not only current in courtly and scholarly circles but in mercantile ones as well. If the Portuguese way to India was intended to be a secret, it was certainly not well kept, as the Declaration of Obedience offered to Pope Innocence VIII on behalf of the Portuguese Crown in 1485 attests. In this published speech the Portuguese announced their latest voyages along the African coast and reaffirmed their view that the Atlantic and Indian Oceans were connected by water. A policy of secrecy may have applied to making globes and nautical charts showing the

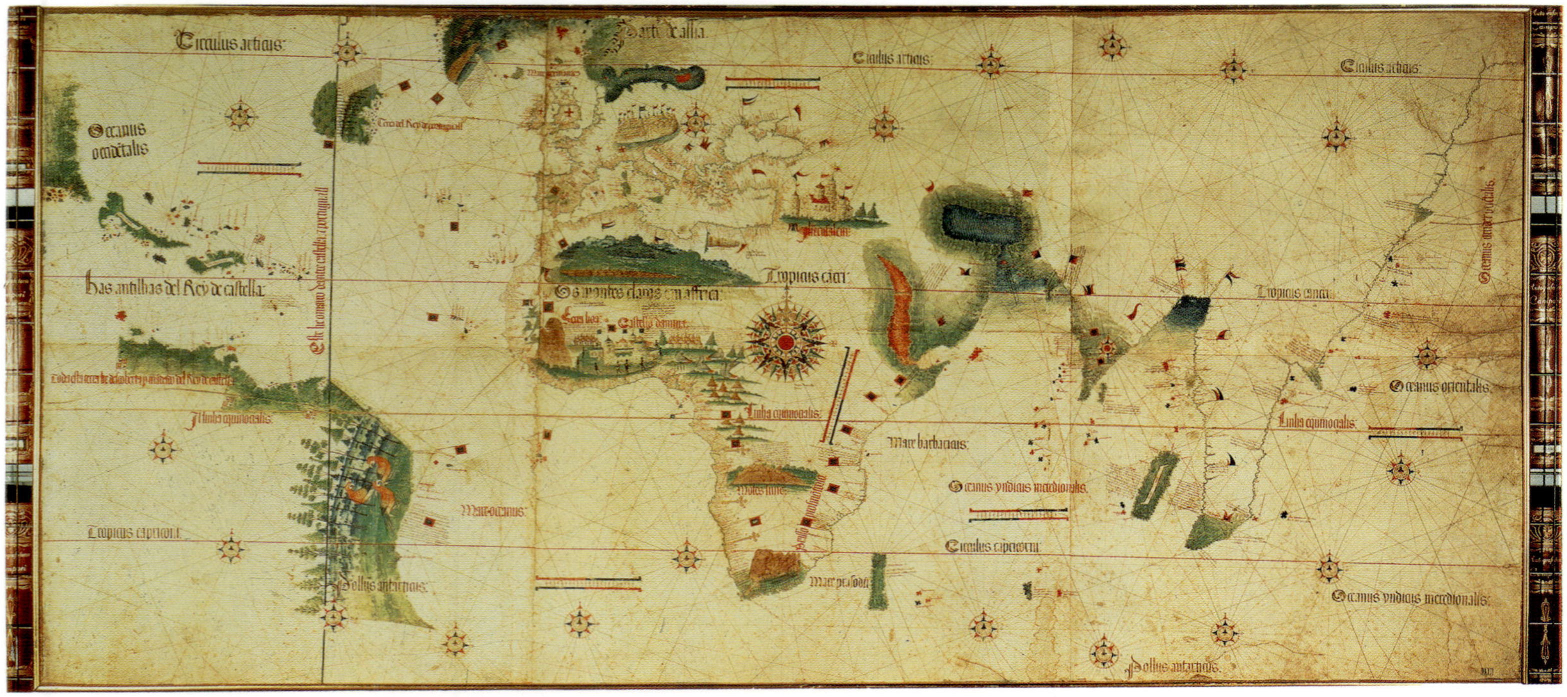

African coast beyond the Zaire River, as a charter of 1504 decrees, but this does not seem to be a restriction that can be generalized to broad Portuguese strategy in the Indian Ocean.

The role of Prince Henry is also controversial. Opinion now seems to weigh on the side that his scientific expertise in astronomy and navigation was grossly exaggerated, and that he does not warrant the sobriquet 'the Navigator' bestowed on him in later centuries. There is no evidence, for example, that Henry founded a 'school' for navigators and astronomers at Sagres in 1419, since he came to settle there more or less permanently only during the final years of his life. Although, as the discoveries unfolded, he may well have surrounded himself by experienced navigators with knowledge of Africa and the Atlantic, there is no evidence that this exchange of information constituted an established institution such as the so-called School of Sagres. We do know of other institutions that were founded in Portugal to support trade and overseas administration, beginning with the Casa de Ceuta in Lagos shortly after 1415, succeeded around the middle of the century by a Casa da Guiné and a Casa da Mina. After Vasco da Gama's return, these were merged into the Casa da Guiné, Mina e Indias or, as it was simply called, the Casa da India.

The supervision of nautical activities was concentrated in the Armazém da Guiné (literally the Depot of Guinea), which already existed as a separate storage facility in the early years of the reign of João II, when it is known to have included a repository of navigational instruments. By the beginning of the sixteenth century, the Armazém was carrying out cartographic duties, including the maintenance of a *padrão de navegar,* or master map, about which the chartmaker Lopo Homem (?–1565) wrote: 'the charts that the King's Armazém requires for its fleets and voyages to India are made in agreement with such a *padrão*'.[15] The master map no longer survives, but the so-called Cantino map of 1502 made for Ercole d'Este, Duke of Ferrara (1431–1505), may have been based on it (plate 2.8). The Spanish had their own equivalent of the Armazém. A master world chart, known as the *padrón general*, was ordered by the Spanish Casa de la Contratación ('Board of Trade') in 1508 to record geographical information as it became known. What this map might have looked like is suggested by manuscript maps made in the 1520s, such as three by Diogo Ribeiro (*fl.* 1519–33), a Portuguese by birth working for the Spanish Casa from about 1519.

However controversial and complex early Portuguese imperial aspirations may have been,

2.8
'Cantino' map of the world
Anonymous

Ink and colours on vellum
Portugal, 1502

Biblioteca Estense Universitaria, Modena

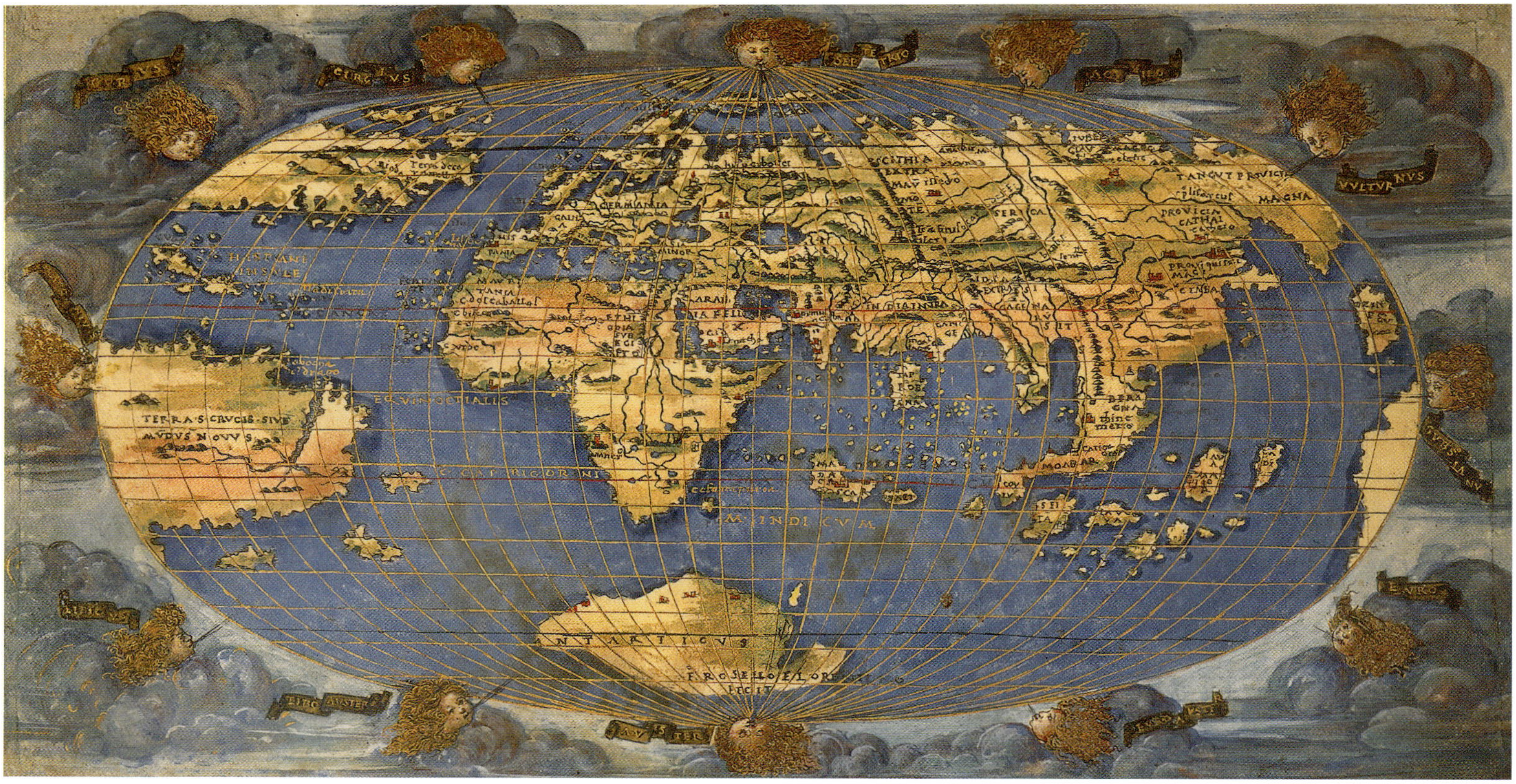

2.9
World map
Francesco Rosselli
Hand-coloured copperplate engraving on paper
Italy (probably Venice) *c.* 1508
National Maritime Museum, London

2.10 opposite, above
Theatrum Orbis Terrarum
Abraham Ortelius
Copperplate engraving on paper
Belgium (Antwerp), 1570
British Library, London

2.11 opposite, below
World map (detail)
Giacomo Gastaldi
Woodcut
Italy (Venice), 1561
British Library, London

a Portuguese trading presence was quickly established in the Indian Ocean at the beginning of the sixteenth century, with Goa as its headquarters. The principal trading centres at either end of the route were Hormuz (Ormuz) in the Persian Gulf and Malacca on the Malay peninsula. By the end of the sixteenth century, however, the empire had become over-extended and could not compete with the Spanish seaborne empire and the fiercely competitive Dutch and English East India companies.

The Spanish had chosen a westward route to Cathay and the Spice Islands. Columbus's landfall in the West Indies in 1492 thus created a huge confusion over the relationship of this newly discovered land with the continent of Asia. The uncertainty is eloquently illustrated by Francesco Rosselli's small map of the world of *c.* 1508 (plate 2.9). Because Rosselli made a map of the *whole* world, 360° from east to west and 180° from north to south, an amazingly innovative idea, he was forced to reconcile the relationship between the lands described by Columbus, Amerigo Vespucci, Pedro Alvarez Cabral and John Cabot with the traditional Ptolemaic view of Asia. On Rosselli's map, names of places discovered by Columbus on his fourth American voyage (1502–04) along the coast of present-day Panama, Costa Rica, Nicaragua and Honduras dot part of the coast of South-East Asia, revealing the uncertainty as to whether or not Columbus had reached Asia. These names are mixed with those that classical and medieval geographers used for places in Asia, such as Catigara (Cape Cattigara), Seila[n] (Ceylon) and Iava Maior. Cape Cattigara is usually found at the southernmost promontory of the peninsula called the Golden Chersonnese, the hooked crescent shape of which is one of the diagnostic characteristics of maps derived from Ptolemy's *Geography*. It should be added that these names are not visible on the Greenwich version of the map illustrated here as they have been painted over.[16]

A much larger world map by Giacomo Gastaldi, made in 1561, illustrates how Europeans' knowledge of China grew during the next 50 years. Gastaldi lived and worked in Venice from 1539 to his death in October 1566. He attained great fame there, becoming a member of the prestigious Accademia Veneziana. In the 1550s, Gastaldi produced maps for the three volumes of the *Navigationi et viaggi* (1550–56) of Giovanni Battista Ramusio (1485–1557). Ramusio was the major link between the information provided by explorers and the Italian academic publishing scene. A diplomat in the Venetian service, Ramusio was also secretary of the Council of Ten, the ruling body of the Republic. His compilation of voyages and travels reflected his belief that geographical explorations were the greatest achievements of recent centuries.

In 1559 Gastaldi received a commission from the Venetian Senate for a large map of the three parts of Asia, which appeared between 1559 and 1561. The three-part map of Asia – Asia Minor, South Asia, and East and South-East Asia – was used as the basis for at least three other maps, including Abraham Ortelius's large 1567 map of Asia. The sources of information for the representation of the Indian Ocean and South-East Asian islands in Gastaldi's maps were the Portuguese and Spanish voyages. There is no truth to Ortelius's exotic assertion that Gastaldi used an Arab geographer named Taqwim Albudan. *Taqwim Albudan* is the title of a fourteenth-century geographical lexicon by Abu'l-Fida, which would have been of no use to Gastaldi for his mapping of Asia.[17]

Gastaldi's maps of Asia were used for the large undated 10-sheet woodcut map of the world with the title *Cosmographia universalis* that bears the unusual form of his name 'Jacopo a Castaldio' (plate 2.11). It is centred on the Fortunate Islands (the Canaries), resulting in Asia being split into two sections. It is the first map to identify a strait between Asia and the Americas, named the Strait of Anian, a hypothesis that would not be confirmed by western exploration until the eighteenth century. Gastaldi's maps of Asia were among the sources used by Abraham Ortelius in his world atlas of 1570, perhaps the single most influential publication to form the public's geographical image of the world in the late sixteenth century (plate 2.10). Ortelius acknowledges Gastaldi in the unusual list of authors at the beginning of the atlas. Mapmakers and publishers in the Netherlands took over leadership in the map trade from Italy from this time, and provided the bulk of commercial maps, charts and globes until the end of the seventeenth century. Perhaps the best-known cartographer was Gerardus Mercator, whose world map of 1569 was drawn on the famous Mercator projection.

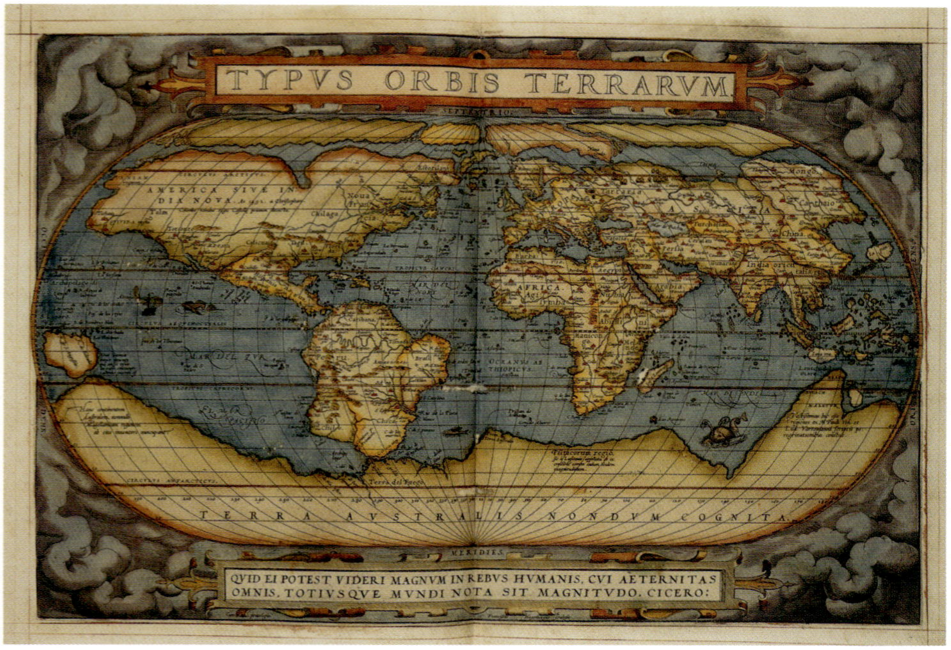

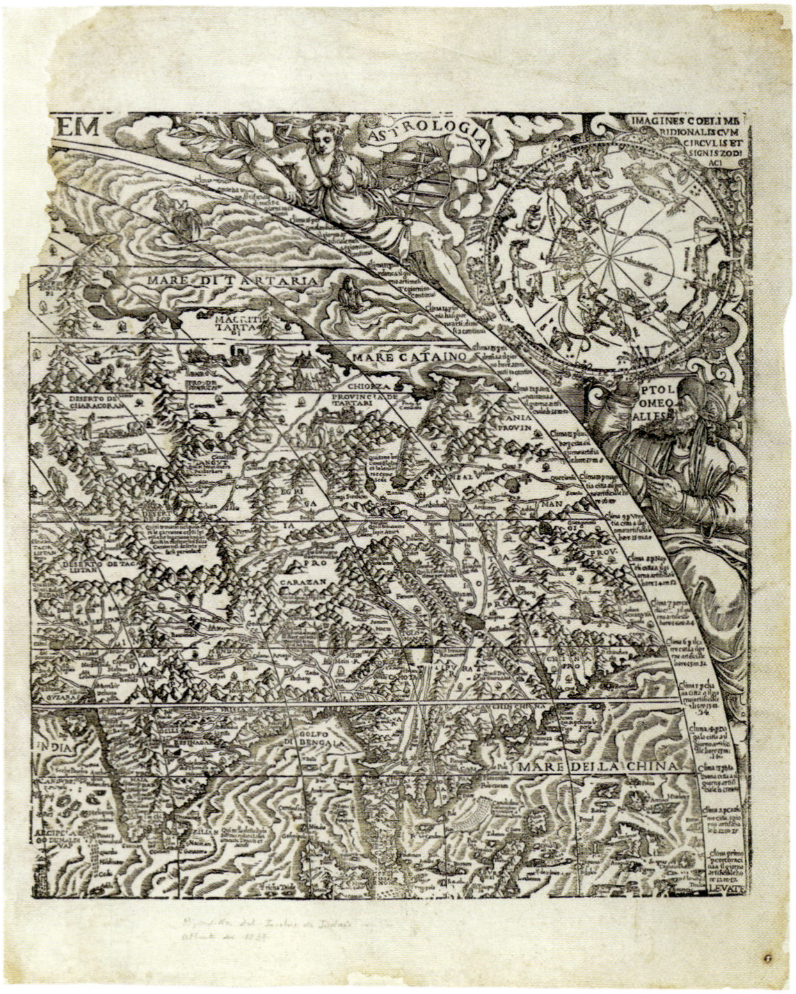

ASIAN MAPPING OF THE WORLD

A comparison of the Fra Mauro *mappamundi* and the roughly contemporary *Kangnido*, a Korean map of 1402 (known from a copy dating to *c.* 1460) illustrates the difference in European and East Asian cartographic representations of the world (plate 2.12). *Kangnido* is short for *'Honil kangni yoktae kukto chi to'*, which means 'Map of integrated lands and regions of historical countries and capitals'. The *Kangnido*, or map of the integrated regions, is the most significant East Asian map of the known world before 1600, and the recent works of Gari Ledyard have brought it to the attention of English-speaking readers.[18] It was compiled in 1402 by Yi Hoe, at the request of Kwōn Kūn, a leading Confucian scholar in the Korean court.

We know that the *Kangnido* was intended to cover the whole world from Kwōn Kūn's text on the face of the map, which states that it was difficult to achieve precision when compressing into a single sheet a world 'tens of millions of *li*' (a *li* was about half a kilometre, so the estimate was unrealistic to say the least) from China in the centre to 'the four seas at its outer limits'. It is a remarkable map, the only East Asian one from this period to show the continents of Africa and Europe beyond. Africa can be easily identified from the representation of the Nile with its source in the famous 'Mountains of the Moon', which, in this map, feeds into the Red Sea and not the Mediterranean. The Mountains were found in maps of the world accompanying Ptolemy's *Geography*, but the concept had been adopted by Islamic mapmakers such as al-Idrisi in the twelfth century and ibn Khaldun in the fourteenth. It is highly probable that the compilers of the *Kangnido* derived their information about Africa from Arabic world maps,

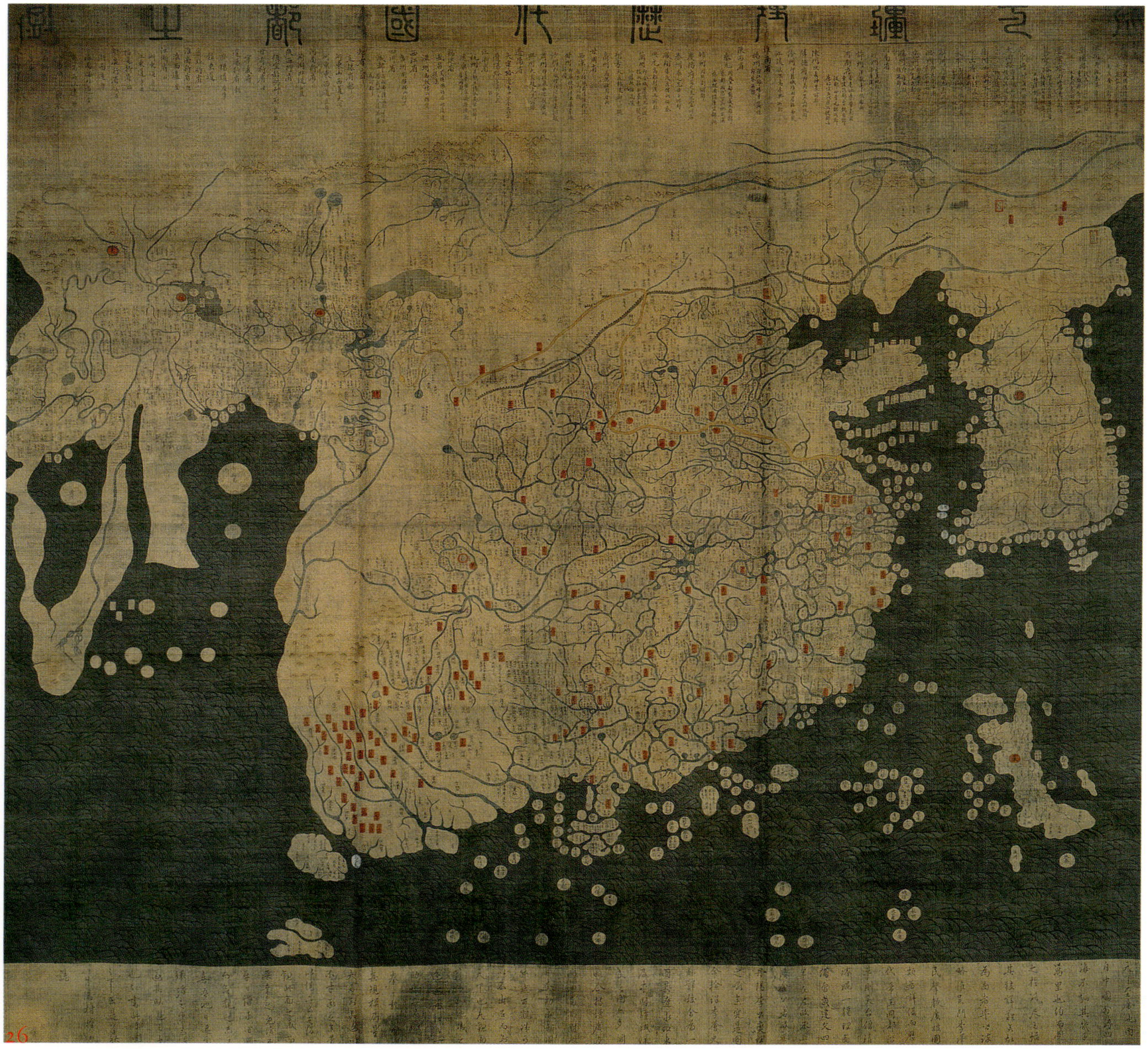

2.12
Copy of Yi Hoe's *Kangnido* of 1402

Ink on silk
1460

Ryūkoku University Library, Kyoto

for the transcribed name of the Mountains of the Moon on the map is *Zhebulu hara*, derived from the Persianized Arabic *Djebel al-kamar*. In the interior of Africa is shown a huge inland sea that feeds the Nile and a westward-flowing river, a conflation perhaps between reports of Lake Chad and the two lakes that were thought to feed the Nile in classical geography. What the *Kangnido* clearly did not adopt from the Greco-Roman and Arabic mapmakers, however, was the notion of the closed Indian Ocean, for there is a clear navigable way around the southern tip of Africa, giving the land-mass a recognizable shape. Africa is, however, not drawn to the same scale as the representation of China, and certainly not Korea, being about the same size as the latter. As in the Fra Mauro map, the Indian peninsula is mysteriously absent. The *Kangnido* folds it into the Asian mainland to such an extent that it is hidden, although its shape would be approximately correct if the east bounding river were transformed into the Bay of Bengal. The representation of Europe – in which the Mediterranean, the Iberian peninsula, the Italian peninsula and the Adriatic Sea can clearly be seen – is noticeably more reliable than the representation of China, and especially Korea, on the Fra Mauro map. Four place-names have been identified as derived from the al-Idrisi world map of 1154, but the remaining approximately 100 names still await close study. This is surprising considering the importance of the document. The *Kangnido* was copied often in the fifteenth century; the earliest of three surviving copies, in Japan, dates from around 1460.

The *Kangnido* is unusual, as East Asia maps of the world were usually maps of the Chinese empire (known as the Middle Kingdom) in which the emperor's domains are central, with other countries of the world represented as islands and scattered around the periphery. From at least the Zhanguo period (480–221 BC), the traditional diagram that associated China with the rest of the world was in the form of five concentric squares, with the largest 5,000 *li* on a side. At the centre were the royal domains; at the edge the 'wild zone'.

In East Asian world maps there was no evidence of interest in the concept of mathematical projections, such as that espoused by Ptolemy in the West, because the notion of a flat Earth provided a satisfactory empirical framework for the kinds of maps needed by administrators and scholars in China. The grids found on such dramatically accurate maps of the river systems in the Song dynasty, such as the

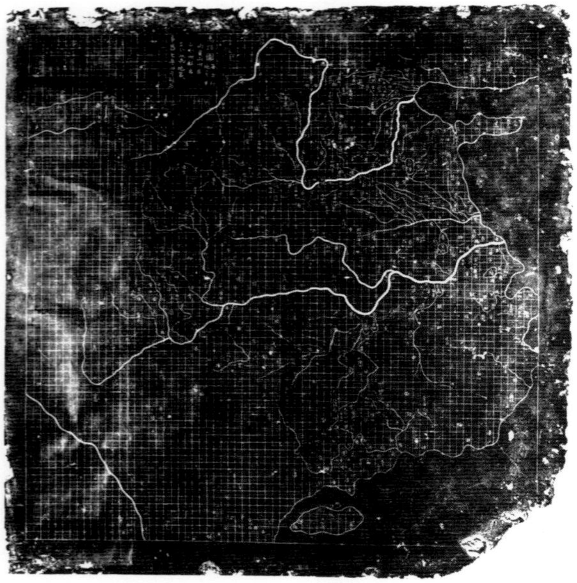

2.13
Rubbing of the *Yu ji tu* of 1142

Cao Wanru, Institute for the History of Natural Sciences, Academia Sinica, Beijing

many versions of the mid-twelfth-century *Yu ji tu*, are demonstrably not projection grids of longitude and latitude (plate 2.13). And it is important not to confuse the frequent references to the measuring of latitude in the Yuan dynasty (such as in *Survey of the Four Seas* by Guo Shoujing [1231–1316]) as being for Earth-measuring purposes, as their primary intention was to calibrate sundials for calendars.[19]

Early world mapping traditions in East and South Asia were more cosmographical in nature, in the sense that they represented not the metrical geography of the world but the traditional religious image of Asia. In this sense, they were similar to the *mappaemundi* of the Christian Middle Ages. Two types will be discussed here, one based on a Hindu, Jain and Buddhist tradition and the other based overwhelmingly on the *Shanhai jing* (*Classic of Mountains and Seas*). The Hindu-Jain-Buddhist world map, of which versions were made in India, China and Japan, represents a pear-shaped world island known as *Jambudvipa*, literally 'Rose-Apple Island', from the Jambu tree that was believed to grow at its centre. Such maps frequently show Mount Meru as the *axis mundi* or centre of the world (commonly associated with either the Pamir range in Tajikistan or the sacred Mount Kailas in Tibet). Around the centre were often placed four continents, one in each cardinal direction, usually represented as lotus leaves.[20] In Japan, a version of this cosmographical map was known as the 'Map of the Five Indias', or *Gotenjiku zu*. The map represents the famous

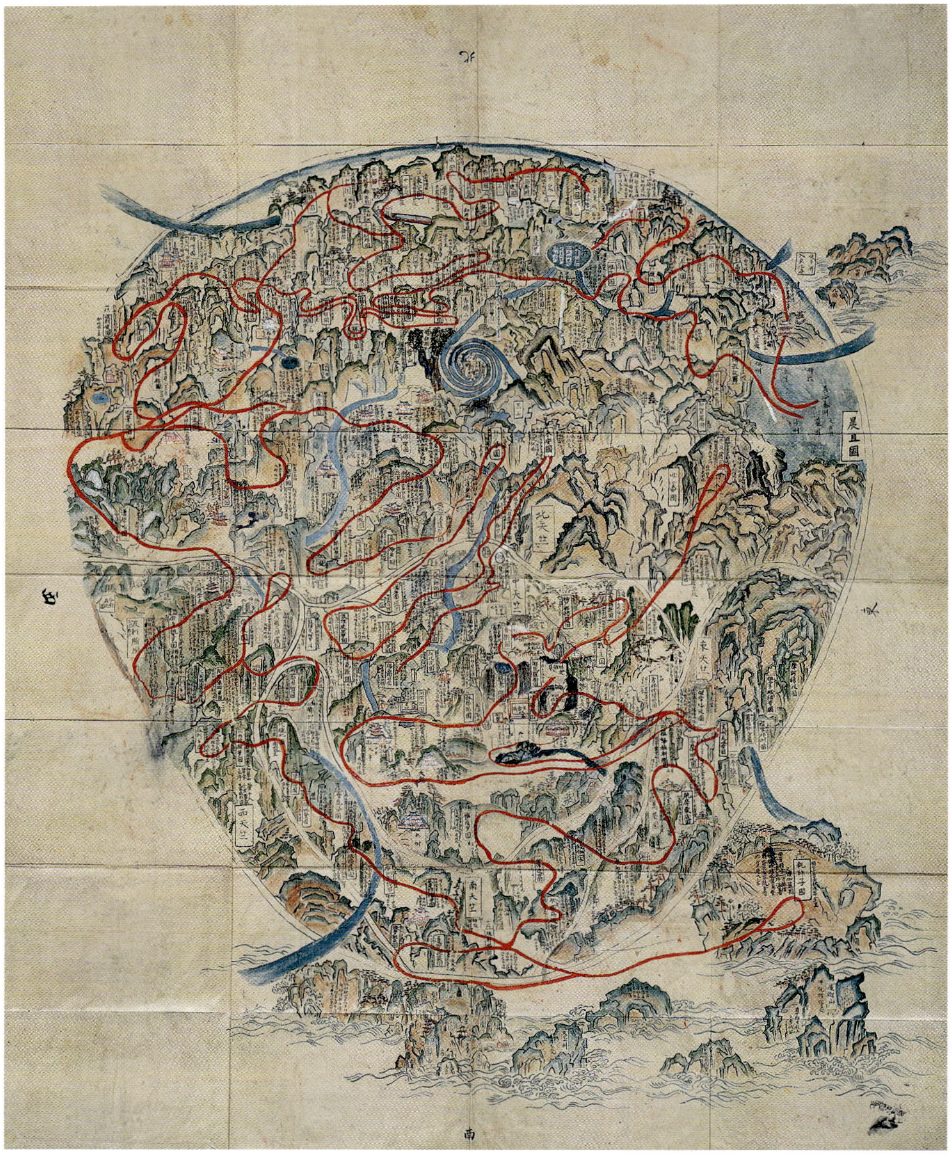

2.14
Nansenbushuzu
Copy of the 14th-century *Gotenjiku-zu* in the Horyu-ji, Nara
Ink and colours on paper
Japan, late 18th–early 19th century
Museum of National History, Sakura

2.15
Ch'onhado
Woodcut on paper
Korea (Seoul), 1800
British Library, London

pilgrimage of the Chinese priest Xuanzhuang to India, and its survival in many Buddhist temples is due to its importance as an object of veneration (plate 2.14).[21]

An example of a hybrid of traditional cosmographical knowledge and geographical knowledge acquired through European contact is afforded by a world map with text in the Marathi language (plate 2.16).[22] Most of the map concerns the rivers and mountains of India, and two pilgrimage places, Badrinath and Kedarnath, are seen near the source of the sacred Ganga. It focuses on the lands of the Maratha Confederacy, and beyond them the space is drastically summarized and stylized in all directions. Three islands west of the Arabian Sea appear to represent Europe: England, France and 'other hat-wearing islands'. Apart from two even smaller islands representing China, East Asia is totally ignored. Above the two trans-Eurasian mountain ranges a small symmetrical view of the world reflects traditional wisdom in the Puranic Hindu legends handed down by performance from AD 300 to 1200 and preserved in Vedic texts. This part is written in the relatively little-known Modi script and has yet to be adequately studied.

Another mapping tradition, followed mainly in Korea, was known as the *ch'onhado* (map of all under heaven) (plate 2.15). The maps are found in small woodcut atlases, and it is this genre rather than the *Kangnido* type of map that persisted in Korea, being enormously popular up to the nineteenth century.[23] A main continent containing China and Korea occupies the middle of such maps and is surrounded by an ocean filled with islands, beyond which is a ring-shaped continent with fictional countries, mountains and other features. The place-names in this continent can be overwhelmingly traced to the *Shanhai jing*, an ancient Chinese geography, as well as being named after prominent trees that appear in the eastern and western margins of the map.

INTRODUCTION OF WESTERN MAPS TO ASIA

The extent of westernization of Chinese cartography is a controversial issue. When Matteo Ricci (1552–1610) went to China in 1583, he was following in the footsteps of two other Jesuit missionaries – Alessandro Valignano (1539–1606) and Michele Ruggieri (1543–1607). They all believed that the most effective way of converting the Chinese to Christianity was to adapt Chinese values and beliefs to their message. When the Chinese were curious to know where Ricci had come from, he produced a map to show them. He also used maps to introduce western science and technology, hoping to demonstrate its advantages to the Chinese scholarly elite. On the wall of the Zhaoqing mission, Ricci had hung a map of the world in European characters that elicited such interest that a new version was drawn in Chinese, printed in 1584. No examples of this version survive, but its appearance is known from a later copy (plate 2.17).

Ricci had difficulty persuading the Chinese that the Earth was round, with neither beginning nor

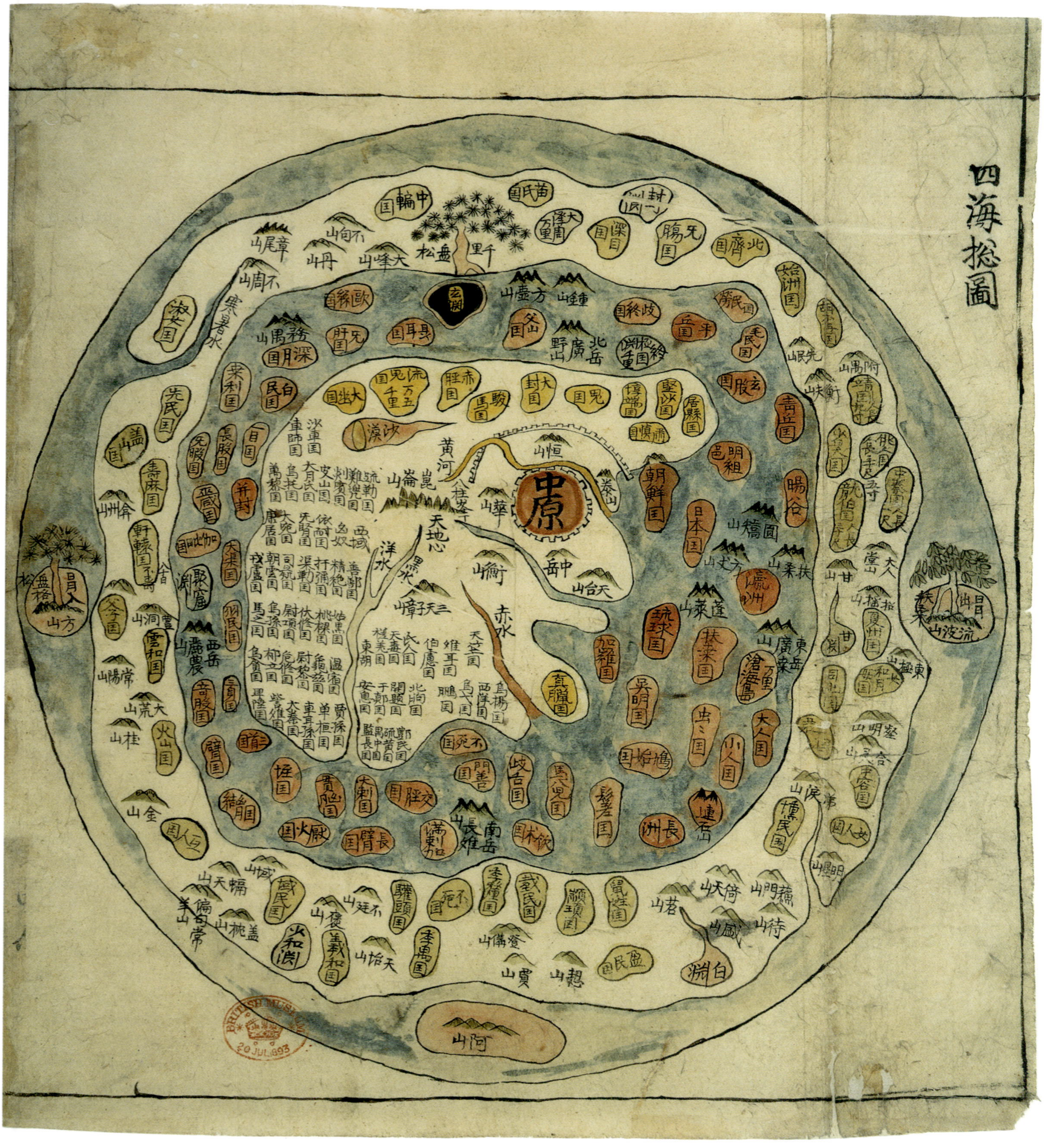
四海摠圖
中原
朝鮮国
日本国
黄河
赤水
崑崙山
天地心
琉球国

3

RARITIES AND NOVELTIES

Annemarie Jordan Gschwend

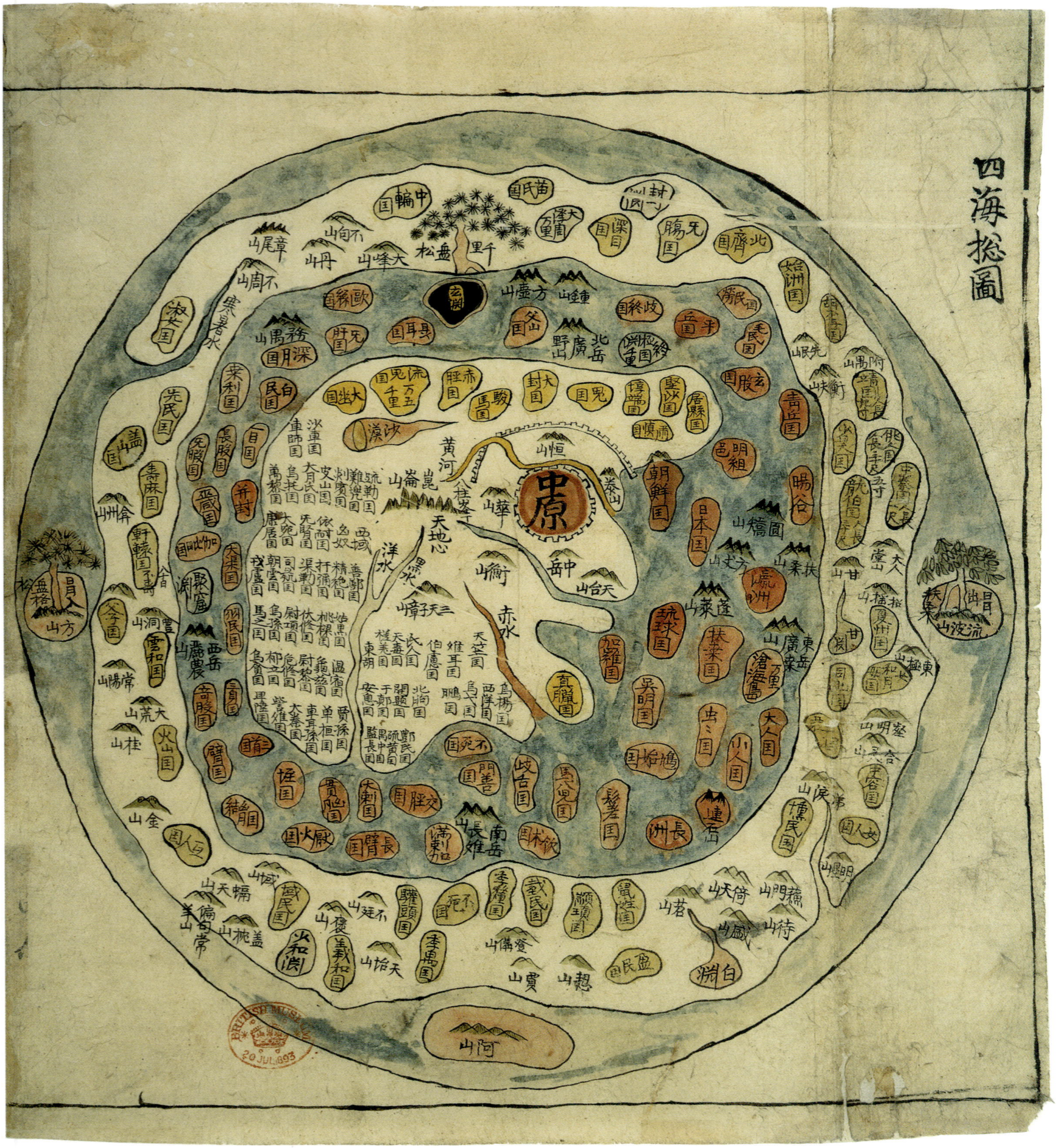
四海摠圖
中原
朝鮮国
日本国
琉球国
黄河
赤水

3

RARITIES AND NOVELTIES

Annemarie Jordan Gschwend

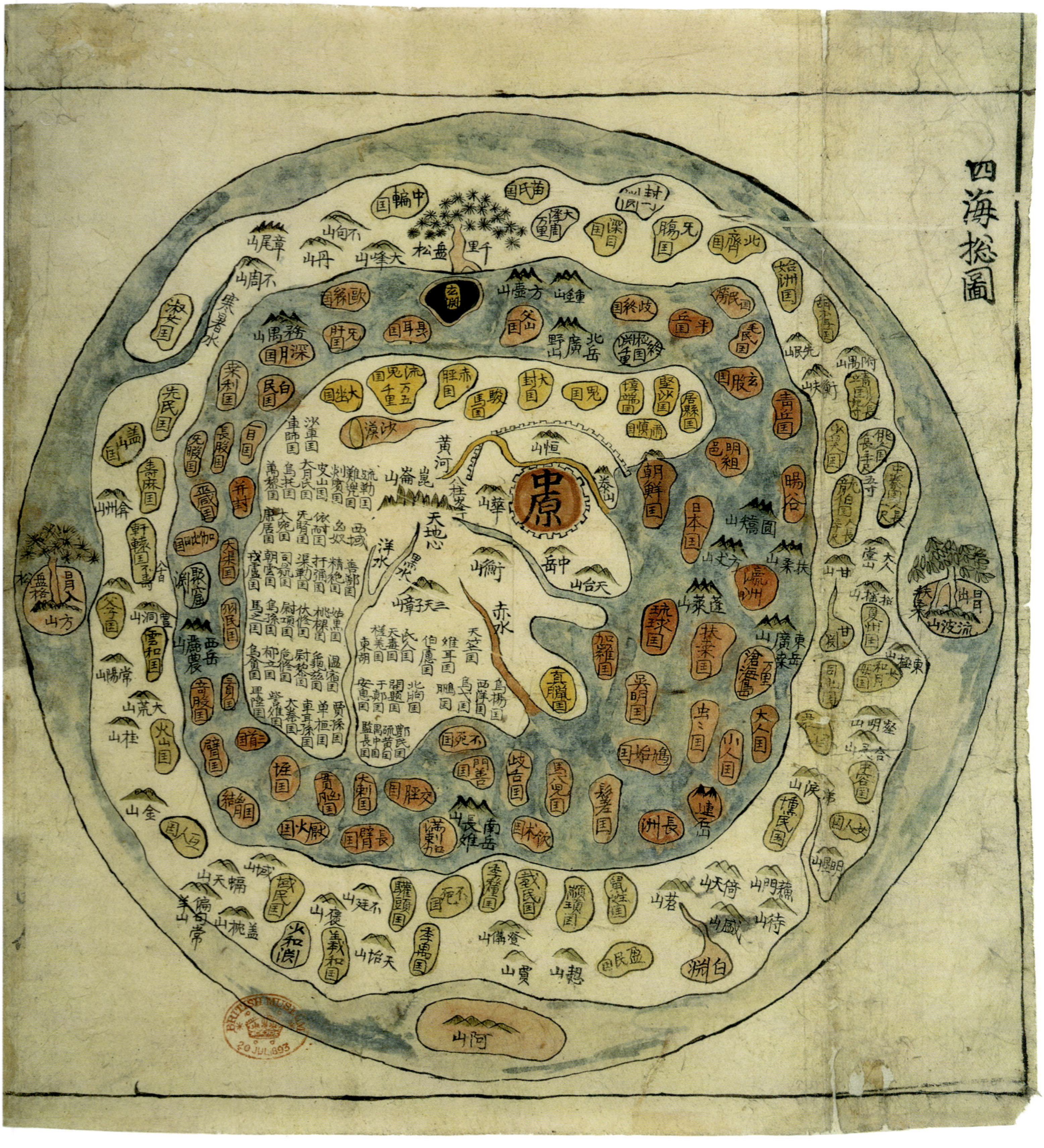
四海總圖
中原

3

RARITIES AND NOVELTIES

Annemarie Jordan Gschwend

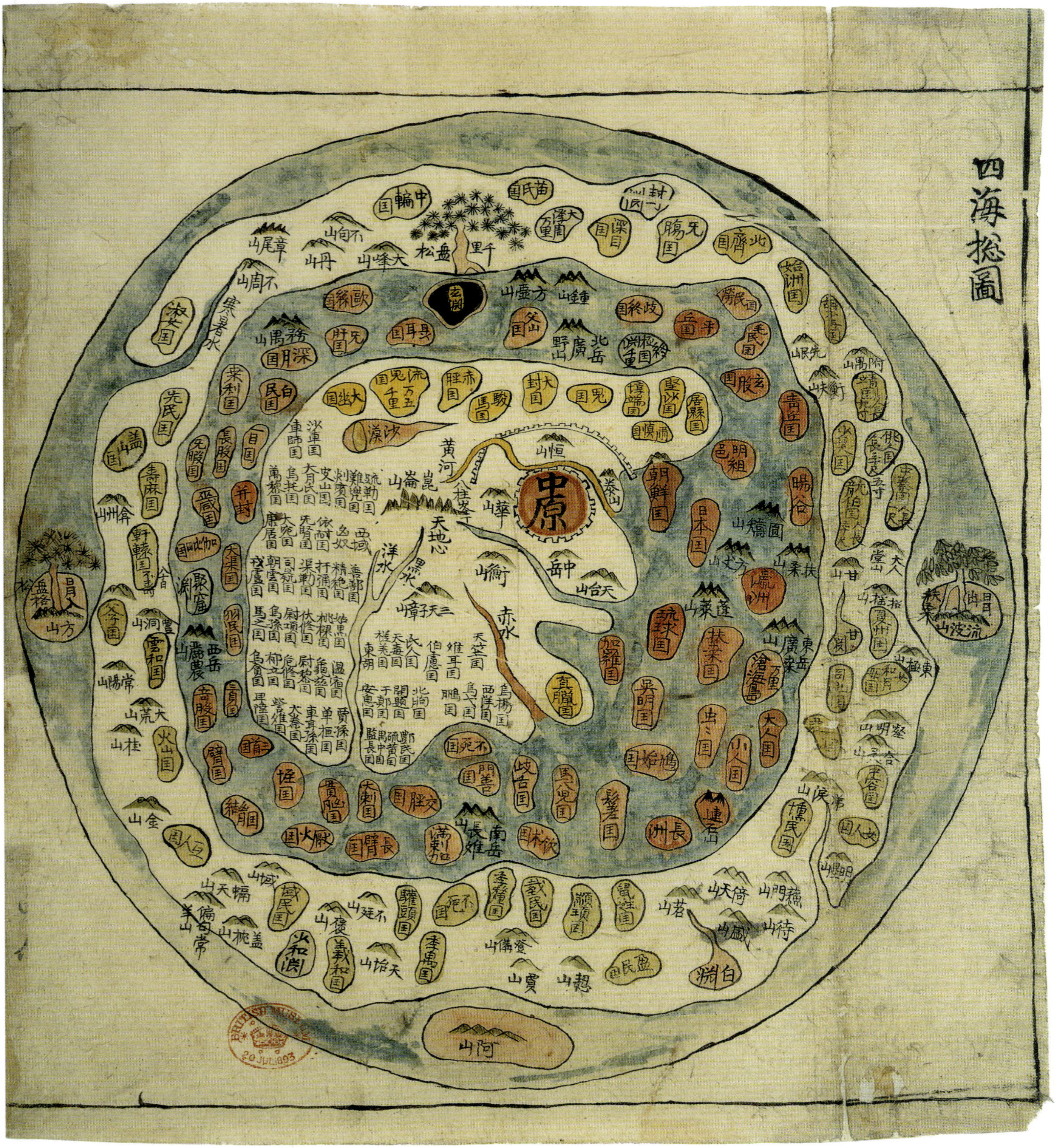
四海捴圖
中原
朝鮮国
日本国

2.16
Marathi world map
Ink on paper
India, late 18th– early 19th century
British Library, London

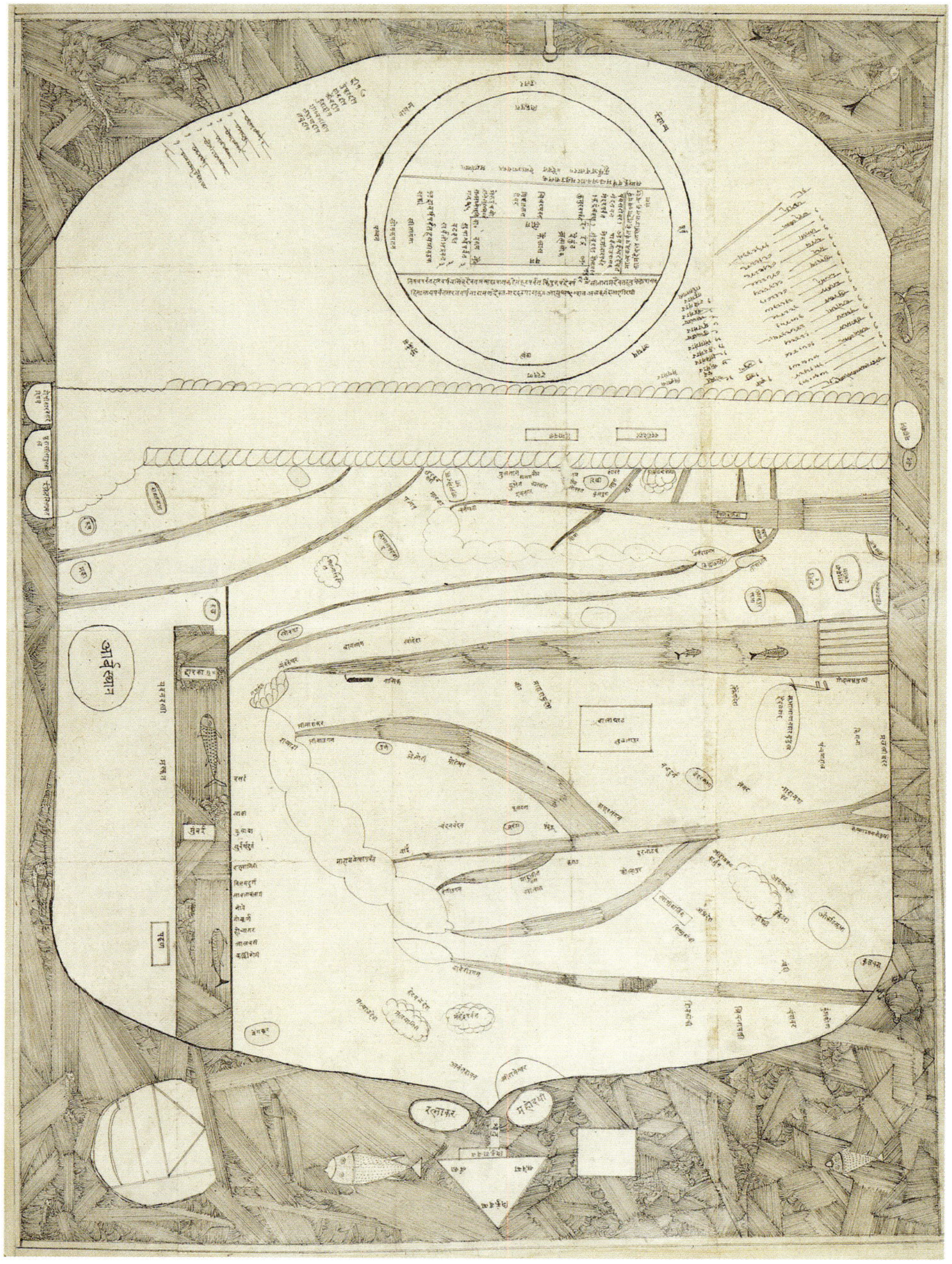

end. They could not understand the need for a map projection, since their own maps compiled a flat Earth surface on to a flat map surface. Distance and direction were all that was necessary to plot the correct positions of objects in the world. The proportions could be scaled down with the square grid. It was the map's analogy with Chinese astronomical maps that helped convince some Chinese intellectuals that Ricci's use of projection was necessary. For example, according to Feng Yingjing (1555–1606):

> It fixes the surface of the terrestrial sphere by means of the degrees of the celestial sphere; by means of the trajectory of the sun it differentiates the cold zones from the warm zones; it fixes the confines (of the world) by means of the Five Great Continents, and adds to them the specialities of products and the singularities of customs of peoples. What a nice thing![24]

The first globe made in China dates from 1623, and was not the creation of native cartographers, but of Jesuit missionaries working at the imperial court (see plate 23.1).The representation of China as one small country in a world covered mostly by water caused greater conceptual difficulties among a Chinese audience. They interpreted the great distances between Ricci's homeland and their own as mere deceit to make it seem as if Europe was not a threat to them. It has been suggested that Ricci centred his projection at 180° in the Pacific rather than 0° in the west to accord with the Chinese view that China was close to the centre of the world. There may be some truth to this suggestion, but the point has to be made that the map is not actually centred on China. Indeed, Wei Jun criticized Ricci for *not* placing China at the centre of the world. Furthermore, in the Chinese Buddhist world map tradition, the centre is traditionally located at Mount Kunlun, west of China. And the term 'Middle Kingdom', which is sometimes used to imply that the Chinese believed themselves to be at the geographic centre of the world, could just as well imply cultural or political centrality.

Ricci recorded that several versions of his map were engraved on wood or stone. A few Chinese scholars included versions of them in their own works, but introduced severe discrepancies in place-names and understanding of the longitude/latitude net. But despite this fairly wide circulation, Ricci's maps had no lasting impression on Chinese cartography. Except for the slavish reproductions, no Chinese map in the Ming dynasty perpetuated the use of Ricci's coordinate system. There were several reasons for this. Certainly, the geographic

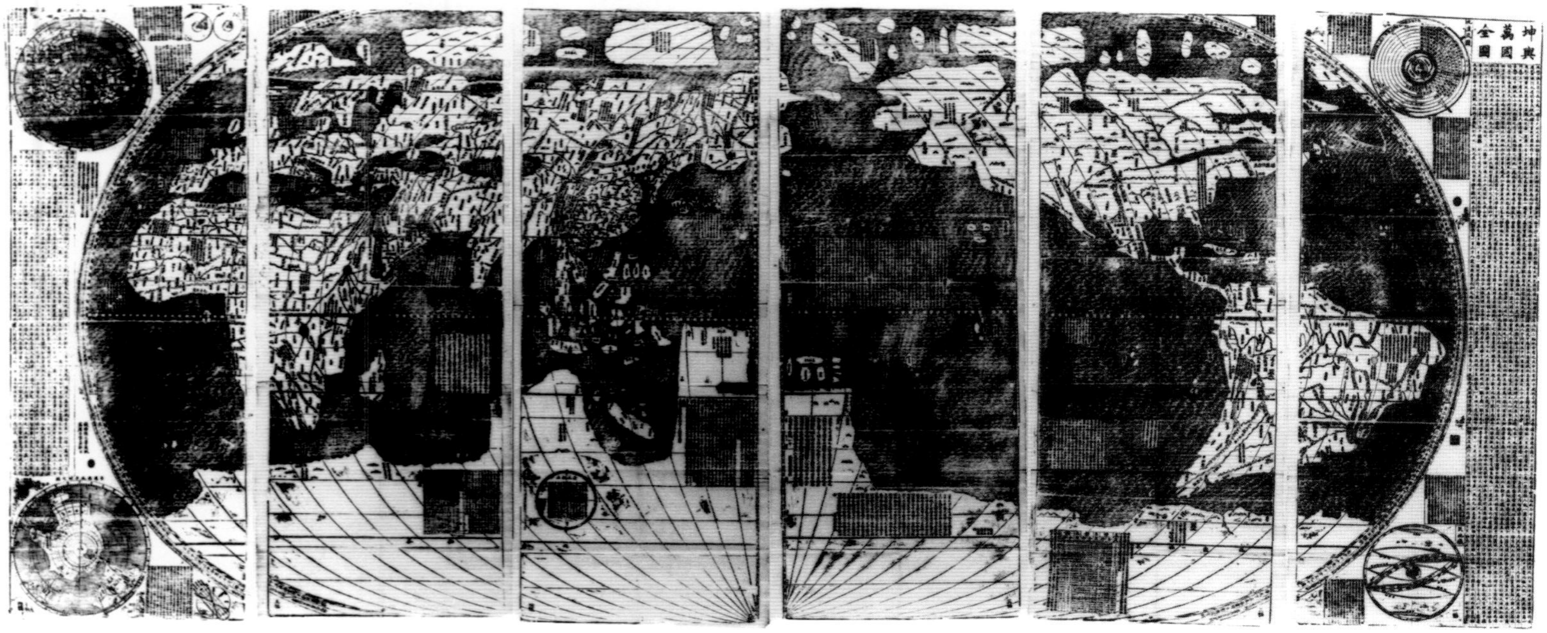

information about China was superior in Chinese maps. Although Ricci had made some longitude and latitude observations of prominent landmarks, he over-estimated the number of *li* in a degree of latitude by about 22 per cent (250 instead of 194). The Chinese rightly believed that they could learn little from the West on the geography of their own country, longitude and latitude notwithstanding. And perhaps more complacently than correctly, they also believed they had little to learn about the rest of the world as well. Furthermore, a few years after Ricci's death in 1610, Chinese tolerance for Catholicism and things associated with it waned for a period.

Ricci's influence was much greater on the cartographic tradition of Europe than it was on that of China. He was able to provide Europeans with more reliable geographic sources for East Asia than had earlier maps of the area, such as the 1579 edition of a Chinese atlas by Luo Hongxian, a copy of which was brought to Rome by Michele Ruggieri in 1590. In addition to an improved representation of the Chinese mainland, Ricci's map contained a feature that Gastaldi's map had completely ignored: the Korean peninsula, which he derived from Luo's map. It was one of the sources used by Martino Martini's innovative *Novus atlas sinensis* (1655) along with local gazetteers and other Chinese sources. By the beginning of the eighteenth century, the Chinese tolerance for Jesuit knowledge had reawakened as the Kangxi emperor (r. 1662–1722) commissioned a survey of the whole empire from French Jesuits led by Jean-Baptiste du Halde (1674–1743), using a combination of local records and astronomically fixed data positions. Du Halde presented his results to the emperor in the form of an atlas in 1718. A copy of the 1721 woodblock edition of the atlas was sent back to France, where Jean Baptiste Bourguignon d'Anville (1697–1782) published it. In the West, d'Anville's maps were regarded as the standard for maps of China until the late nineteenth century.[25]

Although Ricci's map had limited immediate influence in China, Jesuit and Portuguese influence in surveying and navigation instruments and methods did have an impact in other parts of Asia, particularly in Japan. Globes, world maps and copies of the *Theatrum Orbis Terrarum* and the first three volumes of Georg Braun and Frans Hogenberg's *Civitates Orbis Terrarum* were all brought to Japan in the late sixteenth century, and such Dutch models of world maps in various projections were used on Japanese folding screens (see plate 24.23). However, the maps made for administrative purposes remained strongly traditional in China, Japan and Korea until the early twentieth century.

2.17
World map
Matteo Ricci

Xylographic printing on paper
China (Ming Court), 1602

3

RARITIES AND NOVELTIES

Annemarie Jordan Gschwend

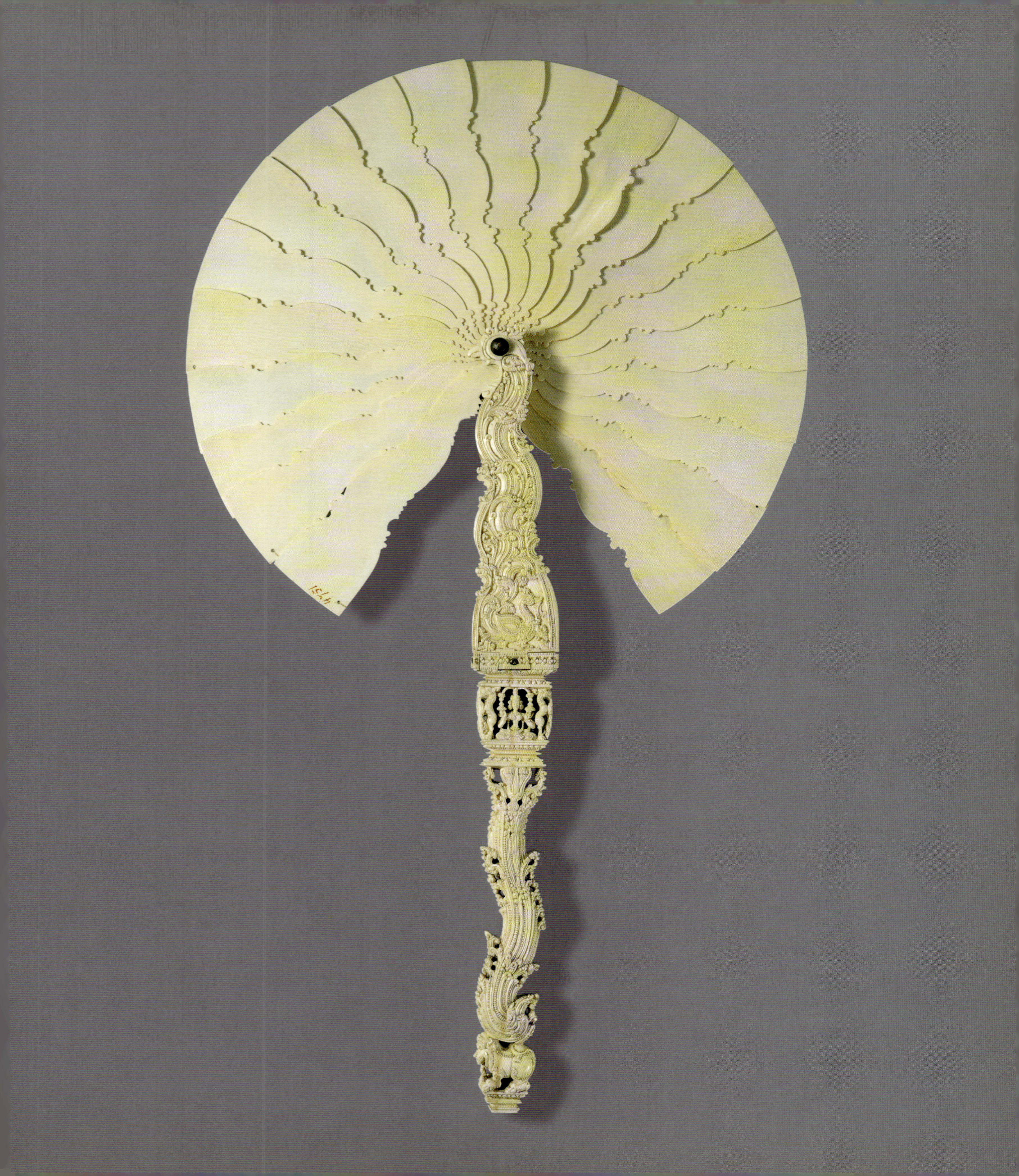

3.1 previous page
Fan
Carved ivory
Ceylon, mid-16th century
Kunsthistorisches Museum, Vienna

Late medieval treasuries, or *Schatzkammern,* were repositories for jewels, regalia, gold plate, rich textiles, ivories and tapestries accumulated by church ecclesiastics and kings. According to medieval aesthetics, art and nature reflected the ideal beauty of God, and the relations of natural and artificial phenomena were rationalized through symbol and allegory.[1] Because of their technical virtuosity, splendour and extreme rarity, such objects were often included in early collections: the wondrous horns of mythical unicorns (actually narwhal whale horns), coral branches, sharks' teeth (presumed to be fossilized serpents' tongues) and bezoar stones (hardened substances found in the stomach of the Persian bezoar goat)[2] were cherished both as wonders and as antidotes against poison. Also collected were relics or objects thought to produce miracles (*mirabilia*), objects made out of prized materials such as rock crystal, and antiquities such as ancient cameos and portrait busts. Occasionally, coconut and nautilus shells made their way to medieval Europe, where they were mounted as vessels or reliquaries (plate 3.2).[3] Particularly prized in early collections was Chinese porcelain, which was considered to possess cosmic and spiritual powers (see chapter 4).[4] To the medieval mind such articles were endowed with innate value and meaning.

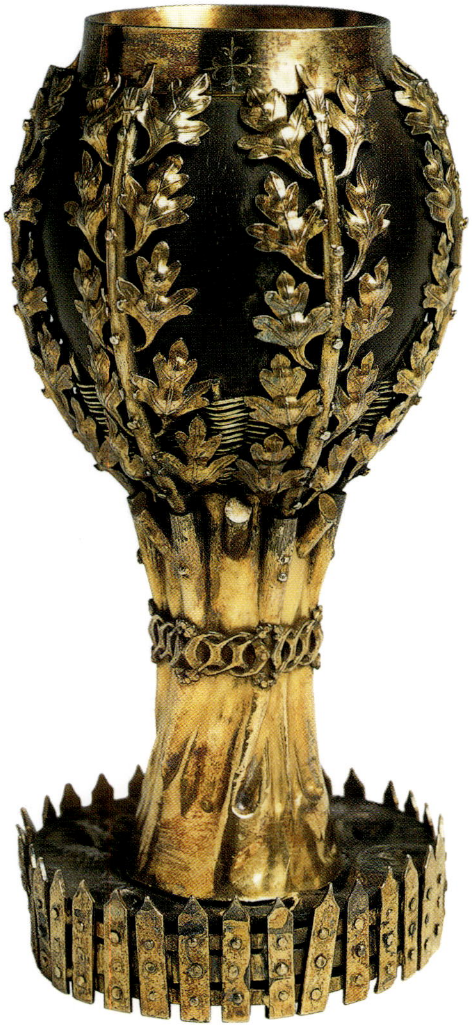

3.2
Cup
Coconut, with mounts of silver, partly gilt
England, c.1475–1500
Warden and Fellows of New College, Oxford

Such rarities arrived in Europe via tortuous trade routes connecting South and East Asia to Cairo and Alexandria by means of the Red Sea, or by even longer roads over land, along the Silk Route. At this time Venice held the monopoly in the eastern Mediterranean for the trade in goods from Asia.[5] This changed with the Portuguese discovery of the direct sea route to India in 1498, after which Lisbon became the pre-eminent marketplace in Europe for exotica, rivalling Seville, Antwerp, Venice and Genoa as commercial hub and entrepôt. Lisbon became synonymous with all imported rarities and novelties: foreign animals,[6] rare plants[7] and seeds, black and Amerindian slaves,[8] Chinese porcelain, precious objects, diamonds, gold and jewellery from India, Ceylonese ivories, gems and mounted crystals, tortoiseshell and mother-of-pearl wares from Gujarat, rhinoceros horn, lacquer, weapons and armour from China and Japan, textiles and embroideries from Cambay and Gujarat (plates 3.1, 3.3, 3.6, 3.8, 3.9). The shopping list seems endless, as an anonymous account written by a Venetian agent in Lisbon in 1568 confirms.[9] Among the goods he mentions are: Oriental pearls from Hormuz (Ormuz), fine diamonds from Bisnaga (Vijayanagara),[10] rubies from Pegu (Burma), musk, camphor, silk[11] and porcelain[12] from China, ambergris from Mozambique, *palo negro* (brazil wood) from Brazil, pepper and ginger from Calicut, cinnamon from Ceylon, nutmeg from the Banda Islands, cloves from the Moluccas and cloth from Bengal.

By the end of the sixteenth century, European rulers, collectors and merchants had long associated Lisbon as the centre for *'cosas curiosas de Portugal'*, as Empress Maria of Austria described the exotica she promised to buy her son, Rudolf II of Prague (r.1576–1612), in Lisbon in 1582.[13] Portuguese caravels returning from distant lands with precious cargoes of exotic merchandise for ever changed life at the Lisbon court as they did elsewhere in Europe.[14] During the Renaissance, Portugal assumed an essential role as intermediary between Europe and Asia, meeting market demands for luxury consumption, as well as diffusing a taste for exotic products and customs.[15] No other city or court was so completely altered by the Age of Discoveries as was Lisbon. The strange, the fantastic, the

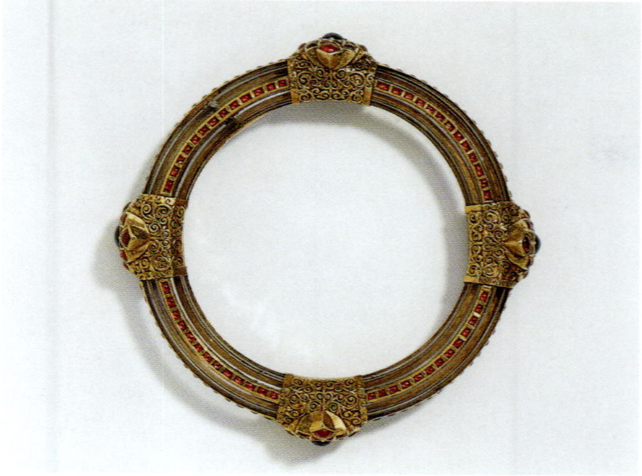

marvellous and the exotic became part and parcel of daily life in Portugal.

Following the discoveries, Humanists and princes alike were inspired by the influx of goods and commodities available in Lisbon and elsewhere in the marketplaces of Europe, and a taste for large-scale collecting developed. The *Kunst* and *Wunderkammer* (literally 'chamber of art' and 'chamber of wonder') designates collections north of the Alps and differs in concept from early Renaissance *studioli* in Italy.[16] Extraordinary objects and luxury goods were juxtaposed with oddities of nature (*naturalia*), such as mounted bezoars and nautilus shells, along with exceptional manufactured objects (*artificialia*), like Chinese lacquer and porcelain (see chapter 4). The underlying precept of such collecting was: the greater the diversity, the better. Some collections were more random in their conceptions, while others were grounded by intellectual and philosophical aims. Late Renaissance collectors sought to create showcases reflecting their universal, encyclopaedic knowledge, where objects reflecting the outer world (macrocosm) were assembled in one space (microcosm).

Renaissance *Kunstkammern* have their roots in medieval treasuries; however, collecting – no longer conditioned by haphazard accumulation – became increasingly systematic. In 1565 a Flemish physician employed at the Bavarian court of Duke Albert V (1528–79), Samuel Quiccheberg (1529–65), set out to organize the ideal collection based on Pliny the Elder's *Historia Naturalis*. His book, *Inscriptiones vel tituli theatri amplissimi* (Munich, 1565), instructed collectors how *Kunstkammern* should be arranged, dividing a collection into categories, classes and sub-categories. He classified high-quality objects, both natural and artificial, according to their materials and in a logical sequence. He then applied Giulio Camillo's current notion of the theatre of the world,[17] or *theatrum sapentiae*, in which the universe, in all its variety, was hermetically contained in one space, its contents decided by diversity, abundance, the irregular, the odd and the uncommon. Quiccheberg defined for the first time a *Kunstkammer* (a chamber for artistic objects) and a *Wunderkammer* (a repository for extraordinary objects).

For Quiccheberg, a collection and its objects defined the character of its owner, while the quality of artwork reflected his honour. For these reasons, a collector engaged skilful painters, jewellers and goldsmiths to carry out important commissions. According to Quiccheberg's principles, a collection was a representation of the outside world symbolically possessed, controlled and understood by its owner, in which objects belonged to a certain tradition of collecting and were selected to underscore and exemplify his status, power and knowledge.[18] A later depiction of an art chamber encapsulates the quintessence of such a *Kunstkammer* collection (plate 3.10). The artist has taken great pains to depict the objects in detail, both man-made (*artificialia*) and natural (*naturalia*). Displayed here are examples of Ming porcelain, incised and mounted nautilus shells, coral branches, a stuffed armadillo, clocks, scientific instruments, weapons, globes, maps, books, religious objects and relics (*mirabilia*), portraits, furniture and sculpture.

The great fortune after 1498 of the King of Portugal, Manuel I (r. 1495–1521), in having direct access to exclusive commodities from Asia, made his the most envied court in Europe. Princes vied with one another to secure his favour, hoping this would enable them to obtain objects for their collections from the Lisbon marketplace. In 1516 the French king, François I (r. 1515–47), despatched his agent, Antoine de Conflans, to Lisbon with the sole purpose of buying elephants and other exotic animals for his menagerie at Amboise. A letter, sent in advance to Manuel I, begged the Portuguese monarch to facilitate the purchase of a male and female elephant and various Oriental products.[19] The French king's interest in foreign beasts had been aroused by the sight in 1516 of Manuel's rhinoceros, which he encountered in Marseilles while it was en route to the papal court at Rome (see plate 3.12).[20] From 1530, through agents in Portugal, Italy and the Levant, François also began to acquire Indian, Chinese and Turkish exotica, books and naturalia for his collection of curiosities at Fontainebleau and the Louvre.

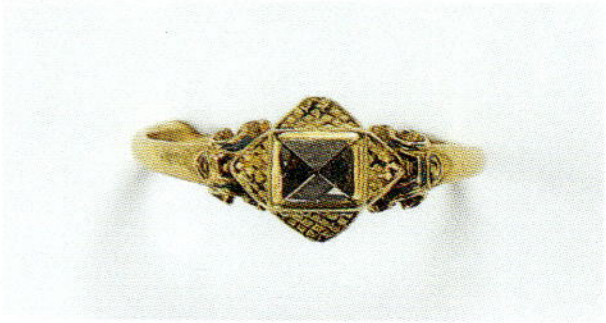

3.3
Ring

Gold, set with diamond
Western Europe, 16th century

V&A: M.220–1975

Until the discovery of diamonds in Brazil in the early 18th century, the world's diamonds were supplied from Indian mines.

3.4 left
Bangle

Rock crystal, set in gold, with rubies and sapphires
Ceylon, early 16th century

Berkeley Castle, Gloucestershire

The bangle was reputedly given by Elizabeth I to her cousin, Henry Carey, 1st Baron Hunsdon.

3.5
Spoon

Rock crystal, set in gold, with rubies and sapphires
Ceylon, 16th century

Kunsthistorisches Museum, Vienna

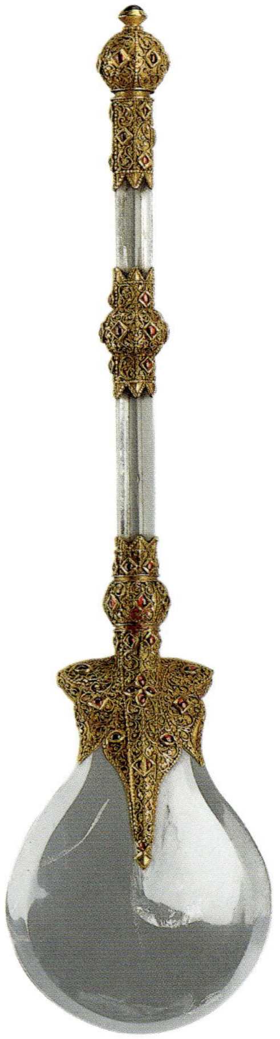

3.6
Cup

Rhinoceros horn, carved and set with gold filigree mounts
Cup: China, early 17th century; mounts: India (Goa), 17th century

Kunsthistorisches Museum, Vienna

3.7 opposite
Nautilus cup

Nautilus shell, with mounts of silver, partly gilt, by Nikolaus Schmidt
Shell: western Pacific Ocean; mounts with Nuremberg town and maker's mark, *c.*1600

The Royal Collection

In 1564 the cosmographer André Thevet (1504–92) was appointed guardian of the French royal cabinet, later called the *Cabinet des singularitez*, which he supervised until his death in 1592.[21] François's wife, Leonor of Austria (1498–1558) (sister of the Habsburg emperor Charles V), had previously lived at the Lisbon court, having been married to Manuel I. This was a bonus for the King of France, whom she must have assisted in the formation of his collection. Leonor herself owned a large group of Indian gems and jewels that Manuel had presented to her in 1518, and which she took with her to France in 1530.[22] A recently discovered receipt in the Archives Nationales in Paris confirms François's purchases of Asiatica in Lisbon. In 1529 he procured from a French merchant based in Lisbon, Pierre Lemoyne, a Gujarati mother-of-pearl chalice with decorative mounts made of black mastic with gold foliage and figures, for his *cabinet* in the Louvre.[23]

An ornate Gujarati mother-of-pearl casket, with silver-gilt mounts added in Paris between 1532 and 1533 by François's court goldsmith, Pierre Mangot, probably came from the king's own collection (plate 3.9).[24] The casket is one of the earliest examples of an Indian object for a princely *Kunstkammer*, transformed in Europe into an objet d'art of the highest quality. Michèle Bimbenet-Privat has argued that the king himself dictated its final, opulent appearance: a combination of Indian and French Renaissance stylistic elements. The brass or silver rivets or

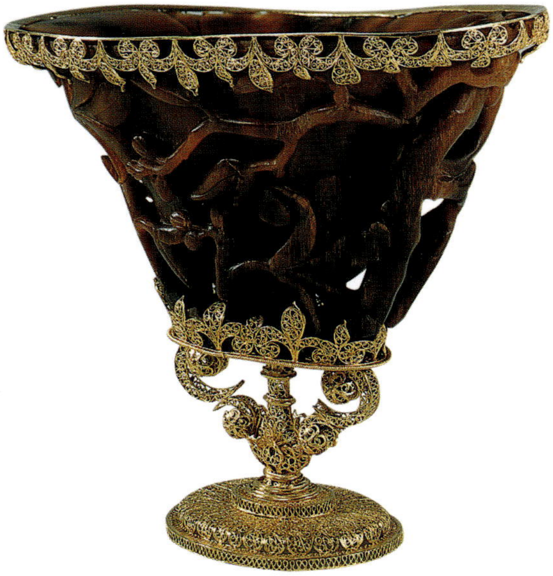

flowers normally seen on such Gujarati caskets have been replaced here by jewelled bosses. The square lock surmounted by a lizard (a symbol for the River Ganges), also typical of Gujarati caskets, has also been transformed, and ball-and-claw feet added.

Dynastic alliances united the Portuguese and Spanish courts in the Renaissance. A double marriage that linked Portugal's royal house of Avis with the imperial court of the Habsburgs was celebrated in 1525 and 1526. Manuel I's son, João III (r.1521–57), married Catherine of Austria (1507–78), while her brother, the Emperor Charles V (r.1516/19–56) married João's sister, Isabella of Portugal (1503–39). The Habsburg family network, which thus bridged Lisbon and Madrid with imperial courts in Brussels and Vienna, was close throughout the sixteenth century. Family relations were fostered over time and great distances with extensive correspondence, diplomatic ties and the exchange of important, costly gifts. Resident ambassadors in Madrid, Lisbon and Vienna made sure that political and family relations were nurtured and communications kept open. For instance, the periodic bouts of illness that Catherine of Austria experienced in her early years as queen alarmed her brother Charles V enough to prompt him to send her, in 1528, a piece of a unicorn horn, valued for its reputed therapeutic properties. The giving of gifts constantly reinforced ties: Catherine delighted in sending her siblings and niece in Brussels (Charles V, Leonor of Austria, Mary of Hungary and Renée, Duchess of Lorraine) gifts of gloves scented with amber, small perfume cakes and aromatic sticks,

3.8
Casket

Tortoiseshell with silver mounts
India, 16th or early 17th century

V&A: M.10–1945

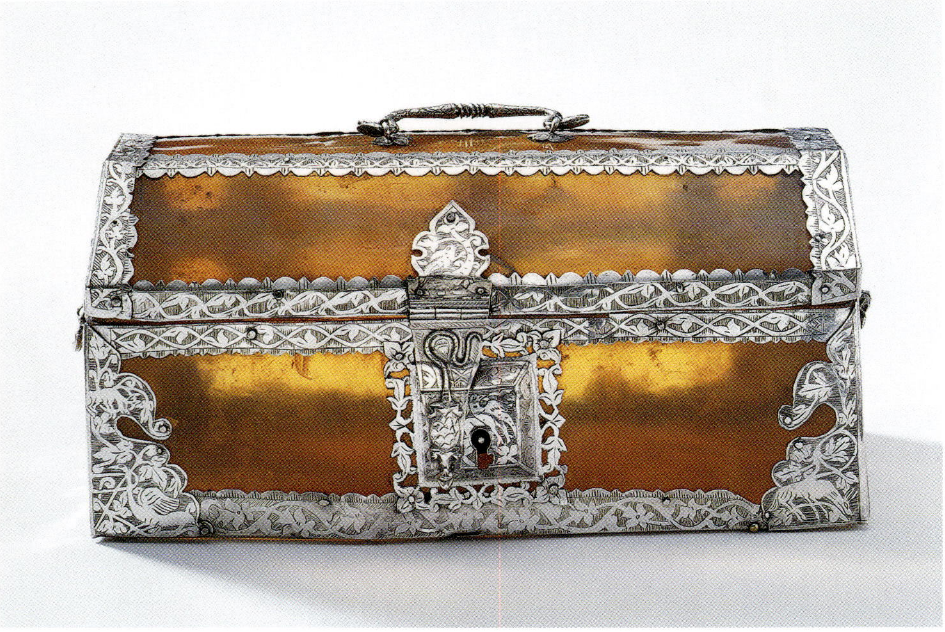

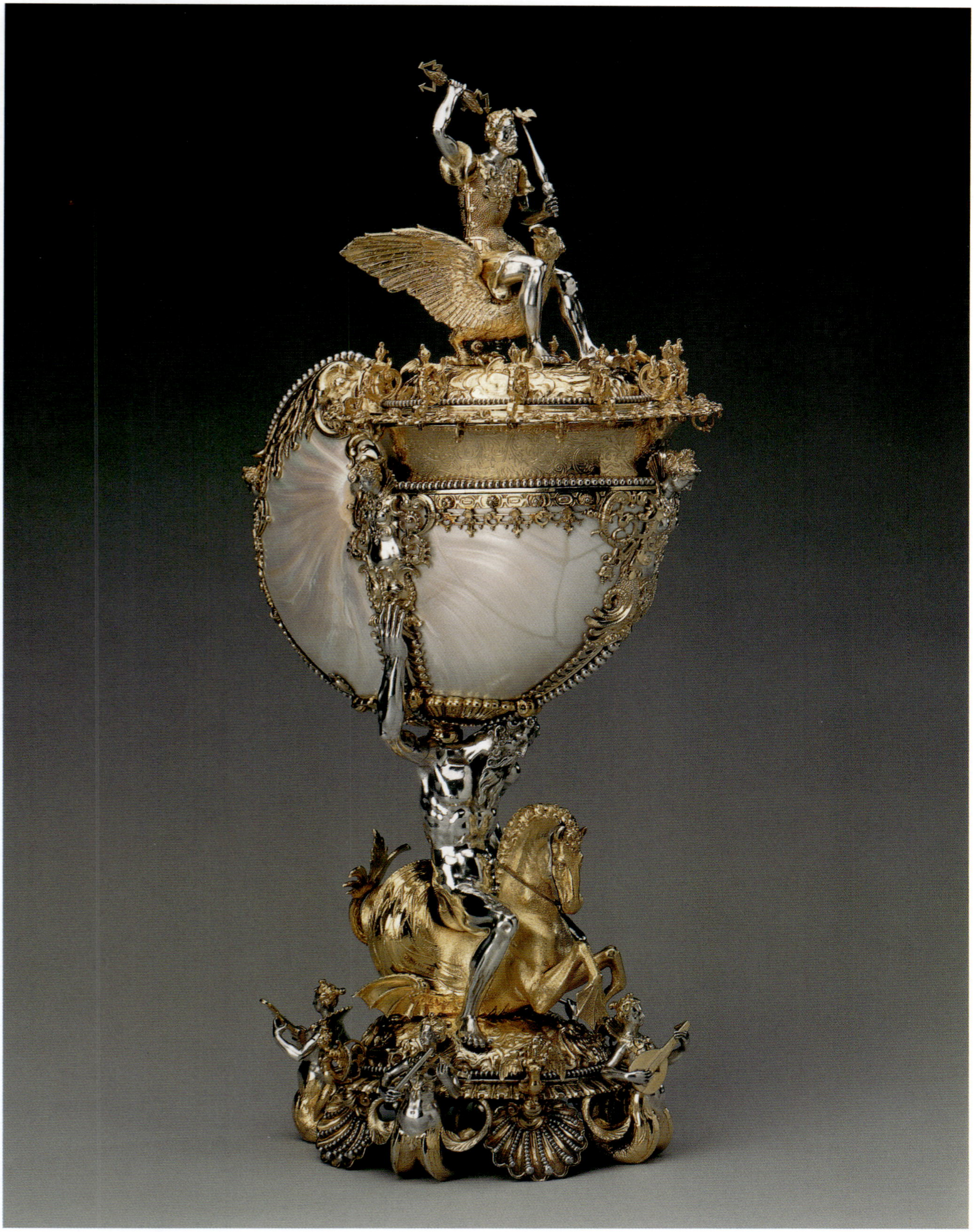

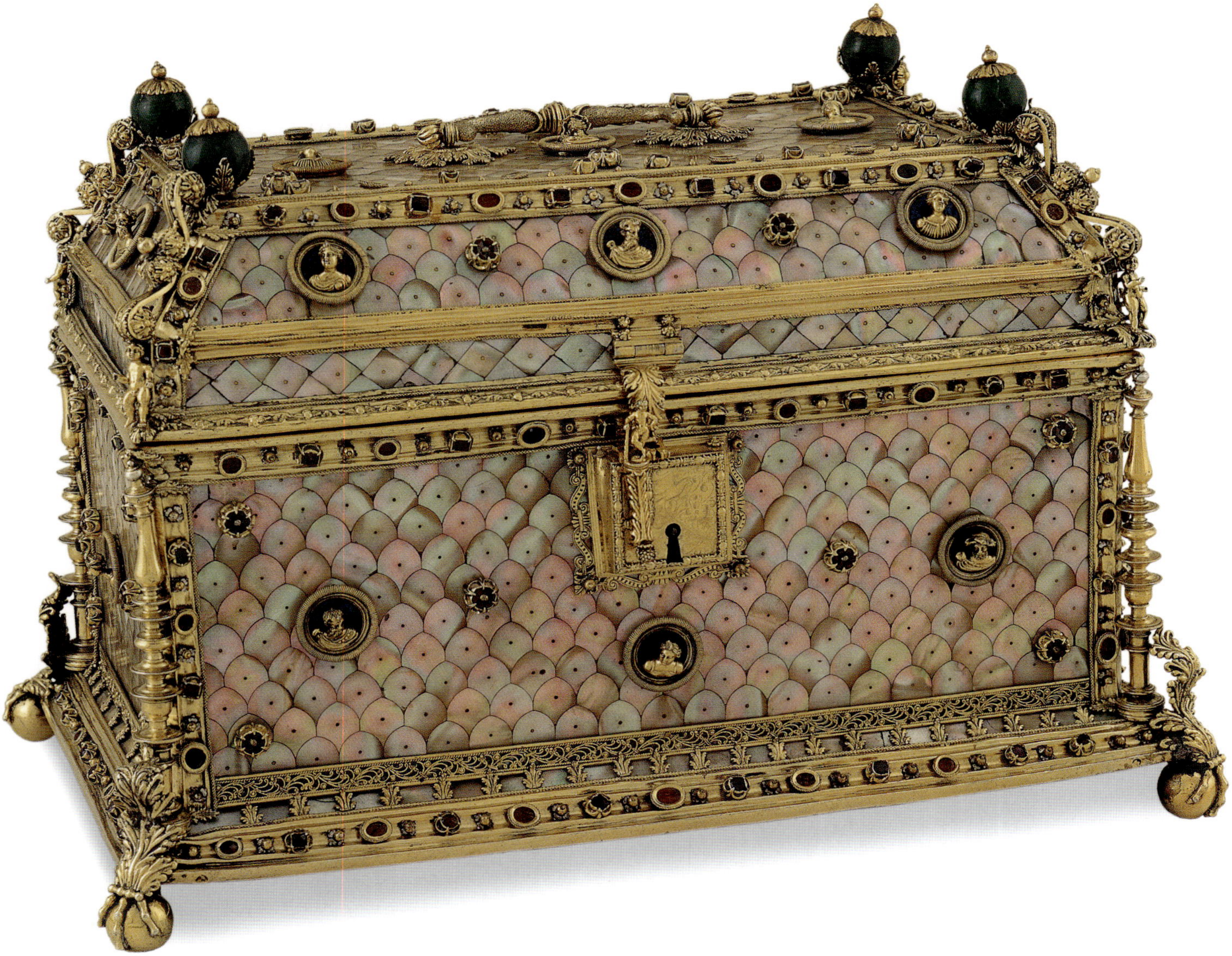

3.9
Casket

Teak, covered with plaques of mother-of-pearl, with mounts of silver-gilt by Pierre Mangot
Casket: India (Gujarat), early 16th century; mounts: France (Paris), 1532–33

Musée du Louvre, Paris

resembling incense, the latter undoubtedly imported from Asia.[25]

Catherine's access to exotica and rarities afforded members of her Habsburg family with the unique opportunity to request and receive Asian commodities and curiosities. In 1542 she sent her nieces in Spain, Juana and Maria of Austria, Gujarati tortoiseshell vessels and a casket with silver bands.[26] The latter gifts were the first Indo-Portuguese wares seen at the Madrid court. In 1563 her brother Ferdinand I (r. 1556–64) asked for 10 pieces of the best amber available in Lisbon. To amuse her brother Charles during his retirement at the monastery of Yuste, Catherine sent him a rare parrot by special courier. In turn, Catherine was given rarities unavailable in Lisbon, such as several claws of a legendary beast known in Vienna as the *Gran Bestia*, sent by her niece, Maria of Austria (1528–1603) as a showpiece for Catherine's *Kunstkammer*.[27]

Catherine's collection, filled with rarities and incomparable items from India, Ceylon and East Asia, was housed in a suite of rooms adjacent to her private quarters in the Lisbon royal palace, the *Paço da Ribeira*. She assembled the first significant *Kunstkammer* in Renaissance Portugal, acquiring more non-European objects before the mid-sixteenth century than any other contemporary collector. The queen was also an astute businesswoman. For instance, she often purchased, at discounted rates, Indian textiles and clothes in Goa to sell in Lisbon, and in turn exported Portuguese wine to Goa, in order to finance her household and shopping expenses.[28] The acquisition of exotica came to embody Catherine's rank and status over the course of her reign, and her *Kunstkammer* defined her social and political position at the Portuguese court. From the outset of her rule, Catherine developed an intricate network of agents who provided her with unique information about acquisitions and procured goods from even the remotest of regions, such as the Ryūkyū Islands in the Japanese archipelago. The queen also recruited Portuguese viceroys in her efforts to amass an incomparable collection. In 1564 the viceroy in Goa, Antão de Noronha, informed the queen of the status of one of her shopping lists, apologising for his delay.[29]

In 1558 Catherine received a shipment from Goa with numerous exotica: three Bengali quilts (*colchas*) (see 20.6), five Indian rugs, perhaps Persian or Turkish in origin, a large coconut in the shape of an Indian boat, a crystal spoon and fork encrusted with rubies from Ceylon and three pieces of Asian lacquer, one of which was a mounted white lacquer bowl painted with gold fish.[30] Catherine's personal servant and agent in Malacca, João Pedroso, sent the queen folding fans and lacquer tables, chairs, caskets and writing desks from China and Japan in 1562.[31] A folding Indian bed (*catre*) was purchased as a gift for her lady-in-waiting in 1555, as were a box of Indian clothes and 320 pieces of Chinese porcelain.[32]

Other *Kunstkammer* objects in the queen's collection were sent to her as prestigious diplomatic gifts, as in 1528 when Catherine was presented with Bengal cotton, Asian fans[33] and coconuts from an Indian potentate.[34] During the 1540s she received a number of exceptional Ceylonese ivories, commissioned expressly for the Lisbon court as unique diplomatic gifts offered by the emperors Bhuvaneka Bahu (r.1521–51) and his grandson, Dharmapala (r.1551–97). These ivory caskets, combs and folding fans symbolize the close political, commercial and artistic ties that Catherine cultivated with Ceylon. A Sinhalese casket executed around 1557 is the first of such ivory caskets to depict Christian motifs, and was probably a gift to commemorate the conversion of Dharmapala to Christianity, underscoring his close ties with the Portuguese court (see plate 6.10). In that year Dharmapala sent a Sinhalese delegation to Lisbon and it is probable that the casket featured among the gifts to João III.[35]

In a world of rulers who were also collectors, the exchange of gifts became the centre of diplomatic activity.[36] During the Renaissance many Habsburgs (male and female) became obsessive collectors and consumers of things Asian, exploiting their family connections to acquire the best and novel on the market for their own consumption and for their *Kunstkammern*. These Habsburgs became true connoisseurs of Asiatica and exotica. Habsburg family identity focused on a cult of the dynasty, and their significance as a ruling family, whose power was literally global, was enhanced by the exchange of exotic gifts – rarities that raised the notion of a family collective. Hugh Trevor-Roper's seminal study of patronage at the Habsburg courts characterized their collecting as a typical family tradition passed down from generation to generation, reflecting distinctive tastes and patterns.[37] Similarities exist in the objectives, goals and patterns of collecting between male and female members of the Habsburg house. A family ideology motivated many Habsburg collectors and select *Kunstkammer* objects were singled out, in a political sense, to represent the family and dynasty. In a recent essay on Central European *Kunstkammern*, Thomas DaCosta Kaufmann outlines the motivation behind these collections. He emphasizes that cultural politics and an ethic of magnificence were fundamental to Habsburg collectors.[38]

In 1564, by royal decree, Catherine's brother, Ferdinand I, gathered together the imperial collections scattered among various residences into one central location, thus formally establishing a *Kunstkammer*. This was the first institution of its kind in Central Europe.[39] Vienna was chosen as the permanent seat to house the objects that Ferdinand deemed sacred to the Habsburg dynasty. Two objects – a unicorn horn and an antique Roman agate bowl (thought then to be the Holy Grail) – were prohibited from being sold or dispersed, and with this decree were safeguarded for ever. These family heirlooms

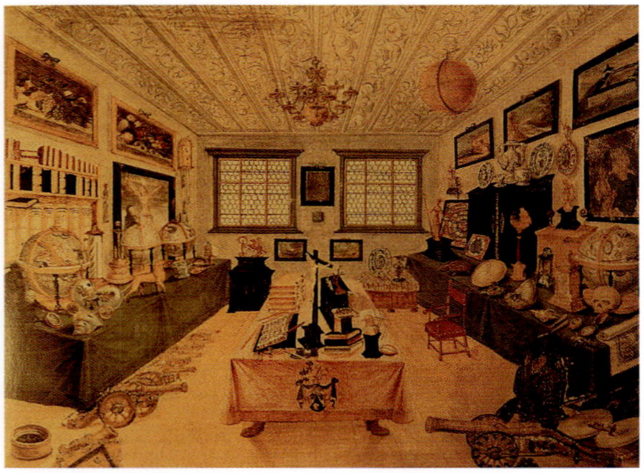

3.10
A Kunst and Naturalia Chamber
Joseph Arnold

Oil on canvas
Germany, 1668

Ulm Museum, Ulm

formed the nucleus of what became a Habsburg museum. Ferdinand's formal establishment of a centralized collection set an unprecedented example for his immediate family. For example, his sons Maximilian II (r. 1564–76) and Ferdinand II of Tyrol (r. 1564–95), his grandson Rudolf II of Prague, and his nephew Philip II of Spain (r. 1556–98) all formed outstanding collections and *Kunstkammern* filled with Asian curiosities and exotica (plates 3.1, 3.5). A collection (no matter how large or how many objects it contained) was understood by its symbolic content: not just merely as a microcosm, resembling the world itself, but also from a cosmic point of view, which advanced the political claims of the owner. In the case of the most famous of Habsburg collectors, Rudolf II, his *Kunstkammer* in Prague was understood by its owner and his court to represent the emperor's symbolic mastery of the world; the idea of *representatio* being its principal message.[40]

No object exemplifies this concept more than the Seychelles coconut that Rudolf II obtained from the Dutch admiral Wolfer Hermanszen in 1602 (plate 3.11). The virtuoso mount was commissioned from Anton Schweinberger and the relief work carved by Nikolaus Pfaff. The *coco-de-mer*, believed then to be extremely rare with mysterious origins, was given European embellishments of the highest quality. The *Triumph of Water* is the allegorical theme encircling the nut in relief, while Neptune victoriously rides his sea horse above. This cup pays symbolic tribute to the mythological lord and master of the oceans, at the same time being resonant of the maritime heritage of the sixteenth century, without which the cup would never have reached Prague.

3.11
Cup

Coco-de-mer shell, carved in relief by Nickolas Pfaff; mounted in silver by Anton Schweinberger. Cup: Seychelles; mounts: Prague, *c.*1602

Kunsthistorisches Museum, Vienna

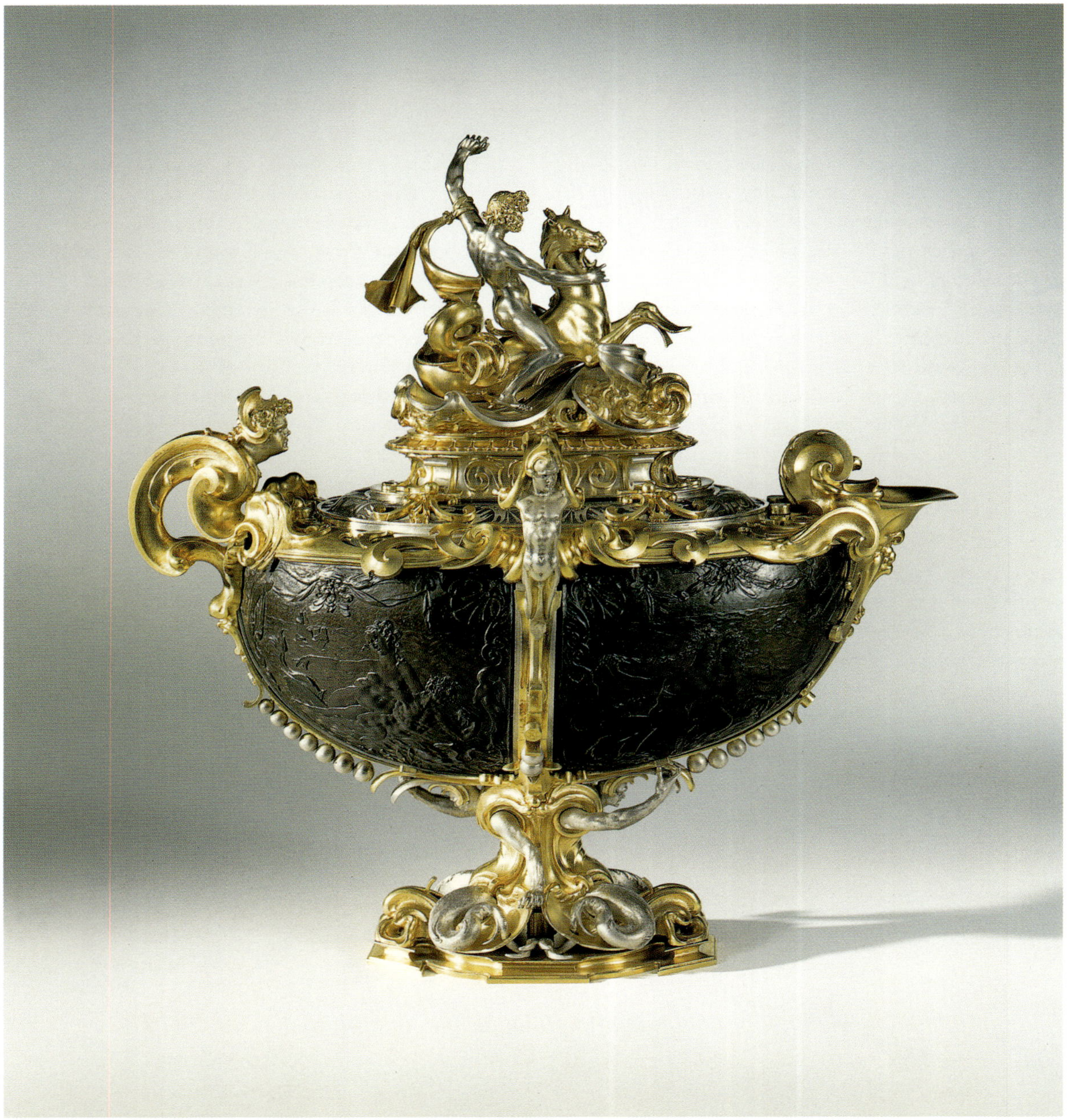

Neptune symbolizes Habsburg hegemony and rule over the world and its seas. The magnificent setting also pays tribute to the discerning taste of Rudolf, who commissioned its transformation from *naturalia* to *artificialia* of the highest level. In a microcosmic fashion, this coconut synthesizes what Rudolf's collection in a macrocosmic way represented for its owner: power, prestige and, like Neptune, a similar mastery of his world. Such objects and exotica from far-flung territories brought their owners closer to other worlds separated from them by geographical distance.[41]

In 1580, two years after the death of Catherine of Austria, Philip II of Spain annexed Portugal and its overseas territories. Lisbon remained the mercantile capital of Europe and a brisk trade in Asian products and spices continued well into the early seventeenth century, although, as part of the Spanish empire, Portugal inherited new enemies. The Dutch were encroaching in Asia, and the Portuguese were beginning to lose ground, suffering losses in their monopolies. Despite such setbacks, Asiatica continued to flood the Lisbon market, and all levels of Portuguese society from aristocracy to clergy were affected by a craze for Asian luxury goods. The Madrid court took over Catherine's role as liaison, supplying family members in Austria, the Low Countries and Bavaria with the appropriate exotica they needed.

The recent publication of a series of documents from the Archivo General de Simancas confirms that a regular flow and traffic of Asiatica was conducted between the courts of Madrid, Lisbon, Vienna, Prague, Graz, Innsbruck, Munich and Brussels, and this for over a period of 50 years, from the 1570s until 1615.[42] These collectors were knowledgeable, well informed and insatiable; money, time and expense were of little concern. As Albert V, Duke of Bavaria, emphatically stated in a letter to his relative, Philip II of Spain, in 1572, he was intent on acquiring as many curiosities as possible for his Munich *Kunstkammer*, a collection that rivalled that of his Habsburg relatives in Madrid, Vienna and Prague.

In this endless quest for exotica, diplomats, commercial agents and merchants played an increasing role in satisfying the demands of their royal and princely patrons. One of the most important personages was the imperial ambassador to the Spanish court, Hans Khevenhüller (d. 1606). His arrival at the Spanish court in 1574, and his long residency in Spain, had a marked effect on Habsburg collecting in Vienna, Prague, Innsbruck and Graz. His vast network, connections, expertise and knowledge played an influential role in the manner in which his Habsburg patrons collected and shaped their collections. He was their exclusive agent in Iberia. The high-quality, rare pieces of exotica – extant today in the Kunsthistorisches Museum, Vienna, and Schloss Ambras, Innsbruck – are there thanks to Khevenhüller's superb eye and exquisite taste. A majority of the objects in Rudolf II's famed *Kunstkammer* were obtained through Khevenhüller and reflect how the ambassador encouraged the emperor in his acquisition of rarities and curiosities. Khevenhüller superimposed his imagination and taste upon Rudolf's collection: the Prague *Kunstkammer* could never have developed without this diplomat. Khevenhüller played a key role, changing for ever the conception of collections, gardens and menageries in Central Europe.

Khevenhüller corresponded with and shopped regularly for Ferdinand II of Tyrol, Rudolf II, Archdukes Ernst and Mattias, Empress Maria of Austria, Elisabeth of Austria (the former Queen of France), Archduchess Maria of Bavaria, in Graz, and her brother, Wilhelm V, in Munich. Besides relying on the services of his well-trained, experienced employees, he recruited the services of Fugger and Welser agents with offices in Seville and Lisbon, to keep him constantly informed of the arrival of ships from overseas and the contents of their cargoes. Nothing was too small or insignificant for him to seek out and buy. He purchased everything from seeds to elephants for the Habsburgs, making sure they were shipped and safely transported to Central Europe: no small feat in the sixteenth century.

Exotic Animals in Sixteenth-Century Europe

Annemarie Jordan Gschwend

WILD AND DOMESTIC ANIMALS from Africa and Asia formed a large percentage of the cargo that Portuguese ships brought back to Lisbon during the sixteenth century. Exotic animals and the formation of princely menageries and aviaries became a fundamental part of the self-imaging of Renaissance courts.[1] The more exotic the animal, the more highly it was prized. The acquisition of foreign, often bizarre, animals became synonymous with the level of luxury and majesty that courts cultivated. Renaissance theorists believed that by taming wild animals, monarchs demonstrated their power and magnificence over the forces of nature.[2]

Manuel I of Portugal (r. 1495–1521) collected Asian elephants, parading through the streets of Lisbon with no fewer than five. Albrecht Dürer (1471–1528) immortalized in a woodcut the first rhinoceros seen in Europe since Antiquity, which Muzafar II, Sultan of Gujarat, sent the king in 1515 (plate 3.12). A combat between this beast and an elephant was staged in a courtyard of the Lisbon royal palace; the elephant fled in fright and the rhinoceros was declared victorious by default. Manuel sent this rhinoceros to Pope Leo X (r. 1513–21) in 1516 as a royal gift. Earlier, in 1513, he sent the elephant Hanno to Rome with a formal embassy led by Tristão de Cunha.

The tradition of sending exotic animals as diplomatic gifts to cement relations between princely courts continued under later Portuguese rulers.[3] In order to strengthen political ties with Vienna, in 1552 Catherine of Austria (1507–78) and João III (r. 1521–57) sent their nephew, Emperor

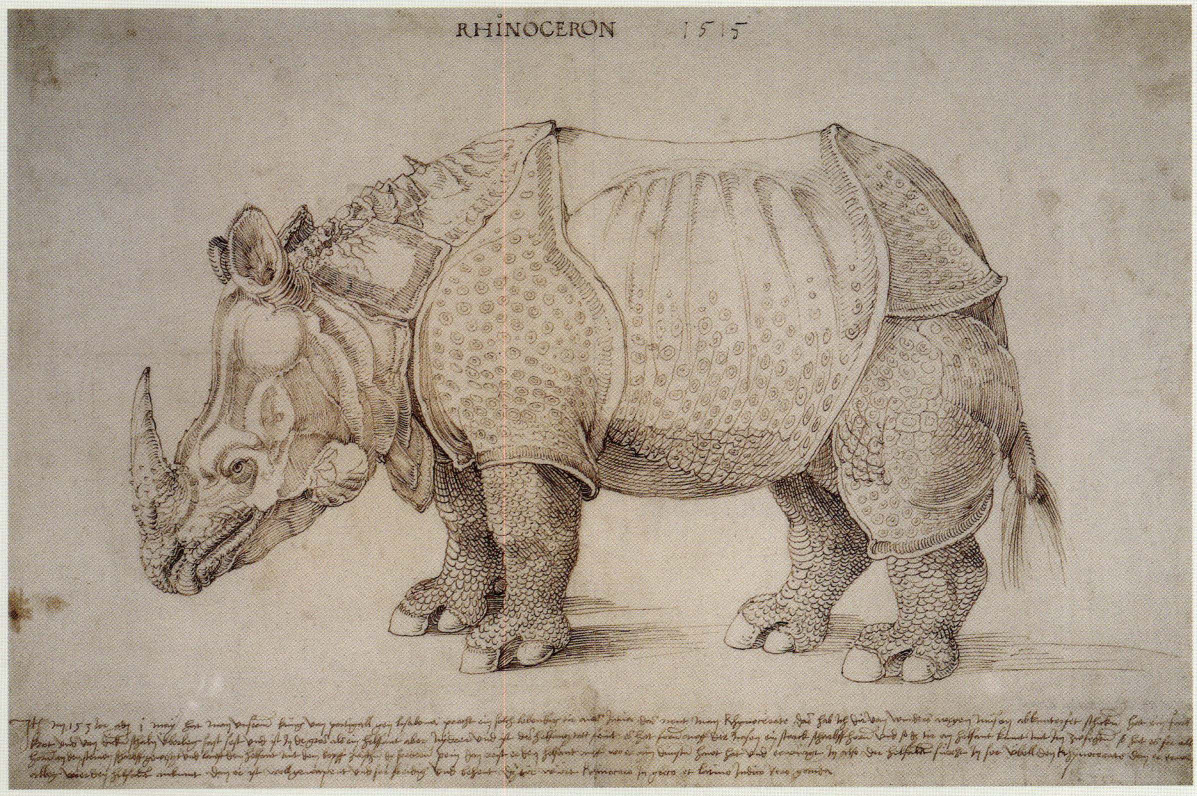

3.12 below left
The Rhinoceros of Cambay
Albrecht Dürer, after a drawing by Valentim Fernandes sent from Lisbon to Nuremberg between 3 June and 1 July 1515

Pen and ink on paper
Germany (Nuremberg), 1515

British Museum, London

3.13
Stool right, above

Engraved with the arms of Maximilian II (r. 1564–76); elephant bone
Austria (Vienna), 1554

Benediktschrift, Kresmünster Abbey

3.14 right, below
Labor: Allegory of Autumn
Georg Hoefnagel

Watercolour on parchment
Vienna or Prague, 1576

Musée du Louvre, Paris

3.15 far right
The Allegory of Earth
Giuseppe Arcimboldo

Oil on panel
Austria (Vienna), 1570

Private collection, Vienna

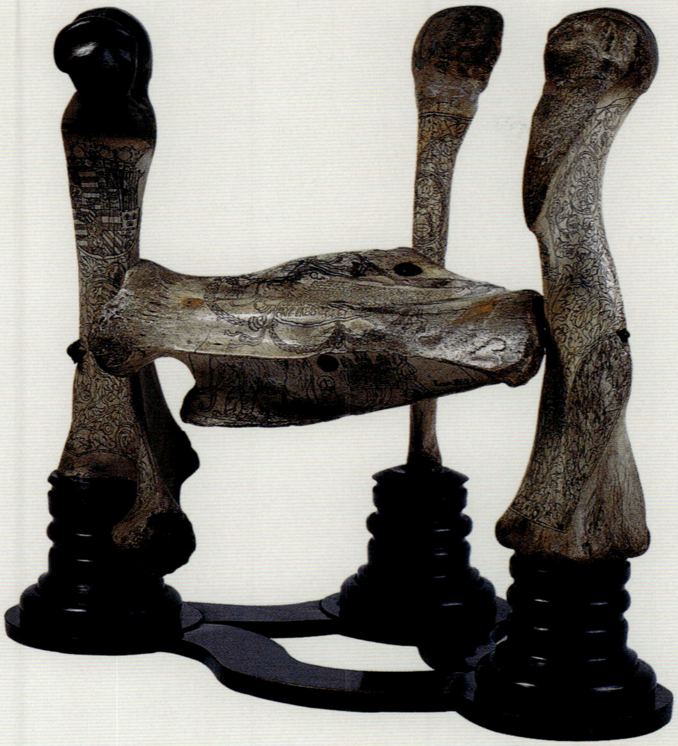

Maximilian II (r. 1564–76), an Indian elephant. It was the first one ever seen in Austria. It died one year later and some of its bones were fashioned into a stool bearing Maximilian's coat of arms (plate 3.13). Through family ties with Portugal, the Habsburg court benefited emblematically from the prestige of an allied kingdom whose power and rule extended over the flora and fauna of a vast overseas empire. Catherine of Austria sent her grandson, Infante D. Carlos (1545–68) of Spain, an African zebra in 1555, the first imported to Europe since ancient times. African and Brazilian monkeys headed princely shopping lists, as did African civet cats, prized for their musk, South American or African parrots and hunting falcons from the Americas (*Aplomados* and *Tagarotes*) (plate 3.14).

Archival documents testify to the quantity of exotic animals exported from the Iberian peninsula to imperial menageries in Vienna and Prague between 1560 and 1621. Many were documented by Maximilian II's court painter, Giuseppe Arcimboldo (1527–93), in his 1570 commission, *The Allegory of Earth*, in which the emperor's animals are depicted, including the elephant sent to him in 1552, a rhinoceros, an Indian antelope (*Cervicapra*), monkeys, a lion, a dromedary, a cheetah and a tiger (plate 3.15).[4] Exotic beasts fired the imaginations of rulers and princes, colouring daily life and festivities at European courts, where they were kept in early zoos, tamed and used for hunting or immortalized in paintings, frescos and illuminated miniatures in royal collections and palaces.

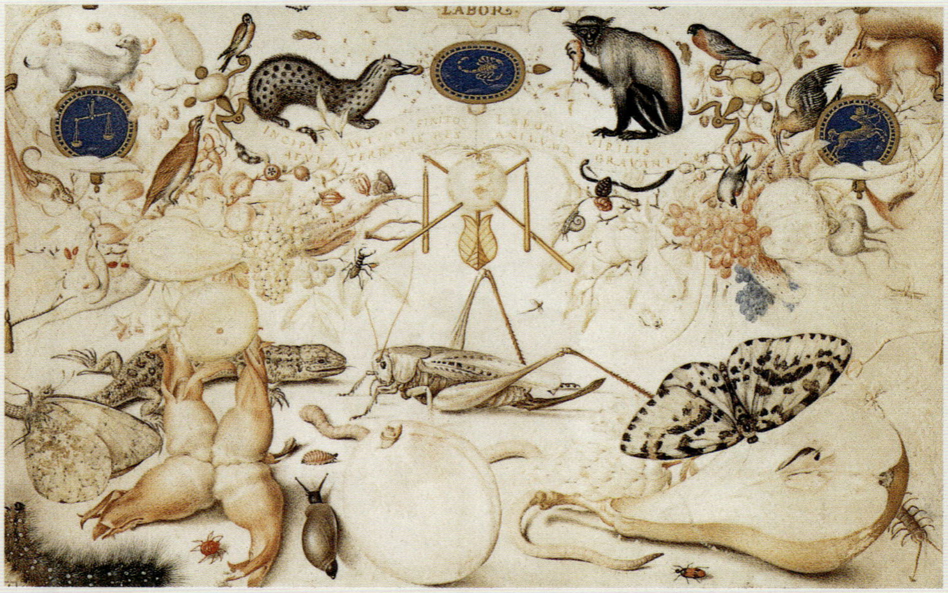

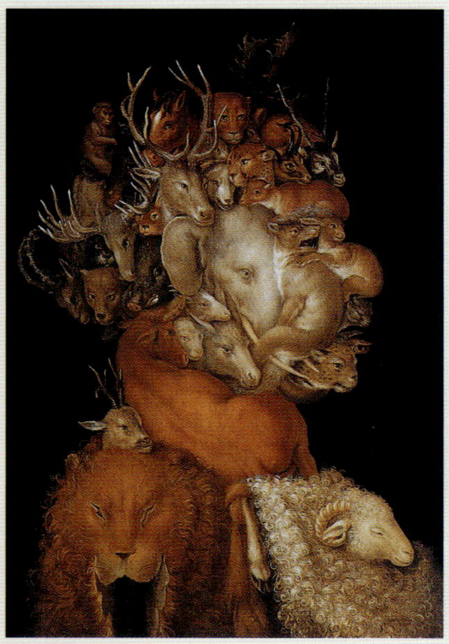

4

CHINESE PORCELAIN IN EARLY EUROPEAN COLLECTIONS

Rose Kerr

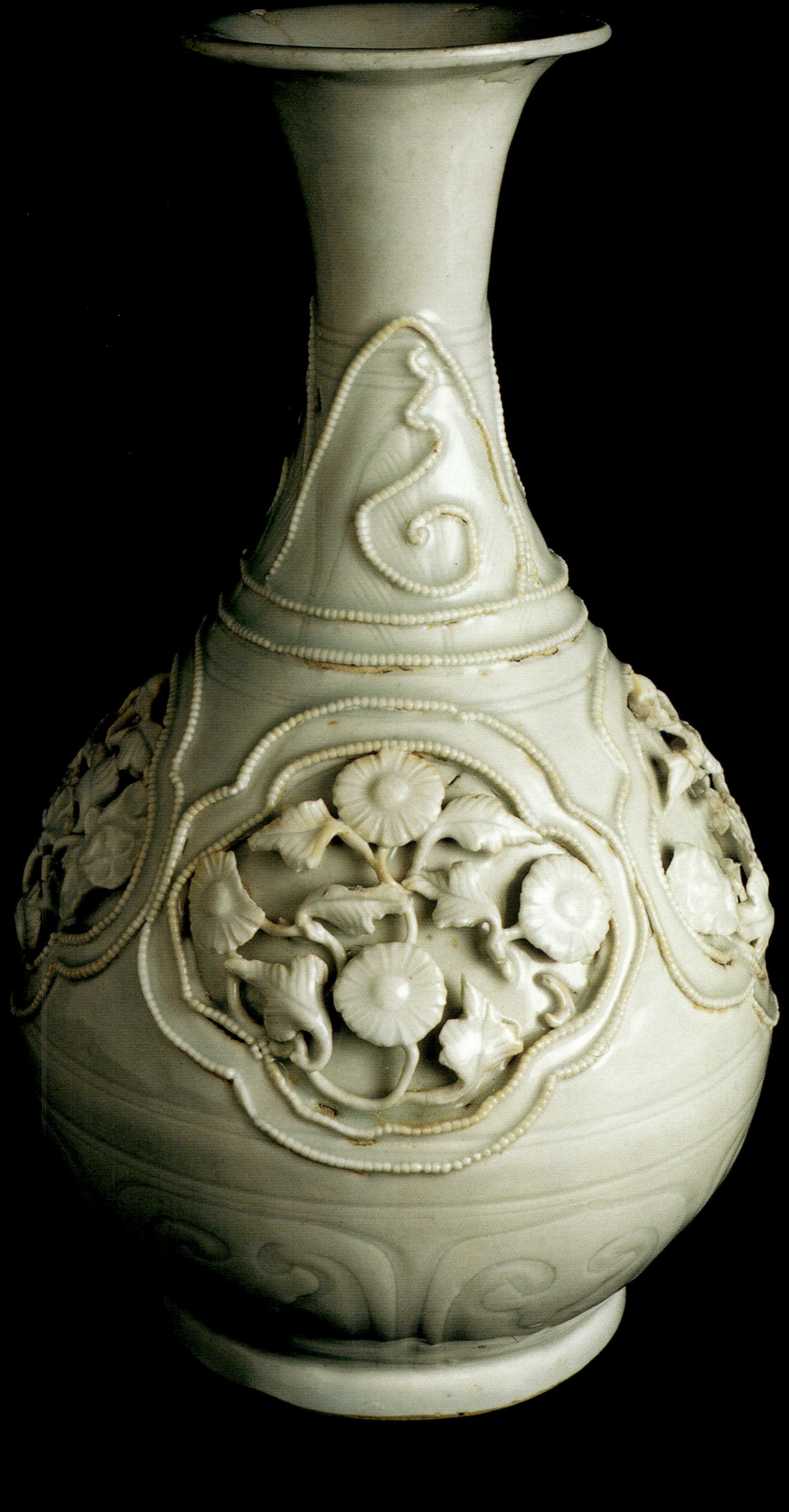

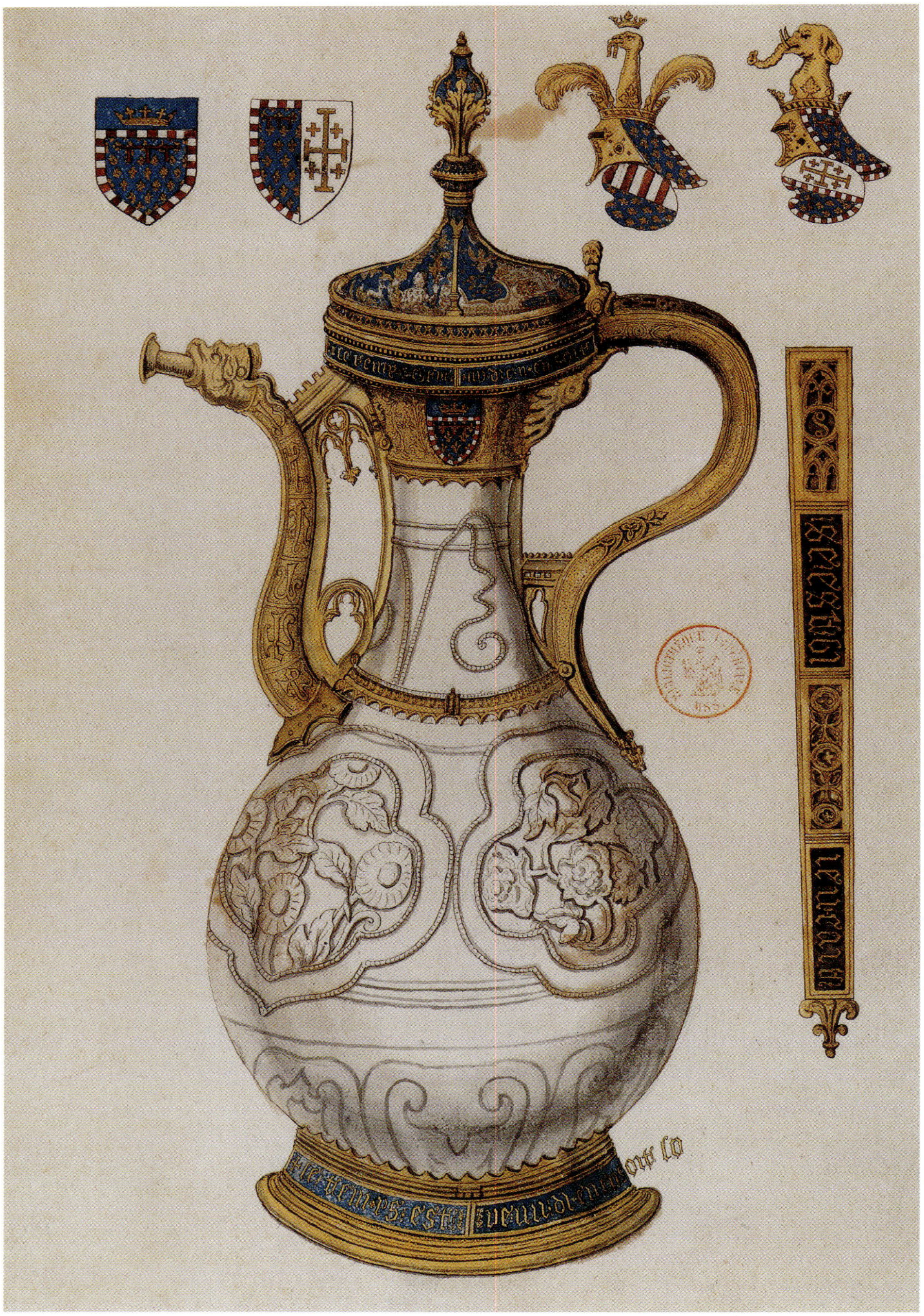

4.1 previous page
Gaignières-Fonthill Vase

Porcelain with bluish-white *(qingbai)* glaze
China, Yuan dynasty (*c.*1300–30)

National Museum of Ireland, Dublin

4.2
Drawing showing the vase transformed into a ewer with silver-gilt and enamelled mounts

Watercolour on paper
France (Paris), *c.*1713

Bibliothèque nationale de France

PORCELAIN IS ONE OF the most curious materials ever to have been created by man. Its appearance has been likened to silver, or white jade, but unlike those two substances it requires several crucial stages of intervention and change to achieve finished perfection. In contrast to the superficial working required of precious metal or stone, porcelain must be rendered down from solid rock and manipulated into workable clay, formed, decorated, glazed and fired in a kiln hot enough to transform its physical substance. In this transmutation by fire an extraordinary process is achieved, for the igneous rock from which much porcelain clay is derived is recreated in the heat of the kiln. Thus porcelain can be seen as being derived from solid rock, and as being in its own essence a refired rock.

Of course, such considerations were absent from the minds of most people who delighted in porcelain. All they could see were pure, white, translucent vessels, light in weight, fragile, graceful and easy to clean. Imagine the pleasure of holding a porcelain cup in your hand for the first time, if you had previously known only clumsy pottery or wood, or even simple leaves. It is not surprising that early commentators speculated that porcelain was some sort of precious stone, or that it was a marvellous liquid that solidified underground, or a mixture of water and crushed eggshells and seashells. Arab traders who dominated Asian maritime routes before the coming of Europeans in the sixteenth century first propounded such theories. These ideas were promulgated by the first Portuguese mission to China in 1510, and were subsequently published by Italian scholars in the mid-sixteenth century.[1] The theory that porcelain was made of crushed shells was still believed in England as late as 1646.[2]

Such notions were prevalent because for a long time after porcelain was first manufactured in the late sixth century, China held the monopoly on its production. Even the Japanese did not make porcelain before about 1610, while in Europe technological problems were not resolved until 1709 (see p. 224). Long before Europeans became involved in trade with China, porcelain was a valuable export commodity to Japan, South-East Asia, the Middle East and as far west as Africa. For example, the site of Fustat (Old Cairo) in Egypt has been extensively excavated and has yielded tens of thousands of broken pieces of porcelain dating from between about 800 and 1450.[3] Egypt stood at the westernmost end of the great trade routes from Asia, and at the

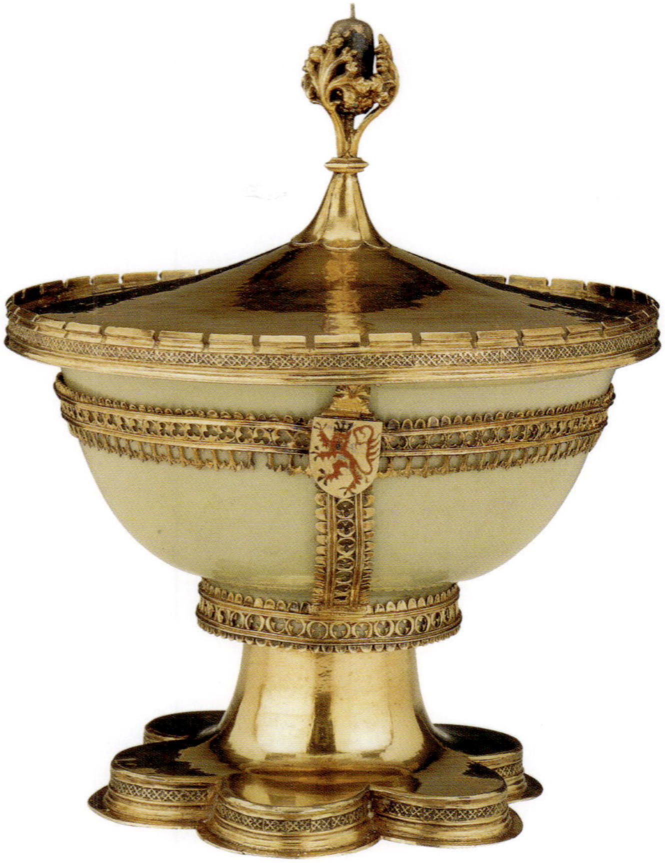

4.3 left
Bowl

Porcelain with celadon glaze and silver-gilt and enamel mounts
China (Longquan), early Ming dynasty (late 14th–early 15th century); mounts: Germany (Rhenish workshop), *c.* 1434–53

Landesmuseum, Kassel

4.4 below
Von Manderscheidt Cup

Porcelain decorated in underglaze blue, enamels and gilding with silver-gilt mounts
China, Jiajing period (1522–66); mounts: Germany, *c.* 1583

V&A: M.16–1970

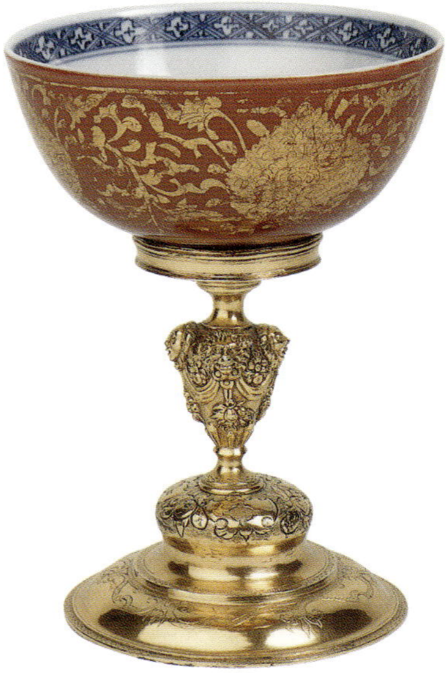

crossroads of commerce between the Levant, the Arabian peninsula and the East African coast. At Alexandria, trade goods were transhipped onto vessels that plied the Mediterranean and supplied the cities of Western Europe. It is significant that some of the earliest Chinese porcelains that reached the West were gifts from the rulers of Egypt to the doges in Venice and the Medici in Florence.

Europeans did not begin to trade directly with China until the early sixteenth century, when Portuguese mariners mastered the great ocean voyage round Africa and on to the East Indies. Prior to that, individual items found their way to Europe by circuitous routes. One of the earliest documented Chinese porcelains to reach the West was the so-called 'Gaignières-Fonthill Vase' (plate 4.1).[4] This object was made in China *c.* 1300–30 and first appeared in Europe in the collection of Louis the Great, King of Hungary (r. 1342–82). He probably acquired it in 1338 when an embassy sent by the Nestorian Christian community of China to Pope Benedict XII passed through Hungary on its way to Avignon. In 1381 the king had the vase enriched with silver-gilt and enamelled mounts and sent as a gift to King Charles III of Naples (r. 1381–86). The vase resurfaced in France and is probably one of the pieces of porcelain described in the inventory of the Duc de Berry in 1416. In 1689 it was recorded among the collection of Chinese porcelain formed by the Grand Dauphin, heir to Louis XIV. It appears in a drawing of about 1713 commissioned by the collector Roger de Gaignières for the king (plate 4.2). The vase was thought to have perished in the French Revolution, but was actually purchased by the English collector William Beckford, on one of his shopping trips to strife-worn Paris in the 1790s and early 1800s. After the sale of Beckford's collection in 1823, and before its appearance as 'damaged' in an inventory of 1844, the vase was vandalized by robbers, who presumably removed its metal mounts to melt them down.

The addition of European precious mounts to Chinese porcelains was by no means uncommon, particularly for pieces intended to grace art chambers and cabinets of curiosities (*Kunstkammern*). The oldest extant documented collection of Chinese porcelains is from the *Kunstkammer* of Archduke Ferdinand of Tyrol, now at Schloss Ambras outside Innsbruck.[5]

Central Europe, with its wealthy principalities and well-established scientific traditions, was richly endowed with scholarly collectors. At Kassel, in present-day north-western Germany, is preserved a Chinese celadon bowl with late Gothic silver-gilt mounts (plate 4.3).[6] The bowl, with rounded walls and gently everting rim, is of quite ordinary quality, of a type mass-produced for export to Asia and the Near East in the period 1375–1425. Tradition states that it was brought back by Count Philipp von Katzenelnbogen from a pilgrimage to the Holy Land in 1433–34. It was transformed into a chalice by a high metal foot, the latter being attached by means of complex strapwork mounts that encircled the body. On either side is a shield with the Katzenelnbogen arms as borne before 1453: a rampant lion in red and black enamel on a golden ground. The imposing lid has a tall knop whose central curling leaves enclose a blue enamelled acorn.[7]

The 'Von Manderscheidt' cups provide an example of German mounts on Chinese porcelain of the Jiajing reign (1522–66). On one of the cups the silver-gilt mounts are plain, but bear an inscription recording that the cup was brought from Turkey by Count Eberhart von Manderscheidt in 1583, and mounted in memory of his brother Count Hermann, to remain permanently in the Blankenheim line.[8] Count Hermann and Count Eberhart von Manderscheidt-Blankenheim were respectively the eldest and sixth sons of that noble family. Count Eberhart (1542–1608 or 1610) held various ecclesiastical offices in the Archdiocese of Cologne, Trier and Liège, and undertook a pilgrimage to Jerusalem in 1582, probably purchasing the cups en route in Turkey. On the pair to this cup, now in the V&A's collection, the mounts are not inscribed, but are more elaborate and engraved with arabesques, flat-chased and marked designs of alternating strapwork and clusters of fruit, with lion and grotesque masks on the shoulders, connected by swags and with clusters of fruit hanging from them (plate 4.4). The cups are more luxurious than most of the Chinese porcelains that reached Europe at this time. Painted with a simple blue diaper border and chrysanthemum medallion centre, the cup shown here has an exterior enamelled in red and gilt in a style known as *kinran-de*, Japanese for 'gold-brocaded'. The gold is composed of carefully cut foil, bonded to the surface with lacquer adhesive. Such sumptuous, heavily gilded porcelains were admired in the Near East and especially in Japan, where sets of *kinran-de* cups are preserved in collections.

The value and prestige attached to Chinese porcelain is graphically illustrated in paintings of the late fifteenth and sixteenth centuries.[9] One of Giovanni Bellini's most famous works, *The Feast of the*

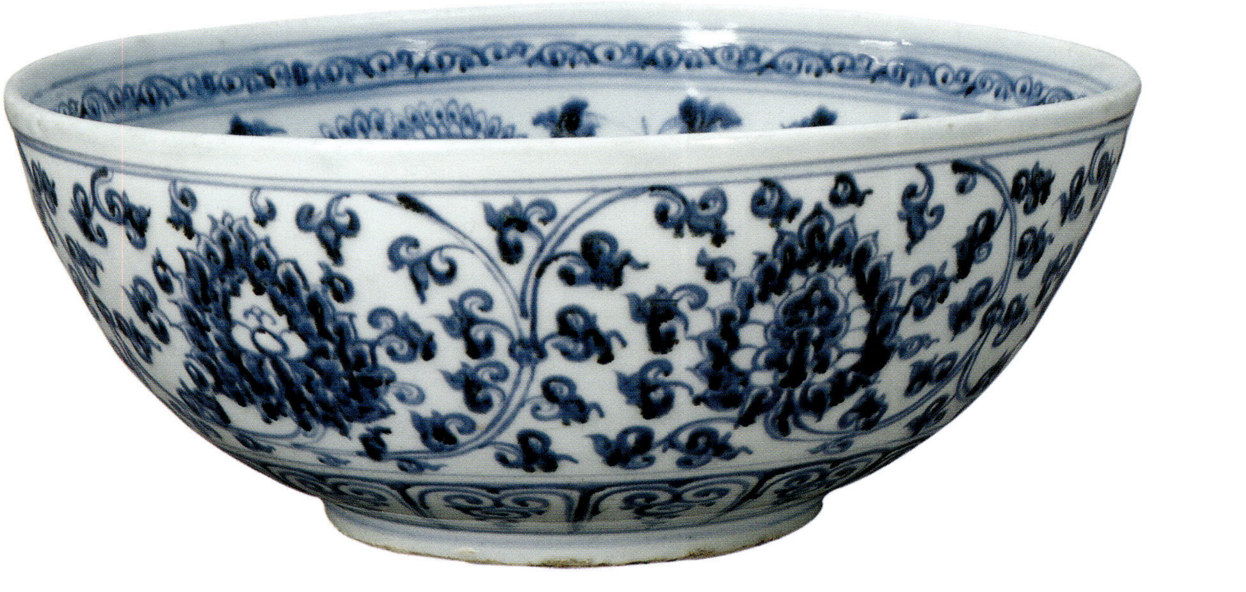

4.5
Bowl

Porcelain decorated in underglaze cobalt blue
China, Hongwu period (1368–98)

V&A: C.18–1957

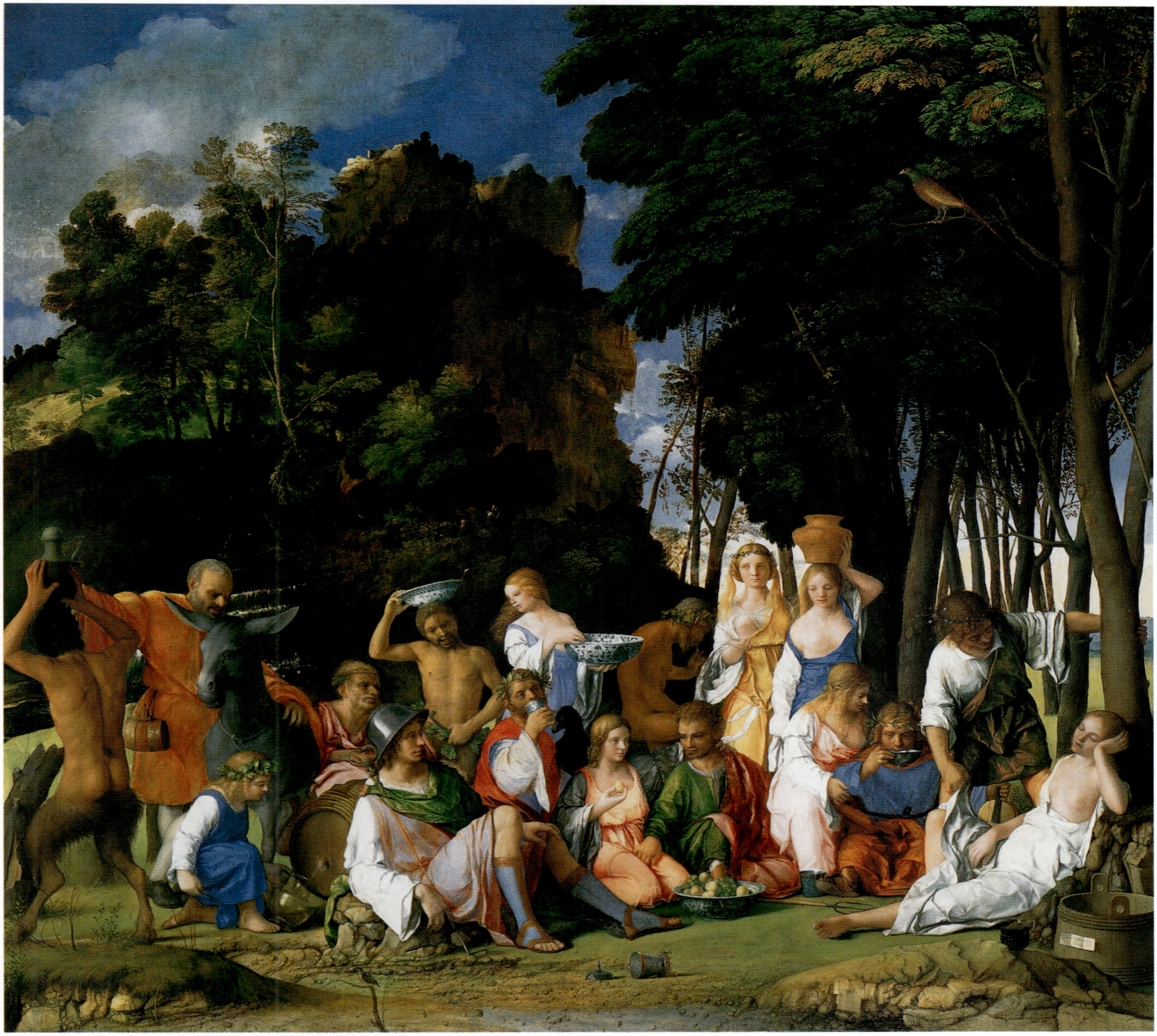

4.6
The Feast of the Gods
Giovanni Bellini
with additions by Dosso Dossi and Titian

Oil on canvas
Italy (Venice), 1514; overpainted in 1521–22 and 1529

Widener Collection, National Gallery of Art, Washington

4.7
Bowl

Porcelain with white glaze, the inside decorated in underglaze cobalt blue, with silver-gilt mounts
Bowl: China, Jiajing period (1522–66);
mounts: England (London), hallmarked 1569–70

Percival David Foundation of Chinese Art, London

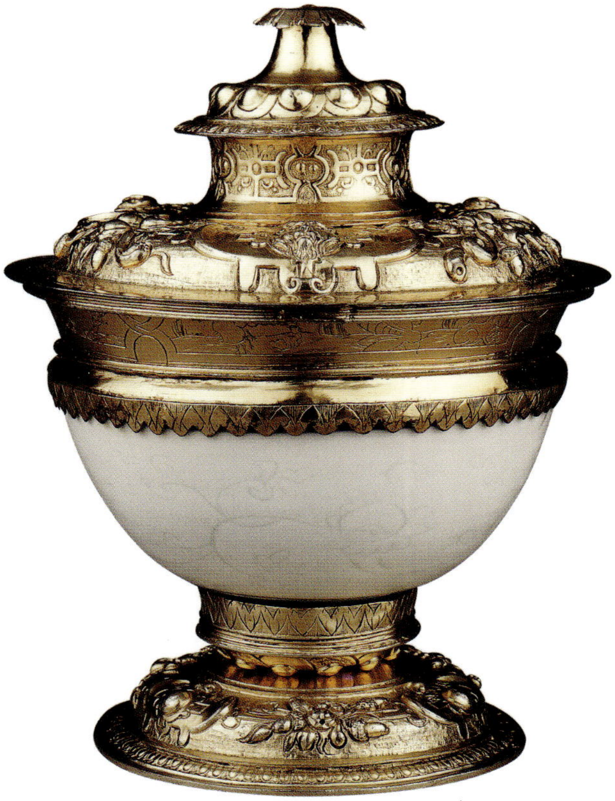

4.8 below
Dish

Porcelain decorated in underglaze cobalt blue
China, early 16th century

Topkapi Saray Museum, Istanbul

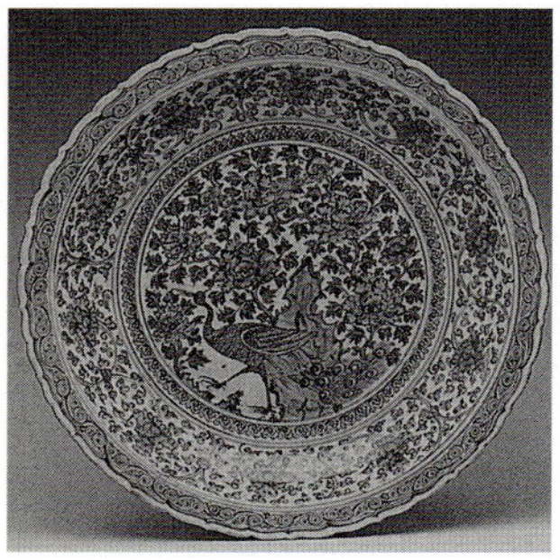

Gods (with later additions by Titian and Dosso Dossi), depicts a sumptuous winter celebration (plate 4.6). Its ribald theme derives from a poem called *The Feasts (Fasti)* by the Roman author Ovid (43 BC–AD 17). The scene, a banquet given by Bacchus, the god of wine, and attended by beautiful nymphs, gods and goddesses, provided sensual and luxurious decor for the private study of Alfonso d'Este, Duke of Ferrara (1476–1534). No expense was spared in the creation of the picture, which used copious quantities of costly pigments such as ultramarine blue, composed of lapis lazuli.[10] This blue was employed to depict valuable commodities like silk, and the blue-and-white Chinese porcelain used for feasting. No fewer than three porcelain vessels are depicted, and they are large, showy pieces. The deep bowl presented by a naiad (nymph of streams and brooks) in the centre of the painting has a scrolling lotus painted inside and out. A satyr to her left balances a deep dish on his head. Its lotus-scroll decoration and form with flattened rim are similar to those of another dish in the foreground of the painting, loaded with luscious fruits. It is possible that the valuable porcelains depicted in Bellini's picture date to the early Ming period (late fifteenth century), like a large bowl with scrolling lotus decoration, in the V&A (plate 4.5). It is more likely, however, that they are near-contemporaneous with the painting, for many large bowls and dishes for communal dining were exported to the Middle East at that time. The kitchens of the Topkapi Saray in Istanbul contained several closely related examples (plate 4.8).[11]

Britain came late to the acquisition and embellishment of Chinese porcelain, when from the 1560s a very few pieces arrived in Tudor England. Many items were acquired by plunder from Portuguese and Spanish ships, as privateer Captain Burroughs recorded when he captured the heavily laden *Madre de Dios* off the Azores in 1592: 'The principal wares after the jewels ... consisted of spices, drugges, silks, calicots, quilts, carpets and colours ... the rest of the wares were many in number but less in value; as elephants' teeth, porcelain vessels of China, coconuts, hides, eben wood as black as jet.'[12]

A white bowl with silver-gilt mounts, bearing London hallmarks for 1569–70, is known as the 'Lennard Cup', as it was owned by Samuel Lennard (1553–1618), lord of the manor at Wickham Court, West Wickam, Kent.[13] It has a translucent, shell-like appearance highly attractive to Westerners, though it would have been unremarkable to Chinese eyes (plate 4.7). The outside is white, with incised decoration of scrolling lotus. On the inside, normally hidden by the precious-metal cover, is depicted a hare reserved in white against a blue rock with pine and bamboo. One can imagine the bowl's owner opening the lid to peep at this enchanting vignette, although it is unlikely that he would have understood the commendatory mark on the bottom, whose Chinese characters read 'Long life, riches and honour'. The mounts are elaborate, although the lower part seems to have been truncated. The spreading foot is embossed with strapwork and trophies of acorns, apples and pears, and the rim bears four strapwork panels enclosing animals and insects, such as beaver, salamander, snake, fox, horse, rabbit, frog, wasp and scorpion. The domed cover is richly embossed with designs of Renaissance masks in strapwork panels alternating with trophies of mixed fruit. Its central knop, whose finial is missing, bears chased strapwork and embossed cable patterns surmounted by a formal flower.[14]

A ewer in the V&A, also with London hallmarks, embodies a meeting of cultural styles (plate 4.9). Its form derives from Persian metalwork of the thirteenth to fifteenth centuries, while its decoration of boys playing is wholly Chinese, representing the birth of sons and hence of good fortune. It was mounted in London in 1585–86 with silver-gilt mounts elaborately worked with fruit, foliage and animals. The unknown goldsmith who carried out the work was expert, and was commissioned by a wealthy and discriminating customer. The ewer itself was treasured, for repair to some damage was carried out in silver in the late seventeenth century.[15]

From the early seventeenth century, as the power of Portuguese traders in the East waned and the influence of Dutch merchants increased, a gradual change in the shapes and decorations of porcelain took place. Western elements of design became more pronounced, and European forms were increasingly commissioned, paving the way for a mass export trade that flourished in the later seventeenth and eighteenth centuries.

4.9
Ewer

Porcelain decorated in underglaze cobalt blue, with silver-gilt mounts
Ewer: China, Wanli period (1573–1620);
mounts: England (London), hallmarked to 1585–86;
silver spout, lip and neckband: late 17th century

V&A: 7915–1862

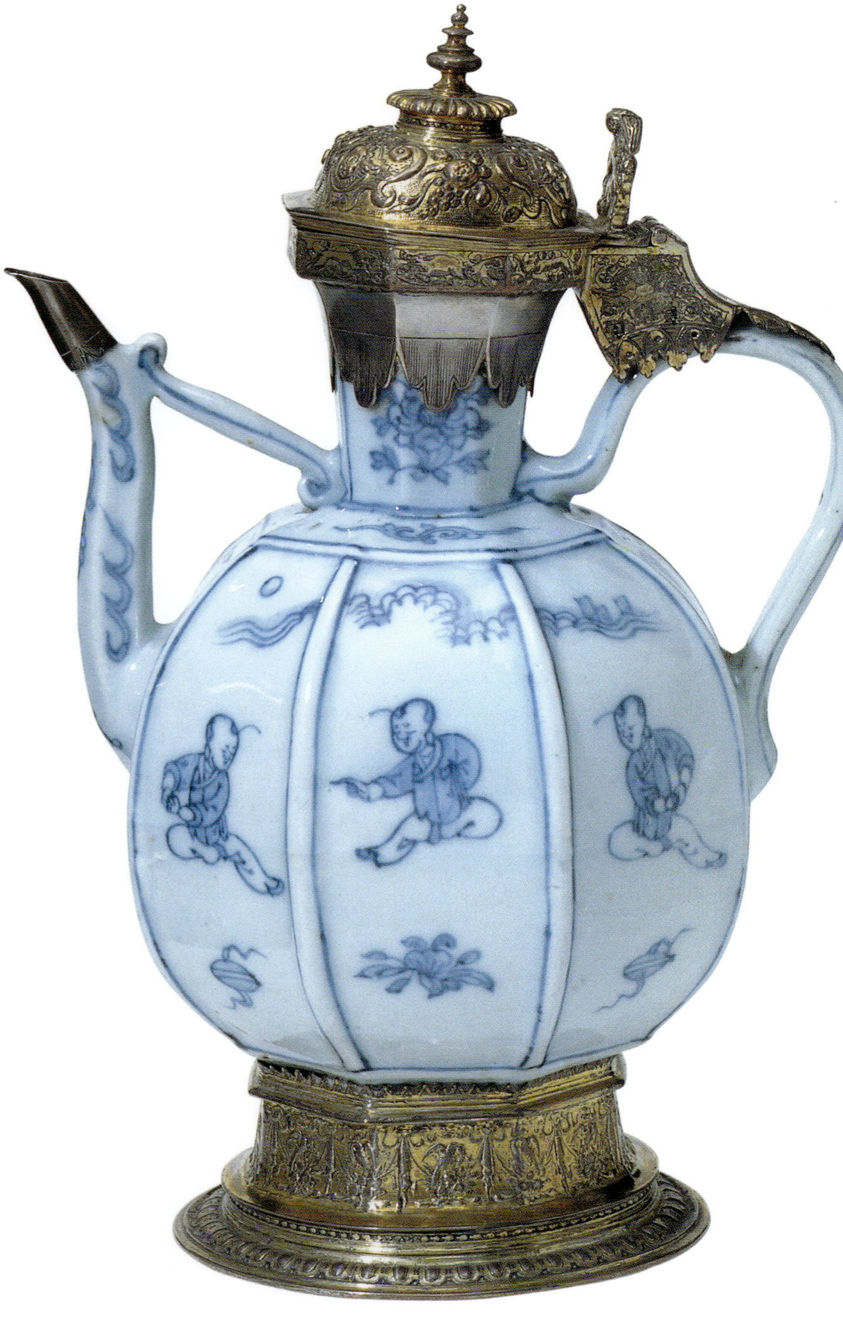

5

ASIAN TRADE AND EXCHANGE BEFORE 1600

John Guy

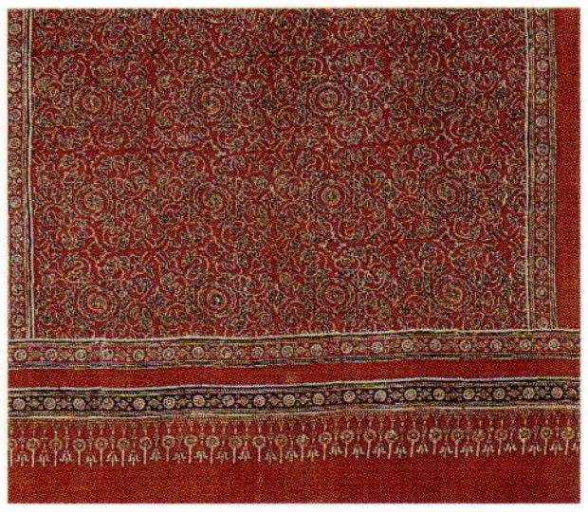

5.1 previous page and above
Ceremonial cloth

Recovered in Indonesia; cotton, block printed and dyed
India (Gujarat), radiocarbon dated 1510 +/– 40 years

V&A: IS.94–1993

5.2
Muslim Horse Merchants in an Arab Dhow

From a mural on the interior of Sri Narumpunadasvami, Tiruppudaimarudur, Tamil Nadu; wall painting
India, 17th century

THE ASIAN TRADING WORLD stretches from the coastal ports of southern China and Japan in the east to the western limits of the Indian Ocean and Arabian Sea. It is a vast region united by sea-lanes that have provided an inexhaustible opportunity for trade and cultural contact. From an early period these oceans were seen not as a barrier to contact, but as an aid. The principal constraints were ship technology and navigation skills; as these advanced, so too did the possibilities for exchange. Arabic speakers sailing the dhow, a remarkably resilient vessel of stitched and lashed construction, appear to have been among the first to master these waters and dominate this long-distance sea trade (plate 5.2). Arabic literature reveals that Arabic-speaking mariners and merchants were trading in South-East Asian waters from around the sixth century. The surviving sources are compilations of travellers' accounts, of which the *Akhar al-Sin* is believed to be the oldest: although published in AD 851 (AH 237), it clearly contains information from much earlier periods.[1] Ports such as Basra (serving Baghdad) and Siraf (serving Shiraz) were active at this time. A merchant from Basra is recorded visiting China around 775, and the perilous journey, trading and collecting goods en route to India and South-East Asia, was a regular occurrence for Gulf merchants throughout the next two centuries. Indians and South-East Asians also sailed these waters, linking West Asia to the Indian subcontinent, South-East Asia and China, the great economic engine of the Asian world.

The cosmopolitan nature of early Asian maritime trade can best be judged from the records of the foreign communities resident in the southern port cites of China.[2] Fuelled by the Southern Sea (*Nanhai*) trade, the cities of Hangzhou, Ningbo, Quanzhou, Zhangzhou and Canton (Guangzhou) all grew in economic importance. Malays, Chams, Indians and Asians each occupied their own quarter (*fan fang*) in each city. The most populous were the Arabs and Persians, together with the non-Muslim Persians, notably Jews and Nestorian Christians. The dominance of West Asian merchants is most evident in the emergence of Arabic as the *lingua franca* for the Asian maritime diaspora. Words from both Persian and Arabic entered the Chinese maritime vocabulary in this period. In addition, the Caliphate gold dinar emerged as the common currency of trade, a position it held from its introduction in 695 until the eleventh century, when Chinese copper coinage usurped its position.

By the ninth century maritime Asia was experiencing a boom, stimulated by the partial disintegration of the overland Silk Route. China actively encouraged the use of sea routes, which gave access to the markets of India, West Asia and the Mediterranean world. The unification of China in the tenth century under the Song dynasty accelerated its direct participation in this trade. Major advances in ship technology resulted in the development of the ocean junk, with its multiple sealed bulkheads, a hull structure secured with iron-nails, flexible rigging and stern rudder. The Chinese junk and the Arab dhow dominated Asian sea trade for the next half-millennium, only being challenged in the course of sixteenth century by the arrival of heavily armed and highly manoeuvrable European ships.

SPICES AND AROMATICS

Like those who had come to South-East Asia before them, the European merchant-adventurers and diplomats (and the quasi-official trading companies that followed a century later) had a simple agenda. Their quest was to secure reliable and affordable sources of the South-East Asian spices so highly prized in the kitchens and dining tables of Europe. The spices (cloves, nutmeg and mace) were the exclusive products of a few isolated islands in eastern Indonesia; pepper was indigenous to southern India, but appears also to have been introduced to western Indonesia by the tenth century. These spices were highly valued, and their scarcity ensured that they

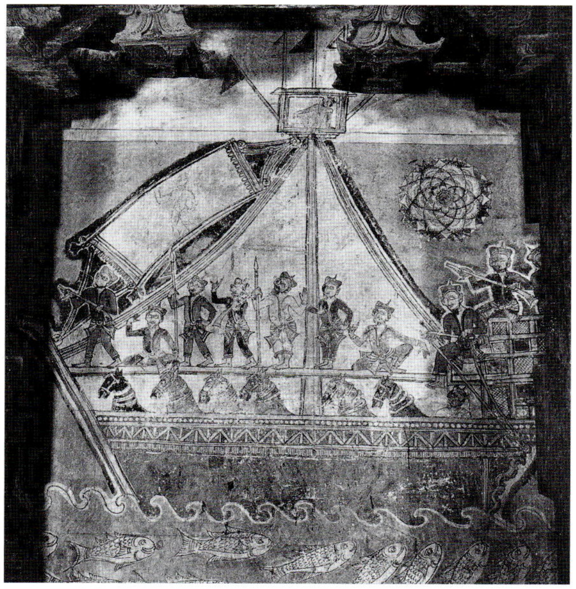

commanded exceedingly high prices on the metropolitan markets of the world. Over time, they became the mainstay seasonings for most of the world's great cuisines.

The spice trade was an ancient one, encouraged by both the Roman empire in the Mediterranean and the Han kingdom in China, which together generated unprecedented demand. Malabar pepper had been sought-after in the Roman world, and rare South-East Asian spices, worth more than their weight in gold, also appear to have found their way west. Even in Anglo-Saxon Britain, the Venerable Bede (AD 673–735) was moved to comment on the expense of spices, listing pepper and incense amongst his few prized possessions.[3] Eleventh- and twelfth-century Jewish trade records of Fustat, Egypt, confirm that one merchant used a store of cloth as payment against customs duty on a large consignment of pepper, presumably from the Malabar coast.[4]

As far as can be judged from the highly selective sources embedded in Chinese dynastic histories, the early Asian trade was largely in exotics and rarities, evocatively characterized in the seventh-century *Sui Shu* as the 'strange and precious'.[5] For China it was the seemingly insatiable appetite for spices and aromatics that drove much of the sea-route trade; in exchange, China supplied precious metals, silk and lacquer wares. Ceramics make their appearance as a significant international trade item towards the end of the Tang dynasty, in the eighth and early ninth centuries.[6]

Accounts of Arab geographers are an invaluable supplement to the Chinese sources, providing a less official view of the Asian trading world. Their histories and geographies were largely compiled by authors typically based in Basra or Siraf in the Persian Gulf, from accounts gleaned from mariners and merchants. Spices feature prominently in these accounts, along with printed textiles and dyestuffs employed in local textile production. Mas'udi (d.956) wrote largely from direct experience of this trade. He noted the emerging role assumed by Chinese shipping in the *Nanhai,* recording the impact of Chinese vessels sent to South-East Asia in search of pepper, spices and aromatics.[7]

Up until the capture of Constantinople by the Ottomans in 1453, Europe had been obliged to get its supplies via the Arab ship and camel trade. Thereafter Europe, led by Portugal and Spain, undertook a series of expeditions intended to discover the location of the 'Spiceries' and so secure independent access to them. It was the voyage led by Ferdinand Magellan (*c.* 1480–1521) that finally succeeded in this quest, arriving in the Moluccas in eastern Indonesia in 1521 and returning to Lisbon with a cargo of spices.[8]

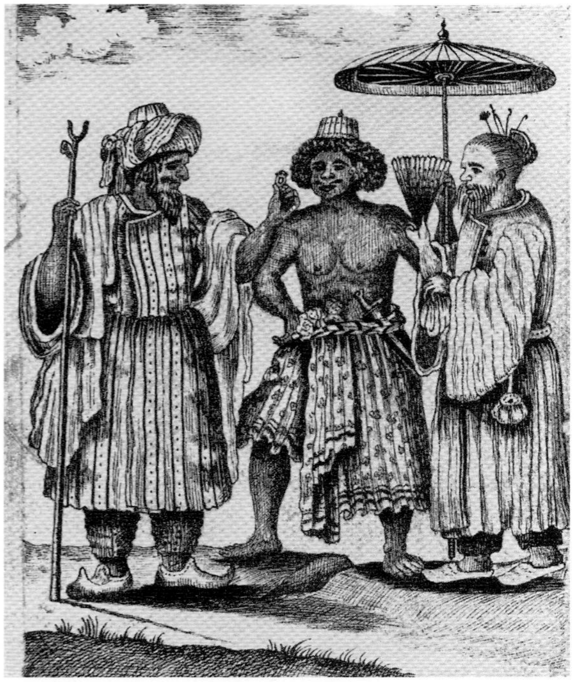

5.3
An Arab, Javanese and Chinese Merchant at Bantam

From J. P. Cortemunde, *Dagbog fra en Ostindiefart, 1672–75*
Engraving

V&A: Asian Department Library

PAINTED TEXTILES

Despite growing Chinese competition, Indian Muslim traders maintained their dominance of the Asian spice trade until the fifteenth century, employing Indian textiles as a key exchange commodity. Archaeological records make clear that these activities stretched from the Red Sea to the Indonesian islands, with western India at the hub of this exchange. The largest and probably the oldest export market for Gujarati textiles lay in Arab lands. Archaeological finds of Gujarati printed cotton textiles in Lower Egypt, mostly at burial sites and at port locations along the Red Sea, point to an extensive and protracted international trade system at work, in all probability dating from the early centuries AD. The arrival of Islam in India and its later introduction into South-East Asia was inextricably linked with this commerce and the presence of Muslim merchants in these regions (plate 5.3).

The scale of the textile trade is hinted at by the recovery of large quantities of Indian cloth at Fostat (Old Cairo), retrieved from medieval cemeteries where such textiles ended their days as wrappers for the dead (plates 5.4, 5.5). This trade is documented to a remarkable degree by the Geniza records, the contents of an archival storehouse (*geniza*) attached to a synagogue at Fustat. They include a wealth of documents from the eleventh to thirteenth centuries.[9] Fustat was the capital of Abbasid Egypt (AD 750–969) until the Fatimids established their capital a short distance to the north at Cairo. Fustat nonetheless retained its commercial importance for several centuries, as the Geniza records demonstrate.[10] The historic Indian textiles found in Egypt span the ninth to the fifteenth centuries.[11] Technical studies have established that these coarse cotton fabrics, block-printed and resist-dyed in indigo blue and mordanted red, were manufactured in Gujarat, and samples with Kufic script in their borders make clear that designs were customized for the Islamic market.[12] Significantly, these finds represent the earliest dated Indian dyed textiles recorded in an archaeologically documented context.[13]

Comparisons of motifs and styles in other media in fourteenth-century Gujarat support these datings. Close parallels can be found with western Indian manuscript paintings, most notably Jain *Kalpasutra* folios.[14] Most instructive perhaps are stylistic parallels that can be drawn from an unexpected source – dated Gujarati tombstones. It is a measure of the degree to which Gujarati Muslim mariners and traders were entrenched in the Asian maritime diaspora that they distributed marble tombstones around their trading realm, which no doubt served as useful ballast en route. The tombstones are dated from the late thirteenth century onwards and have been identified from sites as diverse as the Arabian peninsula and coastal East Africa, the west coast of India and the Maldives, and western Indonesia.[15] The material, a high-grade white marble, and the distinctive vocabulary of decorative ornamentation and calligraphic style of the Arabic inscriptions, establish that these tombstones were the products of architectural workshops around Cambay, Gujarat's major port.[16]

The dedications on the tombstones record that many were used by Gujarati or other Indians who died abroad, as for example by Malik Ibrahim (d. 1419), an Indian Muslim buried at Gresik, Java, who seems to have held high civil office there; or the Tamilian Kling merchant, Na'ina Hussam al-Din ibn Na'ina Amin, whose grave is at Pasai, northern Sumatra. Other tombstones were ordered by non-Indians, wealthy merchants and local rulers, belonging to the Indian Ocean diaspora.[17] This is most clearly demonstrated by a tombstone in the Victoria and Albert Museum, which is from a cemetery at Salalah in Dhofar (medieval Zafar), Oman, on the southern Arabian peninsula (plate 5.7). This headstone (and a second tombstone that served as the footstone, also in the V&A) is inscribed with the name of al-Wathiq Nur al-Din Ibrahim, governor of Dhofar, who died in 1311 (AH 711). The headstone appears to have been ordered in al-Wathiq's lifetime, complete with his personalized inscription – apart from the date of his death, which was added in another hand at the appropriate time.[18]

5.4
Textile fragment

Recovered at Fostat, Lower Egypt; cotton, block-printed and dyed
India (Gujarat), 10th–12th centuries

V&A: T.253–1958

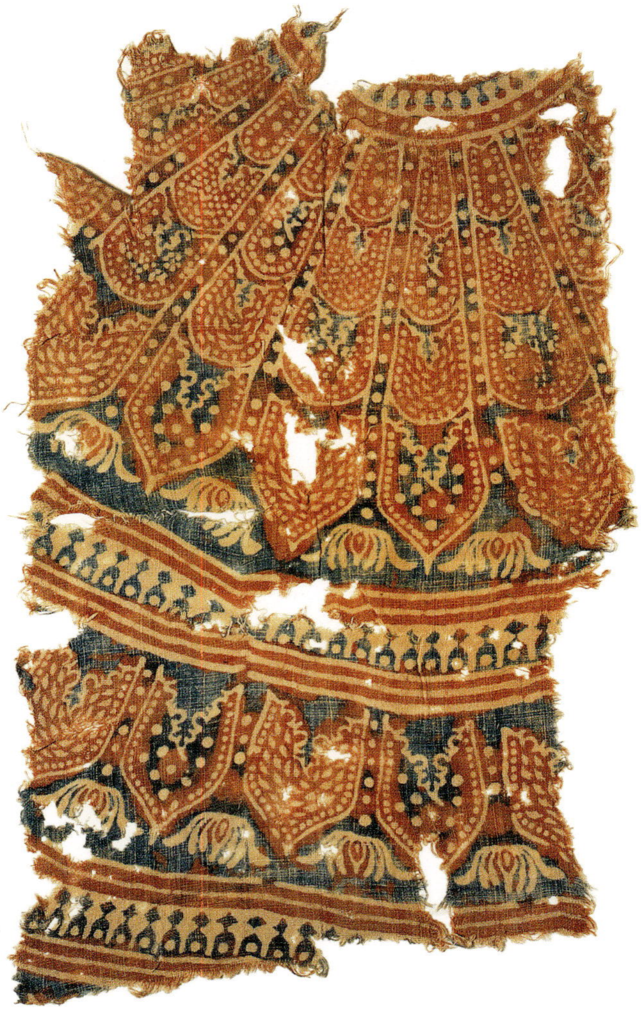

5.5
Textile fragment, possibly part of a canopy

Recovered at Fostat, Lower Egypt; cotton block-printed and dyed
India (Gujarat), *c.* 14th century

V&A: IS.72–1972

The circulation of these made-to-order tombstones vividly illustrates the highly organized nature of Indian Ocean trade. In addition, their designs clearly establish, in the context of securely dated monuments, the repertoire of motifs and styles prevalent in fourteenth- and fifteenth-century Gujarati applied arts. The flowering tree and plantain are recurring motifs, as seen most impressively on the tomb of Ahmad al-Kazaruni at Cambay, dated 1333 (plate 5.6). The designs on his tomb bear close comparison to the Gujarati textiles traded to the Arab world (plate 5.5).[19] This leading Iranian businessman was referred to as the 'king of the merchants', perhaps the *shahbandar* of Cambay, by his contemporary Ibn Battuta (*c.* 1304–68), the most remarkable of fourteenth-century Muslim travellers.[20]

The Indian textiles that formed part of the Red Sea trade assume a further significance in that they have direct parallels with Gujarati cloths recovered from South-East Asia. The dyed cottons of Gujarat were clearly exported to both markets, and in the pre-1500 period were often of the same design (plates 5.8, 5.9). This remained the pattern of intra-Asian trade some centuries later, as confirmed by Tomé Pires (d. 1540), who served as a 'factor of drugs' at Goa, the headquarters of the Portuguese Asian empire, and wrote the most detailed account of the mechanics of this Asian trade at the beginning of the sixteenth century. Stationed at Malacca (Melaka) shortly after its conquest by the Portuguese in 1511, Pires was able to observe at first hand the interdependence of the trading system, and the central role that Indian textiles played in securing supplies of Moluccan spices. Pires wrote of the axial role played by Malacca and the Gujarati port of Cambay in western India, which together formed a chain of international trade:

> Cambay chiefly stretches out her two arms, with her right arm she reaches out towards Aden, and with the other towards Malacca … Malacca cannot live without Cambay, nor Cambay without Malacca, if they are to be very rich and very prosperous … [From Gujarat] they bring cloths of thirty kinds, which are of value in these parts.[21]

That Pires was describing a long-established trading system is demonstrated by two Fustat fragments depicting wooded landscapes, radiocarbon-dated *c.* 1265 +/– 40 years and *c.* 1340 +/– 40 years respectively, which may be closely compared to a group of spectacular textiles found in Indonesia, of which the most complete example is in the V&A (plate 5.8).[22] This, the most impressive of the Indonesian sourced examples, has yielded a radiocarbon date of 1340 +/– 40 years, contemporary with many of the comparable Gujarati textiles recovered from the Red Sea–Fustat region. Flowering trees, plantains, mango and date palm can be discerned in the design. The wooded landscape designs are all decorated in a block-printed dyed design in the red and blue typical of Gujarati cloths of this period. The surviving section represents one half of the complete piece, the original dimensions being 2 × 5 metres. This is far too large for dress and was no doubt intended to serve as a backdrop for ceremonial occasions.

The reception of Indian cotton goods in South-East Asia contrasted with that in the West Asian markets, where they were consumed by a broad cross-section of society. In South-East Asia they were objects of conspicuous consumption, serving as the preferred attire of the elite, from the raja and sultan to the village headman. Both court and village culture shared a belief in the power of cloth and saw textiles as a personal statement of social status. They were willing to invest a substantial part of their surplus wealth in cloth. A corollary of this was that textiles served as a form of currency, a store of wealth, portable and convertible through trade. It was this

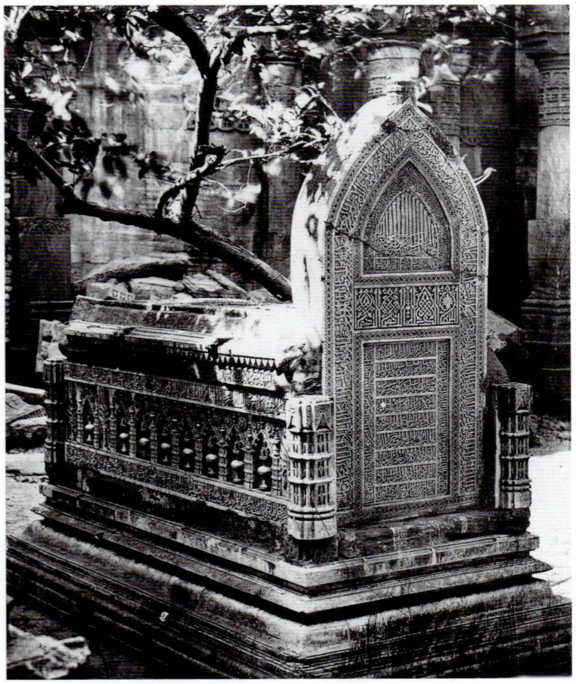

5.6
Tomb of Zaki al-Dawlah wa-'l-Din Umar b. Ahmad al-Kazaruni, known as Parviz Malik (d. 1333)

Jami Masjid, Cambay; marble, carved
India (Gujarat), early 14th century

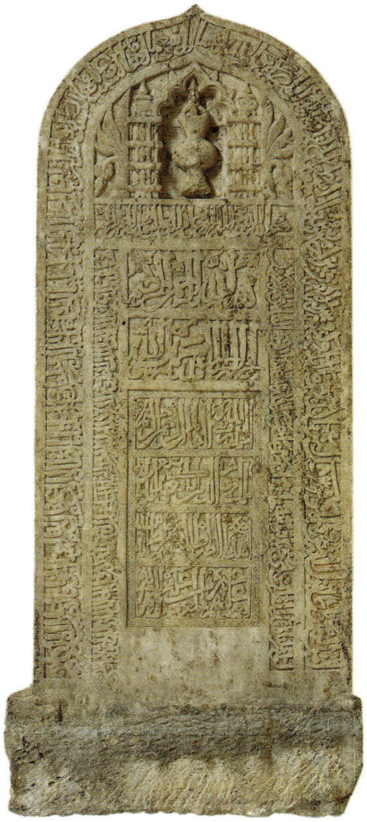

5.7
Tombstone of al-Wathiq Nur al-Din Ibrahim (d. 1311), dated Wednesday 20 Muharram AH 711 (8 June 1311)

Found at Dhofar, Oman; marble, carved
India (Gujarat), late 13th–early 14th century

V&A: A.12–1933

5.8
Ceremonial banner

Recovered in Sulawesi, Indonesia; cotton, block-printed, mordant-dyed and painted, resist-dyed India (Gujarat), radiocarbon dated 1340 +/– 40 years

V&A: IS.96–1993

5.9
Ceremonial cloth *(patolu)*

Silk, resist-dyed yarns (double ikat) India (Gujarat), date uncertain

V&A: IS.74–1993

special status, overlaid with later mythologies and associated supernatural powers, that enabled these fabrics to survive the rigours of the tropical climate for some 500 or more years. Secreted away in storage baskets in the rafters of communal houses and reverently cared for, these textiles defied the normal demands of use and climate.

The sixteenth century saw the foundations being laid for later European monopolistic control of the South-East Asian spice trade, and of attempts to control trade in other goods. It is a measure of the scale and strength of the Asian trading system that, despite these attempts, the European presence made only a modest impact during this period. The Europeans were obliged, if they were to profit from these ventures, to act as participants in the Asian game. The long-term viability of the Portuguese and later the Dutch, English, French and Danish trading companies was determined by their ability to engage in intra-Asian trade. That is, to buy goods in one part of Asia and to offer them for sale at profit in another Asian market. Jan-Pietersz Coen, the first director-general of the Dutch East India Company (VOC) in Asia, clearly understood this and wrote from Bantam to his directors in Holland in 1619 (plate 5.10):

> Piece goods [cloth] from Gujarat we can barter for pepper and gold on the coast of Sumatra; rials and cottons from the [Coromandel] coast for the pepper in Banten [Bantam]; sandalwood, pepper and rials we can barter for Chinese goods and Chinese gold; we can extract silver from Japan with Chinese goods … and rials from Arabia for spices and various other trifles – one thing leads to another.[23]

Local rulers were encouraged to cooperate in various ways, and the Dutch proved skilled at combining bribery with coercion. Headsmen in the Spice Islands were presented with the most prestigious of trade cloths, the western Indian silk *patola.* Such items were often combined with gifts that celebrated western technology. In 1644 the Prince of Pattingaloang, Makassar, extracted from the Dutch in exchange for trading concessions, two world globes and two atlases.[24] Such 'state gifts' not only strengthened the local standing of the ruler, but also served (in the minds of the Dutch at least) to demonstrate European technical superiority and civilization. They also disseminated awareness of the rapidly advancing science of cartography, which continued to prove so essential to securing commercial advantage in the trade wars characterizing Europe's Asian intervention.

Patola textiles were especially favoured as an expression of status, specifically as confirmation of a ruler's ability to attract highly prized objects from beyond his realm. They retained this role into recent times. The antiquity of the most famous of trade *patola* designs, with confronting pairs of caparisoned elephants, is unclear (plate 5.9). The appearance of this design in the famous Iranian samite weave silk known as the Shroud of St Josse, datable prior to 961, secures an early provenance for such designs. The earliest Portuguese sources confirm the presence and status of *patola* in South-East Asia from the sixteenth century; undoubtedly the Gujarati merchants ensured its availability in the region much earlier. The Dutch employed these textiles as high-prestige gifts to local rulers, building on the status that such cloths already held in South-East Asian societies.

The pre-eminence of Malacca and Bantam was increasingly challenged in the course of the sixteenth century by Ayutthaya, the riverine port-capital of the emerging Siamese kingdom. The Siamese created their capital as a centre of Asian trade, in which the European traders could only participate as minor players. The Siamese court skilfully maintained a high level of centralized control of the kingdom's international trade, and actively cultivated diplomatic relations with its trading partners. Fifteenth-century Siamese relations with China are recorded by, amongst others, Ma Huan, the commentator of Admiral Zheng He's 'Ming Voyages', which lasted from 1405 to 1433.[25] The *Rekidai Hoan,* the history of the royal household of the Ryūkyū islands to the south-west of Japan, records a brisk trade with a number of South-East Asian countries. Siam appears in the records as early as the 1380s and by the mid-fifteenth century is supplying Indian textiles for the Japanese market, as well as aromatic woods and dyestuffs.[26]

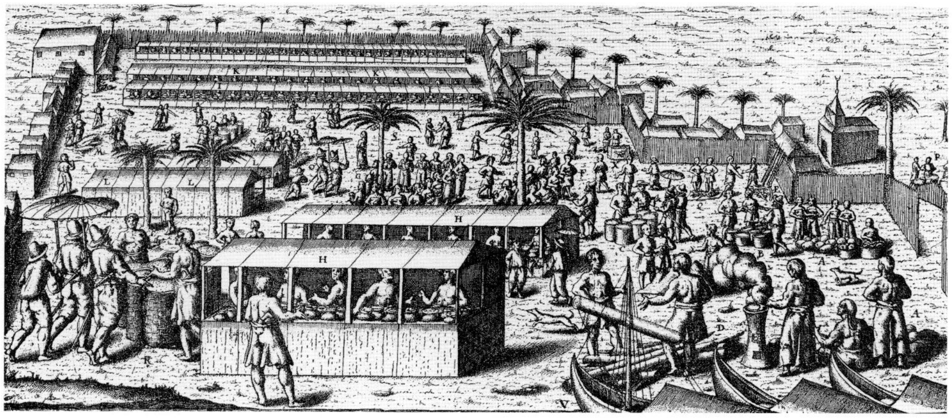

5.10
Market at Bantam

From Jan Huyghen van Linschoten, *Itinerario: Voyage oft schipvaert van Jan Huygen van Linschoten naer Oost ofte Portugaels Indien, 1579–1592*, engraved by Baptista van Doetecun (after a drawing by Linschoten), published by Cornelius Claesz, Amsterdam, 1596
Engraving on paper

This image illustrates the diversity of products sold by local and foreign merchants at Bantam. European merchants, with umbrellas, are shown inspecting sacks of spices while the mosque outside the palisade serves to record the important role played by Muslim traders.

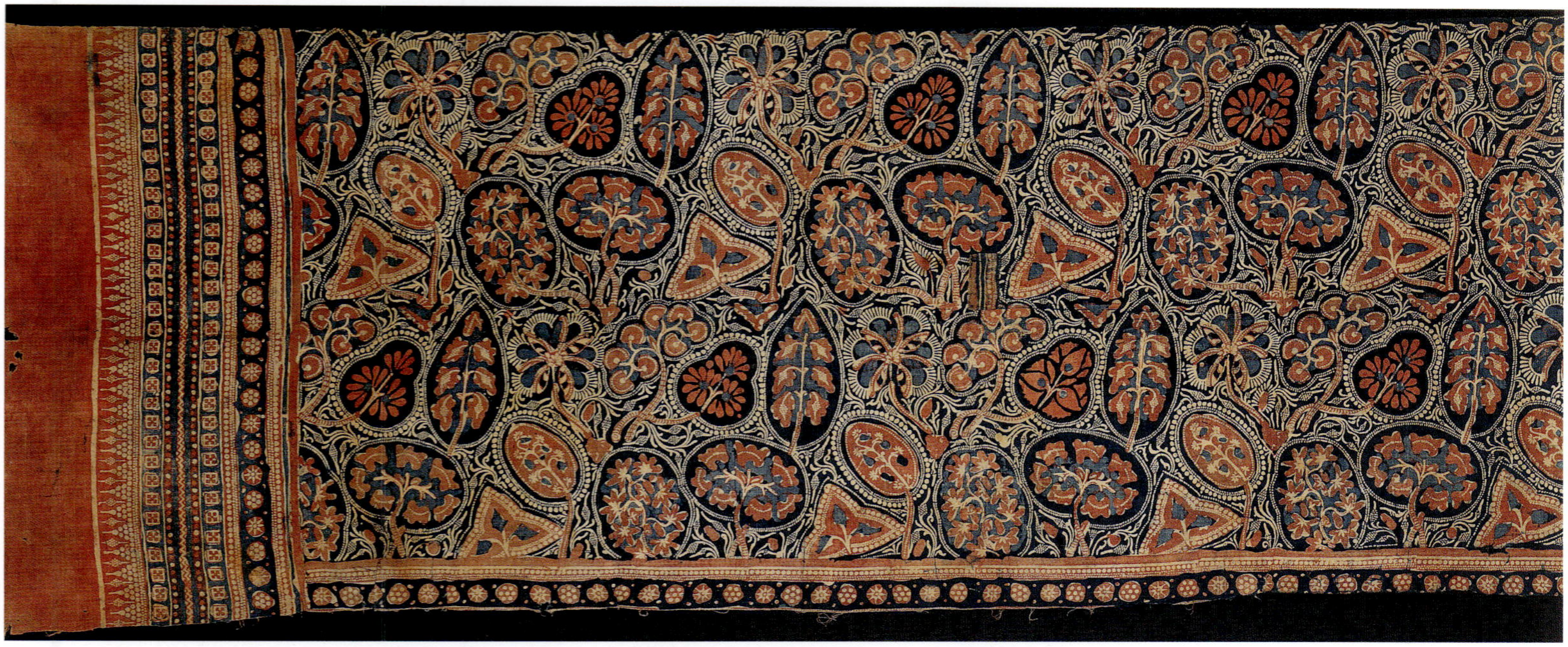

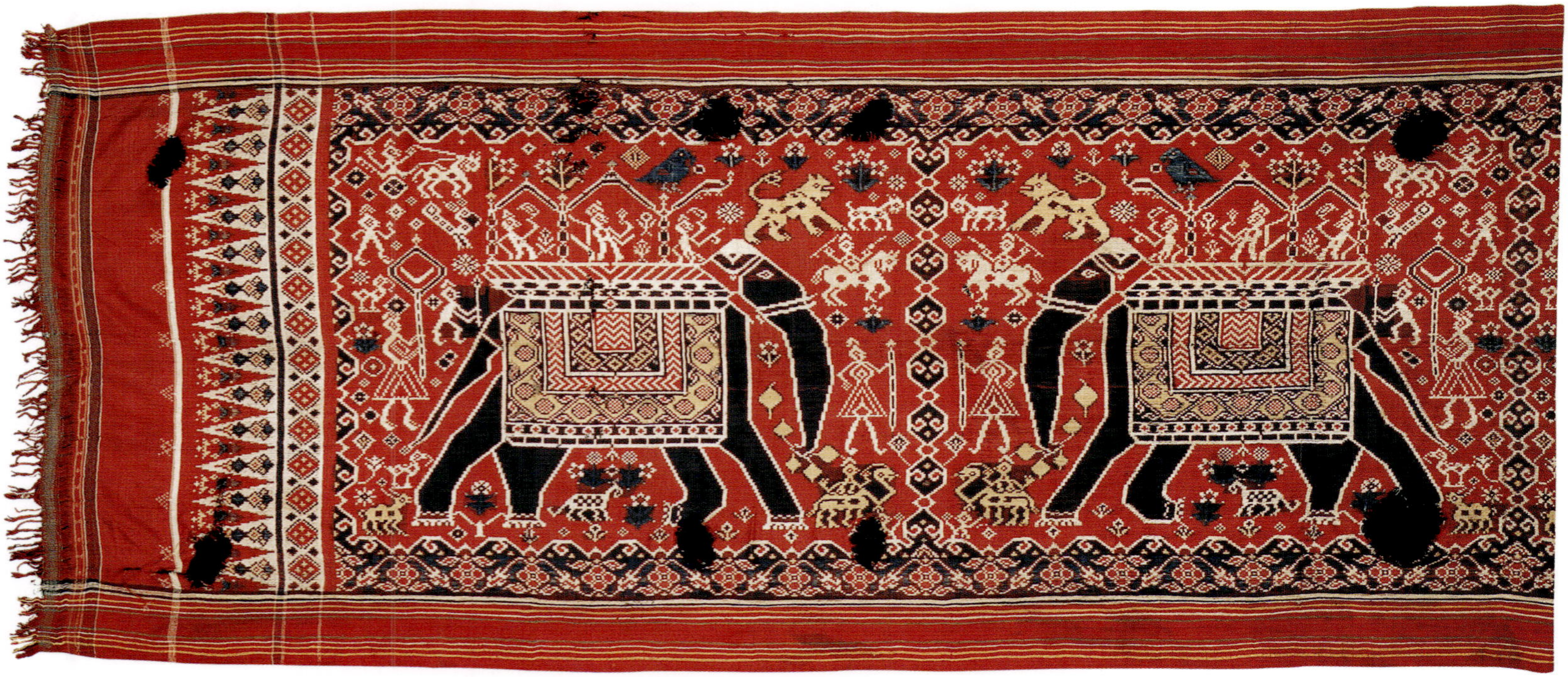

Siamese diplomatic missions were sent as circumstances required to China, Japan and the Ryūkyūs, and to courts in India and Iran. Tributary relations were established with lesser neighbouring states in mainland and peninsular South-East Asia. The supply of natural and forest products marketable in international trade was a required part of these relationships. A key commodity in Ayutthaya's Asian trade was glazed ceramics, sourced from China, Vietnam and from Siam's own production centres in north-central Thailand.

THE ASIAN CERAMIC TRADE

Textiles and aromatics were without doubt the leading trading commodities of medieval Asia, but both are readily consumed: cloths rot and aromatics are burned. High-fired ceramics are unique among historical trade commodities in that their physical resilience ensures they survive in conditions where no traces would remains of less robust goods. The discovery in the late 1990s of a shipwreck off the coast of central Vietnam led to the recovery of a spectacular cargo of late fifteenth-century Vietnamese export ceramics. The shipwreck was located by fishermen off the coast of Cu Lao Cham (the 'Cham Islands'), near the historic port city of Hoi An.[27] The vessel was found to contain a cargo of an estimated quarter of a million pieces, of which more than 150,000 intact pieces were recovered and inventoried, together with another 100,000 fragmentary items. This cargo provides the single most important body of evidence discovered for the understanding of the contribution of the kilns of northern Vietnam to the Asian ceramic trade. As a direct result of the controlled recovery of this vessel and its contents, it has been possible to establish a profile of this ship: its port of origin and destination, the ethnicity of its crew and the nature of its cargo.

The Hoi An ship's hull is well preserved, with clearly discernible Chinese-style bulkheads. Chinese ships are traditionally constructed of pine; the Hoi An vessel employs teak, a timber plentiful in mainland South-East Asia, but unavailable in China. The butted and dowelled construction technique is associated with South-East Asian ship-building. This suggests a hybrid type of vessel resembling a Chinese junk, but with local construction methods; such ships were built in a number of South-East Asian ports to service the South China Sea trade. A South-East Asian provenance for the Hoi An ship is further supported by the presence of lime-containers associated with betel-chewing, a South-East Asian custom, and the presence of large-scale glazed stoneware storage jars recovered from the ship's upper deck. These are of Thai manufacture and are a common feature of ceramic cargoes recovered from wreck sites in the Gulf of Thailand.[28]

The archaeological evidence makes it possible to hypothesize that the ship was Siamese-built, operating on the Ayutthaya–Tonkin route, and embarking on its homeward journey after having spent the spring and summer months in the Red River delta at one of the riverine ports in the Hai Duong area, where it had purchased its large cargo of high-quality glazed ceramics, probably at or near the town of Chu Dau, the epicentre of Vietnam's ceramic export industry in the fifteenth and sixteenth centuries. The ship was probably destined for Ayutthaya, where the cargo would have been sold to secondary traders. It is also feasible that the ship intended to chart a course from southern Vietnam across the South China Sea via Tioman Island, direct to Java, a well-established market for Vietnamese and other Asian trade ceramics.

The Vietnamese chronicle, the *Dai Viet Su Ky Toan Thu,* records the presence of trading ships from 'Xiem-la' ('Siam'), arriving in 1434 (one carrying massive trunks of the aromatic, sandalwood), 1437 and 1467. An edict issued in 1485 by the Thang Long (Hanoi) government regulating such trade clearly points to a growing volume of trade with Siam and other South-East Asian kingdoms.[29] The Hoi An cargo makes clear that a major commodity in this trade was high-fired Vietnamese ceramics. Vietnamese export ceramics were designed to compete with the Chinese wares that were saturating the markets of South-East Asia and those further westwards. The Hoi An cargo demonstrates the extensive range of wares being produced at the end of the fifteenth century. Underglaze blue-decorated wares represent the largest group, containing a number of rare and remarkable wares, with polychromes and monochromes forming other significant groups. They are high-fired stoneware – that is, they do not achieve vitrification of body and glaze, as in true Chinese porcelain. However, they often surpass their Chinese counterparts in the exuberance and invention of their painted decoration (plates 5.11–12). The popularity of polychrome wares is attested by the number that have been recovered in island South-East Asia, especially from Indonesia.

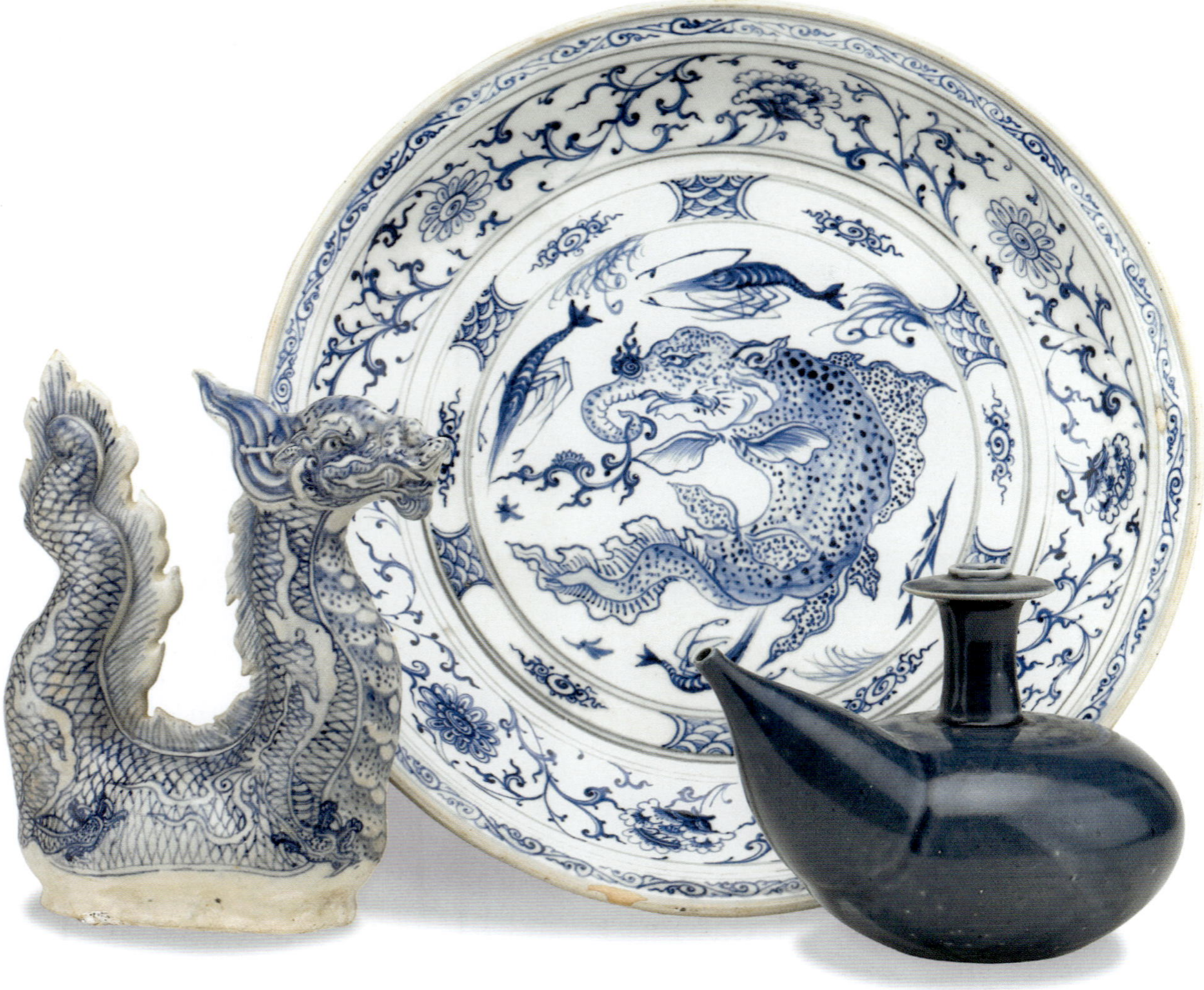

5.11
Ewer

Recovered from Hoi An shipwreck cargo, excavated 1998–99; stoneware decorated in underglaze blue
Vietnam (Red River delta), late 15th century

British Museum, London

5.12
Serving dish

Stoneware decorated in underglaze blue
Vietnam (Red River delta), late 15th century

British Museum, London

5.13
Kendi

Recovered from Hoi An shipwreck cargo, excavated 1998–99; stoneware with monochrome blue glaze
Vietnam (Red River delta), late 15th century

British Museum, London

Yet it is the Middle East that has yielded the largest number of high-quality Vietnamese blue-and-white wares to date. It must be remembered that much of the impetus for the Chinese move into the commercial production of large-scale serving dishes, jars and drinking vessels, decorated in underglaze blue, came from the traders serving Islamic markets in Asia. These merchants are believed to have been instrumental in the initial supply of the cobalt necessary for painted underglaze blue, and dictated the forms needed for these markets. Arab merchants had long known of Vietnam as an important staging port on the sea route to China, and may well have served the potters of the Red River delta in similar fashion, supplying cobalt and ordering wares appropriate to their western markets. In addition to the large serving dishes for communal eating (as seen in the Ardabil Shrine, near Tehran), they also produced spectacular storage jars (for example, see the bottle dated 1450 in the Topkapi Saray Museum, Istanbul), and drinking vessels, of which the spouted *kendi* became the most ubiquitous. The cargo has a number of fine *kendi* of classic Vietnamese form – squat with a vertical neck and large mammiform spout – decorated in both painted underglaze blue and monochrome blue (plate 5.13).

Many of the items on the Hoi An wreck would not have been out of place in a well-appointed Middle Eastern household, as is evident in the Constantinople and Tehran royal collections.[30] On one occasion a Vietnamese ceramic comparable to a jar from the Hoi An cargo even penetrated the households of the aristocracy of sixteenth-century Europe; a large blue-and-white bowl is recorded in the 1595 inventory of the Zwinger palace, Dresden, having been received by the Prince-Elector of Saxony in 1590 as a gift from Ferdinand I, Grand Duke of Tuscany. The presence of the Vietnamese bowl in a European royal collection was probably the result of Italian trade with Ottoman Constantinople.[31] A further example related to a Hoi An cargo jar was found in Yemen, one of the destinations for export of ceramics noted by Ibn Battuta.[32] He reveals that from the bazaars at Zaiton (Quanzhou) porcelain was exported to all parts of China, to India and to Yemen.[33] It would seem that Vietnamese wares were collected en route and traded in the West, where their precise identity would quickly have been concealed, an example of product substitution so common in long-distance trade.[34]

The richest range of Vietnamese export ceramics in South-East Asia has been recovered from east Java, where the Majapahit kingdom was a major consumer of imported ceramics in the fifteenth and early sixteenth centuries. Fragments of vessels recovered from the royal centre of Majapahit are very similar to several spectacular wine ewers from the Hoi An cargo, which are in the form of fantastic mythological creatures, notably the phoenix and the dragon (plate 5.11). The trade of Vietnamese ceramics to Java included high-quality wares customized to local requirements. This demand-led production is vividly illustrated by the architectural tiles made expressly for use in the region of the Majapahit capital, some of which display designs expressly Javanese in origin. That these tiles were made to order is most clearly demonstrated by an example with an underglaze blue-and-white design of a mythical protector (*kala*) (plate 5.14).[35] *Kala* lintels at Candi Surawono in Kediri district, from *c.* 1400, provide the closest dated model for this design.[36] We can only presume that painted models were sent from east Java to northern Vietnam for the pottery artists to follow, just as 200 years later the Dutch VOC carried from Vietnam to Japan painted wooden models of ceramics to be commissioned on behalf of the 'King and Princes of Tongking'.[37]

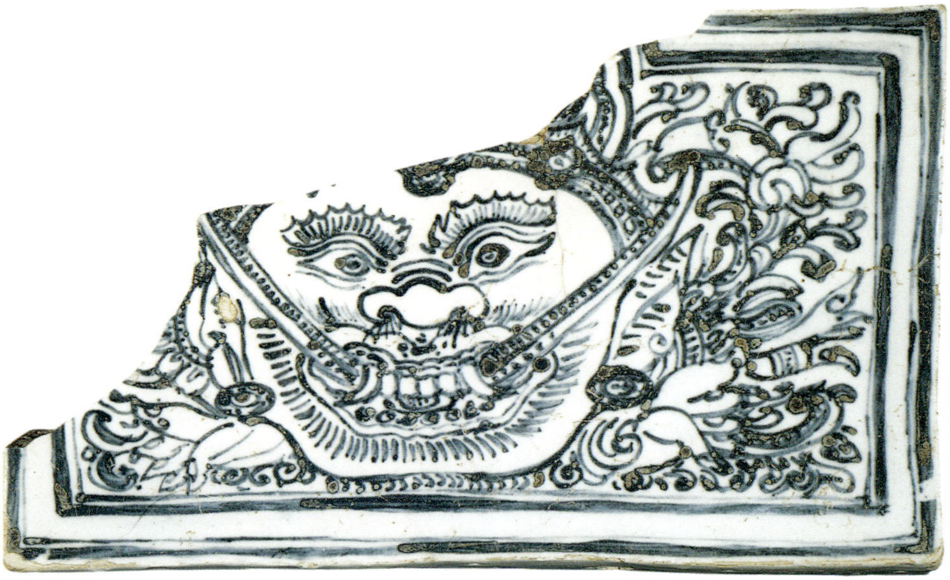

5.14
Wall tile

Glazed stoneware
Vietnam (Red River delta), 15th century

Private collection, London

CHINESE PORCELAIN IN INDIA

Large quantities of Chinese porcelain were also finding their way to the courts of the Indian subcontinent. In a letter written in 1615 to the Earl of Southampton, Sir Thomas Roe (1581–1644), ambassador of James I to the Mughal court, wrote, 'I thought all India a China shop and that I should furnish all my Friendes with rarietyes . . .'.[38] Roe was expecting to encounter all the riches of the East in India. Chinese porcelain was one such marvel, a technical miracle newly introduced to the households of the nobility of Europe. Roe did find Chinese porcelain in abundance in courtly circles in Mughal India, but also found that demand was such that pieces were not readily for sale and, when available, were very expensive. Chinese porcelain was prized in Europe, but in this period in West and South Asia the collecting of such rare and precious objects was altogether more advanced and sophisticated. The rulers of India and their Middle Eastern peers had long shared a passion for porcelain, acquiring and gifting the finest-quality wares that China would permit to enter the international export trade.

Timur (Tamerlane, 1336–1405), the great Mongol ruler, was – in common with other Central Asian rulers – infatuated with Chinese porcelain. His appreciation of this material was witnessed by the Spanish ambassador Ruy Gonzalez de Clavijo at the ruler's capital, Samarkand, in 1403–06. Clavijo described the regular use of Chinese blue-and-white porcelain on Timur's table.[39] Such wares were evidently highly prized and passed down from generation to generation. A number of the finest examples of Chinese porcelain that survive from West Asian and Indian collections bear inscriptions establishing that they once formed part of imperial households; in some cases the pieces predate the inscriptions by more than 200 years.

Blue-and-white porcelain was the product of imperial kilns operating at Jingdezhen in the Yuan and early Ming periods, an era spanning the mid-fourteenth to the early fifteenth centuries.[40] The Yuan dynasty was contemporary with the Afghan Tughlaq Sultanates of Delhi. Both had a common ancestry in Central Asia, and it is perhaps for this reason that they shared a taste for Chinese porcelain. Mughal taste for such wares was also established in Central Asia, at the dynasty's ancestral home of Ferghana on the Silk Route. Large numbers of Yuan blue-and-white sherds have been recovered at Karakorum and at the ruined city of Khara-Khoto, centres marking overland trade routes reopened by the Mongols.[41] The Mongols of Ferghana would have had access to these sources.

One of the earliest descriptions of the Chinese porcelain trade to India is provided by Ibn Battuta. In 1341, when he visited China, he observed that at Zayton (Quanzhou, Fujian) there were 'junks about to sail for India. Among them was a junk belonging to al-Malik al-Zahir, the lord of al-Jawa [Sumatra]. Its crew were Muslims.'[42] Upon his return to India, Battuta recorded seeing 13 Chinese ships at the western Indian port of Calicut – India's main port for the China trade – laden with porcelain and other goods. Some of the porcelains went north to Cambay, and hence to the sultanate court at Delhi; others to vessels destined for Persian Gulf and Red Sea ports.

Ibn Battuta was the first commentator to provide a picture of how Chinese porcelain was used in Indian court life. In the 1340s he resided at Tughlaqabad, the Delhi sultanate capital, as a guest of Sultan Muhammad bin Tughlaq (r. 1325–54), and described a large quantity of Chinese porcelain in use at receptions and dinners in the palace. No traces of these wares have been found in excavations of the fort, suggesting that these highly prized utensils were transferred to nearby Firuzshah Kotla, the fort of the sultan's son and successor, Firuzshah Tughlaq (r. 1354–88), where, some years later, they appear to have been intentionally destroyed, most probably as an act of Islamic iconoclasm. Both Tughlaq sultanate fort-palaces were ravaged in 1398 by Timur, as part of the Mongol campaign that led to the destruction of the Afghan sultanate in Delhi.

A hoard of 72 fragmentary pieces excavated in 1960 in the grounds of the Firuzshah Kotla bears witness to what must have been the largest collection of mid-fourteenth-century Yuan porcelain to have existed in India.[43] However, it was not the only great collection of Chinese porcelain in the Islamic world. The Topkapi Saray imperial Ottoman collection in Istanbul is the most extensive collection preserved today of ceramics that formed part of the China–Middle East trade; inventories exist from 1495. A similar collection once existed in the Chihl Sutun, Isfahan. The Ardabil Shrine collection was assembled by the Iranian royal household and presented to the family's Shi'ite shrine in 1611 by Shah Abbas. Yet none of these imperial collections seems to have rivalled that of the Delhi sultanate, be it in quantity or the variety of designs represented.[44]

This passion for Chinese porcelain was shared by other Muslim rulers in the subcontinent, and the scale of their collecting was also impressive. When the Golconda minister Khajeh Jahan received his sultan in 1471, he 'presented him with so many rich curiosities ... One hundred Faghfoori [Chinese] dishes and cups not to be seen but in the palaces of a few great princes.'[45] Frequent diplomatic exchange with China had ensured a reliable supply of porcelain, which grew significantly in volume. The early Ming emperor Hongwu (r. 1368–98) sent embassies to the Coromandel coast in 1369–70, offering opportunities for trade, as did the renowned voyages of Admiral Zheng He, which took place in the reign of emperor Yongle (1403–33).[46] In 1405, on his first voyage, Zheng He reached Calicut, carrying porcelain as one of the principal cargo items. He also visited Indian ports in Bengal, the Coromandel and Malabar coasts, and Gujarat on his voyages to the 'Western Ocean' (*hsi yang*). Porcelain was a regular feature of this trade mission.

Timur's descendant Babur (r. 1526–30), founder of the Mughal empire, and his successors Humayan, Akbar and Jahangir, were all keen collectors of Chinese porcelain. The peripatetic lifestyle of the early Mughals does not appear to have dissuaded them from collecting and enjoying fine porcelain. The *Baburnama*, the official history of Babur's reign, recounts a series of misadventures involving porcelain, such as a pack animal carrying the royal kitchen's Chinese bowls being successfully rescued during a hasty strategic retreat. References abound to the collections and display of Chinese porcelain in the residences of the Mughal emperor and members of his nobility. The *Baburnama* provides the first description of a *Chinikhana* (China Room), built by Babur's grandfather Ulugh Beg to display his Chinese porcelain collection: 'In the [same] garden he also built a four-doored hall, known as the Chinikhana

5.15
Akbar Receiving the Iranian Ambassador
Double-folio from the *Akbarnama*; composition by La'l; left page by Ibrahim Kahar; right page by Nand, son of Ram Das

Opaque watercolour on paper
Mughal India, 1590–95

V&A: IS.2–1896 28/117, 27/117

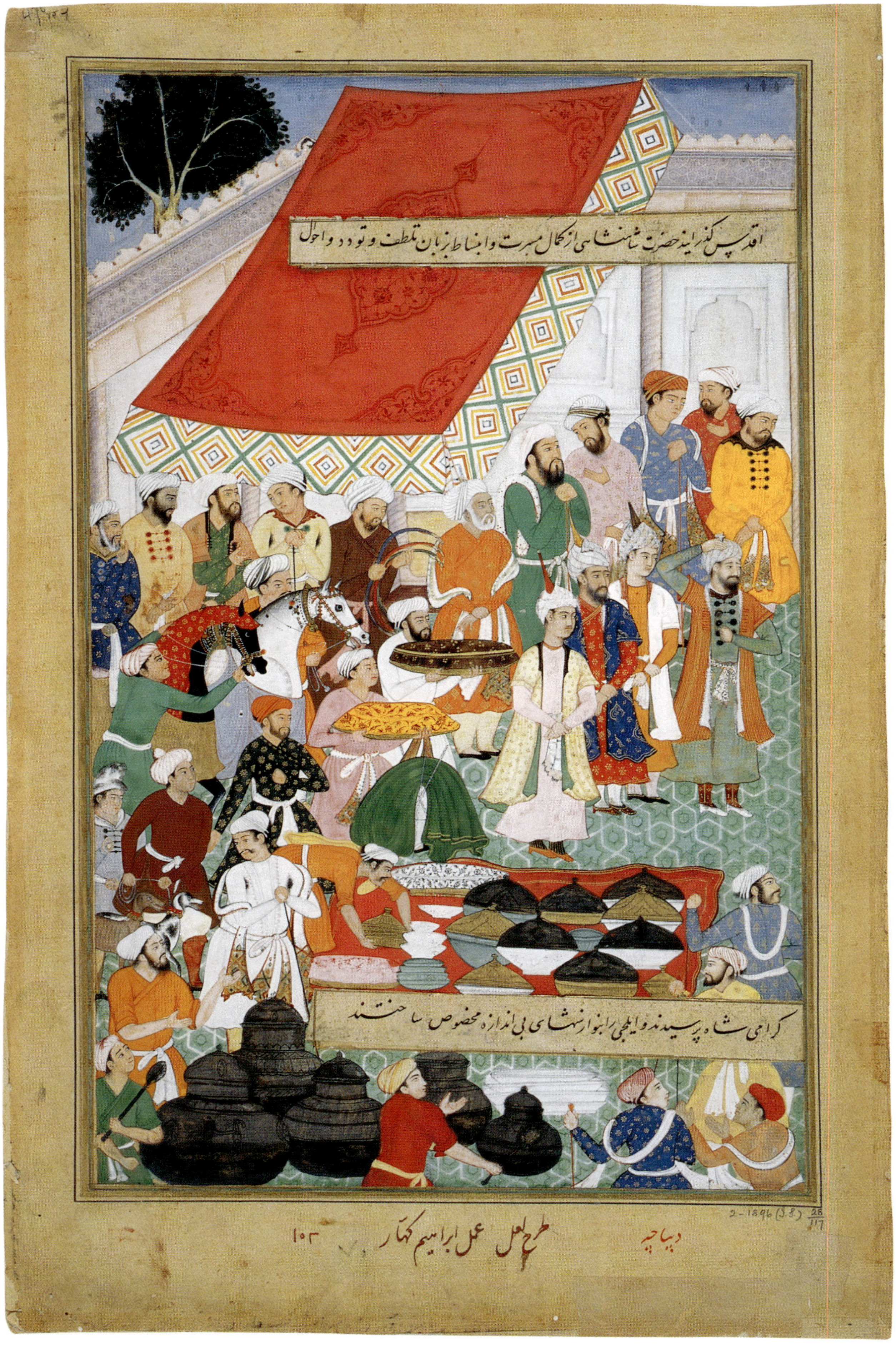

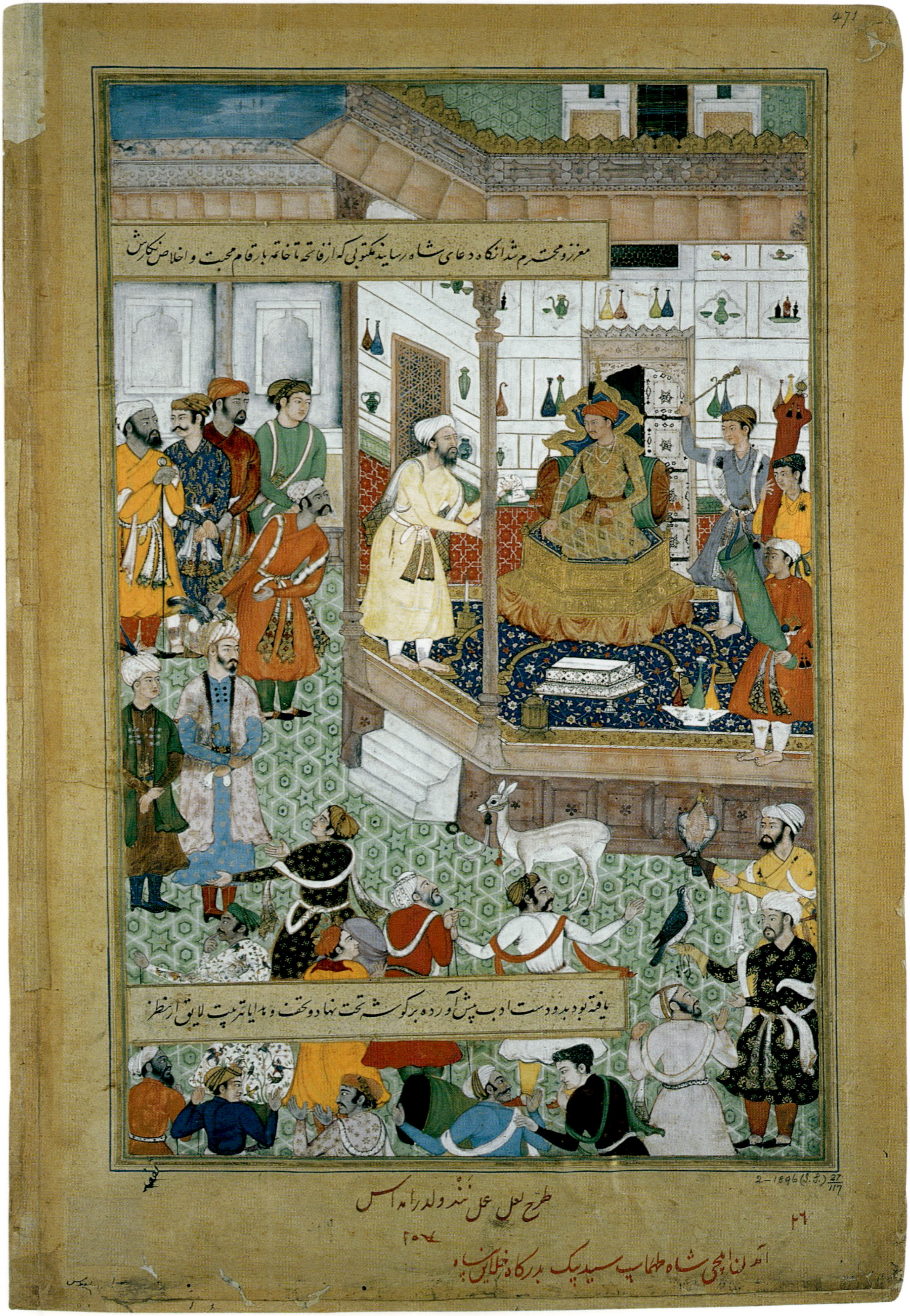
471
معزز و محترم شد انگاه دعای شاه رسایند مکتوبی که از فاتحه تا خاتمه بارقام محبت و اخلاص نگارش
یافته بود بدو دست ادب پیش آورده برگوشه تخت نهاد و تحف و هدایا ترتیب لایق از نظر
2-1896 (I.S.) 27/117
طرح لعل عل نند ولد راهه اس
۲۶
۲۵۷
آمدن ایلچی شاه طهماسپ سید بیک بدرگاه خلایق پناه

5.16
Serving dish (with back view below)

Inscribed with circular *waqf* seal of Shah 'Abbas Safavi and engraved 'Shah Jahan son of Jahangir Shah, 1053' (1643–44); porcelain, with decoration in underglaze cobalt blue
China (Jingdezhen), Xuande period (1426–35)

Anonymous loan, Brooklyn Museum of Art, Brooklyn

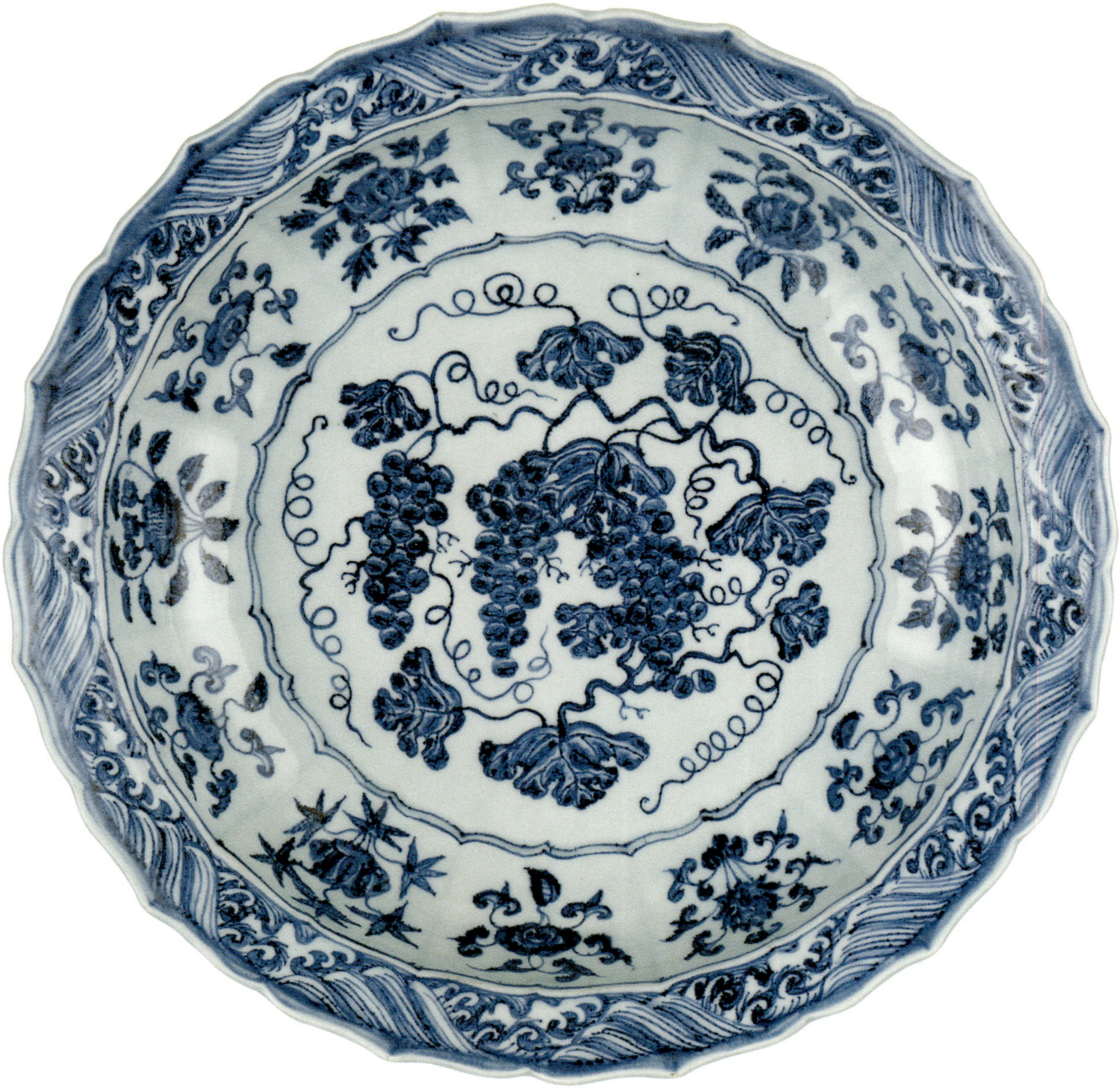

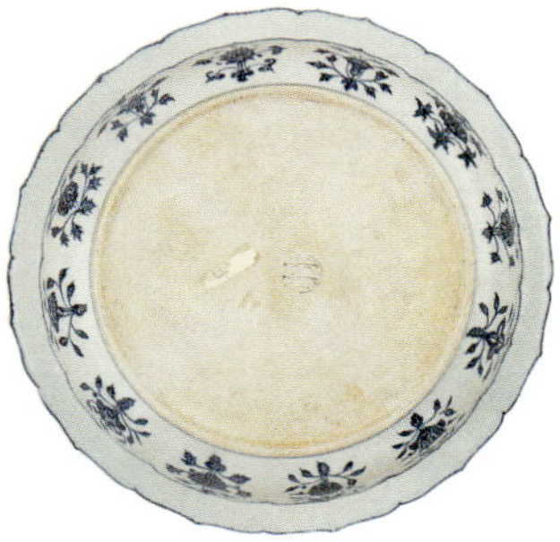

because its izara are all of porcelain; he sent to China for the porcelain used in it.'[47]

By the reign of Akbar (1556–1605) porcelain utensils were a regular feature of court life, as witnessed by contemporary paintings (plate 5.15). The *Akbarnama*, which chronicles the life of the eponymous emperor, includes pages that depict palace interiors in which Chinese porcelain features prominently, both in use and for display. Akbar created China Rooms expressly for the display and enjoyment of the imperial Chinese porcelain collection. Abu'l Fazl, the emperor's official biographer, recorded that the Imperial Treasury contained '25 lakhs worth of the most elegant vessels of every kind of porcelain and coloured glass'.[48] Little survives of these Mughal interiors, apart from some bare niches at Agra Fort and Fatephur Sikri. Mughal and Iranian court miniatures reveal that such displays were a common feature of the finest palaces, where Chinese porcelain was proudly displayed alongside Syrian and Iranian glass and metal objects in vogue at the time. Such court tastes were immediately mimicked by ministers, regional governors and wealthy merchants.

The emperor Jahangir (r. 1605–27) continued this passion for Chinese ceramics, acquiring antiquarian pieces of the highest quality, such as a superb wine ewer of a type now archaeologically linked to the imperial kilns at Jingdezhen (plate 5.18).[49] Sir Thomas Roe wrote that the emperor valued porcelain highly and that among the gifts presented by the ruler of Bijapur were 'Chinawares and one figure of christall which the king accepted more than that masse of wealth'.[50] Roe himself presented two China cups to Prince Khurrum (later Shah Jahan; r. 1628–58) when they met on 12 October 1617. He despaired at the lavish gifts the VOC representative presented at court: 'a great present of Chinaware, sandalwood, parrots and cloves', commodities presumably all sourced via Bantam, the VOC's Asian headquarters in west Java. Nor would Roe's modest gifts have made much impression when set beside the large dish of imperial quality that entered Shah Jahan's collection in 1643–44 (plate 5.16). This piece bears the personal seal (*waqf*) of Shah 'Abbas I of Iran (r. 1588–1629), establishing that it had formed part of the group of porcelain presented to the Ardabil Shrine prior to 1611. Such an imperial provenance does much to establish the status of high-quality Chinese porcelain in the Muslim courts of West Asia and the Indian subcontinent.

According to Abul Fazl's *Akbarnama,* an active overland trade was maintained with Kabul, as well as the regular sea trade via Surat, the leading port serving the Mughal capital. Kabul continued to hold its prominence as a market for luxuries such as Chinese ceramics into the early seventeenth century; according to Jahangir's memoirs, the *Tuzik-i-Jahangiri*, he received among his New Year gifts in 1612 'porcelain from China … and other valuable presents procured in Kabul'.[51] The *Tuzik-i-Jahangiri* praises Jahangir for his expertise in Chinese ceramics. When the emperor was presented with gifts of porcelain, two types were distinguished, *Khata* from northern China and *Faghfuri* from other regions. Such was the level of connoisseurship of Chinese porcelain prevailing in India at the beginning of the seventeenth century.

5.17 below left
Flask

Inscribed 'Aurangzeb', dated AH 1070 (1659–60); porcelain, with decoration in underglaze blue
China, Ming dynasty (early 15th century)

British Museum, London

5.18
Wine ewer

Inscribed as part of Shah Jahangir's household and dated AH 1038 (1628); porcelain, decorated in underglaze cobalt blue
China (Jingdezhen), Xuande period (1426–35) or earlier

Private collection

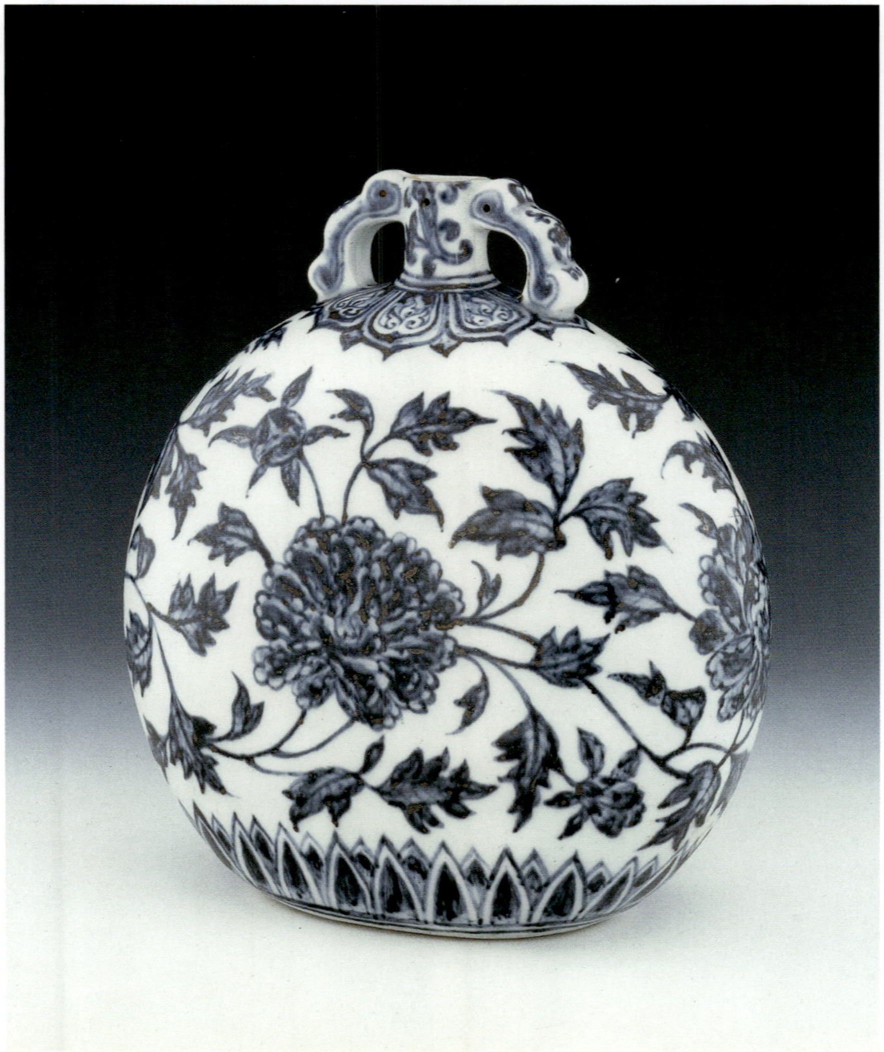

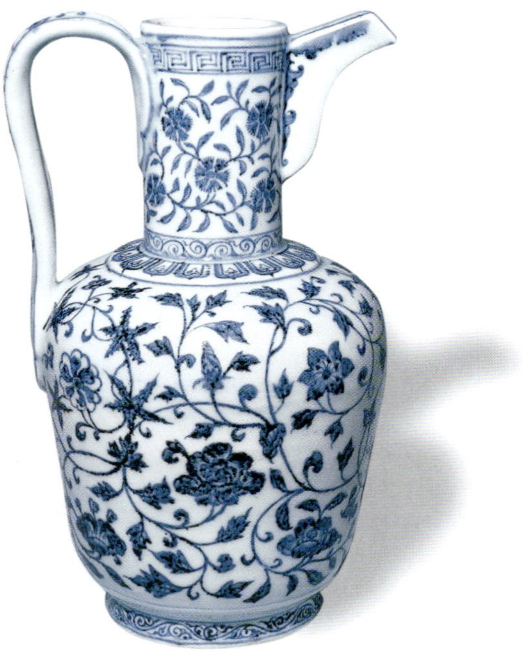

Thai Ceramics and Shipwrecks in South-East Asia

John Guy

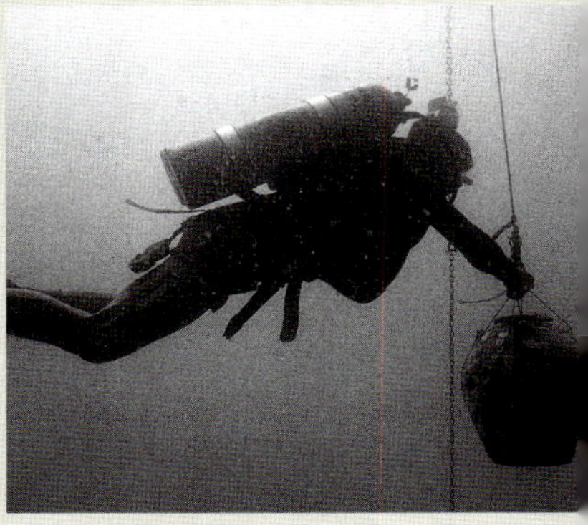

5.19
Diver recovering a Thai storage jar from a shipwreck
Gulf of Thailand, 1985

SHIPWRECKS AND THEIR CARGOES are one of the best sources of information for understanding intra-Asian commerce. Ceramic cargoes survive largely intact, unlike the more perishable textiles, spices and aromatics that were also traded. Often significant portions of the hull of the vessels are sufficiently well preserved to allow construction techniques and timber sources to be studied. These archaeological remains have allowed a more complex picture of Asian trade to emerge than historical data alone would suggest. The period *c.* 1400–1600 was marked by the active participation of South-East Asian ceramic producers in the region's trade, alongside the Chinese merchants who had traditionally dominated this market. A brisk trade operated out of Ayutthaya, the Siamese capital.

The majority of wrecks identified in South-East Asian waters over the past two decades have been ships involved in the Ayutthayan ceramic trade. Those found to be carrying a mixed Thai and Chinese ceramic cargo have proved to be vessels originating in South-East Asia. Shipbuilding yards operated widely in South-East Asia, constructing a type of modified Chinese junk for the regional trade. These vessels incorporated non-Chinese hull construction techniques (notably dowelled hardwood planking)

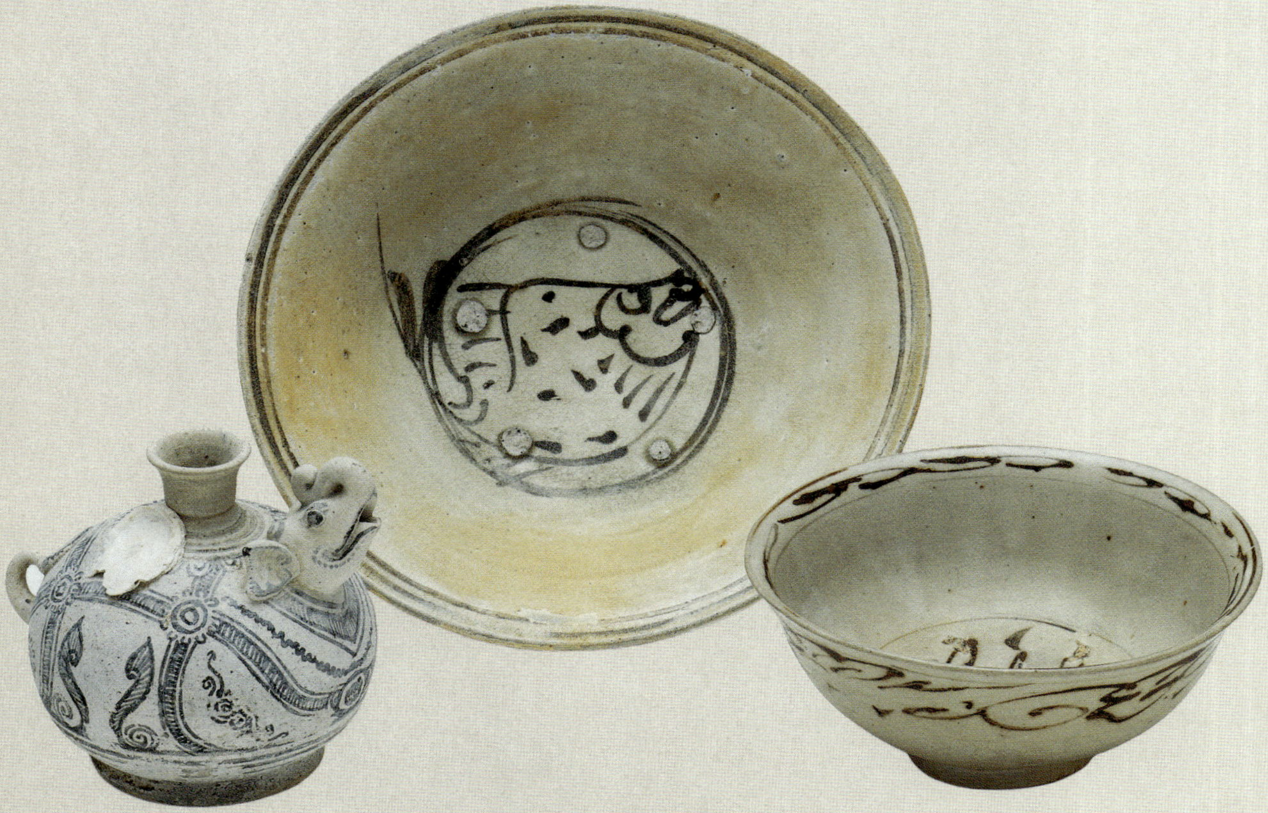

5.20
Thai and Vietnamese ceramics
Recovered from the *Singtai* and *Turiang* shipwrecks, South China Sea, 1998–2000; stoneware, with decoration in underglaze iron
Elephant kendi, Thailand (Si Satchanalai), 16th century; fish-design dish, Thailand (Sukhothai), 14th–early 15th century; bowl, Vietnam (Red River delta), 14th– early 15th century
V&A: elephant kendi, *Singtai*, V&A: IS.91–2002; fish dish, *Turiang*, V&A: IS.101–2002); bowl, *Turiang*, V&A: IS.102–2002

5.21
Thai ceramics

Recovered from the *Royal Nanhai*, *Nanyang* and *Longquan* shipwrecks, South China Sea, 1995–98; stoneware with green (celadon) glaze
Thailand (Si Satchanalai), 15th century

V&A: small jar, *Nanyang*, V&A: IS.77–2002; small jar, *Royal Nanhai*, V&A: IS.72–2002; bottle, *Longquan*, V&A: IS.82–2002; dish, *Royal Nanhai*, V&A: IS.67–2002; jar, *Nanyang*, V&A: IS.75–2002

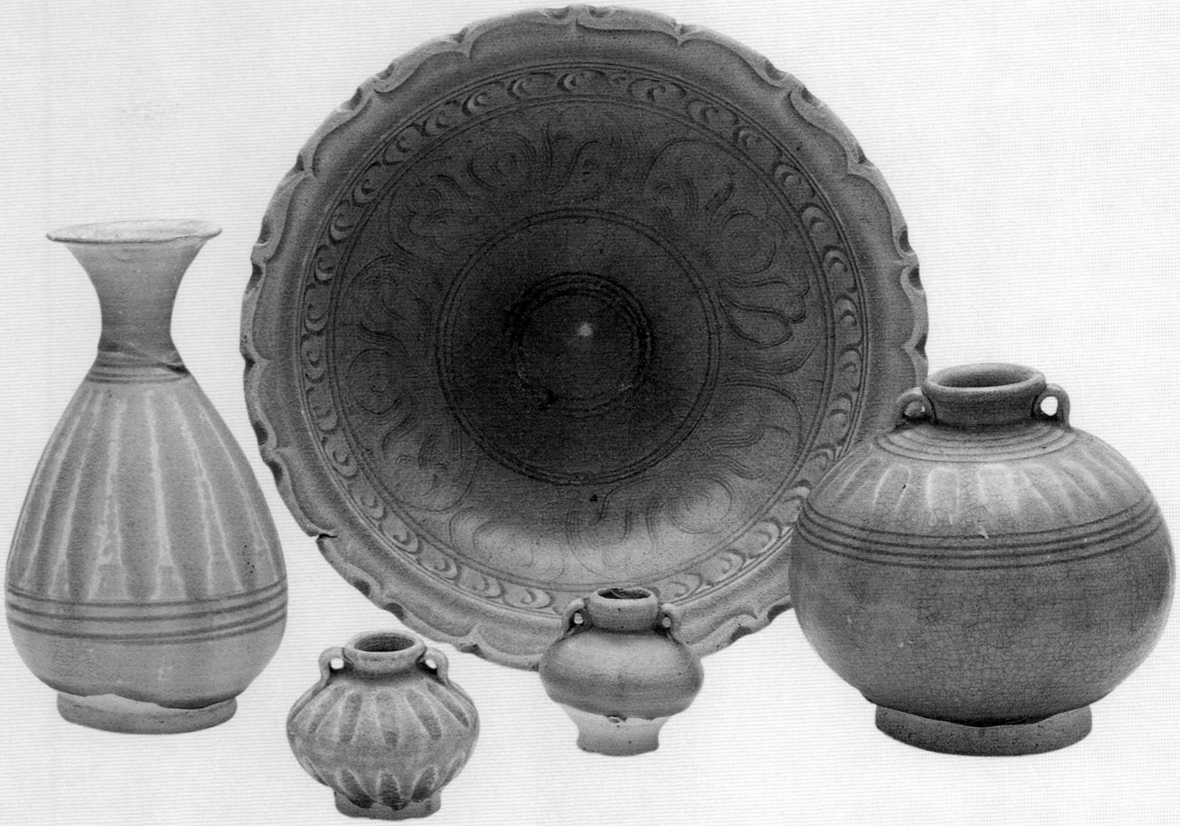

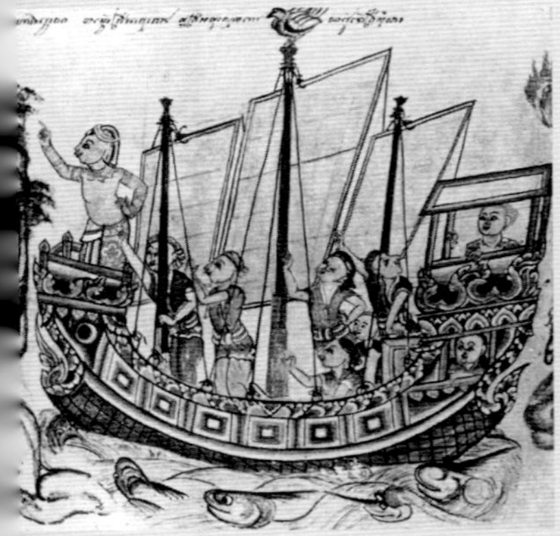

5.22
Sino-Thai Junk

From a Thai Buddhist manuscript, *Pritsana tham Thai*
Watercolour on khoi paper, late 18th century

National Library, Bangkok

into an essentially Chinese-junk design (plate 5.22). This vessel-type is associated with fifteenth- and sixteenth-century ceramic cargoes. The *Royal Nanhai*, a mid-fifteenth-century vessel in all probability built in the Gulf of Siam, typifies this type of trader. It was loaded predominantly with Thai celadons from Si Satchanalai and brown-glazed storage jars from Singburi, the latter's kilns being near Ayutthaya, where both consignments would have been assembled to form this cargo (plate 5.21).

In 1998 the *Turiang* shipwreck was located and excavated 160 kilometres off the Malaysian coast. Unusually, the remains of the softwood hull and the presence of iron nails identify the vessel as a Chinese junk. Yet the majority of the ceramic cargo consisted of Thai wares, from both the Sukhothai and Si Satchanalai kilns of north-central Thailand (57 per cent), together with a significant number of Chinese green-and-brown glazed wares (35 per cent), the remainder being from the Red River delta region of Vietnam. The Thai ceramics were iron-decorated brown-and-white wares and celadons; no blue-and-white ceramics were present (plate 5.20). This indicates an early date for such a cargo – perhaps the late fourteenth or early fifteenth century, when the circulation of Chinese blue-and-white was still limited. It is significant that a Chinese vessel was carrying a cargo composed predominantly of Thai rather than Chinese ceramics. This suggests that the ship may have begun its journey in southern China, off-loading much of its cargo in Ayutthaya, and restocking with Thai wares for the island run. Alternatively, Thai wares may have been used to supplement shortages of Chinese ceramics.

The Thai succeeded in selling their own distinctive styles of wares for two centuries until a combination of domestic instability – which disrupted production and distribution – and revitalized Chinese competition saw them withdraw from this international trade. When Europeans began observing the intra-Asian ceramic trade, it was once again largely a Chinese affair.

Imported Ceramics and Japanese Tea Drinking

Rupert Faulkner

THE JAPANESE CULTURE of tea drinking was closely associated with the collecting of ceramics imported via the intra-Asian trade network linking Japan with China, Korea and South-East Asia. Jesuit missionaries reporting from Japan in the late sixteenth and early seventeenth centuries frequently commented on the prevalence of, and importance attached to, tea drinking. Tea was barely known about in Europe at this time, its regular importation by the Dutch and then the English not taking place until the mid to late 1600s. Tea in Europe was prepared by steeping in the Chinese manner. Steeped tea was also drunk in Japan from the late sixteenth century onwards, but the principal method of preparation was by adding hot water to powdered green tea and mixing it with a bamboo whisk.

Whipped tea, as this form of the beverage is known, was a Chinese invention of an earlier period introduced to Japan at the end of the twelfth century. It was initially drunk in Zen Buddhist temples, but as time went by it came to be enjoyed by the populace at large. Tea also played an important role in formal social interchange between members of the ruling military aristocracy for whom, during the Muromachi period (1336–1573), its consumption was related to the appreciation of, and expression of authority through, Chinese art objects.

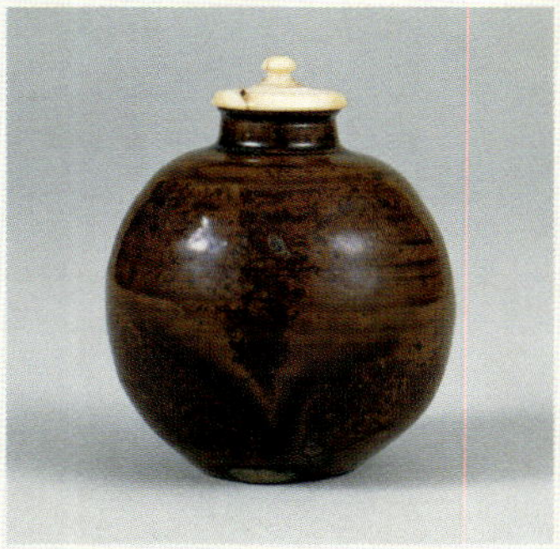

The three most important ceramic items used for tea drinking were the tea jar (for dried tea leaves), the tea caddy (for powdered tea made by grinding dried tea leaves) and the tea bowl. Chinese black-glazed wares from the Jian kilns in Fujian province were

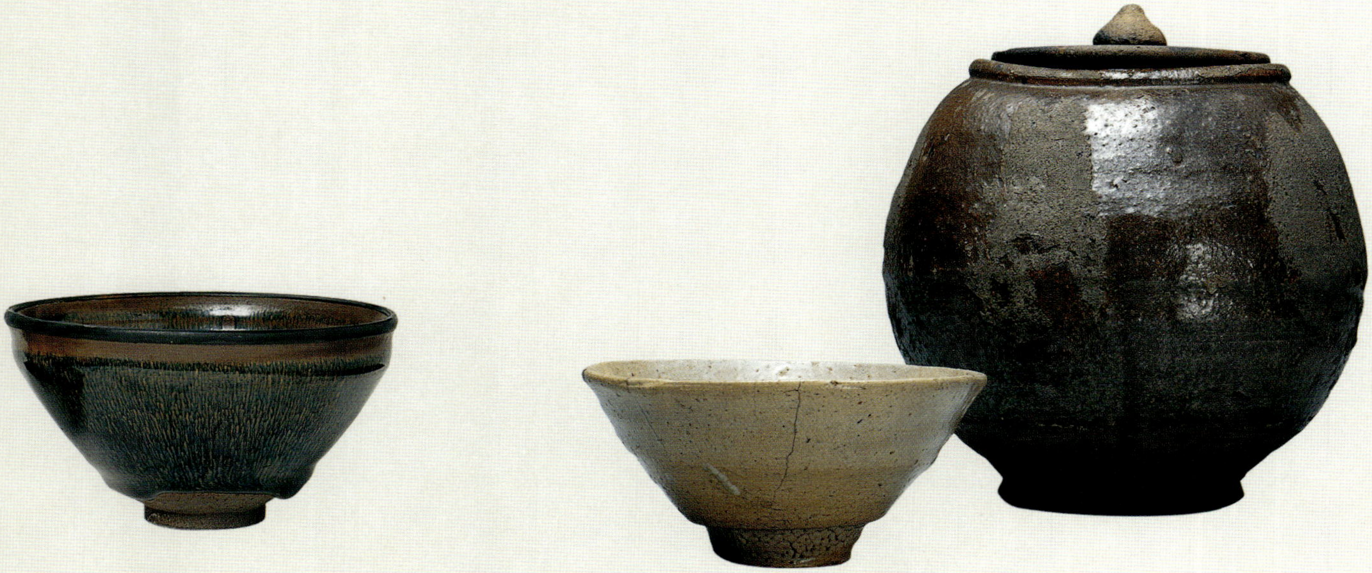

5.23 left, above
Tea caddy
(Bunrin type)
Stoneware with brown glaze
China (probably Fujian province), 13th–14th century
Nezu Institute of Fine Arts, Tokyo; designated as Important Art Object

5.24 far left
Tea bowl
Stoneware with 'hare's fur' *(togōsan)* glaze
China (Jian kilns, Fujian province), 12th–13th century
V&A: C.841–1936

5.25
Tea bowl
***(Ao-ido type)* known as 'Shibata'**
Glazed stoneware
Korea, 16th century
Nezu Institute of Fine Arts, Tokyo; designated as Important Cultural Property

5.26
Fresh-water jar
(Nanban Imogashira type)
Glazed stoneware with earthenware lid
Vietnam, 16th–17th century
Nezu Institute of Fine Arts, Tokyo

the favoured variety of tea bowl (plate 5.24). Tea jars and tea caddies imported from southern China were also highly sought after and exchanged hands at enormous prices (plate 5.23). Tea jars were given individual names, and tea caddies, carefully classified by shape, were kept in bags made from expensive imported textiles. The ruling Ashikaga *shōguns* employed cultural advisers whose various duties included the drawing up of detailed codes of etiquette for the use and display of tea utensils and other Chinese treasures, known generically as *karamono* (literally 'Chinese things').

While the taste for *karamono* persisted throughout the sixteenth century and beyond, the rise of *chanoyu* (the tea ceremony, literally 'hot water for tea') saw the incorporation into the tea-utensil repertory of a wide range of alternative ceramic types. Domestically produced wares, both glazed ceramics copying Chinese imports and rough unglazed stonewares, were avidly collected by influential tea masters such as Murata Shukō (1423–1502), Takeno Jōō (1502–55) and Sen no Rikyū (1522–91). Attention was similarly paid to lesser and hitherto disregarded products of southern Chinese kilns, and there was a particular vogue for Korean bowls and Vietnamese jars (plates 5.25–6).

With its dual championing of the perfection of *karamono* and the rusticity of the kitchen crock, *chanoyu* was a major stimulator of artistic experimentation. Initially the preserve of wealthy merchants in Kyoto, Nara and port cities such as Hakata and Sakai, by the late sixteenth century it was widely practised by the military elite. Growing demand for tea utensils led to the placing of orders at Japanese kilns. This triggered the extraordinary flourishing of domestic ceramic production for which the Momoyama period (1573–1615) is legendary. Orders were also placed abroad, notably in Korea and China, where ceramics were produced in distinctly Japanese taste (plate 5.27).

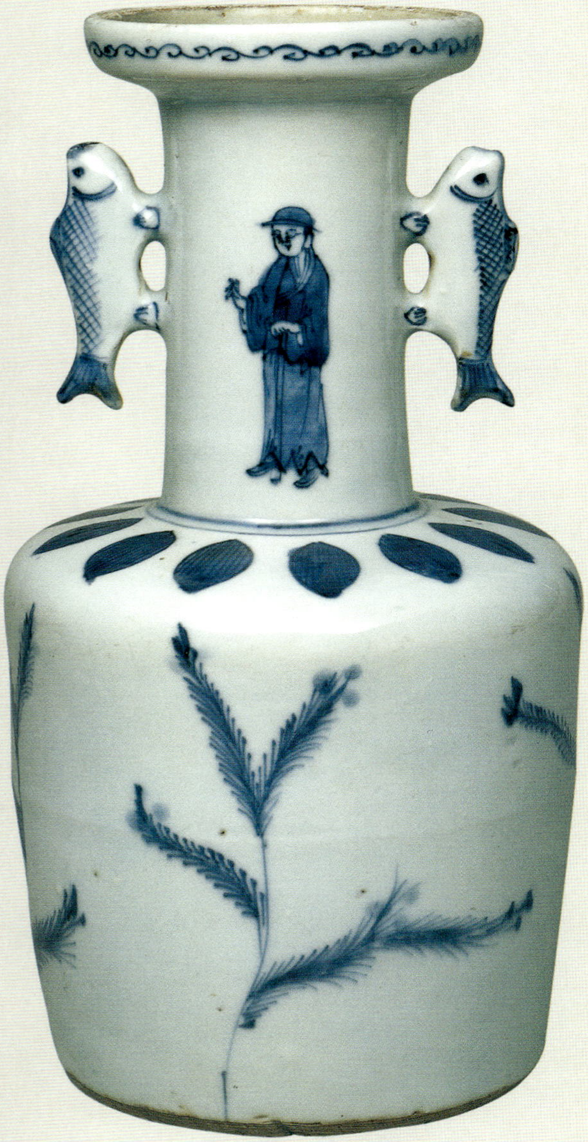

5.27 right
Vase
(Takasago type)
Porcelain with decoration in underglaze cobalt blue
China (Jingdezhen); early 17th century
Nezu Institute of Fine Arts, Tokyo

PART TWO

Encounters

6

DIPLOMATIC ENCOUNTERS: EUROPE AND SOUTH ASIA

Amin Jaffer

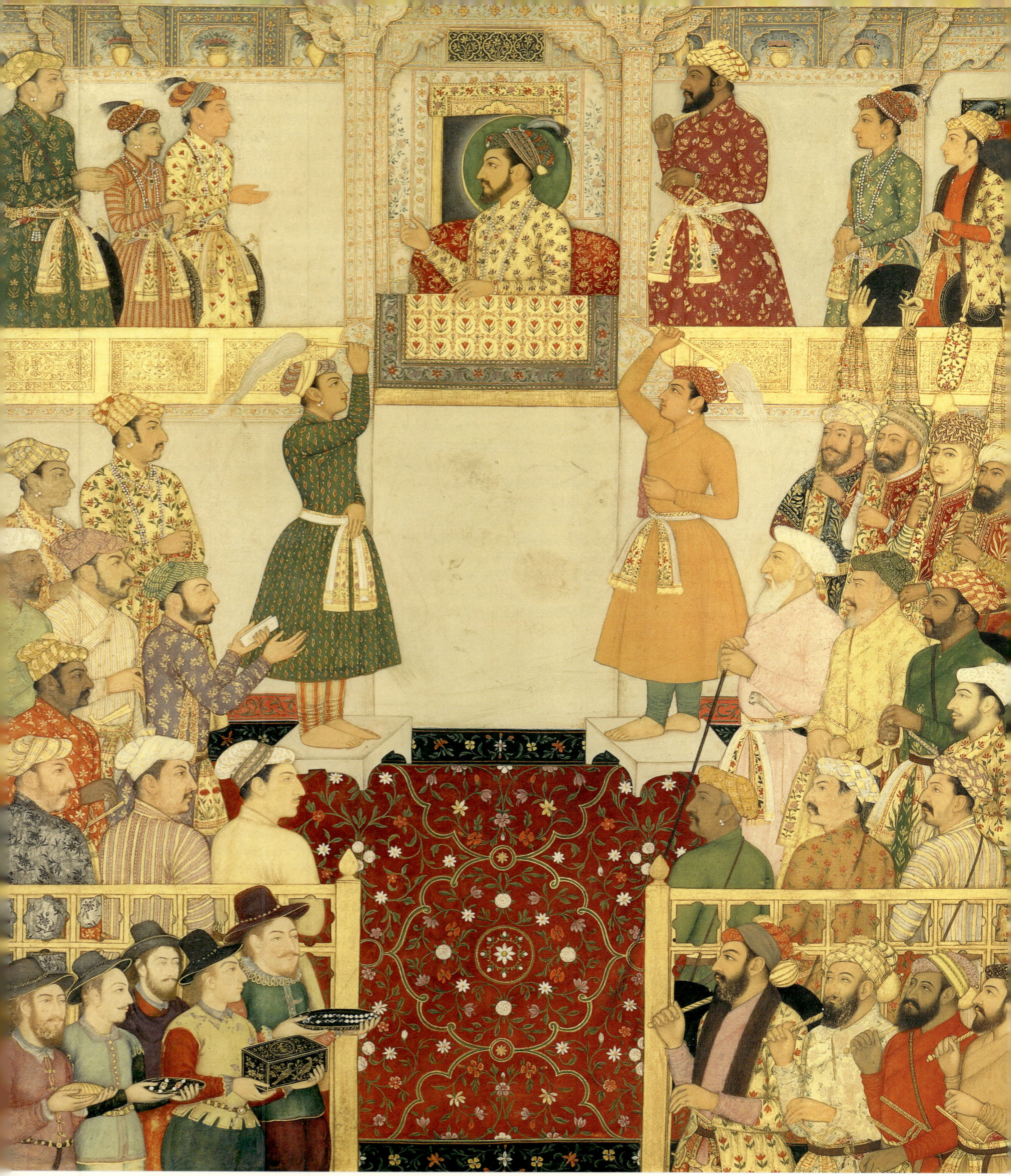

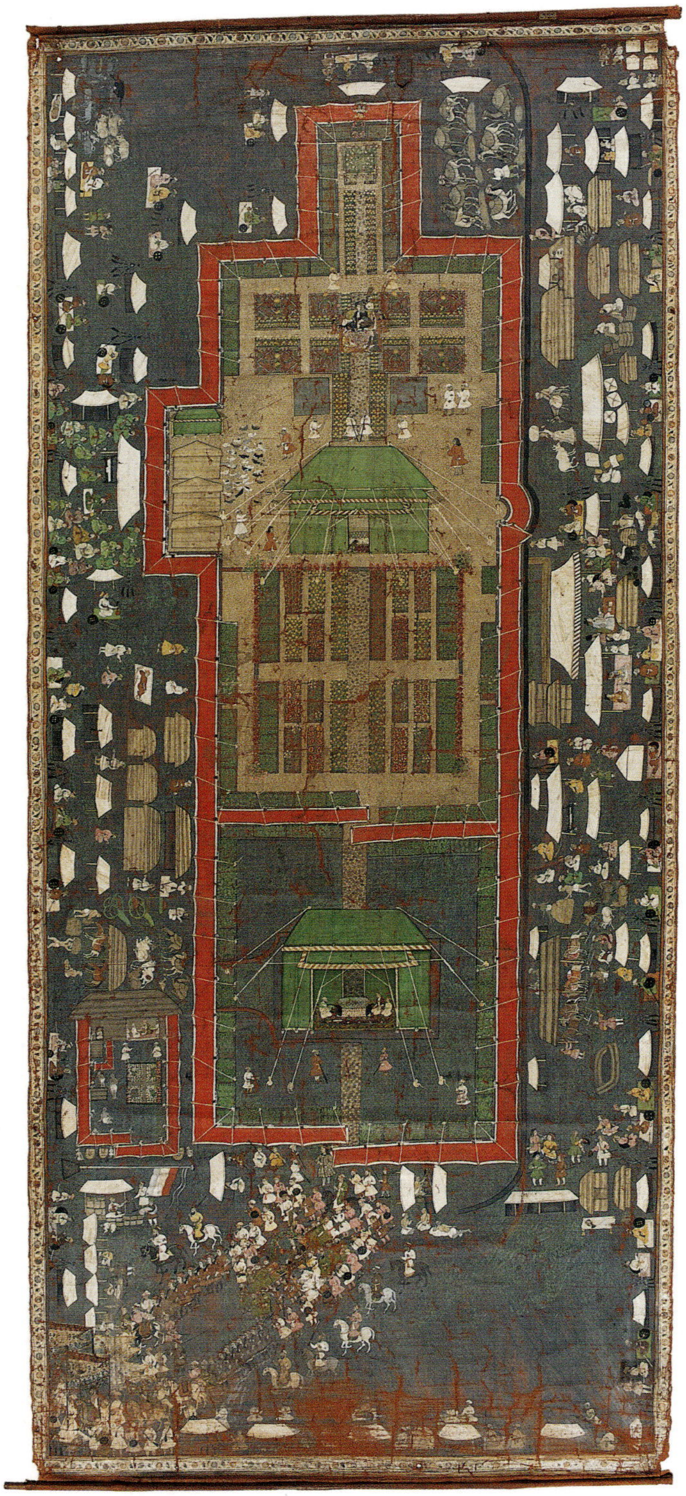

6.6 above and detail opposite
The Embassy of Johannes Bacherus en route to the Court of Aurangzeb
Colours on cloth
India (Golconda), late 17th century
Tropenmuseum, Amsterdam

As Europeans came to dominate trade routes from the Persian Gulf to South Asia, they were in the enviable position of having access to Arabian horses, which were much sought after in India. Exotic animals were also desired by Asian princes, and contemporary papers reveal that the various European trading powers were much occupied in finding and transporting these. Jahangir, for example, demanded an English horse and dogs.[37] Bloodhounds, greyhounds and mastiffs were sent all over South Asia, where people marvelled that they 'can be tought to fetch, or find things lost'.[38] Many times these beasts did not survive the long journeys that they were forced to endure. In 1639 a VOC embassy to Golconda had no choice but to stop because of the death of the presents: an elephant and two horses.[39] Charles Ware Malet's mission to Poona in 1786 was likewise diminished by the death of one of the gifts: a 'large griffin bird'.[40]

Exchanging arms was standard practice among princes in early modern Europe and Asia. Europeans at Asian courts perpetuated this tradition and in doing so helped to introduce western arms and armour to South Asia (see p.325). Admiral Beaulieu gave the King of Achin ceremonial weaponry comprising 'The complete armour of an horseman engraved and gilt; a German hanger, with a carved and gilt hilt, to which hung a pistol, six muskets, the barrels of which were partly engraved and partly gilt, the butt ends enriched with mother of pearl; two heads of pikes enamelled and gilt'.[41] The size and imposing appearance of cannons meant that they were regularly given as showy gifts.[42] South Asian rulers regularly requested gifts of western arms and armour. In the late 1630s Abdulla Hussain Qutb Shah, Sultan of Golconda (r.1626–72), demanded presents from the Company including a suit of armour 'yf possible muskett proofe'.[43] Apart from the presents that they received, Asian rulers were also keen to acquire an understanding of European war technology. In 1666 Aurangzeb asked the VOC and East India Company to provide 'five gunfounders and two engineers or pioneers, that have skill in millitary affaires and giving directions for digging mines and contriving workes for the advantageous assaultong or worsting the enemy; requiring expresly that they be very experienced practical men'.[44]

The gifts presented by Europeans also included luxury goods from other parts of Asia, notably China and Japan. For presentation to Jahangir, for example, Roe was advised that instead of English 'cloth and ill

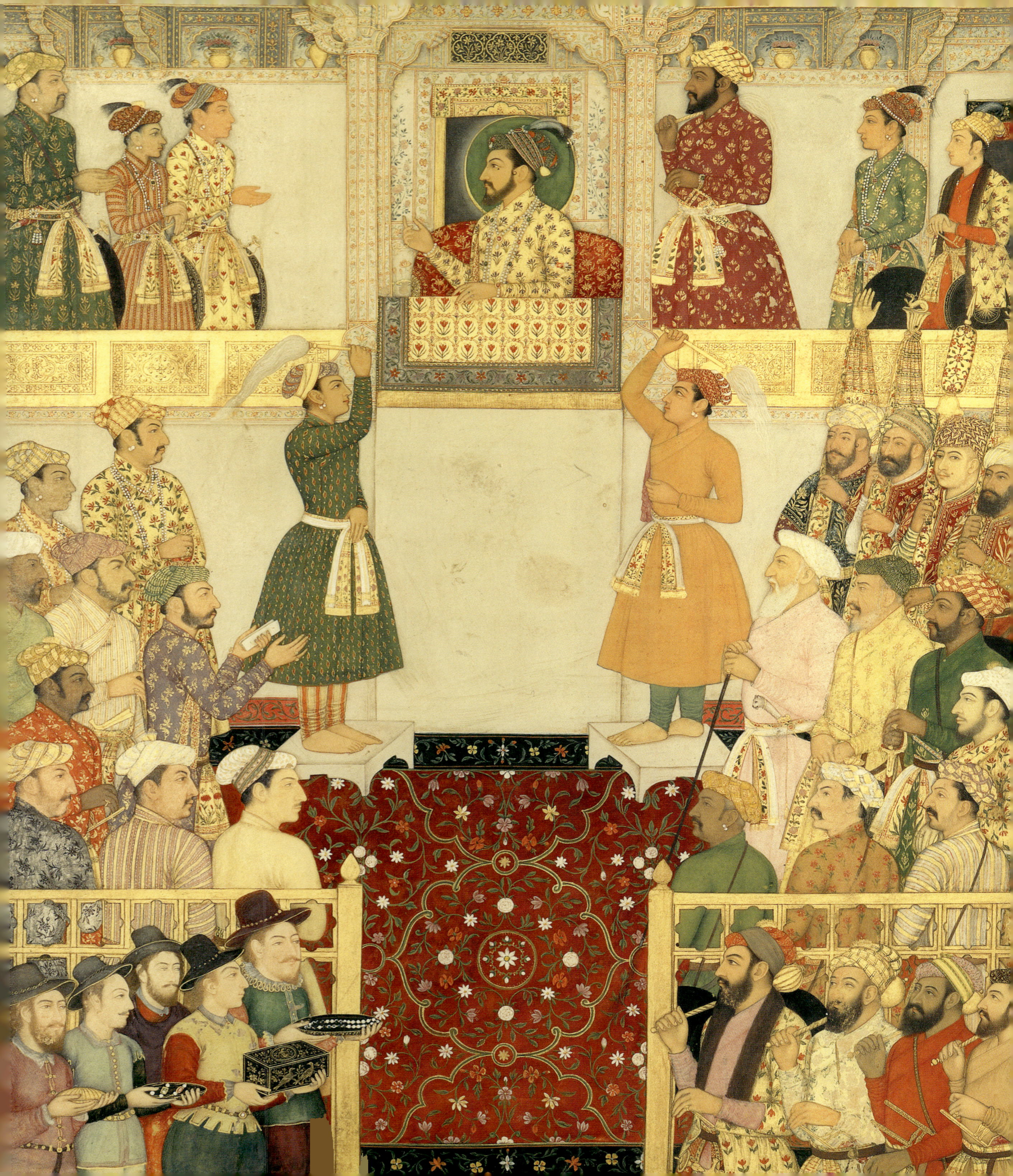

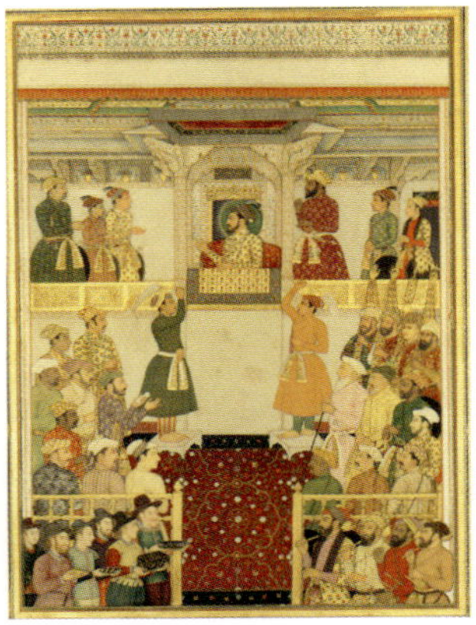

6.1 previous page and above
Europeans Bring Gifts to Shah Jahan
From the *Padshahnama* manuscript
Opaque watercolour on paper
Mughal India, *c.*1650
The Royal Collection

'My Lord, in *Asia*, the great are never approached empty-handed,' wrote French physician François Bernier (1620–88) after 12 years of experience of the Mughal court.[1] His advice was intended for Jean-Baptiste Colbert (1619–83), founder of the *Compagnie des Indes Orientales*, the vehicle for French commercial enterprise in Asia. Alas, Bernier's words arrived after the *Compagnie* had already despatched a mission to the Mughal emperor Aurangzeb (r. 1658–1707). Its envoys arrived at court without any presents and as a result they 'had neither respect nor countenance shewed them, but tossed from post to pillar; and although they have been there some monthes, cannot procure an audience'.[2] By failing to recognize the central role that gifts played in Indian diplomacy, the *Compagnie* was repeating a mistake that Vasco da Gama (*c.* 1460–1524) had himself committed on his first voyage to India. Gama had failed to take rich presents with him and when he landed at Calicut was able to present its ruler with only a meagre offering, among which were 12 pieces of striped cloth, six hats, four strings of coral, a case of sugar, two casks of oil and two casks of honey.[3] This was considered less than adequate by the king's stewards, who, 'when they saw the present … laughed at it, saying that it was not a thing to offer to a king, that the poorest merchant from Mecca, or any other part of India gave more'.[4] The gift seemed particularly insulting since Gama had described himself as an ambassador from the King of Portugal, whom he claimed was 'Lord of many countries and the possessor of great wealth of every description, exceeding that of any king of these parts'.[5]

These incidents illustrate how in South Asia, much more than in Europe, gift-giving was crucial in assuring the success of a diplomatic meeting. But it was only one of the conventions of diplomacy that Europeans needed to master in order to establish their credibility with local princes. The India that Europeans encountered in the sixteenth century was not a single centrally controlled state, but a collection of kingdoms and principalities of vastly differing capabilities. The region was far from homogenous, but throughout the subcontinent there did exist basic conventions for regulating diplomacy. The obstacle confronting early Europeans on the scene was that of establishing and endorsing a place in the hierarchy of local powers. A corresponding problem on the South Asian side was that of determining the status and motives of the Europeans who arrived at court.

Westerners came to South Asian courts not to establish political alliances but to secure or renew rights to conduct business under favourable conditions. Where minor coastal principalities were concerned, they were able to conclude trade agreements relatively easily with diplomacy, or, if necessary, with a show of superior western firepower. However, powerful kingdoms had less reason to take Europeans seriously. While envoys were often endorsed or even accredited by a European monarch, they were usually representing the interests not of a king but of a chartered trading company or the commercial arm of a state. From an Asian perspective, differentiating king from company was a continual problem. This confusion began with Vasco da Gama, whose behaviour was perceived by the Zamorin of Calicut to be more those of a merchant than of a diplomat.[6] The need to ascertain the precise position of the Europeans they encountered was a problem for Indian rulers even as late as the close of the eighteenth century, when Muhammad Ali Wallajah, Nawab of Arcot (r. 1749–95), complained that 'neither his Father, nor himself in their first connexions with the English understood anything about a distinction between the King and the Company … That both had done great favours to the Company supposing they were shewing friendship to the Nation.'[7]

Even before the arrival of Europeans, South Asian rulers were familiar with the phenomenon of foreign merchants who would come to court pretending to be ambassadors in order to enjoy diplomatic privileges.[8] Although they would be expected to offer gifts, these pretend diplomats realized that, according to convention, they would receive presents of value equal to or greater than those which they themselves had given. Contemporary chroniclers reported that in 1664 ambassadors from Mecca, the Yemen and Bassora (Basra) arrived simultaneously at the Mughal court in Delhi. They were all given short shrift since 'every one suspected they came merely for the sake of obtaining money in return for their presents, and of gaining still more considerable sums by means of the numerous horses, and different articles of merchandise, which they introduced into the kingdom free of duty, as property belonging to ambassadors'.[9] Ambassadors from Europe were especially suspect since the claims they made about their countries could not easily be verified. Typically it was the richness of their presents that was used to gauge whether or not they were legitimate royal representatives. Sir Thomas Roe (1580–1644),

James I's ambassador to the Mughal court, noted in 1618 how 'The new pretended Spanish ambassador is refused audience … principally because his presents were not of great valew.'[10] Roe's comment about the 'pretended' ambassador is ironic given that, prior to his own arrival, envoys who had visited the Mughal court representing the English Crown were seriously doubted because of their inadequate gifts and obvious commercial interests.[11]

Credentials were essential in establishing the legitimacy of a royal representative. These were typically conveyed in the form of a letter from one ruler to another, which stated the name of the bearer and specified his rank. Presenting credentials was a convention in ancient Indian diplomacy and was prevalent throughout Asia at the time that Europeans arrived there.[12] Ordinarily an envoy was expected to offer his credentials the first time he was presented to a ruler. However, on his first encounter with the Zamorin of Calicut, Gama merely announced himself as ambassador, explaining that he had been entrusted with two letters from the King of Portugal, which he would deliver later. Gaspar Correa claimed that these letters did not exist, but were made up by Gama and his brother, who apparently forged them together in Calicut.[13] Later diplomats would avert this situation by leaving home with several letters, some left blank so that they could be filled out in case they unexpectedly found themselves in a situation where credentials were needed. For example, James I sent Nicholas Downton (1561–1615) to India with letters for the Mughal emperor, the King of Achin, the Emperor of China, and three letters which the king signed, but with names and titles left blank.[14] A letter of this kind in the British Library was carried by Sir Henry Middleton to Asia in 1619, but was brought back unused (plate 6.2). The Middleton letter was written in English, although diplomatic letters from English kings to Asian rulers were sometimes also prepared in Latin, as was Charles II's missive for Aurangzeb.[15] The Portuguese, by contrast, recognized that Arabic was the *lingua franca* of the Indian Ocean world and routinely despatched letters in that language as well as in their own.[16]

According to Bernier, in order to succeed at court nothing was more important 'than a good and faithful interpreter, thoroughly experienced and familiar with the methods of procedure in the country'.[17] But to what extent were Europeans prepared to trust foreign interpreters to represent them? Vasco da Gama entered the Arab-dominated Indian Ocean with anti-Islamic attitudes inherited from Portuguese centuries of struggle against the Muslim occupiers of the Iberian peninsula. While at Calicut, Gama refused the facilities of a Muslim interpreter, demanding instead an Arabic-speaking Christian.[18] The idea that fundamental differences between the two religions would naturally colour dealings between peoples of the two faiths is evident from Bernier's diplomatic advice, in which he implored Colbert to 'get it clearly into your head that they are Muhamadans and we are Christians and that in consequence they hate us at least as much as we hate them'.[19] Sir Thomas Roe's writings also betray his mistrust of the motives of foreign interpreters, but this was due more to a fear that they might secretly be working for rival Portuguese interests.[20] Conflicting claims from other Europeans, and indeed from their own countrymen, sometimes impeded the success of Westerners trying to build stable relationships with local rulers. For example, in order to thwart the success of John Mildenhall's audience with Akbar (r. 1556–1605), the emperor's Portuguese interpreters informed the ruler that the English were all 'theeves'.[21] And when, under William III, a New East India Company was created, the ambassador it sent to Aurangzeb's court was not recognized by servants of the original or 'Old' Company, who informed Mughal authorities that he was 'no King's Ambassador, but merely the representative of a Company of merchants'.[22]

6.2
Letter from James I to an Asian ruler
Dated 30 March 1619; carried by Sir Henry Middleton on the East India Company's Sixth Voyage
Ink and colours on vellum
British Library, London

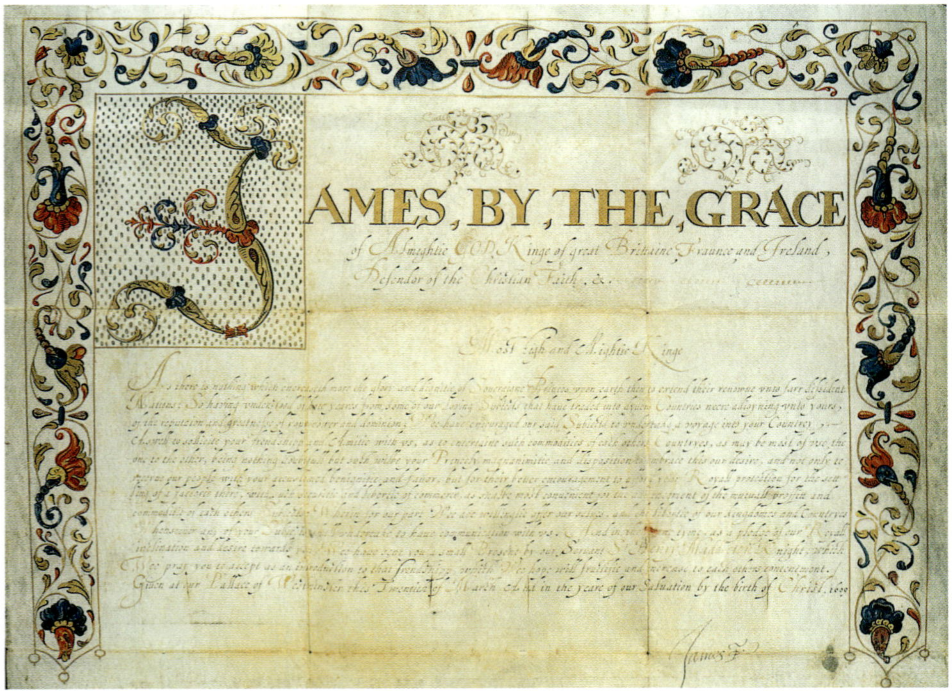

6.3
The Meeting of the King of Kandy and Joris van Spilbergen

From *'t Historiael Journael van tghene ghepasseert is …*
Engraving on paper
Delft, 1605

Rijksmuseum, Amsterdam

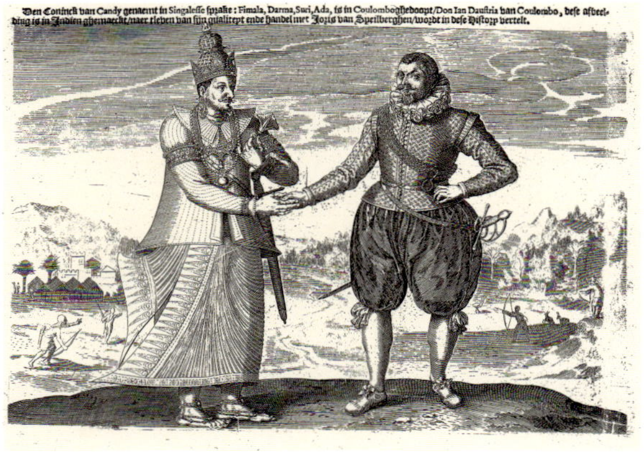

A print of the envoy Joris van Spilbergen with Vimaladharmasuriya, King of Kandy (r. 1591–1604), Ceylon, intentionally distorts the meeting of the two figures in the hope of assuring investors in the VOC (Verenigde Oostindische Companie) that a satisfactory working relationship had been established between the Dutch and the king; what better way is there of doing this than by showing Spilbergen and the king shaking hands (plate 6.3)[23] In reality, in South Asia a ruler's body was considered sacrosanct, and approaching it, let alone touching it, would have required special permission. Even credentials and letters were never given directly by ambassadors to Asian kings, but offered to them via court dignitaries, who in this sense absorbed the pollution of the outsider.[24] The practice of carefully demarcating the physical space of the ruler from those around him was based on the Hindu tradition of representing a monarch as a divine being.[25] The way he was arrayed in *durbar* derived entirely from the manner in which deities were shown in the inner chamber of Hindu temples: richly adorned, placed on a throne of rich textiles, protected by a parasol (*svetatapatra* or *chhatri*) and flanked by attendants holding a fly whisk (*chowrie*) and a fan of peacock feathers (*morchal*). For Hindus, *darshan*, or the sighting of a deity, marked the high point of the physical aspect of their encounter with the divine. In viewing their king, Hindus also experienced *darshan*, for, in Joanne Punzo Waghorne's words, 'when the raja sat in durbar he sat there as a "God"'.[26]

A major bone of contention for Europeans was the manner in which they were expected to salute South Asian rulers. In the western world the convention was to bow to a king, and on presentation to kneel and kiss his right hand, whereas in much of Asia it was obligatory to prostrate before the throne.[27] Most Europeans at Asian courts were understandably reluctant to bow down submissively before a foreign king when their own sovereign would not expect them to perform such a demeaning act. However, as Bernier recognized, in Asia prostration before a king was not a degrading act but a polite form of greeting.[28] Indian princes themselves regularly performed such acts when meeting their superiors. For example, in 1606 Jahangir (r. 1605–27) noted how on visiting his mother he observed 'the rites of … prostration (*sijda*)', which he regarded as 'the formalities the young owe their elders under the terms of the Genghis code and Timurid law'.[29]

Thomas Roe objected to prostrating before Jahangir, and in his diary claims to have persuaded the emperor to allow him to salute in his own manner, a privilege only accorded ambassadors from Persia, whose empire the Mughals regarded as equal to their own.[30] Roe's description of a Mughal *durbar* comes alive in a miniature painting from the *Padshahnama* manuscript in which Europeans are shown outside the inner railings of the court with offerings for Shah Jahan (plate 6.1):

> At the *durbar* I was led right before him, at the enterance of an outward rayle, where mett mee two principall noble slaves to conduct mee nearer. I had required before my going leave to use the customes of my country; which was freely granted, soe that I would performe them punctually. When I entred within the first rayle I made a reverance; entering in the inward rayle a nother; and when I came under the King a theird. The place is a great court, whither resort all sorts of people. The King sitts in a little gallery over head; ambassidors, the great men and strangers of qualety within the inmost rayle under him, raysed from the ground, covered with canopyes of velvet and silke, under foote layd with good carpetts; the meaner men representing gentry within the first rayle, the people without in a base court, but soe that all may see the King. The sitting out hath soe much affinitye with a theatre… [31]

6.4
Hooghly Factory (detail)
Hendrik van Schuylenburgh

Possibly commissioned by Pieter Sterthemius, VOC director of Bengal; oil on canvas, 1665

Rijksmuseum, Amsterdam

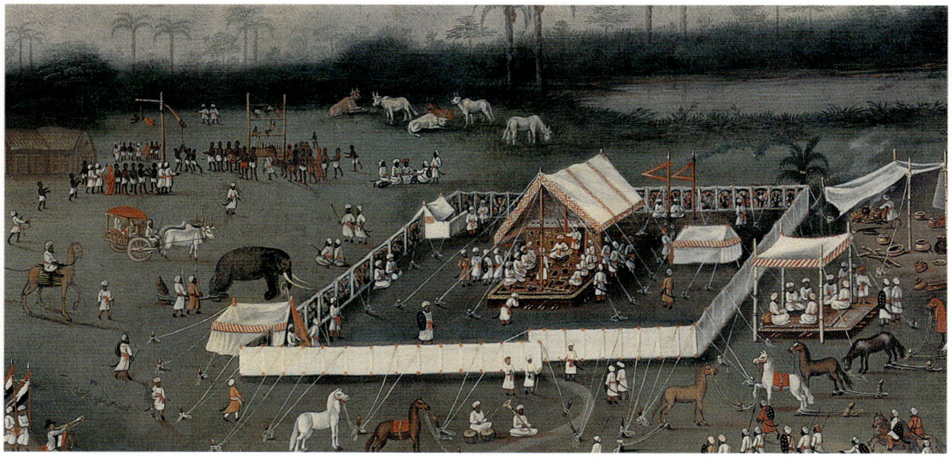

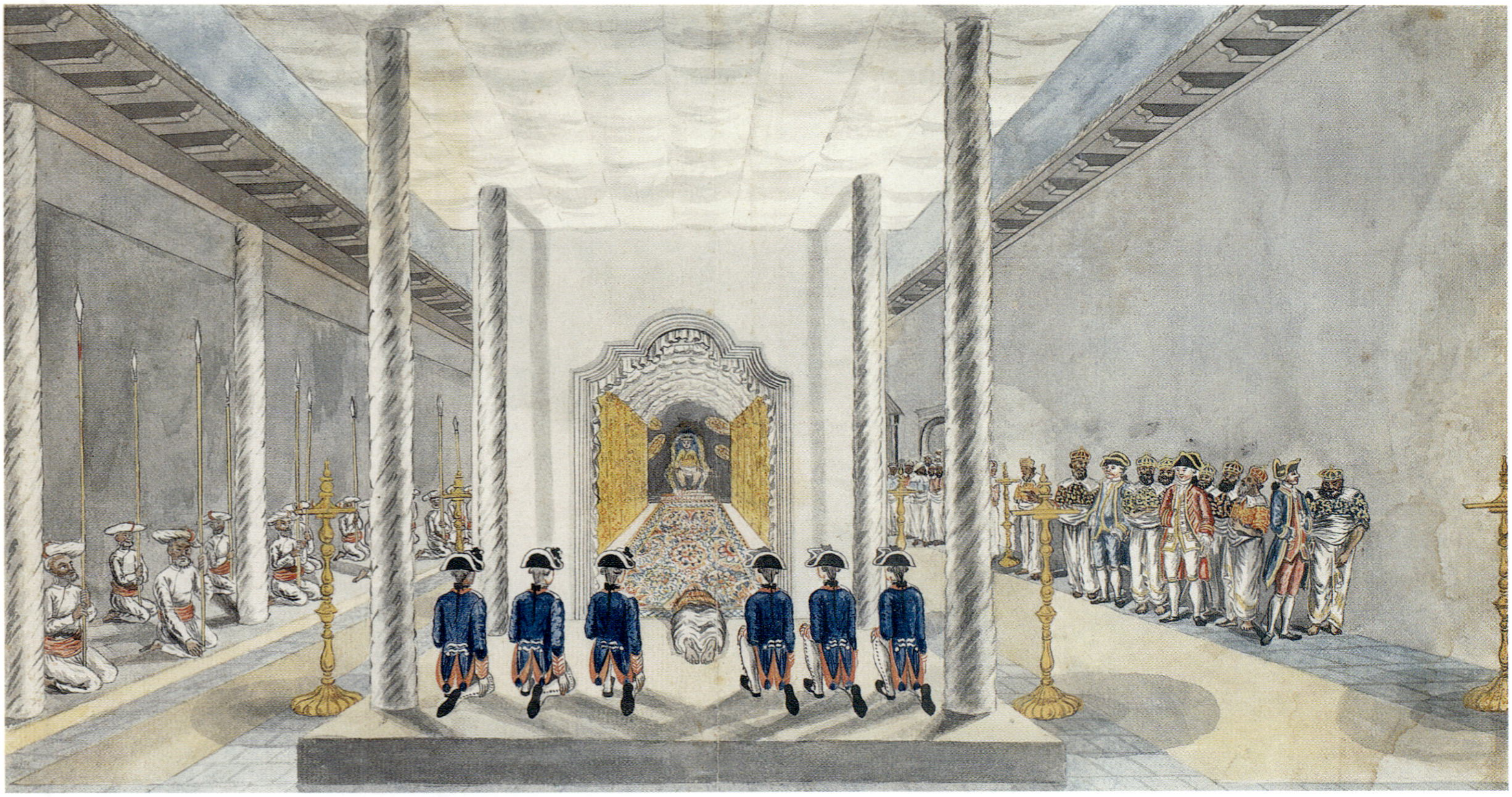

6.5
A VOC Mission to the King of Kandy
Revd Jan Brandes, from the Brandes Album

Watercolour on paper
Ceylon, 1785–86

Rijksmuseum, Amsterdam

The watercolour probably illustrates one of the two audiences granted by Rajadhi Rajasinha (r. 1782–98) to VOC ambassador Cornelis de Cock.

Roe's claim that he was readily permitted to salute Jahangir according to the 'customes of my country' seems unlikely. A refusal to prostrate before the Mughal emperor would not have been well received and this was the case in lesser courts as well, such as that of the kings of Kandy (plate 6.5). When, in 1762, John Pybus visited the court of the King of Kandy, Kirti Sri Rajasinha (r. 1747–63), he was told that he would have to kneel before the ruler 'which I premptorily refused to comply with'.[32] In the end Pybus agreed 'because I would not give any Interruption to the Business I came upon', but he made it clear that 'the English Nation would never submit' to such humiliating treatment. By the time that General Macdowal led an embassy to Kandy in 1800, British control over much of the Indian subcontinent was assured. Consequently he refused point blank to perform any 'degrading tokens of submission', a position that the king had no choice but to accept.[33] When first in India, the Company did not possess such leverage. On his mission to secure trading rights from the Mughal governor of Bengal in 1633, William Cartwright twice refused, but eventually consented to kiss the governor's foot 'as a gesture of respect'.[34]

The thirteenth-century *Adab-u'l-Harb* by Fakhr-i-Mudabbir specified gifts considered appropriate for diplomatic exchange between (principally Muslim) rulers in Hindustan. This began with the Qur'ān and commentaries of the Qur'ān, followed by slaves (both 'cultured' and 'slave-girls' of diverse origin); textiles (embroidered with gold and silver, linen and woollens, mats and prayer carpets, velvet and raw silk); animals (horses, camels, elephants, falcons, lions, tigers, leopards and dogs); animal trappings (saddles, bridles and horse armour); arms and armour (swords, shields, bows, arrows, knives, helmets); precious materials (sandalwood, aloewood, ebony, ivory, ruby, turquoise, agate, jasper, musk, camphor, furs); and 'China vessels'.[35] Some of these presents Europeans were unable to provide, among them Qur'āns, slaves and women. For example, in 1651 the Company was forced to turn down the request of Shah Abbas II (r. 1642–66) for Englishwomen for his harem. Instead they offered him a dozen beaver hats, a somewhat unsatisfactory substitute.[36]

But apart from these lacunae, the types of presents offered by Europeans conformed quite closely to the sorts of gifts that Asian rulers exchanged amongst themselves. Animals were at the top of the list.

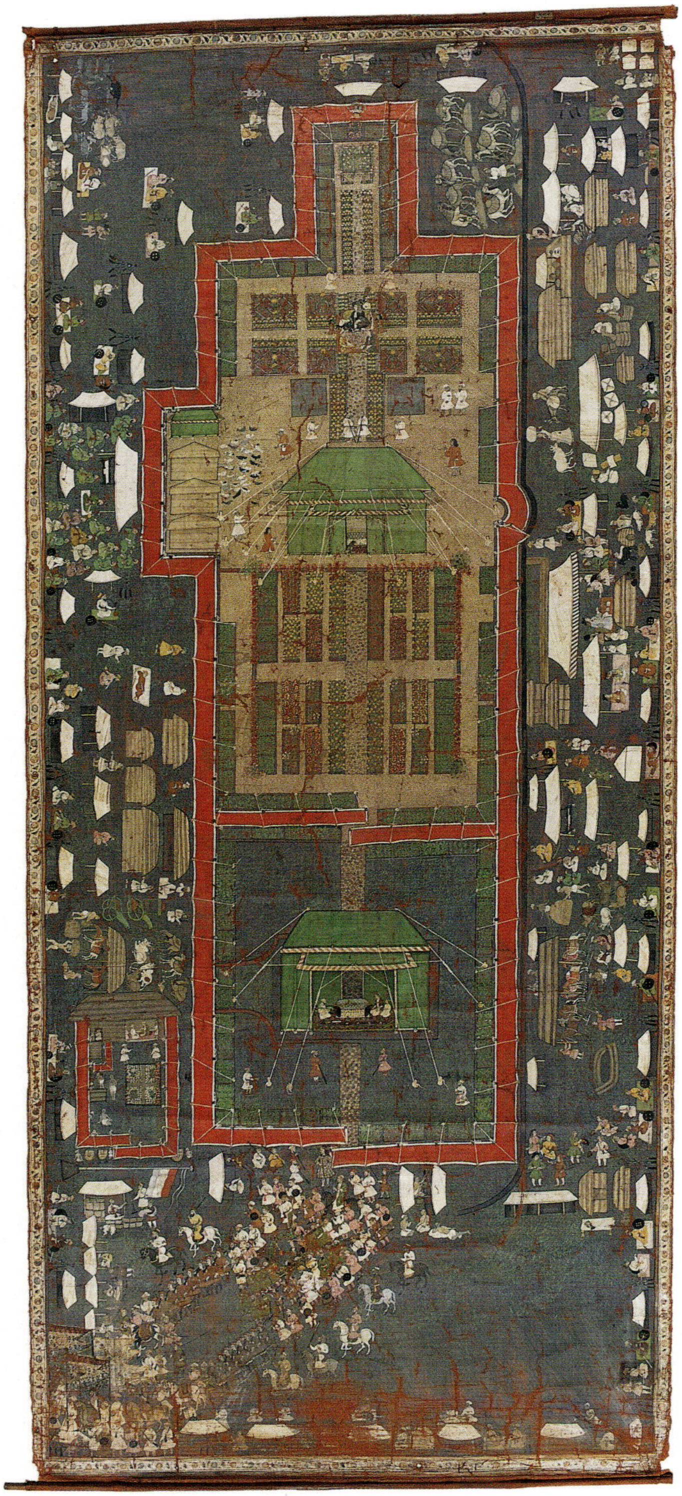

6.6 above and detail opposite
The Embassy of Johannes Bacherus en route to the Court of Aurangzeb
Colours on cloth
India (Golconda), late 17th century
Tropenmuseum, Amsterdam

As Europeans came to dominate trade routes from the Persian Gulf to South Asia, they were in the enviable position of having access to Arabian horses, which were much sought after in India. Exotic animals were also desired by Asian princes, and contemporary papers reveal that the various European trading powers were much occupied in finding and transporting these. Jahangir, for example, demanded an English horse and dogs.[37] Bloodhounds, greyhounds and mastiffs were sent all over South Asia, where people marvelled that they 'can be tought to fetch, or find things lost'.[38] Many times these beasts did not survive the long journeys that they were forced to endure. In 1639 a VOC embassy to Golconda had no choice but to stop because of the death of the presents: an elephant and two horses.[39] Charles Ware Malet's mission to Poona in 1786 was likewise diminished by the death of one of the gifts: a 'large griffin bird'.[40]

Exchanging arms was standard practice among princes in early modern Europe and Asia. Europeans at Asian courts perpetuated this tradition and in doing so helped to introduce western arms and armour to South Asia (see p.325). Admiral Beaulieu gave the King of Achin ceremonial weaponry comprising 'The complete armour of an horseman engraved and gilt; a German hanger, with a carved and gilt hilt, to which hung a pistol, six muskets, the barrels of which were partly engraved and partly gilt, the butt ends enriched with mother of pearl; two heads of pikes enamelled and gilt'.[41] The size and imposing appearance of cannons meant that they were regularly given as showy gifts.[42] South Asian rulers regularly requested gifts of western arms and armour. In the late 1630s Abdulla Hussain Qutb Shah, Sultan of Golconda (r.1626–72), demanded presents from the Company including a suit of armour 'yf possible muskett proofe'.[43] Apart from the presents that they received, Asian rulers were also keen to acquire an understanding of European war technology. In 1666 Aurangzeb asked the VOC and East India Company to provide 'five gunfounders and two engineers or pioneers, that have skill in millitary affaires and giving directions for digging mines and contriving workes for the advantageous assaultong or worsting the enemy; requiring expresly that they be very experienced practical men'.[44]

The gifts presented by Europeans also included luxury goods from other parts of Asia, notably China and Japan. For presentation to Jahangir, for example, Roe was advised that instead of English 'cloth and ill

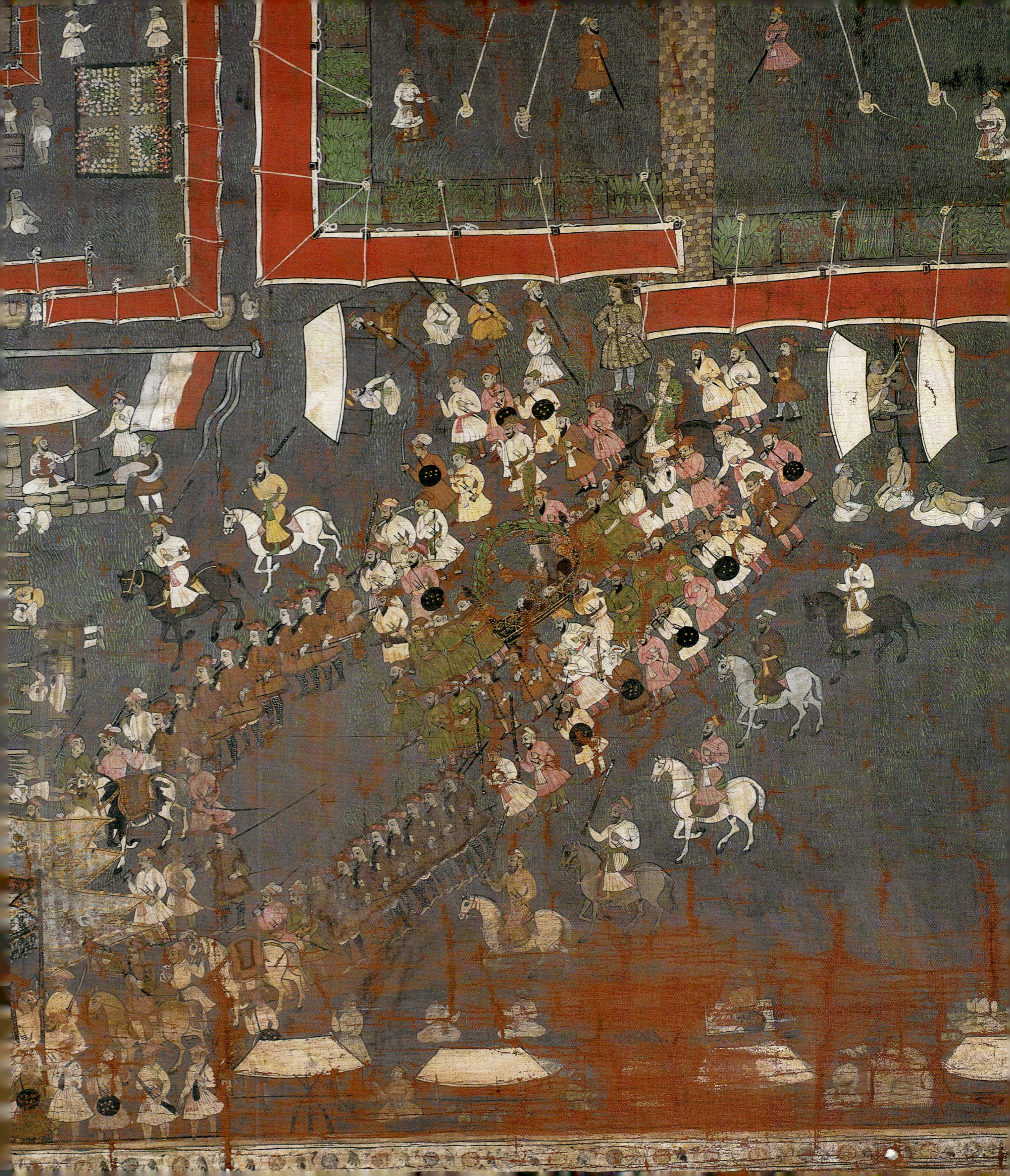

swords' he should offer 'all of the raretyes' of East Asia, which 'were more acceptable here than gould'.[45] With its monopoly of trade with Japan after 1639, the VOC was in a unique position to commission lacquer, which was much admired in India. When, in 1662, Dirk van Adrichem led an embassy to Aurangzeb, he brought as presents objects from East Asia, including 'a plakey [palanquin] and a Tack-ravan [*takht-e-ravaan*], or travelling throne, of exquisite beauty and much admired'.[46] Contemporary documents confirm that these were of Japanese lacquer.[47] More standard gifts were 'truncks' or cabinets 'of Japan', which, according to Roe, 'are here rich presents' (plate 6.1).[48] Objects made in Asia out of precious metals also won approval. Francisco Pelsaert recommended commissioning the following presents in silver reales of eight or gold: aftabas (ewers), bed legs, betel boxes, fan handles, handles for fly whisks.[49] He also suggested gold chains as suitable presents to Asian rulers. An example was given by the VOC to the Sultan of Golconda in Pieter Smith's embassy of 1671–72.[50] What this chain might have looked like is difficult to determine, but it must have been an impressive piece of jewellery, if a gold chain given by the VOC to the Sultan of Ternate in 1675 is anything to go by (plate 6.7).

Examples of European craftsmanship and objects made in the West out of precious materials also featured among the gifts given to Asian princes. For example, the second Portuguese voyage to Calicut, led by Pedro Alvarez de Cabral (1460–1526) in 1500, made up for Gama's paltry offerings with 'a wrought silver bason gilt, a fountain of the same, a silver cup with a gilt cover, two wedges of silver, four cushions, two of cloath of gold, and two of crimson velvet, a cloth of state of the same velvet striped, and bound with gold lace, a very fine carpet, and two rich pieces of arras'.[51] In Thomas Roe's interview with Jahangir in 1616 the emperor enquired 'what kynd of curiosityes' he might expect from England. Roe clarified that these consisted not of jewels and precious stones, but 'as excellent artifices in paynting, carving, cutting, enamelling, figures in brasse, copper, or stone, rich embroderyes, stuffs of gold and silver'.[52] 'Stuffs' or textiles were indeed staple presents from Europeans to South Asian rulers, and these ranged from, at their richest, cloths worked with gold or silver to 'fine scarlett', velvets, damask and broadcloth.[53] Sculpture, painting and tapestries with narrative scenes also had tremendous appeal among both Muslim and Hindu rulers.[54] A list of suitable presents for Jahangir compiled by Muqarrab Khan for Thomas Roe included 'any figures of beasts, birds, or other similes made of glass, or hard plaster, of silver, brasse, wood, iron, stone or ivorye'.[55] South Asian rulers also admired and collected western pictures, which were often displayed or incorporated into interior decoration.[56] It also became habitual for European rulers to send portraits of themselves to Asian princes as a way of cementing relations. For example, as well as numerous canvases painted with biblical and classical scenes, Nicholas Downton gave Jahangir likenesses of James I and Anne of Denmark, as well as of Sir Thomas Smythe, governor of the Company.[57] The Prince of Orange sent the King of Kandy a portrait of himself on horseback with Joris van Spilbergen's embassy in 1602,[58] and in 1699 William III sent Aurangzeb a picture of himself by Godfrey Kneller.[59]

Products of western technology were also regular gifts. Mirrors, lenses and glass, for example, often appear in lists of presents. Company presents for the King of Kandy in 1664 featured 'some looking-glasses'[60] and for the Sultan of Golconda in 1639 comprised 'fayre large looking glasses' as well as 'an excellent perspective and multiplyinge glass'.[61] The VOC embassy led by John Joshua Ketelaar (1659–1718) to the Mughal emperor Shah Alam Bahadur (r. 1707–12) at Delhi also included six microscopes, two spyglasses and telescopes with instructions, as well as a supply of cannons, Japanese lacquer, 10 elephants, 26 horses and 33 birds of paradise.[62] Clear glass was also prized. For example,

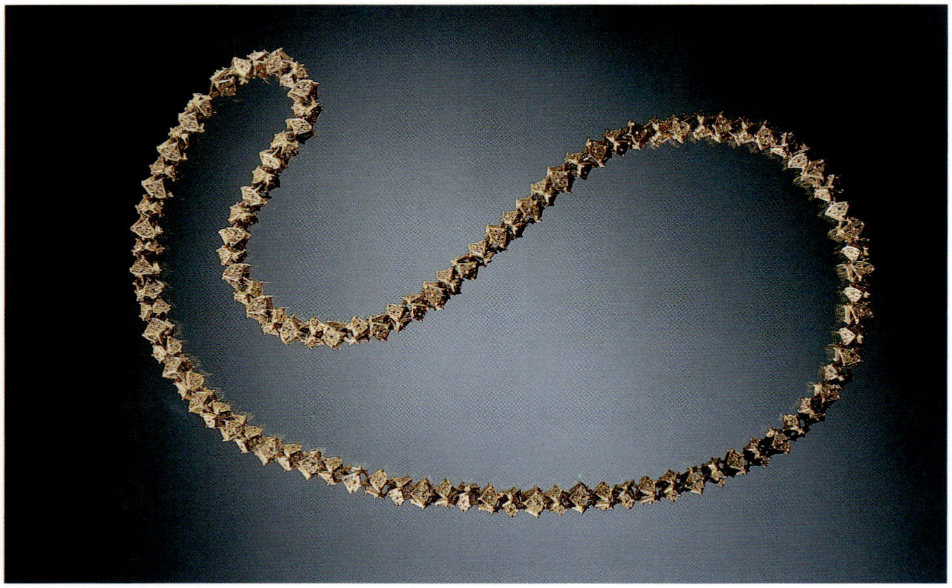

6.7
Chain

Gold
Batavia, *c.*1675

Rijksmuseum, Amsterdam

The chain was originally accompanied by a medal with an engraved inscription that translates: 'On behalf of the Dutch East India Company from the Governor-General in honour of King Quitchily Amsterdam, commemorating his coronation and succession in the Kingdom of Ternate with confirmation and friendship of its honourable members on the first of February, 1675.'

Aurangzeb expressed his interest in glass to 'New' East India Company ambassador William Norris, who presented the emperor with a few examples to his taste.[63]

Western time-keeping devices also won favour among Indian princes and were regularly in demand, even though they can only have been impractical to people who did not mark time in the western manner. In 1616 Roe offered Prince Khurrum (later Shah Jahan) 'a silver watch very small, which hee tooke kyndly'.[64] Some of the time-pieces given to Asian rulers were extravagant works, such as the 'table clock set with precious stones' which the Company sent to the Mughal emperor in 1715, along with a unicorn's horn and a map of the world.[65] Clocks and watches were also made in Europe specifically for Asian users. For instance, in 1699 consul John Pitt presented Nawab Mahdi Khan at Masulipatam with a 'watch with persian characters'.[66] Since such articles were so well received, in 1650 the Company resolved always to stock a 'few rarities of low price ... such as globes, glasses, multiplying glasses, and four or five good substantial house clocks'.[67] Some Asian rulers developed a deep appreciation of western mechanics. Nicholas Downton found that the King of Socotra had formed a collection of 'celestiall and terrestriall globes ... which he had gotten (bought or presented) of former fleets, and every yeare increasing his stocke by English, Dutch, Portugals, and Spanish that came that way'.[68] Not all rulers understood the nature of the gifts they were given. The copy of Mercator's atlas that Thomas Roe offered Jahangir was returned on the grounds that the emperor 'did not understand the language in which that book was written'.[69]

Thomas Roe's diary while at the Mughal court conveys the degree to which the ambassador depended on presents in order to achieve success. Many of his letters to the Court of Directors in London express his embarrassment at the poor quality of gifts with which he was furnished. In 1615 he wrote: 'The presents you have this yeare sent are extremely despised by those [who] have seene them.'[70] So poorly chosen and of such base quality were the gifts that 'they laugh at us for such as wee bring'. How could Roe compete with embassies from the likes of Persia, which brought the finest Asian and European manufactures; or with gift-giving at a court where at New Year's (Nauroz) and on his birthday the emperor was weighed against gold and given tokens of homage from his nobles which regularly included 'costly Jewels and curious Rarities they can any where meet with'?[71] Jahangir's memoirs provide a glimpse of the gifts offered to him for Nauroz in 1610:

> The offerings of several amirs were submitted for inspection. Khan A'zam presented a pearl worth four thousand rupees. Miran Sadr-i-Jahan offered for my inspection twenty-eight hunting birds – hawks and falcons – along with other rarities. Mahabat Khan presented a small chest of European manufacture, the sides of which were sheets of crystal and mother-of-pearl. Anything that was put into the chest could be seen from the outside as well as though there were nothing there. Kishwar Khan presented twenty-two elephants, male and female. And so on, every one of the court servants presented the rarities and offerings they had. [72]

The crystal casket offered by Mahabat Khan was of a type much sought after. Roe himself ordered two from London in 1616–17 as gifts, and the VOC also presented such objects to Asian rulers, including the *shōgun* in Japan (see plate 7.10).

One-upmanship in gift-giving between the various European powers was intense. Roe was regularly told that he 'brought not so curious toyes for the King as did the Portugall' and 'that the Portugalls in one frigatt gave more' than the English ambassador during his long time at court.[73] In assessing Roe's gifts, Jahangir also pointedly asked Jesuits at his court 'whether the King of England were a great Kyng, that sent presents of so small valewe'.[74] Knowing that their gifts were being compared created intense competition between the various European powers. For example, in 1639 Company servants at Masulipatam noted that the Dutch were planning to give the Sultan of Golconda substantial presents: 'their large guifts and our emptie hands shall procure the former respect and us disgrace'.[75] Interest in western objects was in some cases so strong that their supply was a condition of trade in treaties between Europeans and Indian rulers, great and small alike. The treaty between James I and Jahangir stipulated that the English 'shall bring and furnish the said almighty King with all the rarietyes yearly that they can find',[76] and in the agreement signed between the Company and the Raja of Ikkeri in 1637, the ruler likewise specified that he desired the English to supply him with rarities from Europe and China.[77]

In South Asia diplomatic gift-giving was not a one-way street; in fact embassies to the richer courts expected to come away with gifts and subsidies worth more than those they had presented. European embassies, of course, were motivated by the prospect of securing favourable trading conditions, which

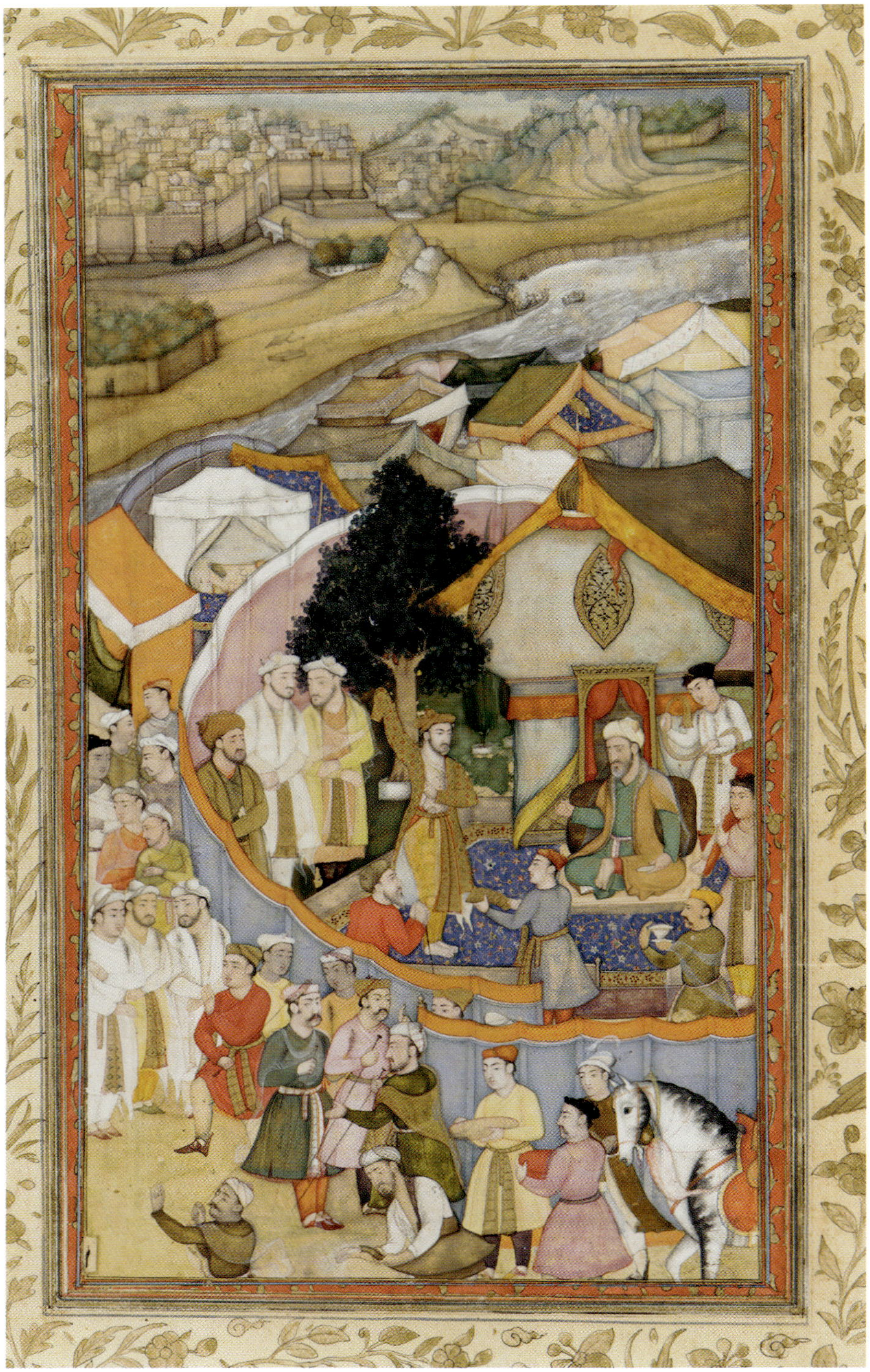

6.8
Da'ud Receives a Robe of Honour from Mun'im Khan

Folio from an *Akbarnama*
Opaque watercolour and gold on paper
Mughal India, *c.*1604

Freer Gallery of Art, Smithsonian Institution, Washington, DC

yielded their own substantial returns. But, of the return gifts bestowed on ambassadors by rulers, the most significant was a *khil'at*, a ceremonial gown or suit of clothes. The convention of presenting these existed throughout the subcontinent. For example, on leaving the King of Vijayanagar in 1517, Christovão de Figueiredo was presented with 'a *cabaya* (tunic) of brocade, with a cap of the same fashion as the king wore'.[78] Jan Nieuhof received from the King of Kalkolang 'a very fine Brocado silk gown, made according to the Indian fashion',[79] and European visitors to the Mughal court frequently describe the 'robes of honour' given them by the emperor on taking leave.[80] While the composition of these suits varied, their symbolic meaning was the same; a *khil'at* embodied the *baraka,* or essence of a ruler, and by wearing it the recipient acknowledged his authority.[81] In this sense accepting a *khil'at* meant taking a pledge; wearing one imposed an allegiance, much as did wearing a medal or badge from an order of knighthood.[82] By offering a *khil'at* in *durbar*, a ruler formed a public bond with ambassadors who nominally, at least, accepted his superiority.

In South and much of South-East Asia formal encounters, whether diplomatic or social, came to a close with the offering of *paan* (a combination of betel leaf, areca nut, lime and spices taken as a digestive), rosewater and *attar*. Niccolò Manucci (1653–1708), who was attached to the Mughal court in various capacities, noted that:

> It is an exceedingly common practice in India to offer betel leaf by way of politeness, chiefly among the great men, who, when anyone pays them a visit, offer *betel* at the time of leaving as a mark of goodwill, and of the estimation in which they hold the person who is visiting them. It would be a great piece of rudeness to refuse it.[83]

Paan sets owned by Clive of India (1725–74) at Powis Castle are testament to the fact that Europeans in India participated in these indigenous courtly procedures. More significantly, they used them in establishing and perpetuating their own authority in the subcontinent.[84] For example, when, as governor-general, the Marquess of Hastings (1813–22) received Indian rulers, he simply re-enacted Mughal court rites. In 1814 he noted in his diary that 'I held a durbar … attended by all the principal natives resident at Benares', at which he presented local rajas with *khil'ats* and gifts of pearls and arms.[85] At Masulipatam, Hastings concluded a meeting with a local raja by pouring 'some rose-water on his hands, for which

6.9
A Prince Holding Court and Receiving Gifts

Opaque watercolour with gold on paper
Mughal India, *c.*1590

British Library, London

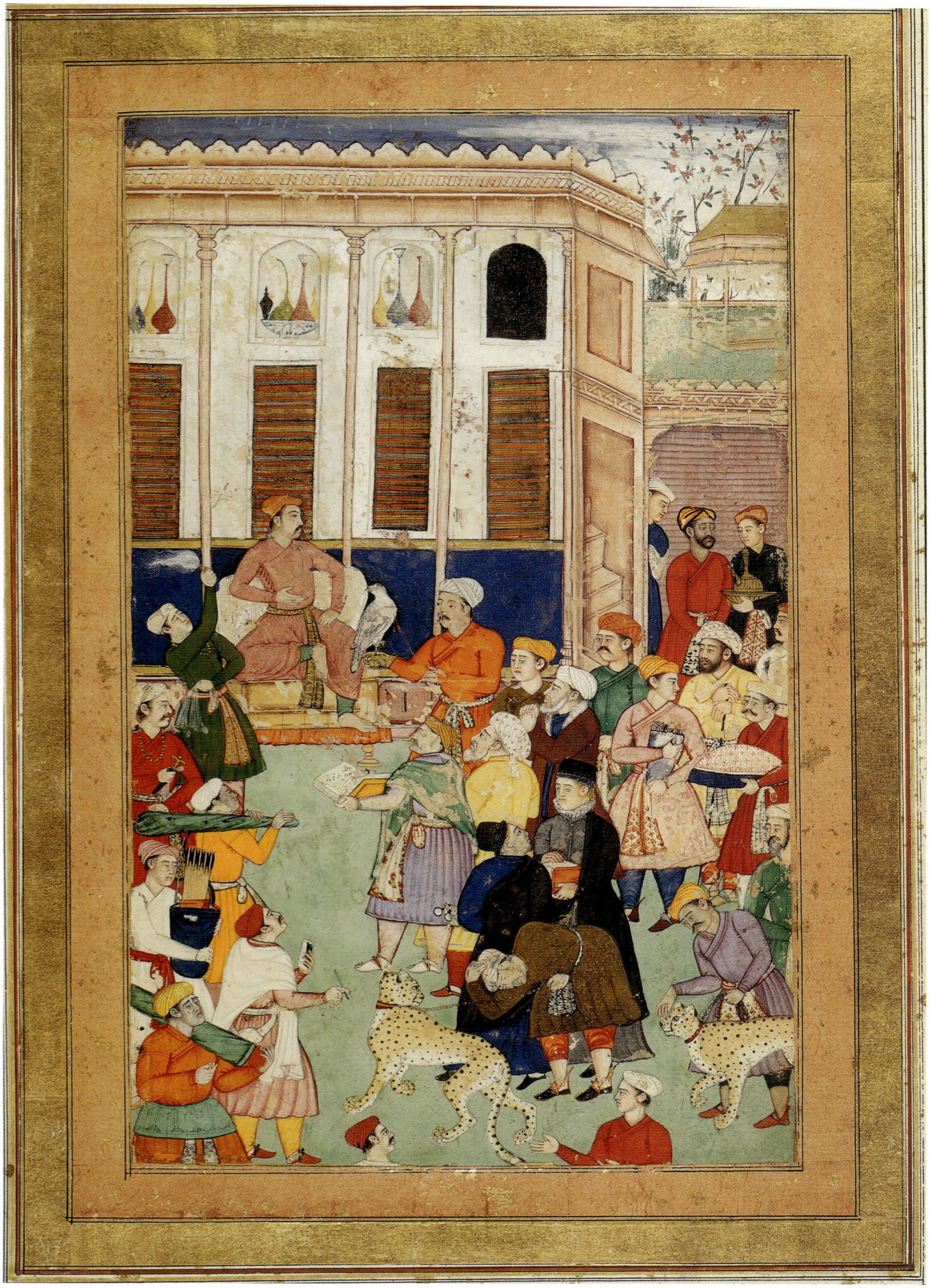

6.10
Robinson Casket

Ivory, carved, with silver-gilt hinges; the lock and handle of gold filigree set with sapphires
Ceylon (Kotte), *c.*1557

V&A: IS.41–1980

6.11 opposite
Muhammad Dervish Khan
Elisabeth Vigée-Lebrun

Oil on canvas
France (Paris), 1787

Marnier-Lapostolle Collection, France

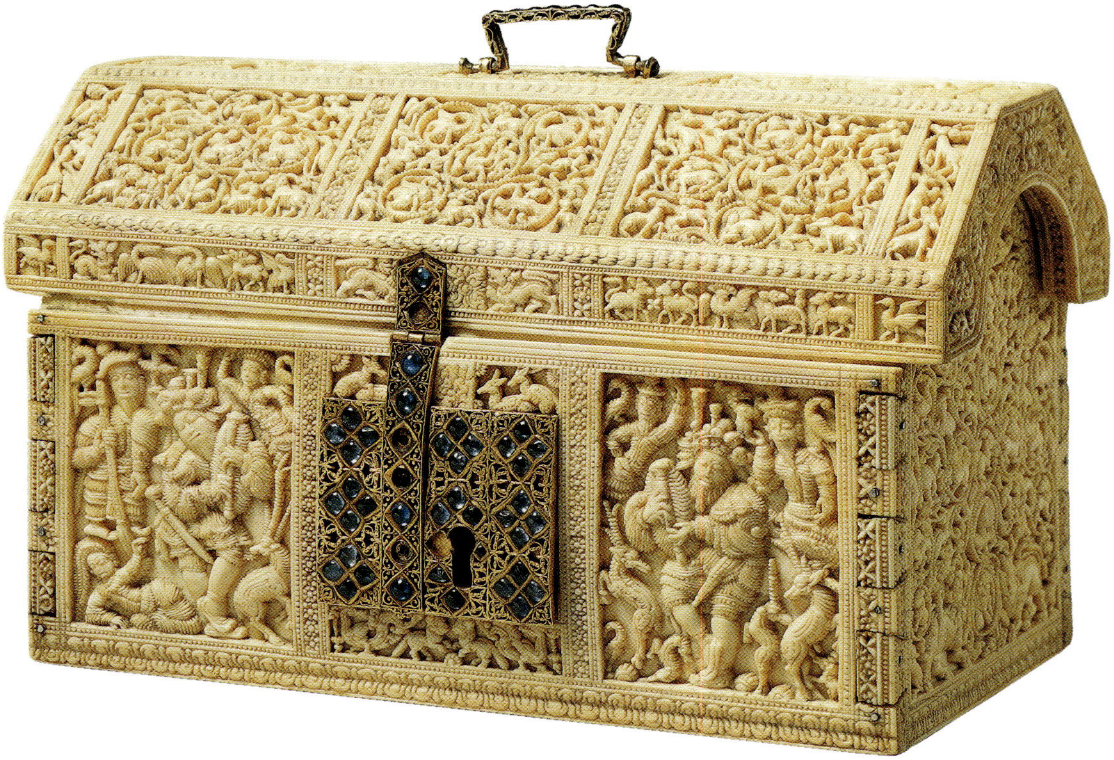

he expressed much gratitude'.[86] Europeans also introduced their own devices for reinforcing relationships with their Indian allies. In 1663, after the Dutch conquest of Cochin, the VOC gave the new king a 'crown which was of gold having cypher of the East India Company graven on its side'.[87] With their growing political and military importance, the modes of behaviour of the British were also adopted by South Asian rulers. In the early nineteenth century Lord Valentia found on visiting a raja that, after offering each other 'salaam', the ruler 'held out his hand'.[88] This hybridity was also evident in the design of court furniture, with rulers often substituting traditional textile (*musnud*) or platform (*takht*) thrones for western-style throne chairs.[89]

Early diplomatic encounters between Europe and South Asia seem one-sided, but this was not always so, particularly in the case of the Portuguese, whose outright conquest of Goa in 1510 established them as a local force to be reckoned with. Rulers who witnessed Portuguese power attempted to forge alliances with these foreigners. For instance, Vira Narasimha, King of Vijayanagar (r. 1503–09), sent an embassy to Francisco de Almeida (1450–1510) in Cananoor in which he offered his sister in marriage to a prince of the Portuguese royal family, a proposal that was not accepted.[90] The Portuguese, and later the VOC and Company, also bound weaker South Asian rulers into tribute relationships. The Ceylonese kings of Kotte, for example, turned to Portugal for recognition and for military support against local contenders to the throne. King Bhuvaneka Bahu (r. 1521–51) and his grandson Dharmapala (r. 1551–97) sent Dom João III (r. 1521–57) of Portugal solid ivory caskets as diplomatic gifts to mark important moments in the relationship between Kotte and Portugal (plate 6.10). These included the conversion to Christianity of Dharmapala (renamed Dom João Perya Bandara) and his queen (rechristened Dona Catherina). In a similar spirit, Tipu Sultan of Mysore (r. 1783–99) despatched an embassy to Versailles in 1787, requesting military support from Louis XVI against impending threat from another local power, the East India Company. While in Paris, one of Tipu's ambassadors, Muhammad Dervish Khan, consented to sit for the celebrated portraitist Elisabeth Vigée-Lebrun (1755–1842) (plate 6.11). Although the envoys returned to Mysore with many presents, among them examples of Sèvres porcelain in European and Asian forms, they failed to secure any assurance of French support.

By the late eighteenth century Europeans in South Asia fully understood local diplomatic conventions; it was in fact the aptitude of East India Company officials at negotiating with Indian princes that was partly responsible for British successes in the scramble for power that ensued with the collapse of the Mughal empire. Even though Company servants continued to participate in acts of submission and homage, such as wearing *khil'at* and accepting *paan,* these were only superficial practices designed to assure a semblance of continuity amidst rapidly changing times in which it was clear that Europeans had the upper hand. For example, Clive of India paid homage to the Mughal emperor Shah Alam, but thwarted the emperor's embassy to George III by ensuring that the appointed ambassador set sail for England without the requisite letter and gifts, which Clive later presented as his own.[91] In this period of decline South Asian rulers experienced the same anxiety that had been evident in the words of Westerners, who, a century earlier, attempted to gauge where they stood at powerful Indian courts.[92]

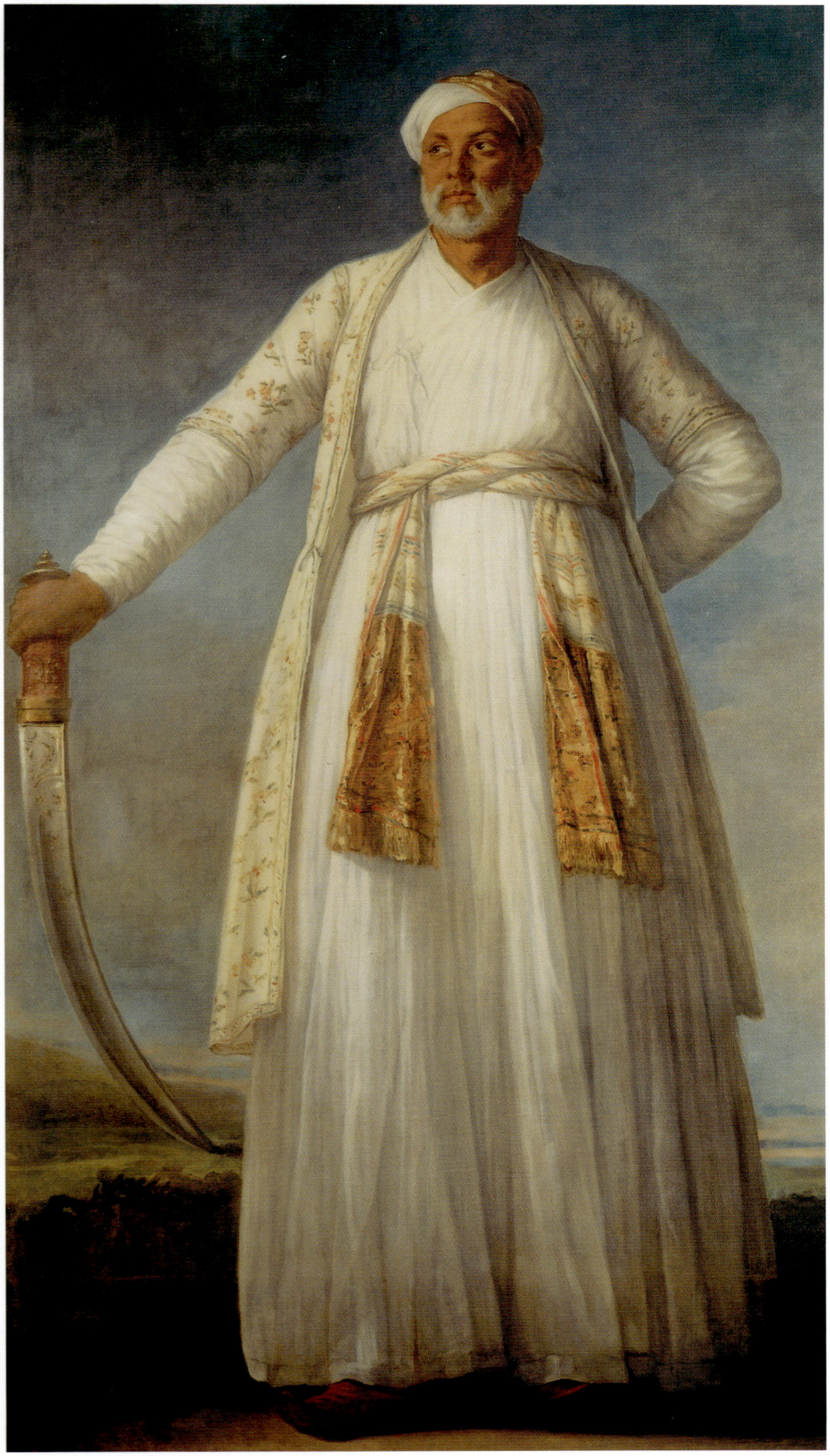

Siamese Embassies to the Court of the Sun King

John Guy

In the second half of the seventeenth century the kingdom of Siam was a cosmopolitan centre of international standing. Its ruler, Phra Narai (r. 1656–88), was both intellectually curious and politically astute and he actively sought to promote his capital, Ayutthaya, as a centre of Asian commerce. Siam had been engaged in diplomatic relations within Asia for several centuries, exchanging missions with China, the Ryūkyū Islands, Japan, India and Persia, as well as its immediate neighbours in mainland and peninsular South-East Asia. Phra Narai's interest in nurturing international relations coincided with those of Dutch and French entrepreneurs acting under royal and state licence: both sought opportunities for profitable trade.

The Portuguese had been present in Siam from the 1520s, but it was the overtures of the Dutch East India Company (VOC) that inspired the first Siamese diplomatic mission to Europe in 1608. After a number of misadventures, diplomatic missions to Europe were revived with unprecedented vigour during the reign of Phra Narai. The most spectacular missions were those that he exchanged with Louis XIV of France (r. 1643–1715). The Siamese king was encouraged in these ventures by his favourite adviser on foreign relations, the Greek Constantin Phaulkon. Following the receipt of letters from the French king and the pope, Phra Narai despatched his first mission to Versailles and the Vatican in 1680. His ambassador carried letters that were engraved on gold leaf, as well as 50 cases of presents and two young elephants. Tragically this mission was lost at sea off the African coast, but a second mission successfully arrived in Paris in October 1684.

The French reciprocated in 1685 with a large mission led by the Chevalier Alexandre de Chaumont (*c.* 1640–1710). Louis XIV sent an array of scientific instruments, particularly those associated with astronomy, including two large globes and contemporary maps. This scientific assemblage was accompanied by highly educated Jesuit scholars, newly admitted to the French Academy of Sciences, whose role was to impress the Siamese court with European culture, learning and religion. The French also sent six specialist craftsmen to enter the service of the King of Siam, opening up an opportunity for the transfer of skills. For France, Siam was a portal to China and Japan, which were seen as bigger prizes for both trade and evangelism. For Siam, diplomatic missions to Europe had a clear commercial agenda: the instructions of the 1684 mission to Portuguese Goa expressly referred to models of goods which the Siamese king hoped the Portuguese could supply.

The third Siamese embassy to France arrived in June 1686. The mission, led by Kosa Pan (plate 6.12), a senior nobleman (*khunnang*) and close confidant of the king, marked a high point in the kingdom's diplomatic relations with the West. The ambassador was granted an audience with Louis XIV at Versailles on 1 September, at which he presented his king's golden letter and abundant gifts, carefully itemized (plate 6.13). This is one of the best-documented diplomatic receptions in East–West relations. The Siamese kept meticulous diaries – a fragment of Kosa Pan's still survives – and the French court recorded the Sun King's pleasure in engravings, medallions and paintings. The Siamese gifts included many gilded textiles along with other fineries, and the dispersal of these gifts to courtiers and others generated a vogue in late seventeenth-century France for '*les siamoiseries*'. Louis XIV's gift of six master craftsmen to Phra Narai in turn generated a ripple of French influence in Siamese court arts at Ayutthaya.

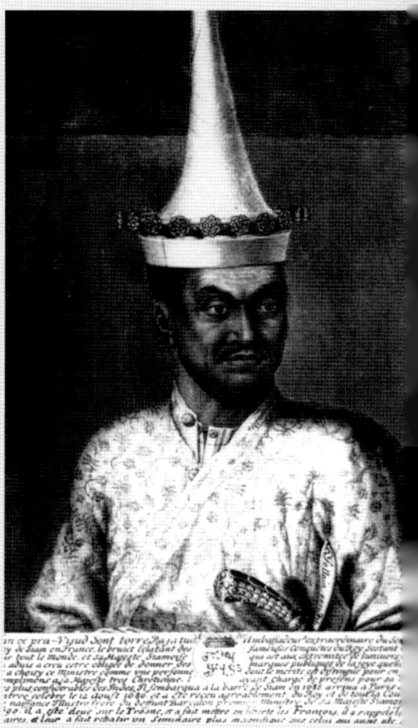

6.12
Portrait of Kosa Pan, Siamese ambassador to France
J. Hainzelman

Engraving on paper
France (Paris), c.1686

Cabinet des Estamps, Bibliothèque nationale de France

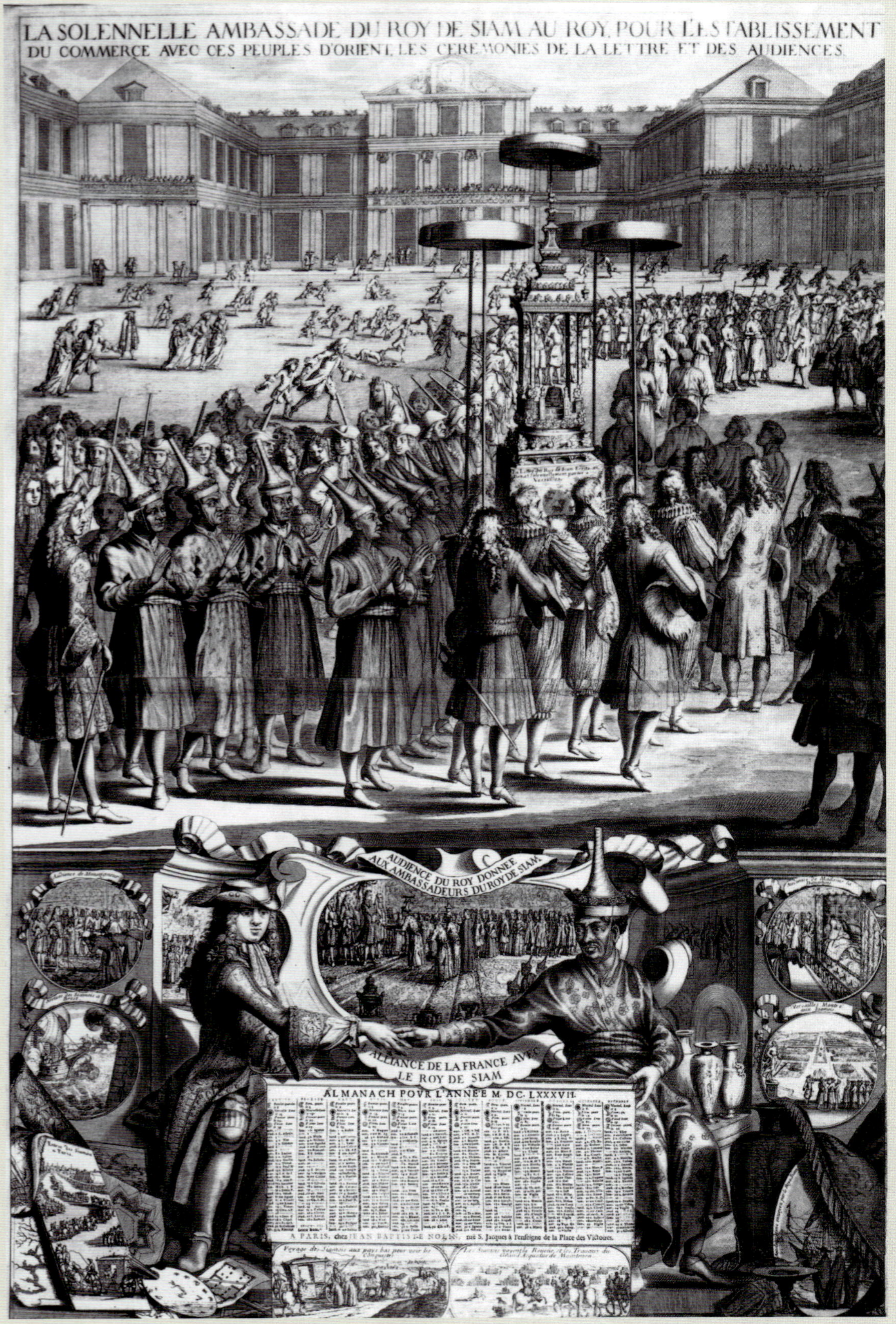

6.13
The Siamese Embassy Processing a Letter from Phra Narai to Louis XIV at Versailles, 1 September 1686
J. Hainzelman

Engraving on paper
France (Paris), c.1686

Cabinet des Estamps, Bibliothèque nationale de France

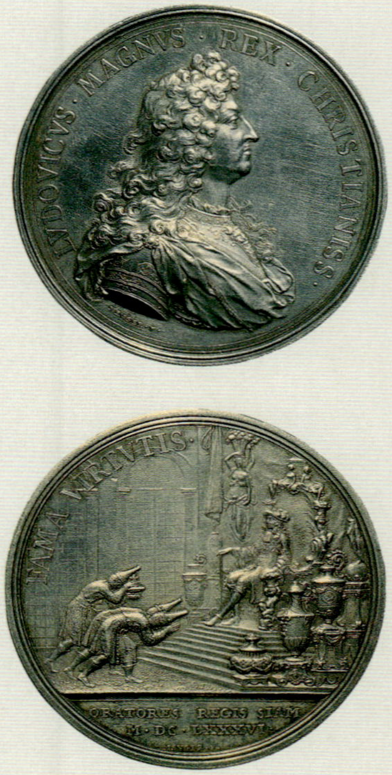

6.14
Medallion commemorating the Siamese embassy to Louis XIV
Jean Mauger

Silver
France (Paris), 1687

Bibliothèque nationale de France

7

DIPLOMATIC ENCOUNTERS: EUROPE AND EAST ASIA

James L. Hevia

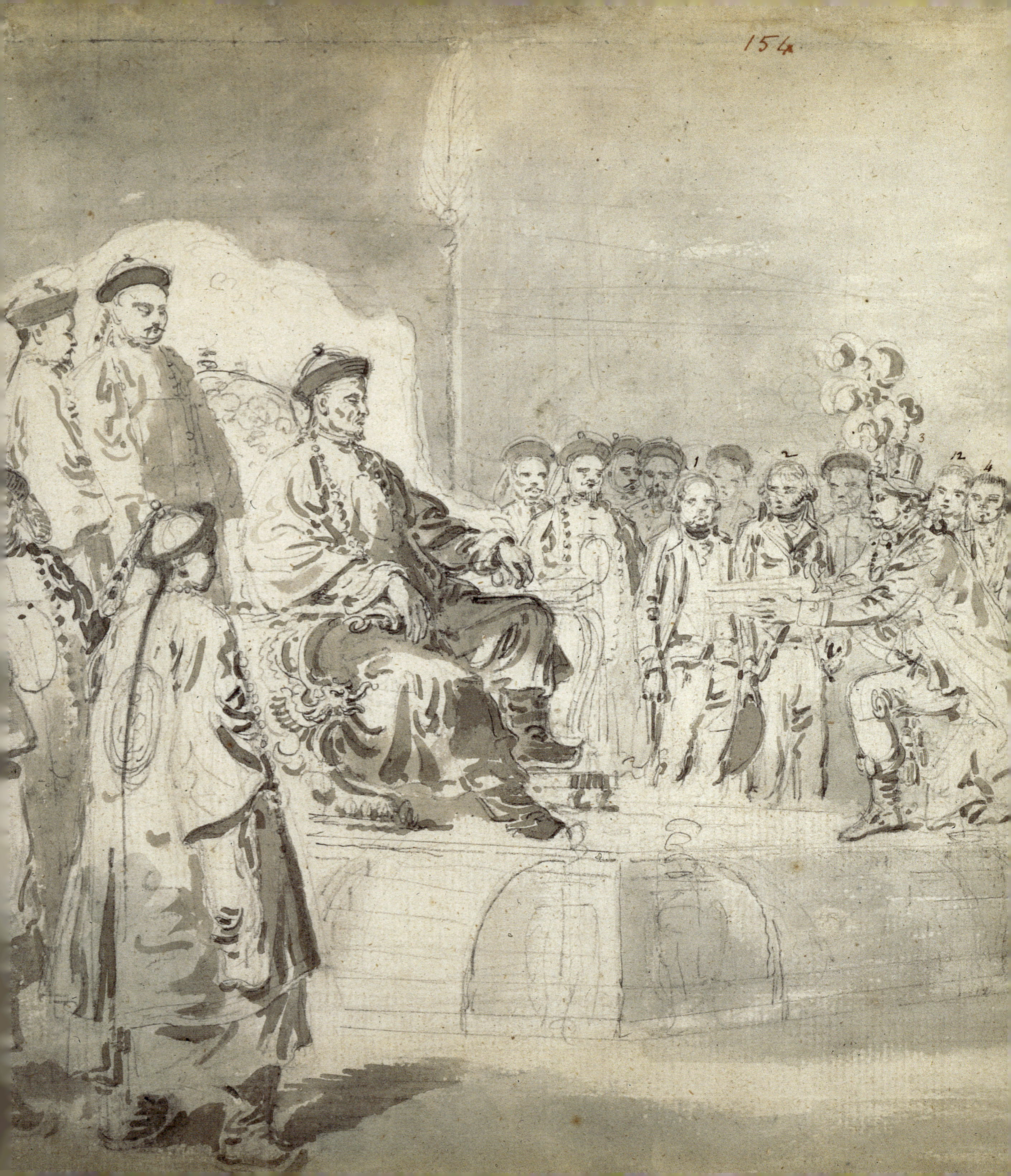
154
1
2
3
12
4

Detail of 7.1 previous page

In a letter written sometime in the 1470s advocating a western route to the Indies, the Florentine astronomer Paolo Toscanelli (1397–1482) described the pearls, gems and gold-coloured temples in Japan and the even greater wealth of China. The latter, he explained, is a country 'worthy to be sought by the Latins, not only because thence may be obtained vast gains of gold and silver and gems of every kind and of spices that are never brought to us; but also because of the wise men, learned philosophers and astrologers, by whose genius and arts that mighty and magnificent province is governed …'[1] The significance of these observations lies in the image that it conjures of an Asia of immense commercial wealth and a political order governed by learned men. This fantasy of China would provide all the motivation necessary to send three centuries of European traders, missionaries and adventurers to what came to be called the Far East.

Toscanelli's views were far from fanciful, however. In search of wealth and power, sixteenth-century Europeans entered a vast world of commercial and intellectual exchange.[2] Until the early 1500s, trade with eastern Asia was controlled by powerful Islamic kingdoms that dominated the overland trade route – the Silk Road – across Asia. Under the sponsorship of the Portuguese Crown, navigators sought to break this monopoly by finding a maritime route to the East. Portuguese adventures rounded the Cape of Good Hope and reached the Indian Ocean in 1498, China in 1514 and Japan in 1543. After wresting control of the Arabian Sea from Arab rivals, the Portuguese established the first European trading post in Asia at Goa off the west coast of India in 1510. A year later they captured Malacca at the tip of the Malay peninsula, opening the way for control of the greater Indian Ocean spice trade. Better ships and armaments account for these successes, but because they lacked attractive goods to exchange, the Portuguese were unable to completely monopolize trade with Asia, a pattern that would repeat itself for other European commercial empires. However, the maritime technological edge allowed the Portuguese to insert themselves into existing commercial patterns. Some resorted to piracy or sold protection from other pirates; others became primary carriers of goods between the markets of China, Japan and South-East Asia.

Not satisfied with these limited arrangements, King Manuel I (r. 1495–1521) of Portugal despatched an embassy to the Ming court to expand trade and announce that he was now the overlord of Malacca. This first European embassy to China was led by Tomé Pires, a pharmacist who was also charged with gathering information and samples of Asian medicinals to send to the king. Pires arrived in Peking (Beijing) in the early summer of 1520. While he waited to be granted an audience with the Zhengde emperor (r. 1506–21), the Ming court gathered information about the Portuguese. Reports indicated that they had deposed the King of Malacca, a loyal Ming tributary, and were a troublesome people who desired a trading post on the China coast. There were delays. In April 1521 the emperor died suddenly and all foreigners were ordered to leave the country. When word of this decree reached Canton (Guangzhou), Portuguese traders refused to embark because they had not assembled their export cargo. Altercations ensued; one Portuguese ship was sunk and several merchants and sailors killed. When Pires arrived from Peking in September, he was arrested and forced to write letters to his king and the Portuguese authorities in Malacca, bearing the Ming government's order to return the kingdom to its rightful ruler. For the next several years, the Ming mustered fleets to guard against a Portuguese return to south China waters.

Given this inauspicious beginning, it is surprising that within 40 years Portuguese traders had established a foothold on the Chinese mainland at Macao. According to local lore, this shift in fortune was brought about by Portuguese collaboration with Ming authorities in suppressing piracy along the China coast. A more likely explanation was the success of Portuguese merchants in accommodating themselves to the interests of local Ming officials. By 1562 there were approximately 900 Portuguese residents at Macao, and the cooperative policy had worked so well that local Canton officials urged a second embassy to the Ming court. In 1562 the Viceroy of Goa despatched Diogo Pereira as ambassador. When he arrived in Canton two years later, officials queried him about the situation in Malacca. Since no change was evident, the embassy was not allowed to proceed to Peking. For the remainder of the Ming dynasty, Portuguese trade would thrive at Macao, but no formal relationship would exist between the King of Portugal and the Emperor of China.

If Portuguese adventurers had only limited success in penetrating Asian markets, other forces unleashed by Iberian expansion were altering the dynamics of

political and economic power in East Asia. More significant than the trade was the infusion of New World silver into the European–Asian commercial equation. Silver from Latin American mines was shipped across the Pacific to the Spanish colony in the Philippines and into the carrying trade between Japan, China and the Philippines.[3] New World silver proved to be the one commodity Asian merchants were willing to take for their spices, teas and luxuries, and it remained the basic fuel of East–West commerce into the eighteenth century.

Yet if silver resolved the basic issue of exchange, it did not lead to the creation of a commercial united front in Asia. For much of the seventeenth century, the Portuguese and Dutch fought a global war for control of the Asian spice and the Atlantic sugar and slave trades.[4] The Dutch won this contest, only to find themselves challenged, at the end of the seventeenth century, by the English. Such contests made East Asian political powers wary of dealing with Europeans, especially when individually they often sought exclusive commercial privileges and special tariff rates, to the detriment of their rivals and other long-established trading partners.

In China and Japan there were also significant changes. Weakened by corruption, ineffectual leadership and peasant unrest, the Ming dynasty collapsed in the middle of the seventeenth century. Into the resulting power vacuum came the Manchus, a warrior group from north of the Great Wall, who established the Qing dynasty in 1644. In Japan, almost a century and a half of feudal civil war came to an end in the early 1600s. With the aid of European military weapons, Tokugawa Ieyasu (1543–1616; r. 1603–05) defeated his rivals and established a military rulership (*shōgunate*) that united Japan and ruled in the name of the emperor.

With two robust new political entities dominating China and Japan, Europeans were forced to operate from a position of economic and military weakness. Both Tokugawa and Qing rulers used their advantage to adopt policies not unlike those of mercantilism in Europe: foreign trade was a means to enrich the state. In Europe this had produced royally chartered monopolies, such as the Dutch and English East India Companies. In China and Japan it led to state-managed trade organized through specially sanctioned merchants. By the middle of the seventeenth century, European commerce was confined to the single port of Nagasaki in Japan and, shortly thereafter, to Canton in China.[5] European traders were only allowed to trade at designated times of the year and their movements were strictly limited. These changes induced European powers or their colonial outposts in Asia (Goa and Batavia on Java) to launch embassies to the courts of China and Japan.

Spanning the reigns of the first four Qing emperors – Shunzhi (r. 1644–62), Kangxi (r. 1662–1722), Yongzheng (r. 1723–35) and Qianlong (r. 1736–95) – 18 European embassies in all made their way to Peking before 1800. These included four from Portugal (1670, 1678, 1727, 1753); four from Holland/Batavia (1656, 1667, 1686, 1795); six from Russia (1656, 1660, 1676, 1693, 1720, 1726); three from the papacy (1705, 1720, 1725); and one from Britain (1793). Encounters were sometimes fraught with tension and confusion. Europeans often thought that by presenting gifts of tribute to Asian rulers, they would obtain the commercial concessions they sought. Although special gifts might be bestowed on such occasions, Qing and Tokugawa rulers seldom altered commercial relations, which, from a European perspective, appeared little improved. This was because, in the eyes of the Chinese and Japanese courts, embassies were about establishing formal relations of superiority and inferiority between themselves and foreign princes. Commerce, so important to Europeans, had a subordinate place in the construction of relations of power and authority in East Asia.

European embassies to the Qing court were organized into the same set of ceremonial protocols that governed imperial relations with East, South-East and Central Asian kingdoms, and Mongol khanates. The protocols incorporated foreign rulers into the overlordship of the Qing emperor (*huangdi*, supreme ruler, and *qagan*, khan of khans). Such quasi-feudal arrangements were cemented through correct

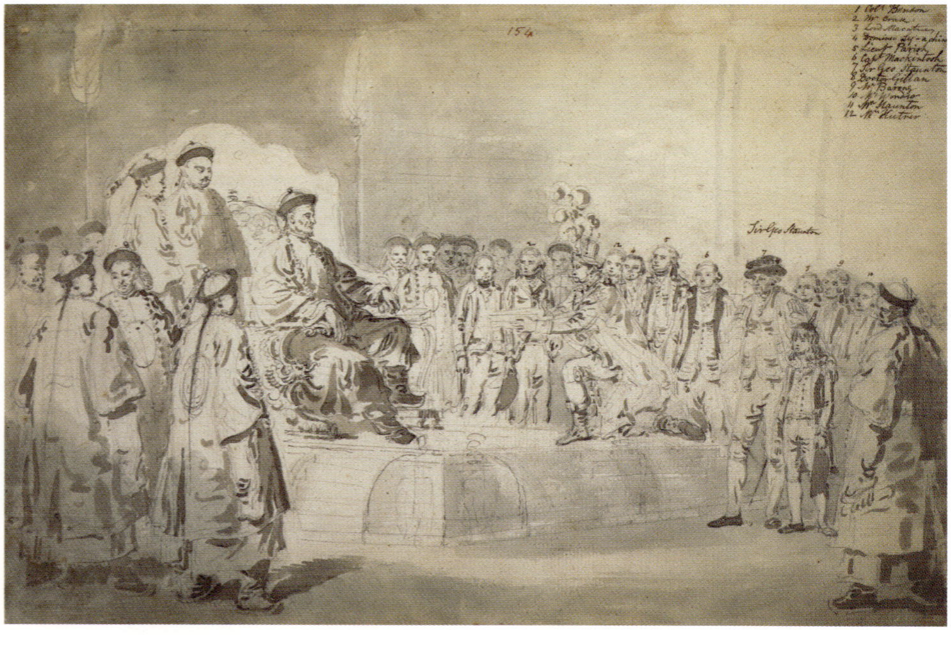

7.1
The Reception (detail)
William Alexander

Watercolour on paper
China, 1793

British Library, London

7.4
Hanging

The poem reads:
For many years the Portuguese have come, presenting gifts
Now the English have arrived in all sincerity
Their journey is akin to that of the legendary travellers Shu Hai and Heng Zhang
The fame of our august ancestors has extended across the vast ocean.
While they appear ordinary, their hearts are good and true
Yet their gifts are not precious, but curiosities, whose subtleties have been exaggerated
Still, in cherishing men from afar, no matter how meagre their offerings,
We treat them with generosity.

Tapestry weave silk
China, *c.*1793

National Maritime Museum, Greenwich

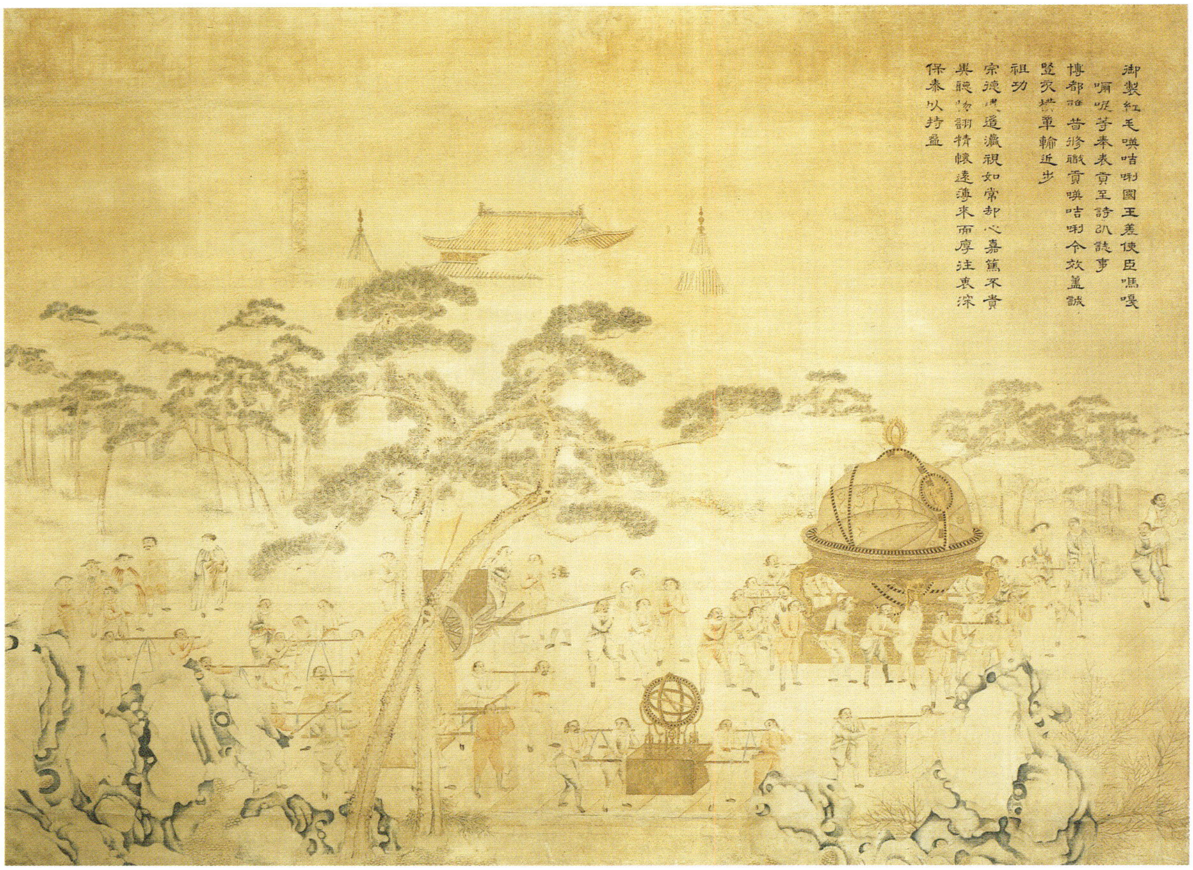

themselves had been treated generously.[13] These references were to the great show that Macartney had made of the scientific instruments George III had sent to Qianlong.

Unaware of the court's view of him, Macartney pressed for broader political contacts and expanded commercial exchange. Qianlong and his advisers interpreted these actions as signs of arrogance, and became concerned that the British had ulterior motives; perhaps they had come to spy or sow dissent among the European merchants at Canton. The upshot was that the Qing elite became convinced they had encountered the most dangerous Europeans ever to have arrived in their empire.[14]

The British encounter with the Qing court demonstrated the great importance of gift exchanges in shaping the diplomacy of embassies. Chinese-language sources are often quite meticulous about precisely what was exchanged. For example, records from the first Portuguese embassy of 1670 indicate that they presented swords, daggers, a portrait of the King of Portugal, coral and amber strings, a box made of gold and amber, cloves, elephant tusks, incense and rose water, calambac wood, four rhinoceros horns and carpets.[15] Imperial bestowals appear in court records in the following form:

To the king: 3 bolts each 4 clawed dragon satin, adorned satin, iridescent satin, and Japanese satin; 1 bolt of gold flecked satin; 10 bolts of brocade; 5 bolts of hat satin, blue satin, and green satin; 14 bolts of damask and 14 skeins of spun silk thread and 300 taels of silver.

To the ambassador: 1 bolt 4 clawed dragon satin; 2 bolts of adorned satin and Japanese satin; 1 bolt of hat satin; 6 bolts of brocade; 5 bolts of blue satin; 4 bolts of damask and 4 skeins of thread; 2 bolts of thin silk and 100 taels of silver.

To the retinue: 1 bolt of adorned silk, 2 bolts of damask, 1 bolt of thin silk and 50 taels of silver.[16]

These bestowals then provided a precedent for later Portuguese embassies. In subsequent visits, the amounts allotted in each category increased, indicating the recognition of a more significant relationship with the Portuguese prince. As noted, the embassy of 1753 provided a precedent for the first British embassy in 1793, which was then consulted for arranging the Dutch embassy of 1795. Moreover, in 1793 a new item was added to the

political and economic power in East Asia. More significant than the trade was the infusion of New World silver into the European–Asian commercial equation. Silver from Latin American mines was shipped across the Pacific to the Spanish colony in the Philippines and into the carrying trade between Japan, China and the Philippines.[3] New World silver proved to be the one commodity Asian merchants were willing to take for their spices, teas and luxuries, and it remained the basic fuel of East–West commerce into the eighteenth century.

Yet if silver resolved the basic issue of exchange, it did not lead to the creation of a commercial united front in Asia. For much of the seventeenth century, the Portuguese and Dutch fought a global war for control of the Asian spice and the Atlantic sugar and slave trades.[4] The Dutch won this contest, only to find themselves challenged, at the end of the seventeenth century, by the English. Such contests made East Asian political powers wary of dealing with Europeans, especially when individually they often sought exclusive commercial privileges and special tariff rates, to the detriment of their rivals and other long-established trading partners.

In China and Japan there were also significant changes. Weakened by corruption, ineffectual leadership and peasant unrest, the Ming dynasty collapsed in the middle of the seventeenth century. Into the resulting power vacuum came the Manchus, a warrior group from north of the Great Wall, who established the Qing dynasty in 1644. In Japan, almost a century and a half of feudal civil war came to an end in the early 1600s. With the aid of European military weapons, Tokugawa Ieyasu (1543–1616; r. 1603–05) defeated his rivals and established a military rulership (*shōgunate*) that united Japan and ruled in the name of the emperor.

With two robust new political entities dominating China and Japan, Europeans were forced to operate from a position of economic and military weakness. Both Tokugawa and Qing rulers used their advantage to adopt policies not unlike those of mercantilism in Europe: foreign trade was a means to enrich the state. In Europe this had produced royally chartered monopolies, such as the Dutch and English East India Companies. In China and Japan it led to state-managed trade organized through specially sanctioned merchants. By the middle of the seventeenth century, European commerce was confined to the single port of Nagasaki in Japan and, shortly thereafter, to Canton in China.[5] European traders were only allowed to trade at designated times of the year and their movements were strictly limited. These changes induced European powers or their colonial outposts in Asia (Goa and Batavia on Java) to launch embassies to the courts of China and Japan.

Spanning the reigns of the first four Qing emperors – Shunzhi (r. 1644–62), Kangxi (r. 1662–1722), Yongzheng (r. 1723–35) and Qianlong (r. 1736–95) – 18 European embassies in all made their way to Peking before 1800. These included four from Portugal (1670, 1678, 1727, 1753); four from Holland/Batavia (1656, 1667, 1686, 1795); six from Russia (1656, 1660, 1676, 1693, 1720, 1726); three from the papacy (1705, 1720, 1725); and one from Britain (1793). Encounters were sometimes fraught with tension and confusion. Europeans often thought that by presenting gifts of tribute to Asian rulers, they would obtain the commercial concessions they sought. Although special gifts might be bestowed on such occasions, Qing and Tokugawa rulers seldom altered commercial relations, which, from a European perspective, appeared little improved. This was because, in the eyes of the Chinese and Japanese courts, embassies were about establishing formal relations of superiority and inferiority between themselves and foreign princes. Commerce, so important to Europeans, had a subordinate place in the construction of relations of power and authority in East Asia.

European embassies to the Qing court were organized into the same set of ceremonial protocols that governed imperial relations with East, South-East and Central Asian kingdoms, and Mongol khanates. The protocols incorporated foreign rulers into the overlordship of the Qing emperor (*huangdi*, supreme ruler, and *qagan*, khan of khans). Such quasi-feudal arrangements were cemented through correct

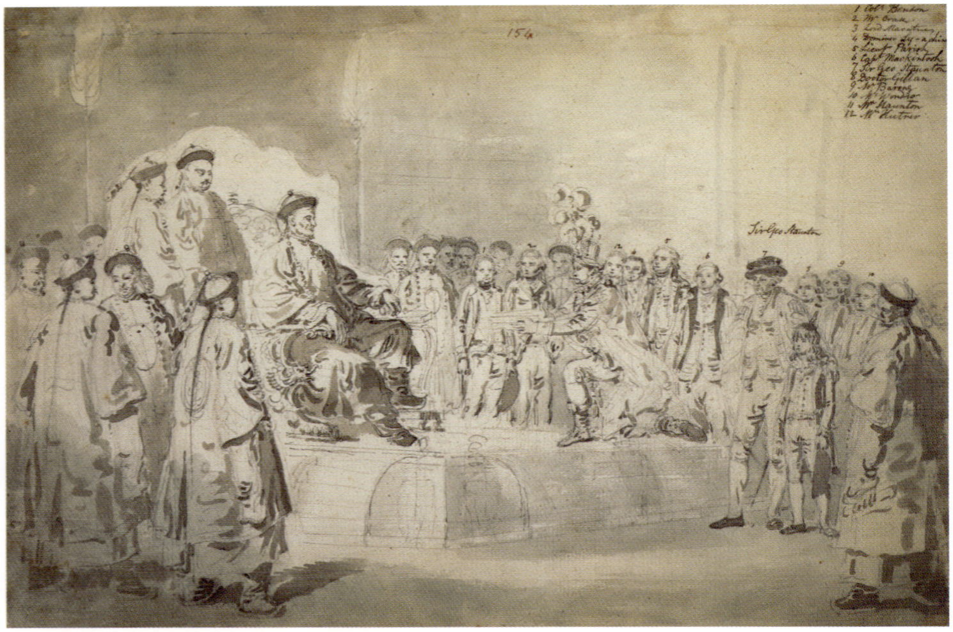

7.1
The Reception (detail)
William Alexander

Watercolour on paper
China, 1793

British Library, London

7.4
Hanging

The poem reads:
For many years the Portuguese have come, presenting gifts
Now the English have arrived in all sincerity
Their journey is akin to that of the legendary travellers Shu Hai and Heng Zhang
The fame of our august ancestors has extended across the vast ocean.
While they appear ordinary, their hearts are good and true
Yet their gifts are not precious, but curiosities, whose subtleties have been exaggerated
Still, in cherishing men from afar, no matter how meagre their offerings,
We treat them with generosity.

Tapestry weave silk
China, *c.* 1793

National Maritime Museum, Greenwich

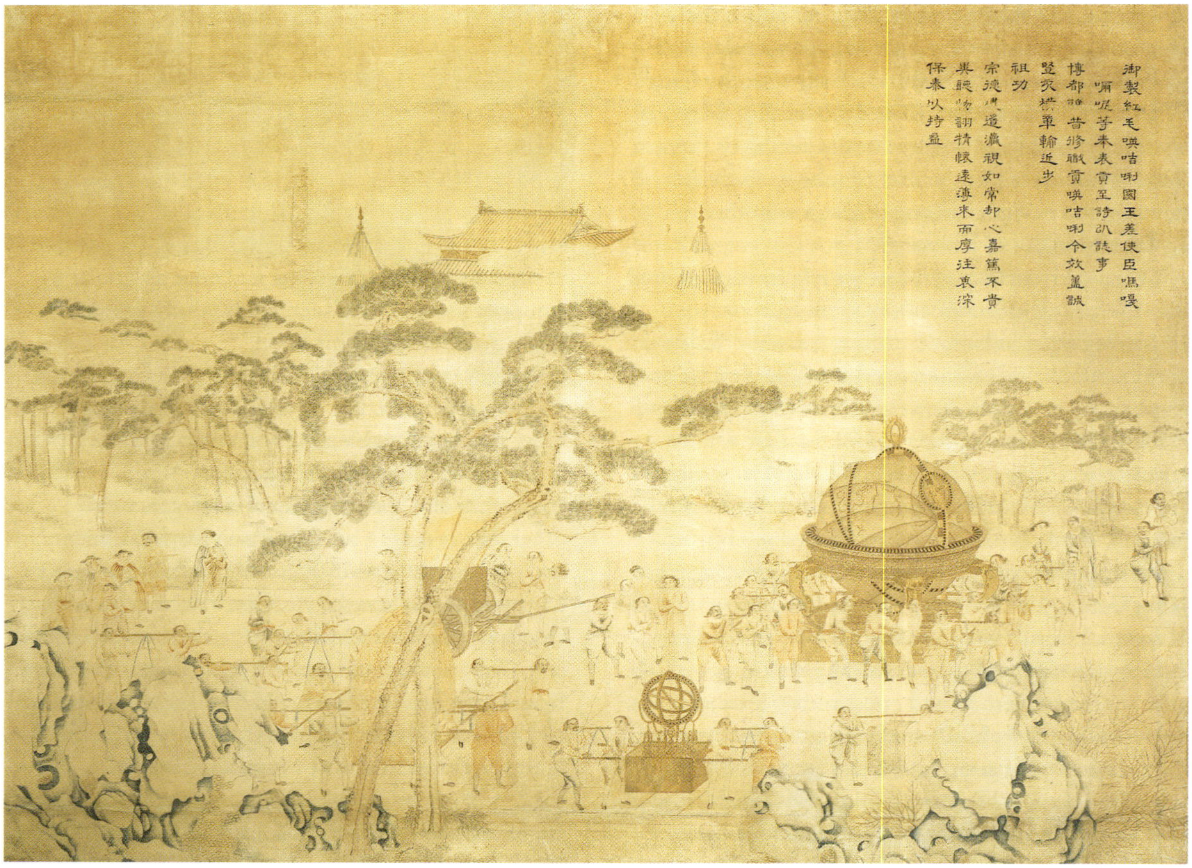

themselves had been treated generously.[13] These references were to the great show that Macartney had made of the scientific instruments George III had sent to Qianlong.

Unaware of the court's view of him, Macartney pressed for broader political contacts and expanded commercial exchange. Qianlong and his advisers interpreted these actions as signs of arrogance, and became concerned that the British had ulterior motives; perhaps they had come to spy or sow dissent among the European merchants at Canton. The upshot was that the Qing elite became convinced they had encountered the most dangerous Europeans ever to have arrived in their empire.[14]

The British encounter with the Qing court demonstrated the great importance of gift exchanges in shaping the diplomacy of embassies. Chinese-language sources are often quite meticulous about precisely what was exchanged. For example, records from the first Portuguese embassy of 1670 indicate that they presented swords, daggers, a portrait of the King of Portugal, coral and amber strings, a box made of gold and amber, cloves, elephant tusks, incense and rose water, calambac wood, four rhinoceros horns and carpets.[15] Imperial bestowals appear in court records in the following form:

To the king: 3 bolts each 4 clawed dragon satin, adorned satin, iridescent satin, and Japanese satin; 1 bolt of gold flecked satin; 10 bolts of brocade; 5 bolts of hat satin, blue satin, and green satin; 14 bolts of damask and 14 skeins of spun silk thread and 300 taels of silver.

To the ambassador: 1 bolt 4 clawed dragon satin; 2 bolts of adorned satin and Japanese satin; 1 bolt of hat satin; 6 bolts of brocade; 5 bolts of blue satin; 4 bolts of damask and 4 skeins of thread; 2 bolts of thin silk and 100 taels of silver.

To the retinue: 1 bolt of adorned silk, 2 bolts of damask, 1 bolt of thin silk and 50 taels of silver.[16]

These bestowals then provided a precedent for later Portuguese embassies. In subsequent visits, the amounts allotted in each category increased, indicating the recognition of a more significant relationship with the Portuguese prince. As noted, the embassy of 1753 provided a precedent for the first British embassy in 1793, which was then consulted for arranging the Dutch embassy of 1795. Moreover, in 1793 a new item was added to the

political and economic power in East Asia. More significant than the trade was the infusion of New World silver into the European–Asian commercial equation. Silver from Latin American mines was shipped across the Pacific to the Spanish colony in the Philippines and into the carrying trade between Japan, China and the Philippines.[3] New World silver proved to be the one commodity Asian merchants were willing to take for their spices, teas and luxuries, and it remained the basic fuel of East–West commerce into the eighteenth century.

Yet if silver resolved the basic issue of exchange, it did not lead to the creation of a commercial united front in Asia. For much of the seventeenth century, the Portuguese and Dutch fought a global war for control of the Asian spice and the Atlantic sugar and slave trades.[4] The Dutch won this contest, only to find themselves challenged, at the end of the seventeenth century, by the English. Such contests made East Asian political powers wary of dealing with Europeans, especially when individually they often sought exclusive commercial privileges and special tariff rates, to the detriment of their rivals and other long-established trading partners.

In China and Japan there were also significant changes. Weakened by corruption, ineffectual leadership and peasant unrest, the Ming dynasty collapsed in the middle of the seventeenth century. Into the resulting power vacuum came the Manchus, a warrior group from north of the Great Wall, who established the Qing dynasty in 1644. In Japan, almost a century and a half of feudal civil war came to an end in the early 1600s. With the aid of European military weapons, Tokugawa Ieyasu (1543–1616; r. 1603–05) defeated his rivals and established a military rulership (*shōgunate*) that united Japan and ruled in the name of the emperor.

With two robust new political entities dominating China and Japan, Europeans were forced to operate from a position of economic and military weakness. Both Tokugawa and Qing rulers used their advantage to adopt policies not unlike those of mercantilism in Europe: foreign trade was a means to enrich the state. In Europe this had produced royally chartered monopolies, such as the Dutch and English East India Companies. In China and Japan it led to state-managed trade organized through specially sanctioned merchants. By the middle of the seventeenth century, European commerce was confined to the single port of Nagasaki in Japan and, shortly thereafter, to Canton in China.[5] European traders were only allowed to trade at designated times of the year and their movements were strictly limited. These changes induced European powers or their colonial outposts in Asia (Goa and Batavia on Java) to launch embassies to the courts of China and Japan.

Spanning the reigns of the first four Qing emperors – Shunzhi (r. 1644–62), Kangxi (r. 1662–1722), Yongzheng (r. 1723–35) and Qianlong (r. 1736–95) – 18 European embassies in all made their way to Peking before 1800. These included four from Portugal (1670, 1678, 1727, 1753); four from Holland/Batavia (1656, 1667, 1686, 1795); six from Russia (1656, 1660, 1676, 1693, 1720, 1726); three from the papacy (1705, 1720, 1725); and one from Britain (1793). Encounters were sometimes fraught with tension and confusion. Europeans often thought that by presenting gifts of tribute to Asian rulers, they would obtain the commercial concessions they sought. Although special gifts might be bestowed on such occasions, Qing and Tokugawa rulers seldom altered commercial relations, which, from a European perspective, appeared little improved. This was because, in the eyes of the Chinese and Japanese courts, embassies were about establishing formal relations of superiority and inferiority between themselves and foreign princes. Commerce, so important to Europeans, had a subordinate place in the construction of relations of power and authority in East Asia.

European embassies to the Qing court were organized into the same set of ceremonial protocols that governed imperial relations with East, South-East and Central Asian kingdoms, and Mongol khanates. The protocols incorporated foreign rulers into the overlordship of the Qing emperor (*huangdi*, supreme ruler, and *qagan*, khan of khans). Such quasi-feudal arrangements were cemented through correct

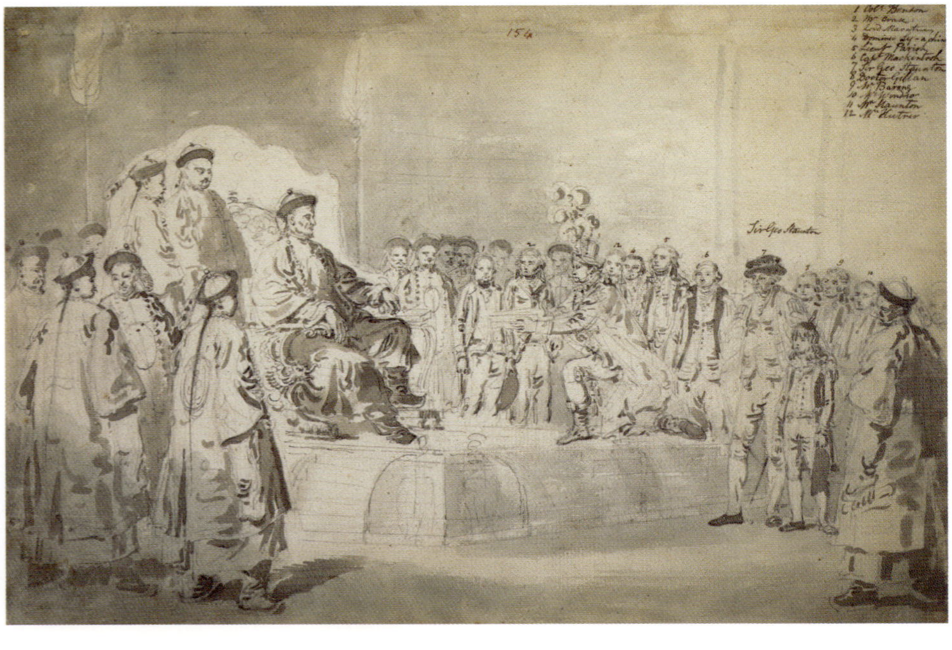

7.1
The Reception (detail)
William Alexander

Watercolour on paper
China, 1793

British Library, London

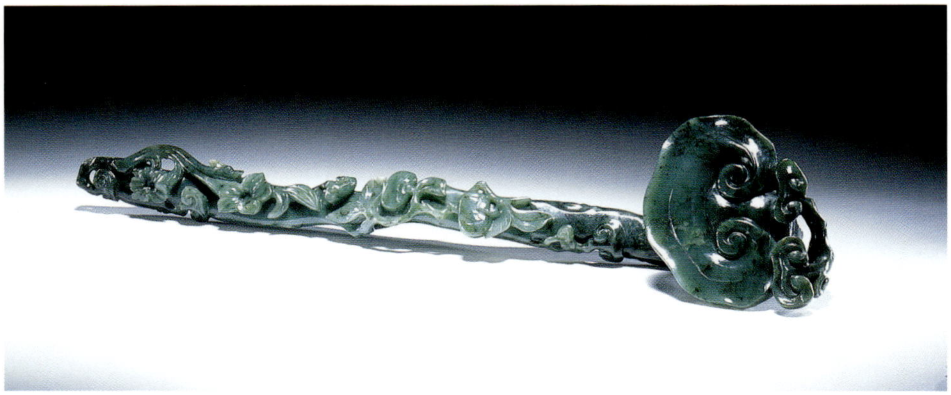

7.2
Ruyi

Presented to George Staunton, Lord Macartney's deputy and minister plenipotentiary to the mission, by the Qianlong emperor in 1793; jade
China, Qianlong period (1736–95)

V&A: A.17–1925

performance of ceremonies, especially court audiences and feasts; and through the offering of local products (*fangwu*) by the embassy and the reciprocal bestowal of gifts by the Qing emperor.

The *Comprehensive Rites of the Great Qing*, a seventeenth-century manual that outlines the protocols for embassy routines, notes that encounters began with a request to enter by the foreign prince, followed by the Qing imperium's response.[6] It continued with greeting the embassy on arrival; the presentation of credentials, a list of gifts, and a ranked list of the members of the embassy; the inspection and translation of all documents; preparation of the embassy for imperial audience; the audience itself, where the relationship between the emperor and the foreign prince was formally constituted; banquets and entertainments; the bestowal of imperial gifts; and the departure of the embassy. At various points in this process the ambassador and his retinue were expected to make obeisance to the emperor by kneeling three times and bowing their heads to the ground thrice. European emissaries often tried to avoid this act (usually translated as the 'kowtow'), but ultimately were unable to, because refusal might mean the dismissal of their embassy. Kneeling and bowing were, however, only one concern in a broader assessment of embassies by the Qing court. Officials scrutinized the whole process of the embassy to determine if the request to form an inferior–superior relationship with the emperor was indeed sincere. If they determined it was not, they might abort the embassy or reduce the amount of gifts to the prince, his ambassador and retinue.

If it was clear that the embassy was more than a commercial enterprise and expressed sincere wishes to forge a relationship with the Qing emperor, then it would be received in audience, banqueted and lavished with gifts. Qing court records are rather perfunctory on the content of imperial audiences and banquets, however. In contrast, European accounts frequently provide rich descriptions of the embassy routine. One of the best of these is by John Bell, a Scottish doctor who accompanied the embassy sent by Peter the Great to Peking in 1719–22. As gifts for the Kangxi emperor, the embassy brought rich furs, scientific instruments, watches, mirrors, horses and hounds, and a portrait of the Tsar. The emperor received the ambassador in the summer palace outside Peking. Breaking precedent, he accepted the Tsar's letter directly from the ambassador. After the embassy's obeisance, the emperor called for a wine ceremony and handed the goblet to the ambassador with his own hand. Such signs of distinction were followed by animated conversations about the Tsar's military campaigns and the affairs of empire, much of which took place in the presence of the emperor's sons and high-ranking dynastic officials. Bell noted that the proceedings, like many that followed in subsequent days, were marked by 'order and decency, rather than grandeur and magnificence'.[7]

This kind of extraordinary care and attention was similar to that accorded missions from Korea, Vietnam and other neighbouring kingdoms. And like them, ceremonies for the Russian embassy helped establish the necessary conditions for dealing with larger geopolitical and commercial issues affecting the relations of the two empires. In 1728, for example, the two parties completed the Treaty of Kyakhta, which regularized border arrangements, allowed for additional commercial interactions and permitted Russia to establish an ecclesiastical mission in Peking.[8] The following year, the Qing reciprocated by sending an embassy to Russia.[9]

Qing rulers seemed to have assumed, moreover, that good relations with other kingdoms were based on extended and repeated contacts from which various kinds of mutual benefit might flow. The Qing–Korea relationship provides a good example. The Korean kingdom had been loyal to the Ming dynasty and was one of the first to submit to the Manchus. After the establishment of the Qing, Korean embassies visited annually for more than two centuries. They came to celebrate the lunar new year, imperial birthdays and the birth of new heirs; to offer condolences on the death of a member of the imperial clan; and to receive the imperial calendar and the investiture documents for new Korean kings. Embassies also came to settle border issues, deal with smuggling and manage trade. While at court, the Korean embassy was fêted on an even grander scale than embassies from Russia. On their side, the Qing despatched embassies to Korea, where they were lavishly received and where matters similar to those listed above were dealt with.[10] Similar reciprocal relations are evident in Qing dealings with the Ryūkyū Islands and Vietnam.[11]

This pattern of imperial foreign relations continued into the late eighteenth century, with European embassies enfolded into the diverse, multi-ethnic configuration that characterized the Qing empire at its peak. By the 1790s, however, signs of change were evident. They came in the form of the first British embassy to China, led by George, Lord Macartney (1737–1806). In addition to addressing commercial matters, the embassy was also designed to impress upon the Qing court the strength and importance of King George III (r. 1760–1820) and his empire. Macartney hoped to use a grand display of the latest British scientific and astronomical technology – all gifts for the emperor – and court audience as an opportunity to establish sovereign equality between the two great monarchs and their dominions. This insistence on equality distinguishes the British from previous European embassies to China.

The embassy was received in Chengde, a summer retreat north of the Great Wall. In order to demonstrate his sensitivity to 'oriental customs and ideas', the ambassador wore a richly plumed hat, a velvet coat, the Order of the Bath, a diamond badge and a diamond star. The audience was held in a large tent in the Garden of Ten-Thousand Trees on 14 September 1793. As soon as the emperor was seated on the throne, Macartney entered the tent and placed a jewelled golden box carrying his king's letter directly into the Qianlong emperor's hands (plate 7.1). In return, the emperor handed him a jade sceptre (*ruyi*). On either this occasion or later, Macartney also presented a telescope to the emperor (plate 7.3).

Assuming that sovereign equality had been established, Macartney took stock of his surroundings. Like Bell and others before him, he was impressed with the 'calm dignity, that sober pomp of Asiatic greatness' that, he averred, 'European refinements have not yet attained'. Yet soon after this admission, Macartney signalled a fundamental shift in European attitudes towards China. This change is exemplified in his characterization of the audience as similar to a puppet show he had seen in his youth, entitled 'King Solomon in all his Glory'.[12] Thus, China was no longer the place of Toscanelli's philosophers and learned governors, but an archaic empire stuck in time, stagnant, unchanging and even childlike.

The Qing record of this encounter was somewhat different. It contained references to other ambassadors, including one from Burma, and organized the British embassy into the events in Chengde at that time of year, the celebration of the Qianlong emperor's birthday. On this occasion, the emperor wrote a special poem recognizing the first British embassy. Appearing in the *Veritable Records of the Qianlong Emperor's Reign* and on a textile hanging in the National Maritime Museum, Greenwich (plate 7.4), the poem places the British within the larger context of Qing relations with European kingdoms and evaluates their behaviour and gifts. After citing the Portuguese embassy of 1753 as the closest precedent, the emperor noted that the arrival of the British was not only a significant journey in itself, but a sign that merit of the founders of the dynasty, Nurhaci (r. 1616–26) and Hung Taiji (r. 1627–35), had extended across the ocean. And while the British appeared ordinary, their hearts were good, true and sincere. The poem then shifted from the appearance of the embassy to their gifts. They were, the emperor explained, not precious (*bugui*) things, but curiosities (*yi*), and their subtlety had been much exaggerated. On the other hand, no matter how meagre their offerings, the British

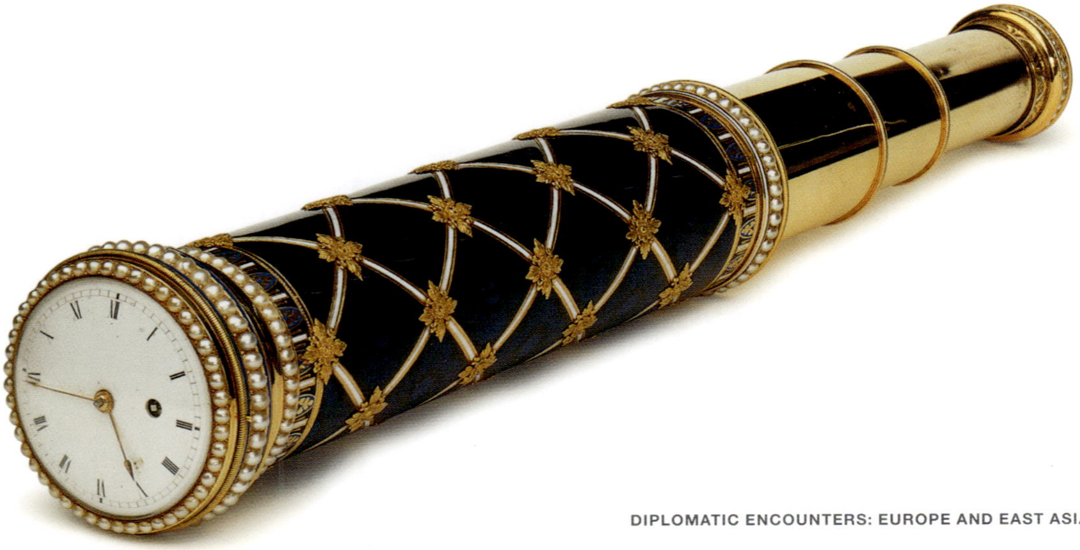

7.3
Telescope
Fraser and Son

Presented by Lord Macartney to the Qianlong emperor in 1793; gold with enamel coating; pearls; glass
England (London), 1790

National Maritime Museum, Greenwich

7.4
Hanging

The poem reads:
For many years the Portuguese have come, presenting gifts
Now the English have arrived in all sincerity
Their journey is akin to that of the legendary travellers Shu Hai and Heng Zhang
The fame of our august ancestors has extended across the vast ocean.
While they appear ordinary, their hearts are good and true
Yet their gifts are not precious, but curiosities, whose subtleties have been exaggerated
Still, in cherishing men from afar, no matter how meagre their offerings,
We treat them with generosity.

Tapestry weave silk
China, c.1793

National Maritime Museum, Greenwich

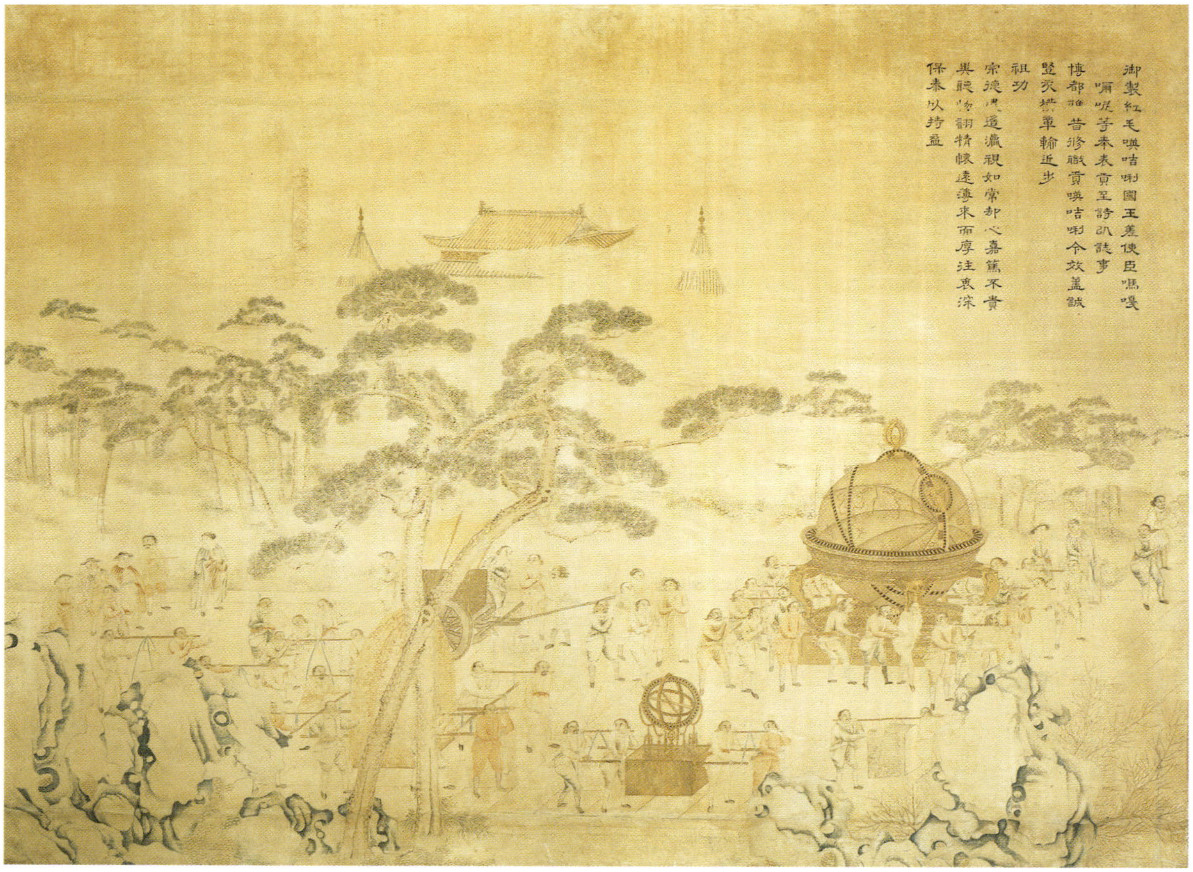

themselves had been treated generously.[13] These references were to the great show that Macartney had made of the scientific instruments George III had sent to Qianlong.

Unaware of the court's view of him, Macartney pressed for broader political contacts and expanded commercial exchange. Qianlong and his advisers interpreted these actions as signs of arrogance, and became concerned that the British had ulterior motives; perhaps they had come to spy or sow dissent among the European merchants at Canton. The upshot was that the Qing elite became convinced they had encountered the most dangerous Europeans ever to have arrived in their empire.[14]

The British encounter with the Qing court demonstrated the great importance of gift exchanges in shaping the diplomacy of embassies. Chinese-language sources are often quite meticulous about precisely what was exchanged. For example, records from the first Portuguese embassy of 1670 indicate that they presented swords, daggers, a portrait of the King of Portugal, coral and amber strings, a box made of gold and amber, cloves, elephant tusks, incense and rose water, calambac wood, four rhinoceros horns and carpets.[15] Imperial bestowals appear in court records in the following form:

To the king: 3 bolts each 4 clawed dragon satin, adorned satin, iridescent satin, and Japanese satin; 1 bolt of gold flecked satin; 10 bolts of brocade; 5 bolts of hat satin, blue satin, and green satin; 14 bolts of damask and 14 skeins of spun silk thread and 300 taels of silver.

To the ambassador: 1 bolt 4 clawed dragon satin; 2 bolts of adorned satin and Japanese satin; 1 bolt of hat satin; 6 bolts of brocade; 5 bolts of blue satin; 4 bolts of damask and 4 skeins of thread; 2 bolts of thin silk and 100 taels of silver.

To the retinue: 1 bolt of adorned silk, 2 bolts of damask, 1 bolt of thin silk and 50 taels of silver.[16]

These bestowals then provided a precedent for later Portuguese embassies. In subsequent visits, the amounts allotted in each category increased, indicating the recognition of a more significant relationship with the Portuguese prince. As noted, the embassy of 1753 provided a precedent for the first British embassy in 1793, which was then consulted for arranging the Dutch embassy of 1795. Moreover, in 1793 a new item was added to the

imperial bestowals – jade *ruyi* for both the British and Dutch monarchs and their ambassadors.

The kinds of things bestowed are worth attention. The bulk of them were high-grade textiles from the imperial storehouses, and occasionally porcelain, jade and lacquerware. Silver, the precious metal that Europeans had brought with them from the Americas, was also prominent. In addition, gifts given by one prince were sometimes bestowed on others, signifying the range of Qing relations. Also noteworthy are the amounts of allotments. Once the Qing had elicited a listing of the ranks of the embassy members, gifts were graded from high to low, with the foreign prince receiving the largest amount in each of the classes of gifts. This pattern was repeated throughout the records of embassies from Holland, Great Britain and Russia, as well as those from Korea, Vietnam, Siam and Burma.

For their part, Europeans brought gifts they thought would impress the Qing court. In addition to items already mentioned, these included telescopes and microscopes, models of ships, crystal, paintings of landscapes and famous places in Europe, and exotica such as elephant, rhinoceros and walrus tusks, ostrich eggs, amber and coral, mechanical toys and clocks (plate 7.5), and black fox, ermine and sable furs. Exotica were designed to stimulate Oriental curiosity in strange things and make Asian courts more amenable to accepting trade in European manufactures such as textiles, knives and swords, rifles and cannons, copper utensils, and pewter and porcelain ware. The hope, which never materialized, was that manufactured products would take the place of silver in Asia–Europe trade. Instead, as the Qianlong emperor noted, the many kinds of things the British brought were lumped together and thought of as curiosities, making them difficult to identify as local products from George III's kingdom.

The Qing ritual emphasis on local items, which was clearly present in the kinds of objects the emperor bestowed, was particularly evident in relations with East Asian domains. With the possible exception of silver, all that the Korean court sent was locally produced or native to Korea. This included various kinds of fine cloth and paper, mats, silks, and leopard, otter, deer and black squirrel skins.[17] Much the same could be said about embassies from Ryūkyū, Vietnam, Burma and Central Asian khanates. We can assume, therefore, that the Qing did not treat objects exchanged as mere commodities. Their emphasis on the local suggests that they may have understood

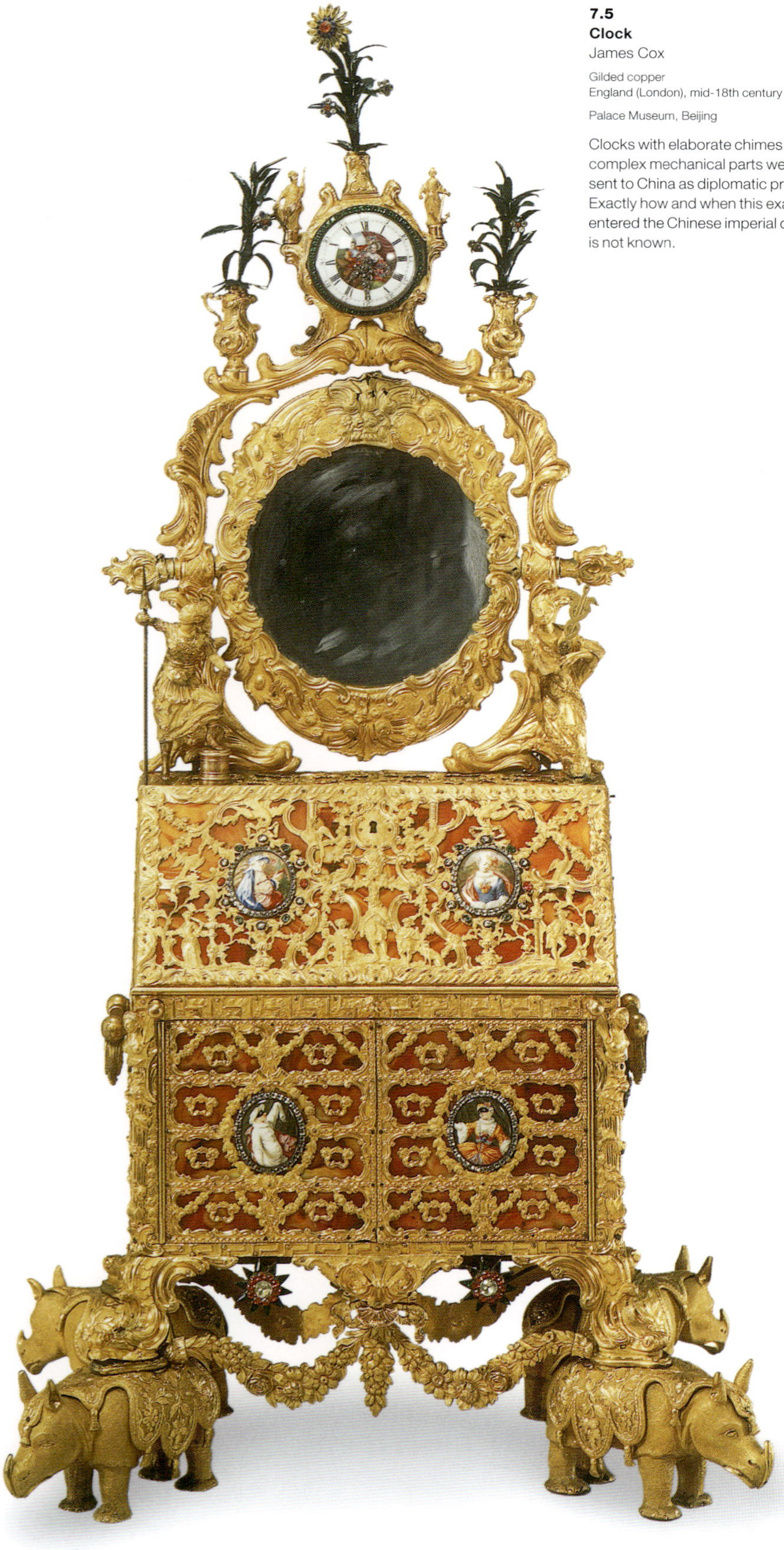

7.5
Clock
James Cox

Gilded copper
England (London), mid-18th century

Palace Museum, Beijing

Clocks with elaborate chimes and complex mechanical parts were frequently sent to China as diplomatic presents. Exactly how and when this example entered the Chinese imperial collections is not known.

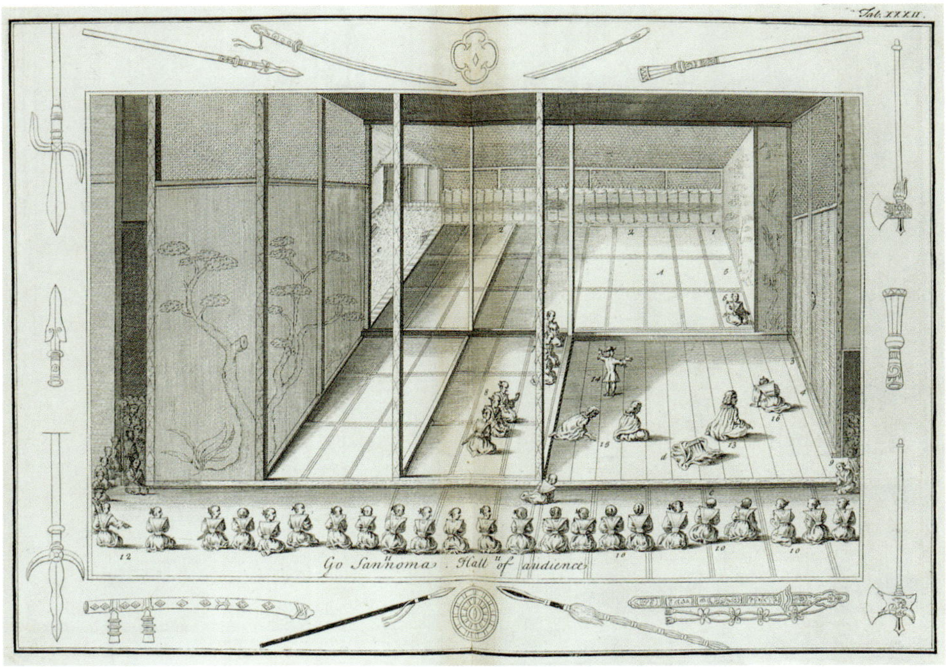

7.6
Engelbert Kaempfer Visiting the Shōgun

From *Kaempfer's Japan*, London, 1727
Engraving on paper

V&A: Asian Department Library

7.7 opposite
Suit of armour
Iwai Yosaemon

Presented by *shōgun* Tokugawa Hidetada to John Saris as a gift for James I; lacquered iron plates with copper, gold, leather and woven silk
Japan, *c.*1613

Royal Armouries, Leeds

native products as material signs of good rulership in their own empire and in the kingdoms of other princes. This point was either never grasped or was overlooked by European embassies, where the profit motive was a predominant reason why embassies were despatched. Moreover, in the case of the British gifts, the Qing court appears to have been somewhat confused by the fact that they could not distinguish many of them – especially the scientific instruments and clocks – from those sent by other European countries. This may explain their mixed reaction to British overtures.

Diplomatic protocol was no less formalized in Tokugawa Japan than in the Qing court, and seems to have followed similar routines and principles of hierarchical relations of rank and status. In Japan, however, actual court audiences, like those in which Bell and Macartney participated, were rare because few actual embassies with official credentials from European courts were ever sent. After the Tokugawa came to power and Portuguese merchants and missionaries were expelled, the Dutch were confined to the island of Dejima in Nagasaki harbour and trade was closely supervised. Their contact with the *shōgunate* was limited to annual visits or 'viewings' at Edo, the capital of Japan.

Because the Dutch were in Japan essentially as commercial agents, their treatment stood in stark contrast to that accorded embassies from Korea or Ryūkyū. Although keenly aware of the differences, representatives of the Dutch East India Company could not finesse the issue of official status and the protocols that went with it.[18] Like Qing emperors, the *shōgun* saw little reason to forge the same sorts of relations with merchants that they would with princes. However, the *shōgunate* also found the Dutch a useful source of revenue and intelligence on the East Asian world. As a reward, Dutch merchants were allowed to come to Edo to be 'viewed', to pay homage to the *shōgun* and to receive instructions on their standing at Dejima.

Engelbert Kaempfer, a Dutch physician, left detailed accounts of the 'viewings' of 1691 and 1692. After their arrival at Edo and preliminary ceremonies, the Dutch delegation, bearing their gifts, was led to an audience hall to await the arrival of the *shōgun*. Officials then escorted the head of the mission into the audience hall. Kaempfer described what then ensued, which he clearly found distasteful.

> As soon as the captain appeared, someone shouted in an exaggeratedly loud voice '*oranda kapitan*' to prompt him to step forward and pay his respects. Thereupon he crawled forward on his hands and knees between the place where the presents had been lined up and the high seat of his majesty as far as they motioned him. Crouching on his knees, he bent his head to the floor and then, like a lobster, crawled back in this very same position, without one word being exchanged.[19]

The audience was followed by a banquet with lower-level functionaries, instructions from the *shōgun*, and dismissal. Occasionally, however, they might be invited to a second audience. On one such occasion, Kaempfer explained that they were asked 'a number of meaningless questions', such as the distance from Holland to Batavia, and from Batavia to Nagasaki; whether the director of the East India Company was more powerful than the Prince of Holland; and what sorts of cures the Dutch might have for certain physical afflictions. After being satisfied with the answers, the *shōgun* or one of the court ladies might then ask the Dutch to remove their cloaks and walk, stand still, dance, jump, play the drunkard, compliment one another, speak broken Japanese, read Dutch, paint and sing (plate 7.6). After performing 'innumerable other monkey tricks', the Dutch were fed and dismissed. Prior to departure, they received a communication from the court that reaffirmed trade relations, urged them to pass peacefully upon the seas, and forbade them to smuggle Portuguese priests into Japan. They thereupon received silk robes as gifts and were allowed to return to Nagasaki.[20]

While this treatment of the Dutch might seem degrading, that was not the intent. Few, if any, commoners were allowed into the presence of a *shōgun*. Moreover, there may well have been genuine interest in Dutch customs, dress, music and so forth. What is significant, however, is that the Dutch were received on the basis of a political understanding of their status. Had they presented a letter from their king, as was the case with an English embassy from James I in 1613, they might have been received in audience in a manner similar to their own court practices, been accorded special trading privileges,[21] and given a suit of armour from the *shōgun* as a gift for their king (plate 7.7). If they had been capable of providing the Tokugawa with political resources beyond the occasional intelligence they brought, regarding movements of commerce and peoples within the East Asian world, they also would have received different treatment.

Such, in fact, was the case with kingdoms understood as important to Tokugawa rule. Korea, the exemplary Qing tributary state, mounted lavish embassies to Japan, which were received as akin to loyal vassals. In one instance, at the very same time as he was establishing relations with the Manchus prior to the founding of the Qing dynasty, the Korean King Injo sent an embassy to Japan. Arriving in 1636, it bore gifts of tiger and leopard skins, falcons and horses, as well as fine silks and clothes like those presented to the Qing emperor. The embassy was celebrated in Japanese paintings and poetry, and large crowds greeted them as they made their way to Edo castle. After being received by the *shōgun*, they diplomatically asked for permission to visit the shrine of the founder of the Tokugawa *shōgunate*, demonstrating that the fame of the ruling house had extended beyond Japan.[22]

Embassies like this one and those from the Ryūkyū kingdom came to cement relations, honour a new *shōgun*, announce a successor ruler in their kingdom or congratulate a *shōgun* on the birth of an heir. Good relations with powerful neighbours were then used by kings in Korea and elsewhere to demonstrate their good governance and, hence, their right to rule. Thus, regardless of the specific reason for embassies, they were all part of the production of rulership in China, Japan, Korea and Ryūkyū. They were also the ways and means by which East Asian monarchs vied for pre-eminence in the region. No European monarch's diplomatic gesture could result in a similar claim.

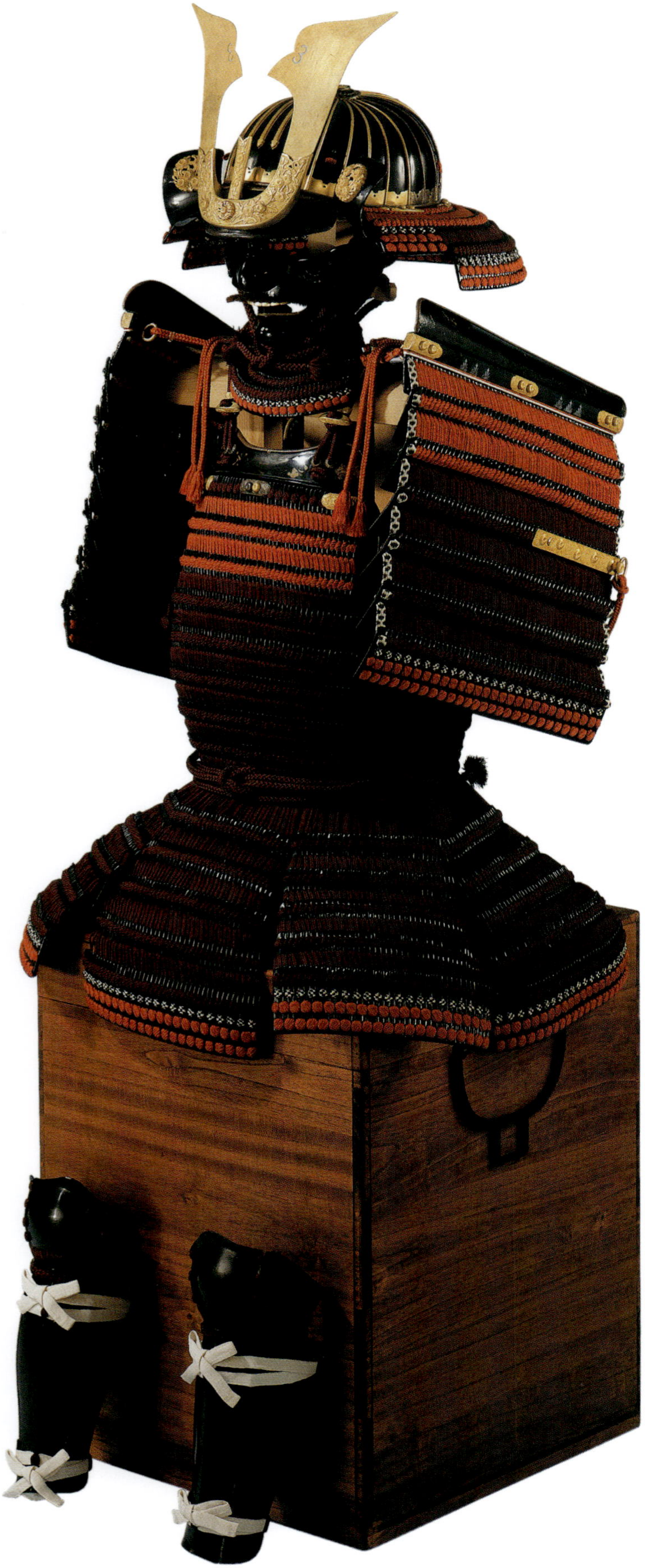

Japanese Diplomatic Relations with Europe

Greg Irvine

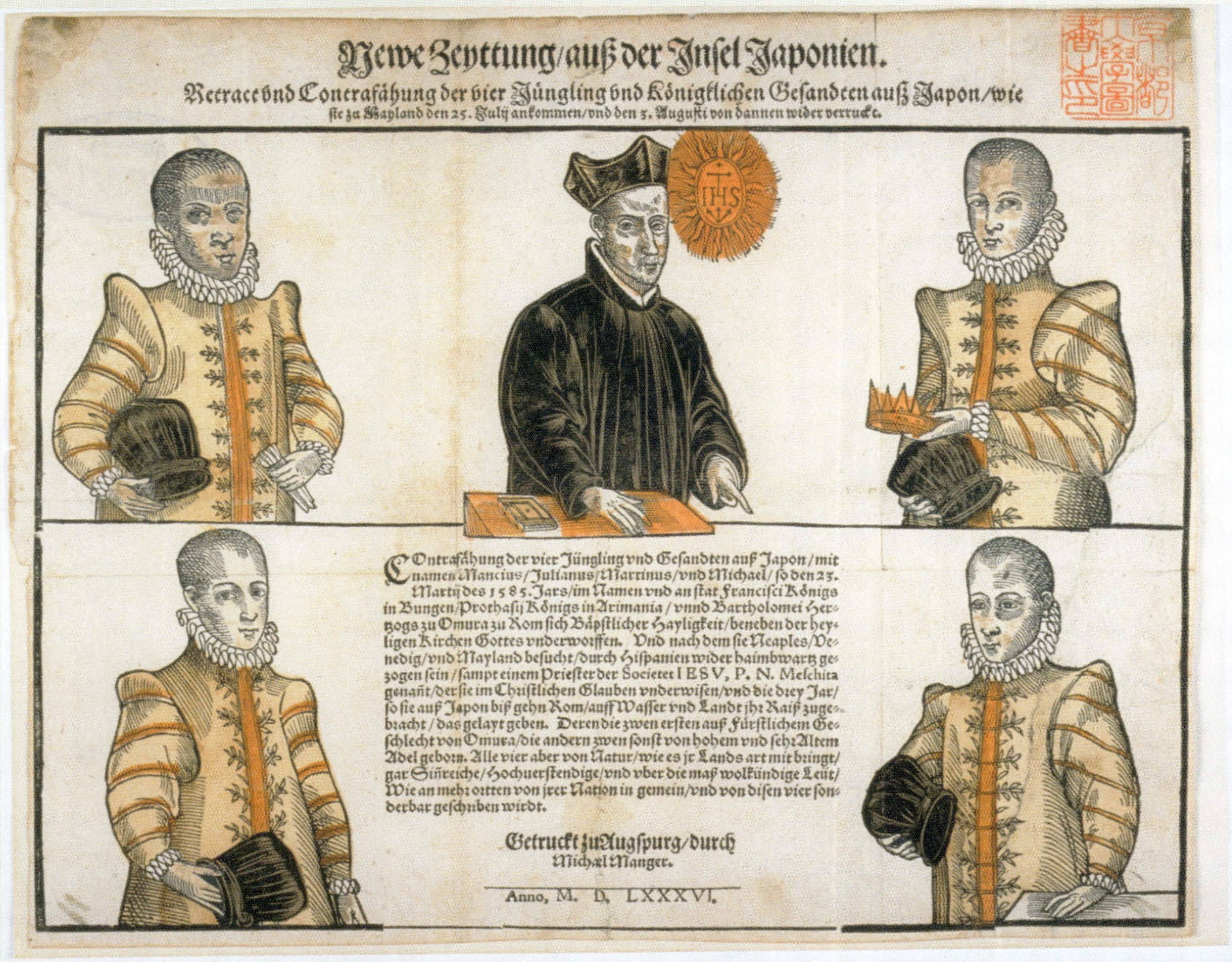

7.8
News from the Island of Japan. Portrait of the young men and royal ambassadors from Japan
Michael Manger

Hand-coloured engraving on paper
Augsburg, 1586

Kyoto University, Kyoto

In February 1582 the Jesuit Alessandro Valignano (1539–1606) organized an official Japanese mission to Europe to win further support for the Jesuit cause in Japan. The envoys were four young men who were relatives and vassals of three Christian *daimyō* in Kyūshū. Mancio Ito, Miguel Chijiwa, Juliao Nakaura and Martinho Hara, themselves Christian converts, were aged between 14 and 15 when they departed. Together with an entourage of priests and attendants, the envoys travelled to Europe via Macao, Malacca and India, arriving in Lisbon in August 1584, two and half years after leaving home.

The envoys were enthusiastically received throughout Catholic Europe, where their appearance aroused much curiosity. In Évora, Portugal, a huge crowd observed the four youths at mass and was struck by their piety. In Madrid, Philip II (r. 1556–98) received the envoys in a manner normally reserved for papal legates and the greatest ambassadors.[1] The youths arrived in Rome in March 1585 and were received by Pope Gregory XIII (r. 1572–85), to whom they offered many diplomatic gifts, including two painted folding screens, a sword in a mother-of pearl sheath, 'its garnishments notched with inlaid gold', two knives, a dagger and three silken garments 'in the Japanese style'.[2] In return the young men were given presents, including eight mirrors and four ivory crucifixes. In Venice they were received by the doge and participated in the annual ceremony marking the acquisition of the body of St Mark, the city's patron saint, from Alexandria. Tintoretto (1518–94) was appointed by the Senate to paint the four young Japanese, but only finished one of these portraits.[3] Engravings of the envoys were also produced in Augsburg in 1586 (plate 7.8).

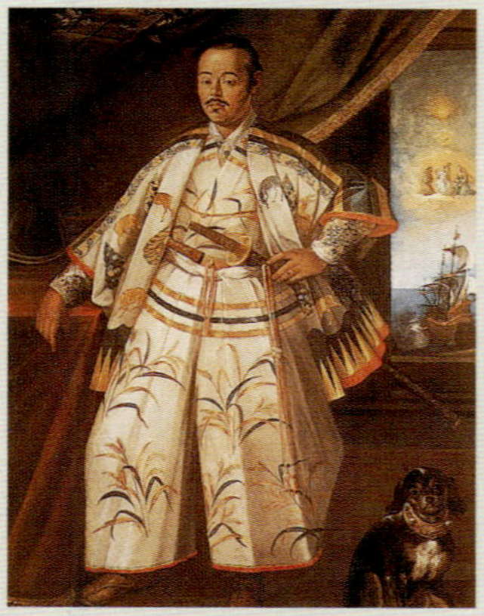

7.9
Hasekura Tsunenaga
Archita Ricci
Oil on canvas
Rome, 1615
Private collection, Rome

On their return to Japan in 1590 the envoys inspired a vogue for western exotica. However, by this time Christianity was facing persecution and the young men were only able to tell of their experiences in Europe to a limited audience in Kyūshū. Nearly 15 years later, in October 1613, Date Masamune, the *daimyō* of Sendai, appointed Hasekura Tsunenaga (1571–1622) to lead a trade mission to New Spain (Mexico) and southern Europe. Accompanied by some 180 Japanese, Hasekura set sail for Acapulco in a vessel constructed by Japanese shipwrights working under Spanish supervision. While in Europe, he converted to Christianity, as is revealed in the iconography of a portrait of the envoy painted in Rome by Archita Ricci (plate 7.9). During Hasekura's absence, however, Tokugawa Ieyasu (1543–1616; r. 1603–05) issued an edict expelling Christian priests from Japan. In Europe, news of the oppression of Christianity led to a hardened attitude towards trade with Japan, and Hasekura's mission ended in failure. He returned home in 1620, and within 20 years Japan decisively adopted a policy of national seclusion.

After the Portuguese were expelled, in 1639, the Dutch remained the only European nation permitted to trade in Japan. The *opperhoofd*, or head of the Dutch factory at Dejima, made regular visits to the *shōgun*'s court in Edo bearing tribute (see p. 98, p. 183 and p. 316). The gifts the Dutch presented included wonders such as rare animals and technical instruments, and objects that were considered exotic in Japan, such as a large Dutch brass chandelier. That this piece was highly prized is evident from the fact that it is preserved at Nikkō Tōshōgu, the mausoleum of Tokugawa Ieyasu, the first Tokugawa *shōgun*. Another Dutch gift preserved at Nikkō, in the treasure house of the Rinnō-ji temple, is a sumptuous late sixteenth-century ivory-veneered casket with an inset relief panel on the lid depicting the biblical story of Susannah and the Elders, and with engraved crystal on the sides (plate 7.10).

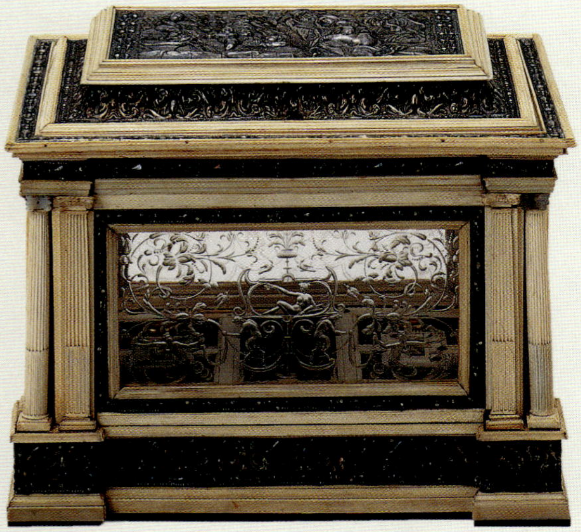

7.10
Casket
Presented by the VOC to the *shōgun*; wood veneered with ivory, with metal and engraved rock crystal panels
Italy, late 16th century
Rinnō-ji, Nikkō

8

RELIGIOUS ENCOUNTERS: CHRISTIANITY IN ASIA

Gauvin Alexander Bailey

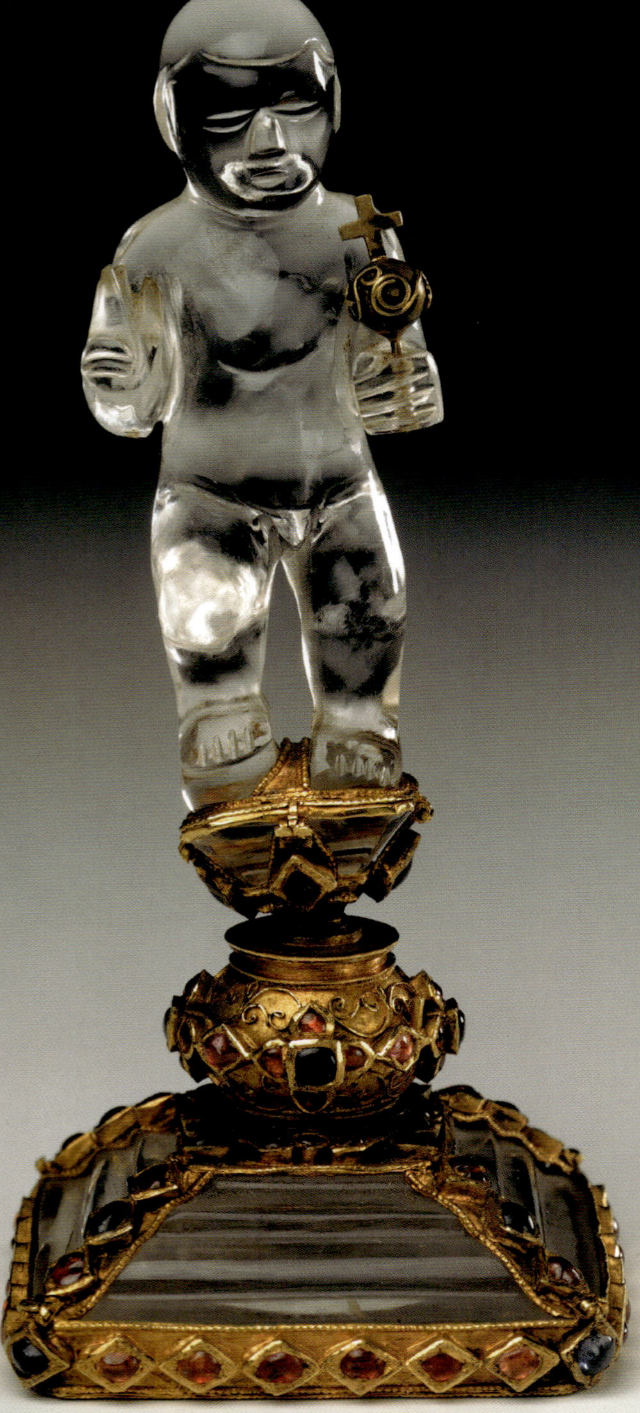

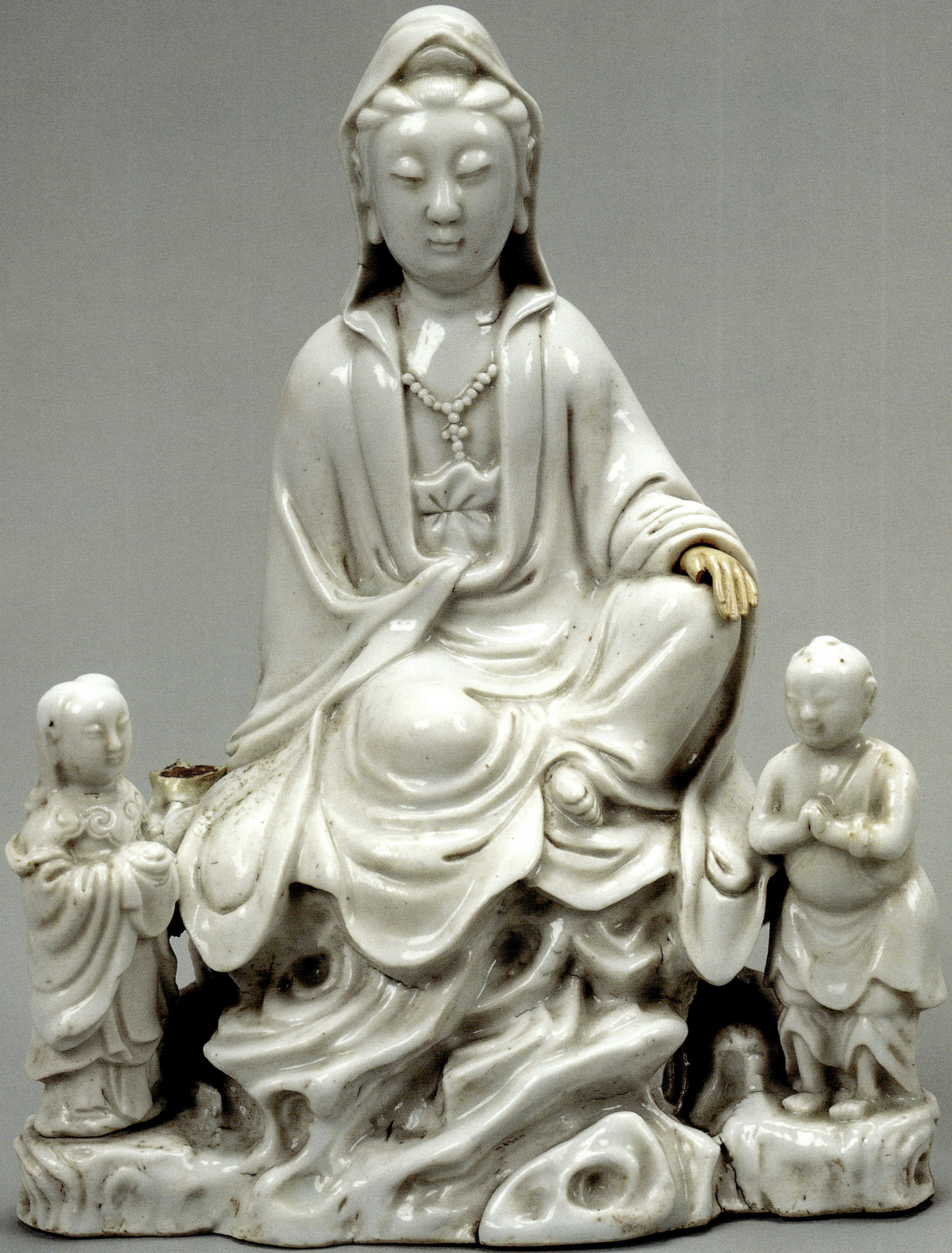

IN THE EARLY MODERN period, Christian missionaries penetrated more deeply into the Asian world than did the European colonial and mercantile powers. Although lacking armies, and preaching a faith that often went against the most basic cultural values of the peoples amongst whom they worked, missionaries were tolerated in some of the most powerful nations in Asia, from Mughal India and Ceylon to Japan and China. From the very beginning, they emphasized the importance of the visual arts in their work, not only to communicate across profound linguistic barriers, but also because they believed that art possessed didactic and miraculous capabilities. But there were two sides to their artistic ministry. Like the missions themselves, their art demonstrates that missionary orders were engaged in an active dialogue with the host culture, borrowing and trading styles, techniques and even symbols, occasionally creating a hybrid visual culture of great subtlety and erudition. In most cases the host cultures responded in kind, adapting elements of European styles and even Christian symbolism to their own traditions, regardless of whether they had any sympathy with the missionaries' religious goals.

By far the most active missionaries were those belonging to Catholic religious orders, predominantly the Society of Jesus (Jesuits), Franciscans and Dominicans. Founded in 1540 in Rome by Ignatius of Loyola (1491–1556), the Society of Jesus rapidly became one of the most extensive missionary orders in the world.[1] Based on a lean and mobile chain of command, it could operate over huge distances with relative ease and maintain a unity of purpose from Chile to Peking (Beijing). The Jesuits became particularly prominent in Asia, moving beyond the Portuguese imperial strongholds into the hinterlands. Founded respectively in 1209 and 1220, the Franciscan and Dominican orders were also leaders in the mission field in Asia, especially in colonial centres such as the Philippines, Macao and Goa, but also in China and Japan where they were often at loggerheads with the Jesuits. Both orders were proud of sending the first Catholic missionaries to Asia, since the Franciscan Giovanni di Piano Carpini (in 1245) and the Dominican André de Longjumeau (in 1248) had led missions to the Mongol court as early as the thirteenth century.[2] Protestant pastors from England and Holland also travelled to Asia during the same period, and preached in places like Batavia, Malacca and northern India, but their activities were largely restricted to East India Company settlements – or to diplomatic intrigue.[3] Typical was the Reverend Edward Terry, chaplain to Sir Thomas Roe, James I's ambassador to the Mughal court between 1615 and 1618, who despite admitting to a certain fondness for his Jesuit rival Francesco Corsi, seized every opportunity to trump him in the presence of the Emperor Jahangir (r. 1605–27).[4] Protestants also had little interest in religious imagery, an iconoclastic attitude that goes back to the origins of the Reformation itself.

Depending upon their order and the personalities and inclinations of their members, Catholic missionaries approached the different regions of Asia with strikingly diverse strategies, sometimes assimilating the clothing, language and customs of the indigenous people, as in the case of the Jesuit missions in Madurai and Japan, and sometimes insisting on the superiority of European ways, as with many of the Spanish-backed orders in the Philippines. The same was true for the visual arts. Some – again particularly the Jesuits – encouraged a blending with local styles, while others insisted on the stylistic inviolability of European sacred art, even in the face of vast cultural differences. The reactions that this art inspired from the indigenous populations were correspondingly varied, from outright rejection and violence to polite curiosity and fervent acceptance.

Early Modern Asia was vast and heterogeneous, with a cultural diversity considerably greater than anything missionaries had faced in Europe. The visual arts were no exception. In Asia, missionaries encountered a spectacular array of artistic traditions, ranging from the intensely figural Buddhist sculpture of Ceylon to the landscape-dominated literati painting of China. At one extreme they came up against an Islamic disinclination for images in parts of India and South-East Asia, while at the other they encountered a Hindu pantheon of imagery that outstripped even the prodigious iconography of Counter-Reformation Catholicism. They also found different approaches to the use of sacred art, whether as a tool for meditation among the Pure Land Buddhists of Japan or as a literal source of divinity among the Tagalog of Luzon. In some cases, missionaries capitalized on advantageous similarities between Christian and indigenous imagery, as in China and Japan, where depictions of the Madonna were merged with those of the Buddhist *bodhisattva* of mercy, Guanyin (Kannon in Japanese) (plate 8.2), while other situations discouraged the use of certain

8.1 page 103
Child Jesus

Rock crystal, carved, with gold mounts and rubies and sapphires
Ceylon, early 17th century

Peabody Essex Museum, Salem

8.2
The Bodhisattva Guanyin

Porcelain with white glaze (Dehua ware)
China (Fujian province), 17th century

Kobe City Museum, Kobe

In Japan figures such as this were worshipped as the Virgin Mary by hidden Christian communities. They were known as 'Maria-Kannon', Kannon being the Japanese term for the Boddhisattva Guanyin.

8.3 below
Basilica of Bom Jesus, Old Goa

Consecrated 1605

8.4 below right
Pulpit

Teak, carved and painted
India (Goa), 17th–18th century

Fundação Medeiros e Almeida, Lisbon

8.5 opposite
Child Jesus

Ivory, carved and partly painted
India (Goa), 17th century

Peabody Essex Museum, Salem

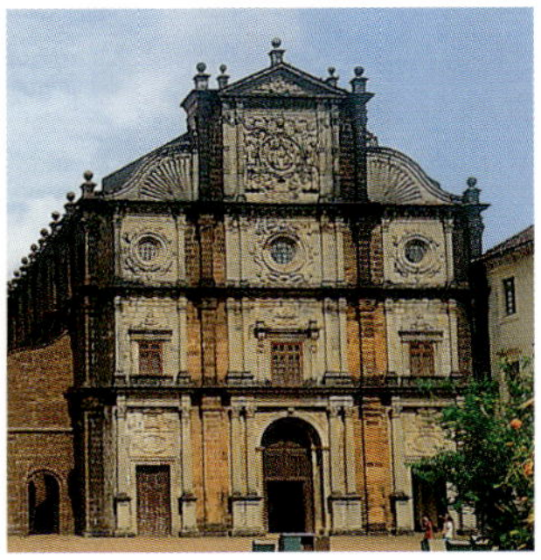

images like the Crucifixion, which was held in revulsion in Ming China. Missionaries even encountered conflicting Christian iconographies from among the existing churches in the East, such as the Armenians of the Mughal empire, the St Thomas Christians of southern India and the Nestorians of China – all of whom descended from traditions at least as old as the Church of Rome.[5]

Missionaries used a variety of art forms in their efforts to convert Asian peoples. Most prominent were engravings and printed books, including treatises on art and architecture. The engravings included some of the most cutting-edge works of European art, from Michelangelo and Raphael to Rubens and Velázquez.[6] Missionaries also imported original paintings and sculpture from Portugal and Italy, where some artists, like the Bavarian Sigismondo Laire (1550–1639), a friend of Caravaggio, and even the baroque master Guercino (Giovanni Francesco Barbieri, 1599–1666), made a lively trade doing paintings exclusively for overseas missions.[7] Occasionally, European painters and sculptors were invited to the missions, and some of them founded art academies in Asia. By training Asian artists to make Christian devotional imagery, they hoped not only to save money, but also to instil the basics of Christianity into the visual memory of the host communities.

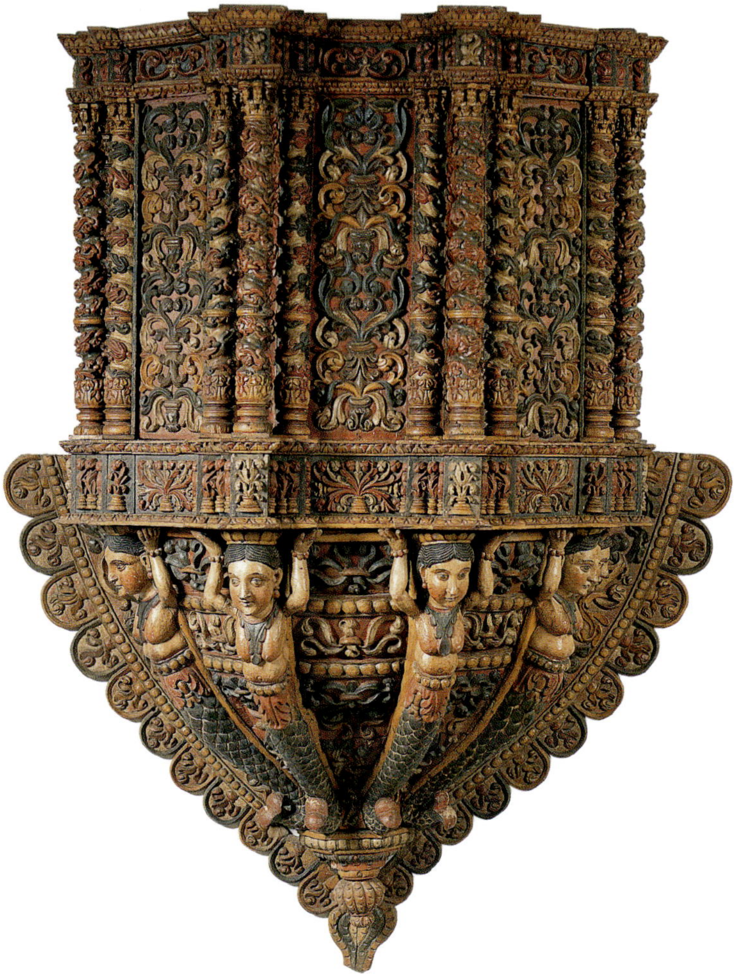

The earliest Catholic missions in Asia were established in Portuguese colonies in southern India. The Dominicans were the first to arrive in Goa, in the retinue of the conqueror Afonso de Albuquerque in 1510, and although they built a church in the fledgling town, they did not devote their energies to converting the local Hindus.[8] This task fell to the Franciscans, who reached the settlement in 1517. Using Goa as a base for missionary work on the mainland and to Indian Ocean islands (including Ceylon), the Franciscans boasted of thousands of converts within eight years of their arrival, and built themselves a grand church in the Manueline style in 1521. But no one equalled the Jesuits in the volume of their missionary activities in the Portuguese colony of Goa. Francis Xavier (1506–62) started the first Jesuit mission in the world when he landed there in 1542. In addition to their massive church of Bom Jesus (1594–1605) (plate 8.3), which now houses Xavier's tomb, the Jesuits founded the College of St Paul between 1560 and 1572, the earliest Catholic university in Asia and a building that predated the Roman Gesù itself.[9] By one reckoning, within a decade of Xavier's arrival, the Jesuits of Goa were responsible for well over a million conversions throughout India, South-East Asia and the Far East.[10] One of the most celebrated Jesuit missionaries was Roberto de Nobili (1577–1656), who lived for 40 years among the Tamils of southern India, adopting their dress, food and manner of living, and writing scholarly treatises in the Tamil vernacular – including one of the earliest European studies of Hinduism.[11]

Although their names are not known, legions of Indian sculptors and painters contributed to Goa's churches, many of them unconverted Hindus from the villages just outside the Portuguese colony. These people brought their centuries-old iconographic traditions to bear on the art they produced for the new religion.[12] The sculpture, pulpits, choir-stalls and other furniture that survive from the seventeenth and eighteenth centuries reveal a blending of European iconography with traditional Hindu and Islamic motifs and figural styles, and they are overwhelmed with rich ornamentation based on indigenous flora and fauna. A richly carved pulpit, from the turn of the eighteenth century, is a case in point, with its lavish decoration of tropical leaves and its circle of caryatids, whose voluptuous nude torsos and jewellery make them look as if they have walked off a Hindu temple (plate 8.4).

Some of the finest testaments to the skills of the southern Indian carvers are the thousands of ivory and rock-crystal religious statues that survive in collections throughout India, Europe and Latin America. Made primarily for export, but also handed out as gifts to new Indian converts, these exquisite objects are among the subtlest and most successful hybridizations found anywhere in Catholic Asia.[13] A seventeenth-century ivory shows the infant Christ holding the globe as the *Salvator Mundi* (Saviour of the World) (plate 8.5). This piece is particularly noteworthy for its monumental size and the crisp carving of the facial features, especially the almond-shaped eyes and the individual tufts of hair. A handful of these pieces are in rock crystal, such as a rare figure of Christ, also as the *Salvator Mundi*, from the early seventeenth century – one of only four presently known (plate 8.1). These figures derived ultimately from a group of engravings by the Wierix brothers (late sixteenth century) of Antwerp, which depict the infant Christ in various adult roles. This kind of imagery was especially well received in southern India and Ceylon, where it recalled traditional iconography of Buddha or of Krishna – the cowherd god revered throughout India.

Indigenous artists who produced these works were desperately needed in the Portuguese colonies, because few European artists made the voyage east, and those who did were often not very good. Such was the Flemish Jesuit priest Father Markus Mach (known as Marcos Rodrigues, d. 1601), whose skills as a crucifix-maker were nevertheless much in demand in colonial Goa.[14] The enigmatic Portuguese painter António Pereira also came to Goa in the late sixteenth century and contributed to some of the large-scale oil-on-panel paintings that adorned the city's great churches – mostly pedestrian copies of Flemish engravings – but nothing survives that can be attributed to his hand.[15] The most famous artist ever to visit Goa was the Flemish painter Michael Sweerts (1618–64).[16] Leaving behind him an extraordinary career in Europe, Sweerts joined the Lazarist missionaries and travelled to Syria and on to India, dying in Goa in 1664. No paintings from this period of his life have survived and his contribution to the artistic life of Goa appears to have been negligible.

Although Goa was a brilliant centre of ivory carving, some of the finest Indo-Catholic ivories

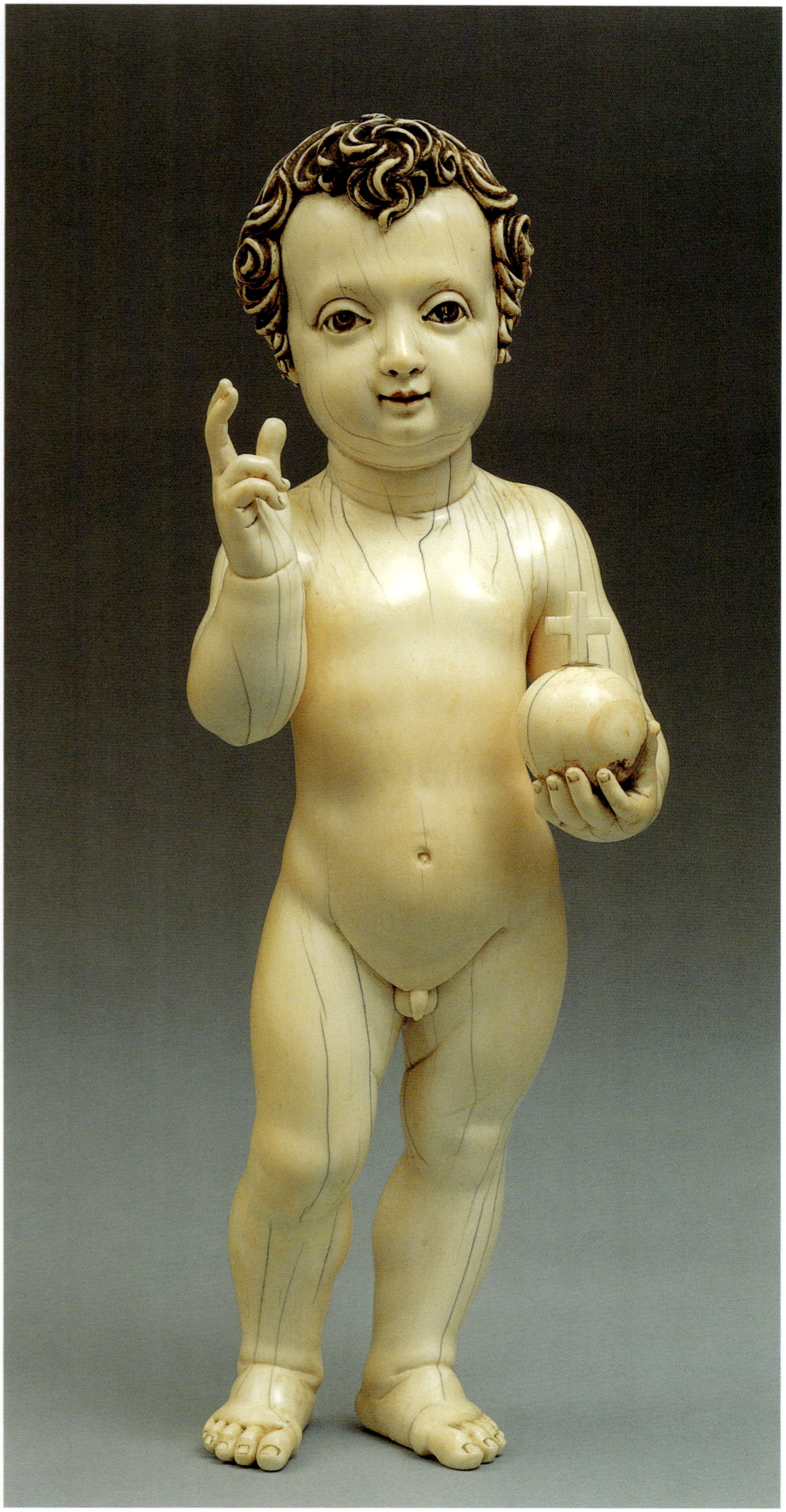

8.6
Akbar Holding Religious Discussions

From the *Akbarnama*

Opaque watercolour on paper
Mughal India, 1604

Chester Beatty Library, Dublin

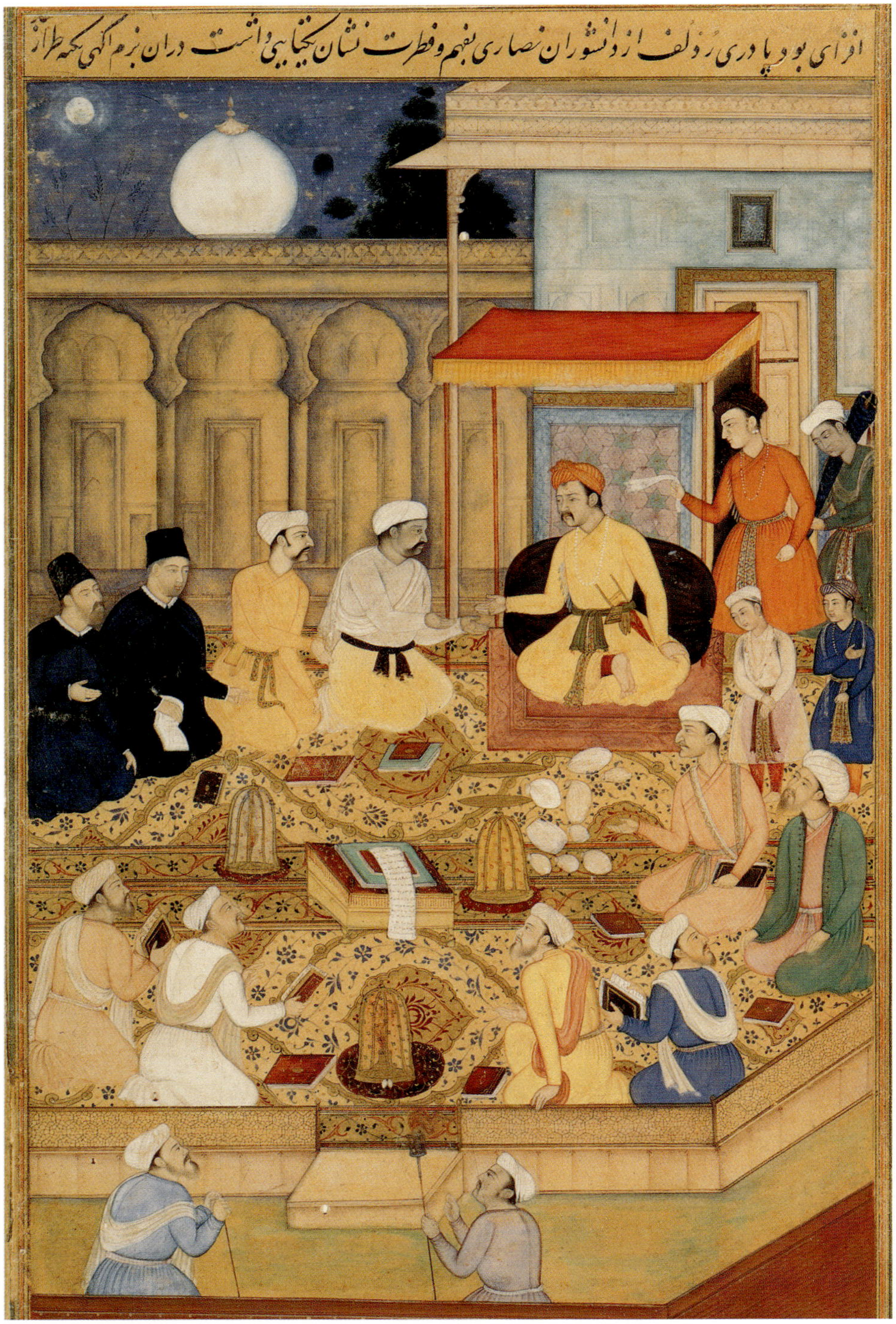

come from Buddhist Ceylon. Ivory carving from Ceylon has always been highly prized.[17] One of the most celebrated and intriguing periods of Ceylonese ivory carving took place during the Portuguese era, beginning with the foundation of the first Portuguese fort at Colombo in 1518–24 and ending with the final expulsion of the Portuguese by the Dutch in 1658.[18] Ceylonese ivory workshops created a new hybrid style that blended traditional Sinhalese forms and motifs with those derived from European engravings and sculptures. Recent scholarship has suggested that the Franciscans played an active role in bringing European imagery to Ceylon, since the friars were the first missionaries to reach the island, in 1543, and they set up schools and basic craft workshops in their convents.[19] The six friars who reached Kōttē in 1543 were granted permission to preach openly and founded missions in the kingdom, and the order soon built churches in several towns on the island, including Colombo and, after 1557, Kandy. Ivory figures and panels of Franciscan saints such as St Anthony of Padua and St Francis of Assisi attest to the activities of the Friars Minor in Ceylonese ivory production. The Jesuits also provided a conduit for European sacred imagery to reach Ceylon.[20] Although Francis Xavier visited the island as early as 1545, the Society of Jesus only founded its first mission there in 1602. When the Jesuits were followed shortly afterwards, in 1606, by the Dominicans and Augustinians, the Portuguese Crown was obliged to divide the island between the four orders, with the Jesuit sphere in the Seven Korales, the area north of Colombo and west of Kandy. The Jesuits founded a college in Colombo in 1620, which served as headquarters for mission activities throughout the Seven Korales, where they claimed 10,000 converts. Like the Franciscans, the Jesuits left their legacy in ivory imagery, including statuettes and relief panels of Francis Xavier and Ignatius of Loyola and depictions of early Christian martyrdoms taken from Jesuit illustrated books.

Ceylonese ivory workers specialized in a kind of decorative casket, some of the earliest of which once belonged to European royal and princely families related to the Portuguese queen Catherine of Austria (1507–78) (see plate 6.10).[21] Made in royal workshops in Kotte, these magnificent caskets are usually rectangular in shape with a pitched lid, a shape that derives from Portuguese boxes of the sixteenth century.[22] A much later casket with a flat lid (early to mid-seventeenth century) features a combination of Catholic iconography and Ceylonese zoological imagery (plate 8.7). This casket features specifically Jesuit symbolism, suggesting that it was made in conjunction with the mission in Colombo, possibly as a gift for the Jesuit provincial in Goa or Portugal, or even for the Jesuit father-general in Rome. The central panel of the lid depicts a Madonna and child derived from Albrecht Dürer's *Madonna by the Tree* (1513), copies of which the Jesuits brought to their mission in Mughal India, and which was copied by the Mughal artist Kesav Das around 1580–85.[23] On the end-panels are depictions of the two most important figures in the history of the Society of

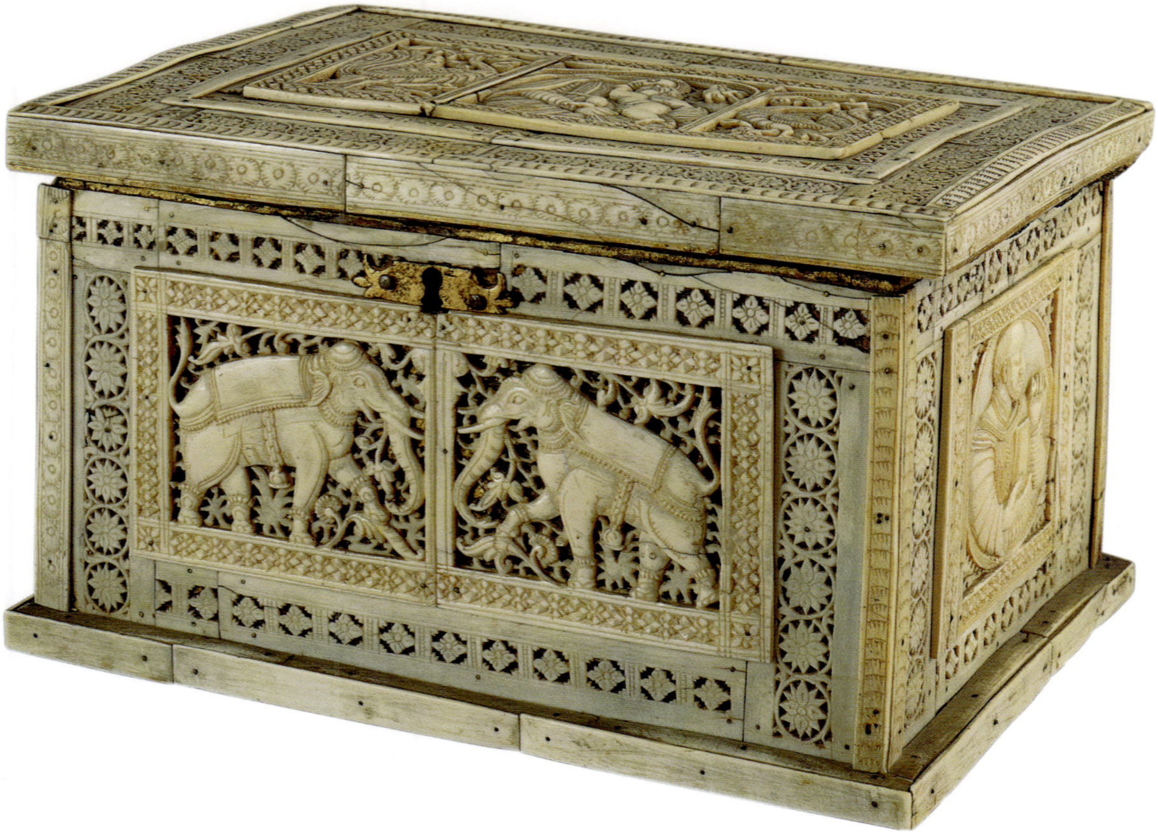

8.7
Casket
Ivory, carved
Ceylon, after 1622
Private collection, Porto

Jesus: Ignatius of Loyola and Francis Xavier. The portrait of Ignatius, in which he is shown holding the *Constitutions* of the Society, is taken from the title page by Cornelis Galle of the 1610 biography *Vita Beati Patris Ignatii Loyolae*.[24] The standing figure of Francis Xavier, the first Jesuit missionary and 'Apostle to the Indies', is taken from another source, this time Peter Paul Rubens's famous double portrait of Ignatius and Francis, printed to mark the 1622 canonization of the two saints by Schelte à Bolswert (1586–1659). Non-European imagery includes a pair of peacocks flanking the Madonna, a pair of elephants on the front, and a pair of mythological creatures on the back, carved with the precise line and bevelled edges typical of Ceylonese sculptors.

At the same time that Catholic religious imagery flourished in the south, it received an extraordinarily warm reception in the Muslim north. Few missionary encounters in Asia were as amicable as the meeting between Jesuit missionaries and the great Mughal emperors Akbar (r. 1556–1605) and Jahangir (r. 1605–27). This intercultural exchange prospered because the Mughals fostered a climate of experimentation, creativity and receptiveness that was remarkable for the time.[25] In an atmosphere recalling Lorenzo de' Medici's Platonic Academy in Florence a century earlier, these enlightened rulers invited scholars and priests from around the world to their court, hosting them in their palaces and fielding weekly interfaith debates into the small hours of the morning. The emperors and their guests expounded on the texts and traditions of faiths as varied as Judaism, Hinduism and Zoroastrianism. Some of the most vocal and influential participants in these debates were the Jesuits, who had been invited by Akbar from Goa in 1580 to serve as representatives of Catholicism, and who would remain at court with a few short interruptions until 1773. In an exquisite miniature by Nar Singh from the *Akbarnama* (*History of Akbar*, *c.* 1604), two Jesuit priests are portrayed at one of these debates, recognizable by their black gowns and caps (the Mughals called them *siyahposh*, or 'blackrobes') (plate 8.6). Although it should be stressed that the Jesuits and the Muslim mullahs rarely agreed on the key tenets of their faiths, the emperors themselves openly tried to bridge the gap between the two religions and bring their teachings into harmony.

The most visual manifestation of this Christian-Muslim encounter can be found in Mughal painting,

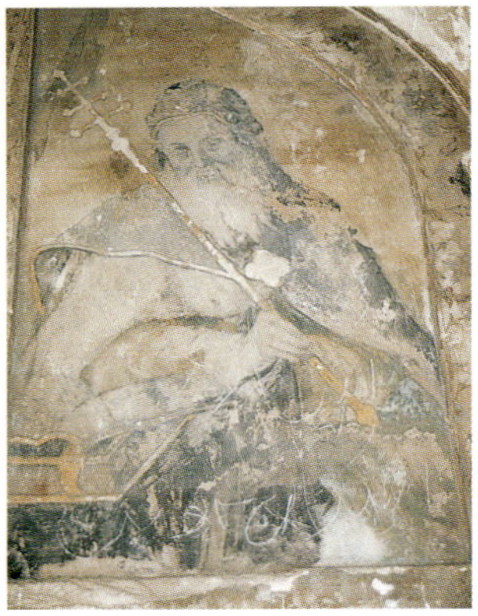

8.8
St Gregory the Great
Wall painting from the Sehdari Pavilion, Jahangiri Quadrangle, Lahore Fort
Mughal, *c.* 1610–20

8.9
The Martyrdom of St Cecilia
Nini, after an engraving by Jerome Wierix
Opaque watercolour on paper
Mughal India, *c.* 1600
V&A: IM.139–1921

precious objects and sculpture. Akbar had been interested in western devotional art since at least the 1560s, especially in its pictorial realism, visual drama and aura of sanctity, and one of the reasons he invited the Jesuits to court was to serve as a conduit for artworks from Europe. The Jesuits were zealous in serving the emperor, bringing engravings, printed books and oil paintings with them to northern India. The third Jesuit mission, which began in 1595, was even accompanied by a Portuguese painter, who tirelessly executed oil paintings on paper for Akbar and his son Prince Salim (the future Jahangir).[26] The emperor demonstrated an immediate fascination with the ritual properties of Christian altarpieces, and the Jesuits reported that he observed and imitated the behaviour of a worshipper, prostrating before an image in the Jesuit chapel. Akbar and his court also emulated the theatrical way in which the Jesuits used curtains, incense and candles to enhance the spiritual power of their images.[27] In fact, in 1581 a member of the royal family displayed one of the Jesuits' altarpieces, draped with rich textiles, in Akbar's audience hall to celebrate his return from a military campaign in Kabul, and Akbar exhibited the same picture on other state occasions, as well as on the Christian Feast of the Assumption (15 August), when he made his courtiers bow before it.[28]

Encouraged by the emperor himself, court artists quickly mastered the late Renaissance style in their book illustrations and album pages – especially western conventions of modelling and perspective, which they adapted to mainstream Mughal painting (see pp. 287–8). Although the mixture of East and West remained eclectic throughout Akbar's reign, under Jahangir it matured into a new manner characterized by an extremely refined naturalism, an enthusiasm for psychological portraiture and a taste for dramatic gesture. Even when he was still Prince Salim, the future emperor Jahangir showed a particular interest in this kind of imagery, assembling a coterie of artists at his court in Allahabad that rivalled that of his father. Salim had a taste for exacting reproductions of European prints, which gained a unique vibrancy through the application of traditional Indo-Persian gouache colours and gold leaf. Such is *The Martyrdom of St Cecilia*, a painstaking copy of an engraving by Jerome Wierix that was itself a reproduction of Stefano Maderno's famous statue of the subject in Rome (1600) (plate 8.9).[29] One of the most noteworthy things about this painting is that it is by a woman. Nini was one of three women painters in Salim's zenana, all of whom signed their work, evidence that some kind of art instruction existed in the zenana and that the artistic enterprises of the Mughal court were also directed towards a female audience.[30]

The new western style and its Christian subject matter soon extended to sculpture and precious objects, such as an extraordinary ruby-encrusted crucifix of jade and its accompanying pair of cruets, an altar set probably made by imperial jewellers as an ambassadorial gift for the Portuguese in Goa, and which once resided in the Portuguese monastery of Alcobaça (plate 8.10). More significantly, the style spread to monumental wall paintings, a handful of which survive today. European visitors to Mughal palaces and tombs in the late sixteenth and early seventeenth centuries were astonished to find them prominently adorned with mural paintings depicting Christ, the Virgin Mary and Christian saints executed in the style of late Renaissance Italy (plate 8.8). The Mughals even adorned their palaces with sculptures depicting the Virgin Mary and other saints, such as the one preserved at Agra Cathedral. The wonderment of these western observers led to false reports of the imminent conversion of the Muslim emperors, and hopeful Portuguese governors, English merchants and Catholic clerics scrambled to forge alliances with this new 'Prester John' (the legendary Christian king believed in the Middle Ages to reign somewhere in the East). Yet despite their cordiality, the Mughals were not interested in conversion, and in fact harnessed Catholic devotional imagery to serve their own propaganda, capitalizing on links between Catholic iconography and Indian and Islamic symbols to communicate their message of divinely sanctioned kingship.[31] Akbar's early experiments in Christian image veneration already show an acknowledgement of the power of sacred iconography and of the ways in which it could be manipulated.

One of the most flourishing missions in Asia, and the site of the most productive mission arts academy, was Japan. The mission was founded by Francis Xavier, who arrived in 1549 with a trunk-load of paintings and other devotional objects.[32] He and his companions wandered the streets, setting up paintings of the Virgin Mary or Christ the Saviour so that they could be seen by a crowd, and he preached in front of them with the assistance of his Japanese translators. Although the Jesuits at first had only limited success in Honshū, dramatic conversions

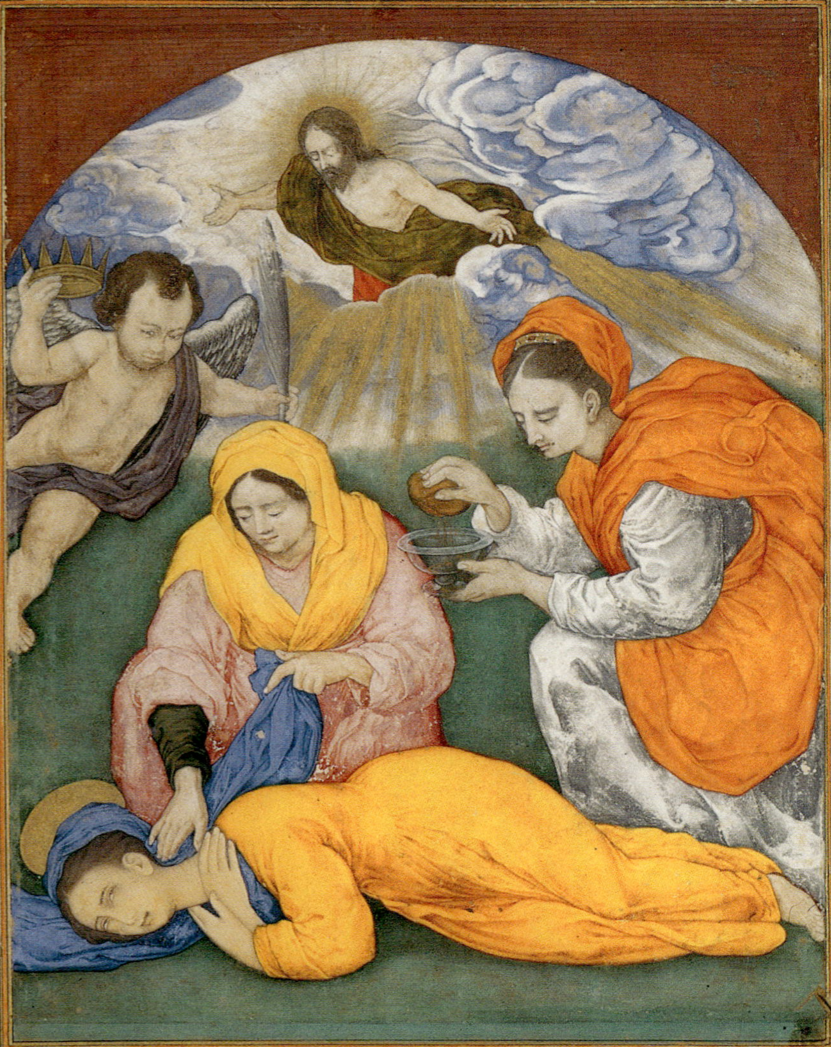

عمل نی نی

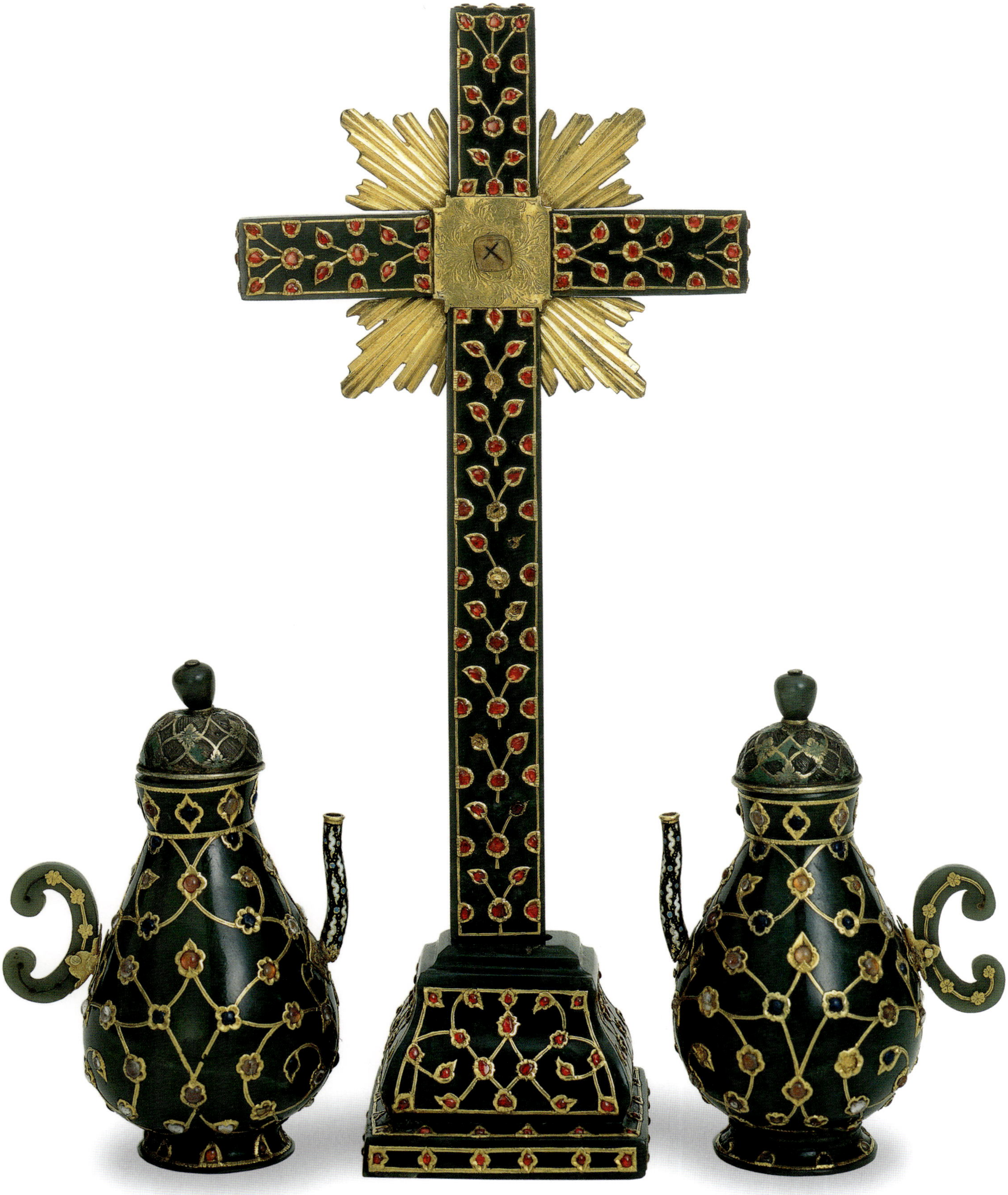

were the rule of the day in Kyūshū, where often, once the *daimyō* accepted Christianity, his people followed suit. Soon the Jesuits also gained a powerful patron in Honshū in the person of Oda Nobunaga (1534–82), the *de facto shōgun*. By 1593 there were 215,000 Japanese Christians, most of them organized into lay confraternity groups, with an independence from clerical assistance that helped Christianity persevere even in the face of later persecutions.[33] Beginning in 1580, the Jesuits operated colleges in Japan modelled on the Collegio Romano in Rome, which were popular not only with converts but with the sons of non-Christian families. Evidence of this Christian era in Japan abounds in the form of personal objects such as crosses or ceramic bowls decorated with Christian imagery (plate 8.11).

Called the 'Seminary of Painters' in documents of the period, the Jesuit art academy in Japan was founded in 1583 by the Italian Jesuit artist Giovanni Niccolò (1560–1626).[34] Although the school did not initially set out to adopt Japanese styles to Christian themes, it did address the iconographic idiosyncrasies of its Japanese audience and, as an increasing number of Japanese and Chinese students swelled its ranks, these artists began to incorporate their own styles and techniques into their work. The school began very modestly, with Niccolò training his Japanese pupils to copy engravings and paintings. However, it soon grew in size, as it welcomed not only Japanese Jesuit brothers but also college students and seminarians. By 1594 the school employed more than 20 artists, a number that may have doubled two years later, when the Bishop of Japan remarked with pride that the academy was 'overflowing with boys and young men who were painters, every one of them with his picture in his hand, painting various images in oil'.[35] By 1603 most of the 70 students at the Nagasaki college were in some way involved with the burgeoning art school.[36]

Students at the Seminary of Painters painted in oils on copper, wood and canvas, and in Japanese watercolours on paper (plate 8.12). There was also a foundry, where students cast copies of European bronze plaquettes, and a printing press, and the school made musical instruments and clocks. The products of the Seminary of Painters display a wide range of responses to their European models. Most of them are predominantly European in style, but show a slight unfamiliarity with western conventions, or traces of Japanese style. Others are a brilliant blend of western naturalism with Japanese technique and colour.

Many of the copper or wooden paintings that survive from the Seminary are set into delicate lacquered wood (*urushi*) triptych frames, which close in front of the image for easy transportation. Called 'hanging' or 'travelling' shrines, these small altarpieces are executed in traditional Japanese black lacquer adorned with silver and gold dust (*makie*) and mother-of-pearl inlay (*raden*) (plate 8.14). Although the frames themselves were made in a separate workshop (presumably by non-Christian Japanese lacquer workers), the patterns and styles are different from more mainstream Japanese pieces, which do not use inlay work and have a looser, freer kind of ornamentation. The patterns may have been supplied by the Seminary of Painters, and they occasionally incorporate Christian motifs, such as Eucharist grapes, or IHS, an abbreviation for the name of Jesus in Greek. These same lacquer workshops produced a wide array of altar furnishings for a Christian clientele, including missal stands,

8.10
Crucifix and pair of cruets

Jade, inlaid and mounted with gold and rubies
Mughal India, 17th century

Museu Nacional Soares dos Reis, Porto

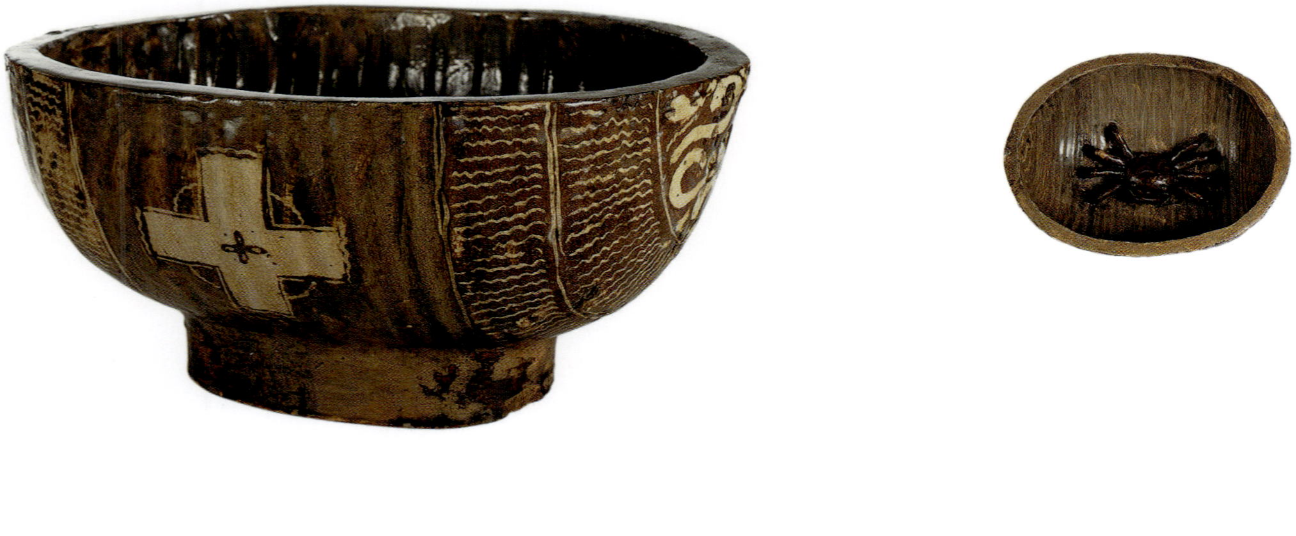

8.11
Bowl

Stoneware with grey-green glaze over incised slip-filled decoration; crab with iron glaze
Japan, early 17th century

Private collection, Porto

The crab inside the bowl refers to the episode in the life of St Francis Xavier when a crab restored to him a crucifix that he dipped, and subsequently lost, in the ocean in order to quell a storm while sailing off the coast of Malacca.

8.12
Madonna of the Snows

Hanging scroll; oil and colours on paper
Japan, after 1583

Twenty-six Martyrs Museum, Nagasaki

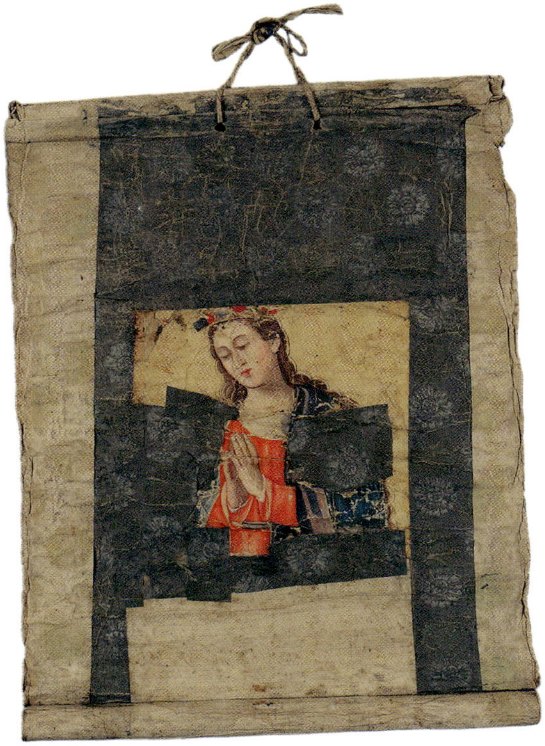

8.13
Writing box

Wood, covered in gold and silver *nashiji*, *hiramakie* and *takamakie*
Japan, late 16th–early 17th century

Namban Bunkakan, Osaka

oratories and boxes, all adorned with similar ornamentation and symbolism (plate 8.13).

The Seminary of Painters enjoyed wide influence outside the Christian community. The presence of a school of western painting in Japan attracted non-Christian painters eager to learn European techniques, and this helped created a general vogue for a hybrid style of painting. Particularly popular were large paper folding screens (*byōbu*), showing landscapes, townscapes, maps and European figures and animals, all in brilliant colours (plate 8.16). A particularly fascinating result of this cultural encounter is a kind of portrait of Zen Buddhist figures, especially the Indian missionary Daruma (Bodhidharma), which uses European conventions of shading and colouring, and sometimes oil paints (plate 8.15).[37] Just as the Seminary of Painters was at its height and its pupils were disseminating Christian devotional art throughout Japan and Asia, the Jesuits' general political situation collapsed. Toyotomi Hideyoshi (r. 1583–98) issued a decree in 1587 expelling the Jesuits from Japan. Although his edict was never carried out, full-scale persecution of Christians began under his successor, the Tokugawa *shōgun* Tokugawa Ieyasu (1543–1616; r. 1603–05), who prohibited Catholic Europeans from Japanese territory in 1614. The second Tokugawa *shōgun*, Hidetada (1579–1632; r. 1605–16), and his successors expelled and hunted down Catholic Europeans and Japanese Christians, staging massacres like the 'great martyrdom' of 1622 and elaborate torture procedures

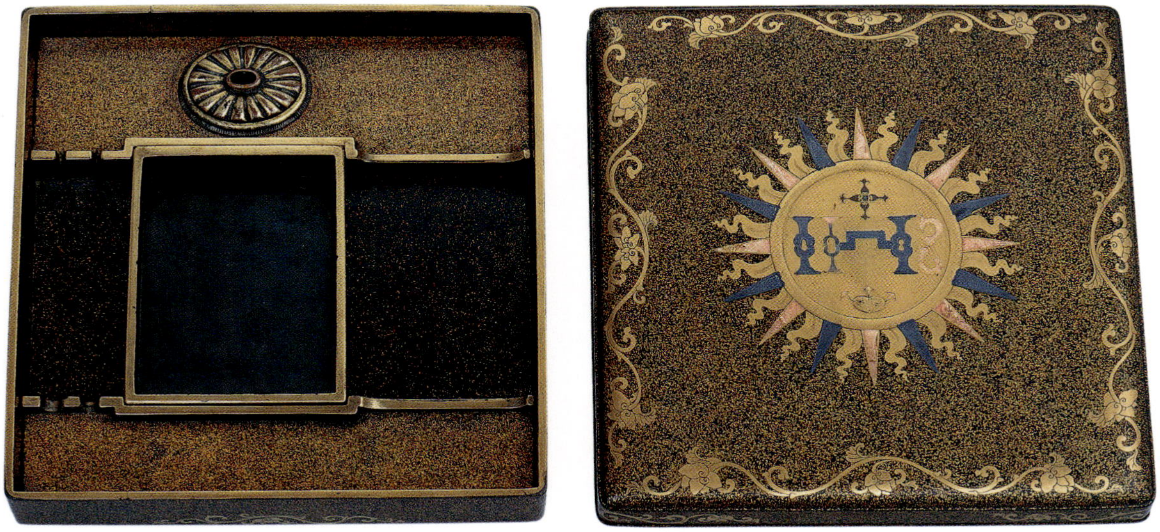

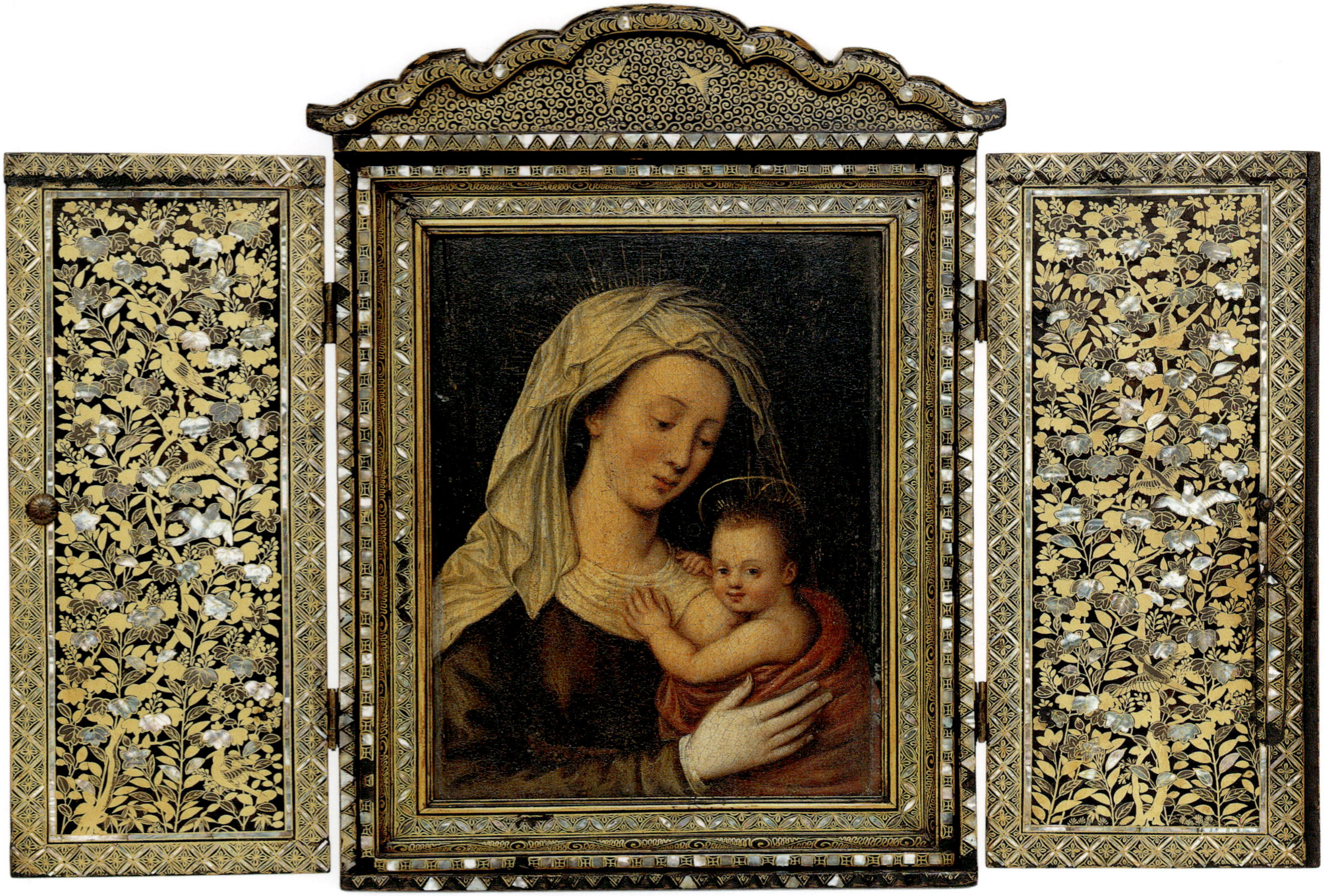

aimed at apostasy (plate 8.17). Despite a few pathetic Jesuit attempts to enter Japan in the early 1640s, the mission would now be Japanese in name alone, based at Macao and administering mostly to South-East Asia and Tibet.

It is an ironic tribute to the Seminary of Painters that the images produced by the academy became the focus of the persecutions of the Tokugawa *shōgunate*. In a famous ceremony initiated by the new regime in 1633, 'foot-treading pictures' (*fumi-e*), or Christian paintings and plaquettes, would be placed on the ground and the citizens of Nagasaki forced to walk upon them as a symbol of their abjuration of Christianity (plate 8.18). Like the iconoclasts of the Byzantine empire or Protestant northern Europe, the Nagasaki police were acknowledging the power of Christian devotional imagery in their desire literally to stamp it out. On the other hand, this same power inspired several groups of crypto-Christians in the islands west of Kyūshū to preserve and worship images, such as a Chinese figure of the *bodhisattva* Guanyin, throughout the era of persecutions until they were discovered by modern-day missionaries in the late nineteenth century (plate 8.2).[38]

Missionaries in China were received very differently from those working in Japan or South Asia. Although the Chinese tolerated their activities, they did so only if the missionaries adapted entirely to Chinese ways.[39] The same imperative went for the arts of the mission, which had to conform as much as possible to Chinese taste and traditions – at least officially. Yet at the same time, in the hope of gaining an export market advantage, non-Christian Chinese artists showed no hesitation whatever in copying

8.14
Portable altar with painting of the Virgin and Child

Altar: wood covered in black lacquer with gold *hiramakie* and mother-of-pearl inlay; painting: oil on panel
Japan, late 16th–early 17th century

Peabody Essex Museum, Salem

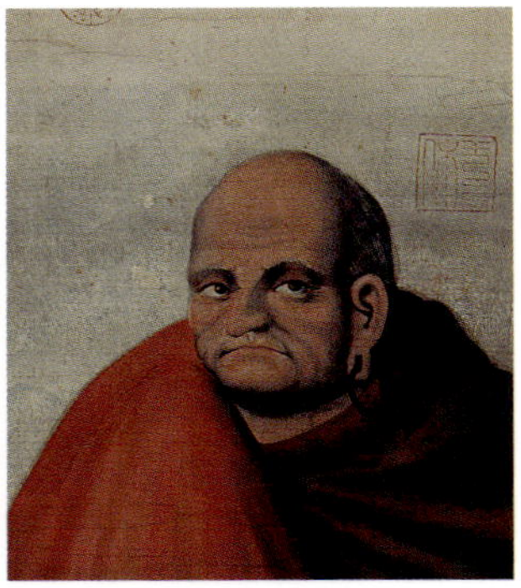

8.15
Daruma

Colours on paper
Japan, first half of 17th century

Namban Bunkakan, Osaka

Christian imagery in a western manner. In December 1561, long before the foundation of the first Catholic mission in China, a Portuguese nobleman wrote a letter from prison describing Chinese craftsmen busily working away on a whole series of Christian devotional paintings in the Flemish Renaissance style.[40] The letter first describes a 'very glorious' processional banner, which the Chinese artists painted 'just as in Flanders', of the sort used by Christian confraternities during parades and other public festivals. The Chinese banner featured the Madonna and Child seated on the globe of the world, with another image of the child Jesus surrounded by Seraphim below it. In the lower image, Jesus handed each of the angels a hat garnished with flower petals and lilies. Below that image the artists depicted a procession of boys from a Jesuit school, led by Francis Xavier's late companion Micer Paolo and an older man with a staff. The entire banner was painted in brilliant colours, presumably indigenous Chinese water-based pigments, against a brilliant gold background. The letter goes on to describe a brisk market in Chinese sculpted ivory crucifixes and paintings on canvas, including standard themes such as the Sacrifice of Abraham, the Nativity, the Three Magi, the Visitation of Saint Elizabeth and the Resurrection of Christ.

This Portuguese *hidalgo* (member of the lesser gentry) was one of the first Europeans to witness the extraordinary Chinese ability to imitate western products in the name of trade. The nobleman wrote with self-righteous disdain that Chinese craftsmen 'never lose an opportunity for profit, which is virtually their only aim', yet this scorn did not prevent his countrymen and their cohorts in the Spanish empire from purchasing thousands of Chinese-made Christian art objects over the next two centuries, to supply their Asian missions and delight their co-religionists in Latin America and Europe.[41] The anonymous Chinese craftsmen knew their market; already a scant four years after the foundation of the first permanent European settlement in China at Macao, Chinese artisans already had a highly sophisticated knowledge of the specific iconographic needs of these strange foreigners who worshipped 'a Barbarian executed in a humiliating fashion during the Han Dynasty', in the words of one anti-Christian Chinese writer.[42]

The southern Chinese produced the greatest volume of Christian ivory carvings for export. Their headquarters was in the province of Fujian on the south-east coast of China, especially the city of Zhangzhou, which was a mere eight days' sail from Manila. The Fujianese wasted no time in capitalizing on commerce with the Philippines' new Spanish overlords. In 1573, a mere two years after the Spanish had founded Manila, junks arrived from Fujian with cargoes of native goods including, according to one report, 'images of crucifixes and very curious seals made like ours [the Spaniards']'.[43] The Fujian craftsmen, and their equally skilled compatriots in Manila's Parián (Chinatown), relied on European models to produce their paintings and ivory sculptures, often adhering very closely to the originals. Nevertheless, they also allowed Chinese style, physiognomy and even iconography to blend with the imported forms. Although most of these pieces were made of ivory, some of them were executed in blanc-de-chine porcelain. The European models that inspired these pieces were almost exclusively engravings from Antwerp, by celebrated sixteenth-century printmakers such as the Wierix brothers or Phillip Galle, either on loose sheets or bound in books.

8.16
Western Scene with Musicians

Pair of six-panel screens; colours on paper
Japan, early 17th century

MOA Art Museum, Shizuoka

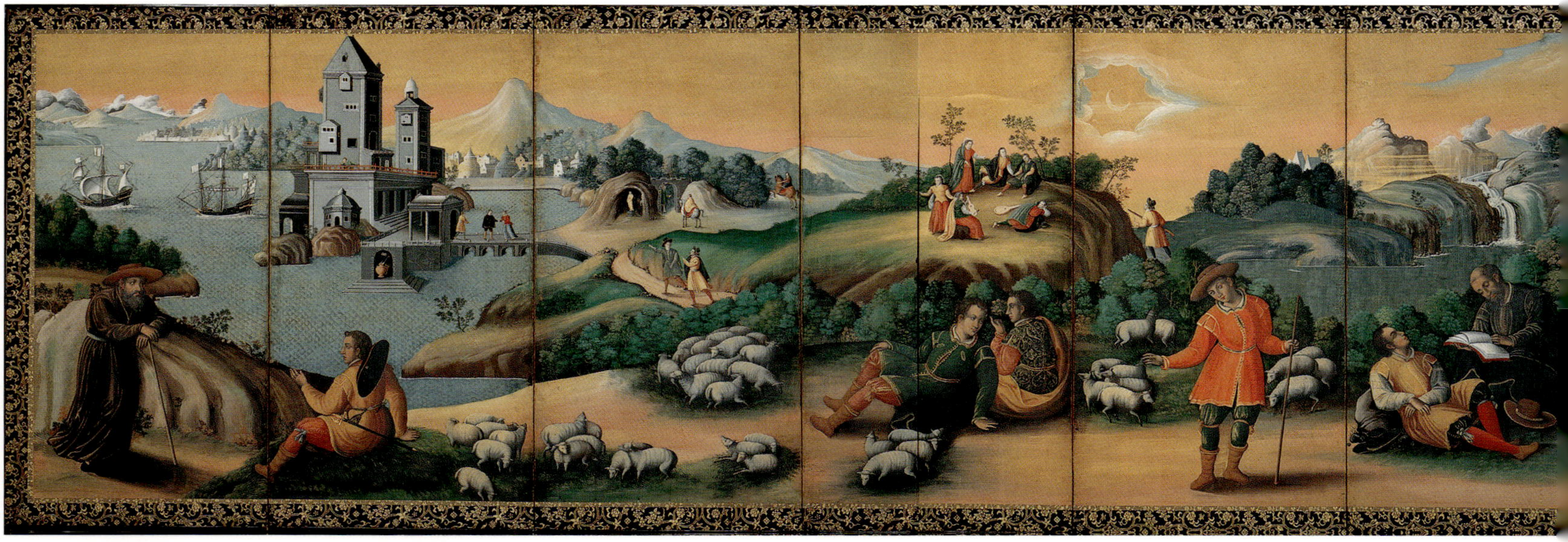

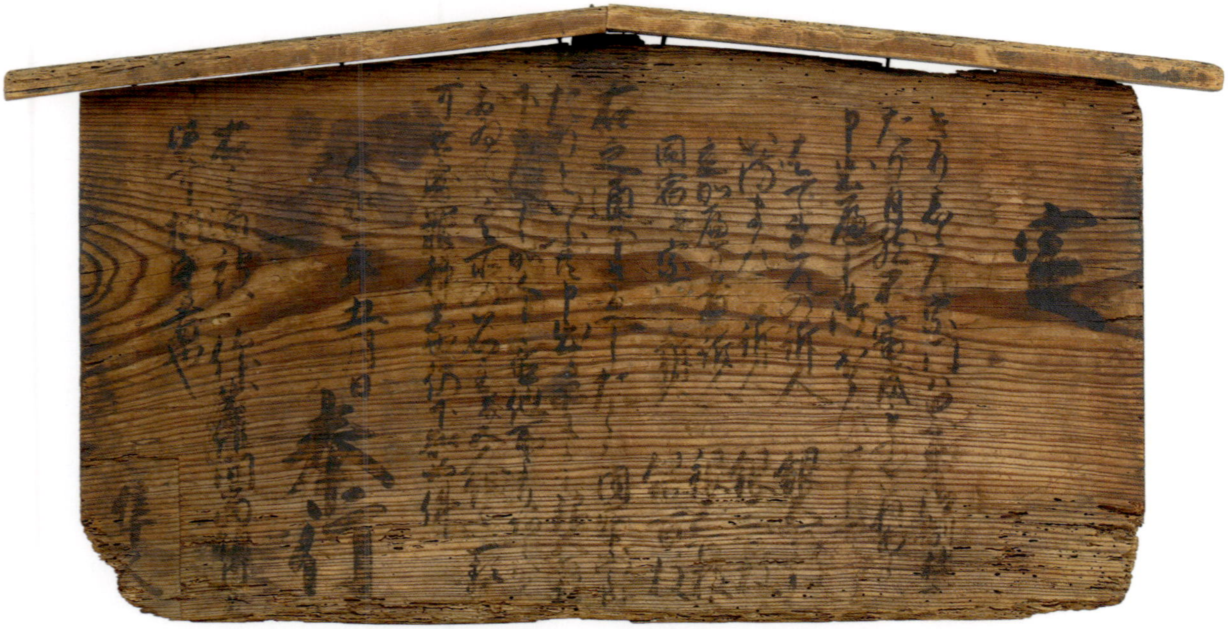

8.17
Edict prohibiting Christianity

Ink on wood
Japan, dated 1682

British Museum, London

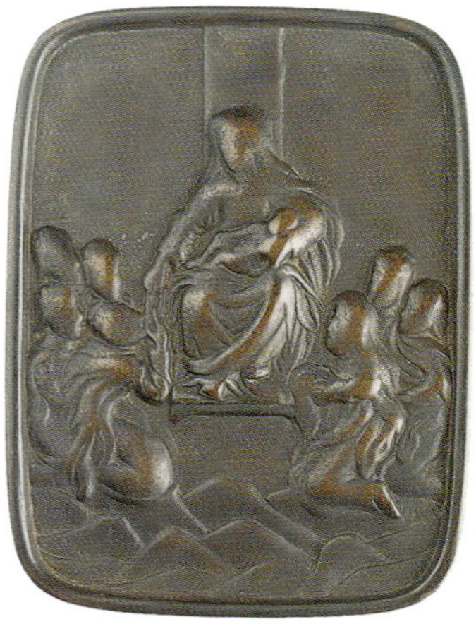

8.18
Fumi-e

Copper, cast
Japan, 17th–18th century

Ethnography Museum, Leiden

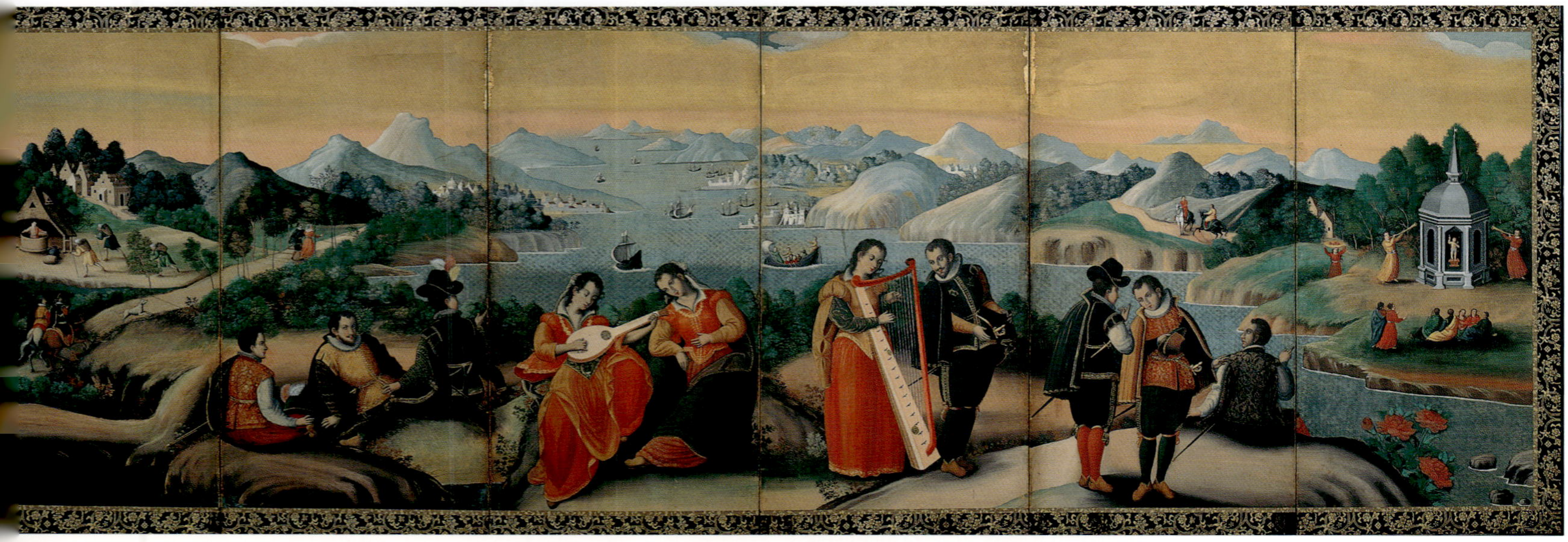

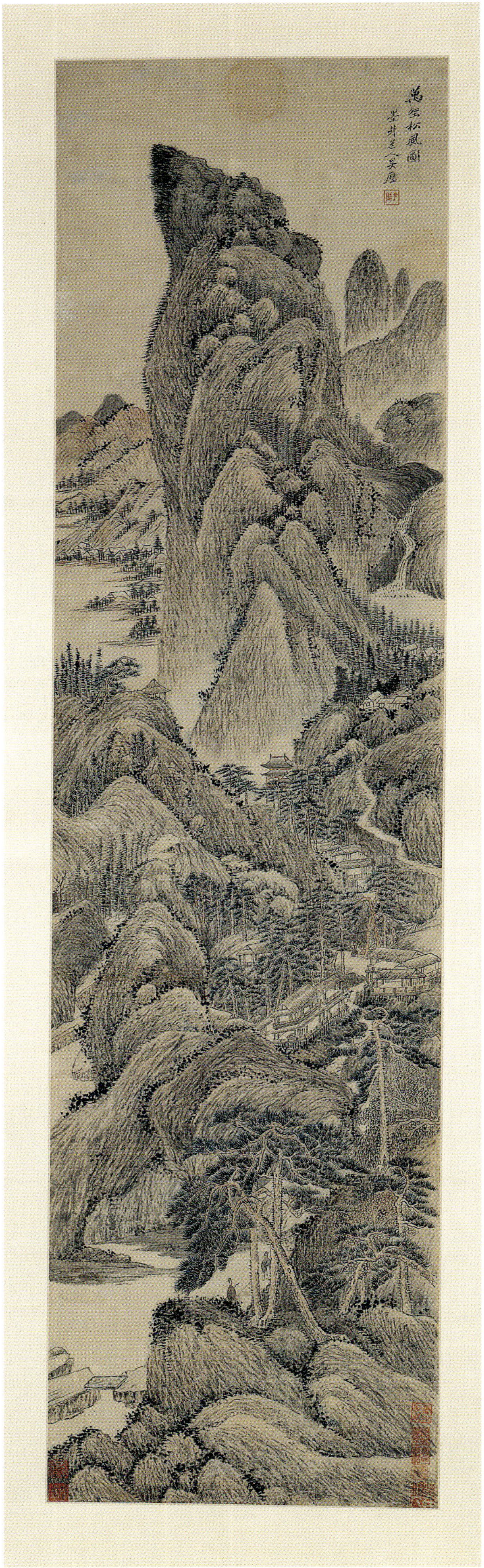

8.19
Pine Winds from Myriad Valleys
Wu Li

Hanging scroll; ink on paper
China, early 18th century

Cleveland Museum of Art, Cleveland

The first permanent Catholic mission on mainland China was established in 1580 by the Jesuits, who quickly learned that they could not use this same kind of overtly European art for their own proselytizing, at least at court and among intellectuals. The most famous early missionary was Matteo Ricci (1552–1610), an Italian polyglot and intellectual who not only acquired an astonishing command of classical Chinese language and Confucianist literature, but was himself a prolific author of philosophical, mathematical and scientific works.[44] Ricci and his followers won the respect of the Chinese literati and soon founded missions in southern China and along the coast, and in the imperial capital of Peking in 1601 (plate 8.20).

Nevertheless, Ricci did not show the same respect for Chinese art, and his attitude created serious setbacks for the mission's visual component. Like most Europeans of his time, Ricci believed in the superiority of western art and ignored Chinese painting traditions, a blunder considering how deeply imbedded painting was in the literary life of China. For the Chinese literati, poetry, calligraphy and painting went hand-in-hand as the 'three perfections' (*sanjue*), and most scholars dabbled in all three. Chinese painting was in consequence very calligraphic in style, and photographic realism was not privileged as it was in Europe. Instead of learning how to paint landscapes with a Chinese brush, Ricci sent letters to Rome asking for the finest Italian oil paintings, works that he hoped would dazzle the emperor and Chinese intellectuals with their naturalism. Instead, the Chinese literati saw them as skilful but superficial, something best classified as a craft. Even the Chinese Jesuit artist Wu Li (1632–1718), one of the most remarkable painters in the history of the Society of Jesus and the author of an entirely new genre of Chinese-Christian poetry,

8.20
Matteo Ricci, Adam Schall and Ferdinand Verbiest

From Jean Baptiste Du Halde's *Ausführliche Beschreibung des Chinesischen Reichs under der grossen Tartarey* [trans. from *Description geographique, historique, chronologique, politique et physique de l'empire de la Chine*'], Book 3, 1749
Engraving on paper

Staatsbibliothek, Berlin

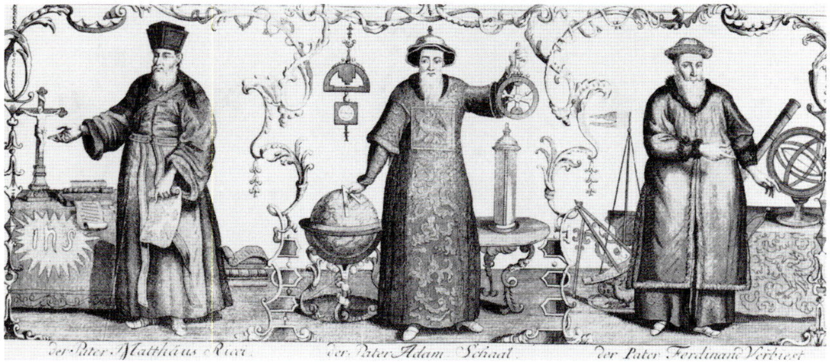

did not show any interest in European art and continued to paint in his literati tradition until his death (plate 8.19).[45]

Shortly before Ricci's death in 1610 the Jesuits quickly changed their policy and 'went native' in the visual arts, accommodating traditions of both the common people and the elite.[46] The popular classes, which made up the majority of converts, were more receptive to devotional art than the literati or court. Daoist and Buddhist artistic traditions endowed these people with a deep familiarity with figural imagery, especially in a domestic setting. As in Japan, Jesuit missionaries made extensive use of devotional pictures when they preached, and circulated copper images, medallions and rosaries to new converts. A few pieces of this more popularist mission art have survived, especially in ecclesiastical collections in Europe. A portable lacquered altar reminiscent of Catholic altar furniture made in Japanese lacquer workshops demonstrates an immediate tendency towards indigenization (plate 8.21). Similarly, a group of *cloisonné* Old Testament figures, although probably based on engravings, was made in a traditional Chinese technique using indigenous colours (plate 8.23). Such a blend of East and West also characterized devotional imagery and altar

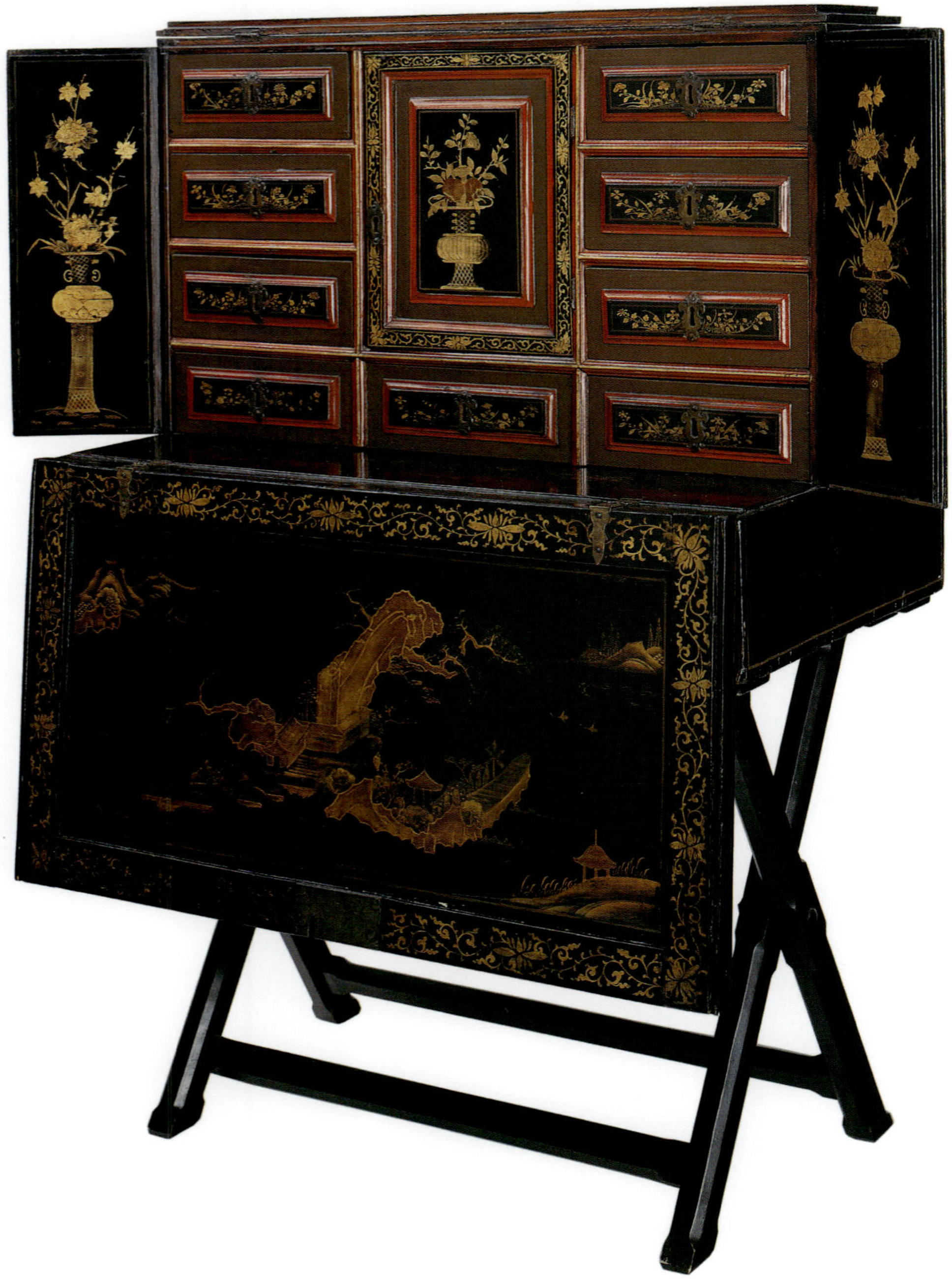

8.21
Portable altar on folding stand

Wood, covered in black lacquer with gold and red lacquer decoration
China, *c.*1700

Private collection, Porto

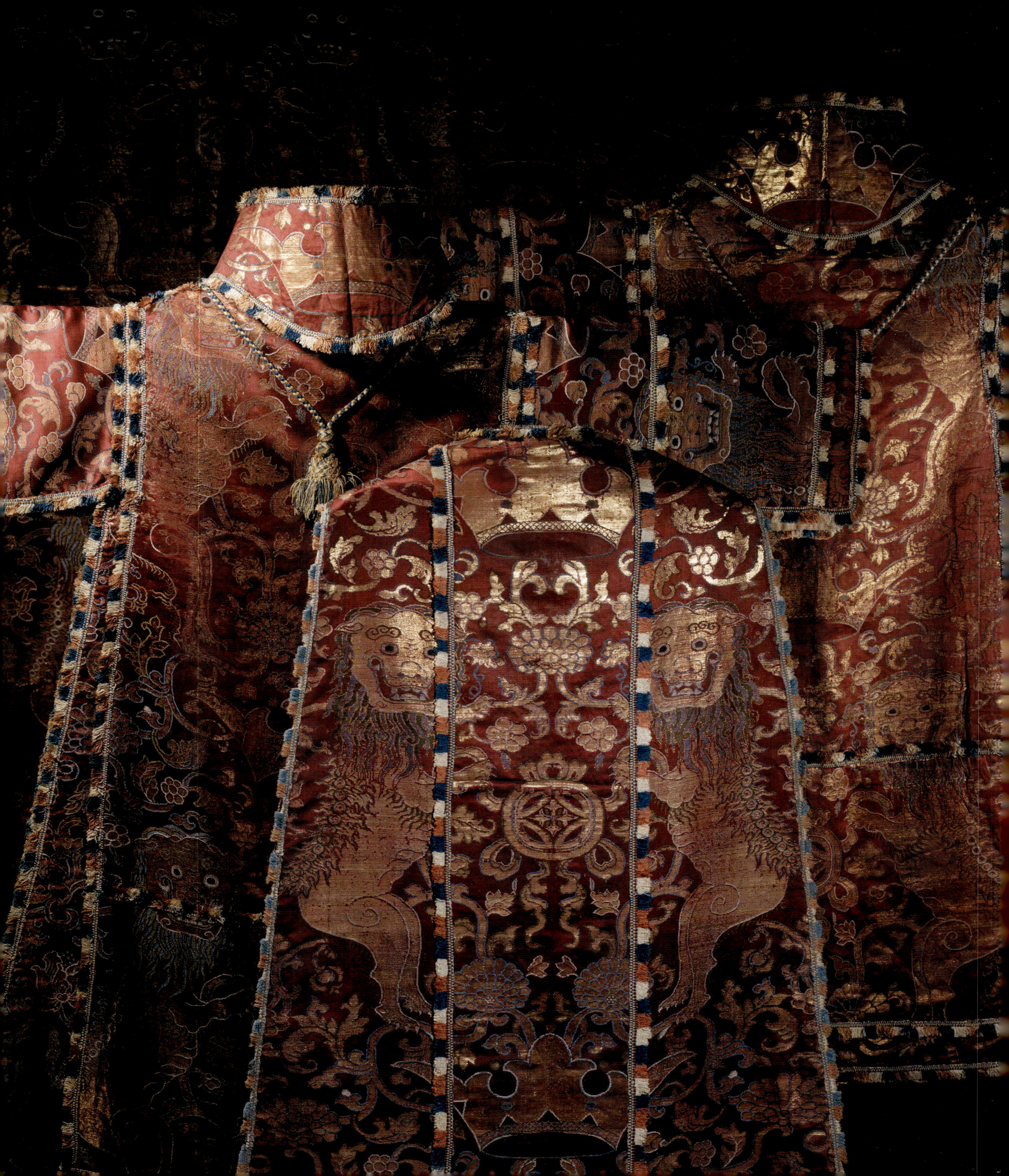

furnishings made in Macao, where painting and textile workshops produced objects for export. A vestment and baldachin probably made in Macao for the western market represents a fusion of Chinese and Euro-Christian sacred imagery. The textile is embroidered in brilliant Chinese colours and the central motifs, pairs of lions, derive from both East Asian iconographic traditions and western heraldry (plate 8.22).

While Sinicized Christian imagery was blossoming at a popular level, the Jesuits tried again to attract the literati, this time with more success. The medium of choice was the woodblock print, an indigenous Chinese printing method that predated that of Europe. Missionaries hired Chinese woodblock printers to carve Christian scenes taken from a Flemish gospel of 1593 by Jerónimo Nadal (1507–80), which were used to illustrate catechisms and Bible stories.[47] Such are the illustrations to a translation of Giulio Aleni's *Life of Christ* (*Tian zhu jiang sheng yan xing ji le*) from 1637 (plate 8.24). These pictures follow their Flemish models almost exactly in subject and composition, but translate virtually every line into its Chinese stylistic equivalent. The artist has removed most of the shading – some Chinese wrote that shading made pictures look 'dirty' – and rendered the images in an entirely calligraphic manner, like traditional Chinese painting. He has often substituted Chinese settings for the Flemish backgrounds of the original, and has even translated clouds and waves into Chinese decorative motifs. The Jesuits eagerly advertised any converts from among the literati, men like Michael Alphonsus Shen Fu Tsung (d. 1691), a young man from a prosperous family who joined the Jesuits in 1688 while on an epic voyage to Italy, France and England, where he helped catalogue Chinese texts at the Bodleian Library and sat for a portrait by the royal painter Sir Godfrey Kneller (1646–1723) (plate 8.25).

The most celebrated period of Jesuit artistic activity in China took place under the Qing dynasty in the first three-quarters of the eighteenth century. Ironically, this period bore little direct relation to Jesuit missionary aims. In an unexpected twist of fate, Jesuit artists and technicians from all over Europe spent years labouring for the Qing emperors as exalted domestic servants. The most famous of these court artists were Giuseppe Castiglione (1688–1766), Jean-Denis Attiret (1702–68) and Michel Benoist (1715–74) (see plate 23.12). The Kangxi emperor (r. 1662–1722) was the first to include Jesuits in his imperial craft workshops, and he and his successors Yongzheng (r. 1723–35) and Qianlong (r. 1736–95) pressed into service any missionaries with artistic

8.22
Vestments and baldachin
Brocaded silk
China (Macao), 1660–65
Peabody Essex Museum, Salem

The vestments were assembled in Europe, probably in Spain, where a European cotton fringe was added.

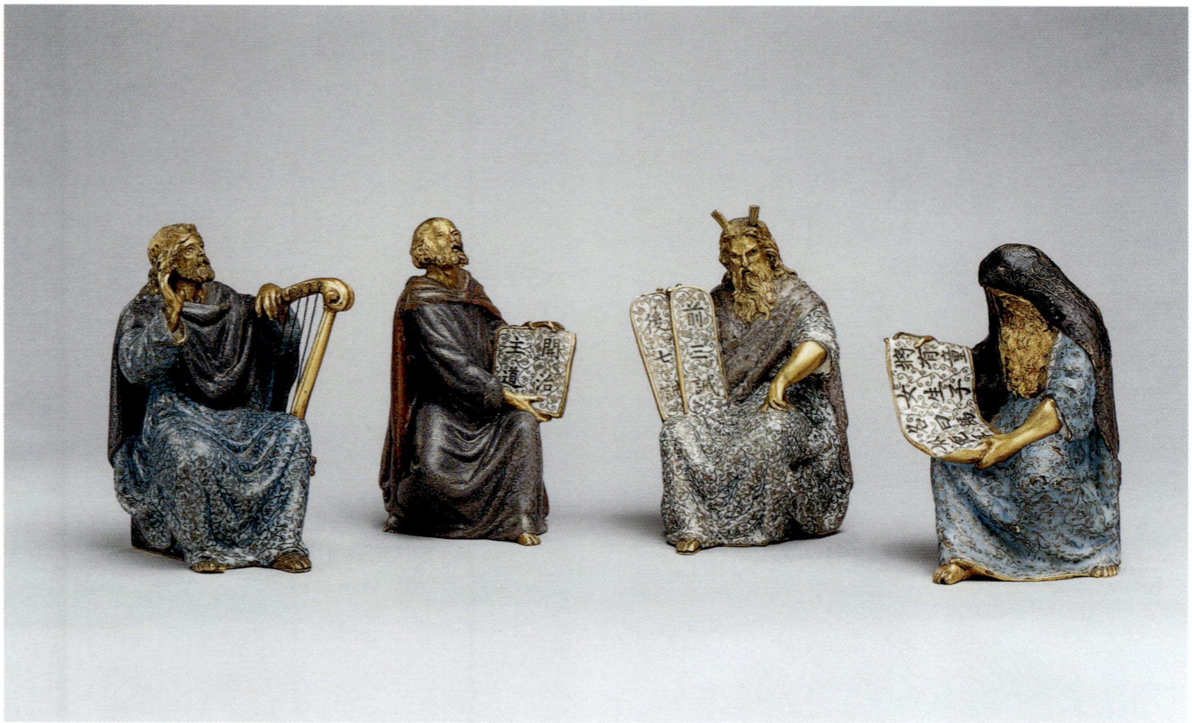

8.23
Figures of David, Young Isaiah, Moses, Old Isaiah
Cloisonné enamel
China, 18th century
Metropolitan Museum of Art, New York

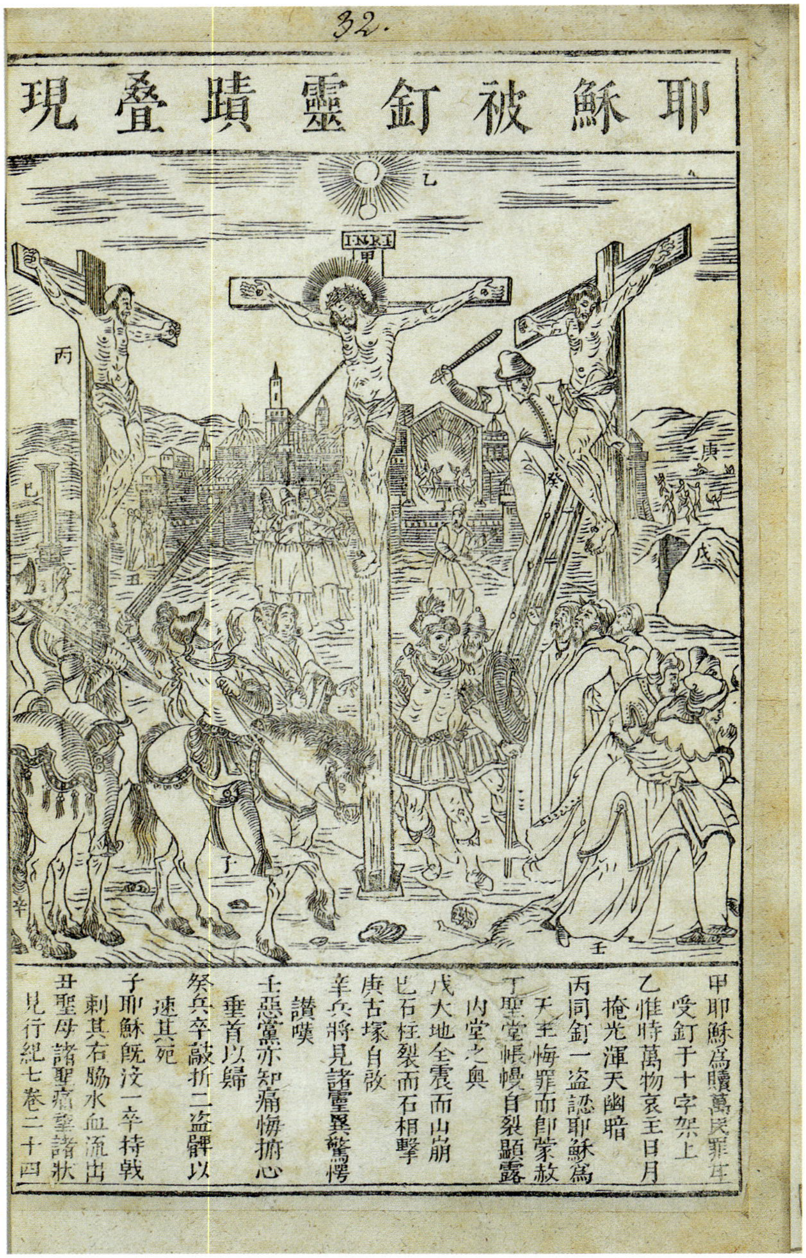

8.24
***Tian zhu jiang sheng yan xing ji le* (Brief Records of the Deeds of God who Became Man)**
Giulio Aleni

Woodblock print on paper
China (Fuzhou), 1637

V&A: NAL C.B.73

skills to produce novelties ranging from fountains and palace pavilions to painted portraits, enamelled metalwork, ceramic ornament and clocks (see chapter 23). The Jesuits only continued to serve under these conditions because their influence at court was essential for their now flourishing mission on Chinese soil. This episode is fascinating, because although the emperor was interested in enjoying the benefits of western artistic technology, he was not interested in European style. Everything had to be done within traditional Chinese parameters. Writing about Father Attiret, a French priest commented bluntly in 1769, 'it is necessary that he abandon his taste and his ideas in many aspects, so that he can accommodate to those of the country'.[48]

It was the pope, not the Chinese emperor, who destroyed the China mission. Due largely to political backstabbing from rival missionary groups, the pope censured Ricci's Confucianist brand of Christianity in 1742 in the conclusion to the infamous 'Chinese Rites Controversy'. Thanks largely to the efforts of the Dominicans, who had been working in China since the 1630s, Pope Benedict XIV (r. 1740–58) condemned the Jesuits' highly effective accommodations to Confucianism, including ancestor veneration and the use of terms like *tian* for 'Heaven' and *shangdi* for 'Supreme Lord'. However, by that time Christian imagery had already made an impact on the wider popular society of the time – and in a way that had nothing whatever to do with religion. Late Ming and early Qing society was increasingly becoming a 'culture of curiosity', ever more fascinated with exotica and foreign societies in a similar way to Europe's own fad for chinoiserie (see chapter 26).[49] In their small but significant way, by serving as a conduit for European art and science during an era when little reached China by other means, the Jesuits helped pave the way for this awareness, and left a legacy – albeit a secular one – to Chinese visual culture.

These cultural encounters throughout Asia not only provide a historical insight, but also offer important lessons about the nature of imagery. The Early Modern period was marked by a deep and lasting encounter between Europe and Asia, made more profound still by the work of Catholic missionaries. With them, Euro-Christian art forms spread around the world, threatening to destroy many of the artistic traditions of Asia. Yet the art that resulted from the missionary encounter was often deeply hybrid, with significant non-European ingredients, and it was frequently informed by traditions that were far from European, or even Christian, in origin. This missionary encounter demonstrates that art can serve as an international language and a way of bridging cultures. But art can also do the opposite, allowing two distinct and even contradictory meanings to coexist in a single image, revealing a cultural diversity which echoes that of the people who made it.

8.25
Michael Alphonsus Shen Fu Tsung
Sir Godfrey Kneller

Oil on canvas
England (London), 1687

The Royal Collection

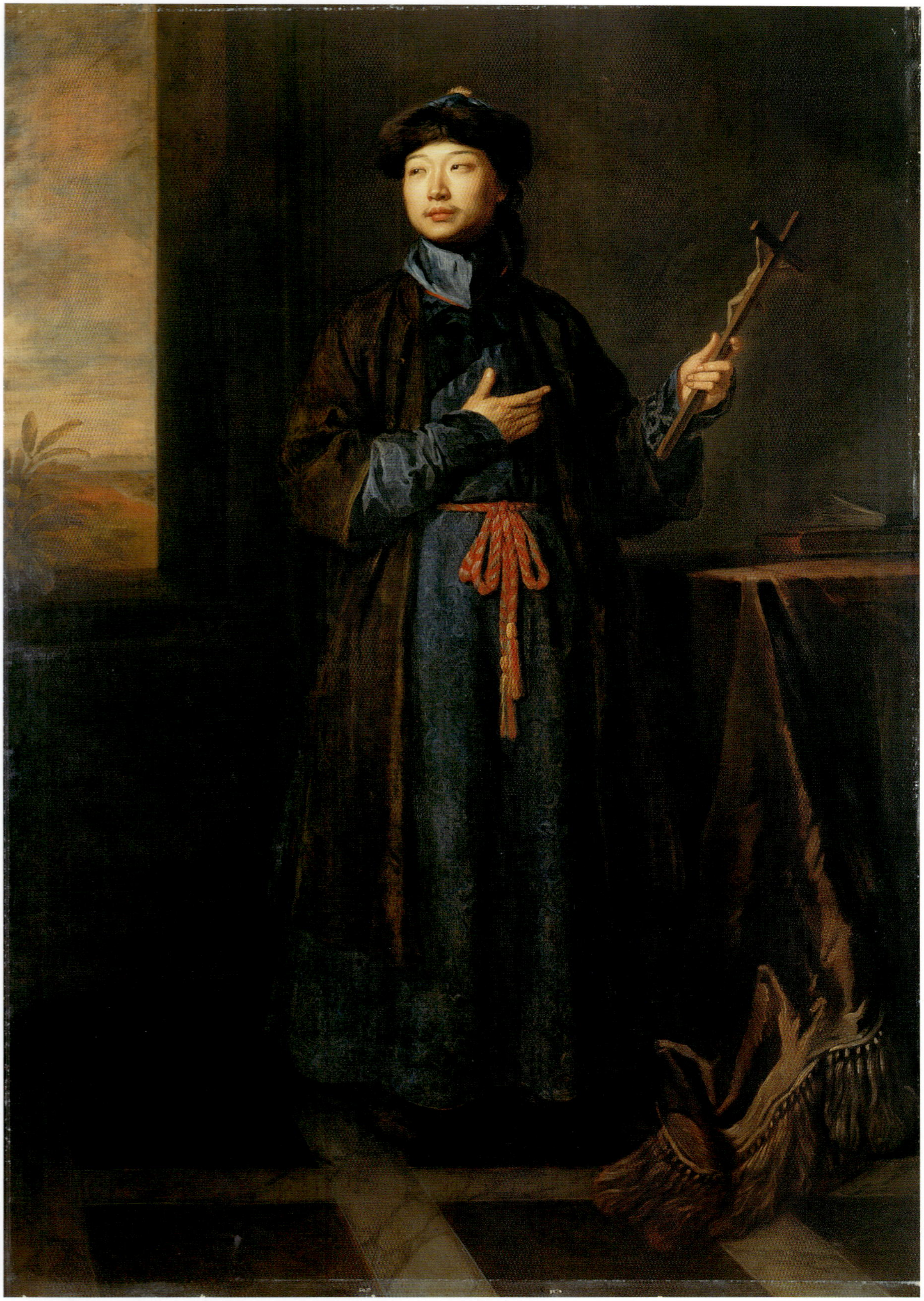

Hastings, Jones and the European Interest in Hindu Traditions

Nick Barnard

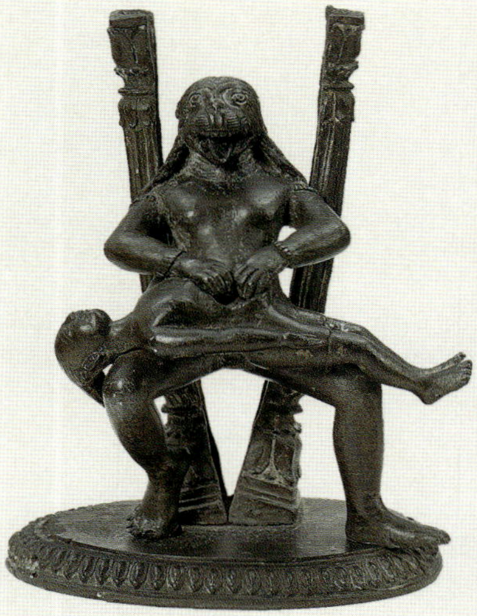

8.26
Narasimha, An Incarnation of the God Vishnu

Commissioned by Charles Wilkins; zinc, cast India (perhaps Varanasi), late 18th or early 19th century

V&A: 586(IS); given to the India Museum by Charles Wilkins

A drawing of this figure was published in Edward Moor's *The Hindo Pantheon.*

The late eighteenth century witnessed the rise of scholarly interest in India's ancient civilization. Warren Hastings (1732–1818), Governor-General of India from 1774 to 1785, recognized that the East India Company could rule more effectively by winning the sympathies of the populace than by governing by force alone. Hastings, who knew Bengali, Urdu and Persian, believed that to achieve this, a familiarity with local languages, customs and culture was essential. Under his influence a group of British scholars emerged in Bengal who were dedicated to exploring India's cultural heritage.

Believing that the judicial system should take account of Indian legal traditions as well as English law, Hastings persuaded Nathaniel Halhed (1751–1830) to translate Hindu legal writings into English. These were published in 1776 as *A Code of Gentoo Laws*. Halhed's Bengali grammar used a typeface for the Bengali alphabet created by Charles Wilkins (*c.* 1749–1836) and was perhaps the first book to be printed in a vernacular Indian language. Wilkins mastered Sanskrit, the courtly and religious language of ancient India, then known to few outside India's priestly class. Hastings, with rapturous praise for the work, persuaded the East India Company to finance the publication of Wilkins's translation of the *Bhagavad Gita*, rendering this Hindu classic into English for the first time.

The arrival of Sir William Jones (1746–94) in India in 1783 as a high-court judge in Calcutta was to revolutionize Indian studies (plate 8.27). He founded the Asiatic Society of Bengal, creating a forum for research, and contributed many papers on diverse subjects to the society's journal, *Asiatick Researches*. A talented linguist, Jones had mastered Persian and Arabic at Oxford and started learning Sanskrit in 1785. After a few months of study he realized that the language was related to Latin and Greek, and more distantly to Germanic and Celtic languages. His 1786 treatise on the subject established the existence of an Indo-European family of languages. His translation of the drama *Shakuntala* by Kālidasā, whom he called the Indian Shakespeare, revealed the glories of Sanskrit literature to the West. It was much acclaimed in Europe and inspired Goethe (1749–1832) and other founders of the

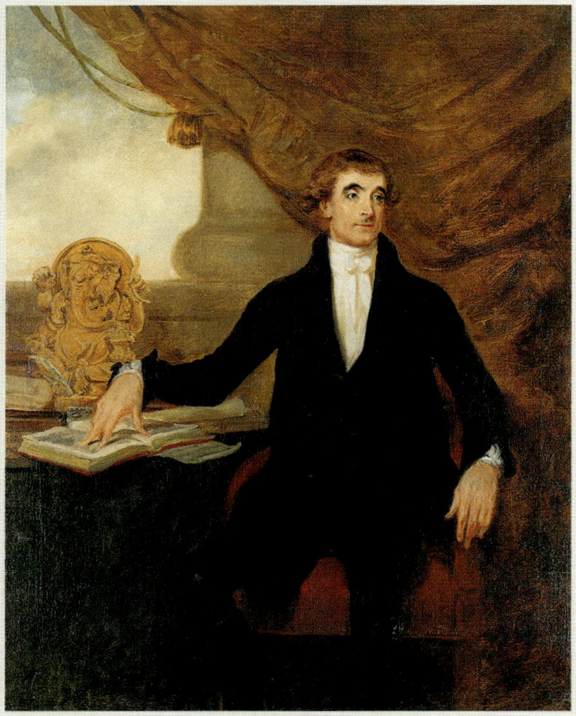

8.27
Sir William Jones
Arthur William Devis

Oil on canvas
India (Calcutta), *c.* 1793

British Library, London

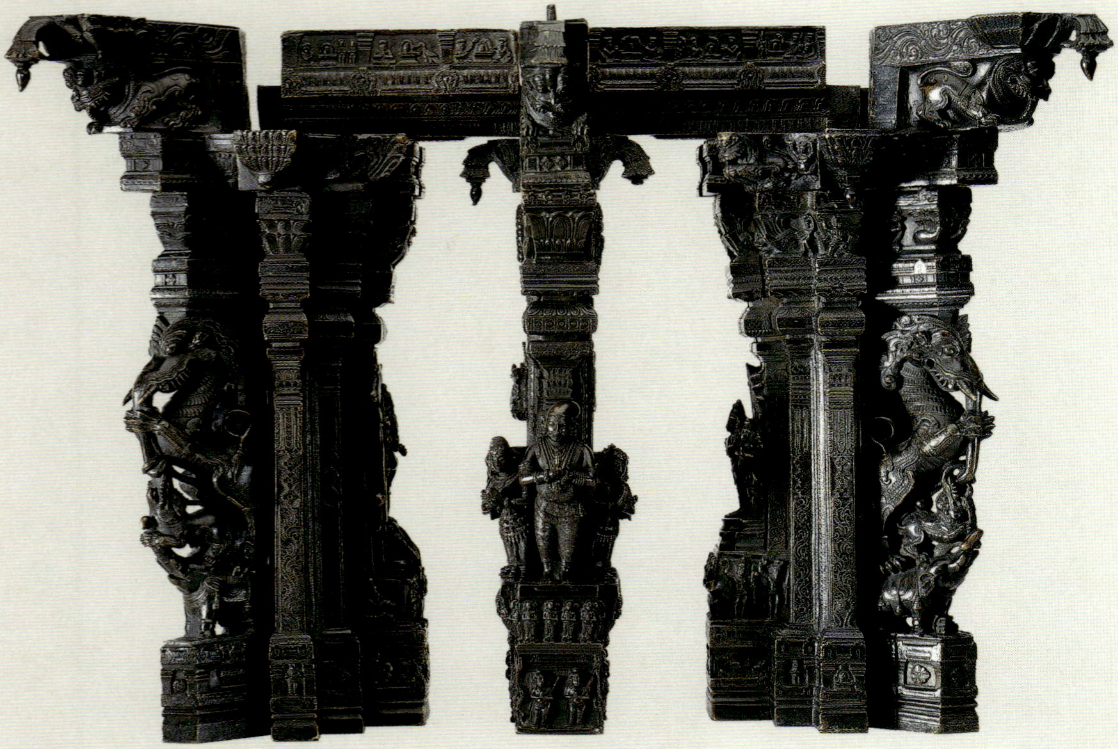

8.28
Model of Pillars in Tirumala Nāyak's Pudu Mandapa

From the Minakshi-Sundareshvara temple, Madurai, commissioned by Adam Blackader; copper alloy
India (Madurai), 1780–89

V&A: 98-98D–1870; given by J Heywood Hawkins

8.29
The Ten Incarnations of Vishnu

Inscribed in English in the top left-hand corner: 'The incarnations of Vishnu. Presented to the R. Asiatic Society 1st December 1828 by Wm Marsden'; watercolour and gold on paper
India (Andhra Pradesh), c.1771 or 1779

V&A: IM.561–1924; given by the Royal Asiatic Society of London

William Marsden probably obtained this scroll on his way to or from Sumatra, where he served as an East India Company writer between 1771 and 1779. It is likely to have been made for him personally.

Romantic movement in Germany. Jones also made important contributions to the study of Indian music and ancient history, establishing its first known date.

Another esteemed Sanskrit scholar, Henry Colebrooke (1765–1836), shed light on current religious practices by studying ancient texts. He published essays on widowhood in Indian society, the caste system and religious ceremonies, as well as on the *Vedas*, which include the most ancient scriptures of Hinduism. Outside Bengal, others were at work. Adam Blackader (*fl.* 1780s), a surgeon in Madurai, commissioned scale drawings and a bronze model of sculpted pillars in a hall at the Minakshi-Sundareshvara Hindu temple (plate 8.28). These were presented before the Society of Antiquaries in London in 1789. From 1796 Colin MacKenzie (1754–1821), an army surveyor, began to amass a vast collection of south Indian manuscripts, inscriptions, images and coins. His essays included possibly the first European account of the Jain religion, revealing to western scholars its separate identity from Buddhism. Meanwhile Edward Moor (1771–1848) was compiling material for his book *The Hindu Pantheon* (1810), the first serious attempt to describe and explain the iconography of Hindu deities to Europeans (plate 8.26).

In this period much was achieved and many branches of Indian history and religion were established as subjects worthy of study. Many of the scholars responsible for this work, known as 'Orientalists', were servants of the East India Company, and their motivations and the effects of their work have been much debated. Nonetheless, in their pioneering admiration for the culture and religion of India they did much to discover and reveal to the West something of the country's rich history and heritage (plate 8.29).

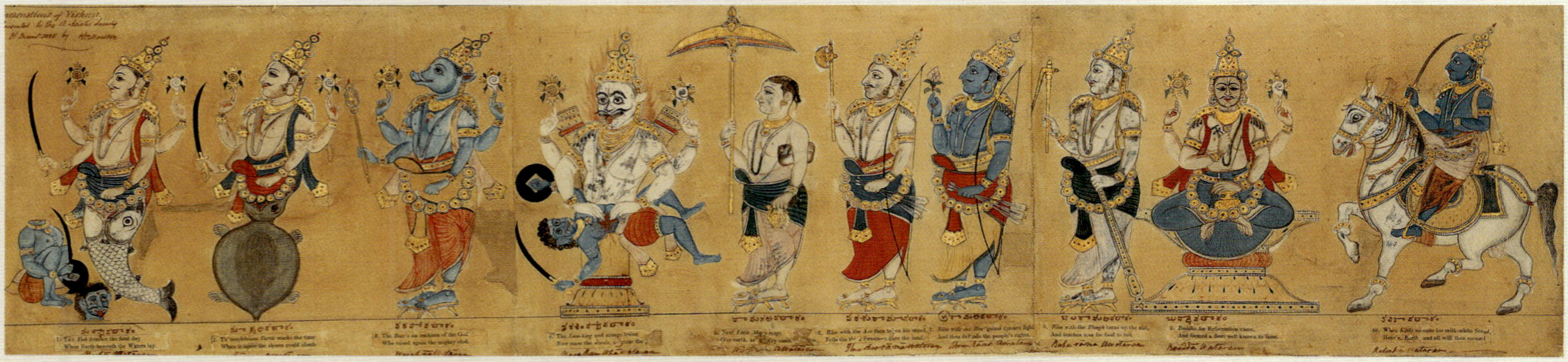

9

PORTUGUESE SETTLEMENTS AND TRADING CENTRES

Paulo Varela Gomes

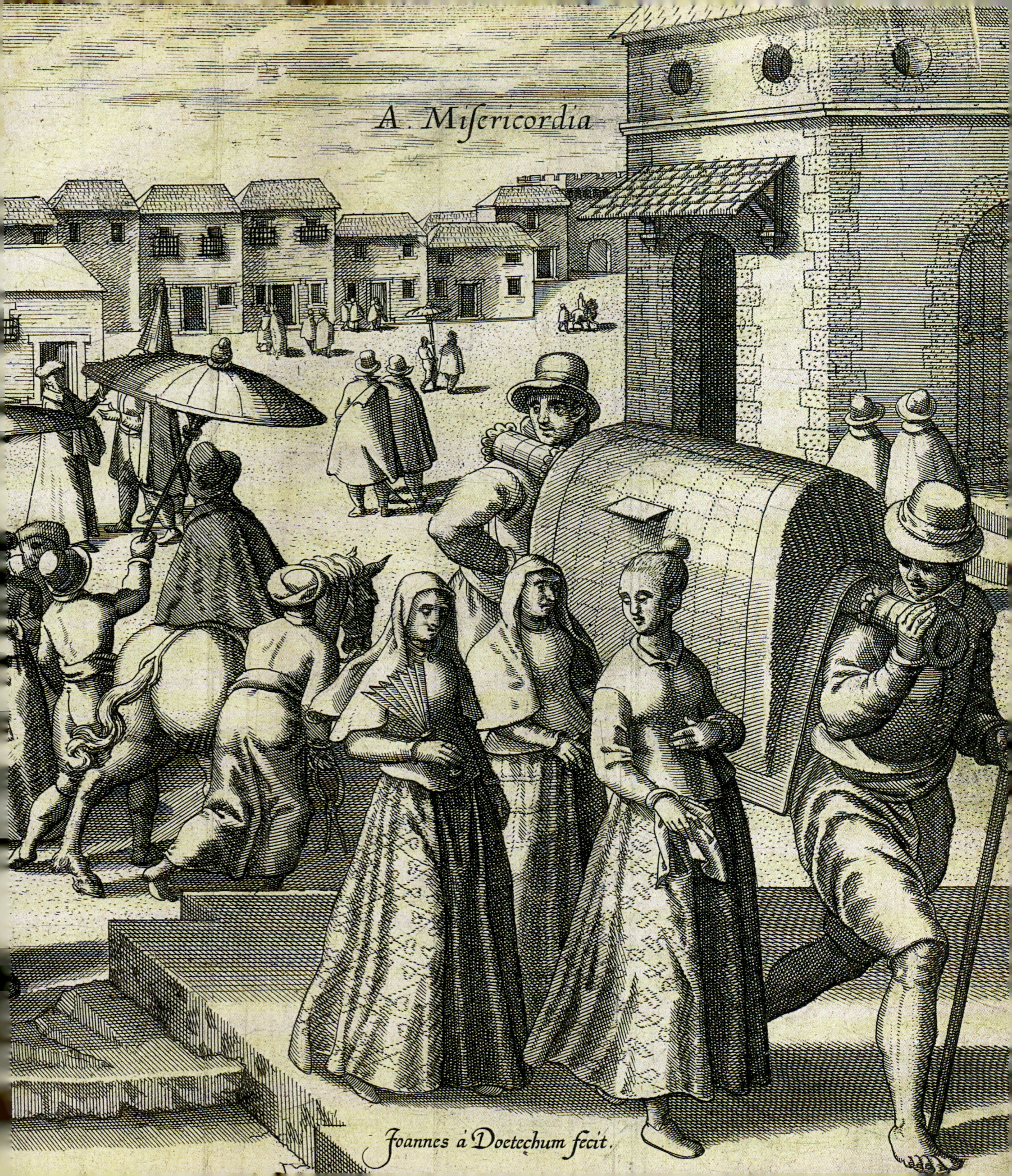
A. Misericordia
Joannes à Doetechum fecit.

Detail of 9.3 previous page

By the end of the sixteenth century the Portuguese controlled a network of more than 100 trading posts and settlements along the coast of Asia. At the centre was Goa, on the Konkan coast of India, the largest European-ruled city in Asia. Goa was part of a territorial enclave some 96 kilometres long by 23 kilometres wide, which was substantially enlarged during the second half of the eighteenth century. The Portuguese also dominated two other territorial settlements: the so-called Northern Province of India, a strip 320 kilometres long between present-day Revdanda (south of Bombay) and Daman; and the lowlands of Ceylon (Sri Lanka), an area comprising about one-third of the island.

However, at first the *Estado da Índia* ('State of India') – as the Portuguese possessions in Asia and eastern Africa were known – was primarily a network of small towns and forts. From Cochin (Kochi; in Portuguese Cochim), Cananor (Konnur), Onor (Honawar) and other places along the Malabar coast of India the Portuguese collected spices, mainly pepper, celebrated as 'the light of our eyes' by Gaspar Correa, a chronicler of the 1540s.[1] Most of the settlements, like Cochin, were fortresses ceded by local rulers with Portuguese towns built around them. Others, like Malacca on the western coast of the Malay peninsula, were the result of outright conquest. There were also settlements governed by the Portuguese under the close surveillance of powerful Asian rulers: Macao on the south China coast was a 'republic of merchants' under its Portuguese town Senate and submitted to the 'realpolitik' of Chinese authorities.[2] This essay begins by looking at some of the ways in which Asian urban forms were perceived by the Europeans and how those perceptions related to Portuguese town planning and building in Asia. Four Portuguese settlements are examined in this light: Diu, Cochin, Malacca and Macao. The issue of the progressive miscegenation of architectural forms in Portuguese Asian collective spaces is then examined to ascertain whether Asian streetscapes were really perceived as Asian.

In his second *Década da Ásia* (1553), the historian João de Barros (1496–1570) described the arrival at Diu in 1509 of the first Portuguese fleet to sail that far north along the coast of India. Diu is a small town located on an island off the coast of Gujarat at the entrance of the Gulf of Cambay. According to Barros, when the Portuguese first saw Diu, they 'longed for the fatherland of which they were reminded by the towers and the beauty of the buildings in the Iberian manner such as they had never seen before in the Malabar Coast ...'[3] Later in his book Barros wrote about Malacca, at the other end of the Portuguese Indian Ocean world. The impression he conveyed was totally different: 'Our people [...] did not encounter walls, towers, majestic whitewashed stone buildings, or any other fortification and beauty of the towns of Iberia [...] The city was almost all made of timber and the houses were covered with palm leaves in the manner of those parts ...'[4] Barros was never in Asia, but the stories he heard about the arrival of the Portuguese at Diu and Malacca would have made perfect sense to him; he knew very well the cities and buildings 'in the manner of Iberia' (*Hespanha*) and especially the Moorish or *Mudejar* architectural features admired by the Portuguese in North Africa or at Sintra, Seville and Cordoba. Diu was (and still is) a walled town of northern Indian type, which is quite different from Malacca or the towns of Malabar. The terms of comparison, the features by which the Portuguese evaluated the monumentality or the beauty of towns, are quite clear in Barros's text. The existence of stone houses is the first thing the Portuguese remarked upon, and the first thing they missed, along the Indian coast where stone and tiled buildings were considered appropriate only for temples and royal households.[5] The Mediterranean types of urban plans and streetscapes were also a key distinguishing factor between what the Europeans liked in Asia and what they did not. The French traveller Pyrard de Laval (*c.*1570–1621), who visited Malabar between 1601 and 1610, was disappointed with the Hindu town of Calicut (Khozikhod): 'The houses are not laid out in order, nor aligned along streets like in Europe, but dispersed here and there.'[6] By contrast, the streetscapes of Chinese towns were enthusiastically praised by sixteenth-century European chroniclers who perceived them as a consequence of the right kind of governance. The Dominican Gaspar da Cruz in his 'Treaty of the Things of China' (1569) wrote many pages about the beauty of Chinese cities, in which he especially liked stone construction and straight streets.[7]

The regularity of the urban layout (which only very seldom meant orthogonality) was something the Portuguese sought to achieve in their newly built Asian settlements through state authority and the activity of military engineers and architects. When the state was not present, as in Macao, spontaneous towns were built. A simple factory was established in

Macao in 1557 as a stop-over in the trade route between Malacca and Japan. The Chinese closely monitored this very rare concession of theirs and collected taxes on both factory and passing ships. In 1575 they built a wall in the isthmus separating the conceded territory from mainland China, but they never allowed the Portuguese to build a complete wall of their own around the whole of the town perimeter.

Macao's urban layout was established by the private initiative of Portuguese merchants – who ruled the factory through the town Senate. Viceregal authority was limited to the brief sojourns in town of the captain of the China and Japan route. This is probably why a source of 1623 described Macao as 'too spread out' because 'each person builds in his own way, without any respect for the common good'.[8] In 1623 the viceroy of the *Estado da Índia* appointed a resident governor, and only afterwards did the town acquire modern European urban features, such as forts protecting some areas of the harbour against Dutch incursions from the sea, large churches and convents which, as in the Jesuits' S. Paulo, dominated the townscape by its elevated location and large frontal staircase.

The first modern colonial town in Asia was lower Cochin on the Malabar coast.[9] The Italian traveller Pietro della Valle (1586–1652) observed in the 1620s that 'in almost all territories of India near the sea-coast there happen to be two places of the same name, one called the higher, or inland, belonging to the natives, the other the lower, near the sea, to the Portugals'.[10] This was the situation in Cochin, the key pepper trading centre, where in 1503 the Portuguese were authorized to build a fort by the local raja. A couple of decades later there was a town extending from the fort to upper or higher Cochin (modern-day Mattancherry), where the Hindu and Muslim communities lived. As in most Malabar Portuguese settlements, the Christian town had a fort by the sea, protecting the harbour, where the governor lived. Outside the fort, there were the streets and houses of the *casados* (Portuguese settlers, mostly married to Asian women) and the Indian Christian community. This city had some broad and almost straight streets, more or less regular squares in front of churches, rectangular-shaped blocks of houses each with its own small garden and orchard (*quintal*).[11]

This type of settlement never really existed in Diu in spite of Portuguese efforts to implement it. Diu is an island some 24 kilometres long, separated from the Gujarati mainland by a canal and a harbour. The Asian fortress that stood at the island's eastern tip was ceded to the Portuguese in 1535. It was subsequently enlarged and modified until it became the most spectacular European fortified site in South Asia. The Gujarati town extended from the fortress to a long 'sea-to-sea' wall, as the Portuguese sources put it, which separated urban Diu from the rest of the island. The Portuguese established a little town inside the fortress, which eventually housed 600 men of arms, many with their families, and created a defensive *non aedificandi* area in the immediate vicinity of the bastions by demolishing all buildings there. The rest, the town close to the sea-to-sea wall, they hardly touched. Portuguese plans or surveys rarely tried to accurately represent its intricate pattern of streets, courtyards and alleys. Most plans, even those designed by such precision experts as the military engineers, represent this area as an abstract maze. It is as if this part of Diu was not important for the Europeans (plate 9.1).

As indeed it was not. From the sixteenth to the twentieth centuries there were several attempts to attract European and Asian Catholic families to Diu. The idea was to build a settlement for Catholics between the fortress and the Asian town. In the second half of the sixteenth century the religious orders – Jesuits, Franciscans and Dominicans – established their churches and convents between fort and town, but away from the *non aedificandi* area. In the late eighteenth century a modern port and

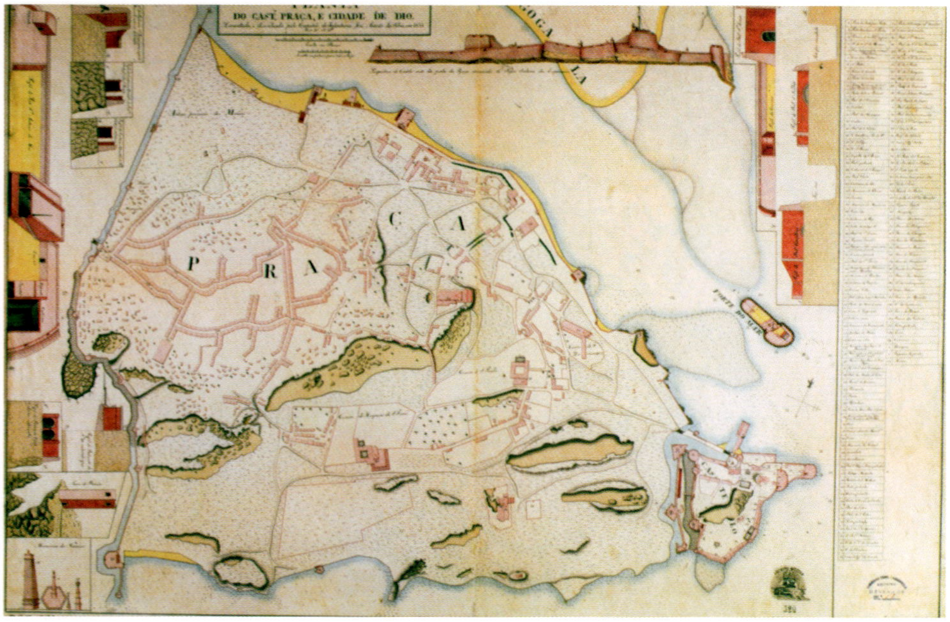

9.1
Planta do Castelo, Praça e Cidade de Diu
José Aniceto da Silva

Watercolour and ink on paper
India (Diu), 1833

Gabinete de Estudos de Arqueologia e Engenharia Militar, Lisbon

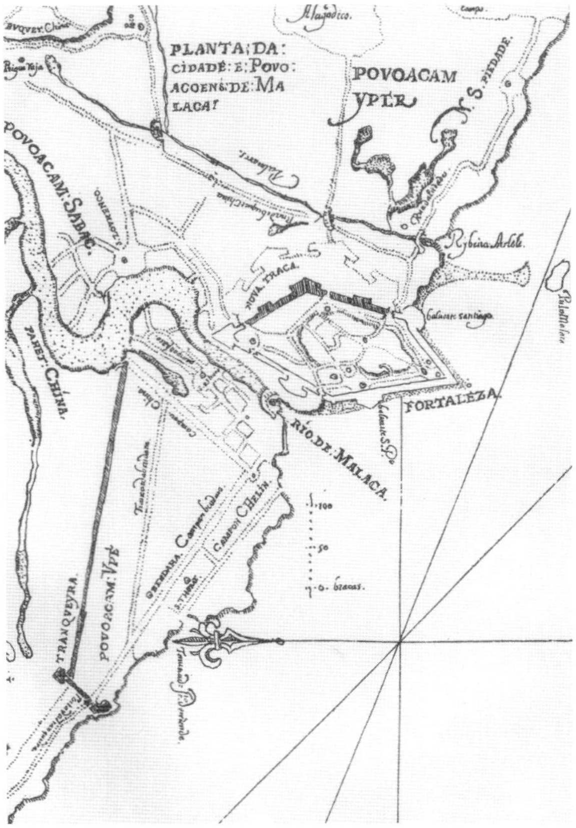

9.2
Plan of Malacca

From Manuel Godinho de Erédia, *Lyvro das Plantaformas das Fortalezas da India*, c.1630
Ink on paper
India (Goa), 1613

Biblioteca do Forte de S. Julião da Barra, Oeiras

market square were built, and later a large straight street and a governor's palace.[12] Yet all attempts to develop the town failed. The growing importance of Surat and, later, Bombay, deprived Diu of its military and economic relevance as the gateway to the Gulf of Cambay. The island survived on its own agricultural and fishing resources and the local trade of Gujarati and Parsi merchants. In spite of the presence of the churches, the *ferenghi wadi* (the foreigners' quarter), as it is still known, inhabited by Gujarati Catholics, was never really anything other than what one sees today: silent monumental buildings partly in ruins, some quiet streets and a handful of houses.

Malacca was much richer than Diu, much bigger and much more diversified in community terms. It was the centre of all trade from Ceylon to Japan, re-exporting Indonesian spices to China and the Bay of Bengal, sending cotton textiles from India to the Indonesian archipelagos, collecting and redistributing Chinese porcelain and copper, and paying for Chinese merchandise in South American, Japanese and Indian silver. The presence of the Portuguese in Malacca lasted from 1511 to the Dutch conquest in 1641. The city was represented in a series of plans dated 1613 (plate 9.2).[13] In Malacca, as in Diu, the Portuguese town was inside the fortress. The plans show that before 1613 a part of the Asian town to the north-east of the fortress underwent an urban planning operation consisting of the erection of a bastionated wall and the opening of straight streets connecting the *kampongs* of two Asian communities: the Chinese and the *Quelins* (Kelings, the Coromandel Tamil merchants), the latter under the authority of their community leader, the *Bendara* (or Bendahara) who acted as a political go-between with the Portuguese governor. This walled town, known as Upeh, and the Chinese quarter undoubtedly had Catholic communities, judging by the presence of churches. Other churches in the Malaysian towns of Yrer (Hilir) and Sabac also represent the conversion efforts of the religious orders. Malacca had about 7,500 Christians in an overall population of around 100,00 people.[14] At the end of the sixteenth century, 600 *casados* lived in the Portuguese town, which had its institutional urban landmarks: the governor's house, the fortified tower with the Europeans' jail, several parish and religious orders' churches and, in common with Portuguese practice in all parts of Asia, three hospitals: the Royal Hospital for the *soldados* (the European soldiers), the Misericórdia for the *casados* and the nobles, and the poor people's hospital (for European and Asian poor). In his famous description of the Royal Hospital in Goa, which he praised as the 'best in the world' because of the quality of its internal organization, cleanliness and efficiency, Pyrard de Laval wrote that it was for 'white people' only, primarily soldiers. But not for all white people: the aristocrats went to the Misericórdia hospital, while the poor civilians – together with the *cristãos novos* (descendants of Jews) and the Christian natives – had a third hospital.[15]

Apart from the hospital in Goa, Pyrard de Laval showed real appreciation of only one other urban feature of Portuguese Asian settlements: streetscapes. The streetscape of Catholic quarters in Asian towns became such a trademark of Portuguese settlements that all European visitors praised their familiar tiled roofs and whitewashed façades. As recently as 1998 the historian K. Chaudhuri, writing about the Gujarati town of Cambay where there was a Portuguese settlement by the end of the sixteenth century, referred to houses 'in the Iberian style' and mentioned the 'obsessive feeling of being in a true Portuguese town'.[16] Pyrard praised the houses of Goa because they were whitewashed and tiled, had a *quintal* behind them and beautiful window panes made of *carepas* – seashells polished to transparency.[17] In 1535 there were already specialized workers in the fabrication and transport of tiles in Goa.[18] In the account of his experiences in Asia in 1583–88 the Dutch traveller Jan Huyghen van Linschoten (1563–1611) illustrated the houses of Goa's *Rua Direita* (main street) as two floored tiled buildings with balconies on the first-floor windows (plate 9.3). These houses were not of northern European type, which is probably why Linschoten represented them so conspicuously. The ethnic variety of people he paraded in front of the houses added to the 'Asian' flavour that made Linschoten's book such a success in Europe.

However, Goa's streets, and more generally the collective spaces of Indo-Portuguese towns, were the stage for constant acts of westernization. Pietro della Valle took part in the feast of the canonization of the Jesuits St Ignatius and St Francis Xavier in 1624, recording that the Goan streets were taken by a 'cavalcade of three squadrons of [Jesuit] collegians representing the Asiatics, Africans and Europeans'. However, the 'Asiatics' were not there as themselves, but as representations of themselves according to the European *topoi*: turbaned, with lavishly arrayed horses.[19] There was a chariot representing European mythology in the shape of Mount Parnassus with Apollo and the Muses, and there were pyramids with Indian participants dressed as – well, as Indians. 'I believe there is no city in the world where there are more processions than in Goa,' concluded della Valle.[20]

The desire of the Portuguese lay and religious authorities to communicate with Asian populations took a while to materialize in the adoption of local architectural features and styles. The Euro-Asian characteristics of Christian and Hindu architecture in the *Estado da Índia* has been much debated.[21] Most writers agree that initially the Portuguese adopted an Asian pattern of life and Asian decorative styles within the home. Linschoten wrote many pages about the way in which the Portuguese and Catholic Indians inhabited their houses. He described the interiors as not furnished in the European way, and he was very interested in the Portuguese women who lived in those houses and who, according to him, behaved like Asians: they 'chew *betele* [*pan*], have bath, use incense and sandalwood perfumes, habits that they have inherited from the gentile Indians [...] In their gardens they have many tanks built in fine carved stone where they have fun swimming.'[22]

The remarks of Linschoten are interesting when compared with those of Muslim chroniclers writing about Portuguese settlements and Hindu towns. Their curiosity was not raised by the architecture or streetscapes as they did not perceive these as

9.3
View of Rua Direita in Goa

From Jan Huyghen van Linschoten, *Itinerario: Voyage oft schipvaert van Jan Huygen van Linschoten naer Oost ofte Portugaels Indien, 1579–1592*, engraved by Baptista van Doetecun (after a drawing by Linschoten), published by Cornelius Claesz, Amsterdam, 1596
Hand-coloured engraving on paper

Koninklijke Bibliotheek, The Hague

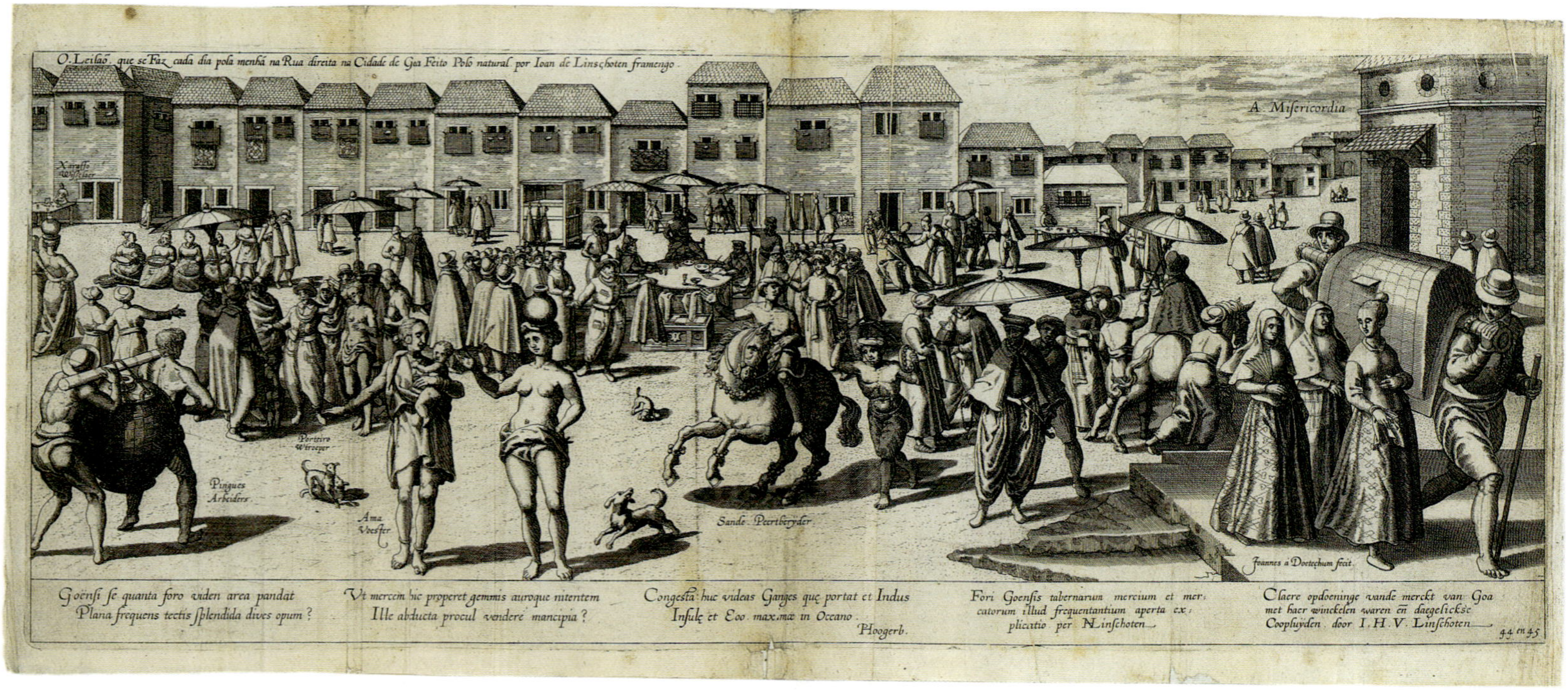

different. Instead, what primarily interested them was the absence of polygamy and the fact that women seemed to rule the affairs of the house. In the Hindu Malabar world they remarked disapprovingly on the existence of polyandry and on the public presence of women.[23]

Linschoten described Goan houses as being 'in the Portuguese manner' and contrasted them to Hindu houses: 'these are very small and low, covered with straw, without any windows, with narrow and low doors'.[24] Pietro della Valle expressed similar views about the Hindu quarters of Calicut: 'He that walks through the city may think that he is rather in the midst of uninhabited gardens than of an inhabited city.'[25] Hindu houses are introverted structures, which function around an internal courtyard and a ritual eating room, the *vasary*. The Christian houses were at first built to a rectangular plan with wide windows and balconies, and with a *quintal* to one of the sides or at the back. Gradually both types of houses changed. The process has been studied in the case of Goa: the courtyard of Hindu houses became surrounded by columns or classical pillars, while the Catholic houses gained internal courtyards or U- and L-shaped plans, had altars placed in the *vasary* and had lobbies (*sadery*) built, where visitors from other castes could be received.[26] Elaborate porches were also built, which separated the house socially from the street while accentuating its urban presence. In the eighteenth and nineteenth centuries the struggle for prominence between upper-caste Goan Catholics led to the erection of the magnificent stately houses that have come to characterize a part of Goan architecture. These had whitewashed façades, high-pitched tile roofs designed to allow hot air to ascend, verandahs of wood and polished seashells – inspired by Mediterranean balconies, which closed with elaborate wood sashes. The Hindu houses acquired a streetscape consciousness by adopting European classical façades with pilasters and cornices, but continued to have only very small windows designed to circulate air rather than afford a view.

However, the first representative buildings in Portuguese Asia to become Euro-Asian along the street fronts were Jesuit churches. At first the Jesuits, like everyone else, built in Asia what they knew how to build in Europe. Such is the case with S. Paulo, their first church in Goa, of which only part of the classical façade remains, and Bassein's (Vasai; in Portuguese Baçaim) college church with its splendid barrel-vaulted single nave and retable-façade. However, at the beginning of the seventeenth century Jesuit architecture in Asia began to change. Nowhere is this more apparent than in Diu's college church, in Goa's Professed House of the Bom Jesus and at Macao's college church façade (all that remains of the building) (plate 9.4). The façades of the Bom Jesus and Macao are four and five orders high respectively – against the canonical two or three of European tradition – and all three buildings are decorated with highly expressive ornamental motifs mixing Flemish decoration with, in the Bom Jesus, volutes that look like Indian decorative spinning wheels (*chakra*) and, in the case of Macao, inscriptions in Chinese.[27] The Jesuit church of Santana de Talaulim, near Old Goa, built at the end of the seventeenth century, is the most Oriental of them all, with an extraordinary white stuccoed interior, profusely ornamented in its compact treatment of the orders (plates 9.5, 9.6). Santana reminds us that in much Asian architecture monumentality is expressed not by size but by the multiplication of elements.[28] During the eighteenth century Christian architectural traits were adopted by Maratha temple builders in Goa who wanted their religious architecture to

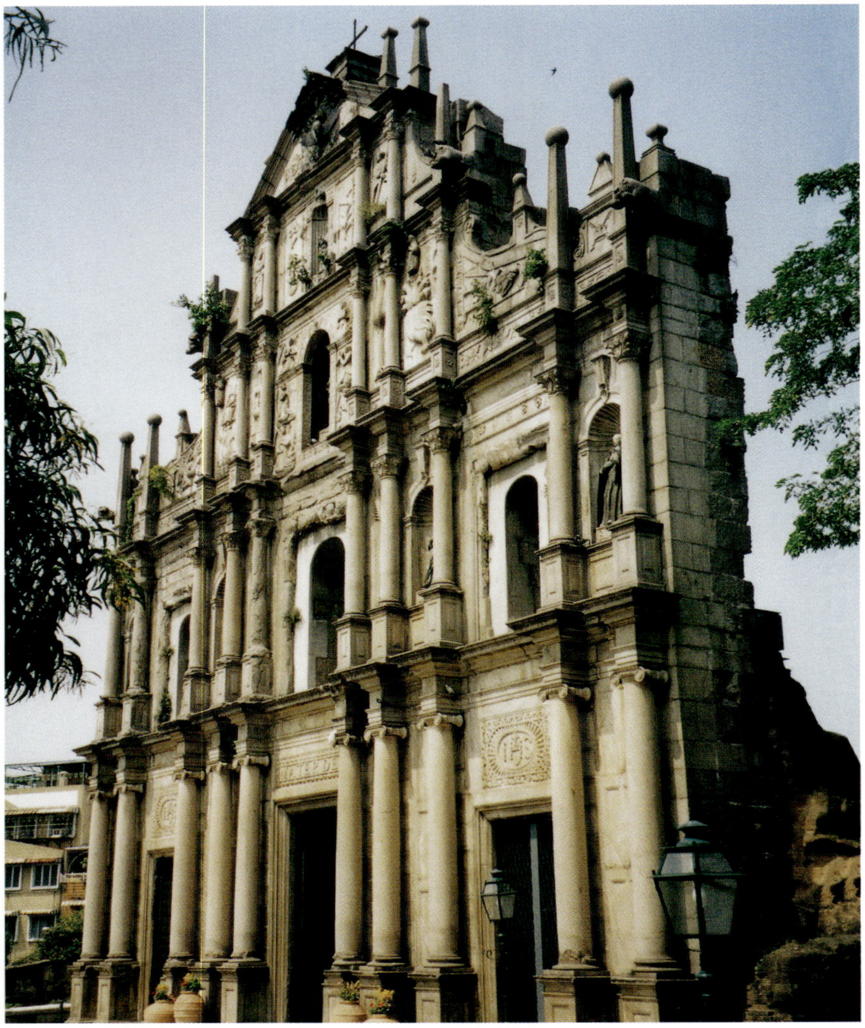

9.4
Façade of the Jesuit college church of S. Paulo, Macao
Designed by Carlo Spinola, SJ
Constructed 1602–40

appear as elaborate as Jesuit churches. The temples appropriated classical European domes over their sanctuaries, pilaster articulated walls, classicizing columns and three-nave porches.

Thus it can be seen that during the sixteenth and early seventeenth centuries Europeans' perceptions of Asian streetscapes and architecture were constructed around the occasional similarity with what they knew in Europe. It was European architecture that they looked towards as a model for the settlements they were to build in Asia. There was no uniform European perception of Asian cities or architecture. For Linschoten, Goa was as alien as Calicut, albeit for different reasons, while for Pietro della Valle, Christian churches in India and Hindu temples were equally despicable in Italian classical terms.[29] The Portuguese perceived Muslim-influenced towns in India as if they were their own, praised Chinese towns as better than the European, and despised Hindu settlements. The political admiration they had for the Mughal and Chinese empires is indistinguishable from their liking of stone walls, tiled roofs, straight streets. This helped to shape the physical aspect of the towns built anew by the Portuguese in Asia. In 1600, for instance, the Portuguese viceroy specifically ordered that all stone houses of Cochin be covered with tiles in order to distinguish them from Hindu houses made of palm leaves or trunks.[30]

Renaissance Europeans in Asia were not observers in the modern sense of the word. They had little interest in difference.[31] As Pietro della Valle, the most modern of them, remarked: 'Indeed the Portugals are not at all curious.'[32] They were more like spies, people who look to use things and information rather than speculate about them. They despised what they could not identify as similar to things European. They identified themselves with the cultural traits they perceived as already known from Europe. Towns were seen as being either 'in the manner of Iberia' or uninteresting. The transformation of houses, churches, streetscapes and of the arts, to incorporate the 'difference' of Asian forms, only took place late in the seventeenth century when a dichotomy was clearly established – that is, when Asian forms began to be perceived as different.

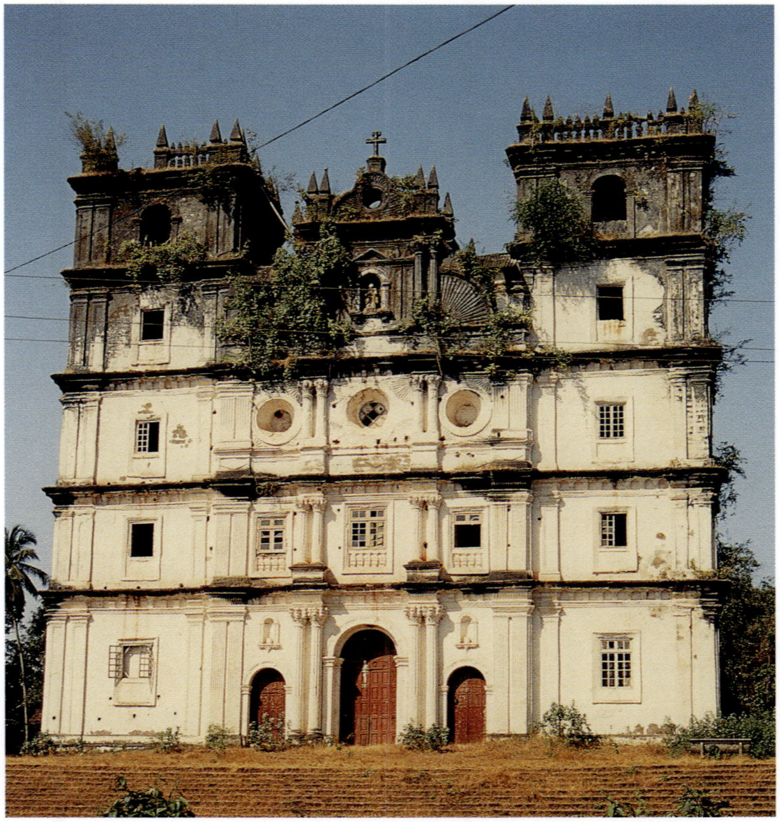

9.5
Façade of the church of Santana de Talaulim, Goa
Designed by Francisco do Rego, SJ, and António Francisco da Cunha, SJ
Constructed 1681–95

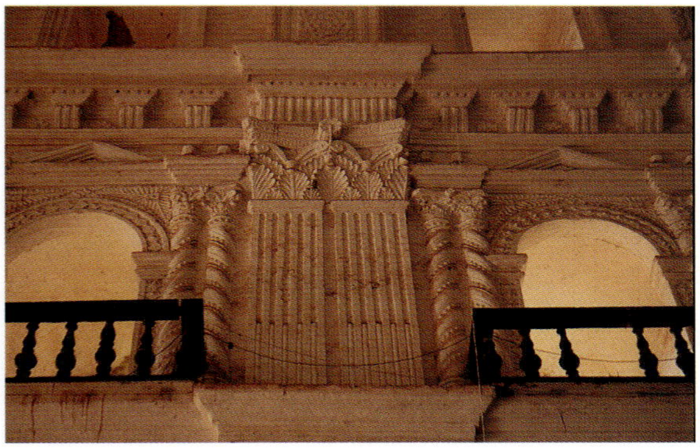

9.6
Detail of the interior of the church of Santana de Talaulim, Goa

10

DUTCH SETTLEMENTS AND TRADING CENTRES

Leonard Blussé

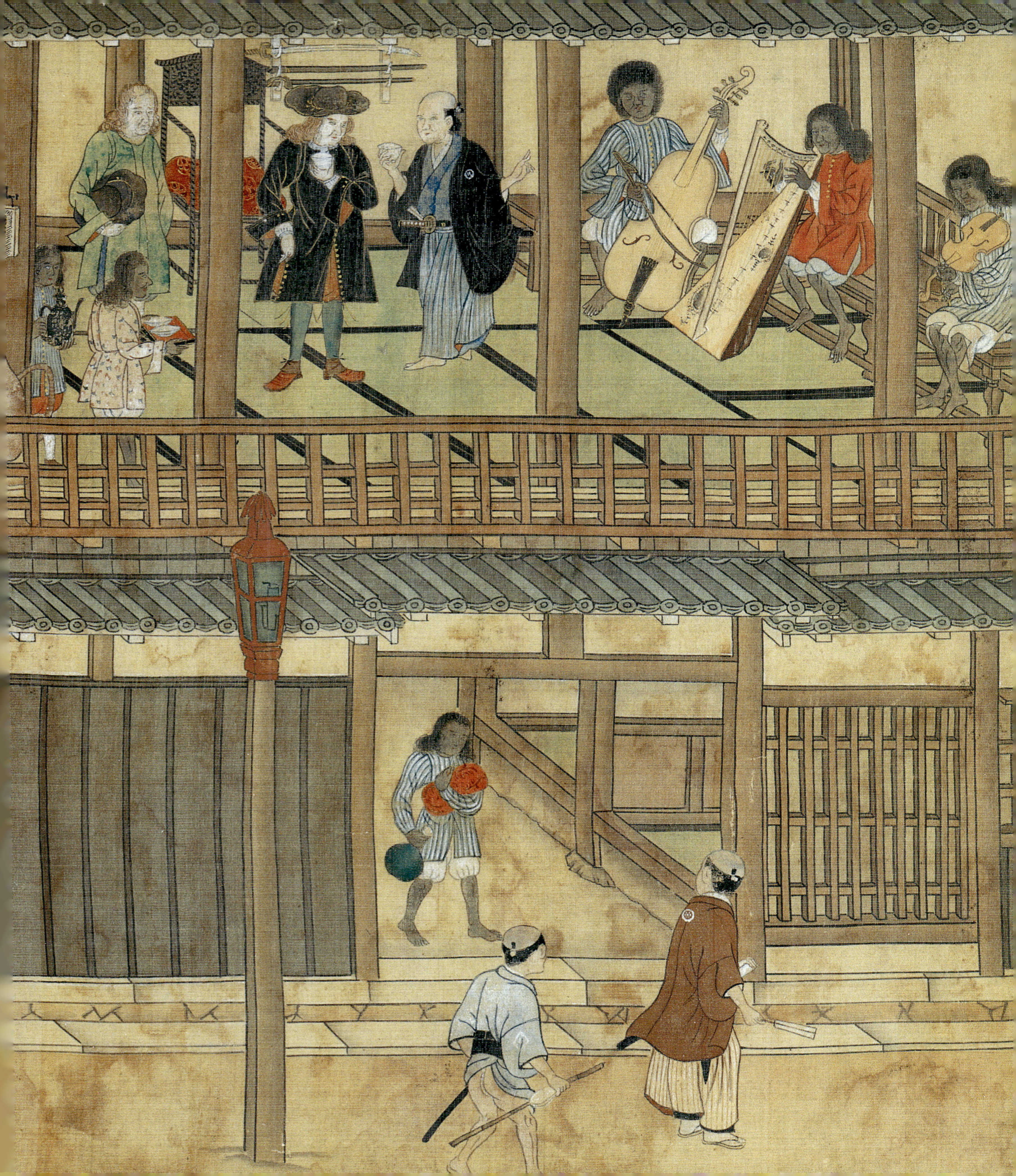

Detail of 10.2 previous page

In its golden age the Dutch Republic was, demographically speaking, a minor player in Europe with a population of well below two million. In a massive historical survey of all shipping movements and the numbers of people on board East Indiamen, it has been calculated that during the 200-year existence of the Dutch East India Company (VOC; 1602–1795) approximately one million people sailed on a total of 4,789 ships bound for the Indies.[1] Half of these voyagers were not from the Dutch provinces themselves, but came from neighbouring countries such as the German princely states or, further away, Scandinavia. Only one-third of all outgoing personnel made it back to the mother country, either because they died in the East or because they preferred to remain there. All people sailing on Dutch ships to Asia were in principle employed by the VOC or were dependants of its personnel. At the height of VOC power, at around the turn of the eighteenth century, some 20,000 personnel were serving this proto-multinational in mercantile and military occupations.[2] '*Jan Compagnie*' was stationed at trading settlements all over Asia, in outposts such as the tiny island of Dejima in distant Japan, where their life was heavily regimented by the local authorities; in the busy ports of Persia and the Indian subcontinent; in various walled towns along the coast or inland military stations in territorial possessions like Ceylon and the Moluccas, where the VOC jealously guarded its monopoly in cinnamon and spices; and of course along the north coast of Java, on the western tip of which Batavia, its headquarters in Asia, was situated.

On a very detailed picture of the VOC factory at Hooghly [Hugli] on a tributary of the River Ganges, painted by Hendrik van Schuylenburgh in 1665, are depicted day-to-day activities typical of this profitable trading post (plate 10.1). Ships are moored in the background, while within the walled compound Europeans and Indians clad in white robes and turbans move in and out of offices, warehouses and the medicinal garden. Outside the walls there is a tank where horses are bathed, and elsewhere elephants and camels parade. Close to the river there are some stray timbers from a shipyard, and a *sati* ceremony in which a Hindu widow joins her deceased husband by throwing herself on the funeral pile. The eye is, however, inevitably drawn to the encampment of a Mughal local official who is ceremoniously greeted by VOC officials who, by handing out frequent gifts, made sure that the *firman* (edict) that allowed them to trade would be continued (see p.76).[3] Yet such Dutch factories were similar to those of other European trading nations in Asia. For this reason this essay focuses on two specific trading establishments, which were felt at the time to be quite unique in outlook and lifestyle: Dejima, the Dutch factory in Japan, and Batavia, the Dutch urban headquarters on the island of Java.

Dejima was a tiny island with a surface area of about two football fields in the bay of Nagasaki. Japanese authorities originally constructed this artificial island in order to house Portuguese merchants, but shortly after the expulsion of the latter in 1639, the Dutch were ordered to dismantle their offices at the nearby port of Hirado and move to Dejima, where they were put under close surveillance. The houses, offices and warehouses on the island were leased to the Dutch by Japanese landlords and were wholly Japanese in appearance. The floors were covered with *tatami* mats and rooms were closed off by sliding doors (*shoji*), but instead of the usual papered panels, which were not very effective in keeping out the cold winter winds, imported glass windows were also installed. Apart from the occasional courtesan from the Maruyama quarter of Nagasaki, no Japanese personnel were allowed to stay overnight on the island (see pp.179–80).[4] About a dozen VOC servants stayed over at the island during the slack winter season after ships had returned to Batavia. They spent their time playing billiards, reading books, talking to occasional Japanese visitors, cultivating the herb garden on the island and looking after imported exotic animals, which were kept to be given as presents to Japanese officials (plate 10.2). In the first month of every year the *opperhoofd*, or chief factor, of the island would embark in the company of a physician and a secretary on a *hofreis*, or court journey, to pay tribute to the *shōgun* at his palace in Edo (present-day Tokyo). By the end of the eighteenth century the volume of trade had shrunk to such an extent that the *bakufu* (military government) approved that these court journeys would be made less frequently, with an interval of four years or an even longer period. The boat trip via the Inland Sea to Osaka, and the overland journey from there by the Tōkaidō route to Edo, often took more than a month in either direction. Along the way the Dutch voyagers had at last some opportunity to meet and talk with curious Japanese, who would visit them at the inns where they passed the night along the road (see p.98, p.183 and p.316).

All this has been duly noted down in the more than 150 travel journals preserved in the Dutch National Archives at The Hague, but probably the best-known court journey in English is the one written by Engelbert Kaempfer (1651–1716), a German physician who served on Dejima between 1690 and 1692. In 1727 his *History of Japan* was published in English, thanks to the patronage of Sir Hans Sloane (1660–1753), one of the founders of the British Museum (see p. 218).[5] There are plenty of Japanese images of life on the isle of Dejima, with its funny-looking and strangely clothed *Orandajin* (literally 'Holland people'), their domestic slaves and the Japanese guards and coolies.[6] Thanks to the artist Shiba Kōkan (1747–1818), we even know what the interior of the house of the Dutch factory chief, Caspar Romberg, looked like (plate 10.3). Kōkan drew a sketch from memory after he had paid a visit to this official who showed him clocks, a barometer, ship models, Dutch furniture, pictures and prints and other typical European gadgets.[7]

Because Dejima was leased to the Dutch by Nagasaki landlords, they were forced to adapt their lifestyle to Japanese customs, but on Java the Dutch were free to build a colonial city according to their own designs, having conquered the kingdom of Jacatra (Jakarta) in 1619. On the ruins of the *kraton* (palace) of the former ruler they built Batavia, the colonial city that came to serve as the headquarters of the VOC in Asia (plate 10.4). The eighteenth-century French traveller Joseph, abbé de la Porte described the town as follows:

> Batavia is situated in between the sea and a mountain chain on a low and level plain, at the rim of a bay, which forms a wide and easy haven. The town is surrounded by walls made of coral stones and is defended by 22 bulwarks, which are named after the most important regions and towns of the Dutch Republic. A wide and deep moat surrounds it in its entirety, which is always filled with water and by high floods represents an invincible defence work. Finally it is provided with all the weaponry needed in a frontier town, and which is aimed in such a way that it covers the most important streets in town, and can take aim at the town itself in case of rebellion. A river with a well-constructed quay of stone lined with rows of planted trees crosses the town, which is about an hour's walk long if one includes the suburbs. The number of its inhabitants [*intra*– and *extramuros*] is estimated at 100,000 people, Asians as well as Europeans. Almost all streets are straight, and about 60 feet wide, lined by double rows of trees, and a footpath of brick for pedestrians. The houses are built of white stone with the same sense of regularity as in Holland, and this town is because of its pleasing site, the beauty of its buildings, and the multitude of its bridges one of the most beautiful in the world. Its most important buildings are the churches, the hospitals, the almshouses, the town hall, the defamatory and the market halls, the castle, the palace of the governor and the buildings of the courts of justice.[8]

10.1
Hooghly Factory
Hendrik van Schuylenburgh

Possibly commissioned by Pieter Sterthemius, VOC director of Bengal; oil on canvas, 1665

Rijksmuseum, Amsterdam

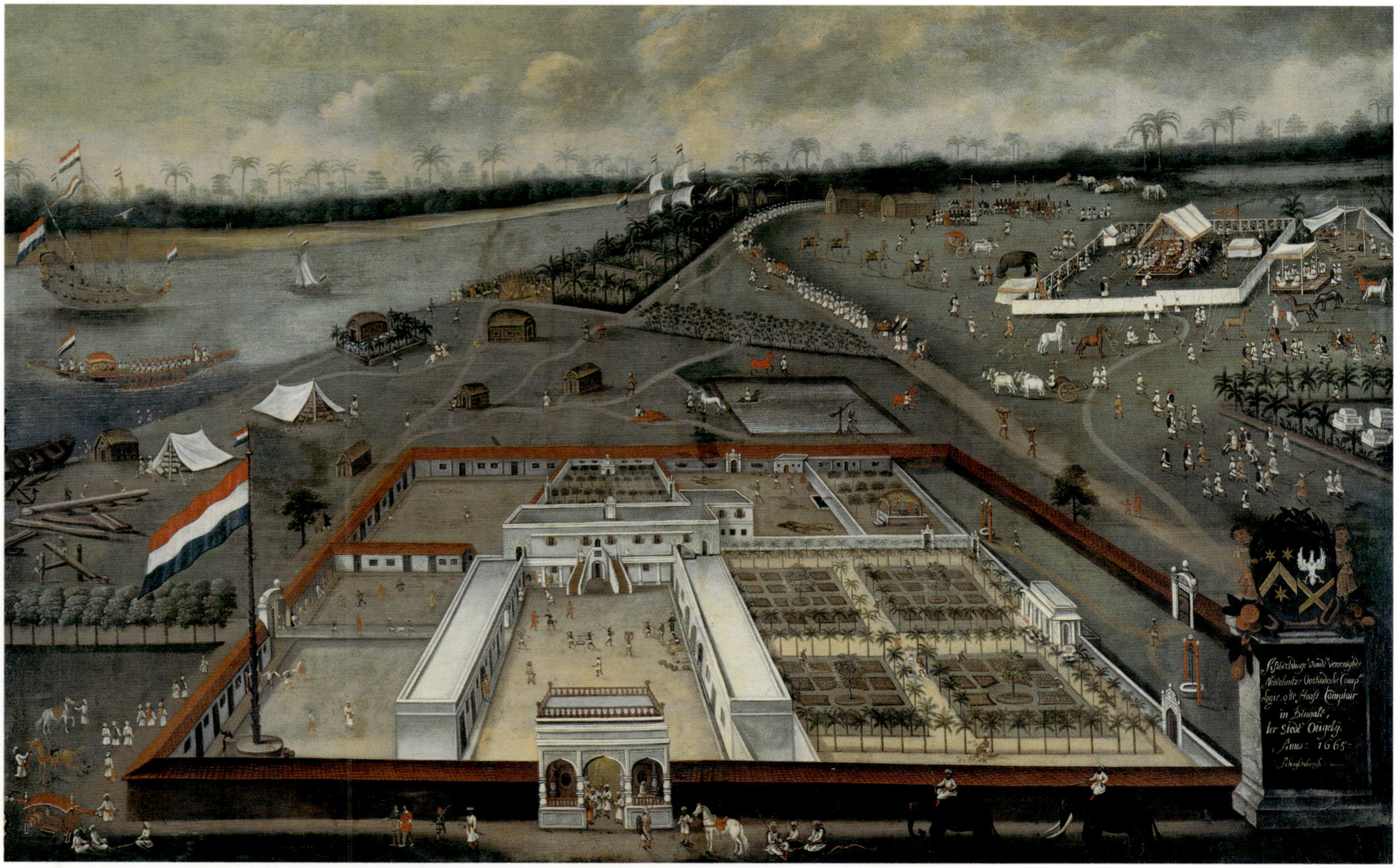

L'abbé de la Porte, a typical 'armchair travel' writer, who compiled travelogues from the writings of real globe-trotters, actually never visited Batavia, but his description of the town is quite representative of what could have been found in contemporary travel literature.

Batavia was a planned city. In reply to the triumphant report of Governor-General Jan Pietersz Coen (1587–1629) about the conquest of the kingdom of Jacatra, the directors of the Dutch East India Company sent him a city plan designed by the famous mathematician, surveyor and fortress builder, Simon Stevin (1548–1620), and suggested using this plan as a 'blueprint' for building the new headquarters in the tropics. City planning was at the beginning of the seventeenth century an extensively studied science in the Low Countries, which were still engaged in their protracted war of independence against Spain. The building of fortified cities was put into practice with great zeal, as is still visible today from the morphology of various cities and fortress towns. Amsterdam, Naarden or Willemstad in the Netherlands and many settlements overseas, like New York or Recife in Brazil, were given part of their characteristic layout and shape in that era. A recent survey by a UNESCO researcher has shown that the design of these settlements has common features.[9] They are built along two axes, along which the main government buildings, public places and churches were situated.

The Dutch were not the first to design and lay out new colonial towns overseas. As in so many other fields of applied science, they were happy to emulate Iberian pioneers. The Spanish had already projected and built many cities in the New World using Roman grid designs. In Asia and Africa the Portuguese put their own stamp on the design of overseas settlements by creating a string of castle towns along the monsoon shipping routes of the Indian Ocean. Fortified settlements like Hormuz, Diu, Goa, Colombo and Malacca all belonged to this 'coastal frontier'. In Asia, Europeans entered a world of strong populous empires. Facing such formidable opponents, they did not even think of challenging them in the way the Spanish had the Maya and Inca empires, although it should be admitted that some over-confident Spaniards proposed conquering China by launching an attack from the Philippines.

Like the Portuguese, the Dutch preferred to construct their settlements on strategic spots that could easily be defended against attacks from land and sea. They protected these with strong fortifications and, of course, with heavily armed ships at the roadstead. During the seventeenth century many of these fortifications built by the *Estado da Índia* ('State of India') in order to control the monsoon trade of Asia were finally conquered by the Dutch, who partly redesigned them by cutting them down in size so that they could be defended in a more economical way. The physiognomy of Portuguese colonial towns often featured a castle adjacent to a walled settlement, for the *soldados* and *casados* (Portuguese settlers, mostly married to Asian women) with their dependants. The Portuguese lived separately from the surrounding settlements, or *kampongs*, of traders of various Asian nationalities. Malacca was a fine example of such a fortified town surrounded by Asian nations, as was Spanish Manila, with its so-called *Parian*, or China town, situated *extramuros*. Although Dutch Batavia, a typical castle town, was to a certain extent modelled after precursors such as Manila and Malacca, it also had special features that set it apart.

First of all, unlike its Iberian sister cities, Batavia was founded and ruled by a large corporation of merchants, the Dutch East India Company. This is evident in the extraordinary amount of space allotted to warehouses and wharves. This storage was needed as the VOC annually sent an average of some 25 ships to and from Asia, and had about 40 ships afloat on the Asian trading routes at any one time. Secondly, the walled town of Batavia, which was built close to the castle where the governing elite was housed, was designed in such a way that it actually *included* those nations on whose military assistance (free Christian burghers of Asian extraction, the so-called *Mardijkers*) and on whose industry (Chinese) the survival of the city depended. Thus, in contrast to Manila where strict segregation between the Spanish and Chinese merchants was enforced, Dutch and Chinese lived within the walls of one and the same town, served by large numbers of domestic slaves from within the

10.2
The Dutch Factory at Dejima

Handscroll; ink and colour on silk
Japan (Nagasaki), *c.*1800

V&A: D.151–1905

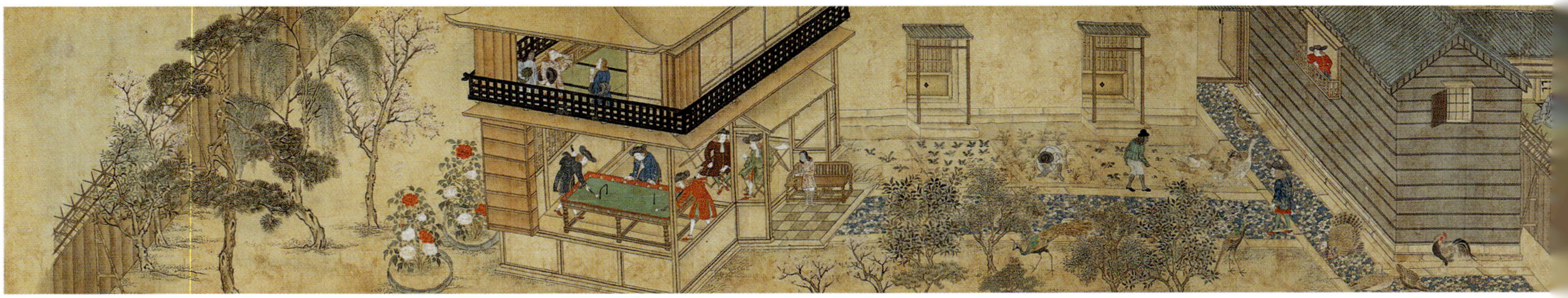

Indonesian archipelago and the Indian subcontinent. In the so-called *Ommelanden* around the city, the VOC designated land where the 'martial nations' were concentrated in *kampongs* of their own – Balinese, Bugis, Madurese and Amboinese – who, when called upon, provided troops for military campaigns elsewhere in the archipelago.[10] Thirdly, the Dutch tried to replicate in their overseas possessions all the well-developed municipal institutions of their burgher society at home. This included typically Dutch construction works such as canal systems lined by rows of trees and neatly built burgher houses. They also erected a town hall, hospitals, a court of justice, churches, reformative institutions and an almshouse.

The extraordinary commercial character of Batavia, its strong defence works, its cultural mix of citizens of various ethnicities, and finally its neat representation of civic liberties and pride (real or imaginary), made the city appear, in the eyes of its visitors, a kind of 'Holland in the tropics' (plate 10.5). For European travellers who had been at sea for six months or more, the town with its neat appearance must have been an amazing sight. L'Abbé de Choisy exclaimed: 'This is the capital of the empire of the Bataves. Their power is formidable and we shouldn't be surprised that they are proud of their own premises', while the English traveller Woodes Rogers remarked in 1710 that he 'was perfectly surpriz'd to see such a noble city and Europeans so well settled in the Indies'.[11]

From the foundation of Batavia in 1619, the Chinese citizens of the city played a major role in its social and economic life. Nearly every European visitor who left a description of Batavia devoted at least a couple of paragraphs to the Chinese inhabitants and the various usages and customs that caught their eye, such as the *wayang wong* (Chinese opera) performances in front of the temples, or the participants of marriage and funeral processions, which almost every day squeezed through the busy streets. The Chinese were the largest ethnic group in the city and, in the absence of a large group of Dutch citizens, formed the industrious middle class upon whom the prosperity of the city depended. The Reverend François Valentijn (1656–1727),

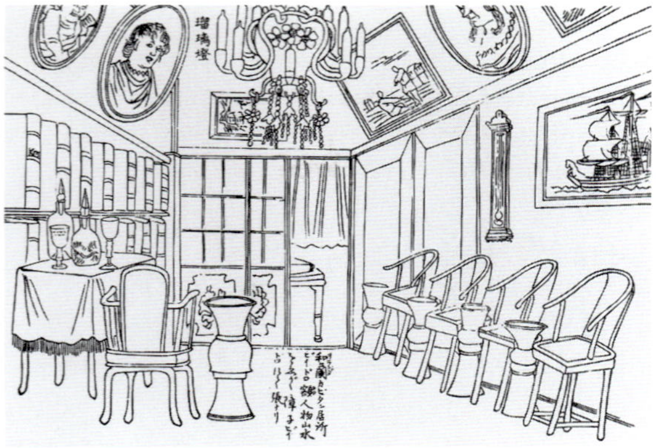

10.3
Chief Factor's Room at Dejima
From Shiba Kōkan, *Edo Nagasaki E Kikō – Saiyū Ryodan (Picture Travelogue Edo to Nagasaki: Travels in the West)*
Woodblock-printed book
Japan (Edo), 1794
Private collection

who visited Batavia on many occasions, had no doubts about the important Chinese contribution to the town's economy:

> Next to the Dutch rank the Chinese; they are an incredibly smart, polite, industrious and attentive people, who pay great services to this city ... all the agriculture rests on their shoulders, there is nothing that one might think of that they do not attempt, and in which they do not trade ... If they weren't here, Batavia would be moribund and devoid of many necessities.[12]

Just as Dutch citizens of the city kept in constant touch with their distant home country through the regular shipping links between the Indies and the republic, so too did the Chinese maintain their ties with their motherland, which could be reached in a sailing ship on the monsoon winds in three to four weeks. Each year, as soon as the north monsoon began to blow, scores of Chinese junks once again dropped anchor in the roads of Batavia. In this fashion, in the months of February and March, the city filled up with thousands of Chinese merchants, immigrants and coolies who had left their own country a month earlier in search of work and adventure. The cargo of the junks consisted mainly of silk textiles, porcelain and tea for the European market, but there were also manufactured goods that were intended for the daily use of the Chinese in the colony. In June or July at the end of the wet monsoon the junks returned to China carrying rich cargoes of tropical products and hundreds of passengers who were returning home, either richer or disillusioned, after a long stay or a brief sojourn in the archipelago.

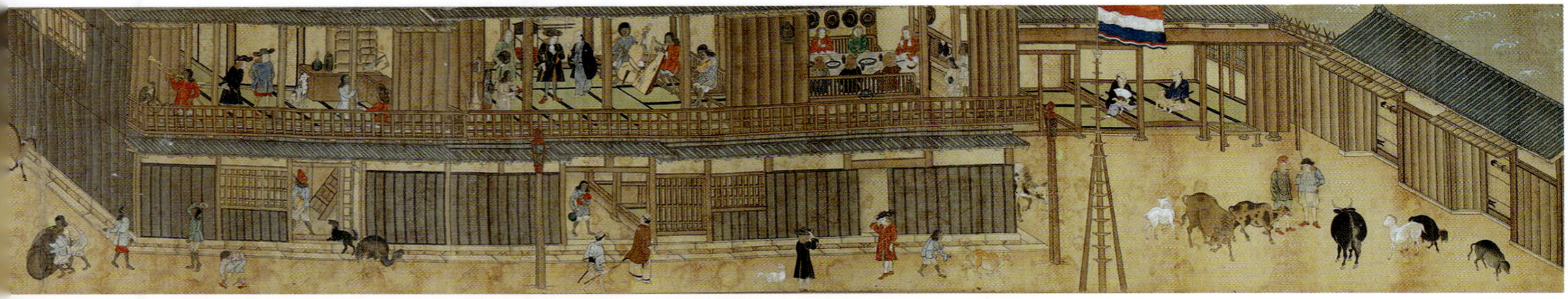

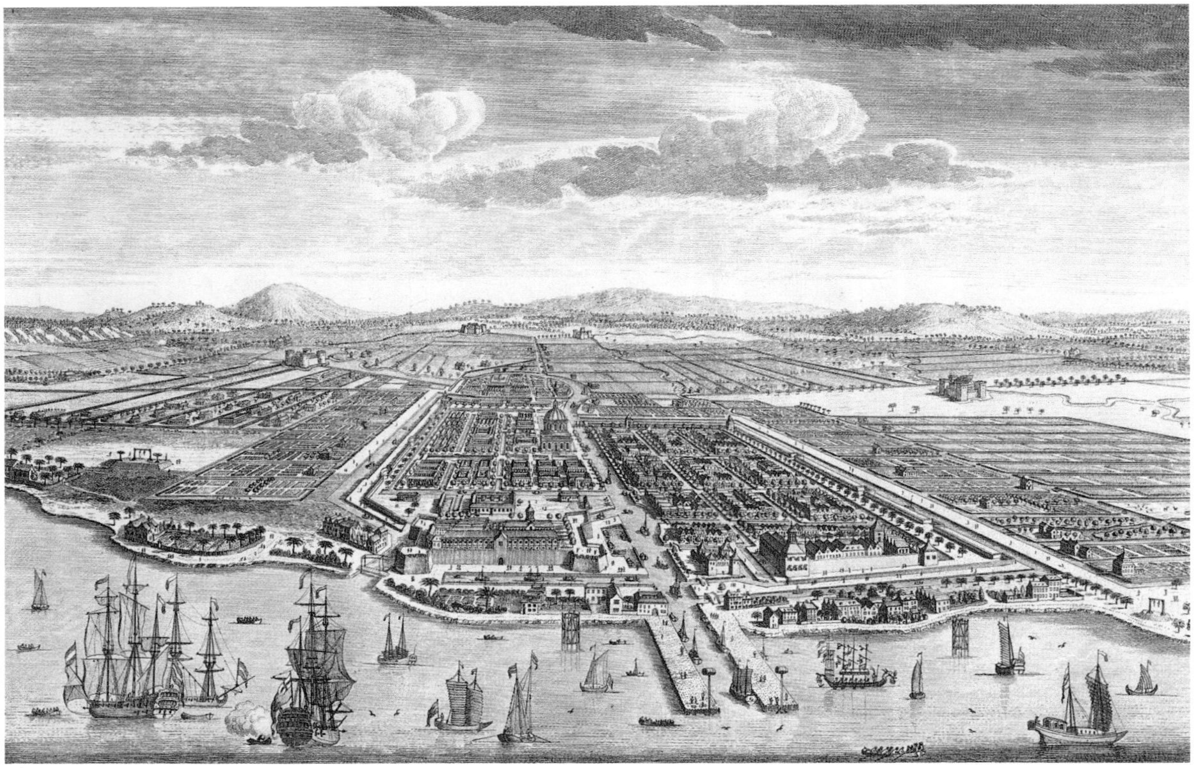

10.4
Batavia
J. van Ryne
Engraving on paper, 1754
V&A: E.494.G.18–1889

Chinese overseas migration was strictly regulated by imperial decree. Not one Chinese woman was permitted to cross the borders of the Middle Kingdom. This is the reason why many Chinese inhabitants of Batavia lived with Indonesian women, whom they had usually bought as slaves. Gradually this practice led to the development of a mixed-blood Chinese *peranakan* population. However, because of the constant stream of *sinkê* or newcomers from China, the typically Chinese character of the group was preserved largely intact. This was also evident in the Chinese houses of Batavia, which were an interesting mixture of Chinese and Dutch architecture, with shops on the ground floor and living quarters above. Living quarters for slaves were constructed at the back of the house. Well-preserved Chinese houses of the VOC period are preserved in modern-day Malacca.

The same rules applied to the architecture of Dutch housing. If the private dwellings in Batavia outwardly resembled town houses along the canals of towns in Holland, the interiors were adapted to the very tropical climate. Dutch ship captain J.S. Stavorinus, who sailed in Asian waters between 1768 and 1778, provides an idea of how they appeared to him:

> The houses at Batavia are mostly of brick, run up in a light and airy manner, and stuccoed on the outside, with sash windows. Within, they are almost all built upon a similar plan, the fronts being, in general, narrow, though there are a few that are more extended. On entering the door, there is a narrow passage, and on one side a parlour, then you come into a large and long room, that receives its light from an inner court, which trenches upon this apartment, and renders its form irregular. This is called the gallery, and is the place where the family usually live, and dine. The floors are of large, square, dark red stones. No hangings are to be seen; but the walls are neatly stuccoed, and whitened. The furniture consists in, some armchairs, two or three sofas, and a great many looking glasses, which the Europeans, in these regions, are very fond of. Several chandeliers and lamps, are hung in a row, along the length of the gallery, which are lit up in the evening. The stairs leading to the upper rooms, are generally at the end of this apartment. Six or seven steps up there is one which stands over the storeroom, or cellar, in which the stock of wine, beer, butter, &c. is kept. Up stairs, the houses are distributed almost similarly as below. They are, in general, but poorly provided with furniture; and the setting out of rooms in order, is not so much in vogue here, as in Holland; nothing is added that is superfluous, or more than is wanted for use. Behind the gallery, are the lodgings for the slaves, the kitchen and so on ...[13]

Without doubt the most beautiful houses in town were those lining the Tijgersgracht, a canal some 750 metres in length. From the end of the seventeenth century, large country houses were also built outside the city walls. What the interiors of houses of the local elite looked like may be gleaned from a letter that the Governor-General of the Indies, Jeremias van Riemsdijk (1712–77), wrote to one of his children in Holland. He reported that his house was 'very wide, so that the side room facing the street side with English sliding windows and a floor of black and white marble tiles, was large enough to seat a company of 40 ladies'.[14] The hallway next to this room led to a gallery or inner room, which drew its light from a large patio. Under the house was a large cellar of 10 or more metres. On the first floor in front there was a large room as big as the one downstairs, and behind it a room of the same size as the cellar, and a couple of smaller rooms that were connected by a 10-metre-deep outer gallery covered by a roof. On both sides of the patio there was a kitchen and a toilet for the owner of the house, as well as a kitchen for the slaves and two levels of slave quarters, two large garages for the various chariots and stables for 20 horses. Two Dutch servants and a cook, and another 200 male and female slaves and their progeny, served van Riemsdijk and his family. In addition to his house he possessed extensive gardens with cupolas outside the city walls, where he kept more horses and chariots and a small fleet of rowing boats and yachts in order to move from one place to another.

Stavorinus remarked that Batavia's houses had less furniture than their Dutch counterparts. Yet it should be noticed that over the years particular styles of colonial furniture developed. Inventories in notarial archives reveal that historical roots of this type of furniture can be traced back to furniture made under Portuguese patronage in the Indian subcontinent (see pp. 256–7).[15] Portuguese artisans in the Indies who had started furniture workshops had also trained local carpenters, who later on, under the management of the Dutch master carpenters, developed a specific Batavian style of furniture, first using ebony from Mauritius and, after 1710 when the Company withdrew from that island, hard woods like *jati* or sandalwood.

Living organisms – real or imagined – like cities or nations, pass through life cycles. Even urban settlements shed their skins like snakes and move their centres accordingly. Goa, Manila and Batavia are each a case in point. What remained of old colonial Manila into the twentieth century was destroyed during the Pacific War. Old Batavia and old Goa, on the other hand, had already fallen into neglect at a much earlier date owing to unsanitary local conditions. In fact, Batavia had become so unhealthy by the end of the eighteenth century that most of its Dutch citizenry had moved *extramuros*, preferring the surroundings of pleasant areas situated away from the coast and on higher land, away from the stench of the torpid canals of downtown Batavia. Various explanations have been given as to why this comparatively healthy town turned into an insalubrious settlement. Contemporaries believed that the Salak volcano, which erupted in 1702, was the main culprit. Its debris transformed the Ciliwong or Great River, which flowed through the centre of the town, into a muddy stream; inevitably its arteries became malodorous pools and gullies. Nowadays researchers not only fault the putrid canals with their heavy stench, but also the Chinese graves and the fish ponds that were laid out in the vicinity of the town. These pools near the grave mounds and the ponds would have served as breeding grounds for teeming colonies of anopheles mosquitoes.

Governor-General Herman Daendels (1762–1818), who was sent to the East in 1807 to implement Napoleonic reforms in the Dutch colonies, dismantled Batavia Castle and moved the administrative centre from downtown to the higher grounds of Weltevreden. Today only a few buildings in downtown Jakarta remind us of the town which, in the seventeenth century, was praised as the 'Queen of the East', until this honorific was gradually replaced in the eighteenth century by the less festive name of the 'Cemetery of the East'. In hindsight it is telling that the life cycle of Batavia was closely tied to that of the Dutch East India Company itself. When the VOC went bankrupt, so did its headquarters in Asia, although not altogether for the same reasons.

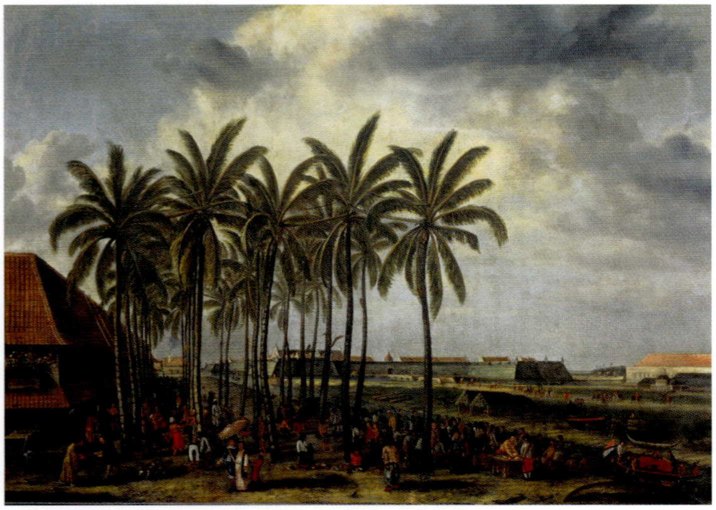

10.5
View of Batavia
Andries Beeckman

Commissioned by directors of the VOC;
oil on canvas
*c.*1661

Rijksmuseum, Amsterdam

Beeckman painted this work in Holland based on sketches he had made while in Batavia. The canvas originally hung in the VOC headquarters in Amsterdam.

II

BRITISH SETTLEMENTS AND TRADING CENTRES

J.P. Losty

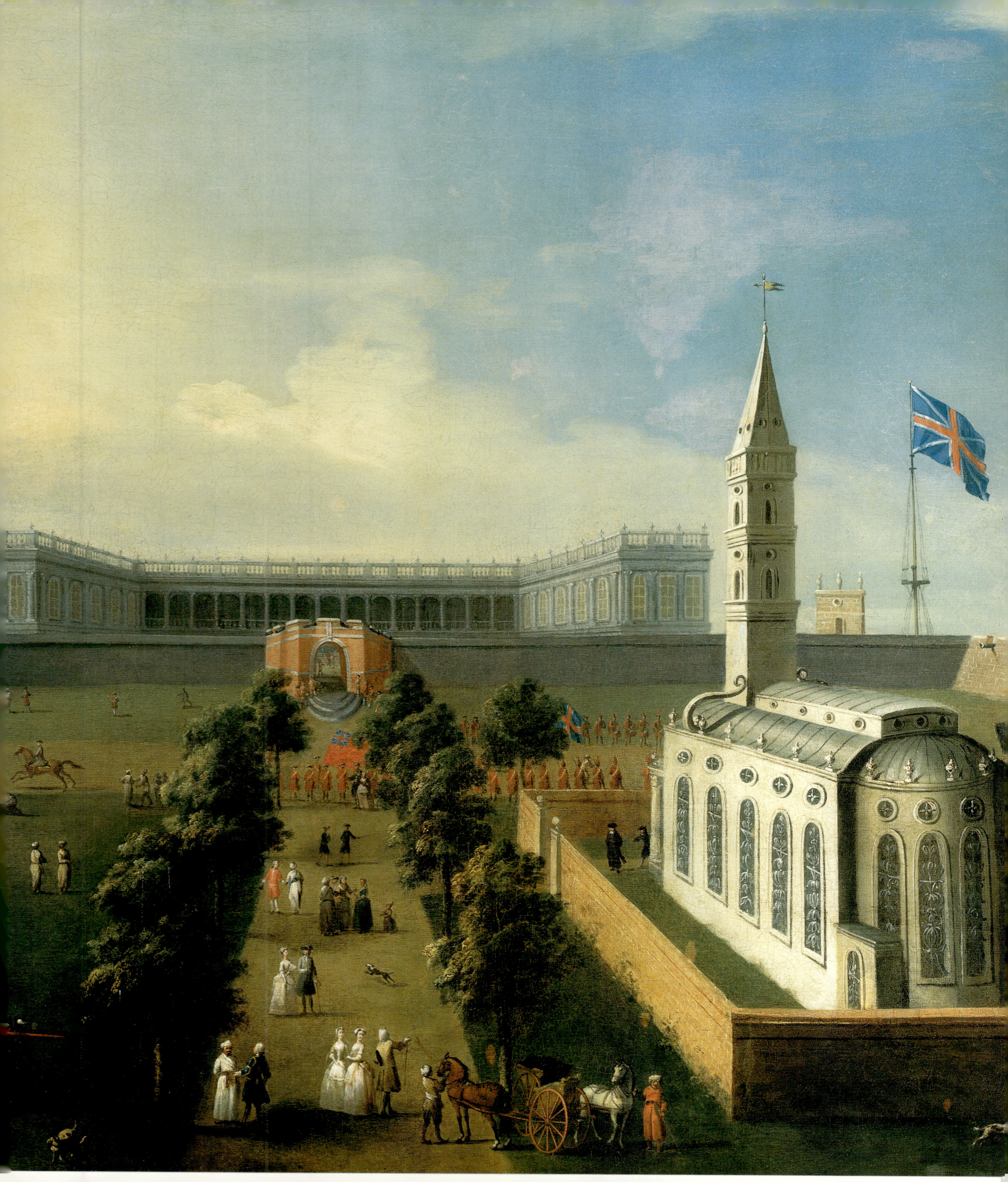

by the Company in London, but of a permanent weakening of the central government. The great nobles who ruled the provinces asserted their independence, and it was with these successor states that the English factories henceforth mostly dealt.

A series of views of the Indian factories, prepared in England but based on now mostly lost earlier sketches, shows the fortifications built around the principal factories of Madras, Bombay and Calcutta. These are of the simplest type: square bastions, some with pepperpot look-out towers, linked by curtain walls, pierced by a land gate on one side and a sea or river gate on the other. Around the small Fort St George, built immediately on the beach at Madras, spread the walled and fortified 'White Town', which was divided into a grid of streets and was built up in regular Georgian terraces. Fryer, who was there in 1673, wrote that 'the streets are sweet and clean, ranked with fine mansions, of no extraordinary height (because a garrison town) though beauty, which they conciliate, by the battlements and terrace walks on every house, and rows of trees before their doors, whose Italian porticoes make no ordinary conveyance into their houses, built with brick and stone'.[12] Governor Pitt's *Prospect* of about 1710 shows the chief buildings rising behind the sea walls:[13] the domed Town Hall (with debtors' prison beneath), the tower and lantern of St Mary's church, the three-storeyed Government Houses behind the Sea Gate, and the tower over the south gate of Fort Square. It also served as the basis for George Lambert's painting of about 1730.[14] The fortified appearance of the houses within the White Town is confirmed by Fryer's earlier description. The English church, consecrated in 1680, and an earlier Catholic church for the 'Portuguese' stood within the town respectively south and north of the fort.[15] The walled 'Black Town' lay outside the main fortifications to the north, where stood the Armenian church. At this period, according to Captain Alexander Hamilton (*fl.* 1688–1723), there were 400–500 Europeans and 80,000 other inhabitants in Madras (plate 11.1).

By the early eighteenth century, when Captain Hamilton visited it, Bombay Castle was laid out similarly to the Madras fort, its walls enclosing the U-shaped old Government House of the seventeenth century.[16] Its guns commanded the little wharf and the approach to the factory. George Lambert

11.2
View of the Factory and Castle of Bombay from the Harbour
George Lambert and Samuel Scott

Oil on canvas
England (London), *c.*1731

British Library, London

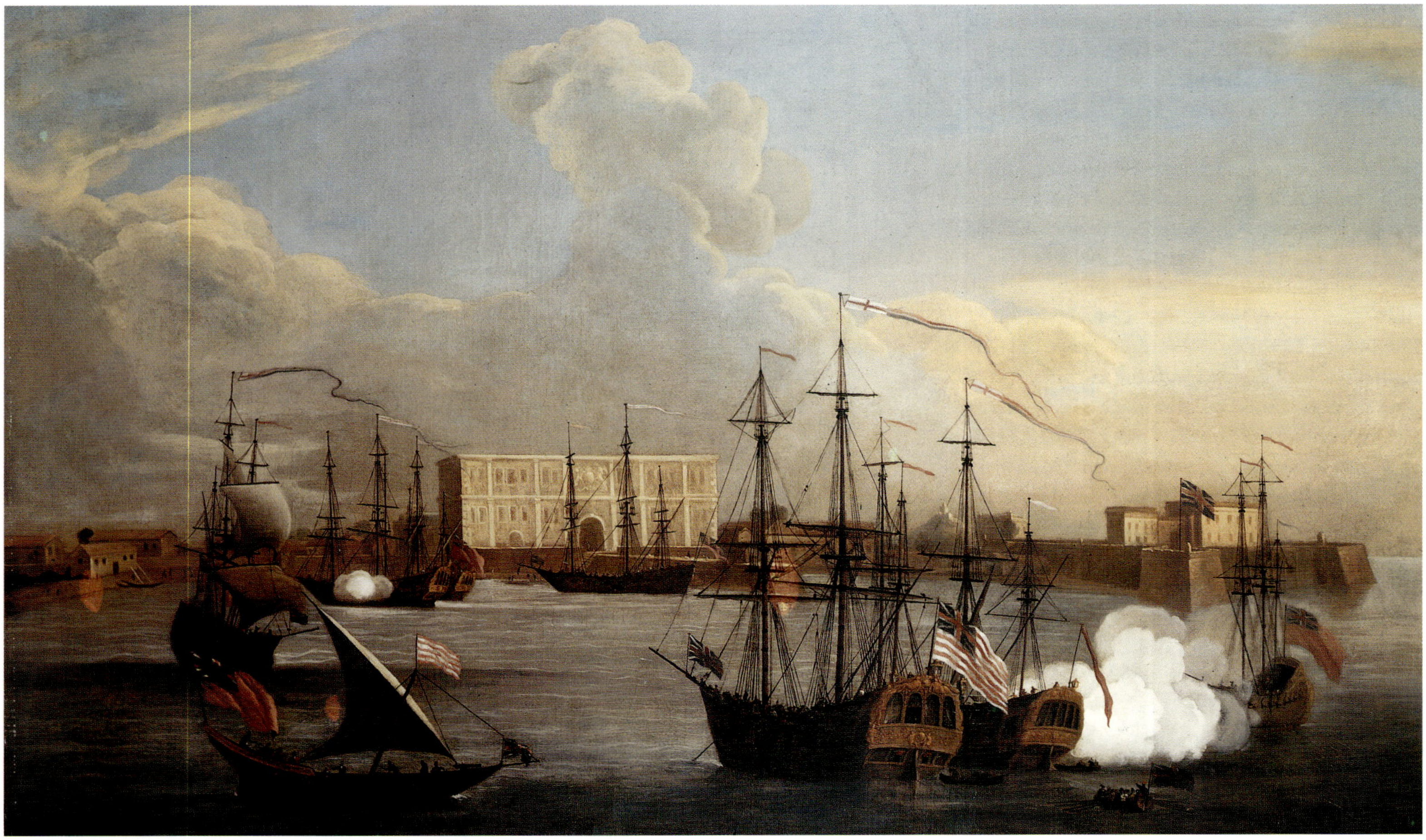

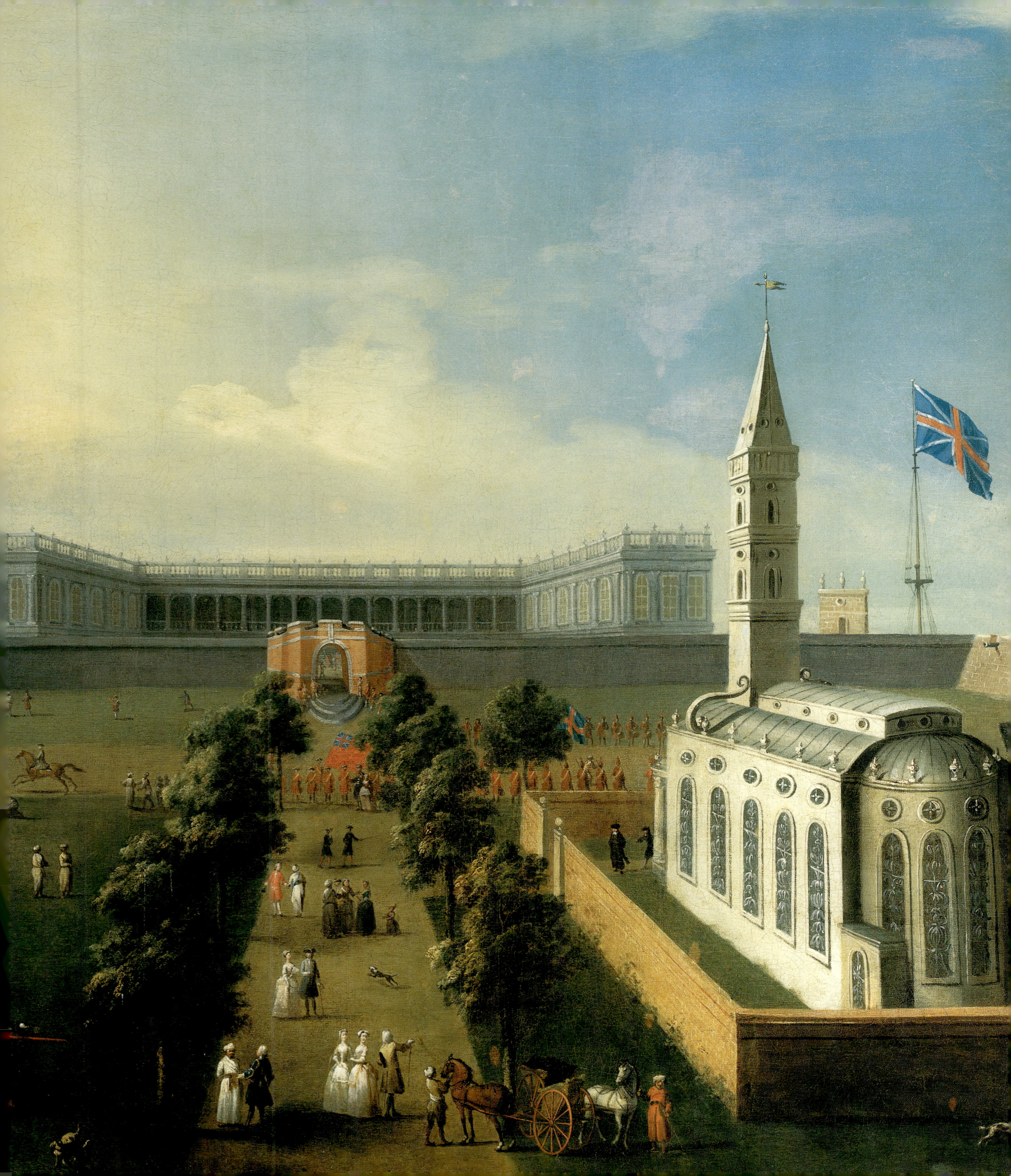

Detail of 11.3 previous page

On 24 September 1600 a group of London merchants incorporated themselves as a company dedicated to trading in the East Indies. The English Company faced difficulties in its early history, mainly due to competition from the Dutch. The home market for eastern products was much smaller than the Dutch one, for Amsterdam had the whole of northern Europe as its trading hinterland. In Bantam, West Java, the centre of the pepper trade, as elsewhere, the English found the Dutch East India Company (VOC) ahead of them. The Dutch soon took over the production centres for the finer spices and, with Japanese connivance, were to monopolize the trade with Japan. The English Company had perforce to look elsewhere in Asia, if they were not to be excluded altogether.

Since Indian textiles were one of the principal commodities of exchange throughout Asia, procuring them in India itself seemed essential also. In order to participate in the textile trade, the Company needed to establish strategically located 'factories', where 'factors' or traders could stay to organize the collection of goods pending the seasonal arrival of ships, and where they were able to sell their own stock. The first of these were established at Surat on the west coast in 1613, and at Masulipatam, on the east coast, in 1611, both for the procurement of calicoes, plain and dyed, and chintzes. Local factories were opened throughout Gujarat near textile-producing centres, and further afield, particularly at Agra, where it was possible to buy indigo, calicoes and carpets, while even the saltpetre of Bengal could be shipped up the Jumna and overland to Surat.

These early factories would have been rented until more certain trade warranted purchasing premises. The Surat factory was 'partly the King's gift, partly hired.'[1] In 1630 Peter Mundy (*c.* 1597–*c.* 1667) described it as one of the 'best sort in town, very fair and strongly built, the roofs in general flat and terraced aloft to walk on ... and below a fair hall, chambers, and rooms for the President and Council, etc., merchants, with complete warehouses, walkes, etc., below'. The garden, 'which for its bigness is the neatest and costliest in all the country heareabouts', was a complete Mughal *charbagh* garden, with a central covered *chabutra* and little fountain beside it.[2] The spacious Dutch factory at Chinsura on the River Hooghly depicted by Hendrik van Schuylenburg in 1665 (see plate 10.1) was built round three sides of a quadrangle, with warehouses in the side wings. This appears to have been the model for the English factory established within the town of Hooghly in 1651 for the procurement of saltpetre and fine muslins and silks. Improvements were made to the English factory in 1676 to increase the married accommodation and to create the necessary offices and Council Chamber.[3] Despite various phases of expansion, the Hooghly site was always going to be desperately cramped and, exposed as it was in the town, rather vulnerable. A better site was identified further downriver at what in 1690 became Calcutta. In 1698 the Company in Calcutta managed to obtain from the *subahdar* (the governor) at Dacca the right to rent the three villages of Calcutta, Suttanuttee and Gobindpore.

Where conditions seemed stable, land could be rented and buildings erected that conformed more closely to what the Company and the factors wanted. Local rulers could be encouraging: in 1639 the factors at Masulipatnam were invited by the Hindu ruler of the coast further south to set up another factory, at a place called Madraspatnam, and he offered the Company half the revenues of the area and permission to build a fort there.[4] The area thus leased by the Company was five kilometres along the length of the coast by one and a half wide. Madraspatnam, commonly abbreviated to 'Madras', was the centre of production of chintzes, which were increasingly in demand as a trade good. It was on this site in 1640 that the Company began work constructing its first properly protected factory, Fort St George. In the meantime, further factories were established all along the Malabar coast, where spices were grown, and around Cape Comorin into the lower Coromandel coast. The general approach to the opening and closure of these smaller factories was flexible, depending on supply and demand.

In 1668 a factory was founded in Bombay, which was considered to be more secure than Surat, where the Company was forced to operate according to dictates of the Mughal governor of Gujarat. This hitherto Portuguese island, which commands the entrance to the finest harbour in western India, was part of the dowry of Catherine of Braganza, who married Charles II (r. 1660–85) in 1661. It was given by the king to the Company in 1668 for a peppercorn rent. Bombay was transferred to the English as a flourishing colony and a thriving settlement, and the Portuguese governor's mansion became the nucleus of Bombay Castle. When John Fryer (*fl.* 1672–98) arrived there in 1673, the fort was being built and the town, although large ('a full mile in length'), had little other than low houses thatched with palms, while 'the Custom house and Warehouses are tiled or plastered, and instead of glass, use panes of oyster-shell for their windows'.[5]

Whereas the Company was able to establish itself firmly along the Indian coast, it faced considerable difficulty elsewhere in Asia. English factories on the mainland of South-East Asia, at which Chinese silk on its way to Bantam could in theory be purchased more cheaply, were unsuccessful, as was the brief period of trade with Japan through the factory at Hirado, from 1613 to 1623. As the VOC increased its hold on the local rulers of Java, the English were ordered out of Bantam in 1682, but the Company was not prepared to lose its staple trade in pepper and managed to establish a factory in 1685 at Benkulen on the south-west coast of Sumatra. This was the only long-lasting English factory in South-East Asia until in 1825, in a very different world, it was exchanged with the Dutch for Malacca.[6]

China produced lucrative commodities such as silks, porcelain and above all tea, which was the new craze in Europe. However, establishing a suitable factory for the Chinese trade took all of the seventeenth century, as China was perfectly satisfied with existing trade arrangements through the Portuguese at Macao. In 1699 the Company finally managed to get a ship through to the great port city of Canton (Guangzhou), but the Chinese originally refused to permit factors to stay there. The first factors were in fact supercargoes sent out with each ship, who negotiated with the customs officials and the merchants of Canton while anchored off Macao; not until all was satisfactorily arranged was the cargo transferred to Canton, where a suitable temporary factory was rented for each season.[7] The foreign factories at Canton seem to have been gradually Europeanized with the introduction of glass windows, solid walls in place of wooden ones and gypsum roofs instead of mats.[8] When, instead of annual supercargoes, a permanent Council was finally established in 1758, it made arrangements with Chinese merchants to rent the same *hongs* for successive years. Two were rented that year; on one of these (the Yee-ho *hong*) they had already undertaken 'repairs'.[9] After 1759, when even stricter trade regulations were imposed, the supercargoes were no longer permitted to remain in Canton after the departure of the ships, but had to retreat to their rented accommodation in Macao until the next trading season. Attempts to travel in China outside of these two areas were absolutely forbidden.

The English factories in India were on a rather different footing. Although the Mughal state was vast, it did not control the entire peninsula, while it was open to both trade and cultural influences from the West. Of the four most important factories, two were ensconced in Mughal towns (Surat and Hooghly), one was in a dependency of the Deccan states (Madras) and one claimed to be a colony on English ground (Bombay). These interlopers on the fringes of empire were tolerated. By 1700 the amount of specie imported to pay for goods had become an important part of the Indian economy; turned into coin by the Mughal mints, it in part paid for the wars of the Mughal emperor Aurangzeb (r. 1658–1707).[10] English command of the Indian seas earned them their trading rights, and the responsibility of protecting Indian shipping from the increasing numbers of pirates. The consequences of failure to respect the Mughal government or to protect the shipping properly brought down the wrath of Aurangzeb on the Company's factories on several occasions.[11] The death of the emperor in 1707 ushered in a period not of chaos, as long feared

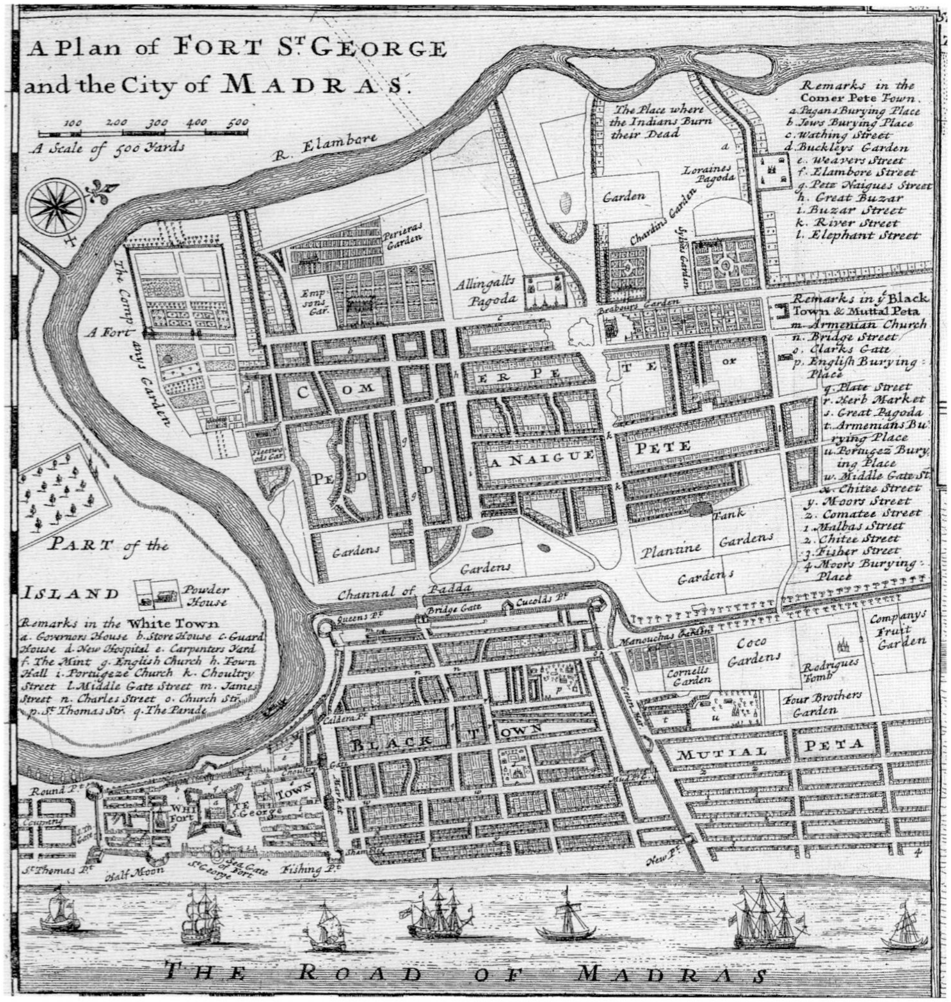

11.1
A Plan of Fort St George and the City of Madras
John Harris

Engraving on paper
England (London), *c.* 1710

Bodleian Library, Oxford

by the Company in London, but of a permanent weakening of the central government. The great nobles who ruled the provinces asserted their independence, and it was with these successor states that the English factories henceforth mostly dealt.

A series of views of the Indian factories, prepared in England but based on now mostly lost earlier sketches, shows the fortifications built around the principal factories of Madras, Bombay and Calcutta. These are of the simplest type: square bastions, some with pepperpot look-out towers, linked by curtain walls, pierced by a land gate on one side and a sea or river gate on the other. Around the small Fort St George, built immediately on the beach at Madras, spread the walled and fortified 'White Town', which was divided into a grid of streets and was built up in regular Georgian terraces. Fryer, who was there in 1673, wrote that 'the streets are sweet and clean, ranked with fine mansions, of no extraordinary height (because a garrison town) though beauty, which they conciliate, by the battlements and terrace walks on every house, and rows of trees before their doors, whose Italian porticoes make no ordinary conveyance into their houses, built with brick and stone'.[12]

Governor Pitt's *Prospect* of about 1710 shows the chief buildings rising behind the sea walls:[13] the domed Town Hall (with debtors' prison beneath), the tower and lantern of St Mary's church, the three-storeyed Government Houses behind the Sea Gate, and the tower over the south gate of Fort Square. It also served as the basis for George Lambert's painting of about 1730.[14] The fortified appearance of the houses within the White Town is confirmed by Fryer's earlier description. The English church, consecrated in 1680, and an earlier Catholic church for the 'Portuguese' stood within the town respectively south and north of the fort.[15] The walled 'Black Town' lay outside the main fortifications to the north, where stood the Armenian church. At this period, according to Captain Alexander Hamilton (*fl.* 1688–1723), there were 400–500 Europeans and 80,000 other inhabitants in Madras (plate 11.1).

By the early eighteenth century, when Captain Hamilton visited it, Bombay Castle was laid out similarly to the Madras fort, its walls enclosing the U-shaped old Government House of the seventeenth century.[16] Its guns commanded the little wharf and the approach to the factory. George Lambert

11.2
View of the Factory and Castle of Bombay from the Harbour
George Lambert and Samuel Scott

Oil on canvas
England (London), c.1731

British Library, London

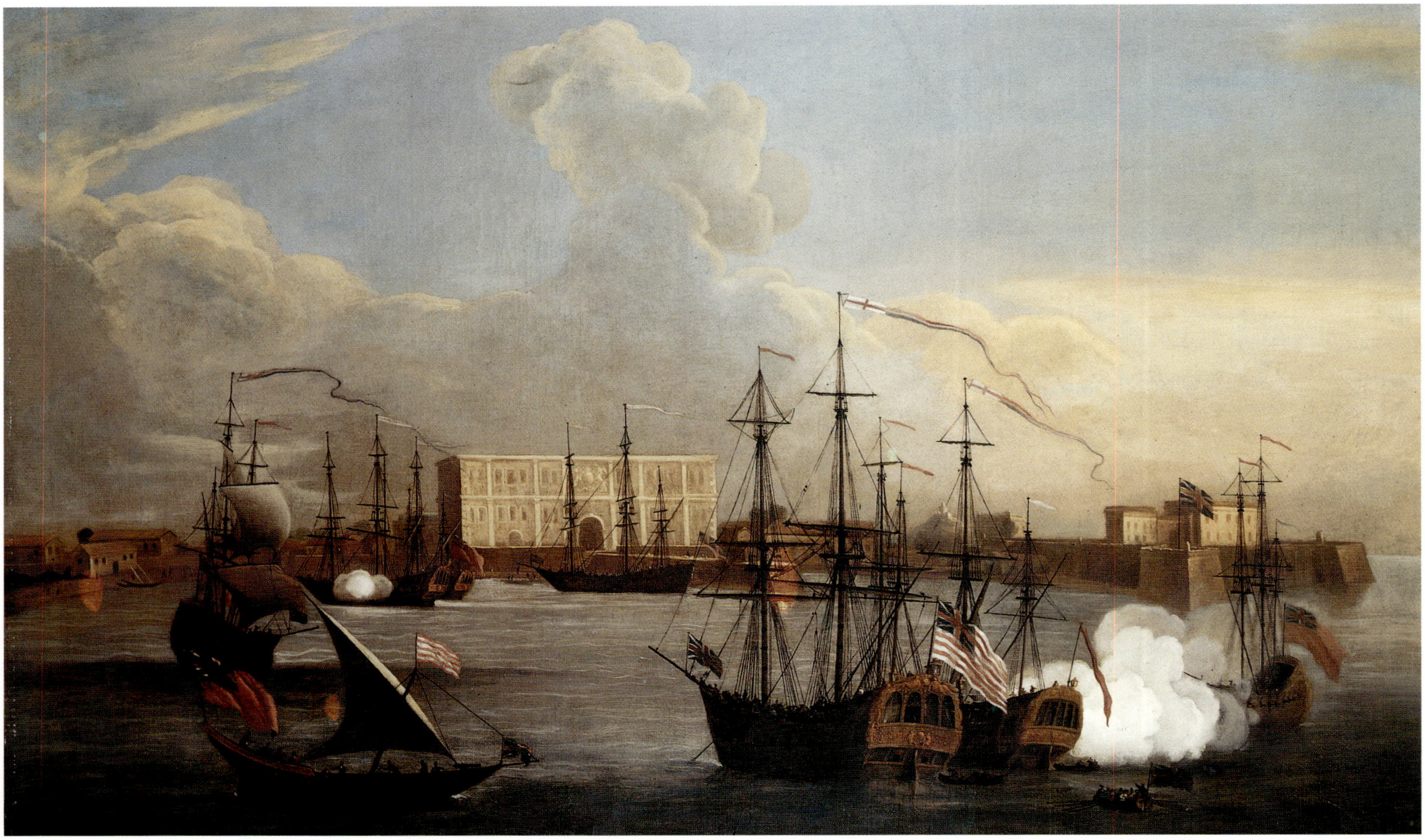

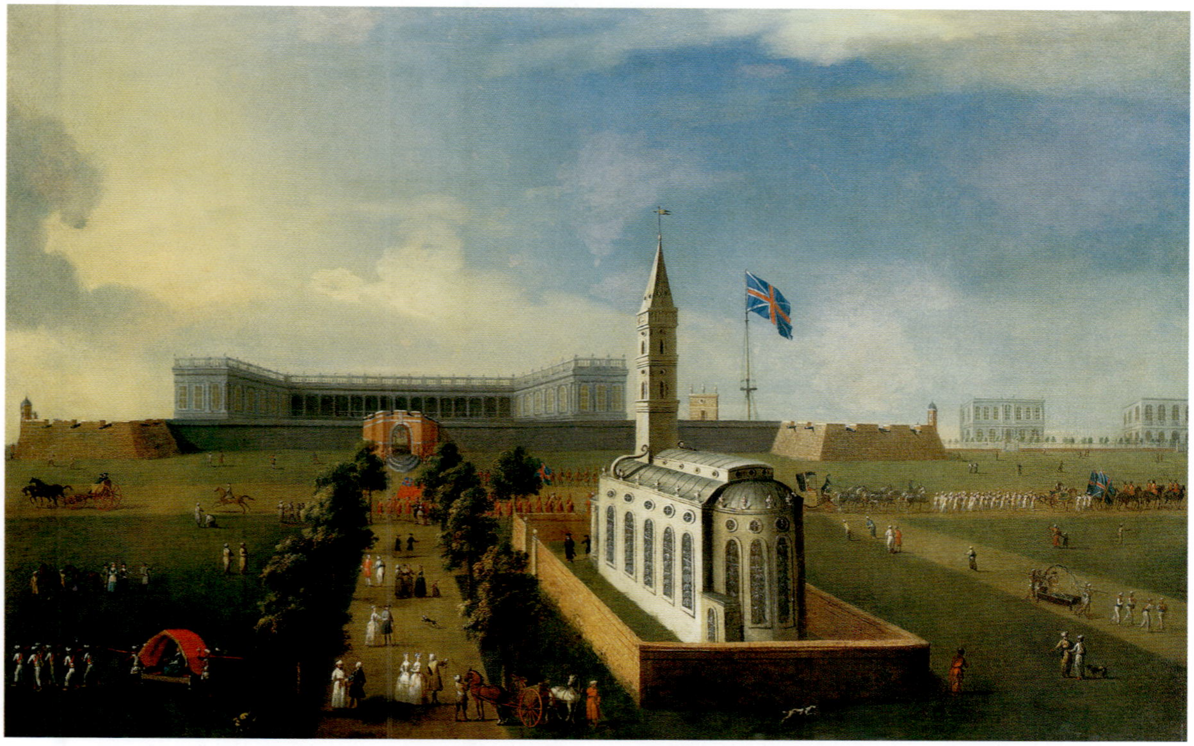

11.3
View of St Anne's church and Fort William, Calcutta
Anonymous

Oil on canvas
England (London), c.1730

Private collection

depicted the factory as the most important piece of architecture in Bombay, a seven-bayed building based on a Roman triumphal arch, with the Company's coat of arms proudly displayed (plate 11.2).[17] An outer polygonal moated wall was built around both the English and the Indian part of town in 1716, with bastions and three strongly fortified gates, and an esplanade of 1,000 metres all around. An open space in the middle of the town was Bombay Green, while the church of St Thomas (built 1672–1718), with tower and lantern, stood further to the west. Unlike Madras, the streets were very irregular. Government House was later moved into an elegant early Georgian house in town.[18]

The factory at Calcutta was described by Captain Hamilton as the 'best and most regular piece of architecture that ever I saw in India'.[19] The arrangement round three sides of a quadrangle was also imitated here, with the central portion fronting the river, and the arms projecting inland. Two paintings of about 1730 make it appear very grand indeed. An anonymous one shows the view from the land of the double-storeyed building, with a central upper pillared verandah and two projecting wings (plate 11.3).[20] The view commissioned by the Company from George Lambert of about 1730 shows the factory from the river, with this side too having short projecting wings, but in the centre a raised imposing entrance block.[21] Contemporary plans of Calcutta show the reality to be much less imposing, with comparatively short projecting wings even on the land side. St Anne's church (consecrated in 1709) was built opposite the main land gate of the fort, in a typical Queen Anne structure. The Armenians and the 'Portuguese' each had their own simple churches in their areas to the north.[22] The Bengali and other Indian merchant communities lived to the north in Suttanuttee. Calcutta was far less organized than Madras or Bombay. The nearest approach to town planning was laying out the park south of the church, with a large tank in its centre. Good two-storey houses in the early Georgian manner were erected haphazardly around the fort. No serious attempt was made to fortify the town with other than simple palisades and defensive ditches, which proved useless in 1756. Hamilton estimated there to be about 1,200 English in his time, and 12,000 people altogether.

The earliest views of the English factory at Canton date from the 1760s.[23] By this time alterations had converted the wide frontage of the *hong* into a palatial Palladian residence. In front was a double-storeyed pillared portico, while behind, the warehouse receded in a series of shallow pitched roofs running across the building. In 1769 it was noted that:

> each supercargo [there were 12 at the time] has four handsome rooms; the public apartments are in front looking to the river; the others go inland to the depth of two or three hundred feet, in broad courts, having the sets of rooms on each side, every set having a distinct and separate entrance with a small garden, and every sort of convenience.[24]

The Company rented two *hongs* at this time, out of the 13 on the waterfront, both of them nearly destroyed in the great fire in Canton in 1773.[25] When William Daniell sketched the scene in 1792–93, the lower storey of the portico had been given an arched arcade (plate 11.4).[26]

The prosperity of the Indian settlements was determined by whether the all-important Indian mercantile classes, tradesmen and their contacts, were prepared to settle there as well. What appears to have been the most important factor in determining this was whether the site was remote and, indeed, protected from traditional centres of power. The instability of the Mughal empire in the early eighteenth century would have enhanced the appeal of these sites. Bombay proved very attractive to Gujarati merchants. Similarly, Fort St George attracted traders away from Masulipatam, as well as more local Tamil merchants and weavers. Suttanuttee was already a thriving mart for Bengali merchants, and the new establishment attracted the mercantile classes from the other commercial centres upriver. The Company went out of its way to attract the Armenian community, long settled in India as traders, and ensured that wherever the Armenians settled they could build a church; and it afforded them the privileges of European status. The 'Portuguese', as the Company liked to call all Indian Christians, likewise had at least to be tolerated, despite their Catholicism, and no objections were raised to their building Catholic churches and supporting Catholic priests. Some of the Portuguese, like the Baretto family in Calcutta, were extremely wealthy.

In Madras, immigrant Indians settled immediately to the north of the fort, in what was called 'Black Town', which was also walled and partially fortified (plate 11.5). Portuguese settlers were also attracted

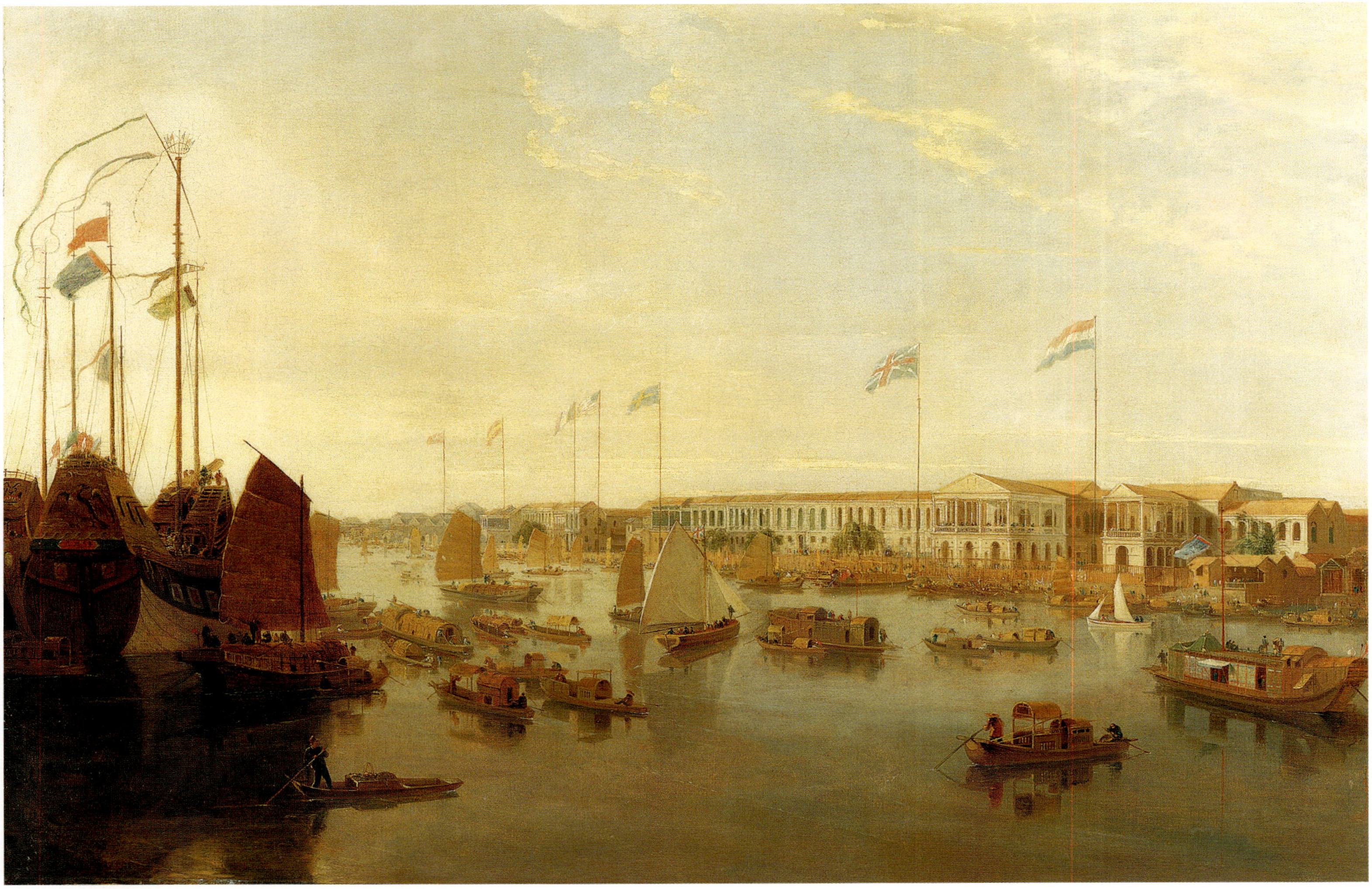

11.4
The European Factories in Canton
William Daniell

Oil on canvas
England (London), *c.*1808, based on an *in-situ* sketch of 1793–94

Yale Center for British Art, New Haven

from San Thomé a few kilometres down the coast. According to Captain Hamilton, 'The Black Town is inhabited by Gentows, Mahometans and Indian Christians, viz. Armenians and Portugueze, where there are temples and churches for each religion, every one being tolerated; and every one follows his proper employment.'[27] As in the White Town, the streets were laid out in a regular grid pattern, with a Great Pagoda in the middle according to Pitt's plan, which makes 'Black Town' correspond to similarly laid-out temple towns of southern India.

Bombay was far from any major centre of commerce or manufacture, and hence needed every incentive to become one. In contrast therefore to Fort St George, Indian merchants were encouraged to settle within the strongly fortified walls, as were Parsi shipbuilders from Surat, who modernized the dockyards. The large numbers of immigrants who came to the town from different religious and caste communities encouraged the creation of separate wards; and within the fortified walls, Indians settled to the north of Church Gate Street and the English to the south. This divide between north and south was officially decreed in 1772, and shortly afterwards the Bombay government started legislating for the appearance of the town.[28] Causeways connecting the various islands that form Bombay, and reclamation of land from the sea between them, were undertaken, which likewise improved the accessibility of the otherwise remote local Hindu and Muslim shrines.

'Bazaar Calcutta' north of Fort William was the most densely populated area of that city, as this division included not only half of the English settlement around the north of the fort, but also the Armenian and Portuguese areas further north, and the Great or Bara Bazaar, the main Bengali area, which had already sprung up between the Christian part of the settlement and Suttanuttee itself.[29] In 1731 one of the largest temples in Bengal was erected by Gobindram Mitter (*fl.* 1720–56) at the northern end of Suttanuttee, while the Kalighat temple to the south had long been famous.

None of the official buildings erected by the Company in its factories and settlements paid much attention to local architectural traditions. The English went into Asia knowing that they were different and were determined to assert this. Factories, fortifications, Government Houses, churches and dwellings were all built along regular European lines. In fact, only in death were the English prepared to compromise. They rather took to the more grandiose

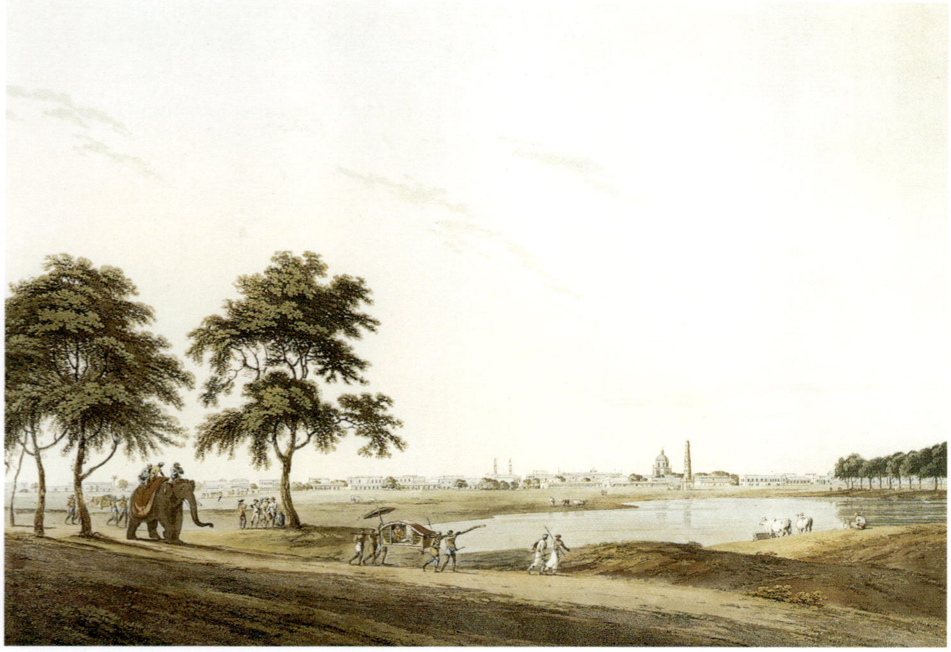

11.5
Part of the Black Town, Madras
Thomas and William Daniell, after Thomas Daniell, *Oriental Scenery*, part II, no. 8, London, 1797, based on an *in-situ* sketch of 1793
Coloured aquatint on paper
British Library, London

Mughal and other Muslim mausoleums which they saw all around them, and were buried like their Dutch counterparts in huge structures – domed chambers with surrounding arcades, which are found in Agra, Surat and Calcutta (plate 11.6).

By late in the eighteenth century, the English in Madras had cast off their austere battlemented façades in favour of a more elegant Palladian appearance. The artist William Hodges (1744–97), arriving in Madras in 1780, described the scene:

> The English town, rising from within Fort St George, has from the sea a rich and beautiful appearance; the houses being covered with a stucco called chunam, which in itself is nearly as compact as the finest marble, and, as it bears a high polish, is equally splendid with that elegant material. The stile of the buildings is in general handsome. They consist of long colonnades, with open porticos, and flat roofs, and offer to the eye an appearance similar to what we may conceive of a Grecian city in the age of Alexander. The clear, blue, cloudless sky, the polished white buildings, the bright sandy beach, and the dark green sea, present a combination totally new to the eyes of an Englishman.[30]

Architecture in Bombay developed along different lines than in Calcutta and Madras. The Palladian style had hardly any impact, either on official or domestic architecture. Partly this was because of the region's own rich architectural traditions, exemplified in wooden multi-storeyed buildings with pitched roofs and carved balconies. Such structures were typical of Gujarat, whence many of the Bombay immigrants came. Under the Portuguese this tradition coalesced into a colonial style with verandahs on several storeys, all under steeply pitched roofs, which were to say the least a good idea in areas of the heaviest monsoon rains. The Bombay factor James Forbes (1749–1819) wrote:

> When I left Bombay [in 1784], the generality of the public buildings were more useful than elegant … The English houses at Bombay, though neither so large nor elegant as those at Calcutta and Madrass, were comfortable and well furnished; they were built in the European style of architecture, as much as the climate would admit of; but lost something of that appearance by the addition of verandahs. or covered piazzas, to shade those apartments most exposed to the sun.[31]

The English adapted this Portuguese style for their own buildings, both official and domestic, thereby imparting a totally different aesthetic to their colonial city.[32]

The transfer of power from Indian to English hands in eastern India after 1757 completely changed the rules of engagement between the two races. Although security considerations dictated the need to build a new fort, in fact it was not essential, since after 1765 the Company was the *de facto* ruler of eastern India. In Calcutta the old Fort William, of which little remained but the outer walls, was abandoned as a fort, but remained a customs house, while a vast new Fort William – large enough to provide refuge for the entire Christian community if threatened again, and embodying the latest European ideas on fortifications – was laid out in what had been the village of Gobindpore along the river to the south. Around the new fort the land was kept clear of buildings to form a great park or maidan; here residents of Calcutta took the air in carriages in the early morning or evening. The settlement around the old fort gradually became the centre of Calcutta's commercial life, although it remained a prestigious address, while more spacious houses were built along the fringes of the maidan around the fort. In the older neighbourhoods, houses had been built in terraces in the regular English Georgian manner. With more space in the newer areas, houses were built in a Palladian style in the centre of compounds and, as in other colonial settlements in warm climates, verandahs were built on each floor behind grandiose colonnades and porticoes. Ground floors contained the offices, reception rooms, and the grandest bedrooms were on the first floor, with other bedrooms above in three-storey houses. Windows were very large, normally unglazed, with Venetian shutters. When one was tired of town, 'the banks of the river are as one may say absolutely studded with elegant mansions' (plate 11.7).[33]

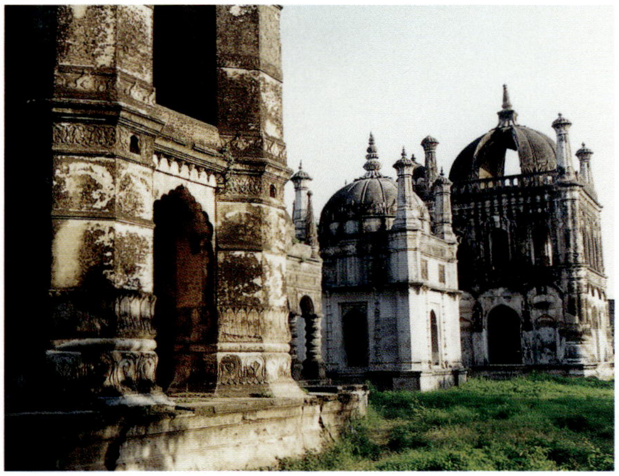

11.6
European cemetery, Surat

Raptures at the first sight of Calcutta from the river became a commonplace of late eighteenth-century travel writing. Hodges, for instance:

> The vessel has no sooner gained one other reach of the river than the whole city of Calcutta bursts upon the eye. This capital of the British dominions in the East is marked by a considerable fortress … superior to any in India … The glacis and esplanade are seen in perspective, bounded by a range of beautiful and regular buildings; and a considerable reach of the river, with vessels of various classes and sizes, from the largest Indiamen to the smallest boat of the country, closes the scene.[34]

Hodges painted this view for Warren Hastings in 1781–83, showing the row of government buildings on the Esplanade of Calcutta from Fort William (plate 11.8). The sharply observant Jemima Kindersley (*fl.* 1764–77) was, however, less easily impressed in 1768:

> I think I have never given you an account of the town of Calcutta; indeed, after Madras, it does not appear much worth describing; for although it is large, with a great many good houses in it, and has the advantage of standing upon the banks of a river, it is as awkward a place as can be conceived; and so irregular, that it looks as if all the houses had been thrown up in the air, and falled down again by accident as they now stand: people keep constantly building; and every one who can procure a piece of ground to build a house upon, consults his own taste and convenience, without any regard to the beauty or regularity of the town; besides, the appearance of the best houses is spoiled by the little straw huts, and such sort of encumbrances, which are built by the servants for themselves to sleep in.[35]

Mrs Kindersley wrote of the appearance and decoration of the interiors of Calcutta houses:

> Paper, or wainscot, are improper, both on account of the heat, the vermin, and the difficulty of getting it done; the rooms are therefore all whited walls, but plastered in panels, which has a pretty effect; and are generally ornamented with prints,

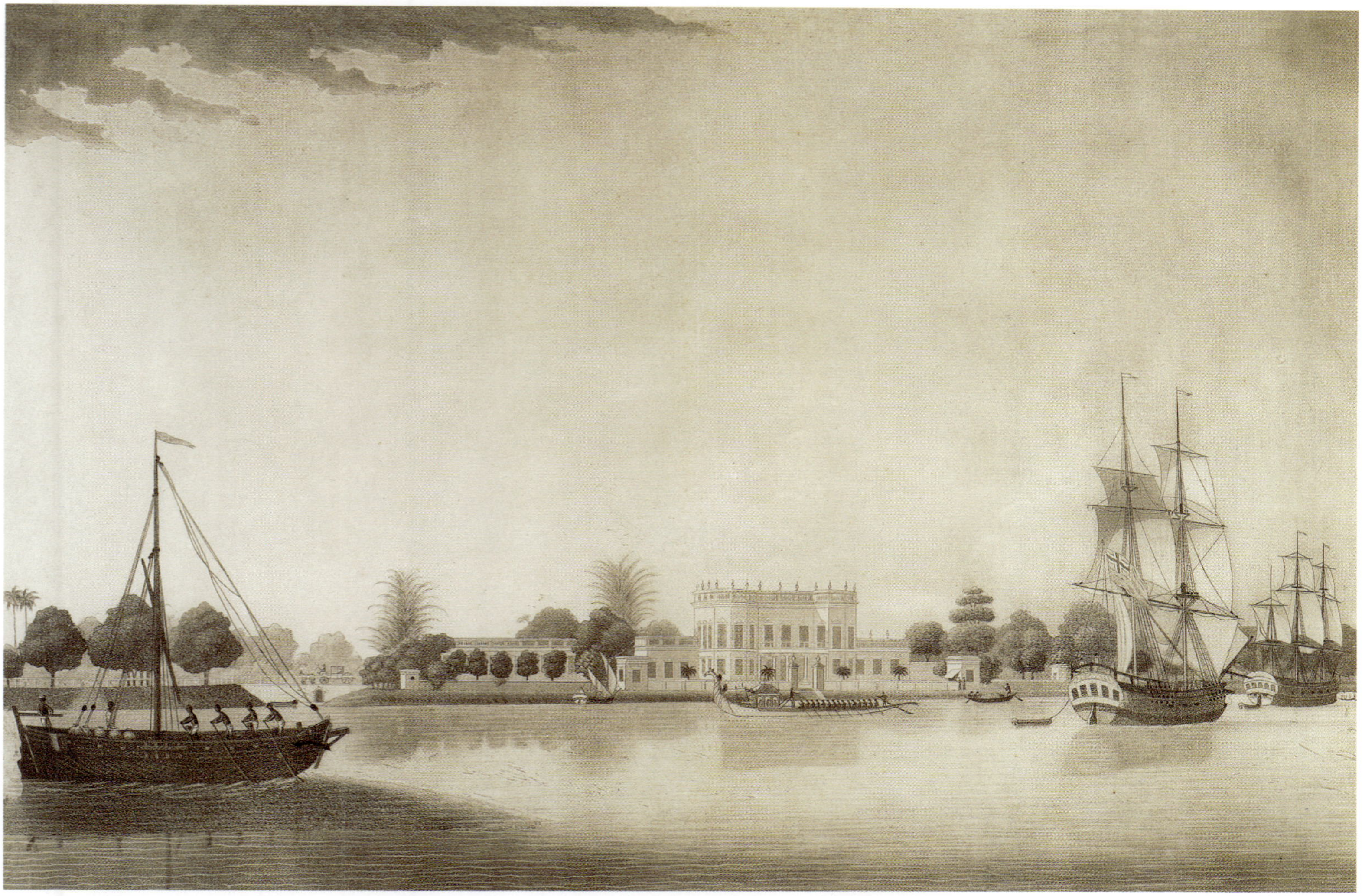

looking-glasses, or whatever else can be procured from Europe; the floors are likewise plaster, covered all over with fine matt, which is nailed down; for although carpets are manufactured in some parts of the country, they are such an addition to the heat, that they are seldom made use of; the rooms are few, but mostly very large and lofty; many of the new-built houses have glass-windows, which are pleasant to the eye, but not so well calculated for the climate as the old ones, which are made of cane.[36]

The description is matched by a contemporary watercolour of the interior of Lady Impey's apartments around 1780 (see plate 21.11).[37]

The church of St Anne was destroyed in the 1756 attack on Calcutta and was not rebuilt; the English Protestant community had to make do with a makeshift chapel made out of some of the rooms in the old fort until a new church of St John was built and consecrated in 1788 in what had been the old burial ground at the south of the settlement. This was like many eighteenth-century London churches, with a portico and steeple at the west end and capacious wooden galleries inside. The churchyard was soon full, and another was opened at the edge of town beside the Maratha Ditch: it was used so frequently that the road to it was known as the Burying Ground Road. The grandiose circular mausoleums of the old churchyard were succeeded in the new cemetery by neoclassical monuments. The Armenian church retained its simple early eighteenth-century appearance, but the Portuguese church (of the 'Virgin Mary of the Rosary') was rebuilt in a very English classical style in 1797–99.[38]

The old Fort William had contained rooms for the president's lodgings and a council chamber. Now that the government of eastern India had fallen into the Company's hands, very much larger premises were required. A planned Government House in the new Fort William never materialized. Instead, the Company resolved in 1764 to build a new

11.7
View on the Banks of the Hooghly near Calcutta, the Country Residence of William Farquharson, Esq.
James Moffat, after a painting by F. B. Solvyns
Aquatint with soft ground etching
India (Calcutta), *c.* 1800
British Library, London

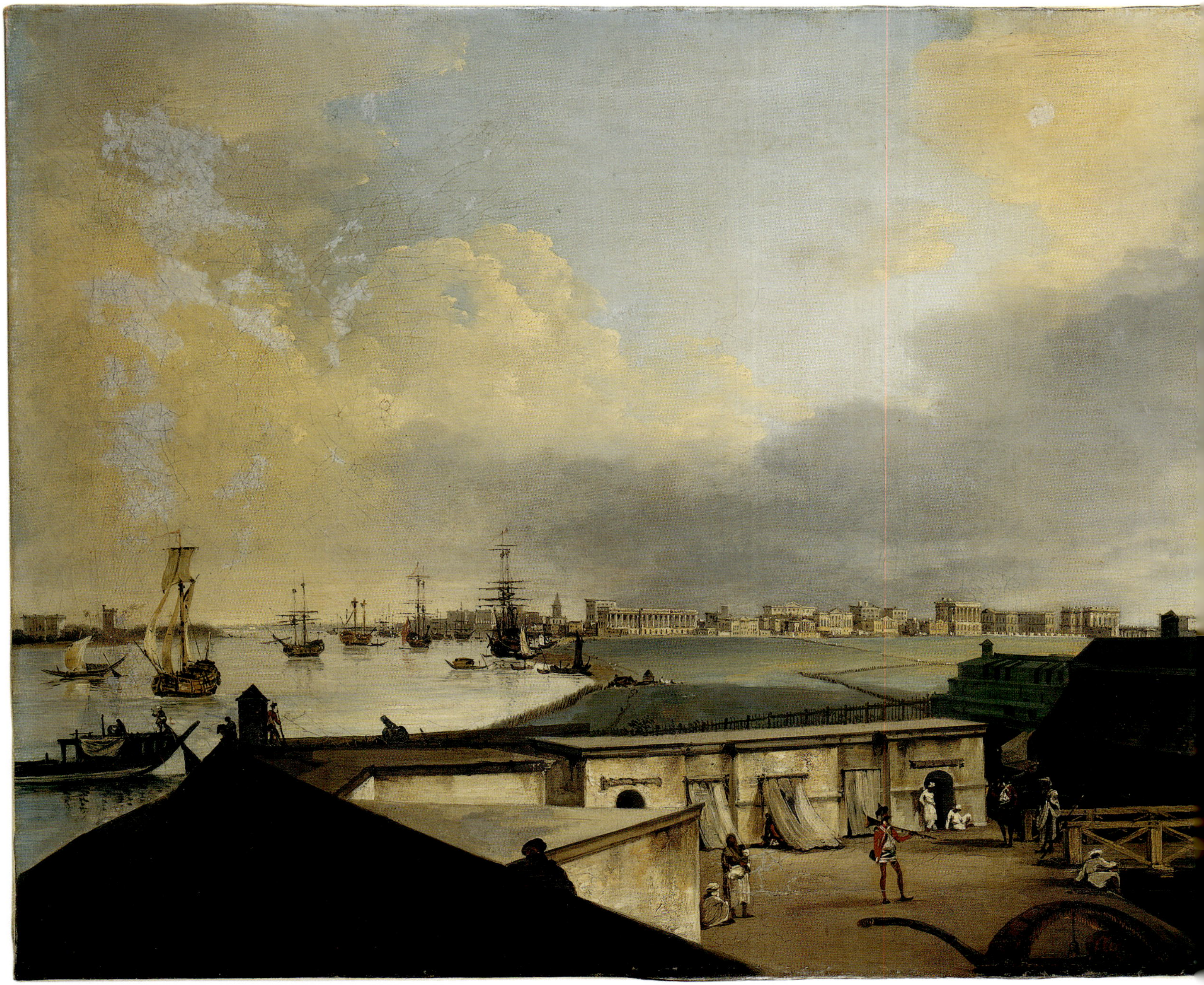

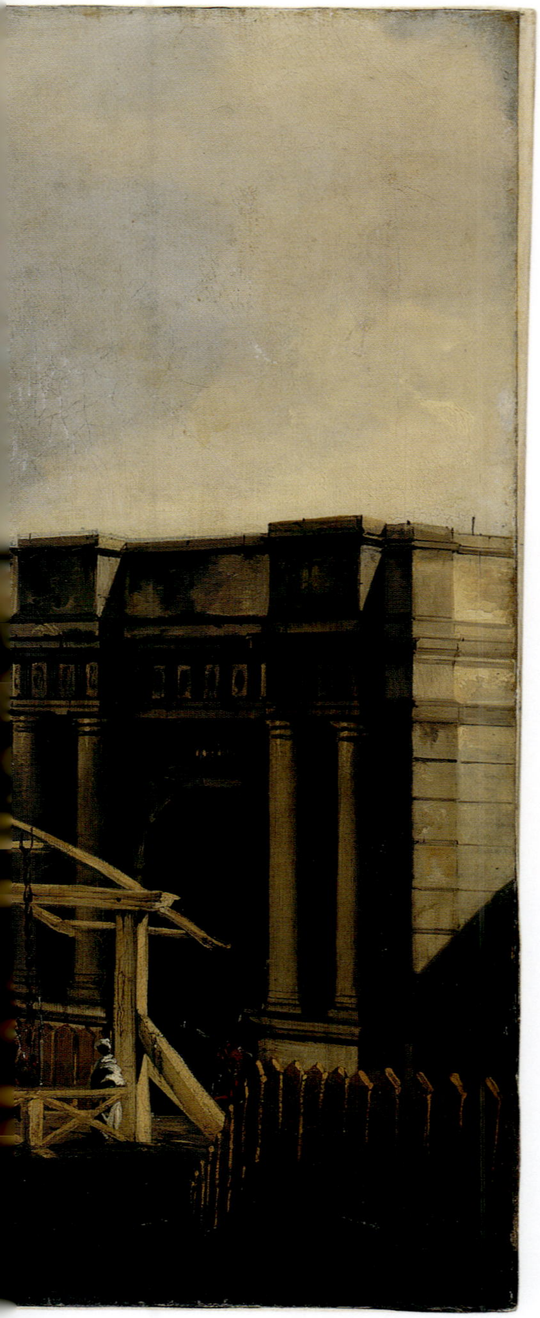

Government House on the northern edge of the maidan, both for the governor's lodgings and the Council meetings and offices; and, this still not being big enough, it leased the neighbouring house owned by a local nobleman, Muhammad Reza Khan. This became the governor's lodgings, while the neighbouring offices became known as the Council House. The latter was a U-shaped building, rather reflecting the factory building in the old fort, with a part-rusticated basement storey and a first floor with a central portico with a row of regular windows with venetians under tall segmental pediments. Government House was also U-shaped with a rusticated office storey, and a *piano nobile* in the main wing with an indented façade with large windows separated by columns.[39] Other governmental buildings along Esplanade Row were the Treasury, next to the Council House, and, further along, the Supreme Court, with a two-storeyed colonnade above a rusticated basement.

Both Government House and the Council House were swept away by Marquess Wellesley (Governor-General of Bengal 1798–1805) at the end of the century to create a huge new three-storeyed Government House. Its central block – the main rooms being a state dining room below and a ballroom above, with entrance porticoes north and south – are connected at both ends by curving passages to wings, all of the same height. The private rooms were in the wings, apart from the north-east one, where the new Council House was. The building of this grandiose palace, whose ultimate model was the idea of an English country mansion, matched Wellesley's expansionist plan for the Company to become the dominant power in India; the transition from a factory for trade to a palace for imperial government was here completed (plate 11.9).

11.8
A View of Calcutta Taken from Fort William
William Hodges

Oil on canvas
India (Calcutta), 1781–83

Private collection

11.9
View of the New Government House, Calcutta
Attributed to Edward Orme, after an aquatint by James Moffat of 1803

Watercolour on paper
England (London), 1804

British Library, London

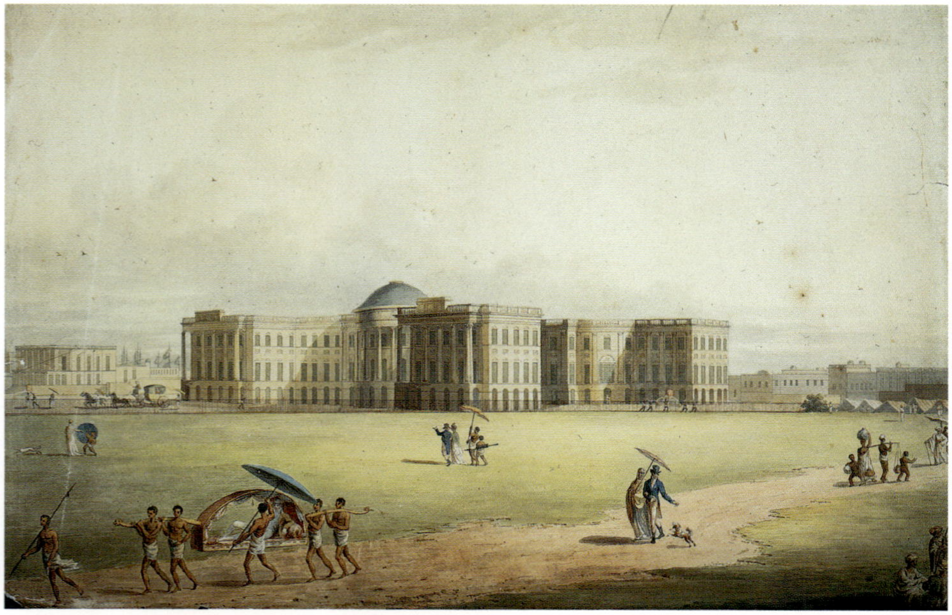

Canton: Centre of Trade

Kee Il Choi, Jr

GUANGZHOU, SITED ON the Pearl River delta about 145 kilometres upstream from the South China Sea, had been an important centre of international commerce between China and the rest of Asia since the Tang dynasty (AD 618–907). It was not until the late seventeenth century that Europeans began to trade there, calling the city 'Cantão', 'Kan-ton' or 'Canton', probably derived from 'Quang-tong' (Guangdong), the name of the province in which it is located.

In 1698 regular, direct trade with Europeans was initiated with the arrival of *l'Amphitrite*, a French vessel belonging to the *Compagnie des Indes*. By the 1730s the ships of trading companies from Britain, Holland, France, Denmark and Sweden called annually at Canton; and vessels from Spain and the United States joined them later in the century. Burgeoning maritime activity reflected a sharp growth in European demand for Chinese commodities such as tea, silk and porcelain, for which the traders paid with silver. The number of East India Company ships sailing annually to Canton, for example, increased from one or two at the beginning of the century to nearly 30 by mid-century. Tea was the most profitable cargo of the trade. By around 1725 the annual purchase of tea by the Company had gradually increased from a few

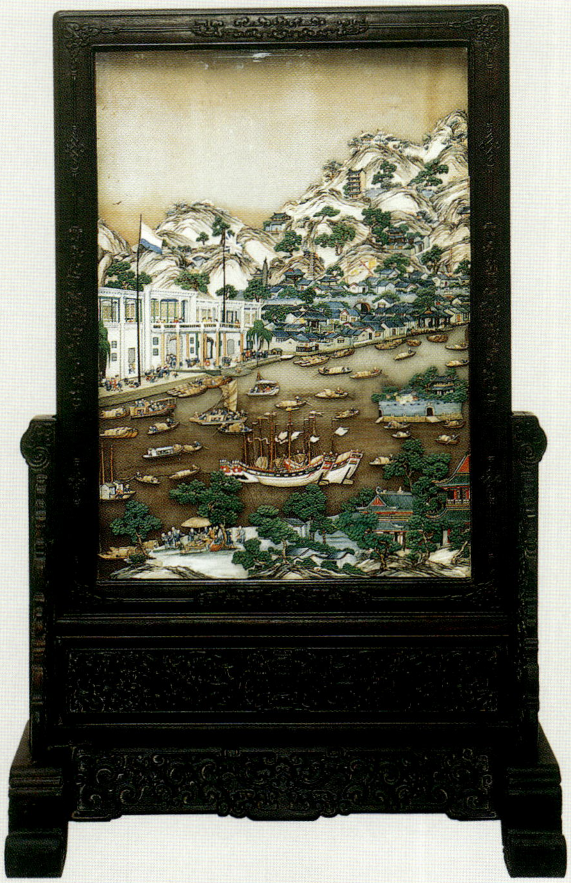

11.10
Table screen with a view of the foreign factories, Canton

Glass, painted in reverse, with carved and stained ivory; frame and stand of zitan
China (Canton), Qianlong period (1736–95)

Palace Museum, Beijing

11.11
Canton

Handscroll; ink and watercolours on paper
China (Canton), *c.* 1730

Royal Collections, Drottningholm, Sweden

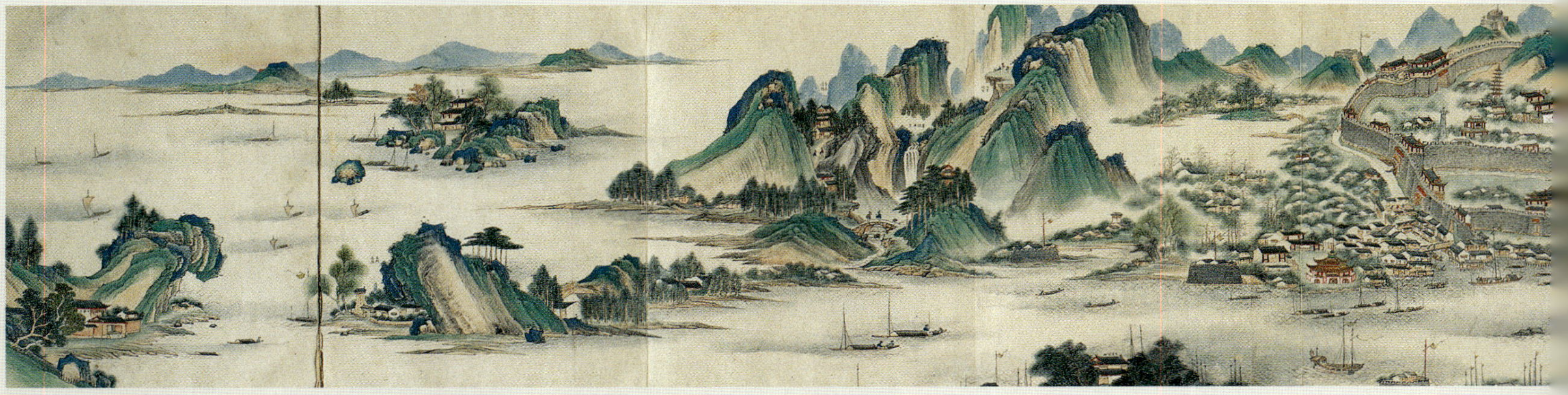

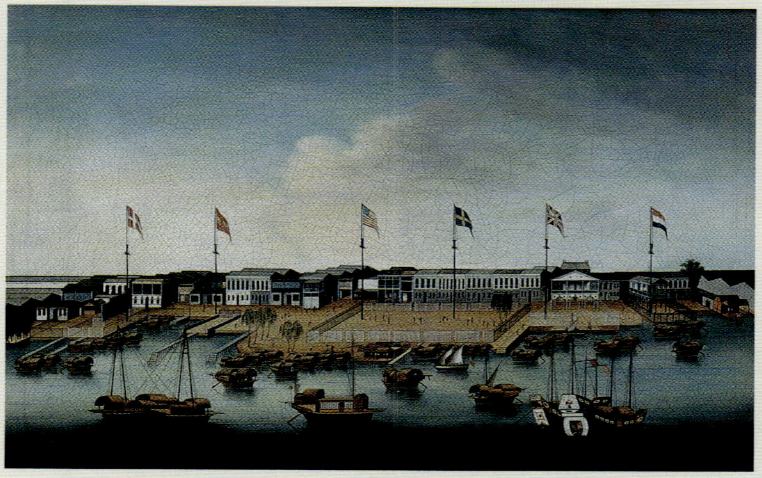

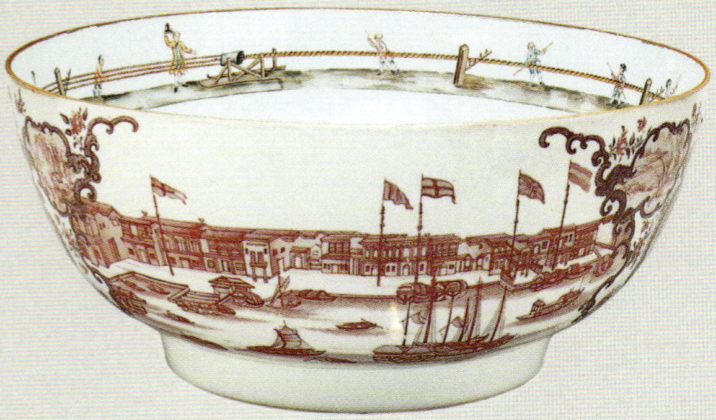

11.12
Foreign Factory Site, Canton

Oil on canvas
China, *c.*1790

Collection of Dr and Mrs John Kurtz

11.13
Punch-bowl depicting views of foreign factories in Canton and the bourse in Copenhagen

Porcelain decorated with overglaze enamels
China (Canton), *c.*1765–75

Collection of Erving and Joyce Wolf

hundred pounds in weight to about 400,000 pounds.

From the start, the conditions of trade were a constant source of tension between the Chinese and the Europeans. Imperial and provincial authorities regulated the conduct of business in Canton through a specially appointed group of merchants. These *hong* (*hang*) merchants were the sole agents of foreign trade and were responsible, simultaneously, for the volume of trade, price fixing and the collection of exactions and customs levies. They also oversaw the personal conduct of the Europeans and rented factories to their trading companies. Conflicts inevitably arose over price and attendant business costs, especially extortions and bribes. Matters came to a head in the mid-1750s, causing the number of ships calling at Canton to plummet as Company merchants, who dominated the trade, sought more favourable conditions and prices for commodities in ports further north. This sudden loss of business impacted upon the local economy and limited the ability of the Cantonese *hong* merchants to pay the required tribute to the imperial court. Consequently they petitioned Peking (Beijing) to raise customs duties at the competing ports. As a result, in 1759 the court decreed that Canton should be the sole Chinese port open to foreign trade, an objective of imperial policy since the late 1720s.

Concurrently, all foreign activity within Canton itself was restricted to a narrow, short strip of land on the river front. This precinct evolved gradually into the foreign factory site (plate 11.12 and endpapers), an architecturally distinct and socially isolated collection of buildings constructed in both native and European styles (see p. 145 and pp. 147–8). The Chinese referred derogatorily to these buildings as 'barbarian houses' (*i-kuan*) and imposed a set of regulations on the traders that aimed to restrict their personal freedom and, as much as possible, prohibit them from fraternizing with the Chinese.

Pre-1750 views of Canton, usually in the form of traditional Chinese scrolls (plate 11.11), presented panoramas of the ancient city and its environs. Beginning in the 1760s, however, demand among European traders grew for souvenirs, rendered in a hybrid style, which depicted the foreign factories exclusively, rather than the whole city (plate 11.13) These images came to mirror the reality of the China trade: westerners were welcome in Canton to do business, but otherwise the Chinese held them at arm's length. By the end of the century, these Chinese export images had grown in popularity and become emblematic not only of the trade, but of China itself.

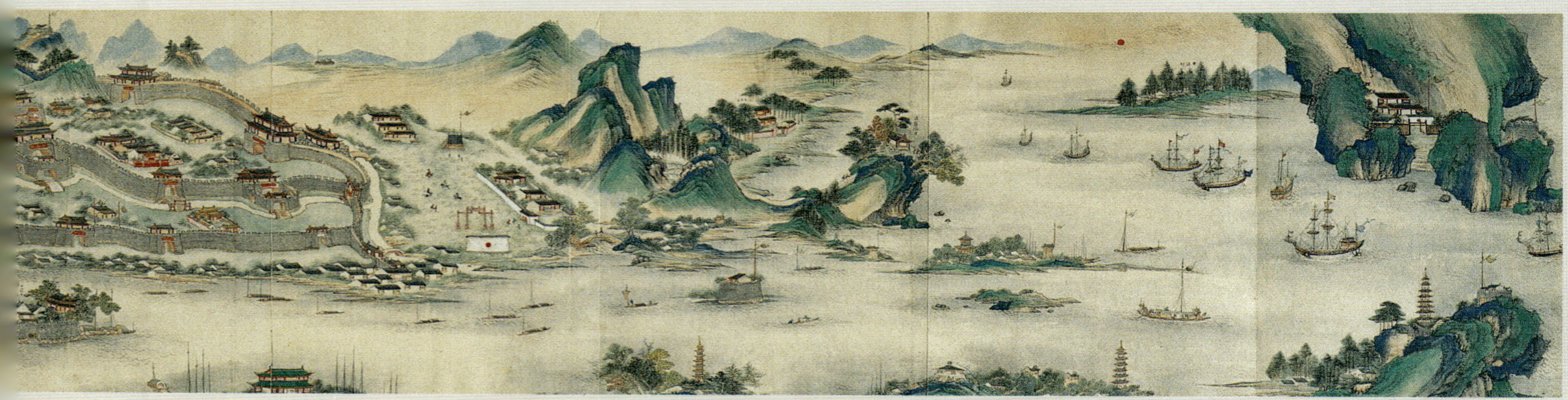

12

PERSONAL ENCOUNTERS: EUROPEANS IN SOUTH ASIA

William Dalrymple

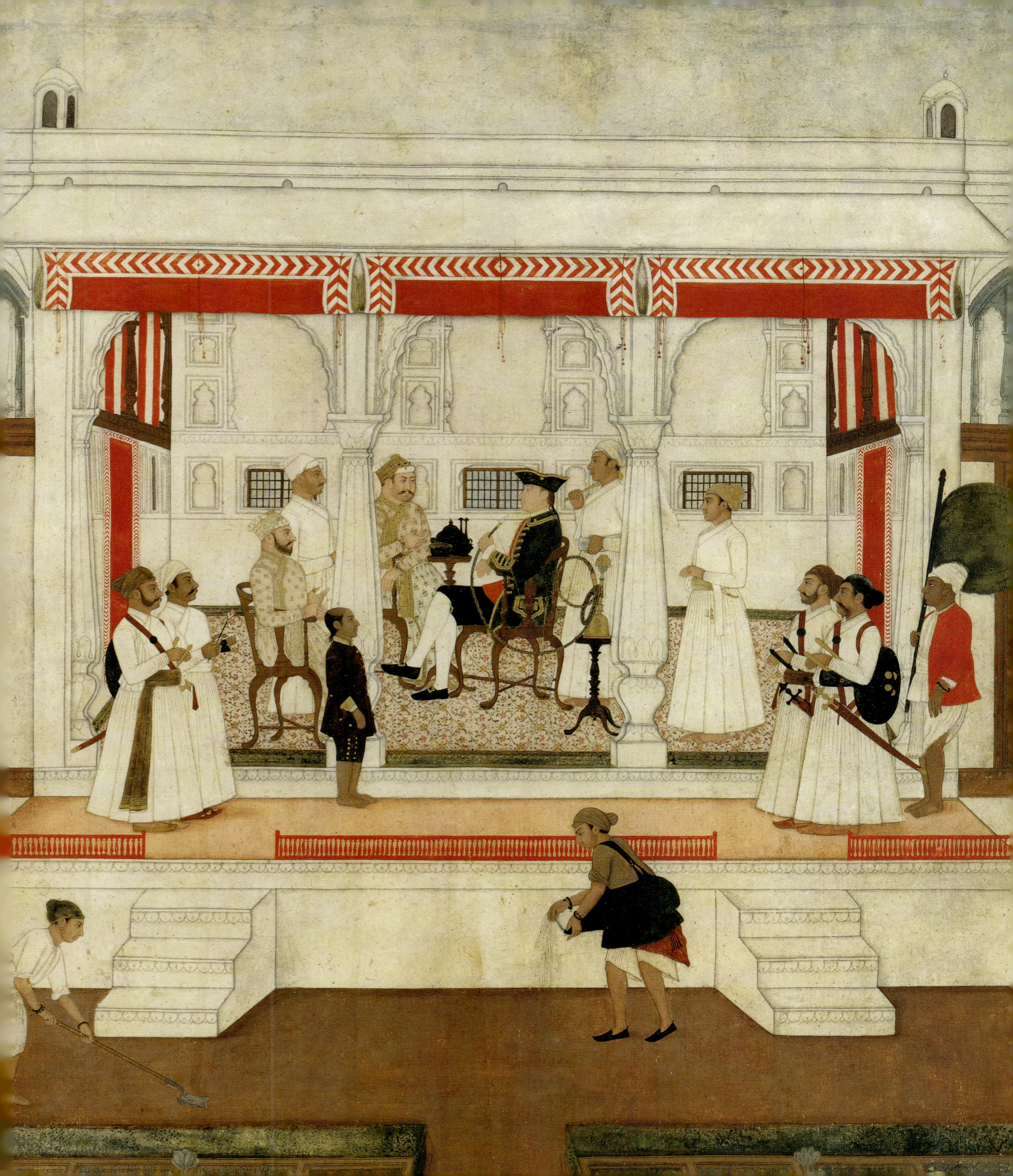

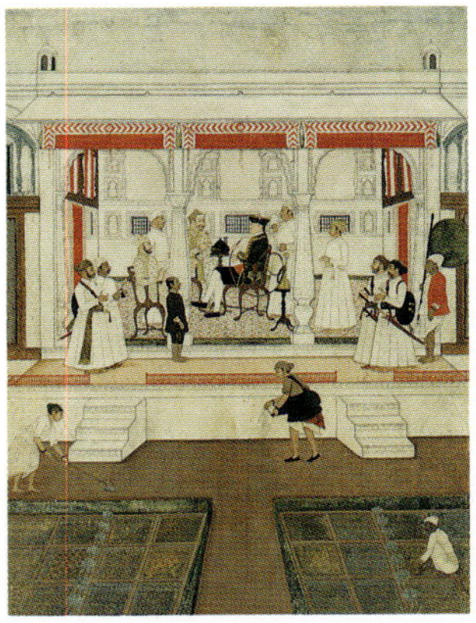

12.1 previous page and above
English Official in Discussion with a Nawab
Opaque watercolour with gold on paper
India (Patna or Murshidabad), 1760–65
Private collection, London

India has a strange way with its conquerors. In defeat, it beckons them in, then slowly seduces, assimilates and transforms them. Over the centuries, many powers have defeated Indian armies; but none has ever proved immune to the strange capacity of the subcontinent somehow to reverse the current of colonization, and to mould those who attempt to subjugate it. So vast is India, and so uniquely resilient and deeply rooted are its intertwined social and religious institutions, that all foreign intruders are sooner or later either shaken off or absorbed.

This 'crossing over' was a process that dated from the very beginning of the European presence in India. The Portuguese were the first to make the transition. After the conquest of Goa in 1510 – some 16 years before the arrival of the Mughals in north India – the Portuguese commander Afonso de Albuquerque (1453–1515) made a point of ordering his men to marry the widows of the Muslim defenders they had massacred during the taking of the city. Albuquerque himself presided at the weddings of these 'fair Mooresses of pleasing appearance' and provided them with dowries.[1] These women were forcibly converted to Christianity, and after baptism, many were made to receive the rudiments of the Catholic faith. But this crude attempt at force-feeding unadulterated Portuguese culture on India proved short-lived.

Over the course of the next half-century, the women, the environment and the sheer distance of Goa from Europe all worked on the new arrivals, so that gradually, generation by generation, the invaders began abandoning the ways of Portugal and taking on instead the customs of India. By the time the Portuguese Inquisition arrived in India in 1560, life at Goa much more closely resembled that in Mughal capitals such as Delhi and Agra than Lisbon or any city in Portugal.

By then, Goan grandees dressed in Oriental magnificence, shielding themselves with umbrellas and never leaving their houses except accompanied by vast retinues of slaves and servants. Travellers reported how the Goan aristocracy kept harems and that even the Christian women wore Indian clothes inside the house and lived as if in purdah 'little seene abroad'.[2] If they had to go out, they did so veiled or in modestly covered palanquins. The men chewed betel nut, ate rice (but only with their right hand) and drank *arrack;* they rubbed themselves with 'sweet sanders',[3] and their doctors prescribed the old Hindu panacea of cow's urine three times a day to their patients 'in order to recover their colour, one glass in the morning, one at midday, and one in the evening'.[4] By 1642, the governor of the Dutch East India Company, Anthon van Diemen (1593–1645), could report that 'most of the Portuguese in India look upon this region as their fatherland, and think no more about Portugal. They drive little or no trade thither, but content themselves with port to port trade as if they were natives and had no other country.'[5] His compatriot, Huyghen van Linschoten (1563–1611), came to the same conclusion: 'The posteritie of the Portingales, both men and women, doe seeme to be naturall Indians, both in colour and in fashion.'[6]

These early descriptions of Indo-Portuguese culture set the tone for what was to come over the next 300 years, in a wide range of encounters between different Indian peoples and various colonial intruders. It is clear from the start that what was happening was not so much a wholesale substitution of one culture for another, so much as a complex process of fusion. The Portuguese in India, and their Indo-Portuguese descendants, did not leave one culture to inhabit another, so much as live in both at the same time, accommodating in their outlook and lifestyles opposing ways of living in and looking at the world.

Perhaps partly because of the Inquisition, a surprisingly large number of Portuguese made the decision to emigrate from Portuguese territory and seek their fortunes at different Indian courts, usually as gunners, cavalrymen and mercenaries. By 1565, according to the Portuguese chronicler João de Barros (1496–1570), there were at least 2,000 Portuguese fighting in the armies of different Indian princes.[7] Not all of them converted to Islam, or even radically changed their modes of living, but it is clear from the sources that a great many did.

Such men were usually from the very margins of Portuguese society; indeed, they were often criminals who had been forcibly exiled from Portugal for crimes at home. They were attracted both by the remarkable religious freedom of India, and by the better prospects and higher and more regular pay. Others were no doubt lured from Portuguese service by the delights of a society in which slavery, concubinage and polygamy were widespread and entirely accepted, and where they could live like the curious figure whom some British sailors encountered at the beginning of the seventeenth century, living it up on the Moluccas 'with as many women as he pleaseth … he will sing and dance all day long, near hand naked ... and will be drunk two days together'.[8]

Most of the men and women who 'crossed over' are only fleetingly visible in the historical record, but occasionally chance circumstances lead to them getting firmly caught in the historian's net. One such was João Machado, who, as a punishment for blasphemy, was abandoned by a Portuguese caravel on the east coast of Africa. Somehow he found his way to Gujarat and from there joined the service of the Adil Shahi rulers of Bijapur. There Machado learned the language, adapted himself to local ways of life, converted to Islam and, as a general in the Bijapur army, sought revenge by leading repeated attacks of his *Firangiyan* (Frankish) cavalry on his old compatriots in Goa. Eventually, he turned coat again, and returned to Goa at a time when the colony was in imminent danger of falling to a Bijapur assault. As a reward for his return at this crucial moment, Albuquerque gave him some land – in the grant he is referred to as 'Joham Machado who was a Turk and now has become a Christian' – but before he had much time to enjoy his new status, Machado was killed in action five years later, ironically in a skirmish with the very Bijapuri cavalry he had once led.[9]

Machado was a man of his times: at the height of the Mughal empire, so many Europeans took service in the Mughal army that a special suburb was built outside Delhi for them called Firingi Pura (Foreigners' Town). The inhabitants of Firingi Pura included renegade Portuguese, English and Frenchmen, many of whom chose to convert to Islam, and who formed a distinct *firingi* (or foreigners') regiment under a Frenchman known as Farrashish Khan.[10]

Often marginalized by their own society, these European renegades became important mediators between the world of Europe and the world of India. Moreover, they demonstrate the remarkable fluidity of the frontier that separated the two. From the mid-sixteenth century, with the advent of wholesale defections from Portuguese Goa, the borderlands of colonial India had taken up the role they would continue to play over the next 300 years: as spaces where categories of identity, ideas of national loyalty, relations of power and the limits of self-transformation were infinitely negotiable and tractable, and where the normal steely dualism of empire – between rulers and ruled, imperialists and subalterns, colonizers and the colonized – almost completely breaks down.

The British were no more immune than any other nation to the social forces that transformed the Portuguese in India. Indeed, it was one of the distinguishing marks of the ragtag assortment of Englishmen who first ventured into the Mughal empire during the seventeenth century that they excelled in accommodating themselves to what at first must have appeared to them as a profoundly foreign society.

Unlike the Portuguese, who usually came out to Goa with the intention of settling in India permanently, the English did in general envisage returning home at the end of their postings, and this profoundly affected the way they looked at the country in which they lived. Nevertheless, the success of the East India Company in its formative years depended as much on contacts across the lines of race and culture as it did on any commercial acumen, and to varying extents the traders, soldiers, diplomats and even the clergymen who ventured eastwards had little choice but – to some extent at least – to fuse themselves with the great diversity that was the Mughal empire.

The great Mughal port of Surat in Gujarat was the focus for the first contacts between British traders and the peoples of the Mughal empire. The first British ship arrived in the Surat harbour area in 1608. Known as Suvali, the harbour area was quickly rechristened 'Swally Hole' by the British sailors, who thus showed early signs of that national talent for linguistic sensitivity that would result in much future British mangling of mellifluous Indian place-names.

Here the British traders inhabited a building that combined elements both of an Oxbridge college and a Mughal caravanserai. On the one hand, the day started with prayers and ended at a communal meal presided over by both the president and the chaplain, the latter's job being to monitor the behaviour of the factors, assure regular attendance at chapel and prevent unchristian behaviour; on the other hand, this cosy English collegiate scene took place within a 'Moor's building' and after dinner the factors could wash and unwind in a 'hummum' (steam bath).[11] As very few European goods were available, the factors quickly adapted themselves to the material culture of India, and it's fascinating to see how soon such specifically Indian luxuries as 'a betle box, two pigdanes [from the Hindi *pikdan,* for spittoon], and a rosewater bottle' begin to turn up on the East India Company inventories.[12] Indian food also made an early appearance on the menu at the factory:

'ordinarily we have dopeage and rice, kegeree and picked mangoes,' reported Peter Mundy, while other early accounts mention 'cabobs' (kebabs), 'dumpokes' (chicken slow-cooked in a *dampakht* oven) and 'mango achar' (chutney).

Nor was acclimatization just a matter of food: in 1630 President William Methwold admitted to London that the factors had almost completely given up using the western drugs that the Company was in the habit of sending out to Surat, preferring to take the advice of local Mughal doctors: 'The utility of the drugs is not to be doubted,' wrote Methwold, 'but being farr fecht and longe kept, applied by an unskilful hand, without the consideration of the temprature of a mans body by the alteration of climats, they peradventure have small or contrary effects.' Rather sheepishly he then admitted: 'wee for our parts doe hold that in things indifferent it is safest for an Englishman to Indianize, and, so conforming himselfe in some measure to the diett of the country, the ordinarie phisick of the country will bee the best cure when any sicknesse shall overtake him'.[13]

John Albert de Mandelslo (1616–44), the ambassador of the Duke of Holstein, visited the English factory in April 1638. His account reveals that, despite the attempts of the factors to portray their establishment as a sort of sober, pious outpost of Oxbridge, washed up on the shores of Gujarat, the factory was in fact a much more lively place than anyone was prepared to let on to London. The factors may have kept to the rule that they should remain unmarried – indeed, there is only one reference in the earliest years to a factor formally marrying an Indian girl, and that caused a major scandal[14] – but that clearly did not stop them dressing in Indian clothes and being serenaded of an evening by troupes of Mughal dancing girls and courtesans. Mandelslo wrote:

> They made the greatest entertainment imaginable; and to come to the height of that country's endearments, they sent for some *Benjan* women, who were very desirious to see my cloaths, which I still wore after the *Germane* fashion, though the *English* and *Dutch* who are settled in the *Indies* go ordinarily according to the mode of the country, and would have obliged me to put them off; but perceiving I was unwilling to do it, and withal that I made some difficulty to accept of the profers they made me to strip themselves naked, and to doe anything that I would expect from persons of their sex and profession, they seem'd to be very much troubled, and so went away.[15]

The further the factors went from the English base in Surat, the more they found themselves adapting to Indian ways, although occasionally there is the odd hint of homesickness: in the small East India Company warehouse at Ahmedabad, for example, inventories show an almost complete lack of European furniture, with the factors choosing instead to sit on the floor on five 'sitternegees' (presumably *shitranji*, coloured cotton carpets); moreover, they have a 'coho pott' at a time when coffee was regarded as a 'Moorish drink'. Nevertheless, they tried to keep some link with home. On the wall were 'two pictures, one of the cittie of London and the other of the King in Parliment'. They also had 'an English coach', which oddly enough appears to have been pulled by oxen.[16]

Elsewhere more dramatic transformations were taking place, as Britons found their national, racial and religious loyalties challenged by the Indian environment that surrounded and at times enveloped them. The letters of the English factories contain many enigmatic entries, such as that of 8 September 1647 about the death of Gilbert Harrison, who was a factor at Thatta, Sindh. Before he died, Harrison had made no will but verbally desired his assistant 'to give his dagger and most of his "Hiendoostane" clothes' to his servant, 'a Hiendooe'. He also requested that a tomb, which was already under construction, be completed 'in the chiefe burying place about Nasserpore', where 'the chief men of Nasserpore' wanted him 'to lye there sepulized'. Would the elders of Nasserpore want a Christian buried in the main Muslim graveyard? It would seem unlikely, as it would be against one of the fundamental tenets of Muslim law, so Harrison must have been regarded, in Thatta at least, as a Muslim.[17]

At the end of the seventeenth century Job Charnock (d. 1693), the founder of Calcutta, adopted the Bengali *lungi* and married a Hindu girl whom he allegedly saved from the funeral pyre of her first husband. The story is told in one of the first English travel books about India, *New Account of the East Indies* by Alexander Hamilton (1688–1723):

> Mr *Channock* choosing the Ground of the Colony, where it now is, reigned more absolute than a *Rajah* ... The country about being overspread with *Paganism*, the Custom of Wives burning with their deceased Husbands is also practiced here. Mr *Channock* went one Time with his ordinary guard of Soldiers, to see a young widow act that tragical Catastrophe, but he was so smitten with the Widow's Beauty, that he sent his guards to take her by Force from her Executioners, and conducted her to his own Lodgings. They lived lovingly many Years, and had several children. At length she died, after he had settled in *Calcutta*, but instead of converting her to *Christianity*, she made him a Proselyte to *Paganism*, and the only Part of *Christianity* that was remarkable in him, was burying her

decently, and he built a Tomb over her, where all his Life after her Death, he kept the anniversary Day of her Death by sacrificing a Cock on her Tomb, after the *Pagan* Manner.[18]

As early as 1672 a military ordinance had to be taken out to prevent English soldiers at Madras dressing in Indian costume. Fifteen years later, in an attempt to prevent the excessive number of illegitimate births for which Madras was becoming notorious, the directors of the East India Company attempted to encourage the Company servants to marry their mistresses: 'Induce by all means you can invent our souldiers [*sic*] to marry honourably with their native woman,' the scandalized directors wrote to the Madras Council.[19]

Another early traveller, Charles Lockyer, reported in 1711 that the governor seemed as Orientalized as his staff and that he:

seldom goes abroad with less than three of fourscore peons arm'd … and Country Musick enough to frighten a Stranger into Belief, the Men were mad; two *Dubashes* [interpreters or angels] attend to cool him with Fans, and drive away the Flies, that otherwise would molest him; he is a man of great parts, respected as a Prince by the *Rajas* of the country, and is in every respect as great; save, those are for themselves, this has Masters.

Nor was it just that the British had decided to observe local diplomatic conventions by holding *durbars* and turning every procession into a spectacle or *tamasha*; for Lockyer also reports that the factors in Madras, like those in Surat, were buried in great domed Mughal tombs carved 'into different Fancies, after the *Indian* manner'.[20]

Many British renegades actually embraced Islam after escaping from the service of the Company and joining one of the regional Indian courts. In 1654, 23 East India Company servants deserted Surat in a single mass break-out. Others soon followed, having first run amok in Surat: 'Their private whorings, drunkenesse and such like ryotts … breaking open whorehouses and rackehowses [i.e. arrack bars] have hardened the hearts of the inhabitants against our very names,' wrote a weary William Methwold (d. 1653). Little wonder that the British were soon being reviled in the streets 'with the names of Ban-chude [literally 'daughter-fucker'] and Betty-chude [literally 'sister-fucker'] which my modest language will not interprett'.[21]

In the course of the eighteenth century, as British power steadily increased both in the Mediterranean and in India, and that of both the Ottomans and the Mughals declined, the incentives to cross cultures for financial betterment steadily diminished; as a result open, voluntary conversions to Islam seem to have become correspondingly less common. But in India at least, as the East India Company gradually transformed itself from a mercantile organization into a colonial government with widespread territorial possessions and its own army, civil service and judiciary, discrete conversions did continue, albeit for rather different motives: by the late eighteenth century conversion was usually a precondition for marriage to any well-born Muslim lady.[22]

There were also a significant number of forced conversions. Between 1780 and 1784, following the disastrous British defeat by Tipu Sultan at Pollilur, 7,000 British men, along with an unknown number of women, were held captive by Tipu in his sophisticated island fortress of Seringapatam. Of these more than 300 were circumcised and given Muslim names and clothes.[23] Even more humiliating, several British regimental drummer boys were made to wear *gagra cholis* (skirt and bodice) and entertain the court as *nautch* (dancing) girls.[24]

These major defeats of the armies of the East India Company by Tipu are a reminder that, even at the very end of the eighteenth century, British military superiority was by no means assured in India. Nevertheless, during the last quarter of the century the attitudes of the British in India were beginning to change, along with the gradual shift in the balance of power. With their new confidence and growing power, the cities of the coast were becoming more

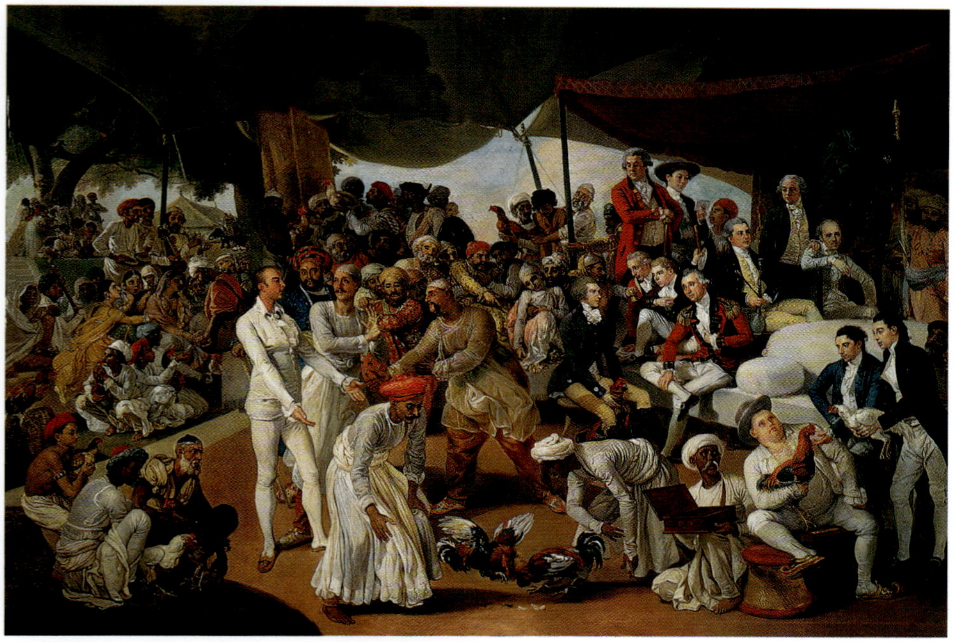

12.2
Colonel Mordaunt's Cock Match
Johann Zoffany
Oil on canvas
India (Lucknow), 1784–86
Tate Britain, London

12.3
Captain John Foote
Sir Joshua Reynolds

Oil on canvas
London, 1765

York City Art Gallery, York

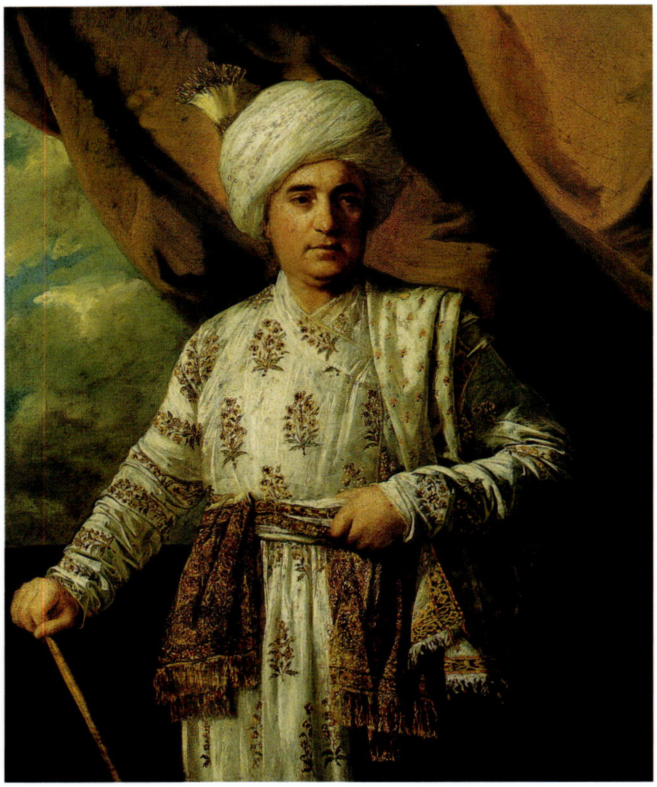

and more British: every year new English theatres and libraries were being built alongside churches almost identical to London's St Martin-in-the-Fields or a governor-general's house based on Kedleston Hall, Derbyshire (see plate 11.9). English newspapers were opened, English card games were played and English balls and masquerades were thrown. It was not an immediate or complete change, and throughout the eighteenth century elements of the old intercultural hybridity continued. Indian dress, for example, remained popular in private and in informal public situations, as a form of undress. Until the 1770s it was not unknown even for members of the Council in Calcutta to wear it for meetings; apart from anything else it was, of course, much better suited to the climate. In the famous image by Johan Zoffany (1733–1810) of a Lucknow cockfight (plate 12.2) some of the Englishmen appear to be wearing a sort of hybrid undress, part western, part Lucknavi pyjamas.

Certainly in eighteenth-century Madras idle young factors could still be found 'in long draws, a banian coat, and slippers' and attending both church and the parade ground in 'Moormen's suits'. The Madras wills and inventories for the period show the quantity of such clothes in Britons' wardrobes. Captain James Cope, for example, bequeathed 'all my Moors clothes' to his *dubash*. Captain Foote's magnificent Indian clothes – *jama* (gown), *patka* (sash) and shawl – in which he was famously painted by Joshua Reynolds (plates 12.3, 12.4; see p. 84), were probably given to him as a *khil'at* by the Mughal emperor and may have been worn for the portrait as much for its exoticism as anything else, but Indian clothes were still certainly worn on a regular basis by the British in the 1760s when Foote sat for his picture.

It was also extremely fashionable in the eighteenth century for the British in India to smoke a hookah, even for the few British women resident in Calcutta, and the diarist William Hickey records that he was told on arrival that '"Here everyone uses a hookah, and it is impossible to get on without [it]".' He added: 'I have frequently heard men declare that they would much rather be deprived of their dinner than their hookah.'[25] Such was their popularity that special places had to be allotted for them in boxes at the theatre in Calcutta.[26] Making little carpets for the hookahs to rest upon even came to be regarded as a suitable pastime for bored British memsahibs.[27] Even Robert Clive (1725–74) – more immune than most of the British to the charms of Indian society and ways of life – was a regular smoker, although his magnificent jewel-encrusted hookah was probably a ceremonial gift (plate 12.7).

The ease with which so many Company servants continued to take on Indian ways is in part a reflection of the open and receptive age at which so many of them arrived in India: no one was officially allowed to join the East India Company after the age of 16, so that any official who had reached the age of 30 had usually spent at least half his life in India.

Yet for all this, an important distinction was beginning to develop between the British who lived in the increasingly European ambience of the three presidency cities (Bombay, Madras and Calcutta) and those who lived in – and to varying extents became part of – the Indian India beyond the walls of the presidency towns. The degree to which an individual was exposed to India depended increasingly on where he was posted, just as the extent to which he reacted to such influences was determined to a great extent by his individual sympathies and temperament.

If the official stayed in Calcutta, Madras or Bombay, or indeed one of the big Bengal cantonments, his exposure to Indian customs could sometimes be very limited indeed. Eighteenth-century Calcutta in particular struck visitors as a dislocated outpost of Europe, as if Regency Bath had been relocated to the Bay of Bengal. In this insular world the only way that a Briton in Calcutta could come into close or intimate contact with Indians and Indian society was if he took an Indian *bibi*, or mistress. In the second half of the eighteenth century the great majority of Company servants still seem to have done this: of the *Bengal Wills* from 1780 to 1785 preserved in the India Office Library, one in three contains a bequest to Indian wives or

12.4 opposite
***Jama* (robe), *patka* (waist sash) and shawl worn by Captain John Foote**

Muslin, embroidered with coloured silks and gold thread
India, mid-18th century

York City Art Gallery, York

This suit was probably given to Foote as a *khil'at*, a type of ceremonial dress presented by Indian rulers to subjects as part of the *durbar* ritual.

companions, or their natural children;[28] and it can be safely assumed that many more kept Indian mistresses without wishing to leave a formal legal record of the fact. This is confirmed by the fact that the mixed-blood Eurasian population was expanding exponentially during the 75 years between 1750 and 1825, so that by 1833 the British in India were well outnumbered by the burgeoning Eurasian population and, of children born in India, Eurasian babies outnumbered 'pure' English infants by six to one.[29]

Certainly the frequency with which the British cohabited with Indian girls struck the Iranian traveller Mir Abdul Lateef Shustari, who passed through Calcutta on his way to Hyderabad in the late 1790s: 'The women of people with no future – of corrupt Muslims and of evil Hindus – of their own accord and desire enter into the bonds of wedlock with the English,' he wrote:

> These Englishmen do not interfere with the religion of their women, nor compel them to leave purdah veiling; when any son born of the union reaches the age of 4, he is taken from his mother and sent to England to be educated. Some daughters are left with their mothers to be trained by them in their own way before being married off to a Muslim who is then given some appointment; the fathers also leave the girls something of their inheritance. When children reach the age of discretion, they are free to choose their religion themselves.

Significantly, Shustari goes on to hint that this sexual intermingling was not one-way, and that he himself had kept a European mistress, letting it drop that 'neither [English] men nor women remove pubic hair, accounting comely to leave it in its natural state [a surprising and even shocking thing for Muslims, who always shave their body hair]. And indeed, most European women have no body-hair, and even if it does occur, it is wine-coloured, soft and extremely fine.'[30]

Despite Shustari's mild Iranian disapproval of the readiness of Indian women to form attachments with Europeans, in India itself Muslim women permanently cohabiting with Europeans were at this period apparently held in no disrespect, there being in Muslim law provision for various degrees of marital attachment. Moreover, although formal, legal marriages were now very much frowned on by the Company, as far as one can tell a great many of these liaisons seem – perhaps surprisingly – to have been faithful and long-standing partnerships: cross-cultural marriages in all but legal name. For example, one women who describes herself in her will as 'Beebee Mehtaub of Bengal, mother of Mrs Colonel Maria Ann Doveton by my late Lord and Master John

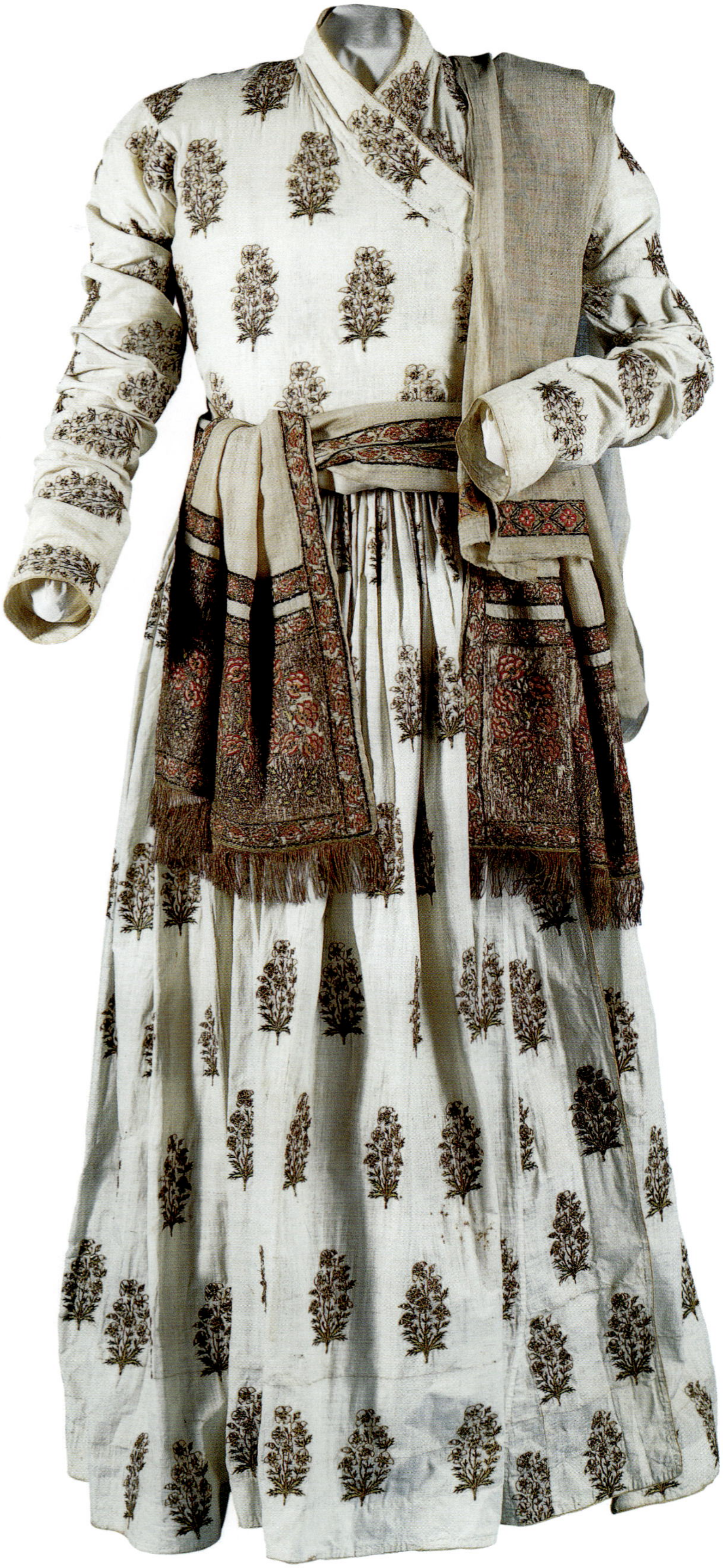

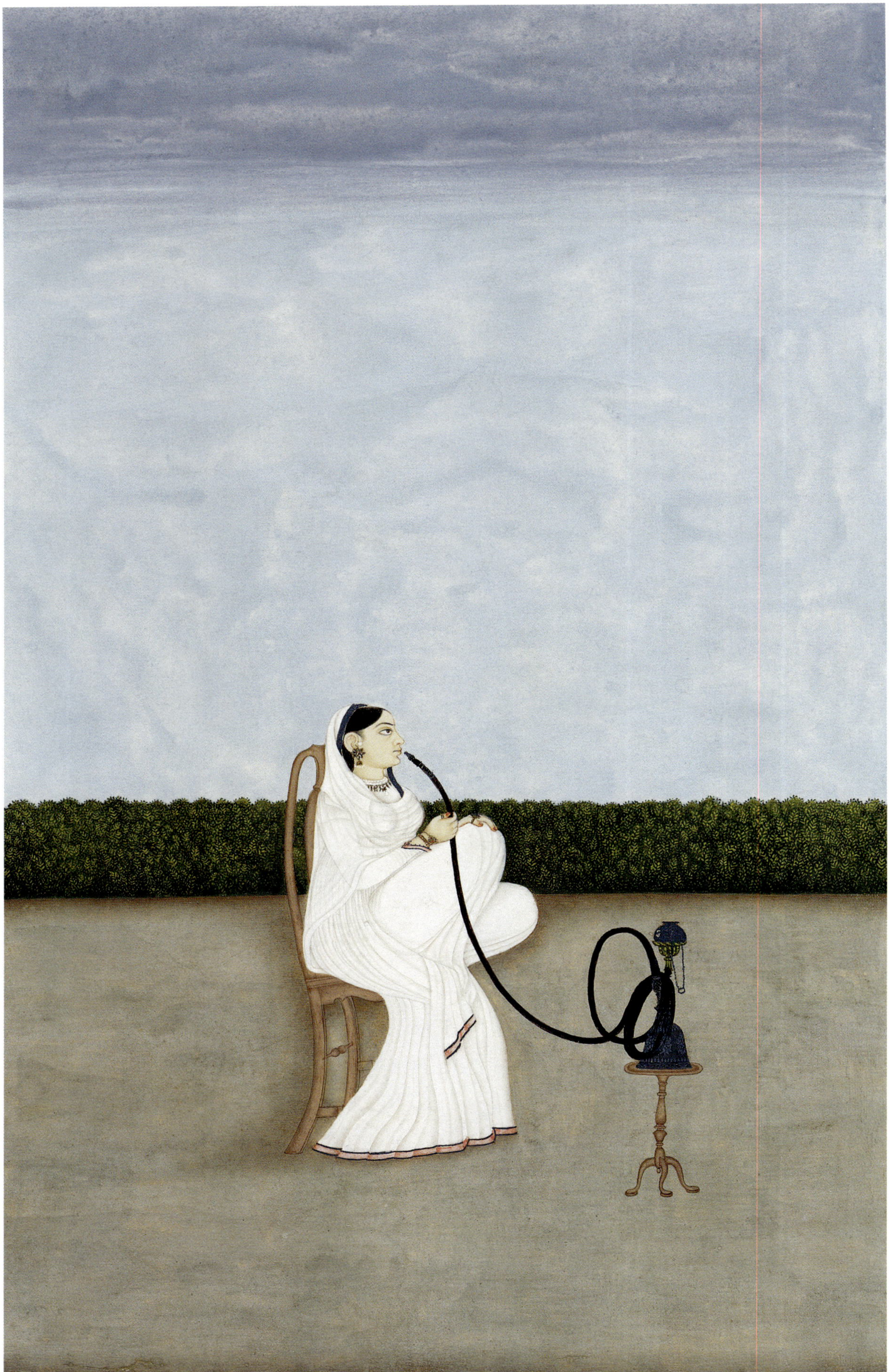

Arnold Knight Companion of Bath' reveals that she had been 'under John Arnold's protection' for no fewer than 58 years.[31]

The East India Vade Mecum (1810), written by Captain Thomas Williamson as a guide to life in Calcutta for young company officials coming out to India for the first time, noted that:

> In India, a woman 'under the protection' of a European gentleman, is accounted, not only among the natives, but even to his countrymen to be equally sacred, as though she were married to him; and the woman herself values her reputation, exactly in proportion as she may have refrained from indulging in variety. Some are said to have passed twenty years, or more, without the possibility for scandal to attach to their conduct ... [By the same token] the attachment of many European gentlemen to their native mistresses is not to be described. An infatuation beyond all comparison often prevails ...[32]

This impression is confirmed by the surviving wills of the period, which show that in most cases the *bibis* had achieved a surprising degree of empowerment, with many inheriting considerable sums and households full of slaves from their English partners. When Major Thomas Naylor died in 1782, for example, he bequeathed to his companion Muckmul Patna 40,000 rupees, a bungalow and a garden at Berhampore, a hackery, bullocks, jewels, clothes and all their male and female slaves.[33] Another Company merchant, Matthew Leslie, left each of his four wives a different house and 20,000 rupees, a very considerable bequest in today's currency.[34]

For all these reasons, the Indian women who formed connections with Europeans seem to have come from across the social spectrum. At the bottom end of the scale, a number of *bibis* were apparently former courtesans, dancing girls or prostitutes: for example, in November 1794 when Richard Blenchynden had a squabble with Jeebun (one of his two *bibis*), she left him and immediately took up work in a nearby Calcutta brothel run by a European woman, where the girls 'would go out for 4 or 8 rupees to whoever sends them'.[35] This prostitute or courtesan background is also indicated by the way in which a number of *bibis* were treated as simple employees, and were effectively paid a salary for their sexual labour.[36] Other *bibis* were slave girls, bought at market. Indeed, roughly one-third of the relationships recorded in the *Bengal Wills* are between the British master of a household and his female employee or slave.[37]

In this context, having an Indian concubine did not of course lead to any automatic sympathy with India or Indian culture on the part of a Company servant. But it was recognized at the time that in practice cohabitation often did lead to a degree of transculturation – even in the transplanted Englishness of Calcutta. Thomas Williamson for one was quite clear as to the effect that taking a *bibi* had on a newly arrived Englishman: '... in the early part of their career,' he wrote, 'young men attach themselves to the women of this country; and acquire a liking, or taste, for their society and customs, which soon supersedes every other attraction'.[38]

Again this was a two-way process. The few surviving wills of the *bibis* indicate that in this hybrid milieu, just as their consorts were picking up Indian habits and ways, so the *bibis* were undergoing a reverse acculturation and picking up European manners and ways of living.[39] According to one scholar who has analysed the lives of these *bibis*, many of them 'wore European clothes, owned European furniture, ate European food [but they also] had brass pots and pans, hookah implements, betel eating accessories and wore saris and shawls';[40] a few even converted to Christianity.

12.5
Indian Woman, Possibly Mutabbey, the Bibi of William Fullerton, Squatting on a Chair

From an album belonging to William Fullerton
Opaque watercolour on paper
India (Murshidabad School), 1760–64

V&A: D.1181–1

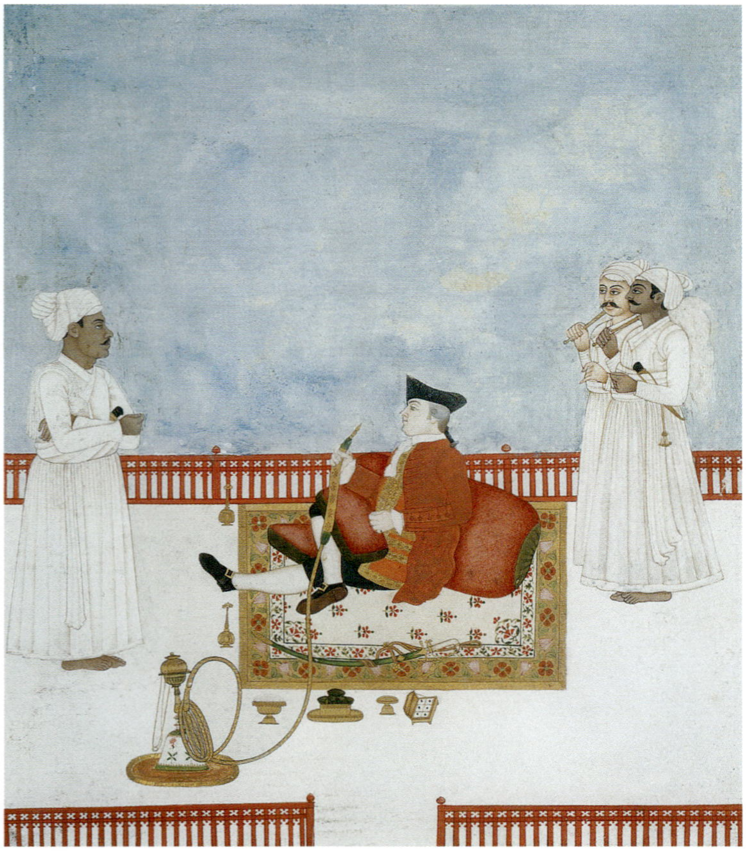

12.6
East India Company Official, Probably William Fullerton, Seated on a Terrace
Dip Chand

Opaque watercolour on paper
India (Murshidabad), 1760–63

V&A: IM.33–1912

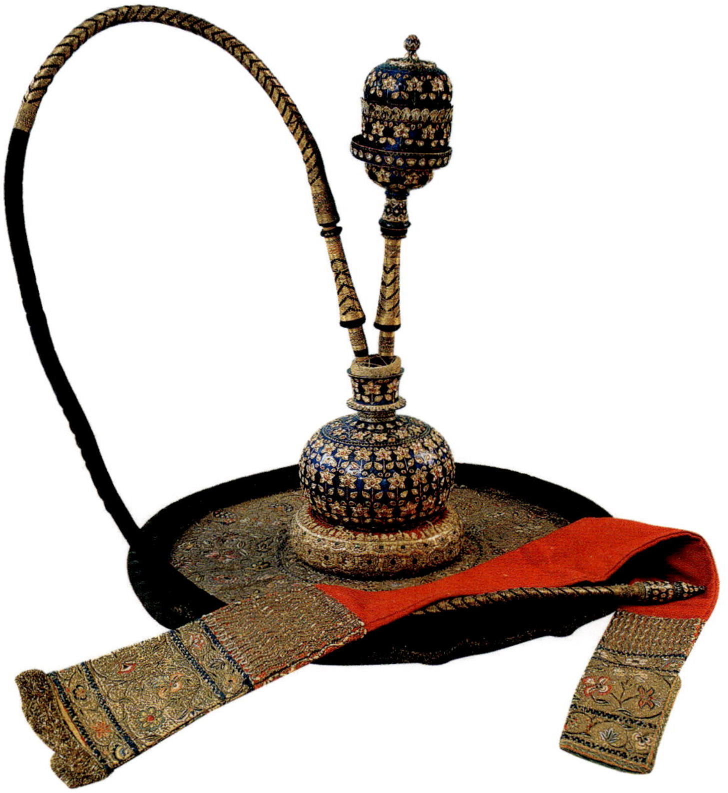

12.7
Hookah
Silver, partly gilt, enamelled and set with diamonds and rubies
India (Lucknow), mid-18th century
Powis Castle, Wales

Others are more difficult to place, and resist any easy racial or religious classification: 'Moosummat Isabella Rawstone, daughter of General Rawstone', was apparently a Muslim woman who had an English general for a father, while 'Beebee Munnoo or Jane Mitchell, native of Hindustan' might have been either Hindu or Christian. But what was the ethnicity of Bett Carnegy, who had 'formerly lived with Alexander Carnegy'? Her inventory – the only clue – shows that she ate from china with silver forks, spoons and knives; she also owned six silver eggcups and a silver toast rack 'with paws'. Yet the same woman also possessed a hookah, a set of silver hookah bottoms, some silver and ivory mouthpieces, a betel box, and a whole range of traditional Indian jewellery, including several gold 'choorees' (bangles), a three-stranded gold chain called a 'chunderhar' and several 'punchlerries' or five-stranded gold chains. As with the world inhabited by the Indo-Portuguese of Goa two centuries earlier, this was clearly a hybrid world of overlapping practices: a fecund multi-cultural, multi-ethnic confusion of different ways and modes of looking at and living in the world. A superb miniature of a *bibi*, almost certainly Mutabbey, the concubine of William Fullerton, a former mayor of Calcutta, encapsulates this hybrid confusion (plate 12.5). Mutabbey chooses to be painted in a European chair, but does not sit in it so much as squat, as she would have, had she been painted on the ground. In order to bring her hookah onto the same level, it has been raised onto a teapoy for easier access.[41]

If the *bibis* took on some European ways, many of their consorts walked a no less complex line between different societies, and there are frequent remarks in the British literature of the period as to 'the alterations that a plain old English acquaintance may undergo by removal to the banks of the Ganges' (plate 12.6).[42] At a time when the British showed no particular enthusiasm for cleanliness, Indian women for example introduced British men to the delights of regular bathing. The fact that the word 'shampoo' is derived from the Hindi word for massage, and that it entered the English language at this time, shows the novelty to the eighteenth-century British of the Indian idea of cleaning hair with materials other than soap.[43] A few Calcutta men were known to have been circumcised in order to satisfy the hygienic and religious requirements of their wives and companions.[44] Under the influence of their Hindu wives, some East India Company servants were even persuaded to become vegetarians. One was the enigmatic Irish general whose collection of sculptures forms the core of the British Museum Indian Collection, Major General Charles 'Hindoo' Stuart (1758–1828). Stuart, who travelled around the country with his Indian *bibi* beside him, his buggy followed by a cavalcade of children's carriages 'and a palkee load of little babes',[45] went as far as employing a group of Brahmins, whose ritual purity he regarded as essential for properly dressing his Hindu family's food.

Not all the relationships recorded in the wills of the period make such happy reading, and there are numerous wills where Indian *bibis* are treated with a chilling carelessness. Likewise, in the letters of the period there is no shortage of Englishmen who clearly regarded Indian women as little more than passive objects of pleasure: Philip Francis (1740–1818), Warren Hastings's unattractive arch-enemy, for example, wrote home boasting to Edmund Bourke that he was sleeping with 'black ladies without end'[46] – and this despite having left his devoted wife, five daughters and son in London. Judging by the wills they left, many Englishmen were serial monogamists, moving on from one partner to another, sometimes at great speed, and a substantial number kept two *bibis* simultaneously.

Indeed, a few had fully fledged harems: Williamson in his *East India Vade Mecum* records the case of one Company servant who kept no fewer than 16 concubines. When asked what he did with them all, he merely muttered, 'Oh I just give them a little rice and let them run around.'[47]

However, such cases are exceptions. The vast majority of the wills suggest ties of great affection and loyalty on both sides, with British men asking their close friends to be executors and to care for their Indian partners, referring to them as 'well beloved' or 'worthy friend', 'this amiable and distinguished lady' and even 'the excellent and respectable Mother of my two children for whom I feel unbounded love and affection and esteem'.

If the British of Calcutta had little close contact with Indians, except for their servants and *bibis*, it was very different for those East India Company officials posted outside the Anglicizing influence of the major Company towns. Often they were the only educated Europeans for several hundred kilometres. In such cases – and especially if they found themselves in a centre of hybrid Indo-Islamic culture, such as Hyderabad or Lucknow, or one of the more lively Rajput courts, like Udaipur – they would by necessity be forced to draw their closest friends, their ways of speaking and thinking, and their sexual partners from their Indian surroundings.[48]

In the late eighteenth century, with Mughal Delhi sinking into headlong decline, Lucknow was at the height of its Golden Age and had usurped the great Mughal capital to become indisputably the largest, most prosperous and most civilized pre-colonial city in northern India. The city's courtly Urdu diction and elaborate codes of etiquette were renowned as the most subtle and refined in Hindustan; its dancers admired as the most accomplished; its cuisine famous as the most flamboyantly baroque. According to one historian, this hedonistic city resembled an Indian version of (pre-Revolutionary) 'Teheran, Monte Carlo and Las Vegas, with just a touch of Glyndebourne for good measure'.[49] It was here in this Bacchanalian atmosphere that some of the most charming images of Anglo-Mughal love and friendship were painted. Johan Zoffany's famous oil of the *Cock Match* (plate 12.2) and a miniature painting of *English Official in Discussion with a Nawab* (plate 12.1) show a world where the friendship between the races was not yet soured by imported European ideas of racialism, nor was an apartheid-like separation of races considered at all desirable.

It was in Lucknow too that Warren Hastings's military secretary, General William Palmer (d. 1814), met his lifelong love Begum Fyze Baksh, in around 1779. Palmer married Fyze according to Muslim law;[50] and the following year the couple had their first child, named William Palmer after his father. Over the next few years, with her sister Nur on hand to play the role of maiden aunt, Fyze produced child after child on an almost annual basis, until the couple had produced a brood of six (four boys and two girls) in eight years. A picture of the family painted in 1785 by Zoffany survives today in the India Office Library in London (plate 12.8).[51] It is one of the most charming images of a family group to survive from the entire Indo-British encounter. Fyze is placed at the centre of the picture, barefoot and dressed in Lucknavi court costume: a magnificent saffron *peshwaz* (robe) and *dupatta* (scarf) over a brief *angia* (halterneck) bodice.[52] She is seated on the ground, surrounded by her children and their *ayahs* and wet-nurses, a calm serene and beautiful young woman in her early twenties, modest and maternal, but hung with the finest Mughal jewellery: sparkling diamond earrings, several strings of pearl necklace and silver *payal* anklets. In her lap she lovingly cradles a new-born sleeping infant. This is her third son, later baptised Charles Palmer, but now still

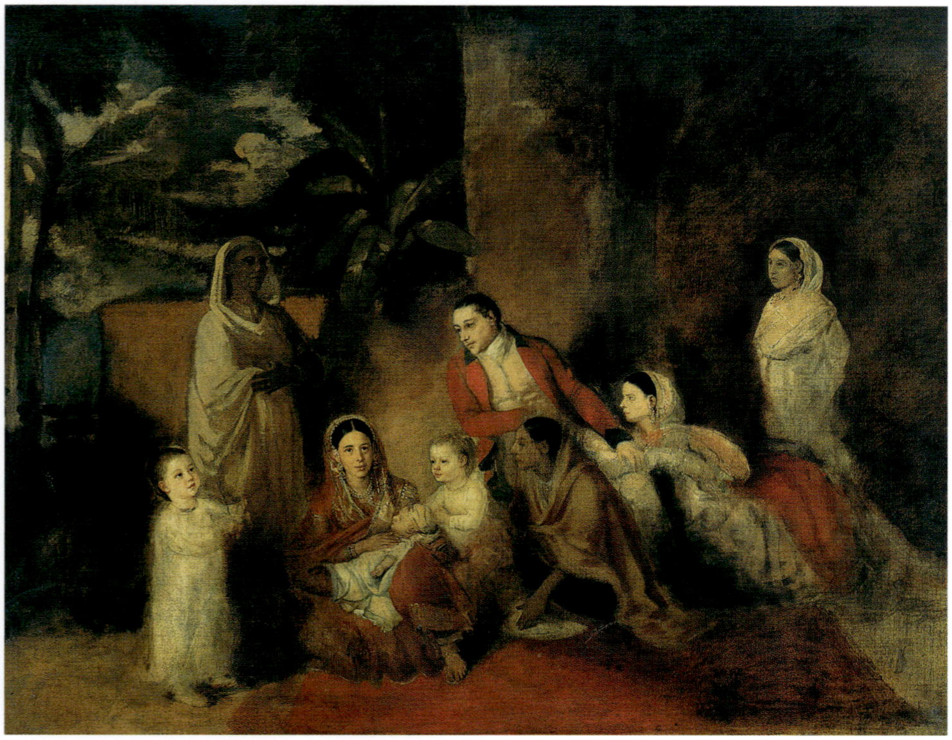

12.8
The Palmer Family
Johann Zoffany

Oil on canvas
India (Lucknow), April–July 1785

British Library, London

wrapped in swaddling clothes and his head covered with an embroidered Muslim *topi*. Charles's two elder brothers, William and Hastings, then aged two and one respectively, look on engagingly from the sides of the canvas in their long flowing Lucknavi *jamas*. To Fyze's left, seated in a European chair and wearing the formal redcoat of his British military uniform, is her husband: a dark, thin, still-handsome man in his early forties. He looks down at Fyze with a long gaze that is at once adoring and protective. To his left, kneeling at William's feet, but with her expression directed at her elder sister, sits Fyze's sister Nur, later to marry General Beniot de Boigne, but then a beautiful girl of around 17, wearing a thin white veil.[53]

In Delhi a similar atmosphere prevailed. There, in the melancholy ruins that surrounded the once magnificent capital of India, the early British residents were a series of sympathetic and severely eccentric figures. The first, the Boston-born Sir David Ochterlony (1758–1825), set the tone. With his fondness for *hookahs*, *nautch* girls and Indian costumes, Ochterlony amazed Bishop Reginald Heber, the Anglican Primate of Calcutta, by receiving him sitting on a divan wearing a *'choga* and *pagri'* (loose robe and turban) while being fanned by servants holding peacock-feather *punkas*. To one side of Ochterlony's own tent was the red-silk harem tent where his women slept, and on the other side the encampment of his daughters, all of them, according to the bishop, 'hung around with red cloth and thus fenced in from the eyes of the profane'.

Although the people of Delhi knew Ochterlony as *'Loony Akhtar' (*or Crazy Star), when in the Indian capital he liked to be addressed by his full Mughal title, Nasir-ud-Daula (Defender of the State), and to live the life of a Mughal gentleman. Though he is reputed to have had 13 wives, one of these – a former Hindu dancing girl who converted to Islam, referred to in his will as 'Beebee Mahruttun Moobaruck ul Nissa Begume, alias Begum Ochterlony, the mother of my younger children'[54] – took precedence over the others.[55] 'Generallee Begum', as she was also known, occasionally appears in contemporary letters, where she is frequently accused of giving herself airs. She offended the British by calling herself 'Lady Ochterlony' – in one letter it is recorded that 'Lady Ochterlony has applied for leave to make the Hadge to Mecca' – and also offended the Mughals by awarding herself the title Qudsia Begum, previously the title of the emperor's mother.[56]

Although Mubarak Begum may have been the senior wife, every evening all 13 of Ochterlony's consorts used to process around Delhi behind their husband, each on the back of her own elephant. Afterwards, Ochterlony would call for his *nautch* girls. A miniature survives depicting an evening's entertainment at the Delhi Residency (plate 12.9).[57] Ochterlony is dressed in full Indian costume and reclines on a carpet, leaning back against a spread of pillows and bolsters. To one side stands a servant with a fly whisk; on the other side stands Ochterlony's elaborate hookah. Above, from the picture rail, portraits of the Resident's Scottish and American ancestors – kilted and plumed colonels from Highland regiments, grimacing ladies in stiff white taffeta dresses – peer down at the group of dancing girls swirling below them.

Beneath this very cheerful exterior, however, seem to have existed certain tensions. One of the most moving of Ochterlony's letters concerns his two daughters, and the question of whether he should bring them up as Muslims or Christians. The letter is written to Major Hugh Sutherland, a Scottish mercenary commanding a regiment of Mahratta's troops, who, like Ochterlony, had married a Muslim begum – and who had opted to bring up his children as Muslims. Ochterlony says he does not know what to do with his two daughters by Mubarak Begum, and asks for advice. If they are brought up as Christians, he fears they will suffer from the racism of the British.

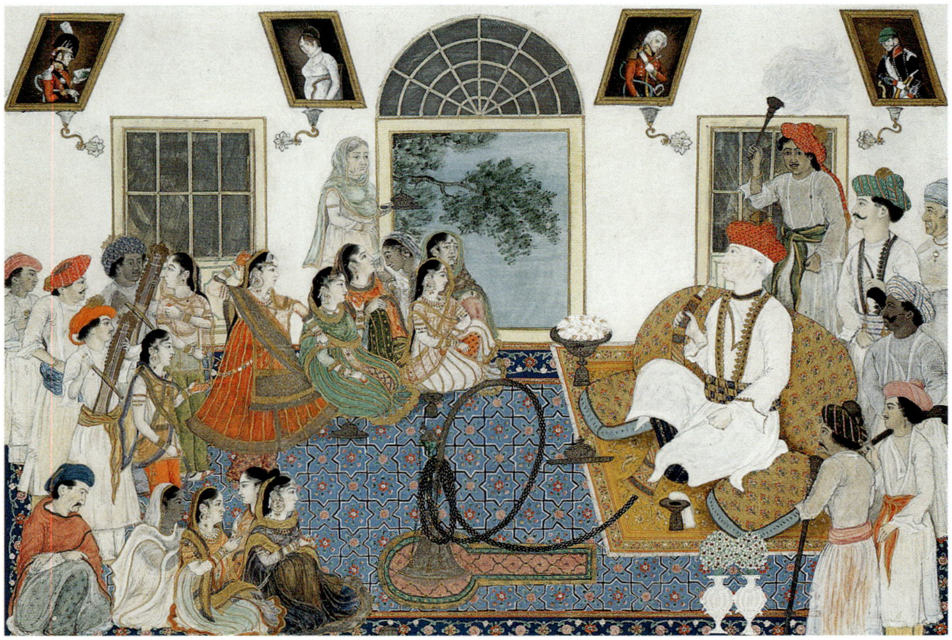

12.9
Sir David Ochterlony Watching a Nautch

Opaque watercolour on paper
Delhi, c.1820

British Library, London

He writes:

> My children dear Major, are uncommonly fair, but if educated in the European manner they will in spite of complexion labour under all the disadvantages of being known as the NATURAL DAUGHTERS OF OCHTERLONY BY A NATIVE WOMAN – In that one sentence is compressed all that ill nature inaction and illiberality can convey of which you must have seen numerous instances during your Residence in this country.

Yet for all this, Ochterlony hesitates to bring them up as Muslims, with a view to them marrying into the Mughal aristocracy, because:

> I own I could not bear that my child should be one of a numerous haram even were I certain that no other Disadvantages attended this mode of disposal & were I proof against the observations of the world who tho' unjust to the children, would not fail to comment on the Conduct of a father who educated his offspring in Tenets of the Prophet.

The letter ends rather movingly: 'In short my dear M[ajor] I have spent all the time since we were parted in revolving this matter in my mind but I have not yet been able to come to a positive Decision.'[58]

By the late eighteenth century, however, men who showed too great an enthusiasm for Hinduism, for Indian practices or even for their Indian wives and Anglo-Indian children were finding that the climate was growing distinctly chilly. David Hare (1775–1842), a Scottish watchmaker who founded the Hindu College in Calcutta, was actually denied a Christian burial when he died of cholera, on the grounds that he had become more Hindu than Christian.[59] Many others found that their Indianized ways led to a block on their promotion. A little later Frederick Shore discovered that his adoption of native dress did not go down well in the increasingly self-righteous atmosphere of Calcutta; indeed, his behaviour scandalized headquarters to such an extent that a government order was issued explicitly forbidding Company servants from wearing anything except European dress. The following year the army issued similar orders forbidding European officers from taking part in the festival of Holi.

Ideas of racial and ethnic hierarchy were also beginning to be aired for the first time in the late 1780s, and it was the burgeoning mixed-blood Anglo-Indian community that felt the brunt of the new intolerance. From 1786, under the new governor-general, Marquess Cornwallis (1738–1805), a whole raft of legislation was brought in excluding the children of British men and their Indian wives from employment by the Company. Cornwallis arrived in India fresh from his defeat by Washington at Yorktown. He was determined to make sure that a settled colonial class never emerged in India to undermine British rule as it had done, to his own humiliation, in America. Thus excluded from all the most obvious sources of lucrative employment, Anglo-Indians quickly found themselves at the beginning of a long slide down the social scale. This would continue until, a century later, the Anglo-Indians had been reduced to a community of minor clerks and train drivers.[60]

These new racial attitudes affected all aspects of relations between British and Indians in Calcutta. The *Bengal Wills* show that it was at this time that the number of Indian *bibis* being mentioned in wills and inventories began to decline: from turning up in one in three wills in 1780–85, the practice of taking *bibis* (or at least acknowledging them in wills) went on a steep decline. Between 1805 and 1810, *bibis* turned up in only one in every four wills; by 1830 it was one in six; by the middle of the century they had all but disappeared. The second edition of Thomas Williamson's *East India Vade Mecum,* published in 1825, had all the references to *bibis* completely removed.[61]

Englishmen who had taken on Indian customs likewise began to be objects of surprise, and even, on occasions, of derision. In the early years of the nineteenth century there was growing 'ridicule' in Calcutta of men 'who allow whiskers to grow and who wear turbans &c in imitation of the Mussulmans'.[62] Curries were no longer acceptable dishes for dinner parties, and for the first time pyjamas became something that an Englishman slept in rather than something he wore during the day. By 1813 Thomas Williamson was writing in *The European in India* how 'The hookah, or pipe ... was very nearly universally retained among Europeans. Time, however, has retrenched this luxury so much, that not one in three now smokes.'[63]

For nearly 300 years Europeans coming out to the subcontinent had been acculturating themselves to India in a kaleidoscope of different ways. That process was now drawing to a close. Increasingly Europeans felt they had nothing to learn from India, and they had less and less inclination to discover anything to the contrary. India was now a place to be conquered, not a place to be conquered by. In the nineteenth century the relationship between the British and their Indian subjects would be radically different from the surprisingly multi-cultural cohabitation which was the mark of the two centuries that preceded it.

13

PERSONAL ENCOUNTERS: EUROPEANS IN SOUTH-EAST ASIA

Leonard Blussé

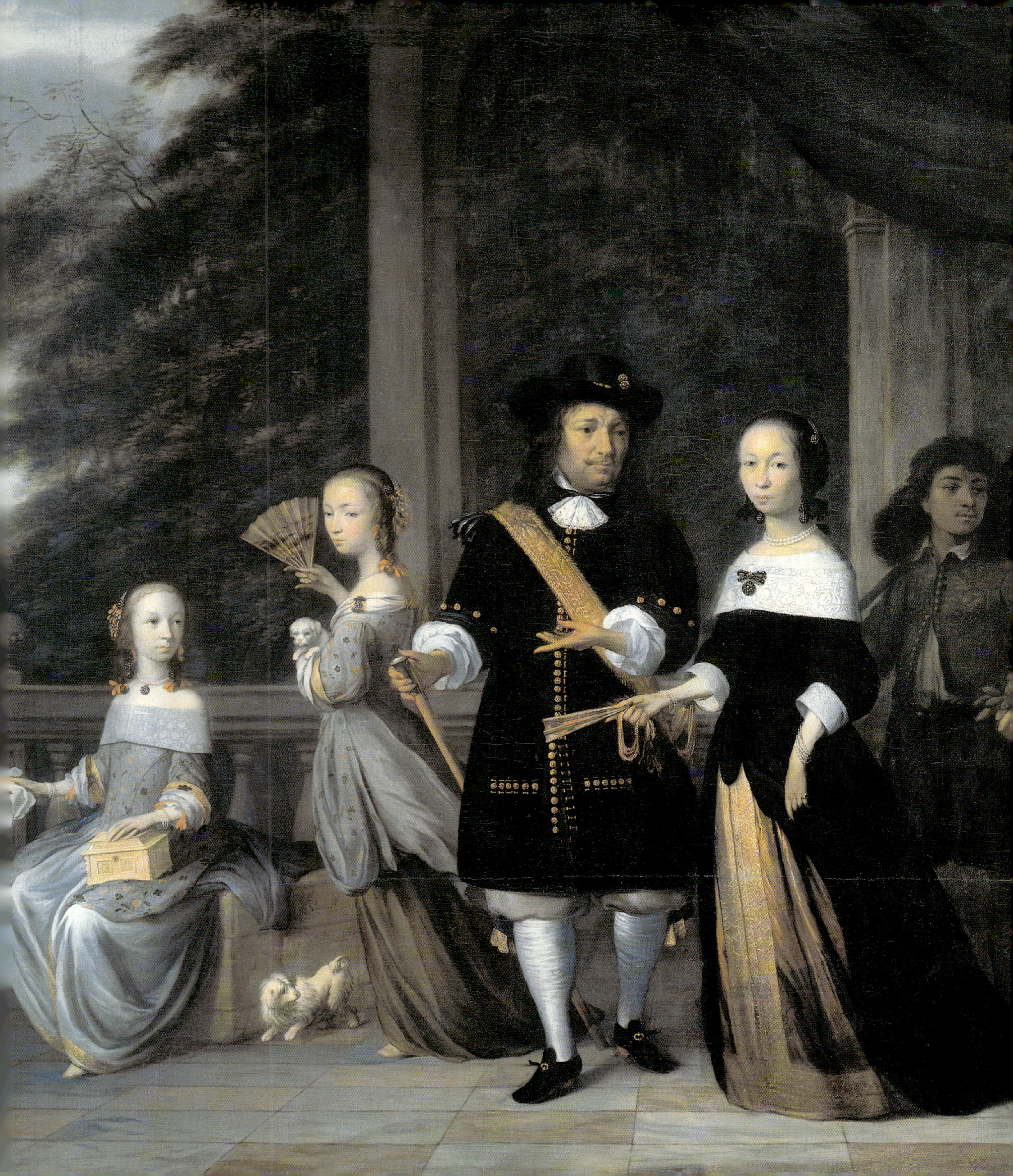

Detail of 13.2 previous page

WHEN EUROPEAN TRADERS began to visit Asian waters more regularly, what thus far had been fairly haphazard encounters with the local populace developed into relationships of a more lasting nature. 'Horizontally', amorous relationships were forged between the sexes, or steady business relationships based on mutual trust evolved between traders of different nationalities. Later the hierarchical and ethnically divisive colonial situation also created 'vertical' relationships between European colonizers and the Asian peoples whom they came to rule. First encounters sometimes grew into steady relationships, but owing to differences of cultural background, violent clashes might also quite suddenly occur, as happened to the unfortunate Captain James Cook (1728–79). He was murdered on his second visit to Hawaii by the same people who had heartily welcomed him on an earlier occasion. It may be safe to say that the way in which these relationships developed depended largely on character, circumstance and the local situation.

In their overseas exploits seventeenth-century Dutch sailors and merchants chanced upon many seemingly 'exotic' peoples on other continents. At this time no European nation sent so many ships to so many different destinations as the Dutch Republic. What is more, Dutch sailors wrote about their adventures in popular travel accounts, which were soon translated into many languages. It is thought that in around 1650 Holland's printing presses published (in various languages) as many books as all of the rest of Europe combined. Melchisédec Thévenot, librarian of Louis XIV and editor of travel accounts, was enamoured of the commonsensical tales of Dutch sailors because, as he jocularly put it, these jack-tars were not burdened by having read what others had written on similar subjects.[1] Even if, in contrast to the Jesuit accounts that Thévenot particularly disliked, the narratives of seventeenth-century Dutch sailors are surprisingly unbiased in religious matters, they nonetheless show how European voyagers in those days pictured the people of the East in such stereotypical terms as sly, haughty, cunning or crafty in behaviour, and black or yellow in appearance. Still, Europeans knew very well that they represented in numerical strength only a tiny minority in Asia. Especially in such large polities as the Persian empire, Mughal India, the Thai kingdom, China or Japan, Dutch East India Company (VOC) servants knew their place and approached local authorities in a very obliging and modest manner. The Amsterdam directorate of the VOC, fearing occasional flares of temper as a result of culture shock, therefore continually admonished the governor-general in Batavia to carefully select personnel for service in Japan: 'Modesty, humility and obedience and an intellect only aimed at commerce are the prerequisites for the continuation of our trade in Japan,' they wrote.[2] As a result, competent diplomats like François Caron (1600–73) and Justus Schouten (d. 1644) not only successfully represented the Company at the courts of Edo and Ayutthaya, but also left fascinating essays on early Dutch relations with the 'mighty kingdoms' of Japan and Siam.[3]

Like sixteenth-century Portuguese writings, seventeenth-century Dutch popular literature was full of tales of shipwrecks and maritime disasters in the eastern seas. Classics within this genre of tragic stories include: tales of the wrecking of the East Indiaman *Batavia* on the Abrolhos cliffs off the west coast of Australia in 1629; the explosion in full sea of skipper Bontekoe's ship in 1619;[4] the adventures of Hendrick Hamel and his crew members, who were shipwrecked on the Korean island of Cheju in 1653 and only succeeded in escaping to Japan after 13 years of captivity;[5] and skipper Schaap and some of his men, who in 1643 were arrested and interrogated for months in northern Japan because they were thought to be Catholic priests in disguise when they went ashore in search of fresh water.[6]

Of course there were also cases of less fortunate sailors who did not survive the first encounters: many were murdered and eaten by natives upon far-away beaches where they had been shipwrecked or had landed in search of fresh drinking water. It was, for instance, discovered that the cannibals of the small island of Lamey, off the western coast of Formosa, had killed and eaten the crews of two Dutch ships in the late 1620s. The act of revenge that followed was brutal. The Dutch governor of Formosa was ordered by his superiors in Batavia to uproot the islanders and banish them to Batavia. It took several expeditions to round up all the islanders, who over and over again managed to escape their pursuers by seeking refuge in caves. When in 1645, after 12 years of hide-and-seek, the last islander was caught, it was estimated that half the population had been killed during this operation. Confronted with this horrendous fact, the directors of the VOC in Amsterdam concluded that their expulsion orders had been carried out in a barbaric fashion that overstepped all limits of civilization: 'It is a natural shortcoming of the people of our

13.1
A Topas or Mardick with his wife

From Johan Nieuhof, *Gedenkwaerdige Zee- en Lant-Reize door de voornaemste Landschappen van West en Oost Indien*, Amsterdam, 1682
Engraving

V&A: Asian Department Library, fascimile copy

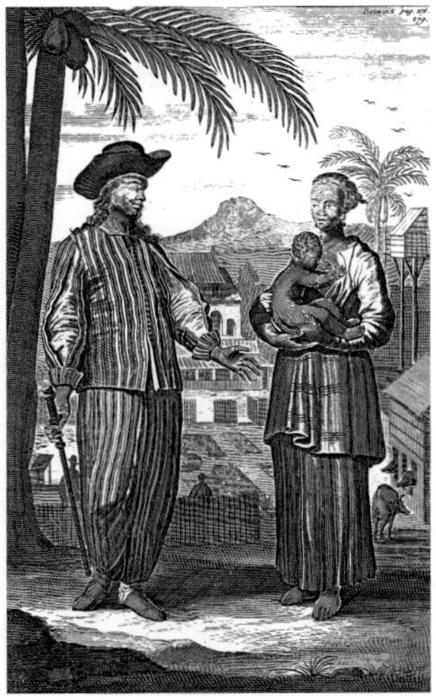

[Dutch] nation to be either too gentle or too severe in their actions when governing the areas that are under their rule; this is amply proven by those living in the East and West Indies.'[7]

Before focusing on European tales of encounters with 'the other', it is worth looking at an early description by a Chinese mandarin of the *hongmau gui*, or 'red-haired devils', as soon as the Dutch showed their freckled faces in Chinese coastal waters. 'Their hair is reddish, their eyes light blue and roundly shaped and standing about ten feet tall,' he wrote, probably without ever having met a Dutchman himself.[8] The Chinese tutor Wang Dahai, who lived from 1783 to 1793 on Java, had ample opportunity to study the Dutch. Although he felt they lacked cardinal virtues such as humanity, a sense of justice, politeness and wisdom, he conceded that they were remarkably sincere. Yet how extravagant they were in their behaviour, spending all their money without thinking of their children; how unfaithful, divorcing with permission to marry again; and how strange were their religious customs:

> [On the seventh day] the Dutch go from nine to eleven o'clock in the morning to their church, in order to pray and stammer incantations, whereby they hang their heads and shed tears as if very emotional. But after half an hour of talking, they are allowed to leave, and soon they are on the way to their garden pavilions to make fun, and spend the whole day in leisure, without caring for their work.

How alienated this learned Chinese felt among these barbarians![9]

The Formosan aborigines of the coastal village of Soolangh were less reserved at their first encounter with Dutch visitors in 1623, as junior merchant Jacob Constant experienced. He reported that:

> They are an amazingly curious people. They examined our body and clothing so closely that it would be shameful to tell. I only disclose here that, with or without our consent, they opened our clothes, jackets, trousers, sleeves and were astonished at the paleness of our skin. Nay, to put it bluntly, they even had a sniff at it, so that there hardly was any part of our naked body which was not looked or sniffed at by men, women or young lasses without the least show of reverence, shame or suspicion.[10]

No less astonished was the average Dutch sailor when he met the Khoi nomadic communities at the Cape of Good Hope, the first non-European people to be encountered on the approximately eight-month voyage to the East Indies. Long before the directors of the VOC – the Gentlemen XVII – finally decided on 26 July 1649 to establish a refreshment station at the Cape, East Indiamen were already anchoring in Table Bay to fetch fresh water and victuals (cattle in particular) and to send ashore sick crew members and passengers so that they could be cured of their illnesses by the skilled, local healers. Nicolaus de Graaff (1619–88), a ship's surgeon, who frequently travelled to the East, visited Table Bay for the first time in 1639 and described it as a 'wild and inhospitable land ... without any fruit trees or cultivated acres'. He called its free-roaming pastoral inhabitants who smeared themselves with lard and the like 'wild, heathen, dirty and stinking people'.[11] He noted, nonetheless, that no words could describe 'the pleasure and joy among the crew when the landfall was sighted ... The lame, the crippled and those who were able to leave their sickbed came on deck to see the land.' According to de Graaff, the destitute sailors were happy because the local inhabitants had an excellent reputation as healers. Hottentot (as the Khoi were called, because of their strange clicking languages) would take care of the sick voyagers, nurturing their patients back to health within the nick of time with concoctions of local herbs. Observing this on every occasion that he passed the Cape, the Dutch physician expressed a profound admiration for his barefoot colleagues from the Cape.

The settlement of Cape Colony also has its own version of the 'Pocahontas story'. It was partly owing to the language skills of Krotoa – a young Khoi girl who was given the Christian name Eva at her baptism, and who had learned to speak Dutch

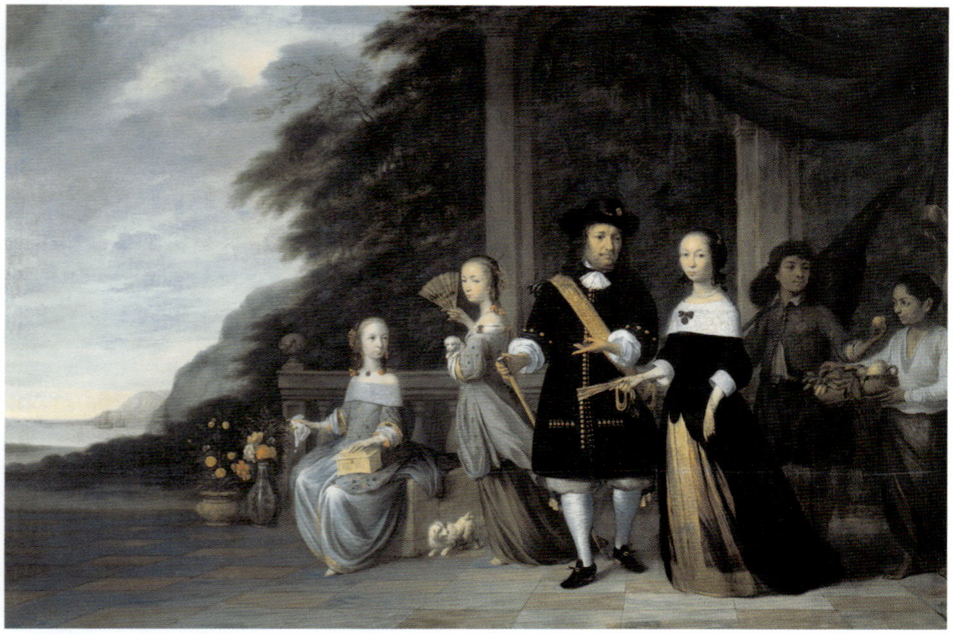

13.2
The Family of Pieter Cnoll
Jacob Jansz Coeman
Oil on canvas
Batavia, 1665
Rijksmuseum, Amsterdam

very well – that more or less peaceful relations were established between the Dutch and the roving local tribesmen, from whom they purchased cattle for the provisioning of passing ships. Almost effortlessly, Krotoa changed from European clothes to cattle skins and back again as the occasion solicited, as she moved between the two camps, until she lost interest and returned to her own people.[12] Nicolaus de Graaff lived long enough to witness the transformation of the settlement in later years. At the foot of Table Mountain arose Cape Town settlement with its teeming vegetable gardens, and in the hinterland region of Stellenbosch wine farms were laid out by Huguenot refugees who settled there after the revocation of the Edict of Nantes in 1685.

No doubt the presence of this *Indische Zeeherberg* ('Indian sea tavern') saved the lives of many sick Dutch sailors. Whatever occasional clashes may have occurred in the years that followed between the Dutch and the Khoi, the latter were never enslaved and were always treated as a free people by the VOC. Indeed, not until the white 'trekboer' with their own herds encroached on the pastures of the Khoi did real tension arise. Tragic was the fate of destitute 'Hottentot' women who, encountering the free-spending lifestyles of the transient sailors, would show their private parts in exchange for some tobacco or small change, in the so-called *kut-kijken* (literally 'cunt-peeking'). This custom led to a whole iconography of Cape women, in which they were depicted in various states of nudity.

The encounters with the local population of the Cape were only fleeting for those who were on their way to Asia. But as soon as VOC servants, soldiers and merchants alike began to settle in the Indies, they were confronted with the fact that, without women, the men could not exist. This is exactly what one of the first governors-general of the Dutch East Indies, Jan Pietersz Coen (1587–1629), pointed out to his directors, the Gentlemen XVII. How else could Batavia, the new headquarters that he founded on Java in 1619, grow into an urban settlement? Coen asked for 'marriageable young women', 400–500 Dutch girls, accompanied by a few older women to chaperone them.[13] According to François Valentijn (1656–1727), who wrote one of the first histories of the Dutch settlement in the Indies, the garrison of Batavia welcomed the first shipload of 'young women' as they would a cargo of 'stewed pears'.[14] Coen, however, was very disappointed, calling the young ladies 'an ungodly bunch making a lot of trouble and causing horror and outrage among many of the natives, who, not seeing any other, better women, think that the entire Dutch nation must be just as godless, unreasonable, and ill-mannered as these creatures'.[15] Attempts by Coen's wife, Eva Ment, to set high standards of civility by training young girls as ladies in waiting also misfired, when one of them was discovered on her bed *in flagrante delicto* with a young soldier; the boy was beheaded and the girl publicly flagellated.[16]

Coen's successors opted for a different, more realistic approach. Henceforth Asian wives were sought, for 'when our (Dutch) men marry native women, strong robust children are produced, who stay alive'.[17] This led to the decision that 'in order to stabilize the headquarters at Batavia, Dutchmen should follow the Portuguese example in India and marry Indian women instead of Dutch women'.[18] In the years that followed, Portuguese-speaking female slaves were brought from India, and after some elementary education and examination by the proper authorities were prepared for baptism and marriage. Because of the large influx of Portuguese-speaking Indians, the Lusitanian language became – together with Malay – the *lingua franca* in Batavian households.

Because wives generally had a longer lifespan than their hard-drinking spouses, there were many widows who remarried more than once and amassed fortunes by inheriting from their deceased husbands. How these women became the target of gold-diggers is well illustrated by the extraordinary story of Cornelia van Nijenrode (1629–92).[19] This daughter of a VOC official and his Japanese concubine was left an enormous fortune by her first husband Pieter Cnoll (d. 1672). A family portrait painted by Jacob Jansz Coeman depicts Cnoll, his half-Japanese wife and their daughters in all their splendour and burgher pride (plate 13.2).[20] After her husband's death, Cornelia married a destitute Dutch lawyer who had lost his wife on the voyage to Batavia. It did not take her long to realize that her second husband was making strenuous efforts to pillage her possessions. This entailed a tug-of-war in which all of Batavia's colonial society became involved. Friends tried to mediate, the church council intervened and finally the Batavian law court sought to administer justice. More than 15 years of quarrelling were settled by a banishment order, whereupon the couple continued their 'war of the roses' at the High Court of Holland at The Hague. Although the Supreme Court's final verdict gave the husband the right to dispose of his wife's belongings as it suited him, Cornelia's sudden death threw a spanner in the works: her testament left her remaining assets to her grandchildren.

Always critical, Nicolaus de Graaff did not have a good word to say about the ostentatious Batavian Eurasian housewives, whom he called 'vain, lazy and sinful', always scolding their domestic slaves.[21] Whatever may have been the case, the Dutch elite at Batavia grew into an ethnically mixed community, which, especially on the female side, was remarkably well adapted to the local lifestyle. This did not particularly please Thomas Stamford Raffles's first wife Olivia (1771–1814) when she initially invited local Batavian ladies for tea. When they showed up in their homely *sarong kebaya*, she sent them home to change into European dresses.[22]

There was, however, a hitch in the marriage policies of the VOC. If an employee who had married 'a native black woman' wanted to return to the Netherlands at the end of his term of service, his wife and children were not allowed to accompany him. It is hardly surprising then that the Dutch employee of *Jan Compagnie* was more likely to take a concubine than a wife. Should he wish to return to Holland, he could buy off his obligations to his mistress and any children whom he had produced with her. The church authorities in Batavia refused to sanction concubinage – no matter how well the system seemed to function – because it was at odds with the concept of Christian matrimony. Baptism and marriage were the reins by which the church held the urban population in check, for those who were not baptized could not marry, and those who were not married could not have their children baptized.

Batavia with its plural society was in a way a laboratory of social relations where all kinds of cross-cultural encounters were constantly occurring. Various different ethnicities lived within and without its walls. Personal encounters between Europeans and Asians can perhaps be best illustrated by examining the lives of two people who are representative of their respective communities. So Bing Kong, known as Bencon (d. 1644), was appointed first headman or captain of the Chinese by Governor-General Jan Pietersz Coen immediately after Batavia was founded in 1619. He and his successors were given remarkable room to govern their own countrymen according to Chinese norms and values. Coen often went to see Bencon at his home, and together the two friends developed their plans for promoting prosperity in Batavia and fostering trade with China. Bencon, the Chinese pioneer, was greatly honoured in life and death; his tomb has been preserved until the present day. Under VOC rule, all ethnicities were ordered to maintain their own customs and forms of dress, and it was not until the nineteenth century that these regulations were commuted. Yet the Chinese community of Batavia continued to be represented by its own Chinese officers, and managed its own temples and cemeteries until the beginning of the Pacific War.[23] Almost all European visitors were in awe of the conspicuous consumption displayed by the Chinese, who formed the biggest population group in the town.

Another group of people in Batavia who left their mark on the city's public life were the *Mardijkers* or *orang merdeka*, Christian free-burghers of mixed race who were descended from Portuguese-speaking freemen and slaves from the Indian subcontinent, the Moluccas and Malacca. While the enterprising Chinese were indispensable for the Batavian economy, the *Mardijkers* supplied the main force for the urban militia who had to defend the town. With their distinctive dress and lifestyle, the *Mardijkers* formed a colourful element in Batavia's multi-cultural society. *Majoor* Augustijn Michels (1769–1833), who like so many of his nation was descended from a freed slave from Bengal, was typical of his community. During the eighteenth century the Michels family struck it rich when it acquired a plot of land with a swallows' nests cave, which produced countless edible birds' nests for the Chinese market. Augustijn, nicknamed Jantje Michielsz, rose to the post of major of the militia in 1807. By then, however, the population of *Mardijkers* had already shrunk considerably, and so had the use of the Portuguese language. Majoor Jantje is fondly remembered for the way he entertained the many dignitaries whom he wined and dined at his domain of Tjitrap. During dinner his orchestra of 30 musicians played a type of Portuguese-inspired music, marching around the table wearing semi-military costume. Out of this tradition sprang so-called *kroncong* music, which is still very popular in Indonesia today.

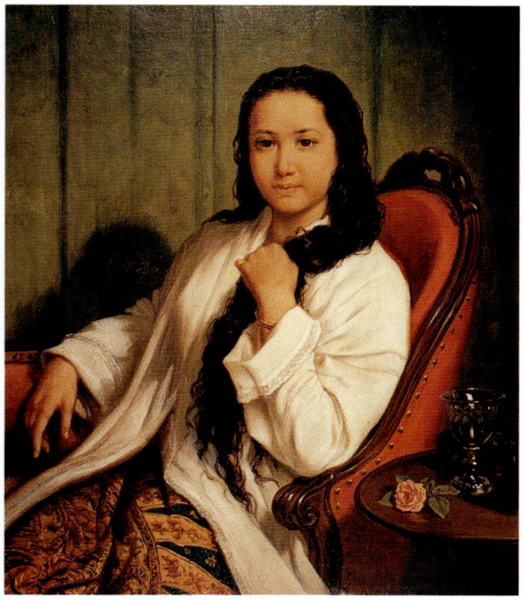

13.3
Portrait of a Dutch East Indian Lady
J. D. Benyon

Oil on canvas
Batavia, *c.* 1857

Royal Tropical Institute, Amsterdam

14

PERSONAL ENCOUNTERS: EUROPEANS IN EAST ASIA

Rupert Faulkner

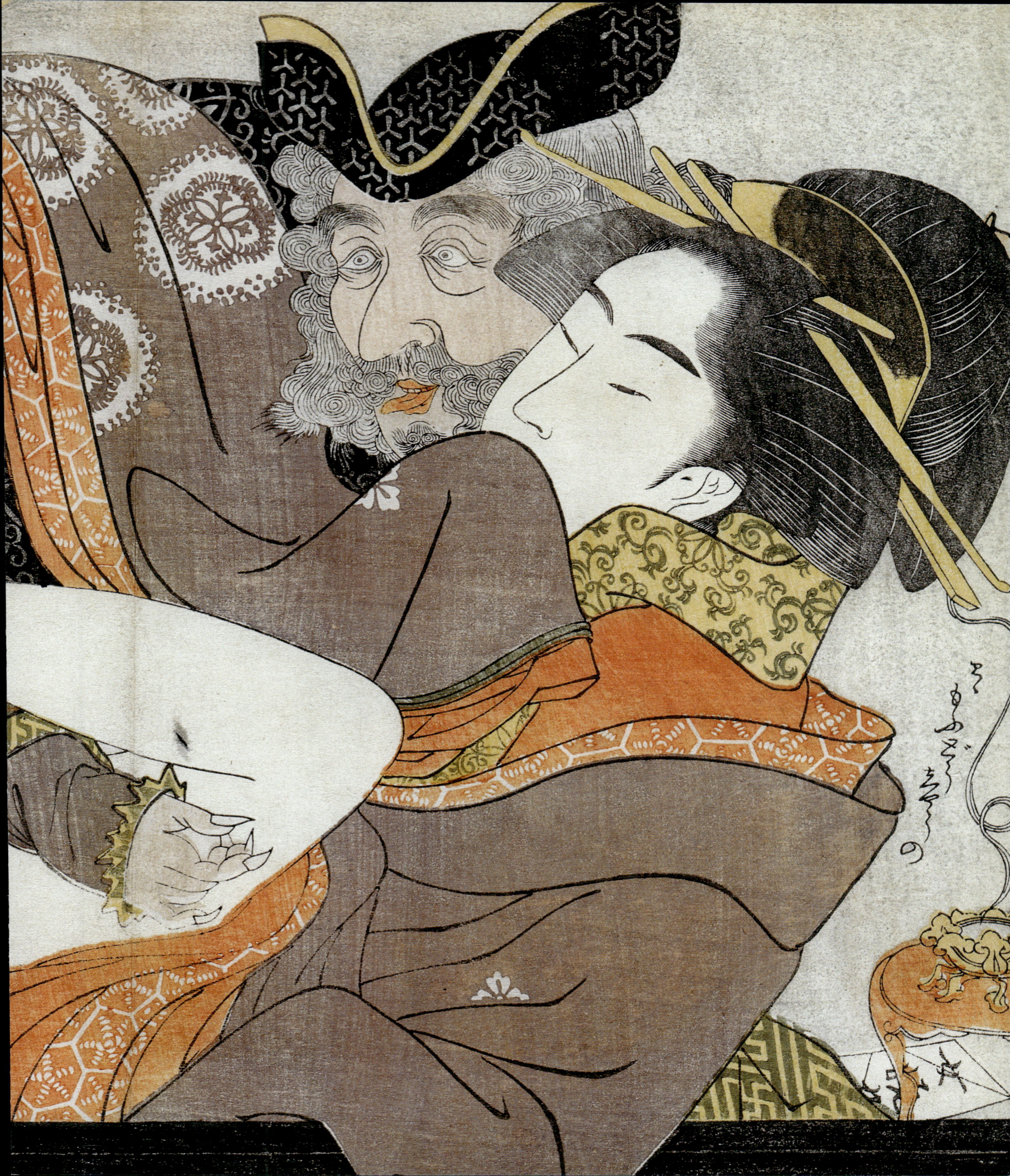

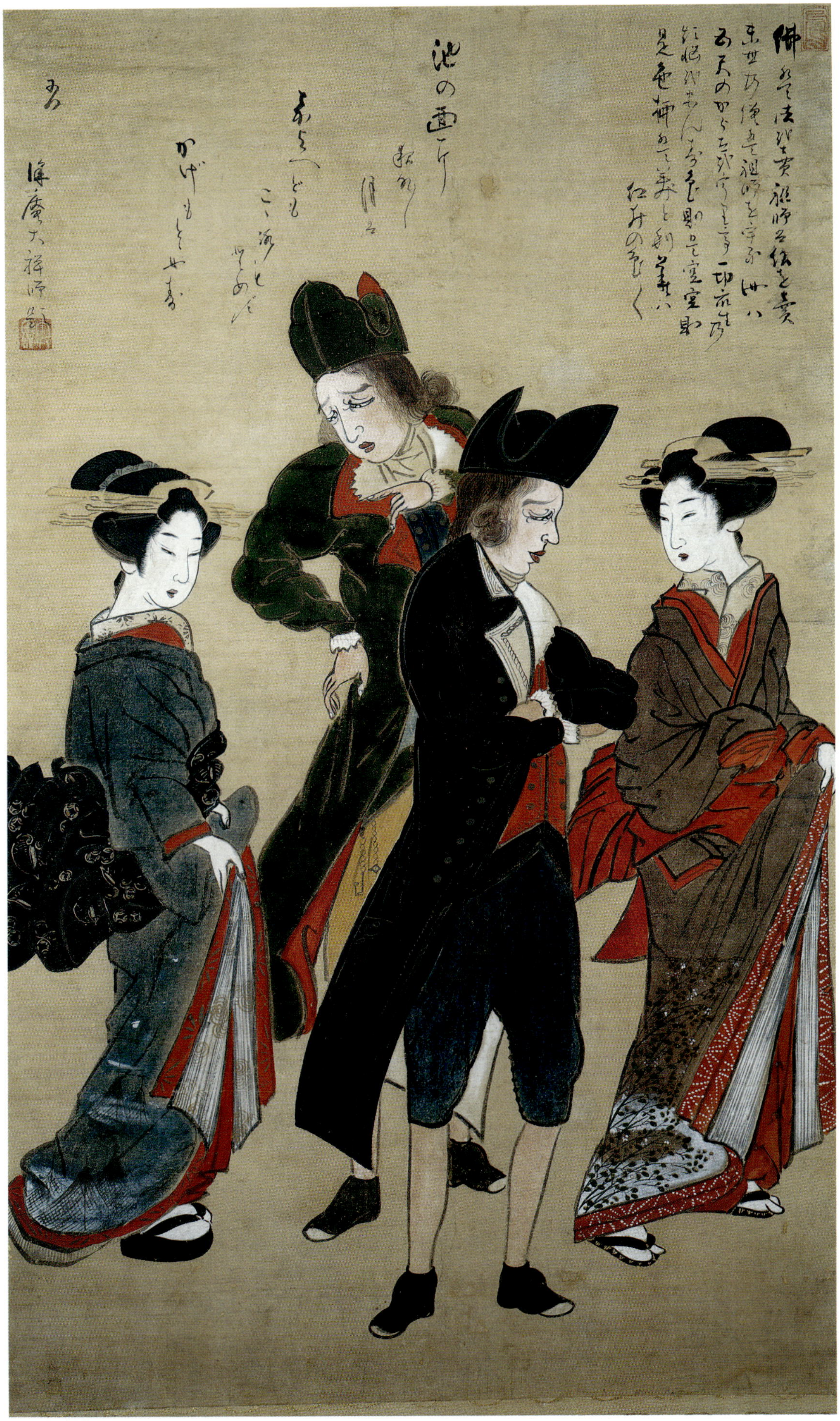

'I can't understand what you are saying at all,' says the woman in Chōkōsai Eishō's depiction of a Dutchman copulating with a Nagasaki prostitute (plate 14.2). 'Push!' she urges, 'Do it harder!' The man, gripping her thigh with a claw-like hand, responds to her entreaties with a stream of gibberish, 'Oken kera kera kera kenkera tou yoka yoka yoka yoka.'[1] Behind them, to the right, burning incense wafts upwards to disguise the rancid body odour of the meat-eating barbarian.[2]

In September 1769, 20 years or so before Eishō (*fl.* 1790–1800) set about titillating the more libidinous vein of Japanese fascination with the Dutch residents of Dejima, William Hickey (1749–?1830), a young Englishman visiting Canton (Guangzhou) after a short period in the service of the English East India Company in Madras, embarked on a boat trip to Whampoa. The outing was proposed by Bob Pott, a precocious 13-year-old who had befriended Hickey on his arrival in Canton, and one of its purposes, as Hickey recorded in his memoirs, was to visit the prostitutes of Lob Lob Creek:

> When we were off Lob Lob Creek one of the boatmen, opening the cabin door, peeped in and said, 'Master, Caree Lob Lob?' to which Bob directly answered, 'Yes,' holding up two fingers. In five minutes a little open boat came paddling towards us, and two very pretty girls jumped in at our window. Bob retired with one to the after cabin, leaving me with the other. We had been a very short time together when the same man opened the door again, quickly crying out, 'Chop Chop Lob Lob, mandarin dee come.' Regardless of him or his words, which I did not understand, I continued the business I was engaged upon; which when finished I called to Bob, who desired me to come in, and I found him and his companion sitting very quietly together. Having dismissed our Lob Lob ladies, we continued our voyage to Whampoa…[3]

Shortly after returning to Canton, Hickey's memoirs continue, he was invited to two parties at the country residence of the Cohong merchant Pankeequa. The first was 'a dinner, dressed and served *à la mode Anglaise*, the Chinamen on that occasion using, and awkwardly enough, knives and forks, and in every respect conforming to the European fashion'. For the second party, held the following day, 'everything was Chinese, all the European guests eating, or endeavouring to eat, with chopsticks, no knives or forks being at table. The entertainment was splendid, the victuals superiorly good, the Chinese loving high dishes and keeping the best of cooks.'[4]

Although Eishō's print and Hickey's colourful recollections of his stay in Canton are the outcomes of rather different sets of circumstances, they both provide valuable insights into the realm of personal as opposed to religious, diplomatic or other more formal kinds of encounter. Sex and prostitution are central focuses of concern, but they also touch upon and reflect other important issues such as language, cross-cultural attitudes and the embracing of foreign manners and forms. Hickey's description of Pankeequa's parties shows how Canton merchants were willing to adopt, if only in the interests of furthering trade, European modes of dining; and how their European counterparts were prepared to negotiate the use of chopsticks out of respect for their Chinese hosts. In Eishō's print the claw-like hand and stench-repelling incense reflect the popularly held view of Dutchmen as otherworldly monsters; at the same time, as the existence of the print and others of its kind attests, there was a clear desire on the part of Japanese consumers of pornography to appropriate them into their world of sexual fantasy.

The furtiveness of Hickey's encounter with the ladies of Lob Lob Creek indicates that the Chinese authorities took a dim view about such liaisons, if not about prostitution more generally. Indeed, Hickey noted that there were 'no more than six women to satisfy the lusts of a fleet of five-and-twenty ships, the consequence of which had already shown itself, a number of their junior officers being diseased'.[5] This suppression of sexual services would have been especially frustrating when combined, as it was, with the ruling that no foreign women were allowed at Canton.[6]

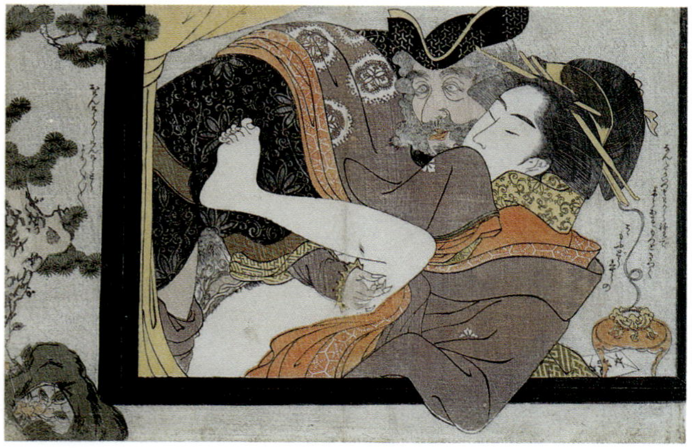

14.1 opposite
Two Dutchmen and Two Courtesans
Hanging scroll; ink and colours on paper
Japan (Nagasaki), c.1800
Private collection

14.2 page 177 and below
Dutchman and Maruyama Courtesan
Chōkōsai Eishō
Woodblock print on paper
Japan (Edo), 1790s
V&A: E.170–1954

The unyielding position of the Chinese at Canton was in marked contrast to the provisions made by their Japanese counterparts in Nagasaki. The Dutch, who had been confined to Dejima since 1641 – in a similar way to the manner in which English and other European merchants (with the exception of the Portuguese outpost at Macao) were restricted to Canton from 1760 onwards – were also not permitted to have their own women with them. They were, on the other hand, allowed to consort with the prostitutes of Nagasaki's Maruyama and Yoriai brothel districts (plate 14.1). Engelbert Kaempfer (1651–1716), a German physician who served on Dejima from 1690 to 1692, famously recorded that one of the regulations posted on the bridge connecting the island to the mainland read: 'Whores only, but no other women shall be suffer'd to go in.'[7]

Policy in Edo-period (1615–1868) Japan was to contain prostitution within officially prescribed red-light districts at a distance from main centres of population. Nagasaki was unusual in that the prostitutes were allowed to go out to their clients, who included both the Dutch on Dejima and the more numerous Chinese who, from 1689 onwards, were likewise forced to reside in specially designated quarters. Prostitutes were initially allowed to stay at Dejima for only one night. This was extended to three nights in 1713 and later to five.[8] During the eighteenth century the Dutch, like the Chinese, were also permitted to leave Dejima in order to visit the brothel areas.[9]

These relaxations of rules, minor concessions though they were within the rigid system of control exercised by the Nagasaki authorities, led to a number of close relationships being formed between Dutchmen and Japanese women. The children born of such unions were considered to be Japanese. During their early years they were allowed to remain with their parents, but when they were old enough to be educated they were transferred to the care of others (their grandparents, for example) and made subject to the same restrictions imposed on other Japanese in their dealings with foreigners.[10] In this respect the situation never reverted to the more liberal conditions that had obtained prior to Japan's adoption of its 'Closed Door' policy in 1639.

Earlier records from the Dutch and English factories at Hirado show that Europeans enjoyed sexual freedoms inconceivable at home.[11] Many of them whored their time away, there being little else to do by way of recreation, and many drank to excess. Some, however – and this was especially true of the chief factors – formed stable relationships with Japanese women, numerous progeny being born as a consequence. Cornelia, the gracefully attired woman who appears with her husband and two daughters in the family portrait by Jacob Coeman (see plate 13.2), was the daughter of Cornelis van Nieuwenroode, chief of the Dutch factory at Hirado from 1623 to 1633, and his Japanese concubine Surushia.[12] François Caron (1600–73), who arrived in Hirado in 1619 and rose through the ranks to become chief of the Dutch factory from 1639 to 1641, sired no fewer than six children during his time in Japan.[13] Two of them, Daniel and François, grew up to study theology at Leiden.[14] Richard Cocks (1565?–1624), who came to Japan in 1613 and served as chief of the English factory until its closure in 1623, was less happy in love. Despite his best efforts to keep his Japanese consort Matinga in the style he felt suitable for the daughter of a *samurai* retainer of the locally powerful Matsuura family, she proved too fickle for him. In 1620, having become aware of her 'villany & that she had abused herself w'th vj or 7 p'rsons', he brought their relationship to an end.[15]

Arrangements in Nagasaki, where the Portuguese were based from 1571 until their expulsion in 1639, were similarly accommodating. Francesco Carletti, a Florentine merchant in Portuguese service who visited Japan in the late 1590s, observed that as soon as the Portuguese arrived, pimps would come to their lodgings and 'enquire whether they would like to purchase … a girl, for the period of their sojourn, or to keep her for so many months, or for a night, or for a day, or for an hour, a contract being first made with these brokers, or an agreement entered into with the girl's relations, and the money paid down'. He also explained that this practice did not 'in any way interfere with a girl's chance of marriage. Indeed, many of them would never get married, if they had not by this means acquired a dowry.' Despite this acknowledgement of locally pertaining exigencies, Carletti concluded that 'the country is more plentifully supplied than any other with these sort of means of gratifying the passion for sexual indulgence, just as it abounds in every other sort of vice'.[16] With European and Japanese sexual mores being as different as they were, one can understand Carletti's disapproving tone. At the same time it is hardly surprising that the vast majority of European merchants and sailors coming to Japan should have cast off whatever inhibitions they might have had and indulged themselves as fully as they evidently did.

If Nagasaki and Hirado were so obliging in catering to the needs of European men, what of Macao, settled by the Portuguese in 1557 at the other end of the profitable China–Japan trade route? Some of the most interesting information about life in Macao is contained in a series of European reports written in the late 1630s, shortly before the expulsion of the Portuguese from Japan and the decline in Macao's fortunes that ensued as a result. One of these records that there were 850 *casados*, Portuguese men married to native or half-caste women, and a similar number of married Chinese, many of whom worked as interpreters. It also noted that there were large numbers of unmarried Portuguese sailors and traders.[17] A report written later in the seventeenth century, which relates how 60 women, expelled for having 'earned their living with their bodies', perished when the ship carrying them from Macao was lost at sea, indicates that their sexual needs must have been more than adequately met.[18]

One aspect of Chinese and Japanese sexual behaviour that Europeans frequently commented upon was the prevalence of homosexuality and male prostitution. The disapproval they expressed reflected the severity with which such practices were condemned in their home countries. Whether they were as principled in deed as in word is something of a moot point, for the environments in which mariners, merchants and missionaries operated were often populated, with the obvious implications this would have had, largely or solely by men. While one can only speculate as to what actually took place, surviving European records referring to Chinese and Japanese homoeroticism are unremittingly critical. Matteo Ricci (1552–1610), for example, who was rarely censorious towards the Chinese, was noticeably harsh on the subject.[19] His Jesuit contemporaries in Japan were similarly concerned at the local penchant among men of all classes and callings for sodomizing young boys. Alessandro Valignano (1539–1606), visitor to the Jesuit missions in the East, wrote of the 'great dissipation' of the Japanese 'in the sin that does not bear mentioning', laying much of the blame on Buddhist monks, who 'teach that not only is it not a sin but that it is even something quite natural and virtuous'.[20]

Male prostitution in China appears to have declined during the Qing dynasty (1644–1912), possibly because of the more puritanical attitude of the Manchus compared with their Ming predecessors.[21] In Japan, on the other hand, *nanshoku* or 'man sex' continued to be widely and openly practised well into the nineteenth century.[22] The Dutch were no less shocked by this than the Jesuits and others before them, something that was remarked upon by Morishima Chūryō (1756?–1810) in his *Kōmō Zatsuwa* (*The Red-Hair Miscellany*) of 1787. In an entry entitled 'Prohibition of *Nanshoku*', Morishima commented on the ferocity of the strictures that applied in Europe, how *nanshoku* was believed to run counter to human ethics, and how offenders were known to have been burned at the stake or executed by drowning.[23]

Like the nearly contemporaneous print by Eishō, the *Kōmō Zatsuwa*, which takes the form of a series of short entries on intriguing facts about Europe, was

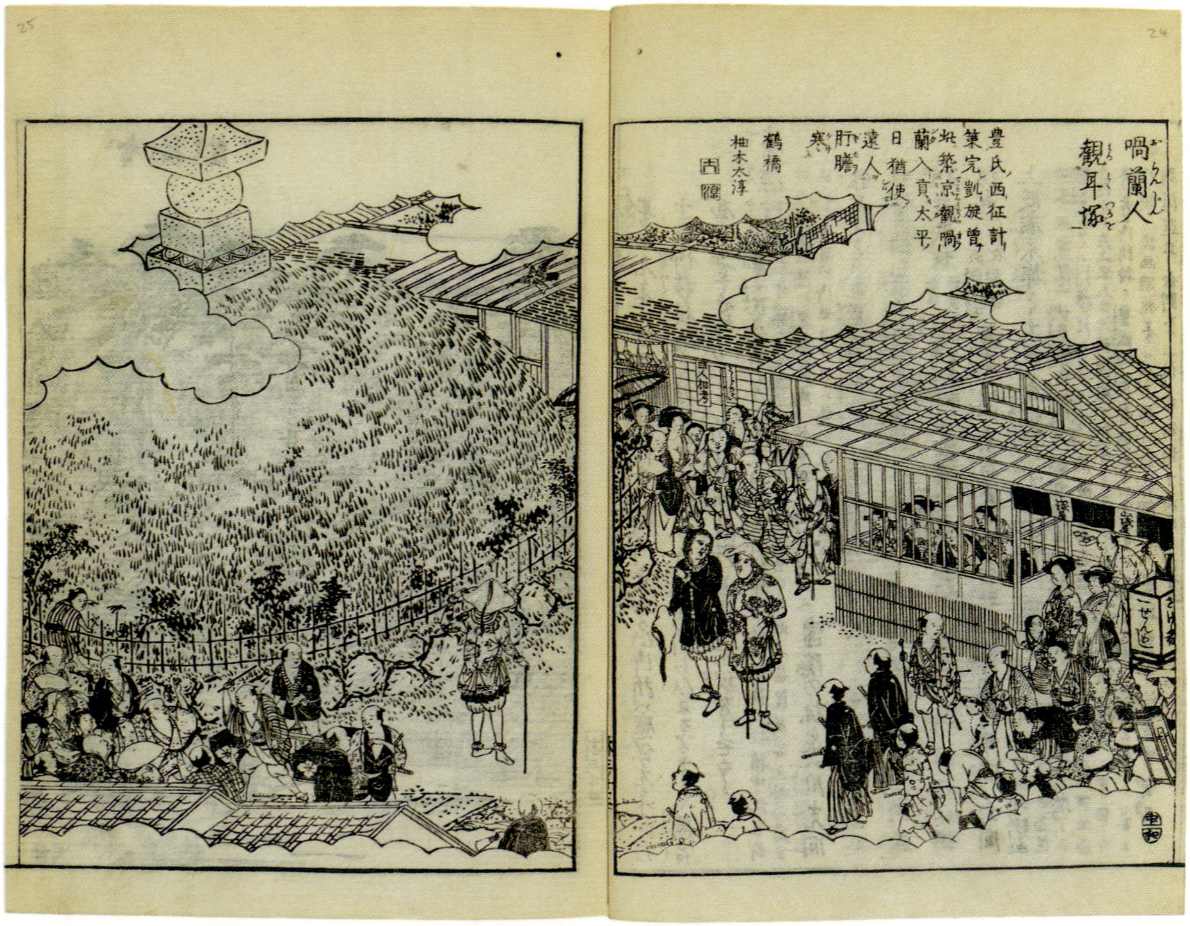

14.3
Japanese Crowd Looking at Dutchmen Visiting the Mimizuka in Kyoto
From the *Miyako Rinsen Meishō Zue (Illustrated Record of Famous Places in Miyako [Kyoto])*, vol. 3, written by Akisato Ritō and illustrated by Sakuma Sōen et al.

Woodblock-printed book
Japan (Edo), 1799

V&A: E.2242–1925

14.4
Blood Circulation in the Human Body

From *Kaitai Shinsho (New Anatomical Atlas)*, translated by Sugita Genpaku et al. and illustrated by Odano Naotake, 1774
Woodblock-printed book
Japan (Edo)

British Library, London

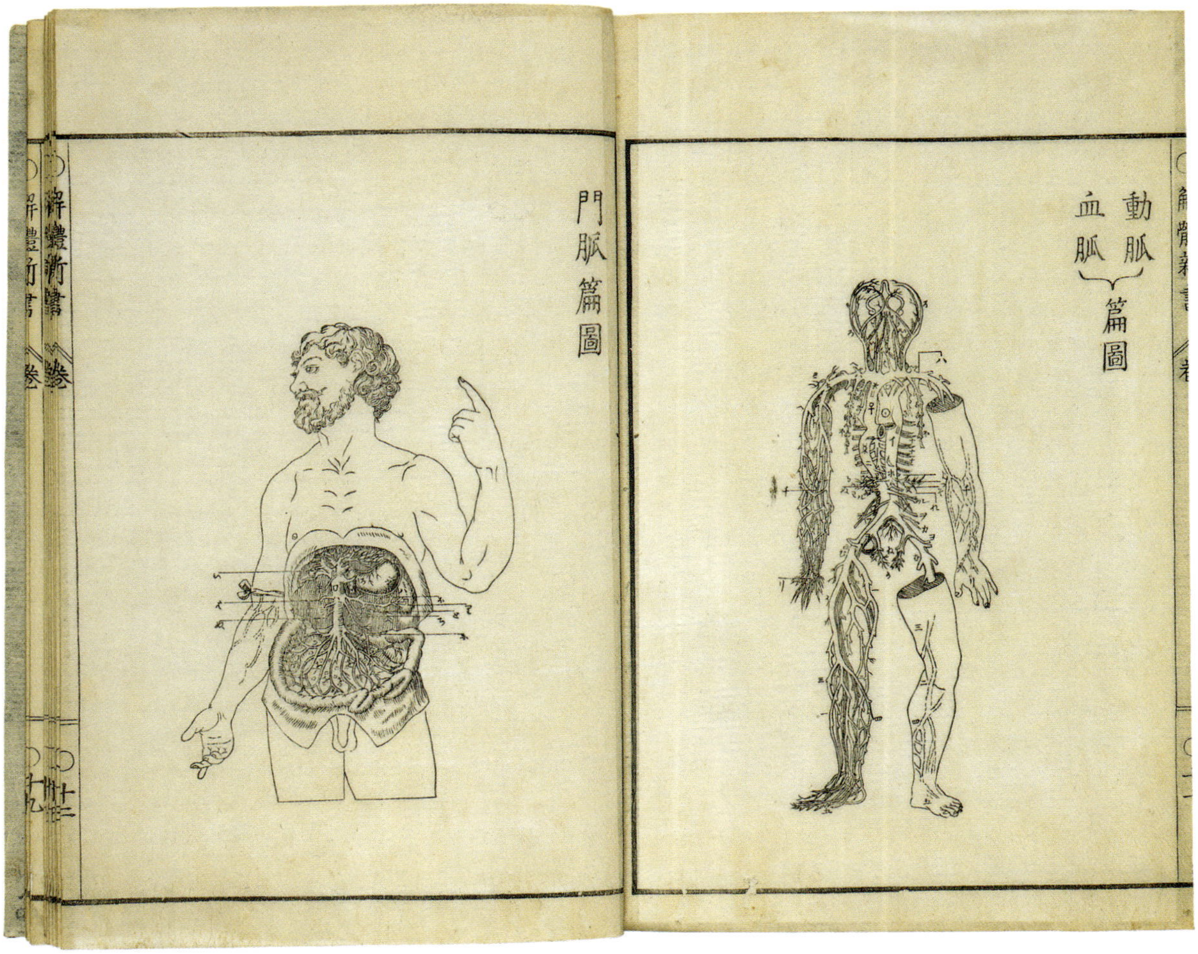

the product of growing Japanese interest in the West. Popular fascination with the inhabitants of Dejima, whose senior members (the chief factor, the secretary and the physician) made annual visits to the *shōgun*'s court in Edo and were thus seen by many Japanese other than those living in Nagasaki, paralleled the rise of *Rangaku* (Dutch learning) in the second half of the eighteenth century (plate 14.3). Morishima was indeed a prominent *Rangaku* scholar, one of whose various claims to fame was the compilation of the first Japanese–Dutch dictionary, the *Bango-sen* (*A Lexicon of Primitive Words*), published in Edo in 1798.[24]

Mastery of Dutch was essential to the *Rangaku* project, whose main concern was to understand and translate into Japanese European treatises on medicine and science. The challenge this presented was enormous, as we know from the *Rangaku Kotohajime* (*The Origins of Rangaku*) of 1815 by Sugita Genpaku (1733–1817), in which he describes the immensely laborious process that he and his fellow physician Maeno Ryōtaku (1723–1803) went through in producing the seminal *Kaitai Shinsho* (*New Anatomical Atlas*) (see p. 318) (plate 14.4). Published in 1774, this was a Japanese translation of a 1734 Dutch version of the *Anatomical Tables* of Johannes Adam Kulmus, first published in German in 1725.[25] The translation took Sugita and Maeno four years to complete, on some days it not being 'rare that we would be thinking and staring together till sunset and yet unable to decipher a line or even a sentence one or two inches long'.[26]

Elsewhere in the *Rangaku Kotohajime*, Sugita recounts how some years previously he and Maeno had been put off learning Dutch by Nishi Zenzaburō (d. 1768), the senior interpreter accompanying the Dutch delegation staying at the Nagasaki-ya, their official lodgings in Edo. Nishi went to considerable lengths to explain how difficult it was to master Dutch, with the result that the impatient Sugita returned home convinced that it would be a waste of time to burden himself 'with such a troublesome job'.[27] It has been suggested that Nishi's discouragement of Sugita and Maeno may have been motivated by a concern to guard the study of Dutch as a professional secret, the Nishi being one of numerous hereditary families of interpreters employed at Dejima.[28]

The system of *oranda tsūji,* or Dutch interpreters, to which the Nishi family belonged was a highly organized one. When the Dutch moved to Dejima in 1641 they brought with them the Portuguese-speaking interpreters they had employed at Hirado. These were joined by the interpreters who had formerly worked for the Portuguese. Together they became local officials in the employ of and responsible to the Nagasaki authorities. Dutch gradually replaced Portuguese as the working language, and in 1695 a guild for the complement of 150 interpreters who worked at Dejima was established.[29]

The job of the interpreters was not easy. They had to learn a foreign language at a time when grammars and dictionaries did not exist, and when there were no dedicated teachers to turn to. They were not allowed to fraternize with the Dutch, but, on the contrary, were expected to spy on them. Kaempfer described them as people 'employed to assist us and to discourage foreigners from learning the language, so that they can be kept ignorant of and blind to internal conditions', and 'by whose crooked and false mouth our substantial trade must be pursued and annually be conducted'.[30] Although such conditions were hardly conducive to the development of close friendships, the Dutch and the interpreters were in constant contact with one another, one of the interpreters' tasks being to ensure that the Dutch were supplied with all their daily needs, women included. It is difficult to imagine, given these circumstances, that some degree of warmth and understanding did not develop between them, particularly after the attitude of Japanese officialdom towards the Dutch began to relax in the late eighteenth century.

In connection with language and the procurement of women, there is an interesting survival in the form of a Dutch–Japanese phrasebook compiled by a Nagasaki interpreter for the owner of the Ebi-ya, the inn in Kyoto where the Dutch delegation stayed on their way to and from Edo. It dates from about 1770 and consists of 80 short phrases written in Dutch with *katakana* transcriptions and Japanese translations. These range from simple greetings such as 'Good morning' and 'Please come in' to more complex expressions like 'I drank too much last night and have a hangover'. A sequence of seven phrases is specifically to do with hiring the services of women: 'Please look at that pretty girl over there'; 'Yes, she is a pretty girl'; 'Do you like that girl?'; 'Yes, I like her a great deal'; 'Would you like me to make appropriate arrangements?'; 'Yes, please do'; 'Understood'.[31]

With the growth of *Rangaku*, the interpreters' language abilities and the knowledge of western medicine and science that several of them had gained through working alongside the Dutch began to be called upon, as we have seen, by the likes of Sugita Genpaku and Maeno Ryōtaku. Whenever the Dutch came to Edo, not only was the Nagasaki-ya swarmed by inquisitive townspeople (plate 14.5), but it was visited by a steady stream of scholars hungry for foreign knowledge. The burgeoning of *Rangaku* coincided with and was stimulated by the posting to Dejima of Isaac Titsingh (1745–1812) and Carl Thunberg (1743–1828), who, with their predecessor Engelbert Kaempfer, were among the more highly educated Europeans to come to Japan during the

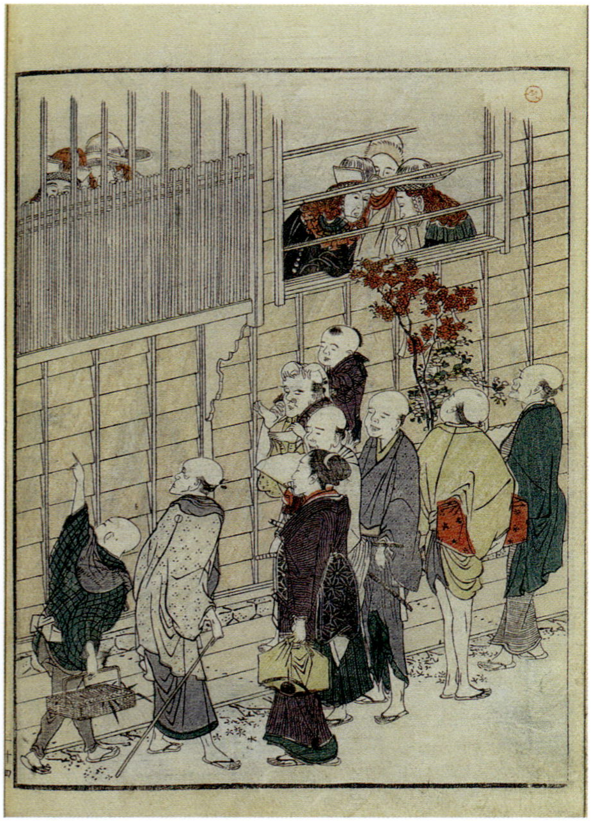

14.5
Dutchmen in the Nagasaki-ya
Katsushika Hokusai
From *Ehon Azuma Asobi (Picture Book of Places of Entertainment in the Eastern Capital)*, 1802
Woodblock-printed book
Japan (Edo)
V&A: E.2675–1925

Edo period. Titsingh was chief factor three times between 1779 and 1784. Renowned as a collector and scholar of things Japanese, he was also famous for having wooed the high-ranking Maruyama courtesan Ukine.[32] His success in this was, it has been suggested, partly due to the fluency of his Japanese.[33] Thunberg, a Swedish physician of considerable distinction who served at Dejima from 1775 to 1776, was also a proficient linguist. His ability to converse in Japanese was a major factor in the close and lasting friendship that he formed with Katsuragawa Hoshū (1754–1809), Morishima Chūryō's elder brother, who was later to become private physician to the *shōgun*.[34]

Thunberg and Titsingh were not the first members of the Dutch East India Company with Japanese language abilities. When the Dutch were at Hirado in the early seventeenth century, before the ban on learning Japanese alluded to by Kaempfer was imposed, there were several capable linguists. François Caron, mentioned earlier, was one.

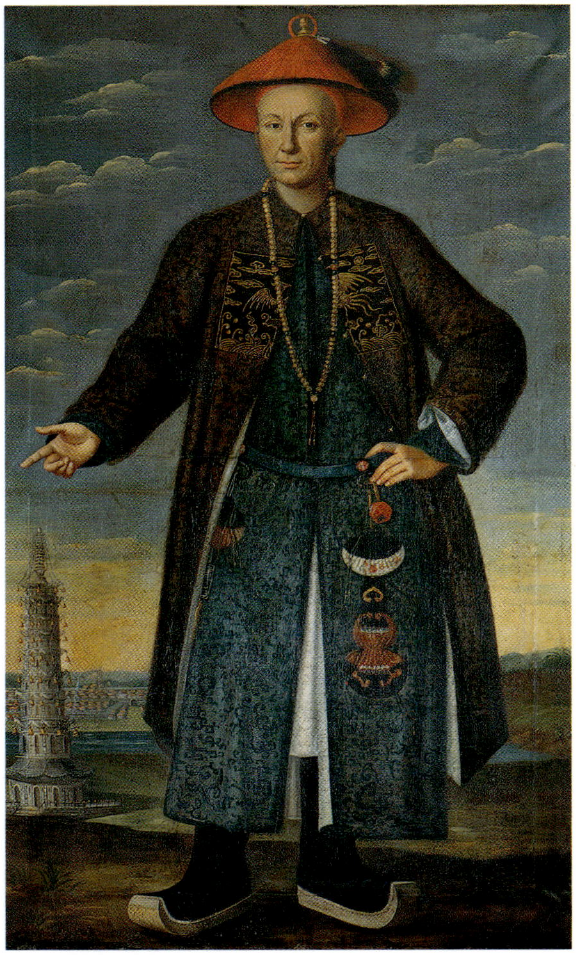

14.6
European Wearing Chinese Dress
Oil on canvas
England, c.1690
Collection of Jonathan Lourie

Jacques Specx, the first chief factor, was another. Without their mastery of Japanese, it is unlikely that the Dutch would have been as successful in establishing themselves in Japan as they were. Another notable figure of this period was the Englishman William Adams (1564–1620), who arrived in Japan in 1600 on board the Dutch ship *De Liefde*. Befriended by Tokugawa Ieyasu (1543–1616; r. 1603–05), whom he served as informal adviser and by whom he was granted an estate and an annual stipend, Adams's interpreting skills helped smooth the way for the establishment of the Dutch and English factories at Hirado.

The linguistic achievements of Adams and his Dutch East India Company contemporaries were considerable, but they pale in comparison with those of the Jesuits. The policy encouraged in Asia by Francis Xavier (1506–62) was that priests should master the language of the people among whom they worked, rather than assume – as had tended to be the case with missionary activity before his time – that the embracing of Christianity implied learning to speak and effectively becoming Portuguese. Translation of Christian texts into local languages was, he believed, the key to missionary success.[35] In Japan he took the further step of actively learning about Japanese culture, establishing a precedent that informed Alessandro Valignano's subsequent formulation of a new and radical approach to missionary work in East Asia.[36] Accommodation, as this is termed, was premised on the Jesuit and indeed more broadly European view of the Chinese and Japanese as white races equal to themselves. It required missionaries to adapt to and work within the framework of the other culture rather than impose Christianity from a position of assumed superiority outside. Highly developed communication skills were, as Valignano repeatedly stressed, critical to its success.

Records of the Jesuit mission in Japan include listings of Europeans competent in Japanese, as well as information about the preaching abilities of Japanese Christians. A catalogue drawn up by Valignano in 1592 mentions several individuals who 'all know the language very well, and can preach and write in it'.[37] The most fluent of these was João Rodrigues (*c.* 1561–1633), who travelled to Japan at the age of 15, became a Jesuit in 1580 and later served as interpreter to Toyotomi Hideyoshi (1537–98; r. 1583–98) and Tokugawa Ieyasu. He was closely involved in the compilation of the famous

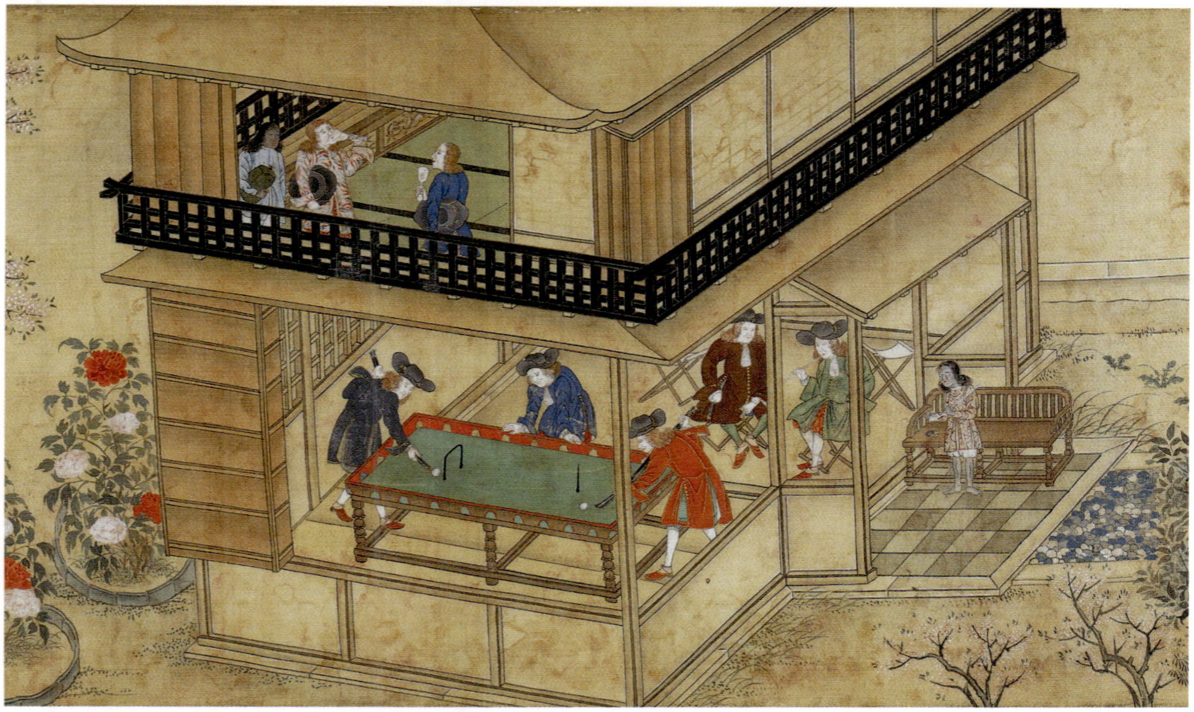

14.7
The Dutch Factory at Dejima (detail)
Handscroll; ink and colour on silk
Japan (Nagasaki), *c.* 1800
V&A: D.151–1905

Japanese–Portuguese dictionary, the *Vocabulario da Lingoa de Japam*, published by the Jesuit mission press in Nagasaki in 1603, and wrote an important Japanese grammar entitled the *Arte da Lingoa de Japam*.[38] There was also Luis Frois (1532–97), the Jesuits' most capable Japanese speaker prior to Rodrigues, who was well known for having been befriended by Oda Nobunaga (1534–82) and for the exceptional detail of his many reports on Japan.

Matteo Ricci, the co-founder of the Jesuit mission in China, was an equally if not even more talented linguist. Ricci died in 1610, 27 years after arriving in China, and was buried in Peking (Beijing), where his tomb can still be seen today. His Chinese was so fluent that he was able to engage in philosophical debate with China's most eminent thinkers, who knew him by the Chinese name Li Madou. His profound grasp of Confucianism – the accommodation of Christianity to which became the focus of his endeavour – was based on his extensive reading of the Chinese classics and the knowledge he gained through translating the *Sishu* (*The Four Books*). Ricci also published in Chinese, both original books and translations of western texts.[39] His translation of the first six books of Euclid's *Elements of Geometry* was especially important. Through this and his work as a cartographer he set the Jesuit mission in Peking on the path to becoming renowned among Chinese intellectuals as a conduit for western scientific learning (see pp. 298–301).

Ricci and his successors were also famous for dressing like literati scholars. This sartorial gesture was an assertion that the Jesuits belonged firmly within, and in the upper echelons of, the hierarchical structure of Chinese society. Ricci had initially worn Buddhist dress. In so doing he was following the precedent of the Jesuits in Japan, who, although they did not wear Buddhist attire as such, were urged by Valignano to deport themselves with the dignity and gravity of Zen priests. Ricci's decision to recast himself in the Chinese literati mould was the outcome of his deepening engagement with Confucianism and his realization that the Buddhist priesthood was not as widely respected in China as he had originally thought.[40] His determination in this was directly influenced, it has been suggested, by Qu Rukuei, a young gentleman scholar whom he befriended in Shaozhou after moving into a newly built Chinese-style residence there in 1589.[41]

The adoption by the Jesuits of Chinese and Japanese modes of behaviour and living was central to the principles of accommodation advocated by Valignano. Acculturation was, in short, an integral part of a missionary's job. This was not the case with other Europeans in China and Japan, most of whom were there for mercantile reasons. In the close-knit

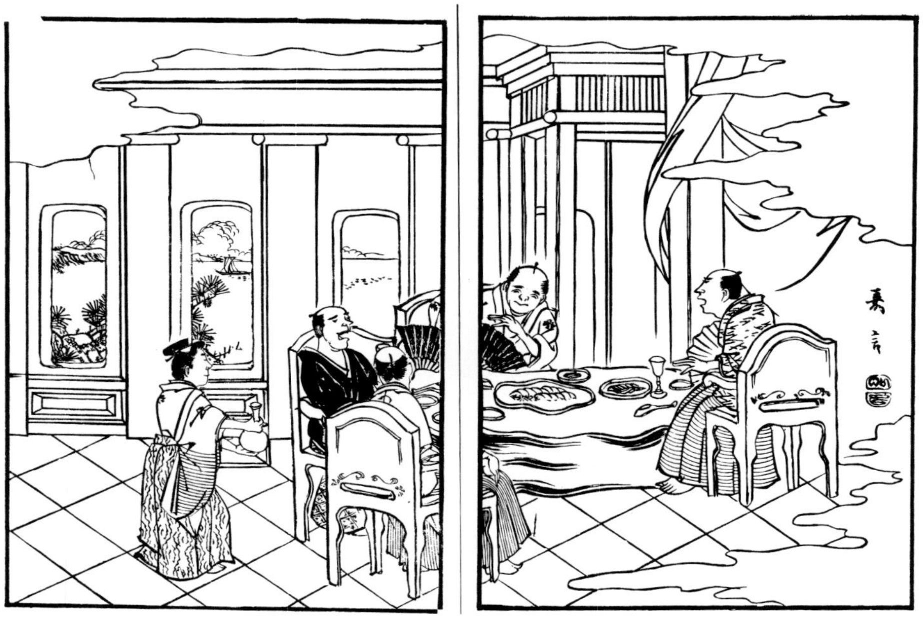

14.8
Western-style Room in Yoshida Kōsaku's House

From *Hokusō Sadan*, written by Tachibana Nankei and illustrated by Ichiyanagi Kagen

Woodblock-printed book
Japan (Edo), *c.* 1831

National Diet Library, Tokyo

Sino-Portuguese community of Macao, there would have been a high degree of mutual borrowing and hybridization of cultural forms. Macao was the exception to the rule, however. We know from William Hickey's account of his stay at Canton that the Europeans maintained as far as possible the style of living they would have enjoyed at home. Hickey describes 'a capital dinner' at the English factory 'consisting of fish, flesh and fowl, all of the best, with a variety of well-dressed made dishes, being served up in two courses, followed by a superb dessert, the wines, clarets, Madeira, and hock, all excellent, and made as cold as ice'.[42] His observation, noted earlier, about the difficulty that the Europeans at Pankeequa's dinner party had in using chopsticks indicates, furthermore, that they rarely ate in the Chinese manner. Such evidence suggests that the late seventeenth-century portrait of a European merchant dressed as a Chinaman is less a reflection of any kind of day-to-day reality than a pronouncement about the fact of having travelled to and experienced China (plate 14.6).

The detailed depiction of the Dutch factory in a late eighteenth-century handscroll suggests that the situation in Dejima was much the same as in Canton, with the Dutch closely preserving the lifestyle they were accustomed to in Europe, albeit in Japanese-style buildings (plate 14.7). The sketch by Shiba Kōkan (1747–1818) of the chief factor's room shows how it was fitted out in European style with paintings, chairs, spittoons, a chandelier, a barometer and an arrangement of decanters and glasses on a table in front of two rows of bound ledgers (see plate 10.3). Kōkan, who visited Dejima while staying in Nagasaki in late 1788, was also shown what he thought was a guest room where, he recorded, there 'was a table for pocket billiards – a game that Dutchmen play just as Japanese play dice games'.[43] The depiction of the billiard room in the Dejima handscroll matches Kōkan's description exactly.

While in Nagasaki, Kōkan met a number of important local residents, including the interpreter and *Rangaku* scholar Yoshio Kōsaku (1724–1810), who was well known for living in a two-storey house built in western style. It featured a room with a dining table and chairs in which Kōsaku treated his guests to exotic repasts using glassware and other novel appurtenances (plate 14.8). It also had a western-style bath and a flight of stairs with green-painted woodwork, rather than the ladder-like arrangement usually found in Japanese buildings.[44] Kōsaku's house and his style of entertaining were extreme instances of the widespread fashion for things Dutch that paralleled the rise of *Rangaku* in the second half of the eighteenth century. This was an almost exact repeat of what had occurred when Portuguese merchants and Jesuit missionaries were in Japan two centuries before.

Painted screens from this earlier period show how fashion-conscious Japanese men wore a hybrid form of dress with clearly western elements such as ruffs and full, big trousers in the style of *calsan* (plate 14.9). Crucifixes and rosaries often feature in depictions of this kind, where they function as fashion accessories charged with a flavour of the exotic. A Jesuit report of 1594 noted that Hideyoshi:

> has a great liking for Portuguese clothing, and the members of his retinue, in emulation, are often attired in the Portuguese style. The same is true even of those *daimyōs* who are not Christian. They wear rosaries of driftwood on their breasts, hang a crucifix from the shoulder or waist, and sometimes even hold a handkerchief. Some … have memorized the Our Father and the Hail Mary, and recite them as they walk in the streets. This is not done in ridicule of the Christians, but simply to show off their familiarity with the latest fashions.[45]

A report of the previous year had observed in connection with Hideyoshi's return to Kyoto from Nagoya in Kyūshū that:

> all the *daimyōs* … [and] their retinues … [were] attired in the manner of our country. The tailors of Nagasaki are all so busy that they have not a moment to spare, yet they also accompanied him. Recently, amber jewelry, gold chains, and buttons have become popular among them. Our foods are to their liking, particularly hen's eggs and beef, which the

Japanese used to detest … It is quite astounding how so many things of the Portuguese have come to have such good report among them.[46]

It is a matter of speculation what might have happened had the Tokugawa regime not enforced its 'Closed Door' policy in 1639. Throughout its history, Japan has been receptive to external influences, notably Chinese, but also other Asian and, as has been shown, European ones. The relaxation of controls in the eighteenth century was followed very quickly by the rise of *Rangaku* and the burgeoning of popular interest in things Dutch. In China during the same period the Qing emperors, who came to power in 1644, employed Jesuit missionaries for their knowledge of western mathematics, astronomy, philosophy, warfare, cartography, shipping and navigational practices. They also employed Jesuit missionary artists as court painters and, in the case of Giuseppe Castiglione (1688–1766), as an architect as well (see pp. 343–5).[47] The paintings and buildings thereby created are the subject of another essay, but of pertinence here is the fact that their commissioning reflected on the part of the Qing court a profound interest in what Europe had to offer. To the extent that it was the Japanese elite, both in the late sixteenth century and the late eighteenth century, who led the way in Japan's appropriation of the West, there were similarities with China. There was, on the other hand, a difference in the degree of popular engagement with the foreign. Qing court patronage may have given rise to splendid depictions of imperial concubines in European attire (see plate 26.1), but conditions in China were not such that there was widespread domestic demand for the kind of exotic erotica produced in Japan by Eishō and his ilk.

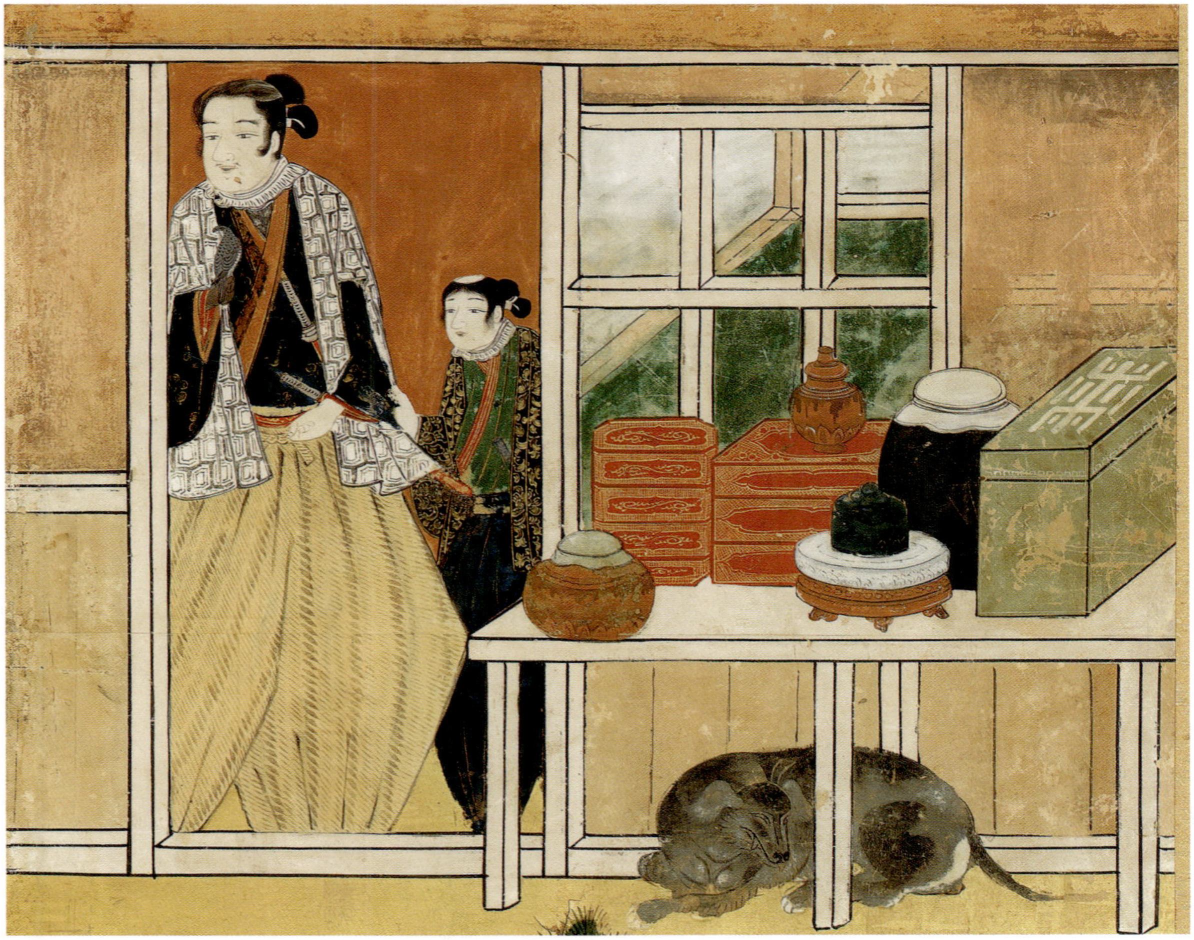

14.9
Japanese wearing *nanban* fashions

Detail from a pair of six-panel screens depicting the arrival of the Portuguese in a Japanese port; ink, colour and gold-leaf on paper
Japan, early 17th century

Asian Art Museum of San Francisco, The Avery Brundage Collection, B60D77+ and B60D78+. Used by permission

15

VISUAL RESPONSES: DEPICTING EUROPEANS IN SOUTH ASIA

Rosemary Crill

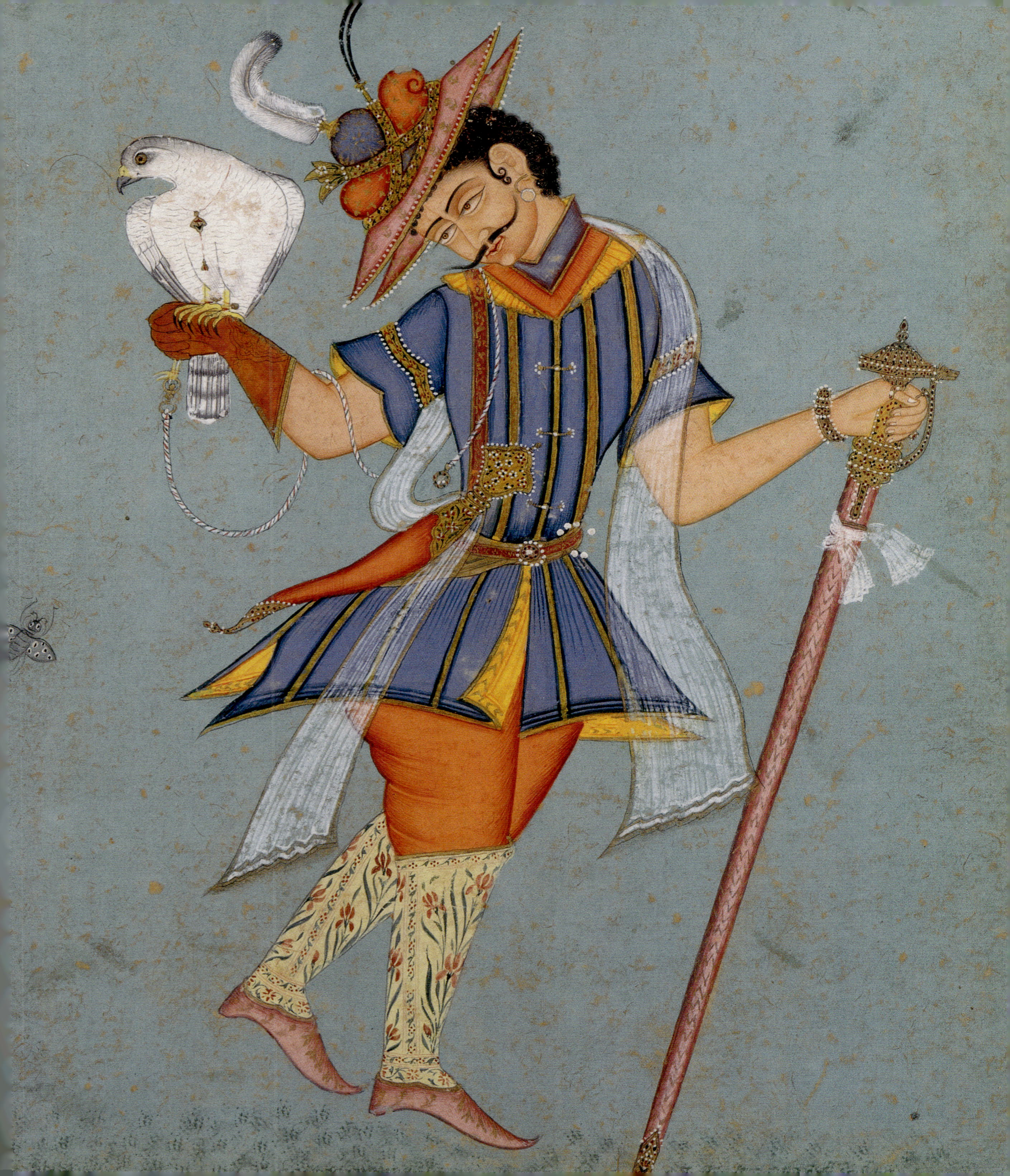

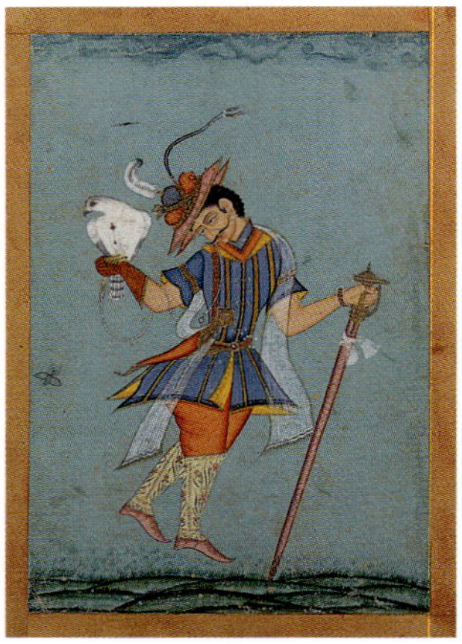

15.1 previous page and above
A European with a Falcon

Opaque watercolour on paper
India (Mewar), *c.* 1740

Private collection

15.2
A European

Opaque watercolour on paper
Mughal India, *c.* 1610–20

V&A: IM 9–1913

The Portuguese are a race of people very white in colour and of great beauty; they wear jackets and hats of iron and pace up and down without resting for a moment.[1]

The Sri Lankan chronicle *Rajavaliya* (*The Roll of Kings*) is one of the few South Asian literary sources to suggest the visual impact made by the Portuguese on the local inhabitants of the area. The curiosity aroused by the physical appearance, manners and dress of Europeans is evident in this passage describing the first contact between Sri Lankans and Portuguese in Colombo in 1506. This fascination is revealed in the works of art produced in a variety of media by South Asian artists and craftsmen from the sixteenth to the nineteenth centuries, and it is mainly through visual rather than written sources that we can assess the South Asian reaction to Europeans.

While western images of the East were almost entirely based on idealized perceptions of luxury and pleasure, depictions of Europeans by Indian artists derived far more from the observation of individuals, whether or not they were actually represented from life. The people portrayed in Indian paintings and textiles are typically envoys, traders and later religious figures and, in at least one instance, a gunner working for the Mughal army;[2] these were the first Europeans seen in Indian society (plate 15.2). Probably the earliest Indian depictions of Europeans are found in a series of watercolours in the Biblioteca Casanatense in Rome, dating to about 1540 and presumably executed for a Portuguese patron.[3] The paintings show the types of inhabitants in areas of Portuguese maritime expansion, including Arabs, Indians, Indonesians and Chinese. One section of the series, however, deals with the Portuguese themselves as they appear in India, and the curiosity which their appearance and activities arouse in the Indian artist is evident, particularly in the splendid scene of Portuguese men and women seated on folding, Portuguese-style chairs around a dining table set up in a stepped water-tank (plate 15.3). The Portuguese caption translates as 'Portuguese people from Ormuz. They are eating in the water as the land is too hot.'[4] Other illustrations from the same manuscript include a procession in which a splendidly dressed, bearded Portuguese gentleman rides a white horse accompanied by Portuguese and Indian attendants, while his wife, wearing a high-necked dress and a snood, is carried in a palanquin by Indian servants.[5] If such images are uncommon, three-dimensional depictions of Europeans from this period are even rarer; a southern Indian bronze lamp with a central figure of a Portuguese horseman is perhaps unique (plate 15.4).

Merchants seeking trading rights were the first Europeans to make contact with the Mughals: the Englishman Ralph Fitch (d. 1611) had visited Akbar's court at Fatehpur Sikri in 1585. Although neither Fitch nor any other Europeans can be convincingly identified in manuscripts or miniatures of Akbar's reign, western figures continue to turn up from time to time in illustrated manuscripts from about the 1560s onwards. European figures appear in pages from the *Tutinama* of 1560–65,[6] and in the story of Duvan Rani and Khizr Khan, completed in 1567.[7] They are also included in the border of a page of about 1605 from the so-called Jahangir Album,[8] and a figure in a flamboyant hat who could well be an Italian merchant appears in a *Tuzuk-i Jahangiri* page of about 1620.[9] These European subjects are depicted with careful attention to detail, and some would have been copied faithfully from western paintings. But when Europeans are included in court or crowd scenes, they are always portrayed among lesser-status groups than the Mughal courtiers, as is evident from their lower position in the composition of the page (see plate 6.1). Furthermore, as Ebba Koch has pointed out, Westerners are frequently depicted in the 'unprestigious' three-quarter view, as opposed to the strict profile of the higher-status Mughals.[10]

The arrival of Jesuit missions provided further subject matter for Mughal artists. The Jesuits had been in India since 1542 and were invited by Akbar (r. 1556–1605) to his court, where they arrived in 1578. Known as *Siyahposh* ('black-clad'), they made a strong impact at the Mughal court, and Jesuit priests in their sombre garb were depicted in several Akbar-period paintings, as figures in a crowd (as in the *Tuzuk-i Jahangiri* page),[11] as single subjects[12] or in the Chester Beatty Library's famous depiction of Akbar debating doctrine with a group of priests (see plate 8.6).[13] As well as portraits recording actual Jesuit individuals at court, figures in Portuguese or Jesuit dress are, not surprisingly, frequently seen in the Christian illustrated manuscripts that Akbar had translated into Persian. Perhaps the most notable of these is the *Dastan-i Masih*, which tells the life of Christ and which was translated into Persian by the Jesuit Father Jerome Xavier in 1602. Rather as in Renaissance painting, the Disciples and other attendant figures in the stories are shown as

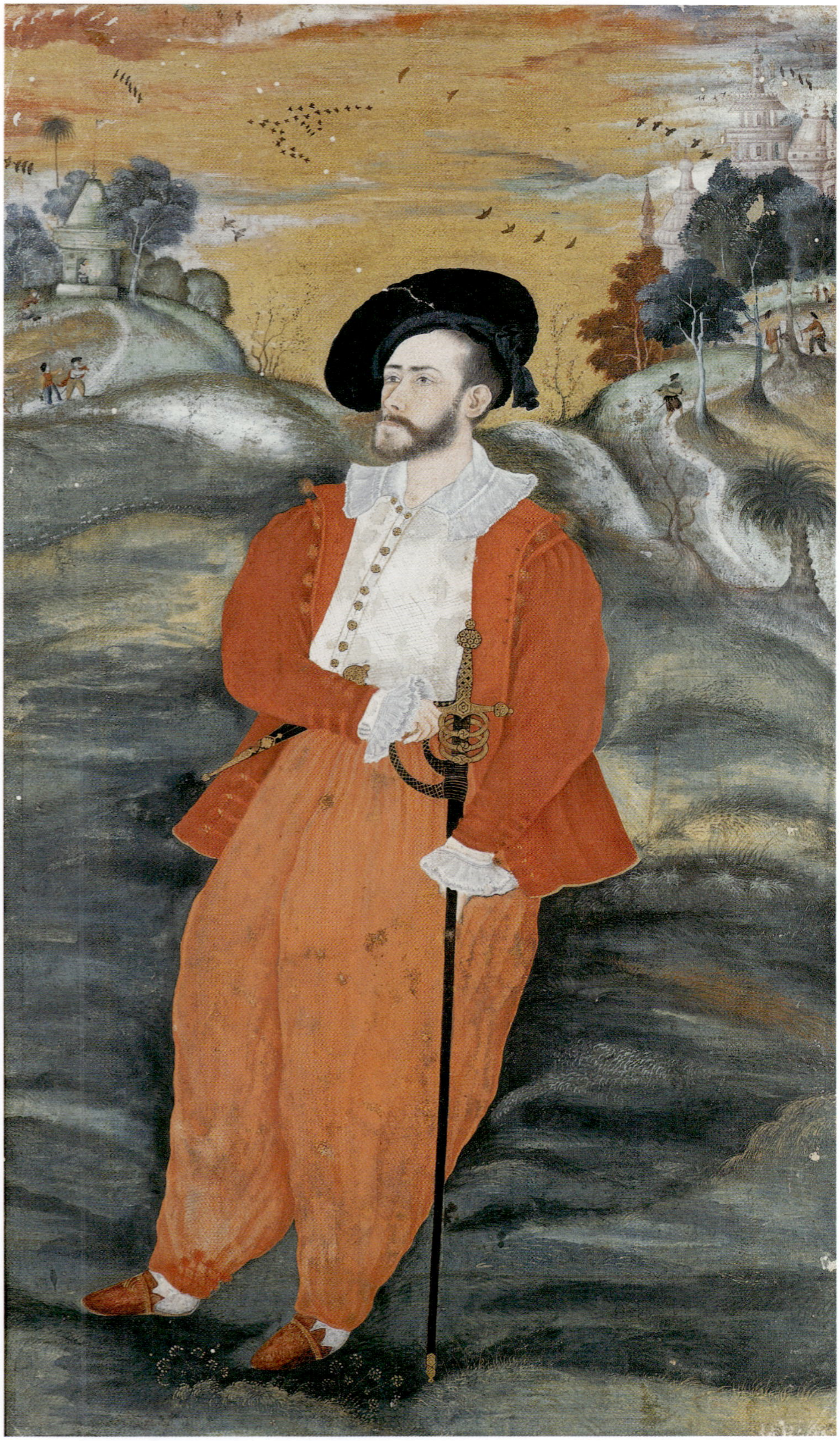

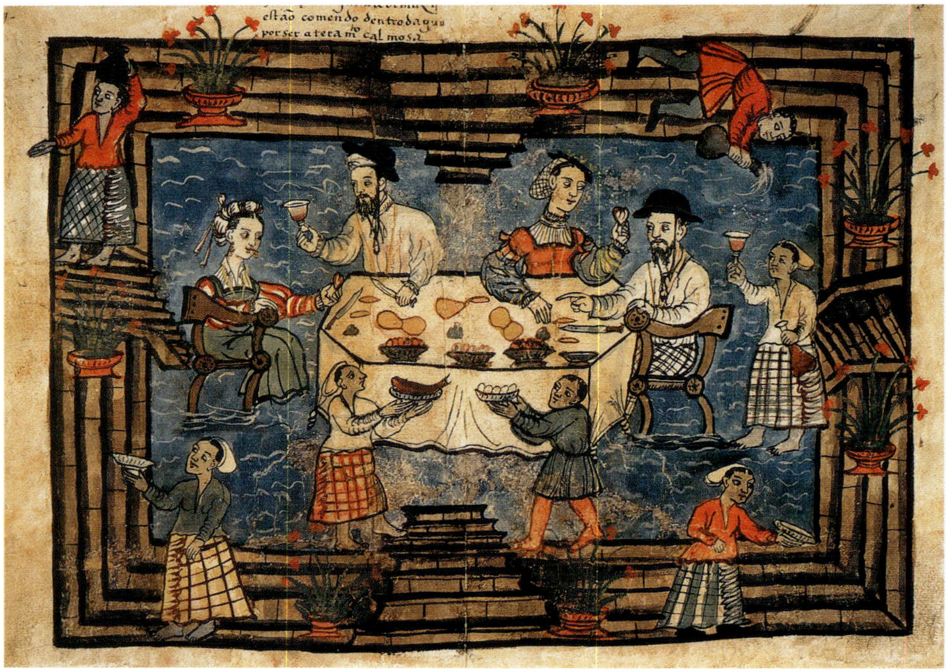

15.3
A Group of Portuguese Dining in a Water-Tank
From the *Codice Casanatense*
Watercolour on paper
India, *c.* 1540
Biblioteca Casanatense, Rome

15.4
Oil lamp in the form of a Portuguese horseman
Cast bronze
South India, possibly 16th century
British Museum, London

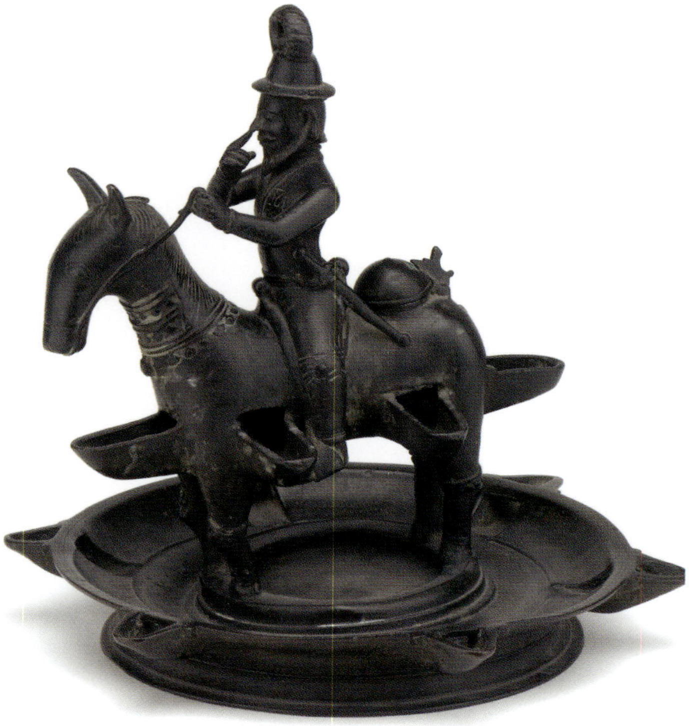

sixteenth-century Europeans,[14] probably drawn from contemporary Portuguese visitors to the court, or based on figures in imported prints. A parallel tradition developed in Bengal, where characters from biblical scenes embroidered on quilts of the late sixteenth and early seventeenth centuries are also shown in Portuguese dress.

The Europeans shown in Mughal paintings from the later sixteenth and seventeenth centuries are mostly male (although several are notably androgynous in appearance). It was not generally until the late eighteenth century that women started to accompany their menfolk to India in large numbers, although Portuguese society seems to have been exceptional in this matter. Women are clearly shown on the Portuguese side in a painting of the capture of Hooghly in 1632 in the *Padshahnama*,[15] in the painted manuscript belonging to the Biblioteca Casanatense (plate 15.3),[16] and in Jan Huyghen van Linschoten's images of 1596. Women depicted in Mughal paintings were usually drawn from European images rather than from life (plate 15.5). Representations of the Virgin and Child in particular were often used as a basis for secular as well as religious subjects, which sometimes imparted an erotic element to the scene that strikes the western viewer as incongruous.[17] Differing concepts of both male and female modesty obviously intrigued people on both sides of the encounter. Western commentators frequently remark on the 'nakedness' of the (Hindu) Indian population, 'saving only that they have a cloth bound about their middles'.[18] Indian artists, for their part, were obviously aware of the contradictory conventions of seventeenth-century western female dress, which appeared cumbersome and constrained, but also allowed for erotic possibilities such as exposure of the bosom.

European dress, and in particular hats, trousers and shoes, was fascinating to Indian observers. Hats came to be so closely associated with the *firingi* that these foreigners even became known by the term *topiwala* or 'hat-wearer',[19] and European visitors to the Mughal court can be identified in miniature paintings by their distinctive headgear. 'Frankish' hats even enjoyed a vogue amongst Mughal courtiers: a page from the *Padshahnama*, depicting a lion-hunt in 1630, shows two Mughal attendants wearing unmistakably European hats on top of their turbans.[20] Jahangir (r. 1605–27) had been so impressed with the hats brought to court by the English envoy Sir Thomas Roe (*c.* 1581–1644) that he accepted them as gifts and appropriated Roe's own hat, saying, according to Roe, 'yours I will return if you need it'.[21] The unidentified western travellers shown in late Akbari and early Jahangiri paintings are frequently dressed as if for the Elizabethan or Jacobean court, in full panoply of hat, ruff, doublet, breeches and elaborate stockings.[22] Others, perhaps Dutch or Portuguese rather than English, are shown in the wide-legged trousers gathered at the ankle which the British did not adopt (plate 15.2). Some images of Westerners are evidently the product of a certain amount of misunderstanding on the part of the Indian artist: a portrait inscribed in Persian *Padshahzade-i farang* ('European prince') appears to depict a European woman dressed as a man (plate 15.7). It is likely that, in the process of being copied from a western painting, some confusion has set in: the costume is essentially English dress of around 1630–40, but certain elements (the sleeves of the jacket, the embroidered leggings) have been misinterpreted by the artist, who has also been misled by the long, curling hair and jewelled earring to suppose that the subject is female.[23] While these portraits may be based on somewhat earlier western paintings rather than drawn from life, it is reasonable to suppose that standard western dress would have been current amongst Europeans in India. These people made few concessions in their dress to local customs or climate. This adherence to western clothes imparts to these Europeans a distinct identity as temporary visitors, unlike their compatriots of the eighteenth and early nineteenth centuries, who frequently became absorbed into Indian society to the extent that they adopted elements of its dress and culture (see plate 12.3).

Elaborate male dress and hairstyles are characteristic of several seventeenth-century depictions of Europeans in painting and textiles. A painted casket from Golconda decorated by Rahim Deccani[24] and a page by the same artist dating from about 1660[25] both include foppish and elegant western gentlemen as part of their decoration, beautifully rendered in exquisite detail with hats, trousers and shoes of the period (plate 15.6). Their attitudes, one seated on a rock playing the flute and another standing holding a wine-flask, are reminiscent of the equally effeminate youths of seventeenth-century Persian painting by artists such as Riza 'Abbasi, who were also incorporating western elements into their work, with which Rahim Deccani would no doubt have been familiar.[26]

Less romantic but equally elegantly dressed Europeans appear in the finely detailed painted cotton hangings (called *kalamkari* or 'pen-work') produced in south-eastern India in the mid-seventeenth century. A superb example in the Musée des Arts Décoratifs, Paris, appears to relate to a diplomatic or commercial encounter involving representatives of the Dutch and Danish East India Companies, accompanied by Indian merchants and musicians (plate 15.8).[27] In this textile, western dress and furniture are treated with elaborate precision, in keeping with the mass of decorative detail on the Indian floral fabrics and of the ground patterns. Many other *kalamkari* textiles from seventeenth-century south-eastern India illustrate courtly activities, usually in Mughal, Deccani, Persian or southern Indian styles and with human participants appropriately dressed for these contexts.[28] In a few cases, however, European rather than Indian figures are central to the designs. In one of the most intriguing of these pieces, one of a set of seven

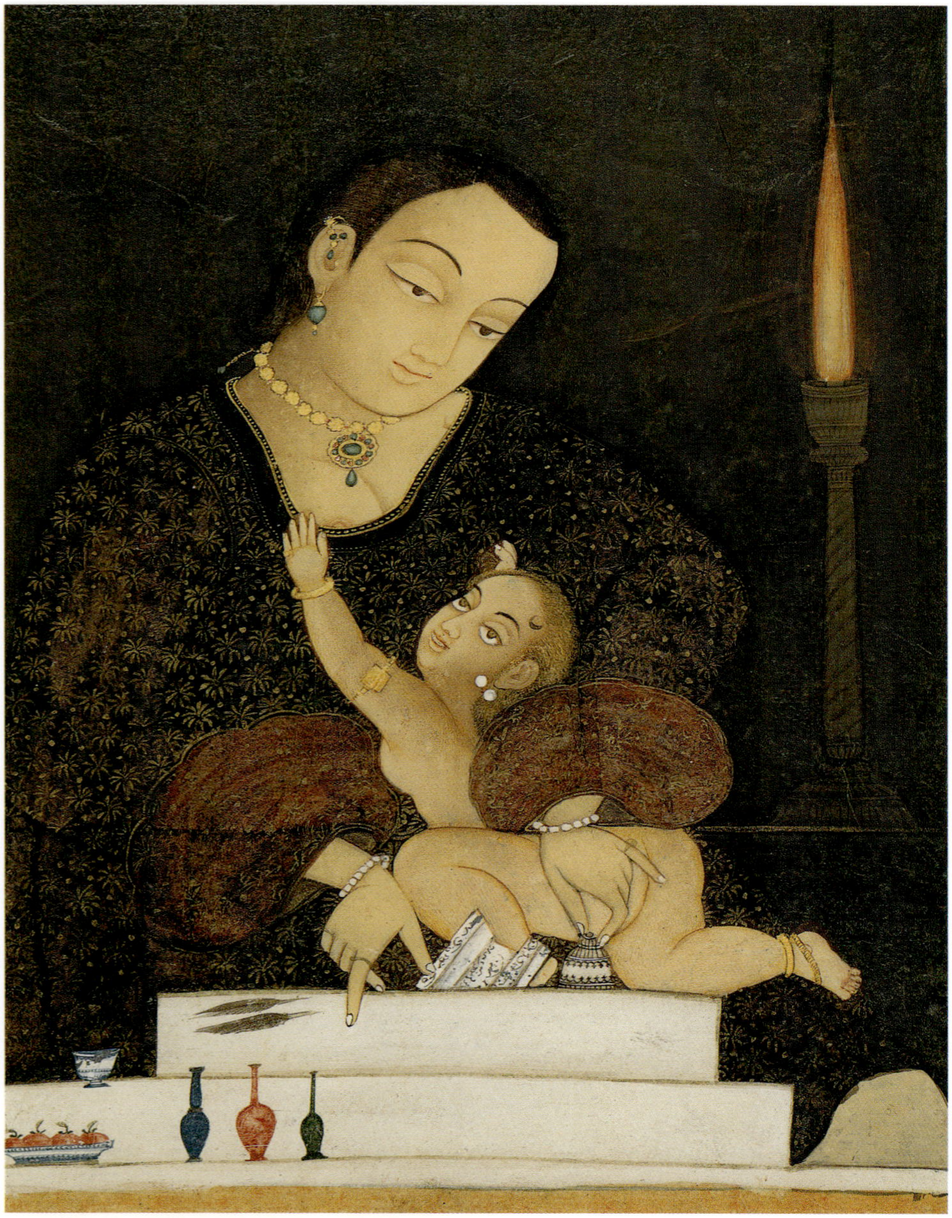

15.5
Mother and Child
Attributed to Chokha

Opaque watercolour on paper
India (Mewar or Deogarh), c.1810

Philadelphia Museum of Art, Philadelphia, Collection of Dr. Alvin O. Bellak

15.6
A European Youth Playing a Flute
Panel from a painted box; painting attributed to Rahim Deccani

Papier mâché, painted and varnished, with pierced ivory base moulding
India (Golconda), late 17th century

V&A: 851–1889

15.7
Padshahzade-i farang (European Prince)

Opaque watercolour on paper
Mughal India, early 17th century

Private collection, Porto

arched panels dating from the early seventeenth century, Europeans (probably Portuguese) are the main subjects of the scenes (plate 15.9). Some are seated, cross-legged or with one leg dangling in Indian style, on raised seats conversing with standing compatriots. Women are also included, but whether they are European or – perhaps more likely – Indian is unclear. The *kalamkari* artist's attention to detail, especially when depicting Westerners' dress, is striking: hats, trousers and doublets are sufficiently clearly rendered to identify them with styles popular in Europe between about 1590 and 1620,[29] although the patterns on the fabrics of their dress seem to be purely fanciful. A pair of seventeenth-century *kalamkari* hangings also made in south-eastern India (now divided between the V&A and Metropolitan Museum, New York), depicting Westerners as well as Indians, can be dated to a few decades later. The faithful rendition of the European hairstyles and costumes (if not the designs on them) is equally marked, as is the attention to detail seen in the depiction of Venetian glass and other tableware.[30]

The fascination with certain elements of dress is evident even in the overtly erotic paintings of Europeans that enjoyed a vogue in the eighteenth century: even in his most intimate moments, the Westerner can be sure to keep his hat firmly on his head, at least in the artist's imagination (plates 15.11).[31] A rare example of a late seventeenth-century erotic painting, probably done in Bikaner in Rajasthan, shows a European (probably Portuguese) man, naked but for strings of pearls and a tall-crowned European hat, in an embrace with a companion of indeterminate race and gender. The painting bears a Persian inscription that translates as 'The private pleasure of the Portuguese commander-in-chief' (plate 15.12).[32] The conventions for depicting eighteenth-century Westerners, especially Dutchmen, were quite rigidly observed. As Andrew Topsfield has pointed out, the manner of depicting the Dutchman and his dress, especially the wide-brimmed hat and full-bottomed wig, is derived from images of the Dutch emissary Johan Josua Ketelaar, made during his visit to Mewar in 1711–13.[33] In an eighteenth-century Mewar painting, the western male is naked but for his hat and some items of Indian-style jewellery, including a jewelled armlet (*bazuband*). He is entwined with an Indian woman who is wearing only a profusion of jewellery, and they stand pointing at the gathering monsoon clouds, a classical symbol of romance in Indian love scenes (plate 15.11)[34]. The lovers are treated in a manner that completely conforms to the conventions of illustrations of love poetry in India at the time, which apply equally to

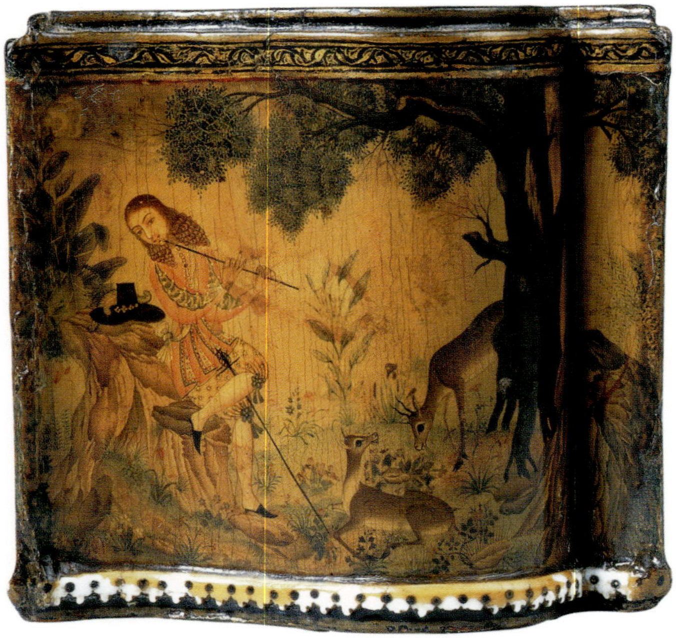

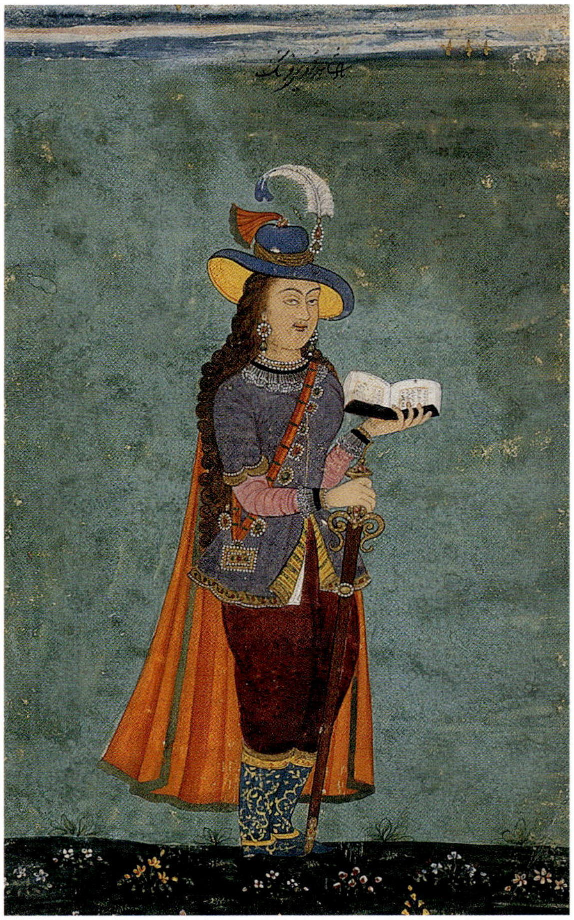

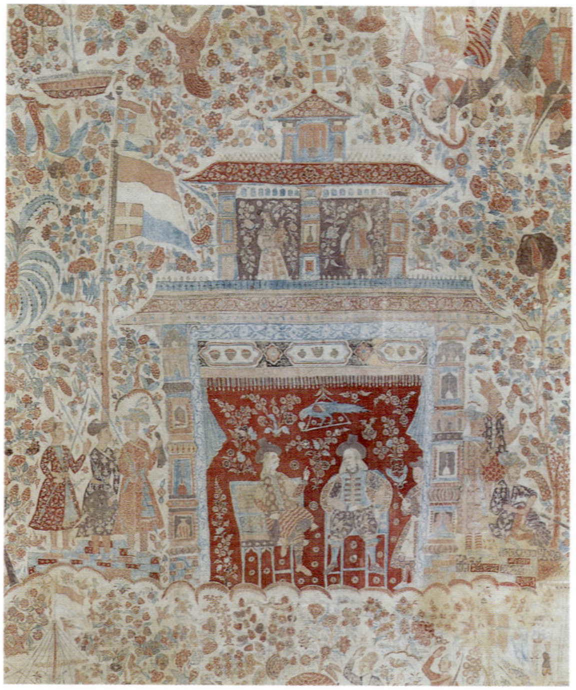

15.8
Detail of a hanging
Cotton, painted and dyed
India (Golconda), *c.*1654
Musée de la Mode et du Textile, Paris

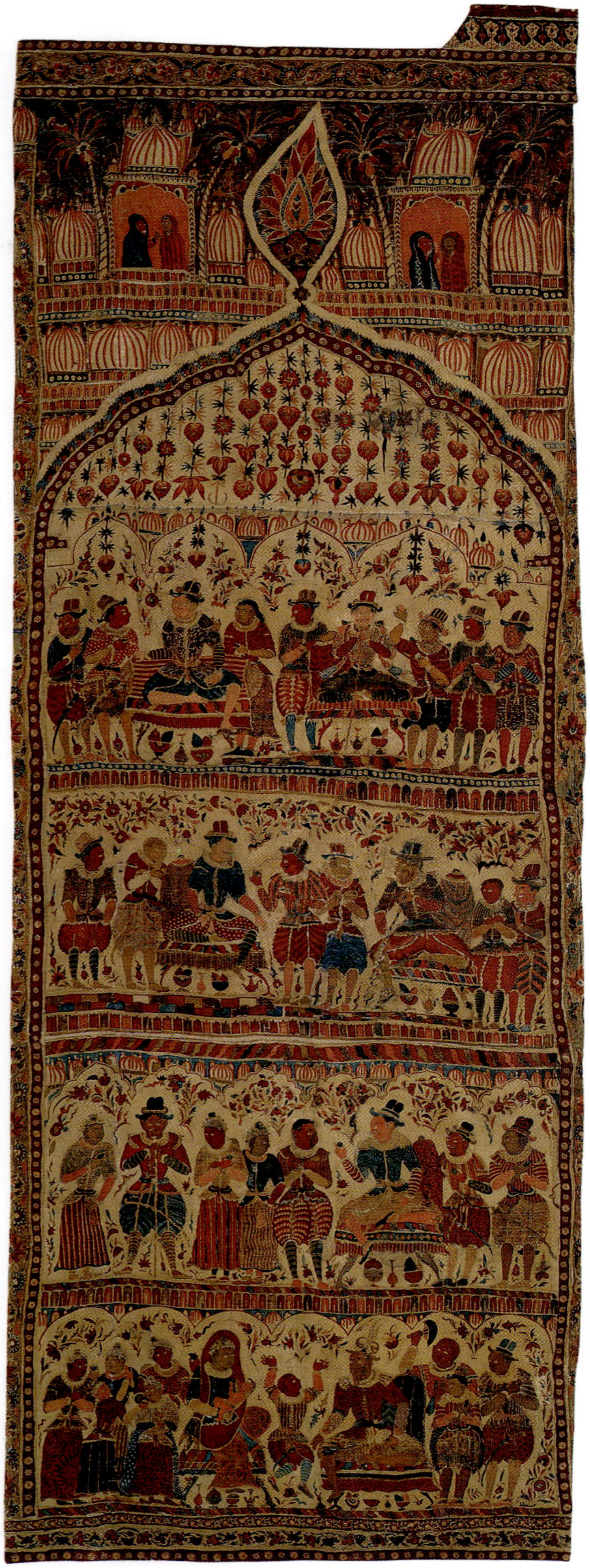

15.9
Detail of a panel from a set of hangings
Cotton, painted and dyed
India (Coromandel coast), *c.*1620
Brooklyn Museum of Art, Brooklyn

religious contexts (in particular Radha and Krishna) and secular ones, in which the ruler or other patron often appears as the main protagonist. In this case, the western lover would not have been the commissioner of the painting, but he and his companion would have been used as a variant on the theme of the archetypal lovers (*nayaka nayika*), even though they fall outside the highly systematized categorization of types of lover found in Indian literature.

These curious portrayals of the exotic incomer as a sexual being are only a short step away from a more overtly humorous or satirical genre of Rajasthani painting that includes Westerners as one of several categories of people who were evidently considered fair game for jokes: old women, the obese (especially Brahmins), the skinny, opium addicts and Africans ('Habshis') were all equally open to ridicule. One striking example is a painting in Philadelphia Museum of Art in which three grotesquely caricatured Westerners (all apparently male) are arranged in a rather sinister scene that must originally have been taken from two or more western sources (plate 15.10).[35] Subtexts of bizarre sexual encounters with possibly frightening outcomes are typical of a particular taste in some schools of Rajasthani painting in the late eighteenth century. Other humorous or satirical images of Westerners are much kinder, and

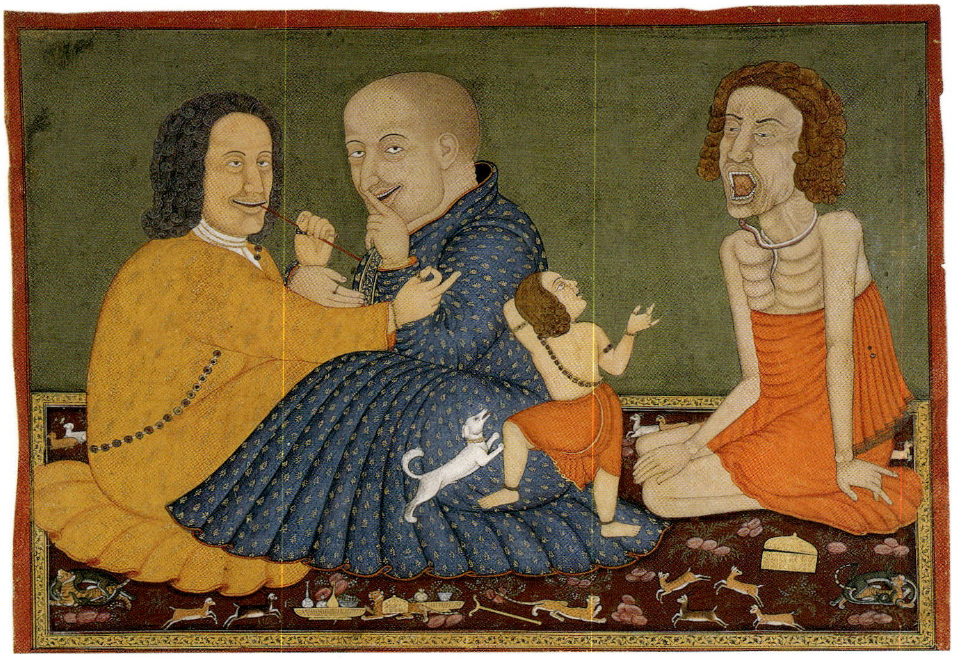

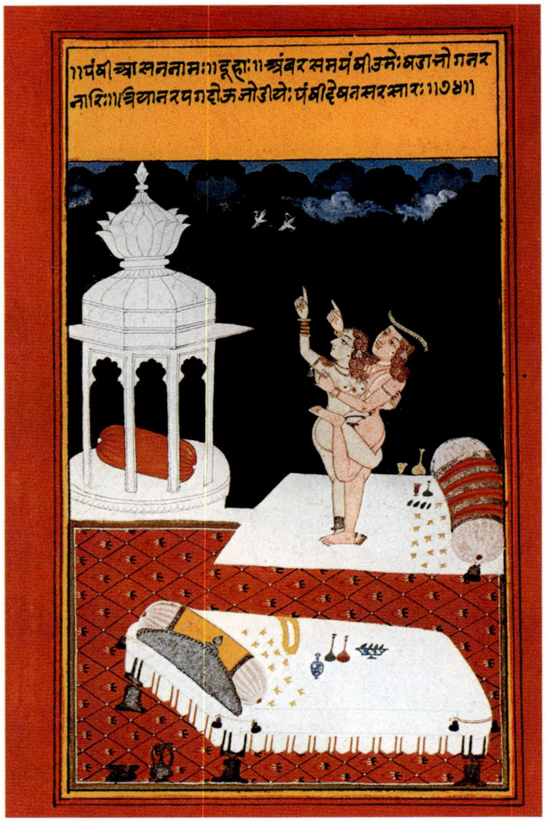

15.10
Three Grotesque Europeans and a Child

Opaque watercolour on paper
India (Mewar), *c.*1760

Philadelphia Museum of Art, Philadelphia, Collection of Dr. Alvin O. Bellak

15.11
Dutchman and an Indian Woman Embracing

Opaque watercolour on paper
India (Mewar), *c.*1720–30

Private collection

some enter the realms of myth: one even depicts a Dutchman as an equivalent to a *peri,* or angel complete with wings (plate 15.13).[36] A South-East Asian (probably Thai) ivory carving of two seated Dutchmen, complete with clogs, is also in this vein of mild humour (plate 15.14). The object itself, a sort of elaborate spirit-level with a finely balanced pointer, reflects an element of whimsy that suits the depiction of Europeans, but also relates to the Asian image of Europeans at the time as bringers of technology and precision instruments.

The line between observation of Europeans and satirical comment on their habits is sometimes an indistinct one. A group of three eighteenth-century Rajasthani paintings, each of a European with a hunting falcon, fall into this quasi-humorous category (plate 15.1).[37] The main figure seems to be based on earlier depictions of Portuguese subjects. Although it has been suggested that the exaggerated pose of the man in two of the pictures (one is a later version of the other) is the result of drunkenness, it is more likely that his posture merely reflects the Indian perception of western behaviour as bizarre and outrageously foppish. It is also possible that the images were inspired by stylized figures in French fashion plates. The man in the earlier version is, curiously, shown wearing a transparent muslin *jama* (robe) and scarf as well as his complete western attire, while the later version has dispensed with this cross-cultural complication.

As the European presence in India grew and diversified, soldiers and administrators took over from traders, priests and diplomats as the prime subjects of paintings. The development of the 'Company' style allowed for their incorporation into depictions of work and life in the subcontinent that had not previously been possible (see pp. 282–3). The southern Indian artist of the Boileau Album of *c.*1785, for example, includes a very elegantly turned-out French officer being handed his large black hat by his *dubash*, or translator (plate 15.15).[38] Other French and British administrators and military men of the eighteenth and early nineteenth centuries, such as William Fullerton (d. 1805), are depicted in a more naturalistic manner, drawing heavily on the European traditions of portraiture that were becoming more and more familiar to Indian artists through the work of western artists working in India (see plate 12.6). With the influx of British women into India in the late eighteenth and early nineteenth centuries, they also become included in Company paintings and in other

15.12
The Private Pleasure of the Portuguese Commander-in-Chief

Opaque watercolour on paper
India (Bikaner), *c.*1660

Fitzwilliam Museum, Cambridge

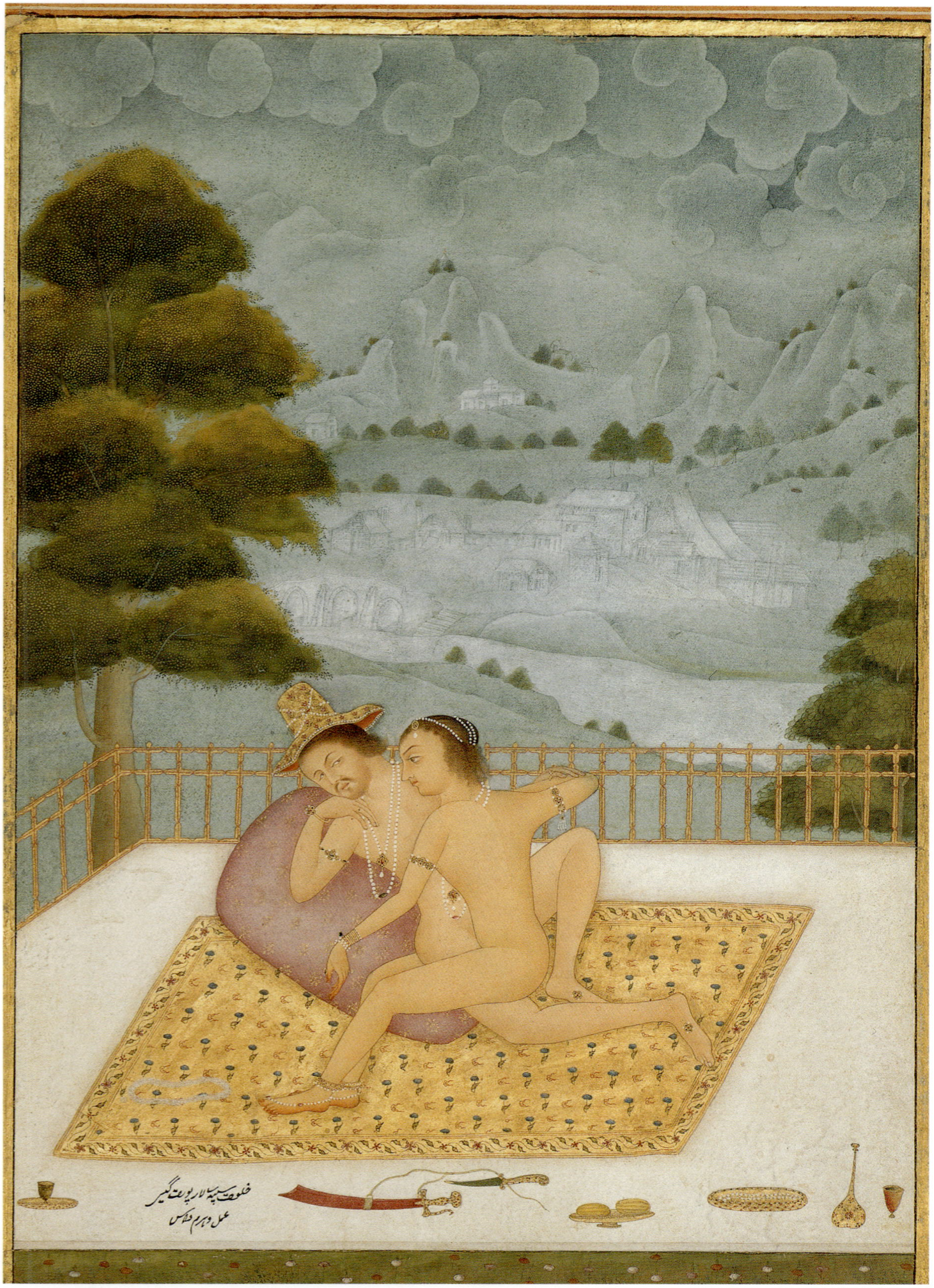

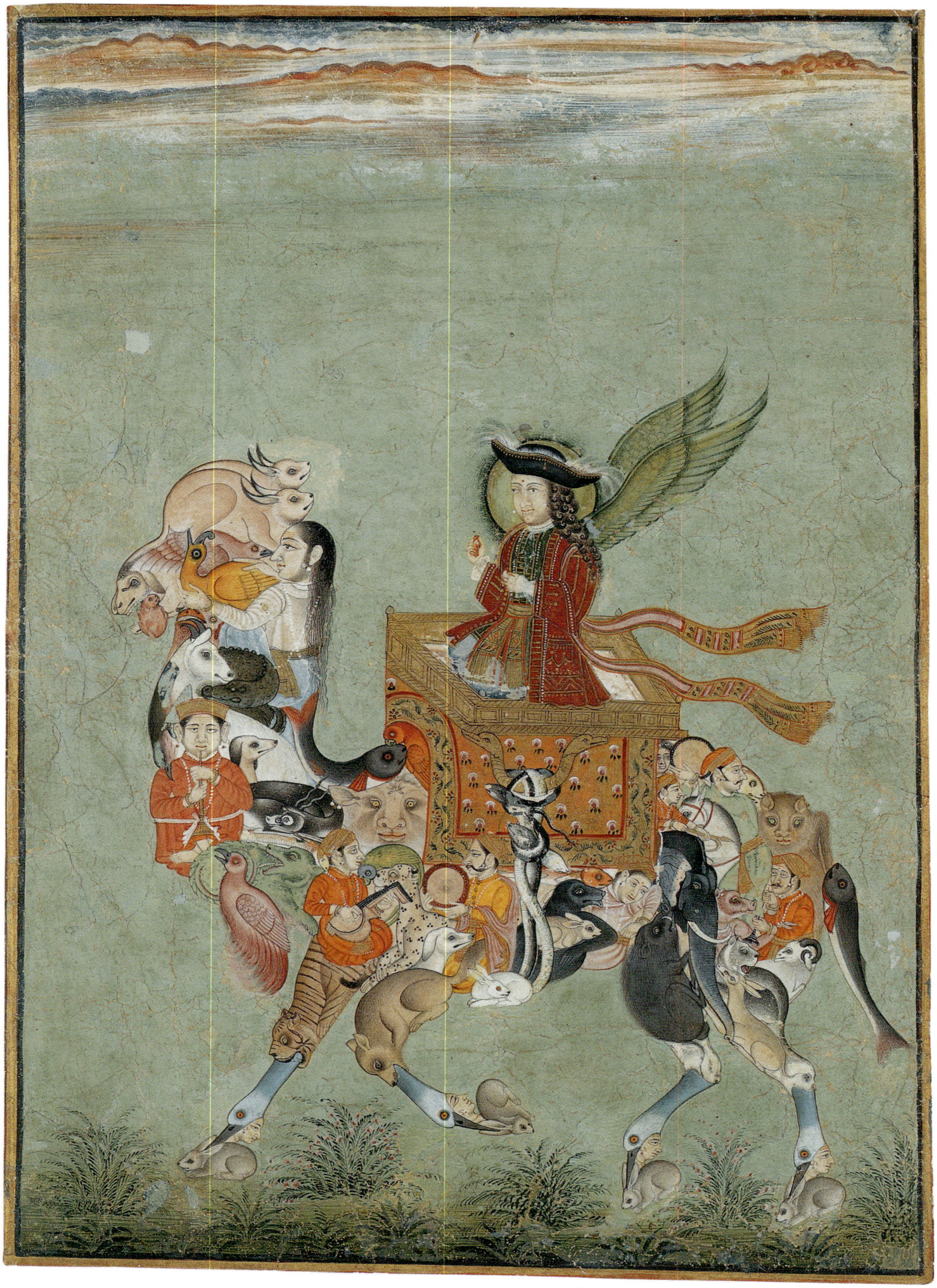

15.13
A Winged Dutchman Riding a Composite Camel

Opaque watercolour on paper
India (Mewar), *c.*1710–25

V&A: IS.10–1947

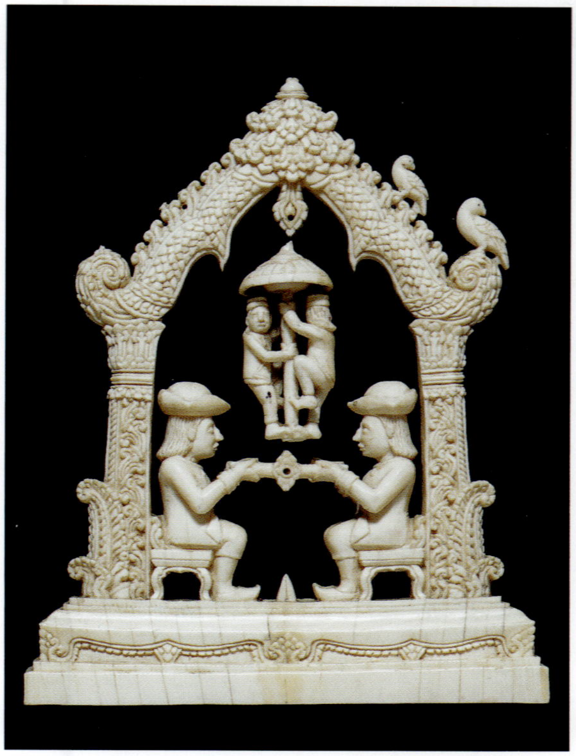

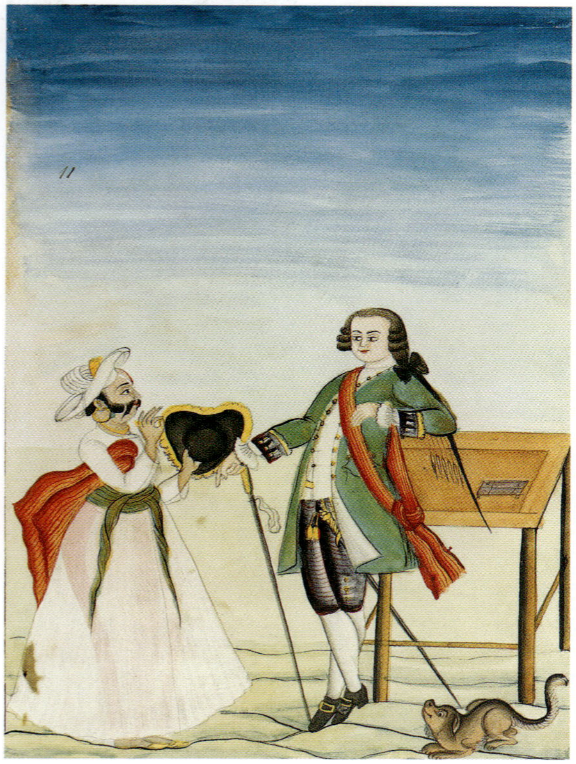

15.14
Spirit level depicting two Dutchmen

Ivory, carved
Thailand, early 19th century

V&A: 432–1894

15.15
A French Officer with His Servant

Page from the *Boileau Album*
Opaque watercolour on paper
India (Madras), 1785

V&A: IS.75:11–1954

15.16
Border of a petticoat (detail)

Cotton, painted and dyed
India (Coromandel coast), 1750–75

V&A: IS.42–1950; gift of G. P. Baker

media, such as chintz (plate 15.16). These two areas of export art were now the main ones to incorporate the Westerner as a pictorial element, although Europeans, elaborately dressed as usual, were also popular as design elements on certain items for local use. Notable among these are the Baluchar saris of Bengal,[39] a region that had also drawn on western figures for designs on earlier embroidered quilts (see plate 20.6) and terracotta bricks for its seventeenth- and eighteenth-century temples.[40]

The treatment of Europeans in Indian art may be said to have progressed through several phases since the Portuguese first entered the visual repertoire in the sixteenth century. Curiosity and even admiration in the sixteenth and seventeenth centuries – when Westerners are recorded in documentary fashion, or with emphasis on their elaborate dress, coiffure and furnishings – gave way to caricature in the eighteenth and nineteenth centuries, when the peculiarities of western life were exaggerated and ridiculed. The final phase was one of acceptance, when Europeans had become so deeply entrenched in Indian society that they could be portrayed realistically, or even incorporated as a stereotype into the decorative arts repertoire.

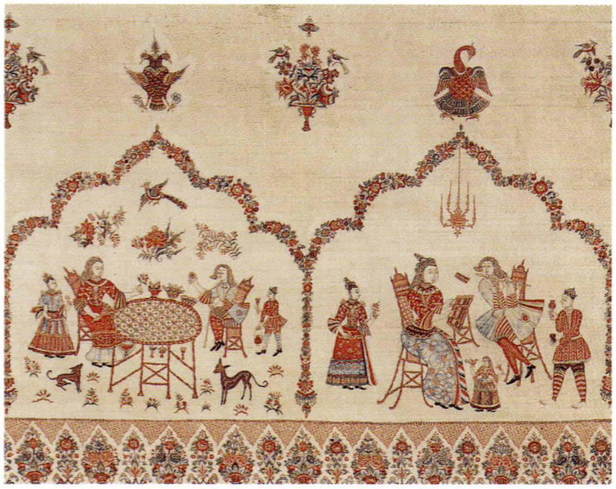

16

VISUAL RESPONSES: DEPICTING EUROPEANS IN EAST ASIA

Anna Jackson

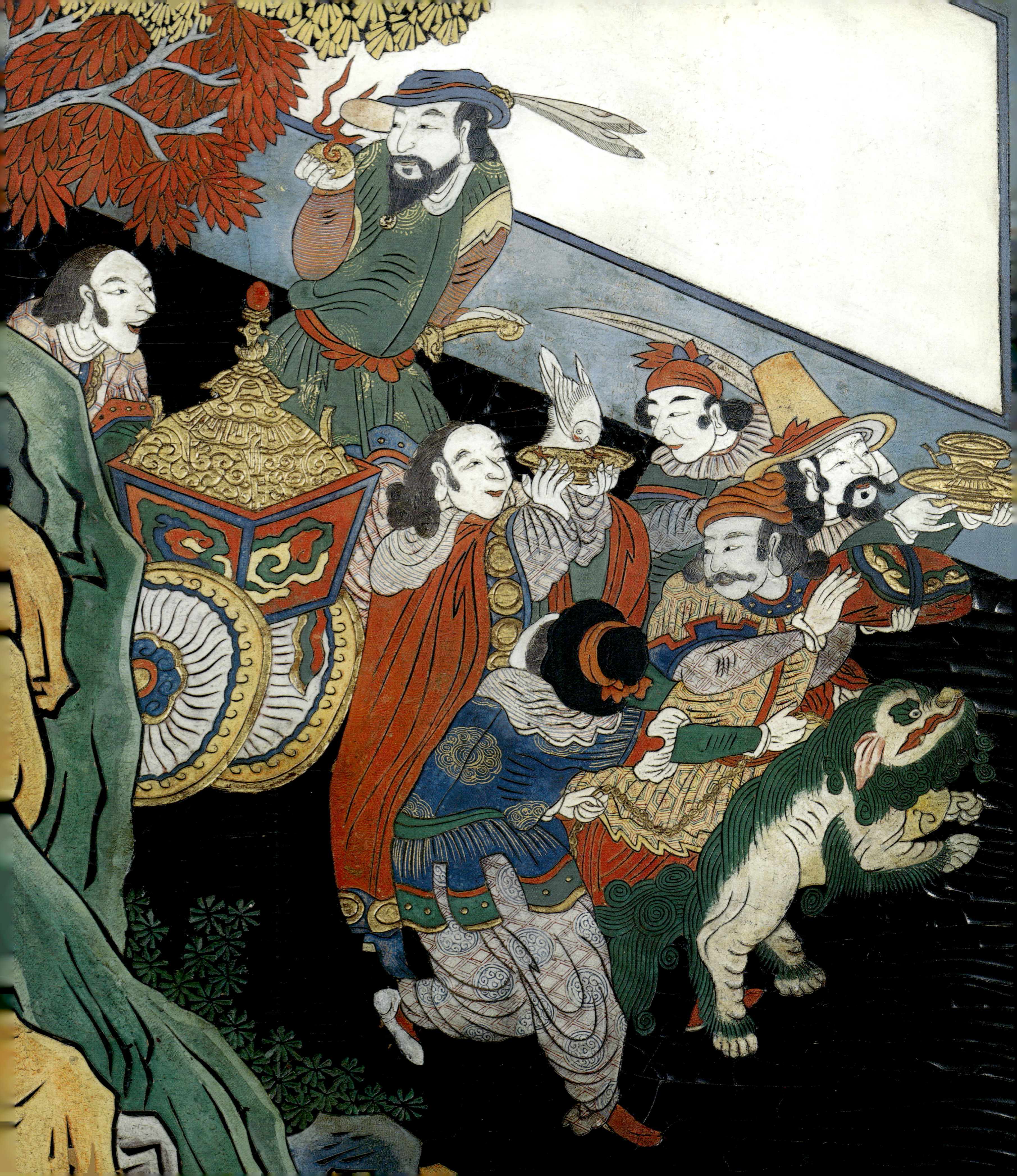

Detail of 16.6 previous page

In the reign of Mikado Go-Nara no In ... A Southern Barbarian trading vessel came to our shores. From this ship for the first time emerged an unnameable creature, somewhat similar in shape to a human being, but looking rather more like a long-nosed goblin or the giant demon Mikoshi Nyūdō. Upon closer inspection it was discovered that this being was called a Bateren. The length of his nose was the first thing that attracted attention: it was like a conch shell. His eyes were as large as spectacles and their insides were yellow. His head was small. On his hands and feet he had long claws. His height exceeded seven feet, and he was black all over ... What he said could not be understood at all: his voice was like the screech of an owl. One and all rushed to see him, crowding all the roads in a total lack of restraint.[1]

THIS ANONYMOUS JAPANESE text, written in 1639, records the mixture of fear and fascination that had greeted the arrival of the first Jesuit *bateren*, or 'padre', some 90 years earlier. Although the religion that the Portuguese brought to Japan was to prove too much of a threat to the authority of the country's military rulers, any initial feelings of alarm caused by the actual appearance of these *nanbanjin*, or 'southern barbarians', were soon overshadowed by their exotic appeal.[2] The curiosity aroused by the strange physical features and outlandish costumes of the Portuguese is evident in Japanese visual arts of the late sixteenth and early seventeenth centuries. A six-fold screen depicts in wonderful detail the arrival of a Portuguese ship in a Japanese port (plate 16.1). Scenes portrayed on Japanese screens are usually read from right to left, but in keeping with its 'exotic' subject, the scene on this screen moves from left to right.[3] On the left a three-masted ship is anchored, its dark form silhouetted against a large expanse of gold. On board are the captain-major, seated on a throne-like chair beneath a canopy, richly dressed merchants, a group of Jesuit missionaries, whose Christian emblems flutter in the breeze, and, in the poop deck, crew members playing backgammon. Overhead small figures dismantle the rigging with acrobatic flair, while boats ferry passengers and their cargoes to shore. Moving along the screen to the right, the captain-major, walking beneath a parasol that signifies his status, is welcomed by Jesuit missionaries, two Spanish priests (a Franciscan and a Dominican), and some Portuguese officials. Below them, groups of Japanese eagerly examine items that the foreigners have brought with them: Chinese

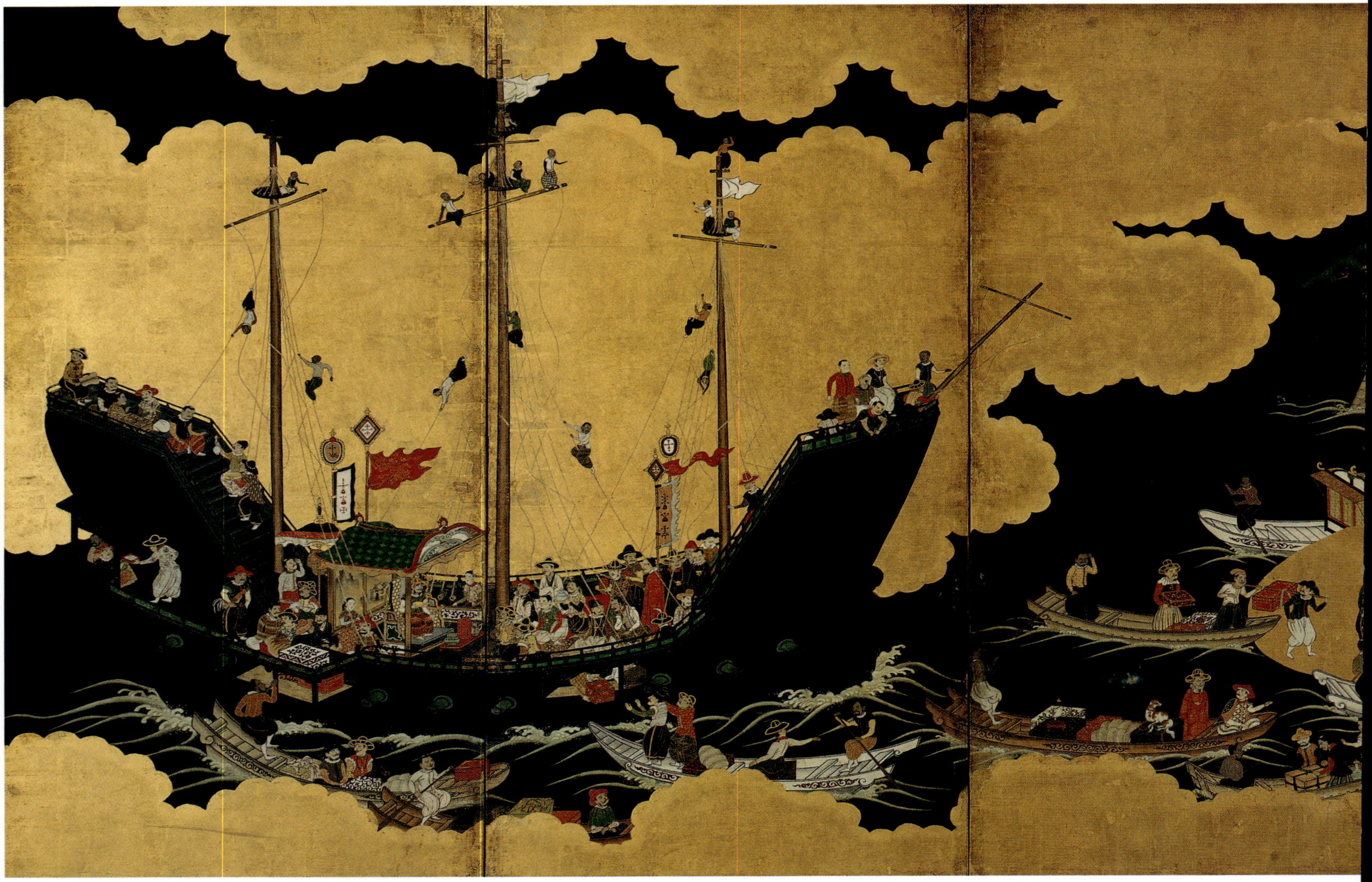

16.1
Six-panel screen depicting the arrival of a Portuguese ship

Ink, colours and gold-leaf on paper
Japan, *c.*1630s

Private collection, New York

ceramics, bolts of cloth, books and, at the far right, a tiger skin. Two Portuguese carry a pair of peacocks in a cage, while others lead a horse laden with more goods. At the back of the street is a group of shops, one offering turtle shells, rhinoceros horn, coral and goldfish. Next door, a Portuguese sits on a Chinese carpet negotiating the exchange of gold, visible in his money bag beside him, for taels of silver, while further along are two establishments selling cloth, ceramics and bronze vessels. Other figures animate the scene: a Portuguese merchant buys rice balls from a stall, a barber shaves the tonsure of a priest, an old woman hobbles past a woman suckling her child, and a Japanese merchant peers out from his doorway curtain to watch a group of *samurai* greet a traveller on horseback. Above the lively street a more serious scene takes place, as a group of Portuguese pay court to the local feudal lord (*daimyō*).[4]

This is one of nearly 70 surviving examples of single or paired screens that depict the arrival of the Portuguese in Japan.[5] With the exception of those depicting scenes in and around Kyoto (a genre known as '*rakuchū rakugai*'), this is the largest group of Japanese screens on one subject, an indication of the enormous popularity of the theme. The screens can be categorized into three main types. The most numerous are those in which the left-hand screen shows the arrival of the ship, and the right-hand screen the procession of a captain-major on shore. In the second group these two scenes are compressed in the right-hand screen, and on the left screen the ship's departure from an imagined foreign port, probably meant to represent Goa or Macao, is depicted. In the third group the left-hand screen shows horse racing, or other activities, in another foreign country, possibly China.[6] The screen illustrated here is likely to be the right screen of a pair of one of the latter two groups. What is unusual in this example is the scene of the Portuguese with the *daimyō*, which replaces the more commonly depicted Jesuit seminary. This suggests that the screen dates from after the 1614 ban on foreign proselytization and before the final persecution of Christianity and the expulsion of the Portuguese in the late 1630s, after which screens such as this were no longer painted. The central theme of this screen is certainly

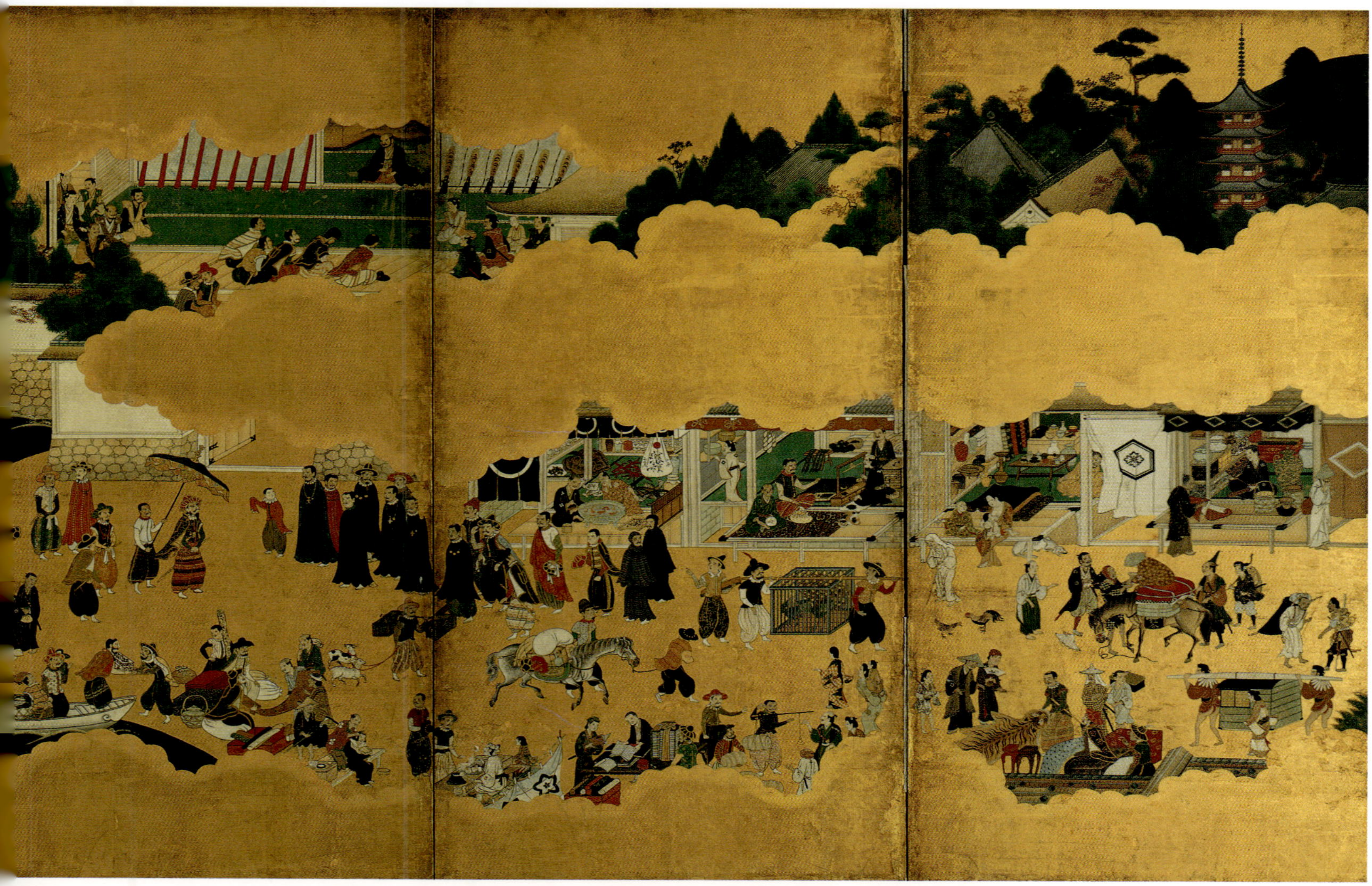

16.2
Votive plaque *(ema)* of a Sueyoshi ship
Painted wood
Japan, 1633
Kiyomizu Temple, Kyoto; designated as Important Cultural Property

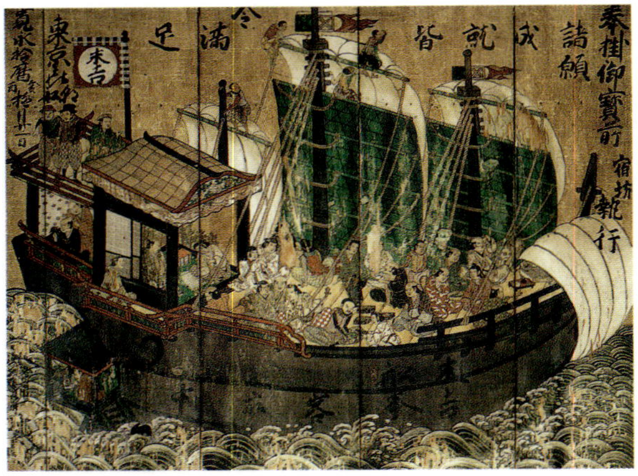

not religion, but trade and the harmonious interaction of Japanese and Europeans.

The production of such screens was part of the fashion for *nanban*, or 'southern barbarian', culture that was inspired, at least in part, by the return of Alessandro Valignano (1539–1606) and four young Japanese who had travelled to Europe (see p. 101). In March 1591 Valignano led the envoys, accompanied by sumptuously dressed Portuguese officials, in a lavish procession through the streets of Kyoto (known at the time as Miyako) to the court of Toyotomi Hideyoshi (r. 1583–98). Another important event in the development of the *nanban* craze was the gathering of more than 30 *daimyō* and more than 100,000 soldiers at the newly built Nagoya Castle in Hizen, Hideyoshi's headquarters for the Korean campaign of 1592–93. The castle's proximity to Nagasaki meant that many *samurai* were able to experience the 'southern barbarians' at first hand. The artist Kanō Mitsunobu (1561/5–1608) was employed in producing *fusuma* (painted doors) for the castle and, as one of the earliest *nanban* screens is attributed to him, it is possible that he also took the opportunity to travel to Nagasaki and make sketches on which his screen was based.[7] Some scholars have cast doubt on this theory, however, for there is no evidence that he, or any other Kanō-school artist, ever visited Nagasaki, nor is there anything in the screens to suggest that the port depicted is actually Nagasaki.[8]

The images on these screens are not rooted in any specific reality, but are a reflection of the tastes and interests of those for whom they were painted. The emphasis is on the exotic appearance of the foreigners and the exciting goods they bring on their ships.[9] Like the map screens produced in the same period, the arrival screens signal a new Japanese view of the world and an interest in what it has to offer (see plate 24.23). However, the map screens are western-style works produced in Jesuit workshops for Christian *daimyō* patrons. The arrival screens are painted in a Japanese style, the majority by lesser artists of the Kanō school working in Kyoto.[10] Research by Takamizawa Tadao into the provenance of the screens has revealed that most of them were commissioned by wealthy merchants and shipping agents in port towns on the Japan and Inland Sea coasts.[11]

While taking Europe and Europeans as their ostensible theme, the subjects depicted on the screens relate to traditional Japanese iconography. The *nanban* ship represents a treasure ship (*takara-bune*) bringing wealth and happiness from over the seas, an auspicious motif that would have been particularly treasured by a merchant engaged in maritime transportation. Elements of the ship in the screen illustrated here, such as the Chinese-style canopy on deck, are very similar to those of a vessel, carrying both Japanese and Europeans, depicted on a votive plaque (*ema*) in the Kiyomizu-dera, one of Kyoto's most important temples (plate 16.2). This *ema* is one of four such ship paintings donated to the temple between 1621 and 1634 by two families engaged in the very profitable 'vermillion seal trade' (*shuinsen bōeki*), the officially licensed Japanese trade with south China and South-East Asia that took place in the period 1590–1630. By donating such images to the temple, the Suminokura family of Kyoto and the Sueyoshi family of Osaka hoped to invoke divine protection and encouragement of their business interests.[12]

Portuguese ships were painted with tar and in *nanban* arrival screens are always depicted as black in colour. As Kuroda Hideo has pointed out, however, black had a symbolic resonance in Japan. The colour represented impurity and signified the outer border of the known or knowable world, while white represented centrality and purity. Chinese ships were called 'white ships' (*shirofune*), while Portuguese vessels were always known as 'black ships' (*kurofune*).[13] Black carried the negative connotations of a frightening world inhabited perhaps by the 'long-nosed goblins' of the opening quotation.[14] Yet in this world's very mysteriousness also lay its appeal, as it was from here that exotic treasures came. Japanese popular belief held that anything washed ashore was a treasured gift from another world: if it was a corpse of someone unknown it was honoured as a deity.

Such beliefs were personified in Ebisu, one of the seven gods of good fortune (*shichifukujin*), and the god of merchants. His name literally means 'barbarian' or 'foreigner'. Such notions of otherworldliness inform representations of *nanbanjin* as alien-looking creatures possessing superhuman powers. The striking figures that decorate this lacquer food box carry wishes for good fortune and suggest that unusual, possibly foreign, delicacies are contained within (plate 16.3), while the *samurai* who commissioned these stirrups would have hoped that the inlaid silver figures would imbue him with divine strength (plate 16.4). Such beliefs explain why, even after the ban on Christianity, key elements of *nanban* iconography survived as symbols of protection and prosperity (plate 16.5).

The symbolic link between Portuguese figures and the gods of good fortune can be seen on a pair of screens in the Kobe City Museum, which have cherry-blossom festivities as their theme. *Nanbanjin* are depicted on the right and a masquerade of two of the gods, Daikoku and Ebisu, are shown on the left. Figures in European dress can be found on quite a number of seventeenth-century screens painted with genre subjects, including those depicting scenes in and around the capital (*rakuchū rakugai*). There is some debate as to whether such figures are actually supposed to be Portuguese or whether they represent Japanese indulging in the *nanban* vogue for dressing up. Such questions are interesting but in many ways irrelevant, for what such scenes ultimately reveal is the way in which the 'exotic other' has been absorbed into the Japanese 'self'. Anything foreign became '*nanban*', with the connotations that this carried. This is seen in later arrival screens, where Chinese figures and elements mingle with those of Europe.[15] After the expulsion of the Portuguese, their distinguishing features – beards, hats, frilled collars, ballooning trousers – were used to characterize depictions of Japan's more familiar 'others', the Chinese, Koreans and Ryūkyūans. As Ronald Toby has pointed out, in art produced prior to the encounter with the Portuguese, foreigners were always depicted in an alien land. After the arrival of Europeans, the 'other' was no longer 'out there', but a pervasive presence on the Japanese visual landscape.[16]

Japan had first felt the impact of the foreign in the sixth century when the language, religion and culture of continental China reached its shores.[17] The coming of the Portuguese in the sixteenth century offered the Japanese an alternative 'other' by which to measure themselves, although Chinese culture remained the dominant influence. Japan's long history of interaction with, and absorption of, foreign elements helps explain why the country was fairly receptive to the European encounter. The Portuguese had also arrived in Japan at a time of civil war when *daimyō* vying for power were happy to use anything the Europeans had to offer that might give them an advantage over their rival, whether it was God, trade goods or, most especially, guns (see pp. 324–5) After Japan was unified under the control of the Tokugawa family in the seventeenth century, China provided the model for the way in which the *bakufu* (*shōgunal* government) organized its official relations with foreign countries (see pp. 98–9). However, the *daimyō* still enjoyed considerable autonomy and were able to pursue their own interests, as long as these were not Christian.

When Portuguese ships first entered East Asian waters, China, in contrast to Japan, had a highly centralized bureaucracy and an established set of

16.3
Tiered food box
Wood covered in black lacquer with gold *takamakie* lacquer and gold and silver foil
Japan, 1600–25
Museu Nacional de Arte Antiga, Lisbon

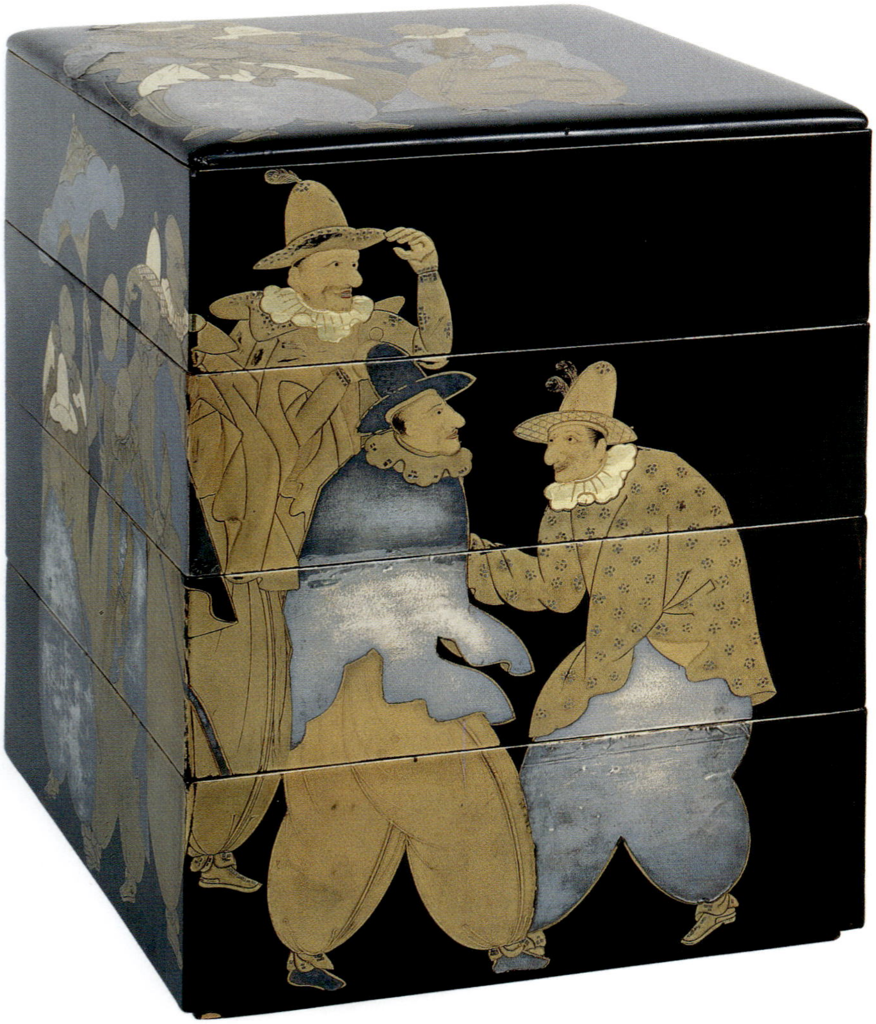

rituals that organized relations between the emperor and the rulers of other countries. Late Ming China was not hostile to foreign trade and influence. In fact there was quite a taste for exotic imports, ranging from lacquerwares from Japan to turkeys from the New World.[18] However, early European visitors to East Asia noticed a difference of reception in Japan and China, João Rodrigues (1561–1633) commenting that the Japanese 'show to foreigners much welcome and kindness, and they are very trusting in allowing them to enter their country. In this respect they are very different from the Chinese ... who despise foreigners and are very jealous of their kingdom.'[19] This view of China and its attitude towards outsiders was to become firmly entrenched in the European mind over the succeeding centuries. As recent research has shown, however, what was perceived as 'jealousy' was more the result of pragmatism: Chinese policy towards foreigners was based not on exclusion, but on management.[20]

In 1644 the Manchu assumed power in China, adopting and adapting the institutions and systems of their Ming predecessors. The Qing perceived the world as a place of numerous rulers over whom the Manchu emperor was positioned as the *huangdi* or 'supreme lord', within whose being the Earth and cosmos were conjoined. The preservation of this world order was centred around what western historians have termed the 'tribute system'. As a wise and benevolent ruler, the emperor welcomed lords from outside his domain and, through a series of guest rituals, maintained a hierarchical, harmoniously balanced relationship between the centre and the periphery. What is often perceived as China's fundamental distinction between the 'barbarian' foreigner and the 'civilized' Chinese is thus rather misleading, for guest ritual was concerned more with inclusion than with the affirmation of difference.[21] In the art of the Qing period Europeans are invariably depicted bringing tribute and thus symbolically incorporated into Chinese ritual order (plates 16.6, 16.8).

The set of four handscrolls, *Huangqing Zhigongtu (Illustrated Tributaries of the Qing Empire)*, was commissioned by the Qianlong emperor (r. 1736–95) in the fifteenth year of his reign and perfectly encapsulates the imperial vision of the world (plate 16.9). The scrolls illustrate peoples of different ethnicities and nationalities, including those from 'western ocean' (*hsi-yang*) countries. Such depictions of foreign envoys have a history dating back to the Tang period and earlier. However, the Qianlong scrolls differ in a number of important respects: the figures are not envoys bearing gifts, but couples who embody some social custom of the regions they represent.[22] The scrolls also include countries not under the influence of the Qing regime, such as Britain. The representation of the 'other' in these scrolls has a highly charged political meaning, as the whole known world succumbs to the emperor's controlling gaze.

It has been generally believed that Qing-period China had little interest in Europe and Europeans, but the text above the figures on the scrolls, in Manchu and Han Chinese, does reveal a certain curiosity about different peoples and customs.

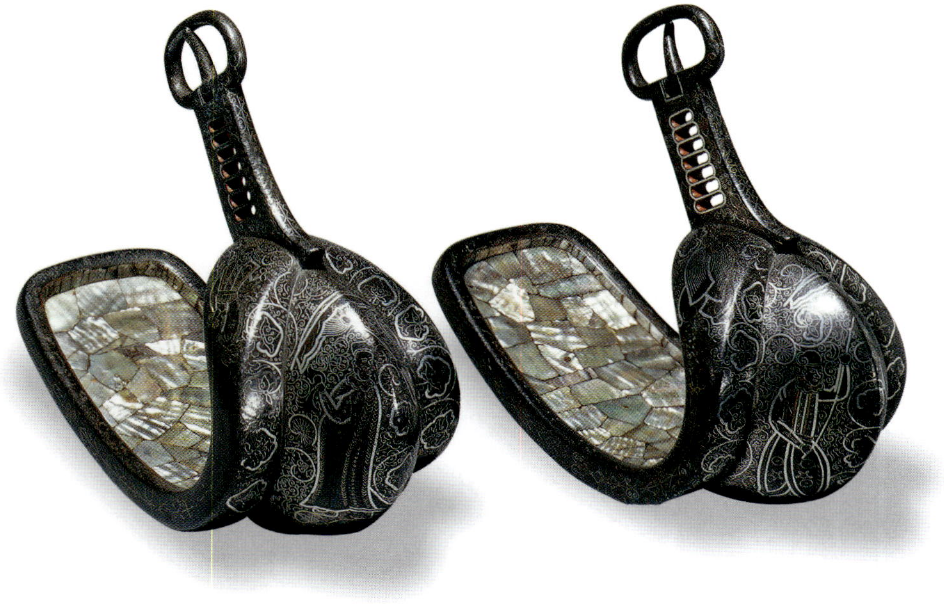

16.4
Pair of stirrups

Iron, with silver and brass inlay; wood linings lacquered in red with mother-of-pearl
Japan, 17th century

Private collection

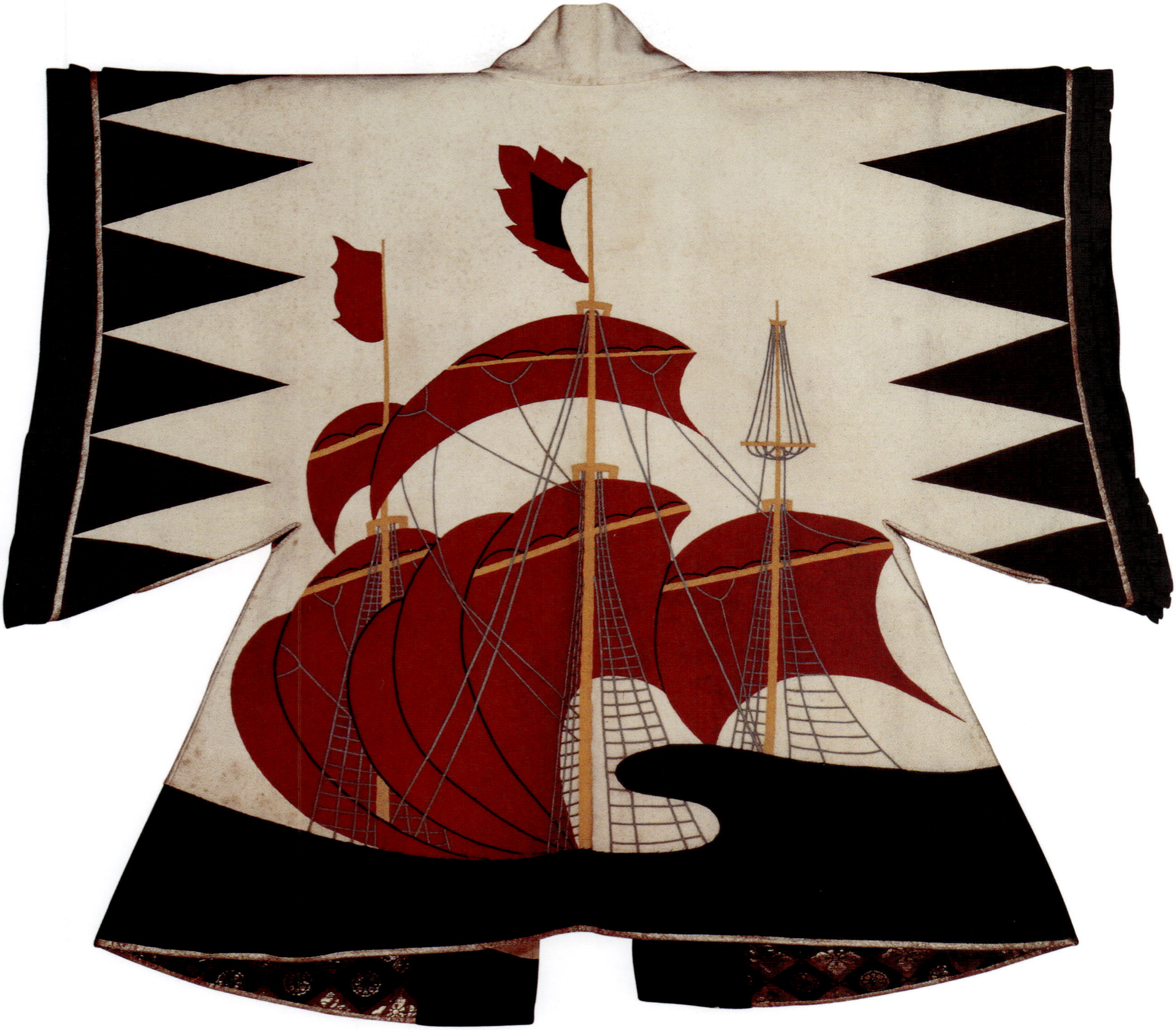

16.5
Surcoat (*jinbaori*)

Woollen cloth *(rasha)*, crêpe silk cuffs and velvet lining
Japan, 1744–48

Maeda Ikutokukai Foundation, Japan

16.6 overleaf
Twelve-panel screen

Wood covered in coloured and incised lacquer
China, dated 1674

Private collection, Toronto

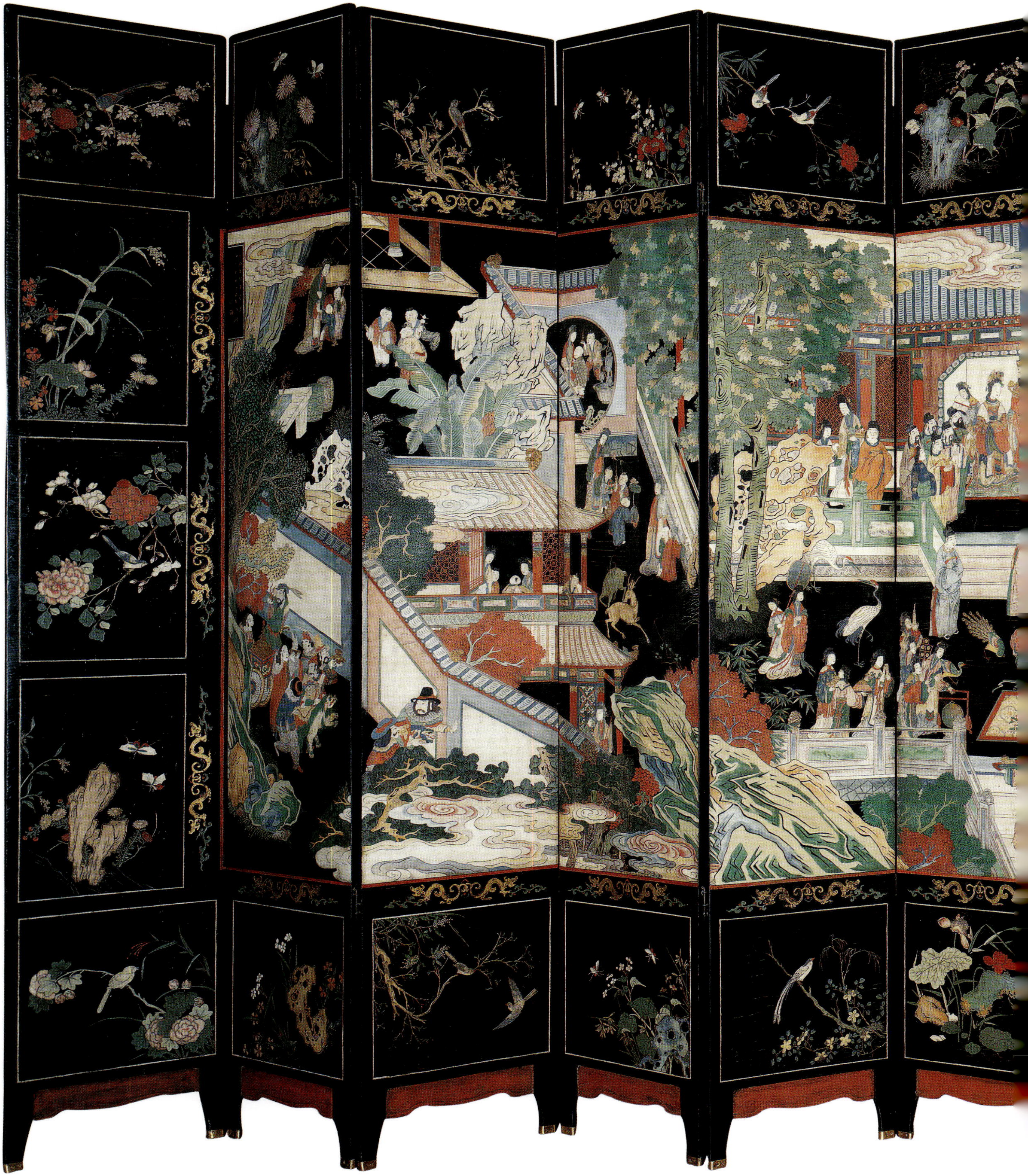

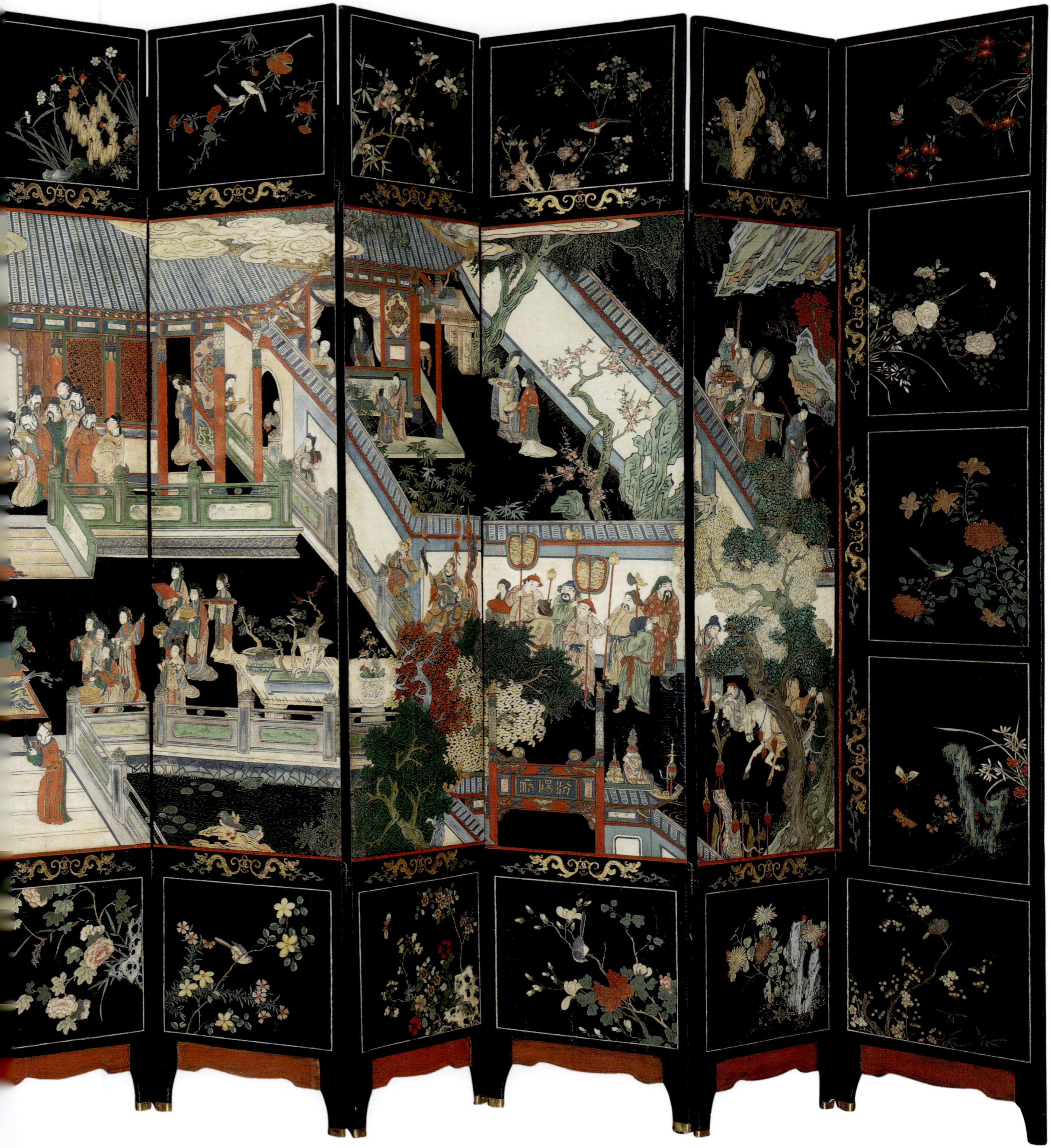

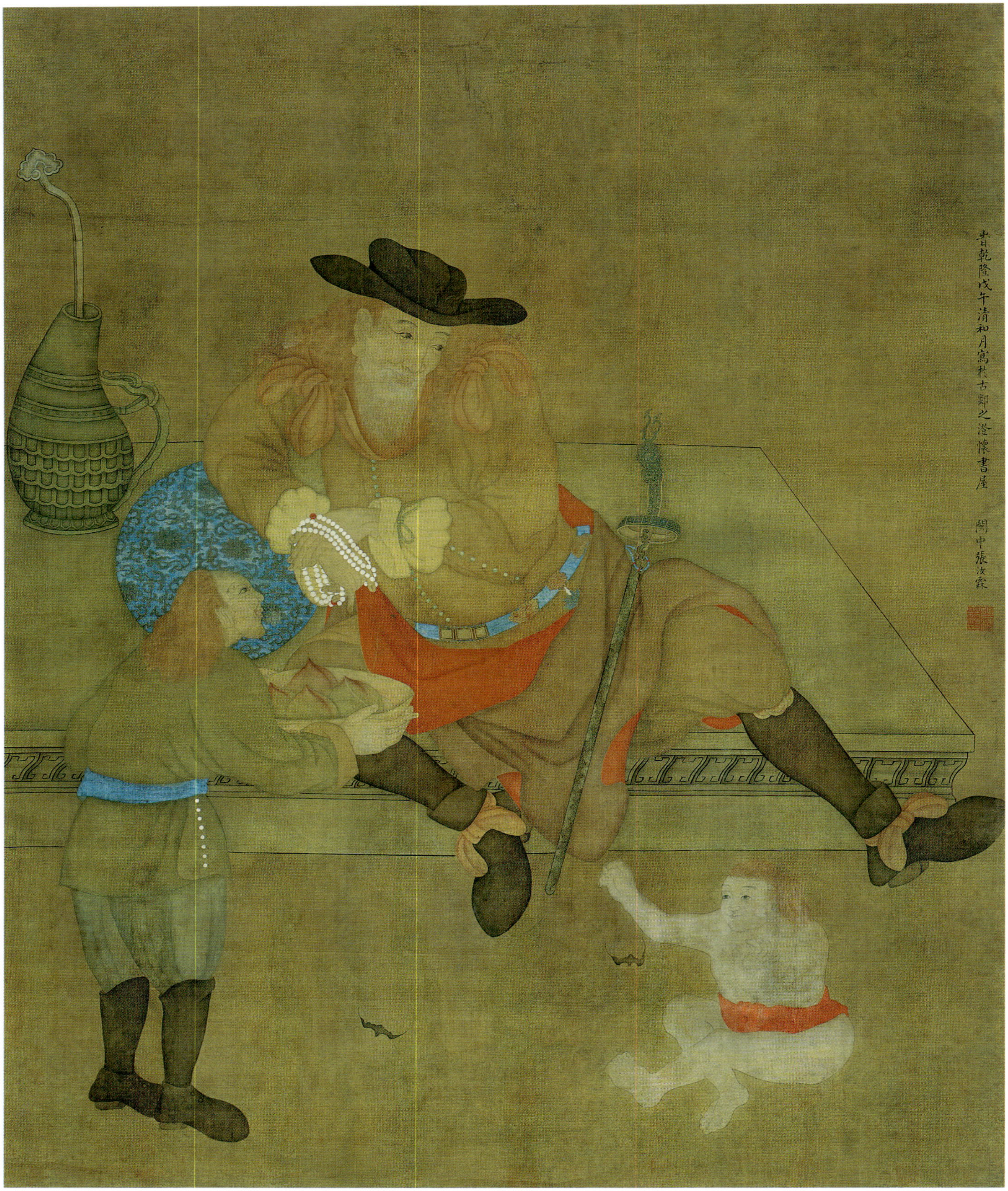
旹乾隆戊午清和月寫於古鄭之澄懷書屋
關中張汝霖

Above the British couple is written: 'British dress is similar to that of the Netherlands. The nation is wealthy. Men are commonly dressed in woollen flannel and like drinking alcohol. Women, before marriage, bind their waists to make them narrow. They wear short tops and long dresses and let their hair flow loosely over their shoulders.'[23] The rather intimate ivory portrayal of two Europeans bearing gifts (plate 16.8) and the animated group of foreigners who appear on the screen (plate 16.6), an object known to have been a gift from one Chinese official to another, also bear testament to the appeal of Europeans, albeit imagined in a safely submissive role. In this screen the 'western ocean' peoples are shown outside the wall, which acts as a physical and symbolic barrier between the Chinese 'inner' world of the emperor and his court and the 'outer' world of the barbarian. However, in another screen in the Nationalmuseet in Copenhagen, gift-bearing Europeans are shown within the palace walls, having processed through the countryside from their ships. But interestingly no Chinese figures are depicted. Nor are Chinese portrayed in the scenes of Europeans riding and hunting, which form another subject of these screens.[24] Visually, at least, the two cultures remain apart.

A far more unusual depiction of a European is found in a scroll painting, dated 1738, in the collection of the Rijksmuseum (plate 16.7). A large, red-haired man with a white beard is shown in western dress

16.7 opposite
The Demon Queller
Hanging scroll; ink and colour on silk
China, 1738

Rijksmuseum, Amsterdam

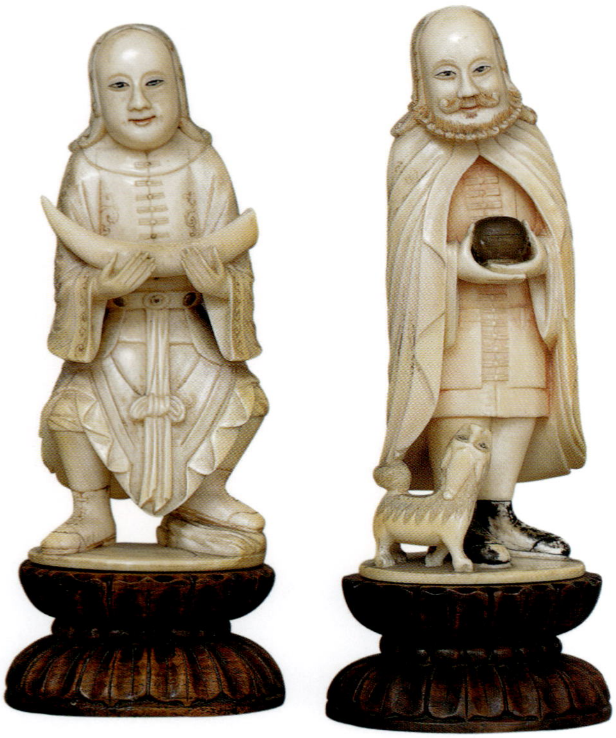

16.8
Two figures of Europeans bearing gifts
Ivory, carved, partly painted and gilded, bases modern
China, early 18th century

Peabody Essex Museum, Salem

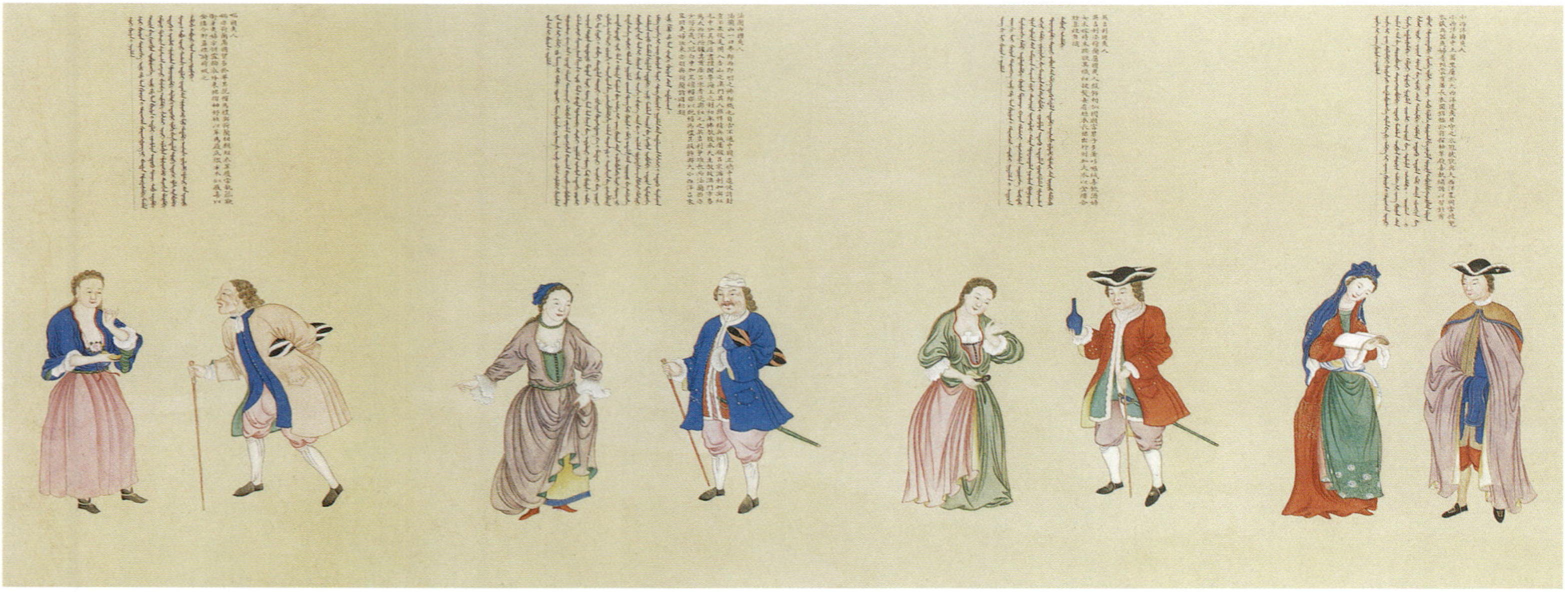

16.9
Illustrated Tributaries of the Qing Empire (detail)
Ding Guanpeng and others
Handscroll from a set of four; ink and colour on paper
China, 1751–75

Palace Museum, Beijing

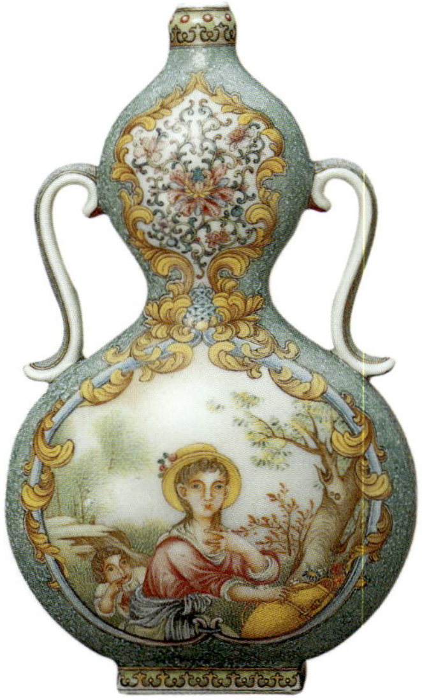

16.10
Vase

Porcelain with overglaze enamel decoration
China (reign and mark of the emperor Qianlong), 1736–95

V&A: C.219–1931

16.11
The Dutch Factory at Dejima (detail)

Handscroll; ink and colour on silk
Japan (Nagasaki), *c.* 1800

V&A: D.151–1905

16.12 opposite
Women with Children

Two hanging scrolls; opaque watercolour on paper
China, late 18th century

Jorge Welsh

sitting on a stone bed. An elaborate sword hangs from his belt and he is being served peaches by a young man of similar colouring and attire, while at his feet a red-haired baby plays with two bats. Behind is a vessel containing a *ruyi* (sceptre). This European is not an envoy bearing tribute, but the auspicious figure of Zhong Kui, the legendary demon-queller.[25] This incorporation of European figures into Chinese iconography echoes that seen in Japanese art.

The positive, heroic portrayal seen in this painting contrasts with the more popular view of Europeans as ugly, cunning and treacherous.[26] That the demon-queller was depicted as a foreigner is testimony to the extent to which China's elite was receptive to European culture in the mid-eighteenth century. The growing interest in representing Europeans is revealed by the Scottish doctor John Bell, who accompanied a Russian embassy to China in 1720. At the end of a banquet hosted by the emperor's ninth son, Bell's party was entertained by:

> several comical farces … The last character that appeared on stage, was a European gentleman, completely dressed, having all his cloaths dedawbed with gold and silver lace. He pulled off his hat, and made profound reverence to all that passed him. I shall leave it to any one to imagine, what an aukward figure a Chinese must make in this ridiculous habit.[27]

Although this performance was staged for the benefit of European guests, scroll paintings of foreign landscapes and ceramics depicting western subjects were made specifically for Chinese consumption (plate 16.10).[28] Highly decorated porcelains, with images derived from western prints,

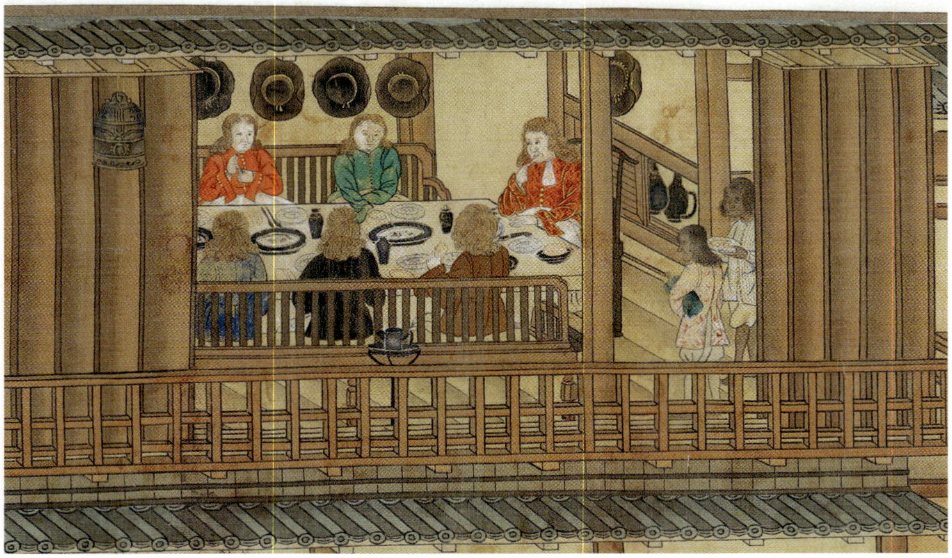

were made for the Qianlong emperor and may have graced the European-style pavilions of the Yuanming Yuan ('Garden of Perfect Clarity') outside Peking (Beijing) (see pp. 343–5).

Such imperial taste for exotica was also revealed in the 'western ocean' festive pavilions erected as part of the empress dowager's 60th birthday celebrations in 1752 and the Qianlong emperor's 80th birthday celebrations in 1790. In her analysis of these temporary buildings, Ellen Uitzinger suggests that ultimately the 'western ocean' fashion was something China wanted only to 'gaze at, but not enter'.[29] A series of scroll paintings depicting women and children in a garden setting implies something slightly different, however, for although the figures are in western dress, they are placed within a Chinese setting (plate 16.12).[30] The facial features of some of the women are European, but on closer inspection other figures, particularly the children, appear to be Chinese. This may not have been the artist's intention, but what these images, and those of the European demon-queller, do suggest is that while China may not have desired to 'enter' western-ocean countries, the latter's people were permitted to enter and become part of Chinese visual culture.

Chinese interest in the foreign was confined to the court and other members of elite society. The influence of some western technologies did spread beyond this limited sphere but, with the exception of those engaged in trade in port cities, the actual presence of Europeans made very little impact on China's great populace. Few people in Japan ever saw a European either, but by the eighteenth century the *kōmōjin* or 'red-haired people', as the Dutch were known, had become both the subject of learned enquiry and part of Japanese popular culture. European figures appear far more frequently in Japanese art than Chinese, evidence less of a concern to exert authority over the 'other' than of a genuine fascination with the foreign and exotic.

Dejima, the island in Nagasaki harbour to which the Dutch were confined, was a natural focus of Japanese curiosity about the *kōmōjin*. A handscroll in the collection of the V&A depicting everyday life in the settlement was probably painted for a senior Tokugawa official to both inform and amuse (plate 16.11)[31] While many Nagasaki painters incorporated western stylistic elements into their work, the unknown artist of the handscroll has used predominantly native methods; the pigments, technique and bird's-eye viewpoint place this work

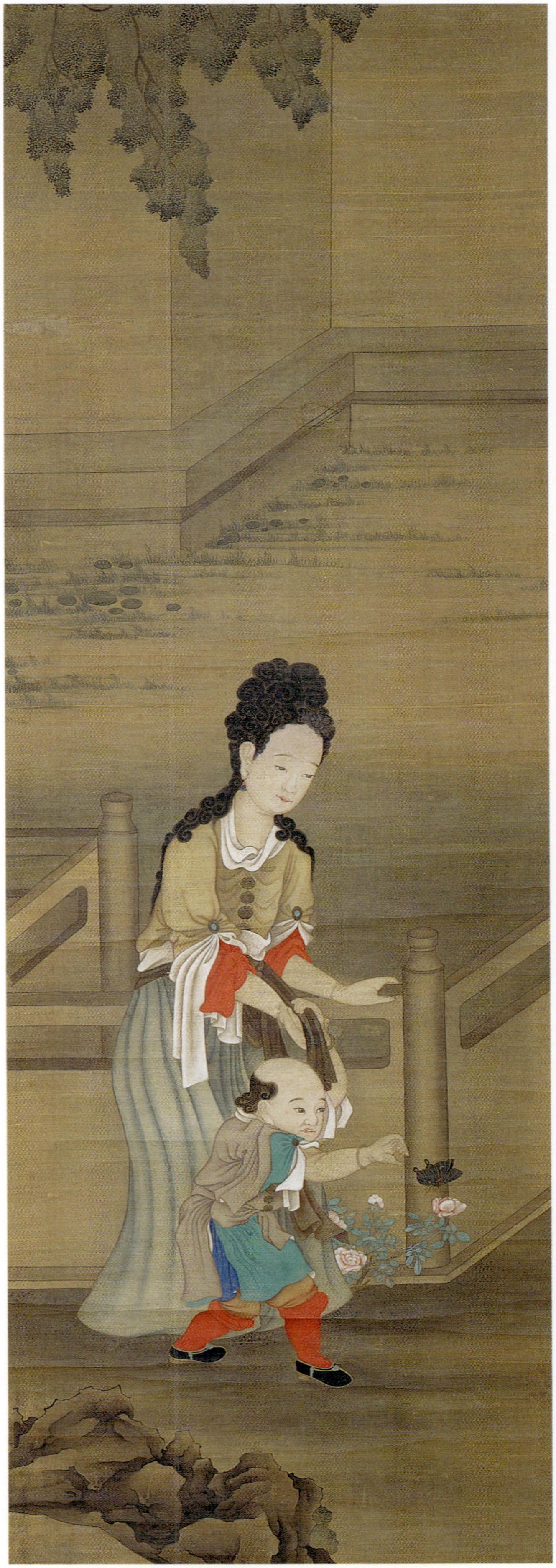
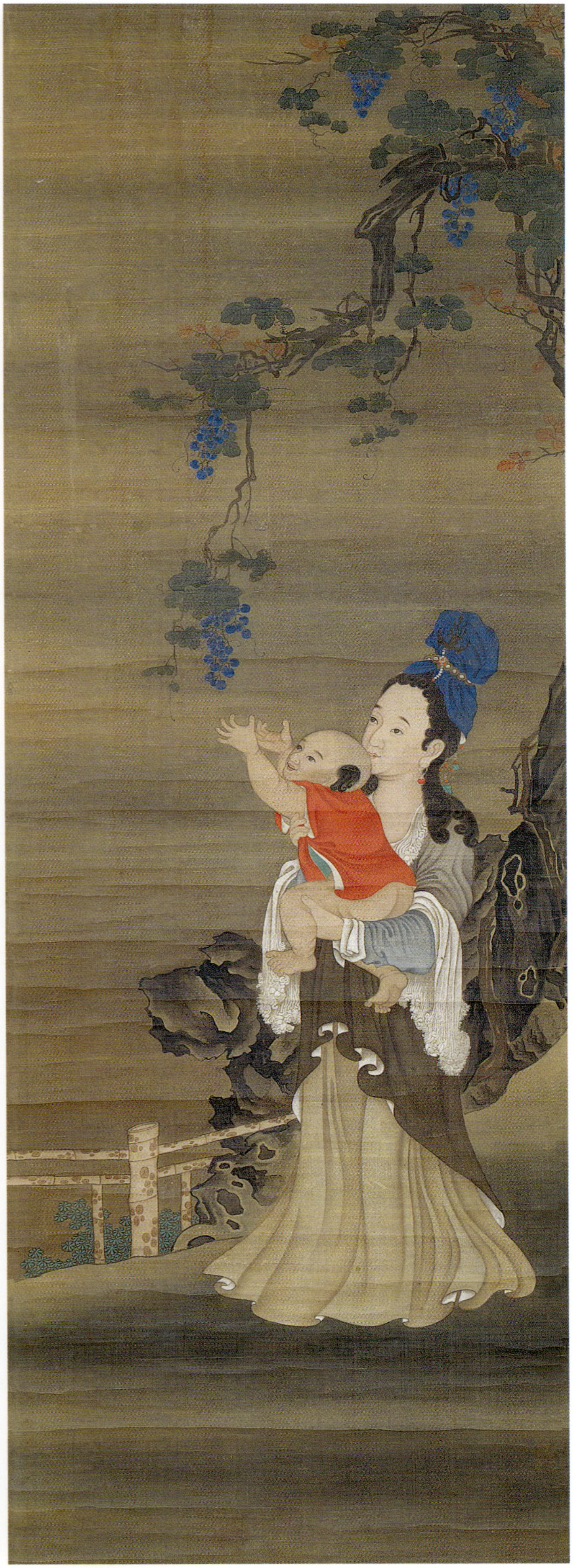

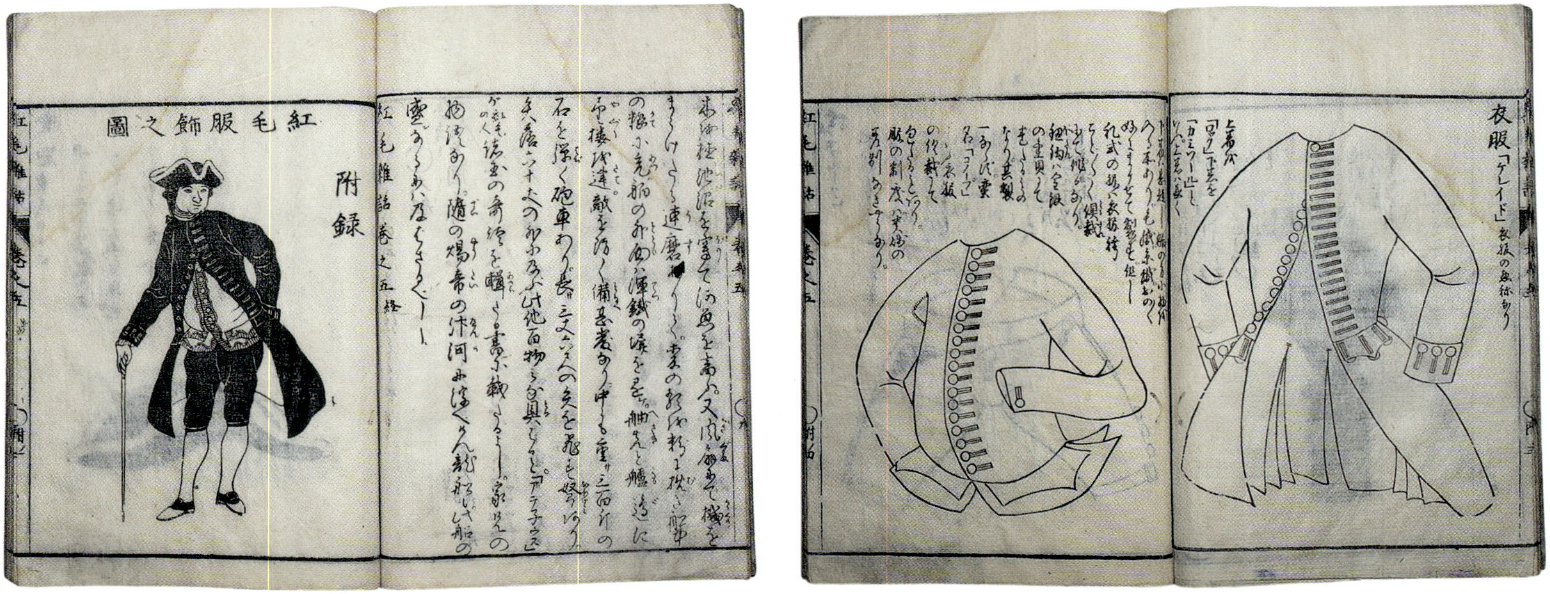

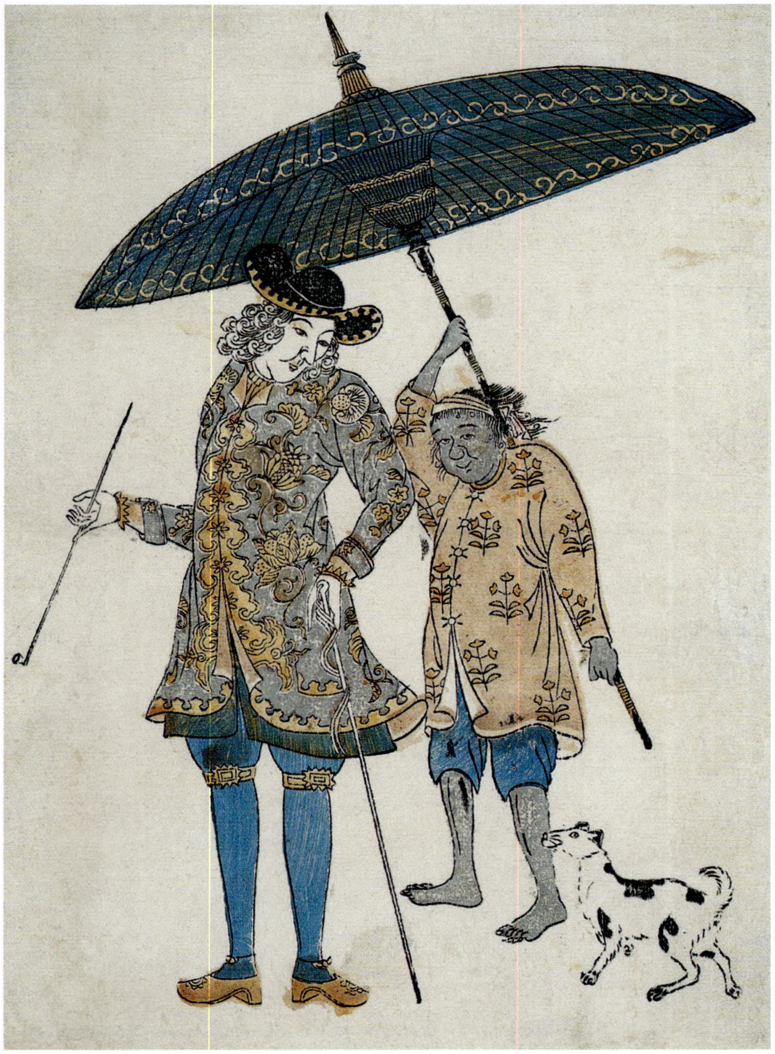

16.13
A Dutchman and His Dress

From Morishima Chūryō, *Kōmō Zatsuwa* (*The Red-Haired Miscellany*)
Woodblock-printed book
Japan (Edo), 1787

Kobe City Museum, Kobe

16.14
Dutchman with Javanese Servant

Woodblock print
Japan (Nagasaki), late 18th century

British Museum, London

within the tradition of Japanese genre painting and, unlike the *nanban* screens of two centuries earlier, the image is read from right to left.

Like others with an interest in the Dutch, Shiba Kōkan travelled to Dejima and recorded what he saw in his diary (see p. 137 and p. 315). Most people who went to Nagasaki would have been disappointed, however, for they were unlikely to have actually seen a Dutchman and certainly would not have been allowed into the Dutch settlement. However, they would still have been able to pick up a pictorial souvenir of their visit (plate 16.14). Nagasaki woodblock prints were rather crude when compared to those of Edo or Osaka but they proved a great commercial success. This image, which shows the *opperhoofd*, or chief of the Dutch factory, smoking a long clay pipe and being protected from the sun by a large parasol carried by a Javanese slave, is the one that was reproduced most frequently.[32]

The iconography of this print bears some similarities to the image of the captain-major on the *nanban* screen (plate 16.1). On the whole, however, the Dutch were perceived and depicted in rather a different way from the Portuguese; the latter had presented themselves as important lords, while the Dutch were merely merchants and thus at the bottom of the Tokugawa social hierarchy.[33] However, they were accorded the rare honour of regular audiences with the *shōgun*, the Dejima *opperhoofd*, secretary and doctor making a 90-day journey from Nagasaki to Edo in order to pay their respects, present gifts and give thanks for the continuation of trade (see p. 98, and p. 183 and p. 316). While in the capital the Dutch were lodged at the *Nagasaki-ya*, the famous image of which by Katsushika Hokusai (1760–1849) reveals the excitement that the presence of the *kōmōjin* created among residents of the city (see plate. 14.5).

Japanese curiosity was also satisfied by a growing number of books about Europe and Europeans. One of the most famous of these is the *Kai Tsūshō Kō* (*On Commercial Relations with China and Barbarians*) by Nishikawa Joken (1648–1724), first published in 1695:

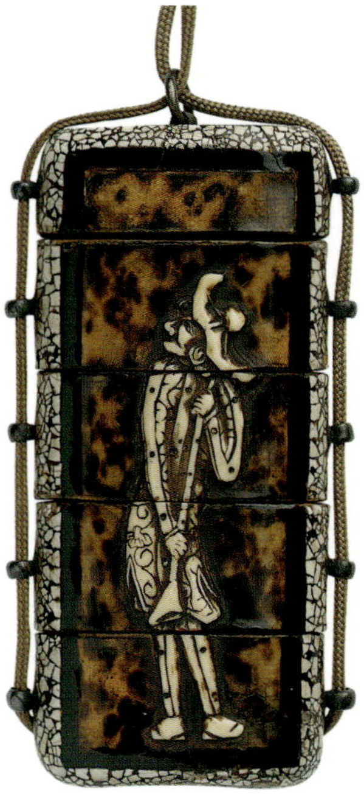

16.15
***Inro* depicting a Dutchman with a matchlock gun**

Wood covered with tortoiseshell, bone and crackled eggshell
Japan, 1650–1750

V&A: W.356–1922

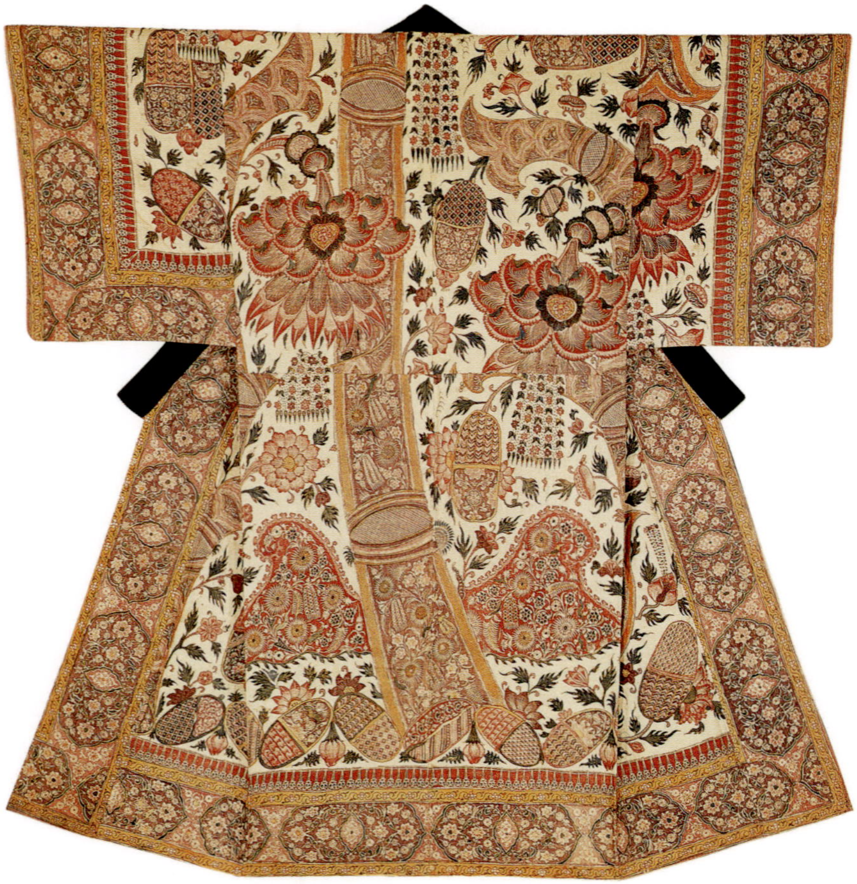

16.16
Under-kimono (*juban*)

Cotton, painted and dyed
Cloth: India (Coromandel coast), 18th century; garment fashioned in Japan, c.1800

Private collection, Kyoto

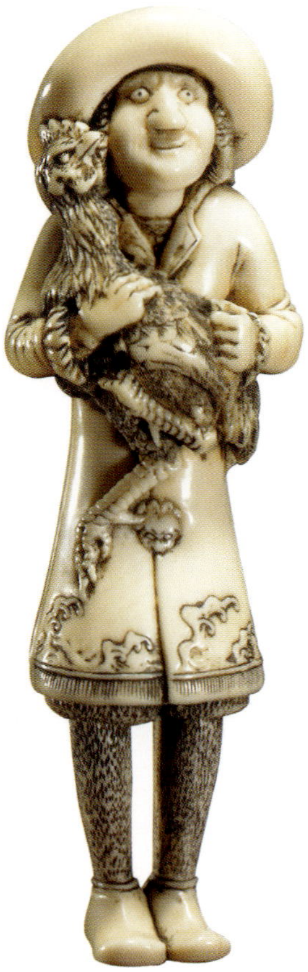

16.17
***Netsuke* of a European figure**

Ivory, carved
Japan, 1700–50

British Museum, London

> The Hollanders have white skins, red and short hair, high noses and the pupils of their eyes are white. Their clothes are usually made of woollen cloth, whilst high and low alike wear beaver hats. Whenever they salute one another, they always remove their hats … The Hollanders are very clever artisans and very skilful in designing various contrivances. They are the best seamen on the ocean seas … well-versed in astronomy, geography and divination. They are also first-class medical scientists.[34]

This description became the basis of many subsequent publications, but other more fanciful aspects were added to the Dutch stereotype: they were believed to have no heels, eyes like animals and to 'lift one leg to urinate like a dog'.[35]

As the interest in Dutch studies (*Rangaku*) grew, many scholars were at pains to change such perceptions (see p. 318).[36] When a *daimyō* remarked to Honda Toshiaki (1744–1821) that 'the Dutch are barbarians … I do not doubt that they are some kind of animal. However … their workmanship is amazingly skilful', Honda replied, 'So, even if they are animals, their workmanship is still precise. You think they use something other than their minds for that?' Honda's words were apparently 'good for more than one laugh'.[37] It was not only the human, or otherwise, characteristics of the Dutch that aroused much interest and debate. Illustrations of western cutlery and furniture appeared in various books, while *Kōmō Zatsuwa* (*The Red-Haired Miscellany*) of 1787 contained a series of images depicting, first a fully dressed Dutchman, and then all the separate items of his clothing, each with its individual description (plate 16.13). European items and attributes were also used in Edo-period haiku. One by Matsue Shigeyori (1602–80) reads:

> Like Dutch letters
> Geese flying
> Across the sky[38]

'*Sekai no zu*', or 'world map', was a fashionable word that found its way into haiku and other forms of poetry, while the image of Dutch ships leaving Nagasaki was sometimes employed as a metaphor for sadness.[39]

Dutch vessels, like their Portuguese predecessors, were much admired in the Edo period (1615–1868) and were another popular subject of Nagaski print artists. The dynamic motif of a ship in full sail decorates the back of a *jinbaori* (surcoat for armour) believed to have been made for the *daimyō* Maeda Shigehiro in the 1740s (plate 16.5). The garment is made from imported wool known as *rasha*, which has been treated and shrunk to give it a felt-like texture. As well as being warm and durable, the fabric, with its European origins, also had an exotic appeal. The curving shape of the *jinbaori* derives from western dress, while the frilled green crêpe on the cuffs emulates Portuguese ruffs. The saw-tooth pattern on the sleeves is inspired by South and South-East Asian painted and dyed cottons imported into Japan by the Dutch. The *opperhoofd* in the Nagasaki print is depicted in a jacket made of such cloth, known in Japan as *sarasa* (plate 16.14). This *sarasa juban* (under-kimono), adapted from an Indian *palampore,* would have been a very expensive garment and was reputedly owned by a rich merchant (plate 16.16). *Sarasa* was more commonly cut into smaller pieces and used as *furoshiki* (wrapping cloths), *obi* (kimono sashes) and tobacco pouches. It was so highly prized that even the smallest pieces were saved and pasted into sample books. The foreign thus became an important part of fashionable dress, something seen not only in garments, but also in dress accessories such as combs, *inrō* (small containers worn by men and suspended from the *obi* [sash] of the kimono) and *netsuke* (the toggle used to hang *inrō* or other articles (plates 16.15, 16.17).

While the *nanban* vogue of the late sixteenth and seventeenth centuries had been limited to the elite, the taste for 'Dutch things' (*Oranda shumi*) was much more widespread and much more varied. For *Rangaku* scholars such as Honda, *Oranda* (or Holland) was a serious matter, but for most people it represented the new and the exotic, something fashionable but also nonsensical. The popular seventeenth-century novelist Iharu Saikaku (1642–93), for example, styled himself *'oranda'* as a mark of his eccentric individualism. *Oranda* came to mean not just

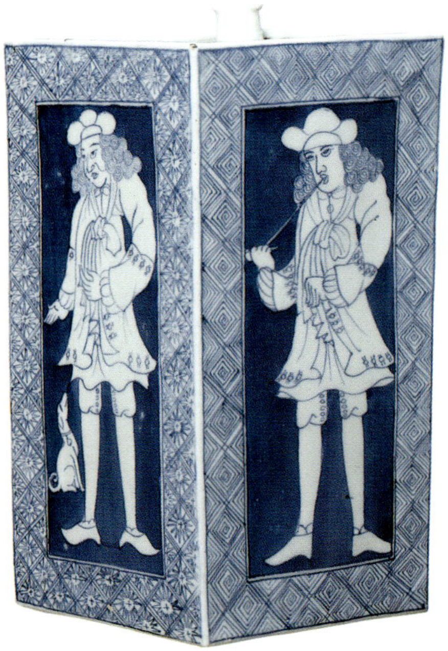

16.18
***Sake* bottle**

Porcelain, with decoration in underglaze blue
Japan (Arita), 1750–1825

V&A: C.64–1963

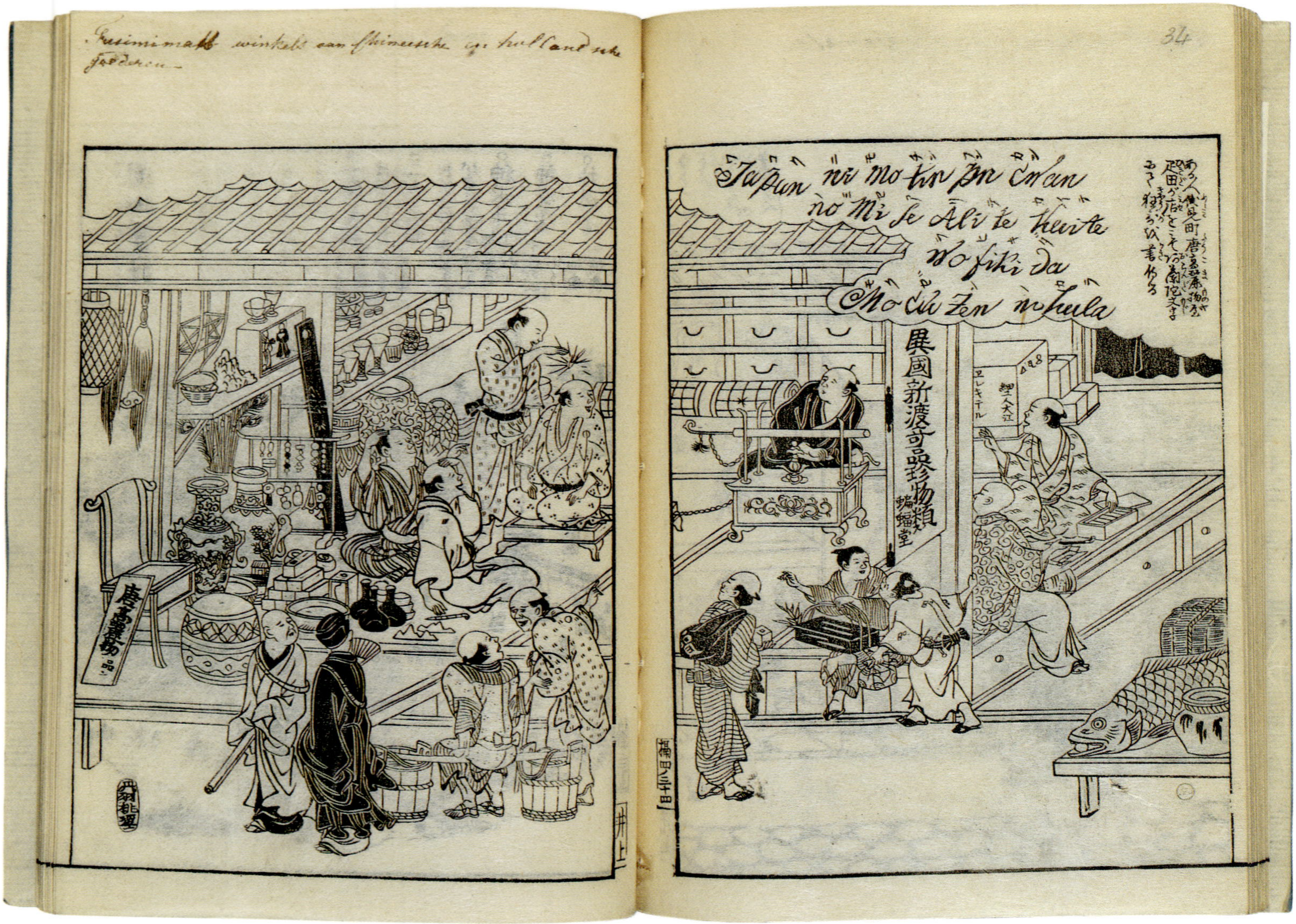

something Dutch, but anything imported, even if it came from China. Foreign goods were sold in special shops such as that depicted in the *Settsu Meisho Zue* (*Illustrations of Famous Places in Settsu Province*) of 1798 (plate 16.19). The horizontal roman letters above the image can be read phonetically in Japanese:

> In our fair land too
> Outlandish nonsense –
> And a shop for it.
> Hikida really pulls the custom in
> Foreignness before their very eyes.[40]

Most of the goods for sale are Chinese, but European wine glasses can be seen on the shelves, and in the centre a static-electricity generator – one of the *kiki*, or 'strange devices', associated with the Dutch – is being demonstrated.[41]

In eighteenth-century Japan, *Oranda* came to occupy the physical and, more importantly, the mental space of leisure and escape; it was the image viewed in a peepbox, part of the world of the fashionable courtesan, or the motif on a *sake* bottle (plate 16.18). As such, *Oranda* was very much part of the alternative culture of *ukiyo,* or the 'floating world', that existed on the periphery of the official Tokugawa state.[42] Like the Portuguese before them, the Dutch had an impact on the realities of Edo-period Japan. At the same time the foreigner and the foreign continued to signify an 'other' world, both a supernatural one of gods and goblins and, more significantly, an imaginary space of excitement, entertainment and exoticism.

16.19
Hikeda's Foreign Goods Shop

Page from *Settsu Meisho Zue*, written by Akisato Rito and illustrated by Takehara Shunchosai | Woodblock-printed book
Japan (Edo), 1796

V&A: E.3011–1925

European Depictions of Asians

Rosemary Crill

WESTERN SOURCES ARE RICH in both visual and textual depictions of Asian people, their beliefs and customs. It was the tales of Marco Polo (1254–1323?) that first planted a vision of the East in the European imagination. Few made such journeys to Asia, however, and images of it – generally relayed through intermediaries – were born more of myth than reality.[1] In the age of discoveries, Europeans were able to travel directly to South and East Asia and returned with first-hand accounts of cultures very different from those of the West.

One of the first European travellers to illustrate aspects of everyday life in India was the Dutchman Jan Huyghen van Linschoten (1563–1611), who lived in the subcontinent from 1583 to 1588.[2] As Donald Lach has noted, the publication of Linschoten's *Itinerario* in 1596 was 'a watershed in Europe's pictorial impression of Asia', for it was the first book to depict the activities, people and architecture of South Asia (plate 16.20).[3] In spite of their exotic subject matter, to modern eyes the figures depicted in these illustrations seem strangely un-Asian, largely because Linschoten's original drawings from life, now lost, were transferred onto copperplate by Dutch printers with no experience of the East.

Western styling is also evident in *China Illustrata* of 1667 by Athanasius Kircher (1602–80) in which Asian and European elements fuse together (plate 16.22). The portrait of the first Manchu emperor shows him in Chinese dress, but depicted in an architectural setting befitting a European monarch. As a Jesuit, the focus of Kircher's book was religion, but in it he presented much other information about China, making the *Illustrata* one of the most popular books of the seventeenth century. Another important publication of the period resulted from the first Dutch embassy to China in 1655–56. *Het gezantschap der Neerlantsche Oost-Indische Compagnie aan den grooten Tartarischen cham*, written by embassy secretary Johann Nieuhof (1618–72), was an encyclopaedic work illustrated with 150 engravings, many based on the author's own sketches (plate 16.21). Although western elements can again be detected, the illustrations provided European readers with relatively accurate images of the landscapes, cityscapes and peoples of China.

The most important seventeenth-century account of Japan was that by Engelbert Kaempfer (1651–1716). Kaempfer was unable to have his manuscript published, but after his death it was acquired by Hans Sloane (1660–1753) who produced

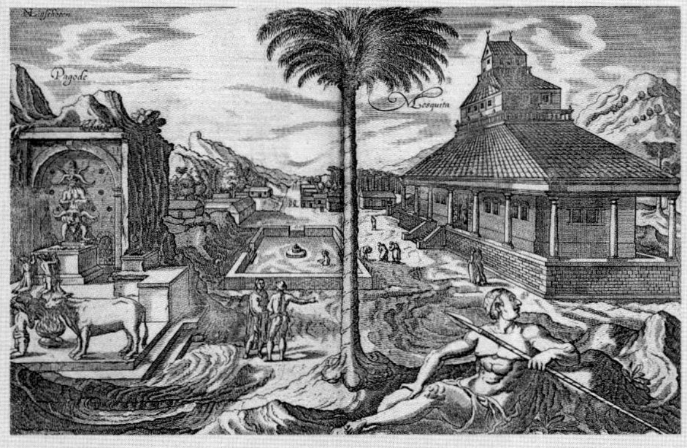

16.20
Plate depicting a mosque and a Hindu temple

From Jan Huyghen van Linschoten, *Itinerario: Voyage oft schipvaert van Jan Huygen van Linschoten naer Oost ofte Portugaels Indien, 1579–1592*, engraved by Baptista van Doetecun (after a drawing by Linschoten), published by Cornelius Claesz, Amsterdam, 1596
Hand-coloured engraving on paper

Koninklijke Bibliotheek, The Hague

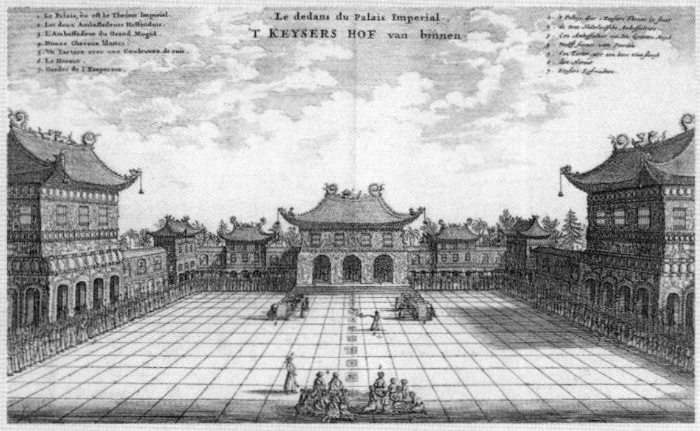

16.21
Reception of Emissaries at the Imperial Court

From Johann Nieuhof, *Het gezantschap der Neerlantsche Oost-Indische Compagnie aan den grooten Tartarischen cham*, 1665
Engraving on paper

V&A: NAL 5.X.36

16.22 right, above
The First Manchu Emperor, Shun-chih (r. 1644–61) at about Eighteen Years of Age

From Athanasius Kircher, *China Illustrata*, 1667
Engraving on paper

British Library, London

16.23 right
A Royal Tamasha at the Mughal Court, Delhi
Willem Schellinks

Oil on canvas
Netherlands, c.1650–75

V&A: IS.30–1892

16.24 far right
The Princely Household at Delhi on the Birthday of the Great Mogul Aurangzeb
Johan Melchior Dinglinger

Gold and silver, jewelled and enamelled
Germany (Dresden), 1701–08

The Green Vaults, Dresden

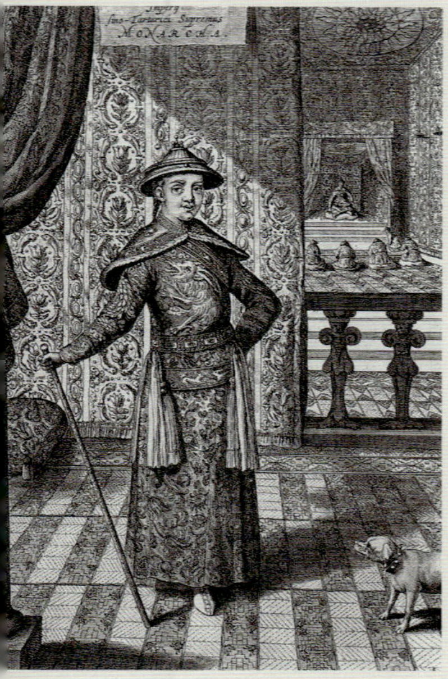

it in English in 1727 with illustrations based on the author's sketches (see plate 7.6). *The History of Japan* became a bestseller and the source of most writings about the country for next 200 years.

Very few Asians travelled to Europe, although those who did aroused much interest and were often painted by leading portraitists of the day (see plates 1.3 and 6.11). The novelty and exoticism of the East described in the accounts of those who travelled there also provided a rich vein of subject matter for artists and craftsmen in Europe. A famous set of 26 tapestry panels 'in the manner of Portugal and India', entitled *The Voyage to Calicut*, was completed in Tournai in 1504 for Manuel I of Portugal (r. 1498–1521).[4] The set celebrated the Portuguese arrival in India in 1498, and its fantastic scenes of exotic animals and figures were derived solely from the designer's imagination rather than from life. The common western perception of life in Asia as one devoted to pleasure is the theme of a group of tapestries made by John Vanderbank (d. 1717) at his Soho factory in London in the late seventeenth century (see plate 27.5).[5] More than 50 of these tapestries 'in the Indian manner' are known: four belonged to Elihu Yale (1649–1721), the founder of the eponymous university.[6] The motifs on the tapestries are an indiscriminate mixture of Indian, Turkish, Persian and Chinese designs. Painters in the West, especially in Holland, also responded to the exotic appeal of the East, particularly to the magnificence of the Mughal court.[7] Willem Schellinks (1623–78) painted elaborate fantasies of the court of Shah Jahan, even incorporating the traditional Indian conceit of composite animals (plate 16.23).[8]

The most extravagant manifestation of the western fascination with Oriental splendour is the enamelled and jewelled gold and silver model entitled *The Princely Household at Delhi on the Birthday of the Great Mogul Aurangzebe* in the Green Vaults, Dresden (plate 16.24).[9] This huge tableau, which measures 142 cm wide, was made in 1701–8 for Augustus the Strong, King of Poland (1697–1706 and 1710–33) and Elector of Saxony (1694–1733) by his court jeweller Johann Melchior Dinglinger (1664–1731) and his two brothers, and is not unlike a three-dimensional, expanded version of the overtly theatrical settings for the Schellinks paintings. The architectural decoration, with its dragons and curly roofs, is typically Chinese in style, as are the elephants, and there is even a Chinese inscription engraved around the top of the walls of the 'stage'. This should not be taken too seriously, however, as Egyptian hieroglyphs are also found decorating the pilasters on either side of Aurangzeb. The Mughal dress of the courtiers, by contrast, is quite accurate; for this element Dinglinger evidently worked from late seventeenth-century illustrations of Indian court life.

The Dresden piece is a classic illustration of how, in western images of the East, Chinese and Indian elements were intermingled indiscriminately. By the 1750s the vogue for chinoiserie was in full swing as Asia became the subject of escapist fantasy. By the end of the century, despite 300 years of interaction between East and West, the European image of Asia was more one of fiction than of fact.

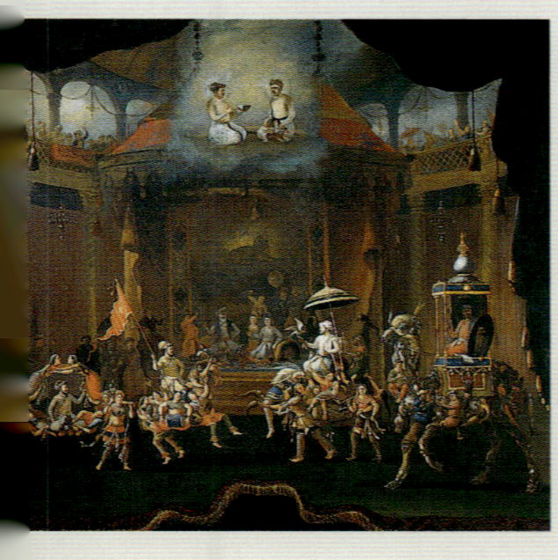

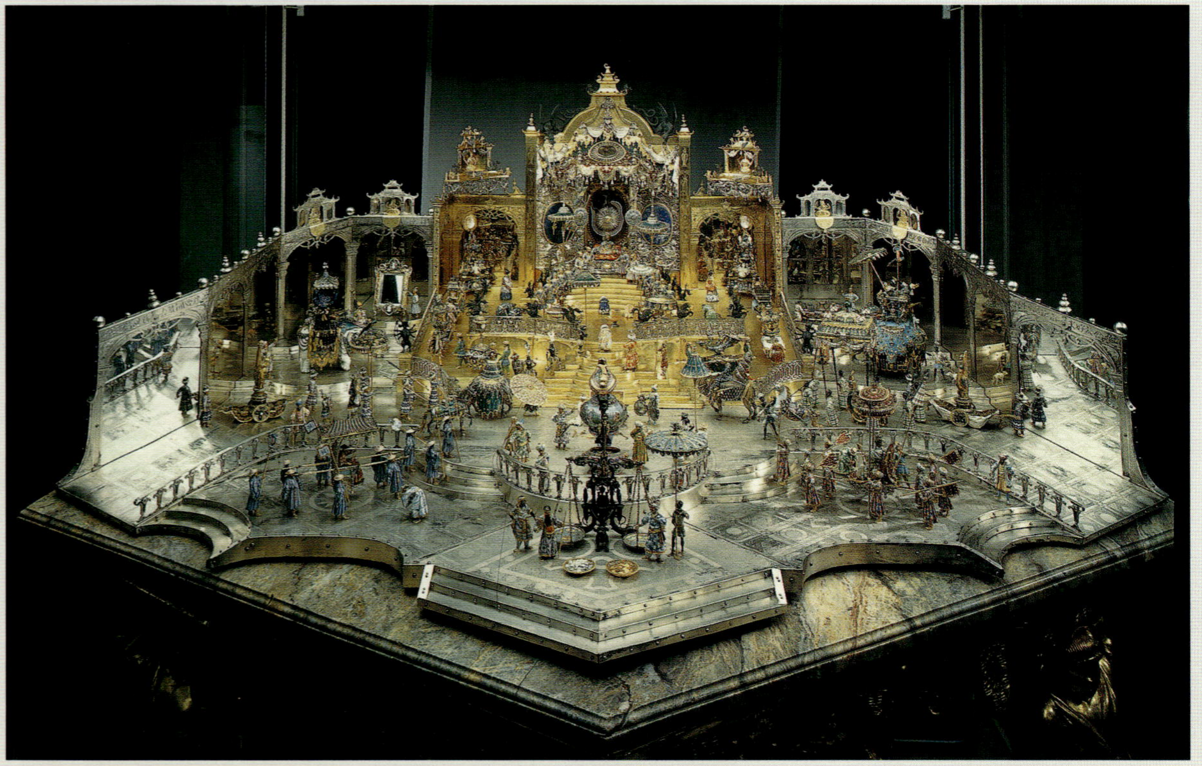

PART THREE

Exchanges

17

ASIA IN EUROPE: PORCELAIN AND ENAMEL FOR THE WEST

Rose Kerr

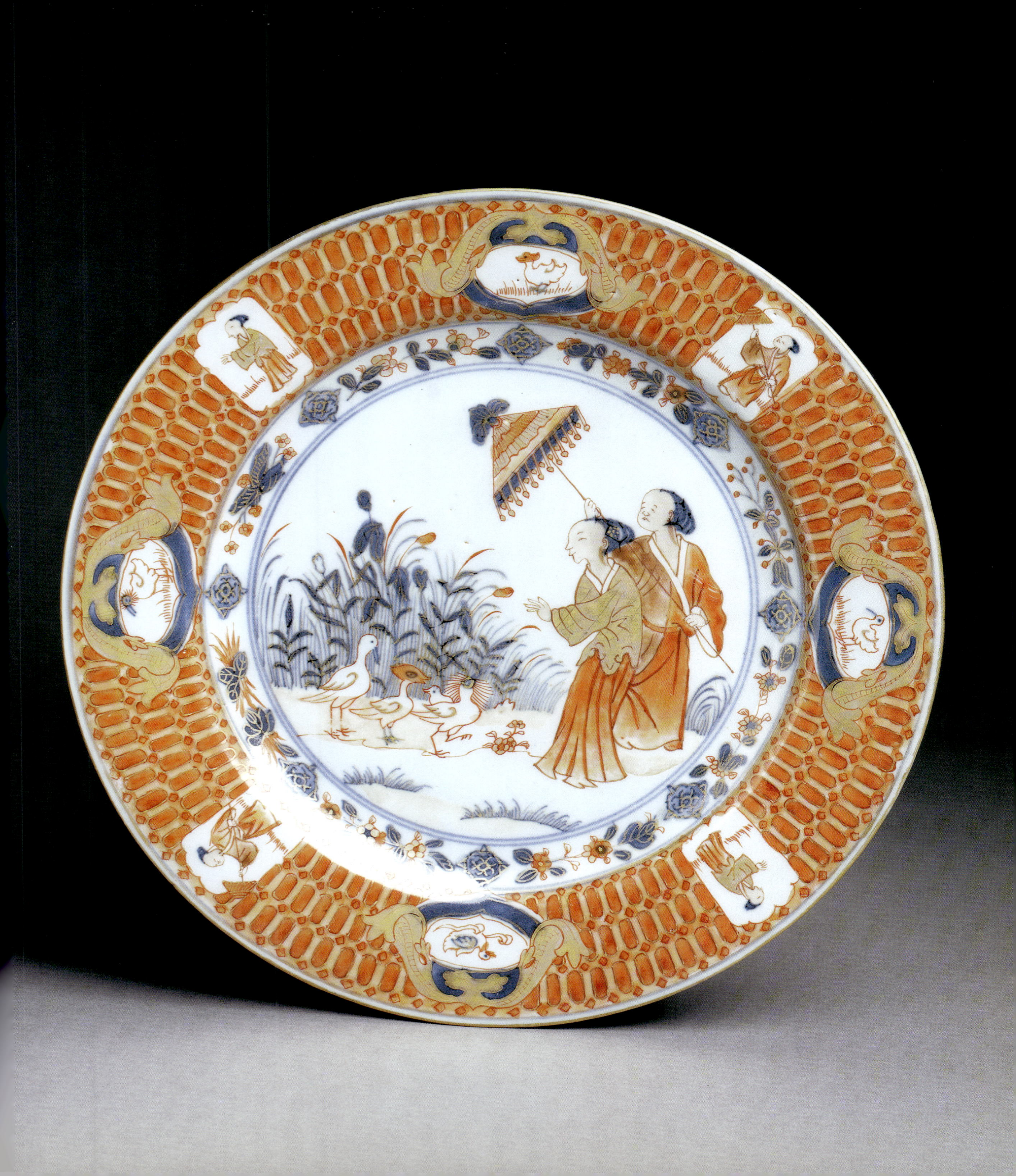

17.1 previous page
Plate from a 'Dame au Parasol' service

Porcelain, decorated in underglaze blue, iron red and gilding
China (Jingdezen), 1736–38

Jorge Welsh

One reason why East Asian ceramics were so highly prized in the West was that for many centuries European potteries were unable to imitate them. Initial efforts to do so were made in Florence in the sixteenth century, the result being the so-called 'Medici porcelain'. Lorenzo de' Medici ('the Magnificent', 1449–92) was a noted collector of Chinese porcelain,[1] and it was his great-grandson the Grand Duke Francesco I de' Medici (1541–87) who supported this early and short-lived experiment to manufacture porcelain between 1575 and 1587.[2] Although the material produced cannot be called true porcelain, its delicate and beautiful glassy surface simulated the effect of Chinese wares (plate 17.2).[3] However 'Medici porcelain' was expensive to make and often deformed during firing, and production seems to have halted with the grand duke's death, with only about 60 items surviving around the world.

While one European country attempted to make its own porcelain, another had already blazed a trading route direct to Asia. Portuguese mariners reached India in 1498 and China in 1513, and initiated profitable commerce in both countries. Chinese ceramics were one of the luxury goods they imported, and the arrival in Europe of greater quantities of such wares initiated a huge vogue for porcelain. Although the Portuguese never developed an extensive mass market in porcelain, they were adept with special orders. A mid-sixteenth-century ewer (plate 17.3) may originally have been made for the Middle Eastern market, as its form and contemporary Persian silver mounts suggest. As no pre-existing export wares in European shapes could be found, Portuguese clients often adapted such items, as the coats of arms on this ewer demonstrate. Europeans liked to embellish luxury furnishings and fittings with such devices, to denote their rank and status. A coat of arms not only identified an individual, but also made reference to his illustrious forebears, by incorporating elements that related to judicious marriages and strategic alliances. The arms on the ewer are those of António Peixoto, a navigator and merchant who traded on the south China coast and was one of the first Portuguese to reach Japan in the early 1540s.[4] The ewer is finely painted in shades and washes of rich cobalt blue, the quality of both porcelain and painting affirming it as an expensive item.

Of less good quality is a bottle with a commonplace Chinese decoration of ducks in a lotus pond and a mark on the base reading *Da Ming nian zao* 'Made in the great Ming dynasty' (plate 17.4). What distinguishes this everyday Chinese vessel is a double

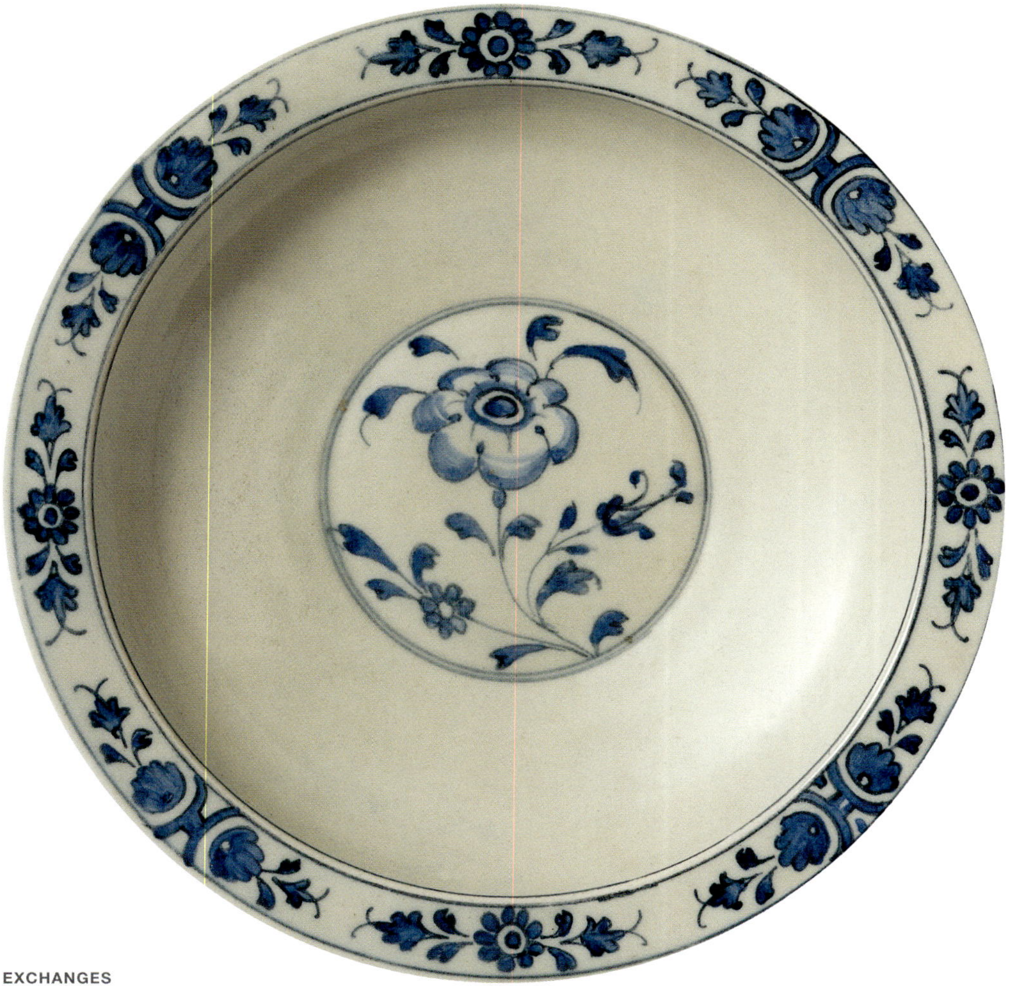

17.2
Dish

Soft-paste 'Medici porcelain', decorated in underglaze blue
Italy (Florence), 1575–87

V&A: 7700–1862

register of Portuguese words around the shoulder, written upside down and with many errors: 'ISTO MANDOU FAZER JORGE ALVARES NA ERA DE 1552'. This is one of six bottles presently known, all bearing different designs and inscriptions referring to Jorge Alvares.[5] Alvares was a naval captain, merchant and friend of the Catholic missionary (and later saint) Francis Xavier (1506–62).[6] He was on the first Portuguese voyage to China in 1513, subsequently acted as factor at the entrepôt in Malacca, revisited China in 1518 and died there in 1552.

From the early seventeenth century, other European countries laboured and fought to consolidate their East India ventures. This was the era when bulk export of porcelain began, but it was also a time when special luxury products entered the markets of Europe in increasing numbers, there to be imitated in local factories. One type of Chinese ceramic much admired and copied was red stoneware from the Yixing kilns in central southern China. The quality of iron-rich clays in that region was especially suited to the brewing of tea, for they maintained the colour, aroma and taste of the drink while providing good insulation. Yixing was a connoisseurial ware in China, formed by hand and consequently not mass-produced like porcelain. It was never exported in quantity, or directly commissioned by Europeans. Indeed, many Yixing teapots that found their way to the West seemed initially to have been intended for a Chinese clientele. A teapot with European silver-gilt mounts is just such a piece (plate 17.5, left). It has a three-line inscription on the base in Chinese characters, recording that it was made in the *dingmao* year of the Tianqi reign (1627) by a potter called Mengchen for the Hall of Friendship. Hui Mengchen was a renowned Yixing potter, and the Hall of Friendship was probably the studio name of one of his clients.[7] The sprig-moulded decoration of *Prunus* branches on both sides of the teapot was a standard Chinese design that was much imitated in Europe.

Yixing objects reached Holland and England in the 1670s. The Dutch soon copied the ware, while in England John Dwight at Fulham obtained a patent in 1684. Dutch silversmith brothers John Philip and David Elers, whose father and uncle were involved in the East India luxury goods trade in London, moved to Britain in the 1680s. After discovering a seam of iron-bearing clay with good casting properties at Bradwell Wood in Staffordshire, they started to make high-quality red stonewares of Yixing type in 1690 and to sell them through David Elers's shop in

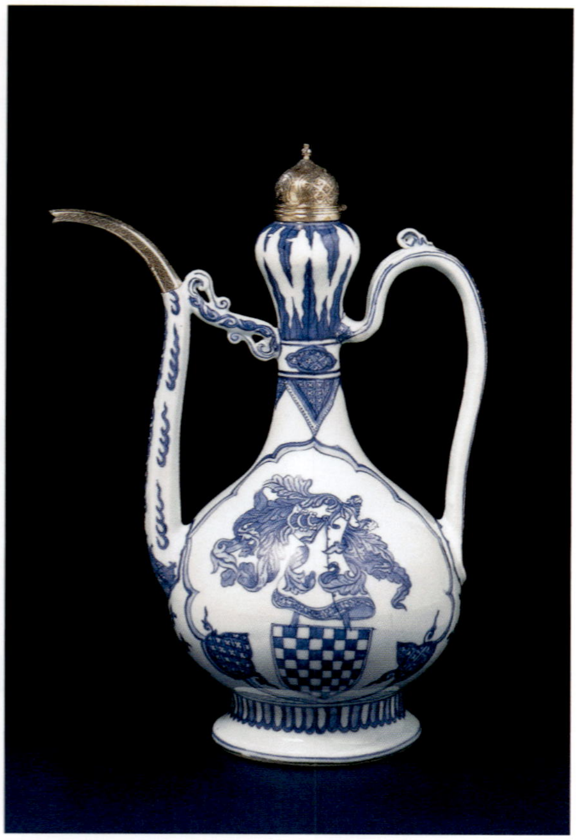

17.3
Ewer with the arms of the Peixoto family
Porcelain, with decoration in underglaze blue; with contemporary silver Persian mounts
China, mark and reign of the emperor Jiajing (1522–66)
V&A: C.222–1931

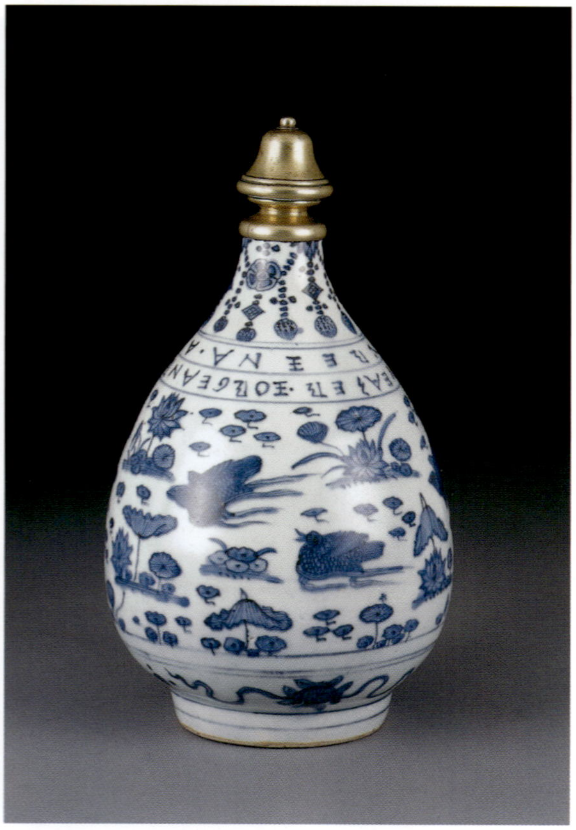

17.4
Bottle with Portuguese inscription
Porcelain, with decoration in underglaze blue
China, 1552
V&A: 237–1892

18

ASIA IN EUROPE: LACQUER FOR THE WEST

Julia Hutt

modelled and carefully painted in brilliant enamel colours. The large figure of a woman in Dutch costume captures both clothing and western features quite accurately (plate 17.13). She may have been modelled from illustrations of Europeans made by Chinese for their own edification, the original information deriving from western prints and engravings.[19]

The comparison of graphic images from Europe and China seems to have been the main purpose behind the commission of a series of rare and beautiful large plaques in the Rijksmuseum, Amsterdam (plate 17.14). Ten porcelain and eight copper plaques are decorated with meticulous artistry to depict scenes copied from western and Chinese prints. The metal plaques are objects known as 'Canton enamels', and as their name suggests were decorated in that southern port through which most European export trade flowed. They must have been part of a special order or orders, for their exquisite quality matches that of copper plaques decorated in enamels with western subjects, which were made as tribute gifts from the authorities in Canton to the imperial court in Peking (Beijing).[20] The Rijksmuseum plaques, however, came from the collection of the Dutch lawyer Jean Theodore Royer (1737–1807), the greatest sinologist of his day. Although he never travelled to China himself, Royer collected objects avidly through a network of contacts among the VOC in Canton. His chief aim in collecting was to document China reliably and clearly, an interest that exemplified the mutual fascination that Europeans and Asians had for one another in the pre-modern period.[21]

European influence was chiefly felt at the apex of Chinese society, at court (see pp. 340–5). Emperors of the late seventeenth and eighteenth centuries played with elements of western adornment, experiencing both wonder and scorn at those oddly dressed and strangely behaved barbarians of the western oceans. Certain western scientific and technological feats were admired and promoted. In the case of porcelain and enamel decoration, this was manifested in the early eighteenth century by the introduction of a new palette of colours in which pink and opaque white predominated.[22] Pink enamel derived from gold had a long history beyond China, and its use was stimulated both by European missionary and diplomatic visits to Peking and by contact with foreigners in Canton.[23]

The effect of western trade on the rest of the vast population of China was negligible. Until the first

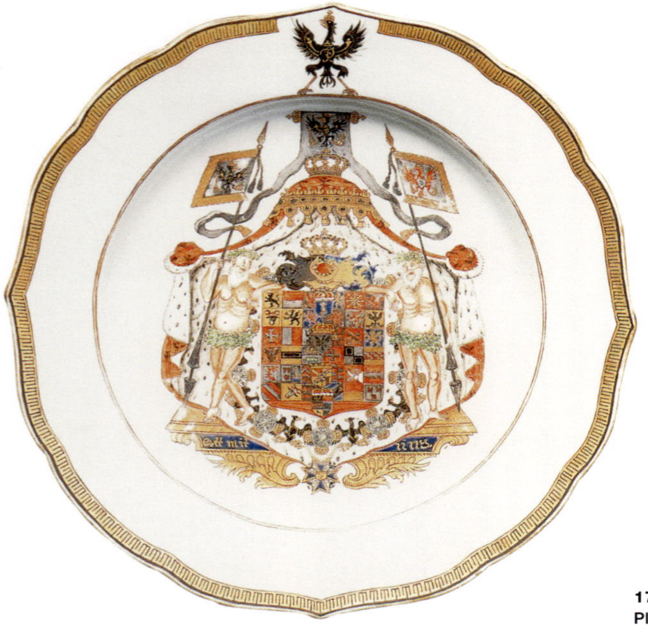

17.10
Plate decorated with the arms of Frederick the Great

Porcelain, decorated with overglaze enamels and gilding
China (made at Jingdezen; decorated at Canton), *c.*1760
V&A: C.73–1963

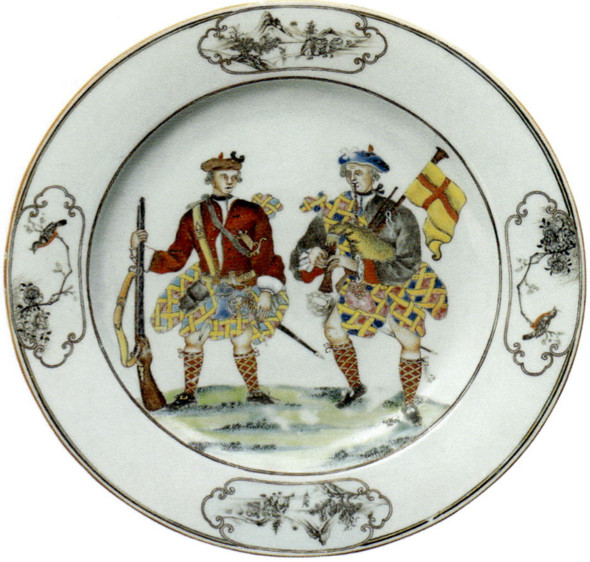

17.11
Plate

Porcelain, decorated in overglaze enamels
China (made at Jingdezen; decorated at Canton), *c.*1745
V&A: C.29–1951

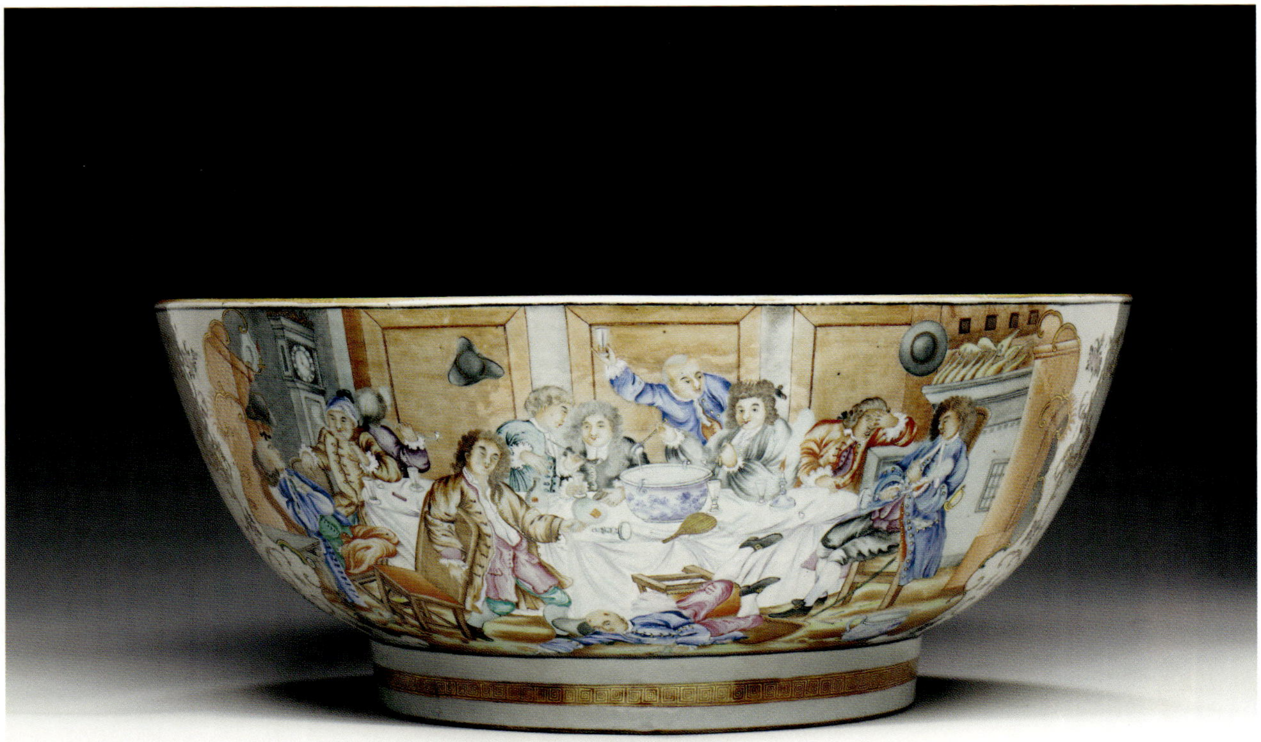

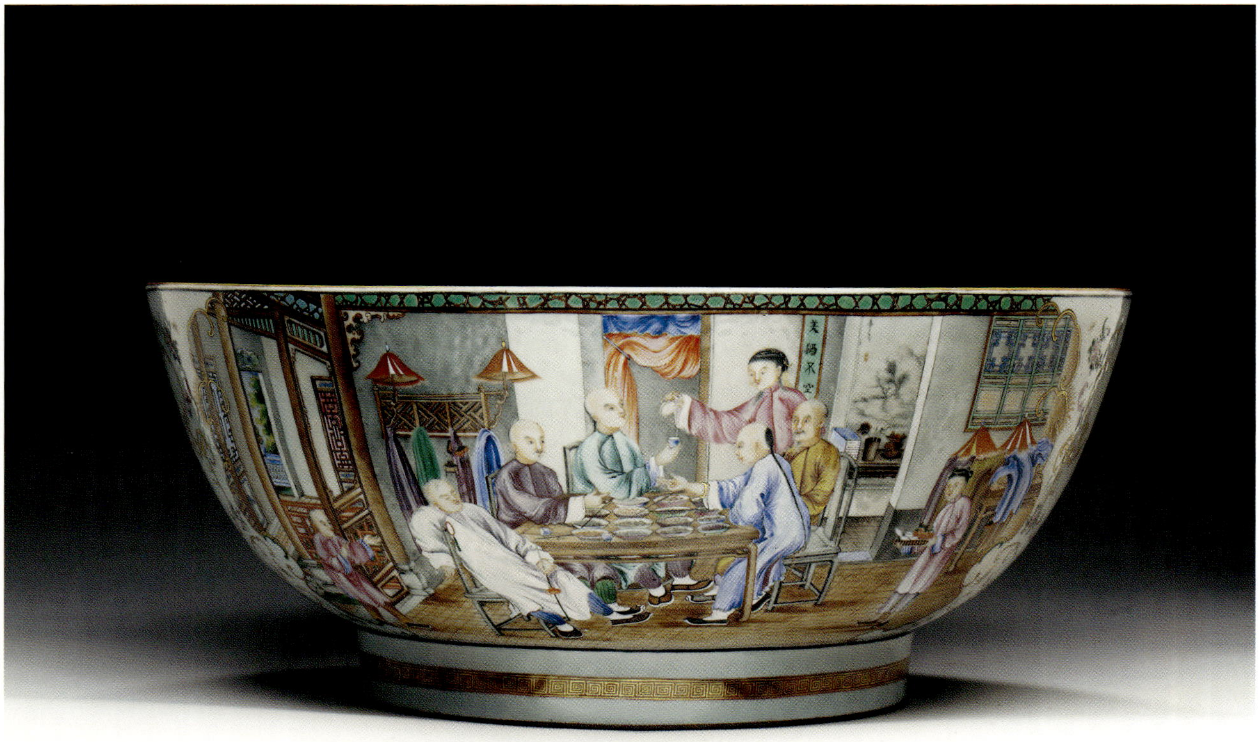

17.12
Punch-bowl

Porcelain, with overglaze enamels and gilding, depicting tavern scenes derived from William Hogarth, *A Midnight Conversation*, 1733, and a Chinese interior screen
China (Jingdezen), 1750–75

Private collection

Opium War of 1840, the official view of trade was that Europeans were tribute bearers, envoys to the Middle Kingdom whose activities on the margins of empire were tolerated because they brought silver to imperial coffers. Foreign trade was strictly controlled and restricted to an enclave in Canton, so that the few Chinese actually affected by western requirements were officials, merchants, decorators at Canton and manufacturers at Jingdezhen. Potters and painters copied directly, often not understanding the patterns they reproduced, as the depiction of Scotsmen in kilts in plate 17.11 shows. At Jingdezhen an experienced workforce was willing to imitate whatever forms foreign trade demanded, for it had been satisfying South-East Asian and Middle Eastern markets for more than 500 years before Europeans arrived. Export porcelain in whatever forms was not deemed useful or attractive, however, as a local scholar called Lan Pu wrote in the late eighteenth century: 'Foreign vessels are specially manufactured for export and sold by merchants in Canton. Foreign devils fill up their markets with them. Their shapes are very odd and every year different designs are wanted.'[24]

At the peak of demand in the eighteenth century in China, and in the mid-seventeenth to mid-eighteenth centuries in Japan, the volume of export ceramics made for Europe led to the opening of new kilns and workshops to satisfy orders. But, as with any trade boom anywhere in the world, retrenchment was necessary when trade declined. No records are available to chart exact patterns of growth and decline, but in both countries the effect was to switch production back to local requirements. European influence disappeared, leaving only scant traces in East Asian product design.

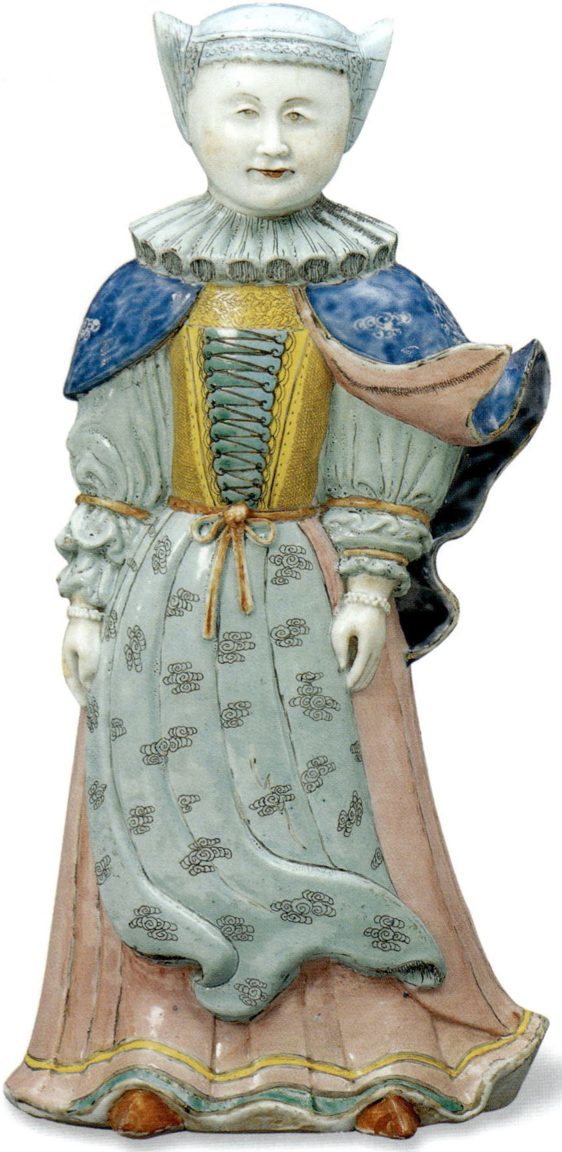

17.13
Figure of a Dutch woman
Porcelain, decorated in overglaze enamels
China, 18th century
V&A: C.94–1963

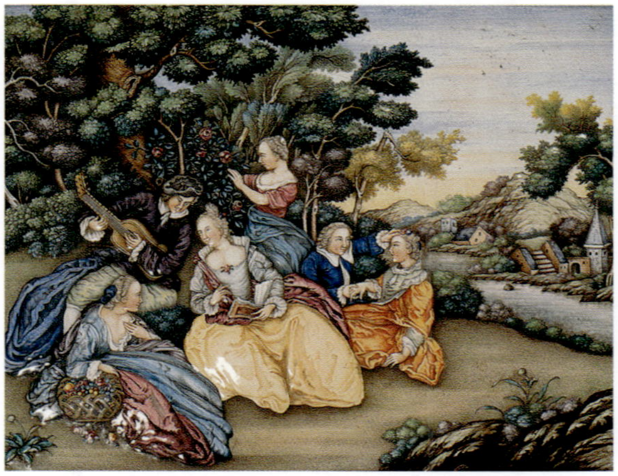

17.14
A European scene derived from Pierre Filloeul, *Le concert amoureux*, 1739
Enamel on copper
China (Canton), 1770–90
Rijksmuseum, Amsterdam

East Asian Metalwork for the Export Market

Greg Irvine

WHEN EUROPEANS ARRIVED in China, the country already possessed a highly evolved tradition of working with precious metals; this had first flowered as early as the Tang dynasty (AD 618–907). In the Early Modern period, deposits of silver and gold drawn from Chinese mines were further enriched by vast quantities of silver specie of Central and South American origin, brought to the country by Europeans who exchanged it for silk, porcelain and tea. The abundance of New World silver and low labour costs meant that in China objects made of precious metals were available at prices that were substantially lower than those in Europe.

The earliest documented piece of Chinese silver brought to the West is a hexagonal teapot, long thought to be English because of its London mark of 1682, which was almost certainly applied when the piece arrived in England (plate 17.18). It is decorated with reserve panels of asymmetric branches of pine, bamboo and plum, motifs that strongly appealed to the contemporary European taste for Oriental designs. In the West such Chinese decoration was copied in various media, including silver, as is evident from the decoration of a small box bearing the London mark 'PD' and an inscription of 1685 indicating that it was a gift from Charles II (r. 1660–85) to his mistress Nell Gywn (1650–87) (plate 17.16).

Surfaces divided into reserve panels with Chinese motifs are also typical of *sawasa*, a form of metalwork made from a copper alloy with black lacquer and fire gilding. The rich contrast of black and gold on *sawasa* objects was much admired by Europeans, who commissioned it for prestige gifts such as sword hangers, hilts and tobacco boxes (plate 17.17). Although originally applied to objects manufactured

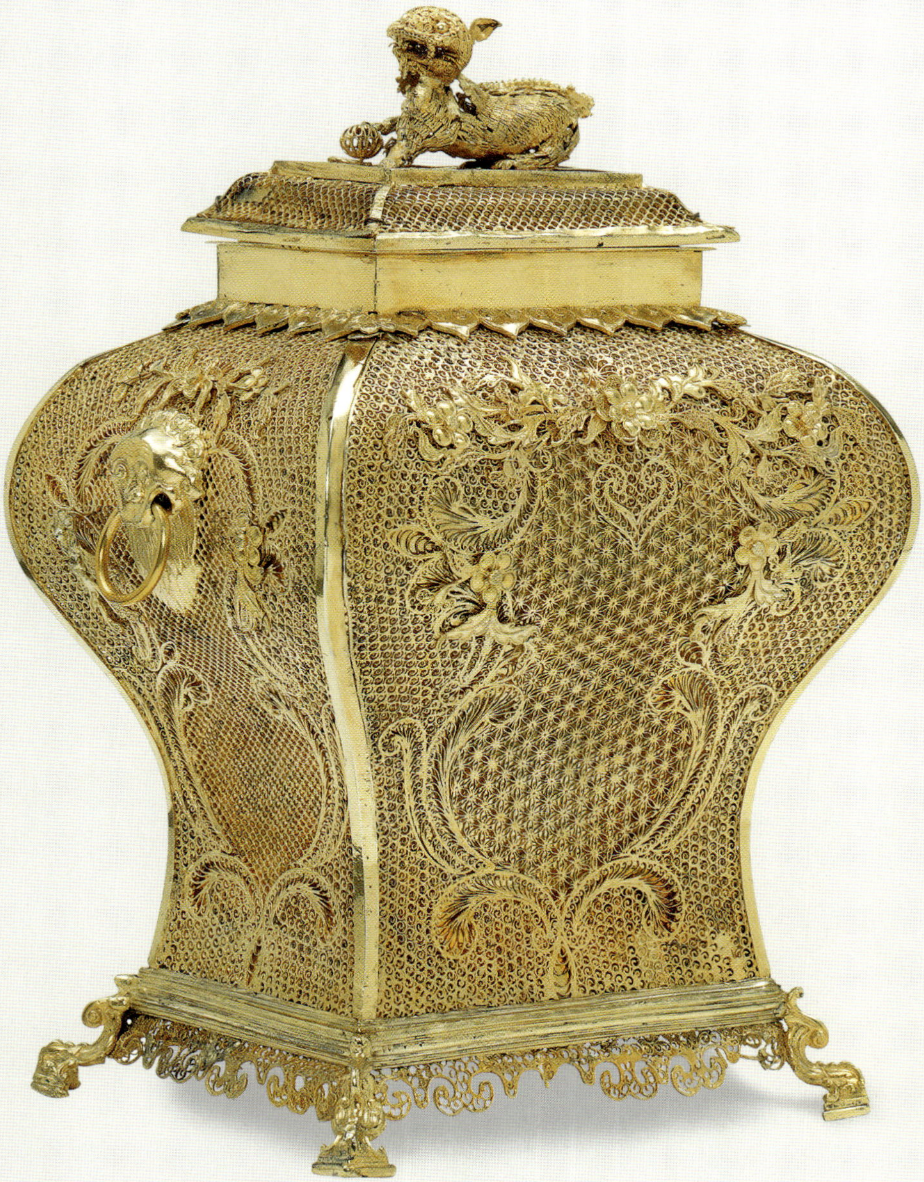

17.15
Tea caddy
Silver-gilt filigree
China (Canton), *c.*1760
V&A: M.114–1919

17.16
Snuff box, with a design derived from Chinese lacquer

Silver, cast and chased, the underside engraved: 'The gift of K Charles 2 to Mrs Gwin. Her son Charles Duke of St. Albans gave this to me Lawrence Answorth 1720 who had then the honour to be head butler to him.'
England, 1670–80

V&A: M.700–1926

17.17
Tobacco box

Sawasa
East Asia, possibly Japan, 18th century

Peabody Essex Museum, Salem

17.18
Teapot

Silver, cast panels with chased and applied decoration
China (probably Canton), c.1679
Sponsor's mark TA and London hallmarks for 1682

Peabody Essex Museum, Salem

in Japan, where it imitated *shakudo* (a gold and copper alloy traditionally used for sword furniture), *sawasa* was eventually produced in Tonkin (north Vietnam), Batavia and possibly even Canton (Guangzhou). Differentiating *sawasa* from these centres is difficult, as is ascertaining the correct origin of another contemporary metalwork technique, filigree, which was also made in different parts of Asia for export. The leading centre of production for such work was Canton, where filigree objects were made out of silver and, less frequently, silver-gilt, in shapes suited for diverse Asian and European markets. A rococo-style tea caddy almost certainly made in Canton epitomizes the skill with which Chinese craftsmen interpreted western forms and decoration in this technique (plate 17.15).

In contrast to these pieces, which were clearly admired for their exotic techniques and ornament, most eighteenth-century silver objects and flatware made in China for export to the West conform so closely to western prototypes that until recently their true origin was not recognized. Today, the pseudo-hallmarks, cast rather than stamped, and the heavier weight of such pieces have helped to identify their Chinese manufacture. It is clear from contemporary accounts that silversmiths in Canton were well provided with western silver designs. According to James Wathen, who visited workshops there in the early nineteenth century, 'articles in silver were well executed, many with English cyphers and coats of arms upon them'.[1] Chinese metalworkers also fashioned western-style objects, especially furniture mounts, from paktong, an alloy of copper, nickel and zinc, which closely resembled silver, but was less expensive and did not tarnish as easily. The material was also imported and worked by silversmiths in the West, including Matthew Boulton (1728–1809), who tried unsuccessfully to produce the alloy.

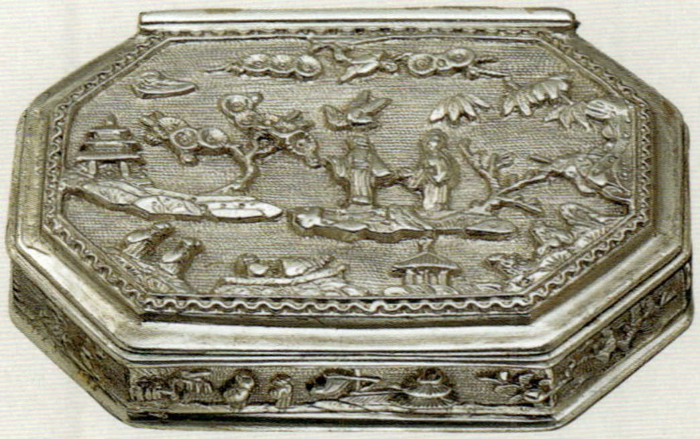

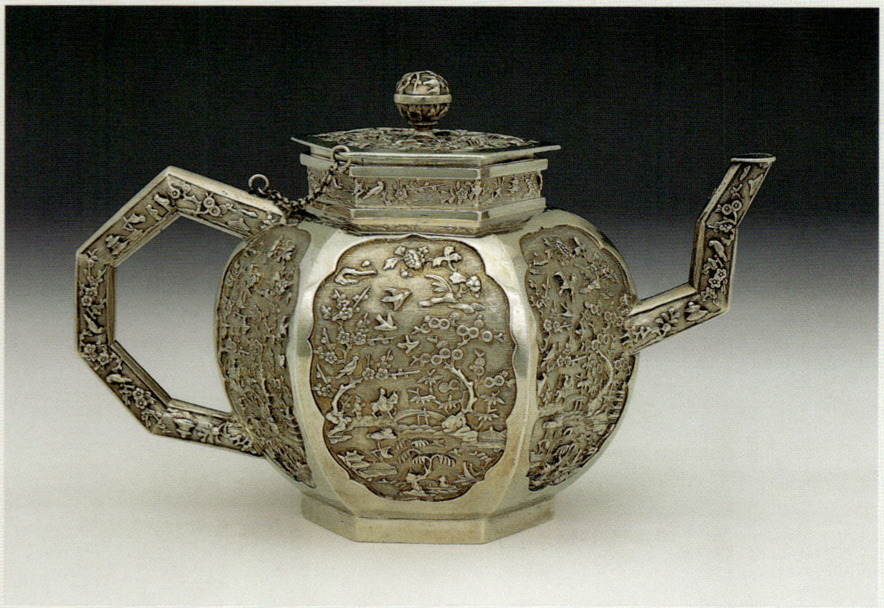

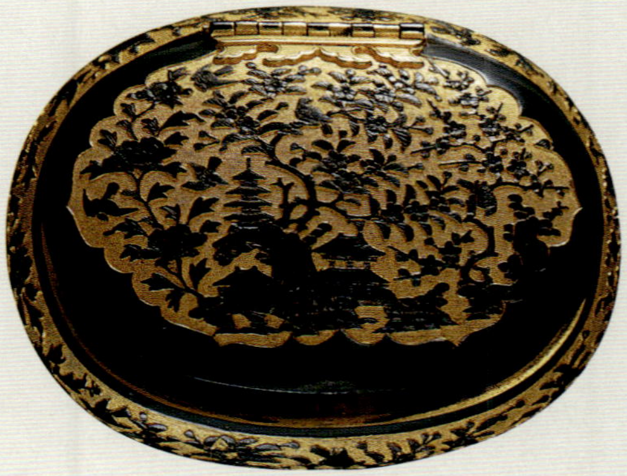

18

ASIA IN EUROPE: LACQUER FOR THE WEST

Julia Hutt

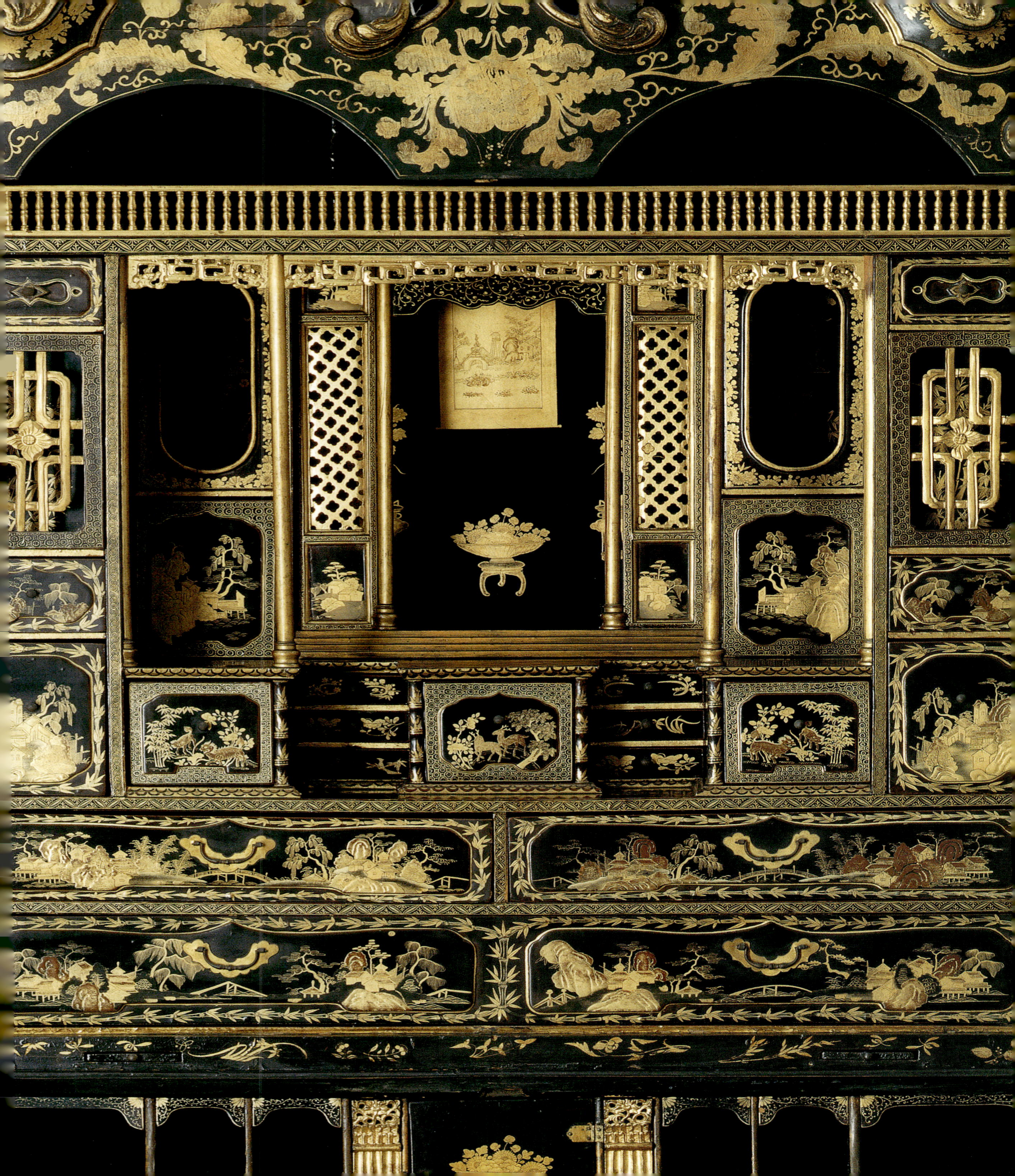

Detail of 18.8 previous page

Lacquer has always played an important part in luxury trade and diplomatic exchange within Asia.[1] Even countries that were renowned for producing high-quality lacquered objects imported examples from elsewhere. True lacquer is the sap from various trees of the *Rhus* genus, the most suitable for art objects being *Rhus vernicifera*. Since this is indigenous throughout China, Japan and Korea, these countries have always occupied a leading role in lacquer production. Other species grow in parts of South-East Asia, giving rise to lacquer-working traditions there: *Gluta usitata* in Thailand and Burma; *Rhus succedanea* in Vietnam; and *Gluta laccifera* in Cambodia. When there was a shortage of raw lacquer in Japan, it was sometimes supplied from Siam and Cambodia.[2] The term 'lacquer' ultimately derives from the Hindustani word *lac*, adopted by the Portuguese as *lacca*. Since lacquer trees are not native to India, there the term *lac* referred to a solid resin that resembled true lacquer, which was secreted by the *Coccus lacca* insect on certain Indian and Indo-Chinese trees. In a dried form, it is known as shellac, a substance that has been used to simulate the effect of lacquer.

Before the European encounter with Asia, lacquer was unknown in the West. Europeans marvelled at this new material, admiring its hardness, lustre and decorative potential.[3] In 1575, for example, the Portuguese Jesuit Father Cosme de Torres wrote, 'the Japanese … produce things with this varnish that resemble shiny smooth leather'.[4] Similarly, of Chinese lacquerwork, Father Jean-Baptiste du Halde (d. 1743) wrote in 1735 that polished black lacquer 'resembles a looking-glass'.[5] Chinese and Japanese lacquered objects first arrived in Europe as individual items of exotica. It was not until after the Portuguese reached Japan in 1543 that organized trade of lacquerware with Europe began. While the Portuguese dominated this trade during the sixteenth century, the Dutch took over thereafter, sharing the trade in Japanese export lacquer with the Chinese. Even at the height of the Dutch trade with Japan, however, lacquer exports were always secondary in importance to porcelain, for although they were highly prized, they consisted mostly of large objects that were not profitable given the proportion of cargo space needed for transport. The Dutch East India Company (VOC) records for 1664, for example, state that roughly 45,000 pieces of porcelain were exported, compared to only 101 items of Japanese lacquerware.[6]

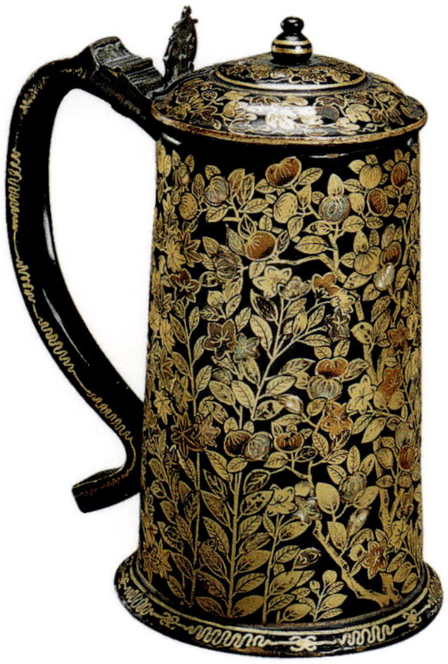

18.1
Tankard

Wood, covered in black lacquer with gold *hiramakie*, inlaid with mother-of-pearl
Japan, late 16th–early 17th century

V&A: FE.23–1982

The early phase of Japanese export lacquerwork for European markets is generally termed *nanban* (literally 'southern barbarian'). Even though this term is widely used in other contexts, it is convenient for referring to lacquerwork made at the time when Portuguese influence was paramount in Japan and to the style that continued for a short time afterwards. *Nanban* lacquerware is likely to have been made as early as the 1570s, but the first example known to have reached Europe is a cabinet, now in Schloss Ambras, near Innsbruck, which was inventoried in 1596 as part of the collection of Ferdinand II of Tyrol (r. 1564–95), to whom it was probably given by his Iberian relations (see pp. 40–4). Rather than supplying the Portuguese with items in Japanese taste, lacquer craftsmen evolved a style of decoration they considered appropriate for Westerners. This *nanban* lacquerwork was in a hybrid style that combined western forms with decoration derived from both foreign and Japanese traditions. The majority of these pieces were domed coffers and cabinets, initially of the fall-fronted type (plate 18.2; see plate 19.2). These gave way to cabinets with doors that were hinged at the sides. That such pieces differed from indigenous Japanese furniture is apparent in the lack of appropriate terminology, resulting in such made-up terms as *kanabokogata* ('boxes in fish-sausage shape') to describe a coffer. Other forms included cups, dishes, tankards, and sets of basins and ewers, shaving basins, tables and backgammon boards (plate 18.1). Although finished *nanban* lacquerwork looked impressive, by Japanese standards it was made with comparatively little time and care, particularly in the preparation of the base layers. This often involved such shortcuts as omitting the textile layer on the base or edges of an object, and using relatively simple lacquer techniques, such as *hiramakie* ('flat sprinkled picture').[7]

Nanban lacquerwork is characterized by gold *makie* on a black lacquer ground, inlaid with a profusion of somewhat thick pieces of mother-of-pearl shell, either precisely or crudely cut to shape (plate 18.1; plate 8.14). Although Japanese lacquer has a long history of inlaid shell work, the extensive use of mother-of-pearl on *nanban* wares owes more to Chinese traditions of the Yuan (1279–1368) and Ming (1368–1644) dynasties, as well as to those from the late Koryō dynasty (918–1392) onwards in Korea. These were combined with Indian decorative elements, such as inlaying wood with ivory and exotic woods, and decorating surfaces with plaques

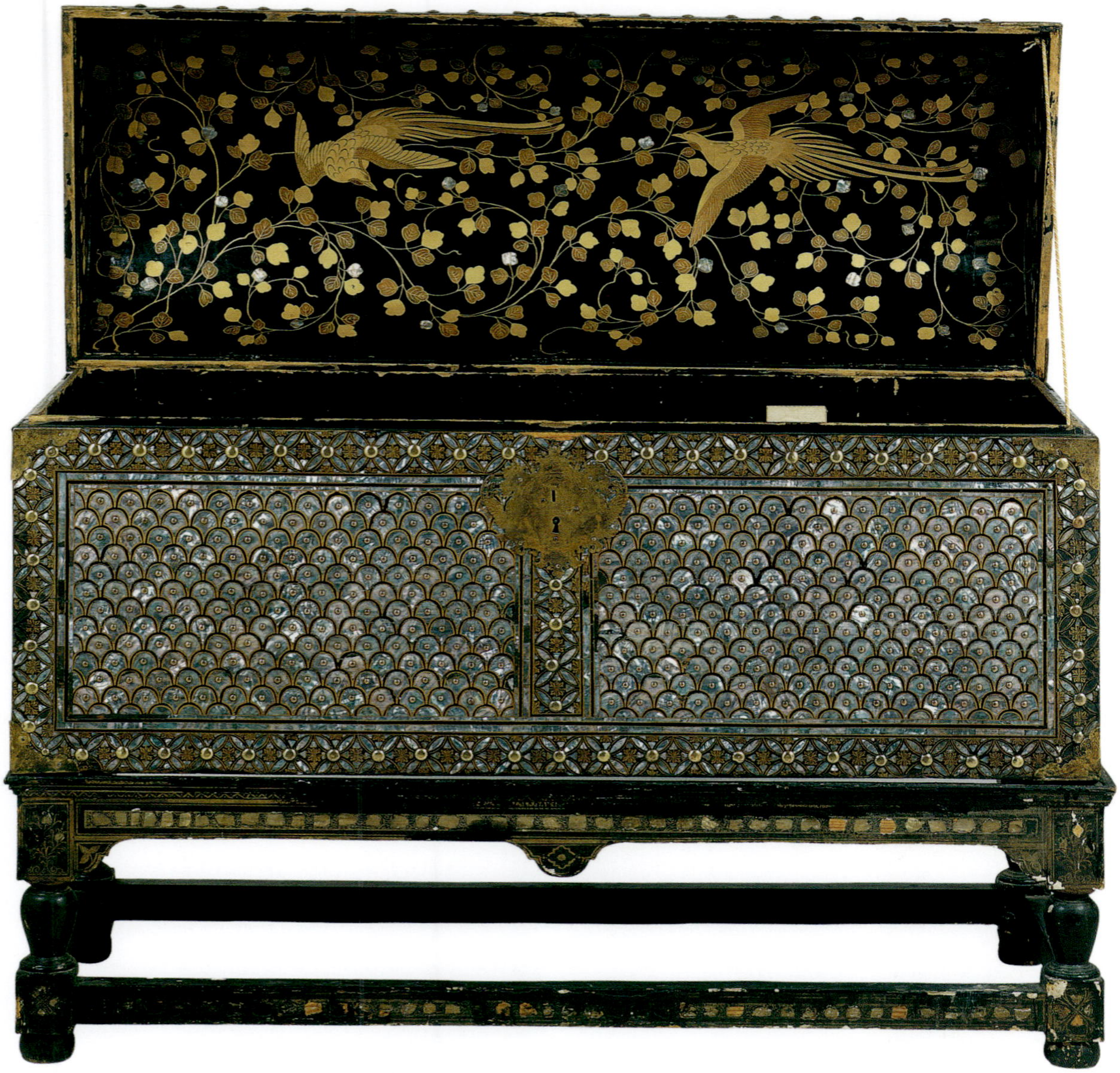

18.2
Domed coffer

Wood, covered with plates of mother-of-pearl held by gilded copper rivets; and black and gold *hiramakie* lacquer
Japan, late 16th–early 17th century

V&A: FE.33–1983

of mother-of-pearl, techniques practised in Gujarat and Sindh, whose ports were regularly visited by Portuguese vessels (see plate 19.1).

The most striking feature of *nanban* lacquerware is decoration that covers the entire surface of the exterior. This was commonly in the form of geometric designs or trees, plants and flowers, with occasional birds, animals and, more rarely, human figures.[8] Cartouches were frequently used, often enclosing a pictorial scene and set against a contrasting geometric ground. The distinctive ogival cartouche so common on *nanban* lacquerware appears to have originated in China. The earliest consistent use of this motif is on a group of eight lacquer *sutra* caskets, datable to the early fourteenth century, all but one of which are in Japanese collections.[9] This *horror vacui*, undoubtedly the result of influences from Chinese, Indian and Islamic art, is totally alien to Japanese aesthetics. Also contrary to the conventions of Japanese art history is the extensive use of decorative borders, such as the key fret, zigzag, dog-tooth, chequered pattern and, in particular, the distinctive '*nanban* scroll'.[10] This practice undoubtedly derived from Chinese ceramics and had an influence on Japanese lacquer and ceramics made for export.

It is widely accepted that when lacquerware first reached Europe in bulk, it met with immediate and wholesale approbation. A recent analysis of VOC

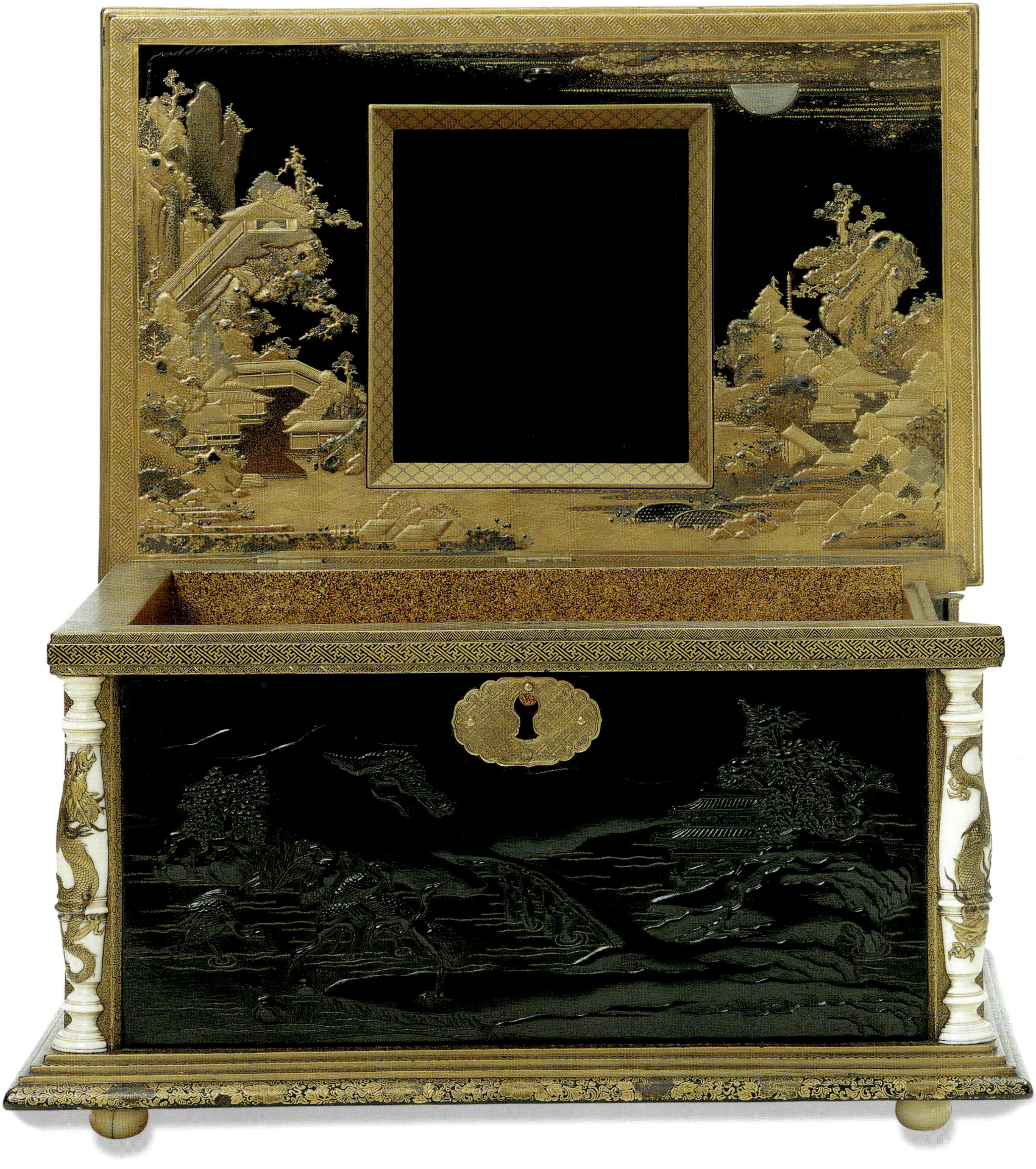

records, however, suggests that this was only partly true. While lacquerware appears to have triggered something of a fashion in much of Europe, in Holland caution was expressed as to its saleability.[11] Such anxiety was confirmed when various items failed to sell at auction in 1614, causing the governors of the VOC to order the Japanese factory to send no further lacquerwork.[12] Since orders took at least two years to be fulfilled, items of lacquer continued to arrive until 1618, after which lacquerwork was not commissioned again until 1634. The reason for this was partly that *nanban* lacquerware was primarily in Portuguese (and Spanish) taste, and partly that it was too expensive.

What was it that stimulated the Dutch demand for lacquerwork once again in the early 1630s? The answer seems to lie in a small group of high-quality pieces that were specially commissioned in a completely different style.[13] Although these continued to use geometric borders and ogival cartouches, their narrative decoration derived from the eleventh-century classic of Japanese literature, *Genji monogatari* (*The Tale of Genji*), and was carried out in complex and expensive lacquer techniques, such as *takamakie* ('high sprinkled picture'). The objects themselves include flat-topped chests and caskets based on Renaissance forms (plate 18.3). Two of these wares are boxes associated with VOC officials, Philips Lucasz, who was the director-general from 1635 to 1639, and Anton van Diemen (1593–1645), who was governor-general of the Dutch East Indies from 1636 to 1645 (plate 18.6).[14] One of the boxes is inscribed with the name of Pieternella Buys, the maiden name of Lucasz's wife, and thus was likely to have been ordered before the couple were actually married in 1634. The other is inscribed with the name of van Diemen's wife, Maria. It is worth noting that craftsmen unfamiliar with the western alphabet and Dutch names misspelled Pieternella's name as Pieternallae, while van Diemen was spelt as Uan Diemen. Since this full name involved three parts, help was given to the lacquerers in correctly spacing it by the addition of commas. That these were copied onto the finished article shows a complete misunderstanding of their purpose.[15] An additional piece in the same style, a small wedding casket, was quite possibly also commissioned for Lucasz's wedding in 1634.[16]

Significantly, both the van Diemen and Buys boxes are in a Japanese form, decorated in a style closer to domestic Japanese wares. This might well suggest that they were commissioned by Japanese officials for

18.3 opposite
Casket
Wood, covered in black lacquer, and ivory, with gold *hiramakie* and *takamakie* lacquer, and gold and silver details
Japan, 1630s
V&A: 628–1868

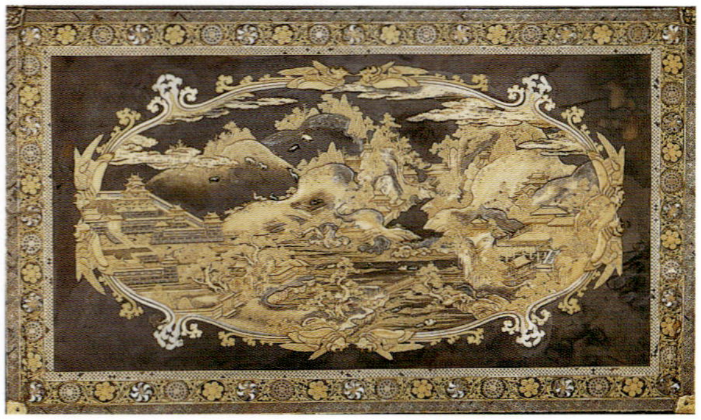

18.4 left, above
The Mazarin Chest (top)
Wood, covered in black lacquer with gold and silver *hiramakie* and *takamakie* lacquer; details in gold, silver and *shibuichi*; gilded *shakudō* fittings
Japan, *c.*1630s
V&A: 412–1882

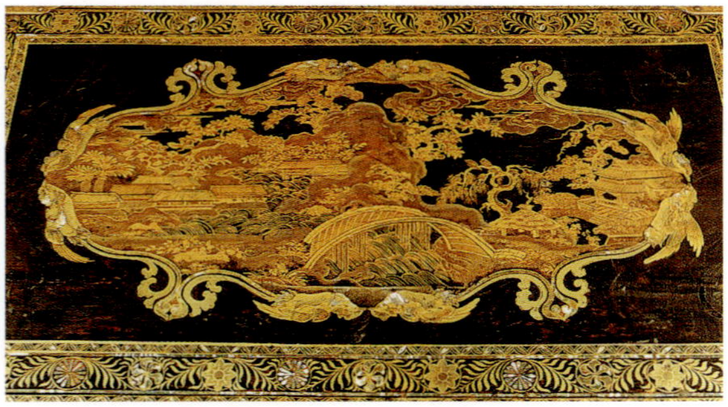

18.5 left below
The Charlottenburg Cabinet (top)
Wood, covered in black lacquer with gold *hiramakie* lacquer
Japan, *c.*1630s
Charlottenburg Palace, Berlin

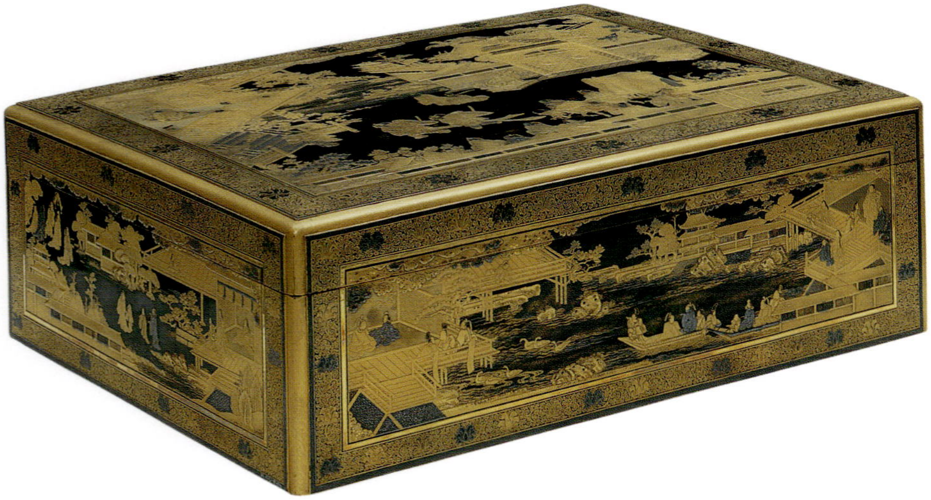

18.6 below
The Van Diemen Box
Wood, covered in black lacquer with gold, silver and red *hiramakie* and *takamakie* lacquer, and gold and silver details
Japan, 1636–39
V&A: W.49–1916

18.7
Cabinet

Wood, covered in black lacquer, with coloured and incised lacquer decoration
China, *c.*1700; stand: English, *c.*1800

V&A: FE.39–1981

their Dutch counterparts. It is likely, moreover, that certain Dutch officials had already seen high-quality domestic wares and found them to their liking. It may well have suited them to associate themselves with a different manner of decoration that was distinct from the *nanban*, or Portuguese style. It is worth noting, however, that not all items from this group were of exceptional quality. The Charlottenburg cabinet (plate 18.5), and dismembered panels from another related chest in the V&A,[17] for example, are stylistically very close to the Lawrence and Mazarin chests (plate 18.4), two very similar chests subsequently named after the collections to which they belonged.[18] Although obviously from the same workshop, the former are of lesser quality than the Lawrence and Mazarin chests. Since objects decorated in this style were only produced for around 10 years, it is possibly more appropriate to call this a 'transitional' group of lacquerwork, rather than 'high-quality' or 'fine', as has become common practice.

Although the transitional group existed alongside *nanban* wares, the latter waned in importance, ultimately disappearing altogether by the late 1630s, around the time of the expulsion of the Portuguese from Japan. Executing high-quality lacquer of the type seen on the transitional group was prohibitively expensive and unsustainable for trade goods. These wares were succeeded by a more realistic version, in which the use of borders and mother-of-pearl began to diminish, until they disappeared altogether, and the technique of *takamakie* was employed to provide height and visual variety. As the seventeenth century progressed, the decoration became increasingly sparse and asymmetric. Could this simpler style have been a response to increasing demands by the Dutch to reduce costs? From 1685 onwards, Dutch officials and Japanese middle-men were constantly haggling over the prices of lacquerwork. The Japanese tried to reduce costs as far as possible, but ultimately were unwilling to sacrifice their craft any further. As a result there are no orders for lacquerware after 1693, when the official trade of lacquerware with Japan effectively ceased. A limited number of small items, however, continued to be carried by officials and sailors as permitted personal trade. It was not until 1733 that the VOC started to buy lacquerware from China, continuing sporadically until 1763. It should be remembered that even after 1639, when the Dutch were the only Europeans permitted to remain in Japan, the Chinese continued trading there on far more advantageous terms, supplying the bulk of Japanese lacquerware to the rest of Asia and Europe.

During the seventeenth and eighteenth centuries China also produced distinctive lacquerwork that was largely associated with the export market, but which – unlike that of Japan – was also made for domestic consumption (see plate 16.6). *Kuan cai* (engraved polychrome) in Chinese, it was referred to as 'Bantam ware' in England, after the South-East Asian port through which it was shipped. At a later date the distinctive wares were exported to Europe from India's Coromandel coast, from which they acquired the name 'Coromandel' in France, a term that subsequently became widespread in England. Coromandel lacquerwork was formed by covering a wooden base with a mixture of brick dust, pig's blood and raw lacquer a few millimetres thick on a whitish foundation of clay.[19] Layers of black or brown lacquer were then applied, into which the design was cut intaglio until the white layers were revealed; the surface was further enriched by applying coloured lacquer or oil paint. Coromandel lacquerwork made for the export market was predominantly in the form of multi-leafed screens and cabinets (plate 18.7).[20] During the last quarter of the seventeenth century, Coromandel lacquerwork had become a familiar luxury in England. By 1688, however, it was recorded that Bantam work was 'now almost obsolete, and out of fashion'.[21]

Although both Chinese and Japanese lacquerware was well known throughout Asia, the latter was considered far superior, a sentiment echoed by several contemporary western observers. In 1575, for example, Father Cosme de Torres wrote of lacquering: 'of all the nations, the Japanese are outstanding in this art'.[22] Similarly in 1699 East India Company instructions specified that 'None of the wares are to be sent but what are lacquered in Japan.'[23] Since the VOC had ceased bulk-trading in Japanese lacquerware, the Chinese began to imitate the Japanese black-and-gold work that was in such demand throughout Asia and Europe. As with its seventeenth-century Japanese prototypes, Chinese black-and-gold export lacquerwork mainly depicted landscapes, surrounded by decorative borders, in the form of geometric designs, scrolls and stylized flower heads, sometimes resembling Japanese family crests (*mon*). Chinese painted and sprinkled gold lacquerwork can be distinguished from Japanese *makie* by the uniform size and type of gold powder, which results in a somewhat dull and regular appearance. Western forms were again most

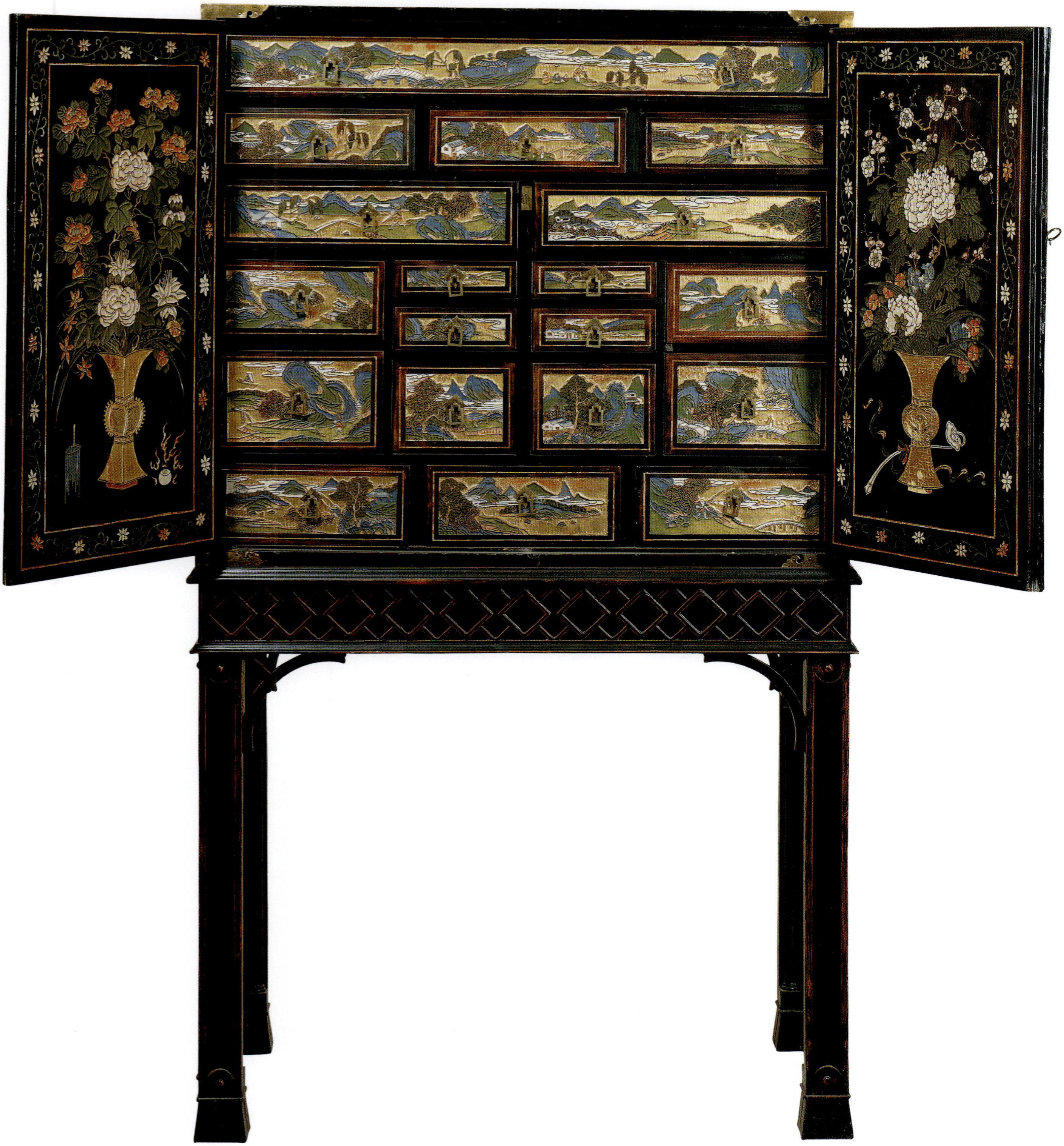

18.8
Bureau-cabinet

Wood, covered in black lacquer with gold lacquer decoration
China, c.1730

V&A: W.28–1935

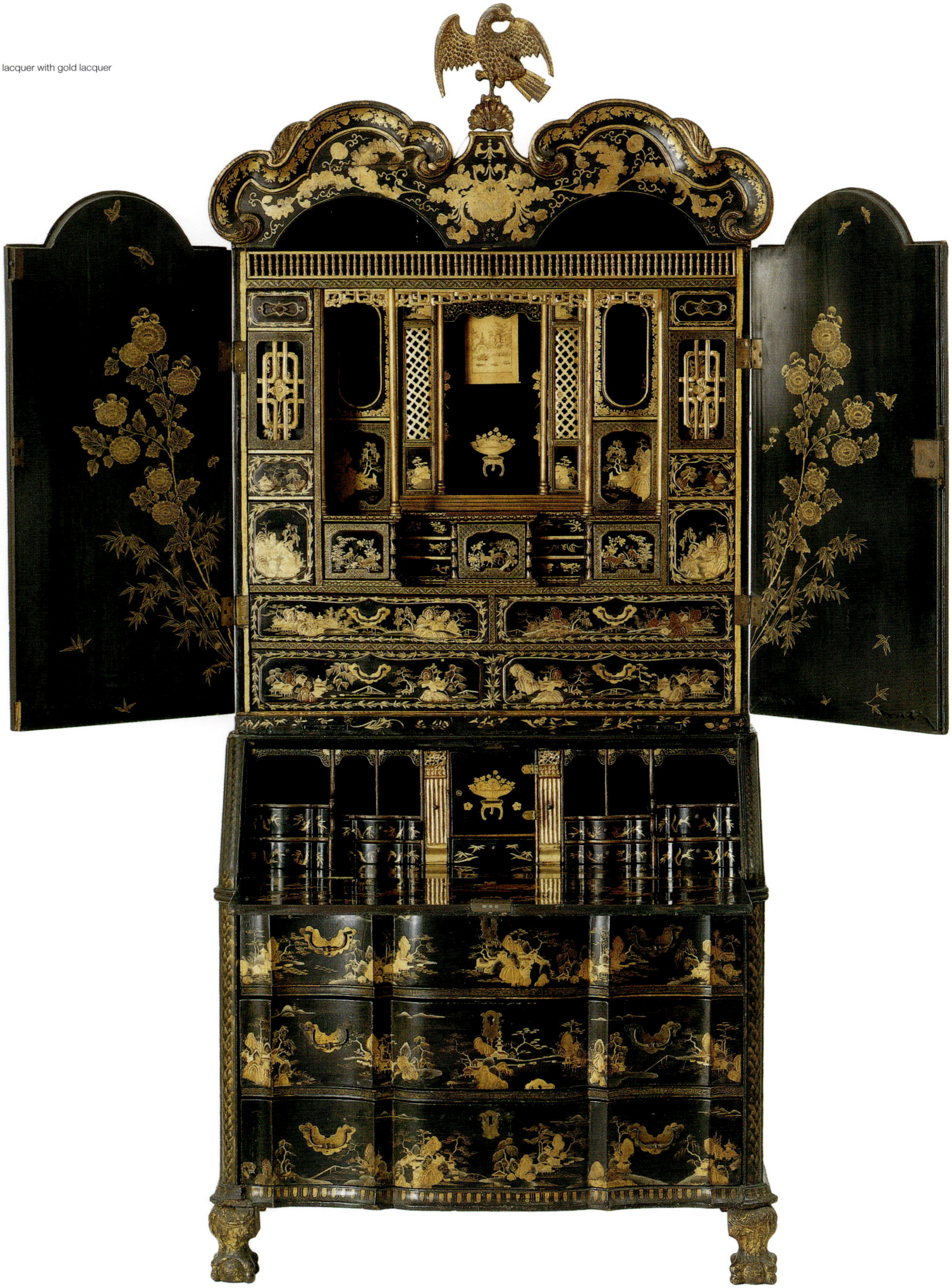

common, with items of furniture being manufactured to the latest fashions (plate 18.8). An interesting Chinese stepped toilet glass for export is clearly influenced by stylistic elements of Japanese striped lacquerwork of more than 100 years earlier (plate 18.10)[24] This is cleverly combined with the distinctive diagonal line that was used on Kōdaiji wares to separate two contrasting areas, suggesting familiarity with Japanese originals.[25] Although the lacquer decoration on the toilet glass is of a high quality, on the whole the mass-produced lacquerware in eighteenth-century Canton (Guangzhou) had earned the port a reputation for inferior goods made in haste. Since ships were reliant on trade winds, they were in port for insufficient time to allow craftsmen to perfect high-quality lacquer decoration. As du Halde pointed out in 1755, 'It is very uncommon for the Chinese to have any [lacquerware] beforehand, or that has lain for some time, for they almost always wait for the arrival of ships before they begin, that they may conform to the taste of the Europeans.'[26]

Lacquerware from Japan and China was regularly being imported into England by the second half of the seventeenth century. In 1661, for example, Samuel Pepys (1633–1703) wrote in his diary that he saw in the Duke of York's closet 'two very fine chests covered with gold and Indian varnish, given him by the East India Company of Holland'.[27] Nearly two decades later, in 1679, John Evelyn (1620–1706) dined at the Portuguese ambassador's house, where he saw 'costly furniture belonging to the *Ambassador*, especially the rich *Jopon Cabinets* of which I think there were a dosen'.[28] By 1698 the seventeenth-century English economist John Pollexfen noted, 'From the greatest gallants to the meanest cookmaids nothing was thought so fit to adorn their … closets like China and lacquered ware.'[29]

Eighteenth-century Europe witnessed the emergence of important lacquer collectors, particularly in France, where figures such as Madame de Pompadour (1721–64) and Marie Antoinette (1755–93) developed a taste for Japanese lacquer, not only of the type made for export, but also the extremely fine lacquer produced for domestic consumption. These objects were sometimes mounted to suit European tastes (plate 18.9). At this time only a few items of Japanese lacquerwork reached Europe, yet the lacquer craze continued unabated. To make up the shortfall, earlier items of lacquerwork, whether in poor disrepair or not, were frequently cut up and reused, often as panels in furniture (plate 18.11). Europeans also met the demand for lacquer by imitating it. As lacquer trees did not grow in the West, the only answer was to try and reproduce lacquer artificially, using high-gloss varnishes (plate 18.13). Although Japanese lacquerware started to reach Europe in significant quantities via the Portuguese, it was Dutch rather than Portuguese or Spanish craftsmen who first attempted to simulate it. In 1609, a year before the first recorded shipment of VOC lacquerware arrived in Holland, William Kick is noted as making japanned furniture. The quality of his work was such that, in 1612, a chest from his workshop was presented to the Sultan of Turkey along with genuine Asian lacquerwork.[30] Similarly in England the arrival of the first ship with lacquerwork in 1614 inspired craftsmen to copy the technique.[31] It was not until

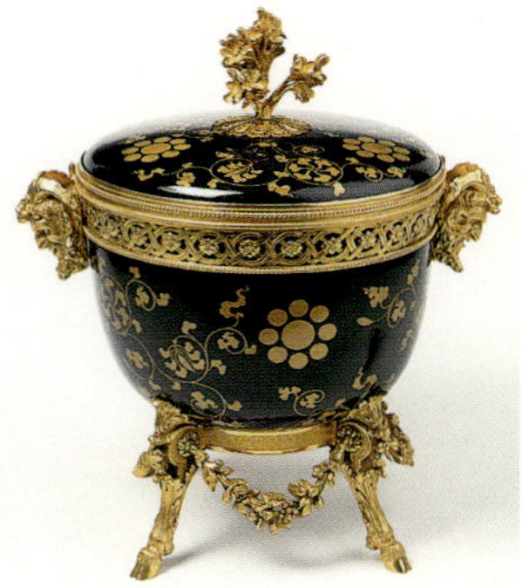

18.9
Pot-pourri holder

Composed of a rice bowl and cover with later feet and decorative mounts
Wood, covered in black lacquer, with gold *hiramakie* lacquer and ormolu mounts
Bowl: Japan, late 17th century; mounts: France, mid-18th century

V&A: 158–1879

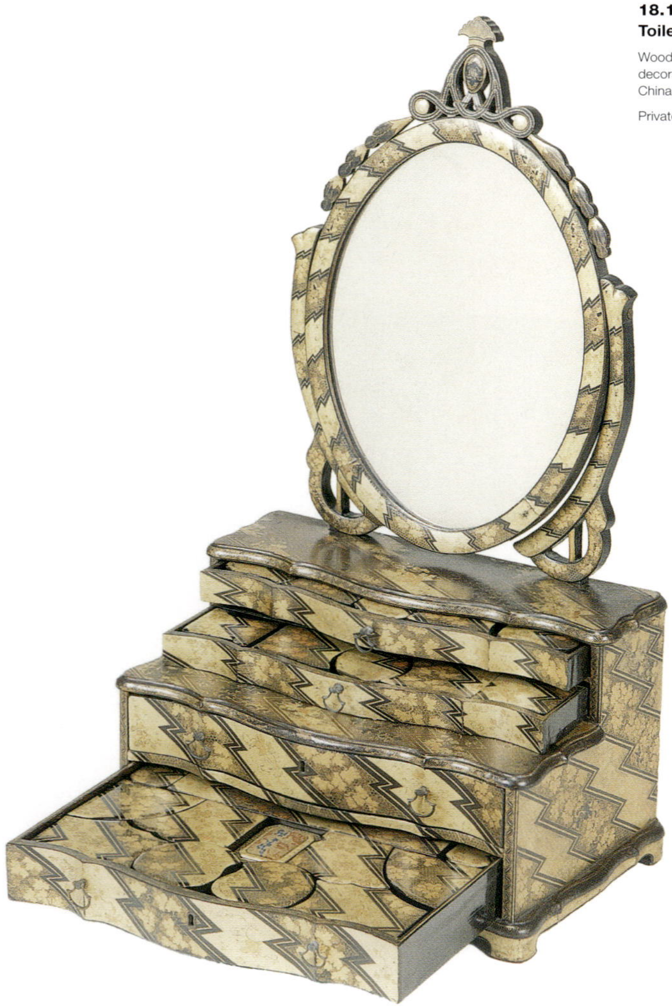

18.10
Toilet glass

Wood, covered in black lacquer with gold lacquer decoration
China, *c.*1790

Private collection, Boston

1688, however, that practical advice became available to aspiring craftsmen in the form of *A Treatise on Japanning and Varnishing* by John Stalker and George Parker. This work provided recipes for a lacquer substitute based mostly on sandarac (a natural resin from the sandarac tree),[32] together with designs considered suitable for their decoration.[33] But it was not until the publication of *Trattato Sopra la Vernice* by Father Filippo Bonanni in 1720 that the constituents of lacquer were correctly identified. He also realized the practical limitations of acquiring and working with lacquer in Europe, recommending instead the use of substitutes. Throughout Europe, the main centres of early japanning evolved around collections of East Asian lacquerware. This is exemplified by the collection of Japanese lacquerware in the Royal Danish Kunstkammer, while the Rosenborg Castle in Copenhagen has the oldest surviving 'lacquered' room, dating from between 1663 and 1665.[34]

Whereas most of the lacquerwork that reached the West originated in Japan and China, the technique was also used in other parts of Asia, though identifying it is problematic. In the 1690s, for example, Engelbert Kaempfer (1651–1716), the Dutch physician, wrote that 'The Chinese and Tonguinese [Vietnamese], with all their care and industry, never came up to that skill and dexterity which the Japanese have in composition of their varnish, as well as in the laying of it on.'[35] Despite several references of this type, it has been impossible to identify Tonkinese lacquerwork. Was the workmanship so fine that it has been mistaken for Chinese or Japanese, or has it simply perished in humid summers? In the case of South Asian lacquerwork, there are more surviving objects, though their provenance is difficult to prove. In general, true lacquer was not produced in India, since trees of the *Rhus* genus are not native to the area. At the beginning of the twentieth century, however, lacquer trees of the *Gluta usitata* species grew at Manipuri, Assam, while the manufacture of lacquered objects in the region suggests that an earlier lacquer industry might have existed.[36] This manufacture may well have been influenced by nearby Burma, where there was a flourishing lacquer industry similarly based on *Gluta usitata*.

Further evidence for the production of lacquerwork in India is provided by a group of objects that have common characteristics. They are predominantly in the form of boxes or large lidded

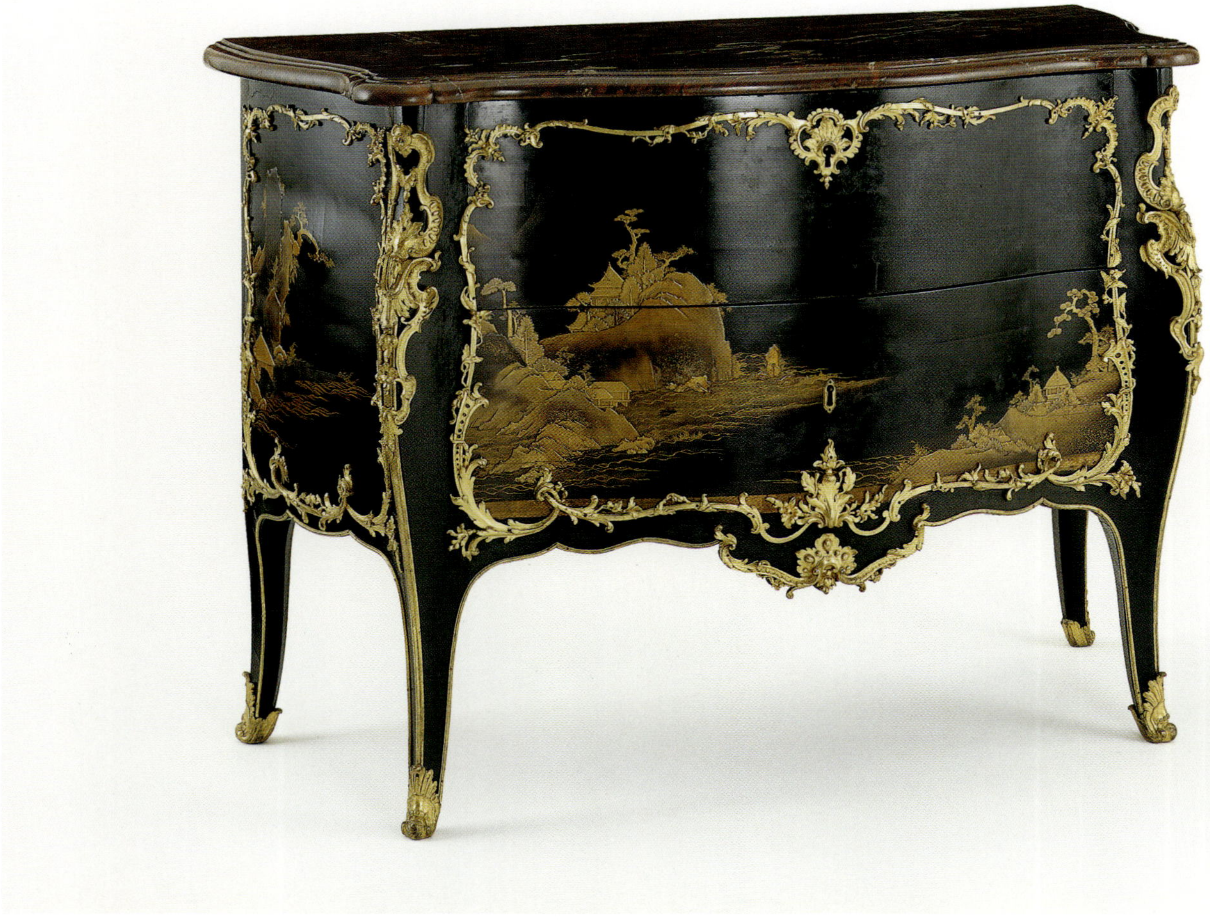

18.11
Commode

Wood, veneered with panels of black lacquer and gold *hiramakie* lacquer decoration, with ormulu mounts
France, 1755–65; lacquer: Japan, late 17th century

V&A: 1105–1882

chests with drawers, which were made for the European – probably Portuguese – market during the second half of the sixteenth and early seventeenth centuries (plate 18.12).[37] The main characteristics of this group are objects with low-relief carving, lacquering and gilding, though some are of plain angely-wood (*Artocarpus hirsutus*), with or without black lacquer. Some interiors are decorated in gold on black lacquer, resembling Burmese lacquerwork, while others reveal gold on red, which bear striking similarities to Chinese lacquerwork.[38] The close similarity of these Indian examples to the *hakue* (gold-leaf picture) technique of Ryūkyūan lacquerware is explained by the close contact between China and the Ryūkyū Islands during the fifteenth and sixteenth centuries. Objects of this group as a whole reveal hybrid influences, in techniques, materials, subjects and designs, from Europe, Asia and the Islamic worlds. Of those pieces that have been analysed, the lacquer is *Gluta usitata*, which was used in Thailand and Burma, but there is no evidence to suggest they were made in either country, while this type of lacquer has known connections with Assam. The wood carved in low relief, moreover, suggests an affinity to carving traditions of India.[39] Recently, the Bay of Bengal and the Coromandel coast have been proposed as their place of manufacture.[40] The evidence, however, is inconclusive. It would seem highly likely that these objects were made at some, as yet, unidentified part of South Asia, though variation between the groups suggests different workshops. The other unanswered question is whether they were made by Chinese or Japanese lacquerers working in South Asia or whether, like *nanban* lacquerwork, the objects were made in a hybrid style on the basis of some of the many foreign influences in India at the time.

Similarly there are other items of lacquerware that cannot be securely attributed, such as the four pairs of basins with jugs in the form of elephants in the National Museum of Denmark, which were first mentioned in Danish records in 1689 (plate 18.14).[41] Sets of ewers and basins were made in the *nanban* style for washing hands in between courses at mealtimes, a custom common both in Europe and the Islamic world. The provenance of the four Danish sets is by no means clear, though it was generally assumed that they were made in India and sent to Japan to be decorated. The basins, however, are decorated in a pseudo-Japanese style, with the

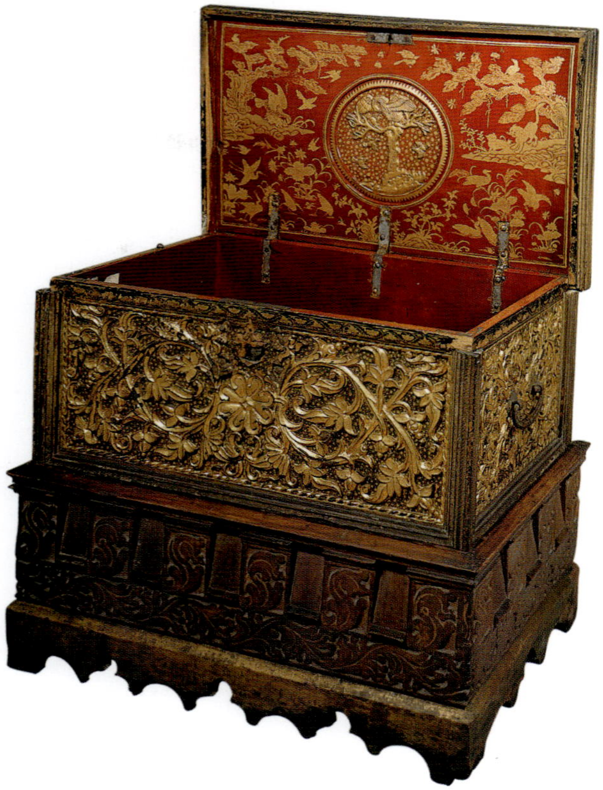

18.12
Pope's Chest
Wood, carved, lacquered, gilded and with gold lacquer decoration
South Asia, late 16th–early 17th century
Museen des Mobilendepots, Vienna (Frazenburg Laxenburg), inv. no. MD 047590

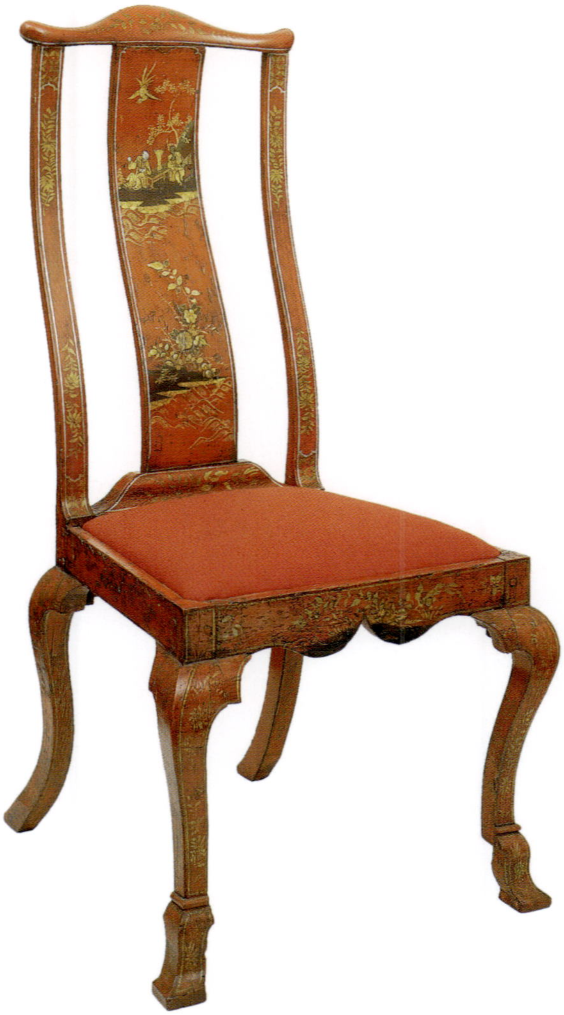

18.13
Side chair
Beechwood, japanned in red with green and gold decoration
England, *c.* 1700
V&A: W.44–1938

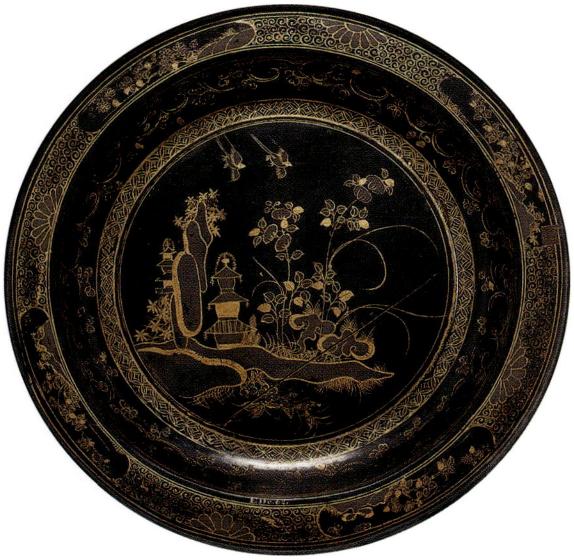

18.14
Ewer and basin, from a set of four pairs
Wood, covered in black lacquer with gold lacquer decoration
India, mid-17th century
National Museum, Copenhagen: Edc64a&b

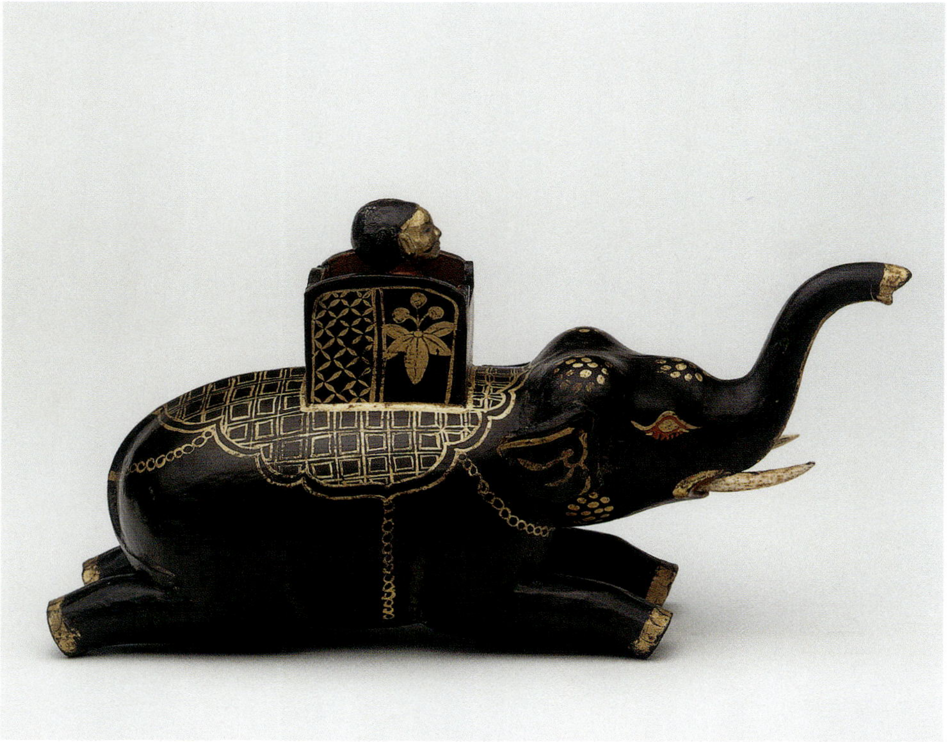

decoration of certain border motifs and howdahs on the elephants suggesting mock *mon*. It is with the Chinese interpretation of the Japanese export style, however, that they have most in common. The fact that details of the central design are quite crude, and suggest that the lacquerer was executing designs in a technique he did not fully understand, implies that they are not of East Asian manufacture. Indeed, an analysis of four samples of diverse wood from different parts of one ewer and basin suggests that these are not native to China or Japan, but to South-East Asia.[42] It seems likely, therefore, that these sets are extremely rare examples of datable Indian workmanship that has survived in a northern climate.

An interesting example of the high demand for Japanese lacquer throughout Asia can be found in the production, under Dutch patronage, of circular shields based on Islamic models. Apart from providing protection in close combat, in the Islamic world these shields were customarily presented as gifts and were considered as a badge of office. The earliest reference to such items in VOC records dates to 1656, when the Dutch factory in Bengal ordered 178 from Japan. That such shields were already known in Japan is evident from a pair of *nanban* screens attributed to Kanō Naizen (1570–1616) and dating from *c.* 1603–10, which depict two black-and-gold shields of this form (plate 18.15). Whether the base for these shields was made in Japan or not is uncertain. However, by the second half of the seventeenth century the VOC was sending shields made in Bengal of thick, convex hide to Japan to be lacquered and decorated with *makie*. VOC orders to the Japanese for the year 1662 requested that some shields be decorated without human figures, animals or birds, suggesting that these were intended for Islamic markets. Shields were also ordered for European consumers, and these were mostly decorated with coats of arms, usually with surrounding plants, birds and insects.[43] One such shield, accompanied by a sword, bears the arms of Johan van Leenen, a VOC official at the Persian court in Isfahan between 1689 and 1692 (plate 18.16). These were presented to him for bringing to a satisfactory conclusion a previous arrangement whereby the Dutch were obliged to purchase large amounts of expensive, poor-quality Persian silk in return for permission to sell spices in Persia.

The majority of export lacquerware was made in western forms that were unfamiliar to Asian

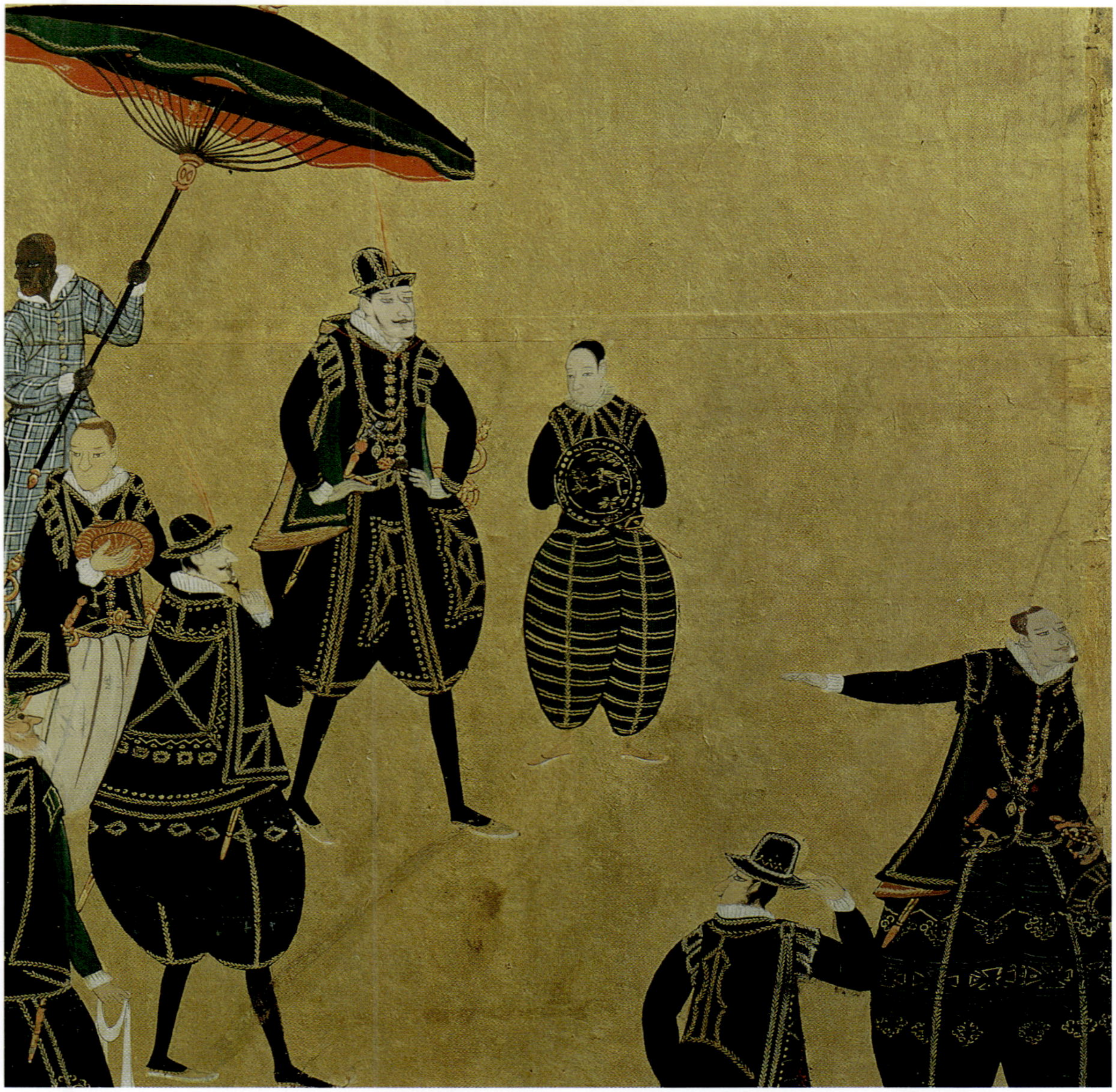

18.15
Six-panel screen depicting the arrival of a Portuguese ship (detail)
Kanō Naizen

Ink, colour and gold-leaf on paper
Japan, *c.*1603–10

Museu Nacional de Arte Antiga, Lisbon

18.16
Sword

Commissioned by the VOC as a gift for Johan van Leenen; steel blade, with *sawasa* hilt and mounts; and scabbard of wood, covered in lacquered rayskin
Blade: Holland; mounts and scabbard: Japan, late 17th century

Rijksmuseum, Amsterdam

Shield

Probably comissioned by Johan van Leenen; hide, rhinoceros or buffalo, covered in black and gold lacquer
Hide: Bengal; lacquer: Japan, late 17th century

Rijksmuseum, Amsterdam

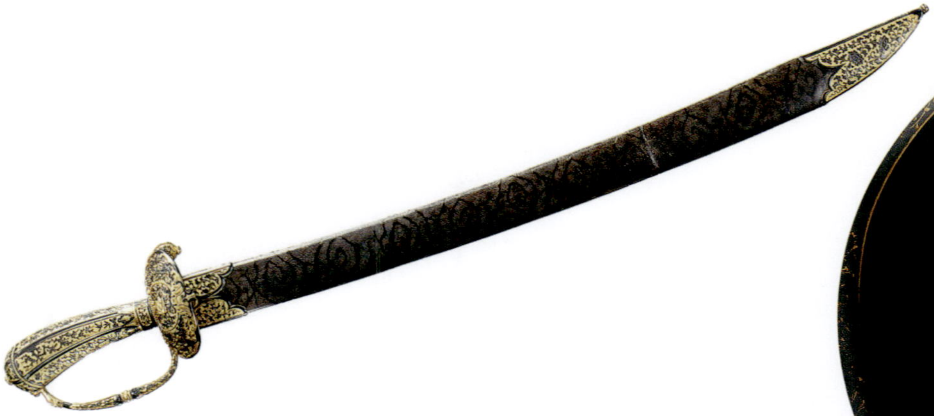

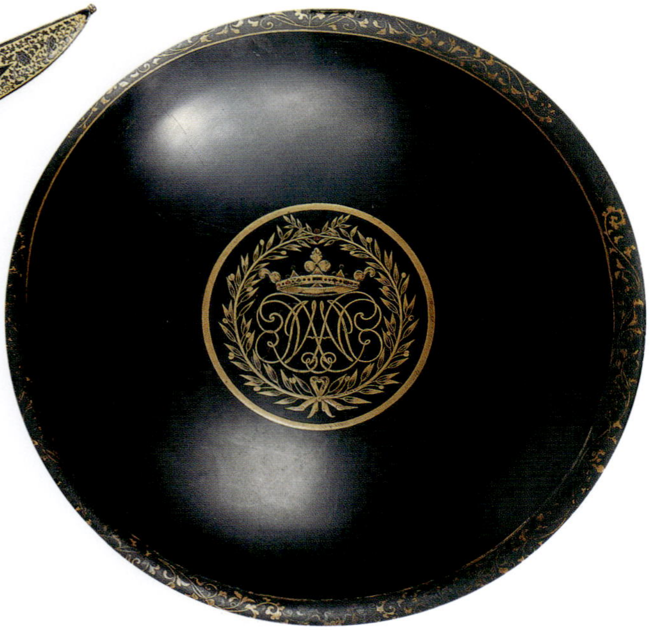

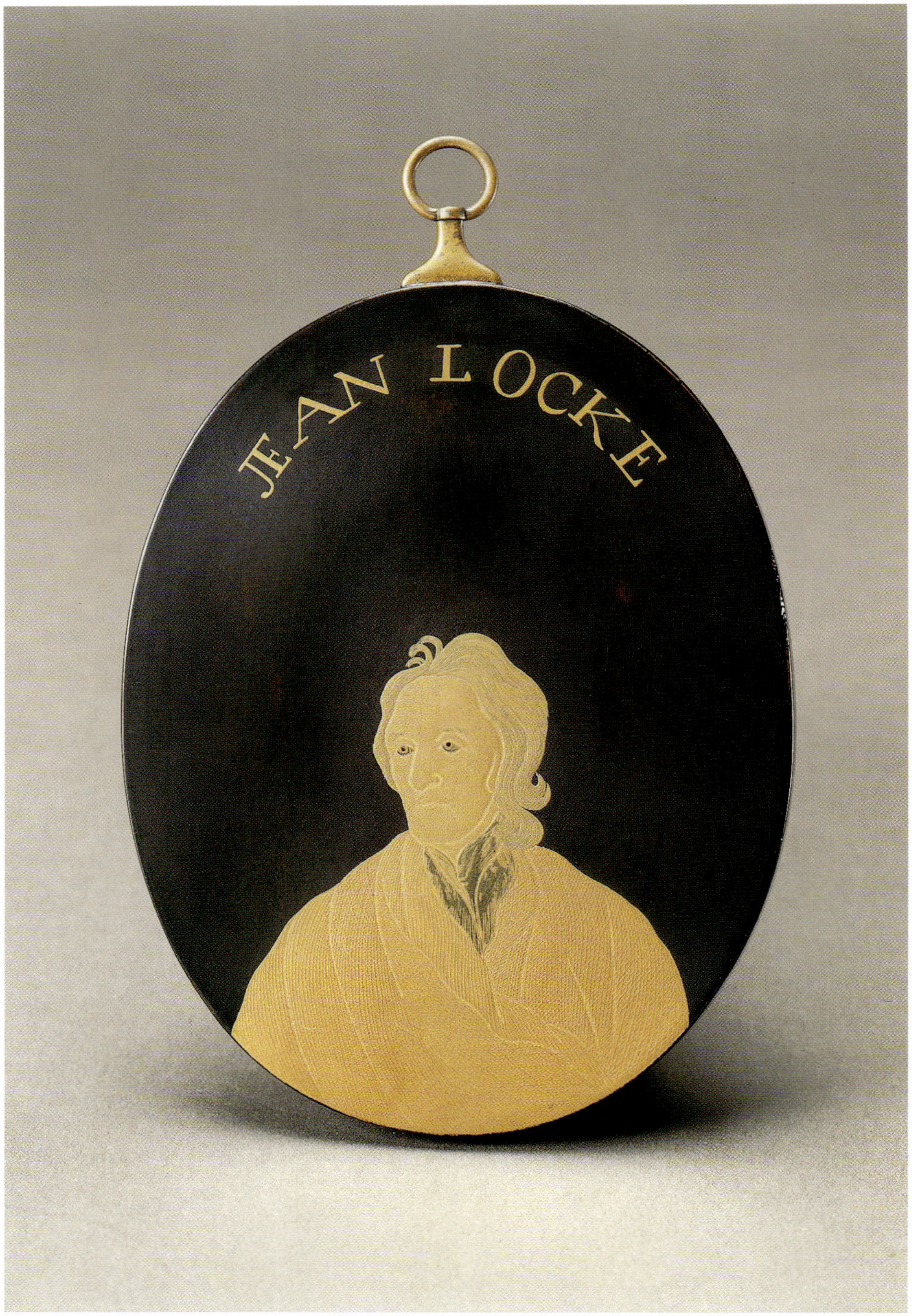

18.17
Plaque with a portrait of Jean [John] Locke

Copper, covered in black lacquer, with gold *hiramakie* decoration and gold details; inscribed top: 'Jean Locke'; and back: 'Philosophe: né en 1632, mort en 1704'
Japan, late 18th century

V&A: FE.29–1985

craftsmen. As a direct result, drawings, wooden models or, more rarely, wooden carcasses were sent to aid them.[44] The Swede Olof Toreen, who was in Canton in 1751, wrote, 'The joiners copy everything that is shown them.'[45] Language was a perennial problem, with traders and officials relying on middlemen. In Japan from the seventeenth century onwards many wholesale dealers in lacquerware had agents or dealers in Nagasaki, who would both take orders and sell the wares of a workshop in Nagasaki, Osaka and, especially, Kyoto, where the main lacquer workshops were situated.[46] Since orders were mostly seasonal, lacquerers worked together in ateliers specializing in export wares as and when required. In the case of a particularly large or important order, craftsmen could be hired from workshops that supplied the domestic market. In 1617 at the height of the *nanban* trade, Will Adams wrote to Richard Wickham, 'I have been at Meaco [Miyako, the capital – Kyoto] and talked with the makeman [*makie*-man] who hath promised that in a short time he will have done. He hath fifty men that worketh day and night: that, so far as I can see, he doth his endeavour.'[47] Allowing for slight exaggeration, the scale of the undertaking was impressive.

Officials working in Japan also ordered lacquerware for their own use. In particular Reede van de Parkeler, the head of Dejima between 1786 and 1788, may have been responsible for initiating the fashion for copper oval plaques when he sent two to his father in 1793.[48] Such plaques were lacquered with famous Europeans and Roman emperors taken from *L'Europe Illustré*, a French work published between 1755 and 1765 (plate 18.17). This first use of western designs in Japanese lacquerwork was an enormous success and led to the manufacture of plaques decorated with western battle scenes and city views. A significant number of them are signed Sasaya – believed to be Sasaya Kisuke, a wholesale dealer in lacquerware who worked in Kyoto, but who had an agent or outlet in Nagasaki.[49] This type of work was increasingly inlaid with mother-of-pearl in a style termed 'Nagasaki lacquer'. This is characterized by very thin inlays of mother-of-pearl, which were specially selected for their colourful hues, often being further underpainted. According to tradition, a certain Aogai Chōbei is said to have learned the technique from the Chinese in Nagasaki in around 1620. A set of four lacquer trays (plate 18.18), recorded in the Royal Danish Kunstkammer in 1689, but probably of an earlier date, are possibly the oldest surviving examples of Nagasaki

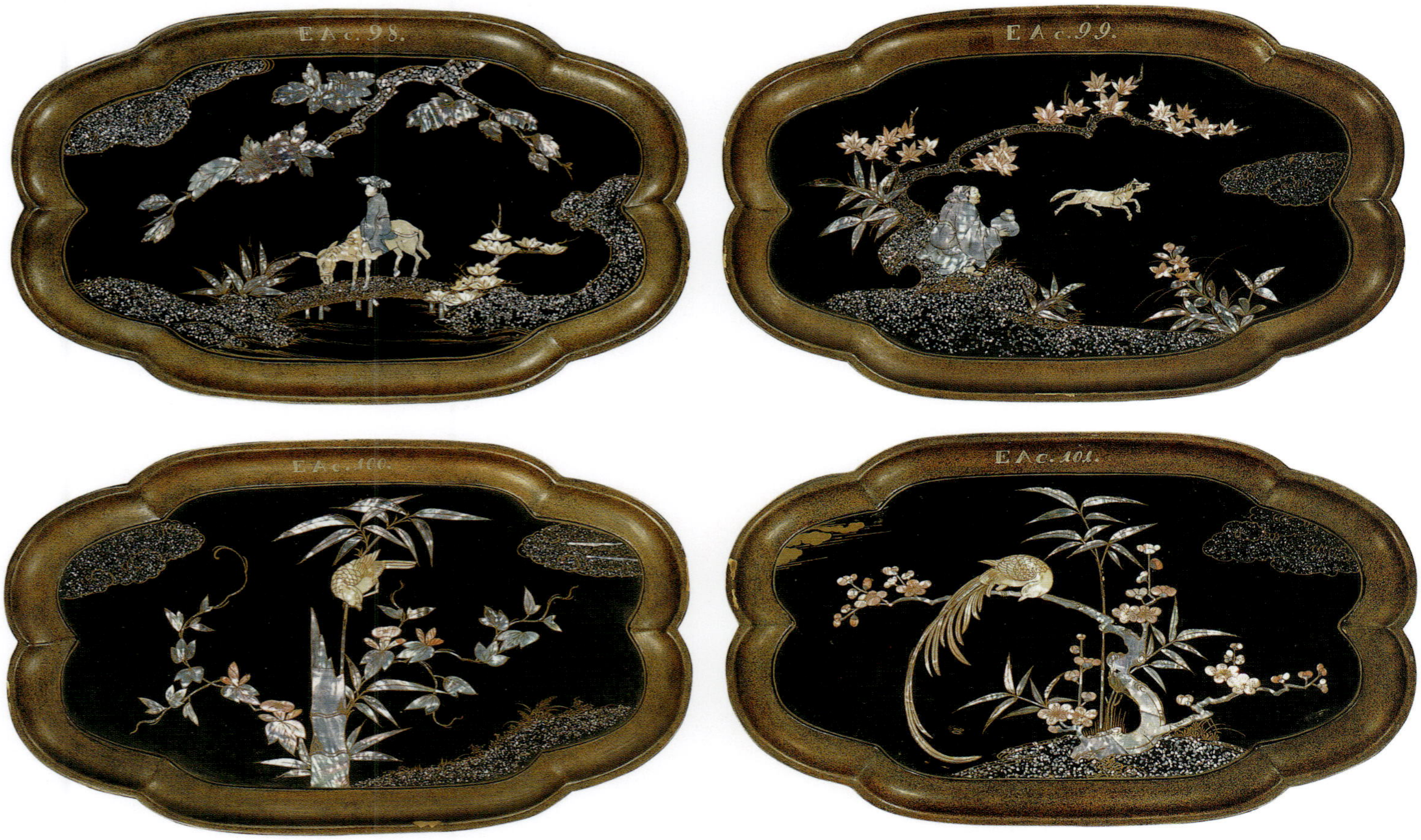

18.18
Trays

Wood, covered in black lacquer and inlaid with shell, some underpainted
Japan, mid-17th century

National Museum, Copenhagen

lacquerwork.[50] This became the dominant late eighteenth- and early nineteenth-century style of Japanese export lacquerware.

The main producers of lacquer, both for consumption within Asia and for export to Europe, were Japan and China. It is an interesting phenomenon that the high cost necessary to maintain the supreme quality of Japanese lacquerware ultimately put an end to the official bulk trade with the VOC. The antithesis was true in China, where corners were cut to remain competitive. This led to a sharp decline in standards, for which Europeans were largely responsible. As du Halde aptly summarized in 1735, 'There is no reason why lacquer objects made at Canton should not have been as beautiful and as good workmanship … It is … that those who undertake the work do it too hurriedly and if they please the eyes of the Europeans they are content with it.'[51]

19

ASIA IN EUROPE: FURNITURE FOR THE WEST

Amin Jaffer

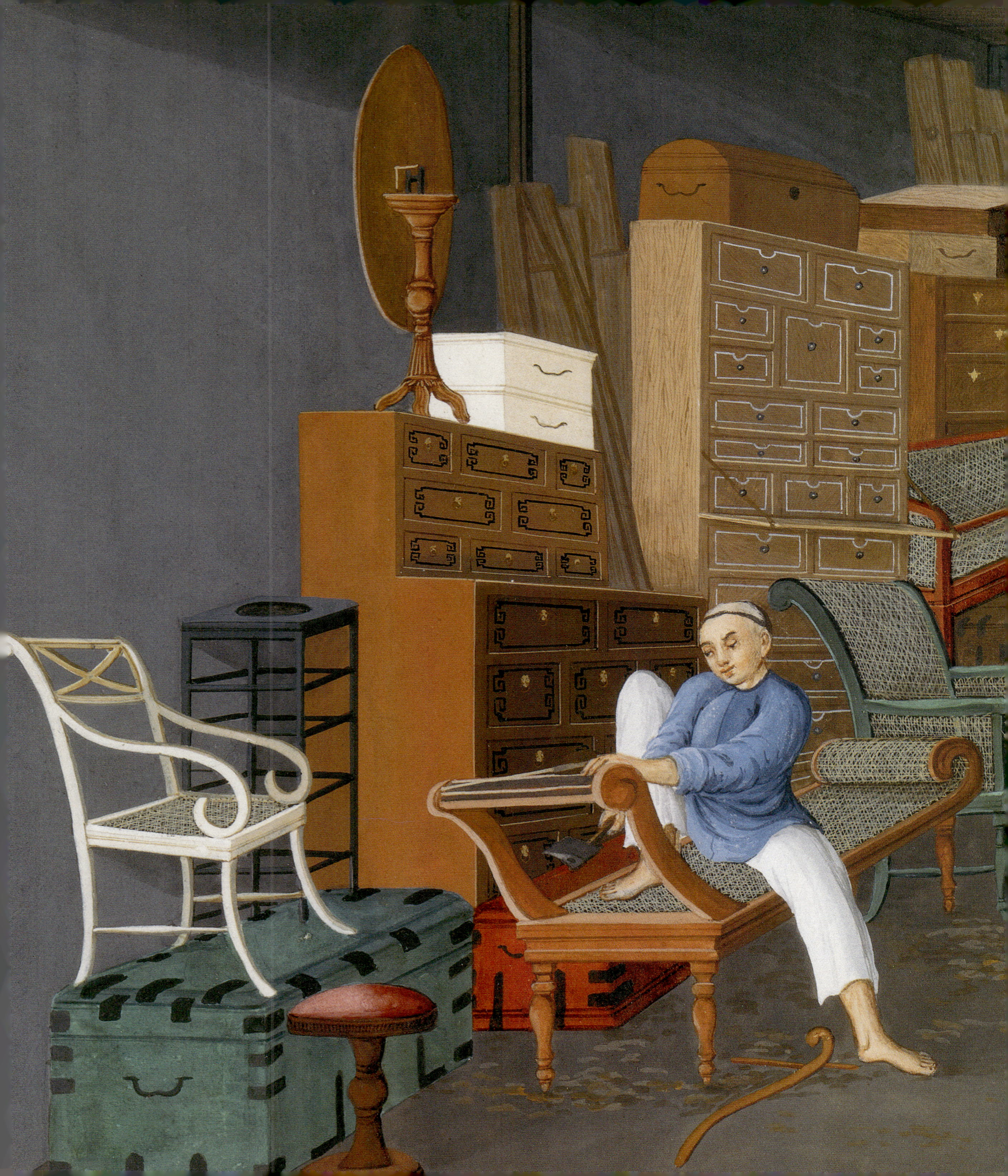

Detail of 19.7 previous page

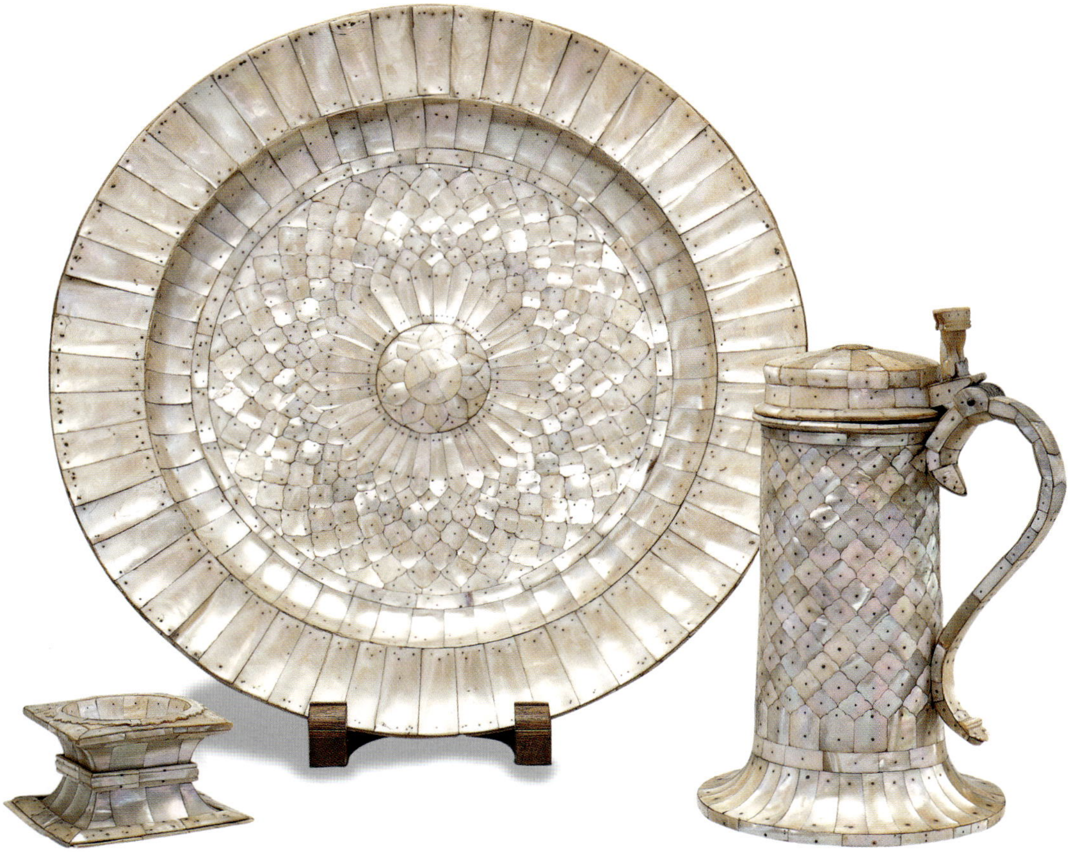

19.1
Tankard, dish and salt cellar

Wood, covered with plaques of mother-of-pearl, secured with metal rivets
Gujarat, early 17th century

Private collection

In his account of sixteenth-century Japan, João Rodrigues (*c.* 1561–1633) observed that rooms there were unfurnished; this was because the Japanese sat cross-legged on the ground 'and indeed this is the usual fashion of the whole of Asia for they do not use chairs in their houses'.[1] When Europeans first landed in Asia they found that there existed neither western-style elevated chairs nor furniture used at chair height, such as tables for eating and writing. It was precisely furniture of this type that they needed, and so began to commission examples from local carpenters, initially based on pieces they had brought out as cabin furniture. By the early seventeenth century there had developed, in the parts of Asia where Europeans established settlements, workshops producing furniture either for use by Westerners locally or specifically for export to Europe. Although such pieces were never traded between Asia and Europe in the same quantities as were textiles and porcelain, they nevertheless travelled regularly from East to West as valued presents, special commissions and private trade cargo.

Frenchman Pyrard de Laval's recollections of the market in early seventeenth-century Goa capture the contemporary European appreciation of the skills of Indian craftsmen at producing western-style furniture:

> Among other things I should mention a great number of cabinets of all patterns, in the fashion of those of Germany. This is an article the most perfect and of the finest workmanship to be seen anywhere; for they are all of choice woods, and inlaid with ivory, mother-of-pearl, and precious stones; in place of iron they are mounted with gold.[2]

A range of accounts reveal that de Laval's effusive praise was not unique. For example, the 'state bed of rich and very curious workmanship' that was brought from India as a present for Queen Charlotte (1744–1818) was described by *Lady's Magazine* of September 1784 as exceeding 'for grandeur, anything ever seen in this kingdom'.[3] Superlatives are also apparent in the writings of John Albert de Mandelslo (1616–44), who thought that the painted furniture of Gujarat was of 'such a lustre, as none yet could ever imitate in Europe'.[4] The approbation evident in these writings is confirmed in the collecting habits of European elites, who admired the exotic materials and decoration of furniture made in Asia, whether of indigenous or western form. For example, Philip II of Spain (r. 1556–98), arguably the most powerful king in Christendom, owned – as well as a group of 'Indian' desks – a pair of Chinese folding chairs, which he apparently used when receiving ambassadors.[5] The Portuguese royal family favoured their relations throughout Europe with presents of caskets and cabinets from Asia, which they acquired through official channels (see pp. 36–8). Even princes without a foothold in Asia were able to acquire such pieces through agents in Lisbon, as well as through the medium of diplomatic exchange, as did Albrecht V (1528–79), who in 1572 received from the Medici a *'Tavolere da giocare composto di madrperla indiana'* (a gamesboard of Indian mother-of-pearl).[6]

Tantalising references to extravagantly decorated furniture abound, but only in exceptional circumstances can they be linked to surviving objects. Some idea of the richness of such pieces is apparent from a casket once owned by François I (r. 1515–47) (see plate 3.9). Constructed of wood, the casket is covered entirely with plaques of mother-of-pearl, whose lustrous and iridescent surface glow in shades of pink and green. The piece was made in Gujarat, western India, where workshops fabricated articles of mother-of-pearl for local markets as well as for export to the Middle East and the east coast of Africa.[7] These were either entirely overlaid with pieces of mother-of-pearl, such as this casket; or covered with a dark mastic inset with pieces of mother-of-pearl in vegetal, geometric and, less frequently, figurative designs.[8] Dutch traveller Jan Huyghen van Linschoten (1563–1611) described the range of furniture that Indians made with mother-of-pearl:

> they make divers things of them, as deskes, tables, cubbards, tables to play on, boxes, staves for women to beare in their hands and a thousand such fine devises, which are all inlaid and covered with this Chanco or Mother of Pearle, very faire to beholde, & very workmanlike made, and are in India so common that there is almost no place in those countries but they have of them. It is likewise much carried abroad, both into Portingale, and elsewhere …[9]

In Europe it became fashionable to further enhance the appearance of mother-of-pearl articles by setting them in elaborate mounts by virtuoso goldsmiths. The casket is richly embellished with mounts by French court goldsmith Pierre Mangot, dated 1532–33, making it one of the earliest documented Gujarati mother-of-pearl objects known in Europe.[10] Its early date and traditional Asian shape suggest that the piece was of a form that workshops were already producing when the Portuguese arrived in Gujarat. By the close of the sixteenth century *firingis* ('Franks' or foreigners) were certainly commissioning mother-of-pearl craftsmen to produce objects based on western forms. European input into indigenous design is very apparent in a garniture of early seventeenth-century mother-of-pearl vessels, plates and candlesticks at Chicheley Hall, Buckinghamshire (plate 19.1). How these pieces came to Britain is unknown, but they may have arrived as exotic luxuries of the type imported by merchants such as John Clerk of Penicuik, who is recorded buying plates and dishes of mother-of-pearl in Paris in the 1640s.[11]

The shape of the tankards from the Chicheley garniture relates closely to that of lacquered vessels made for the export market in the same period in Japan (plate 18.1). That Europeans were commissioning craftsmen in different parts of Asia to produce similar types of objects is not surprising. What is interesting, however, is that under western patronage craftsmen as far apart as Kyoto and Cambay entered into a stylistic dialogue. The use of mother-of-pearl plaques on a range of *nanban* objects is the prime example of how the aesthetic of Gujarati mother-of-pearl influenced lacquerwork in Japan. This is perhaps most strongly articulated in a fall-

19.2
***Scrutore* (fall-front cabinet)**
Wood, the exterior covered with plaques of mother-of-pearl secured with silver rivets; the interior covered in black lacquer with gold *hiramakie* and mother-of-pearl inlay; with silver mounts
Japan, early 17th century
Kobe City Museum, Kobe

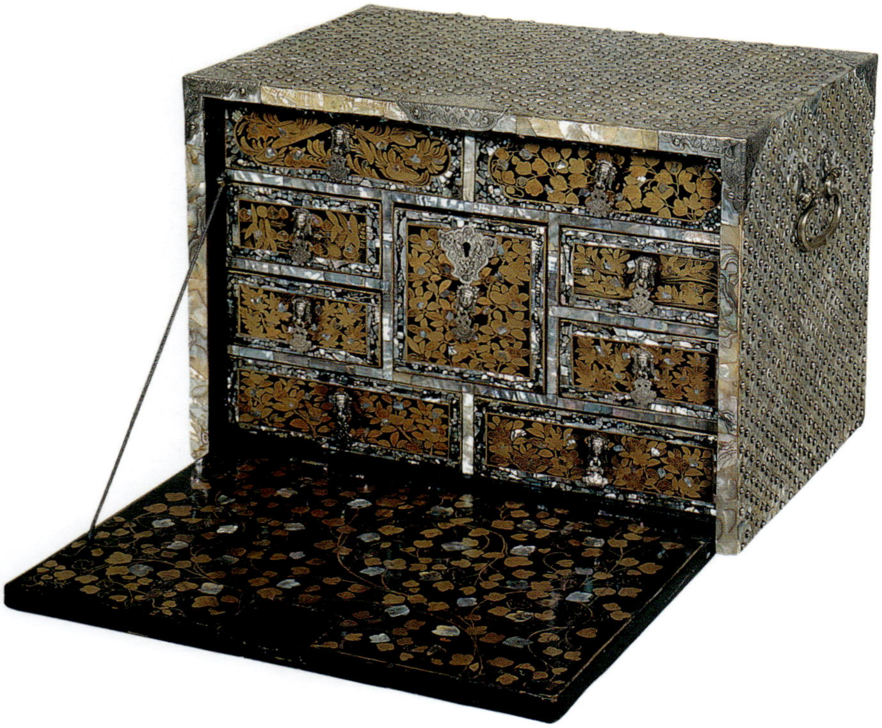

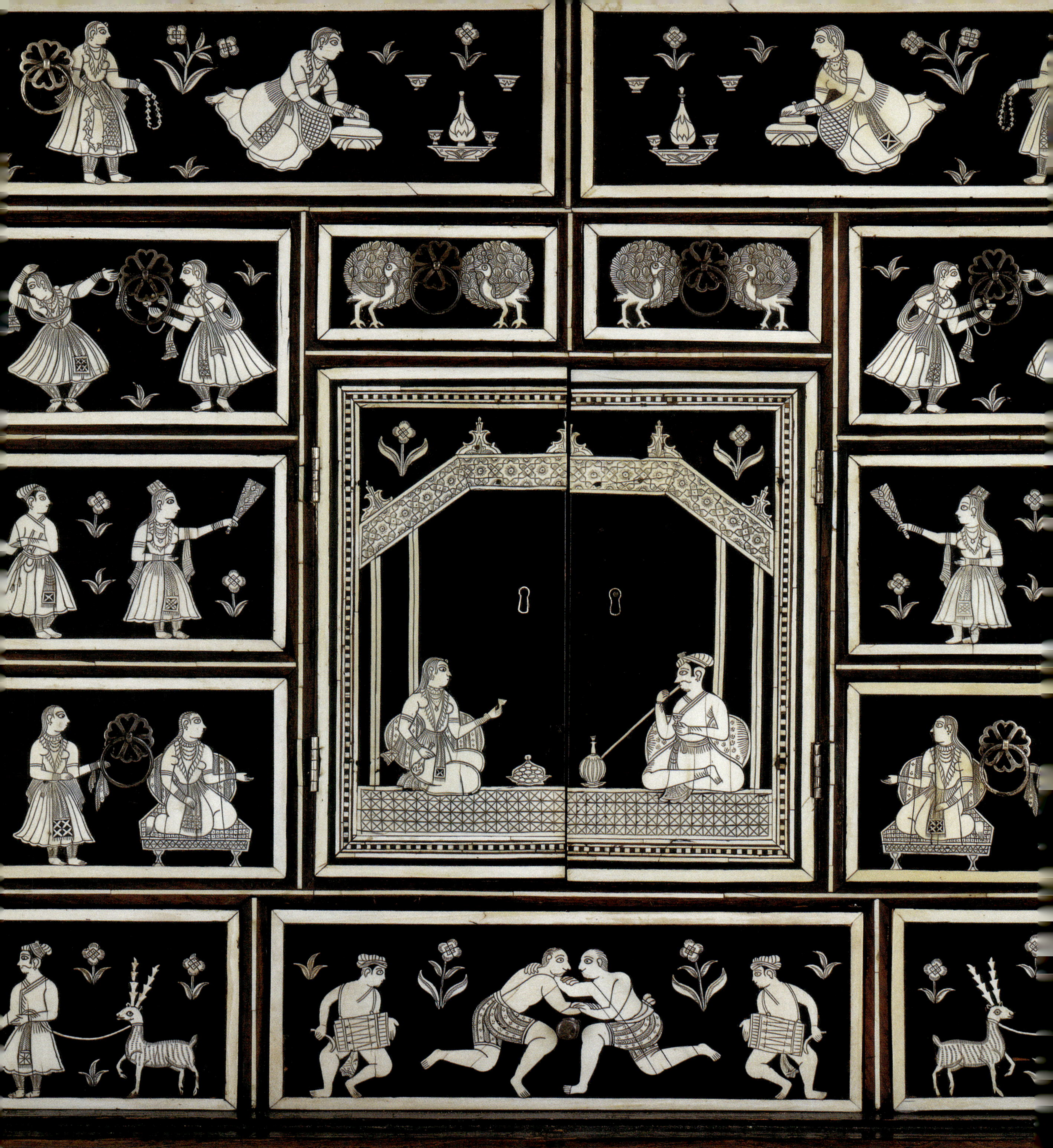

EXCHANGES

front cabinet, or *scrutore*, in the Kobe City Museum whose exterior is entirely overlaid with plaques of shell in Gujarati style, but whose interior is typical of *nanban* lacquerwork (plate 19.2). The shape of the piece is based on a standard type of portable cabinet, which performed the equivalent function of a modern-day briefcase. Such an object would have been an essential part of the equipage of any European official or merchant in Asia and was much reproduced in Gujarat and Sindh, typically in wood inlaid with hardwoods, ivory and micro-mosaic in fanciful designs drawing on a repertoire of Indo-Persian, Hispano-Moresque and European ornament.[12] A degree of cross-influence between South and East Asian decoration was likely to occur, as *scrutores* made both in Japan and in diverse parts of India were available at the international ports of Surat and Goa, which were centres of the trade in western-style goods made in Asia.[13]

A casket of typically Portuguese shape constructed of panels of solid ivory represents one of the first instances of the use of western print sources by Asian craftsmen (see plate 6.10). The piece is one of a group fashioned in the kingdom of Kotte (in present-day Sri Lanka) as diplomatic presents for the kings of Portugal. They are richly carved with narrative scenes and a mixture of European and Sinhalese images symbolic of the relationship between the two royal houses. This casket, for instance, was almost certainly made in 1557 to mark the birth of an heir to the King of Portugal and the conversion to Christianity of King Dharmapala (r. 1551–97) in the same year.[14] A programme of carefully chosen images celebrates the birth and spiritual rebirth occasioned by these two significant events. The front of the casket is carved with bagpiping shepherds drawn from an Albrecht Dürer (1471–1528) woodcut of 1514, while the right end of the casket depicts the Tree of Jesse, apparently copied from a Book of Hours by Thielman Kerver in print from as early as 1499 to at least 1546. The back is carved with scenes from the cycle of the birth of Christ: the Betrothal of the Virgin on the left, and the Rest on the Flight to Egypt on the right.

The Kotte caskets established a precedent for the output of Ceylonese ivory carvers, who were responsible for a large group of ivory and ivory-veneered cabinets and caskets based on western forms decorated with foliage and narrative scenes obviously drawn from European sources. Among the most familiar pieces from this oeuvre is a group of cabinets veneered with ivory panels that depict scenes

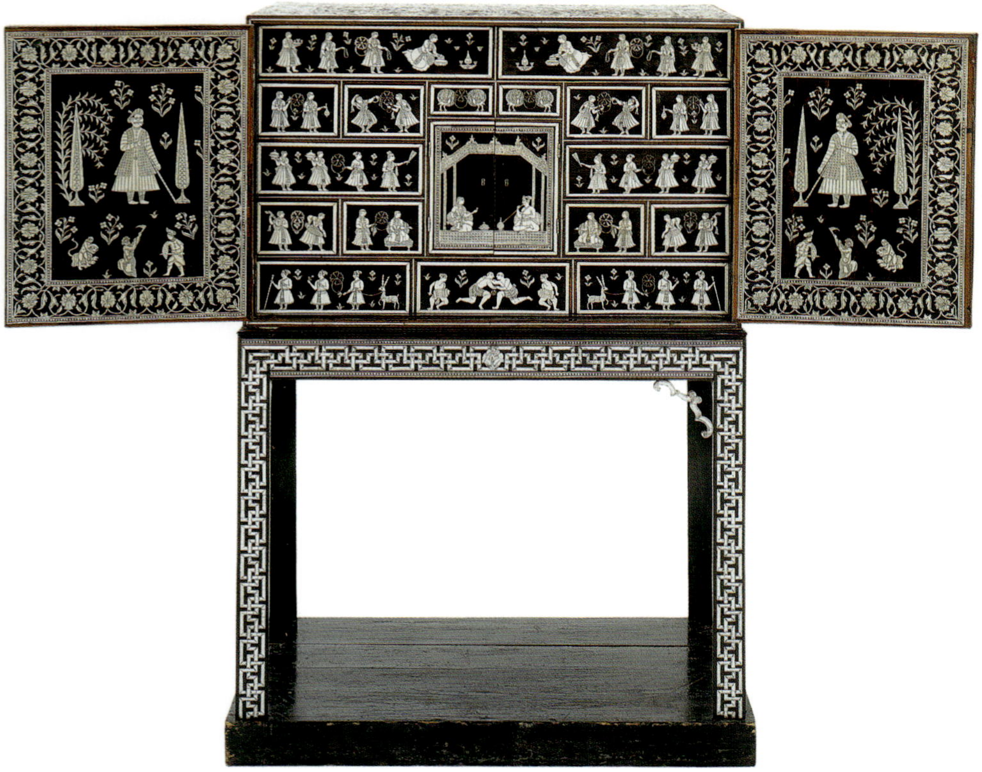

19.3
Cabinet on stand above and opposite (detail)

Wood, inlaid with ivory, incised and highlighted with lac
Cabinet: western India, mid- to late 17th century; stand: England, mid-18th century

V&A: Poteliakhoff Loan

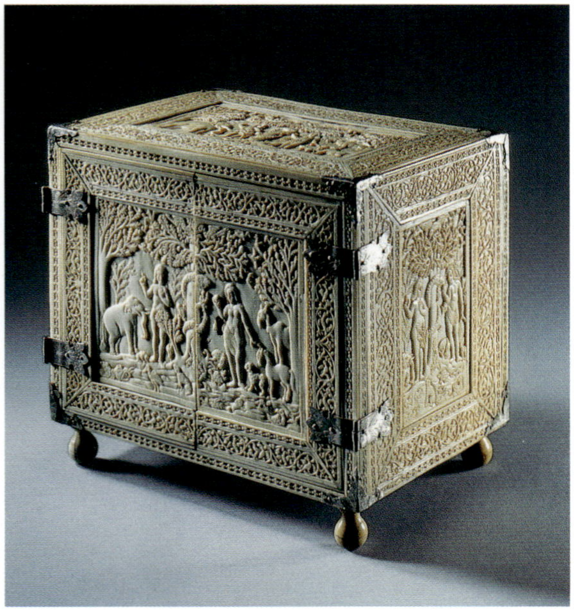

19.4
Cabinet

Wood, veneered with panels of carved ivory, with silver mounts
Ceylon, mid- to late 17th century

Private collection, London

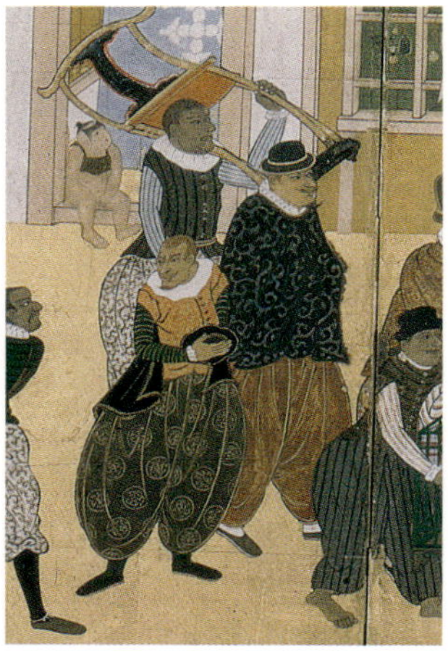

19.5
Six-panel screen depicting the arrival of a Portuguese ship (detail)
Ink, colours and gold-leaf on paper
Japan, *c.*1630s
Museu Nacional de Arte Antiga, Lisbon

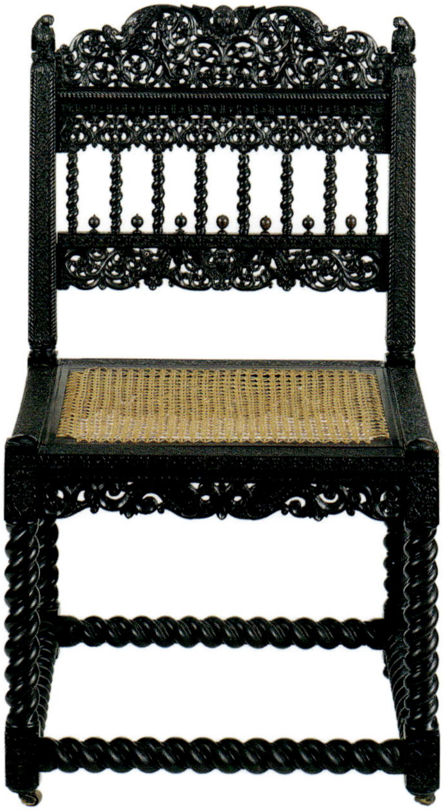

19.6
Side chair
Ebony, carved and pierced
India (Coromandel coast), mid-17th century
V&A: IS.6–2000

of Adam and Eve in the Garden of Eden (plate 19.4).[15] The methods of construction of these pieces was standardized, as were the sizes of the narrative panels and the borders into which they were inserted, suggesting that workshops routinely produced such pieces. References to them appear in the writings of contemporary travellers to Ceylon, such as François Valentijn (1656–1727), who noted among the work of local artisans 'entire cabinets covered with ivory and very ingeniously carved'.[16]

Furniture made for export markets, mainly cabinets inlaid with ivory, was a speciality of western India, as observed by numerous travellers.[17] A substantial two-door cabinet of tropical hardwood inlaid with ivory is a particularly fine late example from this school (plate 19.3). The method of dating such pieces relies heavily on the evolution of their shape, which follows the development of the cabinet form in Europe. The size of this piece reflects the mid– to late seventeenth-century European taste for using large cabinets as showpieces and mounting them on stands, as was this piece after its arrival in Europe. The cabinet's date is further supported by the exterior decoration of the piece, which is of rows of windswept flowers in the high Mughal style. The interior marries a profusion of figures and motifs drawn from provincial Mughal painting of the period, Deccani textiles and images of Europeans drawn from engravings or narrative tapestries.[18]

During their time in Asia, Europeans found that only in China did people sit upright on chairs, a custom introduced in the tenth century. The absence of elevated furniture in most of Asia rendered early Europeans there dependent on the sophisticated hardwood and lacquered furniture of the Middle Kingdom, which they are regularly shown using, for example, on painted *nanban* arrival screens (plate 19.5). Contemporary accounts confirm that the Europeans regularly brought Chinese furniture to other parts of Asia, partly for their own use and partly as a commodity for sale in local markets and for export to Europe.[19] For the most part such references are to lacquered furniture, but eventually hardwood and bamboo furniture also figured in this trade. Vessels bound for Europe from East Asia called in at South and South-East Asian ports, where the dearth of furnishings suitable to western living rendered these imports in high demand. The chronicler Fray Sebastien Manrique (*fl.* 1629–43), for example, wrote that among the goods regularly imported by the Portuguese from China to their settlement in Hooghly, Bengal, were 'great quantities of porcelain and many kinds of gilt articles, such as bedsteads, tables, boxes, chests, writing-desks'.[20] The export of furniture from China to other parts of Asia was certainly well established by the late seventeenth century. Inventories from Batavia during this period indicate that Dutchmen who lived there were using a wide range of furniture of East Asian origin.[21] For instance, the inventory of the estate of Cornelia Teulings (1688) included '6 black Chinese chairs',[22] while that of Cornelia Linis (1690) listed '2 Chinese chairs' and '1 Chinese screen'.[23] East Asian furnishings also figure in some of the surviving Bombay, Calcutta and Madras inventories from the early eighteenth century. For example, the 1725 inventory of the possessions of George Shelton (probably from Calcutta) listed '1 China Hand Escritoire',[24] while a contemporary estate from Madras included '1 China Escritoire' and '1 China Screen'.[25]

The Coromandel coast was another centre where furniture was produced for consumption by Europeans locally, and for export to other parts

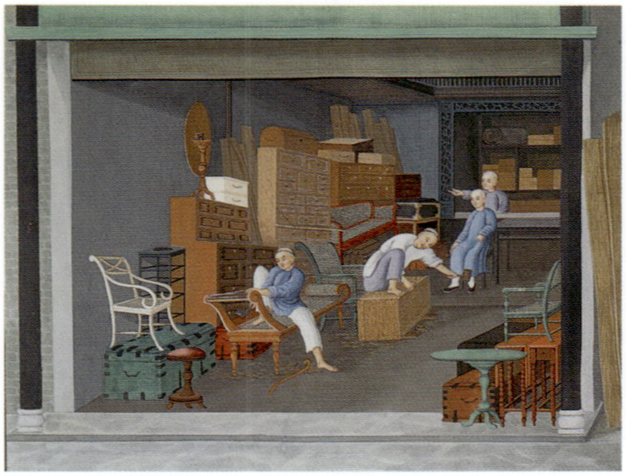

of Asia and to Europe (plate 19.6). Thomas Bowrey noted in *c.* 1669 that at the region's premier port, Masulipatam, could be found 'Chairs and tables of that admirable wood Ebony, Chests of drawers' and that such pieces were carried to 'parts of India, Persia, Arabia, China and the South Seas, as well as to England and Holland'.[26] Ebony furniture produced along the Coromandel coast in the second half of the seventeenth century was evidently made in some quantity, and it appears in Dutch East India Company (VOC) inventories from Batavia and is also referred to in English country-house records.[27] Based on the location of surviving examples and on documentary and stylistic evidence, scholars have been able to confirm that such pieces were not only exported to Ceylon and the Dutch East Indies, but were also much copied there.[28] The VOC was simultaneously moving slaves and craftsmen from the Coromandel coast to their settlements in the East Indies, and as these immigrant communities were sometimes occupied in making furniture, it is difficult to distinguish between what they made and the coastal originals that they copied.

When commissioning furniture in South Asia it was the convention to provide craftsmen with a 'muster' or pattern of some sort, which ranged from a drawing or engraving to a three-dimensional model.[29] Less is known about how western designs were communicated to carpenters in East Asia. In his research on export porcelain, Christiaan Jörg illustrates the sort of two-dimensional drawings sent out to Canton (Guangzhou) workshops, and it is known that such designs were employed in the manufacture of tea trays.[30] Although the trade in furniture was never very significant in commercial terms, furniture nevertheless featured regularly in the private enterprises of European merchants, who had an interest in ensuring an accurate rendition of designs by Chinese makers by sending them models. The demand for European furniture throughout Asia meant that pieces could be taken there as cabin furniture, used as a model, and sold off at profit to Europeans in the East or even to *hong* merchants, some of whom began to furnish their houses after the western manner.[31] Furniture that could serve as a model was sometimes found in the most unlikely places. When Joris van Spilbergen went to Kandy in 1602 he was surprised to find that the king's great hall was 'furnished with Spanish chairs and a table, where everything appeared to be in the Christian style'; such references to western furniture at Asian courts are not unique.[32]

In the 1680s examples of English furniture were sent to Tonkin (northern Vietnam), where the East India Company attempted to have lacquered copies made for the London market more cheaply than those available from China and Japan.[33] Further evidence that prototypes were being sent to East Asia to be copied is found in Pollexfen's *A discourse of Trade, Coyn & Paper Credit*, published in London in 1697, which stated that 'some artisans were sent out to introduce patterns suitable for sale at home'.[34]

19.7
Interior of a Canton Furniture Shop
Opaque watercolour on paper
China (Canton), *c.* 1820
Peabody Essex Museum, Salem

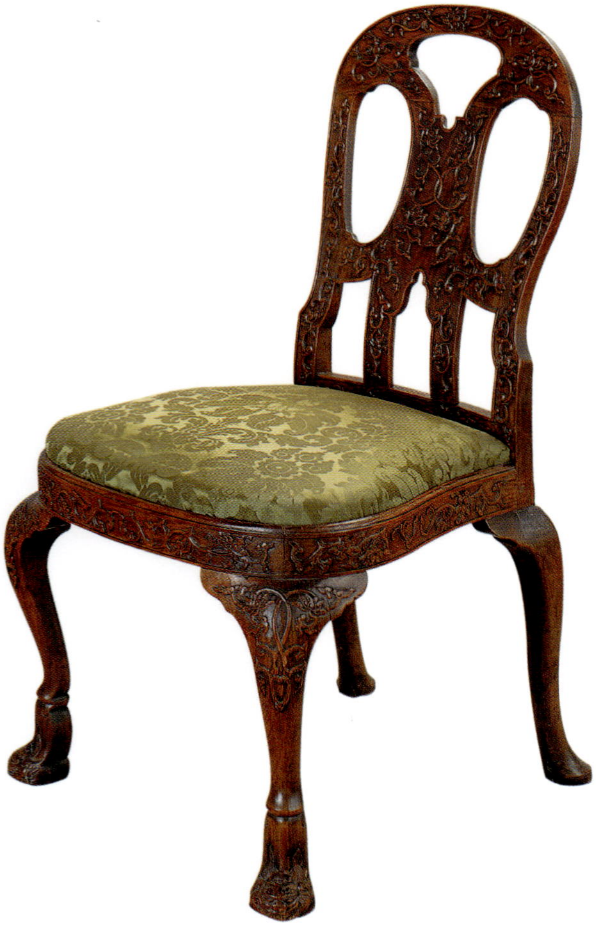

19.8
Side chair
Wood, carved, with slip seat, later upholstery
China, *c.* 1740
Peabody Essex Museum, Salem

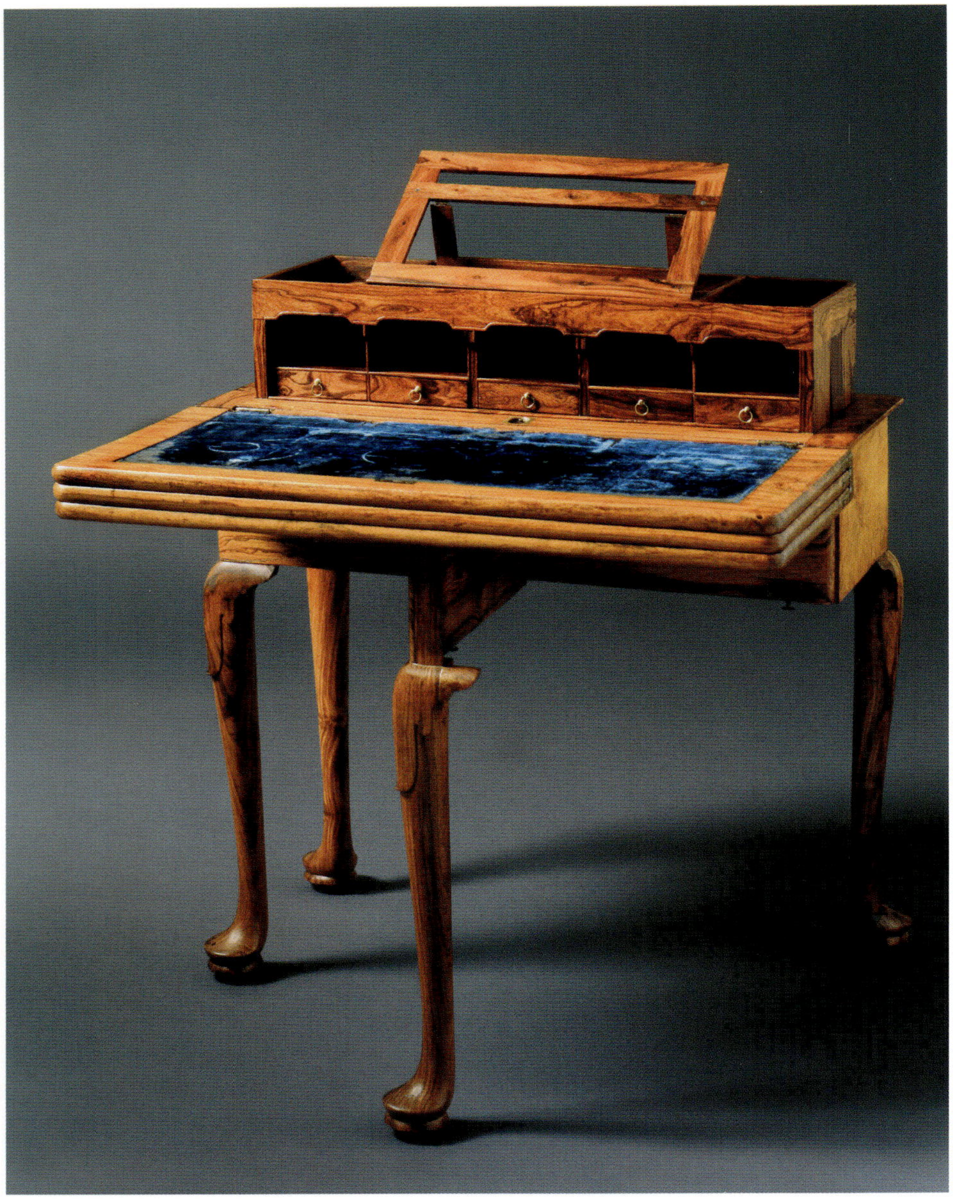

19.9
Harlequin games table
Wood
China (Canton), *c.*1737
Fredensborg Castle, Denmark

The 'Petition of the Joiner's Company', presented in 1700, similarly indicates that London merchants despatched furniture to the Indies to serve as models:

> … several Merchants, and others, Trading to the East-Indies, and to several Ports and Places thereabouts, have procured to be made in London, of late Years, and sent over to the East-Indies, Patterns and Models of all sorts of Cabinet Goods; and have Yearly return'd from thence such great Quantities of Cabinet-Wares, Manufactured there after the English Fashion, by our Models …[35]

By the eighteenth century Chinese carpenters were routinely producing western-style furniture specifically for export (plate 19.8). These pieces were frequently acquired by private traders who speculated in furniture as part of their ventures in country trade. On his trips to Canton in the early eighteenth century, the Madras-based merchant John Scattergood regularly purchased furniture. For instance, in 1711 he bought '1 Excretore large with draws', 'a small chest 2 large boxes and four small ones of silver' and a 'looking glass' from Buqqa Goldsmith[36]; and in 1719 he bought four chairs and a bed, as well as presents to be delivered to England for his wife, which included '2 Tea Tables … 6 China Pictures, 20 China Flowered papers, two Do. Dressing Boxes'.[37] Besides custom-ordered pieces, large consignments of Chinese export furniture reached Indian ports from the third quarter of the eighteenth century as part of commercial ventures. The range of furnishings imported is demonstrated by an advertisement in the *Madras Courier* of 1793:

> Candle Screens, Paper Covers, Rattan Furniture, Bamboo Couches, Chairs and Stools, Paintings, Ivory Snuff-boxes, Tortoiseshell Boxes, Yellow-wood, Black-wood and Rose-wood Furniture of all kinds, Ivory work Baskets, Sandle-wood Furniture, Bureaus and Book-cases, Sham wood Wash-hand Stands, Ditto, Nankeen-backed Couches, Manilla-wood Tables, Ditto Trefoil, Ditto, Backgammon and Chess Tables, Manilla-wood Escrutores, Ditto, Knife Cases, Ditto Wash-hand Stands, Writing-desks, do.do., Tables, Camphor-wood Chests, &c.&c.&c.[38]

At Canton, western merchants were able to obtain furniture directly from shops that stocked western-style pieces in anticipation of the winter trading season. A gouache from the 1820s of a furniture-maker's shop conveys an idea of what such a store might have contained (plate 19.7). Furniture could also be commissioned, in which case patron and craftsman benefited from direct discussion about design and price.[39] Substantial orders could be completed within the few months that Europeans were in port, and from what we know about the production of porcelain and pictures, it would seem

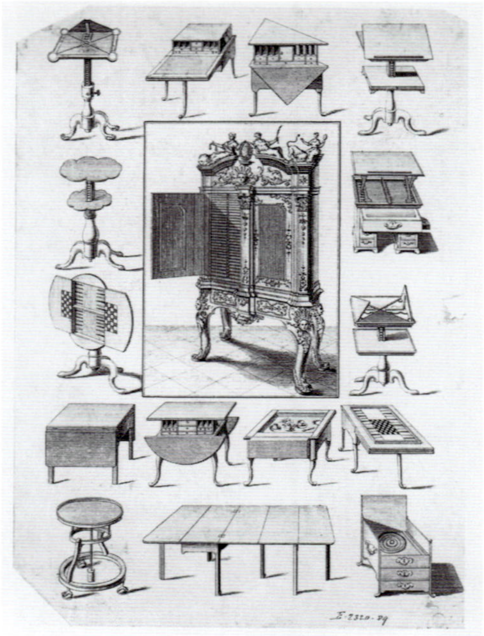

19.10
Advertisement
Engraving
England, 1730s
V&A: E.2320–1889

19.11
Toilet glass
Sandalwood, veneered with ivory, incised and highlighted with lac, with silver mounts
India (Vizagapatam), late 18th century
V&A: IS.31–1975

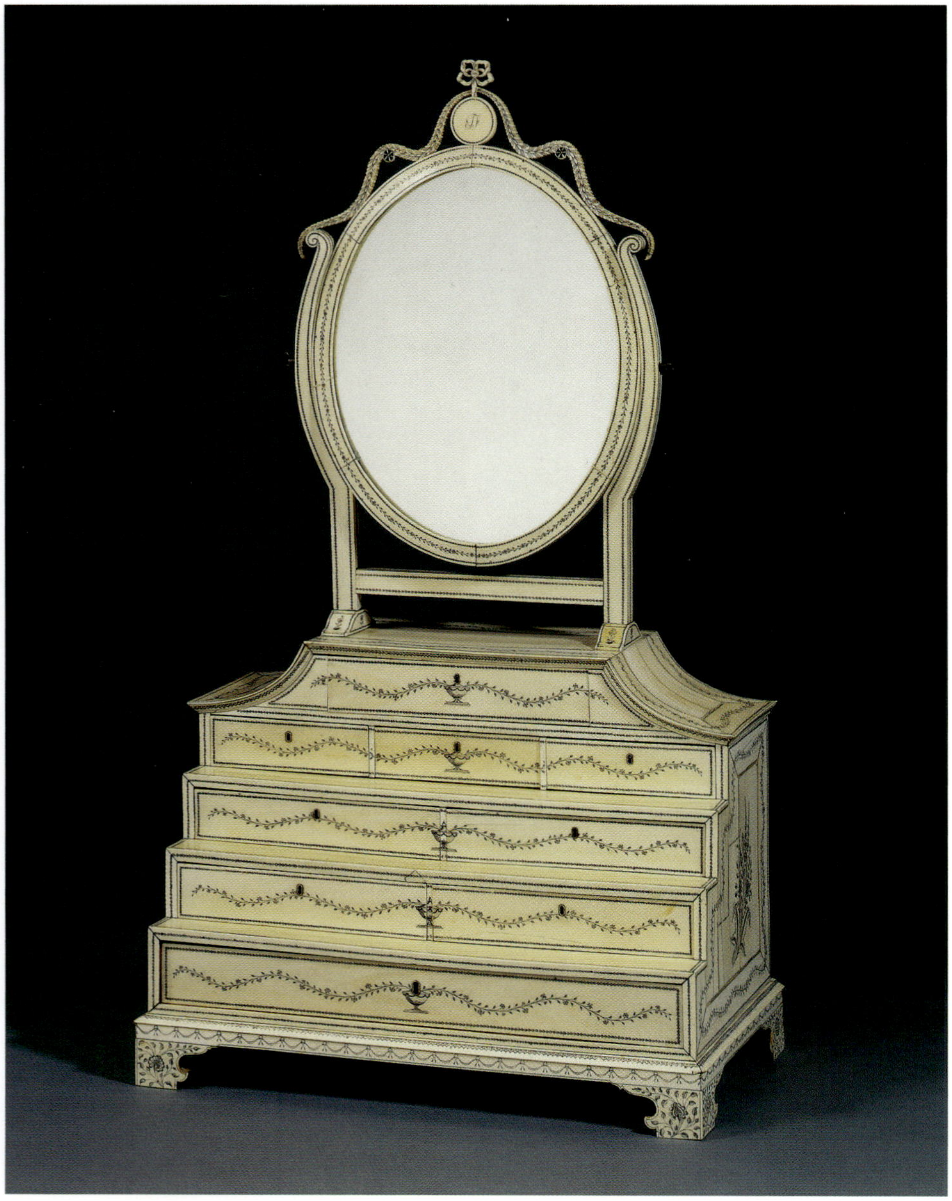

that cabinet-making workshops operated on a large scale with a high degree of division of labour, a conclusion supported by the Chinese markings on furniture components.[40]

While pieces of furniture made in Asia for the European market are traditionally dated several years after the development of the western prototype that inspired them, the actual time required to relay furniture after specific designs could be as little as one trading season – that is, within one year. For instance, in 1737 Danish captain Zacharias Allwelt supplied Christian IV with a harlequin games table precisely like that advertised by London cabinet-maker Thomas Potter in the late 1730s, and fashionable in London at least for the next decade (plates 19.9, 19.10).[41] That furniture made in Asia conformed to metropolitan fashions is evident from a watercolour of about 1780, which depicts Lady Impey, wife of Calcutta chief justice Sir Elijah Impey (1732–1809), examining a hat in a sizeable room furnished with furniture en suite (see plate 21.11). The wheel-backed chair and commode are of types that were certainly fashionable in England at the time when the gouache was painted. That the designs of such furniture were *au courant* is explained by the fact that it was made in Patna by Indian artisans working under a Mr Knight, who, according to his own advertisements, had such pieces made after 'Europe patterns'.[42] Furniture designs from Europe were

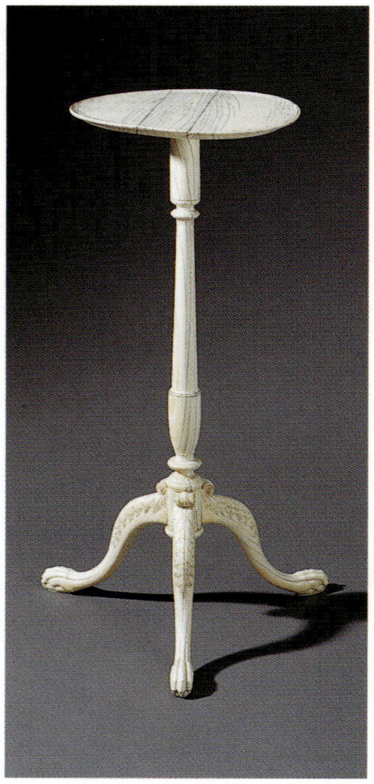

19.12
Candlestand (teapoy)
Solid ivory, turned, carved and partly gilt
India (Murshidabad), late 18th century
V&A: IS.12–1991

19.13
Chair
Wood, veneered with ivory, with modern caned seat
India (Murshidabad), late 18th century
V&A: 1064b–1882 Jones Bequest

certainly being used by furniture-makers in India, as is evident from surviving objects and documentary evidence. For example, in 1785 a copy of Thomas Chippendale's *The Gentleman and Cabinet Maker's Director* was remaindered by the Calcutta Library; the designs that it contained were clearly out of fashion![43]

Patterns, engravings and European expertise were all central to the production of furniture at Vizagapatam, a port on the east coast of India where from the late seventeenth century craftsmen were applying traditional skills of working with ivory to western forms. Examples were brought back to England by leading Company officials such as Clive of India and Warren Hastings. The intricate inlaying and veneering of ivory over wooden carcasses established Vizagapatam wares as luxury furniture, even if towards the close of the eighteenth century workshops began to restrict pieces to portable cabinets and boxes, which were made in larger and larger numbers. Early Vizagapatam furniture was admired for its intricate inlaid decoration, usually of exotic flowers derived from Coromandel coast chintzes. In Europe these textiles were highly fashionable for dress and upholstery; although much rarer, furniture worked with identical motifs must have been just as keenly sought after.

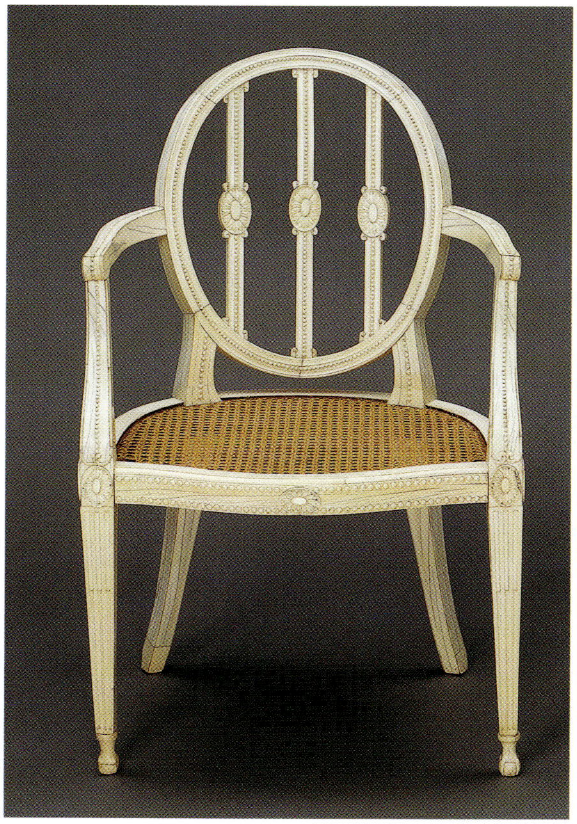

By the late eighteenth century, when this toilet glass was made, Indian motifs were no longer in fashion among Europeans in Asia (plate 19.11); by that time the vogue was for furniture whose decoration and form simulated as closely as possible current tastes in Europe. Although quintessentially neoclassical in appearance, the shape of this toilet glass is more a product of the dialogue between Vizagapatam and Canton than between Vizagapatam and Europe (see plate 18.10). The stepped and pagoda-shaped base does not a have a precedent in English furniture, but may have been loosely inspired by two-tiered English toilet-glass bases. Toilet glasses of related design – with crested oval mirrors on stepped cabinets – were stock products of Canton lacquer workshops during the late eighteenth century, and it is very likely that Canton prototypes inspired the manufacture of this particular form at Vizagapatam. Although it appears to conform to a western model, the stepped base is so high that, if placed on a dressing table, it would be impossible to look in the mirror while seated.

As is evident from surviving examples, schools of furniture-making in Gujarat, Canton, the Coromandel coast and Vizagapatam all produced pieces in some number. But there also existed in parts of Asia frequented by Europeans smaller ateliers that turned their attention to the production of western-style furniture, even if such pieces were not made for export in the true sense of the word. One of these places was Murshidabad, where for generations ivory carvers had produced Indian courtly articles such as fly-whisk handles, combs and fans. In the third quarter of the eighteenth century they began to execute furniture out of solid ivory or of wood veneered with ivory, embellished with finely carved ivory decoration. The oeuvre of these craftsmen, which consists principally of chairs, small tables and candlesticks, cannot have been large; presumably such pieces were available only on a commission basis. A set of four ivory-veneered chairs, bequeathed to the South Kensington Museum in 1882 by John Jones, testifies to their skill at interpreting western furniture and its ornament (plate 19.13). On these chairs the ivory veneer is secured to the wooden frame with ivory rivets configured as rows of decorative pearling, a clever manipulation of western decoration for practical purposes. A solid ivory candle-stand from Murshidabad brought to

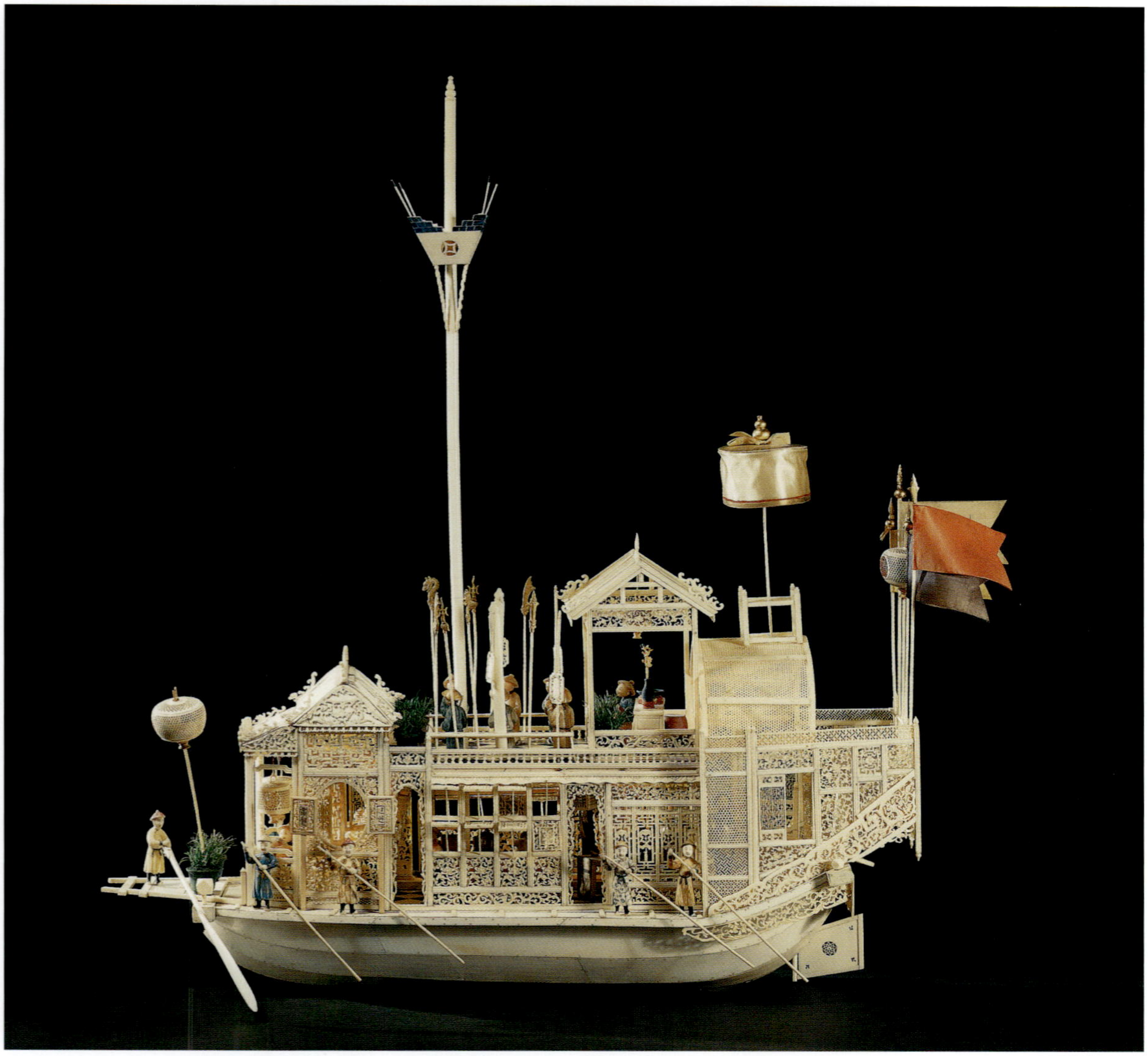

19.14
Model of a boat

Ivory, carved and painted, with clockwork motor
China (Canton), c. 1800

V&A: A.6–1936 Hall Bequest

England by Lord Amherst, Governor-General of India from 1823 to 1828, attests to the artisans' sensitive approach to and naturalistic handling of carving (plate 19.12). Canton artisans were equally known for the skill at handling ivory, which was regularly imported to China as a raw material from South and South-East Asia. By the late eighteenth century craftsmen had begun to produce a range of souvenirs and gifts made of ivory and intended specifically for Europeans at Canton. Among the more elaborate examples were ivory figures, animals and models of Chinese junks propelled by clockwork motors (plate 19.14). An example of the last type is in the collection of the V&A and was acquired in Canton by Richard Hall (1764–1834), who served as chief supercargo until 1803.

In furniture, perhaps more than in any other type of object, it is possible to discern how skilled were Asian artisans at producing goods entirely foreign to their own culture. In much of Asia there did not exist any tradition of elevated seat and case furniture. Nevertheless, Asian woodworkers proved remarkably adept at copying western furniture from models and two-dimensional design sources and applying to it traditional forms of ornament, creating objects that belong to the visual culture of both East and West. In Europe it was the foreign decorative techniques and rare materials of such furniture that rendered it fashionable. In this sense, western-style furniture from Asia was exotic both in the eyes of the Asian artisans who made it and of the Europeans who used it.

20

ASIA IN EUROPE: TEXTILES FOR THE WEST

Rosemary Crill

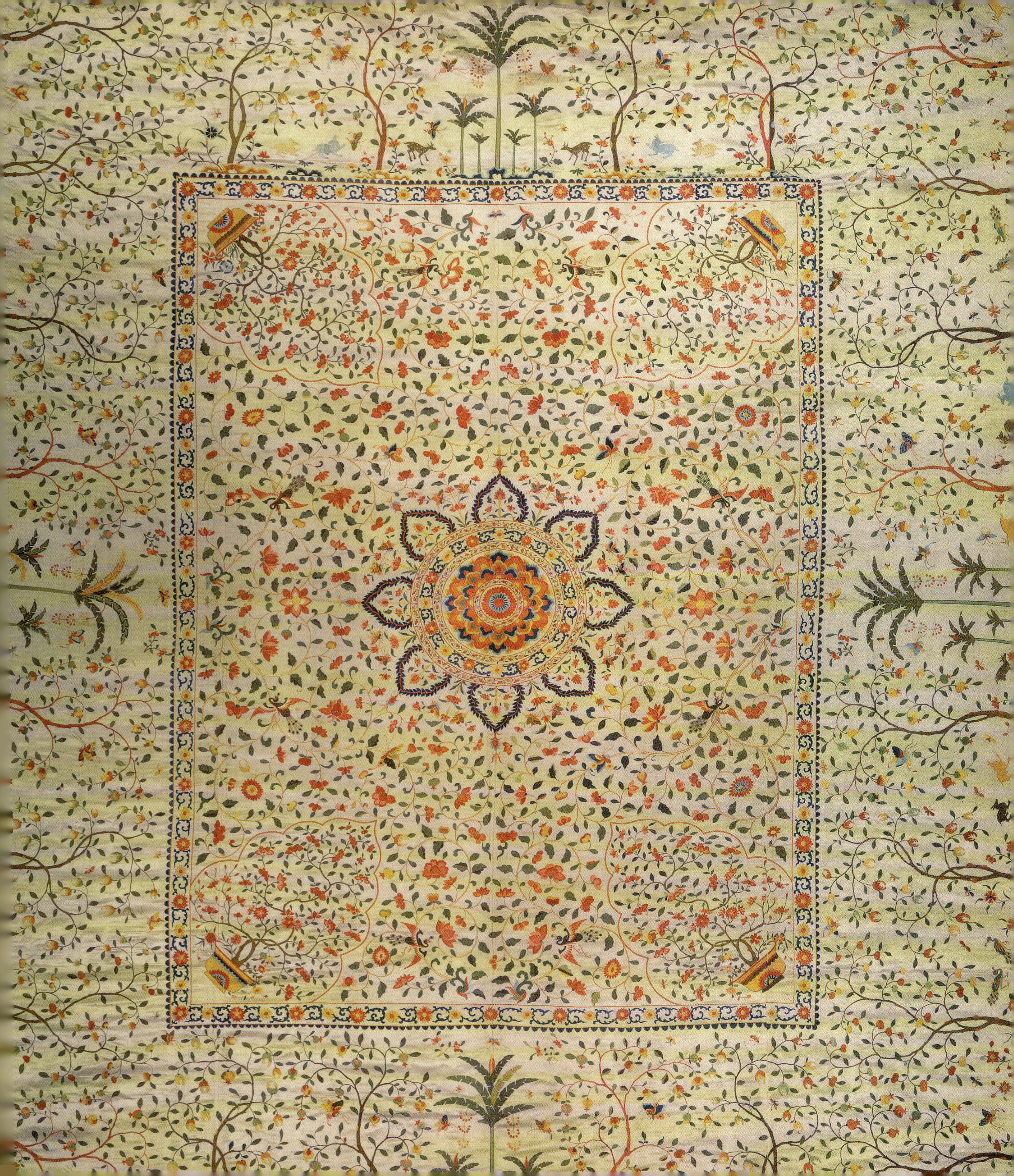

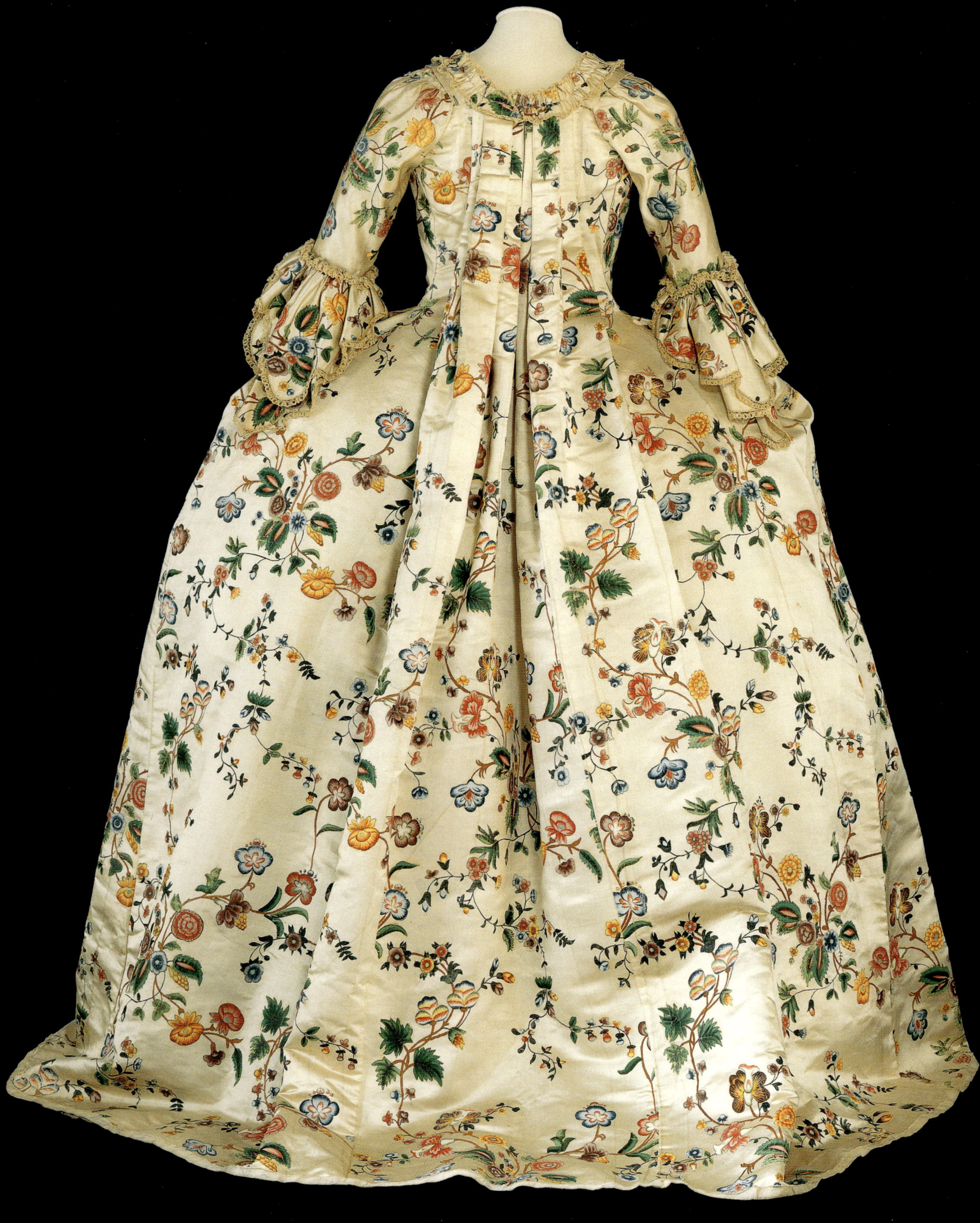

The later seventeenth century witnessed a massive boom in the popularity of Asian textiles in Britain. Part of the generic craze for all things eastern – which included flirtations with Turkish and Persian dress as well as japanned furniture and Chinese porcelain – Indian chintz dress and furnishings, together with Chinese silk fabrics, contributed a strong element of the exotic to an already lively mixed aesthetic. Samuel Pepys (1633–1703), always a useful barometer of upper middle-class taste of the later seventeenth century, bought chintz wall hangings and a chintz gown for his wife in 1663, when the fashion for these painted Indian cottons was at its height. In 1666 he hired an 'Indian gown' for himself, in which to have his portrait painted (plate 20.3). While this seems, from the evidence of the portrait, to have actually been a robe of Chinese silk, or perhaps a Japanese silk kimono, it evidently fell into the category of what Pepys regarded as Indian.[1] Pepys's confused geography was typical of the western response to the new Indian and Chinese goods, with 'Indian' and 'Chinese' often being used interchangeably for exotic furnishings and curiosities.

The confusion is a natural one, given that this period also saw the beginnings of the trade in Chinese silk, in the form of both unwoven yarn and finished textiles. Although Chinese and Indian decorative textiles for the western market share many characteristics, such as a predominantly floral design repertoire that incorporates eastern and western elements, the techniques, materials and designs of the two regions are in fact quite distinct. As with the Indian cotton trade, the bulk of the China textile trade was in less spectacular plain silks and unwoven yarn, but there was also a strong market for beautifully painted and embroidered silk fabrics, used for women's gowns and for bed hangings (plates 20.2, 20.1). French or Italian silk was still *de rigueur* in Britain for formal wear, partly because it was more expensive and hence more prestigious than Indian cotton, but also because the distinctive rustling sound of a generously cut silk gown was still considered a *sine qua non* of female fashionable wear. Here Chinese silks especially showed their worth and could compete with the French and Italian versions. Some eighteenth-century dresses made of Indian cotton even have plain silk under-skirts (which might also be of Indian silk from Bengal), so that the all-important 'frou-frou' could be achieved while wearing a fashionable but disappointingly silent chintz.

When used as furnishings rather than dress, Chinese painted and embroidered silks, like the Indian painted cottons, were mostly employed in bedrooms and dressing rooms, and cream and yellow were considered the suitable colours for this purpose. Surviving beds with Chinese hangings at houses like Osterley Park, Middlesex, and Erddig, near Wrexham in north Wales, confirm this preference.[2] Chinoiserie in general, whether in its Chinese or Indian manifestation, was seen as a playful and essentially informal style. The portrait of 1764 by François-Hubert Drouais (1727–75) of Madame de Pompadour (1721–64), for example, is very clearly meant to show the subject in an informal setting (plate 20.4), unlike the formal portraits of her in which she is always shown in sumptuous silk dresses. In the few informal English portraits of society ladies, the same preference for chintz dresses is evident.[3] The immensely popular man's informal robe known as a *banyan* or Indian nightgown, based on a kimono-style T-shaped cut and made of chintz or any exotic fabric, was also essentially something to wear at home (plate 20.5). It was a matter of slightly shocked comment when gentlemen appeared in them out of doors – something that could only really happen in

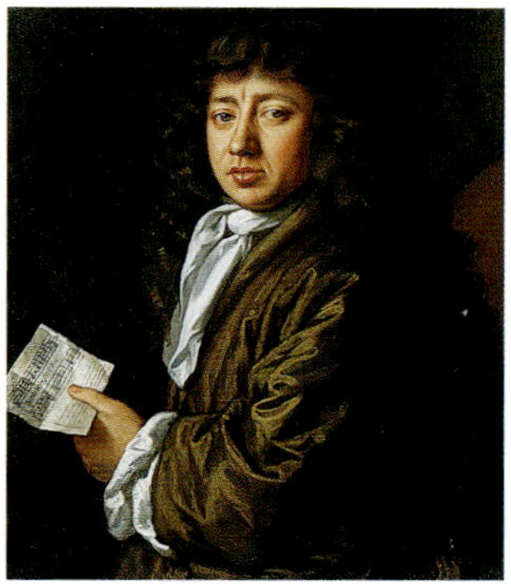

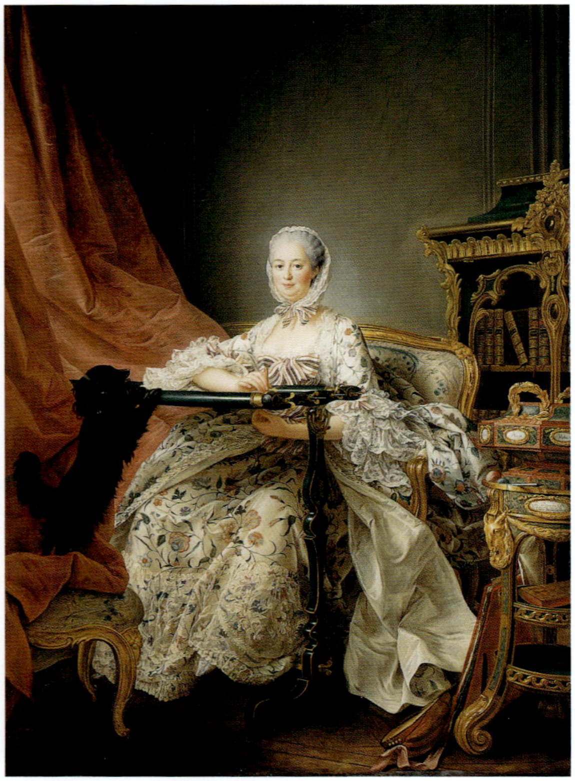

20.1 page 263
Bedcover
Silk, embroidered with coloured silk thread
China, late 18th century
V&A: FE.12-2004; supported by the Friends of the V&A

20.2 opposite
Sack-back gown and petticoat
Painted silk
Cloth: China, c.1760; garment: England, 1760–70
V&A: T.115-1953

20.3 above
Samuel Pepys
John Hayls
Oil on canvas
England (London), 1666
National Portrait Gallery, London

20.4
Madame de Pompadour
François-Hubert Drouais
Oil on canvas
France, 1764
National Gallery, London

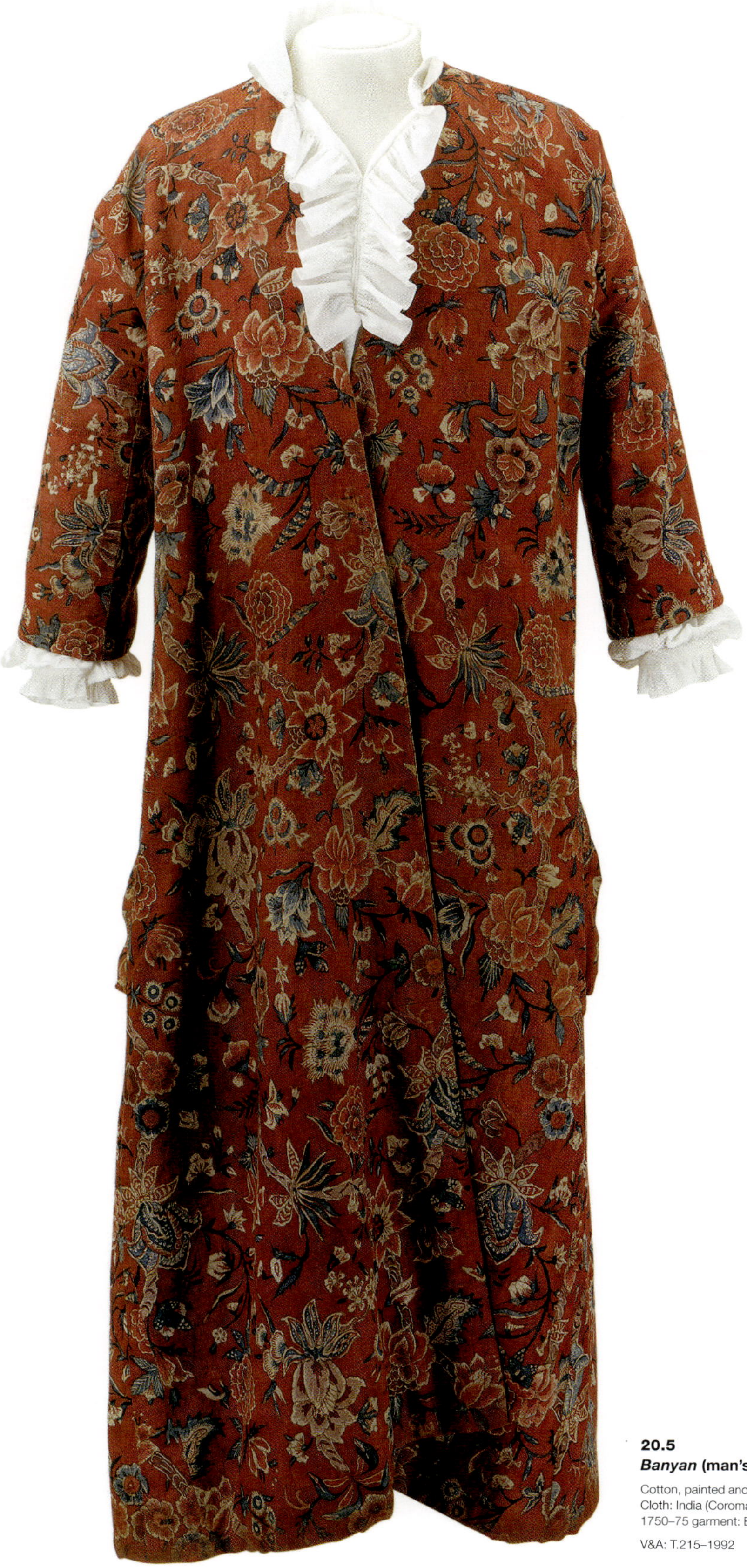

20.5
***Banyan* (man's robe)**

Cotton, painted and dyed
Cloth: India (Coromandel coast), 1750–75 garment: England, 1750–1800
V&A: T.215–1992

places of notably relaxed habits such as Bath, where a certain amount of undress was to be expected.[4]

In striking contrast to this almost bohemian use of exotic fabrics for dress and furnishing, both Indian and Chinese decorative textiles were also used extensively for Christian vestments, for use by Christian communities in the East and in the new colonies in South America (see plate 8.22). Chinese woven, painted or embroidered vestments actually constituted the largest category of ready-made garments from East Asia and were sent to South America from Manila – a standard sea route that was plied by Spanish galleons. Indian chintz vestments were mainly destined for use in Portugal and its colonial outposts, and many examples are still to be found in Portuguese collections.[5]

While chintzes were to become the most enduring symbol of the Asian textile trade, it should also be remembered that they were by no means the first type of Indian cloth to be marketed in the West in the period of European presence in the subcontinent. The Portuguese had been impressed by the embroidery of Bengal and they commissioned large, robust quilts of cotton embroidered in monochrome tussar silk with biblical and mythical scenes.[6] Designs on these quilts were derived from a variety of prints and illustrated Bibles that they had brought with them to their trading posts at Hooghly and other centres. Such embroideries were sent to Portugal, often additionally embellished with the coats of arms of the noble Portuguese families for whom they were intended (plate 20.6). These same 'Bengalla quilts' also found favour in England, certainly by 1618, when they appeared at a sale in London, at which they did remarkably well. Even earlier, that redoubtable Elizabethan, Bess of Hardwick (*c.* 1527–1608), had two Indian embroideries listed in an inventory of the contents of Hardwick Hall in 1601, one of which could well be the splendid Bengali quilt that still survives there, although sadly deteriorated.[7]

Also brought to Europe by the Portuguese were painted cottons called *pintados*. These were the forerunners of what came to be known as 'chintz', a term coined in the seventeenth century by the Dutch and English, who added the plural 's' and later 'z' to the northern Indian word '*chit*' or '*chint*', which simply means 'spotted' or 'coloured'. The earliest *pintados* would have made no concession to western taste, but would have been painted and dyed cloths like those traditionally made as hangings in palaces and temples in southern India. The same craftsmen were already profitably engaged in making painted cottons for the South-East Asian trade (see pp. 55–60). It was only when the Dutch and British started to realize that the painted cottons might sell well in Europe, with some modification for western tastes, that the Indian designs began to reflect an Indianized version of the European patterns or 'musters' that were sent out to be copied. These were at first based largely on crewel-work embroideries that were the standard medium of bed hangings in the seventeenth century, but which were themselves already a hybrid of western and eastern designs, with their exotic blossoms and lush foliage obviously not based on any local English flora (plates 20.8, 20.9).

The flowering tree, usually growing in several branches from a rocky mound at its base, was already established as a popular design in Elizabethan England, and the chintz and embroidered versions were able to slip easily into the English repertoire of furnishings. Although no chintzes firmly datable to the seventeenth century survive, those usually dated to the very beginning of the eighteenth show the progression into ever more elaborate forms of these tree designs (plate 20.7). As the eighteenth century advances, the influence of Chinese porcelain (and later, wallpaper) begins to make itself very clear. Instead of the generic, multi-blossomed tree of the early part of the century, there appear specifically Chinese motifs such as bamboo and peonies, as well as exotic birds like the quail and pheasant.[8] Representations of porcelain vases decorated in Chinese style frequently supplement the rocky mound at the base of the tree.

Floral designs with staggered rows of single flowers were popular during the seventeenth and early eighteenth centuries for embroidered English furnishings and items of dress; these too were translated into chintz and embroideries in India. By 1730, however, these simple designs had become less popular, and East India Company officials requested their associates in India to 'send us some [chintz] in running flowers, and not in single sprigs'.[9] The same letter goes on to stipulate 'the colours must be full, the purple lively, and the cloth well whiten'd. Those sent us from Patna this year we approve of.'[10]

The popularity of western floral paintings also had a huge impact on Indian chintz designs. Large, exuberant Dutch still lifes with vases of tulips, iris, roses and carnations make an unexpected appearance in the works of Indian cotton painters. These were

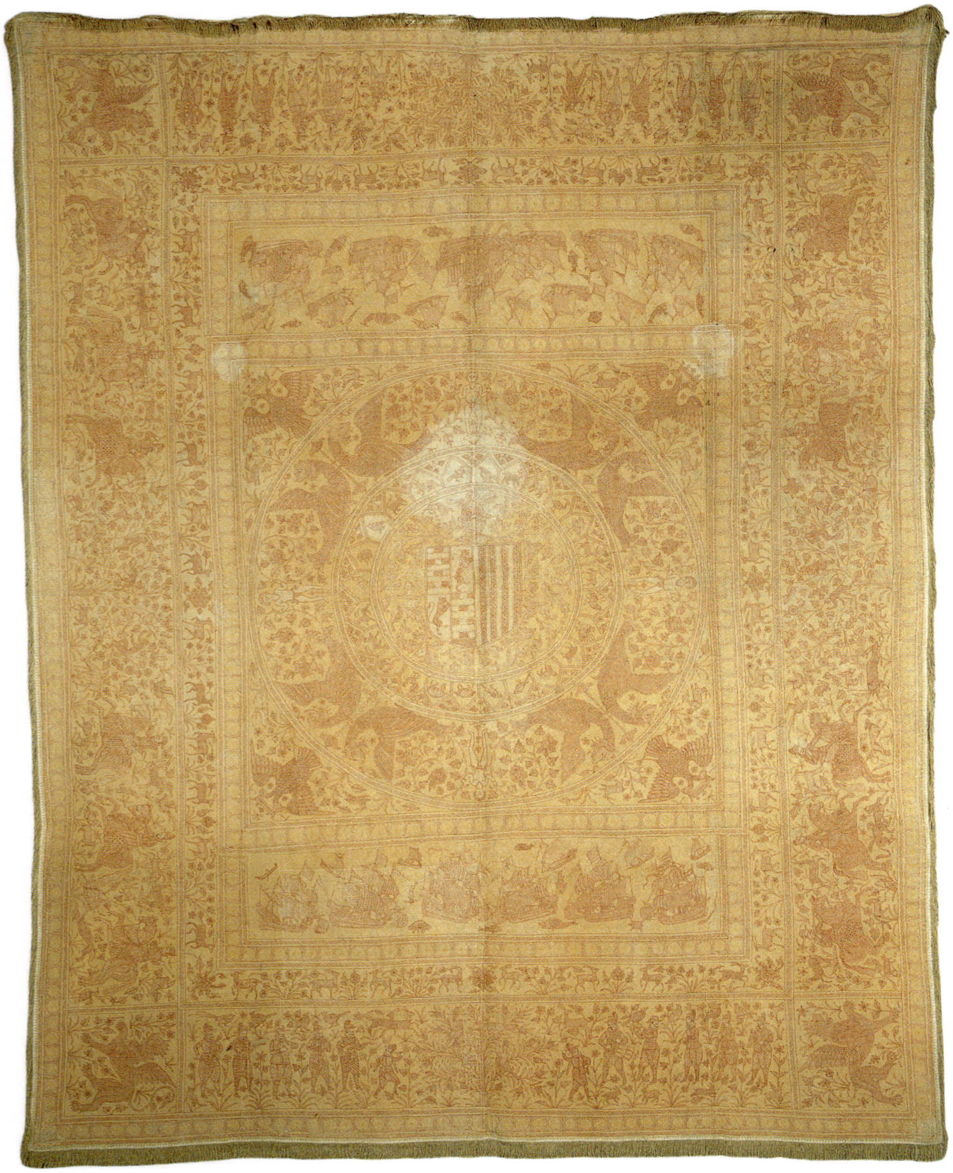

20.6
***Colcha* (quilted bedcover)**

Cotton, quilted and embroidered with silk
India (Satagon, Bengal), 1600–25

V&A: 438–1882

The bedcover is decorated with the coat of arms of the Portuguese family Lima de Vila Nova de Cerveira.

20.7
***Palampore* (bedcover or hanging)**
Cotton, painted and dyed
India (Coromandel coast), mid-18th century
V&A: IS.30–1966

often filtered through the medium of engravings, which were obviously easier than paintings to send to India to be copied. The use of engravings as the basis for the painted design is also apparent in the stippling and cross-hatching used by the cloth painters in their attempt to emulate the effect of prints. Engraved book illustrations provide an even more unexpected source for chintz paintings, with large scenes composed of human figures that make an odd contrast to the floral designs with which they are usually combined.[11]

Engraved ornament of a markedly different kind provided the inspiration for chintz hangings and bed furnishings that were particularly popular with the French market. These were based on the designs of Jean Bérain (1640–1711), who from 1674 held

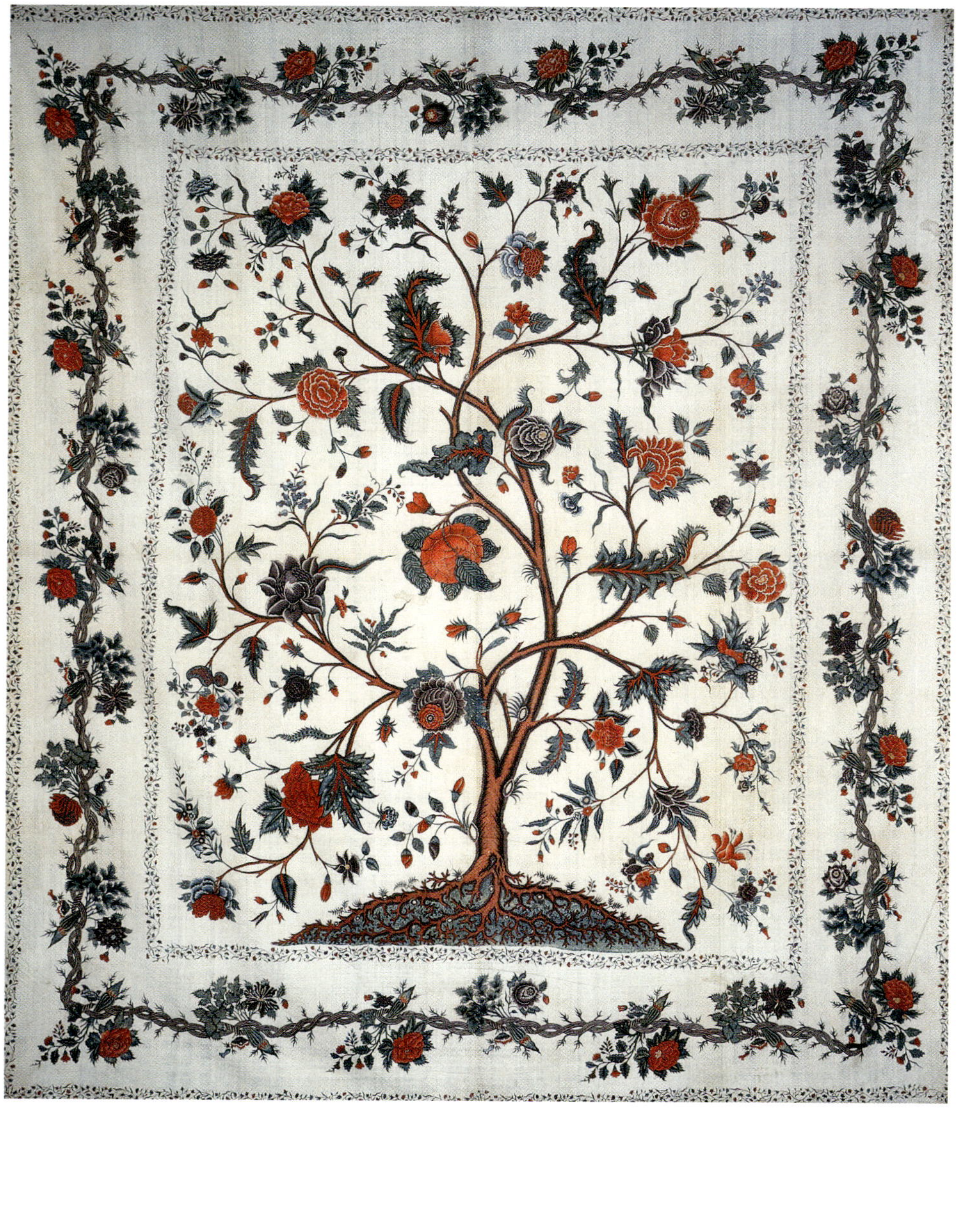

the position of 'Dessinateur de la Chambre et du Cabinet du Roi' under Louis XIV and whose works were immensely influential in his own time and throughout the eighteenth century. Bérain's designs incorporate grotesques and strapwork patterns that were inspired originally by the decoration of classical buildings such as the Domus Aurea in Rome. Indian chintzes with motifs derived from ancient Rome surely represent the longest cultural journey made by any of the patterns that returned to the West (plate 20.10).[12]

Another notable French contribution to the repertoire of the Indian chintz painter (and to the Indian designers of embroidery and Chinese silk painters working for the western market) was that of woven silks, and in particular the so-called 'bizarre' silks made in France in the early eighteenth century (plate 20.11). Characterized by a strong diagonal movement in a predominantly floral design, these silk fabrics projected such a sense of the exotic that some authorities have gone so far as to suggest that they originated in India, a hypothesis that has been rejected by specialists in Indian rather than European textile history.[13] The high status of woven silks, especially those from France, easily explains the popularity of the 'bizarre' and other woven designs as prototypes for export chintzes and embroideries.

The development of the immense export market for Indian textiles took place remarkably rapidly after the establishment of the East India Company in 1600 until, by 1664, textiles accounted for nearly 75 per cent of the entire export trade from India. The correspondence between the Company directors in London and their representatives in India and, from 1699, Canton (Guangzhou), in the huge East India Company archive held at the British Library in London, reveals something of the mechanics of this trade. Minutely detailed instructions were sent out from London in response to every shipment of cloth that was received from the East, specifying changes to be made to the colours and designs of the cloth, as well as assessments of the products of the various centres. While good-quality textiles receive a terse acknowledgement of approval from London, there are frequent complaints in Company correspondence about the variable quality of other 'assortments', as they were known. In 1727, for example, 'various mulmulls' (muslins) were ordered, but 40,000 pieces were left unsold and the Company writer complains bitterly that the Indian factory is 'overloading us with unprofitable goods'.[14]

With regard to selection and quality control, exactly the same type of correspondence took place between England and Canton as between England and India. A letter of 1730 to Canton, for example, urges the eastern representatives to send 'fewer of the dark dirty greens' in silk, just as a letter to India almost 100 years earlier rejects the cotton cloths with 'sad red grounds'.[15] It is interesting to note that the same 'sad red grounds' evidently appealed to Dutch – if not to English – taste, as by 1675 Company representative William Puckle in Masulipatam wrote that 'ye Dutch have taken up and bespoke all ye red cloaths'.[16] This assiduous quality control and the subtle responses to changing tastes of London consumers are all the more impressive when one considers the distances and time-lag involved in acting on the Company's instructions.

Rather than dealing directly with the thousands of craftsmen producing textiles for these orders, the Company employed powerful local merchants as middle-men, or *dubashes,* through whom to convey their instructions. Tamil Nadu records, in particular, have yielded much information about the extent of these 'prime merchants' and their powers and responsibilities.[17] As early as the 1620s, William Methwold, the English factor at Masulipatam, listed the various levels of merchant who facilitated the Company's trade. The foremost were the Komatis, a Telugu term that simply means merchant – as does Chetty, the community from which most of these merchants came. These people were major traders in their own right, under whom a pyramid of lesser merchants farmed out work to the weavers and cotton painters scattered throughout the hinterland of the Coromandel area, and ensured that the Company's orders were filled. A famous merchant called Malaya Chetty, described by one recent commentator as 'the foremost merchant capitalist of his time',[18] was the principal agent for the Dutch trade from his base in Pulicat from 1608 until his death in 1634 (as well as having his own lucrative trade with South-East Asia), and built himself such an imposing house that it appeared on charts as a landmark for ships.

The majority of the Indian cloth imported into Britain by the Company was plain, mundane, cheap yardage, intended for workers' shifts, under-shirts and other underclothes, bed sheets and covers and other utilitarian purposes. Sent out in the early days of the Company mainly from its first headquarters at Surat in Gujarat, and produced in the hinterland of north-west India, the Coromandel trade became at least as significant from the later seventeenth century. Company records are full of lists of different types of cloth; the precise definitions of most of these are now sadly lost. Even if it is not possible to say exactly what these textiles looked like, it is obvious from the quantities and prices that for the most part they were not expensive goods. In 1675, for example, the invaluable William Puckle records that a consignment from Madapollam included 20,000 'ordinary Sallempores' as well as 10,000 pieces of 'long cloth, ordinary' and 10,000 Dungarees, and 1,500 fine salloes made at Golconda, which were obviously a more expensive item.[19] While these piece-goods are precisely the type of cloth that so improved the lives of many of the poorer members of British society – providing them with underclothes for the first time, for example – it is not these that we associate with the Indian textile trade, but the beautiful painted chintzes and embroideries that adorned fashionable homes and bodies from the mid-seventeenth century until the late eighteenth.

The enthusiastic adoption of new fabrics from India can be explained only partly in purely practical terms. Obviously cotton cloth was pleasant to wear and live with, and could be kept clean with unprecedented convenience. But the hunger for novelty was perhaps an even greater incentive for acquiring cotton, and this appetite was common to all levels of society. For the first time the new and sought-after goods were cheap enough that even the less affluent were able to participate in the craze. Traditionally fashions had trickled down, in increasingly dilute form, from the court to the street; but the fashion for cotton was the first that allowed everyone to own examples of the real thing rather than cheap local variations. It should also be borne in mind that in the late seventeenth century, when the Indian cotton craze reached its first peak, fashion and prestige were embodied at least as much in the actual cloth from which a garment was made as in its cut or decoration. The appeal of Indian chintz fabric endured well into the eighteenth century, as is apparent in the 1763 and 1764 portraits of the supremely fashionable Madame de Pompadour, who is depicted wearing gowns of chintz that appear to be at least 50 years old (plate 20.4).[20]

So popular were the imported Indian cottons that English, French and Dutch weavers of wool

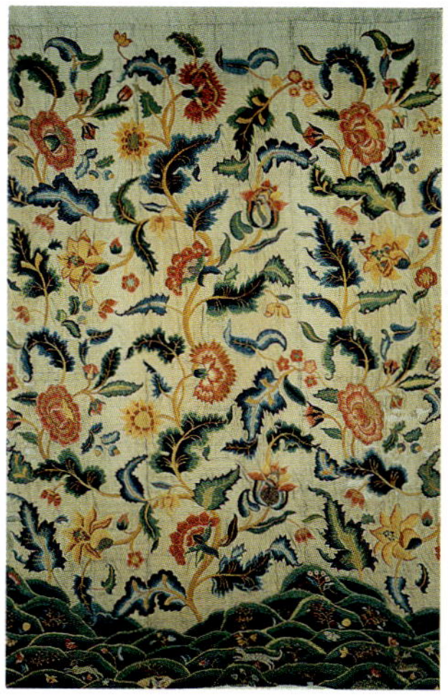

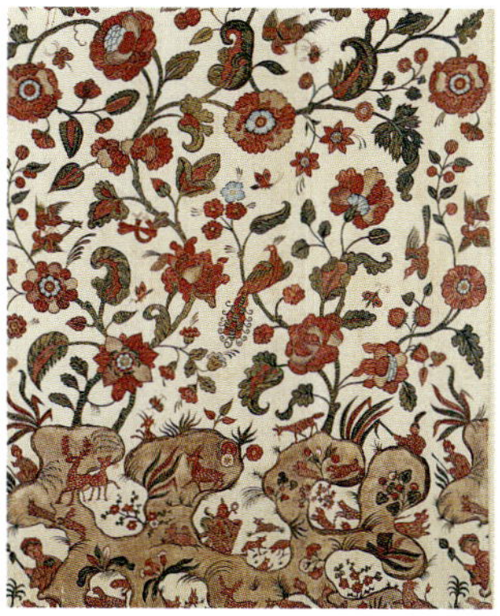

20.8
Bed hanging

Linen and cotton, embroidered with wool
England, *c.*1700

V&A: 72c–1897

20.9
Bed hanging

Cotton, painted and dyed
India (Coromandel coast), *c.*1700

V&A: IS.156–1953

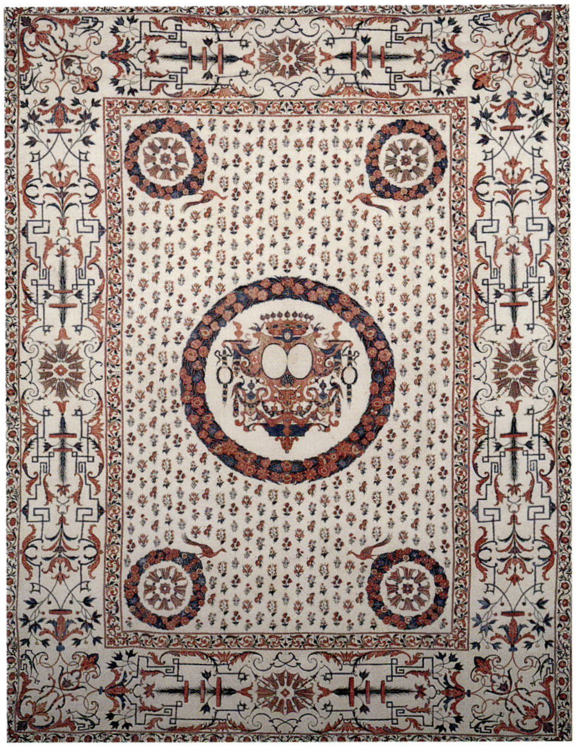

20.10
***Palampore* (bedcover or hanging)**

Cotton, painted and dyed
India (Coromandel coast), early 18th century

V&A: IS.4–1968

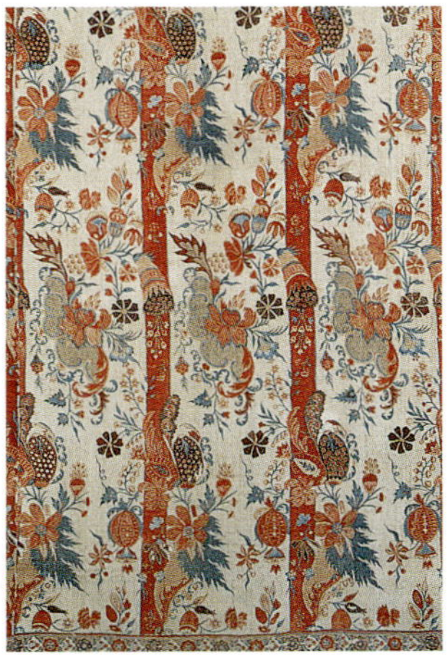

20.11
Length of dress fabric

Cotton, painted and dyed
India (Coromandel coast), *c.*1715–25

V&A: 342–1898

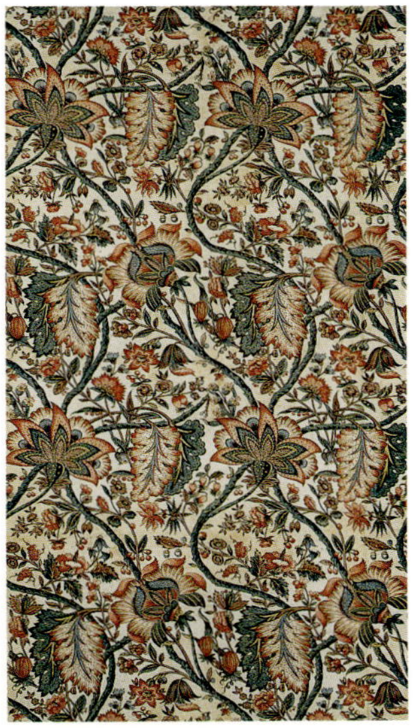

20.12
Length of furnishing fabric

Cotton, block-printed
England, *c.*1795

V&A: 422–1887

and linen cloth feared for their livelihoods. Their concerns were well founded, as it soon became obvious that once the public had experienced cotton clothing and furnishings, 'moved to it as well for the Cheapness, as the Lightness of the Cloth, and the Gaiety of the Colours',[21] they would never want to return to the local woollen and linen fabrics. The British government, desperate to save the local weavers' trade, attempted some extreme measures to force people to wear wool. A law was passed in 1678, for example, decreeing that all English corpses must be buried wrapped in local woollen cloth. A bill of 1689 intended to enforce the wearing of wool for six months of every year failed, not surprisingly, to become law, as did another that would force female servants to wear hats of English felt. In the end, the government had to take the extreme step of prohibiting the import of Indian cotton in two Acts of Parliament of 1700 and 1721, the second of which extended to the importing of plain Indian cloth, which would then be printed in imitation of Indian chintz by increasingly skilled English printers. These English imitations were almost as much of a threat to the weavers as the genuine Indian chintzes, and the printers were denigrated as 'Britain's unnatural children' by Daniel Defoe (1660–1731), a great champion of the weavers' cause.[22]

Prohibition of Indian cloth did not of course diminish the desire for it, and smuggling was rife. Dramatic scenes in which weavers tore chintz clothing from ladies' backs were part of the so-called 'Calico Wars' of 1719, while the war of words between the pro– and anti-calico factions was conducted in Parliament and in print. The situation changed dramatically and permanently in 1771 when Richard Arkwright (1732–92) invented a machine that was capable, for the first time, of spinning the fine Indian cotton yarn. This led to the repeal of the import restrictions in 1774, and both weaving and printing of Indian cotton then took off in Britain in an unprecedented way. Printing technology as well as weaving made great advances, notably with the introduction of metal blocks that enabled larger pattern repeats and finer detailing than wooden ones. From the evidence of sample- and scrapbooks like Barbara Johnson's album, it is clear that, by the 1770s, Indian and English chintz dress materials were practically indistinguishable (plate 20.12).[23] In France, where attempts had been made to imitate Indian painted cottons since the late sixteenth century,[24] even more dramatic advances in printing were being made in the 1770s and 1780s. Foremost among the printers was C.P. Oberkampf, who produced some of the finest printed cottons in his factory at Jouy near Paris, many of them in direct imitation of Indian chintz designs.[25] The success of these European imitations, following on from the crippling blow dealt to the Indian cotton trade by prohibition, effectively spelt the end of the craze for genuine Indian chintz in Europe.

Chintz fabrics had been part of a trend towards increasingly informal dress from the late seventeenth century onwards, in which rigidly tailored garments for both men and women were replaced by styles depending for their effect on looser draperies. Even when the fashion for chintz had waned at the end of the eighteenth century, this desire for ease and comfort in dress continued at an even greater pace, emerging in the neoclassical style of the 1780s. Inspired in part by the statuary of ancient Greece and Rome, the new fashion was epitomized by light cotton gowns falling around the body in an unstructured way, held around the high waist with a simple sash and accompanied by a soft shawl draped around exposed shoulders. This style was ideal for the Indian imports of Bengali muslin and Kashmiri shawls (plate 20.13).

Muslin, often known by the anglicized Indian term 'mulmull', had been one of the staples of the Bengali cotton trade, and had been used mainly for accessories like women's neckwear and undergarments. Now it was being appreciated in its own right as a perfect material for the new, light fashions. Although British women in India dreaded the onset of the hot season, as a condemnation to months of boring white muslin dresses, from the 1780s muslin started to become fashionable wear in France and Britain. Championed by such influential figures as Emma Hamilton in England and Madame Recamier in France, the so-called 'Empire' style catapulted Indian muslin into the forefront of fashion. Simple white or silver-thread embroidery was also sometimes used to embellish it lightly without eroding its virginal appeal, and its pairing with the newly fashionable Kashmir shawl ensured the popularity of both.

Kashmir shawls were too expensive, and made in too small a quantity, ever to become a significant part of the East India Company's textile trade, and most of the commerce in shawls was done through individuals. Many of these were moonlighting British administrators and French military officers who, through their commissions in the Punjab, had access to the shawl weavers who sold their wares in Lahore and Amritsar.[26] Although Kashmir shawls already had high status in the courts of northern India, and had long been exported to Iran, Turkey and Egypt, they only started to make an impression in Britain at the end of the eighteenth century. The shawl's real moment of glory arrived in about 1800 when it was taken up by the Empress Josephine (1763–1814), who reputedly had a collection of more than 1,000 examples. Several paintings show her draped in shawls, and other fashionable French women soon followed suit. A shawl became an essential accessory and, with increasingly exuberant designs, continued to be in fashion until about the 1860s. But undermined, like chintz, by clever local imitations, the shawl fell from favour and, where once it had been an essential part of a fashionable bride's trousseau, it now became an emblem of outmoded taste relegated to covering Victorian pianos.

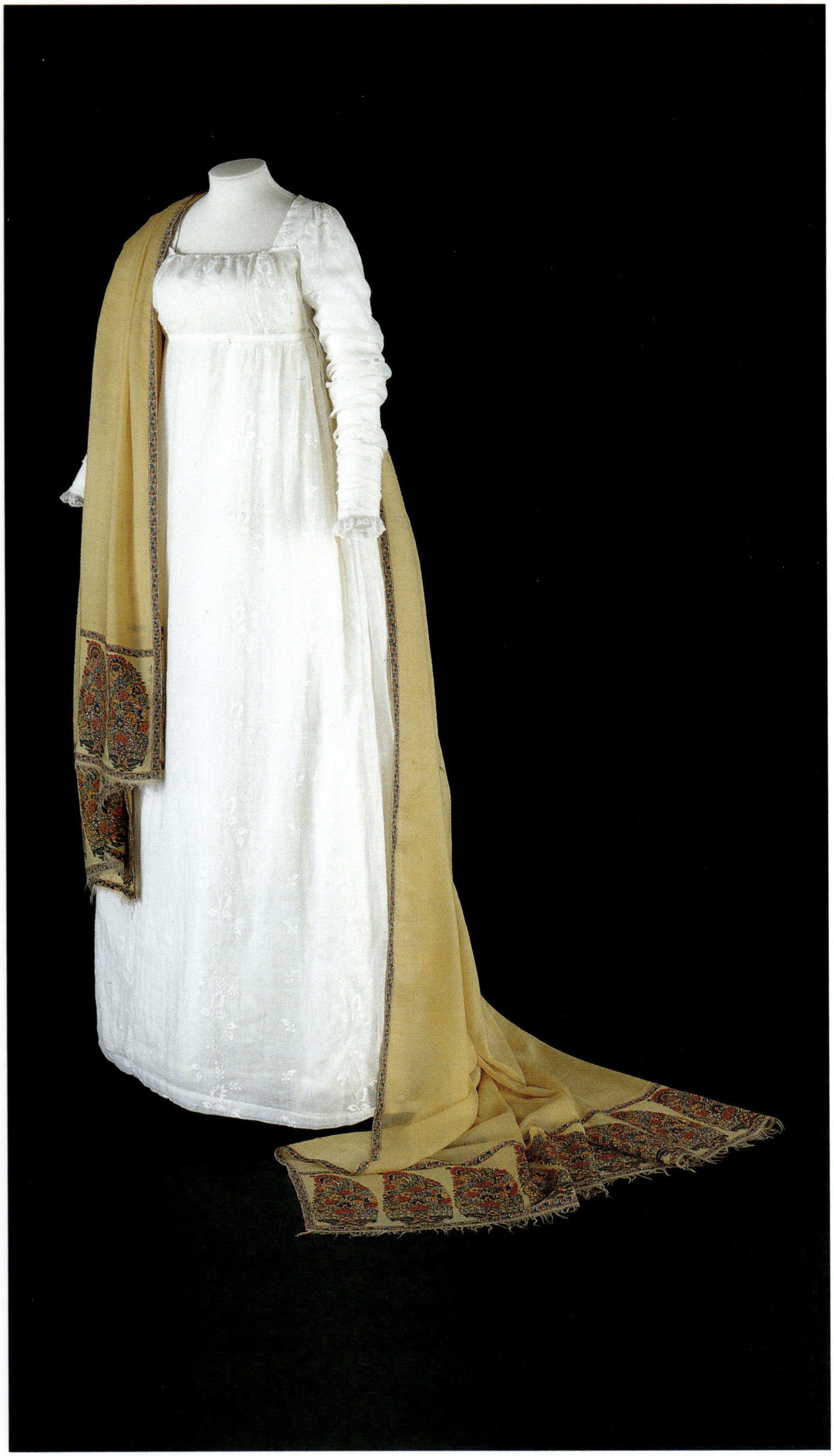

20.13
Gown

Muslin, embroidered with cotton thread and trimmed with lace
Cloth: India (Bengal), c.1800, gown: England, c.1800–08

V&A: 444–1888

Shawl

Woven goat hair (pashmina)
India (Kashmir), late 18th century

V&A: IS.83–1988; gift of Mrs M. Jacquet

21

ASIA IN EUROPE: CHINESE PAINTINGS FOR THE WEST

William R. Sargent

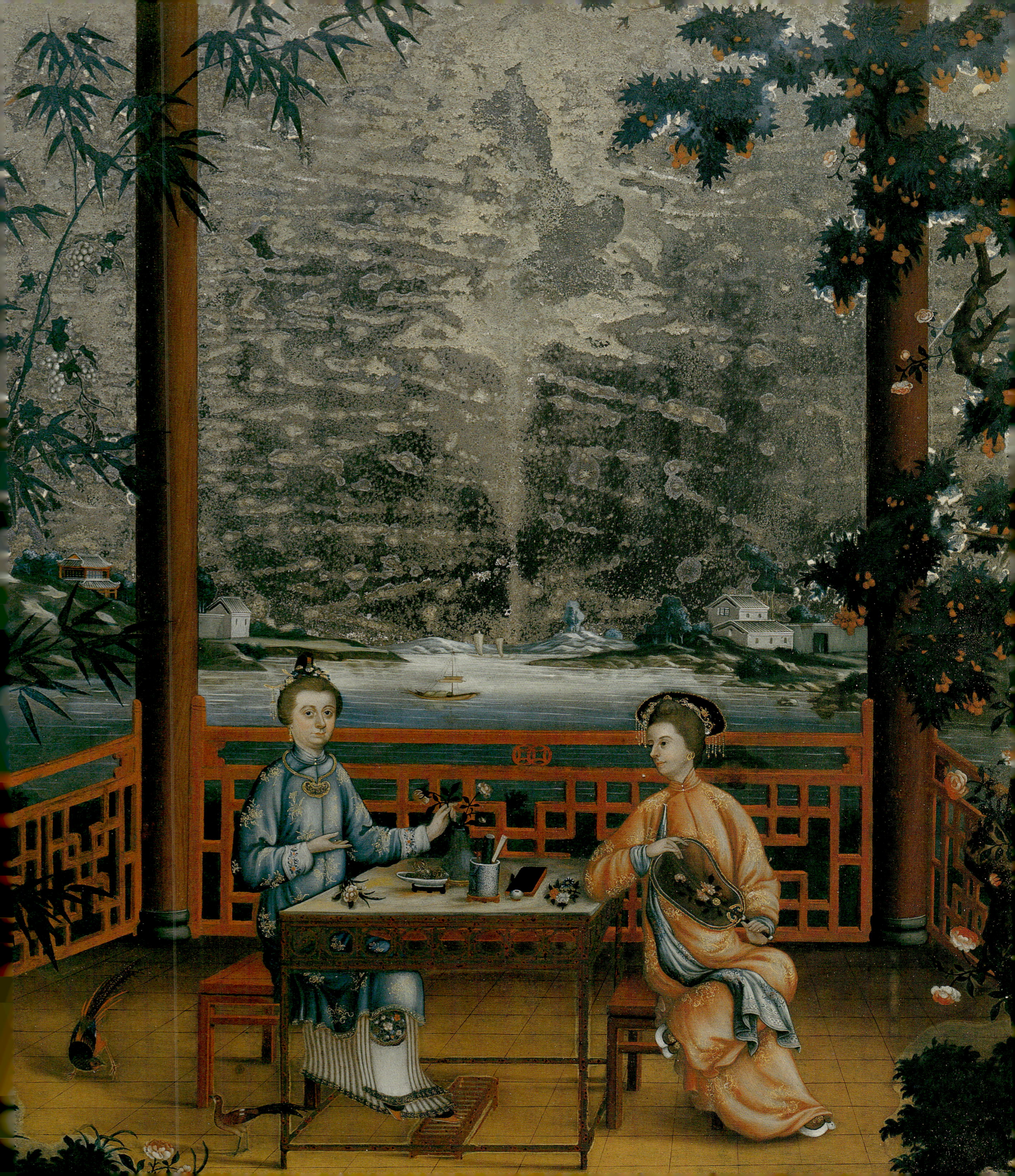

21.1 previous page
Mrs and Miss Revell
Reverse painting on glass
China (Canton), *c.* 1800
Peabody Essex Museum, Salem

INSATIABLE WESTERN CURIOSITY about Asia created a wide market for visual documentation. This interest began with the writing of Marco Polo's travels in 1297–98, and reached its peak in the sixteenth to eighteenth centuries. The desire to record the characteristics and peoples of China was satisfied first by western artists and then by artists native to China. The works of the latter, produced through a complex mix of Chinese and European influences, have yielded a body of art documenting China's landscape, flora and fauna, architecture, people, daily life, trades, manufacturing techniques and customs, including weddings, funerals, birthdays, religious celebrations and even punishments. These illustrations also served as an important design source for western architects, craftsmen and interior and landscape designers. Painting was the perfect medium for conveying information about China as it was quick to produce, relatively inexpensive and easy to transport.

Chinese scroll paintings were known to have been brought to Europe by the Franciscans during the *Pax Mongolica* (*c.* 1250–1350) and it has been conjectured that these scrolls may have been 'the catalyst for this naturalistic breakthrough wrought by Giotto and his contemporaries'.[1] Cesare Vecellio's *De gli habiti antichi, et moderni*, published in Venice in 1590, derives four examples of Chinese dress from original drawings; the Copenhagen University Library contained books in Chinese by 1623; paintings – probably of a type exported from China to Japan – were included in the cabinet of curiosities of Archduke Ferdinand II of Tyrol (r. 1564–95); and John Evelyn (1620–1706) mentioned in his diaries that an English Jesuit showed him paintings from China of '… Landskips, of their Idols, Saints, Pagods, of the most ougly, Serpentine, monstrous and Hideous to which they paie devotion; Pictures of men, and Countries rarely painted on a sort of gumm'd Calico transparent as glasse'.[2] Another notable extant example of Chinese art in the West is the *Section of a Chinese painting*, *c.* 1730, depicting a Manchu wedding procession through a village, found in the *Livre des desseins chinois* (1735) by Jean-Antoine Fraisse (1680?–1738/39), with additions attributed to Fraisse.[3] Yet none of these works can be called 'export' in the true sense – that is, they were not produced specifically for the western market.

By the late seventeenth century, with the sea route to Asia well established, luxury goods from China were exported to Europe in large quantities and these included paintings on paper, wallpaper, glass and canvas. Thanks to the burgeoning global economy of the eighteenth century, such works found their way into great country houses in Europe, and even America, many of which would have had at least one room decorated in an Oriental style, reflecting the enormous interest in Asia that existed at the time.

Although the best source of visual information about the Asian culture that created them, paintings were never a significant part of commercial trade between Europe and China. They were, instead, traded privately or purchased as souvenirs. The earliest date for the importation of what might be Chinese export paintings appears to be 1727, when 'Pictures, 4 Cases' was listed as the private trade of Captain Francis Gostlin of the *Prince Augustus*.[4] Three years later, in 1730, there is a reference to a box of pictures containing 400 loose sheets – obviously works on paper.[5] Although these may have been painted specifically for westerners, without detailed descriptions to confirm this, it is just as likely that they were simply Chinese paintings or prints collected as curiosities. In fact it is not until the nineteenth century that the ordering of paintings by Westerners is well documented.

Two factors were instrumental in the dissemination of western art in Asia: one was religion, the other commerce. Religious art from Europe, in the form of engravings, oil canvases and illustrated Bibles, was first introduced to Asia in the sixteenth century by Jesuits, who used such visual material in their efforts to spread the Christian message (see chapter 8). This initiated a period of artistic cross-fertilization, wherein European originals were used as models for the production of religious arts for Christian communities, both local and foreign. Artists attached to religious missions were succeeded by those accompanying mercantile voyages, who documented raw materials and manufactures in the hope that these could be exploited for commercial advantage.

Exactly how Chinese artists learned western techniques and what their attitudes were towards their customers is not known, but a new generation of Chinese scholars is beginning to address these issues.[6] There are no records of East Asian artists studying under western teachers, other than in schools established in Asia by the Church specifically for the production of religious art. However, European artists did visit Asia, and their presence in coastal trading ports eventually influenced local imitators. It is more likely, however, that Asian artists learned western techniques from copying prints, book illustrations or other secondary sources (plate 21.2).

The module system of production was universal but most prevalent in China, and it enabled the production of paintings in large quantities and of great variety.[7] This system allowed for the widest creative expression in any given art form, using a limited number of component parts that could be combined in varying ways to produce what appears to be a unique work of art, whether this was in painting, furniture, bronze or ceramics. Based on the division of labour, it facilitated speedy production, quality control, serial production and standardization. But such production by reproduction often led to anonymity and a repression of artistic expression. The mass production of paintings using the module system is often remarked on by European visitors in the nineteenth century. Monsieur La Vollée, a French writer, wrote in 1849:

> Lam Qua then introduced us into the outer apartment which was a sort of workshop. Here were twenty youths copying drawings upon great rolls of white or yellow paper, or upon that fine pith we in Europe obstinately call rice-paper although there is no rice in it ... It would take a day to pass in review the pictures, the rolls of drawings and albums heaped up in the shop of Lam Qua. This picture business in China is immense.[8]

As in western artisan traditions, anonymity was fairly normal in the export arts of Asia. In the later eighteenth and nineteenth centuries individual names were sometimes attached to paintings. While these may indicate the actual artist, it is more likely that they identify his studio, for it was common for each artist who gained individual recognition to establish his own business. Identical works of art with the signature of a single artist can vary stylistically, implying that each was painted by various artists working under a studio name. Nearly identical scenes known to be from different studios reflect the constant exchange of influences within the artisan community.

The tradition of painting with water-based paints on paper was common to both eastern and western cultures, and was used both for fine arts and commercial purposes within the courts and among commoners. But the technique was especially useful for the export markets because of the low cost of materials and the speed with which works in this media could be produced. Albums depicting methods of production of ceramics, silk and tea proved to be among the most popular themes for Chinese export paintings (plate 21.4). Such albums were generally

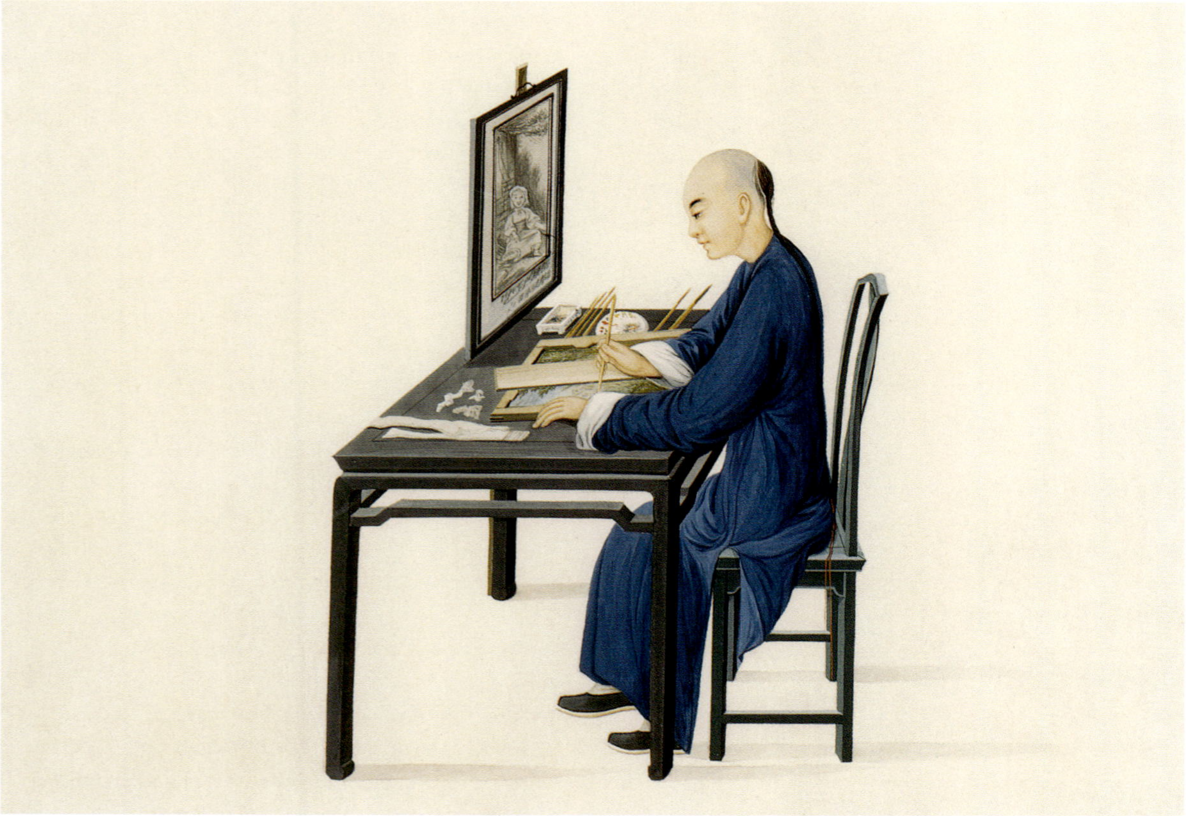

21.2
Artist Copying a European Print onto Glass

Pu-Quà workshop, from a set of 100 plates depicting trades and occupations
Opaque watercolour on paper
China (Canton), *c.* 1790

V&A: D.107–1898

21.3
Liang, the First Minister

From an album depicting Chinese figures
Opaque watercolour and watercolour on paper
China (Canton), *c.* 1735

Peabody Essex Museum, Salem

21.4 below
European Visitors to a Tea Warehouse

From an album of 23 plates depicting tea production
Opaque watercolour on paper
China (Canton), 1780–90

V&A: D.1090–1898

21.5 opposite
Wallpaper panel

Opaque watercolour on paper
China (Canton), 18th century

Peabody Essex Museum, Salem

painted in sets of 24 and closely followed Chinese originals first published in the *Yuzhi Gengzhi Tu* (*Pictures of Tilling and Weaving*) commissioned by the Kangxi emperor in 1696, and the *Taoye Tushuo* (*Illustrated Description of Ceramic Making*) commissioned by the Qianlong emperor in 1743. The printed sets made for the Chinese market consisted of 20 views. The additional views in sets made for export generally depict packing, shipping and display of the final products, which would have been of particular interest to western merchants. Production views were not popular merely because they satisfied curiosity, but also because it was hoped they might offer insights into manufacturing methods that could be replicated in the West. The paintings provided only minimal information, however, because they followed conventions established by the imperial albums that 'glorified the production of rice and silk under a benign ruler ... [and] the purpose was to portray the workers as a happy lot in pleasant surroundings, not to illuminate technical details'.[9]

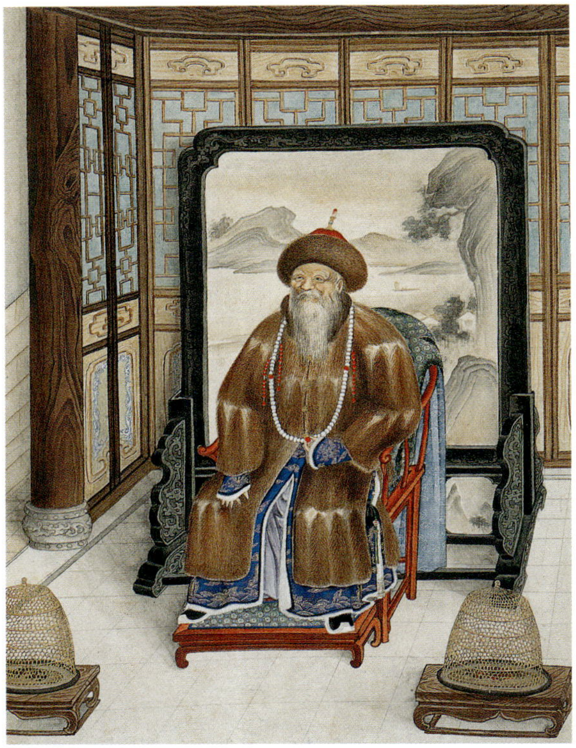

Perhaps the earliest documented album representing Chinese people for the western market

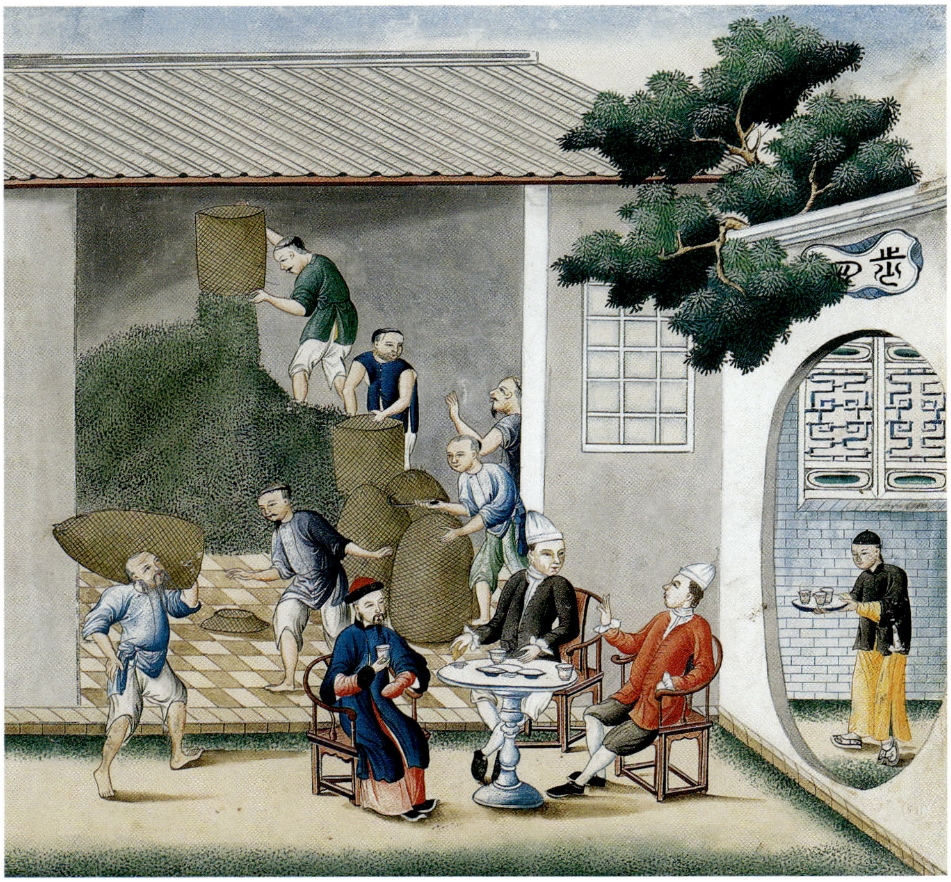

is one of 30 Chinese figures in domestic settings, *c.* 1735, bound in leather and bearing the book plate of Thomas Philip, 2nd Earl Grey, from his estate at Wrest Park, Bedfordshire (plate 21.3). An inscription is written on the inside board: 'I bought these Chinese Drawings for 16 Guineas at the Auction of Mr. Martin the Supercargoes effects in March 1747 / P. Yorke.' Originally there were 34 paintings, only 30 of which remain, and two extra paintings not part of the original series have been added.[10] The album, which depicts historical characters, members of the royal household, a monk, student, doctor, and so on, was keyed with a description of each illustration in French, and this was later annotated by 'Che Qua, a Chinese modeller, who was in England in 1769, [and] read & explained the Characters in this book, /which he said were in the Mandarine language ...'[11]

In Europe, wallpaper – a form of decoration unknown in China – was first used as a less expensive alternative to covering walls with tapestries, silks or cottons. Chinese export examples were known in Europe by at least 1693, when an advertisement in the *London Gazette* announced the sale of paper hangings of 'Indian and Japan figures'.[12] By 1724 a parlour at Wanstead, in Essex, was described as 'adorned with China paper, the figures of men, women, birds, flowers, the liveliest I ever saw come from that country'.[13] In the eighteenth century papers were imported throughout Europe, but were most common in Britain, where they embellished rooms decorated entirely in a Chinese style. 'China' rooms could be found in many a great house, such as Chatsworth or Osterley Park.[14] Lady Beauchamp Proctor described such a room in 1772: 'The lodging rooms are in the atticks and are furnished with the finest Chintzes, painted Taffatys, Indian paper and decker work, and such a profusion of rich China and Japan, that I could almost fancy myself in Peking.'[15]

Papers were usually produced in sets of 25 or 40 panels – about 3.6 metres long and 0.9–1.2 metres wide – which, when lining the walls, created a continuous scene. The themes depicted on Chinese wallpapers can generally be divided into three categories: the earliest is of flowering trees, shrubs and plants; the second of daily life in China; the third of landscapes or country scenes with figures. Of the first category, the botanist Sir Joseph Banks (1744–1820) observed in 1771 that 'Some of the plants common to China and Java, as bamboo, are better figured there than by the best botanical authors I have seen.'[16] The second type includes production views of porcelain, silk and tea, not unlike those found in albums. The finest surviving example of the third type is the panoramic view of Canton (Guangzhou) of *c.* 1780 that once hung in the Ladies' Room at Strathallan Castle at Auchterader, Scotland (see endpapers).

As early as 1737–38 American colonial records indicate that Chinese wallpapers were being imported from London. An example depicting the production of porcelain said to have been brought to America in 1770 lay unopened in a house in Marblehead, Massachusetts, until the twentieth century and is now in the collection of the Peabody Essex Museum, Salem (plate 21.5). Another set of wallpaper still *in situ* in America was installed in the Samuel Dexter house in Dedham, Massachusetts, in 1761.[17]

There are also documents attesting to the use of Chinese pictures in interiors, where they were pasted above fireplaces and on walls. In 1742 Lady Cardigan bought 88 'Indian pictures' and had them pasted 'all over the walls of a dining room' by Benjamin Goodison (*c.* 1700–67), the renowned cabinetmaker.[18] This technique was used to decorate the Chinese Room at Erddig, near Wrexham, in the 1770s (plate 21.7), and that at Clifton Hall, Nottinghamshire. When there were not enough Chinese originals, English imitations were used to fill in the spaces.

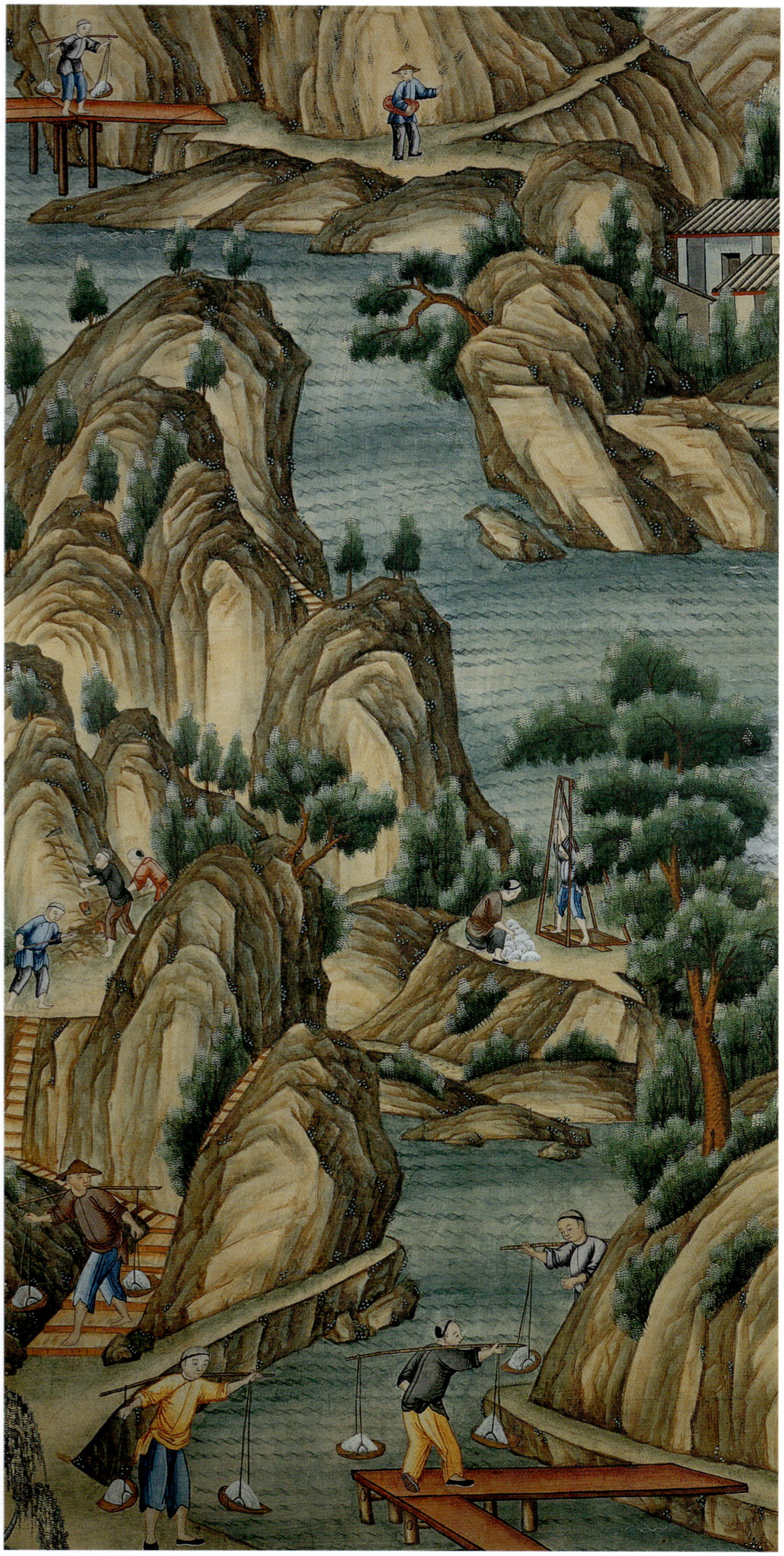

21.6
Portrait of the Late Shuja-ud-Daula and His Sons

Reverse painting on glass
China (Canton), *c.*1800

Peabody Essex Museum, Salem

On the subject of Chinese artists, Alvarez Semedo wrote in 1655 that 'in painting they have more curiosities than perfection. They know not how to make use of oyles or shadowing in this art, and do therefore paint the figures of men without any grace at all; but trees, flowers, birds and suchlike things, they paint very much to the life.'[19] It was the Jesuits who first introduced painting with oils to local artists working at Asian courts. By the late eighteenth century the technique was employed by Chinese painters producing works commercially, although this had more to do with contemporary western demand than with the influence of the earlier Jesuit artists. Oil on glass was the first development, followed by oil on canvas – the perfect medium for recording port views, ships and people.

Reverse paintings on glass had been produced in Europe since the early seventeenth century, centred in the Low Countries. It is generally accepted that the technique was brought to China by the Jesuits. In a letter of November 1743 Father Jean-Denis Attiret (1702–68) (who had joined Giuseppe Castiglione in Peking [Beijing] in 1738) wrote that he painted in watercolours on silk, or in oil on glass.[20] The mirror base for such paintings could not be produced successfully in China, as was confirmed by an eighteenth-century observation: 'Looking glasses and glass mirrors have been manufactured there [Canton], quicksilvered in the European manner, but this undertaking has not proved successful.'[21] Instead, mirrors were imported from Europe. Before the application of paint, the silvering on the mirrored surface was removed with a steel tool and designs in oil substituted. Artists gradually began to utilize more and more of the glass until paint covered most of the surface. By the late eighteenth century they were to dispense with mirrors altogether and paint directly on clear sheets of glass. The technique of reverse painting required the artist to literally paint in the reverse way used on canvas, paper or panel; that is, the foreground was painted first and the background last. The technique, also known in the West as 'back-painting', was described in the *Dictionarium Polygraphicum* of 1735 as 'quite contrary to that of limning or painting on cloth or wood'.

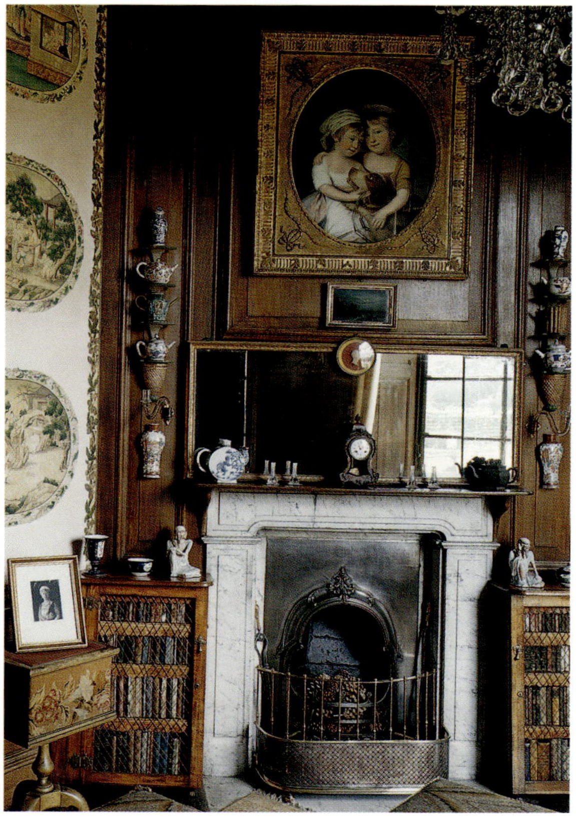

21.7
Chinese Room, Erddig, Clwyd

The National Trust

In 1739 Captain Bottle of the East India Company ship *London* imported, on his own account, six reverse paintings on glass.[22] Although originating in Europe, the technique seems to have been fairly unknown in France by 1745 when an artist wrote:

> When I was in Port Louis … I saw a Chinese mirror … whereon was seen a Chinese lady at her toilet; above her in one corner a parrot on its perch, and behind it a monkey. Overcome by the beauty of the mirror and the skill of the workmanship, I tried eagerly to discover by what means I could imitate it.[23]

Again it is only in the nineteenth century that we first find a record of a direct observation of painters on glass, this time by Toogood Downing, a member of the Royal College of Surgeons writing in 1851:

> It may be mentioned in this place that the Chinese are very famous for their paintings on glass. This is an art which is almost lost in Europe, but is very successfully practised in this country. This style of painting suit the Chinese artists very well as it exhibits the splendour of their colours. Painted glass must be very extensively used in China for ornamenting the houses, &c., as, even in the suburbs without the walls of Canton, great numbers of shops for the sale of this single article are collected together, so that the foreigners have given the locality the name of Painter Street. Our Jack-tars are much caught by this showy material, and generally carry away some trumpery specimens to dazzle the eye of the fair dame of Shadwell and Blackwall.[24]

The imported glass, once painted, was reshipped to Europe, sometimes in frames of hardwood or lacquered softwood; or else framed after arrival.

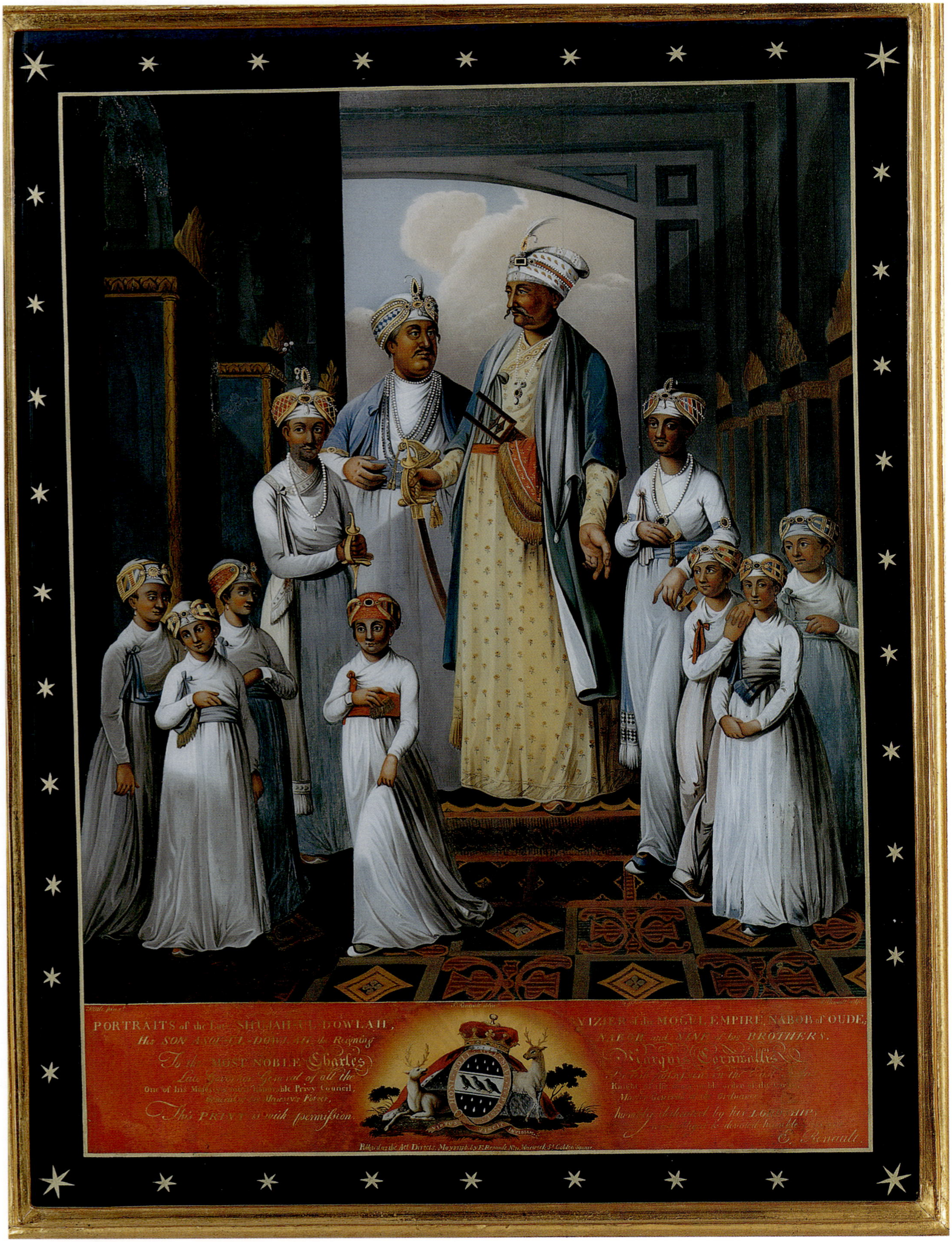

PORTRAITS of the Late SHUJAH-UL-DOWLAH,
VIZIER of the MOGUL EMPIRE, NABOB of OUDE,
NABOB and NINE of his BROTHERS.
To the MOST NOBLE Charles
Marquis Cornwallis
This PRINT is with permission
humbly dedicated by his LORDSHIPS
E. Renault
VIRTUS VINCIT INVIDIAM

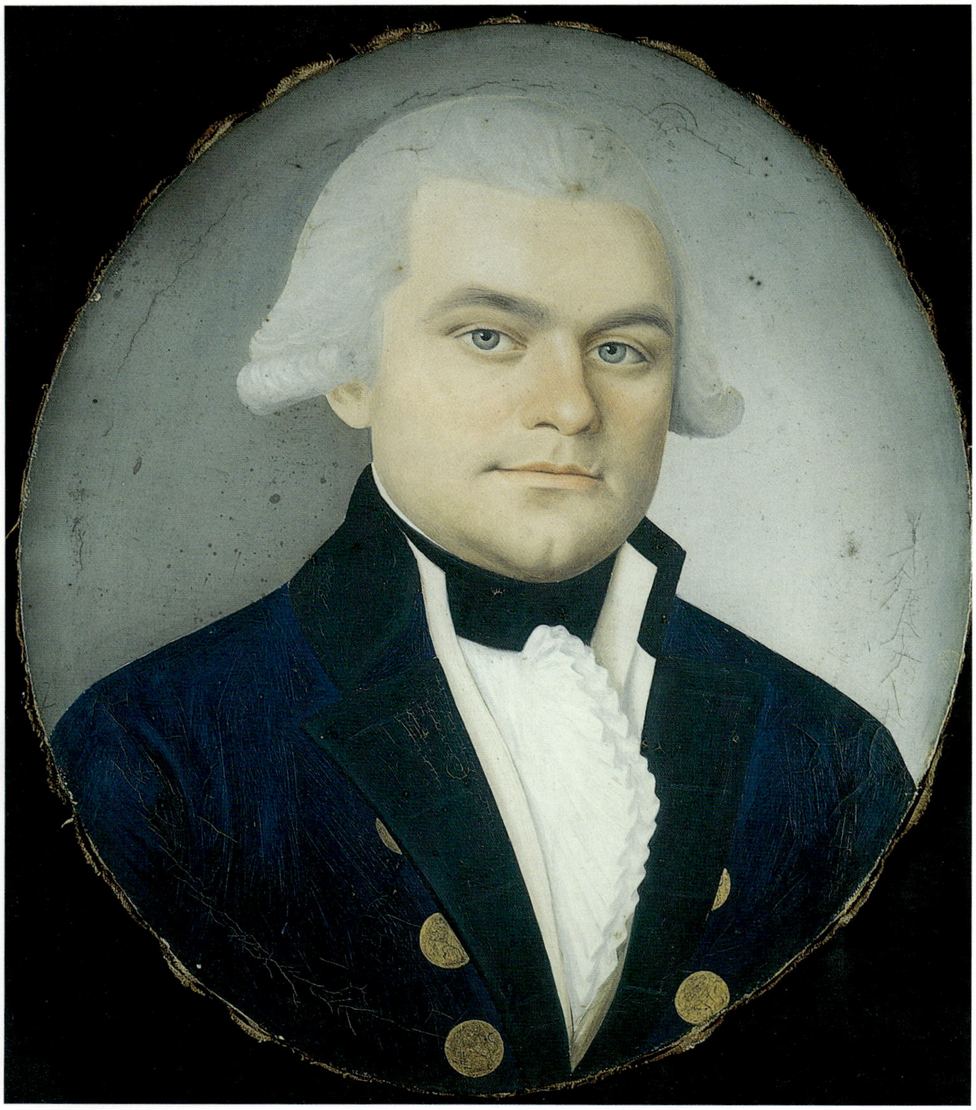

21.8
Captain Roper
Spoilum (Guan Zuolin)
Oil on canvas
China (Canton), late 18th century
Courtesy of Martyn Gregory Gallery, London

The most elaborate frames, always made in the West, were gilded chinoiserie concoctions topped by pagodas, rockwork and phoenix birds. It was not uncommon to mount multiple panels of glass paintings into a complex frame. Reverse-glass paintings were an integral part of any Chinese-style room. Samples were acquired by Admiral Anson for his teahouse at Shugborough, Staffordshire, built in 1747. A painting reminiscent of those belonging to Anson, *Mrs and Miss Revell*, depicts two western women in full Chinese dress seated on a verandah in China (plate 21.1). The faces were obviously copied from miniature portraits of the women and completed in the only way a Chinese artist would have known how, never having seen a western woman, her dress or environment. The painting of *The Late Shuja-ud-Daula and His Sons* portrays the Nawab of Oudh, who was defeated by East India Company forces at the Battle of Buxar in 1764 (plate 21.8). Pictures of the ruler and his family were popular with the British as emblems of their advancing domination of India. This family portrait painted on glass was taken from an aquatint by P. Renault, after an engraving by E. Renault, based on the original oil painting by Tilly Kelly (*c.* 1734–86), and as a direct copy did not allow any interpretation by the Chinese artist who painted it.

Port views were the most common subject for oil paintings on canvas. These export works were generally acquired in sets of four: Macao, Boca Tigris, Whampoa and Canton; later, Hong Kong replaced Boca Tigris, and still later Shanghai, Ningbo or Fuzhou were substituted in the set. The accuracy of the paintings of foreign factory sites at Canton is confirmed by descriptions in diaries and other documents of the merchants who worked and lived there and of the travellers who visited. The earliest views of Canton were mid-eighteenth-century scroll paintings on silk mounted on paper. These were succeeded by individual paintings on paper – generally paper of European manufacture – or on canvas (see pp. 154–5). The earliest of these port views established a formula from which the only variations were in the updating of details (the physical structures, placement of flags, etc.) while the format of a low horizon, cloud-filled skies and a variety of Chinese boats in the foreground changed little. By 1849 Monsieur La Vollée found 'several young Chinese were painting upon canvas views of Canton and Macao and interior scenes. These are pictures which Europeans buy in great numbers … There is not an Englishman who on his return to Europe does not take back a view of Canton.'[25]

Portraits in oils on canvas and glass, and miniatures on ivory, first appeared in the late eighteenth century. Spoilum (*fl.* 1765–1805) is the first identified Chinese artist who created portraits, his earliest work being a portrait on glass of Captain Thomas Fry, dated 1774.[26] Spoilum was described in his lifetime as 'The celebrated artist of China, and perhaps the only one in his line throughout that extensive empire.'[27] This reference may be due to the fact that he was the only portraitist, as there were certainly Chinese artists already painting in the western style. A strong European influence, probably Dutch, is seen in his late eighteenth-century portraits, such as that of Captain Roper (plate 21.8). Spoilum's style also relates to American portraiture of the period: his likeness of Captain Benjamin Smith of Boston was for a long time mistaken for an American vernacular painting. Portraits of Chinese merchants, such as Eshing the silk merchant, were also painted by Spoilum and other artists (plate 21.9). These were generally given as souvenirs by the Chinese merchants themselves, or ordered as such by their western counterparts. Later, in the nineteenth century, Toogood Downing observed, 'Most of these strangers who can afford it have their portraits taken by Lamquoi, as they consider that they will have an additional value in the mother country, by having been painted by a Chinaman.'[28]

The initial commercial interest in China trade paintings in all media peaked in around 1800. However, such works have been collected ever since and in recent years they have engendered a new art historical interest. The academic study of Chinese export paintings is in its infancy, and its exact parameters are yet to be fully defined. In the West new art historical theories surrounding export paintings are being formulated, while scholars in China are rediscovering the role of their indigenous artists in the transmission of artistic ideas and styles across the globe.

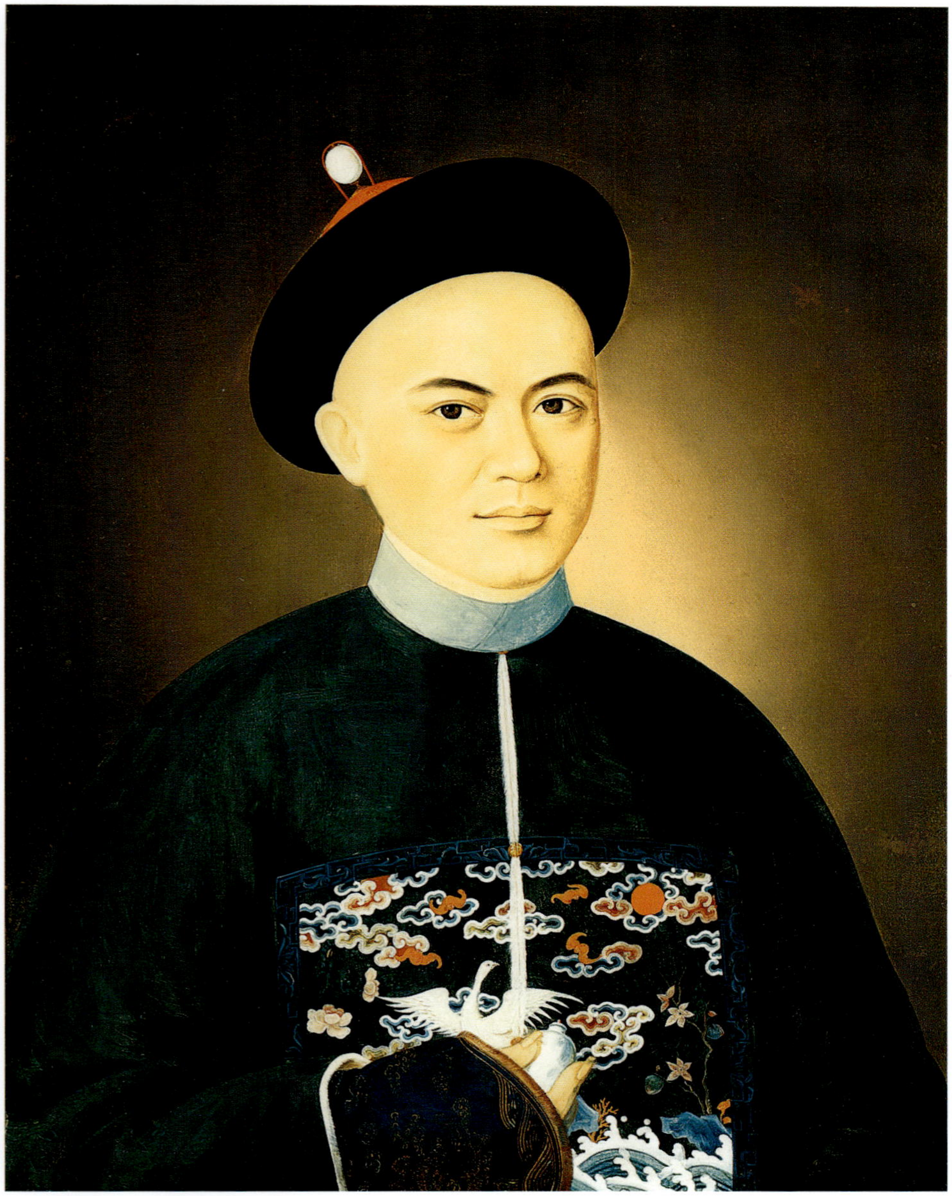

21.9
Eshing
Spoilum (Guan Zuolin)
Oil on canvas
China (Canton), late 18th century
Peabody Essex Museum, Salem

Company School Painting

Graham Parlett

THE TERM 'Company painting' is applied to works made by Indian artists for Europeans who were living and working in the subcontinent, especially British employees of the East India Company. It represents a fusion of traditional Indian artistic styles with conventions and technical features borrowed from western art. The term used in India is *kampani kalam*, meaning Company school or Company style, but in practice the name covers an enormously wide range of different styles, some of them almost indistinguishable from traditional Indian schools of painting, and some that could have been produced by British artists.

The expansion of Company rule in the eighteenth century was paralleled by the need for a greater knowledge and understanding of India in the form of visual representations, and it was in this capacity that Company paintings played a vital role. What the newly arrived British wanted was records of the people and places that surrounded them: portraits of the local dignitaries, depictions of the various castes and trades, the strange-looking deities and temples, the festivals and ceremonies, the animals and means of transport. However, the British also wanted pictures depicted in a manner that they could appreciate. Indian miniature painting, though intricately detailed and colourful, lacked the qualities with which they were familiar, such as a western-style perspective, a sense of proportion and the use of light and shade.

For their part, Indian artists welcomed British patronage at a time when they were losing their traditional sources of income, both through the decline of the Mughal court and through the changing tastes of Indian patrons in favour of work by visiting professional European artists, who had begun arriving in the 1770s. Paintings

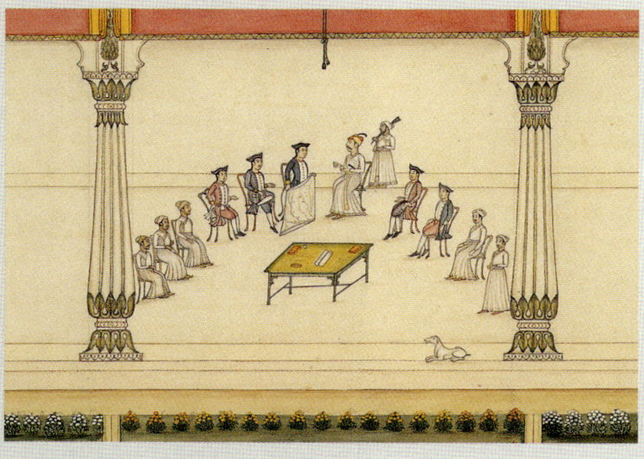

21.10 left
Treaty of the Nawab with the British at Benares in 1765 (detail)

Page from an album showing the customs of the people in India, painted for Colonel Jean-Baptiste Gentil
Watercolour on paper
India (Faizabad), 1774

V&A: IS.25–1980 (f. 20)

21.11 below
Lady Impey Examining a Hat

Opaque watercolour on paper
India (Calcutta), *c.*1790

Impey Family Collection

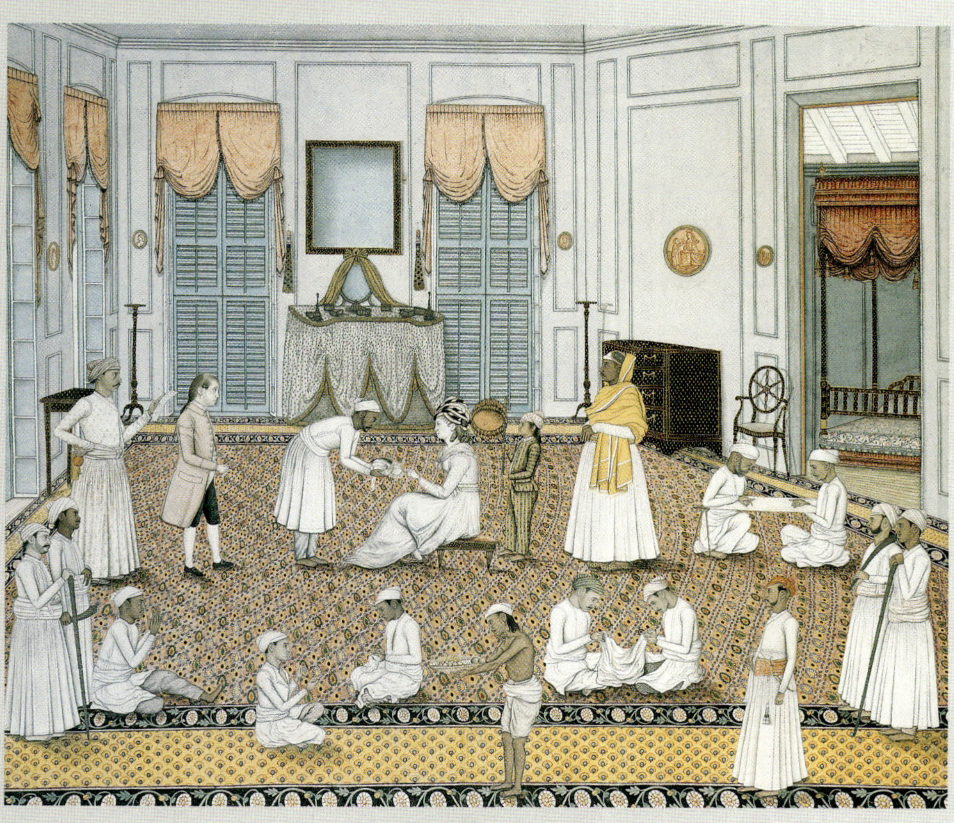

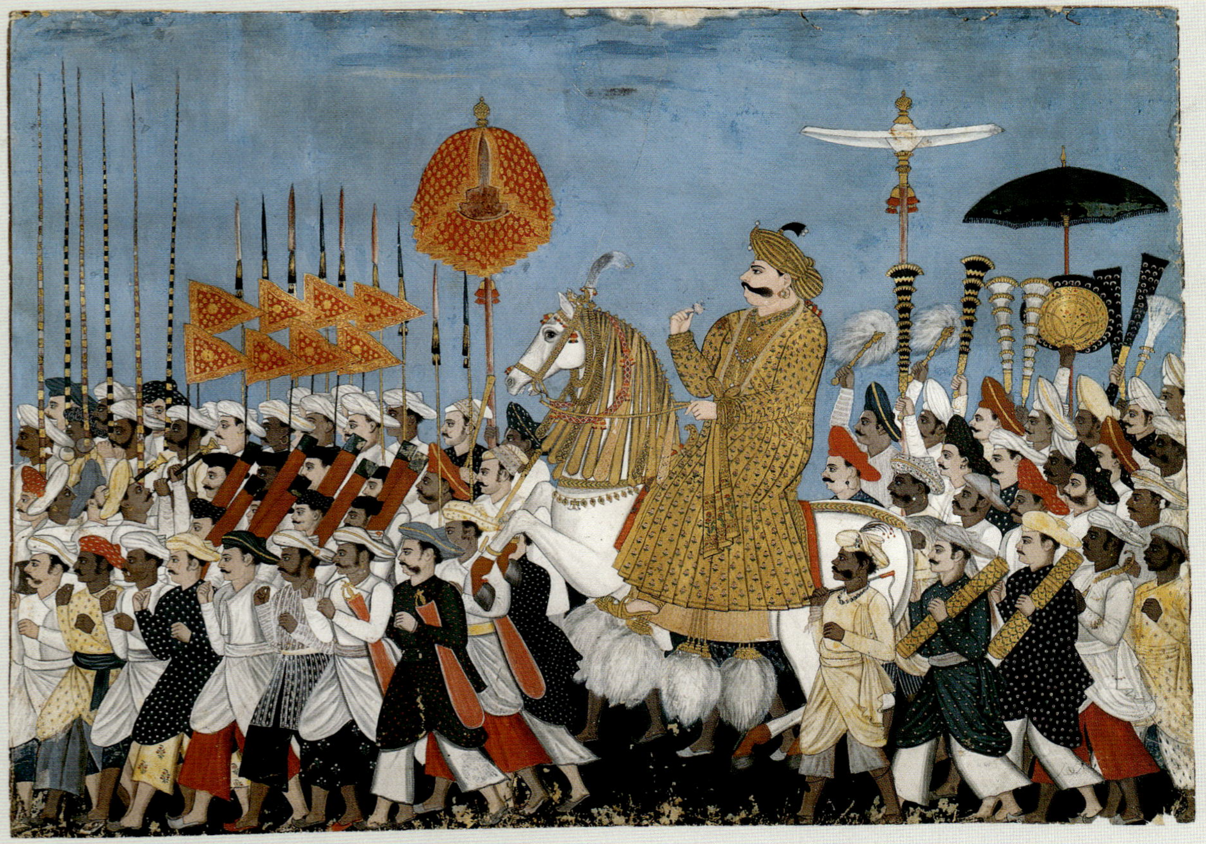

21.12
Raja Tulsaji of Tanjore
Opaque watercolour on paper
India (Tanjore), c.1770
V&A: IM.319–1921

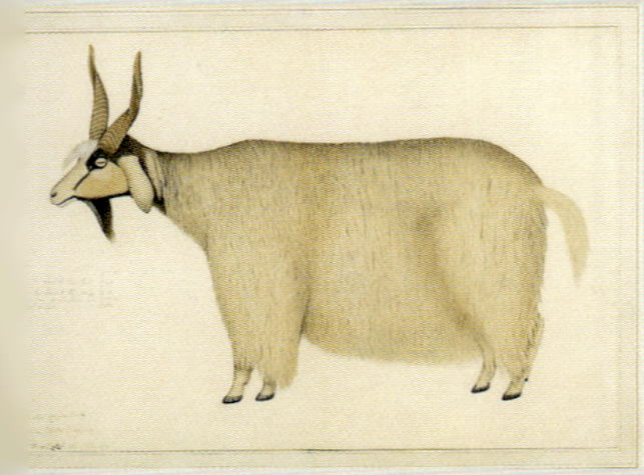

21.13
Shawl Goat from Bhutan
Zayn al-Din
Watercolour on paper
India (Calcutta), 1779
V&A: IS.51–1963

by these newcomers were by no means the earliest instance of European influence on Indian art. The Mughal emperors Akbar (r.1556–1605), Jahangir (r.1605–27) and Shah Jahan (r.1628–58) took a lively interest in European pictures, and themes from classical mythology and the Bible were skilfully copied by court artists; but it was European patronage that encouraged Indian artists to start incorporating western conventions in their work on a large scale.

Among the most generous of British patrons was Sir Elijah Impey (1732–1809), Chief Justice of the Supreme Court in Fort William (Calcutta). He and his wife were especially interested in natural history, and between 1777 and 1782 they commissioned more than 300 paintings from local artists, some of which depicted birds and animals from their private menagerie. The Marquess Wellesley (1760–1842), who also resided in Fort William, had similar interests, and by the time he retired in 1813 he had assembled no fewer than 2,542 Company paintings. Towards the end of the eighteenth century British residents began to move from the centre of the city into the pleasant new suburbs of Chowringhee and Garden Reach, and it was here that Indian artists found substantial patronage.

During the nineteenth century Company painting continued to flourish, and after the 1820s the demand for these works became so great that they were reduced to stock images which were virtually mass-produced. With the coming of photography to India in the 1840s and the demise of the East India Company in 1858, the demand for painted depictions gradually waned. Company painting did survive into the twentieth century, but by then it had long outlived its original purpose.

22

EUROPE IN ASIA: THE IMPACT OF WESTERN ART AND TECHNOLOGY IN SOUTH ASIA

Susan Stronge

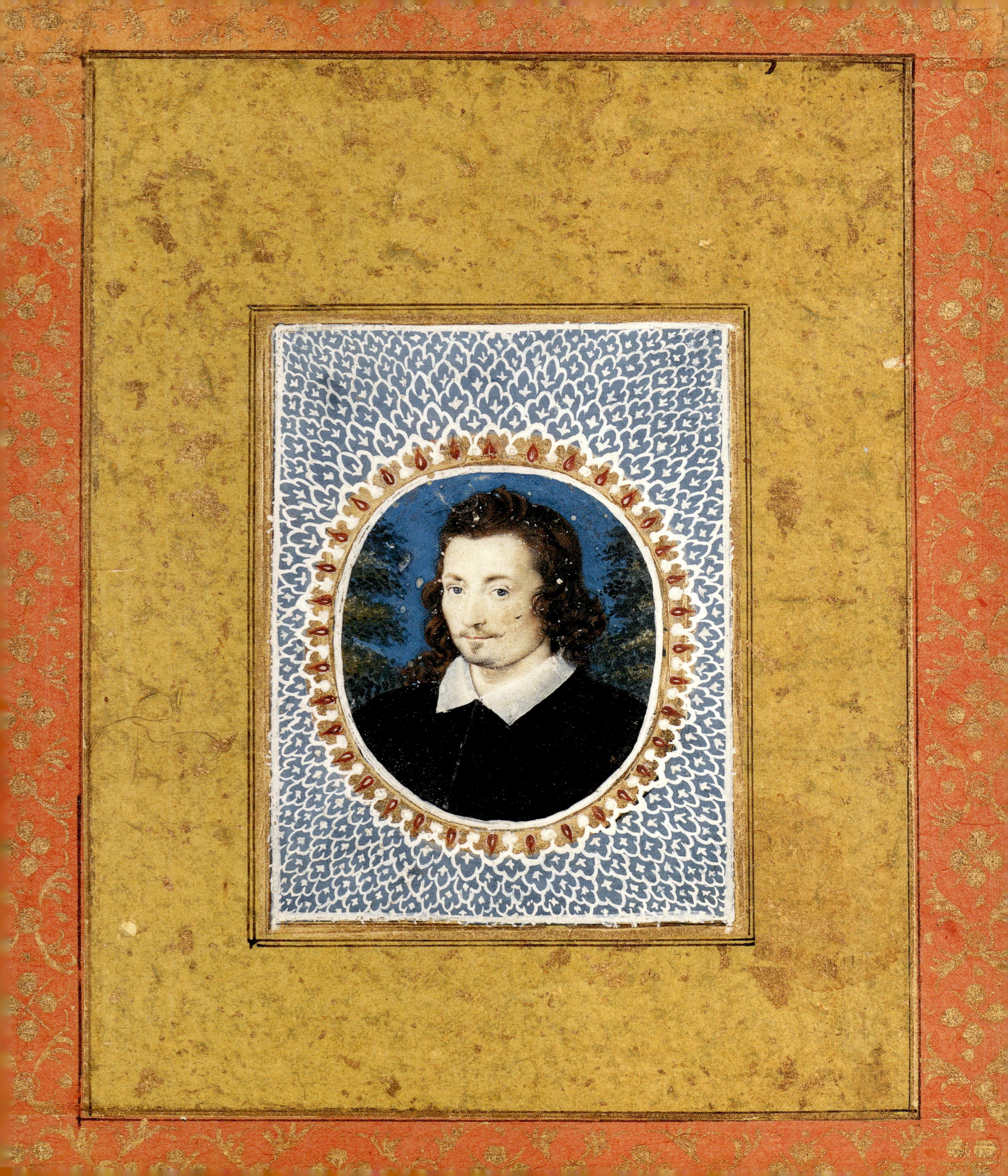

22.1 previous page
Album page incorporating a portrait miniature by Isaac Oliver

Miniature: watercolour on vellum, England, *c.* 1595; mounted on an Indian album page, opaque watercolour and gold on paper, probably late 18th century

V&A: IS.60–1978

That this miniature was mounted in a Mughal album is evidence that western painting was keenly admired and collected at Indian courts.

22.2
Crucifixion
Possibly Kesav Das

Leaf from an album after one or more European engravings
Opaque watercolour and ink on paper
Mughal India, late 16th century

British Museum, London

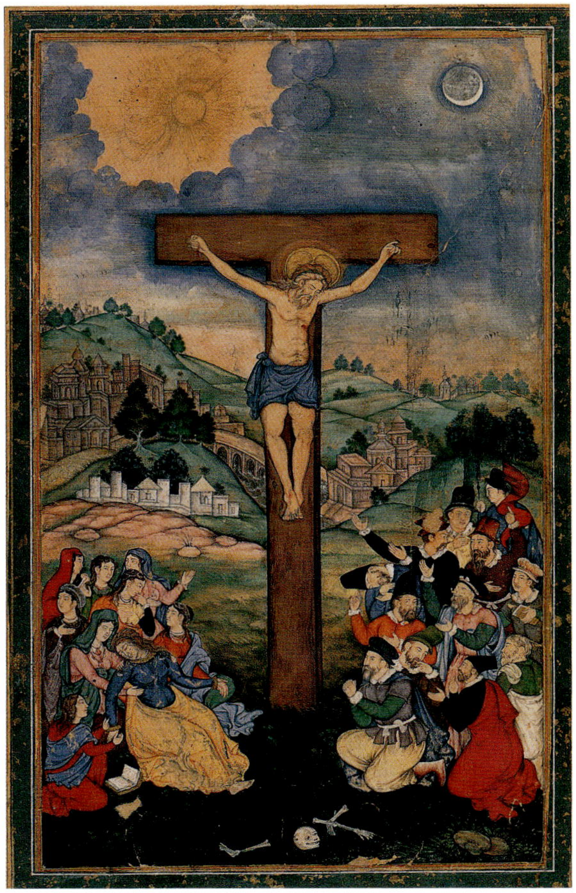

In the final years of the sixteenth century, an English Jesuit lay brother called Alexander living in the southern Indian city of Chandragiri painted the interior of the Jesuit church with images of the Three Magi, the Virgin and Child and St John the Baptist.[1] The reaction of the local population is unknown, but it is unlikely that these exotic images had any influence on the arts of the region.

The reception of similar images at the Mughal court a few years earlier, in 1580, could not have been more different. The members of the first Jesuit mission had shown religious paintings to the emperor Akbar (r. 1556–1605) in their chapel in the royal city of Fatehpur. His enthusiasm for the images of St Luke and the Madonna inspired him to return several times with his sons, senior members of the court and 'his chief painter and other painters', who were later instructed to copy them.[2] Akbar and his son Jahangir (r. 1605–27) energetically collected and avidly studied European paintings and objects of all kinds, regularly ordering their artists and craftsmen to copy what they saw (see plate 8.9). This began to alter Mughal painting fundamentally and irrevocably, and probably also affected the decorative arts, though so little has survived that it is difficult to judge.

In a land as diverse as sixteenth-century India, artistic encounters with the West inevitably had widely differing consequences. Each region of India reacted differently to European visitors and the strange things they brought with them, ranging from profound curiosity to complete indifference. The Portuguese conquered Goa in 1510, and in 1530 made it the official capital of the *Estado da Índia* ('State of India'), which included all Portuguese possessions east of the Cape of Good Hope. The indigenous population of Goa lived and worked with their foreign overlords, sometimes marrying them and adopting their religion (see pp. 158–9). A truly hybrid Indo-European artistic style would develop there in painting, architecture, furniture and other decorative arts.[3] Beyond Goa lay the Mughal empire, which was founded in 1526 and expanded dramatically during Akbar's reign until it dominated the whole of the northern subcontinent. To the south were the Muslim sultanates of the Deccan, where, as in the Mughal empire, Persian was the *lingua franca*. However, Deccani art and culture were more strongly Iranian in character. The southernmost regions of India were a patchwork of mostly Hindu kingdoms, each again with its own distinctive character. Contacts between Europe and India varied in all these regions and took place at many different levels of society.

What little information survives indicates that when language barriers were overcome, educated Europeans and Indians shared a lively exchange of ideas. When the physician François Bernier (1620–88) lived in India in the mid-seventeenth century, he maintained a six-year friendship with Daneshmand Khan, a high-ranking Mughal noble. They discussed geography, astronomy and anatomy, and Daneshmand Khan's interest in philosophy induced Bernier to translate into Persian works by René Descartes (1596–1650) and his former teacher Pierre Gassendi (1592–1655), which were read with great interest.[4] Bernier reported that the medical systems used widely in Hindustan were based on the systems of 'Avicenna' (Ibn Sina: 980–1037) and 'Averroes' (Ibn Rushd: 1126–98), remarking that although Indian medical practices differed greatly from those of Europe, they were appropriate for the conditions of the country.[5]

Such glimpses of intellectual exchange are rare in contemporary sources, which range from accounts of visitors to the Mughal court, to court histories and memoirs in Persian, comprehensive records of the European trading companies, and objects that survive from the period. Outside the court, direct western influence on technology or design is apparent primarily where Indian craftsmen were producing for western markets. As early as 1630, for example, Indian weavers changed the width of their looms to satisfy European requirements,[6] and in 1643 the Court of Directors of the East India Company requested that their factors order bedspreads with a white ground, rather than the standard 'sad red grounds' of the cotton printers, to suit the London market (see p. 269).[7] In areas where there was no western demand, early European influence on local manufacture is almost impossible to determine. Only from the mid– to late eighteenth century, when Europeans were firmly settled in India, did artistic influence and the adoption of technological innovations intensify, often with reciprocal effects.

The most striking area of early European influence on Indian art is in Mughal painting (plate 22.2). The religious works of art brought by Jesuit missions were swiftly followed by examples of western painting and narrative tapestries, which were given to the Mughal emperors by merchants seeking trading concessions. These ranged from portraits of kings and queens to scenes from western mythology, such as a picture of Venus and a satyr, whose nakedness apparently mystified Jahangir.[8] Foreign artists also sometimes came to court in the hope of royal patronage. An anonymous Portuguese artist arrived in Lahore in 1595 with the third Jesuit mission and demonstrated his skills to a fascinated Prince Salim.[9] When he became emperor, Jahangir employed for at least seven years an Englishman who was said to be an excellent artist but who is known only by his surname, Hatfield.[10] Some East India Company factors had modest artistic skills, as demonstrated by the title page to a Persian–English dictionary compiled for Robert Hughes at Ajmer and decorated with his self-portrait.[11] Sir Thomas Roe (1581–1644), the first English ambassador to the Mughal court, was scathing about Hughes's talents, saying 'he did with a pen draw some figures, but very meanly, far from the arte of painting', but Jahangir was nevertheless extremely eager to meet him and see his work.[12] In addition, the Jesuits were occasionally asked to supervise Mughal artists, as Father Monserrate (b. 1536) discovered when he arrived at the palace in Fatehpur in 1580. Akbar had told him 'the painters should paint all that I should tell them, and should be by my side'.[13] Mughal artists used the disparate examples of European painting that they saw in a number of ways, sometimes copying them exactly, occasionally over-painting original engravings, or inserting precise details from prints by masters such as Albrecht Dürer (1471–1528) or Hans Sebald Beham (1500–50) into a broader composition.[14] Soon, paintings were being produced in a European style closer to pastiche than copy.

These various processes introduced into Mughal painting such exotic notions as perspective, almost certainly the result of repeated exposure to pictures rather than knowledge of technical treatises explaining how to create this optical illusion. In European-influenced Mughal painting, textiles billow dramatically and faces are subtly shaded to create a sense of volume; once absorbed, these innovations persisted in Mughal art. In the last quarter of the eighteenth century, in a new wave of outside influence, artists in Delhi and at the court of Oudh demonstrated their mastery of perspective and other western artistic conventions (plate 22.3). Particularly notable for this period are landscapes

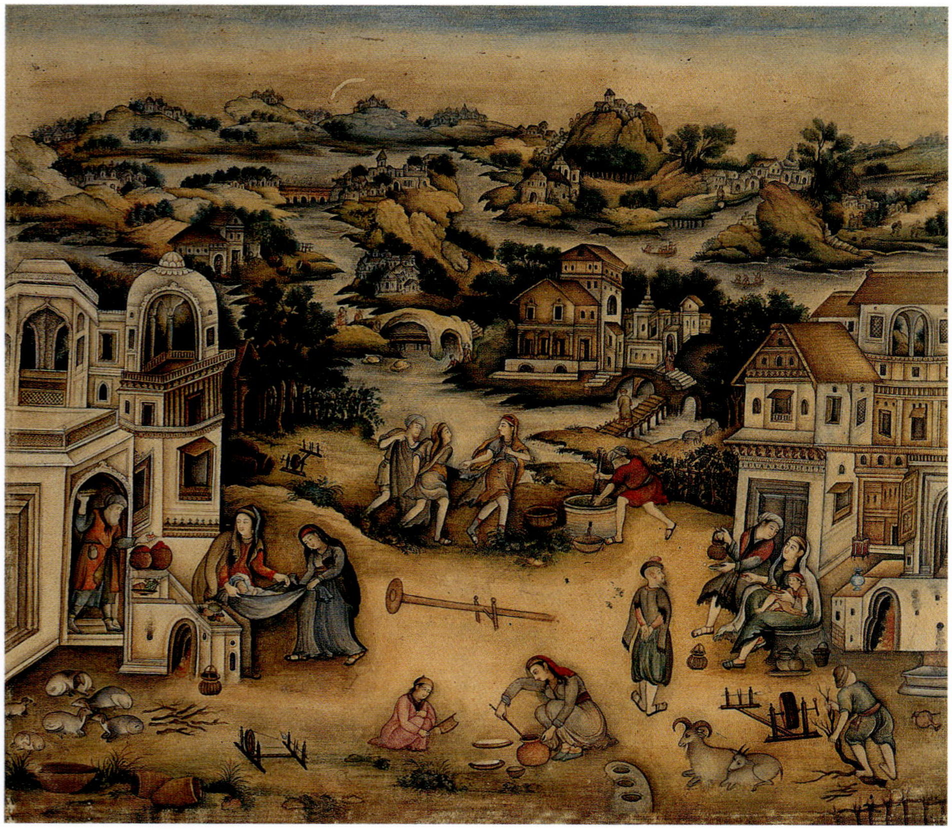

22.3
Village Life in Kashmir
Mir Kalan Khan

Leaf from an album
Opaque watercolour with gold on paper
India (Lucknow), c.1760

British Library, London

22.4
Street Scene

Opaque watercolour on paper
India, late 18th century

British Museum, London

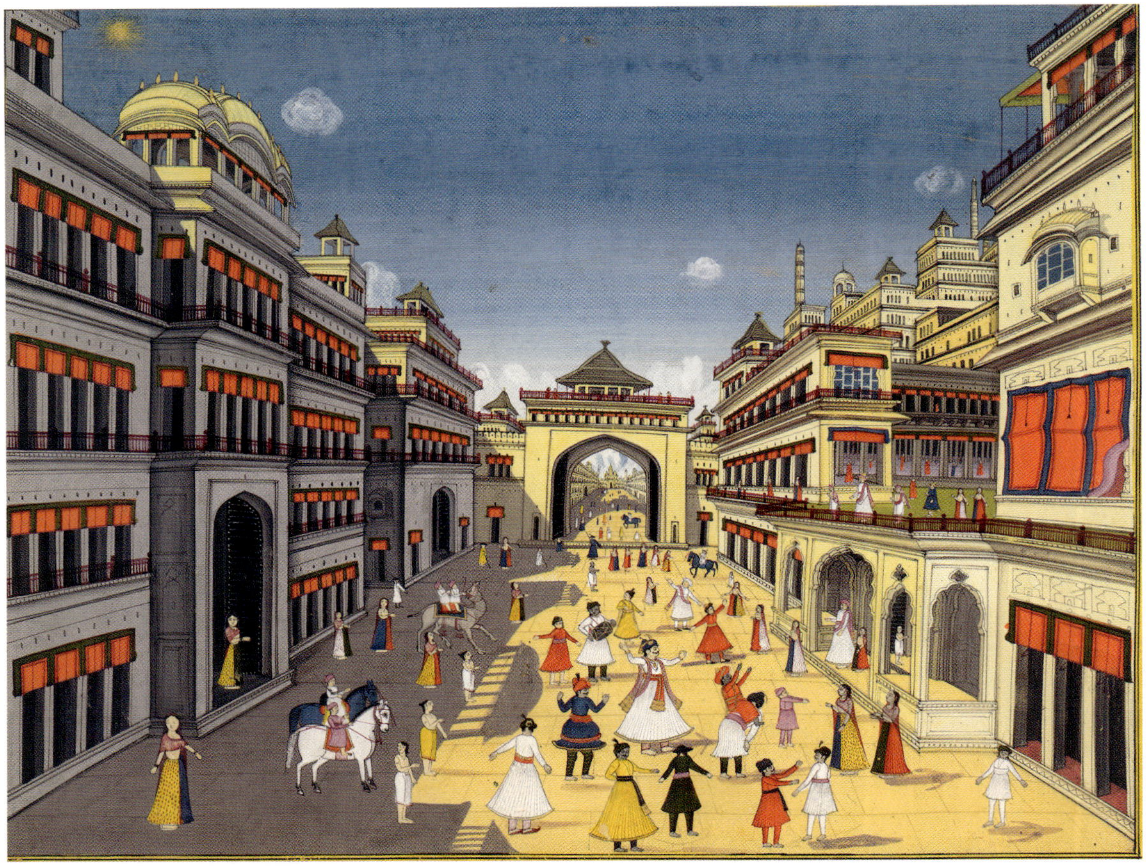

with spectacularly extended vistas, again produced by contact with European prints or paintings in similar style (plate 22.4).[15]

Another western convention became common in Mughal painting in the early seventeenth century: the depiction of the emperor with a European-inspired halo. Although nimbate figures have an extremely long history in South Asian painting and sculpture, those in works for Hindu and Muslim patrons of the sixteenth century follow the specific conventions of Iranian book painting.[16] Jahangir's adoption of western motifs did not indicate any adoption of western ideas: they were simply borrowed to express the fundamental concept of kingship from the Iranian world that shaped Mughal court culture. Royalty was 'a light emanating from God', illuminating the king. The halo represented this *farr-i izadi*, or 'divine light'.[17]

The facility with which Mughal artists copied western models led to greater naturalism in their work, though their intention was probably not European-style realism. A more sensitive depiction of physiognomy, for instance, is apparent in court painting at the end of Akbar's reign and becomes more pronounced under Jahangir, when greater numbers of European portraits reached the court and the emperor sat for his English artist Hatfield.[18] When Sir Thomas Roe showed the emperor a work by Isaac Oliver, Jahangir ordered copies to be made, and less than three weeks later six identical versions were presented to Roe, who was invited to identify his original from the five copies. He claimed he did this with little difficulty despite the high quality of the copies, although his chaplain's hearsay account contradicts this.[19]

Despite the influence of European portraiture, Mughal artists nevertheless worked within an extremely narrow range of conventions when depicting the emperor, his family and leading members of the court. Faces are almost always in strict profile, status is shown through specific details of dress or jewellery, and appearance changes little over time. It would seem that a portrait, once painted, became the definitive image of an individual.

In other courts, the effect of Europe is difficult to gauge because of the relative lack of surviving material. A court painter of Rudolf II (r. 1576–1612), Cornelius Heda, a native of Haarlem and a pupil of

Cornelius van Haarlem, left Prague in 1605 and eventually found his way to the Bijapur court of Ibrahim Adil Shah II (r. 1580–1627).[20] He was said to have painted a study of Venus, Cupid and Bacchus for the king, a keen connoisseur of painting, but no example of his Indian work has survived. In the small corpus of painting that may be securely linked to Bijapur, there is little sign of the absorption of European motifs so prevalent in contemporary Mughal art, apart from a generalized use of shaded faces, the incorporation of a few distant vistas, and modelled draperies, which could as easily have come from Mughal or Iranian painting. By the eighteenth century, traditional styles of portraiture were changing radically. Rulers such as the nawabs of Oudh and the nawabs of Arcot commissioned European artists including Johan Zoffany (1733–1810) and Ozias Humphry (1742–1810) to paint their portraits in oils (a medium of little interest to earlier rulers) and Indian painters adopted their style (plate 22.5).[21]

European craftsmen and other specialists were occasionally taken into royal service. William Leeds, a jeweller, arrived at Fatehpur in 1584 and was immediately employed by Akbar, thereupon disappearing from history.[22] Jahangir commissioned the goldsmith Augustin Hiriart of Bordeaux to design a throne for him, and the craftsman later designed another for Shah Jahan (plate 22.6). Shah Jahan employed a diamond-cutter called Abraham de Duyts for at least 12 years, and the Dutchman's privileged position enabled him to give valuable advice to his compatriots on what presents to bring to court, saying that they need not be expensive, but should be 'artistic', such as paintings and jewels (see p.82).[23]

Most foreign visitors noted that it was imperative to give presents in order to secure an audience with the emperor, the remark made by the English traveller Robert Coverte after his 1609 visit being typical:

> Every stranger must present the king with some present, bee it never so small, which hee will not refuse. And I gave him for a present, a small whistle of gold, waighing almost an ounce, set with sparks of Rubies, which hee tooke and whistled therewith almoste an houre. Also I gave him the picture of Saint John's cut in Amber and Gold, which he also received very gratiously. The whistle he gave to one of his great women, and the picture to Sultane Caroone [Khurram, later Shah Jahan], his youngest sonne.[24]

Such presents may have included examples of recent western technologies, but their impact was extremely limited. While the illustrations in the printed books presented to rulers produced radical changes in painting, the books themselves induced no desire to produce engravings or to set up presses, and their intellectual content similarly had little effect.[25] The Jesuits presented Akbar with Abraham Ortelius's 1570 atlas, the *Theatrum Orbis Terrarum* (see plate 2.10),[26] and Sir Thomas Roe gave Jahangir Mercator's *Atlas*. Akbar's reaction is not known, but Jahangir received Mercator with polite interest, only to return it because 'he had shewed it his *mulaies* [mullahs] and no man could read or understand it'. Roe's chaplain reported a more elegantly phrased rejection: as neither he nor 'his people' could understand it, Jahangir said he would not deprive Roe of 'such a jewel'.[27] To the Mughals, western cartography was unnecessary, therefore of virtually no interest. Although it is not entirely clear how the Mughals mapped their territory, they had good military route maps and knew very precisely the distances between towns, and the boundaries of the subdivisions of the major provinces.[28] It is, however, intriguing to note that all the maps and globes represented in paintings commissioned by Jahangir are European in style,[29] and their careful positioning in relation to the emperor often suggests his

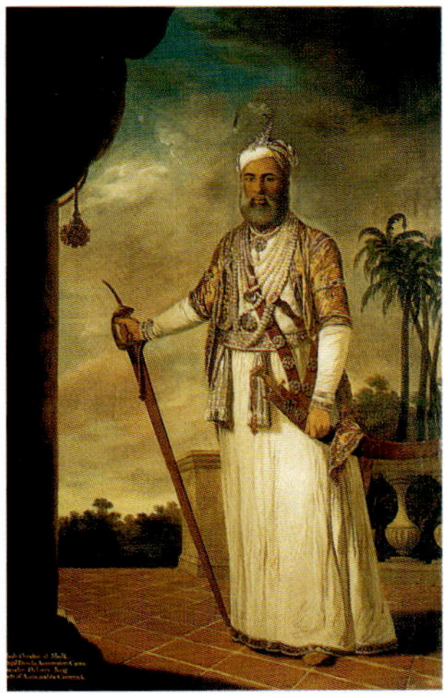

22.5
Muhammad Ali Wallajah, Nawab of Arcot
Tilly Kettle

Oil on canvas
India (Madras), c.1770

V&A: IM.124–1911

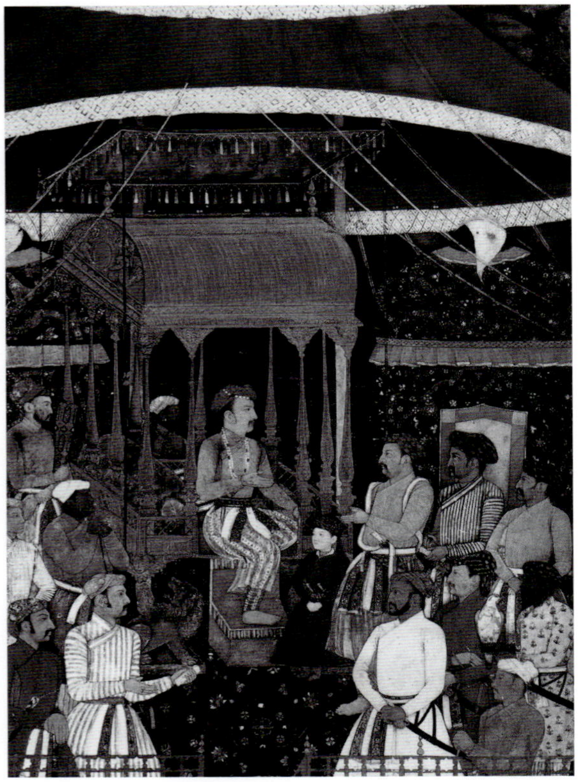

22.6
Jahangir in Durbar

Opaque watercolour and gold on paper
Mughal India, *c.*1620

Private collection

Jahangir sits on a throne possibly designed by Augustin Hiriart of Bordeaux.

22.7
Jahangir Shoots the Head of Malik 'Anbar
Abu'l Hasan

Opaque watercolour and gold on paper
Mughal India, *c.* 1616

Chester Beatty Library, Dublin

22.8 below
Rose-water sprinkler

Lead glass
Probably England, mid-18th century

V&A: IS.13–1893

22.9 opposite
Nawab Mir Qasim Ali Khan

Opaque watercolour and gold on paper
India (Murshidabad), 1760–63

V&A: D.1178–1903

The nawab's hookah base and water sprinkler are of glass.

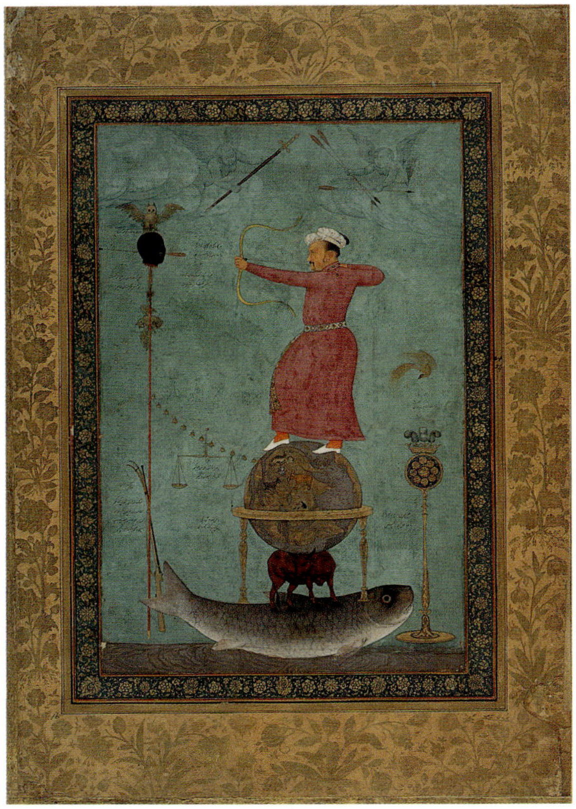

dominion over the earthly realm, thus alluding to his title, which means 'World Seizer' (plate 22.7).

A rare example of a keen Indian desire to obtain western maps, globes and books on astronomy is provided by Maharaja Sawai Jai Singh of Jaipur (r. 1699–1743), builder of a series of observatories in Jaipur and Delhi. He was broadly interested in scientific theory and was presented with western books on mathematics by a Jesuit scientific mission. However, beyond a revision of the imperial calendar, the influence of these books was not long-term.[30] In any case, Sawai Jai Singh's observatories were built according to principles derived from the Islamic rather than the western world and were modelled on Ulugh Beg's 1420 observatory at Samarkand.[31] European clocks were welcome as curiosities, but western time-measurement differed so much from Indian systems that, again, they had little practical use.[32]

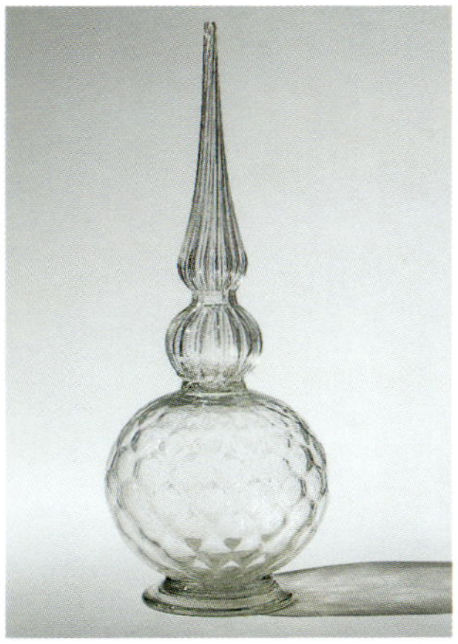

European glass vessels were eagerly received by Indian rulers, partly because indigenous glass was of poor quality. Company records indicate that Venetian glass was exported to India in the seventeenth century, and examples appear in Mughal paintings of the period. Glass from other European countries and Iran also reached India, and in the eighteenth century vast quantities of lead glass were shipped from England, including hookah bases and rose-water sprinklers (plates 22.8, 22.9).[33] Western mirrors were also popular at court, often being embellished with handles of jade or precious metal (plate 22.11) and also came to be used in interior decoration (plate 22.10).

The related art of enamelling also seems to have been an exotic introduction, the most likely source being Portuguese Goa. In 1575 Akbar sent a delegation that included craftsmen to Goa and gave them instructions to copy new techniques, and by the 1590s references to enamellers begin to appear in contemporary chronicles.[34] Pyrard de Laval (*c.* 1570–1621), who lived in Goa from 1606 to 1608, reported that the city was full of lapidaries, goldsmiths and artisans of all kinds from Portugal, Italy, Germany and other western countries.[35] The regular contacts between Goa and the Mughal court may have encouraged the development of the technique, and the raw material was certainly brought to the Mughal court by the Portuguese, as reported by Sir Thomas Roe. In 1618 he wrote that enamel, meaning cakes of glass to be used by enamellers, had fallen in price but would still produce a good profit, and red would sell for twice the price of gold if of very fine quality.[36] However, enamelled artefacts, of superb quality, have survived only from Shah Jahan's reign, and continued to be made at many courtly centres until the nineteenth century (plate 22.13).[37]

European luxury imports such as Italian glass, velvets and cameos brought to the Mughal court by foreign merchants, or purchased by agents in Goa and other major trading centres, superficially enhanced the court setting, but Italian *pietra dura* had a permanent influence on Mughal architectural ornament. In 1648 the emperor formally inaugurated his new city of Shahjahanabad, Delhi, at the centre of which stood a fort-palace complex. The Hall of Public Audience was dominated by a carved marble throne, its marble canopy inlaid with semi-precious stones. Behind the throne, black Italian *pietra dura* plaques are set into the white marble wall, the spaces between inlaid with Mughal *pietra dura* birds and flowering trees. At the top of the entire scheme is a small Italian panel depicting Orpheus playing his lute to the wild animals, which sit peacefully before him (plate 22.12). The decoration is unique in Mughal architecture, though Mughal *pietra dura* had been used on other monuments earlier in Shah Jahan's reign, notably the Taj Mahal. In a detailed study of the

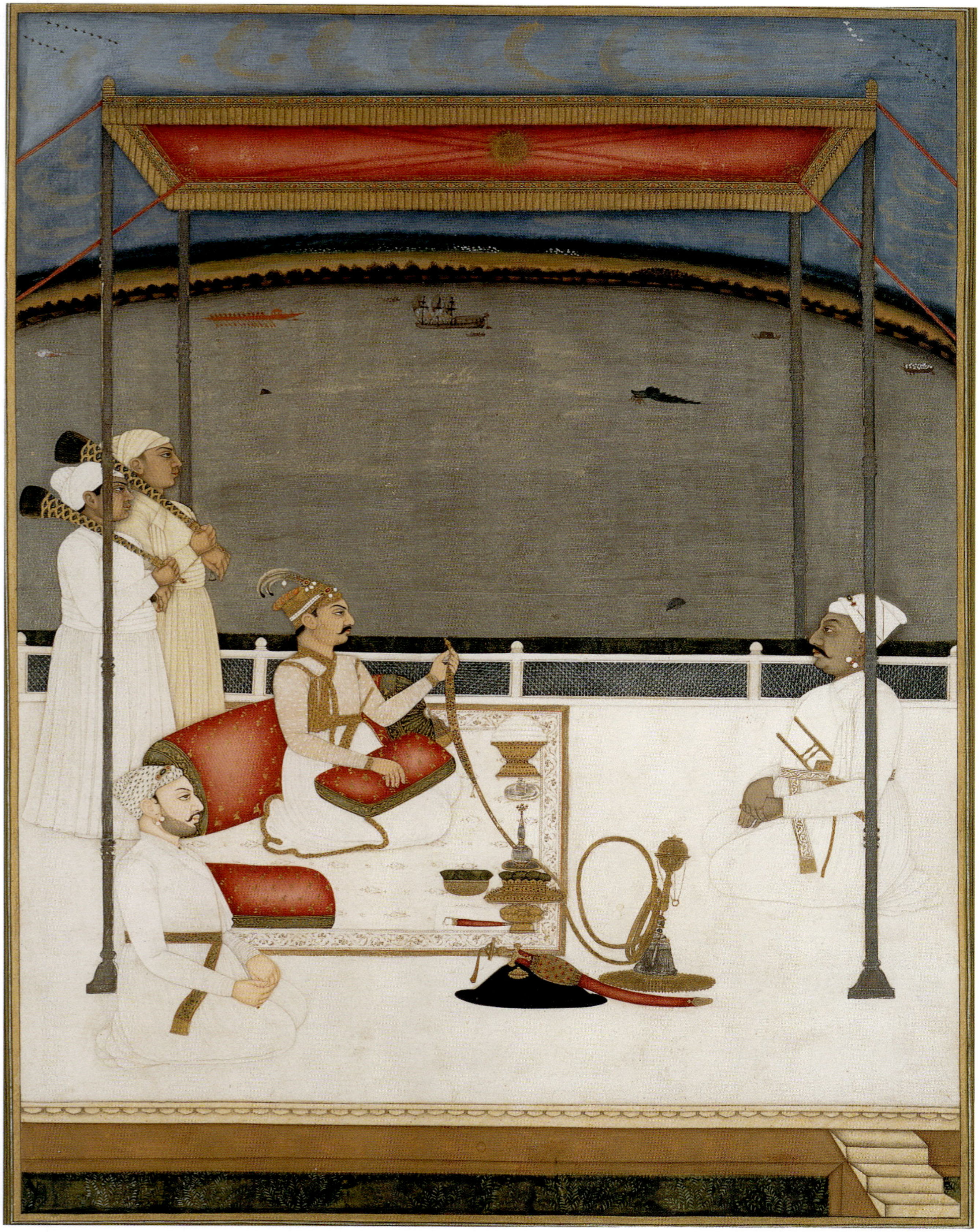

throne and its setting, Ebba Koch concluded that the complex symbolism that combines European and Mughal motifs was chosen to reinforce the identification of Shah Jahan with Solomon, the ideal model of just rule throughout the Islamic world.[38] The Europeanizing character of Mughal *pietra dura* was perhaps the reason why the Augustinian missionary, Father Sebastien Manrique, attributed the decoration of the Taj Mahal to Augustin Hiriart after he had seen it in 1640. Manrique's unreliability is indicated by his confident assertion that Geronimo Veroneo designed the monument itself, despite the names of Mughal and Iranian architects, designers and calligraphers being recorded in Persian sources. Nevertheless, nineteenth-century European commentators repeated the myth.[39]

Western botanical illustrations similarly influenced Mughal architectural decoration. Volumes known as herbals, illustrating plants that could be grown for their medicinal properties, or florilegia, depicting plants from a more decorative point of view, were probably first seen by Mughal artists during Jahangir's reign. At this period, flowering plants derived from Iranian art were first arranged in regular rows with insects hovering over them, as they are in these western illustrations (plate 22.16).[40] The style continued to evolve throughout Shah Jahan's reign, when floral ornamentation pervaded every aspect of court art and architecture. Herbals may have been brought to court by European physicians in Mughal service, such as Jahangir's Venetian practitioner Bernardino Maffei, whose 1628 tombstone records that he was 'Surgeon to the Great Mogul King, who was much esteemed by him and all his court on account of the cures he effected'.[41]

Court physicians, whether European, Indian or Iranian, would have found European plants for their medicine within the Mughal empire, as the Jesuit Father Botelho mentions flowers and plants of Portuguese origin growing in the palace gardens of Agra and Delhi when he visited them in 1646.[42] The introduction by Europeans of the tobacco plant, however, had particularly far-reaching consequences. Tobacco was unknown in the subcontinent until the late sixteenth century, when it appeared in Bijapur, probably introduced from Goa, and independently at the Mughal court at the same time, when a physician brought it as a curiosity for Akbar.[43] However, it was only when a Mughal ambassador to Bijapur in 1604 returned with a hookah, or water pipe, that tobacco smoking quickly spread at court, despite Jahangir's opposition to the habit, a sentiment shared by his contemporary King James I (r. 1603–25). By the eighteenth century it had become the convention to depict elites relaxing and smoking a hookah (plate 22.9). Spherical or bell-shaped hookahs were made in a variety of materials, including glass, jewelled and enamelled precious metals, and base metal. In the eighteenth century manufacturers in England began to export wares suited to Indian customs, so that Indian grandees might inhale perfumed smoke from a Wedgwood-style hookah[44] while Englishmen living in India might order their hookahs locally, perhaps made from the base-metal alloy known as *bidri* and decorated in neoclassical style with silver-inlaid swags.[45] Magnificently decorated hookahs were exchanged as gifts; the richly enamelled and jewelled example given to Robert Clive (1725–74) underlines his status in the rapidly changing balance of power in the eighteenth century (see plate 12.7).[46]

It was perhaps in warfare that the impact of Europe was felt most strongly (plate 22.15). Controversy surrounds the introduction of gunnery into the Indian subcontinent, though it seems clear

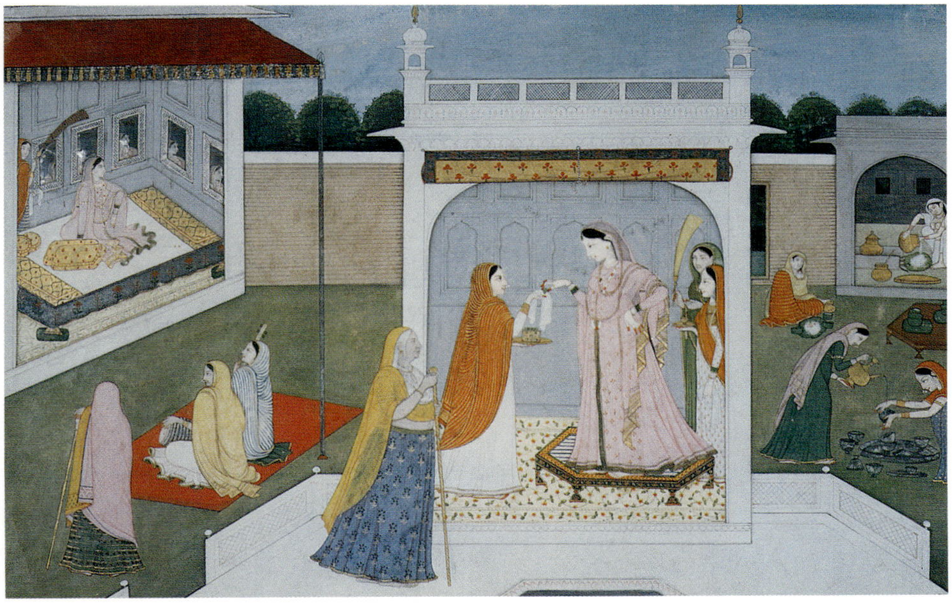

22.10
Scene of Palace Life

Opaque watercolour on paper
India (Kangra), *c.*1790

V&A: IM.4–1912

The pavilion to the left is hung with plates of mirror in which the young woman is reflected.

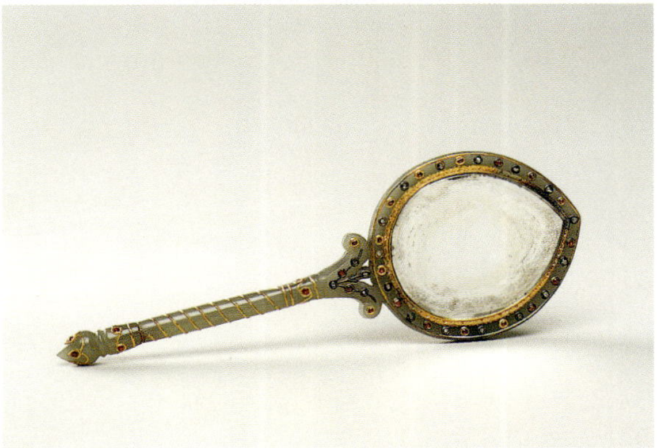

22.11
Mirror

Jade, inlaid with semi-precious stones set in gold
Frame: Mughal India, 17th century; mirror: Europe, 17th century

Musée du Louvre, Paris

that there was more than one channel of entry. The founder of the Mughal empire, Babur (r. 1526–30) brought cannon and firearms to defeat the Delhi sultanate, while the Portuguese found the technology already in the south when they arrived, but almost certainly expedited its diffusion in the region.[47] Akbar introduced major technological advances into weapons manufacture, though there is no evidence for European involvement in the process during his reign.[48] As Irfan Habib has shown, Jesuit reports that Akbar practised the crafts of the blacksmith and armourer in his royal workshops are confirmed by contemporary Persian sources and indicate his informed interest, making the statement by his historian that he invented a device for grinding and boring gun barrels credible.[49]

Nevertheless, European firepower was superior and their skills and weapons were always in demand. In the Deccan, the Portuguese used cannon during two nine-month sieges of the Adil Shahi ruler, which, according to the traveller Pyrard de Laval, were the main reason for his surrender.[50] Pyrard witnessed the extensive manufacture in Goa of cannon and other ironmongery of war at the beginning of the seventeenth century, registering surprise at the number of ironworkers, founders and cannoniers who were 'all, or mostly all, Indians'.[51] The excellence of their work had been noted as early as 1510 by Afonso de Albuquerque in a report made to King Manuel I.[52]

European cannon found a ready market in India. In 1620, for instance, four cannon salvaged from a Dutch ship that had foundered between the Coromandel coast and Surat were sold by the factors to the Mughal Prince Khurram (later the emperor Shah Jahan) for 45,000 mahmudis, equivalent then to 22,500 Dutch guilders. Europeans with a knowledge of firing and maintaining guns became an increasingly important part of Indian armies. The Deccani merchant-prince Mir Jumla, who allied his army with Shah Jahan in 1656, had European gunners in his service, though the quality of these men was not necessarily of the highest.[53] An English factor noted that when Shah Jahan sent his army to Lahore for a new campaign against Iran, it included 'all the drunken English that entertained themselves at Suratt … being of seamen tourned guners'.[54] During Aurangzeb's reign (1658–1707), Niccolò Manucci wrote that the emperor's increasing piety made him prefer to employ Muslims, and he dispensed with his foreign gunners 'and generally with all our Artizans of

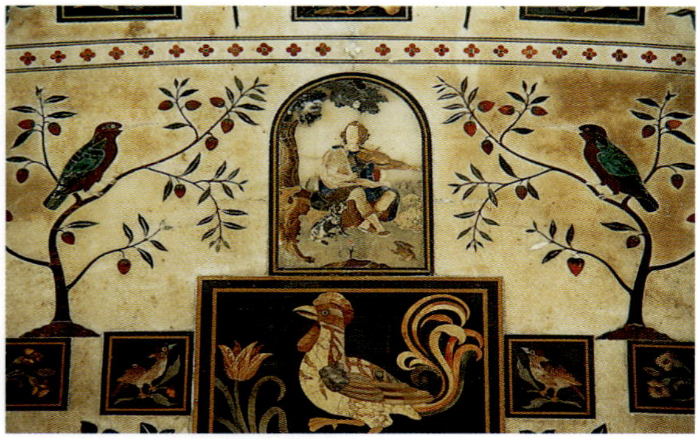

Europe'.[55] Aurangzeb's main adversary, the Maratha ruler Shivaji, had no means of making cannon and regularly purchased them from European sources.[56]

In the second half of the eighteenth and early nineteenth century western expertise was crucial to regional rulers needing to defend themselves against the powerful East India Company army, with its superior technology and discipline. The nawabs of Oudh employed French mercenaries in the 1760s and '70s, though the English forced Nawab Asaf ad-daula (r. 1775–98) to dismiss them on his accession.[57] The swift deterioration in the quality of guns in the nawab's arsenal suggests that the French had been closely involved in their production; in 1773 the Comte de Modave, visiting the capital Faizabad, wrote that the guns were manufactured 'almost as well as in our workshops in Europe', but three years later a British official reported that the Nawab had 'no muskets by him fit for Service and no People capable of making them properly'.[58] When Claude Martin, the Frenchman who became a Company servant, was appointed superintendent of the arsenal in 1776, he employed Indian workmen trained by French officers (plate 22.15).[59] More European expertise was available in Agra, where Benoît de Boigne (1751–1830) established a foundry and arsenal in 1790 and employed French and Irish craftsmen, whose skills in casting cannon and manufacturing muskets were said to be equal to those of the British in India.[60] Benoît de Boigne's remodelling of the army of Gwalior over a period of 20 years gave the Maratha ruler, Mahadji Sindhia (r. 1788–94), unparalleled power,[61] while in the Punjab the Sikh ruler Ranjit Singh (r. 1799–1839) employed French and Italian expertise to establish foundries, as well as to organize and drill his army.[62]

In the south, Tipu Sultan's arsenal was filled with guns made according to western patterns. After his death and the fall of his citadel Seringapatam to the

22.12
Orpheus Playing to the Beasts

Florentine *pietre dure* panel inlaid into the marble wall behind Shah Jahan's throne *jharoka*, Red Fort, Delhi
Italy (Florence), early 17th century

22.13
Turban jewels

Enamelled gold set with diamonds, rubies and a sapphire
India (Murshidabad), *c.* 1757
V&A: IS.3&A–1982

The jewels were presented to Admiral Charles Watson in 1757 by Mir Ja'far, Nawab of Murshidabad.

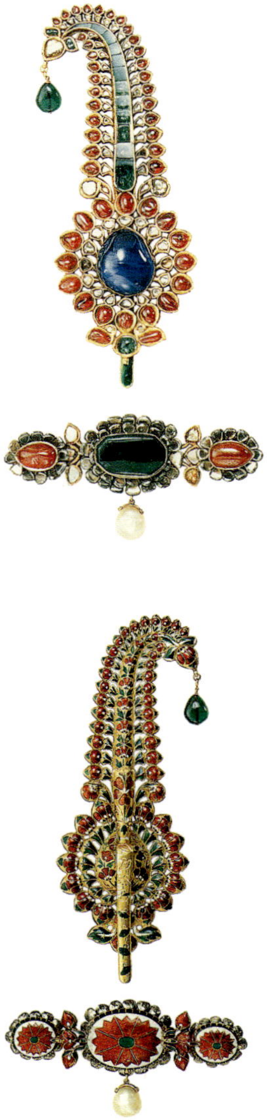

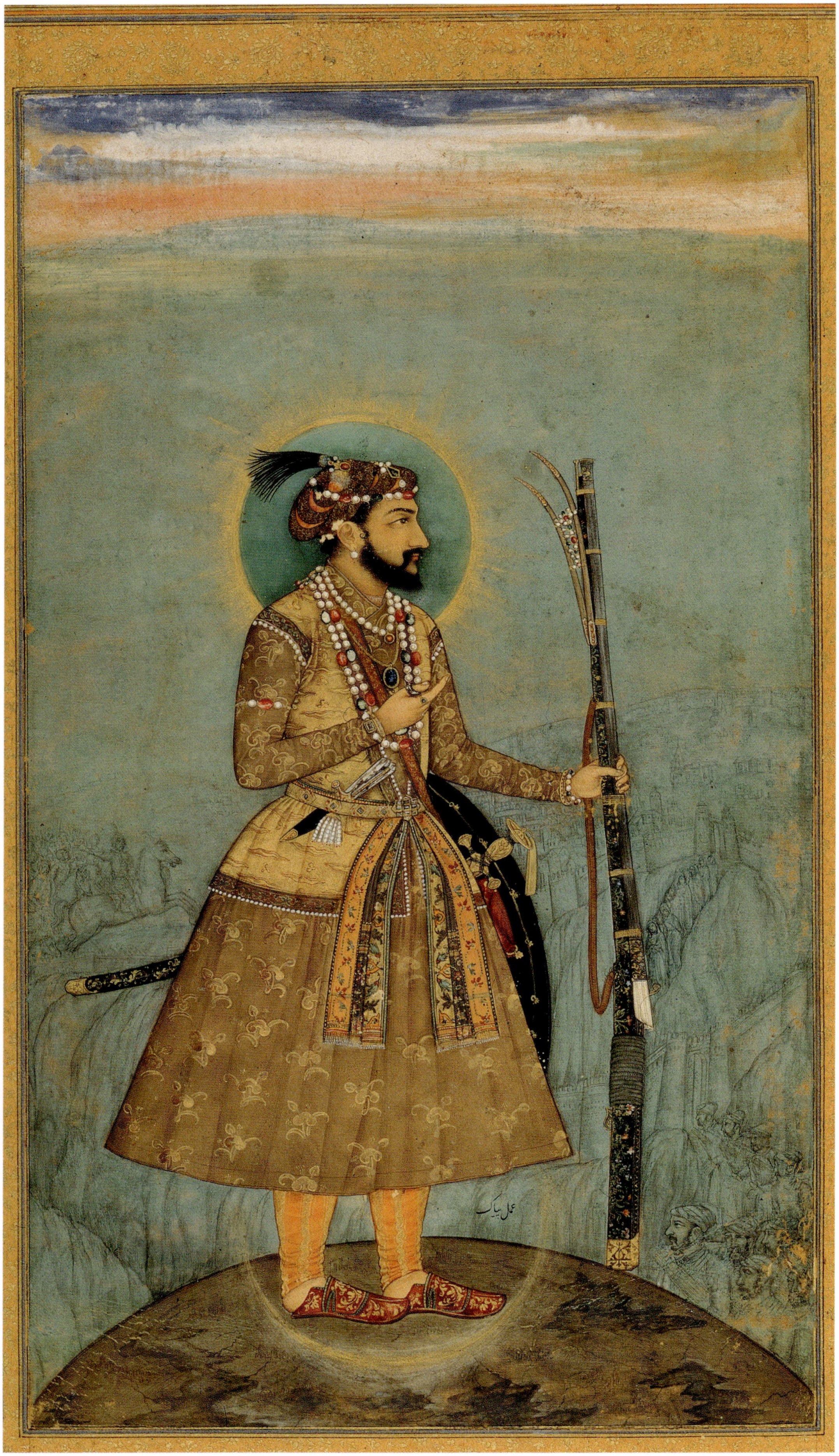

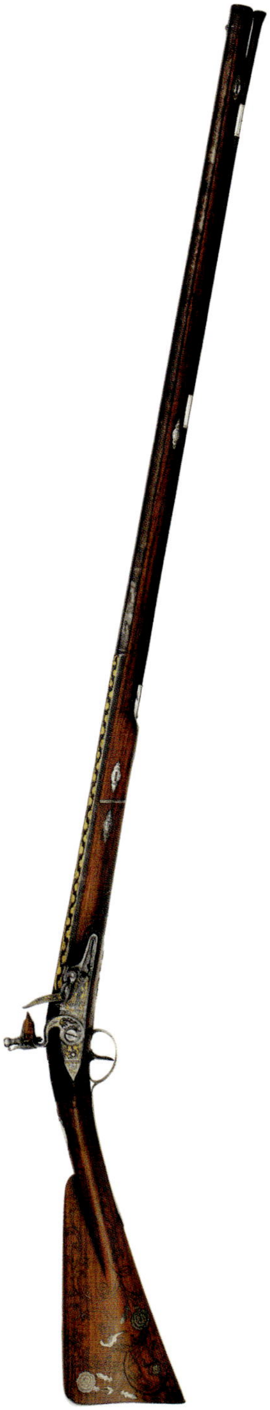

22.14
Shah Jahan with a Rifle
Payag

Opaque watercolour and gold on paper
Mughal India, *c.*1630

Chester Beatty Library, Dublin

22.15
Flintlock gun
Workshop of Major Claude Martin

Forged steel barrel, inlaid with gold, wooden stock with silver inlay
India (Lucknow), *c.*1780

Royal Armouries, Leeds

British in 1799, Tipu Sultan's personal, highly distinctive guns were discovered. Those that still survive include dated examples signed by Muslim smiths, and show familiarity with the almost contemporary work of English gunsmiths such as Henry Nock, though the mechanical workmanship is slightly inferior.[63] As Robin Wigington has pointed out, the British inventory of the arsenal in 1799 recorded that almost all the guns used by Tipu's army were flintlocks, long standard issue in Europe but only gradually being adopted in late eighteenth-century India: of the total 99,000 flintlocks, 52,000 were European, made either in England (15,000) or France (37,000), and the remainder were locally made copies. Only 320 guns were listed as 'matchlocks', all of them unserviceable, demonstrating the relative modernity of Tipu's army compared with other Indian armies, which continued to make and use matchlocks well into the nineteenth century.[64]

These attempts to improve military technology and expertise did not prevent the British advance, and by the mid-eighteenth century the balance of power in India had changed. As British control over the subcontinent tightened, western influence spread over regions as diverse in their nature as they had ever been. Comprehensive surveying and mapping projects were undertaken according to the latest European principles, English replaced Persian as the *lingua franca*, and the numbers of Europeans in India rose. Indian rulers collected western artefacts more avidly than ever before, whether in Lucknow – where the nawab, Asaf ad-daula, indiscriminately collected paintings by Claude Lorrain, vast plate-glass mirrors, cuckoo clocks and furniture (see p. 332)[65] – or Madras, where the nawab, Muhammad Ali Wallajah (r. 1750–95), bought furniture, mechanical toys and mathematical instruments from England in the 1770s.[66]

In general, the latest western technological innovations were readily available in India, as demonstrated by Claude Martin's typically eccentric experiments with a hot-air balloon in Lucknow in 1785, less than two years after the first hot-air balloon flights in Paris.[67] Yet, as shown by the example of Maharaja Sawai Jai Singh of Jaipur and his observatories, when intellectually engaged and able to choose freely, the elite selected only what was useful or necessary from the West. The great mass of the population probably continued to ignore their mildly entertaining foreign residents, until forced to pay attention by involvement in a new, imposed legal system, or war.

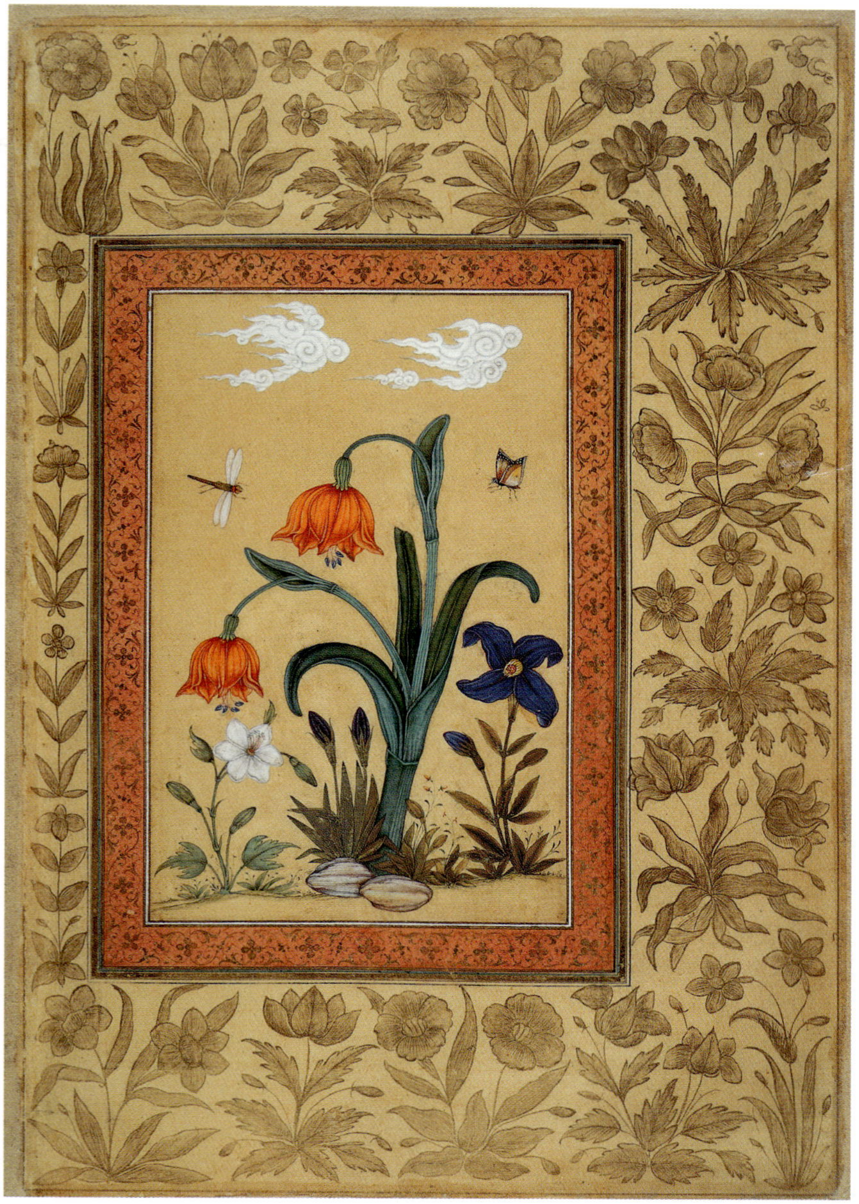

22.16
Exotic Flowers and Insects
From the Dara Shokuh Album; attributed to Muhammed Khan

Opaque watercolour and gold on paper
Mughal India, 1630–35

British Library, London

23

EUROPE IN ASIA: THE IMPACT OF WESTERN ART AND TECHNOLOGY IN CHINA

Catherine Pagani

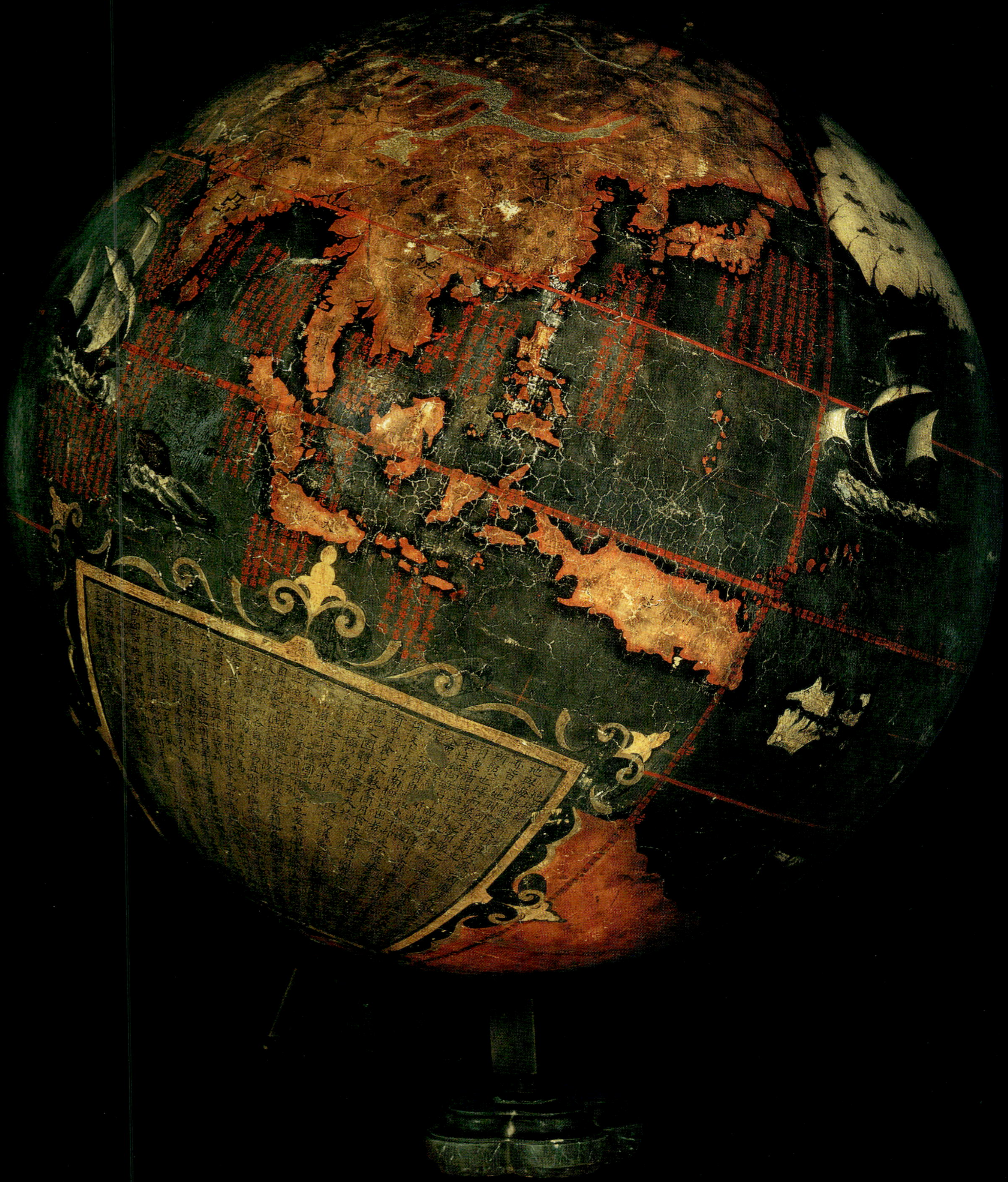

23.1 previous page
Terrestrial globe
Yang Ma-nao (Manuel Diaz) and Long Hua-min (Niccolò Longobardi)

Wood, painted lacquer
China (Peking), 1623

British Library, London

23.2
Page depicting instruments at the Beijing Observatory

From Ferdinand Verbiest, *Lingtai yixiang zhi (Astronomical Instruments in the Observatory)*, preface dated 1674
Woodblock printed on paper

British Library, London

THE LARGE-SCALE transmission of ideas between Europe and China began with the arrival of Jesuit missionaries at the Chinese court in the early seventeenth century. The Jesuits used their knowledge of European technologies, both artistic and scientific, to gain access to the highest reaches of society, in the hope that imperial favour would enable them to establish Christianity on Chinese soil. The Jesuits went beyond simply bringing western objects and technologies, however; they took an active role in teaching these skills to the Chinese by translating western scientific treatises and working with them at the court as astronomers, clockmakers, painters, mapmakers, engravers, architects and mathematicians.[1] It may be said that the Jesuits' most enduring contribution to Chinese culture was not the doctrines of Christianity, but rather the introduction of European technology.

The Jesuit Matteo Ricci (1552–1610) played a fundamental role in this transmission and his contributions to Chinese science were far-reaching. Ricci had discovered the value of European goods in securing a place for the missionaries when he used western objects to facilitate his journey to Peking (Beijing) and obtain an audience with the Wanli emperor in 1601. Among the presents that he brought were Christian religious paintings, a crucifix, a statue of the Virgin Mary, a small clavichord, hourglasses, coins, two glass prisms and two striking clocks. Ricci was a brilliant and versatile scholar: while his strength rested in mathematics (together with the scholar Xu Guangqi he translated Euclid's *Elements* into Chinese), he was also able in the areas of astronomy, mapmaking and clockmaking.[2]

In his efforts to enter the Chinese empire and set up residence in the capital, Ricci used science to promote the faith (*Propagatio fidei per scientias*). This would become the Jesuits' proselytizing strategy in China. They utilized their knowledge in such areas as mathematics, astronomy, geometry and cartography, to enable them to make more conversions.[3] Although this method was unsuitable for large-scale proselytization, it was useful to them in wooing influential Chinese scholars. Discussions would begin with scientific principles and then turn to explain aspects of the faith. Eventually it came to be understood that an acceptance of western science went hand-in-hand with an acceptance of Christianity.

The growing Chinese interest in science aided and shaped this strategy. As the Ming empire entered a period of decline, scholars seeking a cause for the

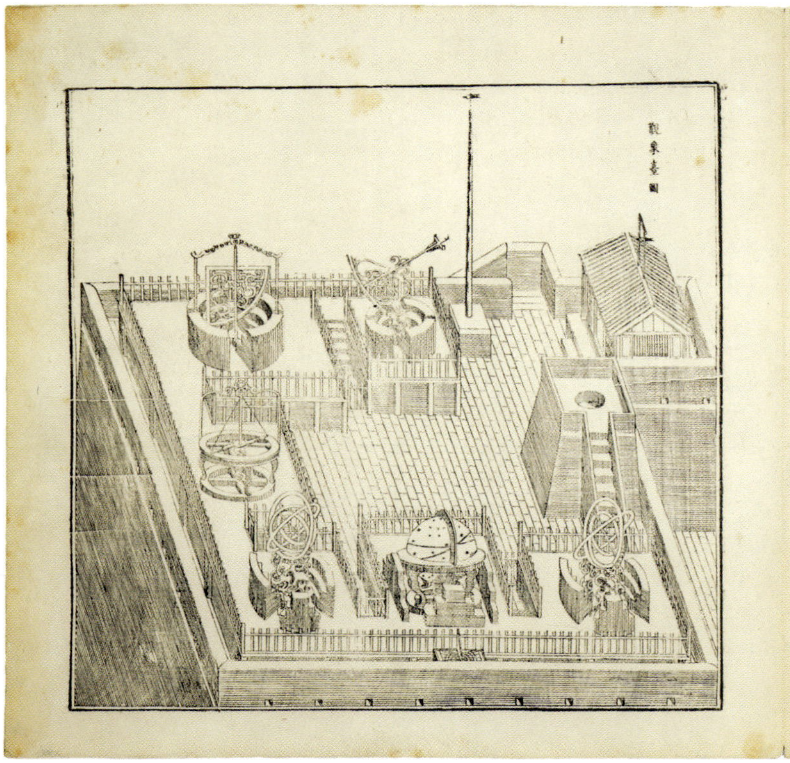

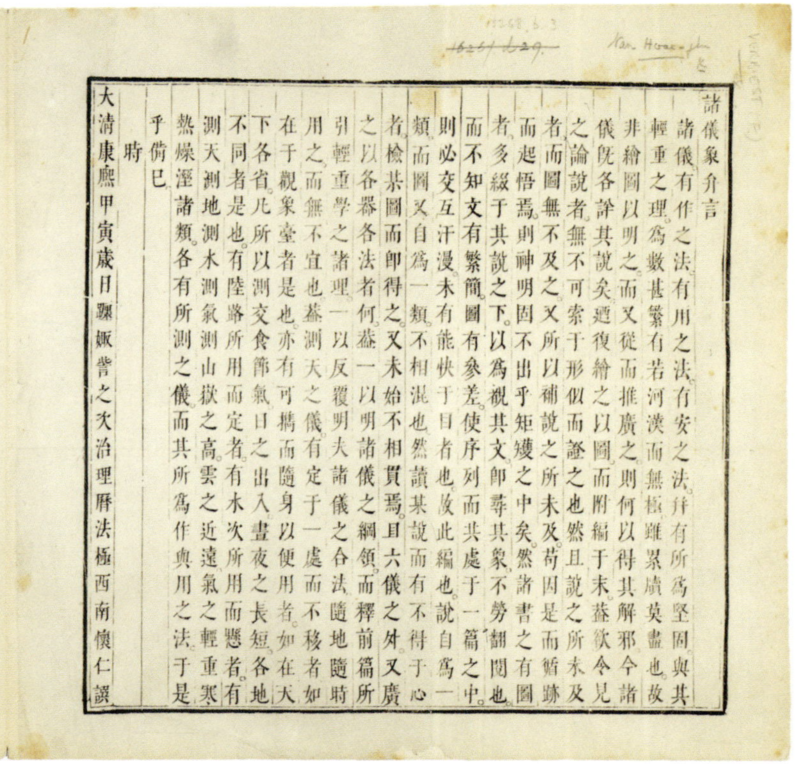

諸儀象弁言

諸儀有作之法有用之法有安之法并有所爲堅固與其輕重之理爲數甚繁有若河漢而無極雖累牘莫盡也故非繪圖以明之而又從而推廣之則何以得其解邪今諸儀既各詳其說矣遞復繪之以圖而附編于末葢欲令見之論說者無不可索于形似而證之也然且說之所未及者而圖無不及之又所以補說之所未及苟因是而循跡而起悟焉則神明固不出乎矩矱之中矣然諸書之有圖者多綴于其說之下以爲覩其文即尋其象不勞翻閱也而不知文有繁簡圖有參差使序列而共處于一篇之中則必交互汗漫未有能快于目者也故此編也說自爲一類而圖又自爲一類不相混也然讀某說而有不得于心者檢某圖而即得之又未始不相貫焉且六儀之外又廣之以各器各法者何葢一以明諸儀之綱領而釋前篇所引輕重學之諸理一以反覆明夫諸儀之合法隨地隨時用之而無不宜也葢測天之儀有定于一處而不移者如在于觀象臺者是也亦有可攜而隨身以便用者如在天下各省凡所以測交食節氣日之出入晝夜之長短各地不同者是也有陸路所用而定者有水次所用而懸者有測天測地測水測氣測山嶽之高雲之近遠氣之輕重寒熱燥溼諸類各有所測之儀而其所爲作與用之法于是乎備巳

時

大清康熙甲寅歲日躔娵訾之次治理曆法極西南懷仁譔

dynasty's problems targeted the writings of the early Ming philosopher Wang Yangming (1472–1528) as the source of the problem. The Chinese literati of the early seventeenth century rejected Wang's notion that the source of moral action came from within one's own body and looked for more practical, outward solutions in the form of *shixue*, 'solid learning' or 'concrete studies'.

In the late seventeenth and eighteenth centuries Chinese scholarship again experienced a change. Interest in personal cultivation at the centre of Song and Ming thinking was replaced by an empirical research methodology known as *kaozheng* (evidential research). In the interest of developing a more rigorous approach to their studies, *kaozheng* scholars turned to certain fields of western learning brought to China by the Jesuits: in particular, mathematics, astronomy and geography.[4] This intellectual environment made the Jesuit strategy of using science to make converts all the more important, for it allowed them to reach the influential literati and created an environment in which these scholars were receptive to Jesuit ideas. In response, the order sought men for the China mission who were trained in specific areas of European technologies.[5] The areas targeted were astronomy and mapmaking, clockmaking, and the visual arts of painting and engraving.

Of the European technologies that the Jesuits brought with them, astronomy in particular captured the attention of the Chinese. At the time that Ricci arrived there was a strong interest in reforming the Chinese calendar. Scholars looked with great enthusiasm to new and improved methods of reconciling the calendar with astronomical observations. The Jesuits were ideally positioned to provide the Chinese with something novel. One of the main controversies of European astronomy of the seventeenth century was between the long-held Aristotelian–Ptolemaic worldview, with the Earth at the centre of the universe, and the heliocentric universe of Copernicus (1473–1543). Galileo (1564–1642), whose discoveries corroborated the heliocentric view, was denounced by the Church in 1633.[6] This ruling was enormously restrictive for the Jesuits, who were well aware of Galileo's findings. Ordered not to expound the theory of heliocentrism, they compromised by telling the Chinese of the work of the Danish astronomer Tycho Brahe (1546–1601), who supported the Ptolemaic view of the sun circling the Earth, but had the other planets circling the sun (the Tychonic system).[7] There were obvious limitations to this theory, and the Jesuits used the controversial ideas of Copernicus on occasion. It was not until 1670, however, that they openly taught the Copernican model to the Chinese.

The most significant European contributions to Chinese astronomy were made in the seventeenth century under two astronomers. Johann Adam Schall von Bell (1591–1666), who had worked under Clavius, arrived in 1622, and in 1626 introduced the concept of the telescope to the Chinese in the *Yuanjing shuo* (*On the Telescope*). In 1645, the year he produced a new Chinese calendar, Schall was appointed by the Shunzhi emperor as director of the Imperial Board of Astronomy, a post that he held until 1665. He was the first of a succession of Jesuits to hold this prestigious position. In 1669 the Belgian mathematician and astronomer Ferdinand Verbiest (1623–88) was appointed to this position.[8] His most visible legacy is found in the set of six large bronze astronomical instruments he had cast in 1669 and illustrated in his *Lingtai yixiang zhi* (*Astronomical Instruments in the Observatory*) (plate 23.2). Based on designs by Brahe, they stand today at the Ancient Observatory in Peking (plate 23.3).[9] Verbiest was not immediately succeeded by another European, but from 1688 until 1694 two Jesuits, Antoine Thomas (1645–1708) and Thomas Pereira (1644–1709), acted as interim directors. The former is best known for his work on the cartographic survey of China that was completed posthumously in 1718. This project resulted in the astronomical determination of the exact measurement of the Chinese *li*, some 90 years before the kilometre was fixed in Europe.[10]

In the eighteenth century European contributions to Chinese astronomy centred around the work of Ignatius Kögler (1680–1746), who served as the sixth director of the Imperial Board of Astronomy from 1720 until his death. Kögler designed the large bronze equatorial armillary sphere that is still present at the Ancient Observatory in Peking. He authored treatises on astronomy and calendrical science, including the *Yixiang kaozheng* (*Imperial Astronomical Instruments*) of 1744. In that year the Jesuits began work on determining new star positions. The project was completed in 1756 and published in 1757 in an expanded edition of Kögler's *Yixiang kaozheng*. With its new star lists, the work came to be known as the Qianlong star-catalogue.

Kögler's association with the Korean scholars An Kukpin and Pyon Chunghwa, who had come

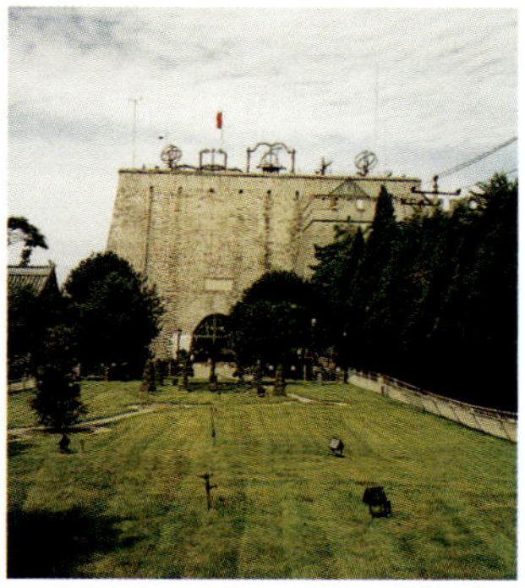

23.3
Observatory, Beijing

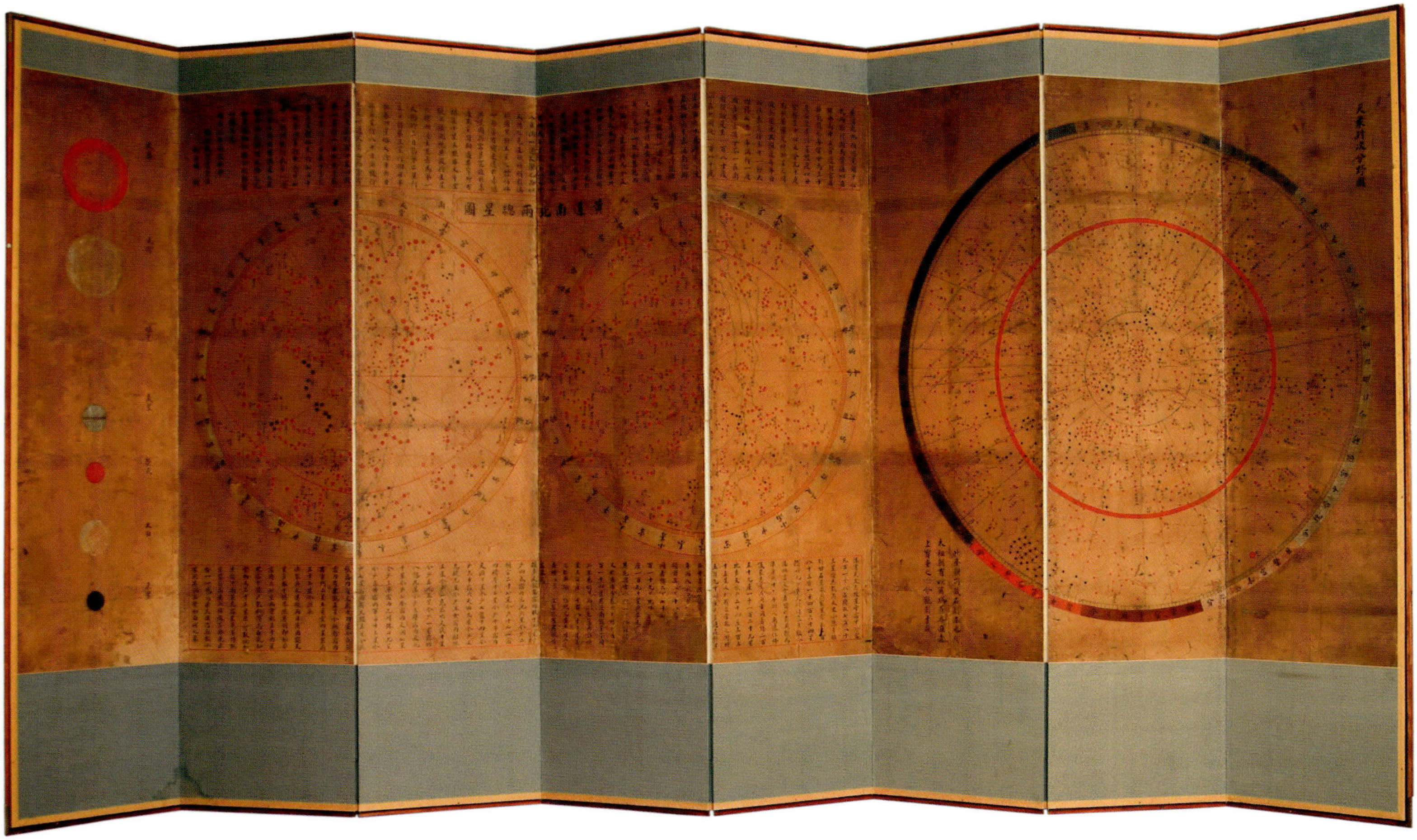

23.4
Astronomical screen

From the Royal Palace of the Yi dynasty, Seoul, Korea; ink and colours on paper
Korea, *c.* 1757

Whipple Museum, Cambridge

to Peking in 1741, brought eighteenth-century Jesuit astronomy to Korea. Evidence of this contact is found on a Korean astronomical screen of *c.* 1757 (plate 23.4) that mentions the Jesuit astronomers Kögler and Verbiest, and on information from the Qianlong star-catalogue.[11] This was not the first contact between Korea and the Jesuit astronomers: as early as 1631 a Korean embassy under Chong Tuwon met Joaõ Rodrigues, a Jesuit priest with a strong interest in astronomy stationed in Dengzhou, Shandong; and in 1644 the crown prince received books, a map and a celestial globe from Johann Adam Schall von Bell.[12] Western scientific knowledge was now transmitted beyond the Chinese court.

In addition to introducing European astronomy, Ricci was also the first to bring western cartography to the Chinese. In 1584 he produced the first world map in China, based on a European example that he carried with him and had on display in his residence in Zhaoqing.[13] Ricci's map is no longer extant, but the revised version of 1602 survives and has earned the distinction of being 'one of the most celebrated maps in the history of cartography' (see plate 2.17).[14] This was the first of a number of Jesuit world maps produced in China in the seventeenth century. Notable among them are the Giulio Aleni (1582–1649) map and treatise, *Zhifang waiji* (*Account of Countries Not Listed in the Records Office*) of 1623; the Francesco Sambiasi (1582–1649) map of 1648, based on the earlier work by Ricci; and Verbiest's *Kunyu quantu* (*Complete Map of the Terrestrial Globe*) of 1674, which built on Aleni's work and included a Chinese version of a contemporary map of Europe. Also of importance among the Jesuit mapping projects is the lacquered Chinese globe made at the court in 1623 by Manuel Diaz (1574–1659) and Niccolò Longobardi (1565–1655) (plate 23.1). This earliest surviving terrestrial globe made in China draws both on European knowledge, by including newly discovered lands, and on the Chinese discovery of terrestrial magnetism, a concept known in Europe only with the findings of Isaac Newton (1642–1727).

The Jesuits also focused on producing maps of China, largely as a means of providing information on China for a European audience. The first effort was undertaken by Martino Martini (1614–61), who collated data from a number of Chinese sources in his *Novus Atlas Sinensis* (published in Europe in 1655). In 1687 the arrival in China of French Jesuits who had training in cartography resulted in the first accurate, scientific survey of China. These Jesuits convinced the Kangxi emperor (r. 1662–1722) of the need for a comprehensive map of the expanded Qing empire. He first asked them to map the area surrounding Peking, followed by the northern area of the Great Wall. These projects involved a number of Jesuits, including Antoine Thomas, Joachim Bouvet (1656–1730), Jean-Baptiste Régis (1663–1738) and Dominique Parrenin (1665–1741). Then, in 1708, the Jesuits began their 10-year imperially sponsored and exhaustive survey of China. In 1717 the *Huangyu quanlantu* (*Comprehensive Imperial Geographic Atlas*) was completed. Its 28 maps were woodblock-printed, but in 1719 a manuscript revision of 32 maps was made. From this, Matteo Ripa (1682–1745) engraved the *Yujin Da Qing yitong quantu* (*Modern Complete Geographical Atlas of the Great Qing Empire*) in 44 plates.[15] Copies appeared in Europe and served as the central source of information on Chinese geography (see p. 31).

In 1601 Ricci presented two striking clocks to the Wanli emperor (r. 1573–1620). When he arrived at the court, Ricci found that the Chinese had no apparent knowledge of mechanical clockwork.[16] Viewing Chinese incense and sand clocks, he commented that, 'Their clocks up to now used water and the fire of certain odoriferous fibres made all of the same size; they make also others with wheels that are moved by sand; they are all very imperfect.'[17] The Chinese had used a type of mechanical clock in connection with astronomy as early as the seventh century; however, while the Chinese made great achievements early on, their skill did not progress beyond the technology of the thirteenth century (seen in the great water-powered astronomical clock of Su Song).[18] European mechanical clockwork technology was slower in developing, but its rapid advancements in the sixteenth century allowed for a smaller mechanism that could support accessory functions such as animated figures and music. Having no native counterpart against which to compete, European clocks – called *zimingzhong*, or 'self-sounding bells' by the Chinese – were received by the court with great enthusiasm (see plate 7.5).

From the time the first clocks were brought to China from Europe in around 1582, the Chinese were at a loss as to how to repair and maintain them. Ricci was instrumental in remedying this by initiating a long line of cooperative efforts between Jesuit and Chinese scholars. As a result, the Jesuits were able to exert an influence on both the theory and practice of horology in China, first through the publication in Chinese of western horological principles, and then in the staffing of the imperial clockmaking workshop.

In 1627 a pivotal work was published on the principles of European engineering and mechanics, *Yuanxi qiqi tushuo* (*Diagrams and Explanations of Wonderful Machines of the Far West*). This work, which provided Chinese names for western mechanical terms, was the first to describe a European-style verge-and-foliot escapement, and was co-authored by the Swiss missionary Johannes Schreck (1576–1630) and the Chinese scholar Wang Zheng (1571–1644).[19] In the same year Wang also published a shorter volume, *Zhuqi tushuo* (*Diagrams and Explanations of a Number of Machines*), which contains the earliest account in Chinese of the verge-and-foliot escapement.[20]

However, it was not enough to supply mechanical theory; practical skills were necessary to keep the pieces in good repair. The history of western clockmaking at the Chinese court begins in the early seventeenth century, when the emperor assigned four eunuchs from the College of Mathematics at the palace to study the art of clock maintenance and repair with Ricci. Ultimately the eunuchs were unable to cope with the demands of the imperial court, believing that they could not keep such complex mechanical objects running without the help of the Jesuits. The Wanli emperor therefore arranged to have the Jesuits at court look after the clocks.[21] The eunuchs at the palace who received instruction under Ricci began an association between the Chinese and the Jesuit missionaries that would continue for nearly two centuries. Eventually the Jesuits were able to call upon professional clockmakers, who were then made part of the China mission.[22]

Among the palace workshops established by the Kangxi emperor in 1693 was one devoted to western-style clocks.[23] This office remained active until at least 1879.[24] The workshop allowed the Jesuits to

23.5
Clock
Gilded copper inlaid with enamel
China (Canton), Qianlong period (1736–95)
Palace Museum, Beijing

23.6 opposite
Entertainment Painting of Emperor Yongzheng's Imperial Concubine
Hanging scroll, one of a series of twelve; colours on silk
China (Qing court), Yongzheng period (1723–35)
Palace Museum, Beijing

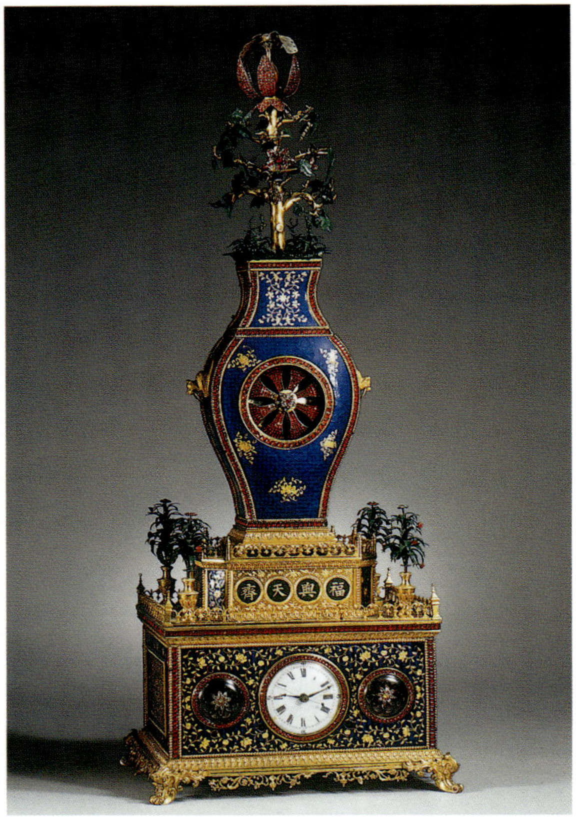

introduce yet another (and highly practical) area of European science and technology to the Chinese that was soon disseminated to other parts of the country with the growth of a native clockmaking industry. European science and technology had now fully penetrated the court circle.

The missionaries were vital to the success of this workshop and, in the course of performing their duties, created extraordinary pieces. Among them was an automaton in the form of a walking lion, which Gilles Thébault (1703–66) was able to construct using the most basic of horological principles, and an alarm clock by Valentin Chalier (1697–1747), which the emperor kept in his own apartments. Sigismondo Mainardi di San Nicolà (1713–67) had planned to make an extraordinary automaton in human form that would be able to walk in a natural manner. It was feared that should Sigismondo succeed (as he was expected to do), the Qianlong emperor would then demand of the missionary: 'You've made it walk, now make it talk.'[25]

Clocks continued to arrive from Europe, joining the Chinese-made pieces from the imperial workshop. Although no accurate count of the clocks in the imperial collection exists, contemporary observations suggest that by the end of the first quarter of the eighteenth century they numbered in the thousands. But these clocks were not collected for their appearance alone. As objects that represented a new and exclusive technology, they were tangible representations of the Qing emperors' power and status (plate 23.6, see also plate 7.5). The Kangxi, Yongzheng and Qianlong emperors all wrote poems in praise of 'self-sounding bells', and during the Qianlong period, clocks were included for the first time in official court documents.[26] Ironically, the Europeans who were associated with the clock trade to China attributed the appeal of these clocks solely to their chinoiserie style, the dominant taste in the decorative arts in Europe at the time. For them, the imperial interest in these fanciful clocks proved that this 'Asiatic splendour' represented true Chinese taste.[27] In fact, the Chinese regarded clocks as the epitome of European design and technology, and not as objects incorporating a European version of Chinese aesthetics.

The emperors were not the only collectors of clockwork at the court. The powerful and opportunistic Grand Councillor Heshen (1750–99), the Qianlong emperor's favourite minister, was famous for his vast accumulation of wealth, which was said to rival that of the emperor himself.[28] His fantastic holdings included 288 large rubies, 4,070 sapphires, 28,000 pieces of jewellery, a 4,288-piece gold dinner service, 38 European clocks inlaid with precious stones, and 140 gold and enamel watches.[29]

By the eighteenth century, perhaps because of their exclusiveness or their association with the emperor, clocks – no matter how simple – seemed to have become an attribute of the elite. Depictions of interior life from paintings and literature represent clocks occupying a prominent place within the home's more public spaces. Throughout the late eighteenth-century novel *Hongloumeng* (*Dream of the Red Chamber*), which follows the story of the wealthy Jia family, western-style clocks are mentioned, providing information on the different types of clocks favoured by the elite, how they were used and how they were regarded. They signified the status of the master of the household and delineated the differences between the urban upper class and the rural non-elite. The elderly Grannie Liu, for example, on first arriving at the mansion from the countryside, noticed a 'boxlike object fastened to one of the central pillars of the room'. As she moved closer to the box to examine it, 'it suddenly gave forth a loud *dong!* like the sound of a bronze bell or a copper chime, which so startled the old lady that her eyes nearly popped out of her head'.[30] What was commonplace for this household was not so familiar outside this wealthy setting.

The demand for clocks encouraged the development of a native industry beyond the palace workshop (plate 23.5). Manufacturing centres developed in other areas of China owing to two factors: the demands by ministers and high officials seeking imperial favour, who chose elaborate clocks as tribute for the court, and the consumption of these items by the elite and official class. The most important of these centres in the eighteenth century was the southern Chinese city of Canton (Guangzhou), although clockmaking came to be practised in Suzhou as well.[31] Such pieces could also be found in Peking households.[32] Canton and Suzhou were also known for making *zimingzhong*.[33] Other, less important centres included Shanghai, Ningpo and Nanjing.[34]

Canton in particular felt the influence of European technologies in the eighteenth century as a direct result of the foreign trade passing through her port. Lists of tribute from Guangdong province tell of the many European items to arrive that were then presented to the emperor by high-ranking officials (plate 23.7). Members of Canton's large craftsman community could study these imported pieces at first hand. The resulting high-quality goods combined European and Chinese elements characteristic of eighteenth-century imperial taste, many of which were also destined as tribute to the Qing court.

The Cantonese artisans did not slavishly copy foreign pieces, but rather developed a style that was a unique synthesis of European and Chinese aesthetics, as seen in a pair of carved ivory hand-mirrors that combine traditional Chinese designs of the 100 deer and *lingzhi* (or fungus of immortality) with European figures in a landscape, found on the mirrors' covers (plate 23.8). These long-handled mirrors also mark a departure in both form and material from traditional Chinese bronze mirrors (plate 23.9). Typically round in shape, bronze mirrors are polished on one side; the designs on the reverse are often cosmological, and there is a central knob for a silk cord. Western glass mirrors also offered new possibilities in size, as evidenced by the painting by Jiao Bingzhen of a woman who looks at herself in a full-length mirror and appears not to believe what she sees (plate 23.10). Similarly, a glass ewer probably made as tribute for

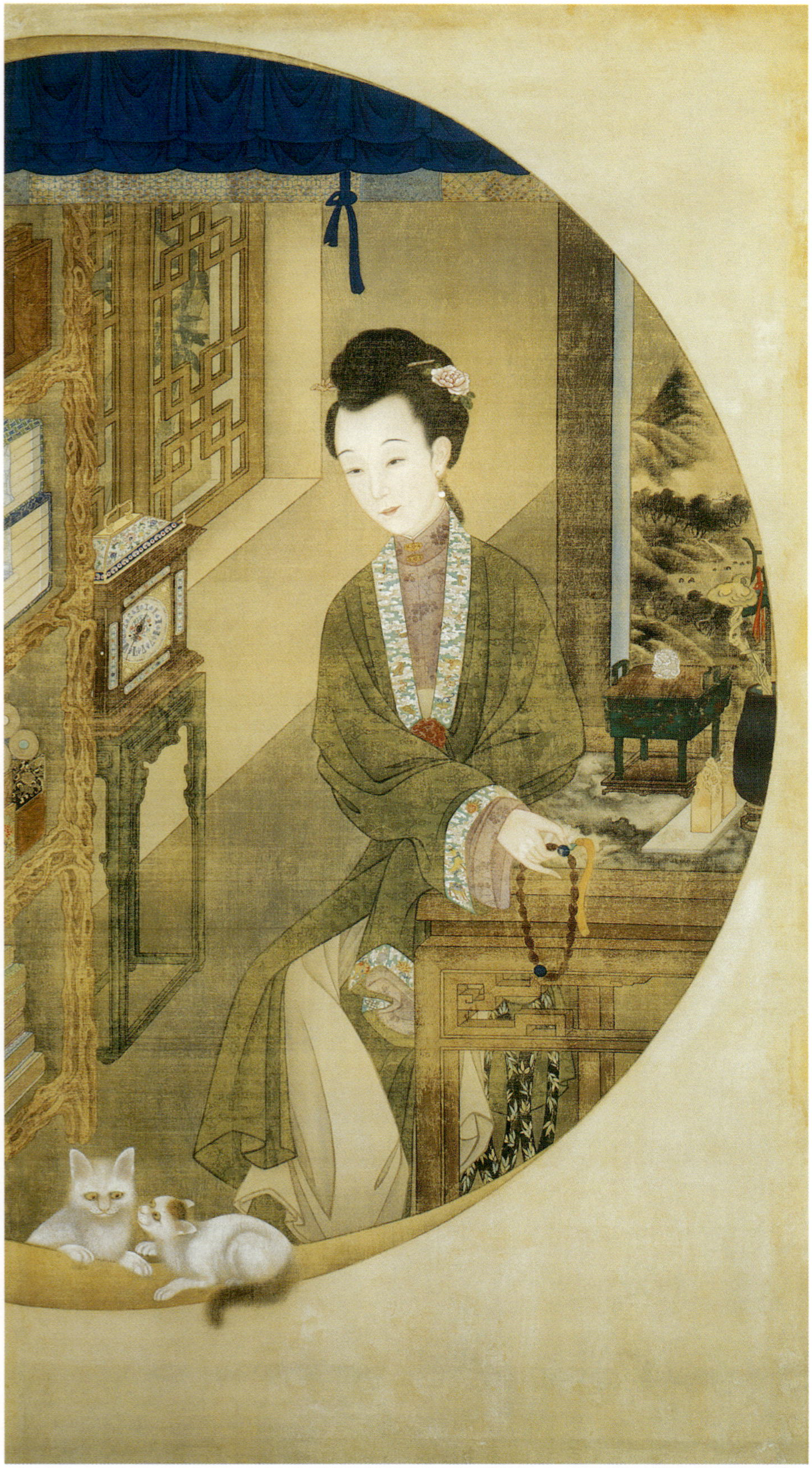

23.7
Telescope

Gilded copper with enamel plaques
England, 18th century

Palace Museum, Beijing

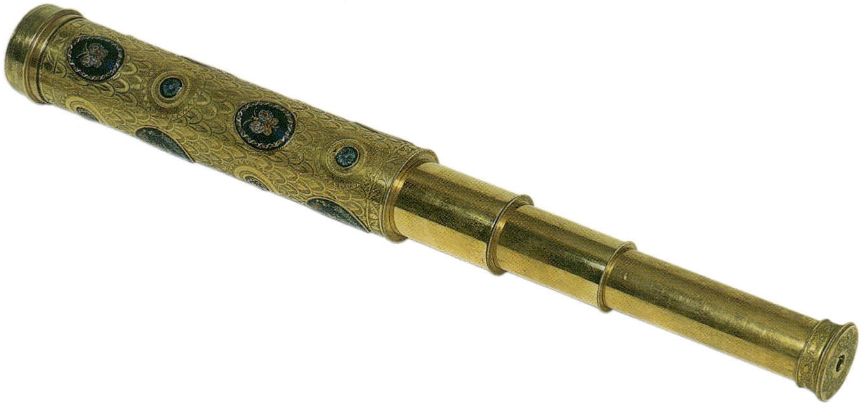

the Qianlong emperor unites a European jug form with Chinese decorative motifs of five-clawed dragons cavorting amid *ruyi*-shaped clouds (plate 23.11) The glass industry in China also owes its later developments to European influence.[35] Jesuit missionaries, knowledgeable about glassmaking, staffed the imperial workshop, where they introduced improvements to traditional Chinese techniques.[36]

Ricci's presentation of two oil paintings of the Virgin Mary to the Wanli emperor marks the beginning of a Sino-western painting style in China. Ricci was not the first to introduce European painting to the Chinese,[37] but his initial efforts were responsible for the steady presence that the European visual arts would maintain at the Chinese court for the next 200 years. European painting conventions were not taken up immediately by Chinese artists, but rather were adopted gradually, in two phases.[38] In the first phase, oil paintings, printed books and engravings brought by the Jesuits to China aroused interest among the Chinese, but did not result in the emergence of a new style of painting: Chinese artists merely copied European works. This phase saw the gradual introduction of Jesuit painters to the court.[39] In the second phase, the presence of

23.8
Pair of hand-held mirrors
Left: back view; right: front view

Carved polychrome ivory
China (possibly Canton), Qianlong period (1736–95)

Private collection, London

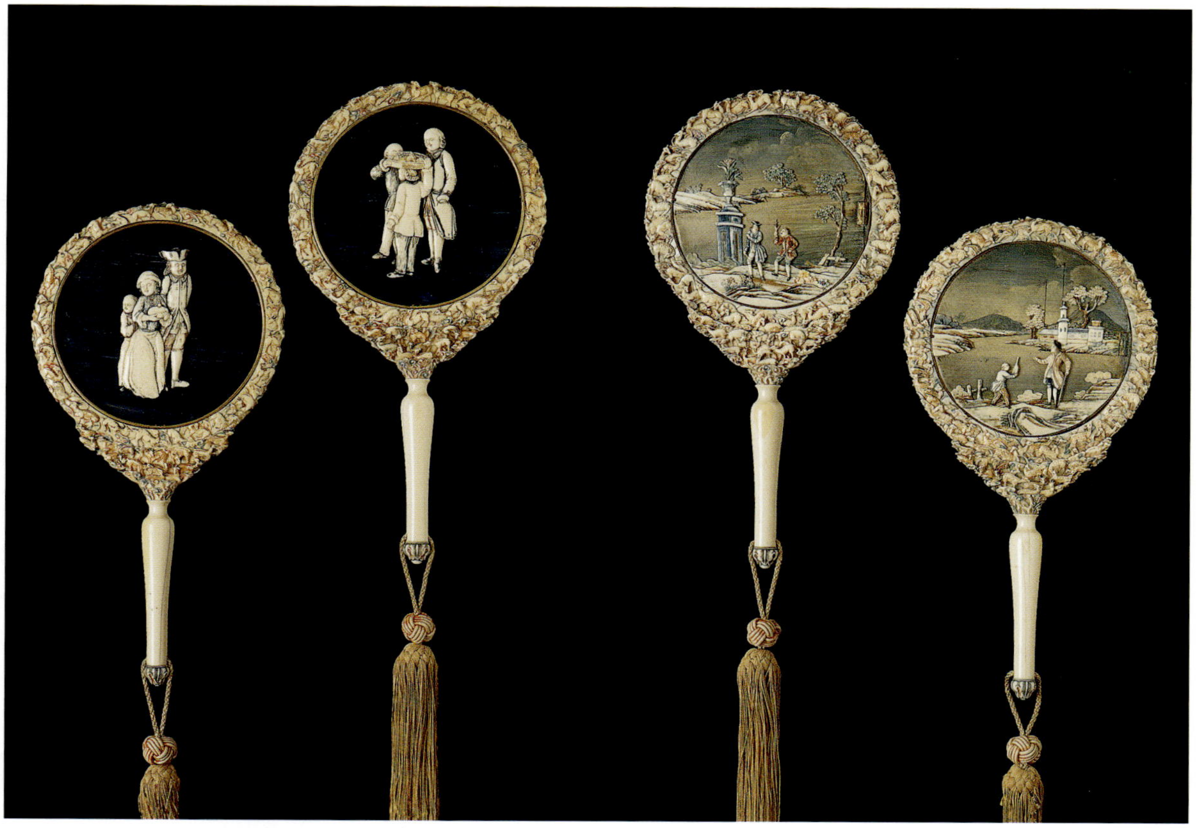

Jesuit painters at the court gave rise to a new painting style that combined western and Chinese elements, which may be attributed to the long tenure at court of the painter Giuseppe Castiglione (1688–1766).

In the late Ming dynasty there were no Jesuits in China trained in painting; the missionaries therefore had to turn to Chinese artists to meet their needs for devotional pictures. Two important early artists were You Wenhui and Ni Yicheng. Both had studied European painting under the priest-painter Giovanni Niccolò (1560–1626), who was now in Japan.[40] You (christened Mañoel Pereira) worked in Peking from 1605 to 1607. He is the likely artist of the well-known portrait of Ricci, of 1610. Now in the Instituto Storico della Compagnia di Jesu in Rome, this work has the distinction of being the earliest painting done in a European style by a documented Chinese artist. Ni (Jacopo Niva), who arrived from Japan to work with Ricci, was the more skilled of the two. His painting, with its use of light and shade, was said to be more like sculpture than painting.[41] Ni decorated churches in Peking and Macao, and in 1610 the wall of the temple that the 'emperor had given as a tomb for Ricci'.[42] Unfortunately, none of his work survives.

European printed works were important sources of imagery in the early seventeenth century. Included among them are Giovanni Rusconi's *Della Archittetura* (1590), Théodore de Bry's *Topographica Urbis Romae* (1597) and Georg Braun and Franz Hogenberg's *Civitates Orbis Terrarum* (1572). Geronimo Nadal's illustrated version of the Gospel, *Evangelicae historiae imagines* (1593), was particularly influential. Giulio Aleni (1582–1649), a priest in Fujian, produced a Chinese version, *Tian zhu jiang sheng you xing ji le* (*Brief Records of the Deeds of God who Became Man,* 1637) (see plate 8.24).[43] Four images of biblical themes were included in the woodblock-printed *Cheng shi moyuan* (*Mr Cheng's Collection of Ink*, 1609), a book of ink-cake designs by Cheng Dayue (see plate 26.2). One of these engravings came from Nadal.[44]

By the mid-seventeenth century the Jesuits understood the value of painting for the missions and sought talented men who could instruct the Chinese court artists in western technique. The first European artist at the Chinese court was the Austrian Jesuit Johann Grueber (1623–80), who came at the request of the Shunzhi emperor in 1659 and stayed in China until 1661. Grueber's first painting was of Johann Adam Schall von Bell wearing the robes of a mandarin of the first rank.[45] Grueber also caught the emperor's attention with a landscape that made use of

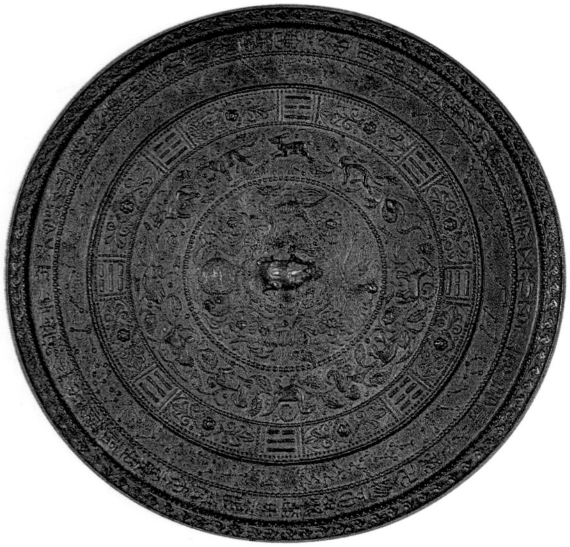

23.9
Mirror

Cast bronze
China, Song dynasty (960–1279)

V&A: 296–1956

The front of the mirror would have been polished to a high reflection.

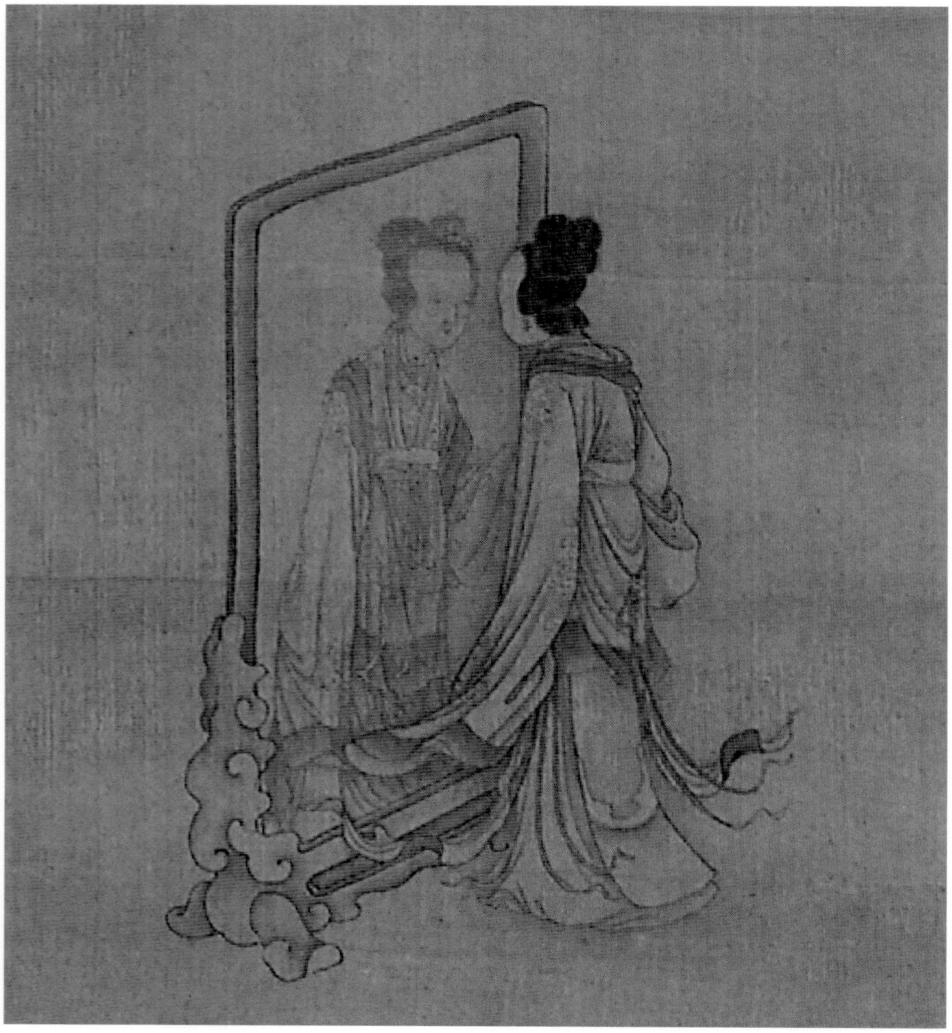

23.10
Lady Looking in a Mirror
Jiao Bingzhen

Ink on paper
China, early 18th century

Museum of Fine Arts, Boston, Marshall H. Gould Fund

23.11
Jug
Carved glass with gilt bronze handle
China (Canton), Qianlong period (1736–95)
Private collection, London

23.12
Shooting Wild Geese
Attributed to Giuseppe Castiglione
Hanging scroll; colours on silk
China (Qing court), *c.*1750
Palace Museum, Beijing

western perspective. At Kangxi's request, in 1700, the lay painter Giovanni Gherardini and the French architect Charles de Belleville (1657–1730) arrived in China. Gherardini was asked to paint the *trompe l'oeil* frescos on the ceiling of the new Jesuit Church of Our Saviour, designed by de Belleville.[46] Simulating a dome, Gherardini's perspective painting fascinated the Chinese. Gherardini also taught students the techniques of western oil painting and perspective. However, in 1704 he returned to France. Although his stay in China was short, Gherardini figured prominently in the advancement of the European arts there.

In 1710 Matteo Ripa (1682–1746), a Neapolitan secular priest sent by the Sacred Congregation for the Propagation of the Faith (*Propaganda Fide*), joined the court of Kangxi, where he served from 1711 to 1723. Ripa, a portraitist by training, is known primarily for being the first in China to make copper engravings. By this time the Kangxi emperor had already been presented with copper engravings executed by the Jesuits in France. When work on his palace complex at Jehol was completed, Kangxi had his court artist, Shen Yu, paint 36 views of the palaces, from which a set of copper engravings were to be made.[47] Ripa had had no experience in engraving, other than once having observed an engraver at work in Italy, but after much experimentation he completed the *Thirty-six Views of Jehol* (1713–14).[48] Subsequently he was given two students to train under him. Following this, Ripa engraved the great Jesuit map of China, Tartary and Korea in 44 plates. On Ripa's visit to London in 1724, George I was presented with a copy, now in the British Museum.

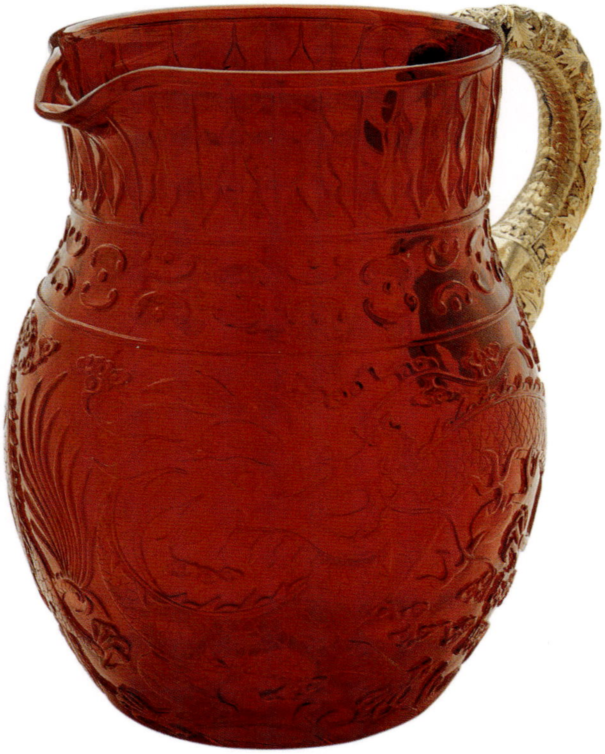

European painting was not fully assimilated by Chinese artists until the arrival in Peking in 1715 of Giuseppe Castiglione (also known by his Chinese name of Lang Shining) (plate 23.12).[49] Castiglione was the most influential – if not the most gifted – of the western artists at court. Known for bringing the European concepts of realism, perspective and chiaroscuro to Chinese painting to yield a cross-cultural hybrid, he served for 49 years under three emperors (Kangxi, Yongzheng and Qianlong).[50] He also collaborated with Nian Xiyao (d. 1738) in the translation into Chinese of Andrea Pozzo's *Perspectiva Pictorum et Architectorum* (1698). *Shixue* (*Visual Learning*) was published in 1729 and again in 1735. Here was the first formal discussion of the techniques involved in rendering a perspective drawing. Castiglione's skill at perspective was put to use when he was appointed chief architect for a new set of buildings in the rococo style at the emperor's summer palace, the Yuanming Yuan (literally, 'Garden of Perfect Clarity') (see plates 26.6–7).[51] These buildings housed Qianlong's collection of European objects, including tapestries, mechanical clocks, furniture and paintings. As a painter at the court, Castiglione served as the Qianlong emperor's official portraitist. Other subjects included the emperor's pets and horses, and occasionally landscapes.

Castiglione achieved a perfect synthesis between European and Chinese styles by blending perspective and shading with Chinese materials and restraint, which gave the emperor 'enough of western realism to delight him, but not enough to disconcert'.[52] Although there would never be another artist at the court of Castiglione's stature, Jean-Denis Attiret (1702–68), who arrived in 1738, rose to become one of the court's most admired artists. During his 30 years serving the emperor, he produced more than 200 portraits and numerous commemorative pictures. Castiglione and Attiret influenced the Chinese artists of the Qing Academy, who produced Chinese works that blended the realism, shading and perspective of European art with Chinese restraint

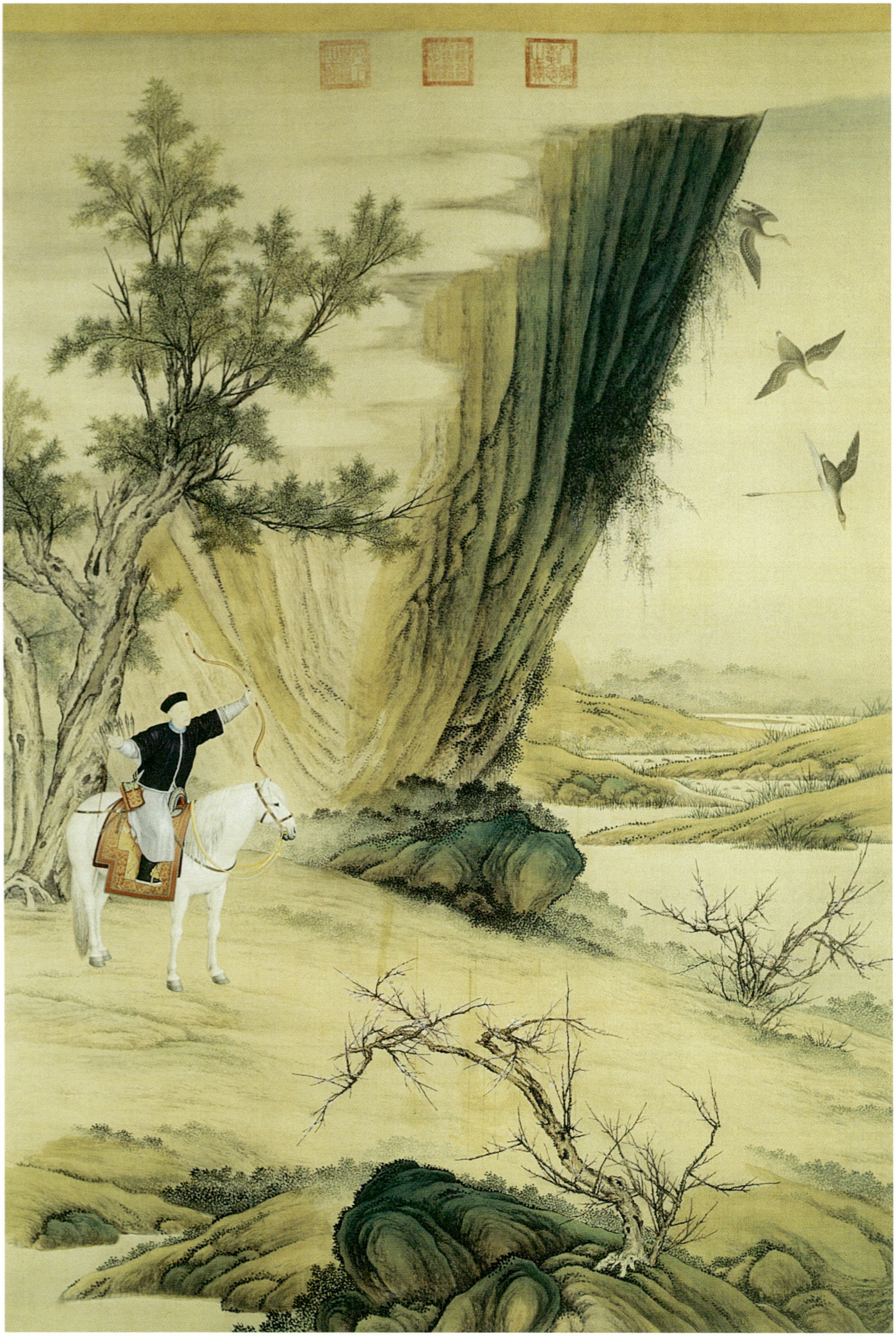

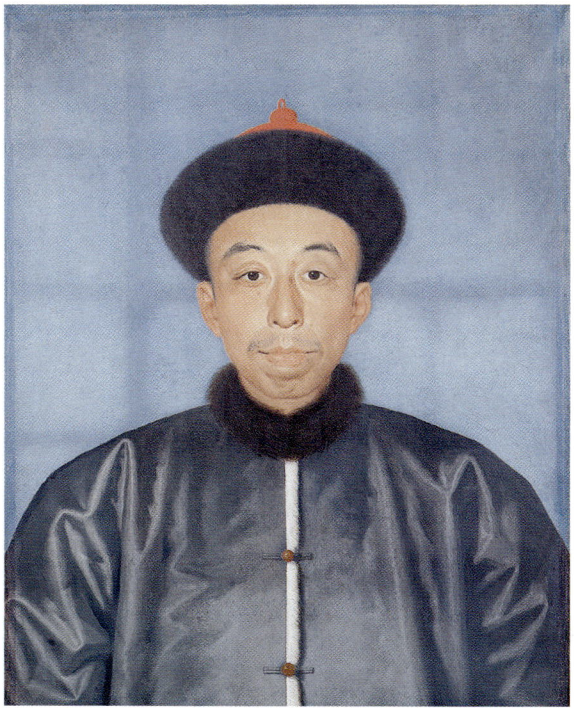

23.13
Hong Yan, Prince Gu
School of Castiglione

Oil on paper
China (Qing court), late 18th century

Courtesy of Martyn Gregory Gallery, London

(plate 23.13). Some of these artists left the court, taking with them their knowledge of a Sino-western painting style that was then disseminated to other parts of the empire. In Suzhou this influence found its way into the woodblock prints produced there (plate 23.14).[53]

But the Jesuits at court were not the only group to introduce western technologies to the Chinese. In the latter part of the eighteenth century, European merchants and residents were exerting their own influence in south China, particularly in the city of Canton. In response to the trade with Europe, Chinese artists and craftsmen developed competency in the mechanical skills and artistic styles needed to keep up with the demands of their European consumers. Thus, although western-style painting was never accepted by the literati as a true art, it maintained a visible presence among the professional artists in south China.

Why were particular western technologies of interest to the Chinese while others were not? And what set certain products apart from other European items? Although easily dismissed as 'exotic' and 'curious', the appeal of western technologies in China was more complex and was not dependent on appearance alone. Some were appreciated for their foreignness: they were unlike anything the Chinese had ever seen. Conversely, other European technologies had native Chinese precedents and were valued because they proved superior to their Chinese counterparts. Clockwork and astronomy illustrate these two views.

European clockwork represented an essentially unknown technology for the Chinese. The Chinese had developed their own clockwork early on. However, it was limited in its potential and the knowledge concerning it was lost several centuries before the arrival of the Jesuits. When European clockwork arrived, it was appreciated for its unusual aesthetics – especially the pieces of the eighteenth century with their gilt-bronze and glass-paste jewels – and for the accessory functions it could support, including moving figures and an ability to chime on its own. Astronomy, on the other hand, had a long history in China, where it was a highly regarded science, particularly for its application to the Chinese calendar. When the Jesuits arrived in China, they were able to demonstrate to the Chinese that their European instruments and methods could surpass those used in China. European astronomy's importance in practical matters led the Chinese emperor to appoint Westerners to the important and highly visible position of director of the Imperial Board of Astronomy, which they held nearly continuously for 150 years. The emperors kept their Jesuits – and Jesuit technology – close at hand.

Western objects, and the men skilled in producing them, were most valuable in promoting the adoption of European technological skills among the Chinese. In addition to the western presence on the Imperial Board of Astronomy, the Jesuits also staffed the imperial workshops. These *zuofang* manufactured luxury and more utilitarian goods for palace use, and operated under the administration of the Imperial Household.[54] Modelled after Louis XIV's Académie Royale des Sciences from Jesuit reports, these workshops employed craftsmen from throughout China. The Jesuits worked alongside the Chinese in the clockmaking, painting, engraving and enamelling workshops. Participation in them kept the Jesuits at the court and allowed them to stay on in China when missionaries in other parts of the country were forbidden on Chinese soil.

However, western technologies were not universally embraced. Although the eighteenth-century painter Zou Yigui was impressed by the use of perspective and shading, overall he found that such painting was 'completely lacking in the mastery of the brush [and] though elaborate, is after all nothing but craftsmanship, and therefore cannot be classified along with paintings of quality'.[55] Zhao Yi, a clerk of the Grand Council, was left similarly unimpressed by European clockwork. 'They break easily,' he wrote, and 'among the court officials, those who own these things forget meetings; or, those at court who do not miss meetings do not own clocks.'[56]

The imperial interest in western technologies was felt beyond the court as centres of production developed in the cities of Nanjing, Canton and Suzhou. European perspective techniques reached the Suzhou suburb of Yangliuqing, known for popular woodblock-printed New Year pictures (plate 23.14). The wide distribution that these prints enjoyed brought western conventions in the visual arts to a large and varied audience. Clockwork introduced important technical skills that provided the basic technology for a fundamental machine. In this way, the Jesuit presence at the Chinese court would have far-reaching implications that would outlast their tenure in Peking.

23.14
Wan-Nian Qiao Bridge
Woodblock print
China (Suzhou), late 18th century
V&A: E.1139–1912

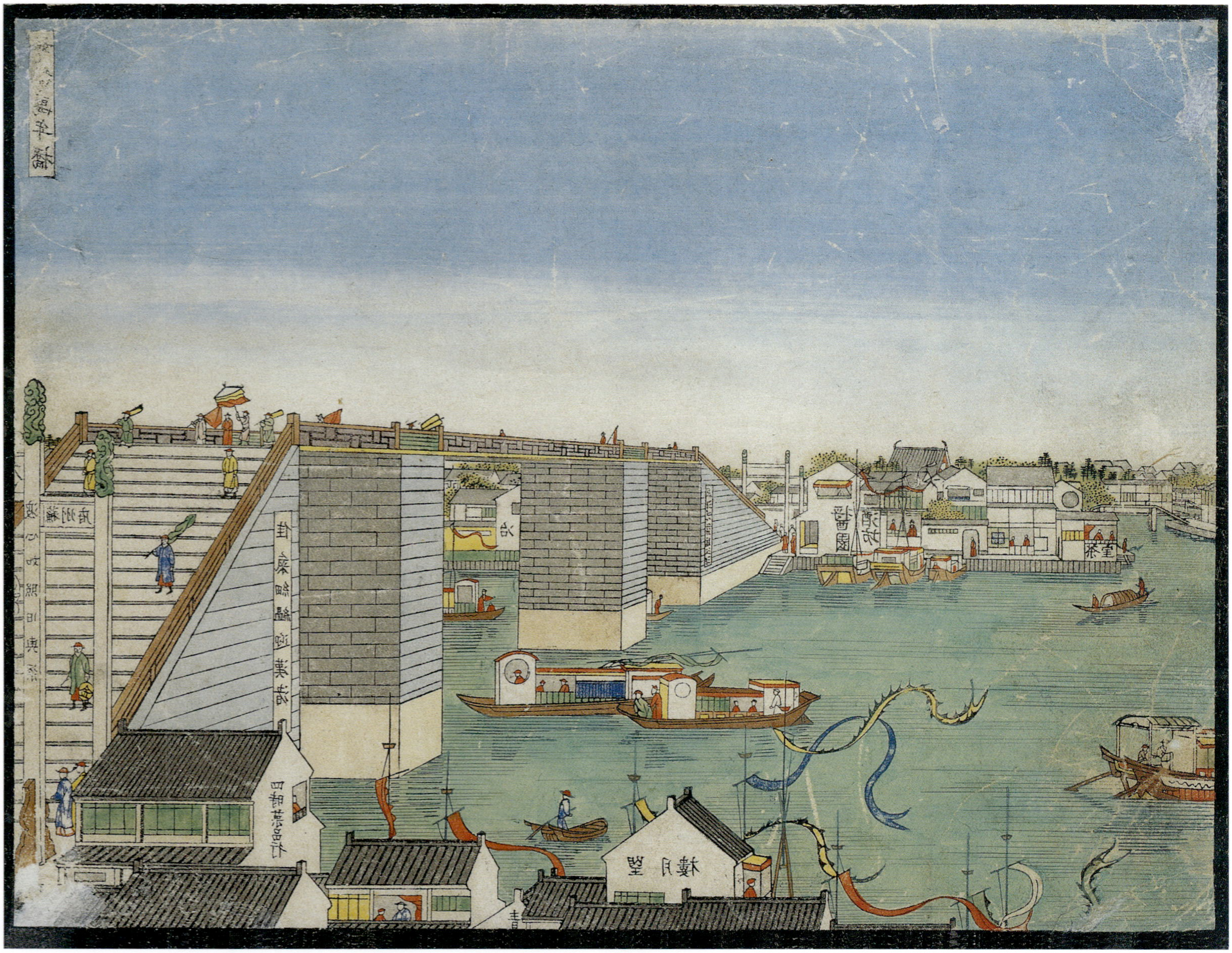

24

EUROPE IN ASIA: THE IMPACT OF WESTERN ART AND TECHNOLOGY IN JAPAN

Timon Screech

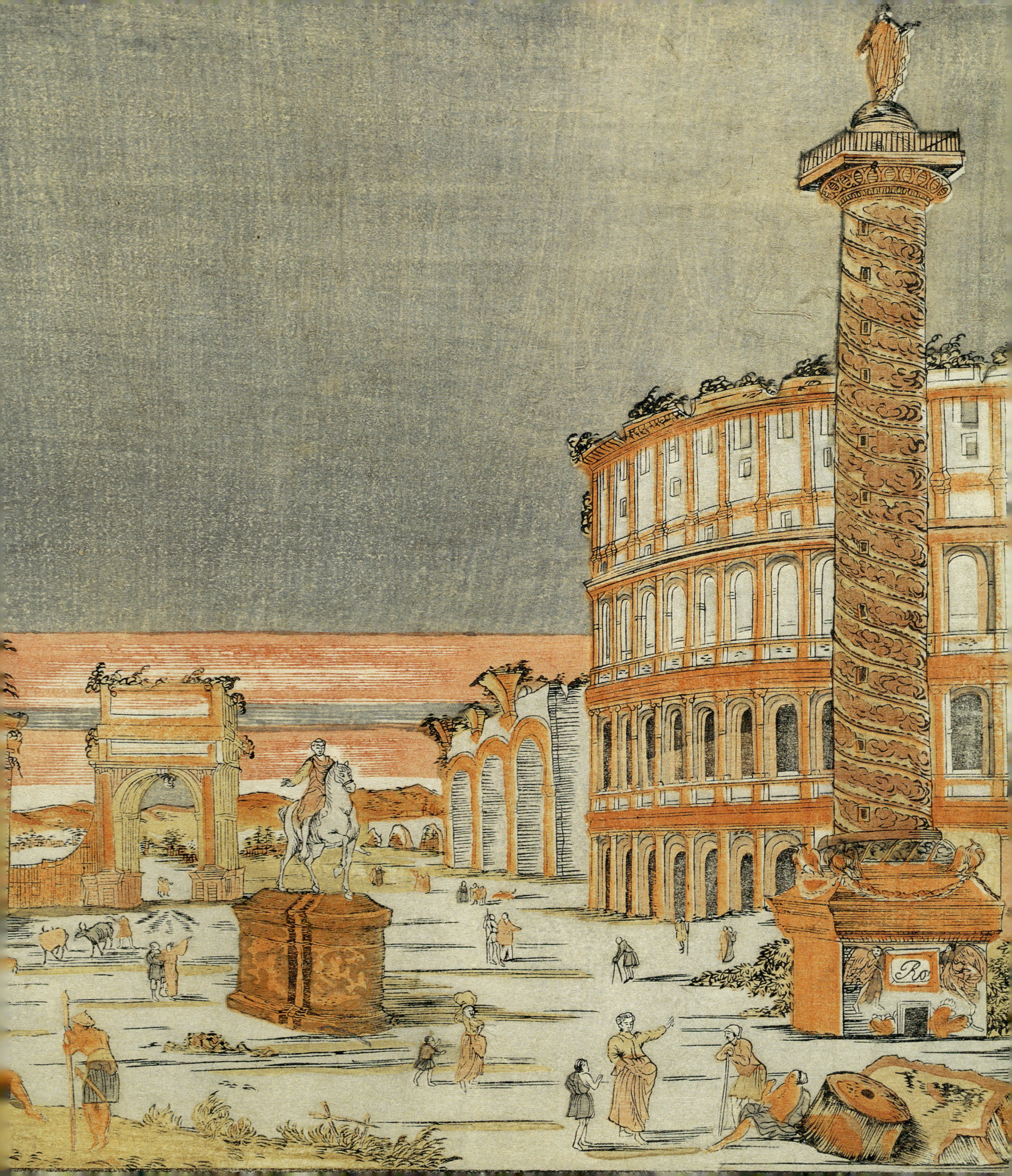
Ro

Detail of 24.8 previous page

Some years ago a Japanese government minister remarked that his country would have liked to import French skiing equipment. But it could not, 'Because Japanese snow is different.' The observation attracted much comment at the time, mostly derisory. But what if he was right?

Historians have increasingly come to recognize that most phenomena, even those that we take as simple givens, are actually fabrications of culture. It might seem extreme to argue this in the case of snow, but actually all the materials and thoughts that surround us and with which we build our lives, however much they appear part of the natural world, are in reality made available to us only through incremental cultural accumulation.

Sometimes this cultural drift comes into rude contact with another world. The shock of unsolicited encounter has occurred more than once in Japanese history, most notably in the mid-sixth century with the arrival of East Asian norms. Internal debate about how to deal with China and Korea (rolled into one in popular Japanese usage as *kara*, 'the Continent') rumbled on throughout the centuries, sometimes bringing Japan into close proximity with the statecraft, science and arts of the Continent, and sometimes acrimoniously distancing it from them. That first precedent was not forgotten when, in the sixteenth century, Europe forced itself abruptly into the Japanese gaze. A debate over this other continent – Europe – began after the arrival of the first Iberians in 1543. To this day a polarity remains in Japan – wilfully, one might argue, given the palpable evidence of hybridity – between the native and the foreign, between the home and the externally derived. As our minister in effect asks: what is Japan? What is the other?

A medieval formulation was available to adjudicate, generally, the taxing matter of how to cope with new cultural forms that arrived, willy-nilly, throughout history along Japan's winding and unpoliceable coasts. The formulation became a veritable trope. It originated in a Nō play attributed to Zeami (1363?–1443?), the genre's finest author.[1] The play told of one specific, if legendary, international encounter: that of the great Tang-period Chinese poet, Bo Jui (772–846) (known in Japanese as Haku Rakuten), with Japanese culture. Haku Rakuten was sent by his emperor to test the Japanese mettle, as a scouting party prior to possible invasion. Being China's foremost poet, Haku Rakuten had as his mission testing the Japanese skill at verse. If they could pass muster in diction and prosody, their polity would be left in place.

Haku Rakuten arrived by sea, sailing self-assuredly into Sumiyoshi Bay, near modern Osaka. Totally unfairly, one might think, he engaged in poetic contest the first person he saw, a humble fisherman labouring over his catch. The courtly Chinese offered a verse that was peerless, of course, and it was then up to the fisherman to riposte. He turned out a very capable offering – indeed, one so accomplished that Haku Rakuten was forced to admit defeat. At this point the audience realizes that this not a fisherman at all, but the god of Sumiyoshi, in the body of a mortal, stepping in to save the nation's honour. The Nō chorus begins to chant:

> Truly, this tranquil realm has its manners and customs!
> Truly, this tranquil realm has its manners and customs!
> And the fisherman had the heart to understand this.
> Truly our traditions must be cherished.[2]

The god then pools his powers with those of his fellows, and the myriad divinities of Japan raise

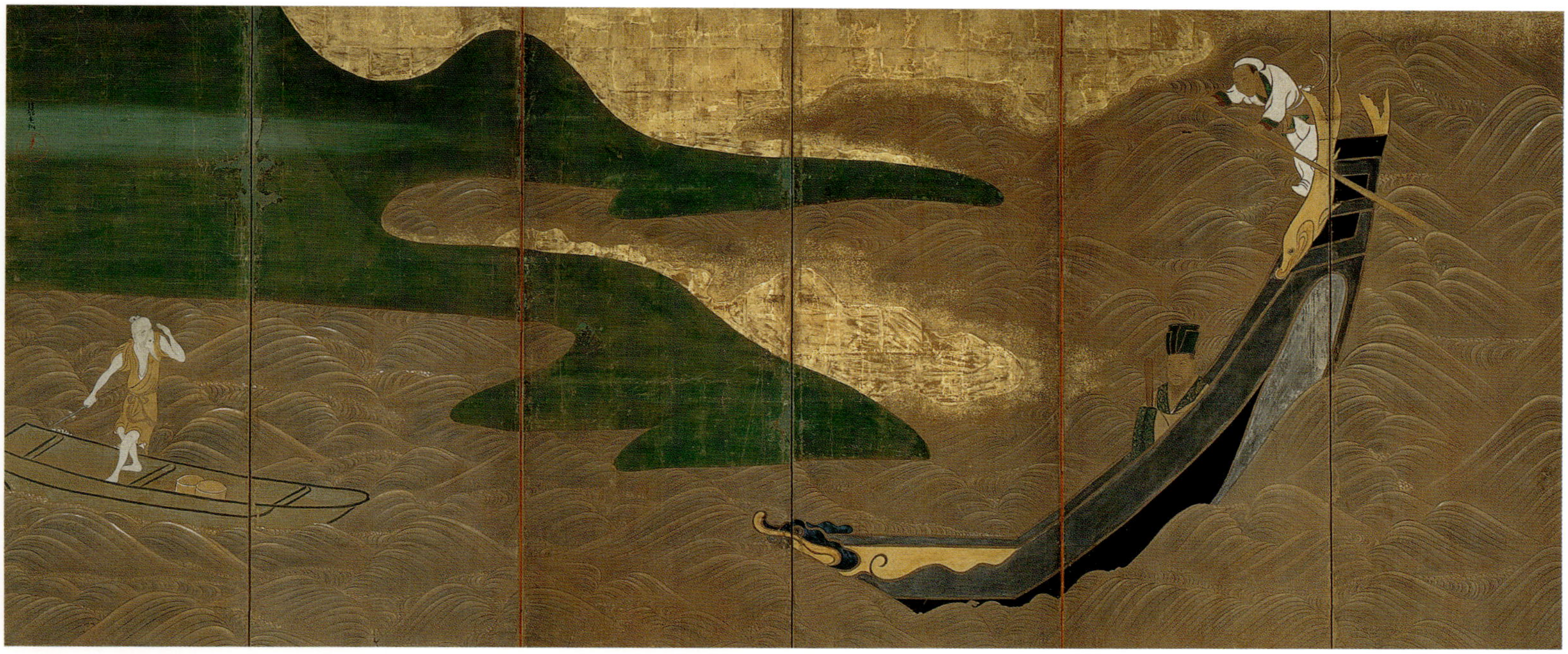

24.1
Hakurakuten
Ōgata Kōrin
Six-fold screen; colours and gold on paper
Japan, late 16th–early 17th century
Nezu Institute of Fine Arts, Tokyo

a *kamikaze* (divine wind) to buffet the startled Chinese back home, where he will report to his ruler that the 'tranquil realm' (*wakoku*) had better be left intact.

The Nō masterpiece continued to be performed and its core tale was recycled in variant forms. Over the centuries it provided meat for many thinkers, both sceptical and enthusiastic about the value of Continental ways. Haku Rakuten's encounter with the god of Sumiyoshi was reworked textually, poetically and visually. A work by Ōgata Kōrin (1658–1716), probably executed about 1690, is among the best-known paintings on the theme (plate 24.1). The six-fold screen shows Haku Rakuten's splendid Chinese boat, its prow in the form of a *baku* (a mythical creature that feeds on dreams) and its stern in the shape of a dolphin. On the other side is the elderly fisherman, unaided by pomp or fine craftsmanship; his beard and clothing catch the breeze as he waves an open greeting at the stranger whose own hands are clasped firmly about his sceptre of office. A balance is thus constructed between the modest and the contrived. One culture reposes itself recessively in nature, the other contests and supplements it. Nature, as if responding, tosses the Chinese vessel, while the Japanese barque is still. The contention is obvious: Japan knows its environment and, embracing it, has built up a culture that is proper to its place. Foreign things, whether poetry or boats, are alien and will not sit comfortably here. But note that Japan is not postulated as better – there is no implication that Haku Rakuten's verse is inadequate (in fact, it was a gem) or that his vessel is infirm; only that, as things from China, they are not right for Japan. Cultures are incommensurable. On the local sea and soil, local things work better.

An inherent problem with the legend, however, was that the innocence proposed for Japan could look dangerously like retardation; over-adherence to nature might be a hindrance to advancement. The trope, which functioned well as a literary or artistic device, hardly encouraged technology transfer. It would not do in the real world to spurn the import of medicines or machines, and the god of Sumiyoshi availed little when real ships arrived in Japanese waters, offering novelties that were useful and exciting, and for which people clamoured. Indeed, at nearly every stage in Japanese history when foreigners came into view, along with them came a rush to import. The foreign compelled attention and the gods very rarely interceded. In fact, they seemed to help. It was a *kamikaze* that brought the first European ship to Japan: the Portuguese had not intended to arrive at Tanegashima, when propelled there by a freak wind. The mission that Francis Xavier (1506–62) established seven years later, in 1549, met with superb success. From Europe, it seemed a vindication of the injunction to 'go out and make all nations disciples of the Risen Christ'.[3]

Christian missionaries arrived at a time when Japan was engaged in one of its periodic civil wars. Usurpation was the order of the day. One of the prime Christian offerings was a legitimization of this, via valuable (and hence validating) goods, along with military hardware and, most importantly, an ideology of the Just War. Any ruthless fighter might carve out a parcel of land and hold it with a tranquil mind, if he underwent baptism and fought under the sign of the Cross. Many did so. In terms of material things, two of the principal imports from Europe were gunpowder and shot; it was with these that, in 1615, the Tokugawa family consolidated its control of the Japanese archipelago and obliterated the rival Toyotomi clan at Osaka Castle.[4] The Tokugawa had assumed the hereditary title of *shōgun* in 1603. They only flirted with Christianity, but had several retainers who converted. The warlord into whose shoes the Toyotomi had stepped (before being ejected from them), Oda Nobunaga, had a church at the foot of his stronghold, Azuchi Castle, and several of his younger lords learned to play deftly on its organ, under the tutelage of Jesuit priests.[5]

Making guns was a skill worth acquiring at the turn of the sixteenth century, and this continued to be so throughout the era known as Japan's 'Christian Century' (1542–1638). The toponym '*tanegashima*', where the Iberians first arrived, became the local word for guns (see plates 24.16–24.17). The Dutch East India Company (VOC) built a cannon foundry beside its trading station at Hirado, and the English merchant Richard Cocks, who saw its Japanese staff in 1620, 'marvelled at their workmanship' and remarked how costs were half those in Europe, and yet the men turned out 'as formal an ordnance as we in Christendom'.[6] Such possibilities for the acquisition of new skills were taken up with alacrity. Weapons were both offensive and defensive, and Tokugawa Ieyasu, the first *shōgun* (1543–1616; r.1603–5), possessed a Portuguese helmet and breastplate, although cunningly adapted with Japanese arm- and neck-guards. There is no incommensurability here.

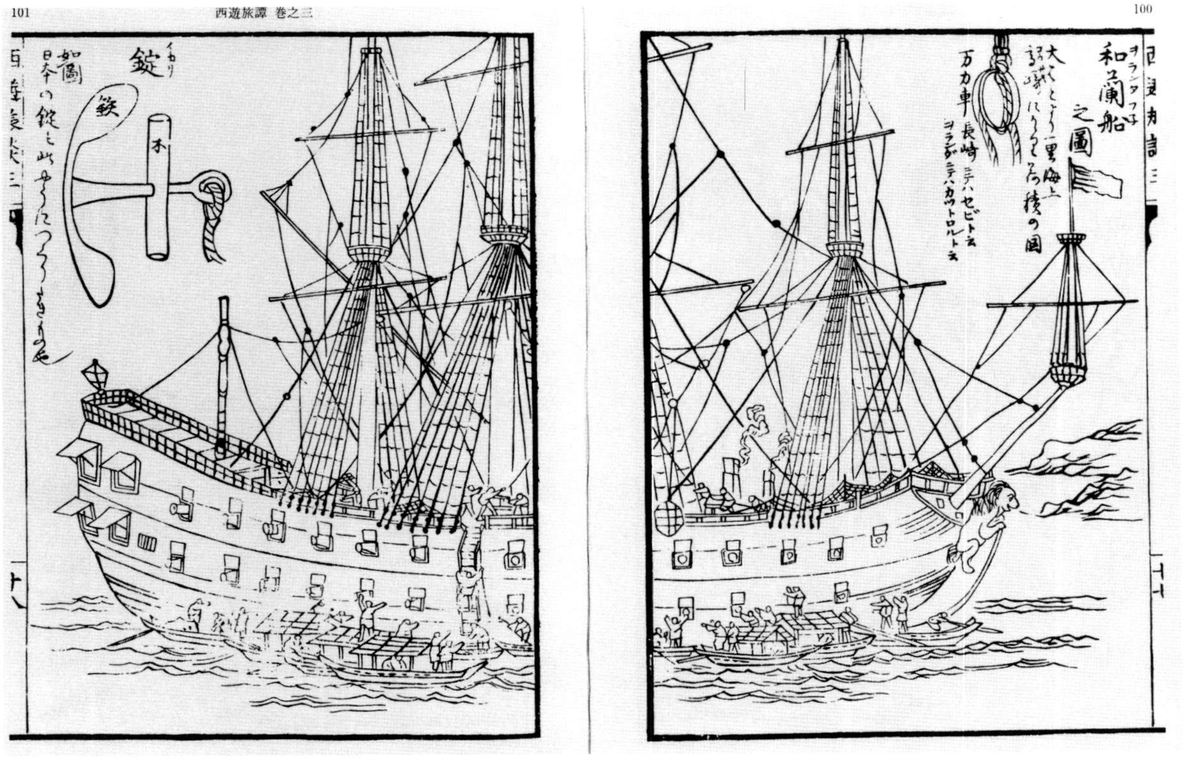

24.2
Dutch Ship

From Shiba Kōkan, *Edo Nagasaki E Kikō – Saiyū Ryodan* (*Picture Travelogue Edo to Nagasaki: Travels in the West*)
Woodblock-printed book
Japan (Edo), 1794

Private collection

Borrowings from the West were not confined to technological matters. It is well known that the founder of kabuki, Okuni, tried out her first louche dances while wearing a crucifix. *Nanban* (or *namban*) apparel became fashionable, as did the 'Christian haircut' (*kirishitan-mage*), with its clerical shaven pate. The missionaries desired to plant ideas, not merely sell goods, and they ensured that things arrived with a degree of background explanation attached. They also set up a painting school in Nagasaki under the veteran master Giovanni Niccolò (1560–1626)(see pp. 113–5).[7] Pictures were very useful in the spread of ideas, whether belligerent, evangelistic or secular .

The 'Christian Century' came to a brutal end. The second *shōgun*, Tokugawa Hidetada (1579–1632; r. 1605–16), began a series of prohibitions which, though intermittently enforced at first, spread fear. In 1623 Hidetada went to Kyoto to perform the ceremony of handing the *shōgunal* office on to his son, Iemitsu (r. 1623–51). Iemitsu's religious suspicions were reinforced in 1637–38 when a Christian uprising broke out, after which all *bateren* (the Japanese garbling of 'padre') were expelled, and all Japanese Christians forced to apostatize or be killed (or both). The English had already withdrawn voluntarily. The Dutch were the only Europeans who chose to stay – although they very nearly lost their trading rights too, in 1646, when suspected of landing Portuguese suicide missionaries.[8] When a Portuguese ship arrived in 1647 asking for renewal of commerce, it was not only denied, but while in dock it was commanded to cover its figurehead and carvings with canvas, such exotic artefacts now being banned.[9] After the mid-seventeenth century, it became hazardous to own an imported object or representation. However, representatives of the Republic of the United Provinces (Holland) remained in Japan ever after. It should be recalled that, as an early multinational, the VOC staff were from many nations, not excluding Portugal and Spain.

The potency of carved figures from European ships is evident from the Japanese treatment of a carving from the first Dutch vessel that came to Japan. The *Liefde* ('charity'; it had previously been called the *Erasmus*) arrived, also unintentionally, in 1600, having been blown to Japan by a freak wind. It broke into pieces. Sections of its woodwork were collected by trophy-seekers. One of its salvaged poop carvings came into the possession of Makino Narisato, evidently a forward-thinking man, as is confirmed by his position as artillery expert to the *shōgun* (a new position).[10] The image is very clearly a representation of Erasmus of Rotterdam, who had died in 1536. In awe, Makino donated the figure to his family temple, the Ryūkō-in (in modern Tochigi Prefecture), where it acquired the label of Kateki-son, the name of the mythical Chinese inventor of ships.

The Dutch three-masted 'East Indiaman' replaced the Portuguese *não* in the seventeenth century. Dutch ships arrived, stayed for a few weeks, and left, with minimal impact, especially after Tokugawa Iemitsu's prohibitions terminated the 'Christian Century'. Standard historiographies see the period from 1638 as one of 'national isolation' (*sakoku*). This in turn is said to have begun to erode some 100 years later in the middle of the eighteenth century. In about 1720, the eighth *shōgun*, Yoshimune (r. 1716–45), liberalized the import of pictures and books. 'National isolation' is perhaps too strong a term, although ship numbers declined steadily and by the early eighteenth century just two were coming per annum, and by the end of it just one. However, much material also arrived from Europe via Chinese ships, which continued to dock in quantity.

European ships seemed embodiments of a prowess that was very much to be welcomed – provided that no Christianity was propagated. They were (and were filled with) stores of knowledge. Pictures of vessels, and admiring descriptions of their appearance and ornamentation, pepper the archives. Those of the VOC bore the corporate figurehead of a golden lion. This was duly noted and the vessels came to be known in Japan as 'lion ships' (*shishigō*).[11] At the close of the eighteenth century, the Edo artist, Shiba Kōkan (1747–1818), sketched a Dutch ship he saw in Nagasaki (almost certainly the *Roosenburg*), and published this in the diary of his trip (plate 24.2). He stated:

> this great ship cannot be adequately described in words; it is coated in black tar with just the railings painted yellow and has twenty-five cannon down either side, making a total of sixty. It has a cabin at the stern with glazed windows so you can look out at the sea. Masts soar in three places and the rigging looks like veritable spider's web.[12]

Kōkan included a couple of insets for clarity: his intentions were scholarly and he preferred to explain rather than confabulate. But many took the opposite view. Kōkan himself noted that cheap, and probably fantastic, prints of Dutch ships were sold in Nagasaki after the arrivals.[13] Pictures of VOC ships always show them enveloped in clouds of smoke, if they are

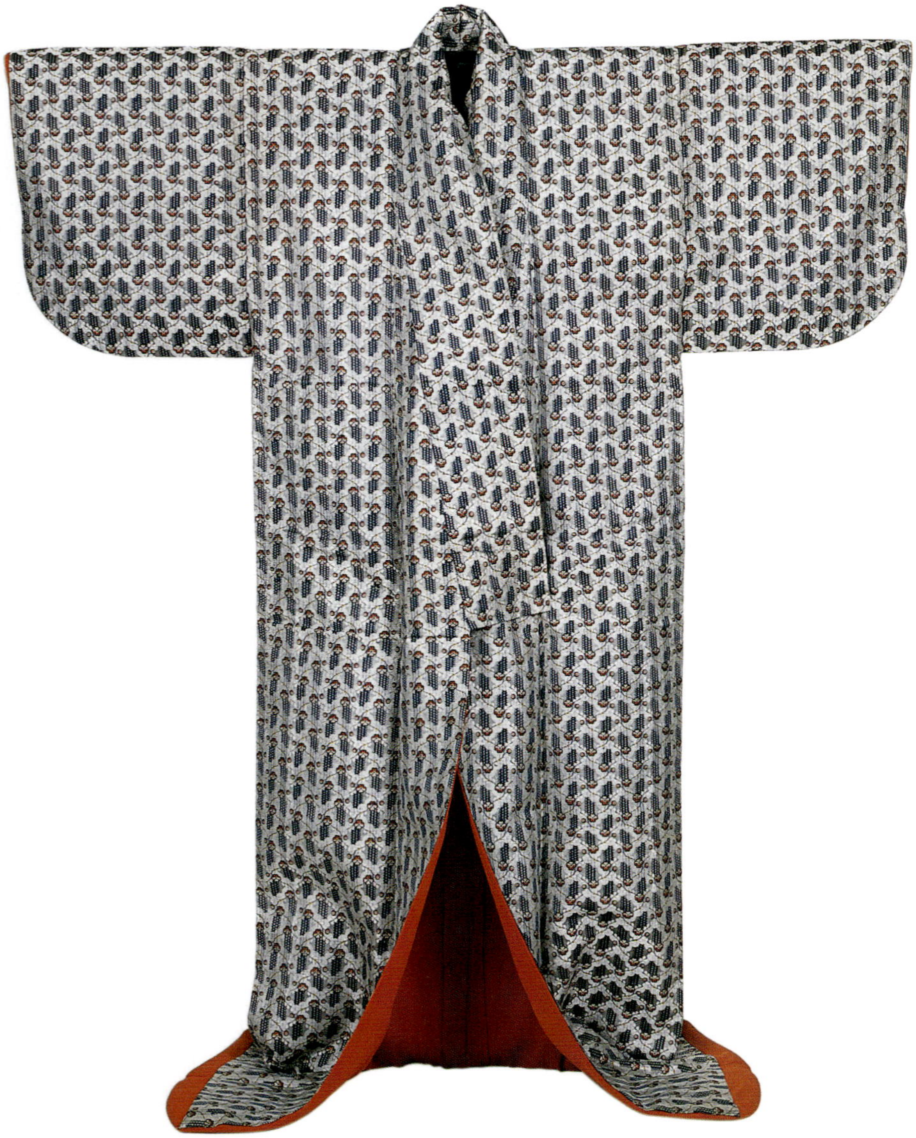

24.3
Outer kimono (*uchikake*)
Woven silk
Cloth: France (Lyon), c. 1760s; garment: Japan, late 18th–early 19th century
Private collection, Kyoto

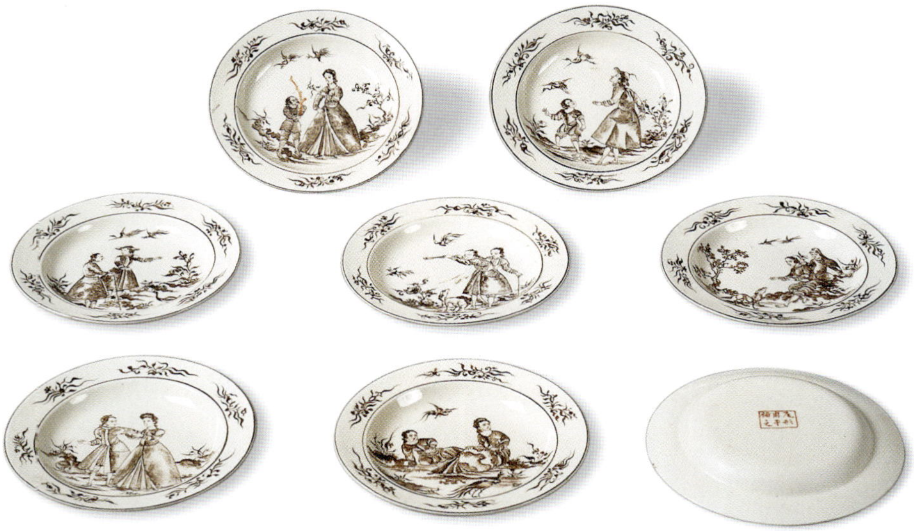

24.4
Plates
Painted by Ogata Shuhei

Creamware, with overglaze decoration
England (Staffordshire), early 19th century; painted in Japan (Kyoto), early 19th century

Kobe City Museum, Kobe

in motion. Few Japanese actually boarded a European vessel and so none could find out how they really worked. It was assumed the guns made them move, but Kōkan (who knew this to be wrong) scornfully wrote, 'the belief that the firing makes the ship move is pure error put about by the people of Nagasaki'.[14]

Artefacts brought from overseas boggled the Japanese imagination. The principal purpose of going from Europe to Japan was to relieve the latter of its vast deposits of gold, silver and copper, and for this, impressive trade goods had to be brought. The best examples of western manufacture came, and of these the finest changed hands on a regular journey made by the VOC to the court of the *shōgun* in Edo (a ritual known as the *hofreis* in Dutch and the *sanpū* in Japanese) (see p.98). It took some three months to get from Nagasaki and back, so for one quarter of each year the Europeans were on a very public transit through Japan. On arrival in Edo, their leader met the *shōgun* (a breathtaking privilege), and there was a giving of gifts. In 1650, to take one example, Iemitsu received one large mirror, one carpet with flowers, one golden telescope, three pieces of Indian cloth, six pieces of coloured woollen cloth, 30 more pieces of Indian cloth, 30 pieces of striped cloth, almost half a kilogram of medicinal mummy, two large artillery pieces and a barrel of Spanish wine.[15] Extant imported items of great worth demonstrate the level of gifts given. Cloth was an ideal present as it was light and easy to transport by ship (although without care, it might rot). But more particularly it could be transformed as they might see fit by its Japanese recipients; cloth arrived in bolts and could be turned into garments that had meaning and purpose in Japanese society (plate 24.3). Other objects given also seem to have been selected with an eye to mutability in a new Japanese context. Lenses were imported loose for setting into Japanese devices, and mirrors came with the intention that they would be smashed for insertion into the same kinds of equipment (plate 24.5). European ceramics also reached Japan. English porcelain blanks were even imported and decorated with 'European' scenes, much as Chinese blanks were imported into Europe and painted with chinoiseries (plate 24.4; see plate 17.7).

One object that should be singled out for mention is the clock. It too underwent adaptation. A vigorous trade in timepieces was enjoyed by the major manufactures of London and Paris (it was not until the nineteenth century that these two cities lost their priority to Geneva). They were sending dozens of very elaborate examples to India and China, and it was natural to wish to expand their trade to Japan. By a quirk of fate the VOC hostel, at Honkoku-chō in Edo, was situated beside Edo's oldest time-bell (*toki no kane*), which would be rung to mark the *koku*. One *koku* is about two modern hours, and Honkoku-chō (though written with *koku* meaning a unit of measurement) probably originally came from the unit of time (*hon* means 'original' or 'true'; *chō* means a city block). Time began here and radiated across the city as other bells echoed its boom. Many were the wits who made a link between the VOC officers, with their fantastic automatic clocks, and the Edo bells. A comic verse in the *senryū* genre ran:

> Here's something he can understand without
> an interpreter!
> The Dutch leader hears it too,
> The Bell of Koku-chō.[16]

The Europeans managed and ordered time in a form which – given that a clock, unlike a bell, has a face and therefore allows the upcoming of the hour to be estimated in advance – was not only accurate, but could also be predicted. The reverberating bell dying to nothing was an established Buddhist metaphor for the impermanence of all things, and in Europe too time had its own symbolism. The use of passion-flower motifs on European clocks was soon noticed, such that even in modern Japanese that plant is called *tokei-sō*, or 'clock-grass'. A passion flower looks like four nails and a crown of thorns, recalling Christ's Passion.

24.5
Telescope

Glass, engraved and painted, with wood and brass fittings
Japan (Nagasaki), late 18th century; with European lenses

Kobe City Museum, Kobe

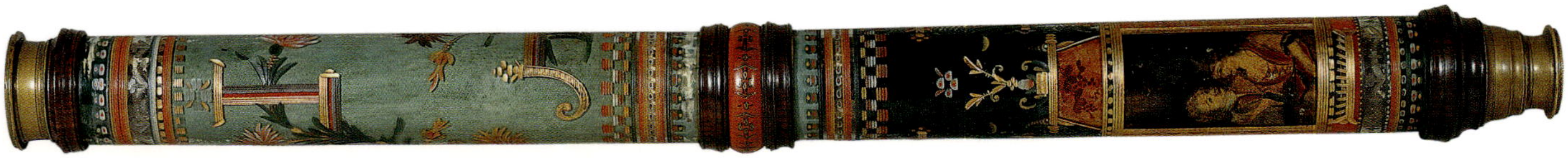

Whether mutual symbolisms were understood in Japan is unclear. A greater problem was that Japanese time could not be told with a western clock, as *koku* were not of equal length: six fell within darkness and six within light, such that a night-time *koku* was rarely the same as a daytime one; moreover, the ratio of difference altered throughout the year. Thus it was that the fashion critic Inaba Tsūryū wrote in 1789 that the best way to treat imported timepieces was to think of them as personal accessories, or as toys (plates 24.6, 24.7).[17]

Tsūryū wrote specifically of what he called 'London clocks' (*rondondokei*). These were pocket watches, much admired although, as he admitted, 'it is barely possible to use one for a whole day without its going wrong'. Japanese-made clocks (always bulky, as minute parts could not be produced) had large tickers to facilitate adjustments, and to be useful a clock master would have to be summoned intermittently to adjust small weights attached to the ticker to retard or speed the mechanism and align the dial with the passing of the *koku*. Western clockwork, in the end, was often used to run automata.

After Yoshimune's liberalization, the presence (and presents) of Europeans attracted ever more attention. The *hofreis* was moved from winter to spring to aid pleasant encounters, and the Dutch found themselves mobbed in the streets by curious Japanese. The great master of *haikai* (better known in the West as 'haiku'), Matsuo Bashō (1644–94), wrote a verse on this in about 1700:

> The Dutch leader too
> Bends his knee –
> Spring time for my lord.[18]

Spring is the time of greatest natural beauty, synecdochical of the cherry blossom, as Bashō wrote in another verse:

> The Dutchmen too
> Have come to view the blossoms.
> Horses' saddles.[19]

Saddles creaked under the weight of gifts for the *shōgun* and other potentates. Many objects also found their way to popular strata, and goods from Europe enjoyed considerable appeal in the burgeoning markets of Japan's major cities. In the words of the

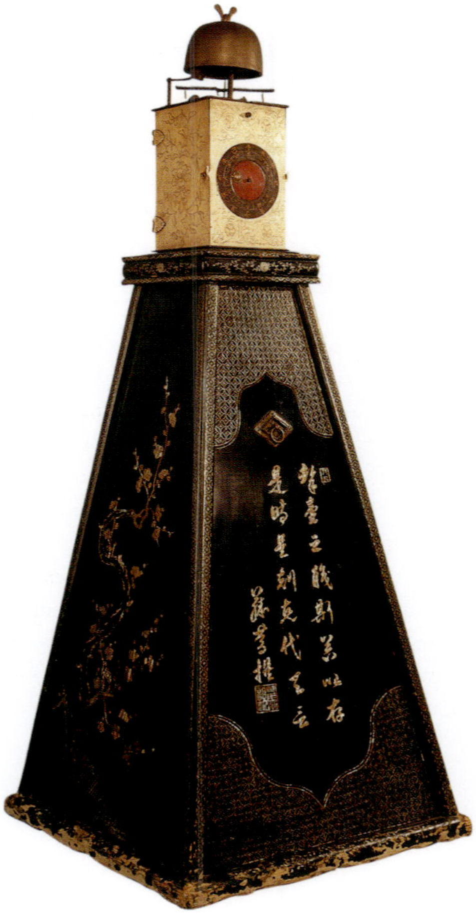

24.6
Clock
Clock: steel, bronze, copper, with engraved decoration; stand: black Somada-lacquered wood, with inlaid mother-of-pearl
Japan, 18th century
British Museum, London

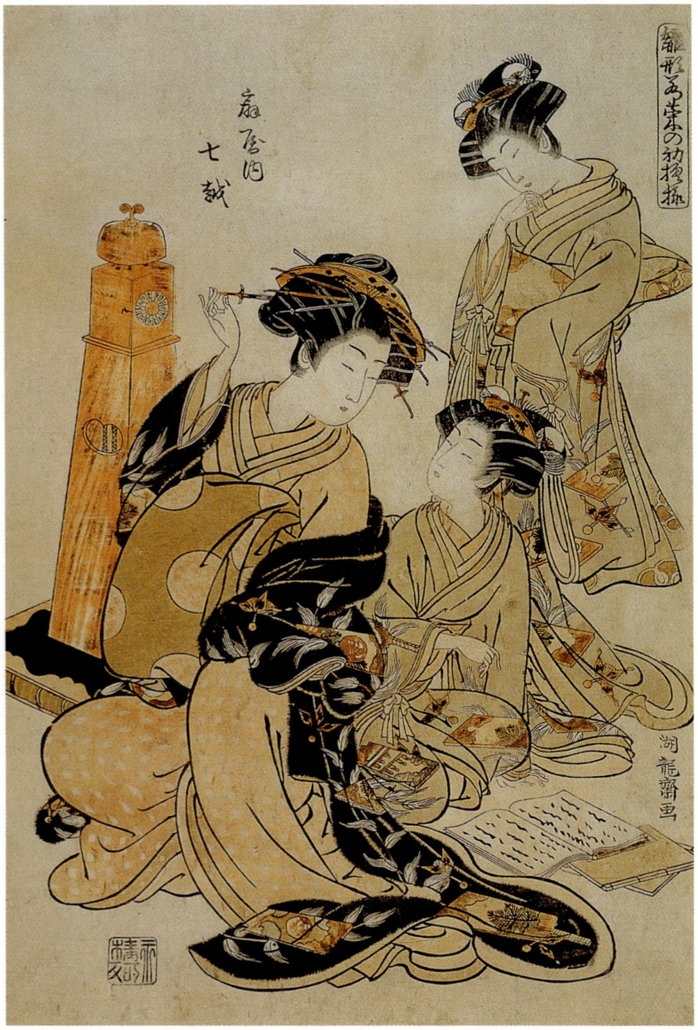

24.7
Nano Koshi from the Ōgi-ya
Isoda Koryusai, from the series *First Designs of Young Leaves*
Woodblock print
Japan (Edo), late 1770s
British Museum, London

important physician, Sugita Genpaku (1733–1817), 'the people of this land adore clever Dutch devices (*oranda kiki*)', although the doctor also pointed out that a good many 'Dutch' items were fakes produced in Edo to cash in on fascination with the West.[20]

In the latter part of the eighteenth century a movement known as *Rangaku* came into being. *Ran* is the abbreviation of *oranda,* Japanese for 'Holland'; *gaku* means an academic discipline. The importance of *Rangaku* in the late eighteenth century cannot be overstated. The first historian of this was Genpaku, who published his still-useful *Rangaku Kotohajime (The Origins of Rangaku*) in the year of his death. According to Genpaku, Yoshimune initiated the movement personally after having seen the illustrations to an imported book; he commented that the 'sideways writing' was to be taught, beyond the confines of the small number of hereditary translator families in Nagasaki. Genpaku was one of the first to undertake this task, although without a teacher or proper primer it was a huge struggle (as he himself admitted).

The year 1774 saw the completion of the first (more or less) integral translation of a European book, openly issued by one of Edo's main publishers. As the work aspired to attention in academic circles, translation was made into pseudo-Chinese (*kanbun*), not Japanese. The resultant book, a medical treatise, was entitled the *Kaitai Shinsho* (*New Anatomical Atlas*) and derived from Johannes Kulmus's none too admired textbook of 1725, *Anatomische tabellen*, known in Japan in the Dutch translation; it was illustrated with a series of woodblock prints copied from Kulmus and assorted other European sources (see plate 14.4). The coordinating editor and head of the translation team was Genpaku. Complimentary copies were sent to top *shōgunal* officials and to some senior courtiers, with the apparent intent not just to secure smooth passage for the book past the censors, but also to encourage the Japanese elite to embrace a novel way of thinking. Anatomy had no role in the Sino-Japanese tradition of *kanpō*, 'the Chinese practice', and lacked metaphorical use beyond medicine. The *ranpō*, 'Dutch practice', which Genpaku and others were now attempting to nurture, was a curative but also a symbolic system. Many of the imports that won most attention in Japan were linked to a new, interiorizing and probing – almost surgical – gaze.

The prints for the *Atlas* were produced by a young *samurai* from the provincial state of Akita, recently arrived in Edo, Odano Naotake (1749–80). The 25-year-old wrote in the illustrator's preface of his huge trepidation and sense of inadequacy at the monumental task on which he was engaged. The illustrations more that the text, however, have stood the test of time. Naotake became one of the foremost painters in the western painting style – designated by many terms, such as *oranda-e* or *horurando-e* (*'e'* meaning picture), but now generally referred to as *Ranga* (*'ga'* also meaning picture). Kōkan was another luminary in this field (plate 24.9), although as a townsman he was beneath the attention of the *Atlas* circle, which consisted of senior *samurai.* Not much love was lost between the two groups of *Rangaku*/*Ranga* scholars. Kōkan complained publicly about the snobbery of the *Atlas,* and its being put into opaque *kanbun* rather than the vernacular. The townsman and *samurai* circles encountered each other, but refused to merge; social expectations of the day precluded it.

The vicissitudes of just one item may be given here to stand emblematically for the use of so many imported things. The object – mechanical and optical – was known in English by a variety of terms, including a 'raree show', and in Japanese as a *karakuri.* It was a peepbox for viewing pictures, and existed in many forms – some enclosed, some little more than a lens on a stand, some elaborate; they also mutated from their invention in about 1610 to their heyday 200 years later. Several are extant in Japan, suggesting a wide circulation (plate 24.12).

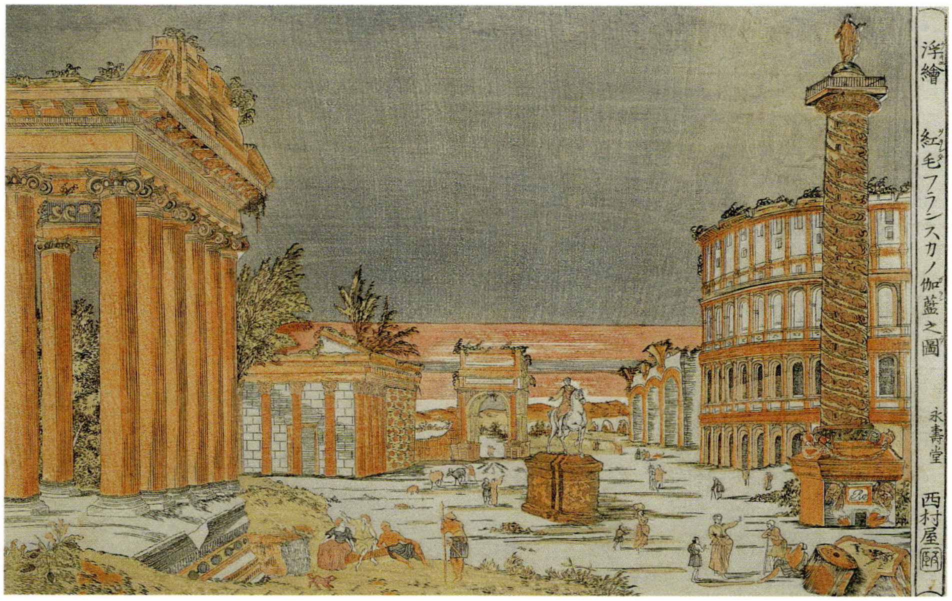

24.8
View of the Forum in Rome
Utagawa Toyoharu

Woodblock print
Japan (Edo), 1770–90

V&A: E.2361–1914

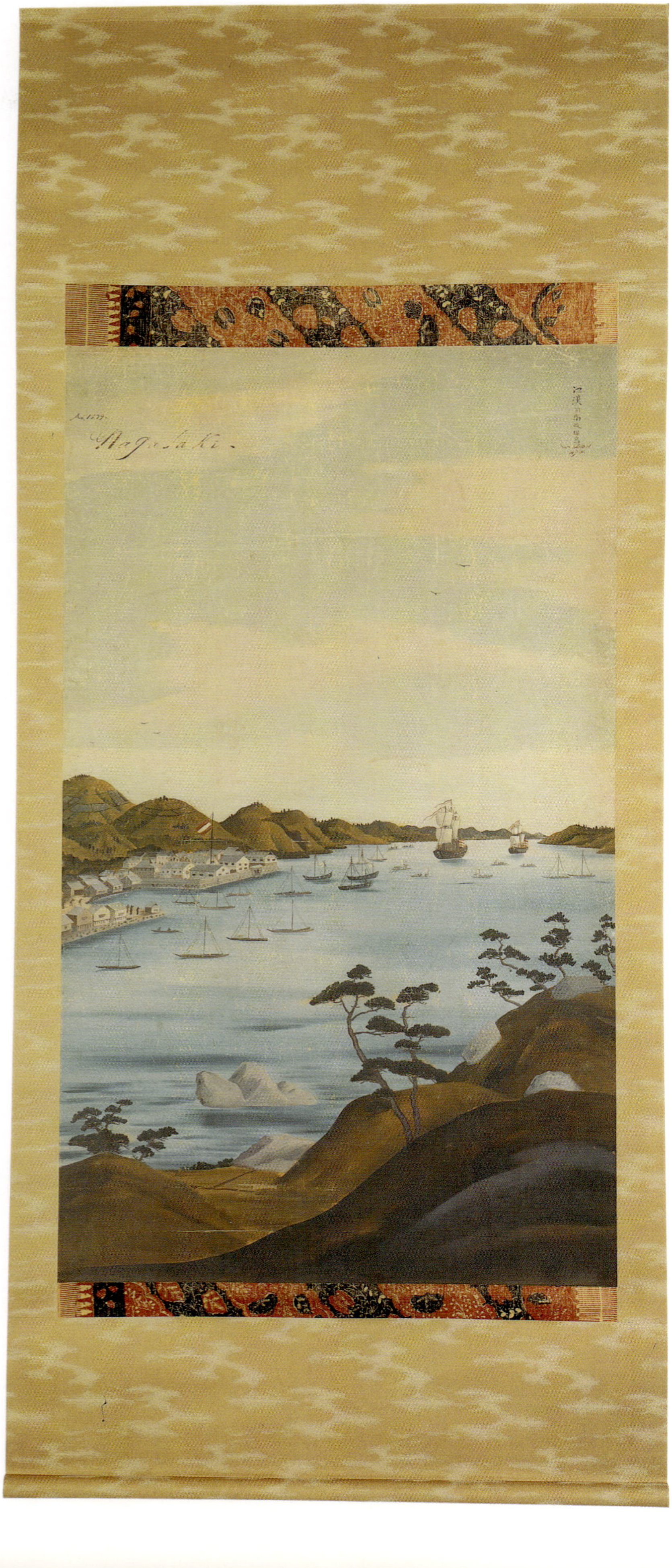

24.9
Nagasaki Bay
Shiba Kōkan

Hanging scroll; ink and colours on silk
Japan, *c.*1799

Peabody Essex Museum, Salem

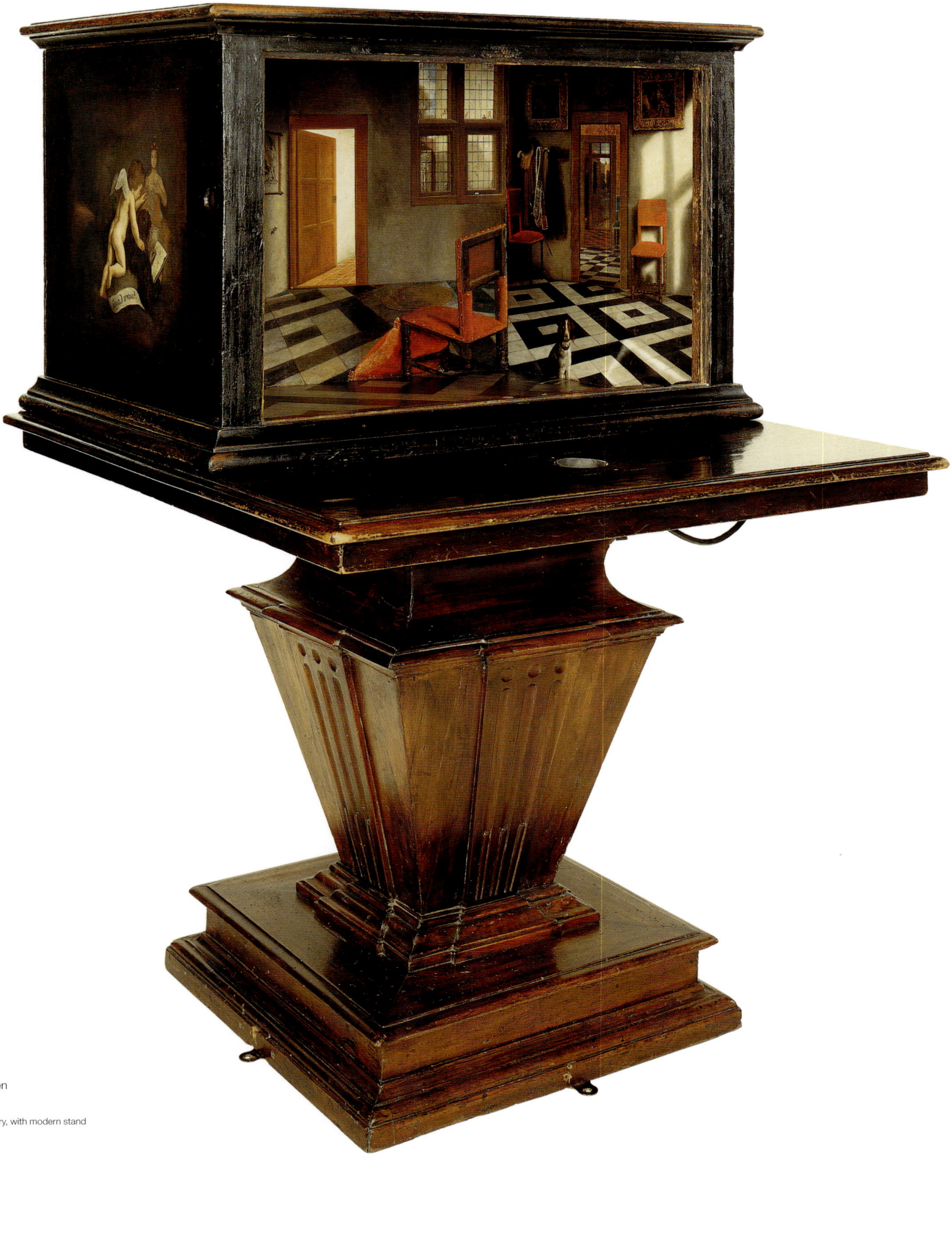

24.10
Peepbox
Samuel van Hoogstraten

Wood and paper
Netherlands, mid-17th century, with modern stand

National Gallery, London

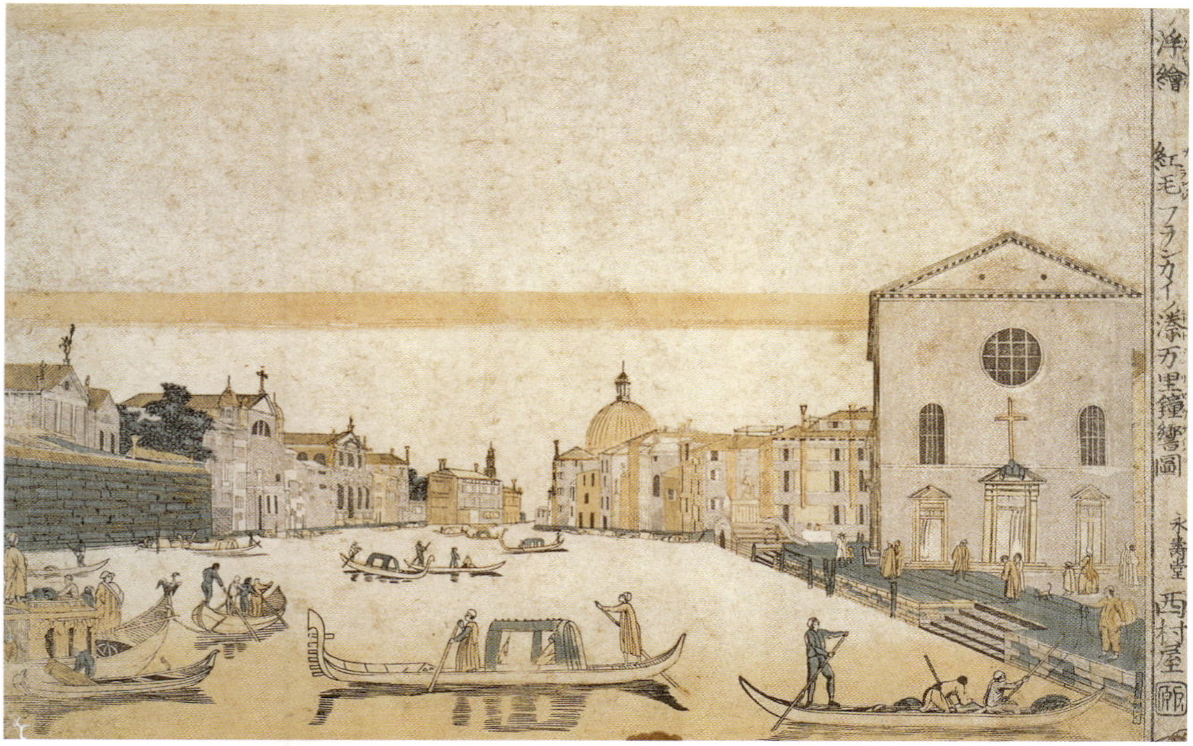

24.11
The Bell Which Rings for Ten-thousand Leagues in the Dutch Port of Frankai
Utagawa Toyoharu

Woodblock print on paper
Japan (Edo), *c.* 1770

Kobe City Museum, Kobe

This print depicts the Grand Canal, Venice.

The VOC imported a sumptuous peepbox in 1646. Their decision was to present it to Iemitsu himself. Once displayed at Edo Castle, it received an ecstatic reception – outdoing even two camels, a cassowary, two white cockatoos, clocks, cups and mirrors that came with it.[21] The Dutch referred to the item as a *perspecteiff cas*, but the Japanese, seeing it for the first time, called it a 'paradise box' (*gokurakubako*):

> the whole [*shōgunal*] castle seemed to be running wild … every nobleman had come to the castle, and all had gathered to view the rarities we had brought; there was not a single open space; they were crowding all about; it was a sight to behold how they were getting in each other's way in a manner that was totally out of proportion. The perspective box drew the most spectators and the most admiration.[22]

The exact nature of this box is hard to tell as few early examples survive, but one of about a decade later and also Dutch, made by Samuel van Hoogstraten (1627–78), is probably similar (plate 24.10). It has a hole for viewing at both ends, the viewer seeing either a devoted housewife going about her chores, or a slattern lying in bed until late in the morning. Antinomies of the vista are given via clever perspective recessions combined with mirrors. Perhaps such objects could also be 'hell boxes'. We know of similarly antithetical images – good and bad, night and day – being made for use with Japanese-designed *karakuri*.

Typically, raree shows had a set of pictures to go with them, so that the view could be switched, not by looking into opposite ends, but by sequential display. Sets either made up a story or just revealed a galaxy of interesting images. In Europe, copperplate printing emerged as the primary source of cheap pictures in the eighteenth century, and pictures drawn in heightened perspective with accentuated lines of recession became common, and were often inserted into raree shows. They were much imported to Japan, and from about 1765 Utagawa Toyoharu (1735–1814) embarked on a probably quite lucrative specialism of replicating them in woodblock, adding this genre to his already celebrated renditions of western cityscapes (plate 24.8); like them, sometimes these were copied *in toto*, sometimes in pastiche (plate 24.11). Pictures had been made in perspective for about a generation, and Okumura Masanobu (1686–1764) identified himself as 'founder' (*kongen*) of what he called 'floating pictures' (*uki-e*) (plate 24.13). But it seems that not until peepboxes appeared were actual Western views attempted

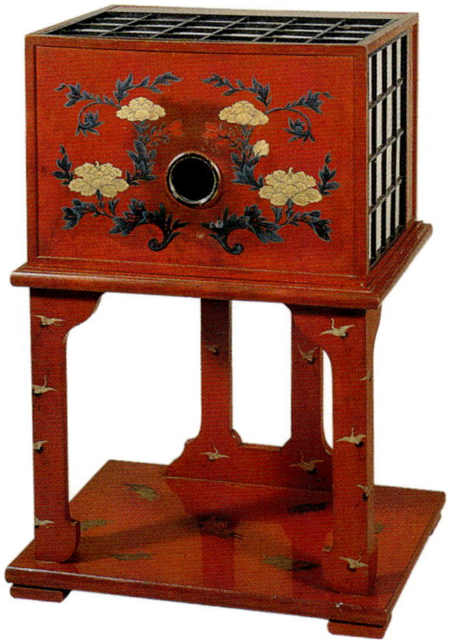

24.12
Peepbox

Wood with red lacquer decorated in gold and colours
Japan, late 18th century

Kobe City Museum, Kobe

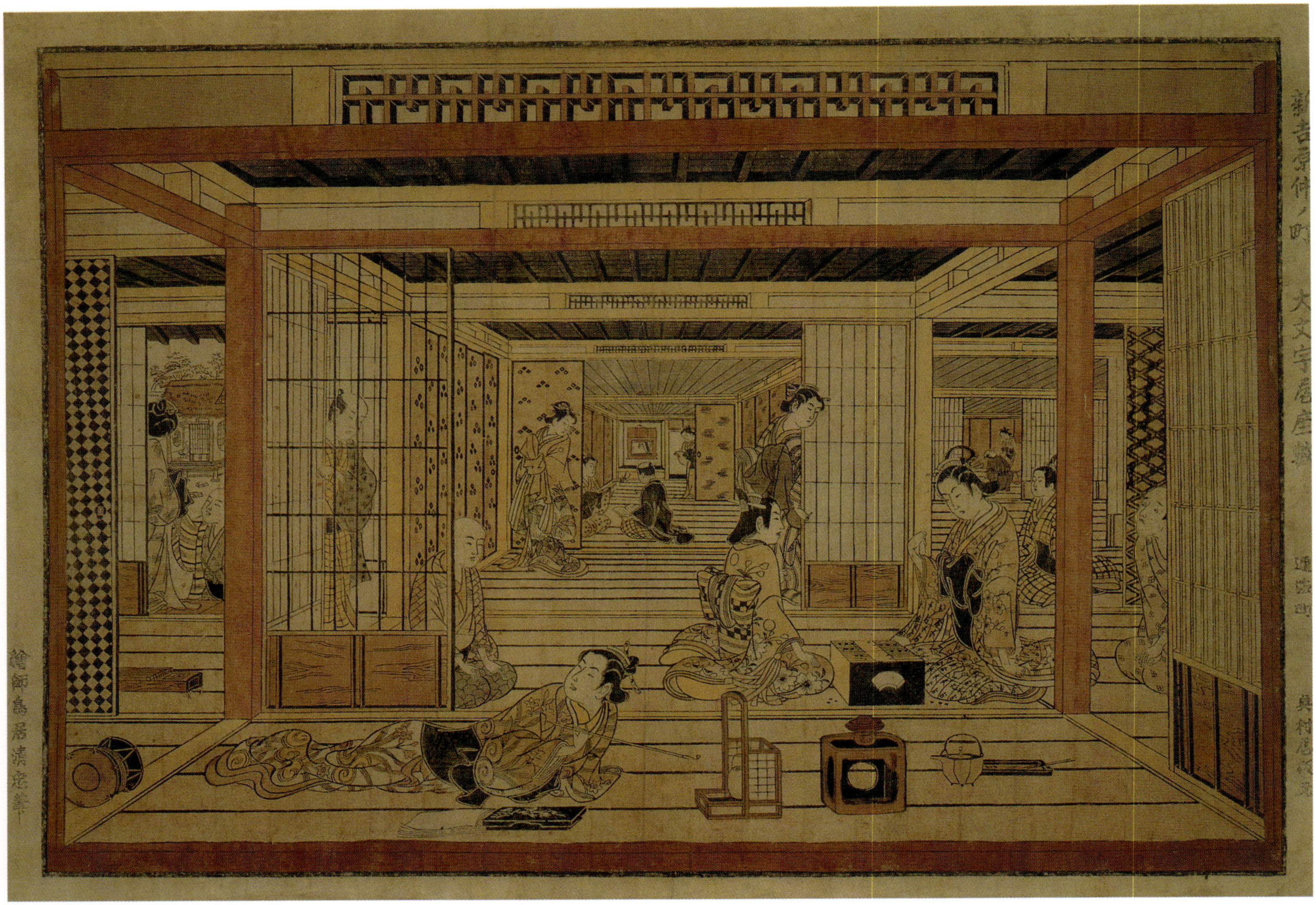

24.13
Daimonjiya Brothel
Okumura Masanobu

Woodblock print
Japan (Edo), *c.*1745–50

British Museum, London

(Masanobu showed only local sites in a somewhat ill-fitting accommodation of vanishing-point perspective). The first Japanese–Dutch dictionary, published in 1788, rendered *gaku* (a framed picture) as 'print', as if Europe had no painting at all, and *seiyō-kei* (western[-style] view) as 'perspective'.[23]

Ranga (western-style painting) artists were scornful of *uki-e* ('floating pictures'), which were marketable because they were exotic and for little other reason. The displacing effect of perspective, as well as its subjects, appealed to viewers precisely because it was baffling. To Naotake and others, *uki-e* were a belly-laugh in the face of the more meaningful *Ranga,* which took the approach that integrating the western style into something that made sense as a picture in Japanese terms was the mature way forward. *Ranga* could hang in the house of an important person, while *uki-e* belonged in the spaces of hubbub. Thus although *Ranga* has an air of the exotic about it, it generally respected established conventions in terms of format, size and theme.

In 1787 Shiba Kōkan made the first Japanese copperplate (previously all prints had been woodblocks). He noted (not entirely accurately) that London was the centre of print production, and accordingly two of his first copperplates were specifically English: the stately homes of Stowe and Cliveden, copied from imported images, though reversed so as to be viable in a mirrored peepbox (plate 24.14).[24] Kōkan also depicted the sites of Edo, done in a similar idiom. He fabricated a mirrored and lensed peepbox and even staged a show for Prince Kan-in, father of the reigning emperor Kōkaku (r. 1779 – 1817) – or so he claimed; the story sounds unlikely.[25] Kōkan certainly funded his trip to Nagasaki by showing off his etchings in the peepbox, at 32 *mon* per session.[26] But he insisted to his punters that this was a new and cogent mode of vision, not just a thrill.

Peepboxes were mostly subsumed into the fairground. The novelist Santō Kyōden illustrated as much in a comic work of 1782, *Gozonji no Shōbaimono (Trade Goods you know all About)* (plate 24.15). The showman bangs a drum to roll-up custom, while children crouch down at the holes. The device is for group viewing. A cyclops has sprung up from inside a candle shade. The operator sits on a box inscribed *uki-e*. Would Kyōden, Kōkan and the *karakuri* users have realized as they peeped in, kneeling in front of a table with candles and a hinged triptych, that it all looked very like a Christian altar? The two wings in Kyōden's picture carry the phrase 'great Dutch *karakuri*', and the text concludes with 'what a wonderful piece of technology [*saiku*] this is!'

The problems raised by new mechanical and visual apparatus, and new conceptions of the body, were vast and complex. Imported exotica such as textiles and ceramics had nothing on telescopes and watches, which brought before the Japanese the plausibility of empiricism as a mode of understanding. Whether foreign ships would topple in Japanese waters or sail steady, and whether foreigners' songs would ring clear in the *shōgunal* land, would have to be thought through again. The trope of Haku Rakuten had become an escape, but was no longer a solution.

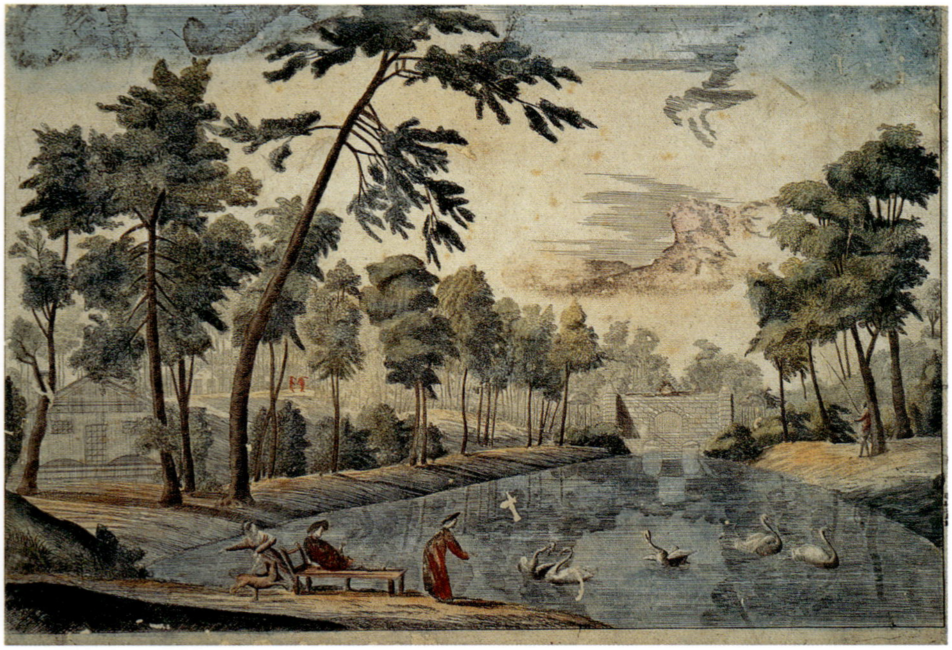

24.14
Serpentine Pond at Stowe
Shiba Kōkan
Hand-coloured copperplate print on paper
Japan (Edo), *c.*1787
Kobe City Museum, Kobe

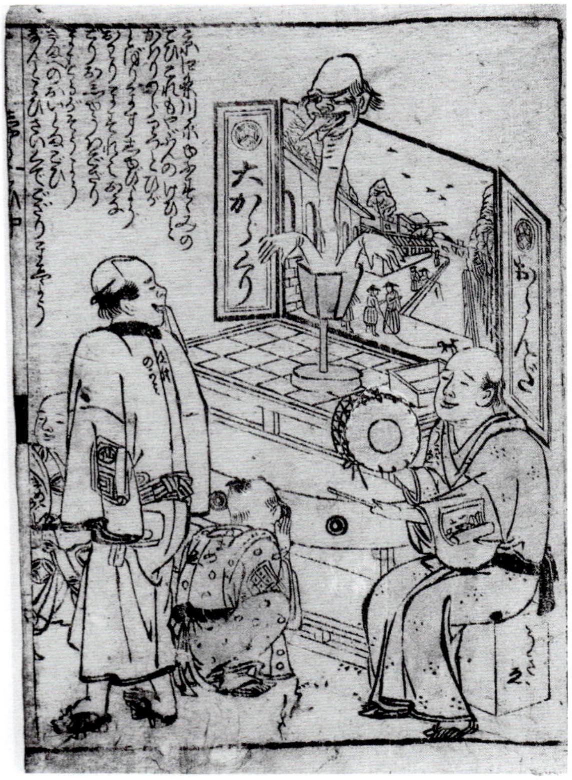

24.15
Page from *Gozonji no Shōbaimono*
Santō Kyōden
Woodblock-printed book
Japan (Edo), 1782
Private collection, Japan

The Impact of European War Technology

Greg Irvine

The greatest impact that Europeans had in Asia was in the sphere of arms and military technology. The Portuguese arrived in eastern waters with matchlock guns (arquebus) and ship-mounted cannon, and the firepower of these weapons far exceeded any of those known in Asia at that time. Deploying these arms, Europeans were able to command the attention of Asian rulers, who immediately recognized the advantages of possessing such efficient weaponry.

It is telling that one of the first Japanese references to Europeans occurs in the 'Teppōki' ('Record of the Musket'), a chronicle that recounts the history of the introduction of firearms into Japan.[1] Japan's feuding warlords recognized the power of this new weapon and the Portuguese were initially welcomed into Japan. For many years afterwards such weapons were known in Japanese as 'Tanegashima', the name of the island on which the foreigners were shipwrecked. Practical guides in scroll and printed book form were produced to explain the many ways to use this novel weapon in different situations (plate 24.17).

The power of the gun was immediately recognized by Japan's feuding warlords; within a decade of its introduction it had become fully incorporated into

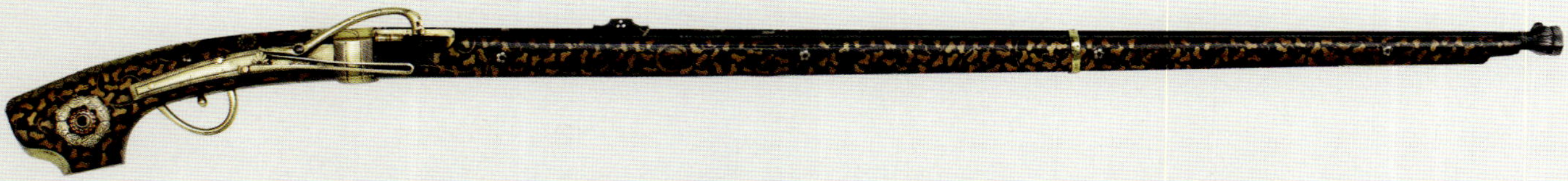

24.16
Matchlock gun
Cast-iron barrel inlaid with gold and silver; lacquered wood stock
Japan (Sakai), 18th century
Royal Armouries, Leeds

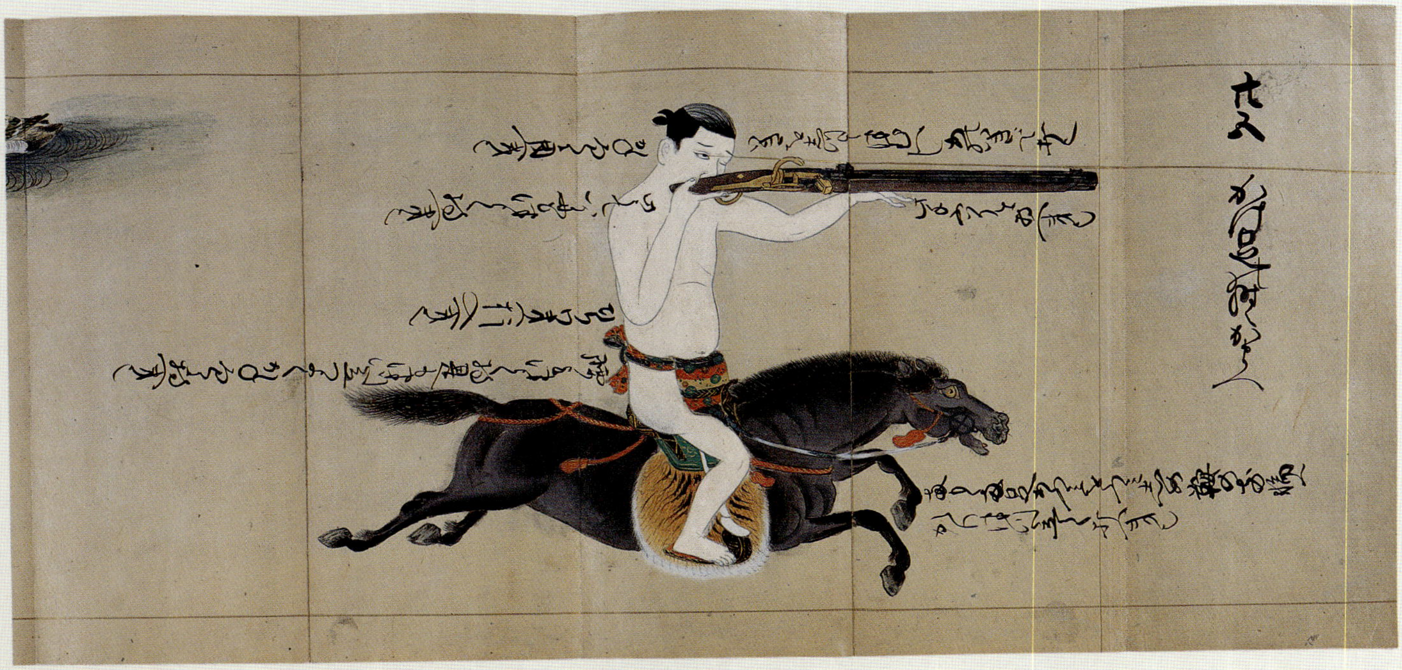

24.17
Secret Teachings of the Inatomi Ryu
Handscroll; ink and colours on paper
Japan, 1606
Namban Bunkakan, Osaka

Japanese warfare. The Japanese overcame technical problems in the manufacture of the weapon and made many useful adaptations to it, including a device for protecting the gun's match from rain (plate 24.16). They produced guns in large numbers, equipping conscripted armies with this weapon, which did not require years of training in order to be used efficiently. The gun had a profound effect on battle techniques, which had previously relied on individual skills with the bow, sword or spear. Now a conscripted farmer could kill a high-ranking *samurai* at a distance.

The great warlord Oda Nobunaga (1534–82) devised a method of using musketeers to superb effect. In 1575, at the Battle of Nagashino, 3,000 of these troops were used in three ranks firing successively in volleys, thereby devastating the *samurai* cavalry of his enemy Takeda Katsuyori. As traditional Japanese armour was ineffective against the gun, heavy western-style plate armour was increasingly adopted (or adapted), both for protection and as a part of the prevailing fashion for western styles (plates 24.18, 24.19).

The Chinese also recognized the advantages of mastering western arms. From about 1520 they began manufacturing weapons based on European prototypes, and later in the century they began to import arms and armour technology through the Portuguese settlement at Macao. Large cannon were introduced to China by the Dutch in around 1604, but in Macao even more powerful cannon were being manufactured in foundries operated by Chinese blacksmiths under the direction of European technicians. In 1642 Johann Adam Schall von Bell (1591–1666), the head of the Jesuit mission at the imperial court, assisted the Ming with the production of cannon in the fight against the invading Qing forces.

In 1526 the Mongol prince Babur (r. 1526–30) won a victory at Panipat in northern India, thereby laying the foundation of the Mughal empire. His success at this battle is attributed to the use of firearms, although it is unclear whether these were of Central Asian manufacture or acquired by him from the Portuguese. What is certain is that subsequent Mughal and other Indian rulers requested guns from Europeans, hired western artillerymen and encouraged the local manufacture of western-style weapons (see pp. 292–5). South Asian artisans also applied traditional decorative techniques in the embellishment of arms and armour and other accoutrements such as powder flasks, which were made for both domestic consumption and for Europeans in Asia. The latter also commissioned local metalworkers to fashion armour that combined western forms with indigenous decoration (plate 24.20).

24.18
Suit of armour
Adapted European helmet and breastplate, with Japanese neckguard and thigh protectors; hammered and engraved iron; leather and silk
Japan, 17th century
Kishu Tōshogu, Wakayama

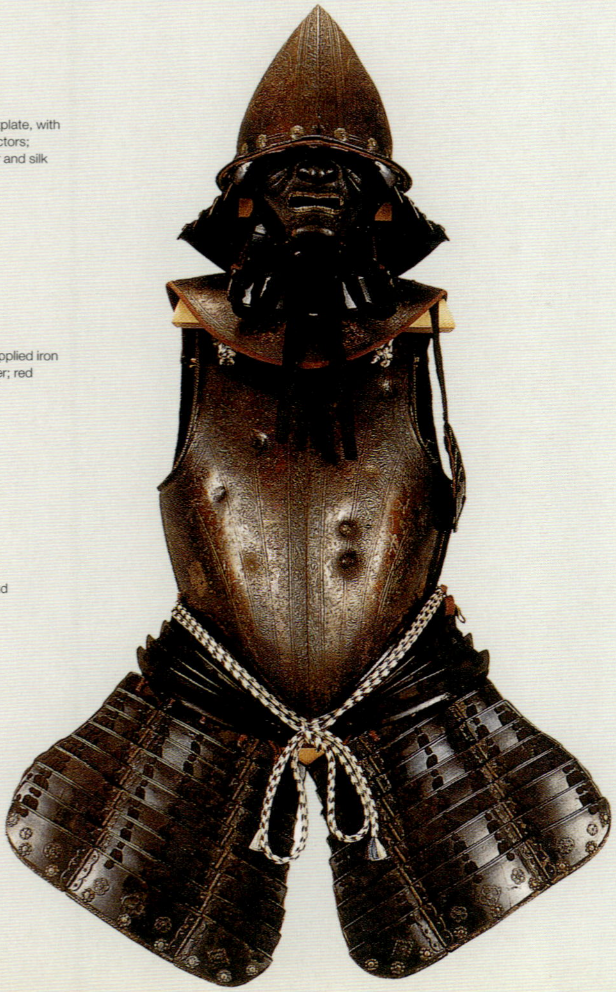

24.19 right, above
Helmet
Hammered iron with silver inlay and applied iron decoration, leather, silk and gilt copper; red lacquered interior
Japan, 17th century
V&A: M.59–1922

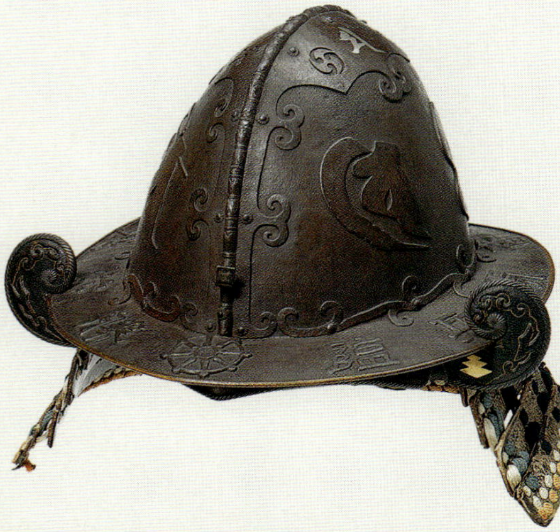

24.20 right, below
Helmet (cabasset)
Gilded copper worked in repoussé and chasing with engraved details
India (probably Goa), c.1580
Private collection

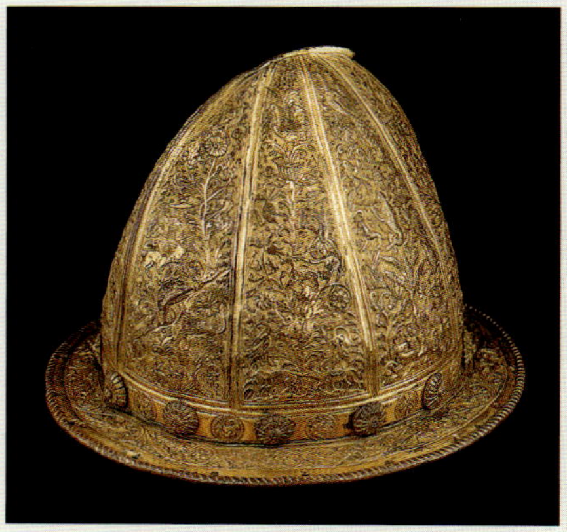

Japanese Map Screens

Miyoshi Tadayoshi

Japan's encounter with the West in the late sixteenth and early seventeenth centuries had an enormous impact on the course of the country's history. Western maps, which were quite different from anything the Japanese had seen before, were introduced alongside similarly revolutionary aspects of European culture such as Christianity and guns. While resented by some for the challenge to traditional orthodoxy that they represented, these maps were generally welcomed for the new and enlightened understanding of the world they brought. Oda Nobunaga (1534–82), for example, is known to have been greatly excited when the Jesuits showed him the route from Europe to Japan on a globe.

It was western cartography that underlay Japanese attempts of this period to depict the world on painted folding screens. Such screens, which are evidence of the extent to which the western worldview was accepted in Japan, are thought to have been painted for wealthy merchants and military leaders engaged in foreign trade. The most sumptuous and detailed pair of screens to have survived are the *World Map and Twenty-Eight Cities* screens in the collection of the Imperial Household Agency (plate 24.23). Their supreme quality suggests that they were made for the *shōgun* or a senior *bakufu* (*shōgunal* government) official. They are based on Pieter van den Keere's 1609 copy of Willem J. Blaeu's world map of 1606–07 (plate 24.21), which dates them to no earlier than the second decade of the seventeenth century. The artist is unknown, but is likely to have been a Japanese painter trained in western artistic techniques at a Jesuit painting workshop.

The left-hand screen depicting the world map is bordered on either side by 42 insets showing different peoples of the world. Not all of these, nor the depiction of cannibalism in the inset at the bottom of the third panel from the left, are derived from the Blaeu–Keere original. This suggests that additional sources were available to the artist. The inset at the bottom of the fourth panel from the right shows a group of figures personifying each of the continents, Europe being represented by the woman in the centre. On the right– and left-hand edges of the map, above and below the equator, there are diagrams illustrating lunar and solar eclipses. The depiction of Japan (right) and its surroundings is particularly well executed and is superior to anything found on other maps of the period. There are markers showing the locations of major cities such as Edo, Kyoto and Osaka. There is also a marker near the Izu peninsula that corresponds to Sunpu, where Tokugawa Ieyasu (1543–1616; r. 1603–05) spent his final years.

The right-hand screen consists of a series of depictions of rulers and cities of the world. Of the 10 rulers and 28 cities that border the original map, eight of the former and 27 of the latter appear on the screen. The 28th city on the screen is Rome, which has replaced the Blaeu–Keere depiction of Gammalamma, the Portuguese spice-trading centre on Ternate Island. The screen also includes a map of Portugal not present in the Blaeu–Keere original. Despite the Dutch origins of the map on which the screens are based, they have very little of the flavour of Holland. Their key messages relate, rather, to Portugal, Christianity and Tokugawa Ieyasu.

The *World Map and Twenty-Eight Cities* screens are a remarkable case of a Japanese artist having assimilated western cartographic conventions and recast them in a traditional painterly format. They are also, as the improved representation of Japan and its surroundings attest, more than blind copies of European sources. Furthermore, the way in which their pictorial language inspired the creation of masterpieces such as the *Foreign Lords on Horseback* screens (plate 24.22) is an indication of the crucial role they played in the development of Japanese art during the first half of the seventeenth century.

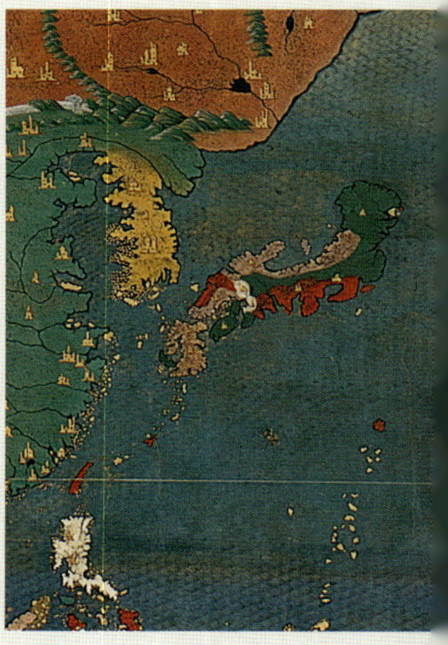

Detail of 24.23

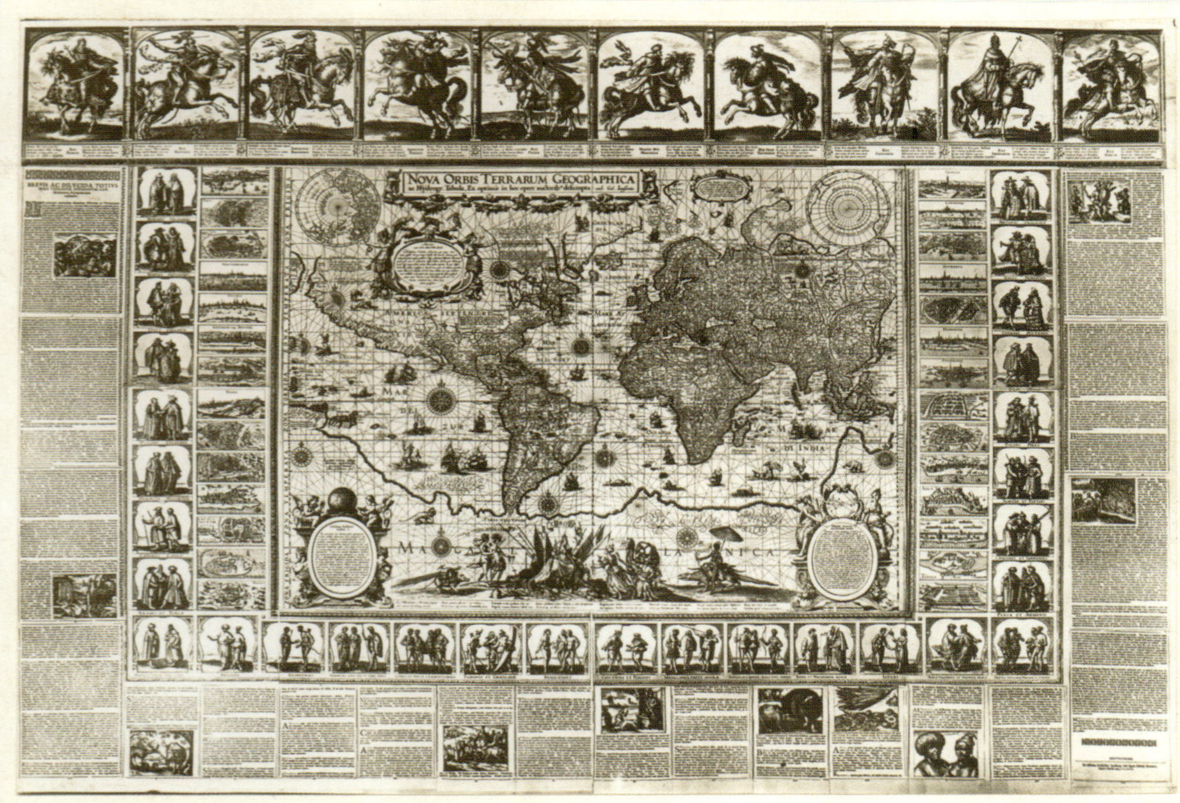

24.21
World map
Willem Janz Blaeu

Amsterdam, 1606–07

Photograph of lost original in the Maritime Museum, Amsterdam

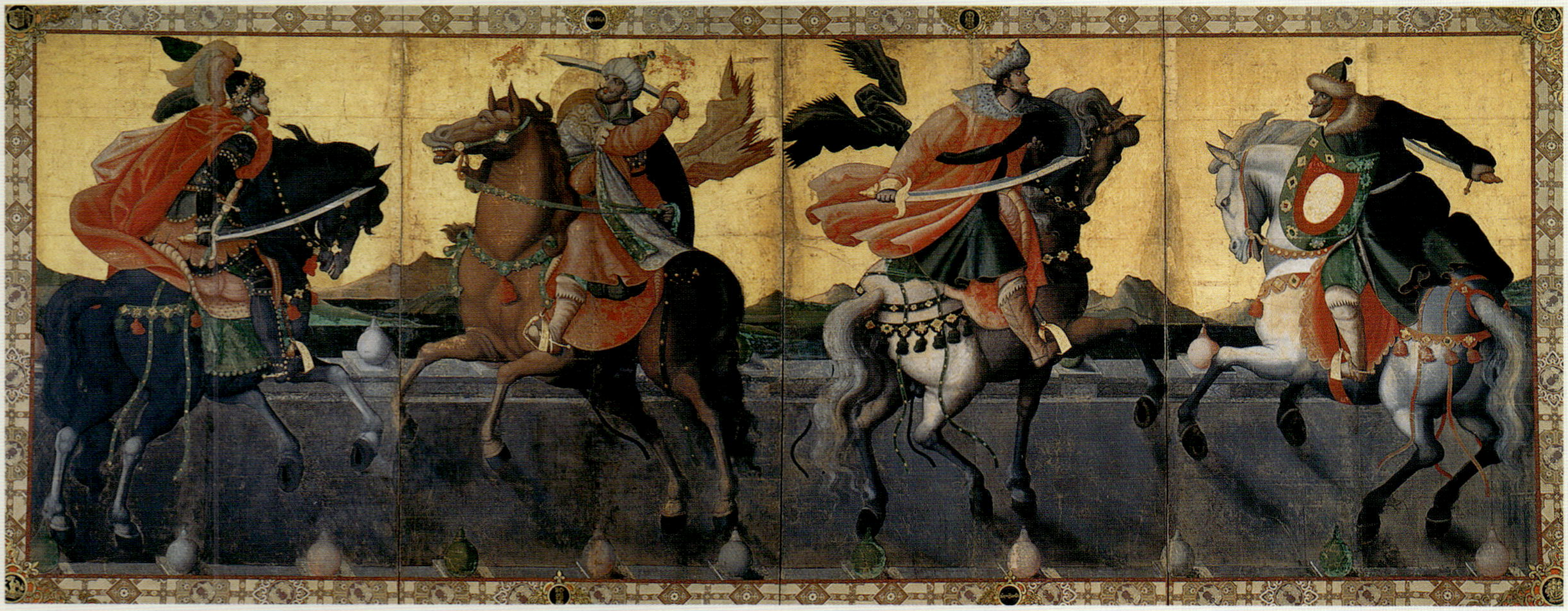

24.22
Foreign Lords on Horseback

Four-fold screen; ink, colours and gold leaf on paper
Japan, early 17th century

Kobe City Museum, Kobe

24.23
World Map and Twenty-Eight Cities

Pair of eight-fold screens; colours on paper
Japan, early 17th century

Imperial Household Agency, Tokyo

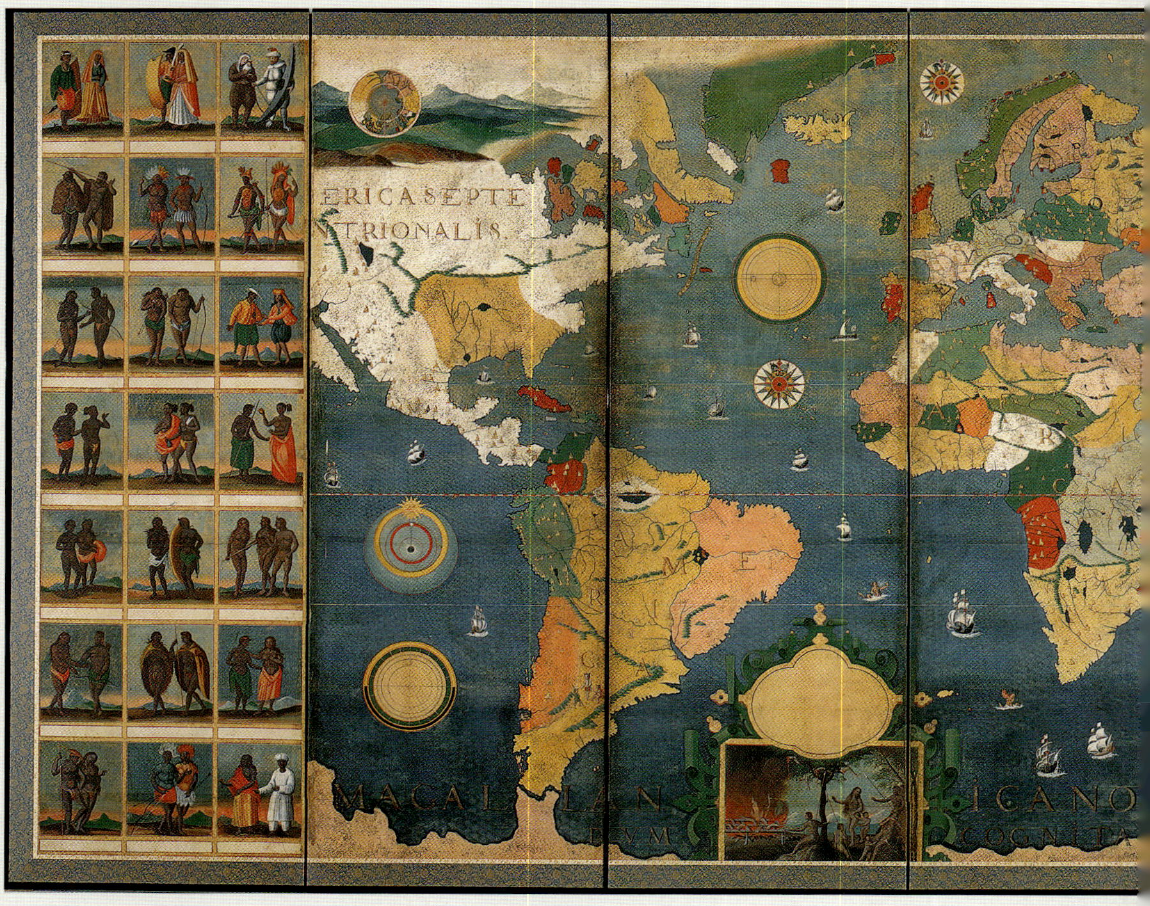

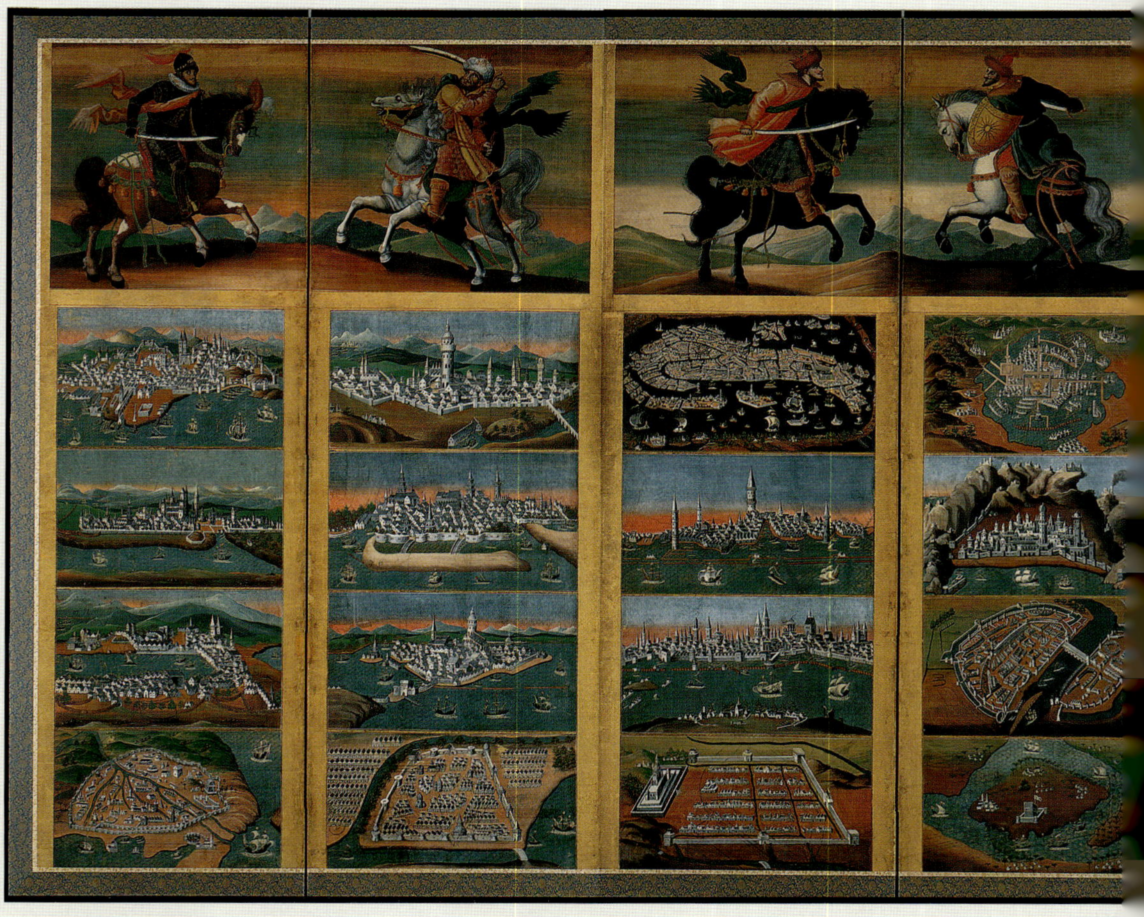

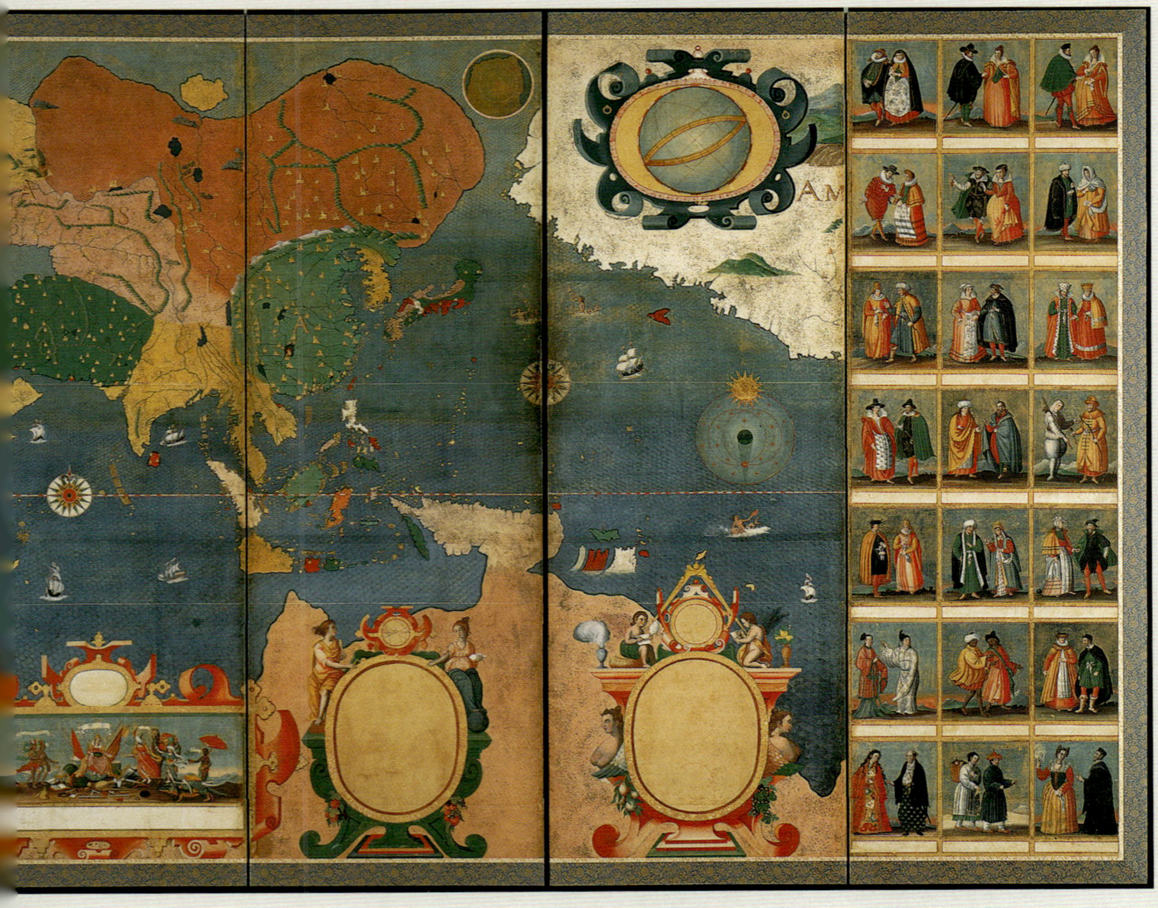

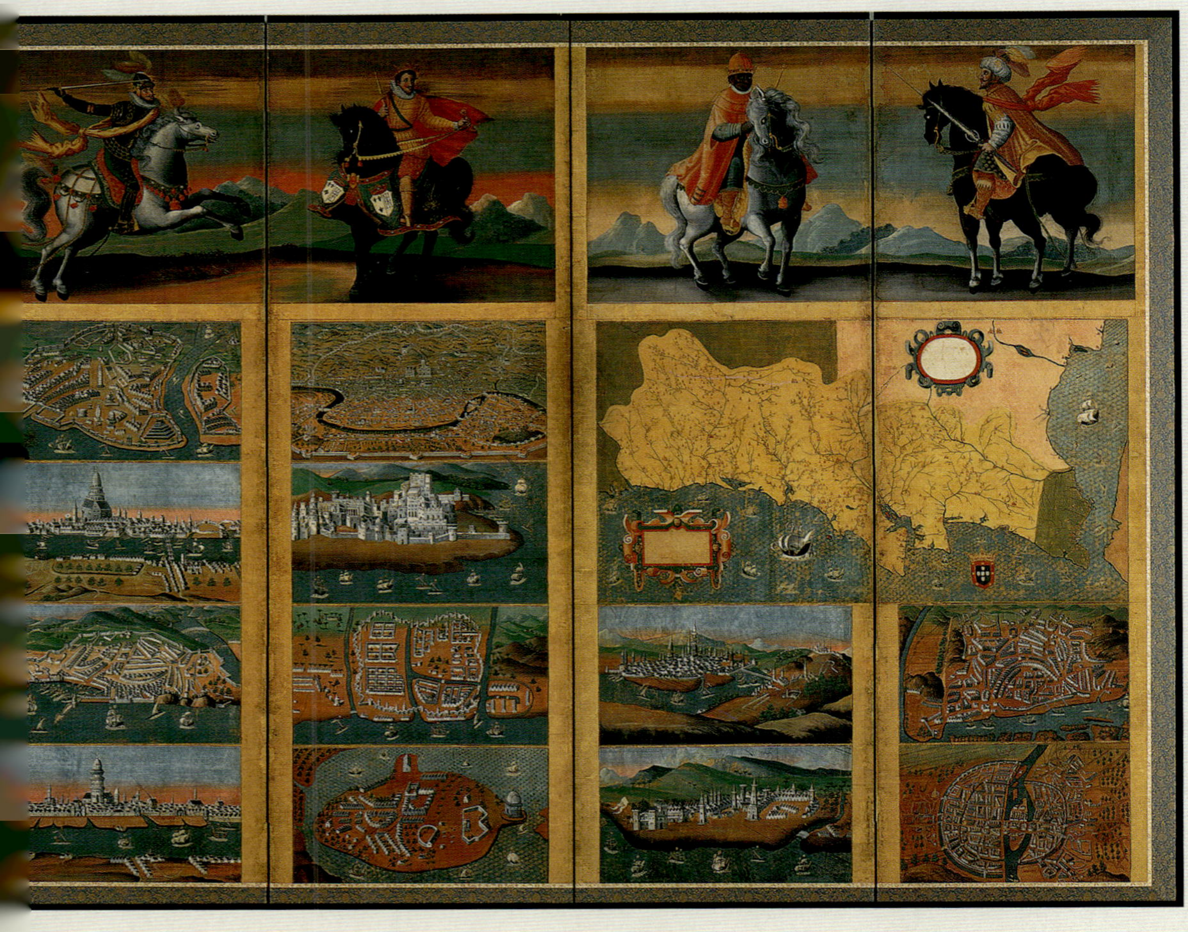

25

INDIAN FANTASIES OF EUROPE

Sally North

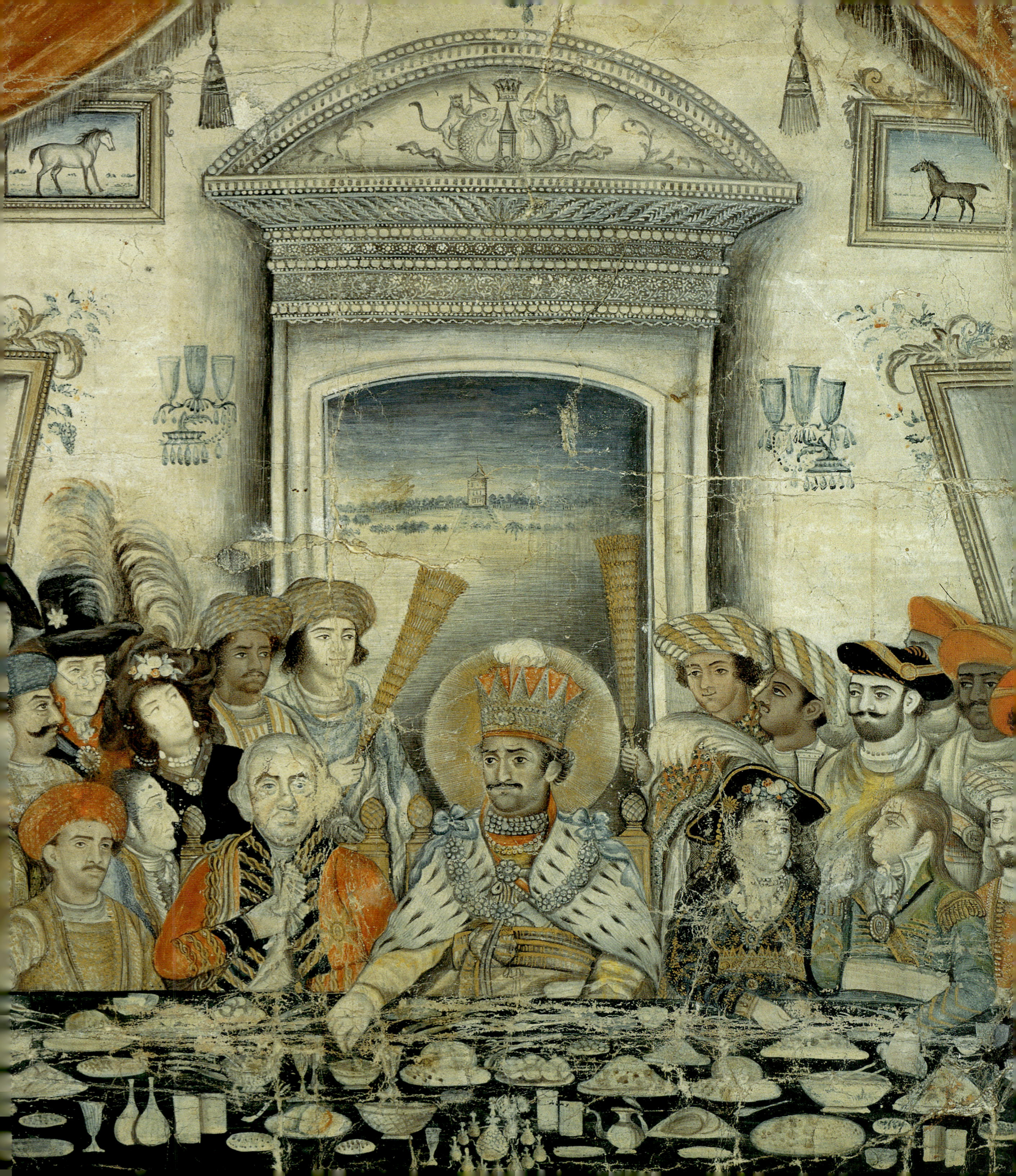

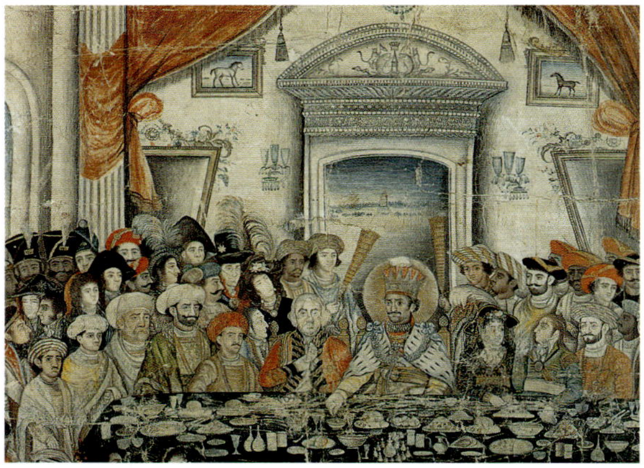

25.1 right and previous page
Ghazi-ud-din Haidar Entertaining Lord and Lady Moira

Opaque watercolour on paper
India (Lucknow), *c.*1814

British Library, London

From their first modern contact with the East, Europeans responded in a variety of ways to the powerful stimulus of new objects, materials, foods and even colours from the fabled cornucopia of the Orient. Goods that flowed westwards, such as spices, chintz, silk, porcelain, indigo and jade, engendered great excitement in Europe, where they epitomized the luxury and appeal of Asia. The Orient also aroused in the western imagination a potent fantasy of itself; a static, dreamy, 'Arabian Nights' world of harems, magic carpets, cruel viziers and wise sages. The role of the East in the formation of western fantasy is clear from even a cursory glance at the cultural productions that it inspired. What is rarely acknowledged is that the reverse was also true; that European objects and artefacts were recontextualized in the East as fantasies, inspiring in Asian peoples a corresponding vision of the mysterious West.

But what is fantasy? Defined as 'caprice', 'whimsical notion' and the 'unreal', the roots of the word are in the Greek *phantazein* – to make visible – a word that connotes a particular kind of visibility related to display.[1] This can be understood as (re)creating objects outside the context that normalizes them: a Chinese folly in the garden of an English country house, or a painting of Europeans in Oriental dress. Asian objects were also used in the creation of miniature Orients; interior spaces that conformed to western notions of eastern life, as seen in Thomas Hope's *Household Furniture and Interior Decoration* (1807), where Egyptian Revival furniture was uneasily juxtaposed with a Turkish ceiling, and in Thomas Daniell's paintings of India. Another important feature of fantasy is the element of transgression and pretence – a mixture and confusion of signals about identity – or a more straightforward 'dressing-up' or masquerade that alters the original identity into something it is not, but still aims to convince.

Initially, Indian contact with European objects and *objets d'art* was limited to diplomatic gifts and the casual small-scale importation of novelty goods by travellers and adventurers. It was inevitable that gradual attempts would be made to assimilate European goods and ideas about Europeans into Indian culture. This was especially so among elites, who, with the mercantile classes, experienced prolonged contact with Europeans. It can be seen, for example, in the various depictions of Europeans, from formal paintings of official *durbars* to portraiture, and even to erotic images of contact between *firingis* and Indian women (see chapter 15). There is no doubt that Europeans who visited Indian courts were considered exotic by Indians, but it would be some time before any exotic dimension would be assimilated sufficiently to be reconstituted into the Indian fantastic.

A conceptual distinction can be made between the first contact, where European objects appear in an unmediated way, such as in straightforward display, and the secondary and fantastic uses of the West, where objects are hybridized and re-presented by Indians. Examples of the former include the decoration of the City Palace, Udaipur, with Dutch tiles depicting biblical scenes, and the installation of western paintings and furniture at the Maratha court at Poona. It is noteworthy that in some places, the display of European objects and the fantastic recreations existed in parallel. The Raja Sarabhoji of Tanjore (1798–1832) had rooms furnished in an English style, complete with bookcases and gilt-framed oil portraits. Visitors were also met in a 'drawing room' furnished with English-style chairs and tables, although the furniture was made in India. In mid-eighteenth-century Kutch, Maharao Lakhpatji (r. 1741–60) erected the '*Aina Mahal*' (literally 'Palace of Mirrors'), which was decorated throughout with European mirrors, chandeliers and clocks.[2] These imports existed alongside Indian-made copies, the palace being a showcase of European objects and influence; it even had a picture collection containing, among other things, a set of William Hogarth's *A Rake's Progress* (1735).

Lucknow, capital of the state of Oudh, was ruled by *nawab viziers* of the declining Mughal empire. Their fantasies of the West included the habit of wearing European clothes and dining 'English-style' with sets of imported china (plate 25.1). One English woman who was invited to share this 'English' feast was scandalized by the unwitting use of chamber pots at the table; they were filled with milk.[3] Nawab Sadaat Ali Khan (r. 1798–1814) also used the West to transgress Islamic dietary restrictions by renaming forbidden foods: pork became 'English venison', cherry brandy 'English syrup', and so on. But it was in their buildings that the nawabs of Oudh so publicly and extravagantly played out their European fantasies through the recontextualization of neoclassical architecture, the sign *par excellence* of the English abroad (see chapter 11). Lucknow is a fascinating example of the sheer diversity of reactions to contact with Europeans, particularly in architecture, which achieved a grandiose scale and stylistic eclecticism unmatched elsewhere, mainly influenced by British and French engineers, and inspired by *Vitruvius Britannicus*.[4] Urban palaces and country houses were used in a fantastic and spectacular way: they were 'picnic palaces' for day trips to the country by the nawabs and court; they were settings for the display of the nawabs' European goods and paintings; and they were also an almost obligatory stop on the tour of Lucknow given to elite European visitors. Perhaps most importantly, they functioned as extravagant signs of the much-proclaimed Anglophilia of the nawabs.

The first buildings in Lucknow to show a definite neoclassical influence were the Bibiapur Kothi and the Residency. The Bibiapur Kothi, a small country house, was commissioned by Asaf-ud-Daula (r. 1775–97) and was used to accommodate the incoming British Resident until he had been officially greeted by the nawab and led in procession into the city. It has been referred to as 'a study in classicism'[5] on account of its regular plan, Romanesque arcading, paired Ionic columns and the plasterwork decoration of the interior. Similarly, early Residency buildings, such as the Banqueting Hall, display an austere classicism entirely suited to the tastes of the British establishment in India, which was accustomed to the grand architecture of Calcutta. In the brief period between 1780 and 1801 a number of palatial houses were built in Lucknow; only the Residency was definitely built by a nawab for a British incumbent.

Although such buildings are described as 'neo-Palladian', which might suggest the influence of English tastes, the early architects of importance in Lucknow were both French. Antoine Polier (1741–94) and Claude Martin (1735–1800) were adventurers originally in the service of Shuja-ud-Daula (r. 1754–75) and his successor. It is not certain which, if any, buildings in Lucknow were erected to the designs of Polier, but one of the most unusual houses in upper India was executed to his design in Faizabad, then the capital of Oudh, in around 1773. The house was ostensibly neoclassical throughout, with pilasters, mouldings and Venetian windows with radiating fanlights. However, it had two technical innovations: the first was a *tykhana*, or underground chamber, with ground-floor-level windows/screens, derived directly from Indian prototypes; the second, seemingly an original idea of Polier, was that of doubled exterior walls, which had a small gap between them to act as an insulating layer against heat and cold.

Musabagh or Barowen (completed in 1803) has been described as a 'perfect synthesis of a European house in the grand tradition with the practical Indian addition of a large open courtyard' (plates 25.2–25.3).[6] Musabagh was an unusual building, not only on account of this synthesis, but also because of the idiosyncratic use of European features in a structure of this type. The house was superficially European and was built on different levels, the front being three storeys high and the back two, with a sunken courtyard. The façade had a large rounded bay in the centre, with pillars of two storeys above the entrance. From the front, the house appeared to be an entirely conventional neoclassical design, albeit without the octagonal towers ubiquitous elsewhere in Lucknow. The open arcaded verandah on the rear ground floor had Adam-style fanlights interspersed with clustered Corinthian columns. The upper storey was composed of tall pilastered bays with french windows, fanlighted, with swags and ribbons in the plasterwork. Unusually, the fanlights on the second

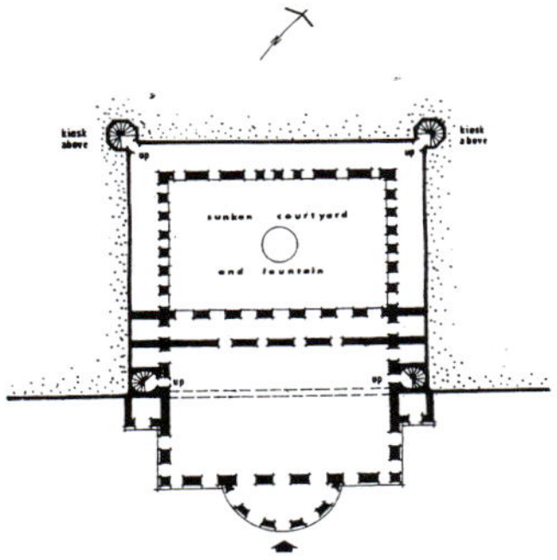

25.2
Plan of Musabagh

Dr Rosie Llewellyn-Jones

25.3
Musabagh or Barowen
Completed 1803

British Library, London

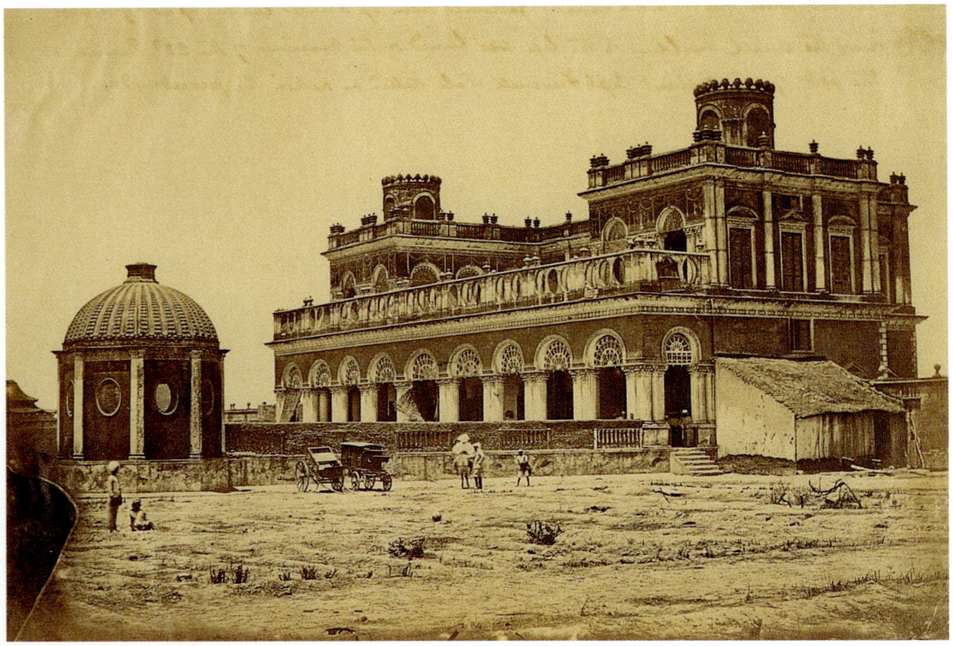

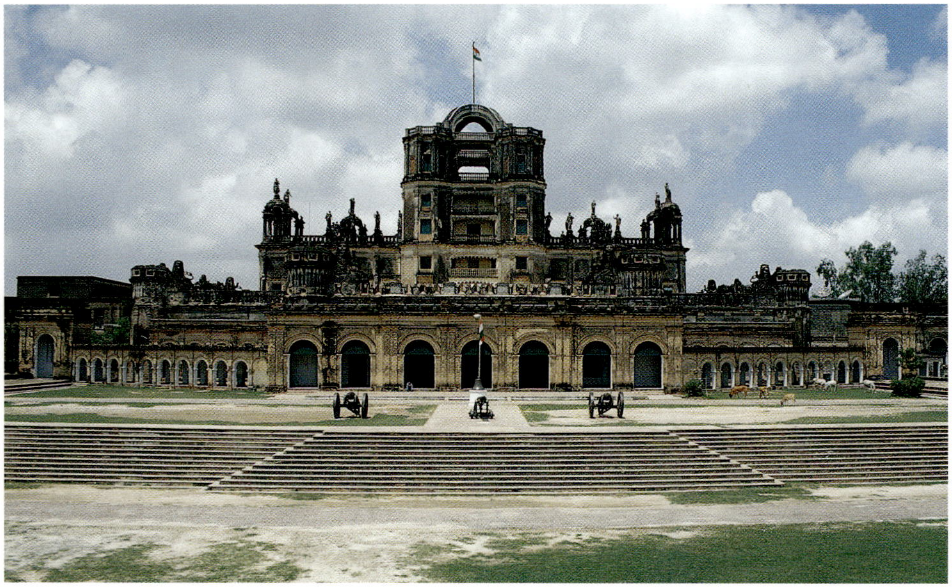

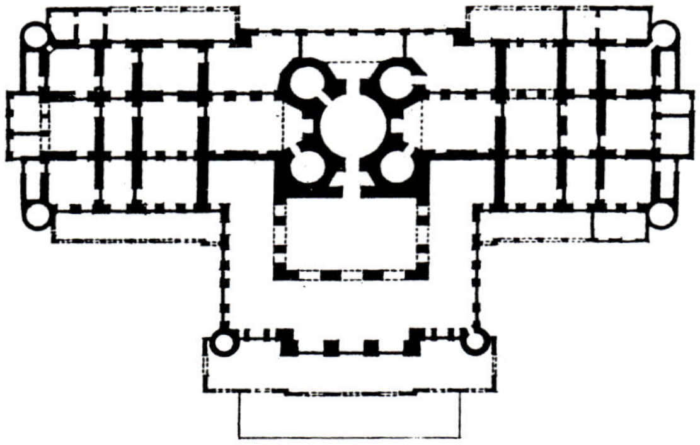

25.4
Constantia from the river side
Completed 1795

25.5
Plan of Constantia
Dr Rosie Llewellyn-Jones

storey were elongated rather than semi-circular. A narrow floral frieze completed each storey.

The courtyard below, reached from the exterior by two circular staircases, had a deep arcaded verandah (plate 25.2, 25.3). At the corners of the courtyard were stairs topped by small kiosks; not the *chattris* of Mughal architecture, but pavilions with classical columns and oval lights. The rooms on this level contained some very fine plasterwork. Elsewhere in the building remains suggest that each storey had elaborately plastered walls and ceilings, decorated predominantly with floral and vegetal motifs. These details and ornaments cleverly disguised the essential Indian aspects of the house, such as the tiny staircases confined to the exterior walls, the wide first-floor terrace, the courtyard and the small rooms that faced the communal yard, all of which replicated features of the *haveli*-style traditional urban house. The plan of the building proper was most likely to have been inspired by *Vitruvius Britannicus*, Wooley Park in Berkshire being an almost perfect match, or perhaps the plan of Doddington Hall in Cheshire. What was extraordinary in the design of Musabagh was the particular amalgamation of European and Indian elements. This was done in such a way that, effectively, the European house was a *mardana* (the part of a house reserved for the use of men and guests) and the sunken courtyard a *zenana* or *haramsarai* (the part of the house reserved for ladies of the family). The change in levels emphatically delineated the two zones. Approaching Musabagh through the unstructured parkland, one would see on a raised piece of ground a small English neoclassical country house, prominently set. Quite hidden, literally underground, and at the rear of the building was a sunken Indian *haveli* where the private and female life of the house took place. The building above was no more than an elaborate and convincing stage for the nawab's fantastic court, with animal fights and firework displays often held in the grounds.

Constantia (1795) is considered to be the exemplar of the grand neoclassical palace in Lucknow, designed and built by Claude Martin as a house, mausoleum and school (plate 25.4). Martin lived here with his Indian wives and adopted children, scandalizing the British establishment in the Residency and in Calcutta. The house consists of a main block (the wings were added later) with receding upper floors, finished by a tower composed of octagonal corner turrets, surmounted by twin arches bisecting the space of a dome. The flat roof created by the recession of the second and third floors supports numerous classical pavilions and is full of statuary: of affectionate couples, 'Greek' goddesses and huge stone lions whose mouths once held lanterns. As at Musabagh, the small balustrades are composed of repeated ovals. From the river side, an even greater similarity with Musabagh can be discerned. The lower floors of both consist of a series of bays with rounded fanlights and interspersed classical columns. The next storey is smaller, creating a terrace by its recession. The method of building upwards and inwards is very similar on both houses, although Constantia is a much larger structure.

The interior of Constantia is very well preserved, the only Lucknow grand house with its period details basically intact. The plasterwork is beautiful and elaborate, but in a decidedly European – even English – style, and includes the use of Wedgwood plaques (or Indian copies of them). Beneath the central portion of the house is a deep basement or *tykhana*, which contains the mausoleum of Claude Martin. It is the unusual plan of Constantia that reveals the truth which the fantastic neoclassical exterior conceals: the central core of the building is a *habsht bihisht*, or eight-fold paradise, a Mughal prototype ultimately derived from Timurid sources (plates 25.5, 25.6). It consists of a square or rectangular plan where four intersecting lines create nine rooms (three to each side), here composed by the clustered towers of the superstructure and the intervening spaces. Even more surprising is the conversion of negative to positive space on each floor of the façade, which only partly disguises the true nature of the building.

Far from being a poor attempt at a Palladian villa, and despite the decidedly European decorative flourishes, Constantia is a fantasy – a clever amalgamation of European grand house and Indian tomb. Perhaps it would be even more accurate to say that it is a Mughal tomb masquerading as an English or French country house. As one approaches the house, even the decorative elements that seem to be so classical appear doubtful. Looking again, one can easily substitute Mughal features for the idiosyncratic classical ones that Martin used. If each french window and blind window on the lower storeys were imagined as an open arch; if the arches were pointed rather than rounded; if the small classical kiosks were seen as *chattris*; if the central cutaway dome were solid – then the process would be complete: Constantia would be a Mughal tomb. This is further emphasized by the corner turrets on the ground floor, which allude to the minars or minarets that would normally be there. Constantia bears a striking resemblance to a type of Mughal tomb, such as those of Akbar in Sikandra and Humayun in Delhi.

Nawab Sadaat Ali Khan carried on the enthusiastic building of his predecessor Asaf-ud-Daula, but with far greater preference for the neoclassical style. During his reign one of the most extraordinary examples of architectural fantasy (or perhaps folly) was built. Dilkusha (literally, 'Heart's Delight') was erected as a hunting lodge in around 1800 and stands in a walled enclosure outside the city. It is an almost exact copy of Seaton Delaval, Northumberland,

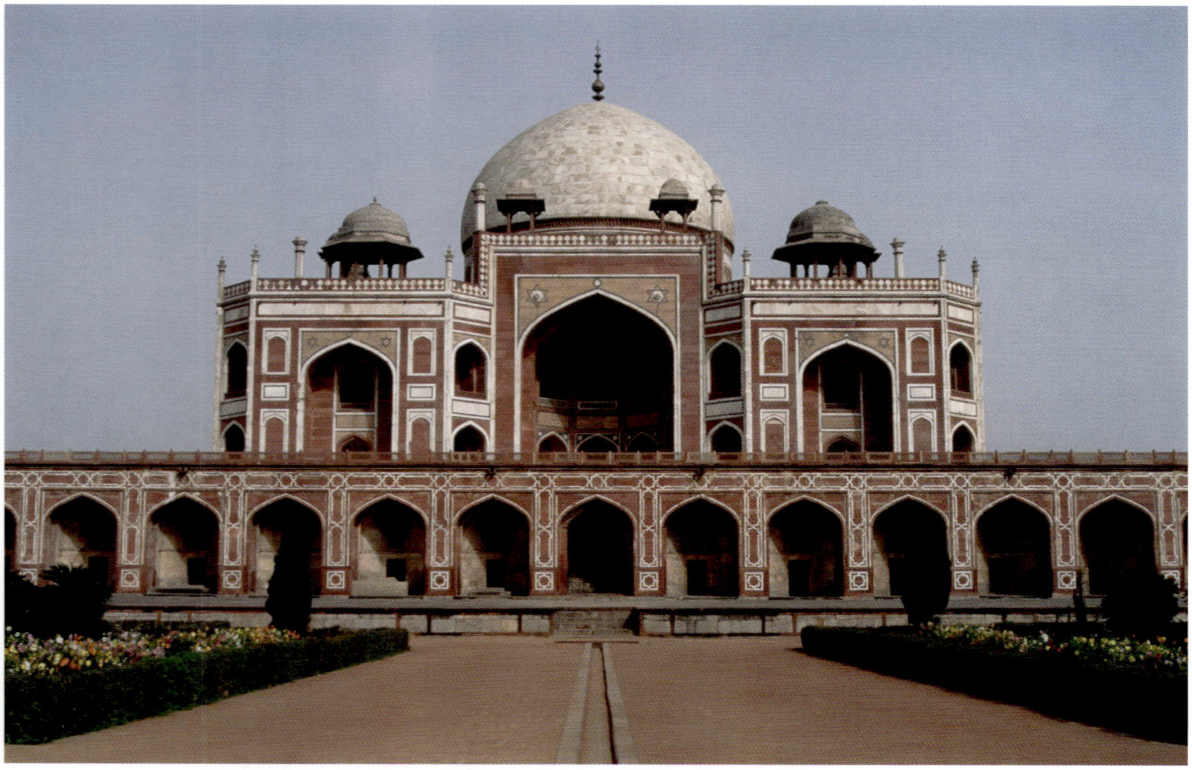

25.6
Tomb of Humayun
Completed 1565

which was designed by Sir John Vanbrugh and built in around 1715 (plate 25.7). How this English country house was known in Lucknow is easy to determine, as it was illustrated in *Vitruvius Britannicus*. Dilkusha is not unique (in terms of British building in India) in that it derived from a book; Government House, Calcutta, was taken from engravings of Kedleston Hall, Derbyshire; and many colonial churches were copied from James Gibbs's St Martin-in-the-Fields in London. Comparisons between the print source and Dilkusha reveal that the latter differs only very slightly, such as in the unusual pointed roofing of the octagonal turrets and the replacement of the pediment with a rooftop pavilion. The similarities are painstakingly rendered (plate 25.8), even to the deep rustication of the lower floors and the rusticated columns on the rear porch. The plans of the two buildings are almost identical, and Dilkusha was also situated in picturesque parkland, rather than a formal Mughal garden. One difference is in the position of the stairs: in Seaton Delaval they are in the mid-section of the side walls. In Dilkusha they are, in typical Indian fashion, located in the octagonal corner towers, as indeed in almost every other Lucknow house.

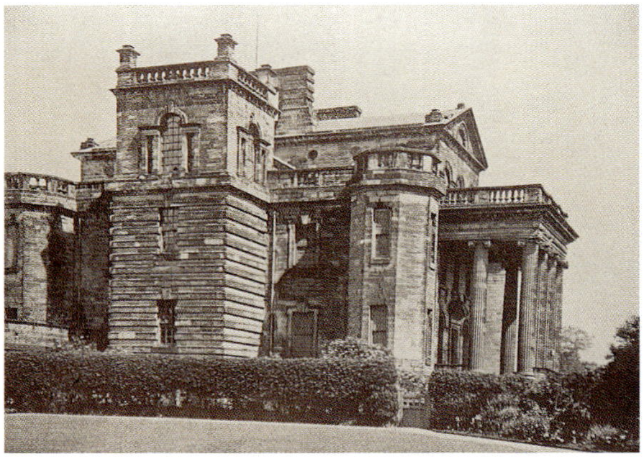

25.7
Seaton Delaval, the garden front
c.1715

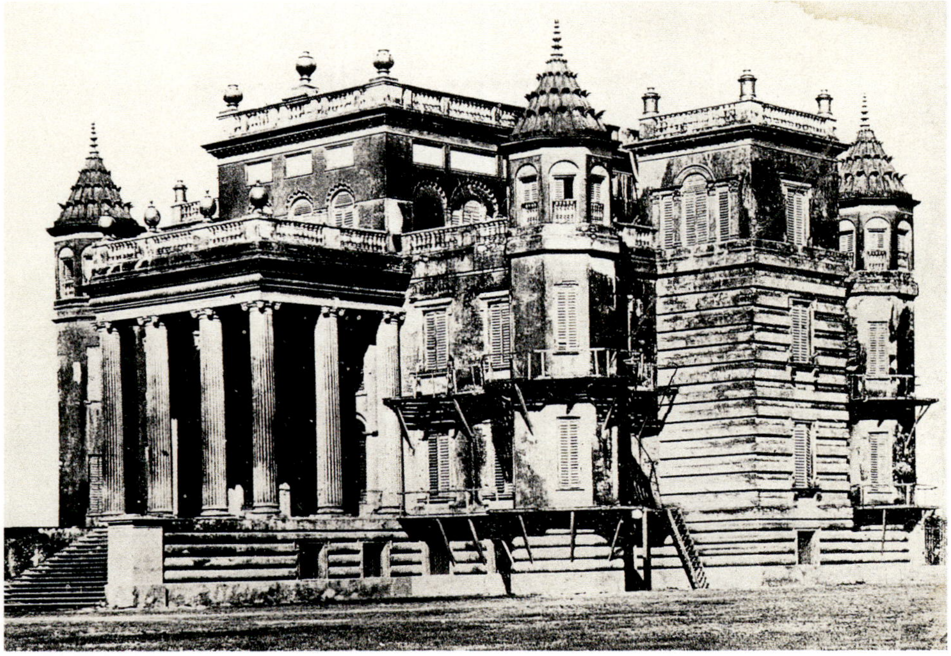

25.8
Dilkusha
c.1800

National Army Museum, London

There is even evidence of a taste for chinoiserie at court, as seen in the unusual turret roofs at Dilkusha (and copied faithfully on the gateway of the Sikanderbagh and the Dilaram Kothi in Lucknow). The upturned concave tiles, set almost horizontally, are strikingly reminiscent of the kind of upturned pavilion roofs seen in Chinese paintings and on export porcelain.[7] Indian elites had long admired and collected Chinese porcelain, which was sometimes displayed in 'China rooms' (see pp.62–7). A late eighteenth-century painting from western India illustrates an interior decorated in a Chinese style. It depicts two women with an African servant in a composition that is common to Indian courtly paintings (plate 25.9).[8] The noble lady is lying on a couch and sitting slightly below her is a female musician, while further down nearer the floor is an African servant (or slave), neatly corresponding to their relative social positions. The decor of the room clearly represents an attempt to invoke a Chinese flavour: the paintings depicted, the blue-and-white jars and the unusual wall decorations form a strikingly 'foreign' impression. This is further underlined by the composition of the paintings themselves – naturalistic outdoor scenes set in the Chinese countryside, which hang in the place where a decorated niche would usually be seen.

The impulse behind the grand project of palatial building in Lucknow appears to be, as with Lucknavi culture in general, an appreciation of the power of spectacle and the appropriation of identity. Transgression and shifting identity were marked features of court culture in Lucknow, and not only in the renaming of forbidden foods or in the wearing of tailored English clothes. Shia Muslims and Hindus celebrated each other's festivals and endowed religious buildings of the other's faith. In both the early and late periods, nawabs were associated with Hindu celebrations, from Asaf-ud-Daula, who enthusiastically celebrated *Holi*, to Wajid Ali Shah (r.1847–56), who donned the saffron robe of a Hindu *sadhu* to inaugurate a yearly fair. During *Holi* palace women broke purdah, dressed up as Englishmen and went about pretending to speak English, no doubt mimicking the East India Company officials whom they could glimpse through the purdah screen.[9] A caste of female entertainers (called *Dominis*) eschewed the traditional *dholak* (a two-headed drum) appropriate to their gender and adopted musical instruments hitherto used only by men.[10] Another group of entertainers, the Kashmiri *bhands*, had a male leader who usually wore female dress. The great Lucknavi Urdu poet Sarshar (1842–1902) composed a comic poem in which the nawab visits a theatre with his mistress, who is dressed as a man, complete with turban. While she is engrossed, the nawab falls in love with one of the performers, a European woman. Another nawab, Nasir-ud-Din Haidar (r. 1827–37) inaugurated a yearly ceremony in which he not only dressed as a woman, but took to his bed to 'give birth' to a child, imitating the mothers of the Shia imams. To this could be added the habit of building what appeared to be impressively large western palaces whose classical features were only a skin concealing something quite different. Furniture, clocks, mirrors, chandeliers and china were imported in large quantities to complete the interiors of these houses, a type of architectural and decorative propaganda testifying to the refinement and Europhilia of the nawabs, disguising – but not obliterating – the 'Indian-ness' beneath.

Most Lucknow palatial architecture conformed to the practical and social requirements of an Indian household while proclaiming a deceptive hybridity or classicism from the exterior walls. The same type of ornament was repeated everywhere in Lucknow: Corinthian columns, pediments, venetian windows, arcades, rustication and fanlights. This suggests that a small number of motifs were considered adequate to convey an *idea* of classical architecture. The idiosyncratic Lucknow version of neoclassicism should not be judged by reference to the canons of European taste. They are emphatically not classical houses, despite the classical signs – and evaluating their appearance without reference to use, both practical and metaphorical, is to ignore the particular political and cultural circumstances that encouraged the trend towards hybridization in palatial architecture. These buildings were composed of classical elements mixed with Indian, as a statement about the nawabs of Oudh and their peculiar intermediary position between two cultures: that of fading Mughal power in Delhi and the newly powerful East India Company in Calcutta. The neoclassical Orient seen in Lucknow is not an attempt to reinvent the West, but to assimilate it, using a type of cultural shorthand on buildings whose essential Indian character can still be determined by reference to the plan and use of the building. Classicism is a surface phenomenon of Lucknow architecture, highly visible but structurally unimportant. As an identity statement, it can be decoded by reference to its associational values. It is modern, civilized, pan-European (especially English) and secular. For the nawabs of Lucknow it provided a repertoire of architecture and ornament which not only proclaimed these values, however purely aspirational they may have been, but also served to separate them from the provincial Mughal style, now a sign of the waning empire and the past. Far from wishing to blindly imitate the West, the nawabs of Lucknow only appropriated it as part of the formation of a new identity, which would declare them, whenever they required, as being neither wholly Mughal nor European. What the neoclassical style in Lucknow served was a spectacular fantasy of Englishness, confidently amalgamated into the local style.

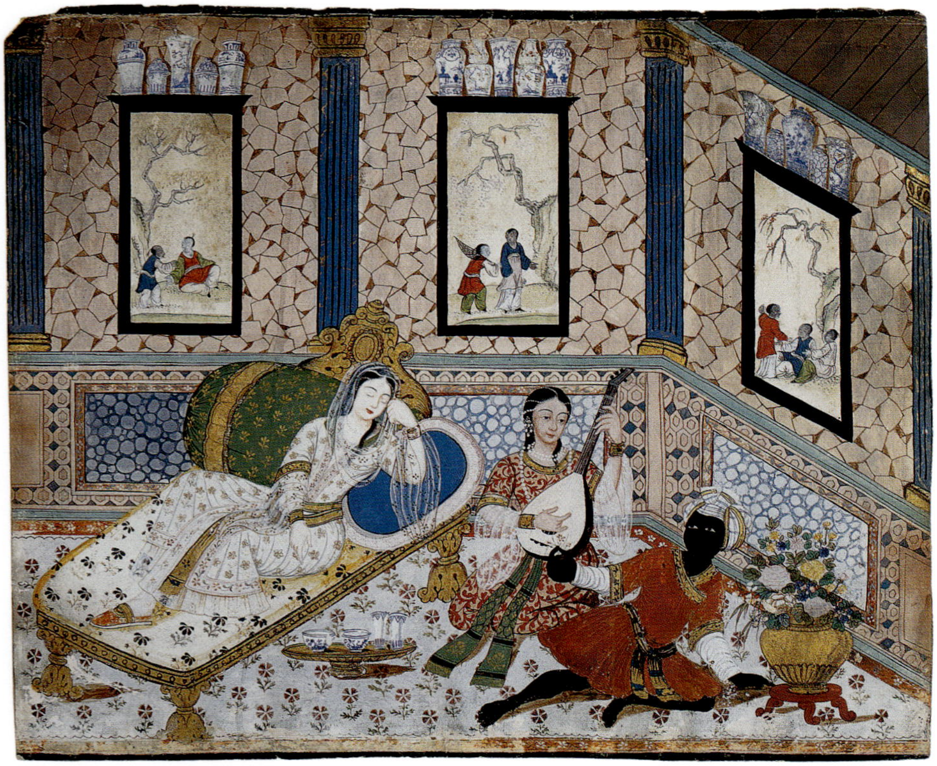

25.9
Two Ladies and a Servant in an Interior

Opaque watercolour on paper
India (Surat?), 1750–1800

On loan to Bristol City Museum and Art Gallery, Bristol

26

CHINESE FANTASIES OF EUROPE

Ming Wilson

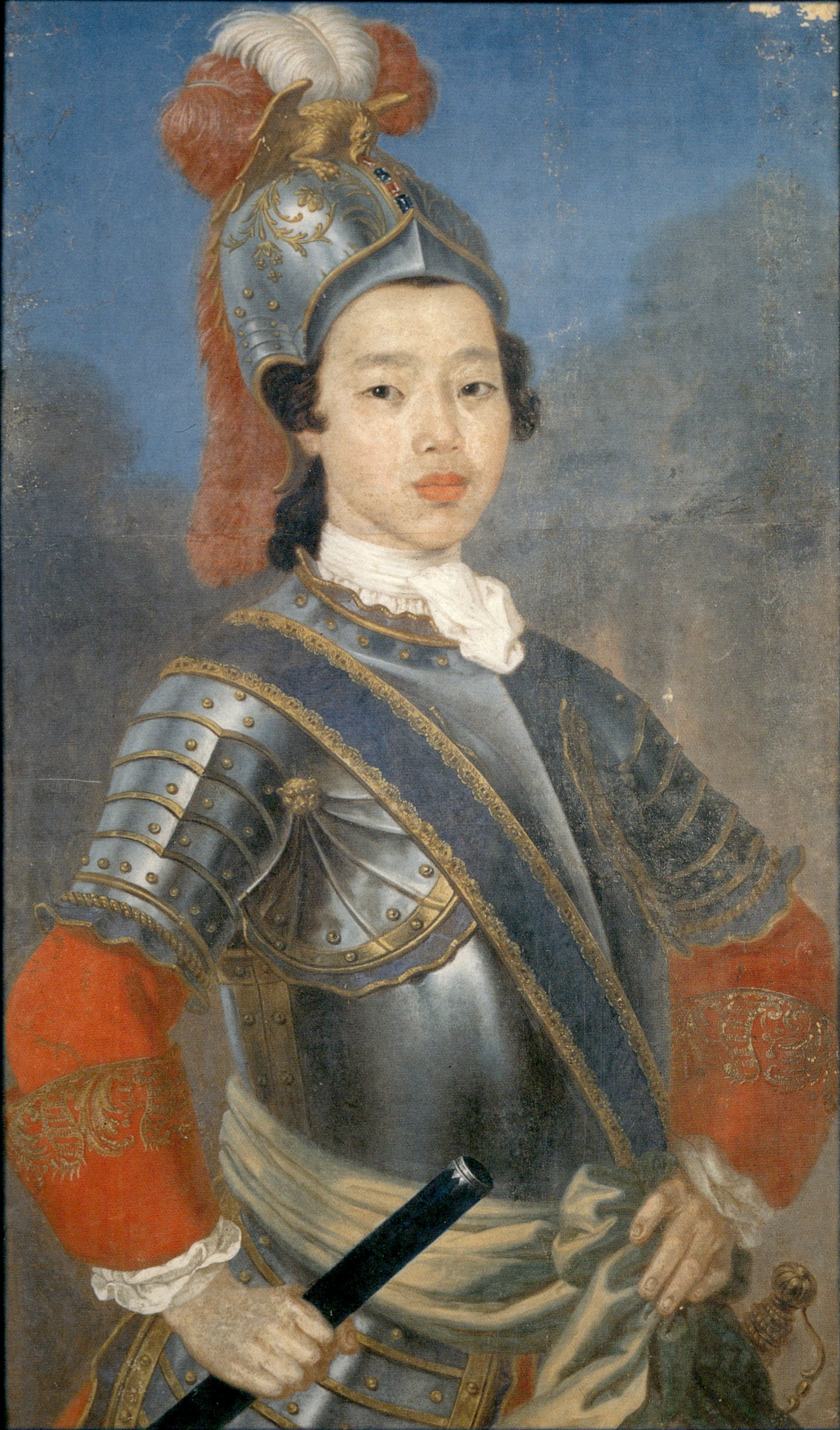

26.1 previous page
Rongfei
School of Castiglione

Oil on paper
China (Qing court), 1760–66

National Palace Museum, Taipei

It is generally agreed that western attempts to interest China in things European met with greatest success in the sphere of scientific instruments. Western consumer goods fared less well. The story of the English carriage presented to the Qianlong emperor (r. 1736–95) by the first British ambassador admirably illustrates that what was treasured in one culture was not always valued in another. Lord Macartney (1737–1806) found the Chinese unsprung carriage extremely uncomfortable, so he believed that the emperor was bound to be impressed by George III's gift of a carriage made by John Hatchett of Long Acre, London.[1] His Lordship would have been much annoyed had he known that Qianlong never rode in the carriage. When Robert Swinhoe (1836–77), British Consul at Amoy (Xiamen) entered the Yuanming Yuan ('Garden of Perfect Clarity') with British troops in 1860 he found it intact, but covered with dust.[2] Apparently this object of Lord Macartney's pride had been put to another use – as a trophy from a foreign land rather than a vehicle in which to travel.

Two hundred years before Lord Macartney, Matteo Ricci (1552–1610) had made similar attempts to impress the imperial court, although his aim was to spread Christianity rather than to secure trade benefits. Ricci's success as a missionary is discussed elsewhere (see pp. 118–9), but the sheer fact that he was a foreigner was sufficient to make an impact on the people of Peking (Beijing). Chinese scholars might have heard about 'red-haired barbarians' forcing their way into coastal cities such as Canton (Guangzhou) or Amoy, but to see a white man in flesh and blood was far more exciting. Furthermore, Ricci could speak and write Chinese, so educated men befriended him even though they were not interested in the religion he preached. The gossiping scholar Shen Defu (1578–1642) wrote about Ricci 10 years after his death, in about 1620:

> When I stayed in Beijing on former occasions I was the neighbour of Li Madou [Chinese name of Ricci]. He was an extraordinary man ... He helped people in need, ate and drank considerably, and the things he made were all very fine. He was not in the money-lending business, yet he never seemed worried about expense, so people suspected he had a formula for gold smelting ... When he was ill he rubbed his entire body with a certain oil. He said that was his country's method of curing ailment ...[3]

It will never be known if Ricci was aware of the fanciful opinion formed about him by the Chinese literati. One ink maker, however, was quick to exploit the 'exoticness' of the man from an unknown land called 'Europe'. Ink making was big business in sixteenth– and seventeenth-century China, not only because every scholar needed ink with which to write, but also because of a flourishing printing industry. Chinese ink was traditionally moulded into cake forms, and to boost sales ink manufacturers developed hundreds of ink-cake designs. Two rival ink makers, Fang Yulu (active 1573–1620) and Cheng Dayue (1541–*c.* 1616), each published his own catalogue of ink-cake designs, known as *Mr Fang's ink album* and *Mr Cheng's ink garden* respectively. The catalogues were intended to be seen as art books, not marketing tools, and famous painters and calligraphers contributed to the volumes. Both men deemed it desirable to add an exotic element to the catalogues. Fang included a page of Sanskrit script in his album, although the number of Chinese conversant with Sanskrit at that time was negligible. Cheng knew Ricci personally, and obtained from him several pages of Gospel text in Chinese, complete with phonetic transliterations into Latin (plate 26.2; see p. 305). Ricci would certainly have known that Cheng was more interested in the Latin script than in the biblical messages that the writings conveyed. Nevertheless he realized that this was a good opportunity to reach out to the Chinese elite, albeit in an indirect way.

Cheng's motives and objectives were obviously commercial. It is less easy to explain, however, why Emperor Yongzheng (r. 1723–35) commissioned a portrait of himself wearing European clothes and a tall wig (plate 26.3). Yongzheng ascended the throne at a time when Giuseppe Castiglione (1688–1766), a Jesuit and skilled artist, was already serving at the Chinese court. It is almost certain, however, that the painting was produced not by Castiglione, but by a Chinese artist who was not at all familiar with European dress. Yongzheng is shown wearing a waistcoat, breeches, a cravat, a long overcoat, stockings and boots. But his European outfit is a mixture of western form and Chinese details. The design of inverted Ys on the waistcoat is a Chinese pattern known as *suozi* (literally 'continuing'). The textile belt is a Chinese accessory that would never have been worn with a European overcoat. The overcoat has no buttons, again an irregularity. The artist had probably not seen many portraits of Europeans wearing a cravat, so the emperor's cravat looks like a shoulder cloth, rather similar to one found on the large stone statue of a warrior erected outside the mausoleum of the Ming emperor Wanli

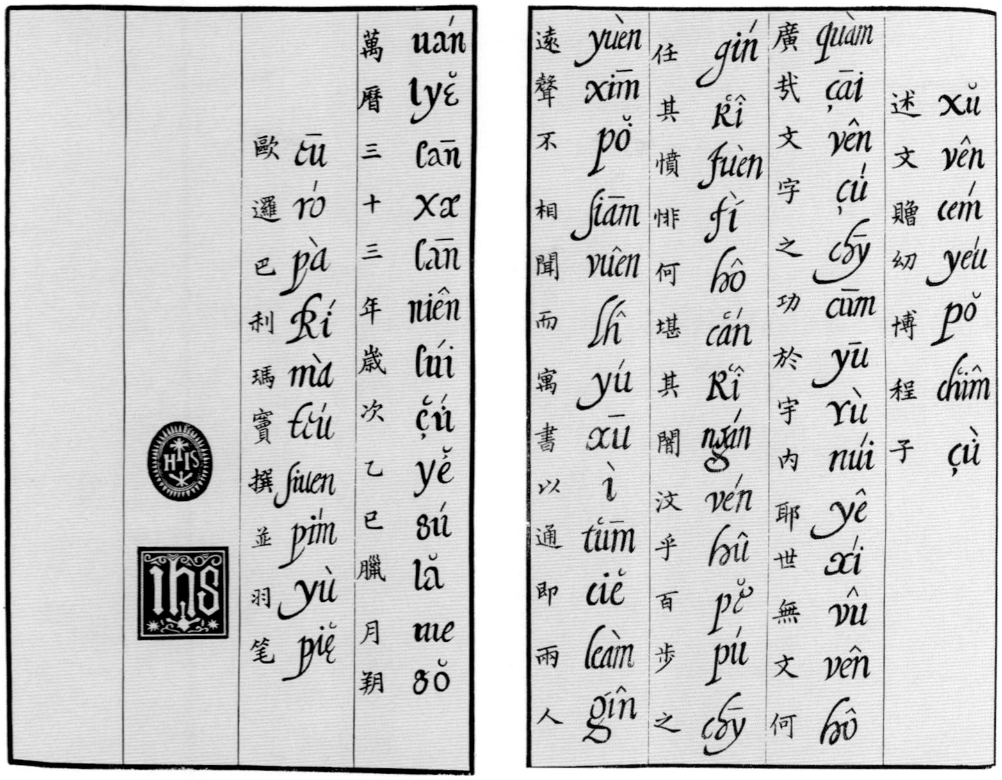

26.2
Page showing Latin and Chinese scripts
From *Mr Cheng's ink garden*, China (Xin-an), 1606

Percival David Foundation, London

(r. 1573–1620). Lastly, the soles of the boots are white, as would have been the case with Chinese soles because they were made of starched cotton or paper. Again the artist was unaware that European boots had leather, and hence dark, soles.

Even more curious is the setting of the scene, as Yongzheng is shown holding a spear and about to attack a tiger. The reason for this hilarious composition has been explained by one modern scholar as the Chinese parallel of a masquerade, which became extremely popular in Europe from the early eighteenth century.[4] As the 14 leaves from the same album to which this image belongs all depict Yongzheng in various guises, including those of a Persian warrior and a Turkish prince, it does seem at first glance that the Manchu emperor was staging a personal masquerade in which he constantly changed dresses and assumed different nationalities and roles.

But all historical records suggest that Yongzheng was a serious man. If he indulged in a game of disguise, he did not do so for amusement. The issue on his mind while commissioning those portraits was probably 'foreigners'. China had always been wary of foreigners. Such apprehension had given rise to a convention of depicting them as tribute-bearers who acknowledged China's cultural superiority (see pp. 206–11). Like all the rulers before him, Yongzheng's primary concern was to ensure that foreigners did not cause a destabilizing effect within the empire. At the same time he realized that he had a much more formidable foreigner to deal with than his predecessors. The presence of European seafarers with a militant temperament, efficiently manned ships and powerful cannon and firearms was regularly reported to him by officials in the coastal cities. To add to his anguish, Yongzheng was aware that, ironically, the Manchu – the race to which he belonged – were foreigners in the eyes of many Han Chinese, the ethnic group that constituted 90 per cent of China's population. Despite the fact that China had been under Manchu rule for 80 years, there was still resentment from some of the Han Chinese, who believed that the 'Northerners from outside the Great Wall' came to the throne by some historical accident. Five years into his rule, in 1728, one of Yongzheng's trusted generals, Yue Zhongqi, received a letter from a scholar called Zeng Jing, urging him to rise in revolt and drive out the 'barbarian ruler who had usurped the precious throne'.[5] Even contemporary European writers called the Manchu 'Tartars' and not 'Chinese'.

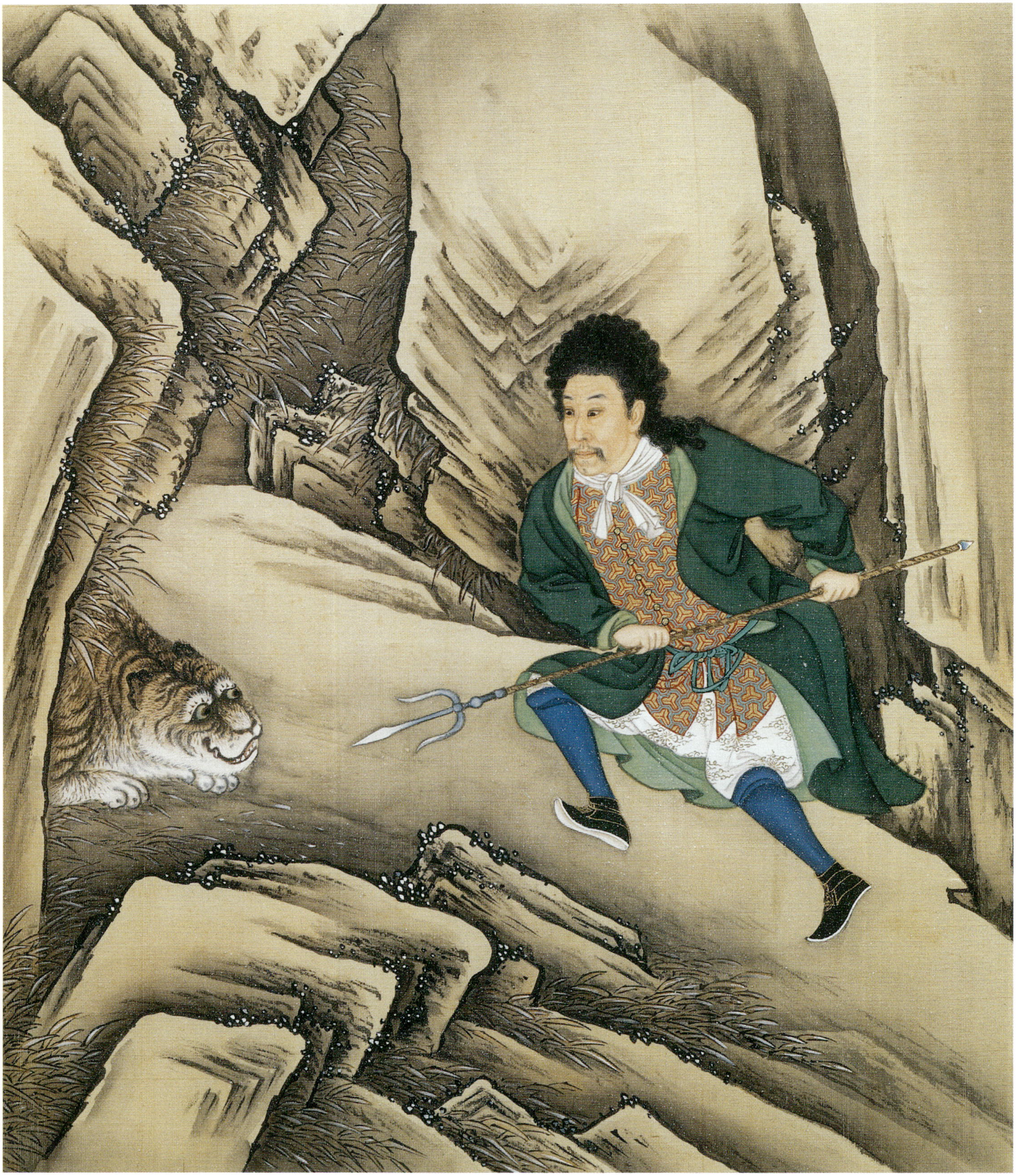

The Chinese habitually used the centuries-old expression 'all under heaven' when they meant 'the Chinese nation'. Yongzheng could no longer pretend that China was the only important nation under heaven. Could he, as Son of Heaven, command respect and allegiance from people outside China, as all his predecessors had believed they had? Here Yongzheng resorted to another centuries-old concept, namely that the Son of Heaven ruled not by force, but by virtue. It did not matter if he were a Manchu or a Mongol, because his valour could match that of any European. Attacking a tiger was another familiar theme to indicate prowess. The other 13 portraits from the album all convey the same message: that the emperor was the personification of wisdom, righteousness, compassion and all other noble attributes. It was a convoluted, even fanciful, way of sending such a message. Perhaps Yongzheng needed to convince himself as much as convince his subjects. The inspiration, however, could well have come from the Jesuits, who told the emperor about masquerades in Europe.

Yongzheng probably never possessed, let alone wore, a European suit of clothes. It is more likely that he merely ordered his court artists to portray him in different guises. His son and successor, the Qianlong emperor, on the other hand, went further than imaginary play-acting. In his vast summer resort outside the capital, the Yuanming Yuan, he built a palace in western style. Unfortunately the Yuanming Yuan was razed to the ground during the second Opium War in 1860. All that is left today are a few architectural components (plate 26.4), 20 engravings of the European buildings and textual accounts about their construction.

It has repeatedly been alleged that the idea of a western-style palace was born when Qianlong saw a European engraving of a water fountain and decided to build one in the Yuanming Yuan.[6] But there could be another reason why Qianlong wanted a palace in the European style. He could have heard about the grand palace and pleasure gardens built by European monarchs and princes. He could also have heard about the vogue for chinoiserie that was sweeping across Europe at the time. Surely the ruler of China should not be eclipsed by monarchs from the western oceans! If Europeans could enjoy Chinese pagodas, then Qianlong could have a maze – something unknown in China.

The initial European section of the Yuanming Yuan consisted of a two-storey building, a water storage tower, an aviary and a maze. All of these, according to modern computation, stood on a ground 320 metres long and 85 metres wide. The water storage tower was necessary because of the fountain in front of the building. The most conspicuous European elements were the outer staircase and the Ionic columns. The paths of the maze were divided by brick walls rather than hedges. Qianlong called the building *Xieqiqu*, meaning 'peculiar delight', an indication that it was the exotic quality that amused him. There is no evidence that the emperor ever lived there. The outward appearance of the building was all he was interested in.

As soon as this phase was completed in 1751, the emperor demanded an extension. Perhaps the two principal architects, the Italian Jesuit Giuseppe Castiglione and the French Jesuit Michel Benoist (1715–74), had by then become more experienced and more confident to embark on something on a grander scale. The extension was 770 metres long and 60 metres wide. The salient feature was the Great Fountain, in front of which a throne was positioned so that the emperor could sit and admire the water gushing – a view that was completely different from

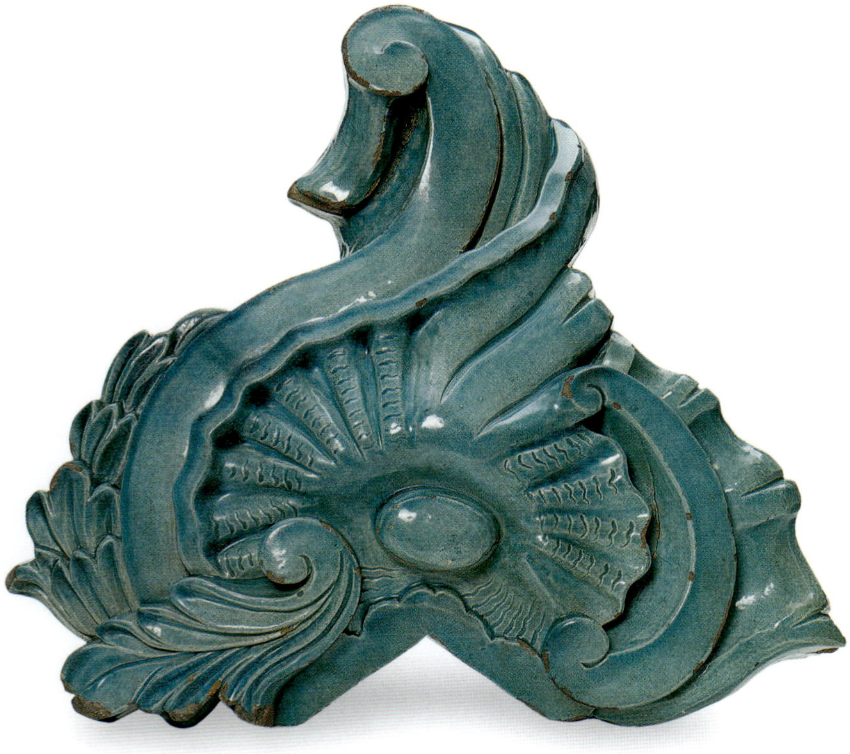

26.3 opposite
The Yongzheng Emperor in European dress

Album leaf from a set of 14; ink and colours on silk
China (Qing court), Yongzheng period (1723–35)

Palace Museum, Beijing

26.4 above
Architectural ornament from a western-style palace in the Yuanming Yuan

Stoneware with turquoise glaze
China, 1747–70

V&A: C.382–1912

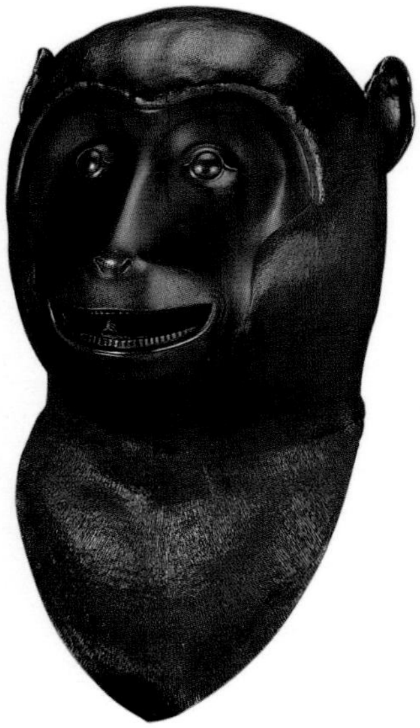

26.5
Fountain head
Bronze
China, *c.* 1750
Private collection

26.6 opposite, above
The Haiyantang (Calm Sea Palace), Yuanming Yuan
Copperplate engraving
China (Qing court), *c.* 1786
V&A: 29452

26.7 opposite, below
Perspective Picture East of the Lake, Yuanming Yuan
Copperplate engraving
China (Qing court), *c.* 1786
V&A: 29452

the running streams in other parts of the Yuanming Yuan. To the west of the Great Fountain was the *Haiyantang* ('Calm Sea Palace'), a building incorporating a curious mixture of European and Chinese features (plate 26.6). There were western-style gables directly above the central doorway, but the roof was typically Chinese. Qianlong's fascination with waterworks was clearly demonstrated by the magnificent clepsydra, a time-keeping device driven by water in front of the Calm Sea Palace. It took the shape of a large basin, with a scalloped shell in the middle and six bronze statues of the Chinese zodiac animals on each side (plate 26.5).[7] The animals had human bodies and were depicted seated. Every two hours water would eject from the mouth of one of the animals, and at noon water would spout from all the animals. It is also interesting to note the juxtaposition of European and Chinese decorative elements along the basin.

At the very eastern end of the palace was a scenic spot known as the *Hudong xianfahua* ('Perspective Picture East of the Lake'). Here Castiglione's mastery of perspective was exploited to create a *trompe l'oeil*, an effect of which Qianlong was extremely fond (plate 26.7). No real buildings had been erected on the other side of the lake; what appear to be Chinese and European houses lining the two sides of the road were in reality part of a scene painted on walls. The emperor could stand on a small hill on the western side of the lake and, looking across a vast stretch of water, imagine himself in some fantastic place where things from the western oceans coexisted with things Chinese.

A description of the interior of the European-style buildings was provided by the Jesuit François Bourgeois (1723–92), who wrote to his friend Louis-François Delatour in 1786:

> The European palaces contain only European ornaments and furniture. It is unbelievable how rich this sovereign is in curiosities and magnificent objects of all kinds from the occident ... He broke up first grade Venetian and French glass to make window panes because he had so many pieces that he did not know where to put them ... In the tapestry hall (70 feet long) there are many pier glasses. It is so full of machines that one can hardly move about in it. Some cost two or three hundred thousand francs, for they are enriched with innumerable precious stones.[8]

The 'tapestry hall' was specially refurbished to house the six Beauvais tapestries known as 'the Chinese set', from a design by the French artist François Boucher (1703–70). Records in the Beauvais manufactory confirm that the hangings were sent to Henri Bertin, then minister and Secretary of State of France, in 1763, for onward despatch to China.[9] The Chinese figures depicted on the tapestries were, of course, fanciful interpretations by the French. Whether or not Qianlong found them amusing will never be known, but at least he did not banish them to some dusty store, as he did with the English carriage. The chair with a scalloped-shell design, on the other hand, would have received full approval from the emperor prior to its manufacture in the palace workshop (plate 26.9). The shell motif matches the overall decorative scheme of the Calm Sea Palace so well that it is without doubt a surviving example of furniture from that building. The fact that it was made of the expensive timber *zitan* also indicates that it was not an object for export.[10]

It is tempting to speculate that the portrait of one of Qianlong's concubines, Rongfei (d. 1788), also known as the 'Fragrant Concubine', once hung on the walls alongside the French tapestries (plate 26.1). The portrait is attributed to Castiglione because it is done in oil, a medium in which very few Chinese court artists excelled. The skilful treatment of the metal armour that the sitter wears is also a hallmark of the Italian master. This favourite Uyghur concubine of Qianlong came from the Kiramet family in eastern Turkestan. When another Muslim family rebelled against the Qing court in 1757, Rongfei's family sided with the Qing troops to suppress the uprising. For their loyalty the Kiramets were handsomely rewarded, and in 1760 Rongfei became an imperial concubine.[11] There is no evidence that she took part in any military action. A portrait of her wearing a suit of western male armour could be intended as recognition of her family's bravery. It could also be a manifestation of Qianlong's attitude towards women.

It would have been improper for Qianlong to show any personal preference of the qualities he admired in women. On the other hand, it is almost certain that he would have heard about European women – their behaviour as well as their appearance – from the Jesuits. Did Qianlong harbour a secret desire to see Chinese women lead a less sedate life? In a male-dominated society such as China there did exist – and very popular they were too – stories of exceptionally courageous women going to battle disguised as men.[12] Men did not feel threatened while such super female beings existed in another place, or another time. The fact that Rongfei was a Uyghur would have made it easier for Qianlong

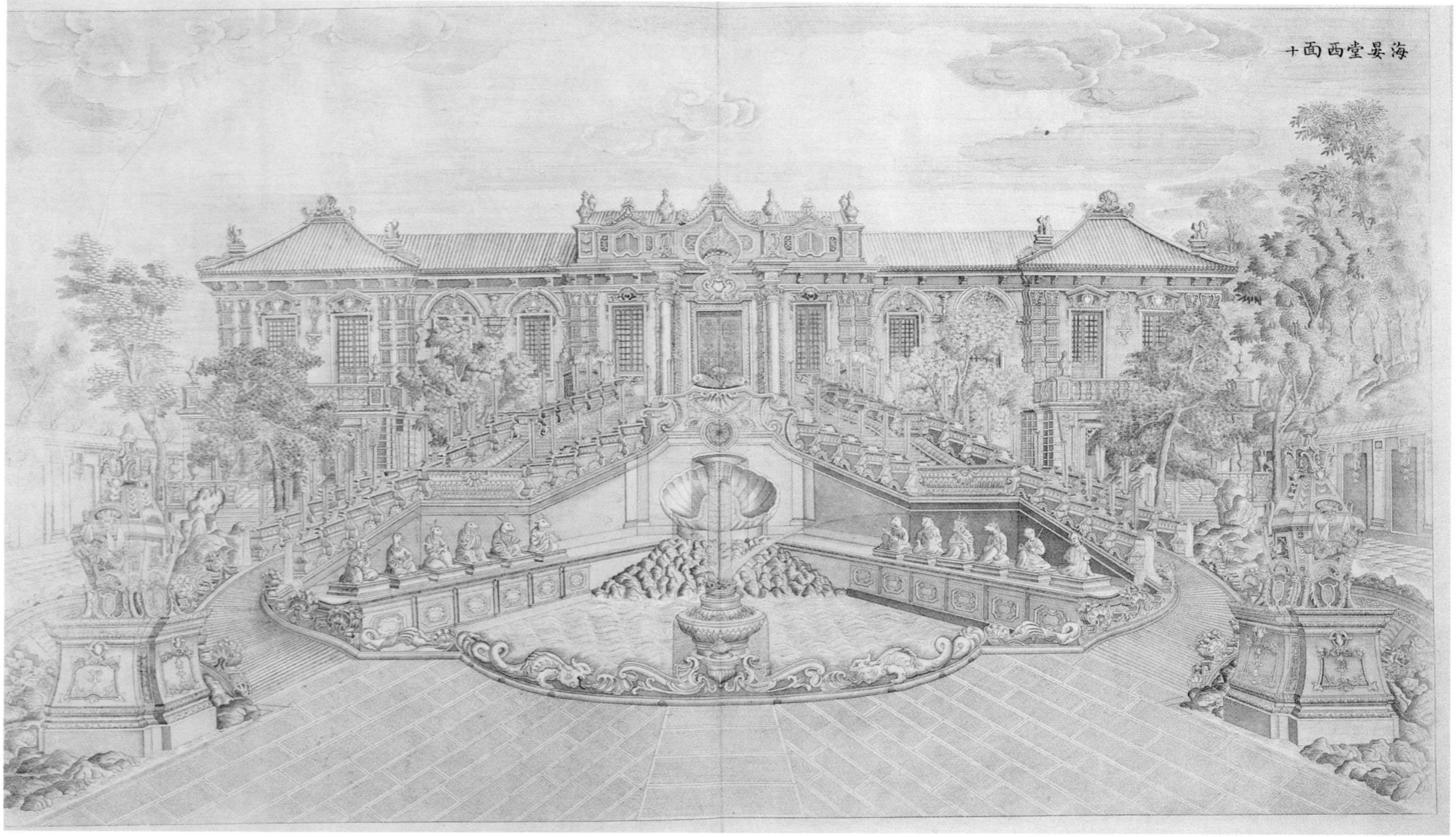
海晏堂西面十

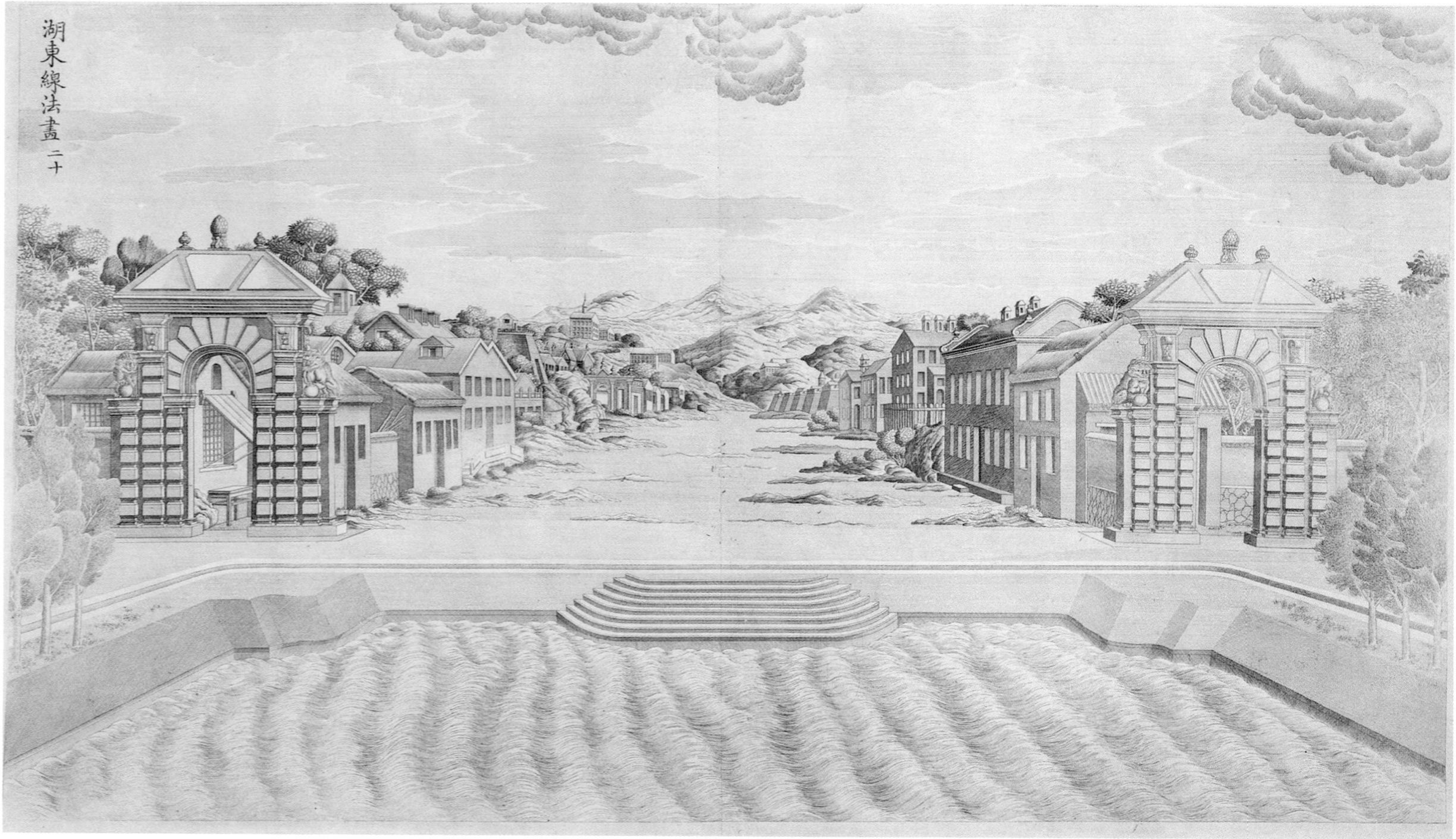
湖東線法畫二十

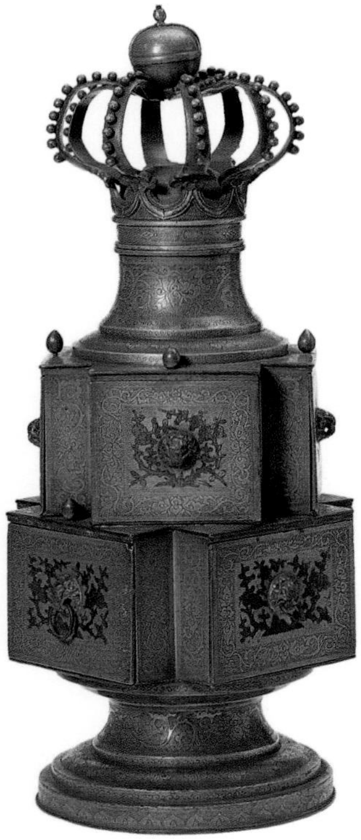

26.8
Treasure box

Pewter, inlaid with brass
China, *c.*1800

V&A 1454–1903

to express such an unconventional sentiment. Outside the court, the Canton scholar Qu Dajun (1630–96) revealed a similar lack of unease when he wrote about the Portuguese women in Macao:

> Women occupy an important position. They manage the family finance and inherit their fathers' properties ... Men are not allowed to have extra-marital relationships. Those who commit such crime are executed without mercy. If a woman is desired by the head priest and bears the head priest's son, the child is called 'god's son' and considered extremely important ... Once a Portuguese woman got herself a Chinese husband. Later the Chinese man wanted to leave [Macao], so the Portuguese woman secretly stained his face black and curled his hair. That man became a true foreigner.[13]

It should be pointed out that the above extract is taken from a serious work, not a fiction designed to provide cheap thrills. Qu was apparently misinformed, but he was not making up stories. Elsewhere in the book he spoke of 'Dutchmen playing musical instruments with metallic strings'. Qu was curious enough to go on board a Dutch ship to gain first-hand experience; thus he did not seem to be a xenophobe. Regrettably, if he found music from metallic strings more appealing than music coming from Chinese silk strings, he made no mention of it, as it would have been out of place to write about personal preferences in an information-gathering book.

Equally, it is tempting to speculate that European goods and customs influenced the tastes of the numerous *hong* merchants who interacted regularly with European supercargoes in Canton. It is difficult to prove that this was the case, largely because there are so few pre-1800 European consumer goods surviving in China today. There is also a convention of indiscriminately sweeping all Chinese products with a trace of western influence into the category of 'Chinese export art', a classification that clouds our understanding of Chinese consumerism. For example, because many Coromandel screens have been found in European palaces and country houses, they have usually been treated as Chinese export items. A long inscription on the reverse of one screen, however, reveals that it was specially commissioned as a birthday present for a high-ranking official in Canton (see plate 16.6). A second example is a large bowl that once belonged to the *hong* merchant Wu Bingjian (1769–1843), better known in the West as Howqua. The bowl is painted with European figures and Near Eastern buildings, and for reasons unknown it found its way into an American collection.[14] The mark on the base of the bowl, reading 'Wu family collection, Garden of Ten Thousand Pines', was overlooked ('Ten Thousand Pines' being the name of Howqua's garden). The bowl changed hands several times, no doubt as one of millions of Chinese export porcelains.

One of the most spectacular expressions of Chinese fantasy is a pewter vessel with a crown-shaped finial (plate 26.8). Chinese emperors did not wear crowns, so to a Chinese, a crown was as exotic as a dragon robe was to a European. The vessel is in fact a Chinese treasure box with western decoration. The Chinese elite, the Qianlong emperor included, commissioned treasure boxes in which they stored small valuable objects such as jades, jewellery, ancient bronzes, miniature scrolls, seals and other toys. The boxes are so skilfully crafted that the compartments are hardly discernible, which is why they are also known as 'secret boxes'. Unfortunately nothing is known about the person who commissioned the vessel, or the date of its manufacture. It is certainly not an export item, since an article of such shape would serve no purpose in a European home. The crown conforms to a German heraldic prototype,[15] but none of the principalities that constituted Germany had a strong commercial presence in Guangzhou in the eighteenth century, although this did not prevent them from ordering export goods (see plate 17.10). The relevant point here is that the *hong* merchants in Canton would have been exposed to all kinds of European patterns and designs. Just as Howqua had chosen to own a bowl decorated with European figures, so an unidentified *hong* merchant might decide to make a treasure box with an exotic appearance. He probably did not know the crown was German, nor may he have cared. Without a documented provenance or other form of evidence, such as an inscription on the pewter box, it has to be admitted that the present attribution is only a guess, but hopefully an informed one. For while Europeans wrote enthusiastically about Oriental curiosities in their diaries and correspondence, the Chinese considered such whimsical products too trivial to mention.

26.9
Chair

Zitan, carved
China (Qing court), c.1759

Palace Museum, Beijing

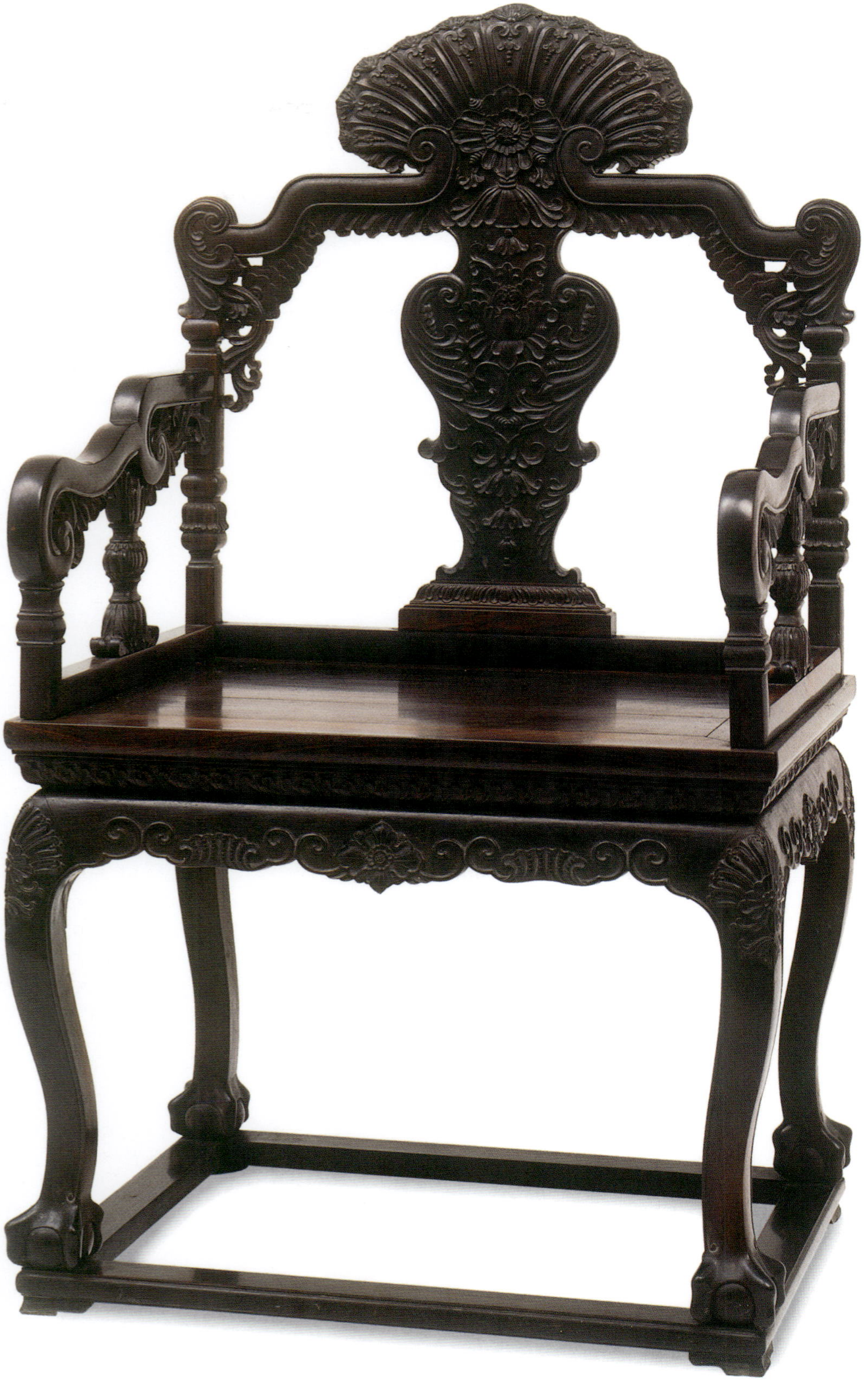

27

EUROPEAN FANTASIES OF ASIA

Steven Parissien

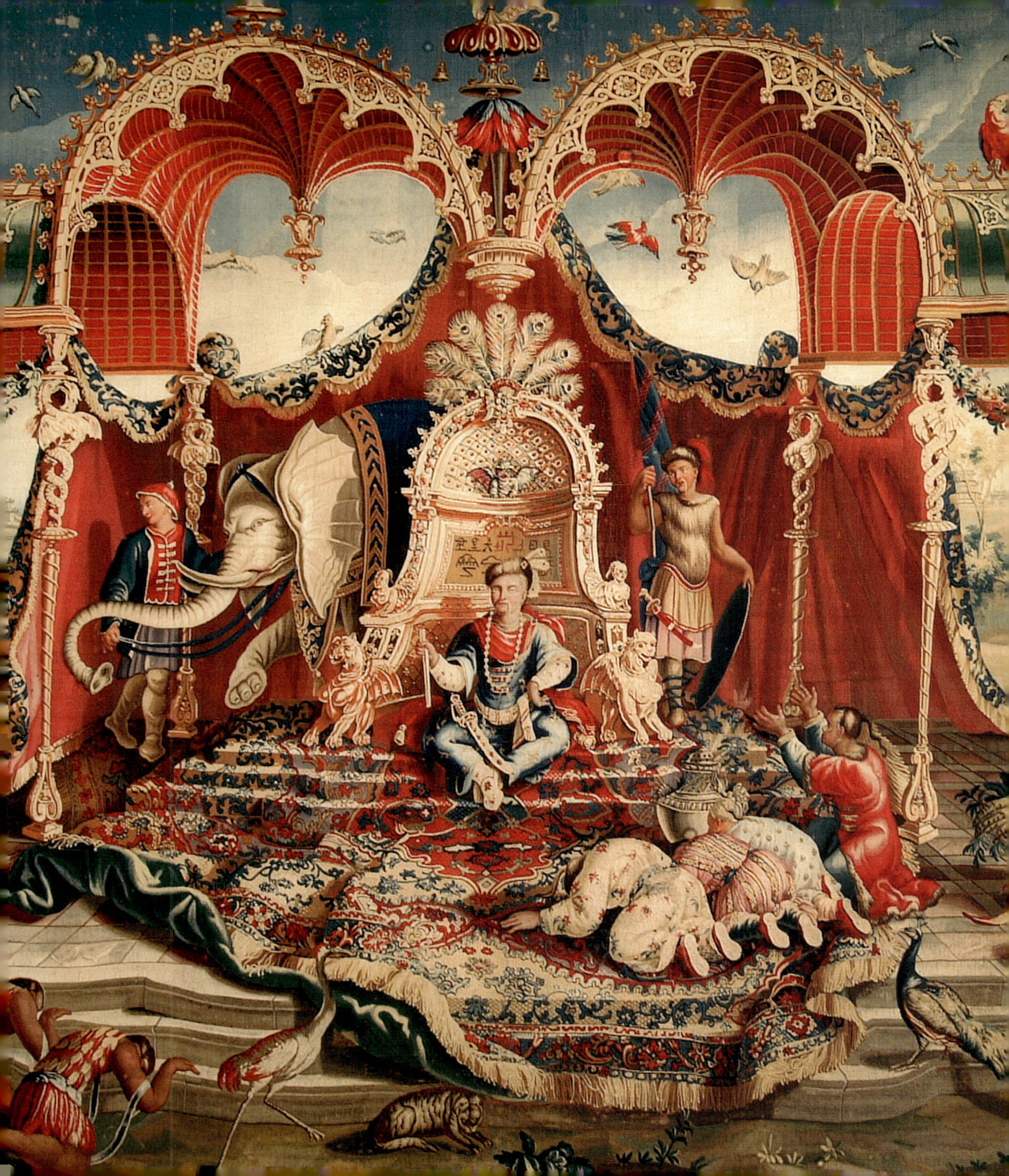

27.1 previous page
The Audience
Tapestry from the series *The Story of the King of China;* woven under the direction of Philippe Béhagle, manufactory director; after designs by Guy-Louis Vernansal, Jean-Baptiste Monnoyer and Jean-Baptiste Belin de Fontenay

Wool and silk, France (Beauvais manufactory), 1690–1705

Ranger's House, Greenwich

As trade links with Asia improved during the seventeenth century, even middle-class Europeans became more familiar with household luxuries brought from the East. Notionally, the fruits of these commercial connections also bred familiarity with eastern landscapes and lifestyles. Ceramics, wallpaper, screens and printed textiles imported into Europe frequently bore painted or printed scenes of what purported to be everyday life in both the Near and Far East. The burgeoning fashion for the East was satisfied not only by these imports but also by locally made pieces inspired by them. This style, known as 'chinoiserie', found its most elaborate manifestations in the early eighteenth century, when prominent European dynasties indulged in their own fanciful recreations of what approximated to eastern environments.

However, such constructions never ventured beyond the realm of fantasy. While blue-and-white porcelain from China was a familiar sight on mantel shelves by 1700, its owners rarely evinced any knowledge of, or indeed any genuine interest in, the realities of life in the Far East. Similarly, while incursions into the Indian subcontinent by European powers increased in number and ambition during the eighteenth century, for the most part these did not prompt a greater appreciation of South or East Asian culture beyond a narrowly mercantile understanding of trading opportunities. The Asians responsible for the exotic imports remained an unknown quantity to most in the West, their homelands far-away countries about which most Europeans preferred to know nothing.

This essay examines the apparent contradiction between the popularity of Asian decorative and applied arts during this period and Europe's reluctance to take the East seriously as a political or cultural reality. The West's obsession with Chinese and Japanese porcelain from the late seventeenth century onwards, the celebrated *Porzellanzimmern* of early eighteenth-century Europe, the short-lived 'Chinese' craze of mid-Georgian Britain – all these phenomena were markedly superficial in execution, with Asian forms or concepts being happily grafted onto western models. Initially conceived as manifestations of a decidedly aristocratic or plutocratic taste,[1] all were predicated on the concept of Asia as a romantic, amusing and, most significantly, passive and unthreatening stereotype.

For most Europeans in the seventeenth and eighteenth centuries the Orient remained very much, to use Edward Said's term, 'a Western projection'.[2] It was a fantasy principally conjured by the northern Europeans who constituted the principal foreign powers in the East after 1600. And its lure became particularly strong at the end of the seventeenth century. By 1700 the craze for Indian objects (particularly in Britain and France) and for all things Siamese (in France), and the Sinomania that enveloped much of northern and central Europe, proved a marked influence on the development of the aristocratic domestic interior.[3] Yet this interest was never particularly academic in its expression. Goods from all these Oriental sources 'were assigned random attributions in a spirit of topographical indifference', with differing pieces and contrasting colours being displayed 'towering and clustering on cabinets and chimneypieces [in] quite un-eastern fashion'.[4]

The sudden explosion of interest in the East was, as has been shown, fuelled by the ambitions of the East India Companies and the expanding commercial horizons of the European maritime nations from which they sprang. And it was a fashion that became particularly noticeable in the 1680s. During this decade numerous silver chinoiserie pieces were made in Europe – executed by different makers but, Charles Oman has speculated, guided by a single engraver well acquainted with Chinese design.[5] At the same time, the import of hand-painted Chinese wallpapers, Chinese porcelain and Indian fabrics into western Europe increased significantly. The surge in interest in Oriental porcelain in turn encouraged the wealthiest dynasties on the continent to concoct fabulous 'Porcelain Rooms' within their existing homes. The Santos Palace in Lisbon was even provided with a ceiling clad in Ming blue-and-white.[6] Further down the social scale, the market for imitative Delftware expanded considerably during the 1680s, as did that for Rouen faience, directly inspired by Imari wares from both Japan and China.

Predictably this flood of imports caused consternation for many European businesses. Thus the explosion in the import of Indian textiles during the 1680s encouraged the French in 1686, and the British in 1701, to prohibit the import of Indian chintz in order to protect their native silk industries. These attempts only succeeded in the short term and could not suppress the rising interest in eastern-styled goods. By 1719 the silk weavers of Spitalfields in the East End of London were rioting in protest against Indian textile imports and ripping the dresses from any women they encountered wearing Indian calicoes (see p. 270). European manufacturers retorted by developing '*soieries bizarres*', locally made fabrics greatly influenced by the exotic plants and almost abstract motifs of Indian textiles.

In the ensuing decades, ground-breaking works such as Engelbert Kaempfer's *History of Japan* (first published in English in 1727, and subsequently translated into French and Dutch) helped to inspire the emerging porcelain works of Meissen and Chantilly, the wallpaper manufacturers of London and Paris, and the tapestry works of Gobelin and Beauvais. And by the 1720s the French were beginning to publish formulae that could supposedly guarantee the production of eastern-style lacquer and porcelain.

The sudden increase in enthusiasm for the Orient during this period can of course be attributed to factors other than Europe's mercantile avarice – including the spread of Huguenot craftsmen, many of whom were pioneering the use of eastern motifs, across Protestant Europe in the wake of the repeal of the Edict of Nantes in 1685; or Mary II's introduction into the English court of her passion for collecting Chinese and Japanese blue-and-white.[7] The demand for eastern luxury goods or their home-grown imitations, however, can at least partly be traced to an important psychological factor: the perceived diminution and neutering of the East as a military threat, and its consequent repackaging as a passive, indolent and benign artistic influence.

The principal catalyst for this dramatic change in western attitudes occurred in 1683. The Ottoman empire had for centuries represented that part of the East with which Europe was most familiar – and by which it was most terrified. Until the late seventeenth century, Europeans constantly believed themselves to be under threat from the Turks' territorial ambitions, with the Ottoman empire being cast as merely the latest in a centuries-old series of brutal eastern invaders. The failure of the Turks' Siege of Vienna in 1683, however, was followed by a complete collapse of Ottoman power in eastern Europe. The Ottoman army suffered a crushing defeat at Mohacs in 1687, losing all of Hungary; Belgrade fell to the Austrians and their allies in 1688; and the empire was ultimately forced to conclude the humiliating Treaties of Karlowitz in 1699 and Passarowitz in 1718, which ejected the Turks from most of their eastern European territories. Sixty years later the diminished status of the Ottoman empire was further underlined by the Treaty of Kutchuk-Kainardji of 1774, which imposed even more drastic territorial forfeits on the impotent Turks.

The humbling of Ottoman power at the eastern frontiers of Europe in the 1680s was, interestingly, paralleled by the crumbling of Mughal hegemony in India. By 1690 the Mughal empire was internally riven, and was on the road to collapse after the death of the Emperor Aurangzeb in 1707. By 1717 the rebellious Jats of Rajasthan were raiding the suburbs of the imperial capital, Delhi, while in 1739 the Persians under Nadir Shah successfully invaded India, defeating the Emperor Muhammad Shah Rangila (r. 1719–48) at Karnaul, emptying the treasury and returning home with the famed 'Peacock Throne'.[8] China, too seemed to be weakening,

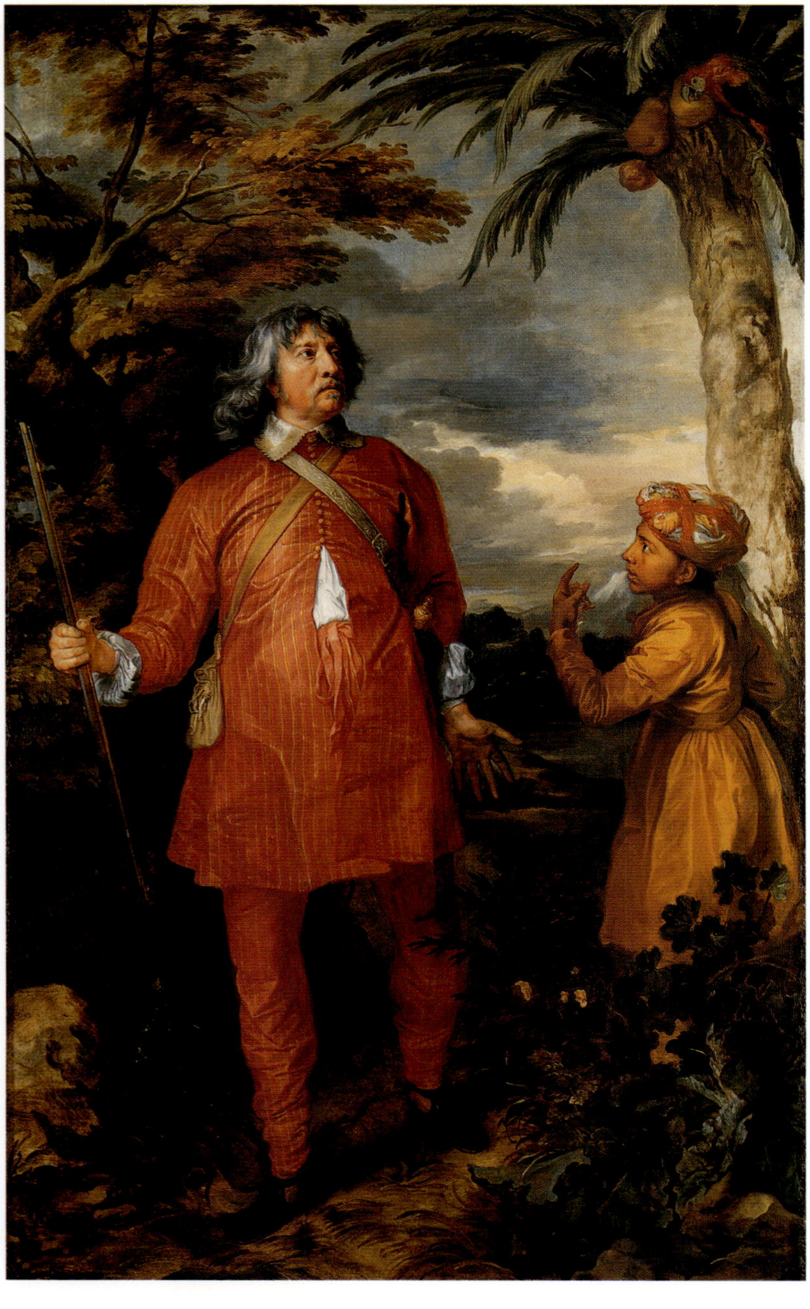

27.2
The Earl of Denbigh
Sir Anthony Van Dyck
England, 1631
National Gallery, London

27.3 opposite
Omai
Sir Joshua Reynolds
Oil on canvas
England (London), 1774
National Portrait Gallery, London

following the long decline of the Ming dynasty (which finally ended in 1644) and the power vacuum created by its fall.[9]

While such imperial withdrawals did not have the psychological impact on the West that the revelation of Ottoman dotage had prompted, they nevertheless helped to raise European confidence regarding commercial and military prospects in the East. Far from posing a threat to western trading aspirations, for example, India in the eighteenth century became a battleground for the European powers themselves. Thus Britain and France were engaged in three protracted bouts over the mastery of the subcontinent after 1740, with the Mughal emperor relegated to the position of an irrelevant doge.

The newly impotent East soon became the subject of popular fiction. Thus, while western works dating from before the Siege of Vienna, such as Hagdron's *Aeyquan* of 1670, Elkanah Settle's *The Conquest of China by the Tartars* of 1676 and John Dryden's *Aureng-Zebe* (also of 1676), portrayed powerful, virile and occasionally merciless eastern empires, by the 1740s most writers took their cue from Thomas Guelette's hugely influential *Moguel Tales* of 1736 – the original basis for the countless retellings of *A Thousand and One Nights*. Guelette's stories were of passive romance rather than aggressive conquest and featured 'a fairyland of stock exotica, where characters use elusive and quaintly overblown rhetoric and employ magic and enchantment liberally'.[10] The association of the East with escapist magic was indeed to permeate western culture throughout the eighteenth century, from Guelette to Mozart's *Magic Flute*, first performed in 1791.

Apparently politically neutered, the East was now considered by Europeans a topic suitable for adapting as a decorative subject for domestic interiors. In these contexts the Orient was pictured as a harmless, picturesque and sometimes magical idyll whose inhabitants were invariably languid, melancholic and indolent, and governed largely by primitive religious obsessions and the excessive consumption of hallucinogens. Despite the imputation of cultural decadence, however, eastern figures as portrayed in western chinoiseries were often strangely androgynous, indicating a European apathy towards individual identities.[11] China became, in western eyes, 'a haven of leisure and luxury, peopled by the gay Chinese of the porcelains who lived in beautiful gardens filled with rounded bridges, temples with curved eaves from which hung tinkling bells, and pagodas stretching skywards'.[12] The Orientals whom François Boucher (1703–70) painted were invariably 'charming and faintly erotic', while in many of his scenes 'the activities of its inhabitants involved nothing more arduous than the playing of weird musical instruments, carrying birds in bamboo cages, and dallying among their fishing tackle or tea-trays' (plate 27.4).[13] For Boucher and his contemporaries, stereotypical images of Chinese – with their long queues, their voluminous sleeves and their strange hats – 'were only reproduced to make people laugh or smile'. What these designers sought to create was a light-hearted fiction, using Asia as an exotic backdrop, innately 'brittle, beautiful and frivolous', which encouraged spectators to suspend disbelief at the drop of a conical hat.[14]

Significantly, the fishing party – a simple, passive and emphatically un-warlike activity – became a favourite theme for chinoiserie designers in the West.[15] Alternatively, eastern landscapes were simply emptied of people and filled with birds and animals – preferably monkeys: diminished, comic semi-humans whose exoticism connoted a wider and geographically vaguer sense of overseas 'other'. Thus was the East tamed and domesticated into an idiom of 'meandering informality' ideally suited to western rococo design.[16]

This shift in the perception of eastern cultures in the late seventeenth and early eighteenth centuries is paralleled in three of the most celebrated Early

27.4
Le Jardin Chinois (detail)
Jean-François Picon after François Boucher
Wool and silk tapestry, c.1750–70
Musée Nissim de Camondo, Paris

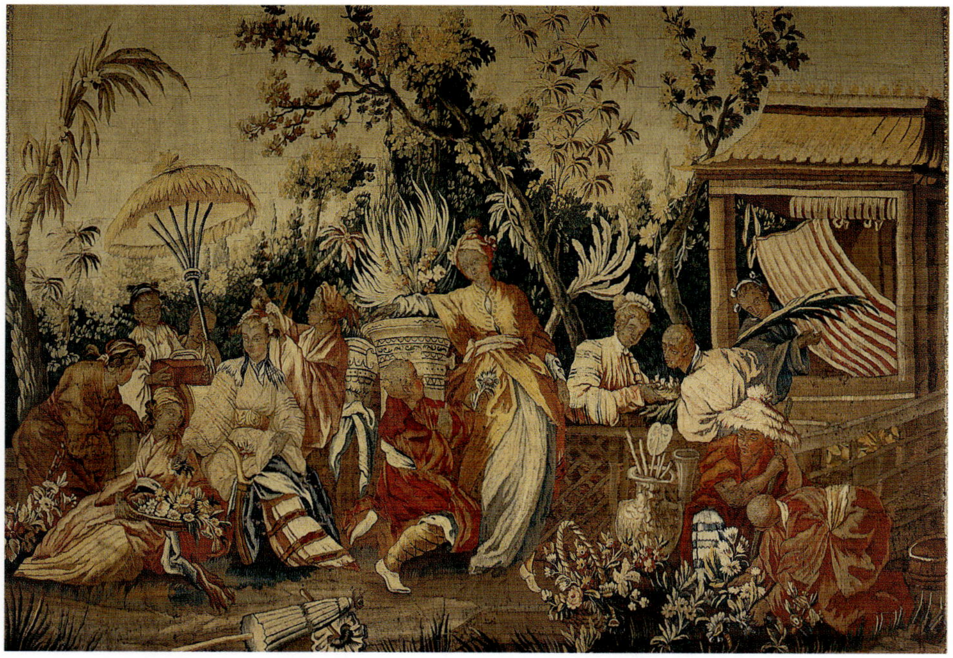

Modern depictions of figures in an eastern context. *The Earl of Denbigh* by Anthony Van Dyck (1599–1641), of 1632–33, clad Denbigh, who had travelled to India as a semi-official ambassador for Charles I in 1631–32, in a fabulous pink silk jacket of the sort then worn by Europeans in India. He gazes in wonderment at the landscape but, nevertheless, is armed with a flintlock. Denbigh is both wary and surprised, and Van Dyck underlines the otherness and implied danger of the East by literally splitting his painting into two worlds, limiting European flora and fauna to the left-hand side and their eastern equivalents to the right (plate 27.2).[17] In sharp contrast is the relaxed familiarity of Captain Foote, as painted by Joshua Reynolds (1723–92) 130 years later, in 1761 (see plate 12.3). Unlike Denbigh, Foote is wearing Mughal court dress 'made of fine Indian muslin, with very long sleeves'.[18] This is possibly a *khil'at,* a ceremonial robe of honour presented to Foote by an Indian ruler and worn by him as a mark of submission or incorporation. However, the expression Reynolds gives the captain is far from being that of a vassal; Foote's confident air instead suggests Britain's recent military success in India – and, perhaps, conquests to come . The idea of a domesticated, westernized Oriental was later celebrated by Reynolds in his full-length portrait of *Omai*, painted in 1776 (plate 27.3). The Tahitian was dressed by Reynolds in his native robes, yet posed in the manner of the Apollo Belvedere, a decidedly Eurocentric reference. Reynolds's *Omai* was certainly no martial threat; indeed, quite the reverse: 'What set Omai apart from the earlier [exotic] visitors was that he seemed to possess an innate sense of what were perceived as civilized values.'[19]

The psychological demilitarizing of the East was crucial in forming eighteenth-century European views of Oriental exoticism and its decorative and literary potential. It encouraged Daniel Defoe's celebrated diatribe against the Chinese in the second part of his *Robinson Crusoe* of 1719, in which China's decaying military and commercial power was compared unfavourably to the might of the maritime powers.[20] But not all eighteenth-century Europeans saw the East as innately decadent or corrupt. By the 1730s many of the emerging French *philosophes* were using the concept of China to critique their own political system. This was not a new idea; Pierre Bayle had exploited the notion of Chinese spiritual tolerance (of which he actually knew next to nothing) as early as 1685, to attack Louis XIV's brutal

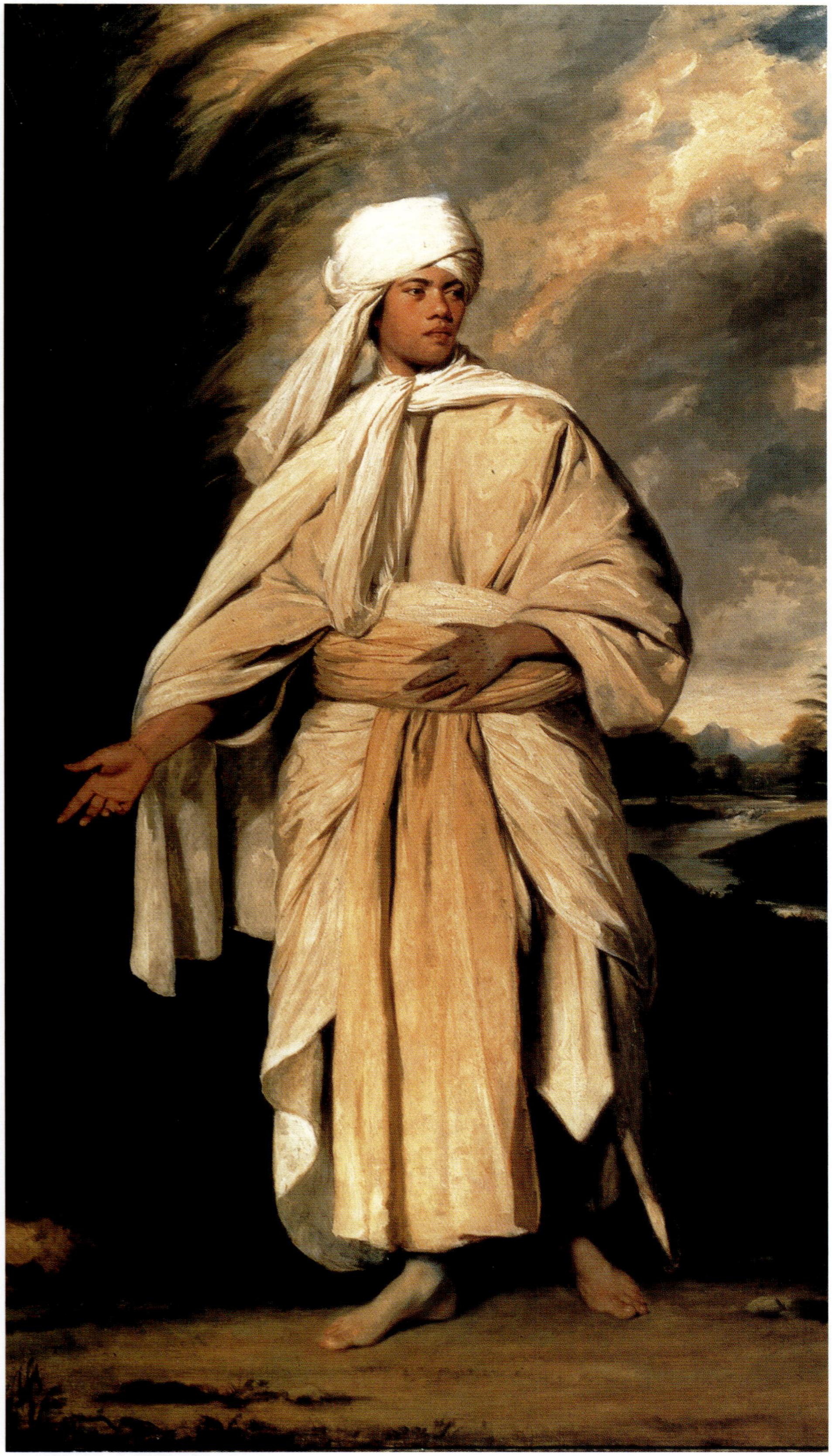

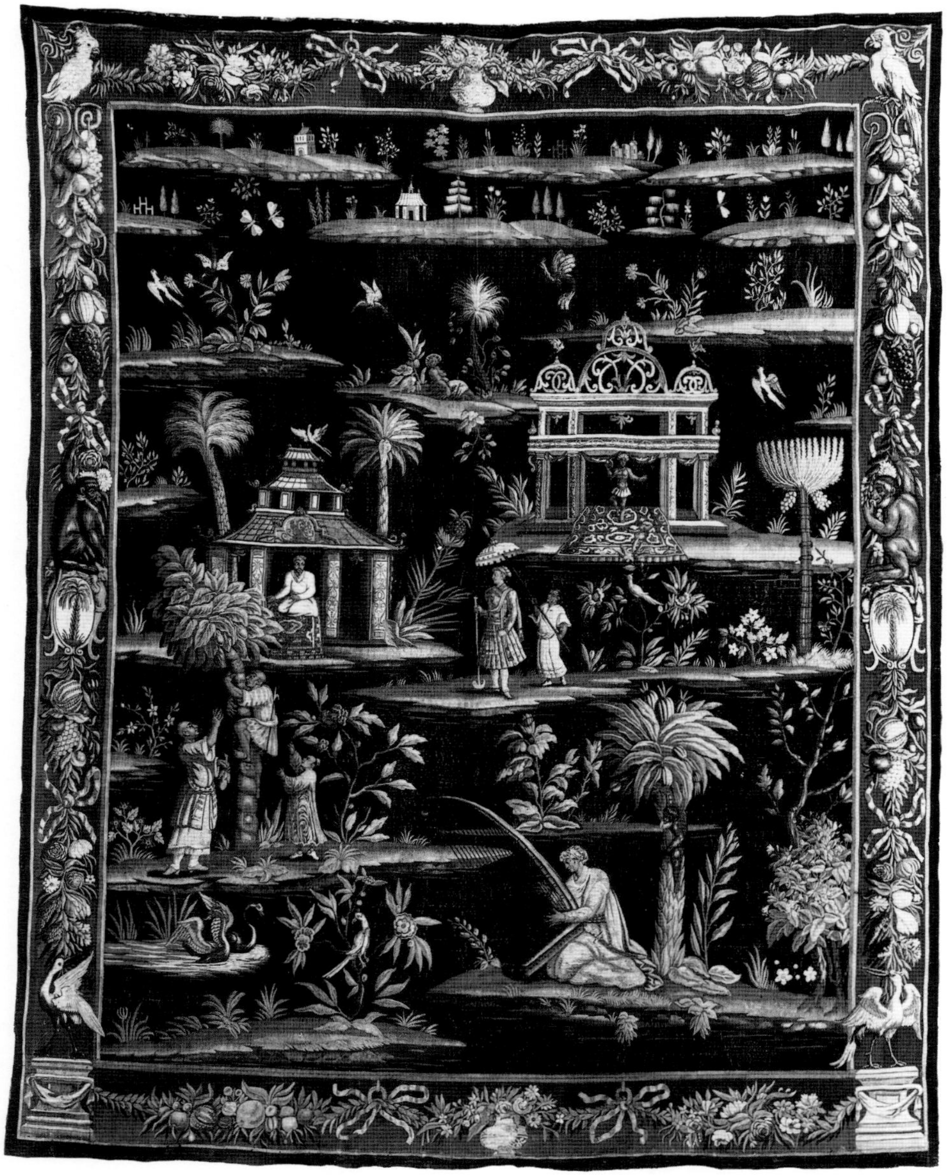

27.5
The Promenade

Wool and silk tapestry
England, late 17th–early 18th century

Yale University Art Gallery

27.6 opposite
The Pagoda

From William Chambers, *Plans, Elevations... at Kew*, London, 1763

V&A: National Art Library

revocation of the Edict of Nantes. Sixty years later Voltaire, following the examples of Diderot and Helvétius, used political and social myths emanating from the East to critique European customs in works such as *L'Orphelia de la Chine* of 1755 and *Essai sur les Moeurs* of 1765, the last of which argued for the inherent superiority of Chinese moral philosophy. Oliver Goldsmith did much the same thing – rather more good-humouredly – in *The Citizen of the World* of 1762.

However, as recent commentators have pointed out, there were always 'strong elements of projection and wishful thinking in [the *philosophes*'] accounts' of China, which originated only through 'Jesuit-filtered images of China' and were interpreted by the French 'in the light of Enlightenment ideas, and as reflecting their own political philosophy and utopian image of a transformed Europe'.[21] By the 1770s, following the expulsion of Christian missionaries from China (an act that served to distance East and West still further), many *philosophes* were actually disowning their former enthusiasm for the East. Rousseau's novel *Julie, ou la Nouvelle Héloïse* of 1761 had already depicted China as an irrevocably flawed civilization, declaring of the Chinese that 'there is no sin to which they are not proud'[22] in language remarkably similar to that soon to be used by western Europeans to connote the failing Ottoman empire.[23] Diderot, too, renounced his earlier Sinomania, 'substituting the idea of the Noble Savage as the ideal for Europe to follow'.[24] This was also true of the German philosopher Friedrich Grimm, who in 1776 declared that China was, after all, an unenlightened despotism, little different to the other decayed and decadent empires of the Orient.

Regarding the East as something remote and easily dismissed relieved designers and craftsmen of the need to be 'authentic' in their reinterpretation of the exotic. Invariably, then, eastern motifs and messages became deliberately jumbled in the hands of their western interpreters, and were cited with little care or concern about social or pictorial realities. Some 'no longer necessarily held an automatic eastern connotation'[25] at all; they were there simply to represent 'exotica' and an impression of 'otherness'. Thus Chantilly porcelain of the 1730s combined sculpted representations of 'Chinese' figures with images from Indian textiles and rococo modelling after Juste-Aurèle Meissonnier (1695–1750), while almost everything in the 'Chinese' scenes painted by Jean-Antoine Watteau (1684–1721)

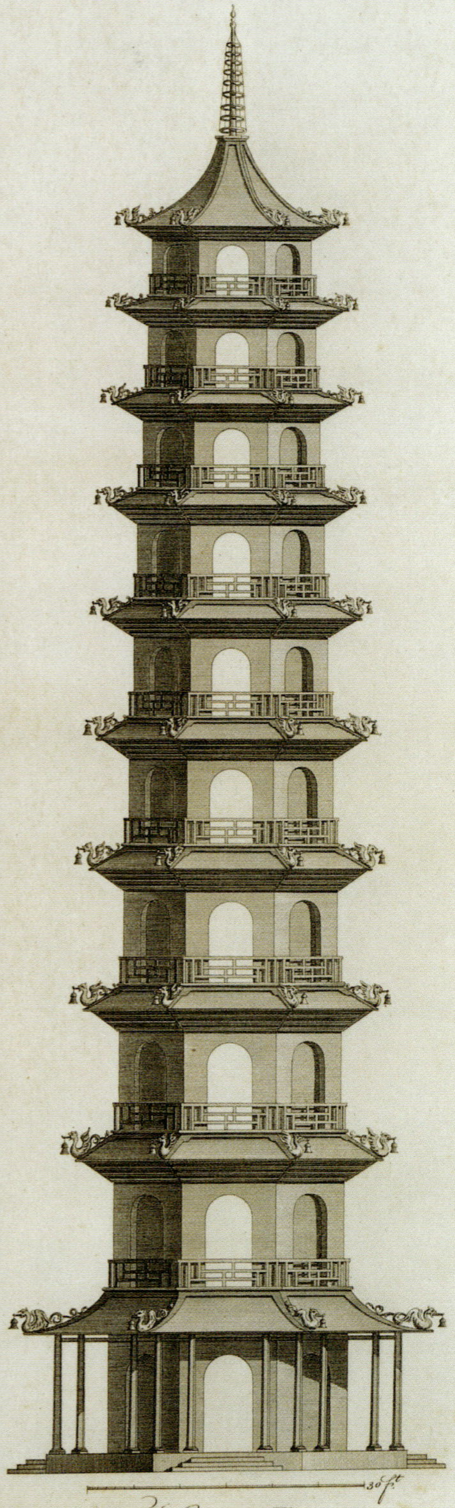

Elevation of The Great Pagoda as first Intended

W. Chambers Architectus — T. Miller sculp.

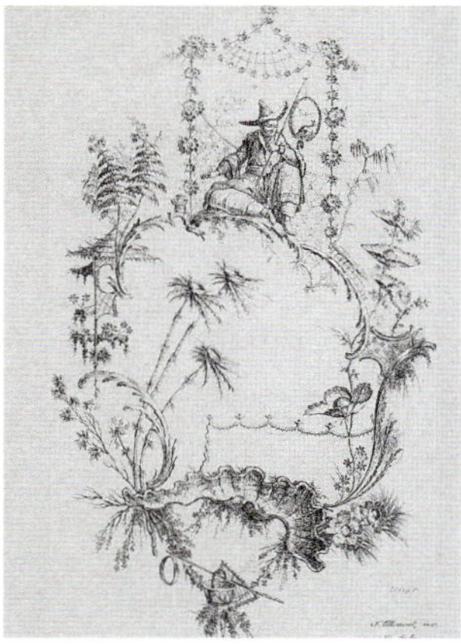

27.7
Page from *A New Book of Chinese Ornaments*
Jean-Baptiste Pillement

Etching on paper
London, 1755

V&A: 28639d

27.8
The Chinese Teahouse, Sans Souci, Potsdam, 1757

Stiftung Preussische Schlösser und Garten, Berlin-Brandenburg

in the 1710s was European in origin – 'the composition, the anatomy, the faces of the figures, the shading, the geometry of the ornaments and the technique'.[26] London wallpaper manufacturers who were advertising 'Japan' papers by the 1750s were in truth marketing a *mélange* of Chinese, Indian and western designs. Chinese wallpaper manufacturers in their turn were cannily flexible in adapting their product for western uses, often supplying extra papers from which 'birds and branches could be cut … and pasted over damaged or discoloured areas, used to fill awkward corners, or simply to embellish the overall effect'.[27] Meanwhile, the new British chinoiserie papers of the mid-eighteenth century – based on comfortingly repetitive, hand-blocked patterns – confined and reduced Chinese compositions for the average Georgian home, making eastern conventions far more easily digestible for western walls. At the same time, Thomas Chippendale (1718–79), in his *Gentleman and Cabinet Maker's Director* of 1754, happily mixed 'Chinese' with rococo and Gothick.

Craftsmen and designers working in the Oriental idiom, whatever the notional geographical inspiration for the piece, were happy to fill any spare space available with Asian stereotypes garnered from all over the continent – elephants, palm trees, monkeys, and so on. Thus the Gobelin series of tapestries *Les Tentures des Indes* of 1690 were 'Completely European in their perspective and composition [and] "Indian" only in so far as their subject matter depicted scenes of exotic luxuriance'; the celebrated Yale tapestries, woven in England for Elihu Yale in 1700, were a bizarre hybrid of Chinese and Indian motifs (plate 27.5); while many of the Beauvais chinoiserie tapestries of the early eighteenth century incorporated the celebrated Italian *commedia dell'arte* figures in Chinese contexts (plate 27.1).[28] Even Jean-

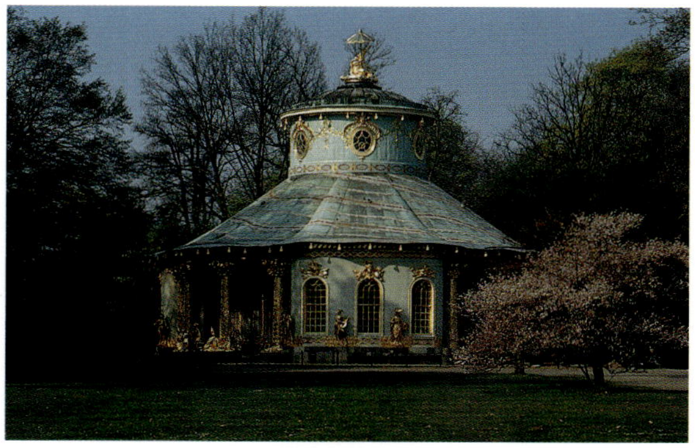

Antoine Fraisse, whose influential *Livre de dessins chinois* of 1735 tried far harder than its contemporaries to reflect actual eastern idioms and conventions, was still happy to combine Mughal and other Islamic motifs with Chinese and Japanese forms. Fraisse never went to the East himself, and even the opening of his book gave away his intrinsic lack of interest in stylistic accuracy – the title page revealing that Fraisse's images were inspired by material from Persia, India, China and Japan.[29] As a recent historian has noted, French chinoiserie of this nature was appreciated only when it was 'integrated into French surroundings, adding some strange seasoning' – an adaptation that, she argues, constitutes 'the very definition of exoticism'.[30]

Unlike Fraisse, the British architect William Chambers (1723–96) *did* travel to the East. Having joined the Swedish East India Company at the age of 16, he travelled at least twice to Canton (Guangzhou) during the 1740s. And at Kew Gardens after 1756, Chambers – under the direction of his powerful and ambitious patron, the Earl of Bute – built two distinctive buildings taken from Chinese sources: the 'House of Confucius' and the Pagoda (plate 27.6). These structures were both far more 'Chinese' in conception than their contemporaries at Drottningholm in Sweden (the Chinese pavilion of 1753) and Potsdam in Prussia (the Chinese teahouse at Sans Souci of 1757) (plate 27.8). However, the Pagoda was inspired not by Chambers's Cantonese experiences, but by the Porcelain Tower of Nanking, as engraved in Nieuhoff's *An Embassy from the East India Company of the United Provinces to the … Emperor of China* of 1669. The same venerable source was also being used by the Boucher-designed Beauvais tapestries of the 1750s and '60s. It is surely instructive that Chambers and Boucher, like many of their fellow artists and craftsmen, preferred to use a century-old European source, rather than more recent scholastic research, to inform their vision of the East.[31] This does suggest a marked lack of intellectual curiosity on behalf of even the most enthusiastic practitioners of chinoiserie. In truth, neither of Chambers's 'Chinese' buildings at Kew was ever intended to be architecturally accurate. Rather, they were devised to form part of an exotic architectural theme park – a concept that embraced not only Chinese, neoclassical and Gothic structures, but also a 'Turkish' Mosque and a 'Moorish' Alhambra. The overall effect of the landscape at Kew was to reveal the vagueness and unconcern with which even

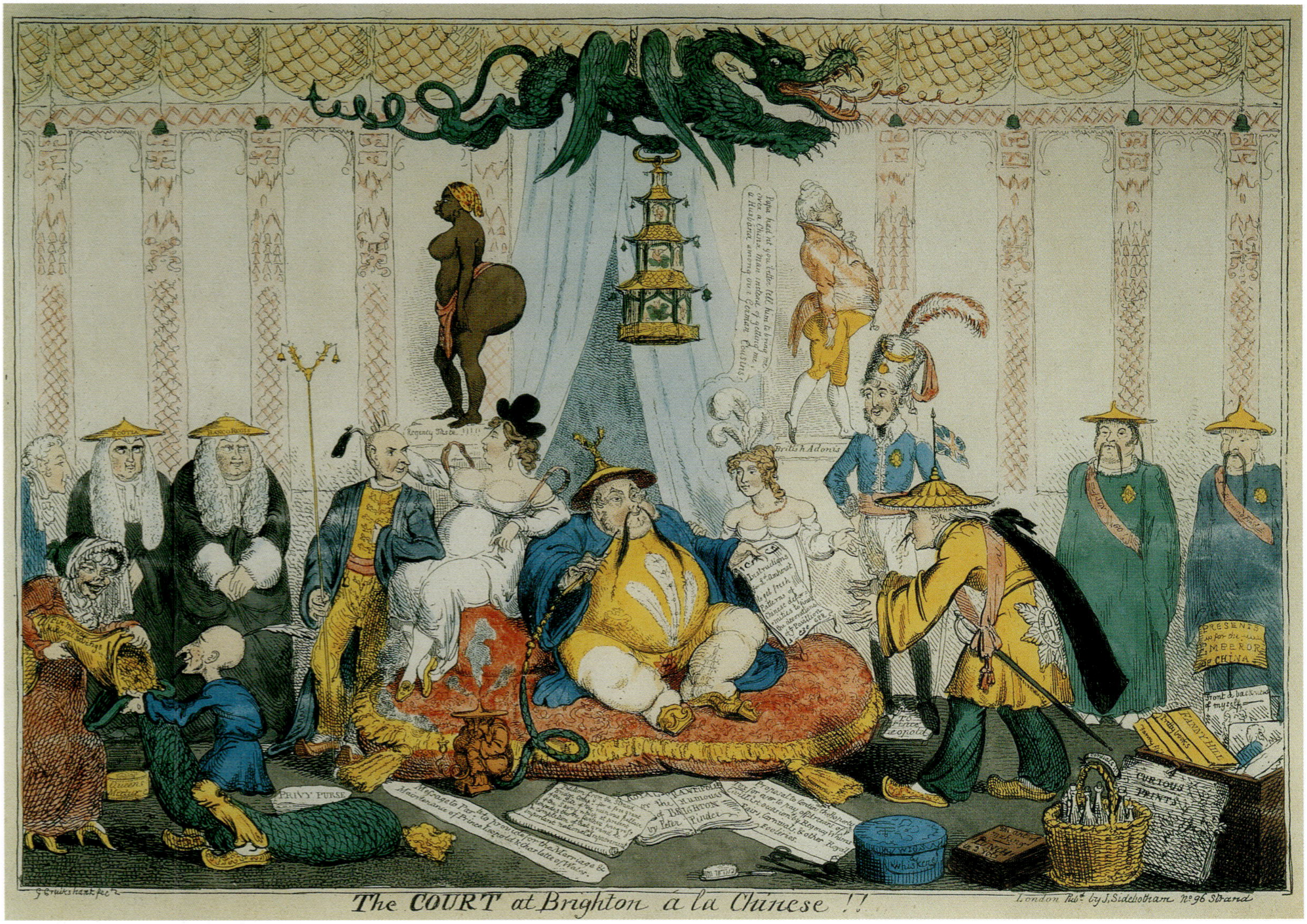

educated and informed Europeans regarded 'Asia'.[32] Rather than representing a genuine attempt to recreate an eastern environment, the buildings at Kew, together with Chambers's pompous pattern-book, *Designs of Chinese Buildings* of 1757, were intended more as a deliberate stylistic snub to the staid, foursquare Palladianism of the court of George II (r. 1727–60).[33] The so-called 'Anglo-Chinese Garden', which Chambers was instrumental in creating, had certainly evolved partly as a reaction against the formalism of the continent and of the early eighteenth-century sensibilities of George II and his staid court. However, even Chambers himself only had a vague grasp of the reality of Chinese landscape. As for the argument that the primacy of nature in imported Chinese wares helped to inaugurate the Romantic Revival of the late eighteenth century, native Gothic traditions were surely far more influential on the development of Romanticism than a transient fashion which, by the 1770s, had become generally discredited.

To designers such as Chambers, 'East' was a movable feast that could be adapted to accommodate all manner of interpretations of an exotic 'abroad'. It was also a construct that was invariably relegated to gardens or structures of relative unimportance. Chambers, though, was by no means the first designer to create such an eastern *mélange*. A decade before Kew, Henry Hoare began assembling an astonishing variety of stylistically themed garden buildings in his landscape at Stourhead, Wiltshire. Fifty years before that, Louis XIV had contemplated

27.9
The Court at Brighton à la Chinese
G. Cruickshank
Hand-coloured engraving on paper
England, 1816
Brighton Museums and Art Gallery

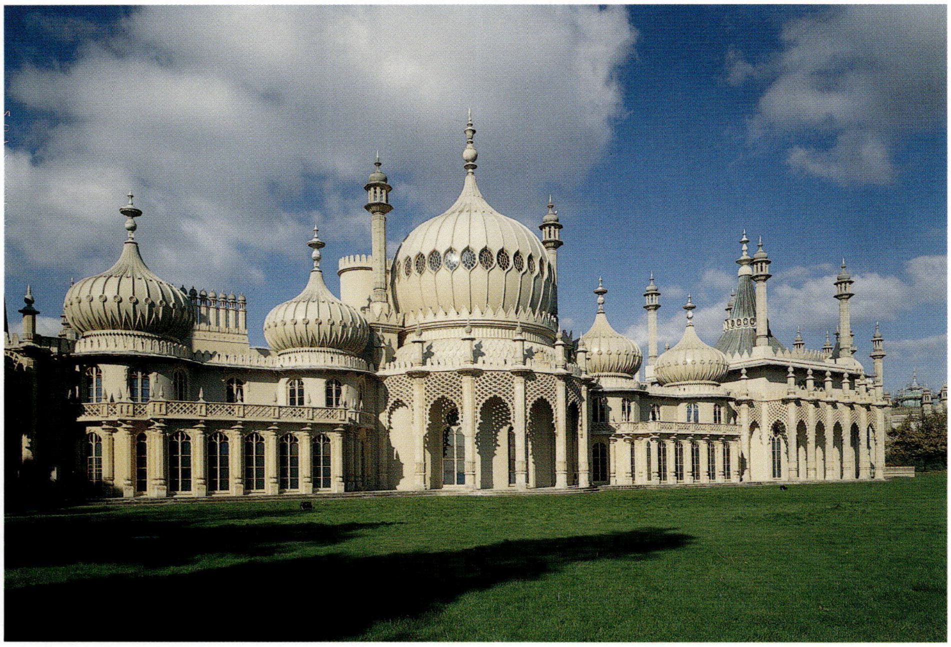

27.10
The east front of the Royal Pavilion, Brighton
John Nash

creating a sequence of rooms at Versailles in different styles – Indian, Chinese, Persian, and so on – in order to underline his 'mastery' of these exotic cultures. Most famously, Johann Dinglinger's astonishing silver centrepiece for Augustus the Strong of Saxony, *The Princely Household at Delhi on the Birthday of the Great Mogul Aurangzebe* of 1701–08 – an astonishing tour-de-force set with jewels and copious amounts of gilding – was intended as 'a glorious celebration of all that is fantastic, exotic and lavish of a partly imaginary East based on intermingled elements of Indian, Chinese, Japanese, Near Eastern and European styles' (see plate 16.24).[34] Revealingly, too, Augustus's own collection of Oriental porcelain was a haphazard accumulation rather than a discerning collection, displayed with no thought for the pieces' eastern purpose or meaning.[35]

Eurocentric imagery was particularly evident in the works of the greatest exponents and popularizers of chinoiserie in mid-eighteenth-century France: François Boucher and Jean-Baptiste Pillement (1728–1808) (plate 27.7). Boucher, as Michael Levey famously noted, happily presided over 'a sort of Cloud-Cuckoo China, with palm trees, doll-like people, feathery hats, and a mass of properties such as fans, parasols, guitars – suggesting a generalized, amusing exoticism'.[36] Even a recent defender of Boucher's chinoiseries has acknowledged that, however heavily the artist relied on genuine Chinese woodblock engravings, his finished designs still represented an 'assimilation of Chinese imagery for French markets'.[37] His 'eastern' scenes featured 'Europeans masquerading as orientals, "in the kind of blue-tinted landscapes that exist only in dreams"',[38] while his figures looked nothing like genuine Chinese. (Indeed, there were no extant studies of eastern physiognomy to fuel any such appreciation.[39])

Pillement's designs, though avowedly more academic in quoting directly from genuine Oriental sources such as Chinese and Japanese porcelain, were also significantly removed from the reality of the East. One recent commentator has noted how Pillement 'exaggerated the wispy, fragile qualities of the style ... as though the world was a fairyland conjured out of gossamer and stalks of grass'.[40] Such a fairyland could easily be dismissed by the West as a passive construct that implied no threat to European lifestyles or European ambitions. Graphic images, such as Chinamen wearing upside-down flowers instead of hats, transmuted what had, a century before, been popularly regarded as a warlike race into a set of harmless cartoon characters.

Only at the very end of the eighteenth century did European cultural attitudes to the East begin to change. Edward Said has defined this development as a move away from the 'appreciation' that characterized the seventeenth and eighteenth centuries towards the 'definition' of the nineteenth century, when 'there emerged a complex Orient suitable for study in the museum, or reconstruction in the colonial office'. William Jones's declaration of 17 August 1787 that 'it is my ambition to know India better than any other European ever knew it' (see pp. 124–5)[41] prefigured a new era of genuine interest in the culture and intellectual potential of the East. Yet William Jones (1746–94) and his contemporary Johann Gottfried Herder (1744–1803) were very much ahead of their time. Their Indophilia was only usefully developed during the nineteenth century, initially by a generation born in the heady, pre-revolutionary days of the 1770s and '80s.

Even at the close of the century, the chasm between East and West still seemed vast. After his embassy to China of 1793–94, British envoy Lord Macartney likened the country to 'an old crazy first-rate man-of-war', which had long overwhelmed her neighbours 'by her bulk and appearance', but was doomed under inept leaders to be 'dashed to pieces on the shore' (see pp. 95–6). Fear of the East had definitely been replaced by contempt – even in such a cultured mind as Macartney's.[42] Significantly, the artist who accompanied Macartney's expedition, William Alexander, 'made no attempt to contact Chinese counterparts or to acquire an understanding of their work' while in China.[43] Instead, Macartney's Britain still preferred the escapist fantasy of a tamed and languid Orient.[44]

Oriental escapism reached its zenith in the person and patronage of the Prince of Wales, later George IV (r. 1820–1830). It is significant that Chinese garb, and the Indo-Chinese architecture of the Brighton Pavilion, were frequently used by caricaturists as a shorthand for the prince's over-indulgence and corruption – vices interpreted by the British public as being inherently eastern (plate 27.9).[45] For the satirists, nothing better illustrated the remoteness of the heir to the throne from his subjects than the bizarre eastern confections of the Banqueting Room at the Prince's Brighton Pavilion, where copper dragons, Chinese vases and chinoiserie figures vied for attention and precedence (plate 27.11). Nevertheless, the Pavilion's bravura interiors, however glitteringly executed, proved a negligible influence on the design of the day. Instead, they merely provided a fitting coda for a century of domestic fantasy.

27.11
The Banqueting Room, Royal Pavilion, Brighton
From John Nash's *Views of the Royal Pavilion*, 1826
Brighton Museums and Art Gallery

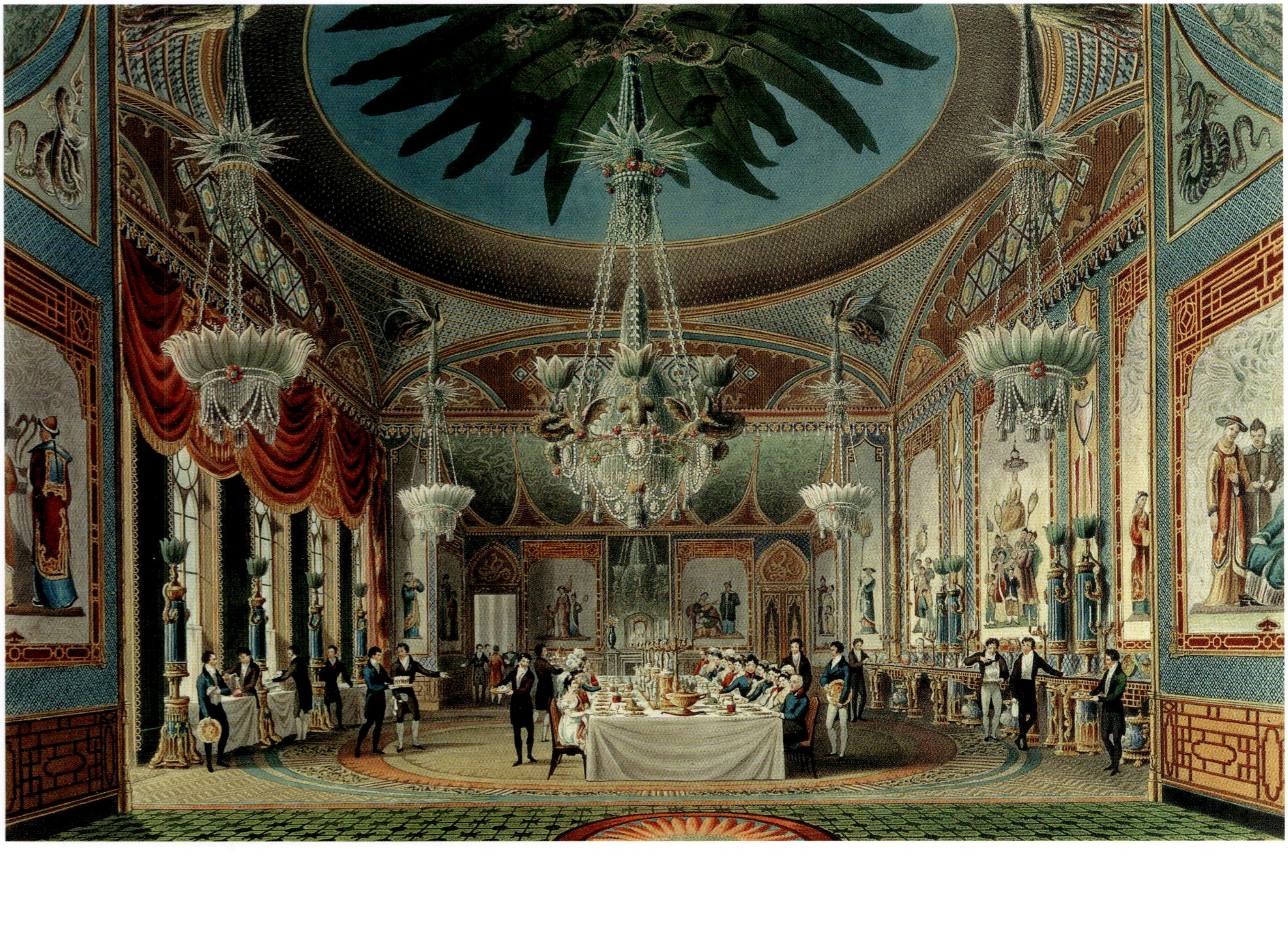

CHRONOLOGY

WORLD

1488
Portgeuse explorer Bartolomeu Dias rounds the Cape of Good Hope

1492
Christopher Columbus lands in the West Indies believing them to be outlying parts of Asia

1494
Treaty of Tordesillas divides the world between Spanish and Portuguese claims

1500
Voyage of Pedro Cabral to the East Indies. En route he lands in Brazil, initiating Portuguese control of the region

1519
Spanish conquistador Hernándo Cortes begins conquest of Aztec empire

1521
Juan Sebastian del Cano completes the voyage around the globe begun by Ferdinand Magellan in 1519

1531
Spanish conquest of the Inca empire begins

INDIA

1398–99
Mughal prince Timur (Tamerlane) invades India and sacks Delhi

1498
Portuguese led by Vasco da Gama reach the Malabar coast

1505
Francisco de Almeida sent out as first governor of the East Indies. During his tenure he establishes forts at Calicut, Cananor and Cochin

1510
Led by Afonso de Albuquerque, second governor of the East Indies, the Portuguese conquer Goa

1526
Battle of Panipat.
Timur becomes first Mughal emperor

1530
Timur succeeded by his son Humayun

1535
Portuguese forces fortify Diu

1539–42
Humayun driven out of India by the Afghan Sher Shah

SOUTH-EAST ASIA

1511
Under Afonso de Albuquerque the Portuguese take Malacca, centre of the spice trade

CHINA

1368–1644
Ming dynasty

1403–33
Series of naval and diplomatic expeditions sent to the southern seas, some under the leadership of the eunuch Admiral Zheng He. China establishes tributary relations with kingdoms as far away as the Arabian peninsula

1513
Portuguese ships anchor in the Pearl River estuary

1520
First Portuguese embassy to the Imperial Court led by Tomé Pires

1522
Portuguese expelled from China

JAPAN

1467–1568
Sengoku ('Warring States') period

1543
Portuguese land on Tanegashima

WORLD

1571
Combined Christian forces defeat the Ottoman navy at Lepanto

1580
Philip II of Spain claims the throne of Portugal

1600
East India Company granted a charter by Elizabeth I

1602
Foundation of the Dutch East India Company (Vereenigde Oost-Indische Compagnie, or VOC)

INDIA

1555
Humayun reclaims Delhi and Agra

1556
Humayun succeeded by his son Akbar

1565
Fall of the Vijayanagar empire

1573
Akbar conquers Gujarat

1576
Akbar conquers Bengal

1578
Akbar institutes public debates on religion

1579
Akbar invites Portuguese Jesuits to religious discussions at the Imperial Court

1586
Mughal conquest of Kashmir

SOUTH-EAST ASIA

1571
The Spanish establish Manila as the capital of the Philippines

1602
The East India Company establishes itself at Bantam

CHINA

1557
Permanent Portuguese settlement established at Macao

1573–1620
Reign of the Wanli emperor

1575
Catholic diocese of Macao created by Holy See and given jurisdiction over East Asia

1582
Matteo Ricci arrives in Macao

1584
Ricci's first map of the world printed

1590
Church of São Paulo built at Macao

1601
Ricci secures the favour of the emperor by presenting him with gifts from the West

JAPAN

1549
Led by Francis Xavier, the first Jesuit missionaries arrive in Japan

1554
A Japanese convert, Bernardo of Kagoshima, becomes the first Japanese to visit Rome

1563
Ōmura Sumitada becomes the first *daimyō* to be baptized

1568
Oda Nobunaga becomes *de facto* ruler of Japan. Beginning of the Azuchi-Momoyama period

1571
Nagasaki becomes main port for foreign ships and the chief centre of Christian missionary activity

1582
The Jesuit Alessandro Valignano leads an embassy of Kyōshō envoys to Europe. Death of Nobunaga; Toyotomi Hideyoshi assumes power

1583
Giovanni Niccolò arrives in Japan and founds the Jesuit art academy

1587
Hideyoshi promulgates the first anti-Christian edicts

1597
26 Christians are crucified at Nagasaki

1598
Hideyoshi dies, passing the reins of power to his son Hideyori

1600
Tokugawa Ieyasu victorious at the Battle of Sekigahara. The Dutch ship, the *Liefde*, arrives in Japan piloted by Englishman William Adams

1601
Japanese converts Sebastião Kimura and Luis Niabara ordained as Japan's first native Jesuit priests

WORLD

1618
Outbreak of the Thirty Years War

1620
English settlers ('Pilgrim Fathers') land at Cape Cod, Massachusetts

INDIA

1603
East India Company representative John Mildenhall arrives at Akbar's court in order to secure trade concessions

1605
Akbar succeeded by his son Jahangir

1609
Dutch factory established at Pulicat on the Coromandel coast

1611
English establish a factory at Masulipatnam on the Coromandel coast

1613
East India Company establishes a factory at Surat

1615–19
Sir Thomas Roe at the Mughal court

1616
The Dutch establish a factory in Surat

1628
Jahangir succeeded by Shah Jahan

1632–53
Building of the Taj Mahal

SOUTH-EAST ASIA

1619
VOC and East India Company found factories in Pegu. VOC founds its headquarters at Batavia on the coast of Java

CHINA

1621–27
Reign of the Tianqi emperor

1624
VOC establishes a trading station on Formosa

1628–44
Reign of the Chongzhen emperor

1630
Jesuit priest Johann Schall von Bell asked to reform the dynastic calendar

JAPAN

1603
Tokugawa Ieyasu assumes the title of *shōgun*. First Japanese–Portuguese dictionary, the *Vocabulario da Lingoa de Japam*, published by the Jesuit mission press in Nagasaki

1604
Printing of the first grammar of the Japanese language, *A arte da lingua Japan* by João Rodrigues

1609
VOC establishes a trading post at Hirado. First 'court journey' (*Edo sanpu*) of the VOC to the *shōgun*'s court in Edo

1613
East India Company factory established at Hirado

1614
Tokugawa *shōgunate* orders expulsions of Christian missionaries

1615
Fall of Osaka Castle, seat of Hideyori; beginning of Edo period

1616
Trade with European ships restricted to Nagasaki and Hirado

1623
English factory at Hirado closes. Court journey of Dutch becomes an annual custom

1633
Beginning of the First National Seclusion Policy, later known as '*Sakuko*' (lit. 'closed country')

1635
Japanese living abroad are forbidden to return to Japan; Japanese forbidden to leave Japan

1636
Portuguese confined to Dejima, island in Nagasaki harbour

1637–38
Shimabara uprising

WORLD

1640
Portugal reclaims its independence from Spain

1648
Treaty of Westphalia; the Netherlands receive their independence from Spain

1652
Cape Town is established by Dutch settlers

1664
Foundation of the French Compagnie des Indes Orientales

1701–14
War of Spanish Succession

INDIA

1638
VOC ousts the Portuguese from Ceylon

1639
East India Company founds Fort St George (Madras)

1658
Shah Jahan overthrown by his son Aurangzeb

1662
Bombay ceded to Charles II as part of Catherine of Braganza's dowry; it is leased to the East India Company in 1668

1674
Compagnie des Indes Orientales establishes a settlement at Pondicherry

1686
Aurangzeb conquers Bijapur

1687
Aurangzeb conquers Golconda

1690
The East India Company founds Fort William (Calcutta)

1707
Death of Aurangzeb. Beginning of the disintegration of the Mughal empire

1717
The East India Company secures from the Mughal emperor exemption from customs and duties on goods traded

1739
Persian ruler Nadir Shah sacks Delhi

1746–48
Anglo-French hostilities break out; concluded by the treaty of Aix-la-Chapelle

SOUTH-EAST ASIA

1644
VOC ousts the Portuguese from Malacca

1664
VOC temporarily secures a monopoly of Siamese foreign trade

1680
Attempted first Siamese embassy to France

1684
Second Siamese embassy to France

1685
First French embassy to Siam

1686
Third Siamese embassy to France

CHINA

1644–1912
Qing dynasty

1644–61
Reign of the Shunzhi emperor

1656
First Dutch embassy to the Imperial Court

1662
Dutch ousted from Formosa

1662–1722
Reign of the Kangxi emperor

1674
Ferdinand Verbiest casts a new set of astronomical instruments for the Peking Observatory

1693
Jean de Fontaney cures the Kangxi emperor with quinine

1715
Jesuit priest and painter Giuseppe arrives at the Imperial Court

1723–35
Reign of the Yongzheng emperor

1736–95
Reign of the Qianlong emperor

JAPAN

1639
Final National Seclusion Policy issued. Portuguese are forbidden to enter Japan

1641
Dutch factory moved to Dejima

1720
Restrictions on the importation of foreign books relaxed

WORLD

1756–63
Seven Years War

1768
Captain James Cook begins exploration of the Pacific

1769
Dissolution of the Compagnie des Indes Orientales

1776
American colonies declare independence from British rule

1789
French Revolution

1799
Dissolution of the VOC

INDIA

1756
Siraj-ud-daulah, Nawab of Bengal, takes Calcutta and imprisons English captives in a storeroom in Fort William (subsequently called the 'Black Hole')

1757
British forces under Robert Clive defeat Siraj-ud-daulah at the Battle of Plassey; Bengal comes under British control

1761
Haidar Ali establishes himself as ruler of Mysore

1763
Treaty of Paris; French possessions reduced to Pondicherry and Chandernagor

1765
Mughal emperor Shah Alam II awards the East India Company the right to collect revenues in Bengal, Bihar and Orissa

1766
First Mysore War between Haidar Ali and the East India Company

1772
Warren Hastings appointed governor-general

1775–82
First Anglo-Maratha War

1780–84
Second Mysore War

1781
Haidar Ali succeeded by his son Tipu Sultan

1787
Tipu Sultan sends an embassy to the court of Louis XVI

1790–92
Third Mysore War

1796
East India Company conquers Ceylon from the Dutch

1799
Fourth Mysore War ends with the death of Tipu Sultan. British control of southern India secured

SOUTH-EAST ASIA

1781
East India Company conquers VOC settlements on the west coast of Sumatra

1783
Treaty of Paris; British return VOC possessions but secure the right to trade throughout the Dutch East Indies

1795
East India Company forces take Malacca

1795–1806
Batavian Republic founded, modelled on France

CHINA

1747
Beginning of construction of European-style palace complex at the Yuanming Yuan under the direction of Castiglione

1759
Restriction of European maritime trade to Canton

1773
The East India Company begins trading Indian opium in Canton

1793
First British embassy to China led by Lord Macartney

1796–1820
Reign of the Jiaqing emperor

JAPAN

1786
Ōtsuki Gentaku founds the Shirandō, an academy for Dutch studies

1790
Court journey reduced to every four years

NOTES

1
INTRODUCTION

1 Ben Jonson, *The Fountaine of Selfe-Love, or Cynthia's Revels* (1601).

2
MAPPING THE WORLD

1 M.W. Lewis and K.E. Wigen, *The Myth of Continents* (1997), pp. 2–3.

2 J.L. Berggren and A. Jones, *Ptolemy's Geography: an Annotated Translation of the Theoretical Chapters* (2000), book 2.1, p. 95.

3 D. Woodward, 'Medieval *Mappaemundi*', *History of Cartography* (1987), vol. 1, pp. 286–370.

4 J.B. Russell, *Inventing the Flat Earth: Columbus and Modern Historians* (1991).

5 C. Yee, 'Taking the World's Measure: Chinese Maps Between Observation and Text', *History of Cartography* (1994), vol. 2.2, pp. 117–24.

6 D. Woodward and H.M. Howe, 'Roger Bacon on Geography and Cartography', in J. Hackett, *Roger Bacon and the Sciences: Commemorative Essays* (1997), pp. 199–222.

7 D. Lach, *Asia in the Making of Europe* (1965), vol. 1, p. 24.

8 Although doubts now exist about Marco Polo's alleged visit to China, as expressed for example by Frances Wood, *Did Marco Polo go to China?* (1995), for balance readers should also consult the book by John Larner that heavily counters it: J. Larner, *Marco Polo and the Discovery of the World* (1999).

9 Larner (1999).

10 See the full description at the Henry Davis Cartographic Images website: http://www.henry-davis.com/MAPS/LMwebpages/249.html

11 F.W. Mote, 'Admiral Zheng He', in J.A. Levenson (ed.), *Circa 1492: Art in the Age of Exploration* (1991), pp. 342–46.

12 The recent book by Gavin Menzies, *1421: The Year China Discovered the World* (2002), uses the Fra Mauro map extensively to support his hypothesis that Zheng He sailed westwards beyond the Cape of Good Hope, but the text on Fra Mauro's map – if it refers to Zheng He at all – suggests that the voyage was confined to the Indian Ocean.

13 R.J. Howgego, *Encyclopedia of Exploration to 1800* (2003).

14 M.F. Alegria, S. Daveau, J.C. Garcia and F. Relaño, 'Portuguese Cartography in the Renaissance', *History of Cartography,* vol. 3 (forthcoming).

15 Bibliothèque Nationale, Paris (Ms. Coll. des Cinq Cents de Colbert, 298, ff. 6–8). The document was published by L. de Matos, *Les Portugais en France* (1952), pp. 318–22.

16 D. Woodward, 'Starting with the Map: The Rosselli Map of the World, ca. 1508', *Plantejaments i objectius d'una història universal de la cartografia (Approaches and Challenges in a Worldwide History of Cartography)* (2001), pp. 71–90.

17 T. Suárez, *Early Mapping of Southeast Asia* (1999), p. 131.

18 G. Ledyard, 'The Kangnido: A Korean World Map, 1402', in J.A. Levenson (ed.), *Circa 1492: Art in the Age of Exploration* (1991), pp. 329–32, and *History of Cartography*, vol. 2.2, pp. 243–49.

19 Yee, *History of Cartography*, vol. 2.2, pp. 46–53.

20 J. Schwartzberg, 'Cosmographical Mapping', *History of Cartography*, vol. 2.1, pp. 332–43.

21 K. Unno, 'Buddhist World Maps', *History of Cartography*, vol. 2.2, pp. 371–76.

22 India Office Library and Records (British Library), London (MSS. Mar.G.28.C-K, f. 1). W. Ouseley, 'Account of an Original Asiatick Map of the World', in *The Oriental Collections*, vol. 3 (1799), pp. 76–77. S. Gole in *Indian Maps and Plans: From Earliest Times to the Advent of European Surveys* (1989), pp. 76–77, reproduces Ouseley's copy and translation. The map has been described at length by J. E. Schwartzberg in 'Geographical Mapping', *History of Cartography*, vol. 2.1.

23 G. Ledyard, 'The Popular "Wheel Maps" of the Ch'onhado Tradition', *History of Cartography*, vol. 2.2, pp. 256–67.

24 C. Yee, 'Traditional Chinese Cartography and the Myth of Westernization', *History of Cartography*, vol. 2.2, pp. 170–77.

25 C. Yee, 'The Influence of Chinese Map Culture on the West', *Plantejaments i objectius d'una història universal de la cartografia* (2001), pp. 265–82.

3
RARITIES AND NOVELTIES

1 A. A. Shelton, 'Cabinets of Transgression: Renaissance Collections and the Incorporation of the New World', *The Cultures of Collecting*, ed. J. Elsner and R. Cardinal (1994), ch. 9, pp. 175–203.

2 Bezoars, narwhal whale and rhinoceros horns were used as antidotes against melancholy, pest, epilepsy and poison. A. Pérez de Tudela and A. Jordan Gschwend, 'Luxury Goods for Royal Collectors: Exotica, princely gifts and rare animals exchanged between the Iberian courts and Central Europe in the Renaissance (1560–1612)', *Exotica. Portugals Entdeckungen im Spiegel fürstlicher Kunst- und Wunderkammern der Renaissance. Die Beiträge des am 19. und 20. Mai 2000 vom Kunsthistorischen Museum Wien veranstalteten Symposiums*, ed. H. Trnek and S. Haag. *Jahrbuch des Kunsthistorischen Museums Wien* (2001), vol. 3, pp. 14–15, fig. 17.

3 These oversize coconuts, found floating in the sea, were thought to have grown on the bottom of the ocean. Nicknamed *coco-de-mer*, they were collected for their natural beauty and scarcity. R. Fritz, *Die Gefässe aus Kokonuss in Mittel-Europa, 1250–1800* (1983).

4 D. Lach, *Asia in the Making of Europe. Book One: The Visual Arts* (1970), pp. 106–07.

5 R.E. Mack, *Bazaar to Piazza. Islamic Trade and Italian Art, 1300–1600* (2002), especially pp. 105–06.

6 A. Jordan Gschwend and A. Pérez de Tudela, '*Exotica Habsburgica.* La Casa de Austria y las colecciones exóticas en el Renacimiento temprano', *Oriente en Palacio. Tesoros asiáticos en las colecciones reales españolas* (Madrid, exhib. cat. 2003), pp. 30–31. Asian elephants were prized as diplomatic gifts between Lisbon and other courts. In 1561 Sebastian of Portugal (r. 1557–78) received word from Rome that, like his predecessor Leo X, Pius IV wished to have one for his menagerie in the Belvedere Gardens. F. M. Sousa Viterbo, 'O orientalismo em Portugal no século XVI', *Boletim da Sociedade de Geografia de Lisboa* (1892–93), vol. 12, nos 7–8, pp. 318–19.

7 Lopo Vaz de Sampaio is credited with bringing the first tulip bulb from Asia (Persia or Turkey) to Europe in 1530. A. Pavord, *The Tulip* (2000), pp. 80–81; Lach, (1970), pp. 12, 86.

8 A. Jordan, 'Images of Empire: Slaves in the household and court of Catherine of Austria', *Black Africans in Renaissance Europe*, ed. K. Lowe and T. Earle (forthcoming).

9 Biblioteca Nazionale Marciana, Venice, Cod. IT. XI, 90 (6774): *Viaggio da Madrid in Portogallo poi a S. Giacomo di Galizia nel 1568*: 'le navi [...] tornano poi l'anno seguinte di luglio et agosto et portano le perle oriental, che si pescano nella procuintia di Armaz [Hormuz] un una terra che si chiama Badem, li Diamante finissimas da Bisnaga, li Rubim dal Pegu, il muschio, la canfora, seda, porcellana della China, l'ambragrisa da Mozzambiche, la negra del Brasil, il pecane et il zenzaro di Calicut, la canela da Zeilan, le nozze muschiade da Banda, li girofili da Maluco et le telle da Bengala, le qual tutte cose stano poco nelli magazzeni per che subito gionte sono levate dalli mercanti de diversi natione et le stano aspetando cudi in Lisbona [...].' Also G. Battelli, 'Lisbona e la corte Portoghese in una relatione Veneta del 1572', *Ateneo Veneto. Riviste di Scienze, lettere ed arti* (1943), CXXXIV, vol. 130, pp. 105–06.

10 Portuguese royals were *cognoscenti* of Indian diamonds and precious stones. Catherine and João III purchased from German factors in Lisbon and Goa who specialized in the sale of Asian pearls and jewels. In 1547 Georg Herwart wanted João to buy a diamond for sale in Narsinga, and in 1549 an extraordinary diamond, worth 30,000 *cruzdaos,* was offered to the Portuguese monarch. Instituto dos Arquivos Nacionais/Torre do Tombo (hereafter IAN/TT), Lisbon, CC I, maço 78, doc. 122; CC I maço 83, doc. 32.

11 In 1518, 2,369 kilograms of Chinese silk alone was exported from the Malabar coast to Portugal. Portuguese merchants (Christian and New Christian) based in Cochin travelled to Malacca to purchase goods from the Far East (porcelain and silk), carrying Gujarati textiles and other Indian goods prized there. J. A. Rodrigues da Silva Tavim, 'From Setúbal to the Sublime Porte: The Wanderings of Jácome de Olivares, New Christian and Merchant of Cochin (1540–1571)', *Santa Barbara Portuguese Studies. Special Issue: The Portuguese and the Pacific II*, ed. S. Subrahmanyam and K. McPherson (1995), vol. 11, pp. 94–134.

12 In 1522 it was decreed that one-third of the cargo of Portuguese ships on the run between China and Goa should contain porcelain (IAN/TT, Lisbon, CC 3, maço 8, doc. 1).

13 Pérez de Tudela and Jordan Gschwend (2001), vol. 3, p. 9, n. 60.

14 *Do Tejo aos Mares da China. Uma epopeia* (Queluz, exhib. cat. 1992); *Indes Merveilleuses. L'ouverture du monde au XVIe siécle* (Paris, exhib. cat. 1993); *A la rencontre de Sindbad. La route de soie* (Paris, exhib. cat. 1994); *Vasco da Gama e a India* (Paris, exhib. cat. 1998).

15 B.W. Diffie and G.D. Winius, *Foundations of the Portuguese Empire 1415–1580. Europe and the World in the Age of Expansion* (1977), vol. 1, p. 380.

16 W. Liebenwein, *Studiolo: Die Entstehung eines Raumtyps und seine Entwicklung bis um 1600* (1977).

17 F. Yates, *The Theater of the World* (1969).

18 E. Scheicher, *Die Kunst- und Wunderkammern der Habsburger* (1979); *The Origins of Museums: The Cabinet of Curiosities in Sixteenth- and Seventeenth-Century Europe*, ed. O. Impey and A. MacGregor (1985).

19 Biblioteca de Ajuda, Lisbon, Ms. 51-5-1, f. 164 (undated). Copy of a letter François I sent Manuel in which the French king desired to obtain 'things which arrive regularly at Lisbon in great abundance from the Province from India'. Cited in L. de Matos, 'Natura intelletto e costumi dell'elefante', *Boletim internacional de bibliografia Luso-Brasileira* (1960), vol. 1, no. 3, p. 46; Lach (1970), p. 31, n. 149.

20 S.A. Bedini, *The Pope's Elephant* (1998), ch. 5, pp. 111–36.

21 Lach (1970), pp. 31–32.

22 Archivo General de Simancas (hereafter AGS), Patronato Real, 50–42 and 50–44.

23 Archives Nationales, KK 100 (Comptes des menus plaisirs de François 1er), l. 109, 24 October 1529: '[...] a Pierre Lemoyne, marchand demourant à Portugal, la somme de 287 livres tournois pour son paiement d'un chalice marqueté à feuillages de nacle de perle faict aux pays d'Indye vernissée de noir et enrichie de feuillages et figures d'or, lesquelz chalice et chaire ledit seigneur a prins et acheptez de luy à ladite somme et iceulx faict mettre en son cabinet du chasteau du Louvre à Paris pour en faire son plaisir.' I am grateful to Michèle Bimbenet-Privat, Conservateur en Chef du Patrimoine, for bringing this document to my attention.

24 I. Toesca, 'Un Coffret Parisien du XVIe siècle', *Gazette de Beaux Arts* (November 1965), vol. LXVI, pp. 309–12; Toesca, 'Silver in the Time of François I', *Apollo* (October 1969), vol. XC, pp. 292–97; *L'Orfèvrerie Parisienne de la Renaissance. Trésors dispersés* (Paris, exhib. cat. 1995), ed. M. Bimbenet-Privat, cat. 73a–73b, pp. 110–12. A related Gujarati casket, slightly larger in size, with mounts also added by Mangot, probably originated from François's collection. See *Exotica. Portugals Entdeckungen im Spiegel fürstlicher Kunst- und Wunderkammern der Renaissance* (Vienna, exhib. cat. 2000), cat. 59, pp. 149–50.

25 IAN/TT, Lisbon, CC 1, maço 93, doc. 54 (15 August 1554).

26 IAN/TT, Lisbon, Núcleo Antigo (hereafter NA) 792, f. 162v.

27 IAN/TT, Lisbon, CC I, maço 106, doc. 147 (10 July 1564); IAN/TT, CC I, maço 107, doc. 140 (13 July 1566). Also Pérez de Tudela and Jordan Gschwend (2001), p. 6, n. 44.

28 IAN/TT, Lisbon, NA 797, f. 114r (1559). The queen sent wine to Goa in April of 1554: IAN/TT, Lisbon, CC I, maço 92, doc. 30.

29 J. Wicki, 'Dokumente und Briefe aus der Zeit des indischen Vizekönigs D. Antão de Noronha (1563–1568)', *Aufsätze zur portugiesischen Kulturgeschichte* (1960), vol. 1, p. 239. Catherine's shopping list covered the extent of trade in Portuguese Asia: diamonds, rubies, emeralds and pearls from Vijayanagara, clothes manufactured in Balaghat (in the highlands of the Deccan), items from China and Pegu, Sinhalese crystal objects, and elephants, which were paid as yearly tribute from the Kingdom of Jaffna.

30 IAN/TT, Lisbon, NA 797, ff. 112r–114v.

31 A. Jordan Gschwend, 'O Fascínio de Cipango. Artes Decorativas e Lacas da Asia Oriental em Portugal, Espanha e Austria (1511–1598)', *Os Constructores do Oriente Português* (Porto, exhib. cat. 1998), pp. 195–227, 406–11.

32 IAN/TT, Lisbon, CC I, maço 96, doc. 147.

33 A. Jordan Gschwend, 'Exotic Renaissance Accessories. Japanese, Indian and Sinhalese Fans at the courts of Portugal and Spain', *Apollo* (November 1999), pp. 25–35; Jordan Gschwend, 'Los primeros abanicos orientales de los Habsburgos', *Oriente en Palacio. Tesoros asiáticos en las colecciones reales españolas* (Madrid, exhib. cat. 2003), pp. 267–71. Catherine began importing fans from North Africa, India, South China and Ceylon after 1528. The first Japanese folding fans, some from the Ryūkyū Islands, made their appearance at her court around 1552. Far Eastern fans became quotidian accessories for elite Portuguese women decades before they were in vogue at other European courts.

34 IAN/TT, Lisbon, NA 792.

35 Jordan Gschwend (Lisbon, exhib. cat. 1996), pp. 103–10.

36 T. DaCosta Kaufmann, 'From Treasury to Museum: The Collections of the Austrians Habsburgs', *The Cultures of Collecting*, ed. J. Elsner and R. Cardinal (1994), ch. 7, pp. 137–45.

37 H. Trevor-Roper, *Princes and Artists: Patronage and ideology at four Habsburg courts, 1517–1633* (1974).

38 T. DaCosta Kaufmann, *The Mastery of Nature. Aspects of Art, Science and Humanism in the Renaissance* (1993), ch. 7, p. 174–94.

39 Margaret of Austria (1480–1530), regent of the Netherlands, was a Habsburg collector supplied by her niece, Catherine of Austria, with Asiatica and exotica. She frequently sent a household official (her *contrôleur* Claude) to Lisbon to buy goods there for her. In 1530 Catherine presented Margaret with 14 chests filled with Asian and Indian goods. AGS, Estado 369, doc. 49 in A. Viaud, *Correspondence d'un Ambassadeur Castillan au Portugal dans les années 1530. Lope Hurtado de Mendoza* (2001), pp. 284, 419. Compare with AGS, Estado 378, f. 11 in Jordan Gschwend and Pérez de Tudela (Madrid, exhib. cat. 2003), p. 35, n. 10.

40 T. DaCosta Kaufmann, 'Remarks on the Collections of Rudolf II: The Kunstkammer as a form of *Representatio*', *Art Journal* (1978), 37, pp. 22–28.

41 DaCosta Kaufmann (1994), ch. 7, pp. 137–54.

42 Pérez de Tudela and Jordan Gschwend (2001), pp. 1–127; Jordan Gschwend and Pérez de Tudela (Madrid, exhib. cat. 2003), pp. 26–43.

EXOTIC ANIMALS IN SIXTEENTH-CENTURY EUROPE

1 Philip II of Spain, for instance, erected an aviary for ostriches and other exotic birds at his palace in Aranjuez in 1584. See Instituto Valencia D. Juan, Madrid, Envio 7, ff. 373r–374r.

2 C. Lazzaro, 'Animals as Cultural Signs: A Medici Menagerie in the Grotto at Castello', *Reframing the Renaissance. Visual Culture in Europe and Latin America 1450–1650*, ed. C. Farago (1995), pp. 197–227.

3 In 1552 Catherine even presented a pair of civet cats to a North African potentate as a display of her queenly power and authority.

4 Arcimboldo's animal and floral compositions fascinated the Habsburg court in Spain, and as a princely gesture Emperor Rudolf II of Prague presented his uncle, Philip II, with two cycles of Arcimboldo's *The Four Seasons* and *The Four Elements* in 1583, which decorated one hall in the Alcázar palace in Madrid. One of the elements included a variation of Maximilian II's 1570 *The Allegory of Earth*. Archivo General de Simancas, Estado (Alemania), leg. 691.

4 CHINESE PORCELAIN IN EARLY EUROPEAN COLLECTIONS

1 R. Lightbown, 'Oriental Art and the Orient in Late Renaissance and Baroque Italy', *Journal of the Warburg and Courtauld Institutes* (1969), vol. 32, pp. 228–79.

2 It was the thesis of Thomas Browne, an English doctor from Norwich, who included it in his published work. See G. Keynes (ed.), *The Works of Sir Thomas Browne* (1929), vol. 2, pp. 154–55.

3 T. Mikami, 'China and Egypt: Fustat', *Transactions of the Oriental Ceramic Society 1980–1*, vol. 45 (1982), pp. 67–89.

4 A. Lane, 'The Gaignières-Fonthill Vase; A Chinese Porcelain of about 1300', *The Burlington Magazine*, vol. CIII, no. 697 (April 1961), pp. 124–32, pls 2–11.

5 H. Garner, *Chinese Export Art at Schloss Ambras*, The Oriental Ceramic Society (1975). Though none of the porcelains Garner illustrates are mounted, a rhinoceros-horn cup (of a type greatly valued in China) has a European silver foot mount; ibid., pp. 14–15, pl. 20.

6 Celadon is a name given by Europeans to ceramics of greyish-bluish-green colour. It derives from the colour worn by a character in a seventeenth-century French play. See R. Kerr, *Chinese Ceramics. Porcelain of the Qing Dynasty 1644–1911*, V&A Far Eastern Series (1986, 1998), p. 83.

7 See *Porzellan aus China und Japan. Die Porzellangalerie der Langgrafen von Hessen-Kassel*, Staatliche Kunstsammlungen, Kassel (1990), pp. 10–11, 216–18.

8 Sotheby's sale in London of 5 February 1970, lot nos 169, 170.

9 Two of the earliest pictures to show Chinese porcelain are a *Madonna and Child* by Francesco Benaglio (1432–*c.* 1492) and a late fifteenth-century *Adoration of the Magi* by Andrea Mantegna (1431–1506). See Dr A.I. Spriggs, 'Oriental Porcelain in Western Paintings 1450–1700', *Transactions of the Oriental Ceramic Society*, vol. 36 (1967), pp. 73–88.

10 D. Bull, *The Feast of the Gods. Conservation, Examination and Interpretation*, Studies in the History of Art 40, National Gallery of Art (1990).

11 J. Ayers, R. Krahl and N. Erbahar, *Chinese Ceramics in the Topkapi Saray Museum Istanbul. A Complete Catalogue, volume 2, Yuan and Ming Dynasty Porcelains* (1986), p. 560, no. 716. A similar large dish is in the collection of the Ardebil Shrine in Persia. John Carswell discusses a possible link with Istanbul and illustrates the porcelain in the painting, in J. Carswell, 'Free for All: Blue-and-White in 1500', *Oriental Art*, vol. XLVIII, no. 5 (2002/03), pp. 10–19.

12 Quoted in P. Glanville, 'Chinese Porcelain and English Goldsmiths *c.* 1560 to *c.* 1660', *The V&A Album 3* (1984), pp. 246–56.

13 S. Pierson, *Percival David Foundation of Chinese Art. A Guide to the Collection* (2003), p. 71, no. 58.

14 I am grateful to Timothy Schroder for bringing the changes to the mounts to my attention.

15 Described in P. Glanville, *Silver in Tudor and Early Stuart England: a social history and catalogue of the national collection 1480–1660*, V&A (1990), no. 98, p. 466.

5 ASIAN TRADE AND EXCHANGE BEFORE 1600

1 J. Sauvaget, *Ahbar Al-sin Wa l-Hind. Relation de la Chine et de l'Inde, redigee en 851* (1948).

2 J. Guy, 'Tamil merchant guilds and the Quanzhou trade', in A. Schottenhamer (ed.), *The Emporium of the World. Maritime Quanzhou, 1000–1400* (2000), pp. 238–308.

3 B. Ward, *The Venerable Bede* (1998).

4 S.D. Goitein, *A Mediterranean Society. The Jewish Communities of the Arab World as Portrayed in the Documents of the Cairo Geniza*, 5 vols (1967–88), vol. I (1967), p. 45.

5 *Sui Shu*, cited in P. Wheatley, 'Geographical notes on some commodities involved in the Sung maritime trade', *Journal of the Malaysian Branch of the Royal Asiatic Society*, vol. XXXII, pt 2, no. 186 (1959), p. 20.

6 J. Guy, 'Early Asian Ceramic Trade and the Belitung ("Tang") Cargo', *Transactions of the Oriental Ceramic Society* (2001–02), vol. 66, pp. 13–27.

7 G. R. Tibbetts, *A study of the Arabic texts concerning materials on South-East Asia* (1979), p. 37.

8 Magellan was murdered on the island of Zebu, in the Philippines, shortly before the expedition reached the Moluccas; the voyage was chronicled by Antonio Pigafetta.

9 Goitein (1967–83).

10 Goitein, vol. IV (1983), p. 185.

11 The earliest example is radiocarbon-dated to 895 +/–75 years, R. Barnes, *Indian Block-printed Textiles in Egypt: The Newberry Collection in the Ashmolean Museum* (1997), no. 241; see J. Guy, *Woven Cargoes. Indian Textiles in the East* (1998), pp. 426, 186, for a summary of radiocarbon-dating results.

12 This technical study was begun by R. Pfister, *Les Toiles Imprimees de Fostat et l'Hindoustan* (1936, 1938); see also G.M. Vogelsang-Eastwood, *Resist-dyed textiles from Quseir al-Qadim, Egypt* (1990). For a summary of dyeing techniques, see Guy (1998), ch. 2.

13 Threads have been recovered from earlier contexts in the Indian subcontinent, but are too fragmentary to allow an identification of dyeing techniques employed.

14 J. Guy, 'Jain Manuscript Painting', in P. Pal (ed.), *The Peaceful Liberators. Jain Art from India* (1995), pp. 89–99.

15 For the first integrated study of the distribution of Gujarati tombstones, see E. Lambourn, 'The decoration of the Fakhr al-Din mosque in Mogadishu and other pieces of Gujarati marble carving on the East African coast', *Azania*, vol. XXXIV (1999).

16 This vogue for Gujarati tombstones was at its height from the early fourteenth to fifteenth centuries; for the Islamic tombs of Cambay and their dated inscriptions, see Z.A. Desai, 'Some 14th century epitaphs from Cambay in Gujarat', *Archaeological Survey of India, Epigraphica Indica, Arabic and Persian supplement* (1971).

17 For the Gujarati tombstone of Gresik and elsewhere in east Java, see J.E. van Lohuizen de Leeuw, 'An Early 16th Century Link Between Gujarat and Java', in Ba Shin et al. (eds), *Essays Offered to G.H. Luce*, Artibus Asiae Supplement XXIII (1966), and for a broader perspective, Lambourn (1999).

18 Al-Wathiq is identified as the third son of Rasulid sultan al-Malik al-Muzaffar, and served as governor of Zafar from 1292 until his death on 8 June 1311; V. Porter, 'Three Rasulid Tombstones from Zafur', *Journal of the Royal Asiatic Society* (1988). E. Lambourn, 'Carving and Re-carving: Three Rasulid Gravestones Revisited', *New Arabian Studies*, vol. 6 (2001), has identified evidence of recutting of the personalized text panels of Al-Wathiq's headstone, indicating that this was a recycled stele, having been prepared initially for a different client. Whether this rededication was done in Oman or Cambay remains unclear, though Gujarat is more likely, as the reuse of tombstones became increasingly the practice in later periods.

19 Compare Guy (1998), pl. 45, 47, 48.

20 Ibn Battuta, *The Travels of Ibn Battuta A.D. 1325–1354*, trans. H.A.R. Gibb , 3 vols (1958–94), vol. IV.

21 T. Pires, *The Suma Oriental of Tomé Pires*, trans. A. Contesao (1944), pp. 42, 45, 270.

22 Ashmolean Museum, see Barnes (1997), nos 821, 1122.

23 N. Steendgaard, *The Asian trade revolution of the seventeenth century* (1973), p. 407.

24 D. Lombard, *Le carrefour javanais: Essai d'histoire globale*, 3 vols (1990), vol. I, p. 108.

25 Ma Huan, *Ma Huan's Ying-yai Sheng-Ian (The Overall Survey of the Ocean's Shores, 1433)*, trans. J.V.G. Mills (1970), p. 87.

26 A. Kobata and M. Matsuda (trans.), *Ryukyan Relations with Korea and South Sea Countries. An Annotated Translation of Documents in the Rekidai Hoa* (1969), pp. 87–92.

27 The controlled excavation was undertaken by the Vietnamese Government during 1997–99; see J. Guy, 'Vietnamese Ceramics from the Hoi An Excavation: The Cu Lao Cham Ship Cargo', *Orientations* (2000 ii), vol. 31, no. 7, pp. 125–28.

28 These jars have been linked to the Ban Rachan kilns of Singburi province, central Thailand. See J. Guy, 'Thai Ceramics in Southeast Asian Trade', in Asian Art Museum of San Francisco, *Thai Ceramics: The James and Elaine Connell Collection* (1993), pp. 10–11.

29 Ngo Si Lien, *Dai Viet Su Ky Toan Thu*, cited by K. Taylor, 'Vietnamese History', in C. Young et al. (eds), *Vietnamese Ceramics* (1982), p. 21.

30 J.A. Pope, *Fourteenth Century Blue and White, A group of Chinese Porcelain in the Topkapi Sarayi Muzesi, Istanbul* (1952); J.A. Pope, *Chinese Porcelain from the Ardebil Shrine* (1956); R. Krahl, *Chinese Ceramics from the Topkapi Saray Museum, Istanbul, A Complete Catalogue*, ed. J. Ayers, 3 vols (1986).

31 The Dresden jar was assumed to be Chinese and was identified as Vietnamese by this author; J. Guy, *Oriental Trade Ceramics in South East Asia: Ninth to Sixteenth Centuries* (1986), p. 52.

32 Bristol City Museum and Art Gallery (N7879, Sedwick Bequest, 1968).

33 Ibn Battuta (1958–94), vol. IV, p. 896.

34 Vietnamese and Thai ceramics recovered by the Egypt Exploration Society in 1891 and deposited in the British Museum were, until recently, catalogued as Chinese; see Guy (1986), p. 65.

35 The Javanese *kala* is an adaption of the classical Indian *kirtimukha* motif, denoting a demonic creature that served to guard the entrances to sacred spaces.

36 For a fuller discussion, see J. Guy, 'The Vietnamese Wall Tiles of Majapahit', *Transactions of the Oriental Ceramic Society*, vol. 53 (1988–89).

37 The seventeenth-century VOC records cite many instances of wooden and clay models, and drawings, being supplied to facilitate the commissioning of ceramics of specific design, to be made to order; see T. Volker, *Porcelain and the Dutch East India Company* (1954).

38 W. Foster, *The Embassy of Sir Thomas Roe* (1926), p. 134.

39 G. le Strange (trans.), *Embassy to Tamberlane, 1403–1406* (1928), p. 224.

40 Yuan blue-and-white was in production in the second quarter of the fourteenth century, and production was revived in the early Ming, most notably in the Yongle (1403–24) and Xuande (1426–35) periods.

41 E. Lubo-Lesnichenko, 'The blue-and-white porcelain of Yuan period from Khara-Khoto', *International Symposium on Ancient Chinese Trade Ceramics: Collected Papers* (1994).

42 Ibn Battuta (1958–94), vol. IV, p. 911.

43 E. Smart, 'Fourteenth century Chinese porcelain from a Tughlaq Palace in Delhi', *Transactions of the Oriental Ceramic Society*, vol. 41 (1975–77), pp. 199–230.

44 For the Ardabil shrine, see Pope (1956); for the Topkapi Saray, see Pope (1952), Krahl (1986).

45 E.H. Hunt, 'Old Hyderabad China', *Journal of the Hyderabad Archaeological Society* (1916), p. 73.

46 Ma Huan (1970), and H. Ray, 'The South East Asian connection in Sino-Indian trade', in R. Scott and J. Guy (eds), *South East Asia and China: Art, Interaction and Commerce* (1995), pp. 41–54.

47 A.S. Beveridge (trans.), *The Baburnama in English*, 2 vols (1922), vol. I, p. 80.

48 A. Aziz, *The Imperial Treasury of the Indian Mughals* (1972), p. 404.

49 Liu Xinyuan, 'Imperial Export Porcelain from late Yuan to Early Ming', *Oriental Art*, vol. XLV, no. 3 (1999), p. 50.

50 W. Foster, *Early Travels in India, 1583–1619* (1921), p. 99.

51 A. Rogers (trans.) and H. Beveridge (ed.), *The Tuzuk-i-Jahangiri or Memoirs of Jahangir from the first to the twelfth year of his reign* (1909–14), p. 206.

6 DIPLOMATIC ENCOUNTERS: EUROPE AND SOUTH ASIA

1 F. Bernier, *Travels in the Mogul Empire A.D. 1656–1668* (1891), p. 200.

2 W. Foster, *The English Factories in India 1665–1667* (1925), p. 158.

3 E.G. Ravenstein (trans. and ed.), *A Journal of the First Voyage of Vasco da Gama 1497–1499* (1898), p. 60.

4 Ibid., p. 60.

5 Ibid., p. 58.

6 Ibid., pp. 59–62.

7 BL, IORC, Mss. Eur. 1 379/3, p. 206.

8 G. Roy, *Diplomacy in Ancient India* (1981), p.123.

9 Bernier (1891), p.134.

10 Sir W. Foster (ed.), *The Embassy of Sir Thomas Roe to India 1615–19* (reprinted 1990), p.454.

11 Ibid., p.xvii.

12 Roy (1981), p.140. In Ceylon (Sri Lanka) and South-East Asia diplomatic letters were seen as manifestations of the royal personage who sent them and were given due respect. For example, in John Pybus's narrative of diplomatic etiquette in Kandy, he recounts how the letter he brought was placed on a silver dish, wrapped in muslin, which he was instructed to carry above his head. While the letter was in his hands, Pybus was instructed to walk on a white cloth while two attendants held a silk canopy over the tray and music was played and guns fired (*The Pybus Embassy to Kandy, 1762*, transcribed with notes by R. Raven-Hart, private circulation copy, [1961?], p.53).

13 Ravenstein (1898), p.58.

14 Sir W. Foster (ed.), *The Voyage of Nicholas Downton to the East Indies 1614–15 as recorded in contemporary narratives and letter* (1939), pp.xv–xvi.

15 N. Manucci, *Mogul India 1653–1708 or Storia do Mogor*, trans. with introduction and notes by W. Irvine, 4 vols (reprinted 1989), vol.1, p.94.

16 S. Subrahmanyam, *The Career and Legend of Vasco da Gama* (1997), p.179.

17 'Minute by M. Bernier upon the Establishment of Trade in the Indies, dated 10 March 1668', *Journal of the Royal Asiatic Society*, part I (January 1933), p.11.

18 Subrahmanyam (1997), pp.81, 138.

19 'Minute by M. Bernier' (1933), p.13.

20 Foster (1990), p.211.

21 Ibid., p.xv.

22 H. Das, *The Norris Embassy to Aurangzib (1699–1702)*, condensed and rearranged by S.C. Sarkar (1959), p.321.

23 K. Zanvliet (ed.), *The Dutch Encounter with Asia 1600–1950* (Amsterdam/Zwolle, exhib. cat. 2002), pp.27–9.

24 M. Athar Ali, *The Mughal Nobility under Aurangzeb* (1970), p.137; Bernier (1891), p.117; Chaumont (1997), p.158.

25 J.-P. Rubiés, *Travel and Ethnology in the Renaissance, South India through European Eyes, 1250–1625* (2000), p.233.

26 J.P. Waghorne, *The Raja's Magic Clothes, Re-Visioning Kingship and Divinity in England's India* (1994), pp.108–9.

27 R.O. Bucholz, 'Going to Court in 1700: a visitor's guide', *The Court Historian*, vol.5, 3 December 2000, pp.204–05.

28 'Minute by M. Bernier …' (1933), p.9.

29 W. M. Thackston (trans. and ed.), *The Jahangirnama, Memoirs of Jahangir, Emperor of India* (1999), p.61.

30 Das (1959), p.324; 'Minute by M. Bernier …' (1933), pp.8–9.

31 Foster (1990), p.87.

32 Pybus (1961), pp.54–5, 60.

33 R. Percival, *An Account of the Island of Ceylon …* (1803), p.402.

34 D.F. Lach and E.J. Van Kley, *Asia in the Making of Europe*, vol.III, *A Century of Advance, Book Two: South Asia* (1993), p.675.

35 K.A. Nizami, *Some Aspects of Religion and Politics in India during the Thirteenth Century* (1961), pp.328–9.

36 W. Foster, *The English Factories in India 1651–54* (1915), p.vii.

37 Foster (1990), p.129.

38 Foster (1939), p.172; W. Foster, *The English Factories in India 1637–41* (1912), pp.182–3.

39 Ibid., p.143.

40 *Poona's Great days, describing the Palace of the Peshwas when they were paramount in India; the British Embassy & its Residents; the Battles of Kirkee & Koregaon* (1944), p.18.

41 *Memoirs of Admiral Beaulieu's Voyage …* (1774), p.162.

42 Das (1959), p.66; W. Foster, *The English Factories in India 1618–1621* (1906), pp.64–5.

43 Foster (1912), pp.182–83.

44 Foster (1925), p.165.

45 Foster (1990), pp.180–1.

46 Lach and Van Kley (1993), p.710.

47 J. Bourne et al., *Lacquer, an International History and Collector's Guide* (1984), p.129.

48 Foster (1990), p.99.

49 *Jahangir's India, The Remonstratie of Francisco Pelsaert*, trans. W. H. Moreland and P. Geyl (1925), p.27.

50 Lach and Van Kley (1993), p.1086.

51 *The Voyage of Pedro Alvarez de Cabral, to the East Indies*, published in *The World displayed …* (1774), p.70.

52 Foster (1990), p.129.

53 W. Foster, *The English Factories in India 1634–1636* (1911), p.297.

54 Lach and Van Kley (1993), p.1010.

55 Foster (1990), p.350.

56 A. Jaffer, *Furniture from British India and Ceylon* (2001), p.111.

57 Curiously, Downton also gave Jahangir a portrait of Tamerlane and of the emperor himself. Apparently the latter was not well received. Foster (1939), pp.xii–xiii.

58 S. Arasaratnam (trans. and ed.), *François Valentijn's Description of Ceylon* (1978), p.292.

59 Das (1959), p.91.

60 W. Foster, *The English Factories in India 1661–64* (1923), p.361.

61 Foster (1912), pp.182–3.

62 Zanvliet (2002), p.126.

63 Das (1959), p.310.

64 Foster (1990), p.227.

65 *Madras in the Olden Time being a History of the Presidency*, compiled from official records by J. Talboys Wheeler, 1861 (reprinted 1993), p.353.

66 Das (1959), p.152.

67 W. Foster, *The English Factories in India 1646–1650* (1914), p.338.

68 Foster (1939), pp.132–3.

69 Roe (1990), pp.380, 383.

70 Foster (1990), pp.76–77.

71 J. Ovington, *A Voyage to Surat in the year 1689*, ed. H. G. Rawlinson (1929), p.111.

72 Thackston (1999), p.107.

73 Foster (1990), pp.49, 151.

74 Ibid., p.99.

75 Foster (1912), p.143.

76 Foster (1990), p.136.

77 Foster (1912), p.6.

78 R. Sewell, *A Forgotten Empire (Vijayanagar)* (1900), p.252.

79 J. Nieuhof, *Voyages & Travels to the East Indies 1653–1670*, with an introduction by A. Reid (1988) p.226.

80 Bernier (1891), p.128.

81 G.G.R. Hambly, 'The Emperor's Clothes: Robing and "Robes of Honour" in Mughal India', *Robes of Honour*, Khil'at *in Pre-Colonial and Colonial India*, ed. S. Gordon (2003), pp.31–32.

82 B.S. Cohn, 'Cloth, Clothes, and Colonialism: India in the Nineteenth Century', in A. B. Weiner and H. Schneider, *Cloth and Human Experience* (1989), p.319.

83 Manucci, vol.I (1989), p.62.

84 M. Archer et al., *Treasures from India, The Clive Collection at Powis Castle* (1987), pp.73–78.

85 The Marchioness of Bute (ed.), *The Private Journals of the Marquess of Hastings, K.G.* (1858), vol.I, pp.126–7.

86 Ibid., p.22.

87 Nieuhof, in Lach and Van Kley (1993), p.919.

88 Viscount Valentia George, *Voyages and Travels to India, Ceylon, the Red Sea, Abyssinia, and Egypt in the years 1802–1806* (1809), vol.1, p.370.

89 Jaffer (2001), pp.115–21.

90 Rubiés (2000), p.187.

91 G. Khan, *Indian Muslim Perceptions of the West During the Eighteenth Century* (1998), p.75.

92 Ibid., p.75.

7
DIPLOMATIC ENCOUNTERS: EUROPE AND EAST ASIA

1 G.F. Hudson, *Europe and China* (1931), pp.208–09.

2 This section is based on J.E. Wills, Jr, 'Relations with Maritime Europeans, 1514–1662', *The Cambridge History of China* (1998).

3 W. Atwell, 'Ming China and the emerging world economy, *c.*1470–1650', *The Cambridge History of China* (1998).

4 H. Furber, *Rival Empires of Trade in the Orient 1600–1800* (1976).

5 R. Hesselink, *Prisoners of Nambu* (2002), pp.6–14, and J. K. Fairbank, *Trade and Diplomacy on the China Coast* (1953), pp.46–51.

6 J.E. Wills, Jr, *Embassies and Illusions* (1984).

7 John of Antermony Bell, *A Journey from St Petersburg to Pekin, 1719–22* (1966), pp.139–72.

8 M. Mancall, *Russia and China: Their Diplomatic Relations to 1728* (1971), pp.249–55.

9 L. Fu, *A Documentary Chronicle of Sino-Western Relations, 1644–1820*, 2 vols (1966), vol.1, pp.160–61, vol.2, pp.516–17.

10 H. Chun, 'Sino-Korean Tributary Relations in the Ch'ing Period', *The Chinese World Order* (1968), pp.90–111.

11 T. Ch'en, 'Investiture of Liu-ch'iu Kings in the Ch'ing Period', *The Chinese World Order* (1968), pp.135–64, and T.B. Lam, 'Intervention versus Tribute in Sino-Vietnamese Relations, 1788–1790', *The Chinese World Order* (1968), pp.178–79.

12 J.L. Cranmer-Byng (ed.), *An Embassy to China* (1963), pp.122–24.

13 *The Veritable Records of the Qianlong emperor's reign*, v. 1434, p.11b. It is impossible to determine if the poem was presented orally by the emperor or by one of his officials at the audience. The poem also appears on a Chinese tapestry, presumably showing the British gifts being brought to the Yuanming Gardens. Needham has argued convincingly that it does not depict the British embassy at all, but an earlier one, perhaps from Holland (1965, p.471). See also J.L. Cranmer-Byng and T.H. Levere, 'A Case Study of Cultural Collision', *Annals of Science* 38 (1981), p.520.

14 For a discussion of the Qing assessment of the British, see J.L. Hevia, *Cherishing Men from Afar* (1995), pp.181–209.

15 Fu (1966), vol.1, p.46.

16 Documents on these and other embassies to the Qing can be found in the Number One Archive, Beijing. Here I have drawn on published sources, the main one being the *Precedents from the Statutes of the Great Qing* (1899). This work is organized chronologically by reign year of the Qing emperors. Fu (1966) provides translations from numerous sources of all the Qing era notices on European embassies to Peking, including Russia.

17 Chun (1968), p.103.

18 R. Toby, *State and Diplomacy in Early Modern Japan* (1984), pp.189–191, and Hesselink (2002).

19 E. Kaempfer, *Kaempfer's Japan* (1999), p.359.

20 Ibid., pp.362–68.

21 M. Parke-Smith, *Western Barbarians in Japan and Formosa in Tokugawa Days, 1603–1868* (1930), pp.17–22.

22 Toby (1984), pp.203–09.

JAPANESE DIPLOMATIC RELATIONS WITH EUROPE

1 D. Lach, *Asia in the Making of Europe, Vol. 1: The Century of Discovery* (1965), pp.692–93.

2 J. Proust, *Europe Through the Prism of Japan* (2002), p.84.

3 Lach (1965), pp.699–700.

8
RELIGIOUS ENCOUNTERS: CHRISTIANITY IN ASIA

1 G.A. Bailey, *Art on the Jesuit Missions in Asia and Latin America, 1542–1773* (1999).

2 C. Dawson, *Mission to Asia* (1980).

3 K. Zandvliet, *The Dutch Encounter with Asia 1600–1950* (2002), pp.31–197.

4 Sir E. Maclagan, *The Jesuits and the Grand Mogul* (1934), pp.62, 76, 86.

5 Christianity came to China as early as the seventh century AD. Indian Christians trace their origins back to the fifth century ad, and in both places there are legends suggesting that the religion had been brought to the East by St Thomas the Apostle.

6 Bailey (1999), p.10.

7 G.A. Bailey, 'Creating a Global Artistic Language in Late Renaissance Rome: Artists in the Service of the Overseas Missions', in P. Jones and T. Worcester (eds), *From Rome to Eternity: Catholicism and the Arts in Italy, ca. 1550–1650* (2001), pp.225–52.

8 J.N. da Fonseca, *An Historical and Archaeological Sketch of the City of Goa* (1878), pp.63–66.

9 D.M. Kowal, 'Innovation and Assimilation: The Jesuit Contribution to Architectural Development in Portuguese Asia', in J.W. O'Malley, G.A. Bailey et al. (eds), *The Jesuits: Cultures, Sciences, and the Arts* (1999), pp.480–504; D. Kowal, 'The Evolution of Ecclesiastical Architecture in Portuguese Goa', in J. Pereira and P. Pal (eds), *India & Portugal: Cultural Interactions* (2001), pp.70–87.

10 Fonseca (1878), p.65.

11 See F.X. Clooney, 'Roberto de Nobili's Dialogue on Eternal Life and an Early Jesuit Evaluation of Religion in South India', in O'Malley, Bailey et al. (1999), pp.402–17.

12 The practice of hiring Hindus became so commonplace that in 1588 fearful church authorities forbade it for fear of doctrinal contamination. Nevertheless, since the edict was repeated many times over the years, it is clear that most people ignored it. Goa State Archives, Panjim, *9529 Provistes a favor da cristandade* (1595), ff.53a–54b.

13 R. Trota José, *Images of Faith: Religious Ivory Carvings from the Philippines* (1990), p.9.

14 Mach, or Maech, was in his own opinion '… quite skillful at [making crucifixes], as my products testify; indeed, the best ones in Asia and Japan, etc., are made by me … My crucifixes are much appreciated in Italy and the rest of Europe; I have, to my great consolation, supplied all the colleges and brothers here with them …' (J. F. Schütte, *Valignano's Mission Principles for Japan*, trans. J.J. Coyne, SJ [St Louis, 1980], vol.I, p.236. The original letter of 1591 is in Archivum Romanum Societatis Iesu [hereafter cited as ARSI], *Goa 14* [*Epp. Goan. et Malab.*, 1590–99], ff.395a–6b.)

15 V. Serrão, 'A pintura na antiga Índia portuguesa nos séculos XVI e XVII', *Oceanos* 19/20 (September/December 1994), p.107.

16 *Michael Sweerts, 1618–1664: Flemish Master of the Sacred and Profane* (2002).

17 Trota José (1990), pp.9–10; J. Tilakasiri, 'Ivory Carving of Sri Lanka', *Arts of Asia* 4 (1974), p.43; C.P. Woodhouse, *Ivories, A History and Guide* (1976), p.72; A. Coomaraswami, *Medieval Sinhalese Art* (1929), pp.2–3, 183.

18 H. Bechert, 'Die Periode der portugiesischen Herrschaft und die Anfänge der römisch-katholischen Kirche auf der Insel Ceylon', in Wilfried Seipel (ed.), *Exotica: Portugals Entdeckungen im Spiegel fürstlicher Kunst- und Wunderkammern der Renaissance* (2000), pp.87–99; D. Alden, *The Making of an Enterprise: The Society of Jesus in Portugal, its Empire, and Beyond* (1996), pp.152, 169, 188.

19 M. A. Schwabe, 'Schatzkunst auf Ceylon', in *Exotica* (2000), p.102; Alden (1996), p.153; E. Peiris and A. Meersmann, *Early Christianity in Ceylon* 1972), p.45.

20 Alden (1996), p.154.

21 Schwabe (2000), pp.101–04; Calouste Gulbenkian Foundation, *Portuguese Expansion Overseas and the Art of Ivory* (1991); A. Jaffer and M.A. Schwabe, 'A Group of Sixteenth-Century Ivory Caskets from Ceylon', *Apollo* (March 1998), pp.3–14; W. Slomann, 'Elfenbeinreliefs auf zwei singhalesischen Schreinen des 16. Jahrhunderts', *Pantheon*,

vol. XX (1937), pp. 357–63; vol. XXI (1938), pp. 12–19; L. Keil, 'Influência artistica portuguesa no oriente: três cofres de marfim indianos do século XVI', *Boletim de Academia de Belas Artes* (1938), pp. 9–43; L. Keil, 'Alguns exemplos da influência portuguesa em obras de arte indianas do século XVI', *I Congresso da historia da expansão Portuguesa no mundo, II secção* (1938), pp. 5–21.

22 See *Exotica*, cat. no. 62; N. Vassallo e Silva (ed.), *A herança de Rauluchantim* (1996), pp. 142–46; cat. nos 3, 5, 6–9, 12, 20–21; B. Ferrão, *Mobiliario Português, India e Japão* (1990), pp. 9–43.

23 G.A. Bailey, *Counter Reformation Symbolism and Allegory in Mughal Painting* (1996), p. 481, fig. 22.

24 For a recent discussion of Xavier imagery in Japan, see M. Wakakuwa, 'Xavier in the "Fifteen Mysteries of the Rosary" at Kyoto University', in *St Francis Xavier: An Apostle of the East* (1999), pp. 210–26.

25 See G.A. Bailey, 'The Catholic Shrines of Agra', *Arts of Asia* (July–August 1993), pp. 131–37; 'A Portuguese Doctor at the Maharaja of Jaipur's Court', *South Asian Studies* 11 (Summer 1995), pp. 51–62; 'The Lahore *Mirat al-Quds* and the Impact of Jesuit Theater on Mughal Painting', *South Asian Studies* 13 (1997), pp. 95–108; 'The Indian Conquest of Catholic Art: The Mughals, the Jesuits, and Imperial Mural Painting', in *Art Journal* (Spring 1998), pp. 24–30; *The Jesuits and the Grand Mogul: Renaissance Art at the Imperial Court of India, 1580–1630* (1998); 'The Truth-Showing Mirror: Jesuit Catechism and the Arts in Mughal India', in O'Malley, Bailey et al. (1999), pp. 380–401; Bailey (1999), pp. 112–41; 'The End of the "Catholic Era" in Mughal Painting', *Marg* 53, 2 (December 2002), pp. 46–59.

26 This anonymous painter is only mentioned in one published letter (Sir E. Maclagan, 'Jesuit Missions to the Emperor Akbar', *Journal of the Asiatic Society of Bengal* 65 [1896], p. 67), and in the history of Du Jarric (P. Du Jarric, *Akbar and the Jesuits*, trans. C.H. Payne [1926], p. 67). I have found two additional letters that mention him (ARSI, *Goa 14*, f. 288a; and *Goa 46I*, f. 30b).

27 For example, J. Correia-Afonso, *Letters from the Mughal Court* (1980), pp. 33–34; A. Monserrate, *The Commentary of Father Monserrate*, SJ, trans. J.S. Hoyland (1922), pp. 59–60.

28 Maclagan (1934), p. 228; Monserrate (1922), p. 176. This tradition of displaying the picture on the Feast of the Assumption was carried on in the years after the first mission left, when there were no longer any priests at the court.

29 A.K. Das, *Mughal Painting During Jahangir's Time* (1978), p. 68; J. Jennes, *Invloed der Vlaamsche Prentkunst in Indie, China en Japan* (1943), pl. IV; for the original Wierix print, see M. Mauquoy-Hendricks, *Les estampes des Wierix* (1978–83), vol. I, p. 75.

30 Prince Salim's women painters included also Nadira Banu and Raqiya Banu (Das [1978], p. 46).

31 See Bailey (1999), pp. 137–41.

32 Xavier records that he brought oil paintings of the *Madonna and Child* and the *Annunciation*, as well as an illustrated Bible, and wrote in a set of instructions to missionaries about the importance of using imagery to communicate with the Japanese. M. Cooper, SJ (ed.), *The Southern Barbarians* (1971), p. 147.

33 Shinzo Kawamura gave a presentation on this topic called 'Jesuit Confraternities in Japan before 1587', at the conference entitled 'The Jesuits: Cultures, Sciences, and the Arts' at Boston College, May 1997.

34 Bailey (1999), pp. 65–67.

35 ARSI, *Jap/Sin 46*, f. 283a; Bailey (1999), pp. 69–70.

36 ARSI, *Jap/Sin 25*, f. 70a.

37 G.A. Bailey, 'The Migration of Forms in the Art of the Jesuit Missions in Japan and China', *Oriental Art* XLVII, 5 (2001), pp. 7–8.

38 See S. Turnbull, *Japan's Hidden Christians, 1549–1999* (2000); Christal Whelan's documentary film *Otaya: Japan's Hidden Christians* (1997), and her translation of the Hidden Christian devotional text: *The Beginning of Heaven and Earth: The Sacred Book of Japan's Hidden Christians*, trans. and ed. C. Whelan (1996).

39 N. Standaert, 'Jesuit Corporate Culture as Shaped by the Chinese', in O'Malley, Bailey et al. (1999), pp. 352–63.

40 J. Ruiz-de-Medina, SJ (ed.), *Documentos del Japón 1558–1562* (Monumentum Historicum Societatis Iesu, vol. 148), pp. 476–77.

41 Ibid., p. 476.

42 J. Gernet, *China and the Christian Impact*, trans. J. Lloyd (1985), p. 124.

43 Trota José (1990), p. 2.

44 For recent assessments of the contributions of Matteo Ricci, see F. D'Arelli (ed.), *Le marche e l'oriente* (1998).

45 On Wu Li, see X. Lin, *Wu Li (1632–1718): His Life, His Paintings* (2001); J. Chaves, *Singing of the Source: Nature and God in the Poetry of the Chinese Painter Wu Li* (1993).

46 Bailey (1999), pp. 99–105.

47 These illustrations are published in P. d'Elia, *Le origini dell'arte cristiana cinese* (1939), and E. Menegon, *Un solo cielo: Giulio Aleni S.J. geografia, arte, scienza, religione dall'Europa alla Cina* (1994).

48 *Lettres edifiantes et curieuses*, vol. IV (1810), p. 129.

49 C. Clunas, *Pictures and Visuality in Early Modern China* (1997), pp. 172–88.

9
PORTUGUESE SETTLEMENTS AND TRADING CENTRES

1 G. Correia, *Lendas da Índia*, 4 vols (1975), vol. I, p. 626.

2 L.F. Thomaz, *De Ceuta a Timor* (1994), p. 231.

3 J. de Barros, *Décadas*, 4 vols (1983), vol. II, book III, pt I.

4 Ibid., vol. III, book VI, pt II.

5 Correia (1975), vol. I, pp. 629–31. About Portuguese perceptions of Indian towns' art and architecture, see P. Varela Gomes, 'Ovídio Malabar. Manuel de Faria e Sousa, a Índia e a arquitectura portuguesa', *Mare Liberum*, 11–12 (1996), pp. 73–90.

6 F.P. de Laval, *Viagem de Francisco Pyrard de Laval*, 2 vols (1944), vol. I, p. 299.

7 R. D'Intino, *Informação das Cousas da China. Textos do século XVI* (1989), pp. 148–254.

8 Quoted by R. Moreira, 'As formas artísticas', *História dos Portugueses no Extremo Oriente* (1998), vol. I, pp. 449–502. See also J. M. Fernandes, 'Macau, da cidade antiga à arquitectura recente', *Arquitectura Portuguesa*, 12 (1988), pp. 62–73; J.M. Fernandes, 'Macau', *Os Espaços de um Império*, catalogue (1999), pp. 211–12; C. Baracho, 'Um percurso ao encontro do medievalismo em Macau', *Revista de Cultura*, 34 (1998), pp. 147–80.

9 W. Rossa, *Cidades Indo-Portuguesas/ Indo-Portuguese Cities* (1997), pp. 35–39.

10 P della Valle, *The travels of Pietro della Valle in India*, 2 vols (1892), vol. II, p. 297.

11 About Cochin, see J. A. R. S. Tavim, 'A cidade portugesa de Santa Cruz de Cochim ou Cochim de Baixo', *Aquém e Além da Taprobana, estudos luso-orientais à memoria de Jean Aubin e Denys Lombard*, ed. L. F. Thomas (2002), pp. 137–89; H. Carita, 'The dock warehouses in Cochim de Cima: continuity within Portuguese-influenced urbanism and architecture in the Cochin area', *Oriente*, 15 (2003), pp. 48–66.

12 About Diu, see W. Rossa, ibid., pp. 69–75; R. Moreira, 'A fortaleza de Diu e a arquitectura militar no Índico', *Os Espaços de um Império – Estudos* (cat. 1999), pp. 139–47; L.F.D. Antunes, 'Diu, espaços e quotidianos', ibid., pp. 149–59.

13 V. de Lima, *Reviver Malaca* (1988); Moreira (1998).

14 S. M. Miranda and C.S. Serafim, 'O potencial demográfico', *História dos Portugueses no Extremo Oriente*, vol. I, pp. 183–215.

15 Pyrard de Laval (1944), vol. II, pp. 11–19.

16 F. Bethencourt and K. Chaudhuri (ed.), *História da Expansão Portuguesa*, 2 vols (Lisbon, 1998), vol. I, p. 491.

17 Laval (1944), vol. II, p. 48.

18 V.A.C.B. Albuquerque, *O Senado de Goa, memória histórico-archeologica* (1909), p. 87.

19 Della Valle (1892), vol. II, p. 402ff.

20 Ibid., p. 415.

21 Some recent titles: D.M. Kowal, 'The evolution of ecclesiastical architecture in Portuguese Goa', *India and Portugal. Cultural Interactions*, ed. J. Pereira and P. Pal (2001), pp. 70–87 (first published in *Mitteilungen der Carl Justi-Vereinigung*, 5 [1993], pp. 1–22); R. Moreira, 'From Manueline to Renaissance in Portuguese India', *Mare Liberum* 9 (1995), pp. 401–07; P. Dias, *História da Arte Portuguesa no Mundo*, 2 vols (1999); J. Pereira, 'The evolution of the Goan Hindu Temple', *India and Portugal. Cultural Interactions* (2001), pp. 89–97.

22 J.H. van Linschoten, *Itinerário, Viagem ou Navegação para as Índias Orientais ou Portuguesas* (1997), pp. 28–34.

23 See Zinadím, *História dos Portugueses no Malabar*, ed. D. Lopes (1898/1998). The book contains excerpts of J. Dowson, *The history of India as told by its own historians, the Muhammadan period edited from the posthumous papers of the late Sir H. M. Elliot* (1867–77).

24 Linschoten (1997), p. 30ff.

25 Della Valle (1892), vol. II, p. 363.

26 H. Carita, *Palaces of Goa* (1995); A.C. Silveira, *A casa-pátio de Goa* (1999); H. Carita, 'Indo-portuguese civil architecture, origins and first models', *India and Portugal. Cultural Interactions* (2001), pp. 99–113; R. Shankwalker, 'The balcão: a Goan expression', *India and Portugal. Cultural Interactions* (2001), pp. 115–23.

27 Moreira (1998), vol. I, pp. 449–502; R. Moreira, 'Uma fachada retábulo em Macau', *El Museo de Pontevedra*, LIII (1999), pp. 159–68.

28 J. Pereira, *Baroque Goa* (1995), p. 41.

29 Della Valle (1892), vol. I, pp. 104, 156.

30 K.S. Mathew and A. Ahmad, *Emergence of Cochin in the pre-industrial Era: a study of Portuguese Cochin, documents from the Biblioteca da Ajuda, Lisbon* (1990), doc. 65.

31 Concerning modern instruments and cultures of observation, see J. Crary, *Techniques of the Observer, on vision and modernity in the nineteenth century* (1992).

32 Della Valle (1892), vol. II, p. 259.

10
DUTCH SETTLEMENTS AND TRADING CENTRES

1 J.R. Bruijn, F.S. Gaastra and I. Schöffer, *Dutch-Asiatic Shipping in the 17th and 18th Centuries*, 3 vols (1987), vol. I, p. 143.

2 F.S. Gaastra, *De geschiedenis van de VOC* (2002), p. 87.

3 K. Zandvliet, *The Dutch Encounter with Asia 1600–1950* (Amsterdam, exhib. cat. 2002), pp. 189–92.

4 L.W. Blussé, W. Remmelink and I. Smits (eds), *Bridging the Divide, 400 Years The Netherlands–Japan* (2000), pp. 35–51.

5 E. Kaempher, trans. Gaspar Scheuzer, *The History of Japan* (1727).

6 W. van Gulik, *The Dutch in Nagasaki – 19th Century Japanese Prints* (1998).

7 Blussé, Remmelink and Smits (2000), p. 144.

8 L'Abbé de la Porte, *De nieuwe reisiger; of beschryving van de oude en nieuwe waerelt*, 28 vols (1767–83), vol. IV, p. 43.

9 R. van Oers, *Dutch Town Planning Overseas during VOC and WIC Rule (1600–1800)* (2000).

10 R. Raben, *Batavia and Colombo, The Ethnical and Spatial Order of two Colonial Cities* (1996), p. 145.

11 F. de Haan, *Oud Batavia*, 2 vols (1935), p. 710, and H. A. Breuning, *Het voormalige Batavia. Een Hollandse stedestichting in de tropen. Anno 1619* (1954), vol. 1, p. 71.

12 F. Valentijn, *Oud en Nieuw Oost-Indiën*, 5 vols (1724–26), vol. 4, p. 249.

13 J. S. Stavorinus, *Reize van Zeeland over de Kaap de Goede Hoop … in de jaren 1768–1771*, 2 vols (1793), vol. 1, p. 116.

14 Breuning (1954), pp. 67–68.

15 Ibid., p. 74.

11
BRITISH SETTLEMENTS AND TRADING CENTRES

1 Dr J. Fryer, *A New Account of East India and Persia* (1698), pp. 83–4.

2 P. Mundy, *The Travels of Peter Mundy in Europe and Asia, 1608–1667*, ed. Sir R.C. Temple (1907–36), vol. 2 (1914), pp. 25–6. A print of the similar Dutch factory in Surat appeared in P. van der Broecke's *Korte Historiael ende Journaelsche Aenteyckeninghe* (1634), reproduced in A. Farrington, *Trading Places: the East India Company and Asia 1600–1834* (2002), p. 75.

3 S. Master, *The Diaries of Streynsham Master 1675–80*, ed. Sir R. C. Temple (1911), vol. II, pp. 47–8.

4 H.D. Love, *Vestiges of Old Madras 1640–1800* (1913), vol. 1, pp. 25–9.

5 Fryer (1698), p. 66.

6 See A. Harfield, *Bencoolen: a History of the Honourable East India Company's Garrison of the West Coast of Sumatra (1685–1825)* (1995), for the history of the factory at Benkulen.

7 H.B. Morse, *The Chronicles of the East India Company trading to China, 1635–1834*, 5 vols (1926, 1929); vol. 1 (1926) chronicles all this.

8 C. Campbell, A *Passage to China: Colin Campbell's Diary of the First Swedish East India Company's Expedition to Canton, 1732–33*, ed. P. Hallberg and C. Koninckx (1994), p. 108.

9 Morse (1929), vol. 5, pp. 73–4.

10 J.F. Richards, *The New Cambridge History of India I, 5: the Mughal Empire* (1993), pp. 196–204, 232–42.

11 J. Keay, *The Honourable Company: a History of the East India Company* (1991), pp. 141–65.

12 Fryer (1698), p. 38.

13 Bodleian Library, Gough Maps 4°, no. 138, reproduced in Love (1913), vol. 1, frontispiece; C. A. Bayley (ed.), *The Raj. India and the British 1600–1947* (1990), no. 64.

14 BL OIOC, F46, M. Archer, *The India Office Collection of Paintings and Sculpture* (1986), no. 92, pl. XX.

15 A. Hamilton, *A New Account of the East Indies* (1727), vol. 1, pp. 363–67.

16 Ibid., pp. 183–89.

17 BL OIOC, F48, Archer (1986), no. 90, pl. XVII; Bayley (1990), no. 62.

18 P. Rohatgi et al., *Bombay to Mumbai: Changing Perspectives* (1997), pt 1.

19 Hamilton (1727), vol. 2, p. 9.

20 Private collection, J.P. Losty, *Calcutta: City of Palaces* (1990), pl. 2.

21 BL OIOC, F45, Archer (1986), no. 91, pl. XVII; Losty (1990), pl. 1.

22 Losty (1990), pp. 11–33, for Calcutta in this period.

23 BL Map Library K.Top. 116, 23, reproduced in Farington (2002), p. 86. A similarly datable view is in the Peabody Essex Museum of Salem; see C. Crossman, *The Decorative Arts of the China trade* (1991), pl. 83.

24 W. Hickey, *The Memoirs of William Hickey*, ed. Alfred Spencer, 4 vols (1925) vol. 1, p. 202.

25 Morse (1929), vol. 5, p. 173.

26 William Daniell exhibited a watercolour of the 'European factories in Canton' at the Royal Academy in 1806, preparatory to the aquatint engraving published in London in 1808. He subsequently based three oil paintings on it.

27 Hamilton (1727), vol. 1, pp. 363–67.

28 S. and M. Dwivedi, *Bombay: the Cities within* (1995), ch. 1, and Rohatgi et al. (1997), pt 1, for good summaries of Bombay's development up to 1800.

29 Losty (1990), p. 18.

30 W. Hodges, *Travels in India during the years 1780–83* (1793), pp. 1–2. For views of Madras, see T. Daniell, *Oriental Scenery* (1797–98), II, nos. 7–12; W. Orme, *24 Views in Hindostan, drawn by William Orme from the Original Pictures painted by Mr. Daniell and Col. Ward* (1802–05).

31 J. Forbes, *Oriental Memoirs* (1813), vol. 1, pp. 152–53.

32 The earliest series of views of Bombay is that by J. Wales, *Bombay views: Twelve Views of the Island of Bombay and its Vicinity… taken in the Years 1791 and 1792* (1800). See also Forbes (1813), and Rohatgi et al. (1997), pp. 94–127.

33 Mrs Fay, *Original Letters from India* (1817, written in 1780), p. 138.

34 Hodges (1793), p. 14.

35 Mrs Kindersley, *Letters from … the East Indies* (1777), pp. 273–78.

36 Ibid., pp. 79–80.

37 Losty (1990), pp. 40–42.

38 Losty (1990), p. 90.

39 Prints and paintings of Calcutta in the 1780s by William Hodges (1744–97), Thomas Daniell (1749–1840), especially in his *Twelve Views of Calcutta 1786–88* and *Oriental Scenery*, vol. II, nos 1–6, and others, give us a very good idea of what the English settlement looked like.

12
PERSONAL ENCOUNTERS: EUROPEANS IN SOUTH ASIA

1 F. Castanheda, *Historia do Descobrimento e Conquista da India peolos Portugueses* (1582), vol. 1, III-43, p. 107, and quoted in M.A.L Cruz, 'Exiles and Renegades in Early Sixteenth Century Portuguese India', *The Indian Economic and Social History Review*, XXIII, 3 (1986), p. 9.

2 J.H. van Linschoten, *The Voyage of John Huyghen Van Linschoten to the East Indies*, 2 vols (1885), vol. 1, p. 205.

3 Ibid., p. 213.

4 J.-B. Tavernier, *Travels in India*, trans. V. Ball, ed. W. Crooke, 2 vols (1925).

5 Quoted in M.N. Pearson, *The Portuguese in India* (1987), p. 87.

6 Van Linschoten (1885), vol. 1, p. 184.

7 See Cruz (1986), p. 11.

8 G.V. Scammell, 'European Exiles, Renegades and Outlaws and the Maritime Economy of Asia *c.* 1500–1750', *Modern Asian Studies* 26, 4 (1992), pp. 641–61.

9 Cruz (1986) and S. Subrahmanyan, *The Portuguese Empire in Asia, 1500–1700, A Political and Economic History* (1993), pp. 251–52.

10 From a manuscript in the OIOC by Mirza Mohd Bux 'Ashoob', *'Tarikh i-Shadaat e Farrukhsiyar va juloos e Mohd Shah'*, f. 266a, quoted by I. Zaidi, 'French Mercenaries in the Armies of South Asian States 1499–1803', *Indo-French Relations: History and Perspectives* (1990), pp. 51–78.

11 Dr J. Fryer, *A New Account of East India and Persian Letters Being Nine Years Travelled Begun 1672 and finished 1681* (1698), vol. 1, p. 83.

12 W. Foster, *The English Factories in India 1624–1629* (1909), p. 360.

13 W. Foster, *The English Factories in India 1630–1633*, p. 99.

14 Foster *1624–1629*, p. 119; pp. 35, 39, 61. The first ever reference to a love affair between an Englishman and an Indian girl is referred to in a letter of 20 February 1626: 'John Leachland having for some years past privately kept a woman of this country and refusing to put her away, in spite of all persuasions, it is debated whether to dismiss him from the Company's service; but as this would only lead to his marrying her and forsaking his country and friends, it is resolved not to adopt this extreme course, in the hope that time will reclaim him, "being otherwise a man of fayre demeanour, sufficient abilities, and clear of accounts with the Honourable Company in India".'

15 J.A. de Mandelslo, 'The Voyages and Travels of J. Albert de Mandelslo', *The Voyages & Travels of the Ambasssadors sent by Frederick Duke of Holstein, to the Great Duke of Muscovy, and the King of Persia*, trans. J. Davis (1662), p. 27.

16 Foster, *1624–1629*, p. 360.

17 W. Foster, *The English Factories in India 1624–1629*, p. 151.

18 A. Hamilton, *A New Account of the East Indies*, 2 vols (1930), vol. 1, pp. 8–9.

19 Cited in H. D. Love, *Vestiges of Old Madras*, 4 vols (1913), vol. 4, p. 533.

20 C. Lockyer, *An Account Of The Trade With India Containing Rules For Good Government In Trade, And Tables: With Descriptions Of Fort St George, Aheen, Malacca, Condore, Anjenjo, Muskat, Gombroon, Surat, Goa, Carwar, Telicherry, Panola, Calicut, The Cape Of Good Hope, And St Helena Their Inhabitants, Customs, Religion, Government Animals, Fruits &C.* (1711), p. 30.

21 Foster, p. 345. Henry Yule, incidentally, includes both terms in *Hobson-Jobson* (1903). He avoids giving direct translations of these still popular Hindustani endearments, saying merely that 'Banchoot and Beteechoot [are] terms of abuse which we should hesitate to print if their odious meanings were not obscure "to the general". If it were known to the Englishmen who sometimes use the words we believe there are few who would not shrink from such brutality.'

22 Kirkpatrick's conversion to Islam is the best attested of such conversions for marriage purposes, but it is clear from his letters that William Gardner also had to undergo a similar ceremony – as, very probably, did William Palmer. It was no doubt a great deal more widespread than is apparent from the sources, which only go into detail on such points in exceptional circumstances.

23 L. Colley, 'Going Native, Telling Tales: Captivity, Collaborations and Empire', *Past & Present* 168 (August 2000), p. 172.

24 P.J. Marshall, 'Cornwallis Triumphant: War in India and the British Public in the Late Eighteenth Century', in L. Freeman, P. Hayes and R. O' Neill (eds), *War, Strategy and International Politics* (1992), pp. 70–1.

25 W. Hickey, *The Memoirs of William Hickey*, ed. A. Spencer, 4 vols (1925), vol. 2, p. 136.

26 A. Jaffer, *Furniture from British India and Ceylon, the collections of the Victoria and Albert Museum and the Peabody Essex Museum* (2001), p. 40.

27 M.M. Kaye (ed.), *The Golden Calm: An English Lady's Life in Mughal Delhi* (1980), p. 125.

28 C. Hawes, *Poor Relations: The Making of the Eurasian Community in British India 1773–1833* (1996), p. 4.

29 Ibid., p. vi.

30 S. A. al-Latif Shushtari, *Kitab Tuhfat al-'Alam* (1802/1847), p. 342.

31 See D. Ghosh, *Colonial Companions: Bibis, Begums, and Concubines of the British in North India 1760–1830* (PhD, 2000), for an outstanding analysis of the position of Indian *bibis*. Bibi Mehtuab is discussed on p. 219.

32 Captain T. Williamson, *The East India Vade Mecum*, 2 vols (1810, 2nd edn 1825), vol. 1, pp. 344, 451.

33 *Bengal Wills* (1782), no. 24, will of Thomas Naylor, probate granted 6 August 1782; OIOC, L/AG/34/29/4.

34 *Bengal Wills* (1804), no. 13, will of Matthew Leslie; OIOC, L/AG/34/29/16.

35 P. Robb, *Clash of Cultures? An Englishman in Calcutta* (1998), p. 46.

36 For girls paid wages, see Ghosh (2000), especially ch. 4 *passim*, and particularly p. 184.

37 Ibid., p. 205.

38 T. Williamson and C. D'Oyley, *The European in India* (1813), pp. xix–xx. See also Williamson (1810/1825), vol. 1, p. 451.

39 Durba Ghosh, in her extensive search through archives in England and India, found only 37.

40 Ghosh (2000), p. 218.

41 The miniature is in the V&A: D. 1181–1903. See Jaffer (2001), pp. 123–4, for both illustration and an excellent discussion.

42 From the 1782 *Monthly Review* cited by K. Teltsher, *India Inscribed* (1997), p. 162.

43 See E.M. Collingham, *Imperial Bodies: The Physical Experience of the Raj c.1800–1947* (2001), pp. 46–7.

44 C.A. Bayly, *Imperial Meridian: the British Empire and the World 1780–1830* (1989), p. 115.

45 Gardner Papers, National Army Museum, letter 119, Sekundra, 12 December 1821 [p. 320].

46 Cited in S.C. Ghosh, *The Social Condition of the British Community in Bengal* (1970), pp. 73–4.

47 Williamson (1810/1825), vol. 1, p. 412.

48 P.J. Marshall, 'British Society under the East India Company', *Modern Asian Studies* 31, 1 (1997), pp. 101.

49 S.C. Welch, *Room for Wonder: Indian Paintings during the British Period 1760–1880* (1979).

50 Palmer is frequently stated to have married Fyze according to Muslim law – for example, by Count Edouard de Warren in *L'Inde Anglaise* (1845), where he says that the general married his wife, 'a well-born Indian lady … according to the Koran, i.e. the rites of her religion', as is confirmed by Palmer family tradition: see the letter from Palmer's great-granddaughter, Mrs Hester Eiloart, of 15 September 1927, in the OIOC, L/R/7/49. Given Fyze's social status, this would in turn imply that, like James Kirkpatrick, Palmer converted to Islam, which apart from anything else would have removed the obstacle of his previous marriage: Muslims are of course allowed up to four wives. But, unlike the case of Kirkpatrick, there is no firm evidence for a conversion and, in Palmer's will, Fyze is merely referred to as 'Beby Fize Buksh Saheb a Begum, who has been my affectionate friend & companion during a period of more than thirty five years' (OIOC, L/AG/34/29/28: *Bengal Wills* for 1816, P297). This formulation, however, leaves the question open, and certainly does not disprove a Muslim marriage: James Kirkpatrick used a similar formulation in his will to describe Khair un-Nissa, despite having been legally married in a Muslim ceremony, because – according to his friend and assistant Henry Russell – he was worried that English law would not recognize the Muslim marriage and he did not wish to endanger his legacy to his children. (See the letter from Henry Russell to his brother Charles Swallow Field, 30 March 1848, in the private archive of JAK's descendants.) It is quite possible that Palmer described Fyze in this way for the same reason.

51 OIOC, I.O. Coll. 597. The Frankfurt-born Johan Zoffany (1733–1810) lived in Lucknow for two and a half years, staying much of the time with Claude Martin, founder of the famous La Martinière School. On his way back to England (where he had settled in the 1750s) he was shipwrecked off the Andaman Islands. Lots having been drawn among the starving survivors, a young sailor was duly eaten. Zoffany may thus be said with some confidence to have been the first and last Royal Academician to become a cannibal.

52 For details of the court costume of this period, see R. Kumar, *Costumes and Textiles of Royal India* (1998). Kumar's book is much the best source for the clothing of the period, but she severely underestimates the degree of intermarriage and cultural cross-dressing that went on.

53 As with much else concerning Palmer's marriage, there has been a great deal of scholarly controversy about the identity of the figures in the picture. A letter written by Palmer's great-great-granddaughter, M.P. Hanley 'of Assam' (now in the India Office Library), maintains that 'the General was a "bad old man" and had two wives, the first being the Princess Fyzun Nissa of Delhi, the mother of Wm Palmer of Hyderabad and the second a princess of Oudh. I have this information from Mr Charles Palmer who tells me he got it from Miss Meadows Taylor who edited Meadows Taylor's *Story of My Life*' (OIOC, L/R/7/49). This version of events was followed by Mildred Archer in her *Indian and British Portraiture* (1979), pp. 281–6, who thought that the figure kneeling to Palmer's left must be the 'Oudh Princess', and that she was 'looking ardently at Palmer and leaning against his knee while he for his part holds her hand' (although this is clearly not the case if you look carefully at the unfinished picture, and represents an almost unique case of the usually super-scrupulous Mrs Archer failing to look closely at a picture: Nur is in fact neither looking at Palmer nor holding his hand). Archer's reading of the picture has been blindly followed by Beth Toibin in *Picturing Imperial Power: Colonial Subjects in Eighteenth Century British Painting* (1999), pp. 113–14. The story seems, however, to have got garbled in the retelling, for while Fyze and her sister appear frequently in Palmer's letters and will, there is never a single mention of a second Indian wife or concubine – though of course the general did in fact have a previous wife, Sarah Hazell, in St Kitts, and here must lie the origin of the confused story. Palmer's 'Begum of Oudh', referred to in a *Times* marriage announcement of 19 February 1925 (taken out by a proud great-grandson of the Begum who was getting married), which Archer believed to be substantiating evidence for a second Indian wife, was of course Fyze herself, who (though born in Delhi) had long been a Lucknow resident. The beautiful bejewelled figure kneeling beside Palmer in the picture must presumably be Nur Begum, as Mrs Hester Eiloart, another great-granddaughter (who sold the picture to the India Office) always maintained, and as Durba Ghosh also concluded in her investigation of the picture (see Ghosh [2000], p. 97, n. 36). This is also the view of the current director of the prints and drawings section in the India Office, Dr Jerry Losty, who, just to add to the confusion, has recently reattributed the picture to the painter Johan Zoffany (Mildred Archer believed it to be the work of Francesco Renaldi, see Archer [1979] and 'Renaldi and India: A Romantic Encounter', *Apollo* 104 [July – September 1976], pp. 98–105). The well-dressed female figure standing on the extreme right of the picture may be another of Fyze's sisters or family members.

54 *Bengal Wills* (1825), OIOC, L/AG/34/29/37, pp. 185–205.

55 For Mubarak Begum's background, see the Muabarak Bagh papers in the Archives of the Delhi Commisoners Office: D.C.O. F.5/1861. Here it is recorded that 'Mubarik ul Nissa was originally a girl of Brahmin parentage, who was brought from Poona in the Deckan by one Mosst. Chumpa, and presented or sold by the said Chumpa to Genl. Ochterlony when 12 years of age. Mosst. Mubarik ul Nissa from that time resided in Genl. Ochterlony's house, and Mosst. Chumpa resided with her there, being known by the name of Banbahi.'

56 Gardner Papers, National Army Museum, letter 16, p. 42.

57 OIOC, Add. Or 1. See M. Archer. *Company drawings in the India Office Library* (1972), pl. D (opp. p. 166) and p. 201.

58 Sutherland Papers, OIOC, Mss. Eur. D. 547, pp. 133–34. The letter is undated, but is probably *c.* 1801–02, and it must immediately predate the Anglo-Mahratta war of 1803.

59 T. Wilkinson, *Two Monsoons: The life and death of Europeans in India* (1976), p. 84.

60 R.B. Saksena, *Indo-European Poets of Urdu and Persian* (1941), p. 21. Hawes (1996), ch. 4.

61 Ghosh (2000), p. 42, for the disappearance of *bibis* from wills, and p. 36 for their disappearance from the *East India Vade Mecum*.

62 Williamson (1810/1825), vol. 1, p. 501.

63 Williamson and D'Oyley (1813), pl. X, 'A gentleman with his Hookah-burdar, or Pipe-bearer'.

13
PERSONAL ENCOUNTERS: EUROPEANS IN SOUTH-EAST ASIA

1 M. Thévenot, *Relations de divers voyages curieux, qui n'ont point esté publiées* (1663–72), vol. 3, foreword.

2 L. Blussé, W. Remmelink and I. Smits, *Bridging the Divide, 400 Years The Netherlands–Japan* (2000), p. 37.

3 See C. Boxer, *A true Description of the mighty kingdoms of Japan & Siam* (1935).

4 W.Y. Bontekoe, *Memorable Description of the East Indian Voyage, 1618–1625* (1929).

5 G. Ledyard, *The Dutch came to Korea* (1971).

6 R.H. Hesseling, *Prisoners from Nambu: reality and make-believe in seventeenth-century Japanese diplomacy* (2002).

7 Letter by Gentlemen XVII to the governor-general and Council in Amsterdam, 14 October 1651, cited in L. Blussé, 'Retribution and Remorse; The Interaction between the Administration and the Protestant Mission in Early Colonial Formosa', in G. Prakash (ed.), *After Colonialism. Imperial Histories and Postcolonial Displacements* (1994), p. 177.

8 Wang Linheng, *Yue Jian Pian* (1601), p. 142.

9 Wang Dahai, *Haidao Yizhi* (1806, republished and annotated by Yao Nan, Wo Langxuan [eds], 1992), pp. 5–6.

10 L. Blussé, N. Everts and E. Frech, *The Formosan Encounter, Notes on Formosa's Aboriginal Society: A Selection of Documents from Dutch Archival Sources* (1999), p. 20.

11 N. de Graaff, *Reisen van Nicolaus de Graaff*, ed. J.C.M. Warnsinck (1930), p. 7.

12 E.C. Godée Molsbergen, *De stichter van Hollands Zuid-Afrika, Jan van Riebeeck* (1912), pp. 141–42.

13 H.T. Colenbrander, *Jan Pietersz. Coen, levensbeschrijving* (1934), p. 199.

14 F. Valentijn, *Oud en Nieuw Oost-Indiën*, 5 vols (1724–26), vol. IV (1726), p. 248.

15 Colenbrander (1934), p. 274.

16 For this so-called Sara Specx affair, see L. Blussé, *Strange Company: Chinese Settlers, Mestizo Women and the Dutch in VOC Batavia* (1986), p. 161.

17 Ibid., p. 162.

18 Ibid., p. 162.

19 L. Blussé, *Bitter Bonds, A Colonial Divorce Drama of the Seventeenth Century* (2002).

20 For a detailed description, see ibid., pp. 23–26.

21 De Graaff (1930), pp. 13–19.

22 E. Hahn, *Raffles of Singapore* (1968), pp. 216–17.

23 L. Blussé and M. Chen, *The Archives of the Kong Koan of Batavia,* 2003.

14
PERSONAL ENCOUNTERS: EUROPEANS IN EAST ASIA

1 T. Screech, *Sex and the Floating World: Erotic Images in Japan, 1700–1820* (1999), p. 284.

2 T. Screech, *O-Edo Ijin Orai* (*The Coming and Going of Foreigners in the Edo Period*), trans. Takayama Hiroshi (1995), p. 101.

3 W. Hickey, *The Memoirs of William Hickey* (1925), p. 131.

4 Ibid., p. 132.

5 Ibid., p. 131.

6 F. Wood, *No Dogs and Not Many Chinese: Treaty Port Life in China, 1843–1943* (1998), p. 10.

7 G.K. Goodman, *Japan and the Dutch, 1600–1853* (2000), p. 22.

8 W.R. van Gulik, *In the Wake of the Liefde: Cultural Relations between the Netherlands and Japan since 1600* (1986), p. 63.

9 Goodman (2000), pp. 22–23.

10 Ibid., p. 23; van Gulik (1986), p. 63.

11 The Dutch and English factories were established in 1609 and 1613 respectively.

12 L. Blussé, *Strange Company: Chinese Settlers, Mestizo Women and the Dutch in VOC Batavia* (1986), pp. 179–82; van Gulik (1986), p. 47.

13 L. Blussé, W. Remmelink and I. Smits, *Bridging the Divide, 400 Years The Netherlands–Japan* (2000), p. 27.

14 Van Gulik (1986), p. 47.

15 D. Massarella, *A World Elsewhere: Europe's Encounter with Japan in the Sixteenth and Seventeenth Centuries* (1990), p. 233.

16 M. Cooper, *They Came to Japan: An Anthology of European Reports on Japan, 1543–1640* (1965), pp. 64–65.

17 C. Willis, *China and Macau*, from the series *Portuguese Encounters with the World in the Age of Discoveries,* general ed. John Villiers (2002), pp. 89–90.

18 Ibid., p. 102.

19 J.D. Spence, *The Memory Palace of Matteo Ricci* (1984), pp. 220–31; J.D. Spence, *The Chan's Great Continent: China in Western Minds* (1998), p. 35.

20 Cooper (1965), p. 46.

21 Spence (1998), p. 50.

22 Screech (1999), pp. 84–86.

23 Ibid., pp. 287–88.

24 T. Screech, *The Western Scientific Gaze and Popular Imagery in Later Edo Japan: The Lens within the Heart* (1996), p. 71.

25 Blussé, Remmelink and Smits (2000), p. 110; Screech (1996), pp. 88–89.

26 G. Sugita, *Dawn of Western Science in Japan (Rangaku Kotohajime),* trans. Matsumoto Ryozo and Kiyooka Eiichi (1969), p. 34.

27 Ibid., p. 16.

28 D. Keene, *The Japanese Discovery of Europe, 1720–1830* (1969), p. 20.

29 Blussé, Remmelink and Smits (2000), p. 117.

30 E. Kaempfer, *Kaempfer's Japan: Tokugawa Culture Observed,* ed., trans. and annotated by B. M. Bodart-Bailey (1999), pp. 193, 201.

31 K. Katagiri, *Oranda-shuku Ebi-ya no Kenkyu vol. I* (*Study of the Ebi-ya Dutch Lodgings*), (1998), pp. 94–115.

32 Blussé, Remmelink and Smits (2000), p. 121; van Gulik (1986), p. 65.

33 Screech (1999), p. 282.

34 Screech (1996), p. 18.

35 A.C. Ross, *A Vision Betrayed: The Jesuits in Japan and China, 1542–1742* (1994), p. 15.

36 Ibid., p. 19.

37 J.F. Moran, *The Japanese and the Jesuits: Alessandro Valignano in sixteenth-century Japan* (1993), p. 184.

38 C.R. Boxer, *The Christian Century in Japan, 1549–1650* (1951/1991), pp. 195–97; Cooper (1965), p. 410.

39 Spence (1984), p. xii.

40 J. Waley-Cohen, *The Sextants of Beijing* (1999), p. 81.

41 Ross (1994), pp. 124–26.

42 Hickey (1925), p. 127.

43 C.L. French, *Shiba Kōkan: Artist, Innovator, and Pioneer in the Westernization of Japan* (1974), p. 65.

44 Screech (1996), p. 15.

45 Y. Okamoto, *The Namban Art of Japan, The Heibonsha Survey of Japanese Art vol. 19,* trans. R. K. Jones (1972), p. 77.

46 Ibid., pp. 71–72.

47 Waley-Cohen (1999), pp. 105, 114–17.

15
VISUAL RESPONSES: DEPICTING EUROPEANS IN SOUTH ASIA

1 A. Disney and E. Booth (eds), *Vasco da Gama and the Linking of Europe and Asia* (2000), p. 282.

2 M. Beach and E. Koch, *King of the World. The Padshahnama: An imperial manuscript from the Royal Library, Windsor Castle* (1997), p. 58.

3 M.M. Mota, 'Codice Casanatense: an Indo-Portuguese Portrait of Life in 16th-Century India', in J. Pereira and P. Pal (eds), *India and Portugal: cultural interactions* (2001).

4 Ibid., fig. 4.

5 Ibid., fig. 8.

6 M. Brand and G.D. Lowry, *Akbar's India. Art from the Mughal City of Victory* (1985), p. 97; illustrated on p. 29.

7 Ibid., p. 97.

8 M. Beach, *The Grand Mogul. Imperial Painting in India 1600–1660* (1978), no. 7 verso.

9 M. Brand, *The Vision of Kings, Art and Experience in India* (1995), fig. 91.

10 Beach and Koch (1997), p. 179.

11 V.N. Desai, *Life at Court: art for India's rulers, 16th–19th centuries* (1985), p. 14

12 For example, a painting of a single seated Jesuit in the National Museum, New Delhi, no. 50.14/27.

13 Brand and Lowry (1985), p. 53.

14 See, for example, *Paintings from the Muslim Courts of India* (exhib. cat. 1976), no. 89.

15 Beach and Koch (1997), p. 58.

16 Mota (2001), pp. 35–45.

17 See, for example, the reclining mother and child in Brand and Lowry (1985), p. 102.

18 B. Frank, 'A European View of Life in 16th-Century Goa: the Images of Jan Huygen van Linschoten', in Pereira and Pal (2001), p. 60.

19 H. Yule and A.C. Burnell, *Hobson-Jobson. A glossary of colloquial Anglo-Indian words and phrases …* (second edn 1903), p. 713, which suggests the term was current before 1808.

20 Beach and Koch (1997), no. 46.

21 Quoted in M. Strachan, *Sir Thomas Roe 1581–1644. A Life* (1989), p. 103.

22 See, for example, S. Stronge, *Painting for the Mughal emperor. The Art of the Book in India 1560–1650* (2002), pl. 105.

23 See C. Brown, H. Vlieghe et al., *Anthony Van Dyck* (1999), pls 93 and 97 for Van Dyck portraits of 1637 and 1638 showing young men in comparable costume and hairstyles. I am greatly indebted to Susan North for her guidance on seventeenth-century European dress in this context.

24 A. Jaffer, *Luxury Goods from India: the Art of the Indian Cabinet-Maker* (2002), pp. 60–61.

25 M. Zebrowski, *Deccani Painting* (1983), p. 204; L. Y. Leach, *Mughal and other Indian Paintings from the Chester Beatty Library,* 2 vols (1995), vol. II, p. 952. The youth in western dress is identified by both authors as a woman, but there seems to be no justification for this.

26 For Persian parallels, see S. Canby, *Persian Painting* (1993), fig. 69; S. Canby, *Princes, Poets and Paladins. Islamic and Indian paintings from the collection of Prince and Princess Sadruddin Aga Khan* (1998), fig. 48.

27 The scene was identified as a Dutch–Danish encounter of 1654 by Ebeltje Hartkamp-Jonxis in a paper given at the 2001 CIETA conference (awaiting publication).

28 See, for example, M. Gittinger, *Master Dyers to the World. Technique and Trade in Early Indian Dyed Cotton Textiles* (1982), nos 100–02 (coverlets) and no. 108 (procession).

29 Ibid., no. 81.

30 J. Irwin, 'Golconda cotton paintings of the early seventeenth century', *Lalit Kala*, vol. 5, pp. 8–48 (1959), figs 4, 5.

31 P. Rawson, *Erotic Art of India* (1977), fig. 35.

32 Fitzwilliam Museum, Cambridge. Two more erotic paintings from the same album – showing Rajput Indian rather than western men with Indian women – are illustrated in C.A. Bayley (ed.), *The Raj. India and the British 1600–1947* (1990), cat. no. 75. It is noticeable that the Rajputs are also naked but for their headgear.

33 A. Topsfield, 'Ketelaar's Embassy and the Farangi theme in the Art of Udaipur', *Oriental Art,* vol. XXX, no. 4 (Winter 1984–85), pp. 350–54.

34 Rawson (1977), fig. 36.

35 Mason (2001), cat. no. 63.

36 A. Topsfield (1984–85), fig. 12. For an earlier winged European, see S. Gahlin, *The Courts of India. Indian Miniatures from the Collection of the Fondation Custodia, Paris* (1991), cat. no. 6. Paintings of winged *peris* riding composite-animal mounts are in the V&A (IS 108–1949) and Chester Beatty Library, Dublin (illustrated in Leach [1995], p. 967).

37 Illustrated in Spink, *The Eye of the Courtier. Indian and Islamic Works of Art* (exhib. cat. 1999), no. 59; Fondation Custodia (2001), cat. no. 30, and Paris (1986), cat. no. 90.

38 J. Guy and D. Swallow (eds), *Arts of India 1550–1900* (1990), p. 200.

39 Ibid., p. 208.

40 G. Sengupta, 'The Portuguese in Bengal', in Pereira and Pal (2001), pp. 30–31.

16
VISUAL RESPONSES: DEPICTING EUROPEANS IN EAST ASIA

1 Quoted in G. Elison, *Deus Destroyed: The Image of Christianity in Early Modern Japan* (1991), p. 321. The first *bateren*, or padre, in Japan was Francis Xavier, who arrived in 1549, during the reign of Emperor (Mikado) Go Nara (r. 1536–57). Mikoshi Nyūdō is a genie who looks like a monk and is of extraordinary size, and the more one looks at him, the bigger he gets. The reference to the *bateren*'s great height is perhaps a distorted memory of Alessandro Valignano, who was exceedingly tall.

2 The term *nanban*, or 'southern barbarian', is derived from Chinese. It is not a particularly pejorative term.

3 To view a Japanese screen, as in a handscroll, you pass along the scene, normally from right to left, but in the case of *nanban* screens from left to right. The protagonist, in this case the captain-major, can appear repeatedly. There is no one fixed viewpoint; you should always be at right-angles to the section you are looking at. Nor is there a fixed vanishing point as in European linear perspective. In Japanese paintings the viewer looks down into the picture.

4 For a full description, see S. Izzard, *Japanese paintings and works of art, Korean ceramics* (2000), pp. 12–19.

5 Originally all the screens would have been in pairs, but in some cases only one has survived.

6 See O. Yoshitomo and T. Tadao, *Nanban Byōbu* (*Namban Screens*) (1970). There is some debate as to whether the different types of screen developed sequentially or evolved simultaneously, but the latter is the more commonly held view.

7 The screen attributed to Kanō Mitsunobu is in the Nanban Bunkakan in Osaka.

8 See, for example, O. Shunroku, *Rakuchū-rakugai zu to Nanban Byōbu (Scenes in and around the Capital to Nanban Screens),Shinpen Meihō Nihon no Bijutsu 25* (1991), p. 68. I would like to thank Kyoko Ando for researching and translating this and other Japanese-language sources.

9 The presence of Jesuits and other missionaries in the *nanban* screens makes Christianity another key element of these depictions, but those who commissioned these screens were not generally Christian converts. Christianity was just another characteristic of the 'exotic', something that is seen, for example, in the wearing of crucifixes as a fashion item.

10 The Kanō school was one of the most influential of the Japanese schools of painting, patronized from the late Muromachi (1333–56) through to the Edo period (1615–1868) by successive military governments. They were particularly famed for their landscape, figure and bird and flower compositions, which synthesized elements from Chinese and Japanese painting styles. The main branches of the Kanō served the *shōgun* and *daimyō*, but *machi-Kanō* ('town Kano') painted works for the merchant classes. It was these artists who painted most of the *nanban* screens.

11 See N. Katsushi, 'Nanban Byōbu no Tenkai' ('The Development of Nanban Screens'), in Kobe City Museum, *Nanban Kenbunroku* (*A Record of Encounter with Nanban Culture*) (Kobe, exhib. cat. 1992), p. 84. The ports include Sakai, Osaka, Tsuruga, Kanazawa, Takaoka and Yamagata.

12 See J. Rosenfield and F.E. Cranston, *Extraordinary Persons: Works of Eccentric, Nonconformist Japanese Artists of the Early Modern Era (1580–1868) in the Collection of Kimiko and John Powers* (1999), vol. 1, p. 272; and Tobacco and Salt Museum, *Ikoku no Kaze: Edo Jidai Kyōto o Irodatt Yōroppa* (*Winds from Afar: European Influences on Edo-period Kyoto*) (Tokyo, exhib. cat. 2000), pp. 22–23. Izumi Mari has established an artistic precedent for the image of a treasure ship and a procession of foreigners in the *tosen zu* (Chinese ship picture) screens produced in the fifteenth century in the era of Japan–China trade. None of these screens survives, but there are echoes of the theme in works from the early Edo period. See Okudaira (1991), p. 69.

13 K. Hideo, *Kyōkai no Chūsei, Shōchō no Chūsei* (*The Boundaries and Symbols of the Medieval Age*) (1986), pp. 108–32.

14 Although the goblins of the opening quote are probably a reference to *tengu*, a Japanese mountain creature.

15 Seen, for example, in the Chinese-style canopy in the screen illustrated here.

16 R. P. Toby, 'The "Indianness" of Iberians and the changing Japanese iconographies of Others', in S.B. Schwartz (ed.), *Implicit Understandings: Observing, Reporting and Reflecting on the Encounters between Europeans and Other Peoples in the Early Modern Era* (1994), pp. 323–51.

17 The first Japanese encounter with China dates back to about the first century, but with the coming of Buddhism in the sixth century the Sinicization of Japanese culture began in earnest.

18 See J. Waley-Cohen, *The Sextants of Beijing: Global Currents in Chinese History* (1999), pp. 57–58, and C. Clunas, *Superfluous Things: Material Culture and Social Status in Early Modern China* (1991), pp. 58–59.

19 M. Cooper (ed.), *João Rodrigues's Account of Sixteenth Century Japan* (2001), p. 125.

20 See Waley-Cohen (1999), pp. 92–96, and J. Hevia, *Cherishing Men from Afar: Qing*

Guest Ritual and the Macartney Embassy of 1793 (1995), pp. 29–56.

21 Hevia (1995), pp. 118–21.

22 See W. Cheng-hua, 'The Qianlong Emperor and his Legacy: the National Palace Museum's 2002 October Exhibition', in *Orientations*, vol. 33, no. 8 (October 2002), pp. 66–67.

23 Quoted in Zhang Hongxing, *The Qianlong Emperor: Treasures from the Forbidden City* (Edinburgh, exhib. cat. 2002), p. 66.

24 There are examples of riding and hunting screens in the Rijksmuseum, Amsterdam, and the Museum of Fine Arts, Boston. I have not studied all screens depicting foreigners, so cannot be entirely sure that Europeans and Chinese are never shown interacting.

25 The description and analysis of this work is based on that by K. Ruitenbeek and published in *Bulletin Rijksmuseum* 37/4 (1989), English summary, pp. 353–54.

26 See W. L. Idema, 'Cannon, Clocks and Clever Monkeys: Europeana, Europeans and Europe in some early Qing Novels', in E.B. Vermeer (ed.), *Development and Decline of Fukien Province in the 17th and 18th Centuries* (1990), pp. 459–88.

27 Quoted in J. Spence, *The Chan's Great Continent: China in Western Minds* (1998), p. 48.

28 See Kobe City Museum, *Ikoku-e no Bōken: Kinsei Nihon Bibutsu ni Miru Jōhō to Gensō (The Admiring of Exotic Art: Intellectual and Creative Images of Japanese Pre-Modern Times)* (Kobe, exhib. cat. 2001), p. 43, for a set of scroll paintings in the Museum's collection that show European figures and buildings within a Chinese-style landscape. A set of scroll paintings in a private collection in London depicts similar figures and buildings, but within a European landscape.

29 E. Uitzinger, 'For the Man who has Everything: Western-style Exotica in the Birthday Celebrations at the Court of Ch'ien-Lung, in L. Blussé and H.T. Zurndorfer, *Conflict and Accommodation in Early Modern East Asia: Essays in Honour of Erik Zürcher* (1993), pp. 216–39.

30 There are similar scroll paintings in a private collection in New York. The works seem to relate to an imperial twelve-fold screen; see C. and M. Beurdekey, *Giuseppe Castiglione: A Jesuit Painter at the Court of the Chinese Emperors* (1972), p. 182. There are also ceramics that depict Europeans in Chinese surroundings (for example, V&A: FE.131–1975).

31 The scroll has a pair that depicts the Chinese settlement at Nagasaki. Other similar versions of the handscrolls can be found in the British Museum, Kobe City Museum and in a private collection in America. The identity of the painter is unknown, but it is possible that he was a member of the *kara-e mekiki* (literally 'Chinese painting expert'), charged with the job of evaluating and making copies of both antique and contemporary paintings imported into Nagasaki.

32 In the collection of Kobe City Museum is an imported Dutch glass bottle that has been painted with the scene.

33 Tokugawa society was rigidly stratified; at the top were the *samurai*, then the farmers, then the artisans and finally the merchants. This neo-Confucian structure did not mirror the realities of the Edo period, for it was the merchants who benefited most from the peace and prosperity both from the demand for goods and from the introduction of a cash economy.

34 N. Joken, *Kai Tsūshō Kō (On Commercial Relations with China and Barbarians)*, first published 1695, quoted in C.R. Boxer, *Jan Company in Japan 1600–1817* (1968), pp. 173–74.

35 T. Ryōan, *Wakan Sansai Zue (Japanese Chinese Illustrated Assembly by the Three Components of the Universe)*, first published 1712, trans. and adapted by Shimada Isao and others in *Tōyō Bunko 456* (1986), pp. 402–03.

36 See, for example, Ōtsuki Gentaku, *Ransetsu Benwaku (Explanation of the Dutch)* of 1799.

37 H. Toshiaki, *Seiiki Monogatori (Tales of the West)*, 1798, quoted in L. Blussé, W. Remmelink and I. Smits (eds), *Bridging the Divide: 400 Years The Netherlands–Japan* (2000), p. 79.

38 Translated in R.H. Blythe, *A History of Haiku* (1963), vol. 1, p. 69.

39 See S. Izuro, 'Ikoku Haishu ki' (*Notes on Exotic Themes in Haiku Poetry*), first published in 1926, in *Shinmura Izura Zenshū (Complete Works of Shinmura Izura)* (1966), vol. 11, pp. 316, 322.

40 Translated in T. Screech, *The Western Scientific Gaze and Popular Imagery in Later Edo Japan: The Lens within the Heart* (1996), p. 29. Hikida was the proprietor of the shop.

41 Ibid., pp. 44–47.

42 Written with the characters meaning 'sad world', the word *ukiyo* was originally a Buddhist term that denoted the painful nature of the transient world. By the second half of the seventeenth century the ephemeral aspect of the world was seen as a cause for celebration rather than sorrow, and the word *ukiyo* was redefined and rewritten with the characters 'floating world'. *Ukiyo* connoted a sense of modernity, stylishness and living for the moment. The floating world had its focus in the licensed pleasure quarters of Edo and other large cities.

EUROPEAN DEPICTIONS OF ASIANS

1 Doubt has been cast as to whether Marco Polo actually travelled to China, although there is no doubt as to the impact of his tales.

2 B. Frank, 'A European View of Life in 16th-Century Goa: the Images of Jan Huygen van Linschoten', in J. Pereira and P. Pal (eds.), *India and Portugal: Cultural Interactions* (2001), pp. 47–69.

3 D. Lach, *Asia in the Making of Europe, Vol. II: A Century of Wonder* (1970), p. 94.

4 Ibid., p. 100, pls 53–4.

5 E.A. Standen, 'English Tapestries "After the Indian Manner"', *Metropolitan Museum Journal* 15 (1981), pp. 119–41.

6 Ibid., fig. 2.

7 Schellinks's contemporary Rembrandt (1606–69) had a collection of Mughal miniatures, of which he made copies. See O. Benesch, *The Drawings of Rembrandt*, 6 vols (1973).

8 P. Pal et al, *Romance of the Taj Mahal* (1989), pp. 195–7.

9 J. Menzhausen, *The Green Vaults* (1968), cat. no. 132.

17
ASIA IN EUROPE: PORCELAIN AND ENAMEL FOR THE WEST

1 The items were dispersed two years after his death.

2 This was a 'soft paste', which resembled Middle Eastern frit ware rather than Chinese 'hard paste' in its composition, being made of fine sand, 15–20 per cent white clay and glazemaker's sinter. Glazemaker's sinter or marzacotta was composed of sand, salt and calcined wine lees. The 'sinter' was a popular ingredient in contemporary Italian tin glazes, and was described by Cipriano Piccolpasso in his 1557 work *The Three Books of the Potter's Art*, trans. R. Lightbown and A. Caiger-Smith (1980).

3 'Medici porcelain' consisted of a mixture of materials available in Italy at the time: white china clay and ground Venetian glass.

4 The ewer has a Jiajing period reign mark (1522–66) and was likely to have been made in a time of flourishing clandestine trade between 1540 and 1549, in spite of the suspension of formal trading relations between China and Portugal from 1522 to 1554. N. de Castro, *Chinese Porcelain and the Heraldry of Empire* (1988), pp. xv and 17, where another ewer with Peixoto arms is shown.

5 The inscription, which is miscopied in a variety of ways on all the Chinese porcelain vessels so far recorded, translates as 'Jorge Alvares had this made in the year 1552'.

6 J. Welsh, *Important Collection of Chinese Porcelain and Works of Art from the 16th to the 19th Century* (October 2000), pp. 4–7.

7 Discussed in M. Wilson, *Rare Marks on Chinese Ceramics* (1998), no. 22, pp. 64–65.

8 Examples of Dutch and English red stonewares with labels and panels describing their circumstances of manufacture are shown in the European Galleries, the British Galleries and the sixth-floor Ceramics Galleries in the V&A.

9 W.D. Kingery, 'The development of European porcelain', *Ceramics and Civilization Vol. 3, High Technology Ceramics – Past Present and Future* (1986), pp. 153–80.

10 The origins and history of Augustus the Strong's collection of Chinese and Japanese porcelain is explored in E. Ströber, *'La maladie de porcelaine'… Ostasiatisches Porzellan aus der Sammlung Augusts des Starken* (2001).

11 The huge kiln complexes at Jingdezhen were situated north-east of the European trading port of Canton, in Jiangxi province. They were the major supplier of Chinese porcelain to both domestic and world markets from the fourteenth century onwards. Regular cargoes of porcelain were transported from Jingdezhen to Canton by water, using an extensive network of canals, rivers, lakes and an inland sea-coastal route.

12 *Hausmaler* were highly skilled artisans who decorated glass and ceramics on a freelance basis. European factories kept their own decorators, but those artisans had to work anonymously and in the approved factory style.

13 The cup and saucer are discussed in more depth by W.R. Sargent, 'A Preissler Decorated Chinese Chocolate Cup and Saucer, 1729–35', *Mélanges en souvenir d'Elisalex d'Albis 1939–1998* (1999), pp. 45–50.

14 D. Howard and J. Ayers, *China for the West. Chinese Porcelain & other Decorative Arts for Export Illustrated from the Mottahedeh Collection*, 2 vols (1978), vol. 1, pp. 292–99.

15 C.J.A. Jörg, *Jan Menze van Diepen Stichting. A Selection from the Collection of Oriental Ceramics. Selectie uit de collectie Oosterse keramiek* (2002), p. 144, see also pp. 143, 145, 201.

16 Howard and Ayers (1978), vol. 1, pp. 239–40.

17 C. Clunas (ed.), *Chinese Export Art and Design* (1987), pp. 64–65; D.F. Lunsingh Scheurleer, *Chinese Export Porcelain. Chine de Commande* (1974), pp. 111, 119.

18 The scenes on the punchbowl are described in detail in *Important Chinese Export Porcelain and Works of Art* (catalogue, May 1988), cat. 55.

19 W.R. Sargent, *The Copeland Collection. Chinese and Japanese Ceramic Figures* (1991), pp. 112–13. See also Howard and Ayers (1978), vol. 2, pp. 612–13.

20 A range of painted enamels in European style are illustrated in *Tributes from Guangdong to the Qing Court* (1987), nos 44–46, 51–55, pp. 84–85, 88.

21 J. van Campen, *Royers Chinese kabinet* (2000), pp. 8–9, 28–29. J. van Campen, '"In 't vuur geschilderd" Geëmailleerde platen van kopper en porselein uit de collectie J. Th. Royer (1737–1807)', *Bulletin Van Het Rijksmuseum* (2002), no. 1, pp. 2–27, 92–95.

22 The palette is best known by the name *famille rose*, a term adopted in the mid-nineteenth century.

23 R. Kerr, 'What were the Origins of Chinese *Famille Rose*', *Orientations*, vol. 31 (May 2000), pp. 53–59.

24 Lan Pu, *Jingdezhen Taolu (An Account of Ceramic Production at Jingdezhen)*, first published 1815, ch. 2, p. 6a.

EAST ASIAN METALWORK FOR THE EXPORT MARKET

1 J. Wathen, *Journal of a Voyage in 1811 and 1812 to Madras and China* (1814), p. 189.

18
ASIA IN EUROPE: LACQUER FOR THE WEST

1 For examples of diplomatic gifts of lacquerware from the Chinese Yongle emperor (r. 1403–33) to the Japanese *shōgun*, Ashikaga Yoshimitsu (1368–1408), see J. Figgess, 'A Letter from the Court of Yung Lo', *Transactions of the Oriental Ceramic Society* (1962–63), vol. 34, pp. 97–100.

2 M. Boyer, *Japanese Export Lacquers from the seventeenth century in the National Museum of Denmark* (1959), p. 21.

3 According to contemporary European written accounts, there was considerable interest and accurate technical information concerning Chinese and Japanese lacquer. Examples include Father Cosme de Torres, 1575, see M.H. Mendes Pinto, *Namban Lacquerware in Portugal: The Portuguese presence in Japan (1543–1639)* (1990), p. 41; for the *Vocabulario da Lingoa de Japam*, dating from 1603, with a supplement of 1604, see L. Leiria, 'The Art of Lacquering; According to the Namban-Jin written sources', *Bulletin of Portuguese/Japanese Studies* (December 2001), pp. 9–26; and for the French Jesuit Louis Lecomte, 1696, see P. De Moura Carvalho (ed.), *The world of Lacquer: 2000 years of history* (exhib. cat. 2001), p. 44.

4 Torres (1575), quoted in Mendes Pinto (1990), p. 41.

5 M. Jourdain and R. Soame Jenyns, *Chinese Export Art in the Eighteenth Century* (1967), p. 17, fn. 4.

6 See Boyer (1959), p. 36.

7 A similar use of labour-saving devices is also apparent in contemporary Kōdaiji *makie* (*makie*, or 'sprinkled picture', wares associated with the Kōdaiji temple); the earliest *nanban* lacquerwork, however, would appear to predate the appearance of Kōdaiji *makie*.

8 In particular the scrolling *kuzu* vine motif, often used on the interior of the domed coffer lid, was highly suited to objects decorated in haste, since it could be adapted with ease to any size or shape with the minimum of planning (see plate 18.2).

9 Such cartouches invariably contain pairs of birds set against a dense background of peony scrolls that cover the entire surface; *nanban* decoration shares many characteristics with these earlier caskets. See J. Figgess, 'A Group of Decorated Lacquer Caskets of the Yuan Dynasty', *Transactions of the Oriental Ceramic Society* (1964–66).

10 The use of the *nanban* scroll also had its immediate origins in Chinese porcelain of the early fourteenth century. It is quite likely that the scroll is a simplified and abstracted version of the simple foliate or half-palmette scroll used in Chinese Buddhist architecture, especially from the late sixth century onwards.

11 O. Impey, 'Namban: Japanese export lacquer for Portugal', in De Moura Carvalho (2001), p. 110.

12 For those that did sell, prices ranged from £4 5s. for a small coffer to £28 for the largest or best *escritorio*, a considerable sum in those days.

13 See J. Earle, 'Genji meets Yang Guifei: A Group of Japanese export lacquers', *Transactions of the Oriental Ceramic Society* (1982–83).

14 See J. Hutt, 'East and West in Japanese Export Lacquerware: Some Problem Pieces in the Victoria and Albert Museum', *Ostasiatische und europäische Lacktechniken/ East Asian and European Lacquer techniques* (dual text) (2000), fig. 1.

15 Another instance of Japanese craftsmen not understanding what they were copying is exemplified by the Coyet shield, made between 1652 and 1662. Instead of the cartouche encircling the coat of arms, they sit one on top of the other. For an illustration, see M. Koyama, 'The *Makie* Shield – A Decorated Lacquered Hide Shield in the "P. A. Garda" Collection', *Shikkoshi* (November 1998), fig. 19.

16 See J. Hutt, 'A Japanese lacquer chest in the V&A; A seventeenth-century wedding casket for the Dutch market', *Apollo* (March 1998), and J. Hutt, 'A Japanese export lacquer chest in the Victoria & Albert Museum; Some further observations', *Apollo* (March 1999).

17 See Hutt (2000), figs 5, 7.

18 Hutt (1998), fig. 4, or Hutt (2000), fig. 6.

19 C. Clunas (ed.), *Chinese Export Art and Design* (1987), p. 80.

20 See Clunas (1987), pl. 62.

21 J. Stalker and G. Parker, *A Treatise of Japanning and Varnishing* (1688, reprinted 1960), p. 37.

22 Torres (1575), quoted in Mendes Pinto (1990), p. 41.

23 Jourdain and Soame Jenyns (1967), p. 23.

24 For an example, see Y. Okada et al. (eds), *Nihon no Shitsugei* (1978–79), vol. IV, pl. 15.

25 Kōdaiji wares are named after the temple for which they were predominantly made. For an example, see Okada (1978–79), vol. III, pls 2–4.

26 Jourdain and Soame Jenyns (1967), p. 19, quoting from J.B. du Halde, *Description geographique, historique, chronologique, politique et physique de l'empire de la Chine* (1735).

27 S. Pepys, *Pepys's Diary*, vol. 1, selected and ed. Robert Lathem (1996 reprint), p. 129.

28 J. Evelyn, *The Diary of John Evelyn: Now first printed in full from manuscripts belonging to Mr John Evelyn and edited by E. S. De Beer* (1673–89, 1955 reprint), vol. IV p. 190.

29 J. Pollexfen, *A Discourse of Trade, Coyn and Paper Credit* (1697), quoted in Boyer (1959), p. 36.

30 C. Jörg, 'Japanese Export Lacquer for the Dutch Market' (2000), p. 43, quoting from T. H. L. Scheurleer, 'Aanbesteding en verspreiding van Japans lakwerk door de Nederlanders in de zeventiende eeuw', Jaarverslagen, *Oudheidkundig Genootschap* (1939–1941), p. 47.

31 One similar piece was a ballot-box, dated 1619, that was used by the East India Company and subsequently owned by the Worshipful Company of Saddlers. For illustrations, see Y. Crowe, 'Echoes of Far Eastern Lacquer in the World of Islam', *Transactions of the Oriental Ceramic Society* (1997–98), vol. 62, figs 8, 9.

32 It has long been a common belief that shellac was the basis of most japanning. Recent scientific research has confirmed sandarac to be the most common constituent (see K. Walch and J. Koller [eds], *Lacke des Barock und Rokoko/ Baroque and Rococo Lacquers* [dual text], [1997], pp. 157, 159, 161–62). I would like to thank Shayne Rivers for drawing this to my attention.

33 At around this time, the effects of lacquerware were also imitated in black glazed Delftwares that were decorated in yellow in-glaze painting. A jar and lid, inventory no. 166–1887, is one such example in the V&A, decorated with designs imitating those on lacquer in yellow on black.

34 See G. Boesen '"Chinese" Rooms at Rosenborg Castle', in *The Connoisseur* (January 1979), pp. 37–39.

35 E. Kaempfer, *The History of Japan, together with a description of Siam* (written 1690–92, but not published until 1727), quoted in O. Impey, 'Japanese Export Lacquer of the 17th Century', in William Watson (ed.), *Lacquerwork in Asia and Beyond* (1982), p. 125.

36 De Moura Carvalho (2001), p. 132, quoting from Sir G. Watt, *The Commercial Products of India* (1908), pp. 779–80.

37 See de Moura Carvalho (2001), pls 67–73.

38 For examples, see Sir H. Garner, *Chinese Lacquer* (1979), pls 154–57.

39 There are few contemporary surviving examples, one exception being an octagonal ebony carving illustrated in B. Dam-Mikkelsen and T. Lundbæk (eds), *Ethnographic Objects in The Royal Danish Kunstkammer 1650–1800* (Danish–English), (1980), p. 128, Edc33; the earliest it was inventoried was in 1689.

40 De Moura Carvalho (2001), p. 140.

41 Boyer (1959), pl. I (5, 6), and pl. II (7, 8), inventory numbers Edc 61a&b–64a&b.

42 E. Tellerup, Appendix I, in Boyer (1959), pp. 147–48.

43 Koyama (1998), vol. 21, pp. 36–57.

44 Impey (1982), p. 138, quotes one such reference in 1649.

45 Clunas (1987), p. 84.

46 O. Impey, 'Sasaya Kisuke, Kyoto "Nagasaki" Lacquer and the woodworker Kiyotomo', *Oriental Art* (Summer 1998), p. 32.

47 Impey (1982), p. 136.

48 O. Impey, 'Japanese export lacquer', *Lacquer: An International History and Collector's Guide* (1984), p. 133.

49 Impey (1998), p. 32.

50 Another probable example is a very unusual *nanban* chest dating from the 1630s and illustrated in Christie's (2002), lot 147. Among the decoration are two roundels with designs inlaid in mother-of-pearl, in a manner similar to the trays, though the ground is gold lacquer.

51 Du Halde (1735), quoted in Jourdain and Soame Jenyns (1967), p. 19.

19
ASIA IN EUROPE: FURNITURE FOR THE WEST

1 M. Cooper (ed.), *João Rodrigues's Account of Sixteenth-Century Japan* (2001) p. 141.

2 F.P. de. Laval, *The Voyage of François Pyrard de Laval*, trans. from the 3rd French edn of 1619, ed. A. Gray, 2 vols (1887–8), vol. II, pt 1, pp. I, 176–77.

3 *The Lady's Magazine* (September 1784).

4 J.A de Mandelslo, 'The Voyages and Travels of J. Albert de Mandelslo', in *The Voyages & Travels of the Ambasssadors sent by Frederick Duke of Holstein to the Great Duke of Muscovy, and the King of Persia*, trans. J. Davis (1662), p. 21.

5 C. Iglesias, *Felipe II, un Monarca y su Epoca* (1998), cat. 23.

6 S. Sangl, 'Von der Aneignung des Fremden. Indische Perlmutt-Raritaten und ihre europaischen Adaptionen in Munchen', *Weltkunst* (1996), pp. 2938–43.

7 S. Digby, 'The mother-of-pearl overlaid furniture of Gujarat: the holdings of the Victoria and Albert Museum', *Facets of Indian Art*, ed. R. Skelton et al. (1986), pp. 213–22.

8 That there exists a small group of objects that has both mastic-inset *and* overlaid mother-of-pearl decoration suggests that Gujarati craftsmen working in the two techniques collaborated or deliberately worked in each other's style.

9 P.A. Tiele (ed.), *The Voyage of John Huygen van Linschoten to the East Indies. From the Old English Translation of 1598* (1885), p. 136.

10 *'L'orfevrerie parisienne de la Renaissance – Tresors disperses'* (1995), p. 112.

11 G. Jackson-Stops (ed.), *The Treasure Houses of Britain: five hundred years of private patronage and art collecting* (Washington, exhib. cat. 1985), p. 169.

12 A. Jaffer, *Luxury Goods from India, the Art of the Indian Cabinet-Maker* (2002), pp. 18–19.

13 S. Seth (ed.), *Indian Travels of Thevenot and Careri* (1949), p. 25; de Laval (1887–88), vol. II, pp. 176–77, 247–48.

14 For a full discussion of these caskets, see A. Jaffer and M. Schwabe, 'A group of sixteenth-century ivory caskets from Ceylon', *Apollo* (March 1998).

15 For a related example, see Jaffer (2002), pp. 20–21.

16 S. Arasaratnam (trans. and ed.), *François Valentijn's Description of Ceylon* (1978), p. 166.

17 Jaffer (2002), pp. 18–19.

18 Ibid., pp. 64–66.

19 BM, Mss. Sloane 197, f. 251. (Pedro Barreto, *Livro de Estado da India*).

20 *Travels of Fray Sebastien Manrique 1629–1643*, introduction and notes by Lt-Col C. Eckford Luard assisted by Father H. Hosten (1927), vol. I, p. 31.

21 J. Veenendaal, *Furniture from Indonesia, Sri Lanka and India during the Dutch Period* (1985), pp. 150–56.

22 Ibid., p. 150.

23 Ibid., p. 151.

24 P. Spear, *The Nabobs* (1991 reprint), p. 177.

25 British Library, IORC, G/40/23, ff. 78–80.

26 T. Bowrey, *Geographical Account of Countries around the Bay of Bengal*, ed. R.C. Temple (1905), p. 71.

27 Jaffer (2001), p. 133.

28 M. van de Geijn-Verhoeven et al., *Domestic Interiors at the Cape and in Batavia 1602–1795* (The Hague, exhib. cat. 2002), pp. 28–34.

29 Jaffer (2001), p. 78.

30 C. Jörg, *Chinese Export Porcelain: Chine de Commande from the Royal Museums of Art and History in Brussels* (1989), p. 33.

31 A. Bulley, *Free Mariner* (1992), p. 74; J. Wathen, *Journal of a Voyage in 1811 and 1812 to Madras and China* (1814), p. 199.

32 Arasaratnam (1978), p. 292.

33 British Library, IORC, E/3/90 pp. 342–43, 345.

34 J. Pollexfen, *A discourse of Trade, Coyn & Paper Credit* (1697), p. 99, quoted in M. Jourdain and R.S. Jenyns, *Chinese Export Art in the Eighteenth Century* (1950), p. 19.

35 Quoted in R. W. Symonds, 'Furniture from the Indies', *The Connoisseur* (May 1934), pp. 283–89.

36 British Library, IORC, Mss. Eur. C. 387/1, p. 3.

37 British Library, IORC, Mss. Eur. C. 387/2, p. 337.

38 *Madras Courier* (17 January 1793).

39 J.B. du Halde, *A Description of the Empire of China*, 2 vols (1738), vol. I, p. 336.

40 C. Clunas, 'Design and Cultural Frontiers', *Apollo* 126 (October 1987), pp. 260–61; P. Conner, *The China Trade: 1600–1860* (1986), p. 112.

41 The invoice for this piece, written in Danish, translates as follows: 'A Chinese table which can be arranged in three ways, made in rosewood and a good and ingenious piece of workmanship, 80 rix-dollars'. T. Clemmensen, 'Some Furniture Made in China in the English Style, Exported from Canton to Denmark 1735, 1737 and 1738', *Furniture History Society Journal* XXI (1985), p. 175; C. Gilbert and T. Murdoch, *John Chanon and Brass-inlaid Furniture, 1730–1760* (London, exhib. cat. 1993), p. 19.

42 *The India Gazette or Calcutta Public Advertiser* (7 March 1785).

43 *The India Gazette* (31 January 1785).

20
ASIA IN EUROPE: TEXTILES FOR THE WEST

1 M.H. Swain, 'Nightgown into dressing gown. A study of Mens' Nightgowns Eighteenth Century', *Costume* (1972), vol. 6, pp. 10–13. T. Screech, 'Dressing Samuel Pepys: Japanese Garments and International Diplomacy in the Edo period', *Orientations* (February 2002), pp. 50–57.

2 See J. Cornforth, 'A role for Chinoiserie?', *Country Life* (7 December 1989), vol. CLXXXIII, no. 49.

3 See, for example, a portrait of Miss Sophia Pelham by Sir Joshua Reynolds dated 1774. A. Ribeiro, *A Visual History of Costume. The 18th Century* (1983), fig. 101.

4 A.M. Buck, *Dress in Eighteenth-century England* (1979), p. 99.

5 See, for example, *De Goa a Lisbo, L'Art Indo-Portugais. XVIe–XVIIIe siècles* (Brussels, exhib. cat. 1991).

6 Tussar or *tasar* silk is a golden-coloured 'wild' silk produced in eastern India from the undomesticated moth *Antheraea paphia*.

7 S.M. Levey, *An Elizabethan Inheritance. The Hardwick Hall Textiles* (1998), pl. 23.

8 See R. Barnes, S. Cohen and R. Crill, *Trade, Temple & Court. Indian Textiles from the Tapi Collection* (2002), nos 42, 43.

9 OIOC, E/3/105, p. 100.

10 Ibid. Patna, not usually a place associated with painted cottons, did produce chintz in response to the overwhelming demand from Europe from the end of the seventeenth century onwards.

11 See, for example, J. Irwin and K. Brett, *Origins of Chintz* (1970), pl. 71, 72; Sotheby's, 18 October 2001, lot 47. The chintz hangings with images from the Don Quixote story have an obvious parallel in the tapestries depicting the same theme made at the Gobelin factory *c.* 1714, and may have been produced in direct response to them.

12 Irwin and Brett (1970), cat. nos 63–69.

13 For 'bizarre' silks, see H.C. Ackermann, *Seidengewebe des 18. Jahrhunderts 1: Bizarre Seiden* (2000), and V. Slomann, *Bizarre Designs in Silks. Trade and Traditions* (1953). For Irwin's rebuttal of Slomann's theories on their origins, see Irwin and Brett (1970), p. 34, n. 26.

14 OIOC, E/3/105, p. 104.

15 For the Canton letter, see OIOC, E/3/105, p. 24. The 'sad red grounds' letter of 1643 is quoted in Irwin and Brett (1970), p. 4.

16 OIOC, G/26/12, 25 August 1675.

17 See K. Mukund, *The Trading World of the Tamil Merchant. Evolution of merchant capitalism in the Coromandel* (1999), *passim*.

18 Ibid., p. 62.

19 OIOC, G/26/12, 30 July 1675.

20 J. Bredif, *Toiles de Jouy* (1989), p. 19.

21 B. Lemire, *Fashion's Favourite: the cotton trade and the consumer in Britain 1660–1800* (1991), p. 39.

22 Ibid., p. 32.

23 N. Rothstein, *Barbara Johnson's album of styles and fabrics* (1987), pp. 10, 21.

24 Bredif (1989), p. 16.

25 Ibid.

26 S. Stronge (ed.), *The Arts of the Sikh Kingdoms* (1999), p. 121.

21
ASIA IN EUROPE: CHINESE PAINTINGS FOR THE WEST

1 L. Arnold, *Princely Gifts and Papal Treasures* (1999), p. 125.

2 C. Clunas, *Chinese-Export Watercolours* (1984), pp. 10–11; G. Boesen, 'Chinese Rooms at Rosenborg Castle', *Connoisseur* 200 (1979), pp. 34–39; R. Whitfield, 'Chinese Paintings from the Collection of Archduke Ferndinand II', *Oriental Art* 22 (1976), pp. 406–16; and E. S. De Beer (ed.), *The Diary of John Evelyn*, 6 vols (1955), vol. III, p. 373.

3 Ink and colour on paper, 30.9 × 335 cm., Cliché Bibliothèque de France, Paris. Rés. V. 86.

4 India Office Library and Records, IOR, G/12/26, p. 38, cited in Clunas (1984), p. 10.

5 India Office Library and Records, IOR, G/12/28, pp. 69–71, cited in Clunas (1984), p. 12.

6 Among the most recent scholars working in this field are: H. Liu, 'The Fragments of Lamqua', *Chinese Art News* (1987), no. 5; G. Hu, *A Study on the Chinese Trade Paintings in the eighteenth and nineteenth Centuries* (1998); Yinghe Jiang (John), Guangzhou; Lee Sai Chong (Jack), Hong Kong; Prof. Huang Shijian, Hangchow.

7 L. Ledderose, *Ten Thousand Things: Module and Mass Production in Chinese Art* (1998), p. 1.

8 C. Crossman, *The Decorative Arts of the China trade* (1991), p. 93, from A.T.E. Gardiner, 'Cantonese Chinnerys: Portraits of How-Qua and Other China Trade Painters', *The Art Quarterly* (Winter 1953), p. 317, quoting Vollée.

9 Ledderose (1998), p. 100.

10 'P. Yorke' may be Philip York, MP 1741–64, a Privy Councillor and Lord Lieutenant of Cambridge. He succeeded as 2nd Earl of Hardwicke in 1764 and died in 1796; his eldest daughter succeeded as Countess De Grey after the death of her mother in 1770. Mr R. Martin was supercargo, 1735, junior on the *Houghton* to Canton, supercargo on the *Haeslingfield*, 1743, and Chief of Council that year; for an armorial service probably related to this Martin, see D.S. Howard, *Chinese Armorial Porcelain* (1974), pp. 319, 904.

11 The Chinese modeller was Chitqua, who came to London from Canton aboard an East India Company ship in 1769 and returned in 1771 after having successfully executed a series of clay portrait figures.

12 M. Jourdain and R.S. Jenyns, *Chinese Export Art in the Eighteenth Century* (1950), p. 25; *London Gazette* (16–20 March 1693).

13 Jourdain and Jenyns (1950), p. 26; J. Macky, *A Journey Through England* (1724), vol. I, p. 2.

14 The V&A has one of the finest collections of these papers; see C. Oman and H. Hamilton, *Wallpapers: A History and Illustrated Catalogue of the Collection of The Victoria and Albert Museum* (1982).

15 O. Impey, 'Eastern Trade and the Furnishing of the British Country House', p. 189, in G. Jackson-Stops et al. (eds), *The Fashioning and Functioning of the British Country House* (1989).

16 Jourdain and Jenyns (1950), p. 29.

17 Crossman (1991), p. 401, colour pl. 135.

18 Jourdain and Jenyns (1950), p. 31; MS account book of the 4th Earl of Cardigan.

19 Jourdain and Jenyns (1950), p. 33; A. Semedo, *The History of the Great and Renowned Monarchy of China* (1655), p. 56.

20 M. Sullivan, *The Meeting of Eastern and Western Art* (1997), p. 72.

21 Jourdain and Jenyns (1950), p. 35; B. de la Martinière, *China, its costume, arts, etc.* (translated 1813), p. 116.

22 P. Conner, 'The Enigma of Spoilum and the origins of China Trade Portraiture', *Antiques* (March 1998), p. 420.

23 Jourdan and Jenyns (1950), p. 35; S. des Bruslons, *Dictionnaire universel de commerce* (ed. 1761).

24 Crossman (1991), pp. 101–02; T. Downing, *The Fan-Qui in China 1836–37*, 3 vols (1838), vol. II, pp. 90–117.

25 Monsieur La Vollée, in 'L'Artiste: Revue de Paris' (1849), trans. in *The Bulletin of the American Art Union* (1850), quoted in Crossman (1991).

26 Conner (1998), p. 421, pl. VI.

27 Crossman (1991), p. 37, quoting J. Meares, *Voyages in the Years 1788 and 1789*, 23 vols (1791), p. 33.

28 Downing (1838), vol. II, pp. 90–117.

22

EUROPE IN ASIA: THE IMPACT OF WESTERN ART AND TECHNOLOGY IN SOUTH ASIA

1 Mentioned in the compilation of Jesuit accounts and letters made by Father Pierre du Jarric, who left in India in 1596 (*Histoire des choses plus memorable advenes tant ez Indes Orientales …, Troisième partie* (1614), pp. 806, 823), quoted in Rev. H. Hosten, SJ, 'European Art at the Moghul Court', *Journal of the United Provinces Historical Society* (May 1922), vol. III, pt 1, p. 183. For details on Father du Jarric and his work, see C. H. Payne, *Akbar and the Jesuits. An Account of the Jesuit Missions to the Court of Akbar by Father Pierre du Jarric, S.J.* (1926), introduction, pp. xxiii–xxxix.

2 J. Carreia-Afonso (ed.), *Letters from the Mughal Court. The First Jesuit Mission to Akbar (1580–1583)* (1980), pp. 31, 59.

3 See G. A. Bailey, *Art on the Jesuit Missions in Asia and Latin America, 1542–1773* (1999), p. 115, for a brief introduction to the general pattern of artistic development. A detailed study of the courtly arts of Goa will be presented in the exhibition *Goa and the Mughal Empire* at the Gulbenkian Foundation, Lisbon, in 2004 (catalogue, ed. N. Vassallo e Silva, in press).

4 A. Constable (trans. and ed.), *Travels in the Mogul Empire AD 1656–1668* (1891), pp. 324–25, 339, 352–53, noted by A.J. Qaisar, *The Indian Response to European Technology and Culture (A.D. 1498–1707)* (1982), p. 9; see Constable, p. xx, for brief mention of Bernier's relationship with Gassendi.

5 Constable (1891), p. 338. For a survey of the medical systems of India, and details on medical practitioners at the Mughal court, see Dr R. Sigaléa, *La Médicine traditionnelle de l'Inde* (1995).

6 R. Manoli, *European Merchant Capital and the Indian Economy. Surat Factory Records 1630–1668* (1992), pp. 24–25.

7 J. Irwin and K.B. Brett, *Origins of Chintz* (1970), p. 4.

8 W. Foster (ed.), *Letters received by the East India Company from its Servants in the East*, vol. IV, 1616 (1900), pp. 207–08, for Venus and the satyr (Jahangir's reaction described by Sir Thomas Roe in W. Foster [ed.], *The Embassy of Sir Thomas Roe to India 1615–19* [1990, reprint of 1926 edn], pp. 386–87); ibid., p. 394, for references to the pictures of the English king and queen displayed at the Mughal court.

9 See Bailey (1999), p. 122 and n. 78 for all known references to the artist.

10 Foster (1990), pp. 447–48, 468–69 and n.

11 The dictionary is in the Bodleian Library, Oxford: Hatton Or. 32.

12 Foster (1990), pp. 187–89.

13 Carreia-Afonso (1980), p. 85.

14 See, for example, E. Maclagan, *The Jesuits and the Great Mogul* (1932), esp. the chapter 'The Missions and Mogul Painting', pp. 222–59; M.C. Beach, *The Grand Mogul. Imperial Painting in India 1600–1660* (1978), pp. 155–57; A. Okada (trans. D. Dusinberre), *Imperial Mughal Painters. Indian Miniatures from the Sixteenth and Seventeenth Centuries* (1992), chapter on 'The Discovery and Impact of Western Art', pp. 95–103; E. Koch, 'The Influence of the Jesuit Missions on Symbolic Representations of the Mughal Emperors', in Koch, *Mughal Art and Imperial Ideology. Collected Essays* (2001), pp. 1–11; Bailey (1999), pp. 118–22, 123–27.

15 Typical examples may be seen in the British Library (an emperor, probably Shah Alam, r. 1759–1806, entering the Hall of Public Audience, Lucknow, *c.* 1780–90): see Norah Titley, cat. 343, p. 160; and bird's-eye views of gardens and palaces given by Colonel Antoine Polier to Ozias Humphry at Lucknow on 11 May 1786: see T. Falk and M. Archer, *Indian Miniatures in the India Office Library* (1981), cat. 343, p. 160 n.

16 Seen, for example, in an illustration depicting the Prophet Ilyas from the *Hamzanama* done for Akbar between *c.* 1562 and 1577 (J. Seyller, *The Adventures of Hamza* [2002], p. 241). Seyller argues for a slightly earlier dating on the basis of numbers he identifies as dates (see pp. 38–39); but cf. A.S. Melikian-Chirvani, 'Mir Sayyed 'Ali: Painter of the Past and Pioneer of the Future', in A. K. Das (ed.), *Mughal Masters. Further Studies* (1998), p. 50, n. 7.

17 See A. Soudavar, *Art of the Persian Courts. Selections from the Art and History Trust Collection* (1992), appendix 3, pp. 410–16, for a detailed commentary on this subject.

18 Foster (1990), p. 468 n.

19 Ibid., p. 200 and n.

20 M. Zebrowski, *Deccani Painting* (1983), pp. 95–96.

21 See M. Archer, *Indian and British Portraiture 1770–1825* (1979), for a comprehensive selection of the work being done at this period by British artists.

22 W. Foster (ed.), *Early Travels in India 1583–1619* (1985, reprint of original 1921 edn), pp. 2, 3, 4, 5, 8.

23 O. Prakash, *The Dutch Factories in India 1617–1623* (1984), pp. 137, 139.

24 R. Coverte, *A True and Almost Incredible Report of an Englishman* (1971, facsimile of original 1612 edn), p. 35.

25 A.H. Qaisar, *The Indian Response to European Technology and Culture (A.D. 1498–1707)*, (1982), pp. 58–64.

26 See G.A. Bailey, 'Jesuit Catechism and the Arts in Mughal India', in J.W. O'Malley et al. (eds), *The Jesuits. Cultures, Sciences, and the Arts, 1540–1773* (1999), p. 385. Bailey provides a list of European printed books in Akbar's library.

27 Foster (1990), pp. 382–83 and n. 2.

28 S. Gole, *Indian Maps and Plans from earliest times to the advent of European surveys* (1989), p. 36.

29 A point made by Gole (1989), p. 26.

30 G.A. Bailey, 'A Portuguese Doctor at the Maharaja of Jaipur's Court', *South Asian Studies* (1995), vol. 11, pp. 51–62, for the story of the Jesuit scientific mission and an assessment of its effect.

31 Bailey (1995), p. 52.

32 Qaisar (1982), pp. 64–69.

33 See S. Digby, 'A corpus of "Mughal" glass', *Bulletin of the School of Oriental and African Studies* (1973), vol. XXXVI, pt 1, p. 86, mentioning the importation of Spanish and Bohemian glass, and a cataloguer's note in a Sotheby sale catalogue referring to the export of 6,306 pieces of English glass in 1737.

34 Colonel H.S. Jarrett (trans.) and Sir J. Sarkar, revised and further annotated, *The A'in-i Akbari by Abu'l Fazl 'Allami* (reprinted 1978), p. 346, mentioning the *minakar*, or enameller, in a list of the kinds of metalworkers found in Hindustan.

35 X. de Castro (ed.), *Voyage de Pyrard de Laval aux Indes orientales (1601–1611)*, 2 vols (1998), vol. II, p. 580.

36 Foster (1990), pp. 449, 460.

37 See M. Keene with S. Kaoukji, *Treasury of the World. Jewelled Arts of India in the Age of the Mughals* (2001), *passim*.

38 C.B. Asher, *Architecture of Mughal India* (1992), pp. 195–96. For a very detailed analysis of the Delhi throne *jharoka*, its symbolism and its decoration, with a comprehensive discussion of the relations between the semi-precious hardstone inlays of Italy and Mughal India, see E. Koch, *Shah Jahan and Orpheus: The Pietre Dure Decoration and the Programme of the Throne in the Hall of Public Audiences at the Red Fort of Delhi* (1988); reprinted in E. Koch, *Mughal Art and Imperial Ideology. Collected Essays* (2001), pp. 61–129.

39 See Asher (1992), pp. 212–13, for the architect and designers, and H.I.S. Kanwar, 'Austin Hiriart de Bordeaux', *Indica* (1968), vol. 5, no. 1, pp. 38–40, for a brief survey of the myths.

40 Robert Skelton was the first to point out the direct copying by a Mughal artist of European herbals in his essay 'A decorative motif in Mughal art', in P. Pal (ed.), *Aspects of Indian Art: Papers Presented in a Symposium at the Los Angeles County Museum of Art, October 1970* (1972), pp. 147–52. He put forward a theory that this was the direct result of Jahangir's trip to Kashmir in 1621 when he was overcome by the beauty of the flowers there and ordered his artists to record them. Although the influence of herbals or florilegia on Mughal design is not in doubt, the evolution of Mughal floral design is more complicated, owing as much to the conventions of Iranian book painting (see S. Stronge, *Painting for the Mughal Emperor. The Art of the Book in India 1560–1650* (2002), pp. 169–73.

41 Quoted in Hosten (1922), pp. 112–13.

42 British Library Add. 9855: f. 22 recto.

43 Qaisar (1982), pp. 118–19.

44 For a Wedgwood-style blue and white jasperware hookah made by Turner & Co., see *The Indian Heritage. Court Life and Arts under Mughal Rule* (1982), cat. 405, p. 127.

45 For example, M. Zebrowski, *Gold, Silver & Bronze from Mughal India* (1997), p. 237, fig. 401.

46 C. Rowell et al., *Treasures from India. The Clive Collection from Powis Castle* (1987), cat. 89, pp. 75–76.

47 For brief notes on the use of firearms and cannon in Gujarat and Ceylon in the late fifteenth and early sixteenth centuries, see S. Digby, 'The Maritime Trade of India', ch. V of T. Raychaudhuri and I. Habib (eds), *The Cambridge Economic History of India*, vol. I: *c.* 1200–*c.* 1750 (1982), pp. 150–51, especially n. 4.

48 For a useful survey of firearms at the Mughal court, and in India generally in the seventeenth century, see R. Elgood, *Firearms of the Islamic World in the Tareq Rajab Museum, Kuwait* (1995), pp. 134–44.

49 I. Habib, *Akbar and his India* (1997), pp. 140–41, where the author provides a new translation of the Persian original and thus identifies for the first time the nature of Akbar's invention.

50 De Castro (1998), vol. II, p. 648.

51 Ibid., p. 573.

52 Quoted in Elgood (1995), p. 133.

53 Manoli (1992), p. 280, n. 8.

54 Letter of 4 December 1656, sent by William Jesson in Agra to Surat (ibid., p. 299).

55 Quoted in Hosten (1922), p. 110, referring to Father Catrou's *General History of the Mogol Empire* (1709), p. 347.

56 Elgood (1992), pp. 144–45.

57 See R. Llewellyn-Jones, *A Very Ingenious Man. Claude Martin in Early Colonial India* (1992), p. 66.

58 Ibid., p. 66.

59 Ibid., p. 132. Elgood (1992), pp. 158–63, provides a detailed summary of Claude Martin's career in relation to the Lucknow arsenal.

60 Elgood (1995), p. 163.

61 J. Boyé, *'L'Extraordinaire Aventure de Benoît de Boigne aux Indes'* (1996), p. 31.

62 S. Stronge (ed.), *The Arts of the Sikh Kingdoms* (1999), p. 89, for reference to improvements to the manufacture of ordnance.

63 R. Wigington, *The Firearms of Tipu Sultan 1783–1799* (1992), p. 32, and cat. TR8, p. 60.

64 Ibid., pp. 32–33, quoting from the *General Return of Ordnance, Ammunition, Military Stores … found in the Fort and Island of Seringapatam*, India Office Library, Boards' Coll. 1115B (F/4/51).

65 R. Llewellyn-Jones, *Engaging Scoundrels. True Tales of Old Lucknow* (2000), pp. 33, 35.

66 M. Archer, *Indian and British Portraiture 1770–1825* (1979), p. 55.

67 Llewellyn-Jones (1992), pp. 129–30.

23

EUROPE IN ASIA: THE IMPACT OF WESTERN ART AND TECHNOLOGY IN CHINA

1 He Zhe, 'Qingdai de Xifang zhuanjiaoshi yu Zhongguo wenhua' ('Western missionaries and Chinese culture in the Qing dynasty'), *Gugong bowuyuan yuankan* (1983), no. 2, pp. 17–26; Ju Deyuan, 'Qingdai Yesuhuishi yu xiyang qiqi' ('The Jesuits and strange Western objects of the Qing dynasty'), pt 1: *Gugong bowuyuan yuankan* (1989), no. 1, pp. 3–16; pt 2: *Gugong bowuyuan yuankan* (1989), no. 2, pp. 13–23; and Zhang Yinlin, 'Ming Qing shi ji xixue shu ru Zhongguo kaolu' ('History of the penetration of Western science and technology into China in the Ming and Qing dynasties'), *Qinghua xuebao* (1924), no. 1, p. 38.

2 For a full biography of Ricci, see L. C. Goodrich and Chaoying Fang (eds), *Dictionary of Ming Biography* (1976), pp. 1137–44.

3 K. Maurice, 'Propagatio fidei per scientias: Jesuit Gifts to the Chinese Court', in Klaus Maurice and Otto Mayr (eds), *The Clockwork Universe* (1980), p. 31.

4 B.A. Elman, *From Philosophy to Philology: Intellectual and Social Aspects of Change in Late Imperial China* (1984).

5 The Jesuits were ideal communicators of information on European science, as the order itself stressed training in this area. Members both taught and studied alongside the best scientific minds of Europe; and certainly the men sent to China were well versed in current theory. In addition to theoretical knowledge, the Jesuits also brought tangible examples of European science to engage the interest of the Chinese, thus taking advantage of an already present Chinese curiosity in objects from the West.

6 Galileo had known for 20 years the Jesuit Christoph Clavius (Klau, 1537–1612), the eminent mathematician who oversaw the final reform of the Gregorian calendar and who confirmed the accuracy of some of Galileo's observations. Clavius was at the famous Collegium Romanum and had taught Ricci.

7 On Brahe, see J.R. Christianson, *On Tycho's Island: Tycho Brahe and his Assistants, 1570–1601* (2000); K. Ferguson, *The Nobleman and his Housedog: Tycho Brahe and Johannes Kepler: The Strange Partnership that Revolutionised Science* (2002); A. Chapman, 'Tycho Brahe in China: the Jesuit Mission to Peking and the Iconography of European Instrument-Making Processes', *Annals of Science* 41 (1984), pp. 417–43; and K. J. Howell, *God's Two Books: Copernican Cosmology and Biblical Interpretation in Early Modern Science* (2002).

8 Verbiest arrived at the capital in 1660 and held the position of director of the Imperial Board of Astronomy until his death.

9 All but one of Brahe's original instruments have been lost; Verbiest's Chinese models offer the only remaining tangible evidence of Brahe's work.

10 The kilometre was determined in 1791. P.Y. Ho, 'China and Europe: Scientific and Technological Exchanges from the Sixteenth to Eighteenth Centuries', *China and Europe: Images and Influences in Sixteenth to Eighteenth Centuries*, ed. T.H.C. Lee (1991), p. 196.

11 See J. Needham and G.-D. Lu, *A Korean Astronomical Screen of the Mid Eighteenth Century from the Royal Palace of the Yi Dynasty (Choson Kingdom, 1392 to 1910)* (1966).

12 There were other encounters between the Jesuits and Koreans in the seventeenth century. See, for example, W.C. Rufus, 'Astronomy in Korea', *Journal of the Royal Asiatic Society* (Korea Branch) 26, 1 (1936), pp. 23–72. In the eighteenth century Hong Tae-yong (1731–83) visited Peking and, owing to his interest in western astronomy, returned to Korea with books on European science given to him by the missionaries at court. He had western astronomical instruments made for the observatory at his home. F. Bray, 'Some Problems Concerning the Transfer of Scientific and Technical Knowledge', in *China and Europe: Images and Influences in Sixteenth to Eighteenth Centuries* (1991), pp. 203–19.

13 Ricci produced this map at the request of visitors to the Jesuit residence. He copied the map, translating the names into Chinese. This map is known as the *Yudi shanhai quantu*. For mapmaking in relation to Ricci's other activities, see W. Franke's entry on Ricci, in Goodrich and Fang (1976), vol. 2.

14 T.N. Foss, 'A Western Interpretation of China: Jesuit Cartography', *East Meets West: The Jesuits in China, 1582–1773* (1988) p. 211.

15 For the full history and detailed discussions of the various editions of this map, see ibid., pp. 223–33.

16 A mechanical clock has an escapement (the mechanism that regulates the driving force of the timepiece) that allows a rotating wheel to turn slowly, continuously and with constant speed.

17 P. D'Elia, *Fonti Ricciane. Documenti Originali Concerenti Matteo Ricci e la Storia delle Prime Relazioni tra l'Europa e la Cina. 1579–1615*, 3 vols (1949), vol. 1, p. 33; 'Delle arti meccaniche di questra terra', translation from A. Forte, *Mingtang and Buddhist Utopias in the History of the Astronomical Clock: The Tower, Statue, and Armillary Sphere Constructed by Empress Wu* (1988), p. 1. The 'odoriferous fibres' to which Ricci refers are incense sticks.

18 *Xinyixiang fayao* (*New Design for a Mechanized Armillary Sphere and Celestial Globe*) by Su Song, 1172 (Shanghai, 1937). J. Needham, Wang Ling and D.J. de Solla Price, *Heavenly Clockwork: The Great Astronomical Clocks of Medieval China* (1960; 2nd edn 1986).

19 Schreck was well versed in the sciences of medicine, mathematics and natural philosophy. In Italy he was a member, along with Galileo, of the Cesi Academy, and was a friend of Johannes Kepler (1571–1630). Needham, Wang and Price (1960/1986), p. 145.

20 This clock is notable as it also contained at the back a traditional Chinese type of timekeeper. Needham, Wang and Price (1960/1986), pp. 146–47.

21 M. Ricci, *China in the Sixteenth Century: The Journals of Matteo Ricci, 1583–1610*, ed. N. Trigault, trans. L.J. Gallagher (1953), pp. 373, 392, 536.

22 So strong was this connection that into the nineteenth century Ricci was regarded by the clockmakers of Shanghai as their patron saint of sorts, being known as '*Li Madou pusa*', the Bodhisattva Matteo Ricci. Needham, Wang and Price (1960/1986), p. 148, and J. Needham, *Science and Civilisation in China* (1958–), vol. IV ii 2, p. 532. All clockmakers belonged to a guild. All guild members were required to participate in religious ceremonies associated with their particular guild. These ceremonies were often designed as worship of the guild's founder, which may explain the 'deification' of Ricci, as he was the first to introduce western clockmaking to the Chinese court.

23 The Office of Self-Ringing Bells (*zimingzhongchu*) was the predecessor of the *zuozhongchu*, the Office of Clock Manufacture. For a more complete description of this workshop, see C. Pagani, *'Eastern Magnificence and European Ingenuity': Clocks of Late Imperial China* (2001), pp. 181–84.

24 The last dated inventory of clocks was the *Zuozhongchu zhongbiao xishu qingce* (*Accurate List of the Detailed Count of Clocks of the Office of Clock Manufacture*) from the *Yuanmingyuan chengnei zuozhongchu zhongbiaodeng xiang qingce* (*Accurate List of the Clocks, Watches, etc., of the Yuanmingyuan and Inner City Office of Clock Manufacture*), archival document no. 404 (Guangxu 5/12/20), housed in the Number One Historical Archives, Beijing.

25 Amiot letter of 1754, in *Lettres Edifiantes et Curieuses, Ecrites des Missions Etrangères. Mémoires de la Chine*, new edn (1771–81), XXIII, p. 362.

26 Illustrations of a clock and watch may be found in the *Huangchao liqi tushi* (*Illustrated regulations for ceremonial paraphernalia of the Qing dynasty*) of 1766.

27 James Cox (d. *c.* 1791), a London maker whose elaborate chinoiserie creations formed part of the Qianlong emperor's collection of clocks and watches, is a case in point. His pieces destined for China did not differ from those made for his London clientele. Cox stated that the popularity of his pieces with the Chinese emperor was proof of his understanding of Chinese aesthetics, which he then used to increase the appeal of his work in the home market, where sales were greatest and reputations were built. For an extended discussion, see Pagani (2001), pp. 167–70.

28 Heshen's fortune was valued at about 10 times the 70 million taels in annual income of China as a whole at that time. Li Jiannong, *Zhongguo jinbainian zhengzhi shi* (*A Political History of China During the Past Hundred Years*) (1948), p. 11.

29 The full list is enumerated in E. Backhouse, E. and J.O.P. Bland, *Annals and Memoirs of the Court of Peking* (1914), pp. 366–67.

30 Cao Xueqin, *The Story of the Stone*, vol. 2, trans. D. Hawkes (1987), ch. 6, vol. 1, p. 158, at Rongguo Palace. Xu Wenlin and Li Wenguang have suggested that the clock that Grannie Liu saw was one that indicated the traditional Chinese double hours. Xu Wenlin and Li Wenguang, 'Tan Qingdai de zhongbiao zhizao' ('On the manufacture of Qing dynasty clocks'), *Wenwu* (1959), no. 2, p. 34.

31 See Xu Wenlin and Chen Kaige, 'Qingdai Suzhoude zhongbiao zhizao' ('On the Manufacture of Suzhou Clocks in the Qing Dynasty'), *Gugong bowuyuan yuankan* (1981), no. 4, pp. 90–94. The most interesting source is *Artistry in Time*, a catalogue of timepieces that were sent from Peking to Walt Disney World, Orlando, Florida, for an exhibition in 1988; 13 of the clocks illustrated were made in Guangzhou; three are of Suzhou manufacture.

32 Xu Wenlin and Li Wenguang (1959), p. 35.

33 Liang Zhangju, *Langji xutan* (*Further Impressions Collected During Official Travels*), *juan* 8. Guangzhou and Suzhou also supplied a workforce for the palace workshops.

34 In the early nineteenth century Xu Chaojun, of Shanghai, published his *Zimingzhongbiao tufa* (*Illustrated Account of the Manufacture of Mechanical Clocks*), and in the preface stated that he came from a long line of clockmakers. His family had been making clocks and watches in European style for five generations. It is possible that Xu was a descendant of Xu Guangqi (1562–1634), who had worked with Matteo Ricci. See Needham, Wang and Price (1960/1986), p. 154.

35 See Yang Boda, 'A Brief Account of Qing Dynasty Glass', in C. Brown and D. Rabiner, *Chinese Glass of the Qing Dynasty, 1644–1911* (1987), pp. 71–86.

36 The Jesuits introduced defects as well. At the end of the seventeenth century European glass suffered from glass disease, or crizzling, caused by an excess of alkali in the formula. Chinese glass produced at the time that the imperial glassmaking workshop was established under Jesuit supervision also suffers from this defect. It appears that by the end of the Kangxi period this problem was remedied. R.S. Jenyns, 'Glass and Painting on Glass', in R. S. Jenyns and W. Watson, *Chinese Art III* (1981), pp. 99–100.

37 Chinese copies of European paintings had been made in the fourteenth century for Jean de Monte Corvino. M. Sullivan, *The Meeting of Eastern and Western Art from the Sixteenth Century to the Present Day* (2nd edn 1989), p. 43.

38 For further information, see H. Kobayashi, 'Chinese Painting and Western Art Introduced by Jesuit Missionaries', *St Francis Xavier: An Apostle of the East, vol. 1: The Encounter Between Europe and Asia During the Period of the Great Navigations* (1999).

39 Yang Boda, 'Qing Qianlong chao huayuan yan'ge' ('The evolution of the art academy in the Qianlong period of the Qing dynasty'), *Gugong bowuyuan yuankan* (1992), no. 1 (55), pp. 3–11, 89.

40 Niccolò arrived at Nagasaki in 1583 and two years later established the Academy of St Luke, 'where he trained young Japanese converts in oil and fresco painting'. Sullivan (1989), p. 8.

41 Niva was the son of a Japanese father and Chinese mother.

42 Sullivan (1989), p. 44.

43 A mathematician and geographer, Aleni was a prolific writer and had an excellent knowledge of Chinese. In addition to his scientific works, he published a world atlas, compiled with Yang Tingyun, based on Matteo Ricci's world map, along with the notes made by other Jesuits. Goodrich and Fang (1976) vol. I, pp. 2–5.

44 Although not considered high art, Nadal's illustrations were highly significant as they provided the Chinese with the European artistic conventions of chiaroscuro and the depiction of three-dimensional space using one- and two-point perspective.

45 This painting was sent to Goswin Nickel, the Jesuit general, on 30 January 1661 and was included in *China Illustrata* (1667). G. Loehr, 'European Artists at the Chinese Court', *The Westward Influence of the Chinese Arts from the 14th to the 18th Century* (1972), p. 33.

46 'Our Saviour' was demolished in 1827 by imperial order.

47 B. Gray, 'Lord Burlington and Father Ripa's Chinese Engravings', *British Museum Quarterly* XXII (1960), p. 41.

48 Sources disagree on the date of completion of the engravings. G. Loehr, in 'Missionary Artists at the Manchu Court', *Transactions of the Oriental Ceramic Society* 34 (1962–63), pp. 51–67, sets it at April 1714, while Gray sets the date at October 1713.

49 C. and M. Beurdeley, *Castiglione: Peintre Jésuite à la Cour de Chine* (1971).

50 Chiaroscuro is the Italian term for light and dark and refers to a form of modelling figures using light and shadow.

51 For a study of the history of photographs of the Yuanming Yuan, see R. Thiriez, *Barbarian Lens: Western Photographers of the Qianlong Emperor's European Palaces* (1998).

52 Sullivan (1989), p. 71.

53 H. Kobayashi, 'Suzhou Prints and Western Perspective', unpublished paper delivered at 'The Jesuits II: Cultures, Sciences, and the Arts, 1540–1773' (June 2002).

54 Gao Zhentian, 'Kangxidi yu Xiyang zhuanjiaoshi' ('The Kangxi emperor and Western missionaries'), *Lishi dang'an* (1986), no. 1, pp. 187–91, and Liu Yufang, 'Qinggong zuozhongchu' ('The clock-making workshop of the Qing palace'), *Gugong bowuyuan yuankan* (1989), no. 4, pp. 49–54.

55 Cited from Zou Yigui's *Xiaoshan huapu* in Mayching Kao, 'European Influences in Chinese Art, Sixteenth to Eighteenth Centuries', in *China and Europe: Images and Influences in Sixteenth to Eighteenth Centuries* (1991), p. 273.

56 Zhao Yi, *Yanpu zaji*, *juan* 2, p. 36.

24

EUROPE IN ASIA: THE IMPACT OF WESTERN ART AND TECHNOLOGY IN JAPAN

1 For a translation, see A. Waley, *The Nō Plays of Japan* (1921), pp. 248–57.

2 Zeami (attrib.), 'Haku Rakuten', *Nihon koten bungaku taikei* (1968), vol. 41, p. 308.

3 Matthew 28: 19.

4 See A. Farrington, *The English East India Company in Japan, 1613–1623* (1991), vol. 1, p. 145 *passim*.

5 See G. Ellison, *Deus Destroyed, The Image of Christianity in Early Modern Japan* (1988), p. 248.

6 See edn of E. Thompson, *Diary of Richard Cocks, Cape-merchant in the English Factory in Japan*, Hakluyt Society, LXVI (1883), vol. 1, p. 34.

7 Like many Japanese towns, modern Kyoto has changed names repeatedly over history. Founded under the name of Heian-kyō, it became known as Miyako in the medieval period, and from the Edo period as either Kyō or Keishi; the name Kyoto had been deployed too over the centuries, mostly in formal parlance, but became standard usage only in the nineteenth century.

8 See R. Hesselink, *Prisoners from Nanbu: Reality and Make-Believe in Early-Modern Japanese Diplomacy* (2002).

9 C. Viallé and L. Blussé (eds), *The Deshima Dagregisters* (2001), vol. 11, p. 296.

10 Sakamoto Mitsuru et al. (eds), *Nanban bijutsu to yōfūga* (1976), vol. 64, p. 419.

11 Ōtsuki Gentaku, 'Hoei mondō', in *Nihon shisō taikei* (1976), vol. 64, p. 419.

12 Shiba Kōkan, *Saiyū nikki* (1986), p. 117.

13 Ibid., p. 118.

14 Ibid., p. 118.

15 Hesselink (2002), pp. 157–58.

16 *Tsūji nashi kite wakaruran, kapitan no kiku kokuchō no kane*, quoted in T. Screech, *The Lens within the Heart* (2002), p. 32.

17 Inaba Tsūryū, *Shōken kishō*, no modern edition, unpaginated.

18 *Kapitan mo tsukubawasekeri kimi ga haru*, quoted in Katsuhara Haruki, 'Haikai no jūhasseiki', in Momokawa Takahito, *Edo bunka no hen'yō: jūhasseiki nihon no keiken* (1994), p. 93.

19 *Oranda mo hana o minikeri uma no kura*; quoted in ibid., p. 93.

20 Sugita Genpaku, 'Rangaku kotohajime', in *Nihon koten bungaku taikei* (1968), vol. 95, p. 482.

21 Viallé and Blussé (2001), vol. 11, pp. 263–64.

22 Ibid., pp. 263–64 (adapted).

23 Morishima Chūryō, *Bango-sen*; no modern edition; original unpaginated.

24 See Tsuruoka Akemi, 'Shiba Kōkan to 18 seiki igirisu fūkei hanga', in *Kokka* 1249 (1999).

25 Shiba Kōkan (1986), p. 202.

26 Ibid., p. 35.

THE IMPACT OF EUROPEAN WAR TECHNOLOGY

1 This was written between 1596 and 1614, but not printed until 1649. See J. Villiers, 'The Portuguese and the Trading World of Asia in the Sixteenth Century', in P. Milward (ed.), *Portuguese Voyages to Asia and Japan in the Renaissance Period* (1994), p. 4.

25

INDIAN FANTASIES OF EUROPE

1 *Chambers English Dictionary* (1988), p. 516.

2 A. Jaffer, 'The Aina Mahal: an early example of Europeanerie', in C. London (ed.), *The Arts of Kutch* (2000), pp. 62–75.

3 A. Deane ('A.D.'), *A Tour through the Upper Provinces of Hindostan* (1823). It seems that, never having seen a chamber pot, the servants assumed it was a milk jug. The narrative describes the droll reaction of Sadaat Ali when his English guests all refused to drink: 'I thought the English were very fond of milk.' A further explanation of the comic value of milk-drinking and Urdu *double entendre* is given in A. Sharar's *Lucknow: the last phase of an Oriental Culture* (1975), p. 201.

4 Produced by Colen Campbell, *Vitruvius Brittanicus*, initially in three volumes between 1717 and 1725 (later expanded to five), was an ambitious publication with plans, sections, elevations and descriptions of the great English architects of Campbell's time. Its *raison d'être* was to persuade English architects that their work was as good as 'the best of the Moderns' (C. Campbell, *Vitruvius Britannicus or The British Architect*, 3 vols [1715–25], vol. 1.

5 B. Tandan, *The Architecture of Lucknow and its Dependencies, 1722–1856* (2001), p. 101.

6 R. Llewellyn-Jones, *A Fatal Friendship, the Nawabs, the British and the city of Lucknow* (1985), p. 44.

7 According to Viscount Valentia, who visited India between 1802 and 1806, the nawab had in his collections Chinese drawings and ornaments.

8 Probably from Surat and dated to the second half of the eighteenth century (A. Topsfield, 'Ketelaar's Embassy and the Farangi theme in the Art of Udaipur', *Oriental Art* XXX, no. 4 [Winter 1984–85], pp. 350–67), from a private collection.

9 H. Amir, *Vanishing Culture of Lucknow* (1983) p. 67.

10 Ibid., p. 74.

26
CHINESE FANTASIES OF EUROPE

1 J.L. Cranmer-Byng, *An Embassy to China, Lord Macartney's Journal 1793–1794* (reprinted 2000), p.145.

2 Ibid., pp.366–67, n. 27.

3 Shen Defu, *Wanli Yehuo Bian*, *c.*1620 (reprinted 1959), ch. 30, pp.783–85.

4 Wu Hung, 'Emperor's Masquerade – Costume Portraits of Yongzheng and Qianlong', *Orientations* (July 1995), pp.25–41.

5 J. Spence, *Treason by the Book* (2001), p.7.

6 M. Pirazzoli-t'Serstevens, 'The Emperor Qianlong's European Palaces', *Orientations* (November 1988), pp.61–71.

7 Three of the 12 bronze zodiac animals from the Great Fountain have surfaced recently and were acquired by a private museum in China. *Art Treasures of Guangzhou Art Museum* (2000), vol.2, p.86.

8 C.B. Malone, *History of the Peking Summer Palaces under the Ch'ing Dynasty* (1934), p.160.

9 J. Badin, *La Manufacture de Tapisseries de Beauvais* (1909), pp.31, 36.

10 Illustrated in Zhu Jiaqian, *Furniture of the Ming and Qing Dynasties, The Complete Collection of the Treasures of the Palace Museum* (2002), p.49.

11 For a concise account of the uprising, see Zhang Hongxing, *The Qianlong Emperor, Treasures from the Forbidden City* (2002), pp.85–86.

12 The best-known story is about Mulan, a young woman who went to battle because her father was too old and her younger brother too young. The tale first took the form of a ballad in the sixth century, based on which several novels and dramas have been written. Mulan was probably a historical figure, but her identity cannot be confirmed.

13 Qu Dajun, *Guangdong Xinyu* (*New Narratives on Guangdong*), *c.*1700 (reprinted 1974), p.38.

14 D. Howard and J. Ayers, *China for the West*, vol.1 (1978), p.344.

15 G. Oswald, *Lexikon der Heraldik* (1984), p.320.

27
EUROPEAN FANTASIES OF ASIA

1 Although, by the 1750s, most British homes of any pretension could at least have afforded a chinoiserie bench in the style of William Halfpenny's *Rural Architecture in the Chinese Taste*, or a bolt or two of cotton *toile de Jouy* with copperplate chinoiseries in the manner of Jean-Baptiste Pillement.

2 E. Said, *Orientalism* (1978), p.95.

3 In truth, Louis XIV's interest in Siam only derived from his interest in using the country as a commercial and military springboard for French expansion in China. Following the failure of the embassies of the 1680s, his roving eye turned westwards once more. See D. Elisseeff-Poisle, 'Chinese Influence in France', in T. C. H. Lee (ed.), *China and Europe: Images and Influences in the Sixteenth to Eighteenth Centuries* (1991), p.154.

4 D. Jacobsen, *Chinoiserie* (1993), pp.31–2.

5 See M. Jarry, *Chinoiserie* (1981), p.225.

6 J. Ayers, O. Impey and J.V.G. Mallet, *Porcelain for Palaces* (1990), p.57.

7 Unfortunately, this bold patronage ended with Mary's death in 1694: her husband, William III, subsequently sold or dispersed much of her collection. Interestingly, the first Chinaman to set foot in England appeared at James II's court in 1685 (see J. D. Spence, *The Chan's Great Continent: China in Western Minds* [1998], p.65).

8 L. James, *Raj* (1997), pp.7–8.

9 J.E. Wills, *1688* (2001), p.101.

10 T.N. Foss and D.F. Lach, 'Images of Asia and Asian in European Fiction', in Lee (1991), pp.172, 176.

11 Strong identification of the Oriental character with sex came only in western publications of the nineteenth century.

12 D.F. Lach, *Asia in the Eyes of Europe* (1991), p.14.

13 Jacobsen (1993), p.73.

14 Elisseeff-Poisle and Foss and Lach in Lee (1991), pp.160, 176.

15 See Jacobsen (1993), p.72.

16 Spence (1998), p.62.

17 Lothar Ledderose also notes the absence of any genuine Chinese setting from Rubens's and Poussins's depictions of 1616–17 and 1641 of St Francis Xavier in the East. See Ledderose, 'Chinese Influence on European Art', in Lee (1991), p.229.

18 Aileen Ribeiro, quoted in D. Mannings and M. Postle, *Sir Joshua Reynolds: A Complete Catalogue of his Pictures* (2000), vol.I, p.198.

19 D. Moore-Gwynn, in *Important British Pictures*, Sotheby's sale catalogue (29 November 2001).

20 'What is their trade to the universal commerce of England, Holland, France and Spain? What are their cities to ours for wealth, strength, gaiety of apparel, rich furniture, and an infinite variety? What are their ports, supplied with a few junks and barks, to … our large and powerful navies?' Quoted in Spence (1998), p.67.

21 J.J. Clarke, *Oriental Enlightenment: The encounter between Asian and Western thought* (1997), pp.43, 46.

22 Ibid., p.52.

23 In 1796 Johann Herder (in *Der Chineser in Rom*) used similar language to describe a Chinaman: 'Proclaims the sick the truly sound, and this/That he, the truly sick, may pass for sound'. The vocabulary is remarkably similar to that used by western Europeans to denote the Ottomans during the crises of the 1870s.

24 Ibid.

25 O. Impey, *Chinoiserie* (1977), p.12.

26 Ledderose in Lee (1991), p.230.

27 G. Saunders, 'The China Trade: Oriental Painted Panels', in L. Hoskins (ed.), *The Papered Wall* (1994), p.49.

28 Jacobsen (1993), p.57.

29 S. Miller, 'Jean-Antoine Fraisse at Chantilly: French Images of Asia', *East Asian Library Journal*, vol.IX, no. 1 (Spring 2000), p.84.

30 Elisseeff-Poisle in Lee (1991), p.160.

31 Boucher's other principal source in 1742 was Arnold Montamous's wildly inaccurate and equally ancient *Atlas Japannensis* of 1669. See Miller, 'Jean-Antoine Fraisse …' (2000), p.188.

32 In a similar vein, the pleasure gardens at Vauxhall, where 'Chinese' pavilions were added in 1751, was equipped with a 'Turkish Tent' – replete with decidedly un-Islamic Ionic and Doric columns – by 1762.

33 The Earl of Bute was not only Chambers's patron and the 'companion' of the dowager Princess of Wales, but also the tutor and mentor of the future George III, whom Bute encouraged to despise his aged grandfather, King George II. And the only buildings that can be associated with George II's personal patronage were Roger Morris's staid, cubic and unmistakably Palladian villas at Marble Hill and Richmond Park of the 1720s.

34 O. Impey in Ayers, Impey and Mallet (1990), p.177.

35 Augustus was always far keener on display than on meaning. In 1709 he happily dressed 'as a Moorish king on horseback accompanied by Moors'. See D. Syndram, *Gems of the Green Vaults in Dresden* (2000), p.112.

36 M. Levey, *Painting and Sculpture in France 1700–1789* (1972), p.164.

37 P. Stein, 'Boucher's Chinoiseries: Some New Sources', *Burlington Magazine* (September 1996), p.604.

38 Jarry (1981), p.26.

39 See Foss and Lach in Lee (1991), p.229.

40 Jacobsen (1993), p.75.

41 Said (1978), pp.7, 78–9.

42 Lord G. Macartney, *An Embassy to China … 1793–4*, ed. J.L. Cranmer-Byng (1926), pp.212–13, quoted in Spence (1998), p.60. Subsequent Chinese accounts of Macartney's presents for the emperor – which allegedly included 'an elephant not larger than a cat, and a horse the size of a mouse; and … an enchanted pillow' (ibid., p.61) – show what a sizeable gap between East and West there was still to cross.

43 Ledderose in Lee (1991), p.228.

44 According to one recent view, aesthetic encounters such as this were always bound to fail, since 'travellers do not know how to observe' and 'readers are imprisoned in their own aesthetic systems'. See Elisseeff-Poisle in Lee (1991), p.160.

45 The prince was frequently portrayed in prints of the day as a slothful, fat and stupefied mandarin or as an exotic despot. See S. Parissien, *George IV: The Grand Entertainment* (2001), pp.346–50.

BIBLIOGRAPHY

MANUSCRIPTS

BRITISH LIBRARY, LONDON
OIOC, L/AG/34/29/4. *Bengal Wills* 1782, no. 24, Will of Thomas Naylor, probate granted 6 August 1782.
OIOC, L/AG/34/29/16. *Bengal Wills* 1804, no. 13, Will of Matthew Leslie

NATIONAL ARMY MUSEUM, LONDON
Gardner Papers, National Army Museum, Letter 119, Sekundra, 12 December 1821

HISTORICAL ARCHIVES, BEIJING
Number One Historical Archive: *Yuanmingyuan chengnei zuozhongchu zhongbiaodeng xiang qingce [Accurate List of the Clocks, Watches, etc., of the Yuanmingyuan and Inner City Office of Clock Manufacture]*, archival document no. 404 (Guangxu 5/12/20)

DISSERTATIONS

BAILEY, G.A., *Counter Reformation Symbolism and Allegory in Mughal Painting* (Ph.D. dissertation, Harvard University, 1996)

BALSIGER, B.J., *The Kunst- und Wunderkammern. A Catalogue Raisonné of Collecting in Germany, France and England 1565–1750* (Ph.D. dissertation, University of Pittsburgh, 1970)

DAVIDSON, S., *African Ivories from Portuguese Domains. Symbols of Imperial Rule in European Courts 1462–1650* (Master's thesis, George Washington University, Washington, DC, 1985)

GHOSH, D., *Colonial Companions: Bibis, Begums, and Concubines of the British in North India 1760–1830* (Ph.D. dissertation, Berkeley, 2000)

JORDAN, A., *Portuguese Royal Collections (1505–1580): A Bibliographic and Documentary Survey*, (Master's thesis, George Washington University, Washington, DC, 1985)

JORDAN, A., *The Development of Catherine of Austria's Collection in the Queen's Household: Its Character and Cost* (Ph.D. dissertation, Brown University, Providence, RI, 1994)

PRIMARY SOURCES

ABU'L FAZL ALLAMI, *The Ain-i Akbari*, trans. H. Blochmann, 2nd edn revised and ed. Lieut-Colonel D.C. Phillott (1927), vol. I

BELL, JOHN OF ANTERMONY, *A Journey from St Petersburg to Pekin, 1719–22* (New York, 1966)

BERNIER, F., *Travels in the Mogul Empire A.D. 1656–1668*, revised and improved by Archibald Constable (London, 1891)

BEVERIDGE, A.S. (trans.), *The Akbarnama of Abu-l-Fazl* (London, 1902)

BEVERIDGE, A.S (trans.), *The Baburnama in English*, 2 vols (London, 1922; reprinted Delhi, 1989)

BLUSSÉ, L., EVERTS, N. and FRECH, E., *The Formosan Encounter, Notes on Formosa's Aboriginal Society: A Selection of Documents from Dutch Archival Sources* (Taipei, 1999)

BONTEKOE, W.Y., *Memorable Description of the East Indian Voyage, 1618–25*, trans. Mrs C. B. Bodde-Hodgkinson and P. Geyl (New York, 1919)

BOWREY, T., *Geographical Account of Countries around the Bay of Bengal*, ed. R. C. Temple (Cambridge, 1905)

BULLEY, A. (ed.), *Free Mariner, John Adolphus Pope in the East Indies, 1786–1821* (London, 1992)

BUTE, MARCHIONESS OF (ed.), *The Private Journals of the Marquess of Hastings, K.G.*, 2 vols (London, 1858)

CAMPBELL, C., *Vitruvius Britannicus or The British Architect*, 3 vols (London, 1715–25)

CAMPBELL, C., *A Passage to China: Colin Campbell's Diary of the First Swedish East India Company's Expedition to Canton*, 1732–33, ed. P. Hallberg and C. Koninckx (Göteborg, 1994)

CASTRO, X. DE, *Voyage de Pyrard de Laval aux Indes orientales (1601–1611)*, 2 vols (Paris, 1998)

CAO XUEQIN, *The Story of the Stone* (reprinted Harmondsworth, 1987)

CHAUMONT, CHEVALIER DE and THE ABBÉ DE CHOISY, *Aspects of the Embassy to Siam 1685 …*, ed. and in part trans. M. Smithies (Chiang Mai, Thailand, 1997)

CHENG DAYUE, *Chengshi Moyuan (Mr Cheng's ink garden)* (China, 1606)

CONSTABLE, A. (trans. and ed.), *Travels in the Mogul Empire AD 1656–1668* (London, 1891)

COOPER, M. (ed.), *They Came to Japan: An Anthology of European Reports on Japan, 1543–1640* (Berkeley and Los Angeles, 1965)

COOPER, M. (ed.), *João Rodrigues's Account of Sixteenth-Century Japan* (London, 2001)

Copy of a letter of the King of Portugal Sent to the King of Castile Concerning the Voyage and Success of India, trans. S. Pacifici (Minneapolis, 1955)

CORREIA, G., *Lendas da Índia*, 4 vols (Porto, 1975)

CORREIA-AFONSO, J., *Letters from the Mughal Court* (Mumbai, 1980)

COVERTE, R., *A True and Almost Incredible Report of an Englishman* (Amsterdam, 1971; facsimile of original 1612 edition)

CRANMER-BYNG, J.L., *An Embassy to China, Lord Macartney's Journal 1793–1794* (London, 2000)

DAHAI, W., *Haidao Yizhi* (1806), republished and annotated by Yao Nan and Wo Langxuan (eds), (Hong Kong, 1992)

DANVERS, F.C. (ed.) (vol. I) and Foster, W. (vols II–VI), *Letters Received by the East India Company from its Servants in the East (1602–17)*, 6 vols (London, 1896–1902)

Da Qing tongli [Comprehensive Rites of the Great Qing], (Beijing, 1824).

DEARE, A., *A Tour through the Upper Provinces of Hindostan* (London, 1823)

DE LA PORTE, L'ABBÉ, *De nieuwe reisiger; of beschryving van de oude en nieuwe waerelt*, 28 vols (Dordrecht, 1767–83)

DELLA VALLE, P., *The travels of Pietro della Valle in India*, 2 vols (London, 1892)

DOWSON, J. (ed.), *The history of India as told by its own historians, the Muhammadan period edited from the posthumous papers of the late Sir H.M. Elliot* (London, 1867–77)

DU HALDE, J.B, *Description geographique, historique, chronologique, politique et physique de l'empire de la Chine* (Paris, 1735; English edn, 1738)

EVELYN, J., *The Diary of John Evelyn: Now first printed in full from manuscripts belonging to Mr John Evelyn and edited by E. S. De Beer, Vol. IV, 1673–89* (Oxford, 1955)

FAY, MRS, *Original Letters from India* (Calcutta, 1817)

FORBES, J., *Oriental Memoirs*, 4 vols (London, 1813)

FOSTER, W., *The English Factories in India 1618–1621* (Oxford, 1906)

FOSTER, W., *The English Factories in India 1634–1636* (Oxford, 1911)

FOSTER, W., *The English Factories in India 1637–1641* (Oxford, 1912)

FOSTER, W., *The English Factories in India 1646–1650* (Oxford, 1914)

FOSTER, W., *The English Factories in India 1651–1654* (Oxford, 1915)

FOSTER, W., *Early Travels in India, 1583–1619* (London, 1921)

FOSTER, W., *The English Factories in India 1661–1664* (Oxford, 1923)

FOSTER, W., *The English Factories in India 1665–1667* (Oxford, 1925)

FOSTER, W., *The Embassy of Sir Thomas Roe* (London, 1926)

FOSTER, W., *England's Quest of Eastern Trade* (London, 1933)

FOSTER, W. (ed.), *The Voyage of Nicholas Downton to the East Indies 1614–15 as recorded in contemporary narratives and letter* (London, 1939)

FROIS, L., *Historia de Japam, Vol. V, 1588–93* (reprinted Lisbon, 1984)

FRYER, DR J., *A New Account of East India and Persian Letters Being Nine Years Travelled Begun 1672 and finished 1681* (London, 1698)

GRAAV, N. DE., *Reisen van Nicolaus de Graaff*, ed. J.C.M. Warnsinck (The Hague, 1930)

HAMILTON, A., *A New Account of the East Indies* (Edinburgh, 1727; reprinted London, 1930)

HICKEY, W., *The Memoirs of William Hickey*, ed. A. Spencer, 4 vols (London, 1925); ed. P. Quennell, 1 vol. (London and Boston, 1975)

HODGES, W., *Travels in India during the years 1780–83* (London, 1793)

Huangchao liqi tushi [Illustrated regulations for ceremonial paraphernalia of the Qing dynasty], (1759; reprinted Taipei, 1976)

IBN BATTUTA, *The Travels of Ibn Battuta A.D. 1325–1354*, trans. H.A.R. Gibb, 3 vols (Cambridge, 1958–71)

JARRETT, COL. H.S. (trans.) and SARKAR, SIR J., revised and further annotated, *The A'in-i Akbari by Abu'l Fazl 'Allami* (reprinted New Delhi, 1978)

KAEMPFER, E., *The History of Japan* (London, 1727; trans. from the Dutch, Glasgow, 1906)

KAEMPFER, E., *Kaempfer's Japan: Tokugawa Culture Observed*, ed., trans. and annotated by B. M. Bodart-Bailey (Honolulu, 1999)

KINDERSLEY, MRS J., *Letters from the Island of Teneriffe, Brazil, the Cape of Good Hope, and the East-Indies* (London, 1777)

LAVAL, F.P. DE., *The Voyage of François Pyrard de Laval*, trans. from the 3rd French edn of 1619, ed. A. Gray, 2 vols (London, 1887–8); also *Viagem de Francisco Pyrard de Laval*, 2 vols (Porto, 1944)

LE STRANGE, G. (trans.), *Embassy to Tamberlane, 1403–1406* (New York, 1928)

Lettres Edifiantes et Curieuses, Ecrites des Missions Etrangeres. Mémoires de la Chine (Paris, 1771–81; reprinted Toulouse, 1810)

LIANG ZHANGJU, *Langji xutan [Further Impressions Collected During Official Travels]*, (reprinted Beijing, 1981)

LINSCHOTEN, J.H. VAN, *The voyage of John Huyghen van Linschoten to the East Indies*, trans. A. C. Burnell, 2 vols (London, 1885; reprinted Delhi, 1988)

LINSCHOTEN, J.H. VAN, *Itinerário, Viagem ou Navegação para as Índias Orientais ou Portuguesas* (Lisbon, 1997)

LINXIANG, W., *Yuejianbian* (1601; reprinted Taipei, 1969)

LOCKYER, C., *An Account Of The Trade With India Containing Rules For Good Government In Trade, And Tables: With Descriptions Of Fort St George, Aheen, Malacca, Condore, Anjenjo, Muskat, Gombroon, Surat, Goa, Carwar, Telicherry, Panola, Calicut, The Cape Of Good Hope, And St Helena Their Inhabitants, Customs, Religion, Government Animals, Fruits &C.* (London, 1711)

MA HUAN, *Ma Huan's Ying-yai Sheng-Ian [The Overall Survey of the Ocean's Shores, 1433]*, trans. J. V. G. Mills (Cambridge, 1970)

MANDELSLO, J.A DE., 'The Voyages and Travels of J. Albert de Mandelslo', in *The Voyages & Travels of the Ambasssadors sent by Frederick Duke of Holstein to the Great Duke of Muscovy, and the King of Persia*, trans. J. Davis (London, 1662)

Memoirs of Admiral Beaulieu's Voyage to the East-Indies. Drawn up by himself (1762), published in *The World displayed; or, a Curious Collection of Voyages and Travels, Selected from the Writers of all Nations. In which Conjectures and Interpolations of Several vain Editors and Translators Are expunged*, 3rd edn. corrected (London, 1774), vol. VIII

'Minute by M. Bernier upon the Establishment of Trade in the Indies, dated 10 March 1668', in *Journal of the Royal Asiatic Society*, part I: January 1933

MONSERRATE, A., *The Commentary of Father Monserrate, S.J., on his Journey to the Court of Akbar*, trans. J.S. Hoyland (London, 1922)

MUNDY, P., *The Travels of Peter Mundy in Europe and Asia, 1608–1667*, ed. Sir R.C. Temple (Cambridge, 1907–36)

NIEUHOF, J., *Voyages & Travels to the East Indies 1653–1670*, with an introduction by A.Reid (Singapore, 1988)

OVINGTON, J.A., *Voyage to Surat in the year 1689*, ed. H. G. Rawlinson (London, 1929)

PELSAERT, F., *Jahangir's India: The Remonstratie of Francisco Pelsaert*, ed. W.H. Moreland and P. Geyl (Cambridge, 1925)

PERCIVAL, R., *An Account of the Island of Ceylon …* (London, 1803)

PIRES, T., *The Suma Oriental of Tome Pires*, trans. A. Contesao, 2 vols (London, 1944)

POLLEXFEN, J., *A discourse of Trade, Coyn & Paper Credit* (London, 1697)

Precedents from the Statutes of the Great Qing [Da Qing huidian shili], (Beijing, 1899)

The Pybus Embassy to Kandy, 1762, transcribed with notes by R. Raven-Hart, private circulation copy (1961)

QU DAJUN, *Guangdong Xinyu [New Narratives on Guangdong]*, (*c.* 1700; reprinted Hong Kong, 1974)

RAVENSTEIN, E.G. (trans. and ed.), *A Journal of the First Voyage of Vasco da Gama 1497–1499* (London, 1898)

RICCI, M., *China in the Sixteenth Century: The Journals of Matteo Ricci, 1583–1610*, ed. Nicolas Trigault, trans. Louis J. Gallagher (New York, 1953)

ROGERS, A. (trans.) and BEVERIDGE, H. (ed.), *The Tuzuk-i-Jahangiri or Memoirs of Jahangir from the first to the twelfth year of his reign*, 2 vols (London, 1909)

SATOW, E.M. (ed.), *The Voyage of Captain John Saris to Japan, 1613*, Hakluyt Society (London, 1900), series III, vol. 7

SAUVAGET, J., *Ahbar Al-sin Wa l-Hind. Relation de la Chine et de l'Inde, redigée en 851* (Paris, 1948)

Shen, D., *Wanli Yehuo Bian*, *c.*1620 (reprinted Beijing, 1959)

Shiba Kōkan, *Edo Nagasaki E Kikō – Saiyū Ryodan [Picture Travelogue Edo to Nagasaki: Travels in the West]*, (1794; reprinted Tokyo, 1992)

Shiba Kōkan, *Kōkan Saiyū Nikki [Kokan's Travels in the West]*, first published 1815, *Tōyō Bunko 461* (reprinted Tokyo, 1986)

Shushtari, Seyyed Abd al-Latif, *Kitab Tuhfat al-'Alam* (written Hyderabad, 1802; lithographed Mumbai, 1847)

Smithies, M. (trans. and ed.), *The Chevalier de Chaumont and the Abbé de Choisy. Aspects of the Embassy to Siam 1685* (Chiang Mai, 1997)

Smithies, M. et al., *The Diary of Kosa Pan* (Chiang Mai, 2002)

Stalker, J. and Parker, G., with an introduction by H.D. Molesworth, *A Treatise of Japanning and Varnishing* (1688; reprinted London, 1960)

Staunton, G., *An Authentic Account of an Embassy from the king of Great Britain to the Emperor of China*, 3 vols (London, 1797)

Stavorinus, J.S., *Reize van Zeeland over de Kaap de Goede Hoop … in de jaren 1768–1771*, 2 vols (Leiden, 1793)

Streynsham, Master, *The Diaries of Streynsham Master 1675–80*, ed. Sir R.C. Temple (London, 1911)

Su Song, *Xinyixiangfayao [New Design for a Mechanized Armillary Sphere and Celestial Globe]*, 1172 (reprinted Shanghai, 1937)

Tavernier, J.-B., *Travels in India*, trans. V. Ball and W. Crooke, 2 vols (Oxford, 1925)

Thackston, W.M. (trans.), *The Jahangirnama, Memoirs of Jahangir, Emperor of India* (New York and Oxford, 1999)

Thévenot, M., *Relations de divers voyages curieux, qui n'ont point esté publiées* (Paris, 1663–72)

Torres, Father C. de, *Historia da Igreja de Jap vo* (1575)

Valentia, Viscount, *Voyages and Travels to India, Ceylon, the Red Sea, Abyssinia, and Egypt in the years 1802–1806*, 3 vols (London, 1809)

Valentyn, F., *Oud en Nieuw Oost-Indiën*, 5 vols (Amsterdam, 1724–26)

Valentyn, F., *Description of Ceylon*, trans. and ed. S. Arasaratnam (London, 1978)

The Veritable Records of the Qianlong emperor's reign [Gaozong chun huangdi shilu (Taipei, 1964)]

Vocabulario da Lingoa de Japam (Nagasaki, 1603; with a 1704 supplement)

Wathen, J., *Journal of a Voyage in 1811 and 1812 to Madras and China* (London, 1814)

Williamson, Capt. T., *The East India Vade Mecum*, 2 vols (London, 1810)

Xu Chaojun, *Zimingzhongbiao tufa [Illustrated Account of the Manufacture of Mechanical Clocks]*, (Shanghai, 1809)

SECONDARY SOURCES

Abd al'-Aziz, *The Imperial Treasury of the Indian Mughals* (Delhi, 1972)

Ackermann, H.C., *Seidengewebe des 18. Jahrhunderts 1: Bizarre Seiden* (Riggisberg, 2000)

Adshead, S.A.M., *China in World History* (London, 1994)

Adshead, S.A.M., *Material Culture in Europe and China, 1400–1800* (Basingstoke, 1997)

Akveld, L. and Jacobs, E.M. (eds), *The Colourful World of the VOC* (Amsterdam, exhib. cat. 2002)

Albuquerque, V.A.C.B., *O Senado de Goa, memória histórico-archeologica*, Imprensa Nacional, Nova (Goa, 1909)

Alden, D., *The Making of an Enterprise: The Society of Jesus in Portugal, its Empire and Beyond* (Stanford, 1996)

Alegria, D. and Garcia, R., 'Portuguese Cartography in the Renaissance', in D. Woodward (ed.), *History of Cartography* (forthcoming, 2005), vol. 3

Alfons, S., 'The Museum as Image of the World,' in *The Archimboldo Effect. Transformations of the Face from the Sixteenth to the Twentieth Century* (Palazzo Grassi, Venice, exhib. cat. 1979), pp. 67–85

Antunes, L.F.D., 'Diu, espaços e quotidianos', in *Os Espaços de um Império Estudos* (Comissão Nacional para as Comemorações dos Descobrimentos Portugueses, Lisbon, exhib. cat. 1999) pp. 149–59

Archer, M., 'British patrons of Indian artists: Sir Elijah Impey', in *Country Life* (18 August 1955), pp. 340–41

Archer, M., 'A Georgian palace in India', in *Country Life* (9 April 1959), pp. 754–56

Archer, M., 'Company painting in South India: the early collections of Niccolao Manucci', in *Apollo* (August 1970), pp. 104–13

Archer, M., *Company drawings in the India Office Library* (London, 1972)

Archer, M., 'Colonel Gentil's Atlas: an early series of Company drawings', in *India Office Library and Records, Annual Report, 1978* (London, 1979), pp. 41–45

Archer, M., *Indian and British Portraiture 1770–1825* (London, 1979)

Archer, M., *Early Views of India: the Picturesque Journeys of Thomas and William Daniell* (London, 1980)

Archer, M., *The India Office Collection of Paintings and Sculpture* (London, 1986)

Archer, M. et al., *Treasures from India, The Clive Collection at Powis Castle* (London, exhib. cat. 1987)

Archer, M., *Company paintings: Indian paintings of the British period* (London, 1992)

Archer, M. and Archer, W.G., *Indian painting for the British, 1770–1880* (Oxford, 1955)

Archer, M. and Falk, T., *Indian Miniatures in the India Office Library* (London, 1981)

Arnold, L. *Princely Gifts and Papal Treasures* (San Francisco, 1999)

Asher, C.B., *Architecture of Mughal India* (Cambridge, 1992)

Athar Ali, M., *The Mughal Nobility under Aurangzeb* (Mumbai, 1970)

Atwell, W., 'Ming China and the emerging world economy, *c.*1470–1650', in *The Cambridge History of China* (Cambridge, 1998), vol. 8, ch. 8

Ayers, J. et al., *Porcelain for Palaces* (London, exhib. cat. 1990)

Ayers, J., Krahl, R. and Erbahar, N., *Chinese Ceramics in the Topkapi Saray Museum Istanbul. A Complete Catalogue*, 2 vols (London, 1986)

Backhouse, E. and Bland, J.O.P., *Annals and Memoirs of the Court of Peking* (Boston and New York, 1914)

Badin, J., *La Manufacture de Tapisseries de Beauvais* (Paris, 1909)

Bailey, G.A., 'The Catholic Shrines of Agra', in *Arts of Asia* (July–August 1993), vol. 23, no. 4, pp. 131–37

Bailey, G.A., 'A Portuguese Doctor at the Maharaja of Jaipur's Court', in *South Asian Studies* (Cambridge, 1995), vol. 11, pp. 51–62

Bailey, G.A., 'The Lahore *Mirat al-Quds* and the Impact of Jesuit Theater on Mughal Painting', in *South Asian Studies* (1997), vol. 13, pp. 95–108

Bailey, G.A., 'The Indian Conquest of Catholic Art: The Mughals, the Jesuits, and Imperial Mural Painting', in *Art Journal* (Spring 1998), pp. 24–30

Bailey, G.A., *The Jesuits and the Grand Mogul: Renaissance Art at the Imperial Court of India, 1580–1630* (Washington, 1998)

Bailey, G.A., *Art on the Jesuit Missions in Asia and Latin America, 1542–1773* (Toronto and Buffalo, 1999)

Bailey, G.A., 'Jesuit Catechism and the Arts in Mughal India', in J. W. O'Malley et al. (eds), *The Jesuits. Cultures, Sciences, and the Arts, 1540–1773* (Toronto, 1999)

Bailey, G.A., 'The Truth-Showing Mirror: Jesuit Catechism and the Arts in Mughal India', in J. W. O'Malley et al. (eds), *The Jesuits. Cultures, Sciences, and the Arts, 1540–1773* (Toronto, 1999), pp. 380–401

Bailey, G.A., 'Creating a Global Artistic Language in Late Renaissance Rome: Artists in the Service of the Overseas Missions', in P. Jones and T. Worcester (eds), *From Rome to Eternity: Catholicism and the Arts in Italy, ca. 1550–1650* (Leiden, 2001), pp. 225–52

Bailey, G.A., 'The Migration of Forms in the Art of the Jesuit Missions in Japan and China', in *Oriental Art*, XLVII, 5 (2001), pp. 2–12

Bao Leshi, *Zhonghe jiaowang-shi* (Beijing, 1989)

Baracho, C., 'Um percurso ao encontro do medievalismo em Macau', *Revista de Cultura*, 34 (Macau, 1998), pp. 147–80

Barbosa, D., *The Book of Duarte Barbosa. An account of the Countries Bordering on the Indian Ocean and Their Inhabitants, 1518*, trans. M. Langworth Dames, 2 vols (London, 1918–21; reprinted Delhi, 1989)

Barnes, R., *Indian Block-printed Textiles in Egypt: The Newberry Collection in the Ashmolean Museum*, 2 vols (Oxford, 1997)

Barnes, R., Cohen, S. and Crill, R., *Trade, Temple & Court. Indian Textiles from the Tapi Collection* (Mumbai, 2002)

Barros, J. de, *Décadas*, Livraria Sá da Costa, 4 vols (Lisbon, 1983)

Bassani, E. et al., *Via Orientalis* (Brussels, exhib. cat. 1991)

Battelli, G., 'Lisbona e la corte Portoghese in una relatione Veneta del 1572', *Ateneo Veneto. Riviste di Scienze, lettere ed arti*, CXXXIV (1943), vol. 130, pp. 102–06

Bayly, C.A., *Imperial Meridian: the British Empire and the World 1780–1830* (London, 1989)

Bayly, C.A. (ed.), *The Raj. India and the British 1600–1947* (National Portrait Gallery, London, exhib. cat. 1990)

Beach, M., *The Grand Mogul. Imperial Painting in India 1600–1660* (Williamstown, 1978)

Beach, M. and Koch, E., *King of the World. The Padshahnama: An imperial manuscript from the Royal Library, Windsor Castle* (London, exhib. cat. 1997)

Bechert, H., 'Die Periode der portugiesischen Herrschaft und die Anfänge der römisch-katholischen Kirche auf der Insel Ceylon', in W. Seipel (ed.), *Exotica: Portugals Entdeckungen im Spiegel fürstlicher Kunst- und Wunderkammern der Renaissance* (Vienna, exhib. cat. 2000), pp. 87–99

Beekman, E.M., *Troubled Pleasures, Dutch Colonial Literature from the East Indies, 1600–1950* (Oxford, 1996)

Benesch, O., *The Drawings of Rembrandt*, 6 vols (London, 1973)

Berggren, J.L. and Jones, A., *Ptolemy's Geography: an Annotated Translation of the Theoretical Chapters* (Princeton, 2000)

Berliner, F., *Europa und die Kaiser von China* (Berlin, exhib. cat. 1985)

Berliner, F., *Japan und Europa 1543–1929* (Berlin, exhib. cat. 1993)

Bethencourt, F. and Chaudhuri, K. (eds), *Historia da Expansao Portuguesa*, 2 vols (Lisbon, 1998)

Beurdeley, C. and M., *Castiglione: Peintre Jésuite à la Cour de Chine* (Fribourg, 1971)

Beurdeley, C. and M., *Giuseppe Castiglione: A Jesuit painter at the Court of the Chinese Emperors* (London, 1972)

Beveridge, H., 'Von Poser's Diary in Persia and India', in *The Imperial and Asiatic Quarterly Review* (January 1910), 3rd series, vol. XXIX, no. 57, pp. 96–100

Bitterli, U., *Cultures in Conflict: Encounters Between European and Non-European Cultures 1492–1800* (Cambridge, 1989)

Blussé, L., *Strange Company: Chinese Settlers, Mestizo Women and the Dutch in VOC Batavia* (Dordrecht, 1986)

Blussé, L., 'Retribution and Remorse; The Interaction between the Administration and the Protestant Mission in Early Colonial Formosa', in G. Prakash (ed.), *After Colonialism: Imperial Histories and Postcolonial Displacements* (Princeton, 1994) pp. 153–82

Blussé, L., *Bitter Bonds: A Colonial Divorce Drama of the Seventeenth Century* (Princeton, 2002)

Blussé, L. and Menghong Chen, *The Archives of the Kong Koan of Batavia* (Leiden, 2003)

Blussé, L., Remmelink, W. and Smits, I. (eds), *Bridging the Divide, 400 Years The Netherlands–Japan* (Leiden, 2000)

Blythe, R.H., *A History of Haiku* (Tokyo, 1963), vol. 1

Boesen, G., '"Chinese" Rooms at Rosenborg Castle', in *The Connoisseur* (January 1979), vol. 200, no. 803, pp. 34–39

Bottomley, I., 'Diplomatic gifts of arms and armour between Europe and Japan during the 16th & 17th centuries', in Nikko Toshogu bulletin (2000)

Bouchon, G., *L'Asie du Sud à l'époque des Grandes Découvertes* (Aldershot, 1987)

Bouchon, G., *Inde Découverte, Inde Retrouvée (1498–1630)*. Études d'histoire indo-portugaise (Lisbon–Paris, 1991)

Bourne, J. et al., *Lacquer, an International History and Collector's Guide* (London, 1984)

Boxer, C.R., *A true Description of the mighty kingdoms of Japan & Siam* (London, 1935)

Boxer, C.R., *The Christian Century in Japan, 1549–1650* (Berkeley, Los Angeles, and London, 1951; reprinted Lisbon, 1991)

Boxer, C.R., *The Great Ship from Amacon* (Lisbon, 1959)

Boxer, C.R., *Jan Company in Japan 1600–1817* (Tokyo and London, 1968)

Boxer, C.R., *From Lisbon to Goa, 1500–1750*. Studies in Portuguese Maritime Enterprise (Aldershot, 1984)

Boxer, C.R., *Portuguese Merchants and Missionaries in Feudal Japan: 1543–1640* (London, 1986)

Boyajian, J.C., *Portuguese Trade in Asia under the Habsburgs, 1580–1640* (Baltimore, 1993)

Boyé, J., *L'Extraordinaire Aventure de Benoît de Boigne aux Indes* (Paris, 1996)

Boyer, M., *Japanese Export Lacquers from the seventeenth century in the National Museum of Denmark* (Copenhagen, 1959)

Braancamp Freire, A., 'Cartas de Quitação del Rei D. Manuel', in *Archivo Histórico Portuguêz* (Lisbon, 1903), vol. 1, pp. 75–76

Brand, M., *The Vision of Kings, Art and Experience in India* (National Gallery of Australia, Canberra, exhib. cat. 1995)

Brand, M. and Lowry, G.D., *Akbar's India. Art from the Mughal City of Victory*, Asia Society (New York, exhib. cat. 1985)

Bray, F, 'Some Problems Concerning the Transfer of Scientific and Technical Knowledge', in T. C. H. Lee (ed.), *China and Europe: Images and Influences in Sixteenth to Eighteenth Centuries* (Hong Kong, 1991), pp. 203–19

Bredekamp, H., *Antikensehnsucht und Maschinenglauben. Die Geschichte der Kunstkammer und die Zukunft der Kunstgeschichte* (Berlin, 1993)

Bredif, J., *Toiles de Jouy* (Paris, 1989)

Breuning, H.A., *Het voormalige Batavia. Een Hollandse stedestichting in de tropen. Anno 1619* (Amsterdam, 1954)

Brook, T, 'Communication and Commerce', in *The Cambridge History of China* (Cambridge, 1998), vol. 8, ch. 10

Brotton, J., *Trading Territories: Mapping the Early Modern World* (London, 1997)

Brotton, J., *The Renaissance Bazaar: From the Silk Road to Michelangelo* (Oxford, 2002)

Brown, C. and Rabiner, D., *Chinese Glass of the Qing Dynasty, 1644–1911* (Phoenix, 1987)

Brown, C., Vlieghe, H. et al., *Anthony Van Dyck* (London, 1999)

Brown, R. and Sjostrand, S., *Maritime Archaeology and Shipwrecks in Malaysia* (Kuala Lumpur, 2002)

Bruijn, J.R., Gaastra, F.S. and Schöver, I., *Dutch-Asiatic Shipping in the 17th and 18th Centuries*, 3 vols (The Hague, 1987)

Bucholz, R.O., 'Going to Court in 1700: a visitor's guide', in *The Court Historian* (3 December 2000), vol. 5, pp. 181–215

Buck, A.M., *Dress in Eighteenth-century England* (London, 1979)

Cameron, N., 'Picturesque portraits of India', in *Orientations* (November 1975), vol. 13, no. 11, pp. 35–43

Canby, S., *Persian Painting* (London, 1993)

Canby, S., *Princes, Poets and Paladins. Islamic and Indian paintings from the collection of Prince and Princess Sadruddin Aga Khan* (London, exhib. cat. 1998)

Carita, H., *Palaces of Goa* (Lisbon, 1995)

Carita, H., 'Indo-portuguese civil architecture, origins and first models', in J. Pereira and P. Pal (eds), *India and Portugal: Cultural Interactions* (Mumbai, 2001), pp. 99–113

Carita, H., 'The dock warehouses in Cochim de Cima: continuity within Portuguese-influenced urbanism and architecture in the Cochin area', in *Oriente* 15 (Fundação Oriente, 2003), pp. 48–66

CARREIA-AFONSO, J., *Letters from the Mughal Court. The First Jesuit Mission to Akbar (1580–1583)* (Mumbai, 1980)

CHAPMAN, A., 'Tycho Brahe in China: the Jesuit Mission to Peking and the Iconography of European Instrument-Making Processes', in *Annals of Science* 41 (1984), pp.417–43

CHAVES, J., *Singing of the Source: Nature and God in the Poetry of the Chinese Painter Wu Li* (Honolulu, 1993)

CHECA, F., *Felipe II. Mecenas de las Artes* (Madrid, 1992)

CH'EN TA-TUAN, 'Investiture of Liu-ch'iu Kings in the Ch'ing Period', in J.K. Fairbank, *The Chinese World Order: Traditional China's Foreign Relations* (Cambridge, MA, 1968), pp.135–64

CHOI, KEE IL, 'Carl Gustav Ekeberg and the invention of Chinese export painting', in *Antiques* (March 1998), pp.426–37

CHRISTIANSON, J. R., *On Tycho's Island: Tycho Brahe and his Assistants, 1570–1601* (Cambridge, 2000)

CHUN, H., 'Sino-Korean Tributary Relations in the Ch'ing Period', in J.K. Fairbank, *The Chinese World Order: Traditional China's Foreign Relations* (Cambridge, MA, 1968), pp.90–111

CHUN, H., *Portuguese Conquest and Commerce in Southeast Asia* (Aldershot, 1985)

CLARKE, J. J., *Oriental Enlightenment: the Encounter Between Asian and Western Thought* (London and New York, 1997)

CLARKE, T. H., *The Rhinoceros from Dürer to Stubbs 1515–1799* (London, 1986)

CLEMMENSEN, T., 'Some Furniture Made in China in the English Style, Exported from Canton to Denmark 1735, 1737 and 1738', in *Furniture History Society Journal* XXI (1985)

CLOONEY, F. X., 'Roberto de Nobili's Dialogue on Eternal Life and an Early Jesuit Evaluation of Religion in South India', in J. W. O'Malley et al. (eds), *The Jesuits: Cultures, Sciences, and the Arts* (Toronto and Buffalo, 1999), pp.402–17

CLUNAS, C., *Chinese Export Watercolours* (London, 1984)

CLUNAS, C. (ed.), *Chinese Export Art and Design* (London, 1987)

CLUNAS, C, 'Design and Cultural Frontiers', in *Apollo* (October 1987), vol.126, pp.256–63

CLUNAS, C., *Circa 1492. Art in the Age of Exploration*, ed. J. Levenson (Washington, DC, exhib. cat. 1991)

CLUNAS, C., *Superfluous Things: Material Culture and Social Status in Early Modern China* (Cambridge, 1991)

CLUNAS, C., *Pictures and Visuality in Early Modern China* (Princeton, 1997)

COHEN, W. I., *East Asia at the Center: Four Thousand Years of Engagement with the World* (New York, 2000)

COHN, B. S., 'Cloth, Clothes, and Colonialism: India in the Nineteenth Century', in A. B. Weiner and J. Schneider, *Cloth and Human Experience* (London and Washington, 1989)

COLENBRANDER, H. T., *Jan Pietersz Coen, levensbeschrijving* (The Hague, 1934)

COLLEY, L., 'Going Native, Telling Tales: Captivity, Collaborations and Empire', in *Past & Present* (August 2000), no. 168

COLLINGHAM, E. M., *Imperial Bodies: The Physical Experience of the Raj c. 1800–1947* (London, 2001)

CONNER, P., *The China Trade: 1600–1860* (Brighton, exhib. cat. 1986)

CONNER, P., 'The Enigma of Spoilum and the origins of China Trade Portraiture', in *Antiques* (March 1998), pp.418–25

COOMARASWAMI, A., *Medieval Sinhalese Art* (London, 1929)

CORNFORTH, J., 'A role for Chinoiserie?', *Country Life* (7 December 1989), vol.CLXXXIII, no. 49, pp.144–51

CORT, L., *Shigaraki Potters' Valley* (Tokyo, New York and San Francisco, 1979)

CRANMER-BYNG, J.L. and LEVERE, T.H., 'A Case Study of Cultural Collision', in *Annals of Science* 38 (1981), pp.503–25

CRARY, J., *Techniques of the Observer, on vision and modernity in the nineteenth century* (Cambridge, MA, and London, 1992)

CROSSMAN, C., *The Decorative Arts of the China trade* (Woodbridge, 1991)

CRILL, R., *Marwar Painting. A history of the Jodhpur style* (Mumbai, 2000)

CROWE, Y., 'Echoes of Far Eastern Lacquer in the World of Islam', in *Transactions of the Oriental Ceramic Society* (1997–98), vol.62, pp.57–67

CRUZ, M.A.L., 'Exiles and Renegades in Early Sixteenth Century Portuguese India', in *The Indian Economic and Social History Review* (1986), vol.XXIII, no. 3

CURVELLO, A., 'Nagasaki: An European Artistic City in Early Modern Japan', in *Bulletin of Portuguese-Japan Studies* (2001), no. 2, pp.23–35

DAENHARDT, R., *The Bewitched Gun, the introduction of the firearm in the Far East by the Portuguese* (Lisbon, 1994)

DALRYMPLE, W., *White Mughals* (London, 2002)

DAM-MIKKELSEN, B. and LUNDBAEK, T. (eds), *Ethnographic Objects in The Royal Danish Kunstkammer 1650–1800* (Copenhagen, 1980)

D'ARELLI, F. (ed.), *Le marche e l'oriente* (Rome, 1998)

DAS, A.K., *Mughal Painting During Jahangir's Time* (Calcutta, 1978)

DAS, A.K. (ed.), *Mughal Masters. Further Studies* (Mumbai, 1998)

DAS, H., *The Norris Embassy to Aurangzib (1699–1702)*, condensed and rearranged by S. C. Sarkar (Calcutta, 1959)

DASH, M., *Tulipomania: The Story of the World's Most Coveted Flower and the Extraordinary Passions it Aroused* (New York, 1999)

DASTON, L. and PARK, K., *Wonders and the Order of Nature, 1150–1750* (New York, 1998)

DAWSON, C., *Mission to Asia* (Toronto, 1980)

De Goa a Lisboa. L'Art Indo-Portugais. XVIe–XVIIIe siècles (Brussels, exhib. cat. 1991)

DELAUNEY, P., *La zoölogie au seizième siécle* (Paris, 1962)

D'ELIA, P., *Le origini dell'arte cristiana cinese* (Rome, 1939)

D'ELIA, P., *Fonti Ricciane. Documenti Originali Concerenti Matteo Ricci e la Storia delle Prime Relazioni tra l'Europa e la Cina. 1579–1615*, 3 vols (Rome, 1949)

DE MOURA CARVALHO, P., 'A group of early lacquered furniture for the Portuguese market and its probable origin in Bay of Bengal and Coromandel Coast', in P. De Moura Carvalho (ed.), *The world of Lacquer: 2000 years of history* (Lisbon, exhib.cat.2001), pp.127–41

DESAI, V.N., *Life at Court: art for India's rulers, 16th–19th centuries* (Museum of Fine Arts, Boston, exhib. cat. 1985)

DESAI, Z. A., 'Some 14th century epitaphs from Cambay in Gujarat', in *Archaeological Survey of India, Epigraphica Indica, Arabic and Persian supplement* (1971)

DESWARTE, S., *Ideias e Imagens em Portugal na época dos Descobrimentos* (Lisbon, 1992)

DIAS, P., *História da Arte Portuguesa no Mundo*, 2 vols (Lisbon, 1999)

DÍAZ, P. J., *El coleccionismo manierista de los Austrias. Entre Felipe II y Rodolfo II* (Madrid, 2001)

DIFFIE, B. W. and W., *Foundations of the Portuguese Empire 1415–1580. Europe and the World in the Age of Expansion* (Minneapolis, 1977), vol. I

DIGBY, S., 'The mother-of-pearl overlaid furniture of Gujarat: the holdings of the Victoria and Albert Museum', in R. Skelton et al. (eds), *Facets of Indian Art* (London, 1986), pp.213–22

D'INTINO, R., *Informação das Cousas da China. Textos do século XVI*, Imprensa Nacional (Lisbon, 1989)

DISNEY, A. and BOOTH, E. (eds), *Vasco da Gama and the Linking of Europe and Asia* (New York and New Delhi, 2000)

DOS SANTOS LOPES, M., *Coisas maravilhosas e até agora nunca vistas. Para uma iconográfia dos Descobrimentos* (Lisbon, 1998)

DU JARRIC, P., *Akbar and the Jesuits*, trans. C. H. Payne (London, 1926)

DWIVEDI, S. and M., *Bombay: the Cities within* (Mumbai, 1995)

EARLE, J., 'Genji meets Yang Guifei: A Group of Japanese export lacquers', in *Transactions of the Oriental Ceramic Society* (1982–83), vol.XLVII, pp.45–75

EDO-TOKYO MUSEUM, *Hizo Kapitan no Edo Korekushon: Oranda-jin no Nihon Shumi [The Kapitan (the Dutch Chief) Collection from the Edo Period: The Dutch Fascination with Japan]*, (Tokyo, exhib. cat. 2000)

EICHBERGER, D., *Leben mit Kunst, Wirken durch Kunst. Sammelwesen und Hofkunst unter Margarete von Österreich, Regentin der Niederlande* (Turnhout, Belgium, 2002)

ELGOOD, R., *Firearms of the Islamic World in the Tareq Rajab Museum, Kuwait* (London, 1995)

ELISON, G., *Deus Destroyed: The Image of Christianity in Early Modern Japan* (Cambridge, MA, 1991)

ELMAN, B.A., *From Philosophy to Philology: Intellectual and Social Aspects of Change in Late Imperial China* (Cambridge, MA, and London, 1984)

Encounters of Cultures: Eight Centuries of Portuguese Mission Work (Vatican City, exhib. cat. 1996)

ENTWISLE, E.A., 'Chinese Painted Wallpaper', in *The Connoisseur* (June 1934), vol.93, pp.367–75

FAIRBANK, J.K., *Trade and Diplomacy on the China Coast* (Stanford, 1953)

FAIRBANK, J.K.., *The Chinese World Order: Traditional China's Foreign Relations* (Cambridge, MA, 1968)

FAIRBANK, J.K.. and REISCHAUER, E.O., *China: Tradition and Transformation* (Sydney and London, 1989)

FARAGO, C. (ed.), *Reframing the Renaissance. Visual Culture in Europe and Latin America 1450–1650* (New Haven, CT, 1995)

FARRINGTON, A., *Trading Places: the East India Company and Asia 1600–1834* (London, exhib. cat. 2002)

FAULKNER, R. (ed.), *Tea: East and West* (London, 2003)

FERGUSON, K., *The Nobleman and his Housedog: Tycho Brahe and Johannes Kepler: The Strange Partnership that Revolutionised Science* (London, 2002)

FERNANDES, J.M., 'Macau, da cidade antiga à arquitectura recente', in *Arquitectura Portuguesa* 12 (Lisbon, 1988), pp.62–73

FERNANDES, J.M, 'Macau', in *Os Espaços de um Império* (Comissão Nacional para as Comemorações dos Descobrimentos Portugueses, Lisbon, exhib. cat. 1999), pp.211–12

FERRÃO, B., *Mobiliario Português, India e Japão*, 4 vols (Lisbon, 1990)

FERRONHA, A. L., BETTENCOURT, M. and LOUREIRO, R., *A Fauna Exótica dos Descobrimentos* (Lisbon, 1993)

FIGGESS, J., 'A Letter from the Court of Yung Lo', in *Transactions of the Oriental Ceramic Society* (1962–63), vol.34, pp.97–100

FIGGESS, J, 'A Group of Decorated Lacquer Caskets of the Yuan Dynasty', in *Transactions of the Oriental Ceramic Society* (1964–66), vol.36, pp.39–43

FINDLEN, P., 'The Museum: Its Classical Etymology and Renaissance Genealogy', in *Journal of the History of Collections* (1989), vol. I, no. I, pp.59–78

FISHER, C.T., 'Portuguese as seen by the Historians of the Qing Court', in A. Disney and E. Booth (eds), *Vasco da Gama and the Linking of Europe and Asia* (New Delhi, 2000), pp.307–21

FONDATION CUSTODIA, PARIS, *Couleurs de l'Inde. Nouvelles acquisitions de la Collection Frits Lugt* (Paris, exhib. cat. 2002)

FONSECA, N. DA, *An Historical and Archaeological Sketch of the City of Goa* (Mumbai, 1878)

FORTE, A., *Mingtang and Buddhist Utopias in the History of the Astronomical Clock: The Tower, Statue, and Armillary Sphere Constructed by Empress Wu* (Rome, 1988)

FOSS, T.N. 'A Western Interpretation of China: Jesuit Cartography', in C. E. Ronan and B.B.C. Oh, *East Meets West: The Jesuits in China, 1582–1773* (Chicago, 1988), pp.209–25

FRANK, B., 'A European View of Life in 16th Century Goa: the Images of Jan Huygen van Linschoten', in J. Pereira and P. Pal (eds), *India and Portugal: Cultural Interactions* (Mumbai, 2001), pp.46–69

FRENCH, C.L., *Shiba Kōkan: Artist, Innovator, and Pioneer in the Westernization of Japan* (New York and Tokyo, 1974)

FRENCH, C.L., *Through Closed Doors: Western Influence on Japanese Art 1639–1853* (Michigan, exhib. cat. 1977)

FU, L., *A Documentary Chronicle of Sino-Western Relations, 1644–1820*, 2 vols (Tucson, 1966)

FUJIOKA, R., *Tea Ceremony Utensils, Arts of Japan 3*, trans. and adapted L. A. Cort (New York and Tokyo, 1973)

FUKUOKA ART MUSEUM, *Nihon Bijutsu no Naka no Seiyo: Azuchi Momoyama – Edo no Nyu Ato [Western Influences on Japanese Art: Azuchi Momoyama Period to the New Art of the Edo Period]*, (Fukuoka, exhib. cat. 1995)

FURBER, H., *Rival Empires of Trade in the Orient 1600–1800* (Minneapolis, 1976)

GAASTRA, F.S., *De geschiedenis van de VOC* (Zutphen, 2002)

GAHLIN, S., *The Courts of India. Indian Miniatures from the Collection of the Fondation Custodia, Paris* (Paris, 1991)

GALLERIA REGIONALE DELLA SICILIA, PALERMO, *Wunderkammer siciliana. Alle origini del museo perduto*, ed. V. Abbate (Palermo, exhib. cat. 2001)

GAO ZHENTIAN, 'Kangxidi yu Xiyang zhuanjiaoshi' ['The Kangxi emperor and Western missionaries'], in *Lishi dang'an* (1986), no. I, pp.187–91

GARCÍA SANZ, A. and JORDAN GSCHWEND, A., 'Via Orientalis. Objetos del Lejano Oriente en el Monasterio de las Descalzas Reales', in *Reales Sitios* (1998), no.138, pp.25–39

GARNER, SIR H., *Chinese Lacquer* (London and Boston, 1979)

GERNET, J., *China and the Christian Impact*, trans. J. Lloyd (Cambridge, 1985)

GHOSH, S.C., *The Social Condition of the British Community in Bengal* (Leiden, 1970)

GILBERT, C. and MURDOCH, T., *John Channon and brass-inlaid furniture, 1730–1760* (London and New Haven, exhib. cat., 1993)

GILMOUR, B. and WORRELL, E., 'Paktong: The Trade in Chinese Nickel Brass to Europe', in *Trade and Discovery: The Scientific Study of Artefacts from Post-Medieval Europe and Beyond* (London, 1995)

GITTINGER, M., *Master Dyers to the World. Technique and Trade in Early Indian Dyed Cotton Textiles* (Textile Museum, Washington, exhib. cat.1982)

GODÉE MOLSBERGEN, E.C., *De stichter van Hollands Zuid-Afrika, Jan van Riebeeck* (Amsterdam, 1912)

GÓIS, D. DE, *Crónica do Felicíssimo Rei D. Manuel* (Coimbra, 1949–55), pts I–IV

GOITEIN, S.D., *A Mediterranean Society: The Jewish Communities of the Arab World as Portrayed in the Documents of the Cairo Geniza*, 5 vols (Berkeley, 1967–88)

GOLE, S., *Indian Maps and Plans: From Earliest Times to the Advent of European Surveys* (New Delhi, 1989)

GOODMAN, G.K., *Japan and the Dutch, 1600–1853* (London, 2000); previous editions published as *Japan: The Dutch Experience* (London, 1986) and *The Dutch Impact on Japan, 1640–1853* (Leiden, 1967)

GOODRICH, L.C. and CHAOYING FANG (eds), *Dictionary of Ming Biography* (New York, 1976)

GORGAS, M., 'Animal Trade between India and Western Eurasia in the Sixteenth Century – The Role of the Fuggers in Animal Trading', in K. S. Mathew (ed.), *Indo-Portuguese Trade and the Fuggers of Germany* (New Delhi, 1997), pp.195–225

GRAHAM, P.J., *Tea of the Sages: The Art of Sencha* (Honolulu, 1998)

GRAND P ALAIS, PARIS, *Rasa. Les neuf visages de l'art indien* (Paris, exhib. cat.1986)

GRAY, B., 'Lord Burlington and Father Ripa's Chinese Engravings', in *The British Museum Quarterly* XXII (1960), pp.40–43

GRAY, B., 'The Export of Chinese Porcelain to India', in *Transactions of the Oriental Ceramic Society* (1964–66), vol.36, pp.31–37

GROTE, A. (ed.), *Macrosomos in Microcosmo. Die Welt in der Stube. Zur Geschichte des Sammelns 1450–1800* (Opladen, 1994)

GUNDESTRUP, B., *The Royal Danish Kunstkammer 1737* (Copenhagen, 1991), vol. II

GUPTA, A.D., *Merchants of Maritime India, 1500–1800* (Aldershot, 1994)

GUTH, C.M.E., *Art, Tea, Industry: Masuda Takashi and the Mitsui Circle* (Princeton, 1993)

Guy, J., *Oriental Trade Ceramics in South East Asia: Ninth to Sixteenth Centuries* (Singapore, 1986)

Guy, J., 'The Vietnamese Wall Tiles of Majapahit', in *Transactions of the Oriental Ceramic Society* (1988–89), vol. 53, pp. 27–46

Guy, J., 'Thai Ceramics in Southeast Asian Trade', in *Thai Ceramics: The James and Elaine Connell Collection* (Kuala Lumpur, 1993), pp. 8–13

Guy, J., 'Jain Manuscript Painting', in P. Pal (ed.), *The Peaceful Liberators. Jain Art from India* (Los Angeles and New York, 1995), pp. 89–99

Guy, J., *Woven Cargoes: Indian Textiles in the East* (London, 1998)

Guy, J., 'Tamil merchant guilds and the Quanzhou trade', in A. Schottenhamer (ed.), *The Emporium of the World. Maritime Quanzhou, 1000–1400* (Leiden, 2000), pp. 283–308

Guy, J., 'Vietnamese Ceramics from the Hoi An Excavation: The Cu Lao Cham Ship Cargo', in *Orientations* (2000), vol. 31, no. 7, pp. 125–28

Guy, J., 'Early Asian Ceramic Trade and the Belitung ("Tang") Cargo', in *Transactions of the Oriental Ceramic Society* (2001–02), vol. 66, pp. 13–25

Haan, F. de, *Oud Batavia*, 2 vols (Bandoeng, 1935)

Habib, I., *Atlas of the Mughal Empire* (New Delhi, 1982)

Habib, I. (ed.), *Akbar and his India* (New Delhi, 1997)

Hahn, E., *Raffles of Singapore* (Singapore, 1968)

Hall, R., *Empires of the Monsoon. A history of the Indian ocean and its invaders* (London, 1996)

Hambly, G.G.R., 'The Emperor's Clothes: Robing and "Robes of Honour"' in S. Gordon (ed.), *Mughal India, Robes of Honour, Khil'at in Pre-Colonial and Colonial India* (Delhi, 2003)

Hardie, P. and Greenstead, M., *Chinese Ceramics: The India Connection* (Bristol, 1982)

Harfield, A., *Bencoolen: a History of the Honourable East India Company's Garrison of the West Coast of Sumatra (1685–1825)* (Barton on Sea, 1995)

Harris, J. and Snodin, M. (eds), *Sir William Chambers: architect to George III* (New Haven, CT, 1996)

Hasan, A., *Palace Culture of Lucknow* (New Delhi, 1983)

Haupt, H. et al., *Le Bestiare de Rodolphe II. Cod. min 129 et 130 de la Bibliothèque national d'Autriche* (Paris, 1990)

Hawes, C., *Poor Relations: The Making of the Eurasian Community in British India 1773–1833* (London, 1996)

Hayashiya, S. et al., *Chanōyu: Japanese Tea Ceremony* (New York and Japan, exhib. cat. 1979)

Hesselink, R., *Prisoners of Nambu* (Honolulu, 2002)

Hevia, J.L., *Cherishing Men from Afar* (Durham, NC, and London, 1995)

He Zhe, 'Qingdai de Xifang zhuanjiaoshi yu Zhongguo wenhua' ['Western missionaries and Chinese culture in the Qing dynasty'], in *Gugong bowuyuan yuankan* (1983), no. 2, pp. 17–26

Historisch Museum, Amsterdam, *Distant Worlds Made Tangible. Art and Curiosities: Dutch Collections, 1585–1735* (Amsterdam, exhib. cat. 1992)

Ho, P.Y., 'China and Europe: Scientific and Technological Exchanges from the Sixteenth to Eighteenth Centuries', in T.C.H. Lee (ed.), *China and Europe: Images and Influences in Sixteenth to Eighteenth Centuries* (Hong Kong, 1991), pp. 189–201

Hood Museum of Art, Hannover, NH, *The Age of the Marvelous* (New Hampshire, exhib. cat. 1991)

Howard, D. and Ayers, J., *China for the West. Chinese Porcelain & other Decorative Arts for Export illustrated from the Mottahedeh Collection*, 2 vols (London and New York, 1978)

Howell, K.J., *God's Two Books: Copernican Cosmology and Biblical Interpretation in Early Modern Science* (Notre Dame, IN, 2002)

Howgego, R.J., *Encyclopedia of Exploration to 1800* (Sydney, 2003)

Hradschin Castle, P rague, *Rudolf II and Prague. The Court and the City* (Prague, exhib. cat. 1997)

Huang Shijian and Sargent, W. R., *Customs and Conditions of Chinese City Streets in 19th Century – 360 Professions* (Shanghai, 1999)

Hudson, G.F., *Europe and China* (Boston, 1931)

Hunt, E.H., 'Old Hyderabad China', in *Journal of the Hyderabad Archaeological Society* (1916), pp. 48–91

Hutt, J., 'A Japanese lacquer chest in the V&A; A seventeenth-century wedding casket for the Dutch market', in *Apollo* (March 1998), vol. CXLVII, no. 433, pp. 3–9

Hutt, J., 'A Japanese export lacquer chest in the Victoria & Albert Museum; Some further observations', *Apollo* (March 1999), vol. CLXIX, no. 445, pp. 22–24

Hutt, J., 'East and West in Japanese Export Lacquerware: Some Problem Pieces in the Victoria and Albert Museum', in *Ostasiatische und europeische Lacktechniken / East Asian and European Lacquer techniques* (dual text), (Munich, 2000), pp. 19–26

Idema, W.L., 'Cannon, Clocks and Clever Monkeys: Europeana, Europeans and Europe in some early Qing Novels', in E.B. Vermeer (ed.), *Development and Decline of Fukien Province in the 17th and 18th Centuries* (Leiden, 1990), pp. 459–88

Impey, O., 'Japanese Export Lacquer of the 17th Century', in W. Watson (ed.), *Lacquerwork in Asia and Beyond*, Colloquies on Art and Archaeology in Asia No. 11, Percival David Foundation of Chinese Art (London, 1982), pp. 124–58

Impey, O, 'Japanese export lacquer', in *Lacquer: An International Hstory and Collector's Guide* (Marlborough, 1984), pp. 123–35

Impey, O, 'Sasaya Kisuke, Kyoto "Nagasaki" Lacquer and the woodworker Kiyotomo', in *Oriental Art* (1998), vol. XLIV, no. 2, pp. 28–32

Impey, O., 'Namban: Japanese export lacquer for Portugal', in P. De Moura Carvalho (ed.), *The world of Lacquer: 2000 years of history* (Calouste Gulbenkian Museum, Lisbon, exhib. cat. 2001), pp. 105–14

Irvine, W., 'Austin of Bordeaux', in *Journal of the Royal Asiatic Society* (London, 1910), pp. 1343–45

Irwin, J., 'Golconda cotton paintings of the early seventeenth century', in *Lalit Kala* (New Delhi, 1959), vol. 5, pp. 8–48

Irwin, J., *The Kashmir Shawl* (London, 1973)

Irwin, J. and Brett, K., *Origins of Chintz* (London, 1970)

Iyer, R. (ed.), *The Glass Curtain between Asia and Europe* (London, 1965)

Izzard, S., *Japanese paintings and works of art, Korean ceramics* (New York, sale cat. 2000)

Jackson-Stops, G. (ed.), *The Treasure Houses of Britain: five hundred years of private patronage and art collecting* (National Gallery of Art, Washington, exhib. cat. 1985)

Jacobson, D., *Chinoiserie* (London, 1993)

Jaffer, A., *Furniture from British India and Ceylon, the collections of the Victoria and Albert Museum and the Peabody Essex Museum* (London, 2001)

Jaffer, A., *Luxury Goods from India, the Art of the Indian Cabinet-Maker* (London, 2002)

Jaffer, A. and Schwabe, M., 'A group of sixteenth century caskets from Ceylon', in *Apollo* (March 1999), CXLIX, no. 445, pp. 3–14

Jardine, L., *Worldy Goods: A New History of the Renaissance* (London, 1996)

Jardine, L. and Brotton, J., *Global Interests: Renaissance Art between East and West* (London, 2000)

Jarry, M., *Chinoiserie: Chinese Influences on European Decorative Arts 17th and 18th centuries* (New York and London, 1981)

Jennes, J., *Invloed der Vlaamsche Prentkunst in Indie, China en Japan* (Leuven, 1943)

Jenyns, R. Soame, 'Glass and Painting on Glass', in *Chinese Art III* (New York, 1981), pp. 95–126

Jervis, J., *Transgressing the Modern: Explorations in the Western Experience of Otherness* (Oxford, 1999)

Jordan, A., 'Images of Empire: Slaves in the household and court of Catherine of Austria,' in K. Lowe and T. Earle (eds), *Black Africans in Renaissance Europe* (Cambridge, forthcoming in 2004)

Jordan Gschwend, A., 'A Crystal Elephant from the *Kunstkammer* of Catherine of Austria', in *Jahrbuch der Kunsthistorischen Sammlungen in Wien* (1991), vol. 87, pp. 121–26

Jordan Gschwend, A., 'Lisbon: Between Spices and Diamonds, 1500 to 1700', in *The Court Historian* (March 1993), vol. 3, no. 1, pp. 16–23

Jordan Gschwend, A., 'Catarina de Áustria: Colecção e *Kunstkammer* de uma Princesa Renascentista', in *Oceanos* (December 1993), no. 16, pp. 62–70

Jordan Gschwend, A., 'In the Tradition of Princely Collections: Curiosities and Exotica in the Kunstkammer of Catherine of Austria', in *Bulletin of the Society for Renaissance Studies* (1995), no. 13, pp. 1–9

Jordan Gschwend, A., 'Uomini Illustri. A série de retratos dos vice-reis portugueses em Goa', in *Tapeçarias de D. João de Castro* (Museu Nacional de Arte Antiga, Lisbon, exhib. cat. 1995), pp. 73–79

Jordan Gschwend, A., 'Marvels of the East. Renaissance Curiosity Collections in Portugal', in *A Herança de Rauluchantim [The Heritage of Rauluchantim]*, (Museu de S. Roque, Lisbon, exhib. cat. 1996), pp. 82–127

Jordan Gschwend, A., 'Jóias e pedras preciosas', in *Nossa Senhora dos Mártires. A última Viagem* (Portuguese Pavilion, Expo 98, Lisbon, exhib. cat. 1998), pp. 253–63

Jordan Gschwend, A., 'O Fascínio de Cipango. Artes Decorativas e Lacas da Asia Oriental em Portugal, Espanha e Austria (1511–1598)', in *Os Constructores do Oriente Português* (Museum, Porto, exhib. cat. 1998), pp. 195–227, 406–11

Jordan Gschwend, A., 'Os produtos exóticos da carreira da India e o papel da corte portuguesa na sua difusão', in *Nossa Senhora dos Mártires. A última Viagem* (Portuguese Pavilion, Expo 98, Lisbon, exhib. cat. 1998), pp. 123–41

Jordan Gschwend, A., 'Exotic Renaissance Accessories. Japanese, Indian and Sinhalese Fans at the courts of Portugal and Spain', in *Apollo* (November 1999), vol. CL, pp. 25–35

Jordan Gschwend, A., 'Mujeres mecenas de la casa de Austria y la infanta Isabel Clara Eugenia', in *El arte en la corte de los Arquiduques Alberto de Austria e Isabel Clara Eugenia (1598–1633). Un reino imaginado* (Madrid, 1999), pp. 118–37

Jordan Gschwend, A., 'Queen of the Seas and Overseas. Dining at the Table of Catherine of Austria, Queen of Portugal', in *Royal and Princely Tables of Europe. Commissions and Gifts. European Royal Tables – International Symposium Acts* (Lisbon, 1999), pp. 14–43

Jordan Gschwend, A., 'Las dos águilas del emperador Carlos V. Las colecciones y el mecenazgo de Juana e Maria de Austria en la corte de Felipe II', in L. R. García (ed.), *La Monarquia de Felipe II a debate* (Madrid, 2000), pp. 429–72

Jordan Gschwend, A., 'A Masterpiece of Indo-Portuguese Art: The Rhinoceros Cup of Maria of Portugal, Princess of Parma (1538–1577)', in *Oriental Art* (2000), vol. XLVI, no. 3, pp. 48–58

Jordan Gschwend, A., 'Los primeros abanicos orientales de los Habsburgos', in *Oriente en Palacio. Tesoros asiáticos en las colecciones reales españolas* (Patrimonio Nacional, Madrid, exhib. cat. 2003), pp. 267–71

Jordan Gschwend, A. and Pérez de Tudela, A., '*Exotica Habsburgica*. La Casa de Austria y las colecciones exóticas en el Renacimiento temprano', in *Oriente en Palacio. Tesoros asiáticos en las colecciones reales españolas*, (Patrimonio Nacional, Madrid, exhib. cat. 2003), pp. 26–43

Jörg, C., *Chinese Export Porcelain: Chine de Commande from the Royal Museums of Art and History in Brussels* (Hong Kong, 1989)

Jörg, C., 'Japanese Export Lacquer for the Dutch Market', in *Ostasiatische und europeische Lacktechniken/ East Asian and European Lacquer techniques* (dual text), (Munich, 2000), pp. 43–46

Jourdain, M. and Jenyns, R.S., *Chinese Export Art in the Eighteenth Century* (1950; 2nd edn Feltham, 1967)

Ju Deyuan, 'Qingdai Yesuhuishi yu xiyang qiqi' ['The Jesuits and strange Western objects of the Qing dynasty'], pt 1, in *Gugong bowuyuan yuankan* (1989), no. 1, pp. 3–16; pt 2, in *Gugong bowuyuan yuankan* (1989), no. 2, pp. 13–23

Kao, M., 'European Influences in Chinese Art, Sixteenth to Eighteenth Centuries', in T.C.H. Lee (ed.), *China and Europe: Images and Influences in Sixteenth to Eighteenth Centuries* (Hong Kong, 1991), pp. 251–303

Katagiri, K., *Oranda-shuku Ebi-ya no Kenkyu [Study of the Ebi-ya Dutch Lodgings]*, vol. I (Kyoto, 1998)

Kaye, M.M. (ed.), *The Golden Calm: An English Lady's Life in Mughal Delhi* (London, 1980)

Keay, J., *The Honourable Company: a History of the East India Company* (London, 1991)

Keene, D., *The Japanese Discovery of Europe, 1720–1830* (Stanford, 1969) (revised and expanded edition of *The Japanese Discovery of Europe: Honda Toshiaki and Other Discoverers, 1720–1798* [London, 1952])

Keene, M. with Kaoukji, S., *Treasury of the World. Jewelled Arts of India in the Age of the Mughals* (London, exhib. cat. 2001)

Keil, L., 'Alguns exemplos da influência portuguesa em obras de arte indianas do século XVI', in *I Congresso da historia da expansão Portuguesa no mundo, II secção* (Lisbon, 1938), pp. 5–21

Keil, L., 'Influência artistica portuguesa no oriente: três cofres de marfim indianos do século XVI', in *Boletim de Academia de Belas Artes* (1938), pp. 9–43

Kensington Palace, London, *Embroidered Quilts from the Museu Nacional de Arte Antiga Lisboa* (London, exhib. cat. 1978)

Khan, G., *Indian Muslim Perceptions of the West During the Eighteenth Century* (Karachi, 1998)

Kobata, A. and Matsuda, M. (trans.), *Ryūkyūan Relations with Korea and South Sea Countries. An Annotated Translation of Documents in the Rekidai Hoan* (Kyoto, 1969)

Kobayashi, H., 'Chinese Painting and Western Art Introduced by Jesuit Missionaries', in *St Francis Xavier: An Apostle of the East, Vol. 1: The Encounter Between Europe and Asia During the Period of the Great Navigations* (Tokyo, 1999)

Kobayashi, H., 'Suzhou Prints and Western Perspective', unpublished paper delivered at 'The Jesuits II: Cultures, Sciences, and the Arts, 1540–1773' (Boston, June 2002)

Kobe City Museum, *Nanban Kenbunroku [A Record of Encounter with Nanban Culture]*, (Kobe, exhib. cat. 1992)

Kobe City Museum, *Ikoku-e no Bōken: Kinsei Nihon Bibutsu ni Miru Jōhō to Gensō [The Admiring of Exotic Art: Intellectual and Creative Images of Japanese Pre-Modern Times]*, (Kobe, exhib. cat. 2001)

Koch, E., *Mughal Art and Imperial Ideology: Collected Essays* (New Delhi, 2001)

Kowal, D.M., 'Innovation and Assimilation: The Jesuit Contribution to Architectural Development in Portuguese Asia', in J. W. O'Malley et al. (eds), *The Jesuits. Cultures, Sciences, and the Arts, 1540–1773* (Toronto, 1999), pp. 480–504

Kowal, D.M., 'The Evolution of Ecclesiastical Architecture in Portuguese Goa', in J. Pereira and P. Pal (eds), *India & Portugal: Cultural Interactions* (Mumbai, 2001), pp. 70–87

Koyama, M., 'The *Makie* Shield – A Decorated Lacquered Hide Shield in the "P.A. Garda" Collection', in *Shikkoshi* (November 1998), vol. 21, pp. 36–52

Krahl, R., *Chinese Ceramics from the Topkapi Saray Museum, Istanbul, A Complete Catalogue*, ed. J. Ayers, 3 vols (London, 1986)

Kunsthistorisches Museum, Innsbruck, *Alle Wunder dieser Welt. Die Kostbaren Kunstwerke aus der Sammlung Erzherzog Ferdinands II. (1529–1595)* (Innsbruck, exhib. cat. 2001)

Kunsthistorisches Museum, Vienna, *Prag um 1600: Kunst und Kultur am Hofe Rudolfs II* (Vienna, exhib. cat. 1988)

Kunsthistorisches Museum, Vienna, *Die Kunst des Steinschnitts. Prunkgefäße, Kameen und Commessi aus der Kunstkammer* (Vienna, exhib. cat. 2002)

Kuroda, H., *Kyokai no Chusei, Shocho no Chusei [The Boundaries and Symbols of the Medieval Age]*, (Tokyo, 1986)

LACH, D., *Asia in the Making of Europe, Vol. 1: The Century of Discovery* (Chicago and London, 1965)

LACH, D., *Asia in the Making of Europe, Vol. 2: A Century of Wonder* (Chicago and London, 1970)

LACH, D. and KLEY, E.J. VAN, *Asia in the Making of Europe, Vol. 3: A Century of Advance* (Chicago and London, 1993)

LAMBOURN, E., 'The decoration of the Fakhr al-Din mosque in Mogadishu and other pieces of Gujarati marble carving on the East African coast', in *Azania* (1999), vol. XXXIV, pp. 61–86

LAMBOURN, E., 'Carving and Re-carving: Three Rasulid Gravestones Revisited', in *New Arabian Studies* (2001), vol. 6,

LARNER, J., *Marco Polo and the Discovery of the World* (New Haven, CT, 1999)

LEACH, L.Y., *Mughal and other Indian Paintings from the Chester Beatty Library*, 2 vols (London, 1995)

LEDDEROSE, L., *Ten Thousand Things: Module and Mass Production in Chinese Art* (Princeton, 1998)

LEDYARD, G., *The Dutch came to Korea* (Seoul, 1971)

LEDYARD, G., 'The Kangnido: A Korean World Map, 1402', in J.A. Levenson (ed.), *Circa 1492: Art in the Age of Exploration* (New Haven, CT, exhib. cat. 1991), pp. 329–32

LEE, T.C.H. (ed.), *China and Europe: Images and Influences in Sixteenth to Eighteenth Centuries* (Hong Kong, 1991)

LEIRIA, L., 'The Art of Lacquering; According to the Namban-Jin written sources', in *Bulletin of Portuguese/Japanese Studies* (December 2001), vol. 3, pp. 9–26

LEMIRE, B., *Fashion's Favourite: the cotton trade and the consumer in Britain 1660–1800* (Oxford, 1991)

LEVEY, S.M., *An Elizabethan Inheritance. The Hardwick Hall Textiles* (London, 1998)

LEWIS, M. and WIGEN, K., *The Myth of Continents* (Berkeley, 1997)

LHOTSKY, A., *Die Geschichte der Sammlungen. I: Von den Anfängen bis zum Tode Kaiser Karls VI. 1740* (Vienna, 1941–45)

LIDIN, O.G., *Tanegashima, the arrival of Europe in Japan* (Copenhagen, 2002)

LIGHTBOWN, R., 'Oriental Art and the Orient in Late Renaissance and Baroque Italy', in *Journal of the Warburg and Courtauld Institutes* (1969), vol. 32, pp. 228–79

LI JIANNONG, *Zhongguo jinbainian zhengzhi shi [A Political History of China During the Past Hundred Years]*, (Shanghai, 1948)

LIMA, V. DE, *Reviver Malaca* (Porto, 1988)

LIN XIAOPING, *Wu Li (1632–1718): His Life, His Paintings* (Lanham, MD, 2001)

LIU XINYUAN, 'Imperial Export Porcelain from late Yuan to Early Ming', *Oriental Art*, (1999), vol. XLV, no. 3, pp. 48–54

LIU YUFANG, 'Qinggong zuozhongchu' ['The clock-making workshop of the Qing palace'], in *Gugong bowuyuan yuankan* (1989), no. 4, pp. 49–54

LLEWELLYN-JONES, R., *A Fatal Friendship, the Nawabs, the British and the city of Lucknow* (New Delhi, 1985)

LLEWELLYN-JONES, R., *A Very Ingenious Man: Claude Martin in Early Colonial India* (Delhi, 1992)

LLEWELLYN-JONES, R., *Engaging Scoundrels: True Tales of Old Lucknow* (Delhi, 2000)

LLOYD, J.B., *African Animals in Renaissance Literature and Art* (Oxford, 1971)

LOEHR, G., 'Missionary Artists at the Manchu Court', in *Transactions of the Oriental Ceramic Society* 34 (1962–63), pp. 51–67

LOEHR, G., 'European Artists at the Chinese Court', in *The Westward Influence of the Chinese Arts from the 14th to the 18th Century* (London, 1972), pp. 33–42

LOHUIZEN DE LEEUW, J.E. VAN., 'An Early 16th Century Link Between Gujarat and Java', in Ba Shin et al. (eds), *Essays Offered to G. H. Luce*, Artibus Asiae Supplement XXIII (1996), pp. 89–93

LOMBARD, D., *Le carrefour javanais: Essai d'histoire globale*, 3 vols (Paris, 1990)

LOSTY, J.P., *Calcutta: City of Palaces* (London, 1990)

LOVE, H.D., *Vestiges of Old Madras 1640–1800*, 3 vols (London, 1913)

LUBO-LESNICHENKO, E., 'The blue-and-white porcelain of Yuan period from Khara-Khoto', in *International Symposium on Ancient Chinese Trade Ceramics: Collected Papers* (Taipei, 1994), pp. 463–81

LUGLI, A., *Naturalia et Mirabilia. Il collezionismo enciclopedico nelle Wunderkammern d'Europa* (Milan, 1990)

LYNN, C., *Wallpaper in America from the seventeenth century to World War I* (New York, 1980)

MACKENZIE, J.M., *Orientalism: History, Theory and the Arts* (Manchester and New York, 1995)

MACLAGAN, SIR E., 'Jesuit Missions to the Emperor Akbar', in *Journal of the Asiatic Society of Bengal* 65 (1896), pp. 38–112

MACLAGAN, SIR E., 'Four Letters by Austin of Bordeaux', in *Journal of the Punjab University Historical Society* (1916), vol. IV, no. 1, pp. 3–17

MACLAGAN, SIR E., *The Jesuits and the Grand Mogul* (London, 1934)

Madras in the Olden Time being a History of the Presidency, compiled from official records by J. Talboys Wheeler (1861; reprinted Madras, 1993)

MALONE, C.B., *History of the Peking Summer Palaces under the Ch'ing Dynasty* (Urbana, IL, 1934)

MANCALL, M., *Russia and China: Their Diplomatic Relations to 1728* (Cambridge, MA, 1971)

MANOLI, R., *European Merchant Capital and the Indian Economy. Surat Factory Records 1630–1668* (New Delhi, 1992)

MANUCCI, N., *Mogul India 1653–1708 or Storia do Mogor*, trans. with introduction and notes by W. Irvine, 4 vols (reprinted Delhi, 1989)

MARSHALL, P.J., 'Cornwallis Triumphant: War in India and the British Public in the Late Eighteenth Century', in L. Freeman, P. Hayes and R. O'Neill, (eds), *War, Strategy and International Politics* (Oxford, 1992)

MARSHALL, P.J., 'British Society under the East India Company', in *Modern Asian Studies* 31 (1997) no. 1

MASELIS, M.-C., BALIS, A. and MARIJNISSEN, R.H., *The Albums of Anselmus de Boodt (1550–1632): Natural History Painting at the court of Rudolph II in Prague* (Tielt, Belgium, 1999)

MASON, D., *Intimate Worlds: Indian paintings from the Alvin O. Bellak Collection* (Philadelphia Museum of Art, Philadelphia, exhib. cat. 2001)

MASSARELLA, D., *A World Elsewhere: Europe's Encounter with Japan in the Sixteenth and Seventeenth Centuries* (New Haven and London, 1990)

MASSARELLA, D., 'Some Reflections on Identity Formation in East Asia in the Sixteenth and Seventeenth centuries', in D. Denoon et al. (eds), *Multicultural Japan: Palaeolithic to Postmodern* (Cambridge, 1996), pp. 135–52

MATHEW, K.S., *Portuguese Trade with India in the Sixteenth Century* (New Delhi, 1983)

MATHEW, K.S., 'German Merchant Financiers in Goa during the 16th and 17th Centuries', in *Goa's External Relations*, ed. P.P. Shirodkar (Panaji, Goa, 1992), pp. 32–41

MATHEW, K.S. (ed.), *Mariners, Merchants and Oceans. Studies in Maritime History* (New Delhi, 1995)

MATHEW, K.S and AHMAD, A., *Emergence of Cochin in the pre-industrial Era: a study of Portuguese Cochin, documents from the Biblioteca da Ajuda* (Pondicherry, 1990)

MATOS, L. DE, 'Forma e natura e costumi del Rinoceronte', in *Boletim internacional de bibliografia Luso-Brasileira* (Lisbon, 1960), vol. 1, no. 3, pp. 387–98

MAUQUOY-HENDRICKS, M., *Les estampes des Wierix*, 3 vols (Brussels, 1978–83)

MAURICE, K., 'Propagatio fidei per scientias: Jesuit Gifts to the Chinese Court', in M. Klaus and O. Mayr (eds), *The Clockwork Universe* (Washington, DC, and New York, exhib. cat. 1980), pp. 27–36

MENDES PINTO, M.H., *Biombos Namban [Nanban Screens]*, (Lisbon, 1988)

MENDES PINTO, M.H., *Namban Lacquerware in Portugal: The Portuguese presence in Japan (1543–1639)*, (Lisbon, 1990)

MENEGON, E., *Un solo cielo: Giulio Aleni S.J. geografia, arte, scienza, religione dall'Europa alla Cina* (Brescia, 1994)

MENZHAUSEN, J., *The Green Vaults* (Leipzig, 1968)

METTE, H.-U., *Der Nautiluspokal. Wie Kunst und Natur miteinander Spielen* (Munich, 1995)

MILLER, S., 'Jean-Antoine Fraisse at Chantilly: French Images of China', in *East Asian Library Journal* IX (Spring 2000), pp. 79–221

MILLER, S., 'Images of Asia in French luxury goods: Jean-Antoine Fraisse at Chantilly, *c.* 1729–36', in *Apollo* (November 2001), vol. IX, pp. 2–12

MILWARD, P. (ed.), *Portuguese Voyages to Asia and Japan in the Renaissance Period* (Tokyo, 1994)

MIRANDA, S.M. and SERAFIM, C.S., 'O potencial demográfico', in *História dos Portugueses no Extremo Oriente* (Lisbon, 1998)

MISRA, A., *Lucknow: Fire of Grace* (New Delhi, 1998)

MITSURU, V. and Y., *Fūzokuga – Nanban Byōbu [Genre Paintings – Nanban Screens], Nihon Byōbue Shūsei [Collection of Japanese Screen Paintings series]*, (Tokyo, 1979), vol. 15

MIYOSHI, T., 'P. Kaerius 1609 Nenban Sekai Chizu o Megutte' ['On the 1609 World Map of P. Kaerius'], in *Kōbe Shiritsu Hakubutsukan Kenkyū Kiyō [Kobe City Museum Research Bulletin]*, (1997), no. 13, pp. 15–43

MIYOSHI, T., *Zusetsu Sekai Kochizu Collection [Illustrated Collection of Old Maps of the World]*, (Tokyo, 1999)

MIYOSHI, T., 'Bankoku Ezu Byobu' no Genzu ni Tsuite – 1609 Nenban P. Kaerius Sekai Chizu no Fukugen' ['On the Original Sources for the "World Map Screens" – A Reconstruction of the 1609 World Map by P. Kaerius'], *Kōbe Shiritsu Hakubutsukan Kenkyū Kiyō [Kobe City Museum Research Bulletin]*, (2003), no. 19, pp. 55–66

MORAN, J.F., *The Japanese and the Jesuits: Alessandro Valignano in sixteenth-century Japan* (London and New York, 1993)

MOREIRA, R., 'From Manueline to Renaissance in Portuguese India', in *Mare Liberum* 9 (Lisbon, 1995), pp. 401–07

MOREIRA, R., 'As formas artísticas', in A. H. de Oliveira Marques (ed.), *História dos Portugueses no Extremo Oriente* (1998)

MOREIRA, R., 'A fortaleza de Diu e a arquitectura militar no Índico', *Os Espaços de um Império – Estudos* (Comissão Nacional para as Comemorações dos Descobrimentos Portugueses, Lisbon, exhib. cat. 1999), pp. 139–47

MOREIRA, R., 'Uma fachada retábulo em Macau', in *El Museo de Pontevedra* LIII (Pontevedra, 1999) pp. 159–68

MORELAND, W.H., *From Akbar to Aurangzeb, a study in Indian economic history* (London, 1923)

MORISHIMA, C., *Kōmō Zatsuwa [Tales of the Red-haired Barbarians]*, (first published 1787; reprinted Tokyo, 1980), Edo Kagaku Koten Sōsho 31 (series)

MORSE, H.B., *The Chronicles of the East India Company trading to China, 1635–1834*, 5 vols (Oxford, 1926–29)

MOTA, M.M., 'Codice Casanatense: an Indo-Portuguese Portrait of Life in 16th Century India', in J. Pereira and P. Pal (eds), *India and Portugal: Cultural Interactions* (Mumbai, 2001), pp. 34–45

MOTE, F.W., 'Admiral Zheng He', in J.A. Levenson (ed.), *Circa 1492: Art in the Age of Exploration* (New Haven, CT, exhib. cat. 1991), pp. 342–46

MUKUND, K., *The Trading World of the Tamil Merchant. Evolution of merchant capitalism in the Coromandel* (Chennai, 1999)

MUROGA NOBUO, 'Atarashii Sekai no Ninshiki' ['Knowledge of a New World'], in *Tanbō Daikōkai Jidai no Nihon [Japan in the Great Maritime Age]*, (Tokyo, 1978), vol. 5, pp. 93–102

MUSÉE DES ARTS DÉCORATIFS, BORDEAUX, *La Route des Indes. Les Indes et l'Europe: échanges artistiques et heritage commun 1650–1850* (Bordeaux, exhib. cat. 1998)

MUSÉE DU LOUVRE, PARIS, *'L'Etrange et Merveilleux en terres d'Islam'* (Paris, exhib. cat. 2001)

MUSÉES ROYAUX D'ART ET D'HISTOIRE, BRUSSELS, *Art Namban: Les Portugais au Japan/ Nambankunst: Portugezen in Japan [Nanban Art: The Portuguese in Japan]*, (Brussels, exhib. cat. 1989)

MUSEU NACIONAL DE ARTE ANTIGA, *Ouro Mundo. Novo Vimos* (Lisbon, exhib. cat. 2001)

MUSEU DE SÃO ROQUE, LISBON, *A Herança de Rauluchantim* (Lisbon, exhib. cat. 1996)

MUSEU DE SÃO ROQUE, LISBON, *Reflexos: Símbolos e Imagens do Cristianismo na Porcelana Chinesa* (Libson, exhib. cat. 1997)

NATIONAL GALLERY OF ART, WASHINGTON, DC, *The Flowering of Florence. Botanical Art for the Medici* (Washington, DC, exhib. cat. 2002)

NATIONAL MUSEUM OF JAPANESE HISTORY, *Tōjiki no Bunkashi [A Cultural History of Ceramics in Japan]*, (Sakura, exhib. cat. 1998)

NEEDHAM, J., *Science and Civilisation in China, Vol. 2: History of Scientific Thought* (Cambridge, 1956)

NEEDHAM, J., *Science and Civilisation in China, Vol. 4: Physics and Physical Technology, Part 2: Mechanical Engineering* (Cambridge, 1965)

NEEDHAM, J., *Science and Civilisation in China, Vol. 5: Chemistry and Chemical Technology, Part 7: Military Technology, the Gunpowder Epic* (Cambridge, 1986)

NEEDHAM, J. and GWEI-DJEN LU, *A Korean Astronomical Screen of the Mid Eighteenth Century from the Royal Palace of the Yi Dynasty Choson Kingdom, 1392 to 1910* (Florence, 1966)

NEEDHAM, J., WANG LING and D.J. DE SOLLA PRICE, *Heavenly Clockwork: The Great Astronomical Clocks of Medieval China* (Cambridge, 1960; 2nd edn with supplement by J.H. Combridge, Cambridge, 1986)

NISH, I. and KIBATA, Y. (eds), *Anglo Japanese Relations, 1600–1858; The History of Anglo-Japanese Relations, Vol. 1: The Political-Diplomatic Dimension, 1600–1930* (Basingstoke, 2002)

NISHIMURA, T., *Nanban Bijitsu [Nanban Art]*, (Tokyo, 1958)

NIZAMI, K.A., *Some Aspects of Religion and Politics in India during the Thirteenth Century* (India, 1961)

OKADA, A., *Imperial Mughal Painters. Indian Miniatures from the Sixteenth and Seventeenth Centuries*, trans. D. Dusinberre (Paris, 1992)

OKADA, Y. ET AL. (eds), *Nihon no Shitsugei* (Tokyo, 1978–79), vol. IV

OKAMOTO, Y., *The Namban Art of Japan, The Heibonsha Survey of Japanese Art*, trans. R.K. Jones (New York and Tokyo, 1972), vol. 19

OKAMOTO, Y. and TAKAMIZAWA, T., *Nanban Byōbu [Namban Screens]*, (Tokyo, 1970)

OKUDAIRA, S., *Rakuchū-rakugai zu to Nanban Byōbu [Scenes in and around the Capital to Nanban Screens]*, Shinpen Meiho Nihon no Bijutsu 25 (series), (Tokyo, 1991)

OLIVEIRA MARQUES, A.H. DE (ed.), *História dos Portugueses no Extremo Oriente* (Lisbon, 1998)

O'MALLEY, J.W. ET AL. (eds), *The Jesuits. Cultures, Sciences, and the Arts, 1540–1773* (Toronto, 1999)

OMAN, C.C. and HAMILTON, J., *Wallpapers: A History and Illustrated Catalogue of the Collection of The Victoria and Albert Museum* (London, 1982)

ORANGE, J., *The Chater Collection: Pictures relating to China, Hongkong, Macao, 1655–1860* (London, 1924)

Os Constructores do Oriente Português (Edificio de Alfândega, Porto, exhib. cat. 1998)

OSWALD, G., *Lexikon der Heraldik*, VEB Bibliographisches Institut (Leipzig, 1984)

O Tempo de Vasco da Gama, ed. D. R. Curto (Lisbon, 1998)

ŌTSUKI, G., *Ransetsu Benwaku [Explanation of the Dutch]*, Seikatsu no Koten Sōsho 6 (1799; reprinted Tokyo, 1972)

P ABELLA DE ESPANA, LISBON, *Las sociedades ibericas y el mar a finales del siglo XV* (Lisbon, exhib. cat. 1998)

PAGANI, C., *'Eastern Magnificence and European Ingenuity': Clocks of Late Imperial China* (Michigan, 2001)

PAL, P. ET AL., *Romance of the Taj Mahal* (New Delhi, 1989)

PALAZZO GRASSI, VENICE, *The Arcimboldo Effect. Transformations of the Face from the Sixteenth to the Twentieth Century* (Venice, exhib. cat. 1987)

PARKE-SMITH, M., *Western Barbarians in Japan and Formosa in Tokugawa Days, 1603–1868* (Kobe, 1930)

PAYNE, C.H., *Akbar and the Jesuits. An Account of the Jesuit Missions to the Court of Akbar by Father Pierre du Jarric, S.J.* (London, 1926)

PEARSON, M.N., *The Portuguese in India, The New Cambridge History of India 1.1* (Cambridge, 1987)

PEIRIS, E. and MEERSMANN, A., *Early Christianity in Ceylon* (Colombo, 1972)

PEPYS, S., *Pepys's Diary*, selected and ed. R. Lathem (London, 1996), vol. I

PEREIRA, J., *Baroque Goa* (New Delhi, 1995)

PEREIRA, J., 'The evolution of the Goan Hindu Temple', in J. Pereira and P. Pal (eds), *India and Portugal: Cultural Interactions* (Mumbai, 2001)

PEREIRA, J. and P. PAL (eds), *India and Portugal: Cultural Interactions* (Mumbai, 2001)

PÉREZ DE TUDELA, A. and JORDAN GSCHWEND, A., 'Luxury Goods for Royal Collectors: Exotica, princely gifts and rare animals exchanged between the Iberian courts and Central Europe in the Renaissance (1560–1612)', in H. Trnek and S. Haag (eds), *Exotica: Portugals Entdeckungen im Spiegel fürstlicher Kunst- und Wunderkammern der Renaissance. Die Beiträge des am 19. und 20. Mai 2000 vom Kunsthistorischen Museum Wien veranstalteten Symposiums, Jahrbuch des Kunsthistorischen Museums Wien* (Mainz, 2001), vol. 3, pp. 1–127

PFISTER, R., *Les Toiles Imprimees de Fostat et l'Hindoustan* (Paris, 1938)

PINDER-WILSON, R., *Paintings from the Muslim Courts of India* (London, 1976)

PINN, K., *Paktong, the Chinese Alloy in Europe, 1680–1820* (Suffolk, 1999)

PIRAZZOLI-T'SERSTEVENS, M., 'The Emperor Qianlong's European Palaces', *Orientations* (November 1988), vol. 19, no. 11, pp. 61–71

POMERANZ, K., *The Great Divergence: Europe, China and the making ot the Modern Industrial Economy* (Princeton, NJ, 2000)

POMIAN, K., *Der Ursprung des Museums Vom Sammeln* (Berlin, 1988)

POMIAN, K., *Collectors & Curiosities: Paris and Venice, 1500–1800* (Venice, 1990)

Poona's Great days, describing the Palace of the Peshwas when they were paramount in India; the British Embassy & its Residents; the Battles of Kirkee & Koregaon (Poona, 1944)

POPE, J.A., *Fourteenth Century Blue and White, A group of Chinese Porcelain in the Topkapi Sarayi Muzesi, Istanbul* (Washington, 1952; revised 1970)

POPE, J.A., *Chinese Porcelain from the Ardebil Shrine* (Washington, 1956; second edition 1981)

PORTER, V., 'Three Rasulid Tombstones from Zafur', in *Journal of the Royal Asiatic Society* (1988), no. 1, pp. 32–44

PRAKASH, O., *The Dutch Factories in India 1617–1623* (New Delhi, 1984)

PROUST, J., *Europe Through the Prism of Japan* (Notre Dame, IN, 2002)

PTAK, R., 'China and Calicut in the early Ming period: envoys and tribute embassies', in *Journal of the Royal Asiatic Society* (1989), no. 1 pp. 81–111

PTAK, R., *China and the Asian Seas. Trade, Travel and Visions of the Other (1400–1750)* (Aldershot, 1998)

QAISAR, A.J., *The Indian Response to European Technology and Culture (A.D. 1498–1707)*, (Delhi, 1982)

RABEN, R., *Batavia and Colombo, The Ethnical and Spatial Order of two Colonial Cities* (Leiden, 1996)

RAWSON, P., *Erotic Art of India* (London, 1977)

RAY, H., 'The South East Asian connection in Sino-Indian trade', in R. Scott and J. Guy (eds), *South East Asia and China: Art, Interaction and Commerce*, Percival David Foundation of Chinese Art, Colloquies on Art and Archaeology, no. 17 (London, 1995), pp. 41–54

RAYCHAUDHURI, T. and HABIB, I. (eds), *The Cambridge Economic History of India, Vol. I: c.1200–c.1750* (Cambridge, 1982)

RIBEIRO, A., *A Visual History of Costume. The 18th Century* (London, 1983)

RICHARDS, J.F., *The New Cambridge History of India I, 5: the Mughal Empire* (Cambridge, 1993)

RIJKSMUSEUM, *Sawasa: Japanese export art in black and gold, 1650–1800* (Zwolle, exhib. cat. 1998)

RIJKSMUSEUM, AMSTERDAM, *Sweerts, Michiel, 1618–1664: Flemish Master of the Sacred and Profane* (Amsterdam, exhib. cat. 2002)

ROBB, P., *Clash of Cultures? An Englishman in Calcutta*, inaugural lecture, 12 March 1998 (London, 1998)

ROHATGI, P. ET AL., *Bombay to Mumbai: Changing Perspectives* (Mumbai, 1997)

ROSENFIELD, J. and CRANSTON, F.E., *Extraordinary Persons: Works of Eccentric, Nonconformist Japanese Artists of the Early Modern Era (1580–1868) in the Collection of Kimiko and John Powers* (Cambridge, MA, 1999), vol. I

ROSS, A.C., *A Vision Betrayed: The Jesuits in Japan and China, 1542–1742* (Edinburgh, 1994)

ROSSA, W., *Cidades Indo-Portuguesas/ Indo-Portuguese Cities* (Comissão Nacional para as Comemorações dos Descobrimentos Portugueses, Lisbon, 1997)

ROSSO, A.S., *Apostolic Legations to China of the eighteenth century* (South Pasadena, 1948)

ROTHSTEIN, N., *Barbara Johnson's Album of Styles and Fabrics* (London, 1987)

ROUSMANIERE, N.C., 'Defining Temmoku: Jian Ware Tea Bowls Imported into Japan', in R.D. Mowry (ed.), *Hare's Fur, Tortoiseshell and Partridge Feathers: Chinese Brown- and Black-Glazed Ceramics, 400–1400* (Cambridge, MA, exhib. cat. 1996), pp. 43–58

ROUSMANIERE, N.C. (ed.), *Kazari: Decoration and Display in Japan, 15th–19th Centuries* (Japan Society, New York and London, exhib. cat. 2002)

ROUSSEAU, G.S. and PORTER, R. (eds), *Exoticism in the Enlightenment* (Manchester and New York, 1990)

ROY, G., *Diplomacy in Ancient India* (Patna, 1981)

RUBIÉS, J.-P., *Travel and Ethnology in the Renaissance, South India through European Eyes, 1250–1625* (Cambridge, 2000)

RUDOLF, K., 'Die Kunstbestrebung Kaiser Maximilian II. im Spannungsfeld zwischen Madrid und Wien. Untersuchungen zu den Sammlung der österreichischen und spanischen Habsburger', in *Jahrbuch der Kunsthistorischen Sammlungen in Wien* (Vienna, 1995), vol. 91, pp. 165–256

RUDOLF, K., 'Exotica bei Karl V., Philipp II. und in der Kunstkammer Rudolfs II. in Prag', in H. Trnek and S. Haag (eds), *Exotica: Portugals Entdeckungen im Spiegel fürstlicher Kunst- und Wunderkammern der Renaissance. Die Beiträge des am 19. und 20. Mai 2000 vom Kunsthistorischen Museum Wien veranstalteten Symposiums, Jahrbuch des Kunsthistorischen Museums Wien* (Mainz, 2001), vol. 3, pp. 173–219

RUFUS, W.C., 'Astronomy in Korea', *Journal of the Royal Asiatic Society* (Korea Branch, 1936), 26, 1, pp. 23–72

RUÍZ-DE-MEDINA, J. (ed.), *Documentos del Japón 1558–1562*, Monumentum Historicum Societatis Iesu, vol. 148 (Rome)

RUSSELL, J.B., *Inventing the Flat Earth: Columbus and Modern Historians* (New York, 1991)

RUSSELL-WOOD, A.J.R., *A World on the Move: The Portuguese in Africa, Asia and America 1415–1808* (New York, 1992)

SAID, E., *Orientalism: Western Conceptions of the Orient* (London, 1978)

SAKAMOTO, M. ET AL., *Nanban Bijutsu to Yōfūga [Nanban Art and Western-Style Painting], Genshoku Nihon no Bijutsu [Japanese Art in Colour]*, (Tokyo, 1970; revised 1980), vol. 20

SAKAMOTO, M. ET AL., *Fūzokuga: Nanban Fūzoku [Genre Painting: Nanban Genre Painting]*, Nihon Byōbue Shūsei 15 (series) (Tokyo, 1979)

SAKSENA, R.B., *European and Indo-European Poets of Urdu and Persian* (Lucknow, 1941)

SANGL, S., 'Von der Aneignung des Fremden. Indische Perlmutt-Raritaten und ihre europaischen Adaptionen in Munchen', in *Weltkunst* (1996), pp. 2938–43

SANSOM, G., *The Western World and Japan: A Study in the Interaction of European and Asiatic Cultures* (Tokyo, 1977)

SANSOM, G., *A History of Japan, 1334–1615* (Folkestone, 1978)

SARGENT, W., *Views of the Pearl River Delta: Macau, Canton and Hong Kong* (Hong Kong, 1997)

SCAMMELL, G.V., 'European Exiles, Renegades and Outlaws and the Maritime Economy of Asia c.1500–1750', in *Modern Asian Studies* 26, no. 4 (1992)

SCHEICHER, E., *Die Kunst-und Wunderkammern der Habsburger* (Vienna, 1979)

SCHEURLEER, T.H.L., 'Aanbesteding en verspreiding van Japans lakwerk door de Nederlanders in de zeventiende eeuw', in *Jaarverslagen Oudheidkundig Genootschap* (1939–1941), vols LXXXII–LXXXIII

SCHILDER, G., 'Willem Jansz. Blaeu's Wall Map of the World on Mercator's Projection, 1606–07, and its Influence', in *Imago Mundi* (1979), no. 31, pp. 36–54

SCHLOSSER, J. VON, *Die Kunst- und Wunderkammern der Spätrenaissance* (Leipzig, 1908)

SCHÜTTE, J.F., *Valignano's Mission Principles for Japan*, trans. J.J. Coyne, SJ (St Louis, MO, 1980)

SCHWABE, M.A., 'Schatzkunst auf Ceylon', in *Exotica*, pp. 101–04

SCHWARTZBERG, J., 'Cosmographical Mapping', in *History of Cartography* 2.1, pp. 332–43

SCREECH, T., *Ō-Edo Ijin Ōrai [The Coming and Going of Foreigners in the Edo Period]*, trans. Takayama Hiroshi (Tokyo, 1995)

SCREECH, T., *The Western Scientific Gaze and Popular Imagery in Later Edo Japan: The Lens within the Heart* (Cambridge, 1996)

SCREECH, T., 'Glass, paintings on glass, and vision in eighteenth-century Japan', in *Apollo* (March 1998), vol. CXLVII, pp. 28–32

SCREECH, T., *Sex and the Floating World: Erotic Images in Japan, 1700–1820* (London, 1999)

SCREECH, T., 'Dressing Samuel Pepys: Japanese Garments and International Diplomacy in the Edo period', in *Orientations* (February 2002), vol. 33, no. 2, pp. 50–57

SEELIG, L., 'The Munich Kunstkammer, 1565–1807', in *The Origins of Museums: The Cabinet of Curiosities in Sixteenth- and Seventeenth-Century Europe*, ed. O. Impey and A. MacGregor (Oxford, 1985), pp. 101–11

SENGUPTA, G., 'The Portuguese in Bengal', in J. Pereira and P. Pal (eds), *India and Portugal: Cultural Interactions* (Mumbai, 2001), pp. 24–33

SERRÃO, V., 'A pintura na antiga Índia portuguesa nos séculos XVI e XVII', in *Oceanos* 19/ 20 (September/December 1994), pp. 102–12

SEWELL, R., *A Forgotten Empire (Vijayanagar)*, (London, 1900)

SEYLLER, J., *The Adventures of Hamza* (Washington, DC, exhib. cat. 2002)

SHANKWALKER, R., 'The balcão: a Goan expression', in J. Pereira and P. Pal (eds), *India and Portugal: Cultural Interactions* (Mumbai, 2001), pp. 115–23

SHINMURA, I., 'Ikoku Haishu ki' ['Notes on Exotic Themes in Haiku Poetry'], in *Shinmura Izuru Zenshū [Complete Works of Shinmura Izuru]* (1926; reprinted Tokyo, 1966)

SHULSKY, L., 'A Note on a possible Spanish-Chinese Connection', in *Oriental Art* (2002), vol. XLVIII, no. 1, pp. 23–24

SIGALÉA, R., *La Médicine traditionnelle de l'Inde* (Geneva, 1995)

SILVEIRA, A.C., *A casa-pátio de Goa* (Porto, 1999)

SKELTON, R. ET AL., *The Indian Heritage. Court Life and Arts under Mughal Rule* (London, exhib. cat. 1982)

SLOMANN, V., *Bizarre Designs in Silks. Trade and Traditions* (Copenhagen, 1953)

SLOMANN, V., 'Elfenbeinreliefs auf zwei singhalesischen Schreinen des 16.Jahrhunderts', in *Pantheon* (1937), vol. XX, pp. 357–63; (1938), vol. XXI, pp. 12–19

SMART, E., 'Fourteenth century Chinese porcelain from a Tughlaq Palace in Delhi', in *Transactions of the Oriental Ceramic Society* (1975–77), vol. 41, pp. 199–230

SOUDAVAR, A., *Art of the Persian Courts. Selections from the Art and History Trust Collection* (New York, exhib. cat. 1992)

SOUSA VITERBO, F.M., 'O orientalismo em Portugal no século XV', in *Boletim da Sociedade de Geografia de Lisboa* (1892–93), vol. 12, nos 7–8, pp. 317–30

SOUTH BANK CENTRE, LONDON, *Exotic Europeans* (London, exhib. cat. 1991)

SPEAR, P., *The Nabobs* (reprinted Calcutta, 1991)

SPENCE, J.D., *The Memory Palace of Matteo Ricci* (New York, 1984)

SPENCE, J.D., *The Chan's Great Continent: China in Western Minds* (New York and London, 1998)

SPENCE, J.D., *Treason by the Book* (London, 2001)

SPINK & CO., *The Eye of the Courtier: Indian and Islamic Works of Art* (London, sale cat. 1999)

STAATLICHE KUNSTSAMMLUNGEN, KASSEL, *Porzellan aus China und Japan. Die Porzellangalerie der Langgrafen von Hessen-Kassel* (Berlin, exhib. cat. 1990)

STANDAERT, N., 'Jesuit Corporate Culture as Shaped by the Chinese', in J.W. O'Malley et al. (eds), *The Jesuits. Cultures, Sciences, and the Arts, 1540–1773* (Toronto, 1999), pp. 352–263

STANDEN, E.A., 'English Tapestries "After the Indian Manner"', in *Metropolitan Museum Journal* 15 (New York, 1981), pp. 119–41

STEENDGAARD, N., *The Asian trade revolution of the seventeenth century* (Chicago, 1973)

STEIN, P., 'Boucher's Chinoiseries: Some New Sources', in *Burlington Magazine* (September 1996), pp. 598–604

STEVENS, H., *Dutch Enterprise and the VOC 1602–1799* (Amsterdam, 1998)

STEVENSON, J. and GUY, J., *Vietnamese Ceramics. A Separate Tradition* (Chicago, 1998)

STRACHAN, M., *Sir Thomas Roe 1581–1644. A Life* (Salisbury, 1989)

STRÖBER, E., *'La maladie de porcelaine …' Ostasiatisches Porzellan aus der Sammlung Augusts des Starken* (Leipzig, exhib. cat. 2001)

STRONGE, S. (ed.), *The Arts of the Sikh Kingdoms* (London, exhib. cat. 1999)

STRONGE, S., *Painting for the Mughal emperor. The Art of the Book in India 1560–1650* (London, 2002)

SUÁREZ, T., *Early Mapping of Southeast Asia* (Hong Kong, 1999)

SUBRAHMANYAN, S., *The Portuguese Empire in Asia, 1500–1700, A Political and Economic History* (London and New York, 1993)

SUBRAHMANYAN, S., *The Career and Legend of Vasco da Gama* (Cambridge, 1997)

SUBRAHMANYAN, S., 'The romantic, the oriental and the exotic: notes on the Portuguese in Goa', in *Stories of Goa* (Museu Nacional de Etnologia, Lisbon, exhib. cat. 1997)

SUGITA, G., *Dawn of Western Science in Japan [Rangaku Kotohajime]*, trans. M. Ryozo and K. Eiichi (Tokyo, 1969)

SULLIVAN, M., *The Meeting of Eastern and Western Art from the Sixteenth Century to the Present Day* (2nd edn Berkeley, 1989; reprinted London, 1997)

SWAIN, M.H., 'Nightgown into dressing gown. A study of Men's Nightgowns Eighteenth Century', in *Costume* (1972), vol. 6, pp. 10–21

SWAN, C., *The Clutius Botanical Watercolors: Plants and Flowers of the Renaissance* (New York, 1988)

SYSON, L. and THORTON, D., *Objects of Virtue. Art in Renaissance Italy* (Los Angeles, 2001)

TACHIBANA, N., *Seiyōki [Travels in the West]*, Shin Nihon Bungaku Taikei 98 (series), (1783; reprinted Tokyo, 1991)

TAKAHASHI, T., 'Nanban Toshi Zu Byōbu kara Kaerius Sekai Zue' ['From Nanban Screens of Cities to the Kaerius World Map'], in *Ezu no Cosmology [Cosmology of Picture Maps]*, (Kyoto, 1988), pp. 248–64

TANDAN, B., *The Architecture of Lucknow and its Dependencies 1722–1858* (New Delhi, 2001)

TANI, S. and SUGASE, T., *Namban Art: A Loan Exhibition from Japanese Collections* (Washington, DC, exhib. cat. 1973)

TASSEL, R. VAN, *Bezoars and the Collection of Henri van Heurck* (1838–1909) (Antwerp, 1970)

TASSEL, R. VAN, 'Bezoars', in *Janus. Revue internationale de l'histoire des sciences, de la medicine, de la pharmacie et de la technique* (1973), no. 60, pp. 241–59

TAVIM, J.A.R.S., 'A cidade portugesa de Santa Cruz de Cochim de Baixo', *Aquém e Além da Taprobana, estudos luso-orientais à memória de Jean Aubin e Denys Lombard*, ed. L.F. Thomas (Lisbon, 2002), pp. 137–89

TAYLOR, K., 'Vietnamese History', in C. Young et al. (eds), *Vietnamese Ceramics* (Singapore, 1982), pp. 14–24

TELLERUP, E., Appendix I: 'Xylometric Examination of Wooden Jug and Basin', in M. Boyer, *Japanese Export Lacquers from the seventeenth century in the National Museum of Denmark* (Copenhagen, 1959), pp. 147–48

TELTSCHER, K., *India Inscribed: European and British Writing on India 1600–1800* (New Delhi, 1997)

TERASHIMA, R., *Wakan Sansai Zue [Japanese Chinese Illustrated Assembly by the Three Components of the Universe]*, trans. and adapted S. Isao et al., in *Tōyō Bunko 456* (1712; reprinted Tokyo, 1986)

THIRIEZ, R., *Barbarian Lens: Western Photographers of the Qianlong Emperor's European Palaces* (Amsterdam, 1998)

THOMAZ, L.F., *De Ceuta a Timor* (Lisbon, 1994)

THORTON, P., *The Italian Renaissance Interior 1400–1660* (London, 1991)

TIAN, J., *Classic Chinese Furniture of the Qing Dynasty* (London, 1996)

TIBBETTS, G.R., *A study of the Arabic texts concerning materials on South-East Asia* (London, 1979)

TILAKASIRI, T., 'Ivory Carving of Sri Lanka', in *Arts of Asia* 4 (1974), pp. 42–46

TOBACCO AND SALT MUSEUM, TOKYO, *Oranda Shumi; Sakokuka no Ekizochizumu Hollandase Smaak [Inspiration from Holland: Exoticism under the Sakoku (Seclusion) regime]*, (Tokyo, exhib. cat. 1996)

TOBACCO AND SALT MUSEUM, TOKYO, *Ikoku no Kaze: Edo Jidai Kyōto o Irodatt Yōroppa [Winds from Afar: European Influences on Edo-period Kyoto]*, (Tokyo, exhib. cat. 2000)

TOBY, R., *State and Diplomacy in Early Modern Japan* (Princeton, 1984)

TOBY, R.P., 'The "Indianness" of Iberians and the changing Japanese iconographies of Others', in S. B. Schwartz (ed.), *Implicit Understandings: Observing, Reporting and Reflecting on the Encounters between Europeans and Other Peoples in the Early Modern Era* (Cambridge, 1994)

TOKITA, T., 'Nanban Sekaizu Byōbu Genzu Kō (Sono 1)' ['Study of Source Maps of Nanban World Map Screens (Part 1)', in *Nagasakidan Sō [Collections of Nagasaki Stories]*, (1974), no. 56, pp. 48–71

TOKITA, T., 'Shoki Yōfuga "Oko Kiba Zu" Genryū Kō – 1606 Nenban Blaue Sekaizu to no Kankei' ['Study of the Sources for the Early Western-Style Painting "Lords and Rulers on Horseback" – Its Connection with Blaue's 1606 World Map'], in *Bijutsushi [History of Art]*, (1980), no. 108, pp. 127–41

TOPSFIELD, A., 'Two early Company albums', in *The V&A Album* (1983), no. 2, pp. 57–62

TOPSFIELD, A., 'Ketelaar's Embassy and the Farangi theme in the Art of Udaipur', in *Oriental Art* (Winter 1984–85), vol. XXX, no. 4, pp. 350–67

Tributes from Guangdong to the Qing Court, University of Hong Kong (Hong Kong, 1987)

TROTA JOSÉ, R., *Images of Faith: Religious Ivory Carvings from the Philippines* (Pasadena, CA, 1990)

TRUONG BUU LAM, 'Intervention versus Tribute in Sino-Vietnamese Relations, 1788–1790', in J. K. Fairbank (ed.), *The Chinese World Order: Traditional China's Foreign Relations* (Cambridge, MA, 1968), pp. 165–79

TURNBULL, S., *Japan's Hidden Christians, 1549–1999* (Surrey, 2000)

UITZINGER, E., 'For the Man who has Everything: Western-style Exotica in the Birthday Celebrations at the Court of Ch'ien-Lung', in L. Blussé and H.T. Zurndorfer (eds), *Conflict and Accommodation in Early Modern East Asia: Essays in Honour of Erik Zürcher* (Leiden and New York, 1993)

UNNO, K., 'Buddhist World Maps', in *History of Cartography* (Chicago, 1994), vol. 2.2, pp. 371–76

UNNO, K. ET AL., 'Sekaizu' ['World Maps'], in *Nihon Kochizu Taisei [A Comprehensive Collection of Japanese Old Maps series]*, (Tokyo, 1975)

VAN DE GEIJN-VERHOEVEN, M. ET AL., *Domestic Interiors at the Cape and in Batavia 1602–1795* (Gemeentemuseum, The Hague, exhib. cat. 2002)

VAN DER CRUYSSE, D., *Siam and the West, 1500–1700* (Chiang Mai, 2002)

VAN DONGEN, P.L.F., *'Sensitive Plates': Nineteen Chinese Paintings on Glass* (Sassenheim, n.d.)

VAN GULIK, W.R. ET AL., *In the Wake of the Liefde: Cultural Relations between the Netherlands and Japan since 1600* (Amsterdam, 1986)

VAN GULIK, W., *The Dutch in Nagasaki – 19th Century Japanese Prints* (Amsterdam, 1998)

VAN OERS, R., *Dutch Town Planning Overseas during VOC and WIC Rule (1600–1800)* (Zutphen, 2000)

VARELA GOMES, P., 'Ovídio Malabar. Manuel de Faria e Sousa, a Índia e a arquitectura portuguesa', in *Mare Liberum* 11–12 (Lisbon, 1996) pp. 73–90

VARLEY, P. and KUMAKURA, I. (eds), *Tea in Japan: Essays on the History of Chanoyu* (Honolulu, 1989)

VEENENDAAL, J., *Furniture from Indonesia, Sri Lanka and India during the Dutch Period* (Delft, 1985)

Via Orientalis (Galerie de la CGER, Brussels, exhib. cat. 1991)

VOGELSANG-EASTWOOD, G.M., *Resist-dyed textiles from Quseir al-Qadim, Egypt* (Paris, 1990)

VOLKER, T., *Porcelain and the Dutch East India Company* (Leiden, 1954)

WAGHORNE, J.P., *The Raja's Magic Clothes, Re-Visioning Kingship and Divinity in England's India* (Pennsylvania, 1994)

WAKAKUWA, M., 'Xavier in the "Fifteen Mysteries of the Rosary" at Kyoto University', in *St Francis Xavier: An Apostle of the East* (Tokyo, 1999), pp. 210–26

WALCH, K. and KOLLER, J. (eds), *Lacke des Barock und Rokoko / Baroque and Rococo Lacquers* (dual text) (Munich, 1997)

WALEY-COHEN, J., *The Sextants of Beijing* (New York and London, 1999)

WALT DISNEY WORLD, ORLANDO, *Artistry in Time: Decorative Timepieces of Imperial China* (EPCOT Center, Florida, exhib. cat. 1987)

WANG CHENG-HUA, 'The Qianlong Emperor and his Legacy: the National Palace Museum's 2002 October Exhibition', in *Orientations* (October 2002), vol. 33, no. 8, pp. 60–75

WARD, B., *The Venerable Bede* (London, 1998)

WATT, SIR G., *The Commercial Products of India* (London, 1908)

WELCH, S.C., *Room for Wonder: Indian Paintings during the British Period 1760–1880* (New York, exhib. cat. 1979)

WELTEN HARMONIE, *Die Kunstkammer und die Ordnung des Wissens* (Herzog Anton-Ulrich Museum, Braunschweig, exhib. cat. 2000)

WHEATLEY, P., 'Geographical notes on some commodities involved in the Sung maritime trade', in *Journal of the Malaysian Branch of the Royal Asiatic Society* (1959), vol. XXXII, pt 2, no. 186, pp. 1–140

WHELAN, C., *The Beginning of Heaven and Earth: The Sacred Book of Japan's Hidden Christians* (Honolulu, 1996)

WIGINGTON, R., *The Firearms of Tipu Sultan 1783–1799* (Hatfield, 1992)

WILKINSON, T., *Two Monsoons: The life and death of Europeans in India* (London, 1976)

WILLIAMS, I. ET AL., *Views from the West: Collection of nineteenth century pith paper watercolours* (Guangzhou, 2001)

WILLIS, C. (ed.), *China and Macau* (Aldershot, 2002)

WILLS, J.E., JR, *Embassies and Illusions* (Cambridge, MA, 1984)

WILLS, J.E., JR, 'Relations with Maritime Europeans, 1514–1662', in *The Cambridge History of China* (Cambridge, 1998), vol. 8, ch. 7, pp. 333–75

WILSON, M., 'Fengshui, opium and bound feet: Chinese watercolours for the West', in *Apollo* (November 2000), vol, CLII, no. 465, pp. 24–28

WINIUS, G.D., *Studies on Portuguese Asia 1495–1689* (Aldershot, 2001)

WOOD, F., *Did Marco Polo go to China?* (London, 1995)

WOOD, F., *No Dogs and Not Many Chinese: Treaty Port Life in China, 1843–1943* (London, 1998)

WOODHOUSE, C.P., *Ivories, A History and Guide* (New York, 1976)

WOODWARD, D., 'Medieval Mappaemundi', in *History of Cartography* (Chicago, 1987), vol. 1, pp. 286–370

WOODWARD, D., 'Starting with the Map: The Rosselli Map of the World, ca. 1508', in *Plantejaments i objectius d'una història universal de la cartografia [Approaches and Challenges in a Worldwide History of Cartography]* (Barcelona, 2001), pp. 71–90

WOODWARD, D. and HOWE, H.M., 'Roger Bacon on Geography and Cartography,' in Jeremiah Hackett, *Roger Bacon and the Sciences: Commemorative Essays* (Leiden, 1997) pp. 199–222

WU HUNG, 'Emperor's Masquerade – Costume Portraits of Yongzheng and Qianlong', in *Orientations* (July 1995), vol. 26, no. 7, pp. 25–41

WÜRTTEMBEGERGISCHER KUNSTVEREIN, STUTTGART, *Exotischen Welten. Europäische Phantasien* (Stuttgart, exhib. cat. 1987).

XU WENLIN and CHEN KAIGE, 'Qingdai Suzhoude zhongbiao zhizao' ['On the Manufacture of Suzhou Clocks in the Qing Dynasty'], in *Gugong bowuyuan yuankan* (1981), no. 4, pp. 90–94

XU WENLIN and LI WENGUANG, 'Tan Qingdai de zhongbiao zhizao' ['On the manufacture of Qing dynasty clocks'], in *Wenwu* (1959), no. 2, pp. 34–35

YANG BODA, 'A Brief Account of Qing Dynasty Glass', in *Chinese Glass of the Qing Dynasty, 1644–1911* (Phoenix, 1987), pp. 71–86

YANG BODA, *Tributes From Guangdong to the Qing Court* (Hong Kong, 1987)

YANG BODA, 'Qing Qianlong chao huayuan yan'ge' ['The evolution of the art academy in the Qianlong period of the Qing dynasty'], in *Gugong bowuyuan yuankan* (1992), no. 1 (55), pp. 3–11, 89

YEE, C., 'Taking the World's Measure: Chinese Maps Between Observation and Text', in *History of Cartography* (Chicago, 1994), vol. 2.2, pp. 117–24

YEE, C., 'Traditional Chinese Cartography and the Myth of Westernization', in *History of Cartography* (Chicago, 1994), vol. 2.2, pp. 170–77

YEE, C., 'The Influence of Chinese Map Culture on the West', in *Plantejaments i objectius d'una història universal de la cartografia [Approaches and Challenges in a Worldwide History of Cartography]*, (Barcelona, 2001), pp. 265–82

YOSHIDA MITSUKUNI ET AL. (eds), *The Hybrid Culture: What Happened When East and West Met* (Tokyo, 1984)

YULE, H. and BURNELL, A.S., *Hobson-Jobson. A glossary of colloquial Anglo-Indian words and phrases* (second edn, London, 1903)

ZAIDI, I., 'French Mercenaries in the Armies of South Asian States 1499–1803', in *Indo-French Relations: History and Perspectives* (Delhi, 1990), pp. 51–78

ZAIN AL DĪN AL-MA'BARĪ, *História dos Portugueses no Malabar*, ed. David Lopes (Lisbon, 1898; reprinted Lisbon, 1998)

ZANDVLIET, K. (ed.), *The Dutch Encounter with Asia 1600–1950* (Rijksmuseum, Amsterdam, exhib. cat. 2002)

ZEBROWSKI, M., *Deccani Painting* (London, 1983)

ZEBROWSKI, M., *Gold, Silver & Bronze from Mughal India* (London, 1997)

ZHANG HONGXING, *The Qianlong Emperor: Treasures from the Forbidden City* (Edinburgh, exhib. cat. 2002)

ZHANG YINLIN, 'Ming Qing shi ji xixue shu ru Zhongguo kaolu' ['History of the penetration of Western science and technology into China in the Ming and Qing dynasties'], in *Qinghua xuebao* (1924), no. 1, pp. 38

ZHAO YI, *Yanpu zaji [Miscellaneous Notes]*, (reprinted Beijing, 1982)

OBJECT LIST

Encounters: The Meeting of Asia and Europe 1500–1800
Victoria and Albert Museum,
23 September – 5 December 2004

Note: the object list is correct at the time of going to press.

The dimensions are only an indication of the size of each object. Display dimensions (in mm) = height × width × depth.

INTRODUCTION

Screen depicting the arrival of a Portuguese ship
Ink, colours and gold-leaf on paper
1180 × 3690
Japan, *c.*1630s
Private collection, New York
PLATE 16.1

DISCOVERIES

World map
Francesco Rosselli
Hand-coloured copperplate engraving on paper
420 × 370
Italy (probably Venice) *c.*1508
National Maritime Museum, London, G201:1/53
PLATE 2.9

RARITIES AND NOVELTIES

Gaignières-Fonthill Vase
Porcelain with bluish-white (*qingbai*) glaze
283 × 160 × 97
China, Yuan dynasty (*c.*1300–30)
National Museum of Ireland, Dublin, NMIDC:1882.3941
PLATE 4.1

Bowl
Porcelain with celadon glaze and silver-gilt and enamel mounts
206 × 168 × 168
China (Longquan), early Ming dynasty (late 14th–early 15th century); mounts, Germany (Rhenish workshop), *c.*1434–53
Staatliche Museen, Kassel, Inv.Nr.BII.240
PLATE 4.3

Von Mandersheidt Cup
Porcelain decorated in underglaze blue, enamels and gilding with silver-gilt mounts
167 × 117 × 117
China, Jiajing reign (1522–66); mounts: Germany, *c.*1583
V&A: M.16–1970
PLATE 4.4

Cup
Coconut, with partly-gilt silver mounts
203 × 90 × 90
England, *c.*1475–1500
With permission of the Warden & Scholars of New College, 1744
PLATE 3.2

Nautilus cup
Nautilus shell, with partly-gilt silver mounts by Nikolaus Schmidt
520 × 170 × 240
Shell: western Pacific Ocean; mounts with Nuremberg town and maker's mark, *c.*1600
The Royal Collection
PLATE 3.7

Spoon
Rock crystal, set in gold, with rubies and sapphires
204
Ceylon, mid-16th century
Kunsthistorisches Museum Wien, Kunstkammer, Inv.Nr.1351
PLATE 3.5

Fan
Carved ivory
430
Ceylon, mid-16th century
Kunsthistorisches Museum Wien, Kunstkammer, Inv.Nr.4751
PLATE 3.1

Cup
Rhinoceros horn (*Rhinoceros sondaicus*), carved and set with gold filigree mounts
155 × 176 × 100
Cup: China, early 17th century; mounts: India (Goa), early 17th century
Kunsthistorisches Museum Wien, Kunstkammer, Inv.Nr.3757
PLATE 3.6

Casket
Teak, covered with plaques of mother-of-pearl, with mounts of silver-gilt by Pierre Mangot
290 × 400 × 260
Casket: India (Gujarat), early 16th century; mounts: France (Paris), 1532–33
Paris, Musée du Louvre, département des Objects d'art, OA 11936
PLATE 3.9

Seat
Engraved with the arms of Maximilian II (r.1564–76)
Elephant bone
820 × 900 × 550
Austria (Vienna), 1554
Stift Kremsmuenster Kunstsammlungen
PLATE 3.13

ENCOUNTERS

A Meeting of Japan, China and the West
Attributed to Shiba Kōkan
Ink, colours and gold on silk
1940 × 700
Japan, late 18th century
Ruth & Sherman Lee Institute, Permanent Collection, 2001.2
PLATE 1.6

DIPLOMATIC ENCOUNTERS

Europeans Bring Gifts to Shah Jahan
From the Padshahnama manuscript
Opaque watercolour on paper
338 × 237 (sheet size)
Mughal India, *c.*1650
The Royal Collection
PLATE 6.1

Gold Chain of the Sultan of Ternate
Gold filigree
1600 length
Batavia, *c.*1675
Rijksmuseum, Amsterdam, NG-394
PLATE 6.7

Robinson Casket
Ivory, carved, with silver-gilt hinges; the lock and handle of gold filigree set with sapphires
400 × 230 × 120
Ceylon (Kotte), *c.*1557
V&A: IS.41–1980
PLATE 6.10

Muhammad Dervish Khan
Elisabeth Vigée-Lebrun
Oil on canvas
2450 × 1610
France (Paris), 1787
Private collection
PLATE 6.11

The Embassy of Johannes Bacherus en route to the court of Aurangzeb
Colours on cloth
20 × 1050 × 2420
India (Golconda), late 17th century
Collection: KIT/Tropenmuseum, Amsterdam, A-9584
PLATE 6.6

Medal commemorating the Siamese embassy to Louis XIV
Jean Mauger
Silver
72 × 72 × 8
France (Paris), 1687
Bibliothèque nationale de France, SR939
PLATE 6.14

Ruyi
Jade
45 × 357 × 85
China, Qianlong period (1736–95)
V&A: A.17–1925, given by the Royal Asiatic Society of London
PLATE 7.2

Telescope
Fraser and Son
Gold with enamel coating; pearls; glass
65 × 320 × 65
England (London), 1790
National Maritime Museum, London, NAV1579
PLATE 7.3

Hanging
Tapestry weave silk
1215 × 1600 × 48
China, *c.*1793
National Maritime Museum, London, TXT0107
PLATE 7.4

Suit of armour
Iwai Yosaemon
Lacquered iron plates with copper, gold, leather and woven silk
1600 × 700 × 550
Japan, *c.*1613
Lent by the Board of Trustees of the Royal Armouries, XXVIA.1
PLATE 7.7

Casket
Wood, veneered with ivory, with metal and engraved rock-crystal panels
244 × 305 × 204
Italy, late 16th century
Rinnō-ji Treasure Museum, Rinnō-ji Temple
PLATE 7.10

RELIGIOUS ENCOUNTERS

Child Jesus
Ivory, carved and partly painted
470 × 160 × 150
India (Goa), 17th century
Peabody Essex Museum, AE85572AB
PLATE 8.5

Child Jesus
Rock crystal, carved, with gold mounts and rubies and sapphires
115 × 50 × 50
Ceylon, early 17th century
Peabody Essex Museum, E85219
PLATE 8.1

Cabinet
Wood, veneered with panels of carved ivory, with silver mounts
220 × 240 × 160
Ceylon, mid– to late 17th century
Private collection, Canada
PLATE 8.7

The Martyrdom of St Cecilia
Nini, after an engraving by Jerome Wierix
Opaque watercolour on paper
575 × 423 × 23
Mughal India, *c.*1600
V&A: IM.139–1921, bequeathed by Lady Wantage
PLATE 8.9

Crucifix and pair of cruets
Jade, inlaid and mounted with with gold and rubies
Crucifix: 281 × 125; each cruet: 120 × 85
Mughal India, 17th century
Museo Nacional Soares dos Reis, Oporto, 120/1-3
PLATE 8.10

The Ten Incarnations of Vishnu
Inscribed in English in the top left-hand corner: 'The incarnations of Vishnu. Presented to the R. Asiatic Society 1st December 1828 by Wm Marsden'
Watercolour and gold on paper
260 × 1130
India (Andhra Pradesh), *c.*1771 or *c.*1779
V&A: IM.561–1924; given by the Royal Asiatic Society of London
PLATE 8.29

The Muharram Procession
Opaque watercolour on paper
395 × 680
India (Murshidabad), 1795–1805
V&A: IS.11:12–1887
PLATE 1.16

Portable altar with painting of the Virgin and Child
Altar: wood covered in black lacquer with gold *hiramakie* and mother-of-pearl inlay; painting: oil on panel
460 × 620 × 100
Japan, late 16th–early 17th century
Peabody Essex Museum, AE85752
PLATE 8.14

Writing box
Wood, covered in gold and silver *nashiji*, *hiramakie* and *takamakie*
310 × 183 × 175
Japan, late 16th–early 17th century
Namban Bunkakan, Private collection of Yoshiro Kitamura
PLATE 8.13

Bowl
Stoneware with grey-green glaze over incised slip-filled decoration; crab with iron glaze
180 × 385
Japan, early 17th century
Private collection
PLATE 8.11

The Bodhisattva Guanyin
Porcelain with white glaze (Dehua ware)
241 × 177 × 110
China (Fujian province), late 17th– early 18th century
Kobe City Museum, Ikenaga 21-42
PLATE 8.2

Edict prohibiting Christianity
Ink on wood
520 × 990 × 90
Japan, dated 1682
British Museum, London, JA1895.7-21.1
PLATE 8.17

Portable altar on folding stand
Wood, covered in black lacquer with gold and red lacquer decoration
590 × 770 × 470
China, *c.*1700; the stand modern
Private collection, Oporto, Portugal
PLATE 8.21

Figures of David, Moses, Young
Isaiah, Old Isaiah
Cloisonné enamel
135 × 85 × 85; 124 × 85 × 83;
121 × 68 × 83; 121 × 83 × 83
China, 18th century
Lent by the Metropolitan Museum
of Art, Gift of Mr and Mrs Edmond
J. Safra, 1997 (1997.115A–D)
PLATE 8.23

Dalmatic
Brocaded silk
1120 × 1230 × 230
China (Macao), 1600–65
Peabody Essex Museum. Museum
purchase with funds donated in part by
the Asian Export Art Visiting
Committee, AE85947.3A-3B
PLATE 8.22

The Anunciation
Giulio Aleni
From *Tian zhu jiang sheng yan xing ji le (Brief Records of the Deeds of God who Became Man)*
Woodblock print on paper
264 × 182 × 24 (closed book)
China (Fuzhou), 1637
V&A: NAL C.B.73
PLATE 8.24

Michael Alphonsus Shen Fu Tsung
Sir Godfrey Kneller
Oil on canvas
2327 × 1699 × 68
England (London), 1687
The Royal Collection
PLATE 8.25

PERSONAL ENCOUNTERS

Colonel Mordaunt's Cock Match
Johann Zoffany
Oil on canvas
1235 × 1695 × 85
India (Lucknow), 1784–86
Tate. Purchased with assistance from
the National Heritage Memorial Fund,
the National Art Collections Fund, the
Friends of the Tate Gallery and a group
of donors, 1994, T06856
PLATE 12.2

Captain John Foote
Sir Joshua Reynolds
Oil on canvas
1232 × 990
England (London), 1765
York Museums Trust (York Art
Gallery), YORAG:216
PLATE 12.3

Jama (robe), *patka* (waist sash)
and shawl
Muslin, embroidered with
coloured silks and gold thread
Robe: length 1530; waist sash:
5590 × 410; shawl: 2560 × 510
India, mid-18th century
York Museums Trust (York Art
Gallery), YORAG: 2003.4
PLATE 12.4

Indian Woman
From an album belonging to
William Fullerton
Opaque watercolour on paper
575 × 423 × 23
India (Murshidabad School), 1760–64
V&A: D.1181–1903
PLATE 12.5

East India Company Official, Probably William Fullerton, Seated on a Terrace
Dip Chand
Opaque watercolour on paper
575 × 423 × 23
India (Murshidabad), 1760–63
V&A: IM.33–1912
PLATE 12.6

English Official in Discussion with a Nawab
Opaque watercolour with gold
on paper
650 × 505 × 17
India (Patna or Murshidabad), 1760–65
Collection Howard Hodgkin
PLATE 12.1

The Palmer Family
Johann Zoffany
Oil on canvas
1340 × 1590 × 170
India (Lucknow), April–July 1785
British Library, London, FOSTER 597
PLATE 12.8

The Dutch Factory at Dejima
Handscroll; ink and colours on silk
351 × 4342
Japan (Nagasaki), *c.*1800
V&A: D.151–1905
PLATE 10.2

Two Dutchmen and Two Courtesans
Ink and colours on paper
975 × 568
Japan (Nagasaki), *c.*1800
Private collection, courtesy of
Sydney L. Moss Ltd, London
PLATE 14.1

Dutchman and Maruyama Courtesan
Chōkōsai Eishō
Woodblock print
533 × 380
Japan (Edo), 1790s
V&A: E.170–1954
PLATE 14.2

European Wearing Chinese Dress
Oil on canvas
1940 × 1200
England, late 17th–early 18th century
Jonathan Lourie, Private collection
PLATE 14.6

Sake Dean Mohamed
Thomas Baynes
Oil on canvas
1040 × 850 × 65
England, early 19th century
The Royal Pavilion, Libraries and
Museums, Brighton and Hove, 000732
PLATE 1.3

VISUAL RESPONSES

Plate depicting a mosque and
a Hindu temple
From Jan Huyghen van Linschoten,
Itinerario: Voyage oft schipvaert van Jan Huygen van Linschoten naer Oost ofte Portugaels Indien…, engraved by Baptista
van Doetecun (after a drawing by
Linschoten)
Engraving on paper
Amsterdam, 1596
British Library, London, 569.G.23
PLATE 16.20

Reception of Emissaries at the Imperial Court
From Johannes Nieuhof, *L'ambassade de la Compagnie orientale des Provinces Unies vers l'empereur de la Chine, ou grand cam de Tartarie, faite par les Srs. Pierre de Goyer & Jacob de Keyser*
Engraving on paper
375 × 248 × 48 (book closed)
Leiden, 1665
V&A: NAL 5.X.36
PLATE 16.21

The Great Bull, an Hindoo Idol at Tanjore
Thomas and William Daniell
Aquatint on paper
530 × 722
England, 1798, based on sketches made
in India in 1792
V&A: E.909–1902
PLATE 1.11

Panel of wallpaper
Probably designed by Mongin
for Jean Zuber
1822 × 698
France, mid-19th century, from a
late 18th-century plate
Hobhouse Limited
PLATE 1.10

Padshahzade-i farang (European Prince)
Opaque watercolour on paper
285 × 215
Mughal India, early 17th century
Private collection
PLATE 15.7

A European
Opaque watercolour on paper
575 × 423 × 23
Mughal India, *c.*1610–20
V&A: IM. 9–1913
PLATE 15.2

Oil lamp
Cast bronze
315 × 330 × 330
South India, possibly 16th century
British Museum, London,
OA1992.6-27.1
PLATE 15.4

Tent panel
Cotton, painted and dyed
3048 × 1245
India (Coromandel coast), *c.*1620
Brooklyn Museum of Art, Museum
Expedition 1913–14, Museum
Collection Fund 14.719.2
PLATE 15.9

Pair of figures
Ivory, carved, partly painted and gilded;
the base modern
150 × 65 × 50; 155 × 60 × 50
China, early 18th century
Peabody Essex Museum,
AE86358.1AB-2AB
PLATE 16.8

Screen
Wood covered in coloured and
incised lacquer
2740 × 5820 (each panel: 2740 × 485)
China, dated 1674
Private collection
PLATE 16.6

Illustrated Tributaries of the Qing Empire
Ding Guanpeng and others
Handscroll from a set of four; ink
and colour on paper
336 × 19413
China, 1751–75
Collection of the Palace Museum,
Beijing, China, GU 6306 1/4
PLATE 16.9

The Demon Queller
Hanging scroll; ink and colour on silk
1225 × 1015
China, 1738
Rijksmuseum, Amsterdam, AK-MAK-
1410
PLATE 16.7

Two hanging scrolls
Opaque watercolour on paper
Each: 1920 × 450
China, late 18th century
Jorge Welsh
PLATE 16.12

Tiered food box
Wood covered in black lacquer with
gold *takamakie* lacquer and gold
and silver foil
270 × 240 × 220
Japan, 1600–25
Museu Nacional de Arte Antiga,
Lisboa, Inv. Nr. 68cx
PLATE 16.3

Pair of stirrups
Iron, with silver and brass inlay;
wood linings lacquered in red
with mother-of-pearl
Each: 170 × 140 × 310
Japan, 17th century
Private collection
PLATE 16.4

Dutchmen in the Nagasaki-ya
Katsushika Hokusai
From *Ehon Azuma Asobi (Picture Book of Places of Entertainment in the Eastern Capital)*
Woodblock-printed book
265 × 175 (book closed)
Japan (Edo), 1802
V&A: E.2675–1925
PLATE 14.5

Inro
Wood, covered with tortoiseshell,
bone and crackled eggshell
114 × 51 × 25
Japan, 1650–1750
V&A: W.356–1922, given
by Richard A. Pfungst
PLATE 16.15

Netsuke
Ivory, carved
115 × 35 × 25
Japan, 1700–50
British Museum, London, JA F.558
PLATE 16.17

Sake bottle
Porcelain, with decoration
in underglaze blue
204 × 106 × 101
Japan (Arita), 1750–1825
V&A: C.64–1963, bequeathed
by Basil Ionides
PLATE 16.18

EXCHANGES

ASIA IN EUROPE

Design for a fan
Oil on board
345 × 510 × 45
Europe, *c.*1700
V&A: P.35–1926
PLATE 1.4

Ewer with the arms of the
Peixoto family
Porcelain, with decoration in
underglaze blue; with contemporary
silver Persian mounts
330 × 225 × 150
China, mark and reign of the
emperor Jiajing (1522–66)
V&A: C.222–1931, bequeathed
by W.G. Gullard
PLATE 17.3

Bottle with Portuguese inscription
Porcelain, with decoration in
underglaze blue
240 × 130
China, 1552
V&A: 237–1892
PLATE 17.4

Dish
Soft-paste 'Medici porcelain',
decorated in underglaze blue
246 × 43
Italy (Florence), 1575–87
V&A: 7700–1862
PLATE 17.2

Casket
Gold filigree
140 × 195 × 96
India (Goa), 1575–1600
Museu Nacional de Arte Antiga,
Lisboa, Inv. Nr. 577 our
PLATE 1.5

Helmet (cabasset)
Gilded copper worked in repoussé
and chasing with engraved details
213 × 260 × 289
India (probably Goa), *c.*1580
Private collection
PLATE 24.20

Tankard
Wood, covered in black lacquer
with gold *hiramakie*, inlaid with
mother-of-pearl
185 × 165 × 105
Japan, late 16th–early 17th century
V&A: FE.23–1982
PLATE 18.1

Tankard, dish and salt cellar
Wood, covered with plaques
of mother-of-pearl, secured with
metal rivets
350 × 229
India (Gujarat), early 17th century
Private collection
PLATE 19.1

Scrutore (fall-front cabinet)
Wood, the exterior covered with
plaques of mother-of-pearl secured
with metal rivets; the interior covered
in black lacquer with gold *hiramakie*
and mother-of-pearl inlay; with
silver mounts
315 × 428 × 290
Japan, early 17th century
Kobe City Museum
PLATE 19.2

Colcha (quilted bedcover)
Cotton, quilted and embroidered
with silk
3203 × 2503
India (Satgaon, Bengal), 1600–25
V&A: 438–1882
PLATE 20.6

Cabinet on stand
Wood, inlaid with ivory, incised
and highlighted with lac
510 × 827 × 498
Cabinet: western India, mid- to late
17th century; stand: England mid-18th
century
V&A: On loan from Dr & Mrs A.
Poteliakhoff
PLATE 19.3

Casket
Wood, covered in black lacquer and
ivory, with gold *hiramakie* and *takamakie*
lacquer, and gold and silver details
200 × 286 × 197
Japan, 1630s
V&A: 628–1868
PLATE 18.3

The Van Diemen Box
Wood, covered in black lacquer with
gold, silver and red *hiramakie* and
takamakie lacquer, and gold and
silver details
157 × 479 × 370
Japan, 1636–39
V&A: W.49–1916
PLATE 18.6

Sword
Commissioned by the VOC as a gift for Johan van Leenen
Steel blade, with *sawasa* hilt and mounts; and scabbard of wood, covered in lacquered rayskin
805 × 120
Blade: Holland; mounts and scabbard: Japan, late 17th century
Rijksmuseum, Amsterdam, NG-1978-99
PLATE 18.16

Shield
Probably commissioned by Johan van Leenen
Hide, rhinoceros or buffalo, covered in black and gold lacquer
580 × 580
Hide: Bengal; lacquer: Japan, late 17th century
Rijksmuseum, Amsterdam, NG-NM-541
PLATE 18.16

Teapot
Porcelain, hand-modelled with applied decoration
132 × 179 × 120
Meissen, 1716–25
V&A: C.112–1940, bequeathed by Arthur Hurst
PLATE 17.5

Plate from a 'Dame au Parasol' service
Porcelain, decorated in underglaze blue, iron red and gilding
230 (width)
China (Jingdezen), 1736–38
Jorge Welsh
PLATE 17.1

Plate from a 'Dame au Parasol' service
Porcelain, decorated in underglaze blue, overglaze enamels and gilding
254 (width)
Japan (Arita), *c.*1738
Jorge Welsh
PLATE 17.8

Cup and saucer
Porcelain, with underglaze blue borders; overpainted in iron, red and gold by Ignaz Preissler, based on designs by Martin Englebrecht
Cup: 75 × 75
China, 1723–30; the painting: Bohemia, *c.*1730
Peabody Essex Museum. Museum purchase with funds donated in memory of Joseph D. Hinkle, AE85558.A-B

Plate decorated with the arms of Frederick the Great
Porcelain, decorated with overglaze enamels and gilding
260 × 260 × 50
China (made at Jingdezen; decorated at Canton), *c.*1760
V&A: C.73–1963, bequeathed by Basil Ionides
PLATE 17.10

Punch-bowl
Porcelain, with overglaze enamels and gilding, depicting tavern scenes derived from William Hogarth, *A Midnight Conversation*, 1733, and a Chinese interior screen
229 × 540 × 540
China (Jingdezen), 1750–75
Sunrider International, Chen Art Gallery, USA
PLATE 17.12

Palampore (bedcover or hanging)
Cotton, painted and dyed
3140 × 2729
India (Coromandel coast), mid-18th century
V&A: IS.30–1966
PLATE 20.7

Length of furnishing fabric
Cotton, block-printed
1840 × 1072 × 47
England, *c.*1795
V&A: 422–1887
PLATE 20.12

Banyan (man's robe)
Cotton, painted and dyed
1530 × 660 × 360
Cloth: India (Coromandel coast), 1750–75; garment: England, 1750–1800
V&A: T. 215–1992
PLATE 20.5

Bedcover
Silk, embroidered with coloured silk thread
3260 × 2740
China, 1760–70
V&A: FE.12–2004; supported by the Friends of the V&A
PLATE 20.1

Sack-back gown and petticoat
Painted silk
1690 × 1180 × 900
Cloth: China, *c.*1760; garment: England, 1760–70
V&A: T.115–1953
PLATE 20.2

Bureau-cabinet
Wood, covered in black lacquer with gold lacquer decoration
2377 × 1120 × 665
China (Canton), *c.*1730
V&A: W.28–1935, given by Lord Riddell
PLATE 18.8

Side chair
Beechwood, japanned in red with green and gold decoration
1152 × 560 × 585
England, *c.*1700
V&A: W.44–1938
PLATE 18.13

Joseph Collet
Portrait figure
Amoy Chinqua
Painted unfired clay on bamboo armature
750 × 400
China (Canton), 1716
National Portrait Gallery, London, NPG 4005
PLATE 1.2

Commode
Wood, veneered with panels of black lacquer and gold *hiramakie* lacquer decoration, with gilt-bronze mounts
845 × 1380 × 540
France, 1755–65; lacquer: Japan, late 17th century
V&A: 1105–1882 Jones Bequest
PLATE 18.11

Pot-pourri holder
Composed of a rice bowl and cover with later feet and mounts
Wood, covered in black lacquer, with gold *hiramakie* lacquer and gilt-bronze mounts
375 × 335 × 246
Bowl: Japan, late 17th century; mounts: France, mid-18th century
V&A: 158–1879
PLATE 18.9

Pair of candelabra
Composed of pieces of porcelain set with later mounts
White-glazed porcelain (Dehua ware) and soft-paste porcelain, with gilt-bronze mounts
Each: 398 × 221
Wine cups and whistles: China, *c.*1700; saucers, candle cups and mounts: France, 18th century
Peabody Essex Museum, E84079.1-2
PLATE 1.9

Teapot
Composed of a bowl and cover with later spout and handle
Rock crystal, with gold mounts
930 × 155
Bowl and cover: Mughal India, *c.*1700; mounts: Germany 1715–20
Metropolitan Museum of Art, New York, Gift of Ruth Blumka, in honour of Ashton Hawkins, 1985 (1985.195.11AB)
PLATE 1.7

Teapot
Composed of a tea canister later mounted with a spout and handle
Silver, partly gilt, with silver-gilt spout and handle
168 × 187 × 67
China, 1680; mounts: England, *c.*1750
V&A: M.69–1955
PLATE 1.8

Shawl Goat from Bhutan
Zayn al-Din
Opaque watercolour on paper
706 × 985 × 4
India (Calcutta), 1779
V&A: IS.51–1963
PLATE 21.13

Lady Impey Examining a Hat
Opaque watercolour on paper
510 × 590 × 20
India (Calcutta), *c.*1790
Impey Family Collection
PLATE 21.11

Gown
Muslin, embroidered with cotton thread and trimmed with lace
1500 × 770 × 850
Cloth: India (Bengal), *c.*1800; gown: England, *c.*1800–08
V&A: 444–1888
PLATE 20.13

Shawl
Woven goat hair (pashmina)
3150 × 1345
India (Kashmir), late 18th century
V&A: IS.83–1988; given by Mrs M. Jacquet
PLATE 20.13

Chair
Wood, veneered with ivory, with modern caned seat
935 × 580 × 450
India (Murshidabad), late 18th century
V&A: 1064b–1882 Jones Bequest
PLATE 19.13

Candlestand (teapoy)
Solid ivory, turned, carved and partly gilt
740 × 390
India (Murshidabad), late 18th century
V&A: IS.12–1991, given by the 5th Earl Amherst of Arracan
PLATE 19.12

Toilet glass
Sandalwood, veneered with ivory, incised and highlighted with lac, with silver mounts
1043 × 573 × 312
India (Vizagapatam), late 18th century
V&A: IS.31–1975
PLATE 19.11

Toilet glass
Wood, covered in black lacquer with gold lacquer decoration
849 × 492 × 299
China (Canton), *c.*1790
Richard Milhender
PLATE 18.10

Model of a boat
Ivory, carved and painted, with clockwork motor
825 × 700 × 699
China (Canton), *c.*1800
V&A: A.6–1936 Hall Bequest
PLATE 19.14

Side chair
Wood, carved, with slip seat, later upholstery
1000 × 560 × 590
China, *c.*1740
Peabody Essex Museum, E81830
PLATE 19.8

Portrait of the Late Shuja-ud-Daula and His Sons
Reverse painting on glass
760 × 585 × 60
China (Canton), *c.*1800
Peabody Essex Museum, AE85329
PLATE 21.6

Artist Copying a European Print onto Glass
Pu-Quà workshop
From a set of 100 plates depicting trades and occupations
Opaque watercolour on paper
471 × 574
China (Canton), *c.*1790
V&A: D.107–1898
PLATE 21.2

Captain Roper
Guan Zuolin (Spoilum)
Oil on canvas
483 × 407
China (Canton), late 18th century
Martyn Gregory Gallery, London
PLATE 21.8

Wallpaper panels depicting Canton
Watercolour on paper
Various sizes
China (Canton), *c.*1780
Martyn Gregory Gallery, London
Endpapers

Large Composition of Architecture Representing Some of the Most Celebrated Hindoo and Moorish Buildings in India
Thomas Daniell
Oil on canvas
England (London), *c.*1799
Private collection
PLATE 1.15

A Capriccio of Chinese Landscape
Antonio Joli
Oil on canvas
1480 × 1560 × 50
Possibly England, 1744–48
Private collection
PLATE 1.14

The Geometric View of the Steine Front, The Royal Pavilion, Brighton
From John Nash's *Views of the Royal Pavilion*, England, 1823
300 × 418
The Royal Pavilion, Libraries and Museums, Brighton and Hove, 206783

The Court at Brighton à la Chinese
G. Cruickshank
Hand-coloured engraving on paper
407 × 560
England, 1816
The Royal Pavilion, Libraries and Museums, Brighton and Hove, 200641
PLATE 27.9

EUROPE IN ASIA

Marathi world map
Ink on paper
780 × 1050 (sheet dimensions)
India, late 18th– early 19th century
British Library, London, MSS MAR G28, c-k, Fol.1
PLATE 2.16

Korean world map (*Ch'onhado*)
Woodcut on paper
310 × 290 (sheet dimensions)
Korea (Seoul), 1800
British Library, London, 9C.27 f.14 sheet 1
PLATE 2.15

Theatrum Orbis Terrarum
Abraham Ortelius
Copperplate engraving on paper
430 × 560
Antwerp, 1570
British Library, London, C2.C3
PLATE 2.10

Terrestrial globe
Yang Ma-nao (Manuel Dias) and Long Hua-min (Nicolo Longobardi)
Wood, painted in lacquer
840 × 592 × 592
China (Peking), 1623
British Library, London, G35
PLATE 23.1

World map
Eight-fold screen (one of a pair)
Colours on paper
1935 × 5136 × 15
Japan, early 17th century
The Museum of the Imperial Collections, Sannomaru Shozokan
PLATE 24.23

Twenty-Eight Cities
Eight-fold screen (one of a pair)
Colours on paper
1935 × 5136 × 15
Japan, early 17th century
The Museum of the Imperial Collections, Sannomaru Shozokan
PLATE 24.23

Jahangir Shoots the Head of Malik 'Anbar
Abu'l Hasan
Opaque watercolour and gold on paper
550 × 400
Mughal India, *c.*1616
Trustees of the Chester Beatty Library, Dublin, In 07A.15
PLATE 22.7

Page depicting instruments at the Beijing Observatory
From Ferdinand Verbiest, *Lingtai yixiang zhi* (*Astronomical Instruments in the Observatory*)
Woodblock printed on paper
35 × 385 × 385
China, 1674
British Library, London, 15268.B.3
PLATE 23.2

Clock
James Cox
Gilded copper
740 × 380 × 280
England (London), mid-18th century
Collection of the Palace Museum, Beijing, China, GU 182838
PLATE 7.5

Clock
Gilded copper inlaid with enamel
830 × 300 × 220
China (Guangzhou), Qianlong period (1736–95)
Collection of the Palace Museum, Beijing, China, GU 183130
PLATE 23.5

Entertainment Painting of Emperor Yongzheng's Imperial Concubine
One of a series of twelve
Colours on silk
1840 × 980
China (Qing court), Yongzheng period (1723–35)
Collection of the Palace Museum, Beijing, China, GU 6458 5/12
PLATE 23.6

Clock
Steel, bronze, copper, with engraved decoration; stand: black Somada-lacquered wood, with inalid mother-of-pearl
1440 × 550 × 550
Japan, 18th century
British Museum, London, CAI.2165
PLATE 24.6

Nano Koshi from the Ōgi-ya
Isoda Koryūsai
From the series *First Designs of Young Leaves*
Woodblock print
558 × 407 × 5
Japan (Edo), late 1770s
British Museum, London, 1906.12-20.090
PLATE 24.7

Blood Circulation in the Human Body
From *Kaitai Shinsho* (*New Anatomical Atlas*), translated by Sugita Genpaku et al. and illustrated by Odano Naotake, 1774
Woodblock-printed book
35 × 320 × 260 (when open flat)
Japan (Edo)
British Library, London, OR.74.C.5
PLATE 14.4

Telescope
Glass, engraved and painted, with wood and brass fittings
522 (length) × 47 (diameter)
Japan (Nagasaki) or China, late 18th century; with European lenses
Kobe City Museum
PLATE 24.5

Telescope
Gilded copper with enamel plaques
37 × 230 × 37
England, 18th century
Collection of the Palace Museum, Beijing, China, GU 141743
PLATE 23.7

Jug
Carved glass with gilt-bronze handle
193 × 150 × 215
China (Canton), Qianlong period (1736–95)
Anonymous
PLATE 23.11

Rose-water sprinkler
Lead glass
280 × 110 × 110
England or India, mid-18th century
V&A: IS.13–1893
PLATE 22.8

Nawab Mir Qasim Ali Khan
Opaque watercolour and gold on paper
575 × 423 × 23
India (Murshidabad), 1760–63
V&A: D.1178–1903, bequeathed by Miss Mary Thompson
PLATE 22.9

Mirror
Mirror mounted in jade, inlaid with semi-precious stones set in gold
215 × 75
Frame: Mughal India, 17th century; mirror: Europe, 17th century
Paris, Musée du Louvre, département des Artes de l'Islam, R.449
PLATE 22.11

Scene of Palace Life
Opaque watercolour on paper, with mica
423 × 575 × 23
India (Kangra), *c.*1790
V&A: IM.4–1912
PLATE 22.10

Mirror
Cast bronze
267 × 267 × 12
China, Song dynasty (960–1279)
V&A: M.296–1956, bequeathed by Dr.W.L. Hildburgh
PLATE 23.9

Pair of hand-held mirrors
Carved polychrome ivory
Each: 325 × 170 × 20
Frame: China (possibly Canton), Qianlong period (1736–95); mirror: Europe, 18th century
Anonymous
PLATE 23.8

Lady Looking in a Mirror
Jiao Bingzhen
Ink on paper
300 × 583
China, early 18th century
Museum of Fine Arts, Boston. Marshall H. Gould Fund, 2002.36
PLATE 23.10

Shah Jahan with a Rifle
Payag
Opaque watercolour and gold on paper
550 × 400
Mughal India, *c.*1630
Trustees of the Chester Beatty Library, Dublin, In 07B.28
PLATE 22.14

Flintlock gun
Workshop of Claude Martin
Forged steel barrel, inlaid with gold and silver, wooden stock with silver inlay
205 × 1420 × 55
India (Lucknow), *c.*1780
Lent by the Board of Trustees of the Royal Armouries, X11/1279
PLATE 22.15

Secret Teachings of the Inatomi Ryu
Ink and colours on paper
250 × 1790
Japan, 1606
Namban Bunkakan, Private collection of Yoshiro Kitamura
PLATE 24.17

Matchlock gun
Cast-iron barrel inlaid with gold and silver; lacquered wood stock
145 × 1310 × 65
Japan (Sakai), 18th century
Lent by the Board of Trustees of the Royal Armouries, XXVIIF.53
PLATE 24.16

Helmet
Hammered iron with silver inlay and applied iron decoration, leather, silk and gilt copper; red laquered interior
315 × 355 × 335
Japan, 17th century
V&A: M.59–1922
PLATE 24.19

Album page incorporating a portrait miniature by Isaac Oliver
Miniature watercolour on vellum, mounted on an Indian album page, opaque watercolour and gold on paper
575 × 423 × 23
Miniature: England, *c.*1595; album page: 18th century
V&A: IS.60–1978
PLATE 22.1

George III
Portrait miniature after the painting by Allan Ramsay
Inscribed in Chinese ('Red-haired Emperor')
Enamel on copper
55 × 45
England, late 18th century
The Khalili Collections, ENG-645
PLATE 1.1

Hong Yan, Prince Gu
School of Castiglione
Oil on paper
788 × 623
China (Qing court), late 18th century
Martyn Gregory Gallery, London
PLATE 23.13

Nagasaki Bay
Shiba Kōkan
Ink and colours on silk
2263 × 960
Japan, *c.*1799
Peabody Essex Museum. Gift of Philip Hofer, M13393
PLATE 24.9

Perspective print showing Wan-Nian Qiao Bridge
Woodblock print
215 × 270
China (Suzhou), late 18th century
V&A: E.1139–1912
PLATE 23.14

Street Scene
Opaque watercolour on paper
508 × 407 × 5
India, late 18th century
British Museum, London, OA1958.10-11,014
PLATE 22.4

Daimonjiya Brothel
Okumura Masanobu
Woodblock print
815 × 610 × 5
Japan (Edo), *c.*1745–50
British Museum, London, JA1922.12-14,09
PLATE 24.13

View of the Forum in Rome
Utagawa Toyoharu
Woodblock print
295 × 404
Japan (Edo), 1770–90
V&A: E.2361–1914
PLATE 24.8

Outer kimono (*uchikake*)
Woven silk
1470 × 1300
Cloth: France (Lyon), *c.*1760s; garment: Japan, late 18th–early 19th century
Private collection, Kyoto
PLATE 24.3

The Yongzheng Emperor in European Dress
Ink and colour on silk
615 × 520
China (Qing court), Yongzheng period (1724–35)
Collection of the Palace Museum, Beijing, China, GU6449
PLATE 1.12

The Haiyantang (Calm Sea Palace), Yuanming Yuan
Copperplate engraving
34 × 521 × 578
China (Qing court), *c.*1786
V&A: 29452
PLATE 26.6

Architectural ornament from a western-style palace in the Yuanming Yuan
Stoneware with turquoise glaze
220 × 365 × 350
China, 1747–70
V&A: C.382–1912
PLATE 26.4

Chair
Zitan, carved
1175 × 660 × 515
China (Qing court), *c.*1759
Collection of the Palace Museum, Beijing, China, GU 208164
PLATE 26.9

Tippoo's Tiger
Automaton with mechanical organ
Wood, painted; with metal and ivory fixtures
710 × 1780 × 610
India (Mysore), *c.*1795
V&A: 2545 (IS)
PLATE 1.13

PICTURE CREDITS

Illustrations have been provided by the following individuals and institutions.

AUSTRIA

Kaiserliches Hofmobiliendepot 18.12

© Ebba Koch 22.12

Kunsthistoriches Museum, Wien 3.1, 3.5, 3.6, 3.11

Private collection, Vienna 3.15

Stift Kremsmunster, Kustodiat der Kunstsammlungen © Norbert Artner 3.13

CHINA

Collection of the National Palace Museum, Taiwan, Republic of China 26.1

Palace Museum, Beijing, China 1.12, 7.5, 11.10, 16.7, 23.5, 23.7, 23.9, 23.12, 26.3, 26.9

DENMARK

By permission of Her Majesty the Queen/Photograph: Thorkild Jensen 19.9

© The National Museum of Denmark, Department of Ethnography 18.14, 18.18

FRANCE

Bibliothèque nationale de France 4.2, 6.12, 6.13, 6.14

Marnier-Lapostolle Collection, France 6.11

Musée de la Mode et du Textile, Paris. Photo: Laurent Sully Jaulmes. All rights reserved 15.8

Musée Nissim de Camondo, Paris. Photo: Laurent Sully Jaulmes. All rights reserved 27.4

Private collection, Paris 1.14

© Photo RMN – Michèle Bellot 3.9; J.G. Berizzi 3.14; Franck Raux 22.11

GERMANY

© bpk, Berlin, 2004, Staatsbibliothek Preussischer Kulturbesitz Berlin 8.20

Germanisches National Museum 2.5

Grünes Gewölbe, Staatliche Kunstsammlungen 16.24

Landesmuseum Kassel 4.3

Stiftung Preussische Schlosser und Garten Berlin-Brandenburg, Fotograf: Roland Handrick 18.5, 27.8

INDIA

Institut Français d'Indologie, Pondicherry 5.2

IRELAND

© The Trustees of the Chester Beatty Library, Dublin 8.6, 22.7, 22.14

National Museum of Ireland, Dublin 4.1

ITALY

Biblioteca Marciana Venice 2.7

By permission of Conte and Contessa Cavazza 7.9

Su concessione del Ministero per I Beni e le Attivita Culturali 2.8, 15.3

JAPAN

Kishu Toshogu, Wakayama 24.18

Kiyomizu Temple, Kyoto 16.2

Kobe City Museum 8.2, 16.13, 19.2, 24.4, 24.5, 24.11, 24.12, 24.14, 24.22

Kyoto University Library 7.8

Imperial Households Collection 24.23

Maeda Ikutokukai Foundation 16.5

Matsuzakaya Co. Ltd 16.16

MOA Museum of Art 8.16

Namban Bunkakan, Osaka 8.13, 24.17

National Diet Library 14.8

Courtesy of the National Museum of Japanese History 2.14

Nezu Institute of Fine Arts, Japan 5.23, 5.25, 5.26, 5.27, 24.1

Private collection, Kyoto 24.3

Private collection, Japan 24.15

Rinnō-ji, Nikkō 7.10

Ryūkoku University Library, Kyoto 2.12

Twenty-six Martyr's Museum, Nagasaki 8.12

THE NETHERLANDS

Den Haag, Koninklijke Bibliothek 9.3

KIT Tropenmuseum 6.6, 13.3

Maritiem Museum, Rotterdam 6.3

National Museum of Ethnology, Leiden, Object 2984-5 8.18

Netherlands Maritime Museum, Amsterdam 24.21

© Rijksmuseum, Amsterdam 6.4, 6.5, 6.7, 10.1, 10.5, 13.2, 16.7, 17.9, 17.14, 18.16

PORTUGAL

Biblioteca do Forta de S. Julião da Barra, Oeiras 9.2

Gabinete de Estudos de Arquelogia e Engenharia Militar, Lisbon 9.1

Instituto Portugues de Museus 1.5, 8.10, 16.3, 18.15, 19.5 (Photo: Francisco Matias)

Medeiros e Almeida Collection, Lisbon, Portugal 8.4

Photo: Paulo Varela Gomes 9.5, 9.6

Private collections, Porto 8.7, 8.21, 15.7

SWEDEN

Copyright Royal Collections. Photo: Alexis Daflos, 1998 11.11

THAILAND

National Library Bangkok 5.22

TURKEY

Image reproduced in *Chinese Ceramics in the Topkapi Saray Museum, Istanbul* by Regina Krahl and John Ayers (Philip Wilson, London, 1986) 4.78

UK

© The Board of Trustees of the Armouries 7.7, 22.15, 24.16

Bodleian Library, University of Oxford, Map Res. 2/151 11.1

By permission of the British Library: Add.Ms.28681, fol 9r, 2.1; Royal MS 7 F Vii, fol. 85r, 2.4; MS. Add. 15760, fols 68v-69r, 2.6; Maps C2 c3, 2.10; Maps C.18.n.1, 2.11; Maps 33.c.13, 2.15; India Office Library and Records, MSS Mar.G28.C-K, fol1, 2.16; OIOC Photo 1000/17, 5.6; Manuscript Collection Add. Ch. 56456 6.2; Johnson Album 8. No. 6, 6.9; WD 961 f.57 (154), 7.1; F840, 8.27; OIOC F48, 11.2; OIOC P943, 11.5; OIOC P2976, 11.7; OIOC WD 476, 11.9; Foster 597, 12.8; OIOC BL Add. Or. 2, 12.9; Or.74.c.5, 14.4; 457.E.3, 16.22; OIOC Add.Or.3, 22.3; Add.Or.3129.f.65.v, 22.16; Maps.G.35, 23.1; 15268.b.3, 23.2; Add.Or.1815, 25.1; PW 6B 25 9, 25.3

Copyright © British Museum 3.12, 5.11, 5.12, 5.13, 5.17, 8.17, 15.4, 16.14, 16.17, 22.2, 22.4, 24.6, 24.7, 24.13

© Christie's Images Ltd 2004 5.18, 17.12, 26.8

© Country Life 25.7

© Eric and David Hosking/CORBIS 25.6

Fitzwilliam Museum, Cambridge 15.12

Impey Family Collection 21.11

Courtesy of Martyn Gregory Gallery, London 21.8, 23.13, endpapers

Photo: Anna Jackson 9.4, 23.3

Photo: Amin Jaffer 8.3, 11.6

Anthony Kersting 27.10

Collection of Dr. and Mrs John Kurtz 11.12

Collection of Jonathan Lourie 14.6

National Army Museum London 25.8

© National Gallery, London 20.4, 24.10, 27.2

© The National Maritime Museum, London 2.9, 7.3, 7.4

© National Trust Photographic Library/Andreas von Einsiedel 12.7, 21.7

National Portrait Gallery, London 1.2, 20.3

Courtesy of the Warden and Fellows of New College, Oxford/Bridgeman Art Library 3.2

Pelham Galleries, London 16.6

Percival David Foundation of Chinese Art 4.7, 26.2

Private collection, image reproduced in *The Erotic Art of India* by Philip Rawson (Thames & Hudson, 1977) 15.11

Private collection, on loan to Bristol Museums and Art Gallery 25.9

Private collections 1.1, 1.10, 1.15, 12.1, 16.4, 19.1, 19.4, 22.6, 23.8, 23.11, 24.20

The Royal Collection, 2004 © Her Majesty Queen Elizabeth II 3.7, 6.1, 8.25

Property of a private collector, courtesy of Sydney L. Moss, Ltd 14.1

Photograph courtesy of Simon Ray, London 15.1

Photo: Brian Richards 5.19

Royal Pavilion, Libraries and Museums, Brighton and Hove 1.3, 27.9, 27.11

By courtesy of Sotheby's Picture Library, London/Guy Morrison 27.3

© Tate, London, 2004 12.2

Jorge Welsh 16.12, 17.1, 17.8

Whipple Museum of the History of Science, Cambridge 23.4

York Museums Trust (York Art Gallery) 12.3, 12.4

USA

Asian Art Museum of San Francisco, The Avery Brundage Collection, B60D77+ and B60D78+. Used by permission 14.9

Anonymous loan to the Brooklyn Museum of Art. L.1991.4 5.16

Brooklyn Museum of Art. Museum Expedition 1913–14, Museum Collection Fund. 14.719.2 15.9

Photograph © 2003 Museum of Fine Arts, Boston, Marshall H. Gould Fund, 2002.36 23.10

© Cleveland Museum of Art John L. Severance Fund, 1954–584 8.19

Freer Gallery of Art, Smithsonian Institution, Washington D.C.: Purchase, F1952.31 6.8

Harvard-Yenching University 2.3

The Metropolitan Museum of Art, Gift of Ruth Blumka, in honour of Ashton Hawkins, 1985 (1985.195.11ab) Photograph copyright 1986 The Metropolitan Museum of Art 1.7

The Metropolitan Museum of Art, Gift of Mr. and Mrs. Edward J. Safra, 1997. (1997.115a-d). Photograph copyright 2003 The Metropolitan Museum of Art 8.23

Image © Board of Trustees, National Gallery of Art, Washington. Photograph by Jose A. Naranjo 4.6

Photograph courtesy of the Peabody Essex Museum 1.9, 8.1, 8.5, 8.14, 8.22, 16.8, 17.7, 17.17, 17.18, 19.7, 19.8, 21.1, 21.3, 21.5, 21.6, 21.9, 24.9

Loan Attributed to Choka, *Mother and Child*, Collection of Dr. Alvin O. Bellak, Philadelphia Museum of Art 15.5

Loan Rajasthan, Mewar, *A European Concoction*, Collection of Dr. Alvin O. Bellak Philadelphia Museum of Art 15.10

Private collection, Boston 18.10

Private collection, New York 16.1

Ruth and Sherman Lee Institute for Japanese Art at the Clark Center 1.6

Collection of Erving and Joyce Wolf 11.13

B1981.25.210, *The European Factories, Canton,* William Daniell, 1769–1837, 1806. Oil on canvas 34 x 50 in (84.0 x 127.0 cm) Paul Mellon Collection, Yale Center for British Art 11.4

Yale University Art Gallery, Gift of Edward S. Harkness, 1997 27.5

Map pp.x–xi: designed by Isambard Thomas. Map relief and borders: Mountain High Maps, copyright © 1995 Digital Wisdom Inc.

INDEX

Names of people – page numbers refer to text. Where there are no names of authors, place of origin is given.

Illustration plate numbers are in **bold** and listed after the page numbers.

Note: names with the prefixes 'van' and 'de' are usually indexed under the main part of the surname e.g. Adrichem, Dirk van

K

L

M

N

O

P

First published by V&A Publications, 2004
V&A Publications
160 Brompton Road
London SW3 1HW

Distributed in North America
by Harry N. Abrams, Inc., New York

ISBN 1 85177 432 7

Library of Congress Control Number
2004103252

A catalogue record for this book is available
from the British Library.

Designed by Isambard Thomas, London

V&A photography by the
V&A Photo Studio under the
direction of Christine Smith

FRONT AND BACK JACKET ILLUSTRATIONS
Six-panel screen depicting the arrival of
a Portuguese ship (detail). See p.202.

FRONTISPIECE
Leaf from the *Padshahnama* manuscript.
See p.76.

ENDPAPERS
Wallpaper panels depicting Canton (detail).
Watercolour on paper.
China (Canton), *c.*1780.
Courtesy of Martyn Gregory Gallery, London.

Printed in Italy

V&A Publications
160 Brompton Road
London SW3 1HW
www.vam.ac.uk

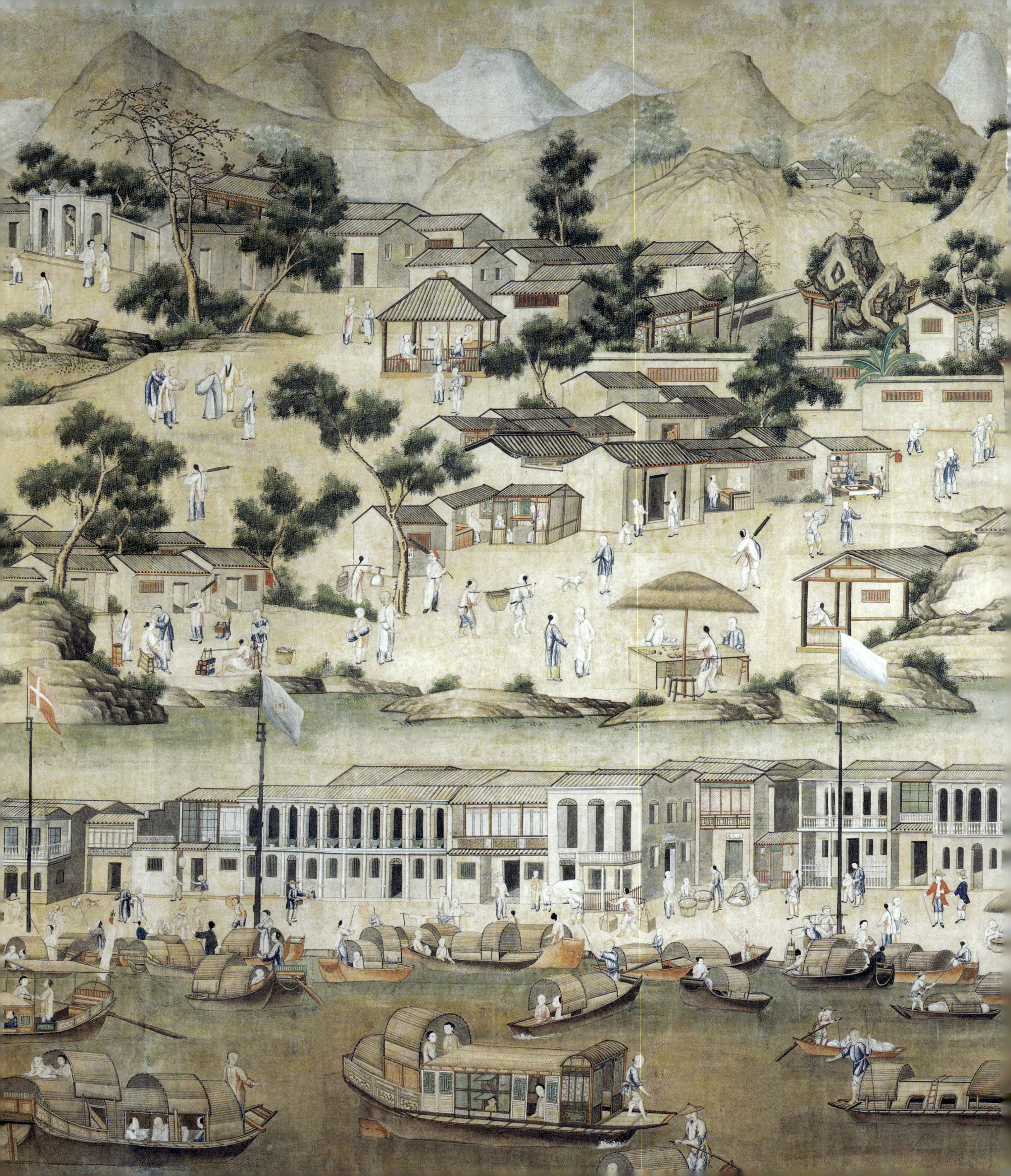